SEVENTH EDITION

Politics and Change in the Middle East

Sources of Conflict and Accommodation

Roy R. Andersen
Robert F. Seibert
Jon G. Wagner

All of Knox College

PEARSON
Prentice
Hall

Upper Saddle River, New Jersey 07458

Library of Congress Cataloging-in-Publication Data

Andersen, Roy.
    Politics and change in the Middle East: sources of conflict and accomodation / Roy A.
Andersen, Robert F. Seibert, Jon G. Wagner.—7th ed.
        p. cm.
    Includes bibliographical references and index.
    ISBN 0–13–140193–9 (paperback)
    1. Middle East—Politics and government.   I. Seibert, Robert F.   II. Wagner, Jon G.   III.
Title.

DS62.8.A5 2004
956.04—dc21

2003056481

Acquisitions Editor: Glenn Johnston
Editor-in-Chief: Charlyce Jones Owen
Assistant Editor: John Ragozzine
Editorial Assistant: Suzanne Remore
Director of Marketing: Beth Mejia
Marketing Assistant: Jennifer Bryant
Production Editor: Joan Stone
Manufacturing Buyer: Sherry Lewis

Cover Art Director: Jayne Conte
Cover Design: Suzanne Behnke
Cover Photo: Miles Ertman/Masterfile Corporation
Composition: Pine Tree Composition, Inc.
Printer/Binder: RR Donnelley & Sons Company
Cover Printer: Phoenix Color Corp.
Typeface: 10/11 Times New Roman

Pearson Education LTD.
Pearson Education Singapore, Pte. Ltd
Pearson Education, Canada, Ltd
Pearson Education—Japan
Pearson Education Australia PTY, Limited

Pearson Education North Asia Ltd
Pearson Educación de Mexico, S.A. de C.V.
Pearson Education Malaysia, Pte. Ltd
Pearson Education, Upper Saddle River, NJ

10 9 8 7 6 5 4 3 2 1
ISBN 0-13-140193-9

To Our Children and Grandchildren
Brynn, Eric, Kyla, Nicholas, Joanna, and Seth
and Our Wives
Corine, Jan, and Marna

Contents

CHAPTER TEN ————————————————————————————————————

Political Leadership in the Contemporary Middle East   **177**

CHAPTER ELEVEN ————————————————————————————————

The Economic Setting   **201**

CHAPTER TWELVE ————————————————————————————————

International Relations in the Contemporary Middle East, 1945–1990   **235**

Contents

Preface

This book has grown out of the authors' conviction that a proper understanding of present events in the Middle East requires knowledge of the cultural, social, and economic, as well as the political, background of these events. It is, more specifically, an outgrowth of the authors' attempts to develop an undergraduate course sequence aimed at such understanding. We found that, despite the abundance of excellent scholarship on the Middle East, there was a paucity of works that brought together the diverse disciplinary perspectives in a way suitable to our pedagogic aims. It is our belief that this book, with its combination of historical and contemporary materials and its integrated perspective, provides something of value that is not elsewhere available to the undergraduate student or educator.

Many profound changes have occurred since the original publication of this book. As we published our first edition in 1982, the first signs were evident of the inevitable decline of the bipolar international system, a system in which the overarching conflict between the United States and the U.S.S.R gave substance and meaning to a wide range of international interactions. Now, the U.S.S.R. no longer exists, replaced by a loose confederation of states, autonomous areas, and de-

pendencies that is only a shadow of the old order. It must now compete for power and influence with its former allies in Ukraine, Belarus, Poland, the Czech Republic, and Kazakhstan, as well as its old enemies in the West. It has been necessary to incorporate these new realities into our analysis of governments and politics in the Middle East. But the long-term consequences of these changes are not yet clear; they are, in fact, in the process of evolution. The new Russia is not the powerhouse that the old U.S.S.R. was reputed to be; but Russia still sees a role for itself in the Middle East. Regaining an element of its dominance in the areas of Central Asia is an emergent theme in its domestic politics—yet another example of the "domesticization of international politics and the internationalization of the domestic."

Changes in the Middle East itself have also been drastic. OPEC, for instance, was in its robust maturity as we began our initial work, a dominant player in the international energy system, capable of ostensible control of both supply and price of petroleum. Indeed it can be demonstrated that as Middle Eastern leaders "played the petroleum card" they were able to extract concessions from East and West. But by 2000, OPEC was not nearly the dominant influence it had been, despite a 1999 rally of prices engineered by OPEC. Its influence was diluted by a combination of new non-OPEC sources of petroleum, new technology squeezing new life and profits out of older fields, and modest conservation measures. The oil-rich monarchies of the Middle East are still rich, it is true; but they now live in an age of tough economic constraints in which important choices must be made, economically and politically. The cushion upon which they have relied for two decades has dramatically thinned.

If ever there was an issue or conflict considered architectonic in the Middle East, it was surely the Arab-Israeli conflict. Many regional issues and prospects were held hostage to this seemingly intractable problem. Parties directly involved in the conflict—Israel and the PLO—seemed inexorably headed in opposite directions. Even moderate Israelis seriously considered the merits of "transfer," a euphemism for the coercive expulsion of all Palestinians from Gaza and the West Bank. Many Palestinians committed themselves to violent confrontation with Israel, joining and working within a range of parties and groups dedicated to the destruction of Israel. Even the heavy-handed intervention of the United States failed to break the emotional and political deadlock between Israeli and Palestinian.

In the spring of 1993, Norway and independent international nongovernmental organizations succeeded where the combined influence of the "great powers" of the world had failed in establishing a framework for negotiating a lasting peace. The signing of the Accords negotiated at Oslo registered not just the willingness of two former adversaries to seek some future negotiated solution to their self-destructive conflict but also registered the relative decline of the superpowers and of their ability to dictate international outcomes. The peace process stalled from 1996 to 1999. Then a new administration in Israel signaled that it was ready to resume the process, this time including Syria on a separate track. That said, the series of negotiations only began a process—a process that was characterized by ambiguity, trial and error, and missed or extended deadlines. The second Palestinian uprising (Intifadah II), along with the Israeli responses, led Amnesty International to accuse both parties of crimes against humanity in a report issued in late 2002. The Oslo Accords have been formally renounced by Israel, and the Palestinian Authority edges closer to administrative inefficacy. The prospects for peace between the two antagonists seemed as remote as at any other time in their shared history.

Other system-level changes should be acknowledged as well. The on-again off-again efforts to discipline Iraq and remove Saddam Hussein introduced serious fault lines into the Middle Eastern system, pitting nominal allies against each other. The proliferation of satellite channels, new personal communication systems, and the geometric expansion of the Internet and access to it have begun to deliver on the promise of a truly global system of communication. These changes may have direct political consequences. The small but serious expatriate challenge to the Saudi royal family, for example, distributes its messages on the Internet, located in a home page originating in London. It is significant that the countries most interested in controlling the information on the Net or access to it include China, the United States, and Germany, three of the most powerful countries in the world. It is also significant that the most innovative and controversial new television outlet in the region, Al-Jazeerah TV, is sponsored by one of the smallest states in the region, the Emirate of Qatar.

Sadly, our work has been also bracketed in time by the assassination of two key Middle Eastern leaders, Anwar Sadat in Egypt in 1979 and Yitzhak Rabin in Israel in 1995. Each leader was assassinated by extremist members of his own polity, and each had personally transcended the history of his previous career in order to explore the possibilities of peace. They both succumbed to the violence engendered by a rising tide of religiously motivated political extremism, a tide evident not just in the Middle East but truly global in scale. Non–Middle Eastern referents could include the Oklahoma City bombing in the United States, the release of poison gas in the subways of Japan, the reemergent political violence in England and Ireland—and, of course, the series of terrorist attacks directed at assets of the United States, culminating in the destruction of the World Trade Center.

The good news is that the religious communities involved in systematic political violence appear to be relatively small and not representative of their religious roots. There are growing movements of moderation and tolerance in the mainstream communities of Christianity, Judaism, and Islam that now strive to offset the influence of their extremist co-religionists. It is instructive that in the aftermath of both Sadat's and Rabin's assassinations, the immediate effect was to reinforce the resolve of their successors to continue the search for peace. We have continued to incorporate discussions of religion and politics in this new edition.

These events have necessitated substantial revisions in the text. In some cases the changes amounted to a straightforward updating. In others, revisions were made so as to give a more thorough background to emerging issues. In particular, more explicit reference to the globalization process and what it seems to imply for the study of the behavior of individuals and nations, and, indeed, the very notion of area studies is sprinkled through the last half of the text. Most significantly, the book continues to be predicated on the value of using a multidisciplinary approach within a conflict and accommodation format.

We have directed our writing to an undergraduate audience not specifically acquainted with the Middle East. In addition, we have made every effort to avoid disciplinary jargon, arcane theoretical concepts, or other devices that would necessitate a sophisticated background in any of the social sciences. This is not to say that we do not introduce any special concepts or terms; but we do so only as necessary, and we do it as painlessly as possible.

One of the characteristic problems in writing about another culture involves the use of language. The words used by Arabs, Turks, or Persians to describe institutions and concepts fundamental to their civilization usually have no direct equivalent in English. We are faced with the dilemma of whether to translate them (which necessarily introduces our own cultural bias) or to use "native" terms (which places on the reader the burden of learning a new vocabulary). Compounding this problem is the more technical matter of how to transliterate Arabic or other languages into the medium of the English alphabet. Our solution has been one of compromise; we have used foreign words when there is no English equivalent or when the nearest English equivalent would be awkward or misleading. Despite our efforts to minimize the use of foreign words, the text has unavoidably made use of a number of them—especially Arabic terms. All these are explained in the text, and whenever possible the explanation accompanies the first appearance of a term, which is indicated by the use of italics. As an extra aid to the student we have also included important terms in a glossary. The terms explained in the glossary are in boldface type the first time they appear in the text. As for the spelling of Arabic and other foreign words, we have omitted the diacritical marks that scholars use to render their transliterations technically correct. We do so on the assumption that the limited number of terms we use can, for the reader's purposes, be determined without these marks. Nearly all Arabic terms appear in several different English forms in the literature; we have tried to hold to those forms that reflect the most frequent current usage among informed scholars who write for a general audience. In personal names especially, we have often departed from the technically correct forms and employed instead the forms used in English for news reportage and popular historical writing.

One further matter that deserves mention here is the definition of the Middle East itself. The term *Middle East* raises some problems, for it originates in recent Western military usage and utilizes present national boundaries that cut across historically significant cultural and geographical divisions. Furthermore, the reference to the region as part of the "East" reveals a European bias; from the larger perspective of the whole civilized area stretching from Western Europe to East Asia, the so-called Middle East is located somewhat toward the West and has close cultural ties with the Mediterranean region as a whole. Despite these problems, we shall follow the (more or less) established convention and define the Middle East as the region bounded on the northwest by Turkey, on the southwest by Egypt, on the southeast by the Arabian peninsula, and on the northeast by Iran. At the same time, it must be remembered that this division is somewhat arbitrary, and that bordering regions like Afghanistan, the Sudan, and North Africa have much in common with their

"Middle Eastern" neighbors. For this reason, we shall include them in our discussions whenever appropriate.

The authorship of this book is genuinely a joint affair; there is no "senior" author. The order of our names on the title page was randomly chosen. One of the authors is an economist with a long-standing interest in economic development; one is a political scientist specializing in political development in the Third World; and the third is a cultural anthropologist specializing in religion and culture change. Each chapter was largely the work of a single author, but each reflects a dialogue that began long before the book was conceived and has continued throughout its preparation and revision.

We cannot hope to name all the people and institutions that have made important contributions to this writing. We wish to thank Knox College for its material and moral support, and particularly for maintaining an atmosphere that nourishes interdisciplinary collaboration and teaching. We are indebted to the United States Office of Education, which made it possible for us to observe at first hand the phenomena of social and political change in two Muslim countries, Egypt and Malaysia, during 1976 and 1977. We also thank Dr. John Duke Anthony, founder, director, and driving force of the National Council on U.S.-Arab Relations, under whose sponsorship we have collectively traveled to Bahrain, Iraq, Jordan, Kuwait, Saudi Arabia, Syria, the U.A.E., and Israel and the Palestinian territories it occupies. There are scores of individuals in each of these countries who gave generously of their precious time and considerable talents in order that we could better appreciate some nuances of highly complex situations. We also owe thanks to Professor John Woods and the Center for Middle Eastern Studies at the University of Chicago. As always, the staff at Prentice Hall, especially Joan Stone, has been supportive and professional. We would like to thank the following reviewers for their helpful suggestions: Masoud Kheirabadi, Portland State University, and Joyce N. Wiley, University of South Carolina. Finally, we thank our students at Knox, whose interest in the Middle East, energy, and enthusiasm give us continued motivation for this work.

Above all, we take this opportunity to express our appreciation to our wives and children for suffering bravely through what is, as every author knows, the seemingly endless task of transforming a set of ideas into a finished book.

Roy R. Andersen
Robert F. Seibert
Jon G. Wagner

Introduction

Events in the Middle East have been capturing worldwide attention since the 1970s. Hefty increases in petroleum prices brought about by the efforts of the Organization of Petroleum Exporting Countries (OPEC), the spectacular rise of the Islamic Republic of Iran, the Iran-Iraq war, and conflicts in Lebanon, the West Bank, and the Persian (Arabian) Gulf have riveted the attention of both the regional actors and the world as a whole. Yet only a couple of decades earlier, many outside the region saw the problems of the Middle East as largely local affairs that rarely affected the world political arena. Today, the Middle East is properly regarded as crucial to world events, and it will continue to be so regarded in the foreseeable future.

The Middle East's geographic position alone, at the junction of Africa, Asia, and Europe, is ample reason for it to command the world's attention. A sign in the Cairo airport proclaims it the "Crossroads of the World," a slogan that rings true for several reasons. Three great monotheistic religions—Judaism, Christianity, and Islam—arose from the same society and culture; the Western and Muslim intellectual heritages have much more in common than is generally recognized. Although some major strands of Western thought can be traced to Greece, much of Greek philosophy and science were preserved and transmitted to the West through the writings of Muslim scholars. In fact, the Middle East served as a repository of Greek thought while Europe languished in the Dark Ages. Also during this time, a great intellectual and cultural florescence occurred in the Islamic world. The development of algebra (in Arabic, *al-jabr*), fundamental advances in the sciences of optics and medicine, and many other intellectual achievements originated in the Middle East. Furthermore, concepts from the Far East were melded into Middle Eastern intellectual and cultural patterns. "Arabic" numerals, the decimal system, and the use of zero—all brought to the Middle East from India—paved the way for profound advances in quantitative thinking. The role of the Middle East in trade and conquest, no less than its intellectual activity, made it a crossroads in every way. The Middle East is not a desert devoid of high culture and rich history; the religion of its peoples is not characterized by wild-eyed fanaticism. The Middle East should not be viewed as an exotic area of intellectual inquiry, but rather as integral to our understanding of the world.

A serious study of the relationship of the Middle East to the rest of the world must introduce a broad array of facts, assumptions, hypotheses, and theories—all of which might threaten to overwhelm the beginning student. And, although Egypt, Saudi Arabia, Iran, Lebanon, and other Middle Eastern states share a common heritage, particular historic, geographic, and economic influences have produced substantial regional diversity. Thus the Middle East cannot be viewed as a monolithic entity; its constituent regions and entities must be studied carefully in order to identify points of commonality and divergence. The welter of information generated by these complexities can create more confusion than understanding, more tedium than excitement. We have therefore selected two themes—conflict (and its resolution) and social change—to make the task more manageable for the beginning student. Although we focus on political systems in the Middle East, we carry our themes across disciplinary lines into other social sciences. We have not, however, attempted a systematic coverage of Islamic art, literature, science, and theology, even though such coverage would indeed lend richness and subtlety to the topics covered in the text. We encourage the student to explore these topics.

POLITICS AND CONFLICT

The first theme of our text centers on the definition of politics employed: the study of conflicts between groups of people and how those conflicts are resolved in human institutions. Conflict is present in all societies and is caused by competing demands for limited resources. The demand for resources embraces a wide variety of valued things, but may include ordinary things such as money, land, and water, or more abstract things such as deference, prestige, or even claims on cultural and religious symbols of legitimacy. The propensity of human beings to demand such things in greater quantity than the supply allows leads to conflict over distribution or consumption. When formal organizations make socially binding decisions regarding such things, they are engaging in the political resolution of social conflict. To sum up, *conflict* arises out of the inevitable competition for scarce resources; *politics* involves the resolution of these conflicts through the formal and informal processes and institutions that constitute government. We consequently equate politics with the formation and resolution of conflict in social

life. Although there are many alternate definitions of politics that could be employed, the one given here is widely used and fits into the major plan of this book.

Conflict and conflict resolution occur at various levels of social organization. For example, conflict over water resources can take place at the local level (which fields are to receive how much water?), or at the regional level (should a dam be constructed in region A or region B?), or at the national level (should a country rely on its existing water sources or explore the feasibility of desalination of ocean water?). Although all of these decisions involve the provision and allocation of scarce resources, the people, institutions, and style of decision making will vary from one level to another. Conflict resolution involving personal discussion among those affected is more likely to occur at the local level than at the regional or national level. The political processes employed depend on the level and arena of conflict.

In this text, we discuss political conflict in terms of the applicable arenas. For example, in a discussion of the elite structure of a given government, we distinguish between the qualities and styles of national and local elites. This is a convenient way of analyzing a nation's political system. However, no nation consists of neatly layered conflict arenas; any given arena interacts with other arenas that are potentially higher, lower, or equal in level. The arenas of conflict in a nation resemble the composition of a multiflavored marble cake in which various colors and flavors dip and swirl irregularly.

As an example, the complex interaction of arenas can be seen in the decisions that led to the construction and operation of the Aswan High Dam in Egypt. Egypt is, as Herodotus said more than 2,000 years ago, the "gift of the Nile." Almost all its arable land lies in the Nile Valley and Delta. Over thousands of years the cultivators of the land have adapted their agricultural techniques and timing to the annual flooding of the river. Regulating the flow of the Nile through the construction of a large dam, it was theorized, would free the farmers from dependence on the caprice of the river, minimize flood damage, and maximize agricultural production.

However, the project brought to light many unanticipated conflicts—some of which had been simmering below the surface of day-to-day events, and some of which were created by the construction and operation of the dam. The major themes of conflict were as follows: (1) The financing and construction of the dam involved superpower interests: The United States had first agreed to finance the project, but backed out of the agreement; the U.S.S.R. then stepped in to fill the breach. (2) The determination of water rights between Egypt and the Sudan had to be resolved, since the lake formed by the dam crossed the border dividing the two countries. (3) Thousands of families had to be relocated from the lake site into existing or new villages and towns. (4) A system for allocating irrigation water to Nile Delta farmers had to be developed. (5) Drainage problems induced by the operation of the dam required individual, village, provincial, national, and finally World Bank intervention. The relationships among various groups involved had to be reworked, sometimes drastically. The Aswan High Dam was—and is—the focal point of conflict in several arenas; it is an example of the tendency for solutions in one arena to generate new problems in another, in a complex cycle of cause and effect.

APPROACHES TO SOCIAL CHANGE

Human social life is changing with increasing speed. Certain trends set in motion only a few centuries ago have accelerated and spread until they have profoundly affected most of the world's societies and have drawn nations into an unprecedented degree of interdependence. Westerners, who have benefited in particular from many of these changes, sometimes take them for granted as part of the natural course of human "progress," without much attempt at a deeper critical understanding. Even the social sciences may be subtly influenced by ethnocentric assumptions. For the Western reader to grasp the essence of these changes and to understand their causes without falling into the trap of cultural chauvinism (or its negative counterpart, cultural self-deprecation) is no easy task.

Many Westerners naively assume that the West has been in the forefront of cultural development for thousands of years, a view that is enhanced by

grafting European history onto that of the Greeks while placing the Middle East in the vague category of "Oriental" or "Asian" cultures. But by any objective standards, Western Europe could not be called a leader in world cultural development until very late in history. Even after the Renaissance, Europe was on no more than an equal footing with the older centers of civilization, and it was only in the eighteenth century that it decisively surpassed the Middle East in technology and commercial power.

What is the nature of the unique change that originated in Western society and subsequently influenced the emerging world order, and why did it occur in Europe rather than in the older centers of civilization? Marshall G. S. Hodgson, in his remarkably insightful work *The Venture of Islam,* has characterized this change as one toward "technicalization."[1] A technicalized society is one in which the interplay of specialized technical considerations tends to take precedence over aesthetic, traditional, interpersonal, religious, or other nontechnical concerns—in short, a society structured by the demands of specialized technical efficiency. This is not to imply that nontechnicalistic societies have no interest in technical efficiency or that technicalistic societies care for nothing else, but only that the unprecedented emphasis on specialized technical considerations has played a key role in the development of modern cultures. The process of technicalization and its ramifications can be seen as central to many of the cultural changes that are taking place in contemporary countries, from the poorest to the most affluent. Some of these changes tend to occur repeatedly in different countries because they are directly related to the process of technicalization; others, such as style of clothing or taste in entertainment, are communicated as part of a growing international cosmopolitan culture. Some changes are predictable and others are not, and some may be fundamental to the technicalization process while others are only incidental to it.

Perhaps the most fundamental elements are economic and technological in nature. The rise of

---

[1] Marshall G. S. Hodgson, *The Venture of Islam,* Vol. 3 (Chicago: University of Chicago Press, 1974), pp. 186–196.

technicalism in Europe was accompanied by certain changes that still seem inseparable from it, and central among these is the institutionalization of technical innovation. The ability to adopt efficient technical innovations was the key to success among the competing private business enterprises of seventeenth- and eighteenth-century Europe, and for that reason traditional European social forces that impeded free scientific inquiry gradually gave way before a cultural outlook that took for granted continuous inquiry and innovation. Such an outlook has had far-reaching consequences in noneconomic realms, but its effect on the techno-economic order has been most immediate. It has led to a rapid development of industrial production, the use of fossil fuels, complex machines, standardized mass production, a highly specialized division of labor and knowledge, and a substantial reinvestment of profits in the machinery of production. This pattern of production has been accompanied by a growth of regional interdependence, so that even nonindustrialized regions tend to become part of a growing network for the exchange of raw materials and manufactured items. This integration may or may not occur on such terms as to facilitate an increase in economic independence and material well-being for a given society; there is nothing in the creation of a world economic system that ensures justice, equality, or a universal advance in well-being.

In addition to its material aspects, the technicalizing trend has had many social and cultural consequences. In society generally, there has been a greater tendency for roles and social status to be achieved rather than ascribed on the basis of gender, age, kinship, or circumstances of birth. The criterion of technical efficiency is applied in politics, where technical competence gradually displaces the more traditional criteria for choosing leaders, while the public becomes increasingly informed and competent in political matters. Mass communication has brought about the possibility of mass public support for political leaders and programs, thus ushering in a new era of participatory politics (or, all too often, active repression of burgeoning popular movements). The institutionalization of change, together with the notion of holding customs and institutions accountable to criteria of technical efficiency, also brings about

new attitudes toward societal rules, which are less likely to be seen as absolute and eternal. And, finally, increased communication and interdependence have helped to create a much more cosmopolitan outlook in which an increasing number of people see themselves, if not as "citizens" of the whole world, at least as actors in it.

The historical reasons for the technicalization of the West are difficult to unravel, but they may include some geographical and ecological components. In fact, some of the ecological conditions that retarded European civilization in earlier history may have aided its more recent rise. Among the most significant factors in the rise of technicalism in the West were the unprecedented importance of capital reinvestment and technological innovation, both of which were being built into the commercial institutions of eighteenth-century Europe. It is possible that entrepreneurial capitalism, which supported this competition for technical efficiency, was discouraged in the older civilizations where irrigation-based agriculture promoted the consolidation of a more centralized governmental control. Europe, by contrast, had an economy based on rainfall agriculture that provided less of a basis for centralized control of the economy, and monarchs and central bureaucracies were therefore less able to thwart and exploit would-be capitalists. The West's economic potential in the eighteenth century may have been bolstered by the fact that it, unlike the land-depleted Middle East, still had virgin countryside into which agricultural production could expand. Whatever the historical reasons for the priority of Europe in making the transition, the West's institutionalization of technical efficiency and technological innovation has done much to determine not only the character of the West itself but of the world order as well.

The West did not set out to conquer the world; rather, each European nation sought to extend its political and economic interests and to protect them, not only from local threats but from other European powers as well. Whatever their nationality, Europeans invariably saw themselves as a progressive people ruling and tutoring the backward segments of humankind, and they were able to support this attitude with a technically efficient military force. Sometimes European domination took the form of direct occupation and political rule; but even when it did not, the pattern of domination remained similar. The European powers intervened as necessary to ensure that local governments kept sufficient order to protect European interests, but not enough power to pose any challenge to European hegemony. Typically, the economic production of the dominated countries was structured to provide a limited range of those raw materials most needed by the dominant power.

In some respects, European cultural domination was just as far-reaching as its political, military, and economic domination. Middle Easterners were classified along with the various Asian peoples as "Orientals," and it was widely held that such people were given to inscrutable peculiarities of thought, blind obedience to tradition, and insensitivity to suffering. Even Middle Eastern nationalism has sometimes been influenced by Western biases in subtle ways; for example, many Middle Easterners have tacitly accepted the classification of themselves as "Orientals," a category that has little meaning except as an expression of European ethnocentrism.

One of the lingering and pervasive effects of Western ethnocentrism is the tendency to confuse "progress" with Westernization, and to hold up middle-class Europe and America as a universal model of "modernity." It is intellectually and morally indefensible to assume that everything non-Western is necessarily backward, especially when much of Western culture comes from a time when Western civilization was less developed than that of the Middle and Far East. Yet it is often tempting, even for the non-Westerner, to equate change with Westernization. The political and economic dominance of the West during the past few centuries has made Westernization a companion of most other changes, so that Westerners and non-Westerners alike sometimes find different types of changes difficult to distinguish from Westernization.

In keeping with the prejudice that Western society sets the course for universal human progress, some Westerners—including certain social theorists—have pictured non-Western societies as stagnant and mired in an unreflective obedience to "tradition." A theoretical view widely accepted a decade or two ago, for example, contrasted the

purportedly inflexible and unimaginative conservatism of the "traditional" Middle Easterner with the open-minded, resourceful, optimistic, and empathetic outlook of the "modernized" person. According to this view, the key to progress and affluence in the Third World is a fundamental change in psychological outlook that comes from exposure to more liberated ways of thinking that originate—of course—in the West. Critics of this now-outdated view have pointed out, with some justice, that it is more self-congratulatory than illuminating. It ignores the great diversity of outlooks that exist within the "traditional" world and the particular historical conditions that have given rise to them. It also overlooks the possibility that cultural attitudes may be understandable responses to political, economic, or ecological realities that cannot be waved away by a change in attitude—realities that include the Western presence itself.

Perhaps the chief oversight of the "modernization" theory, in the context of this book, is its failure to appreciate the political dimensions of human choice in "traditional" settings. Conflict, political strategy, and calculated choice are found in all human societies, even when they result in the reproduction of a relatively stable system— and few if any societies are ever completely stable. Although the Western observer may be tempted by the romantic notion that every "exotic" custom or idea dates from time immemorial, a closer look at cultural history (especially that of the Middle East) reveals a continuous state of flux. The origin and spread of Islam is one good example of the speed and magnitude of change, even in basic beliefs, that can occur in a traditional society. While people everywhere are inclined to accept the beliefs and perspectives with which they were reared, they are everywhere capable of revising and criticizing these traditions when they no longer seem to fill their needs.

While it is true that a "modern" or technicalized setting may present people with a greater range of possibilities than was previously known, it is important not to underestimate the degree to which rational calculation enters into decision making even when "traditional" values are invoked. Indeed, some of the supposed differences between "traditional" and "modern" outlooks may be largely a matter of rhetorical style. For example, a political leader planning the invasion of a neighboring country may seek to justify it in a variety of ways: He may utilize a rationalistic rhetoric that stresses its benefits ("This invasion will bring peace, security, and good government to all concerned"); he may use a traditionalistic rhetoric that looks to the authority of the past ("These people have always been our subjects"); or he may use religious rhetoric ("God will look kindly on us for subduing the infidel"). All these styles of rhetoric have been used throughout history, but the rationalistic style is relatively fashionable in technicalized societies. The use of such rhetoric does not in itself make one's actions particularly reasonable, any more than the use of a religious rhetoric means that one's actions are divinely guided, or a traditionalist rhetoric proves that a given practice is genuinely traditional. It is a mistake, then, to conclude simply from these differences in public rhetoric that one society's motives and actions are in fact more rational than another's.

The perspective of distance almost always makes other cultures look flat, arbitrary, and deterministic compared with our own. Whether we are getting married or getting dressed in the morning, we see our own actions as guided by reason, filled with subtle meaning, and tempered by personal freedom. The corresponding behavior in another culture seems to us simple, stereotyped, and unreflective. "We" put on neckties because we think, and "they" put on turbans because they don't—or so it seems. Yet close studies of traditional peoples have shown them to be more critically aware of circumstances and choices than is commonly assumed. Quite often, behavior that appears motivated by blind conservatism turns out instead to be based on a realistic assessment of the alternatives; thus many people are quite capable of grasping the significance of changing circumstances and are able to adapt to them accordingly. Such choices, however, must always be made within the framework of existing institutions and guided by existing values and assumptions about the nature and purpose of human existence. These values and assumptions are deeply rooted in the cultural heritage of a people; this is as true of the West as it is of the Middle East, and it helps account for the continuing role of religion in both settings. For that reason we have adopted two basic strategies in presenting the material. First, we shall heavily emphasize the historical forces that have shaped the Middle East. To understand what the Middle East is and what it might be requires that one know what it was. The chapters dealing with the history of past centuries, therefore, are best viewed as part of the present landscape and not as a separate story. Second, since the politics of the Middle East are woven together with general social and economic forces, a multidisciplinary approach has been adopted—an approach facilitated by the diversity of the authors' academic training in political science, economics, and cultural anthropology.

Political affairs in the Middle East are treated here as the product of the interaction among social organization, secular values, religion, and the control and allocation of authority and resources at all levels. While the variables must sometimes be isolated for analysis, to remove them permanently from their context is to invite misunderstanding.

CHAPTER ONE

Traditional Cultures of the Middle East

The Cradle of Civilization and Politics

In dealing with "exotic" peoples and cultures, we often form stereotypical images, based on some grain of truth but containing enough distortion and error to make them useless and often even harmful. Popular images of the Middle East are a case in point.

The Middle East is no stranger to the Western imagination. It is the setting of the Jewish and Christian Holy Scriptures. We derive our images of the Middle East partly from these Scriptures and the Hollywood images spun around them, and partly from the news reports of current events. The Middle East is often seen as the primeval wilderness from which our civilization sprang—a wilderness that has since lapsed into timeless stagnation. In the popular imagination it is inhabited mainly by fierce desert nomads who, driven by a childlike attachment to tradition and the fiery narrowness of the barbaric "Mohammedan" faith, spend most of their time menacing each other and impeding peace and progress. With alarming regularity the "Arab" is depicted in film and on television as regressive, sex-crazed, violent, and sinister. News coverage highlights "terrorism," oil profiteering, and other supposed threats, casting Middle Easterners as odious but ineffectual enemies. Thus, we form a composite picture of the

Arab (and all native Middle Easterners are commonly thought to be Arabs) as an evil buffoon. However, the popular notion of the Middle East as a geographic and cultural backwater inhabited by ignorant fanatics is incompatible with even the most elementary knowledge of Middle Eastern culture and history.

Besides the need to dispel these common prejudices, there are several reasons why a look at traditional Middle Eastern culture is useful. For one, it provides a backdrop against which to understand the historical development of innovative social, religious, and political institutions in the region. Furthermore, it allows us better to understand those aspects of contemporary Middle Eastern life that still retain substantial continuity with past traditions. The Middle East today, like any region of the world, has constructed its modern institutions on a base of traditional social arrangements, values, philosophical assumptions, and everyday practices that are deeply rooted in a cultural heritage. And unlike most of the Western world, the Middle East contains regions, or aspects of social life, whose continuity with the lifestyle of two or three centuries ago is in some respects more apparent than are the recent influences of a cosmopolitan, "technicalized" cultural milieu. One must be careful, however, not to fall into the common Eurocentric bias of thinking that all non-Western practices are ancient and lacking in developmental change—a habit of thought encouraged by referring to "tradition" as though it represented some timeless eternality. Except when it is otherwise clear from the context, we shall use the term *traditional* to refer very generally to patterns of social and cultural life that prevailed in the few centuries prior to the massive incursion of European influence and technicalizing changes. But as we shall see, such cultural features are in many respects part and parcel of historical patterns that reach further back and further forward in time.

Contrary to the above-mentioned Western stereotypes about the region, the most significant historical features of the Middle East were not marginality and simplicity, but centrality and diversity. The centrality of the Middle East in history was partly the product of its strategic location at the junction of the three continents of Africa, Asia, and Europe and its consequent pivotal role in trade, conquest, communication, and migration. Middle Eastern cultural diversity has been aided by local geography and by the complexities of cultural adaptation in the region.

The geographical diversity of the Middle East, which depends largely on the relative availability of water, is striking. Although the "desert" image is correct in that the region is predominantly arid, there are sharp contrasts. The Nile Valley and the "Fertile Crescent" of the Tigris-Euphrates region and Mediterranean coast were the sites of the first known farming civilizations and the sources of the images of Eden and of the Land of Milk and Honey. These geographical contrasts have led to diverse but interlocking ways of life suited to different strategies of survival and adaptation.

Another factor contributing to diversity in the Middle East is the region's long and complex cultural evolution. Prior to about 10,000 B.C., all the world's peoples were gatherers of wild foods; the domestication of plants and animals—which set human culture on its path of increasing complexity—originated in the Middle East at about that time. During the ensuing twelve millennia, the Middle East has ranked in the vanguard of social and technological evolution more consistently

than any other region of the world. It is from the Middle East that Europe received not only its basic agricultural crops and techniques, but indeed all the most fundamental social and cultural elements we associate with "civilization," including literacy, urban life, and occupational specialization.

It is especially interesting, in view of this book's political theme, that the Middle East was the site of the earliest states and formal governments. Partly because of the organizational requirements of irrigation systems, the independent villages of the region were soon encompassed in regional forms of political organization, in which the village-dwelling farmers became "peasants" dominated by a nonfarming urban ruling class. This ruler–producer split was the foundation of the state, since it facilitated, through various forms of taxation, a substantial amount of *surplus production*—that is, production that exceeded the subsistence needs of the farming population. This surplus subsidized the power of the state and ultimately allowed the existence of an urban population engaged in various occupations not directly associated with agricultural production, a necessary condition for the specialized accomplishments of "civilized" peoples. The necessity of enforcing peasant taxation and protecting the prerogatives of the ruling classes, regulating trade and exchange, and generally mediating social relationships in an increasingly complicated society gave rise to what we now take for granted as the political apparatus of the state: legal codes, police and military forces, courts, and other instruments of "law and order."

The role of the Middle East in political innovation did not end with the early civilizations; the region was also the birthplace of three world religions, each involving unique contributions to social thought. Yet despite the leadership of the Middle East in political and social development, the region has long been characterized by social conservatism. The everyday lives of most peasants, nomads, and townspeople have until recently been little affected by intellectual and organizational advances in the larger society; instead, these lifestyles have been woven into the fabric of an increasingly complicated plural society.

FOUNDATIONS OF SOCIAL DIVERSITY

While the American "melting pot" ideology views cultural diversity as an accidental and temporary byproduct of history, such diversity has been an enduring and valued part of life in the Middle East. Middle Eastern culture is characterized not only by diversity but also by *pluralism*—the maintenance of diversity as a significant aspect of the social system. The use of cultural diversity, or pluralism, as a structuring principle in society has led some writers to characterize social life in this region as a "mosaic." This mosaic character is particularly difficult to describe because it follows no simple pigeonhole scheme but includes many dimensions, levels, and criteria of variation that often cut across one another. These include six important dimensions of variability and identity that together have shaped much of the character of traditional life in the Middle East: (1) ecological pluralism, (2) regional and local ethnic pluralism, (3) religion, (4) family and tribe, (5) occupational groups, and (6) class distinctions. Although it is sometimes useful to discuss these criteria separately, the reader should remember that in practice they are partly dependent on one another.

Ecological Diversity

Of the many elements that contribute to social diversity in the Middle East, one of the most basic is the relation of people to the land. The vicissitudes of wind patterns, rainfall, and river courses, combined with the effects of irrigation systems, often lead to stark contrasts in the land and its potential uses. In parts of Egypt, for example, a railroad track divides a verdant field producing two or three crops a year from a desert so barren as to discourage even Bedouin herders. Although the arable regions constitute less than 10 percent of the land in the Middle East, their role in the economic and social order of the region has been of the utmost importance since prehistoric times. For several thousand years, since the beginnings of the state and its associated intensive agricultural techniques, a large portion of Middle Eastern farmland and an even larger portion of the farming population and agricultural produce have depended on irrigation systems.

The nonagricultural lands that make up the bulk of the Middle East are by no means uniform in character. Some of these are forested mountain slopes; others are arid steppes capable of supporting nomads with their herds of camels, sheep, or goats; still other regions, like the "empty quarter" of Arabia or Egypt's Western Desert, support virtually no human populations at all. Water is the crucial resource in all these regions, and the utility of a territory inhabited by a group of camel nomads, for example, may change from year to year, day to day, and mile to mile according to variations in rainfall or groundwater. The importance of water is illustrated by the fact that a permanent well, hardly worth noticing in more watered parts of the world, determined the location of the early Arab trading settlement of Mecca, later to become the birthplace of Islam and the spiritual homeland of Muslims around the world.

The geographic division between the desert and the arable lands is a recurrent phenomenon throughout the Middle East, and it has been accompanied by a threefold social division that also spanned the entire region: the division between peasants, nomads, and townspeople. Peasants, who composed as much as three-quarters of the population, were engaged directly in agricultural production and lived in the small, simple villages that dotted the cultivable countryside. Nomads were also engaged in primary economic production, based on the husbandry of camels, sheep, goats, or cattle, usually in those regions incapable of supporting agricultural production. Urbanites, on the other hand, were engaged not in primary food production but in other, more specialized occupations traditionally ranging from government, scholarship, or priestly functions to crafts, peddling, and begging, and more recently including modern industrial, service, and other business pursuits.

Nomads

Nomadic herders captivate the imaginations of Middle Easterner and foreigner alike, and often tend to be seen by both (and by nomads themselves) as the "purest" expression of the region's cultural tradition. In fact, the nomads have been economically and politically marginal throughout most of history, and are becoming more so today. While nomads have traditionally been the sole inhabitants of the region's nonarable land, their population has never been more than a small fraction of the total for the region (in recent times probably less than 15 percent of the population). Nomadic herding was not practiced in the intensive farming regions, and in transitional regions it was combined with village farming. The forms of nomadism varied according to the capacity of the land, which in turn depended on water. Semiarid steppes supported cattle, sheep, and goats, while the true desert sustained only camel nomads such as the **Bedouins** of Arabia. The camel nomads, for all their aristocratic airs, were confined to the most marginal lands, those unusable to anyone else. Their place in politics has been a complex one. They have traditionally been admired for their independence, virility, and simple virtue, and the fourteenth-century Arab sociologist Ibn Khaldoun took note of their role in periodically taking over and revitalizing the leadership of Islamic states, drawing on their qualities of military discipline and tribal solidarity. It is also true, however, that the political influence of nomads was only sporadic, and that much of the time they were peripheral to the sources of state power. In recent decades, national governments have tried to control nomads by promoting their settlement in sedentary communities.

The ruggedness and apparent simplicity of nomadic life have led to the widespread misconception that it was the oldest and most primitive lifestyle of the Middle East and that it involved complete independence from the more settled and sophisticated life of the cities and villages. This was not strictly true, for nomadic herders traditionally depended on settled communities for manufactured items and agricultural products, which they obtained by trading their animal products, and, prior to the control of the modern state, by raiding the villages. When drought made herding less feasible, some nomads were able to shift temporarily or permanently to a more settled life in the city or village. The camel nomadism of the desert has existed only since the introduction of the camel in about 2000 B.C.; even the herding of sheep and goats, which originated much earlier, depended to some extent on the existence of settled populations and probably did not predate them as a general stage of development.

Of all the nomads in the Middle East, the Arab Bedouin has occupied a position of special significance. The Bedouins are Arabian camel nomads who constitute only one of the many nomadic groups in the Middle East, yet they have played a unique role in the cultural consciousness of the region. Prior to the birth of the Prophet Muhammad, the Arabs (that is, the original speakers of Arabic) were a collection of tribes occupying central Arabia. Many were camel nomads, and the others were sailors, caravanners, and townspeople who traced descent from nomadic herders. Islam facilitated the spread of Arabic as the daily language of much of the Middle East and the holy language of all Muslims, and with it came some measure of identification with the Arab Bedouin heritage. Thus, despite the ambivalence that urbanites and villagers have often felt toward the fierce and "lawless" inhabitants of the desert, the Bedouins were at the same time acknowledged as the "truest" Arabs. (In Arabic the term *Arab* refers, in the strictest usage, only to the Bedouin.) A Cairo shopkeeper might underscore his business integrity by referring to his (literal or figurative) Bedouin heritage, and the desert outside modern Riyadh is periodically dotted with the tents of Saudi urbanites celebrating their recent Bedouin past with weekend campouts.

Peasants and Urbanites

Despite the common perception of pastoral nomadism as the primeval Middle Eastern lifestyle, peasants and traditional city dwellers carried on an equally old and well-established pattern of life, one with roots in the early civilizations of Egypt and Mesopotamia. We have pointed out that the historical relation between village-dwelling peasants and urbanites depended on a political organization that taxed the village-dwelling farmers, thus subsidizing the ruling class in particular and the nonfarming urban populations in general. The development of the state, then, entailed two divergent ways of life, the urban and the rural, each of which existed as a result of the other. (In this context, "city" and "urban" refer to permanent settlements of any size whose populace consists primarily of nonfarmers—as opposed to a rural peasant "village" whose inhabitants walk daily to their farms.) From the perspective of the traditional Middle Eastern state, the peasant village existed for the purpose of delivering its tax quota in the form of agricultural produce, money, labor, or some combination of these. For their taxes the villagers rarely, if ever, received such government services as police protection, education, or public works. As long as the village headman delivered the taxes, the village was left to govern itself. Internally, the village was relatively homogeneous, consisting of peasants who exercised little influence on the politics of the state that governed their lives, and who had few, if any, opportunities for social mobility.

Although modern Middle Eastern states are generally committed to changing these conditions, life in peasant villages retains a continuity with the past. Many villagers are still small landholders, sharecroppers, or landless laborers. Each village is divided into families and blocks of related families, and is headed by a patriarch of the most influential family, whose authority is shared with other village elders. Like the nomads, the peasants have been led by the conditions of their lives to a distinctive worldview. Unlike the nomads, whose traditional values emphasized militant independence, peasants were typically fearful of authority, distrustful of the world outside the village (and often of their own neighbors), and pessimistic with regard to social change. The unenviable position of peasants led traditional urbanites and nomads alike to despise them as "slaves of the soil" while continuing to depend on them for the production of basic foodstuffs.

If popular conceptions of the Middle East give undue attention to the nomads because of their romantic image, "historical" treatments of the region tend to place great emphasis on the towns and cities as the locus of rulers and their "high" culture, the source of written documents on which historical scholarship largely depends. Traditional urban life in the Middle East does not lend itself easily to general description, because urbanites were involved in a great variety of occupations

and modes of living. The traditional Middle Eastern cities were, among other things, seats of local and regional government. As such, they were home to political elites and their retinue, including military commanders, civil and legal authorities, government bureaucrats, and religious leaders. In addition to those involved in government, traditional urban life also involved a middle class of merchants, artisans, professionals, and petty officials. The least affluent and least prestigious urbanites were peddlers, laborers, and sometimes beggars. In addition to its role in political and religious leadership, the city has traditionally been a center of crafts and trade, with the **suq**, or bazaar, serving as a distribution point for manufactured wares as well as for the products of the farmers and nomads. Many traditional cities also became producers of wealth in their own right by virtue of their profitable involvement in the trade between Europe, Asia, and Africa.

Although many aspects of traditional Middle Eastern urban life were as ancient as the lifestyles of the village and desert, *ancient* does not imply *simple*. Life in Middle Eastern towns and cities reached a high degree of sophistication and complexity millennia ago. Some urban centers, such as Jericho and Damascus, were already ancient in biblical times. Others, like Baghdad and Cairo, were founded more than a thousand years ago as seats of government and represent landmark achievements in urban planning. Today, of course, Middle Eastern cities are also hubs of modern industrial and commercial activity; yet in many ways the old continues to exist alongside the new.

Ethnic and Religious Diversity

The ecological pluralism of nomads, peasants, and townspeople was only one dimension of traditional cultural diversity, the others being ethnic, religious, familial, occupational, and social class distinctions. Ethnic differences, or differences in historical descent and cultural heritage, have existed both between and within regions. Vast regions of the Middle East are set apart from others by their distinctive language and culture, the most prominent example being the division between the speakers of Turkish, Persian, and Arabic. Each of these groups occupies a major contiguous portion of the Middle East, and each correctly conceives of itself as having distinct cultural roots. The extent of their historical divergence is suggested by the languages themselves, which are classified into different families and differ from one another more than English does from Persian. These regional groups have also exhibited major differences in values, outlook, details of social organization, and, to some extent, religion.

The ethnic diversity of the Middle East would be relatively easy to discuss if it were confined to regional divisions, but the vicissitudes of history have brought about a more complex situation, since migrations have created much cultural diversity within regions. It is difficult to say whether the Middle East has seen more migrations than other regions or whether these are simply better documented due to the region's long tradition of literacy. Waterways and seafaring, land trade, the nomadic ways of some of the inhabitants, and the existence of organized states bent on conquest have all contributed to the physical mobility of peoples. We find, for example, the Sumerians appearing rather suddenly more than 6,000 years ago in the lower Mesopotamian region, creating the world's first literate civilization, and then fading from the scene to be displaced and eclipsed by peoples of other backgrounds. The Jews historically occupied several parts of the Middle East, including Egypt and Palestine, and then many dispersed from the region only to return in this century. During the long career of the Islamic state, Arab ruling classes spread their influence from Spain to Persia; Egyptians were ruled by resident Turks; and much of the region found itself under the sword of Asian Mongols, while the ethnically diverse elites of the Islamic world sought refuge in Muslim India. While such migration resulted in a considerable amount of cultural assimilation, it also gave rise to multiple ethnic communities within regions.

What is especially striking about local ethnic diversity, from the viewpoint of the outsider, is that these ethnic differences have been institutionalized as a stable feature of traditional Middle Eastern life. One reason for this is that ethnic distinctions have often been reinforced by other kinds of traditional diversity, such as religion, occupation, and social status.

Descent, Occupation, and Social Stratification

The traditional importance of family, kinship, and common descent in the Middle East is difficult for a Westerner to appreciate. While the European or American considers the individual to be the basic functioning unit of society, the individual has had relatively little autonomous importance in the traditional Middle East, or for that matter, in most traditional societies. Instead, the individual's status, privileges, obligations, identity, and morality were inextricably tied to the descent group. Traditionally, the minimal descent unit was the extended family, whose structure we shall discuss in the following section. The extended family was part of a larger group of related families, the lineage (in Arabic, *hamula*). The families of a nomadic hamula pitched their tents together, and among sedentary villagers the hamula was (and is) likely to be represented by a clustering of residences. The hamula has served, among other things, as a political unit that resolved internal disputes between families and represented their interests to the outside world. Sometimes the lineages were further united into a "tribe." Each of these units was based on the notion of shared ancestry from some patrilineal founder. The idea of common descent remains important in the contemporary Middle East, and as in the past it extends to larger groupings: All Arabs consider themselves as having a common descent, and for that matter the Jews, Christians, and Muslim Arabs together are thought to share common ancestors in the biblical patriarchs. The more specific and immediate the common descent, the more relevant it is to one's personal obligations and identity. It is hardly surprising, in view of the practical importance of descent, that ethnic groups within a particular region are in no hurry to obliterate their distinctive ancestry.

Another important factor in maintaining ethnic distinctions has been their connection with occupation. In the traditional Middle East, one's occupation was quite often determined by one's family background. Of course, the matter of occupation was relatively simple for the child of a Bedouin or peasant family, but it was scarcely less so for the son of an urban artisan. Membership in organizations that controlled crafts and trades was frequently passed from father to son, as was the requisite training. Since occupation was largely ascribed rather than achieved, certain trades frequently became associated with certain ethnic groups. The continuing relationship of descent to occupation was dramatized in practical terms when, after the formation of Israel, the exodus of the Jewish population of Yemen left the country virtually bereft of blacksmiths, bricklayers, and practitioners of certain other trades traditionally followed by this ethnic group.

As the above example shows, ethnic differences have often been associated with religious affiliation, reflecting differences both within and between the three major religions of the Middle East. Whole regions may be characterized by a predominant religion, as in the concentrations of **Shia** Islam in Iran and parts of Iraq. Many minority religions are also concentrated in specific regions, as with the Christian Copts of Egypt. The integrity of the non-Muslim groups has been reinforced on the local level by the traditional Muslim practice of allowing minority religious communities protection and self-government in return for their recognition of Muslim hegemony.

A final type of social diversity is the division of socioeconomic classes. Since the origin of the earliest states, Middle Eastern society has been stratified into classes that enjoy varying degrees of privilege and wealth. These distinctions are relatively subdued in the countryside, but are quite apparent in the cities, where lifestyles span the extremes from poverty to opulence. Distinctions of class are of course tied in various complex ways to family background, ethnicity, occupation, and ecological situation.

The Patchwork of Pluralism:
Two Historical Examples

Traditional Middle Eastern society, we have argued, was a complex tapestry in which ecological, ethnic, family, tribal, occupational, and class factors were interwoven. The complex way in which these dimensions intertwined can be seen in two different examples of traditional life: the city of Mecca in Muhammad's day, and the Bedouin camp.

The city of Mecca, as Muhammad knew it in about A.D. 600, forms the backdrop of major historical events that we shall discuss in the following chapter. It had been founded two centuries earlier by a tribe of Bedouins who had shifted from nomadism to trading and had located their settlement at the site of a permanent water supply and the junction of two major trade routes. Their social organization and worldview still bore the stamp of Bedouin life, yet even this budding town had begun to manifest a more urban sort of complexity. The formerly egalitarian founding tribe had differentiated into richer and poorer divisions, and the more favored displayed the trappings of aristocracy. Some families of this tribe had begun to control and monopolize religious worship, a practice in which shrines played a large role. Attached to the ruling tribe were subordinate "client" groups, and below them were slaves. The range of occupations was considerable, and many were interwoven with specific ethnic backgrounds. One author makes reference to "Syrian caravan leaders; travelling monks and curers; Syrian merchants; foreign smiths and healers; Copt carpenters; Negro idol sculptors; Christian doctors, surgeons, dentists and scribes; Abyssinian sailors and mercenaries."[1] It should be kept in mind that Mecca was at this time a relatively new and modest-sized trade settlement, a mere upstart in comparison with the more established seats of Middle Eastern government.

Even the traditional Bedouin camp was hardly the simple affair one might expect. In fact, such a camp was likely to include representatives of as many as half a dozen non-Bedouin groups, each performing a separate function as defined by various criteria of descent and cultural tradition. While the Bedouin extended family owned the livestock, the camel herders themselves might

---

[1]Eric R. Wolf, "Social Organization of Mecca and the Origins of Islam," *Southwestern Journal of Anthropology,* VII (1951), 336–337.

have come from another, less "noble" group that lent its services as a form of tribute to the Bedouins, who in turn took the responsibility of fighting to protect the herds from other Bedouin raiders. Members of another ethnic group, the Sulaba, whom some anthropologists recognize as the most ancient inhabitants of the desert, served as desert guides, coppersmiths, leatherworkers, and in various other specified functions. The Sunna, members of a group said to be of partly African origin, served as blacksmiths. African slaves were also part of an affluent Bedouin household; well dressed and well fed, they were reputed to be fierce fighters in defense of their masters' herds. Two sorts of traders were also likely to be found in the Bedouin camp. One of these was the Kubaisi, an ambulatory shopkeeper who supplied the camp with a variety of merchandise; the name is derived from a town on the Euphrates from which at least some such merchants traditionally came. Finally, the 'Aqaili, usually a member of the tribe of 'Aquil, bought camels on behalf of urban firms in return for cash and rifles. In this complex scheme, the Bedouins served primarily as soldiers and protectors, engaging in raids against other Bedouins, defending the group against such raids, and granting safe conduct across their territory.[2]

UNITY IN DIVERSITY

As we have seen, the cultural pluralism of the traditional Middle East was set in a context of unity and integration. The ties that bound diverse segments of society into an integrated whole were based on two principles: the functional interdependence and complementarity of unlike parts; and certain overarching similarities of culture, social organization, and religion.

Traditional nomads, peasants, and urbanites were by no means autonomous groups, nor were they necessarily set apart by competition, although conflicts of interest certainly have occurred between them. Bedouins have depended on peasants for agricultural products and on townspeople for manufactured goods. In the past, they often exacted tribute from peasant villages, sold protec-

tion to caravans, and acted as middlemen in trade. The existence of cities and villages was a further convenience when climate or other factors forced Bedouins into settled life, just as the opposite movement often occurred when conditions were reversed. Although prior to the twentieth century the Bedouins were rarely subject to the sort of constraint and taxation the state would have liked to impose, neither were they entirely exempt from state control. Peasants, on the other hand, were always under direct state rule, which set the conditions that governed their lives. Despite internal village self-government, peasants were expected not only to fill their tax quotas but also to obey all laws of the state, over which they had little say. The peasants were also, as noted above, subject to raiding and tribute demands from nomads. It is difficult to say in what ways the peasants benefited from others, since exchanges between them and urbanites or Bedouins were typically out of their control and somewhat in their disfavor. Just the same, the towns did provide manufactured items and markets where certain of the peasants' needs could be provided for, and the state provided, in principle, military protection.

Because they were not engaged directly in food production, urbanites were in a sense the most dependent of all. Like all urban populations they ultimately depended on the rural production of food and raw materials directed into the towns through taxation and trade. In the Middle East the situation was complicated by the presence of the Bedouins, since the urban marketplace served as an intermediary between two modes of rural production. Clearly the divisions among occupational specialties, like those among ecological niches, have been characterized by economic interdependence and complementarity.

We must also not forget that the Middle East possesses overarching cultural similarities that in some measure unite all its people. If one's identity as an Arab, for example, implies separation from Persians, Turks, Berbers, and Kurds, it also implies a unity of outlook and identity with many millions of other Arabs. Cultural similarity, however, transcends even these broad regional and ethnic groupings; significant features of culture and social organization have traditionally united all Middle Easterners. A list of these features would

---

[2]Carleton S. Coon, *Caravan: The Story of the Middle East* (Huntington, N.Y.: Robert E. Krieger Co., 1976), pp. 191–210.

be very long and would range from the threefold ecological system mentioned above to particulars of material culture like the use of the black hair tent among nomads throughout the region. Most significant, however, are similarities in traditional social organization and cultural values that underlie the region's diverse social types.

Family, Kinship, and Marriage

Throughout the Middle East the traditional family has had a similar structure and function. It was patrilineal—that is, it traced descent principally through the male line. Wives were expected to take up residence with their husbands after marriage. The traditional family was strongly patriarchal, remaining intact until the death of the father, at which time each of the sons became a family head. Typically, then, such a family consisted of three generations of men and their wives, and any unmarried daughters or sisters. The traditionally preferred form of marriage among Muslims is between a man and his father's brother's daughter. Although there are conflicting reports on the actual frequency of such cousin marriages, Muslim marriages do tend to favor patrilineal relatives. The Middle Eastern family has long served as the basic unit for holding property in the form of farmland, herds, or smaller business enterprises; it thus acquired a fundamental economic significance.

The importance of kinship in traditional society did not end with the family. Peasant villagers, townspeople, and nomads alike recognized larger kin groupings among related families. Among the nomads and their recent descendants, these groupings have often been extended to a tribal organization. Tribes varied in size from a single band to a powerful and influential group encompassing numerous bands. Relations among the men of each tribe were relatively egalitarian, leadership being based on the "first among equals" principle. There were frequently, however, marked differences of social standing, or "nobility," among tribes, to the extent that marriage to members of lesser tribes was sometimes forbidden. Today, as in the past, it is in the nomad and nomad-derived groups and their tribal organizations that one finds the strongest development of blood feuds, collective responsibility, group honor or "face" (Arabic:

wajh), and strict rules governing hospitality and sanctuary. (These will be discussed further in the following chapter.)

Traditional marriage and sex mores have shown considerable persistence in much of the Middle East. Despite recent trends to the contrary, marriage is still often arranged by parents, being seen more as a relationship between kin groups than one between individuals. An effort was usually made to match mates in terms of social prestige and background. The traditional position of women was, on the whole, one of subordination to men. Compared with the West, a greater emphasis is still placed on female chastity, purity, modesty, and even complete seclusion and veiling. As in the past (but now for somewhat different reasons), veiling and seclusion tend to be practiced most often among urban elites. The conduct of women has generally been thought to reflect on the honor of the patrilineal family, and men are vulnerable to dishonor by the conduct of their daughters, sisters, or wives. Muslim law permits as many as four wives, but while multiple marriages are a sign of affluence, they have always been infrequent in actual practice. Traditionally, Muslim males could initiate divorce more easily than women could. But despite the patriarchal bias that it shares with other Middle Eastern religions, Islamic law has allowed remarriage of divorced women, ensured women a share in the inheritance of property, and protected their right to own property separately from their husbands. Today, traditional ideas about marriage, the family, and the position of women are being modified in some quarters in response to new interpretations of Islam, as well as secular ideas of individualism, women's rights, and romantic love.

Religion

Of all the factors that unify Middle Eastern culture, none is so fundamental as religion. The Middle East is the birthplace of the three major monotheistic religions: Judaism, Christianity, and Islam; the vast majority of Middle Easterners today, however, are Muslims, or adherents of Islam. This is significant not only because of the unifying influence of one ubiquitous religion, but also because that religion has a remarkably pervasive influence on social and cultural life. Islam permeates the daily life and social norms of the vast majority of the Middle Eastern population that is Muslim. It is a religion whose stated aim at the time of its inception in the early seventh century was the unity of all people into a single social and spiritual community, and it succeeded to a noteworthy degree. Islam brought unprecedented political, intellectual, and spiritual unity to the Middle East and made the region a hub of world power for a thousand years. How and why this happened is the subject of the following chapter.

CHAPTER TWO

The Foundations of Islam

Through the dusty streets of a middle-class residential neighborhood in Cairo echo the sounds of dawn: The first vendors are calling their wares, their chants accompanied by the clopping of hooves and the rattling of cart wheels. Blended with these is a more haunting but equally familiar sound, a singsong of Arabic from the loudspeakers on the minaret of a small local **mosque**:

> God is most great.
> I testify there is no deity but God.
> I testify that Muhammad is the Messenger of God.
> Come to Prayer;
> Come to Salvation . . .

It is the same message that five times daily has called the faithful to prayer in Cairo and its predecessors for more than 1,300 years. That same message, in the same Arabic, emanates from mosques as far away as West Africa and Indonesia, calling one-fifth of the world's population (only a minority of whom are Middle Easterners or Arabs) to pray toward their spiritual homeland in Mecca. The religion of Islam, signified by this call to prayer, is central to an understanding of the Middle East's most salient features—its historical and contemporary influence on other parts of the world, the unity of belief and commitment that counteracts some of its bitterest political divisions, and the religious vitality that infuses every aspect of its social, cultural, and political life.

Ninety-five percent of all Middle Easterners are Muslims, followers of the faith of Islam. For them, religion is not a matter separable from daily life or confined to certain times and places; it is the foundation of all ethics, morality, and family life—ultimately, the blueprint for a righteous and satisfying life. Dismayed by the secularism of both the capitalist and the communist ideologies, Muslims see Islam as an essential element that gives direction to their social aspirations and saves them from the dissipation and immorality they see in the West. They are also keenly aware of Islam's success as a world religion—a religion that has always aimed at the social unity of the entire community of believers, that has led the Middle East to a position of considerable historical influence, and that provided the foundations of a civilization that for many centuries surpassed that of Europe.

CENTRAL BELIEFS OF ISLAM

For the Muslim, Islam is at its root nothing more nor less than the complete acceptance of God and submission to His will. The very word *Islam* means "submission," and *Muslim* means "one who submits." The most important step toward this submission is the recognition that there is only one God, the God of Abraham and Moses, of Christians and Jews as well as Muslims, whose name in Arabic is Allah. Muslims believe that they alone have accepted God completely, and that all their beliefs follow from this acceptance. According to the teachings of Islam, a complete acceptance of God entails recognition of His absolute oneness; a Muslim must reject not only other gods but all alleged "associates" of God, including offspring and other semidivine personages. Christians, they feel, have compromised their monotheism by mistaking one of God's prophets for the "son" of God. The acceptance of God also requires belief in all of God's messages through all His appointed messengers, including not only Jesus and the Old Testament prophets, but also—and most significantly—the seventh-century Arab prophet Muhammad. It is through Muhammad, the "seal of the prophets," that God has sent His final and most comprehensive revelations, placed on the lips of Muhammad by God and recorded in the Holy Scripture, the Koran. Since true belief in God means acceptance of His final revelations, the Muslim declaration of faith (the **shahada**) testifies that "There is no God but Allah, and Muhammad is His prophet." Such a declaration is sufficient to make a person a Muslim, but the conscientious pursuit of the faith demands much more.

The Five Pillars of Islam

Muslims recognize five fundamental ritual obligations that make up the "pillars" of their religion. The first and most important of these is the declaration of faith mentioned above. The second is prayer, which ought to be performed five times a day (before dawn, at noon, in late afternoon, just after sunset, and in mid-evening), facing in the direction of the **Kaaba**, the holy shrine in Mecca. Prayer may be performed anywhere, but the preferred situation is with other Muslims in a special place of worship, the mosque. Prayer involves a complex series of preparations, prescribed movements, and phrases. The most important prayer time is Friday noon, when Muslims participate in a formal service under the direction of a prayer leader (**imam**), who reads from the Koran and may also deliver a sermon and discuss matters of public interest.

The third pillar of Islam is the giving of alms, either in the form of **zakat**, a fixed amount used to meet the needs of the religious community and provide for the welfare of its members, or as a voluntary contribution (**sadaqa**), which brings religious merit to the donor.

The fourth pillar of Islam is fasting during the daylight hours of the month of **Ramadan**. While Islam is not an ascetic religion, Muslims view the abstention from food, liquids, smoking, and sexual relations as a celebration of moral commitment, healthy self-discipline, and religious atonement. Since Ramadan is a lunar month, it rotates through the seasons; and the abstention from food or water from dawn to dusk of a summer day is no small sacrifice. At the same time, it is typical of Islam's relatively practical orientation that the very young, the elderly, the sick, and even the traveler are exempted, at least temporarily, from this obligation.

The fifth and final ritual obligation of Islam, the pilgrimage to Mecca, falls only on those members of a Muslim community whose health and resources permit them to fulfill it. It is a great honor to make the **hajj**, or pilgrimage, and those who have done so carry the honorific title of **hajji**. The center of the pilgrimage is a shrine in Mecca said to have been founded by Abraham. The pilgrimage draws together, both physically and spiritually, persons from various national and cultural backgrounds who represent the farthest reaches of Islam. During the pilgrimage, however, all participants shed the marks of their nationality and social position and don the plain white cloak that signifies the equality of every Muslim before God.

The Koran and the Hadith

The ritual obligations of Islam, important as they are, are only the outward expressions of the system of belief that underlies Muslim life. When

Muslims accept the oneness of God and the validity of Muhammad's revelations as the word of God, they also accept certain sources of authority for religious truth. Foremost among these is the written record of Muhammad's revelations, the **Koran**. The Koran is said to be the exact word, and even the exact language, of God. Approximately as long as the New Testament, the Koran is composed of a series of chapters, or **suras**, of varying length. If we were to compare it with the literary forms familiar to the American reader, it more closely resembles a book of poetry than a narrative or a continuous essay. In fact, the Koran in the original Arabic (the form in which Muslims of all nations know it) is regarded as a masterpiece of poetic literature as well as religion. Its subject matter ranges from terse warnings about the Day of Judgment to long discourses on marriage, inheritance, the treatment of non-Muslim minorities, and the duties of each Muslim in spreading the faith. Of the Koran's message on these points we shall have more to say later in this chapter.

A second source of divine authority is the collection of sayings and practices attributed to the Prophet. The Prophet's personal utterances were not, like the Koran, a direct recitation of God's words, but they are thought to have been informed by the Prophet's divine inspiration. Muslim religious scholars recognize that not all these reports (**hadith**) about the Prophet are equally reliable, and much effort has been devoted to tracing their sources and evaluating their accuracy. Even so, there exist various hadith that can, like the holy texts of other religions, be used to support widely differing positions on many issues. There are several recognized schools of Muslim law that differ on the degree to which analogy, scholarly interpretation, social consensus, and established custom might be used to supplement the Koran and the hadith, but all agree that these two sources together form the basis of the Muslim social and legal code (**Sharia**). In principle, they apply to every life situation that a believer might encounter and provide a guide for every sort of decision.

The Ulema

Since Islam teaches the equality of every believer before God, there are, at least in orthodox **Sunni** Islam, no clergy to act as intercessors with the divine. On the other hand, the emphasis on written texts has given rise to an important class of religious scholars, the **ulema**, who collectively advise the community and its political rulers according to God's word. To the extent that most traditional education in Muslim societies is religious in nature, the ulema have filled the role of academics and teachers; to the extent that Islam recognizes no ultimate division of religion and state, the ulema have been not only legal and political thinkers but a political force in their own right. This is true in the contemporary Muslim world, where Cairo's Al-Azhar, the center of Muslim high scholarship, is also an international forum for the discussion of contemporary issues of Muslim politics and social values.

Unlike most Far Eastern religions, which generally try to divorce themselves from the flow of historical events, Islam resembles Judaism and Christianity in its explicit involvement with society and history. Although it is the ultimate concern of individual Muslims to prepare themselves for the Day of Judgment, that preparation takes worldly form in the pursuit of a just and righteous social life. Perhaps even more than Judaism and Christianity, Islam is intimately concerned with specific social relations and institutions. Our discussion of Islam will therefore take the form of a historical account. Islam arose in a particular social setting, and it directly addressed social problems related to that setting. One of the paradoxes of Islam is that while it goes beyond most other religions in specific references to the cultural institutions of its original setting, it has spread to encompass an astonishing variety of peoples and cultures without sacrificing the relevance of its original precepts. In so doing it has followed a remarkable path of adaptiveness balanced with continuity, operating in some contexts as a revolutionary force and in others as a source of stability and cohesion, or, when its practitioners have seen fit to use it so, as a source of deep conservatism. None of these uses is inherent in the religion itself, but each is the outcome of particular human communities applying Islam to particular historical situations. Because Western readers are likely to see Islam as an essentially conservative ideology, let us consider the radical transformations that Islam brought to its original social setting.

PRE-ISLAMIC ARAB ETHICS

Unlike people who lived in the Persian, Byzantine, and other empires that were the heirs of thousands of years of urbanization and central government, the Arab urbanites of Muhammad's time were in a process of transition to settled life, and their society was still organized on the ethical principles that had served their nomadic Bedouin forebears. It is this traditional Arab ethic, or rather the conflict between it and urban life, that provided the backdrop for Muhammad's teachings. Islam at its inception constituted both a revitalization and a radical reform of the old ethic. For these reasons, it is worthwhile to take a closer look at traditional Bedouin society.

As is usually the case with nomadic peoples, the Bedouins did not have a centralized government or political authority. Such authority would have been impossible to maintain, not only because no centralized power can easily impose itself on peoples of such mobility, but also because there was no economic foundation to support one. Yet Bedouins were by no means isolated in the desert wastes; they were in frequent contact with other Bedouin and non-Bedouin groups, and had need of some measure of political order to regulate cooperation and resolve conflict. In such situations, political organization tended to be built from the bottom up—that is, groups were arranged in a hierarchy of levels that acted to deal with whatever conflicts or common interests were at hand.

There is a saying attributed to the Arabs: "I against my brother; my brother and I against my cousin; my brother and cousins and I against the outsider." The saying signifies a hierarchy of loyalties based on closeness of kinship that ran from the nuclear family through the lineage, the tribe, and even, in principle at least, to an entire ethnic or linguistic group (which was believed to have a kinship basis). Disputes were settled, interests were pursued, and justice and order maintained by means of this organizational framework, according to an ethic of self-help and collective responsibility. If a member of one nuclear family was injured or offended by a member of another family, it was the right and obligation of all members of the injured family to settle the score. If the dis-

putants were members of different lineages, all members of both lineages became involved (in varying degrees, depending on closeness to the offended and offending parties). In the same way, a whole tribe or alliance of tribes might have been moved to defend its interests against another group. The collective duty to take up the disputes of a kinsman meant also that someone might legitimately be killed in atonement for the crimes of a relative. An "even score" might take the form of a life for a life or a theft for a theft, or it might be sought in a negotiated settlement. An inherent weakness in the system emerged, however, when the disputing sides were unable to agree on what constituted an even score, and the situation developed into a blood feud that involved whole tribes and their allies and lasted for generations.

Yet the revenge ethic was not the unbridled play of impulse, but a system designed to keep a modicum of order in a society without centralized legal authority. Since the individual's kin group answered collectively for his transgressions, it exercised considerable power of restraint over impulsive acts. Restraint was required even in revenge, which if excessive could initiate a new cycle of offense and counterrevenge. Revenge could, as already noted, be mitigated through an arbitrated settlement that preserved both the system of order and the honor of the disputants while keeping violence to a minimum. In the end, however, it was the ever-present threat of violent reprisal that acted as the chief deterrent against crime.

Every form of social organization requires a particular kind of value commitment, and the central value of the Bedouin ethic was (and still is) the honor and integrity of the various groups, or rather of the concentric circle of groupings, with which the individual identified. Group honor was often referred to as "face" (*wajh*), the maintenance of which was a central concern of every member of a given group. (It is, incidentally, the enduring concern for the purity of the group through its patrilineal kin line, and the belief that sexual misconduct of its women is one of the greatest blows to a family's honor, that contributes today to the seclusion of Arab women.) The other side of the Bedouin's fierce unity against outsiders was his hospitality toward those who entered his domain with permission and were therefore under his protection. Hospitality, as much as revenge, was the measure of a group's willingness and ability to protect its interests and those of its allies, and was thus a reflection on its honor.

Despite its harshness, the Bedouin ethic had its benign side as well. Not only was hospitality highly valued in Bedouin society, but so was generosity. Arab traditions point to the existence, from pre-Islamic times to the present, of a strong belief in the virtue of generosity and sharing, even with strangers. Generosity to outsiders was a gesture of hospitality that reflected favorably on the strength and honor of the group. The sharing of wealth within the kin group provided for the needy, reinforced the sense of general equality and cooperation essential to the members' mutual commitment, and supported the leader's prestige by emphasizing his benevolence.

Although the Bedouin Arab's system of law and politics was based on the patrilineal kin group, it could be extended in various ways to adapt to varying circumstances. Alliances could be established between tribes, and genealogies might consciously or unconsciously be altered to reflect the new relationships. Other pseudo-kin relations were, in pre-Islamic times, established through adoption. Through the payment of tribute and obedience, one group could become the protected client of another, a status that connoted social inferiority and was therefore undertaken only when necessary. Slavery, a widespread practice throughout the ancient Mediterranean and Middle East, provided yet another set of human relationships that supplemented the family and tribe, and that carried its own set of customary regulations.

In sum, then, the Bedouin system of political and legal organization centered on kin groups and their dependents. Ultimately it depended not on authority imposed from the top, but on the individual's sense of honor, which was invested in an ever-widening series of kinship groupings. While such a system was well adapted to the needs of a decentralized society, it resulted in a relativistic morality, which placed loyalty to the group above all abstract standards guiding human conduct. A deed was evaluated in terms of kin loyalties rather than absolute ethical merit; even the deities were often tied to territories and groups, and thus pro-

vided no means for moral transcendence. The outlook thus created has sometimes been called "amoral familism" because it equated ethics with family interests; it might be better thought of, however, as a coherent moral system centered on kinship, a system that was functional in certain circumstances but carried with it some severe limitations in uniting people under a more inclusive morality.

We have examined the pre-Islamic Bedouin social ethic in such detail for several reasons. It is important to realize that the organizational and moral aspects of the system have persisted not only among Bedouins but also to some extent among settled Arabs to the present time, and that this ethic has influenced Muslim society in a number of ways. It is even more important to realize that the ministry of Muhammad revolutionized the Arab society of its time by subordinating the old familistic ethic to a transcendent system of morality, facilitating a moral and political transformation in Arabia and beyond.

THE SOCIAL SETTING OF MECCA

At the time of Muhammad's birth in about A.D. 570, Arabic-speaking peoples occupied the central Arabian peninsula; they were subject to the influences of several powerful empires. Most Arabs were either Bedouin nomads or their settled descendants who occupied themselves with trade and agriculture. Agriculture in the area did not compare with that of the more fertile regions of the Tigris-Euphrates and Mediterranean coast to the northwest, or of the Yemen[1] to the southeast. Consequently, neither the wealth nor the political organization of the Arabs matched that of their neighbors. At that time Syria (the traditional name for the fertile part of the Middle East bordering the eastern Mediterranean) was under the control of the Byzantine Empire, while the Iraq (the farming region along the Tigris and Euphrates) was controlled by Byzantium's principal antagonist, the Sassanian Empire with its ties to the Iranian highland. The Yemen, home of an

---

[1]The terms "*the*" Yemen and "*the*" Iraq distinguish the historically recognized regions from the modern nations of the same name, Yemen and Iraq.

urban agricultural and trading civilization, was losing its former power and was under the threat of domination by the Christian Abyssinian Empire in Africa, which had already intervened in the region on one occasion. Placed in a delicate situation between several more powerful forces, the Arabs were gradually developing their own urban economy and their own political strategies. Arab groups near the areas of Byzantine, Sassanian, and Yemen influence benefited from an arrangement in which the empires sponsored and subsidized them as "kingdoms" in return for military protection of their borders against the rival empires and their Arab clients. Away from these "buffer" Arab kingdoms, equidistant from the contemporary superpowers, most Arabs remained nomadic while some others were beginning to develop a different source of strength.

Located astride some of the most important trade routes that connected Europe, Africa, and Asia, Arabia moved much of the world's long-distance trade. For several centuries prior to Muhammad's time, Arabs had been assuming an increasingly active part in the trade that crossed their region. The Arab tribe of **Quraish** had founded the trade settlement of Mecca in the **Hijaz** (the mountainous region of Arabia's Red Sea coast) at the juncture of several major trade routes.

Although the Meccans were relatively sophisticated urbanites who were several generations separated from Bedouin life, their society was essentially structured by the Bedouin ethic, with some modifications. The backbone of Meccan organization was the Quraish tribe and its constituent lineages, which had successfully managed to avoid blood feuds only by emphasizing tribal loyalties over more divisive ones. The leadership of the community was vested in the tribal elders, who, as among the Bedouins, had limited powers of enforcement. In order to ensure the much-needed security of the regions through which their trade passed, it was necessary to enter into alliances with surrounding desert tribes, alliances that obliged them to take part in costly disputes with their allies' respective enemies. Meccan trade was sanctified and protected by pagan religious practices, particularly by the Meccan holy shrine of the Kaaba, which drew pilgrims from much

of Arabia. By establishing times and places of truce connected with religious observances, the Meccans were able to protect trade from the threat of feuds among the tribes. Thus, through the selective use and modification of Bedouin organization, the Meccans established a viable urban-mercantile economy. The system brought considerable affluence to the Meccans and allowed them to win influence and respect among other urbanites and merchants in the Yemen and Syria as well as the Hijaz.

Even so, the Bedouin ethic as applied to an urbanized mercantile society was beginning to show its limitations in Muhammad's time, with accompanying strains on Meccan life. Economic inequality had increased between the various lineages of the Quraish, leading to a conflict of vested interests and a growing social stratification that was difficult to reconcile with familial unity. Non-Quraish minorities who had become clients of the Quraish were now reduced to little more than debt slaves. The town of Mecca held a wide range of

Towns and Tribes in Arabia in the Time of Muhammad.
Source: Marshall G. H. Hodgson, *The Venture of Islam,* Vol. 1 (Chicago: University of Chicago Press, 1974).

occupations practiced by several resident ethnic groups, including Copts, Syrians, Africans, and Jews; these also did not fit comfortably into a social structure based primarily on kinship, pseudo-kinship, and slavery. In addition to the problems of inequality and diversity, the Meccans were faced with the ever-present threat of feuding should the unity of the Quraish become disturbed; there was no binding, authoritative central leadership. Located between warring empires and in the midst of feuding tribes, the Meccans lacked convincing assurances that their military strength could always be concentrated against outside threats rather than internal squabbles. In adapting the Bedouin social ethic to their needs, the Meccans were straining it to its limits.

The Confessional Religions

The religious as well as the social life of Mecca was hovering on the brink of significant change. The previous centuries had seen the rise, in an area extending from Asia to Europe, of a variety of religious traditions that, unlike their more ancient counterparts, "looked to *individual* personal adherence to ('confession of') an explicit and often self-sufficient body of moral and cosmological *belief* . . . which was embodied in a corpus of sacred *scriptures,* claiming *universal* validity for all men and promising a comprehensive solution to human problems in terms which involved *a world beyond death.*"[2] Although these "confessional religions" included such widely divergent traditions as Christianity and Buddhism, the forms native to the Middle East exhibited some general similarities. The Zoroastrianism of Persia resembled the major Semitic religions, Christianity and Judaism, in its belief in the oneness of God and of transcendent truth, a single universal standard for righteous conduct, a historical struggle between good and evil, the necessity of practical social action and individual responsibility, and a final divine judgment that holds every person accountable for the actions of his or her lifetime. The implications of such religions are quite different from those of a pluralistic, relativistic, kinship-centered paganism.

These confessional religions had political implications as well as spiritual and intellectual influences. The major political entities of the time were associated with confessional religions—the Persian Sassanian Empire with Zoroastrianism, the Byzantines and Abyssinians with Christianity, and the Yemen with both Christianity and Judaism. These last two religions in particular had been making inroads in central Arabia, and some Arab groups had already converted to them. The cohesiveness that these religions offered was an attractive alternative to pagan pluralism, and it might have seemed in A.D. 600 that many more Arabs would eventually become Jews or Christians.

Inner developments as well as outer pressures were moving the Meccans toward religious change. The Meccans had found it expedient to promote the centralization of worship in pilgrimages such as that of the Kaaba, and that change carried with it the seeds of a more fundamental religious transformation. In Arab tradition, the minor deities of places and social groupings had been the most important forces in daily life. Allah, the God presiding over relations between tribes—and therefore over intertribal pilgrimages, shrines, and truces—began to assume a greater importance as the intertribal character of worship developed. In Muhammad's time the Kaaba was associated primarily with Allah, but the Meccans still recognized a plurality of gods, rites, and cults that separated them from the monotheistic religions by a wide gulf.

MUHAMMAD'S MINISTRY

Muhammad was born into a minor but respectable branch of the Quraish. His father died shortly before his birth, and in keeping with the custom of some Meccan families he spent the first few years of his life in the desert under the care of a Bedouin wet nurse. Muhammad's mother died when he was six, after which he was placed in the care of his uncle, Abu Talib. The young Muhammad tended sheep and sold goods in the marketplace, and by the time he reached adulthood he had gained a reputation as a capable businessman and a person of good character (in Mecca he was known as

[2]Marshall G. S. Hodgson, *The Venture of Islam,* Vol. 1 (Chicago: University of Chicago Press, 1974), p. 125.

al-Amin, "the trustworthy"). At the age of twenty-five he married Khadija, a wealthy widow fifteen years his senior, for whom he had been managing business accounts. She remained his only wife until her death some twenty-five years later. During their marriage she bore him three sons, all of whom died before reaching adulthood, and four daughters.

Had Muhammad been an ordinary man he might have settled into a life of secure prosperity, but he was extraordinarily preoccupied with the moral and religious problems of his time. Like many of his contemporaries, Muhammad was dissatisfied with the religious climate around him. He often retreated to a cave on the outskirts of town, where he meditated. It was during one of these retreats that he received the first of a series of visions in which the Angel Gabriel called upon him to become the Apostle of God. According to his biographers, Muhammad at first doubted the visions, but he accepted his calling after Khadija and a Christian relative of hers pronounced them genuine. These first visions came in about A.D. 610, but it was several years before he began his public preaching. Khadija became his first convert; she was quickly followed by Ali, a younger cousin being raised in his household, and by Zayd, a former slave of Khadija. During the first few years of his ministry, Muhammad's converts were to span the social scale from slaves and tribeless persons to wealthy merchants; for the most part, however, they tended to be young men occupying the less-favored positions within the more respected families.

When Muhammad began his public preaching, his revelations were simple and direct: There is but one God, Allah the Creator, and those who ungratefully turn away from Him to the pleasures of this world will be held accountable on the Day of Judgment. Wealth and social position will count for nothing in the Final Judgment, while justice, piety, and righteousness will count for everything. Every person is equal before God, and righteousness is a matter between the individual and God, not a striving for power and position among kin groups. Pride, the mainspring of the Bedouin ethic, was a vice to be replaced by humility before the Creator. It seems that another central theme in the earliest revelations was the Meccans'

excessive pride in wealth and their unwillingness to share with those in need. Through Muhammad, God accused the Meccans:

> You honor not the orphan, and you urge not the feeding of the needy, and you devour the inheritance greedily, and you love wealth with an ardent love. (Koran, 89:18–21)

There is no evidence that Muhammad supported a communistic system in which all wealth was to be made public, but only that he advocated more compassion and sharing, and less stinginess and pride, than was common among the Quraish. In this, evidently one of the earliest ethical messages in Muhammad's preaching, there is considerable continuity with the Bedouin ethic. The most favored Meccan families had succeeded in cornering a growing portion of the community's wealth and privilege, and they had all but abandoned the traditional obligations of sharing. By attacking the Meccans' greed and calling on them to share their wealth, Muhammad was reasserting a moral principle recognized in the Bedouin tradition, but now in a new context and with new ramifications. In a mercantile society where success depended more on opportunism than kinship, the power of the kin group over the individual was often too weak to enforce such sharing. But in the Koran, these obligations came to be represented as sacred duties for which the individual would answer to an all-powerful God on Judgment Day. In this way, Muhammad's reassertion of a traditional value had a radical twist.

In some respects the revelations of Muhammad were perfectly in tune with the developmental course of Meccan society. As had already been pointed out, the Meccans were in need of a unifying moral-religious system not only to serve their need for internal cohesion, but also to meet the challenge of the other monotheistic religions and the political forces with which they were associated. Yet in other ways, the teachings of the Prophet ran against the grain of the prevailing cultural beliefs and the vested power interests in Mecca. In particular, the Quraish saw in Muhammad's budding sect a challenge to the values that legitimized their own power and a denunciation of the religious observances that they had so carefully structured to serve their political and economic interests. Furthermore, the Prophet himself, as God's appointed leader of the righteous, appeared to be making a personal bid for power that might encroach on their own. Not too surprisingly, the Quraish led the way in persecuting Muhammad and his followers to the extent that part of the Muslim community (but not the Prophet) sought temporary asylum in Abyssinia. Relations between Muslims and non-Muslims were tense in Mecca, and became more so as the Muslims made it increasingly clear that they sought the conversion of all Meccans. The tide seemed to turn against Muhammad in 619 when his wife Khadija, his most intimate personal supporter, and his uncle Abu Talib, who had ensured the support of his lineage against the rest of the Quraish, both died.

The Hijira

Muhammad's followers were saved from an increasingly threatened existence in Mecca by what was to become a turning point in the growth of Islam. In 620 the Prophet was approached by a handful of converts from the town of Yathrib, 200 miles to the north of Mecca. Yathrib had been founded (or revived) as a farming oasis by several Arab Jewish clans, who had later been joined by other families of pagan Arabs. The problems of family ethics in the city had eventually reached a level of crisis, in which blood feuding was so widespread that the community had little peace. The Muslims and others at Yathrib saw in Muhammad an arbitrator whose religious commitments and sense of justice would serve them well; therefore, they promised obedience to Muhammad and safety to the Muslims if the Prophet would agree to relocate in their city. After negotiating during the two following years with a growing delegation of Muslims from Yathrib, the Muslim community emigrated in the year 622. The year of the migration, or **hijira**, subsequently became the first year of the Muslim holy calendar, and the city of Yathrib became thereafter known as Medinat al-Nabi ("city of the Prophet") or simply Medina ("the city").

There is more than a ritual meaning to the hijira date as a demarcation. It was in Medina that the Muslims, cut off from previous kinship ties, established their independent political existence based on the principles of Islam. It was also in Medina that Muhammad was presented with the opportunity to construct a new Islamic social order among his followers. If Mecca was the birthplace of Islam as a religion, Medina was its birthplace as a state and a way of life.

The Koran's Social Regulations

The social problems of Medina had some parallels to those of Mecca, but the differences were considerable. Medina depended on farming rather than trade, and the kinship groups there were still relatively strong. Unlike Mecca, where the domination of the Quraish had given some measure of unity and had helped avert blood feuding, Medina was torn by violent strife among its many kinship groups. The predominantly Arab population of Medina was not entirely pagan but included a substantial and influential Jewish faction, a fact that was to complicate Muhammad's ministry there. While some of the most basic ideas of Islam—including the oneness of God, Final Judgment, humility, and generosity—were preached at Mecca, the longer suras containing the most detailed social regulations came to Muhammad while he was judge-arbiter at Medina, and were first addressed to the people of that city.

For the most part the social regulations of the Koran do not define political institutions as such (even the leadership of the Muslims after the Prophet's death was left unprovided for), but they do emphasize the moral responsibility, autonomy, and dignity of the individual by providing detailed rules by which the righteous can guide their daily lives with a minimum of dependence on the old sources of authority, particularly the tribe and lineage. The required abstention from pork, wine, and gambling was, for example, a matter to which any individual believer could adhere without outside support or resources, thereby placing himself in the community of believers and setting himself apart from tradition by these simple and very personal acts of choice. The blood feud, one of the most sacred duties of the old order, was outlawed; in its place equal penalties were set for specified crimes, regardless of the social status of the parties involved. Similarly the zakat, the alms tax collected by the Muslim community on behalf of the needy, transferred certain duties and powers from the lineage and tribe to the religious leadership, and at the same time gave the powerless a more secure status independent of their kin groups.

Many of the Koran's social regulations concern marriage and the family, and here again the tendency was to favor the rights of the individual and the immediate family over those of tribe and lineage. Numerous forms of marriage prevailed in Arabia prior to Islam; some of them were nothing more than casual relationships in which each partner remained under the control of his or her respective family, while others made wives little more than slaves. The status of marriages and their participants was determined more by family connections, power, and social position than by any universal rules. The Koran universalized marriage forms and family obligations; it discouraged casual forms of quasi marriage and gave equal status in law to all marriages between free persons. The Koran limited the number of wives a man might take to four, and counseled that all wives must be treated equally. Inheritance remained within the immediate family rather than becoming diffused into the larger kin group. The rights of the husband-father (including the right to divorce) were strengthened, not so much at the expense of the wife (who had never enjoyed much power) as at the expense of his and his wife's lineages. The husband's rights included the ultimate custody of children after divorce.

In tune with the theme of personal autonomy and responsibility, the Koran showed its recognition of individual rights in other ways. For example, the right to life was affirmed in the prohibition of infanticide, a practice that had often been used to eliminate girl babies. The Koran spoke strongly for individual property rights, urging respect for the property of even the most vulnerable members of society, including women and orphans. The bride wealth that was traditionally paid by a husband to the wife's family was to become her personal property, and a woman's property was protected from the husband during marriage and retained for the wife in the event of divorce.

Slavery was a firmly entrenched practice in the Middle East (and until recently, in many other places where economic factors favored it).

Nevertheless, the Koran allowed slaves greater rights than those granted in, say, nineteenth-century America, and taught that it is meritorious to free a slave. Muhammad set an example by freeing his own slave, who later became a prominent Muslim.

It has been suggested by some writers that the conception of fairness, individualism, and equality implied in Koranic teachings is derived more from the cultural outlook of the marketplace than from the temple or the palace. If this is true, it may be more than coincidence that such an innovation originated not in the older and more civilized centers of power, but in the new mercantile communities of the Hijaz. In any case, it is difficult to deny that Islam was, in the context where it originated, a major step toward the forms of morality most widely recognized in the modern world.

The Spread of Islam

While Muhammad's position in Medina was that of judge-arbiter and did not necessarily depend on the conversion of the populace, the pagan Arab population of the city increasingly became Muslim. The pressure to convert came from several sources, including not only the attractiveness of the teachings and the prospect of inclusion in a cohesive social entity, but also an increasingly aggressive self-identification on the part of the Muslim community.

A central concept in the Koran is that of the **Umma**. Originally the term referred to the people to whom a prophet is sent, but it soon came to refer to the believers in Islam as a community in themselves. It was to this community that a Muslim's social responsibilities were ultimately directed, and loyalty to the Umma came to be seen as inseparable from loyalty to God. The idea of the Umma expresses Islam's radical departure from the past in a most fundamental way, for membership in this community of believers cut across all traditional distinctions of family, class, and ethnicity. In principle, the Muslim owed allegiance unconditionally to another Muslim, even a foreigner or a person without social standing, and against even a sibling or parent if they were unbelievers.

It does not seem that Muhammad at first had in mind the creation of a new religious community to oppose Judaism and Christianity. Rather, he saw himself as a reformer of those religions, who in the tradition of previous prophets would lead Jews, Christians, and pagan Arabs out of error and thereby revitalize the religion of Abraham. Muhammad at first prayed in the direction of Jerusalem and observed the fast of the Jewish Day of Atonement. He was soon to be disappointed, however, by the unwillingness of most Medinese Christians and Jews to convert to Islam. During the Medina period the religion of Islam came to be defined in a manner increasingly distinct from the other monotheistic religions. Muslim prayer was reoriented in the direction of Mecca, where the Kaaba was eventually to become the central shrine of Islam. The fast of the Day of Atonement was replaced by the month of Ramadan. The Koranic revelations outlined a general policy toward the other religions in Arabia that later came to be applied in other contexts as well. If the message of the Prophet is God's holy word, it applies equally to all who will accept it. Because of Islam's emphasis on the creation of a divinely guided community whose religion is expressed in ethics and justice, the dedicated Muslim cannot rest content with personal enlightenment or salvation.

Jihad and the Djimmi System

The extension of the faith is a holy duty and a struggle from which a conscientious Muslim should never retire. The struggle is represented in the concept of **jihad**, or holy war. Just what is entailed in the Koran's support of jihad has always been subject to various interpretations by Muslims, but the Koran did make it clear that Christians and Jews were "People of the Book" who, though in error, ought not to be converted against their will. As long as they did not oppose the hegemony of the Muslim community in Arabia, they were accorded the status of a protected community, or **djimmi**. Following the Arab traditions of client–patron relationships, these communities were expected to pay a tribute tax and to show deference to the Muslims; but they were protected from harsh treatment, exploitation, and attack by either outsiders or Muslims. The

pagan Arabs were a different case: Muhammad was above all a prophet sent to them, for they had strayed the farthest from God. The conversion of all pagan Arabs, including not only most Meccans but also most Bedouin tribes, was so important that it was to be implemented by whatever use of force proved necessary.

The conversion of the Arabs proceeded apace during the Medina years. After the hijira, Muhammad and his followers began to attack the Meccan caravan trade and to clash in a series of skirmishes and battles with Meccan forces. The success of some of these early engagements, sometimes against unfavorable odds, was widely interpreted in Arabia as evidence of divine favor toward the Muslims. Muhammad offered all converts a share in the booty of war, and the Muslims began to gather a following of Arab tribes that posed a growing threat to the Meccans and their own Arab allies. Under Islam, much of the amorphous realm of the Arabs was crystallizing into a community united by a divine purpose and a sense of community.

The Meccans had been obliged to make so many concessions to the growing power of the Muslims that when the Prophet's army reentered the city, some eight years after the forced emigration, it encountered only token resistance. Muhammad was a benign conqueror, so much so that his veteran followers complained of the material rewards granted the Quraish in return for their support. Mecca became a Muslim city almost overnight. The Kaaba, following the destruction of pagan idols and its "restoration" to Allah as Abraham's temple, became the focal point of Muslim prayer and pilgrimage.

Two years later, in A.D. 632, Muhammad, the messenger of God, died. Unlike most prophets, he had lived to see the basic fulfillment of his mission. The word of God had been delivered and heard, and the pagan tribes of Arabia had at least nominally converted to Islam. The religion of Muhammad's childhood had become virtually extinct. Islam was established as a coherent set of beliefs, ritual practices, and social ethics that had swept much of the world known to Muhammad. This in itself is a remarkable enough accomplishment, and it is unlikely that Muhammad could have anticipated that Islam was to spread its influence farther and more deeply than did the Roman Empire, or that within four generations people from Spain to western China would be praying toward Mecca.

FIVE POPULAR MISCONCEPTIONS ABOUT ISLAM

According to popular notions widespread in the West, Islam is an exotic religion of the desert nomad, a religion characterized by fanatical intolerance of the "infidel," spread "by the sword," and dedicated to an ultraconservative view of human social existence. Such a picture is founded on misconceptions about the nature of Islam and of its historical role in Middle Eastern society.

Islam as an Exotic Religion

Viewed from the perspective of Jews and Christians, Islam is by no means an exotic religion. Each of these three religions embodies many of the same notions of society, history, divine will, and personal responsibility—especially compared with the non-historical, otherworldly orientation of many Eastern religions. Each recognizes the same God, the same early patriarchs, and most of the same prophets; and each originated among Semitic-speaking peoples of the Middle East. There are differences, to be sure, but in the perspective of cultural history the three religions must be seen as very closely related. In some respects the Muslim might see more continuity among the three religions than does the Jew or Christian, since Muhammad's prophecies are believed to be merely an outgrowth of the same tradition that encompasses Jesus and the Old Testament prophets. Muhammad had come into contact with Jews and Christians and was familiar with their verbal renditions of their scriptures. While there is no direct written connection between Judeo-Christian and Muslim scriptures (Muhammad was said to have been illiterate), and certain scriptural events are rendered somewhat differently in the Koran, there can be no question that Islam views itself as the culmination of the Judeo-Christian religious tradition.

Insofar as Muhammad was an apostle to the Arabs, and the Arabs identify ultimately with their

Bedouin heritage, there is some truth to the picture of Islam as a "religion of the desert." In fact, Islam draws selectively on certain ancient Bedouin values, such as sharing wealth and caring for those in need. Nevertheless, at its core Islam is an urban and cosmopolitan religion that in its day undermined the tribal system of ethics and religion and replaced it with a rationalized, universal set of beliefs. Its main thrust is at one with the other confessional religions, and not with "primitive" religions centered on nature and the family. Therefore, to represent Islam as merely an extension of the Bedouin outlook, as is so often done, is fundamentally false.

Islam as a Militant Religion

One often encounters the assertion, even among some historians, that Islam is a particularly militant and intolerant religion, and that it was spread mainly through the use of force—or as the phrase goes, "by the sword." Historically, Islam no more deserves such a reputation than does Christianity. It is true that the scriptures of Islam do not advise believers to turn the other cheek, and that the Koran actually praises those who go to war in defense of the faith. The very concept of jihad, the holy struggle against the unbeliever, seems to the Westerner to suggest a program of ruthless suppression of other religions. It should be kept in mind, though, that the concept of jihad is a complex one for Muslims, and that the idea of struggle can be interpreted and implemented in various ways. In some sense, the duty of spreading the faith and the idea of universal brotherhood and equality before God are but two sides of the same coin. If the message of God is good for all people, then one does humankind a disservice by leaving the infidels to their disbelief. This, however, does not and never has meant that the Muslim community sanctions random acts of aggression against non-Muslims. On the contrary, the djimmi system protected the rights of religious communities that rejected Islam entirely.

As for conversion by the sword, the Western accusation against Islam has an exceedingly weak foundation. The Koranic stand on forced conversions is ambiguous, and one can find hadith that seem to forbid it as well as those that seem to support it. Muhammad took a hard stand toward pagans, the nonmonotheistic Arab tribes, but opposed the forced conversion of adherents of the confessional religions in Arabia. In later times other communities, including the Hindus in India, were extended formal protection as djimmis. As we shall see in the next chapter, the millions who converted to Islam did so for a variety of reasons. Even the pagan Arabs probably converted more often for the sake of various material, social, and spiritual advantages than out of fear. The Muslims of the Far East, whose population today rivals that of the Muslim Middle East, were generally converted through the influence of peaceful merchants. The reader should not forget that despite the teachings of Jesus, Christianity was spread at the point of a sword in much of Europe and the Western Hemisphere. We suspect that if the historical record is examined carefully, it will show that the spread of Islam depended no more consistently on the use of force than did the spread of Christianity.

Islam as an Intolerant Religion

As for religious intolerance, it is instructive to compare the attitudes of Christians and Muslims toward the Jews, who were a religious minority in both the Muslim and Christian worlds. Tensions have often existed between Jewish communities and the politically dominant Muslims or Christians. One reason for this tension lies in the very nature of Jewish existence as a religious and cultural minority, with all the conflicting loyalties, suspicions, and persecutions that frequently accompany minority status. In addition, the presence of an unconverted population seems to thwart the universalistic claims of both Islam and Christianity. Finally, the historical connections of both Christianity and Islam with Judaism have given rise to more specific allegations against the Jews: Christians have traditionally blamed them for betraying Christ, while Muslims have accused them of spurning Muhammad's ministry. Indeed, tension between Muslims and Jews became severe even at Medina, where early attempts to convert the Jewish Arabs of that city came to nothing. The Prophet eventually expelled two of the major Jewish clans and sanctioned a blood bath against

the third for their alleged intrigues against him. During this period, the Koranic revelations upbraided the Jews for their supposed errors and their lack of faith in God's prophet.

Despite the ever-present potential for conflict, the actual history of Jewish minorities in both Christian and Muslim worlds has been quite variable, and it would be difficult indeed to portray the differences in terms of Christian love versus Muslim intolerance. While interethnic relations in both contexts had their ups and downs, the Christian and Jewish minorities under Islam ultimately enjoyed the status of protected communities as defined in the Koran. To be sure, this djimmi status carried obligations of civil obedience, special taxation, and limitation of political independence, but it also exempted minorities from the requirements of jihad and zakat. It can be argued that Jewish minorities in Christendom labored under equally severe restrictions and held a less-secure legal status. It is interesting to note that when the Muslims were expelled from Spain in the twelfth to fifteenth centuries, the Jewish communities that had previously thrived under Muslim rule were subjected by the conquering Christians to persecution, forced conversion, and banishment. Putting aside the ecumenical spirit that has recently appeared in the Christian world, there is little in the historical record to support the Western image of Islam as an essentially fanatical and intolerant religion compared with traditional Christianity. Neither is there much support for the idea that active enmity between Muslims and Jews (or Christians) is inevitable.

Islam as an Ultraconservative Religion

Many Westerners believe that Islam is a more socially conservative religion than is Judaism or Christianity. Some have even referred to the recent revival of religious commitment in Muslim countries as a "return to the seventh century" (as though, unlike Christians and Jews, a Muslim must choose between religion and modern life). It is true that Islam's scriptures are notable for their detailed pronouncements on the conduct of social life, a fact that poses a special challenge to the Islamic modernist. However, Judaism and Christianity are by no means lacking in specific social rules; and the scriptures of these religions date to an even earlier period than the Koran. The social ideas presented in the Koran were in many respects radical departures from the prevailing customs of the time and must be seen in their historical context as innovative.

Throughout history and into the present, Islam like other religions has been invoked to justify a wide variety of social agendas ranging from the restoration of an idealized past to the pursuit of progressive programs of social reform. In the end, it is difficult to make the judgment that Islam, any more than other world religions, is inherently opposed to changes that would allow for a satisfying and effective life in the modern world. Since Islam's position on women's rights has sometimes been used as an example of Muslim conservatism and is often used in demeaning portrayals of Muslim life, let us further examine this subject as a case in point.

Islam as a Sexist Religion

Like Judaism and Christianity, Islam reflects the patriarchal character of Middle Eastern society at the time of its origin. Many of its social regulations presuppose a family in which the male is the chief authority and economic provider, as well as a descent system traced through the husband and father. We therefore find a variety of sexually differentiated rules; for example, men but not women may take more than one spouse; a woman receives only half a man's share of an inheritance; and divorce is easier for a man than for a woman to initiate. In each of these matters, however, Islam may not be as conservative as it first appears. Plural marriage was permissible among pagans, Jews, and Christians until long after Muhammad's day, and the effect of Islam was therefore not to originate plural marriage but to regulate it, to set limits on it, and to define the rights and obligations of each partner. Under Islam a man is allowed no more than four wives, and he is permitted only one if he is unable to treat several wives equally. Men are counseled to treat their wives with kindness, and hadith even criticize men who behave selfishly in sexual intercourse. The Koran advises those with marital difficulties to seek arbitration by representatives of both the wife's and the husband's families, indicating not only that the preservation of a marriage is desirable but also that a woman's grievances ought to be taken seriously. As for property and inheritance, the most significant innovations of Islam were in securing for women the right to inherit property and to receive the bride wealth previously paid to the bride's family by the husband, and in protecting her full rights of property ownership even in marriage and divorce. This right of a woman to control her own property after marriage, established by the Koran in the seventh century, is still being sought by women in some parts of the Western world.

The veiling and seclusion of women, for which Islam is often criticized, is more a matter of folk practice than an intrinsic part of Islam. While the Koran advocates sexual modesty on the part of women, it makes the same requirement of men. The social custom of keeping women veiled or behind closed doors is not specifically Muslim, but reflects traditional Middle Eastern concerns. The purity of the women in a family guaranteed its honor and ensured the integrity of the male line. Furthermore, the impracticality of keeping women in extreme seclusion has caused the practice to be concentrated in, and symbolic of, the traditional urban upper classes (including many Jews and Christians). It is traditional public opinion in favor of female seclusion that, contrary to the practice of Muhammad and the early Muslims, has kept women out of the mosques and away from active religious practice. Over the past century, many Muslim intellectuals have objected to the seclusion of women on the grounds that it is contrary to the tenets of Islam.

The Koran echoes the sentiments of traditional Middle Eastern society and of Judeo-Christian thought in saying that "men are the managers of the affairs of women, for that God hath preferred in bounty one of them over the other" (4:5–52). However, Islamic scriptures do not go as far as the Christian scriptures in asserting the moral inequality of women and men. We do not find in the Koran anything corresponding to Paul's pronouncement about the "shame" of women for having brought sin into the world (in the Koran both Adam and Eve are tempted equally), or to the Christian idea that man is the image and "glory of God" while woman is "created for man." If anything, the Koran goes out of its way to emphasize the moral (as distinct from social) equality of the sexes. Repeatedly it makes clear that its pronouncements stand alike for every believer "be you male or female."

If we can separate the essential religious teachings from social customs that have grown up around them, we will find in Islam no more basis for sexist attitudes than is present in the scriptures of Judaism and Christianity. It is true that a relatively large proportion of Muslims retain close ties with the customs of a premodern age, while many Christians and Jews living in the West have all but forgotten some of the more conservative social customs upheld in their scriptures. Nevertheless, there is no reason to assume that Islam is inherently less compatible with modern life and change than its sister religions. Many Muslim modernists, in fact, view Islam as an essentially progressive religion with regard to sex roles and other social issues, and they chide conservative Muslims for allowing custom and prejudice to distract them from the true principles of their faith. We shall have more to say on this subject in a later chapter.

CONCLUSION

In this chapter we have endeavored to portray Islam as a religious faith and as a product of human history. In so doing we have introduced the reader to the interplay between religion and society. At any given point in history the relationship between religious thought and social practice is likely to be a complex one, with religion acting as both a conservative force and an invitation to social change. As a society develops through time, that relationship is subject to constant revision and reinterpretation, sometimes in differing ways by different members of society. While every religion has fundamental themes and values that ultimately guide its development, the range of possible circumstances, applications, and interpretations is often astonishing.

A fundamental challenge to any religion is to address the universal problems of human existence in a way that transcends the narrow limits of time and place, while retaining enough particularity to give its message substance and social relevance. Islam originally addressed the problems of a very specific society in an exceptionally particular and detailed way, and yet it has subsequently presided over a dozen centuries of cultural development among peoples spanning three continents. While readers should be sensitive to the unifying features of Islam, they should also keep in mind the many contradictions and conflicting interpretations that have occurred within other religious traditions as they adapted to varying circumstances and interests, and expect no more consistency from Islam than from any other living religion.

The Political Legacy of Islam
A.D. 632–1800

Accustomed as Westerners are to the ideal of separating politics from religion, they can easily overlook the extent to which political thought and action throughout history have been expressed in religious terms. In traditional Christianity no less than in Islam, questions of justice, public obligation, class privilege, and even revolution have been inseparable from religious issues. Some writers see this as evidence that until recently humankind was driven by religious urges at the expense of practical considerations; others have concluded that the religious impulse is nothing more than a cloak for self-interest. A more moderate interpretation, which we prefer, is that religion has provided the concepts and the language by which human beings have pursued their immediate interests and defined their ultimate values. For this reason, a religious outlook never remains static. It is, indeed, a continuous dialogue; and the form of that dialogue bears the stamp of general human concerns, the changing circumstances of history, and the special qualities of vision that characterize the particular tradition.

While the social thought of Islam is in itself neither more nor less important than that of other world religions, it is especially significant for the study of Middle Eastern politics. Islam has had a

decisive influence on state politics throughout the region since the death of Muhammad, and today the Islamic heritage is present in new ways. To be sure, Islam is not immune to the influence of contemporary events, and its current political role is different from the one it played in previous centuries. Nevertheless, Islam has a personal and social significance that most contemporary Middle Easterners take seriously, and there is no doubt that the present restructuring of Middle Eastern societies and their interrelations will continue to be based on a common Islamic cultural heritage. Even those who wish to minimize the role of religion in politics must pursue their programs with an acute consciousness of the Islamic milieu.

The revelations of Muhammad introduced a new framework within which to work out the problems of social life. Yet no matter how consistent a statement one makes about the human condition, the attempt to apply it to actual conditions will always lead to contradictions and conflicts, and to resolutions that raise new problems in turn. The difficulties are compounded even further as a religious tradition encounters cultural variation and historical change. As human communities over the past thirteen centuries have explored the implications of the Islamic vision, they have uncovered numerous conflicts and paths of resolution. No simple generalization can do justice to this rich heritage of thought, nor is it possible to catalogue fully the many outlooks that have developed under the auspices of Islam. It is possible, however, to sample some of the issues that Muslims have most often raised, and to indicate the characteristic ways in which these issues have been approached within that tradition.

The ministry of Muhammad had a dual character that arose from his role as a civic leader and a religious visionary. Muhammad made it clear that Islam can be realized only by the creation of a religiously guided community, the Umma. At the same time, such a community exists only insofar as it is defined by Islam. Thus, neither the religion nor the Umma can exist except in terms of the other. Islam requires, by its very nature, a social order that is both politically sound and divinely guided. But the requirements of political efficacy and divine guidance are not always easy to reconcile, at least in the short run; and the problems arising from this contradiction have stimulated much of the political dialogue in Islamic thought. This problem of mediating the demands of faith and politics has manifested itself in more specific conflicts such as power versus justice, privilege versus equality, guidance by the community versus the conscience of the individual, and the need for adaptive innovation versus the enduring vision of Muhammad's model community.

THE ESTABLISHMENT OF THE ISLAMIC STATE

The teachings of Muhammad, concentrating as they did on individual obligations, left unanswered a great many questions vital to the future of his community. Most pressing was that of leadership, for which Muhammad had made no provisions. After the Prophet's death, the community at Medina made preparations to choose its own leadership and expected the Meccans to do the same. Many Bedouin "converts" considered themselves to be personal clients of Muhammad and believed that their obligations ended with his death. At this critical moment in history, the initiative was seized by Abu Bakr and Umar, two of Muhammad's closest associates who were to become the first two **caliphs**, or representatives, of the Prophet. Under their strong leadership, the unity of the Muslim community was aggressively asserted. They declared that there would be no prophets after Muhammad, and that the Umma must unite under a single authority. Bedouins slipping away from the Islamic fold were brought back by force in the **Riddah Wars** ("Wars of Apostasy"); and even as these campaigns were being completed, the energies of the newly united Arab armies were turned against the faltering empires of Persia and Byzantium, thus launching Islam on its fateful course.

The Muslim campaigns against the neighboring empires were phenomenally successful. Weakened by decades of indecisive warfare against one another and by internal strains, the exhausted, stalemated Sassanian and Byzantine empires encountered the greatest threat where they had least expected it. The old Arab buffer states, no longer subsidized by the empires, joined with the Muslim Arab conquerors; other local populations, often religious minorities long persecuted by the established state religions, were less than enthusiastic in defending the hegemony of their old masters. Under Umar's guidance (634–644), the terms of conquest were lenient, even attractive. Establishing a pattern for subsequent conquests, Umar allowed life to go on protected and undisturbed in those cities that submitted willingly; they were subject only to a tax. These taxes, along with revenues from lands won in battle and one-fifth of all other booty, went to the Muslim state, which in turn distributed much of it to its soldiers. Under Umar's leadership, Egypt, the Fertile Crescent, and much of Iran came under Muslim domination; the Sassanian Empire was toppled, and the Byzantines were driven back into Anatolia.

The Muslim Empire, as it took form in the early period, was an Arab military state. Using Bedouin military experience and turning its energies from internal raiding and feuding toward fighting the infidel, the Muslim state rapidly gained power. Under capable administrative leadership, the Arab conquerors instituted an orderly process for collecting revenue and for distributing it by means of the army register, or **diwan**. Conquered people were guaranteed their civil and religious freedom as djimmis in return for their submission to Muslim rule and taxation (often a more attractive arrangement than the older empires had afforded). The Arabs themselves lived in garrison towns segregated from the conquered populace; they had no intention either of blending into the local life or of inviting their new subjects to become like them. Forced conversion of the djimmis was rarely an issue, since the Muslims considered their religion, their Arab background, and their privileged status as conquerors and tax recipients to be inextricably connected. In order to promote religious unity and to safeguard against any possible deviations from the faith, Umar did much to establish the forms of worship and to promulgate knowledge of the Koran in the garrison towns. The center of social life in such towns became the mosque, and the military leader himself emphasized the religious character of the community by personally leading the people in prayer.

The Caliph Uthman (644–656) continued Umar's policies, but with less success, for the Muslim community was now confronting some of the social and moral problems arising from the transition of a religious movement into an organized state. Many malcontents saw Uthman as a symbol of what they thought was wrong with the community: a turning from faith to secular power. For them it was particularly galling that Uthman's kinsmen, the **Umayyads**—who unlike Uthman himself had long opposed Muhammad—were now being favored in administrative appointments. Opposition to Uthman was particularly strong in the Iraq at Kufah, and in Egypt. In 656, Uthman was murdered by a group of his opponents from the Egyptian garrison, and the Prophet's cousin and son-in-law Ali was immediately proclaimed caliph. The rebels, who supported Ali's accession, claimed that Uthman had betrayed Islam and that his murder was therefore justified; Uthman's supporters and others horrified by the killing accused Ali of condoning it, and demanded that he punish those responsible. The situation quickly developed into civil war, with Ali's supporters in the Iraq pitted against Muawiya, the Umayyad governor of Syria. After initial successes, some of Ali's men persuaded him to submit to arbitration as de-

manded by Muawiya, whereupon a faction of Ali's army, the **Kharijites**, turned against him for abandoning the cause. His supporters' loyalties were split, the arbitration was indeed damaging to his position, and Ali's fortunes declined until his death at the hands of a Kharijite in 661.

The death of Ali was a turning point for Islam. The last of the Prophet's close personal followers was now gone. The initial unity of Islam was forever shattered, and the issue was raised—an issue that was to continue to trouble Islam up to the present—of whether civil order within the Umma is more important than the divinely mandated legitimacy of its leadership. The accession of Muawiya established a dynasty of rulers whose ultimate recourse was to secular power, and the religious idealists took on the function, which they have generally had ever since, of a moralistic oppositional force.

THE GOLDEN AGE OF THE CALIPHATE

If Islam had lost some of its purity in the eyes of its more idealistic adherents, it was also coming into its own as a civilization and an empire. Under the Umayyads (661–750), Islam spread across North Africa to Spain; in the east, it spread to the Indus Valley. The structure of the empire remained essentially that of an Arab conquest state, in which Islam remained primarily the religion of a segregated Arab elite. Other trends, however, were beginning to appear.

Despite the ethnic biases of the Arabs, the universalistic, cosmopolitan facets of Islam were beginning to surface as the empire embraced highly sophisticated peoples who were both willing and able to take an active part in Muslim civilization. At first, non-Arab converts to Islam were given only marginal status as *Mawalis,* or clients, of influential Arab families. Indeed, their existence posed economic problems since the empire was set up on the assumption that Arab Muslims would collect taxes from their subjects on the basis of religious affiliation. In practice, non-Arab converts to Islam often found themselves excluded from Muslim economic privileges despite their conversion. But the forces of change were at work. The Arabs with their Bedouin and mercantile backgrounds were now heirs to the traditions of the

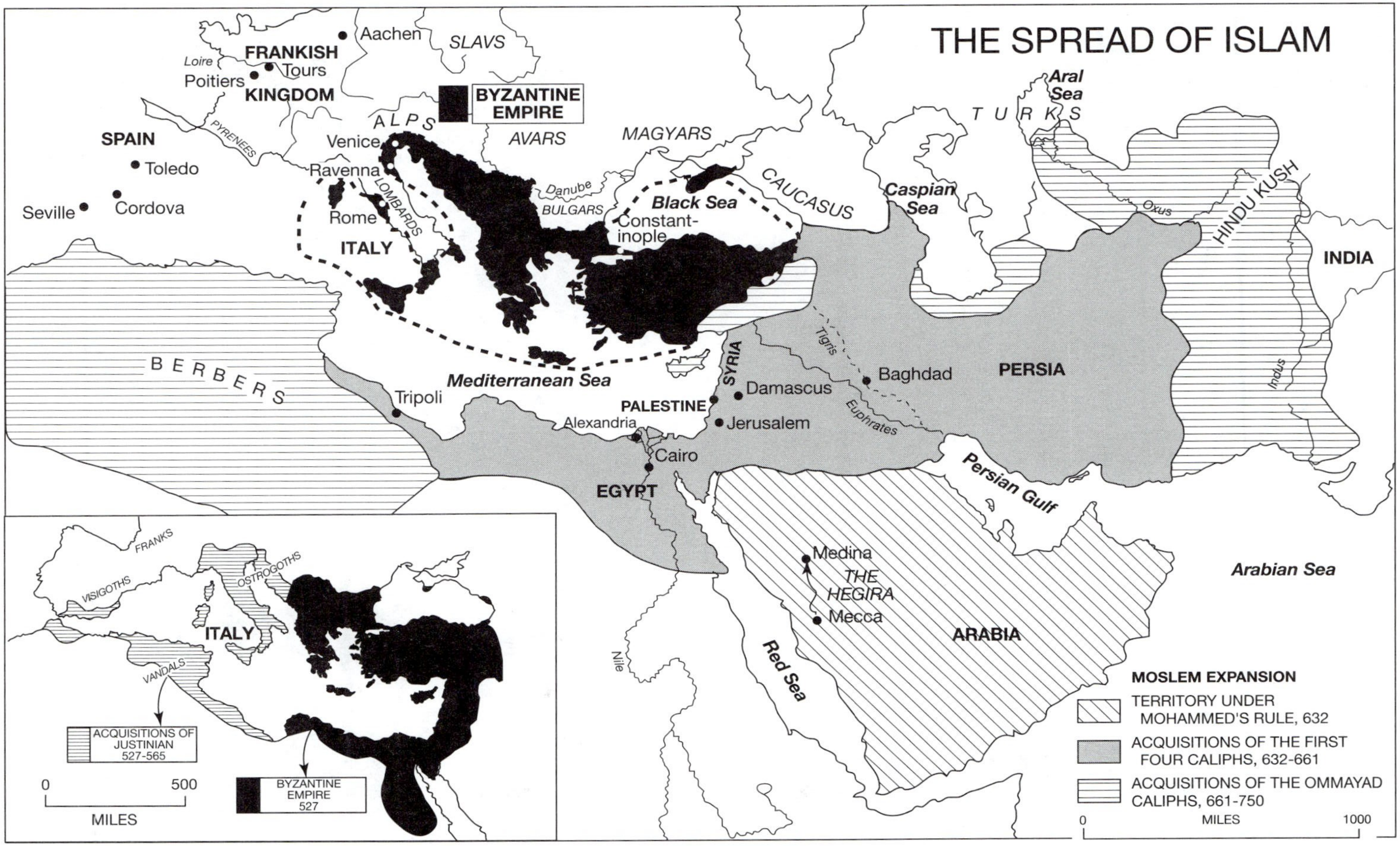
THE SPREAD OF ISLAM
Aachen
SLAVS
FRANKISH
Loire
Tours
Poitiers
KINGDOM
BYZANTINE EMPIRE
SPAIN
PYRENEES
ALPS
Venice
AVARS
MAGYARS
Toledo
Ravenna
Seville
Cordova
LOMBARDS
Rome
ITALY
Danube
BULGARS
Black Sea
Constant-
inople
CAUCASUS
Caspian Sea
Aral Sea
TURKS
Oxus
HINDU KUSH
INDIA
Indus
BERBERS
Tripoli
Mediterranean Sea
SYRIA
PALESTINE
Damascus
Jerusalem
Baghdad
Tigris
Euphrates
PERSIA
Alexandria
Cairo
EGYPT
Nile
Persian Gulf
Medina
THE HEGIRA
Mecca
ARABIA
Red Sea
Arabian Sea
MOSLEM EXPANSION
TERRITORY UNDER MOHAMMED'S RULE, 632
ACQUISITIONS OF THE FIRST FOUR CALIPHS, 632-661
ACQUISITIONS OF THE OMMAYAD CALIPHS, 661-750
0
MILES
1000
FRANKS
VISIGOTHS
OSTROGOTHS
ITALY
VANDALS
ACQUISITIONS OF JUSTINIAN 527-565
BYZANTINE EMPIRE 527
0
500
MILES

The Spread of Islam.
Source: Sydney Nettleton Fisher, *The Middle East: A History,* 2nd ed. (New York: Alfred A. Knopf, 1969).

centralized agrarian state, and the conditions associated with agrarian life came to have more and more sway over them. The Arab ruling class came increasingly to look like any other local gentry, and the caliphs took on the aspect of semidivine emperors ruling at their court in Damascus.

Throughout the period of Umayyad rule, a gathering variety of factions promoted a growing antigovernment spirit. Some disliked the favoring of Syrians over other Arabs; some opposed the distinction of Arabs from other Muslim converts; and some disliked the centralized control over the distribution of revenues, which they felt worked to their disadvantage. Many Arabs despised the pretensions of the caliphs and chafed under the spirit of imperial rule, so incompatible with traditional Arab values. Whatever the specific sources of discontent, the criticisms tended to converge on the accusation that the government was impious, that it had made irreligious "innovations" instead of following the way of the Prophet, and that it had forgotten its communal obligations in favor of material advantages for the few. What was needed, they agreed, was true Islamic guidance for the community. In the 740s a coalition of interest groups and sects, including the Shia (the "party" of Ali, which still bore a grudge against the Umayyads), launched a civil war that ended with the establishment of the **Abbasid** dynasty in 750.

Many of those who had supported the overthrow of the Umayyads were soon to be disappointed. It is true that the bases of the empire were considerably broadened by the change, for the new order with its capital at Baghdad was much more open to the participation and influence of the Iraqi Arabs and especially the non-Arab Persians. Some writers have even gone so far as to characterize the change as one from Arab to Persian domination, because of the decisive participation of Persians at the highest levels of government as well as the increasing influence of Persian language, literature, and culture. Yet in these changes lay the seeds of bitter disappointment for the old opposition. Far from returning to charismatic rule by Ali's inspired descendants, as the Shia had hoped, or even a return to a purer life modeled on the early Umma, as others had advocated, the caliphate continued on its evolution toward agrar-

ian absolutism. Under the Abbasid caliphs, the power of the court reached its peak, with the caliph exercising his own law at his whim, which was enforced on the spot by his ever-present executioner.

The city of Baghdad, which the Abbasids built for their capital, symbolized the trends in government. Unlike the Arab garrison towns located on the edge of the desert, Baghdad was built on the Tigris River on a site that commanded key agricultural land in the Iraq and principal trade routes. It was laid out in a circle; and instead of emphasizing Arab tribal divisions, as the garrison towns had done, the entire city was oriented toward the government complex and the caliph's huge palace. The court of the caliph was the center of an aristocratic high culture marked by strong Persian influences, and Baghdad came to play a dominant economic, political, and cultural role reminiscent of the older Persian and Mesopotamian seats of government.

While absolute despotism was as repugnant to the Bedouin and the ulema as it is to modern taste, it by no means hindered Abbasid civilization itself. Such a monarchy protected the powerless—especially the peasants—against the more grotesque abuses frequently visited on them by decentralized oligarchies and competing petty rulers, and it also brought a degree of order that set the stage for unprecedented material prosperity in the Muslim world. Trade and agriculture flourished, banking and communications were effectively organized across the empire, and government was carefully regulated under a *vizier* (comparable to a prime minister) and an established bureaucracy.

This was the golden age of Muslim civilization, to which Muslims in later times would look for inspiration. Muslim power was unparalleled anywhere in the world, while Islamic art, architecture, literature, and poetry—drawing on Arabic, Persian, Greek, Indic, and other traditions and supported by the courtly high culture—reached their peak of development. Arabic works from this period on mathematics (*algebra* and *logarithm* are Arabic-derived words), chemistry, optics, and medicine put these sciences at such a high state of development that Europeans were still consulting the Arabic sources five hundred years later. The Crusaders who entered the Middle East at the end of the eleventh century, after the decline of the Abbasid caliphate, were seen with some justice as uncultivated barbarians.

Ironically, the golden age of Islamic civilization also signaled the beginning of the decline of the caliphate. For reasons not altogether clear, the Abbasid caliphs began to lose their hold on the vast empire after their first century of rule. In an attempt to bolster their own power against competing factional loyalties, the caliphs by 850 had begun to use private armies. These guards were usually slaves obtained from the Turkic-speaking nomadic tribes of the Eurasian steppes; they were kept totally dependent on the caliph and were loyal, presumably, only to him. The caliphs, however, soon found themselves at the mercy of their own palace guards; by the middle-to-late ninth century, most caliphs were puppets of a Turkish soldier class that was in one form or another to dominate most of Islam for the next thousand years. In the ninth century, some provinces started to assert their independence, and the empire began to devolve into a decentralized civilization with the caliph as figurehead.

Under various dynasties, multiple centers of power developed, and their political control decreased with distance; in some areas there was little more than local civic government. Yet the social unity of the Umma and the norms that governed Muslim life did not depend on a central government and therefore did not decline with the caliphate. Instead, the political disintegration of Islam was accompanied by the continued development of a common, international pattern of Muslim social life that was based on Islamic Sharia law and was overseen by the formally educated ulema.

MONGOL DESTRUCTION AND THE REBIRTH OF EMPIRE

The period from the mid-tenth to the mid-thirteenth centuries saw the militarization of political power. This tendency was brought to an extreme by the Mongol conquests and afterward in the period of the Ottoman and other late empires. Before the thirteenth century, the overall tendency toward decentralized rule by local emirs was reversed only a few times—as in the case of the Seljuk Turks during the eleventh century. The Mongols, however, were able to consolidate pure military power on an unprecedented level. The Mongol invasions were joint efforts involving Turkic-speaking armies recruited among the nomadic tribes of the Eurasian steppes and a Mongol military elite originating in Asia. Due to a complex of historical and technological factors, during the thirteenth and fourteenth centuries the Mongols and their armies were able to conquer most of the civilized world from China to Eastern Europe and place it under the centralized administration of military chieftains. With the fall of Baghdad in 1258 and the execution of the last Abbasid figurehead caliph, political control passed into purely military hands. Although non-Muslim in origin, the Mongols and their Turkish forces converted to Islam; subsequently some of the severest Mongol campaigns under Timur (Tamerlane) were fought in the name of Islamic purity. Destructive as their terrorist techniques were, once established, the Mongols became patrons of Islamic high culture and rebuilders of public works. One of their most enduring influences, however, was the establishment of efficient, highly organized states based on the army. In these states, ultimate control was in the hands of a supreme military ruler whose succession was determined by armed contest within the ruling dynasty; the army organization included not only combat troops but the entire governmental apparatus. So centered on the army were these empires that their capitals were wherever the army and its supreme leader happened to be, and government records were carried into the field on campaigns.

Eventually the effects of Mongol conquest gave way to more homegrown military empires, which in some respects benefited both from the destruction of the old order and from the Mongol military system. Equally important in these new empires was the use of gunpowder, which favored the technically advanced urban populations over the Eurasian nomads and allowed greater concentrations of power to develop. The most important post-Mongol concentrations of power in the Middle East were the Safavid Empire, centering approximately in what is now Iran, and the **Ottoman Empire**, originating in what is now

Turkey. Each arose and achieved much of its glory during the sixteenth century, and each was dominated by a Turkic military elite but used Persian or Turkish as a literary language and Arabic as the religious language. Each followed somewhat similar paths of development, but it is the Ottoman state that is of the greatest interest here, partly because it most directly confronted the growing power of Europe, and partly because it continued as an active force in world politics until the twentieth century.

The Ottoman Empire

The Ottoman Empire, named after its original ruling family of Osman Turks, had its roots in Anatolia during the pre-Mongol period. Located on the frontier of the Byzantine Empire, the Ottoman state had long been associated with the continuing struggle against the infidel; accordingly, it held a prestigious position within Islam and attracted many would-be **ghazis**, or defenders of the faith. A turning point for the Ottomans came with the long-sought conquest of Constantinople in 1453, which they renamed Istanbul and made their capital. Ottoman power grew rapidly as Islamic territories expanded into Hungary and even to the gates of Vienna, which the Ottomans unsuccessfully besieged in 1541 and again in 1683. To the south, Ottoman power encompassed the Levant, Syria, the Iraq, the Hijaz, and Muslim North Africa as far west as Algeria. Rivalry between the Ottomans and Safavids took on religious overtones as the Safavids became more militantly Shia and the Ottomans increasingly Sunni, a conflict that has left the Middle East religiously divided to this day along former Ottoman–Safavid boundary lines.

Like other Muslim empires before it, the Ottoman Empire developed features of an agrarian state with its social stratification and its absolute monarchy, but the Ottoman form remained distinctive. A military ruling family presided over a vast army of **Janissaries**, recruited as slaves and loyal only to the rulers. These slaves were obtained as children from non-Muslim populations, often Christian, and were brought up and trained as Muslims. They formed a class that made up not only the military component of the state but the bureaucracy as well. At first they were not allowed to marry. When marriage was permitted, the offspring of slaves were freeborn and therefore disqualified from government service, and so there was little opportunity for the formation of privileged classes or loyalties at odds with Ottoman interests.

The machinery of Ottoman government was remarkably efficient. Furthermore, the Ottomans accomplished what few Muslim governing powers had done before them: They successfully allied themselves with the ulema. Ottoman success with the ulema was related to the empire's origin as a ghazi state and its devotion to defending the faith against not only the Christian powers but the Shia Safavids as well. It should also be kept in mind that a career as a religious scholar was one of the few paths of prestige open to the freeborn sons of the military-bureaucratic slave class. Under the Ottoman system, the ulema relinquished much of their traditional oppositional role with regard to the ruling powers and came instead to identify with those powers. In return, the government supported the ulema's authority and that of Sharia law, and submitted to some token checks on its power; for example, the ulema could in theory depose the Ottoman sultan if they judged him unfaithful to Islam.

A certain amount of pluralism was built into the Ottoman system. The djimmi communities, or **millets**, were allowed military protection, religious freedom, and self-government under their own chosen leaders, subject as always to a kind of second-class citizenship in the Muslim state. Ottoman provinces relatively distant from Istanbul, such as the Hijaz and North Africa, were also allowed some degree of self-government. For example, the **Mameluks** of Egypt, a Turkish slave class that had ruled Egypt from 1250 until their defeat by the Ottomans in 1517, were allowed to continue in power under minimal Ottoman supervision.

By the eighteenth century, the empire had long since stopped increasing its territories and was beginning to take note of the rapidly growing European threat. Some attempts were made to modernize the Ottoman army, but these were thwarted by more sweeping problems that plagued the empire. The military ruling class had gradually

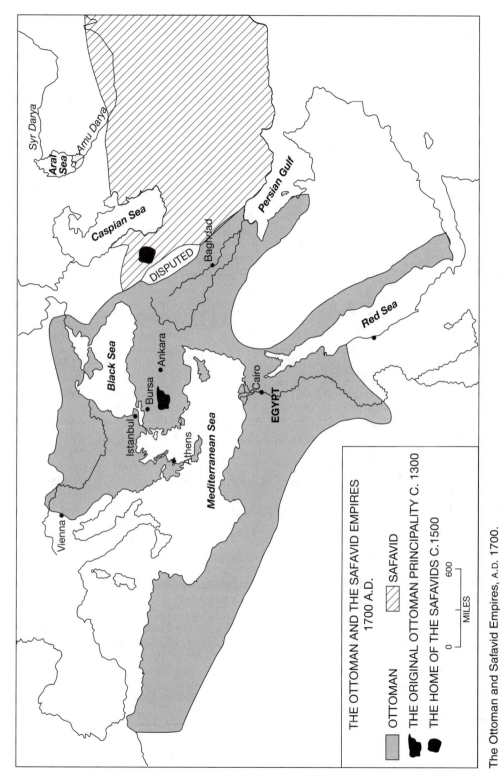

The Ottoman and Safavid Empires, A.D. 1700.

Source: Yahya Armajani, *Middle East Past and Present,* © 1970, p. 161. Reprinted by permission of Prentice Hall, Upper Saddle River, N.J.

Within the map image:

THE OTTOMAN AND THE SAFAVID EMPIRES
1700 A.D.

OTTOMAN

SAFAVID

THE ORIGINAL OTTOMAN PRINCIPALITY C. 1300

THE HOME OF THE SAFAVIDS C.1500

0   600

MILES

Syr Darya

Aral Sea

Amu Darya

Caspian Sea

DISPUTED

Baghdad

Persian Gulf

Red Sea

Black Sea

Ankara

Bursa

Cairo

EGYPT

Istanbul

Athens

Mediterranean Sea

Vienna

become civilized, had suffered a loss of discipline, and had begun to lose even its former structural integrity (army bureaucrats, for example, began to pass their status on to their children). Corruption and demoralization became widespread in government, a condition that many Western observers of the time assumed to be a universal trait of "oriental" governments. When the Western powers began in earnest to move in on the Middle East around the turn of the nineteenth century, they found the Ottoman Empire ill-prepared to resist them.

GROWTH AND DECLINE IN THE ISLAMIC STATE

Many observers have noted that Muslim civilization and Muslim political power seem to have gone through an early period of phenomenal growth and vitality that was followed by a long era of "decline," or "stagnation," ending finally in Western dominance. Often, the rapid growth is attributed to military force driven by religious fanaticism, while the "decadence" that followed is said to reveal the defects either of the "oriental mind" or of Islam itself, both of which are often accused of authoritarianism and resistance to innovation. Such a view is misleading not only because there is no such thing as an oriental mind, but also because the problem of "growth" and "decline" is much too complex to lend itself to such easy generalizations. The Muslim world, like any civilization that endures for centuries or millennia, experienced many different kinds of growth and decline. Indeed, what is decline from one point of view may be growth from another—for example, the decline of centralized government was accompanied by a strengthening of Muslim law that reached across political boundaries. Furthermore, decline in one local region may be offset by growth in another.

The original growth of Islamic civilization actually involved two processes that reinforced one another: the spread of Islam as a religion, and the extension of Muslim political rule (or ties with the centers of Muslim power). The reasons for the spread of Islamic influence varied with the circumstances. In Medina, conversion to Islam was a matter of civic convenience as well as personal conviction. Among the Bedouins of the Arabian peninsula, political advantage and later the threat of force encouraged conversion. The subjects of the Sassanian and Byzantine empires yielded to a well-organized conquering army, but at the same time they were attracted by the promise of being better off as djimmi communities than as Sassanian or Byzantine subjects. Under the Umayyads, non-Arabs converted despite Arab discouragement in order to benefit from the advantages of Muslim social status. In India, political conquest preceded conversion, while conversion itself resulted more often from the attractiveness of Muslim institutions and the personal appeal of **Sufism** (Muslim mysticism) than from the threat of force. In Southeast Asia, which now includes a large segment of the world's Muslim population, Islam spread peaceably as part of an international mercantile culture, again aided by the appeal of Sufism.

The difficulties encountered by the various Muslim political powers after their establishment were due to a variety of causes, but none of these involved turning away from Islam as such. It appears that the Middle East may have been suffering some long-term adverse effects on its ecology, as a result of the ancient and intensive agricultural exploitation of the land. Many Islamic governments followed a policy of assigning "tax farms" as rewards to the military; these temporary revenue assignments were often exploited with little regard for the welfare of the peasants or the condition of the land and irrigation works, thus contributing to the decline of productivity. Coupled with the Mongol invasions and the Black Death during the thirteenth and fourteenth centuries, these trends may have reduced the vitality of agriculture, urban life, and even trade. There is some indication that population may have declined and that nomadism may have increased during the age of the Muslim empires.

In addition to the economic factors, certain political processes seem to involve an inherent dynamic of growth and decline. In agrarian societies, an existing order tends to accumulate vested interests, tax exemptions, and special privileges to the detriment of the overall functioning of the polity, until at last the weakened governmental power is overthrown and the accumulated commitments are wiped away (as happened in the Arab conquest of Byzantine and Sassanian domains). This and other political processes may have contributed to cycles of political disintegration and revitalization both before and during the age of Muslim power.

As for intellectual development, it appears that the creative exploration of new ideas reached a peak during the Abbasid caliphate; afterward the legal, moral, and theological conceptions of the ulema prevailed and became increasingly hostile to innovation, especially after the ulema were integrated into the Ottoman order. While some see this as further evidence of the stagnation of "Oriental" civilizations, one could just as easily see it as the natural consequence of the refinement of the Sharia, and particularly of its institutionalization in the **madrasah** schools where the ulema were trained—features that in turn provided much of the resiliency of Islamic law. The spirit of conservatism that prevailed after the collapse of the caliphate did not in itself cause political decline, nor was it very different from the conservatism that prevailed in Europe before the eighteenth century. The pattern of peaks and valleys in political power and social strength has been common to both regions throughout most of history.

LEGITIMACY IN GOVERNMENT

As stated earlier, the teachings of Muhammad stressed the righteous community that was structured to realize the demands of justice and piety. Since the early caliphate, a central problem in Islam has been to reconcile the demands of political reality and those of faith. The champions of Islamic values needed a workable government in theory, but rarely approved of what they found in practice. The Islamic governments needed the approval of Islam to make them legitimate, but while the Muslim rulers were devout men, they were willing to make only limited concessions to Islamic ideals in government.

In some respects, the first caliphs were able to avoid many of the inherent difficulties of legitimizing Islamic political power. They were personal followers of the Prophet who were intimately acquainted with his words and deeds and who ruled largely by virtue of that knowledge. Like traditional Arab leaders, they also depended largely on their own personal qualities and reputation, and on their close acquaintance with the community (that is, with the core of Muhammad's following). They also acquired much legitimacy through their military leadership (Umar preferred to be called the "commander of the faithful" rather than caliph), a role that was well established in Arab tradition and that carried with it the notion of leadership among men who were essentially equals.

The Political Role of the Ulema

Under Uthman a gap began to develop (or to become apparent) between Islamic ideals and the realities of political power and privilege. The issue of Uthman's murder and Ali's accession became symbolic for Muslims of the conflict between communal loyalty and religious purity. Although the Umayyads won on behalf of political solidarity, they had to face renewed challenges first from Ali's sons and later from a coalition of factions that wished to see Islamic government guided by uncompromising religious ideals. When this coalition failed to reverse the tendency toward secular power, Muslims were obliged to choose between remaining loyal to the protest against government or to the powers that governed Islam, regardless of their faults. While the Shia took the former course, the bulk of the community, later called Sunni, chose in favor of the political unity of the Umma.

As the pious, learned men of the Islamic world began to form into a coherent body of ulema, this body became a kind of loyal opposition, aloof from and critical of the government but not overtly disloyal to it. The ulema generally recognized the legitimacy of the caliphs, even while criticizing their ways. As the caliphs became powerless, they were still invested with theoretical legitimacy as the arbiters of any affairs concerning all Islam, and as the source of authority to the various *emirs,* or local rulers. After the fall of the caliphate, the ulema were inclined to grant at least some legitimacy to the emirs on the grounds that they provided the political order necessary to the community. This trend culminated in the Ottoman theory that whoever can rule the Muslim community according to the Sharia is entitled to be considered the caliph. The Ottoman interpretation completes the transition from the original theory, in which secular power is derived from religious legitimation, to one in which religious legitimation is derived from secular power.

The unique political role of the ulema in Islam deserves special comment. Many traditional agrarian societies had a priesthood, a privileged group of religious practitioners who mediated ritually between the common people and the supernatural, and who tended to be intimately connected with—and supportive of—the political ruling class. The Muslim ulema, however, are scholars rather than priests, and their training in subsidized institutions has been open, in theory, to anyone showing promise. Under the protection of Islam, the ulema have traditionally presented a voice of opposition that attempted to hold political figures accountable to the principles of Islam, principles opposed to privilege and self-indulgence. Even today this heritage influences the relations between the Muslim religious leadership and the politicians. The ulema in Saudi Arabia, for example, retain the right to declare a king unfit to govern, and they exercised this right in 1964 when they approved the deposing of King Saud.

THE SHARIA LAW

The Koran did not provide a complete guide for social life, and after the death of Muhammad the question arose as to how it was to be interpreted and how Muslims should deal with problems it did not directly anticipate. It soon became evident that the secular values of the conquered agrarian states, not to mention the old Arab ways, might reassert themselves unless Islam provided more detailed codes. By gradual steps, religious scholars developed a complex, cumulative set of guiding rules for Muslims that came to be known as the Sharia. At the core of the Sharia is the Koran, but it was necessary to supplement the Koran with reports (hadith) about the sayings and practices of the Prophet and his community. Later, as Sharia thinking attacked more complex problems, the Koran and the hadith were extended by means of the principle of analogy, by reference to the con-

sensus of the Umma (or more specifically, its recognized religious leaders), and by reference to the welfare of the Umma. The relative importance of these various avenues of **fiqh**, or understanding, was debated by leading scholars, and by the ninth century several major schools of legal thinking had developed. Each of these was accorded equal validity, and although they differed somewhat on the methods of arriving at legal codes, their results were similar. Muslims were expected to adhere consistently to one or another of these schools, usually according to the common practice of the locality. Today there are four such recognized schools in Sunni Islam.

Formal training in Sharia law became institutionalized in the madrasahs, Islamic schools supported by privately endowed religious foundations (**waqf**, plural *awqaf*) where any capable person could study free of charge. Such schools helped to determine who was qualified to interpret the tradition, and to standardize the Sharia against indiscriminate reinterpretation. They also made it possible to broaden the Sharia beyond the strict limits of the Koran and hadith without sacrificing its coherence or throwing it open to uncontrolled change. The Sharia, thus broadened and codified, provided a universal law that applied to every Muslim and to diverse aspects of life ranging from the settlement of political and business disputes to the regulation of family life. The application of this code and the qualifications of its administrators were valid in all Muslim nations regardless of political boundaries, which allowed Islam to prosper as an international social order even in times of political decentralization.

Based on the mercantile and Arab values of Mecca and Medina, the Sharia embodied a social philosophy that was opposed to social class or other privilege; it tended to support individual rights and individual social mobility and to protect the weak against the strong. Along with an uncompromising concern for Islamic principles of social justice, however, went a distrust of innovation and of the deviant or the outsider—an inclination that became more and more established in the madrasahs after the fourteenth century. In the madrasahs the methods of teaching became extremely conservative and were aimed at discouraging innovation. Any question that had once been decided upon and accepted by the ulema was no longer open for discussion, and new issues were to be resolved insofar as possible in exact accordance with previous decisions. Even the number of errors was determined—there were six dozen false sects of Islam, and every new heresy could be classified with those already known. Yet without this careful regulation the Sharia probably could not have served its vital function in Muslim life.

The sway of the Sharia was never absolute. Because monarchs often found the Sharia incomplete, irrelevant to certain questions, or excessively "soft" on criminals, they typically established their own courts and legal codes. The peasants and townspeople, on the other hand, sometimes found it in their interest to follow customary law, even (as in the case of some inheritance rules) when it contradicted the Sharia. Despite these auxiliary legal systems, however, the Sharia stood as the supreme expression of legitimacy. It was the core of Islamic social life, to which every Muslim ultimately owed allegiance. Safe from random innovation, local cultural influence, and the tampering of political interest groups, the Sharia provided a means of integrating an international civilization.

THE SHIA

The conflicting demands of political unity and religious purity, which became apparent so early in Islamic history, gave rise to the great sectarian split within Islam—that of the Sunnis and the Shia. While the majority of Muslims are Sunnis, who place loyalty to the established order of the Umma above religious disputation, the Shia, a substantial minority, believe that only a divinely inspired political leadership is worthy of a Muslim's loyalty. The historical split between the two groups is difficult to discuss because the key events of the past have been imbued over the years with complex symbolic significance. At the time of his death, Ali stood for the protest against the supposed corruptions of Uthman's rule, and his defeat was viewed by many Muslims—particularly those in Iraq—as an unfortunate triumph of worldly power over true Islamic piety. Those loyal to Ali and to what he stood for came to be known as the Shia (party) of Ali.

A turning point in the history of the Shia was an insurrection in 680 against the Umayyads under Ali's son Husayn, in which Husayn, abandoned by the bulk of his supporters, was killed. With the rise of the Abbasids in 750, Shia hopes that the new political unrest would lead to a reinstatement of Ali's line were dashed, and the Shia assumed the posture of a minority opposition to the political establishment.

Under the Abbasids the division between the Shia and the Sunnis became more distinct. The Sunni position, even among those who sympathized with Ali's protest and despised Uthman and the fallen Umayyad dynasty, was that devotion to the solidarity of the Umma and obedience to its recognized leadership should transcend religious dissension. By the tenth century, the Shia had developed into a distinct and very influential group that proposed, in opposition to the Sunni view, that Muslims should follow only those authorities who were rightly guided. In the Shia view, this gift of divine guidance (what sociologists call "charisma") was possessed only by a small number of the elect, descendants of the Prophet through his daughter Fatima and his son-in-law Ali. While Husayn was the last of these to make an open bid for power, the Shia believed that secret knowledge and divine inspiration had passed through Ali's line to a succession of rightful leaders.

The Shia movement eventually split over differing interpretations of this line of succession. The largest faction was the "Twelvers," who believed that the twelfth Imam in the succession had gone into hiding from the wicked world, where he would remain until his eventual return as the **Mahdi**, or Muslim messiah. In Twelver Shiism, which predominates in Iran, it has occasionally been possible for religious leaders to claim sweeping powers as representatives of this "Hidden Imam." Another major faction, the **Ismailis**, part with the twelver line in disputing the identity of the seventh Imam. They came to emphasize the esoteric knowledge of a secret religious elite, a knowledge revealed to the pious individuals only by degrees as they ascend in the religious hierarchy. Ismaili Islam reached the peak of its influence in the Fatimid dynasty in Egypt (969–1171), which was renowned for its achievements in government, commerce, art, and learning.

The Shia came to see the majority of Muslims as betrayers of their faith, and temporal power as essentially illegitimate. In this atmosphere of resistance they developed the practice of denying their true beliefs in public when necessary, as well as the idea that the inward truth of the Koran (as opposed to its outward or superficial meaning) is unknown to the community at large and must be interpreted by the Imams or their agents. (The use of the term *imam* can be confusing, since it can refer to a variety of roles ranging from a leader of Muslim prayer to—in Shia thought—a leader of all Islam. Generally, we have capitalized Imam only when it refers to the latter or to a specific historical personage such as the Imam Ayatollah Khomeini.) Another strong current in Shia thought is the tragic view of the fate of the righteous man in an unrighteous society, and a deep sense of guilt over the betrayal and martyrdom of Husayn. Once a year, during the month of **Muharram**, Husayn's martyrdom is commemorated in an outpouring of grief, self-flagellation, and resentment toward the Sunnis. If the ulema of Sunni Islam looked askance at the political establishment, the Shia simply regarded it as illegitimate, to be tolerated only for the time being. Despite the differences in outlook, Sunni and Shia Islam actually developed remarkably parallel institutions, parallel Sharia codes, and even parallel debates over similar issues. Mystical Sufism, which was largely a Sunni phenomenon, developed its Shia counterpart in a particularly inward-turning brand of personal devotion to Ali and Husayn.

Even in Ali's day Iraq was a center of proto Shia resistance. It remained so under the Umayyads as part of the protest against Syrian power; and even after the fall of the Umayyads, Shiism remained strong in the old Sassanian domains—so much that some historians characterize Shiism as a Persian movement against Arabism. Shiism was even more radically localized, however, during the rivalry between the Sunni Ottomans and the Shia Safavids, when nonconforming minorities in each domain were persecuted or driven out. Today, Shiism is largely confined to the Middle East, where more than a fourth of the Muslims are Shia, most of whom live in Iraq or Iran.

SUFISM

If the Sharia was uncompromisingly oriented toward history, justice, and practical responsibility, other elements of Islam addressed very different facets of religious life. Mysticism, that brand of religious awareness that emphasizes the clarifying and enlightening inward experience over conventionalized and verbally communicated ideas, is pervasive in human cultures and was well established in the Middle East before the rise of Islam. Like Christianity and Judaism, Islam has developed its own distinct tradition of mysticism. In early times the mystically inclined Muslims, or Sufis, were a small minority hardly distinguishable from other Muslims, but after 1100 they became more prominent and influential. The Muslim philosopher-theologian Ghazali (d. 1111), though not a Sufi himself, aided the rise of Sufism by arguing that it was not only consistent with the Sharia but was a valuable complement to it.

Sufi mystics used classic techniques of posture, breathing, meditation, music, and dance to induce states of extraordinary awareness that they regarded as closeness to God. In their philosophical writings they emphasized love and cosmic unity, even posing Jesus as the ideal Sufi. Like the Sharia, Sufism was populistic—it took little notice of traditional lines of privilege and was open to all who would pursue it. Unlike the ulema, who were oriented strongly toward the Sharia, the mystics tended to be tolerant of local cultures and customs, of human weakness, and of different levels of understanding. They viewed the Islamic concept of jihad, often translated in English as holy war, as an inward struggle for enlightenment.

Even so, Sufism had its outward, institutional side. After the tenth century, Sufis began to organize themselves into separate orders, or **tariqahs**. Each of these recognized a different line of communication of mystical knowledge, beginning with the private communications of Muhammad to certain followers, and going through a known line of teachers (**pirs**). One could become a pir only by studying under another recognized pir, so that the body of knowledge within each order was preserved and controlled. These Sufi orders had social and political uses, for they often became the organizational core of guilds, young men's military clubs, or even some governmental organizations. One ambitious caliph, shortly before the Mongol invasions, even sought to restore the power of the caliphate through the judicious use of Sufi tariqahs.

Because of Sufism's tolerance, its association in folk religion with local "saints" and their tombs, and its abuse by wandering charlatans or extremists who considered themselves outside the Sharia, the ulema often took a dim view of Sufism. However, despite occasional outbursts of anti-Sufi reaction, as in the thirteenth century, Sufism was established as legitimate by the Sharia principle of consensus. Some ulema scholars were Sufi pirs themselves, and Sufism came to dominate the inward side of religious life in Islam, especially among the Sunnis. The personal appeal of Sufism supplemented the social appeal of the Sharia and contributed greatly to Islam's spread as a religion, and thus indirectly to the political sway of Islam. Furthermore, Sufism remained another potential counterbalance to the outward authority of any "Islamic" government.

ISLAM AND RADICAL POLITICS

Muhammad's ideal of religiously based law and government contained the seeds of religious support for the establishment and of religious opposition to it. The tradition of religious opposition is represented in one way by the ulema, and in quite another by the many radical movements in Islam's history. It is not possible to mention all the major movements that have arisen in Islam, but a few examples will suffice for illustration: The Kharijites, the Ismailis, the Sudanese Mahdi, Twelver Shiism, and the Muwahiddun movement.

THE KHARIJITES

Islam's first civil war began with an insurrection of Egyptian soldiers who murdered the caliph Uthman and justified the act with the accusation that he had departed from Islam and was therefore a usurper. Ali's supporters accepted this line of reasoning, while his opponents accused him of condoning the murder of a believer and of at-tempting to disrupt the community. When Ali agreed to submit the issue to arbitration, his most extreme supporters turned against him to become Kharijites ("seceders"). The Kharijites embodied a radically anarchistic interpretation of Islam, in which personal piety was held to be not only the sole measure of a person's right to lead the community, but the only criterion for membership in the Umma itself. Thus, the impious Uthman was not only a false caliph, but an unbeliever falsely professing Islam; it was therefore the duty of a believer to kill him. In Kharijite eyes, anyone who had committed a "grave" sin was excluded from the Umma, and the most extreme Kharijites did not hesitate to kill non-Kharijites indiscriminately when the occasion presented itself. Even among the Kharijites themselves, on principle no leader was to be trusted, and their "caliph" could be deposed for the slightest transgression. Ali found it necessary to suppress the Kharijites by force, and he was eventually assassinated by one of them. There were more than a score of Kharijite rebellions during Ali's and Muawiya's reigns, and small Kharijite communities have continued to exist down to the present. In their extreme approach to the issue of piety versus political order, the Kharijites severely crippled their own political strength and assured themselves a marginal role in Islamic society.

ISMAILIS AND QARMATIANS

The Shia went in a direction opposite to that of the Kharijites by elevating the charismatic leader to an exalted status, the Ismaili Shia going to the farthest extreme. Their central belief was that a highly esoteric knowledge of the all-important inner meaning of Muhammad's teachings was transmitted through secret communication from the Prophet to certain elect followers. The Ismailis gave rise to a number of movements, but none more fascinating than the **Qarmatians**. Originating in the desert between Syria and the Iraq in the late ninth century, the movement designated its leader as an emissary of God. The Qarmatians were dedicated to the overthrow of the wealthy and privileged, and the Bedouins and peasants who joined the sect apparently held all goods in common. After its suppression by the Abbasids, the movement reappeared in Bahrain, where it became established as an egalitarian, communistic state that lasted well into the eleventh century. It is said that the Qarmatians spurned the Sharia and orthodox forms of worship, and that one of their leaders who was thought to be the Mahdi, or Muslim messiah, set himself above Muhammad (this, however, may be hostile propaganda). In any case, the Qarmatians seem to have regarded other Muslims as unbelievers, and in 930 they succeeded in abducting temporarily the Black Stone from the shrine at Mecca, on the grounds that it was an object of idolatry.

The Mahdi

The Qarmatians were by no means the only Muslims to believe in a Mahdi. Running sporadically throughout Islam is a chiliastic orientation, which holds that the world will eventually be delivered from its wickedness into an age of justice and piety, and the wicked will suffer vengeance from the righteous. The idea of a deliverer, or Mahdi, appears repeatedly in this chiliastic thinking. Of the many persons hailed as Mahdis, one of the most recent and striking examples is the Sudanese Mahdi of the late nineteenth century. Arising in opposition to the inroads of the modernizing Egyptian ruler Ismail, whose stated intention was to make Egypt part of Europe (and the Sudan part of Egypt), the Mahdi drove the Egyptians out of the Sudan and preached a program of Islamic moral reform, not only for the Sudan but for all Islam. The Mahdi appointed his own caliph. Publicized among pilgrims at Mecca, his program seemed to many Muslims an attractive alternative to the weakened and discredited Ottoman leadership until the British finally succeeded in crushing the movement in the 1890s.

Twelver Shiism

Of all the Shia movements, Iranian "Twelver" Shiism has the greatest contemporary relevance. Although it shares with the other forms of Shiism its basic emphasis on esoteric knowledge vouchsafed through the lineage of the Prophet, Twelver Shiism has shown itself to be a persistent factor in the political arenas of the Middle East, alternating between active and passive political activity. Whereas the Ismaili Shia held substantial power only during the Fatimid reign, the Twelver Shia have held dynastic power a number of times, always in the area of Iran and Iraq.

As a consequence of its substantial dynastic experience, Twelver Shiism has developed elaborate doctrines regarding the relationship between faith and the state and between the ulema and the governor. These theories saw contemporary expression during the "Tobacco riot" protests against the Qajar dynasty near the turn of the twentieth century, during the nationalist protests against the shah of Iran in the immediate aftermath of World War II, and most recently in the successful movement against the shah and in the design and implementation of an Islamic republic in Iran. Recent scholarship indicates that a critical turning point in the movement against the shah was Ayatollah Khomeini's successful invocation of the activist symbols of Twelver Shiism, thus effectively transforming Iranian Shia religious activity from quiet protest to political confrontation. In so doing, Ayatollah Khomeini of necessity invoked symbols and myths from the earliest days of Shiism, thus showing anew the relevance of the past to the present.

The Muwahhidun Movement

In Arabia during the late eighteenth century, a former Sufi teacher, Muhammad Ibn Abd-al-Wahhab, came under the influence of the conservative Hanbali school of Sunni Muslim thought, which rejected the role of ulema consensus in the interpreting of the Sharia. He called for the purification of Islam from the influence of evil innovations, which he believed were responsible for the decadence of the Ottoman world. With the aid of Ibn Saud, a local ruler who had converted to the movement, Ibn Abd al-Wahhab set about to promote an extremely puritanical reform of Islam, which opposed all forms of Sufism and pre-Islamic custom and denounced most Muslims as idolators and infidels to be killed. Even after decades of Ottoman attempts to suppress the movement, Ibn Saud's grandson was able to seize Mecca and Medina, to destroy many of Islam's holy shrines, and to massacre the residents of these cities. The movement was temporarily suppressed in 1818, only to reappear in the twentieth century, again championed by members of the house of Saud. This "Unitarian" or **Muwahhidun** movement (a designation preferred by its followers over the more frequently encountered term, **Wahhabi**) was to become the foundation of the modern state of Saudi Arabia. Thus, the deep-lying conservatism of contemporary Saudi Arabia, far from being a continuation of some ancient local heritage, as Westerners often assume, is actually the result of a relatively recent political–religious movement, which by usual Muslim standards can only be regarded as unusually conservative and puritanical.

As these examples show, Islamic political–religious movements have a long history and can take many forms. Like similar movements in Christianity, they tend to adopt a "restitutionist" outlook—that is, they see themselves as restoring the original purity of the religion. The exact nature of that restoration, of course, tends to be partly a projection of the values of the reformers. Despite their unswervingly religious tone, such movements tend to display an acute consciousness of social problems, and to support political programs—some more practical than others—to remedy them. Some such movements bear significant political fruit, as in the case of Muwahhidun influence in Saudi Arabia. The sociology of religion shows that such religious movements often center on charismatic leaders who are thought to have special knowledge of transcendent order and purpose, and they often arise in times of cultural, social, political, and economic upheaval. It should not be surprising, then, if the future sees a succession of charismatic religious movements within Islam, propounding various avenues toward the revitalization of the faith and providing the vehicles for an assortment of social and political reforms. We shall have more to say about Islamic revivalist movements in Chapter 7.

DIVERSITY IN ISLAMIC POLITICAL THOUGHT

The Ayatollah Ruhollah Khomeini, leader of Iran's 1979 revolution, was quoted as saying, "We Muslims are of one family even though we live under different governments and in various regions." While the statement is an accurate reflection of the Muslim ideal of a united Umma, it should not be taken to mean that Islam represents a single, monolithic bloc with a fixed perspective on every significant issue. The recent upsurge of Islamic revival can only be expected to revitalize discussion and controversy among Muslims on the many issues that have always occupied the dialectic of Islamic thought. It is not easy to say, once and for all, what constitutes the Islamic vision of society, law, and government. Almost from its beginning, Islam has had its factions, particularly the Sunnis and the Shia. It has manifested an inward, mystical side as well as an outward set of codes and institutions. Muslims have tried to mediate between the heritage of Middle Eastern civilization, with its despotism and social privilege, and the principles of social equality enunciated in the Koran. Islamic civilization has been deeply influenced in various times and places by diverse cultural traditions, secular philosophies carried on from the Greeks, the aristocratic high culture of the royal courts, and the folk practices that preceded Islam and were independent of formal theology. Cosmopolitan and universalistic in its core outlook, Islam has had to deal with those who chose not to join the brotherhood of Islam. Each one of these conflicts has engendered not one but numerous solutions, depending on historical circumstance.

Yet it would be misleading, despite the change and adaptability of Islam, to see it as entirely amorphous or plastic, lending itself indifferently to every possible interpretation. Throughout the Islamic dialogue run certain recurrent themes that have their roots in the fundamental principles laid out in Muhammad's ministry. One of these is the interdependence of religion and the sociopolitical order, which is built more deeply into Islam than into most world religions. It would be harder for a serious Muslim to accept the separation of church and state than for a traditional Christian, even though the possibility of such a separation was suggested by Egyptian President Sadat's admonition that there should be "no religion in politics, and no politics in religion." Furthermore, Muslim law involves a detailed pattern of everyday life that regulates such matters as alcohol consumption and marriage. Such personal moral regulations existed more informally in traditional Christianity, but in Islam they are part of a literate tradition that will be relatively difficult to change or to separate from political issues. The Sharia is not easily circumvented; strictly speaking, it is open only to interpretation, not legislation. The forces that gave the Sharia and the ulema such independence in the past will probably continue to ensure Islam's role as an active challenge to the political status quo. Westerners observing the dialogue in contemporary Islamic political thought may mistakenly assume that Islam is "waking up" and examining these issues critically for the first time, but nothing could be further from the truth. Whatever the solutions toward which Muslims move, they can be expected to show the influence of previous dialogue within the tradition, a dialogue that will continue to allow for diverse possibilities.

CHAPTER FOUR

Western Imperialism

1800–1914

Imperialism is a familiar word that seems at first to have a clear and straightforward meaning, but on closer inspection it becomes blurred and indistinct. It may mean any one of three relationships in which a relatively powerful country dominates the political, economic, or cultural affairs of a weaker one. In political imperialism, the powerful country controls the major governmental decision making of the weaker, either directly or by proxy through pliant, cooperative officials of the weaker country. Economic imperialism denotes a situation in which a weaker country becomes dependent on stronger countries for income. Cultural imperialism means a situation in which a weaker country adopts the language, manners, and lifestyle of the stronger.

All three kinds of imperialism occurred in the Middle East in the nineteenth century. It is difficult to assess the full consequences of these relationships since many aspects of them have not yet been fully played out and are still active today, but most writers feel that the negative effects of imperialism outweigh the positive. The study of imperialism, however, contains many difficulties in concept, definition, and measurement, and a final assessment is far from certain. For example, it is often difficult to say whether certain commercial transactions between weak countries and powerful ones benefit only the powerful or whether they work to the mutual benefit of both. And while a weaker, less-developed country may chafe at being dependent on a stronger one, its very dissatisfaction may spur it to make some positive reforms that it might not otherwise have made. The effects of imperialism on the weaker country may be shallow or they may be deep. One country may survive a period of imperial stewardship and keep most of its social, cultural, and economic fabric intact. Imperial domination in such a case is only a kind of veneer. In other cases, imperial domination may deeply disrupt a country's social, economic, and political structures.

Nationalism, like imperialism, is another term that most people understand immediately, but on closer study find difficult to apply exactly. Nationalism is not just a matter of simple patriotism born of deep loyalty to an ethnic group, religion, homeland, leader, or set of institutions, although nationalist movements frequently contain a mixture of all these elements. Nationalistic movements give the appearance of solidity because they are often bound together by resentment toward the imperial power. Once the imperial power is removed, the seemingly solid and cohesive nationalist movement often disintegrates into perhaps scores of factional conflicts. We must study such root factions and forces if we are to gain a deeper understanding of a particular country or region. In this chapter we shall examine how European imperialist powers penetrated the Middle East in the nineteenth century, just before the various nation-states in the region emerged. The Europeans did so in a series of powerful, deep-reaching thrusts, and we shall examine how certain areas responded to such battering.

SETTING THE STAGE

For thousands of years, most areas of the world were fairly equal in technology and economic well-being. Major inventions and technological innovations occurred at irregular intervals and in widely separated regions. An innovation that arose at a certain time or in a certain region had little influence on a technology that was being developed in another place or time. It took centuries, even millennia, for ideas and innovations to become uniformly diffused over the large areas of Asia, Europe, and the Middle East. Regions that were late to adopt a particular innovation or bit of technology from abroad had a comfortably long time in which to achieve parity with other regions before the next innovation came along.

During the period from about A.D. 1400 to 1700, however, a set of institutions and cultural forms was developed in Europe that promoted and regularized the flow of innovations. The most important advances occurred in organization and administration, weaponry, and communications. The process by which these innovations were accepted and by which a continuing need for them was institutionalized is still not well understood. The result, however, is clear: Technical innovation became a continuous, irreversible, accelerating process. The time when regions could regain parity because of slow diffusion was at an end; Western Europe achieved technological dominance over the rest of the world, and other regions had no time to catch up.

It is difficult to say just when the West began to penetrate the Middle East or when it finally achieved political and economic dominance. One very important date, however, is 1498. It was in this year that the Portuguese navigator Vasco da Gama sailed around the southern tip of Africa to India, thus opening an important new trade route to the East. Although Europeans had gradually taken control of the Mediterranean sea trade over the preceding 200 years, the opening of this new ocean route to India now assured them of total control over most of the world's maritime trade. The Middle Eastern overland trade routes began to decline. European control of the Mediterranean had already begun to shift the middleman functions from the Arabs to the Venetians and Genoese. Furthermore, Western technical and manufacturing innovations were resulting in the production of better goods. As a consequence, Middle Eastern handicraft production, especially along the southern and eastern Mediterranean coasts, also began to decline.

These developments tore wide rents in the economic and social fabric of the region. For example, Middle Eastern handicraft production was loosely organized in guilds—groups of craftsmen whose taxes provided a source of revenue for the various local governments, and whose presence contributed vitally to the social life of the area. Many of the ulema were either guild members or were supported by guilds. Therefore, a decline in the well-being and consequent leadership role of the religious establishment directly followed the decline in handicraft industries.

European dominance in commerce and production was accompanied by advances in military technology. European armies became powerful instruments of national will. After centuries of successful expansion, the Ottoman Empire began to lose territory to the Europeans.

Some writers claim that the Europeans' technological superiority also gave a sense of moral superiority. While this may or may not be true, Europeans, in their quest for control of the Middle East, often clothed their political and economic motives in the vestments of religion. A belief in the inherent decadence and wickedness of Islam provided generations of Europeans with a strong rationale for imperialistic ventures in the Middle East, and this belief had a strong impact on the various cultures with which they associated.

THE OTTOMANS

By 1800, the decline of the Ottoman Empire was well under way; it would accelerate over the next hundred years. Western technology and military power were having an increasingly strong impact. The Ottoman elite, long used to thinking that Western knowledge was not worth having, realized that it could no longer maintain its sense of superiority. An early sign of this change of attitude is the so-called Tulip Period (1718–1730), during which the Ottoman elite succumbed to a fad for everything Western. It built French-style pleasure palaces, wore Western clothes, sat on Western chairs, and cultivated Western gardens. It developed a mania for tulips, sending the price of tulip bulbs to absurd heights, with high offices being sold for particularly exotic strains.

Aside from these extravagances, the period also saw the tentative beginnings of a new intellectual atmosphere; previously rejected reforms were now being seriously entertained. Most of them were shallow and aimed only at making institutions in the existing framework—especially the military—more effective. Selim III (r. 1789–1807) attempted more fundamental reforms; and while most of these failed or were only partially successful, they did lay the groundwork for later reforms in the nineteenth century. Once antireformist resistance was overcome, particularly that from the traditional military corps, the Janissaries, reform activity quickened. The Janissaries represented the most important group in the nonmodernized army. They viewed the building of a modern army and bureaucracy as a threat to their power; therefore, they were at the forefront of the coalition resisting reform. But Sultan Mahmud II (1808–1839) cleverly built a new coalition loyal to him and in 1826 had the Janissaries killed when they rebelled. This event is called the "Auspicious Incident" because it allowed the sultan to initiate the period of significant reform known as the **Tanzimat** period.

The Tanzimat Period (1839–1876)

The Tanzimat reforms were achieved with no clearly defined master plan other than a mostly unstated desire for greater government central-

ization. During previous centuries, the empire had expanded successfully by means of policies that favored extreme decentralization. By giving local governments large measures of autonomy, the millet system had kept the provinces reasonably satisfied. However, the military in remote areas had begun to look more to its own interests than to those of the empire. Within limits, local authorities had the power to tax the population as they saw fit, as long as they remitted a negotiated amount to the central government; the sultan consequently had little control over the size of the royal treasury. As the empire declined and the booty of conquest stopped flowing into the capital, the Ottoman sultans tried to make up the difference by raising taxes. However, the provincial authorities, having become used to self-rule for several generations, felt no great loyalty to the sultans and firmly resisted them. The sultans therefore saw that it was crucial to reorganize the empire around a strong central authority.

The Tanzimat reforms were many and far-reaching. Ministries were established to impose uniform regulations all over the empire. The military was completely reorganized along Western lines, and its incentive system was restructured to create greater commitment to the empire. The tax collection system was streamlined to allow revenues to flow directly to the royal treasury; local governments had their powers reduced.

Although many Tanzimat reforms failed and many others did not work out exactly as intended, they marked a turning point in Ottoman history. And although the empire continued to lose territory in the nineteenth century, the reforms were a sign of considerable lingering vitality. The Ottoman Empire was far from being the "sick man of Europe," as was said at the time and as was commonly believed well into this century. To be sure, the empire was beset by internal and external difficulties of massive proportions, but there was also substantial positive change. The entrenched powers were understandably opposed to the reforms, but in time they were either accommodated or suppressed. Modern organizational forms and military technology spread to other areas, especially communications and education.

Although the reforms' impact on cultural life was not a central concern during the early years of the Tanzimat period, they had a pervasive and enduring result. Many reforms required that administrators undergo specialized training and education. A new generation of technocrats arose who began to respect the West, for it was there that the needed knowledge was stored. Along with technical knowledge, this new class also absorbed the political philosophies of nationalism and democracy. The lack of qualified personnel within the empire, and the increasing encroachments of European governments and commercial interests, also brought an influx of powerful and active Europeans to the center of the empire.

The Tanzimat reforms took place in an atmosphere of international intrigue. England, France, and Russia (and later Germany) had vital interests in the Middle East which they tried to protect and enlarge. For most of the nineteenth century, the Ottoman Empire had to defend itself against European powers that were pushing and shoving among themselves for competitive advantage. Europe generally did not want to see the Ottoman Empire collapse; the scramble for spoils afterward would certainly have ended in a blood bath and much destruction. So, first one European power and then another supported the empire. But while the Europeans wished the Ottoman Empire a long life, they did not want to see it strong. On the contrary, they chipped away at its edges and blunted many of the effects of the Tanzimat reforms. There is no question that nineteenth-century Ottoman administration was corrupt and inept, but it is questionable whether a smoothly functioning modern organization would have done much better. The European powers had the empire pinioned. The Tanzimat reforms were a significant attempt to adapt to technological realities, and they represented a skillful attempt to resolve the empire's internal conflicts while playing off European interests. But in the end, the Ottomans could not escape the debilitating entanglements imposed on them by Westerners.

As the European powers increased their leverage, responsible parties in the empire grew increasingly dissatisfied with the course taken by the sultan and his inner circle. Various changes of policy were demanded, the most important being representation in the legislative bodies, the adoption of a constitution, and the formation of an Ottoman ideology. Some favored a wholesale adoption of European ways; some sought a return to a past era of Islamic purity; some advocated a host of intermediate positions. The restive attitude of the new technocrats and the role of the Western powers presented the sultan with a problem common to most reforming autocrats—how to control the demands of a new class of people who possess the technical knowledge on which the regime depends. Since the military and commercial presence of the competing Europeans prevented any return to past ways, and since the Europeans could not be expelled, a long series of struggles and partial accommodations took place; this process resulted in the granting of a constitution in 1876 by the shrewd Sultan Abdulhamit (r. 1876–1909). The constitution was suspended shortly thereafter, but was reinstated with significant changes in 1908.

The Young Turk revolution (1908), which prompted the sultan to reconvene the legislative body and activate the constitution, had its ideological roots in various sources of discontent. A significant pan-Islamic and then pan-Ottoman movement, supported by the sultan, arose during the last third of the nineteenth century. The pan-Islamic movement championed the rights of all Muslims. The pan-Ottoman movement was broader; it called for more or less equal rights for all (including non-Muslim) subjects of the empire. But these movements contained many contradictions. Increasingly, waves of ethnic and geographic nationalism developed in reaction to Ottoman hegemony at the same time the sultan was reaffirming the equality of all his subjects. This led to discontent among the military forces, who were asked to support the call for equality while being attacked by its supposed beneficiaries. The ideological reaction was pan-Turkism, the notion that the ethnic identity of the empire deserved first consideration. Turkish greatness and the virtues of the Turkish people were celebrated in a large number of literary works.

The combination of the calls for a Turkish nation, military discontent, millet terrorism, and European pressures put Sultan Abdulhamit in an increasingly defensive position. He responded with many repressive measures. He paralyzed the bureaucracy by insisting on personally approving the smallest changes in policy. A financial crisis sparked a widespread revolt. The revolution of 1908 forced the sultan to agree to demands for a constitution and representation.

The period after World War I was devastating for the empire. The positive effects of some of the modernizing reforms had been undone by a series of crippling conflicts. Furthermore, the Ottoman Empire had aligned itself with the Central Powers during the war; when they were defeated, the empire was dismembered. The Allied forces divided the empire among themselves and imposed a particularly harsh rule on Turkey. But the Turkish nationalist forces that had been successful in 1908 rose to defend the homeland. Led by Kemal Ataturk, they repelled the Europeans and established an independent Turkish state. A remarkable series of reforms followed that would ultimately transform and secularize Turkey.

EGYPT

Long-standing corruption and generally ineffective rule had led to centuries of decay in Egypt. But the power of this weak Ottoman province was to change markedly during the nineteenth century. For the Ottomans of the nineteenth century, Egypt was something to be both feared and imitated.

In the last decade of the eighteenth century, the French were looking at Egypt with increased interest, largely because of their struggle with the British. Egypt could be France's granary, control Middle Eastern military and commercial traffic, and provide a base from which to threaten the British in India. With these aims in view, Napoleon invaded Egypt in July 1798, and with remarkable ease destroyed the Mameluk forces that ruled Egypt under loose Ottoman control. Napoleon presented himself to the Egyptians, and especially the ulema, as a liberator from foreign rule. But his call for cooperation went unheeded, and he was forced to quell a rebellion in Cairo in October 1798.

As all rulers of Egypt knew, control of the Levant was vital to Egyptian security. Consequently, Napoleon invaded Palestine and Syria in 1799. He met with failure, however, as Ottoman forces halted the French advance and the British navy attacked the French fleet. Since the security

of Egypt could not be maintained, Napoleon quickly reassessed his position and quit Egypt in August 1799. The last French forces withdrew by 1801.

The brief French presence in Egypt gave advance warning that European powers would be drawn into Middle Eastern affairs on a much larger scale than previously. It also served as a lesson to the Ottoman rulers and to the future Egyptian ruler, **Muhammad Ali (Mehemet Ali)**, that European organizational and technical skills were superior to those of the Ottoman Empire—so superior that the rulers would have to adapt quickly if the empire were to remain secure.

Muhammad Ali had fought against the French in Syria. Born in Albania, and serving in the Ottoman army, this "selfish, illiterate genius" slowly eliminated his Ottoman rivals in Egypt and assumed control in 1805. He was to rule Egypt until his death in 1849. The lessons of French military superiority were not lost on him. He also realized that the key to building a similar kind of force was a fundamental reordering of the Egyptian economy; the material requirements of a strong military depended on an economy that could supply the needed goods. Although he was officially confirmed as governor in 1806, it was only after beating back a halfhearted British invasion in 1807 and massacring the last serious Mameluk rivals to power in 1811 that Muhammad Ali achieved a secure hold in Egypt. He then began in earnest to modernize Egypt's military. Egyptians were sent to France to learn modern military technology; and foreign advisers, particularly French, were brought to Egypt. Technical knowledge was diffused throughout Egypt by means of training institutes and translations of technical treatises.

Because a strong military was necessary for retaining and expanding power, much of the early effort was directed to meeting the military's basic needs. An army of over 100,000 men, if it was to be modern, needed munitions, communication systems, clothing, and food. Since there was no established industrialist class in Egypt, the government financed and managed its own factories. European industrialists and financiers were invited to provide capital and expertise to supplement the effort. In addition, Egyptian soldiers—

drafted into military service in 1823 for the first time in centuries—were required to learn technical skills. To guard against foreign domination of key positions, European factory managers and technical personnel were needed to train their Egyptian counterparts.

To mount this ambitious drive, the government needed a strong financial base. The 1811 massacre of the Mameluks gave the state control of their vast landholdings. All land rights were subsumed by the government, and the system of tax administration was altered. The traditional system had allowed local leaders to pay a sum to the government in return for the right to tax the **fellahin** under the revised system, the government collected the taxes directly. The government also assumed control of most agricultural marketing, especially of export crops. These policies increased revenues, lessened the power of reactionary local leaders, and partially circumvented an Anglo-Ottoman treaty that limited import and export taxes to 3 percent.

Long-staple cotton was introduced to the Nile Delta in 1821. Although this superior strain of cotton stimulated local textile production, it also tied Egyptian economic fortunes to the vagaries of the international market. Cotton soon became Egypt's leading export, accounting for 75 percent of all receipts by 1860. The Delta, capable of producing a food surplus from a variety of crops, was transformed into a cotton monoculture designed to sustain the textile mills of England. Egyptian dependence on cotton earnings forced more and more land to be turned over to its production, and the country that Napoleon saw as a granary for France was now forced to import food.

Muhammad Ali grew increasingly independent of the Ottoman authorities. The empire saw little harm in this during the early years of his rule. Before Muhammad Ali, Egypt had been a corrupt and militarily weak entity and of little value beyond the taxes paid by Cairo. Under him, Egypt seemed to be undergoing constructive change and developing a credible military force. Muhammad Ali's armies waged various campaigns under the Ottoman banner, the most important being the successful campaigns against the Wahhabis, the conservative expansionist tribal movement in Arabia.

Muhammad Ali's independent actions finally led to a crisis in 1832. Under the pretext of insufficient payment for Egyptian aid in the empire's unsuccessful attempts to stem the Greek rebellion, he invaded and occupied Syria—making Egypt an all but independent political and military force. In 1838, he declared his intention to become king of Egypt. The antiquated military force that the empire sent to displace the Egyptians from Syria was no match for Muhammad Ali's modern troops. After defeating the empire's forces, he toyed with the idea of invading Anatolia proper, but European interests, especially the British, defused the crisis. The British did not want to see Egypt, an ally of France, grow powerful; nor did they relish the possibility of Russia dominating a weakened Ottoman Empire. When the Ottoman sultan Mehmut II died in the midst of the crisis, it seemed that Russian influence in the imperial court would be expanded significantly. The admiral of the Ottoman navy sailed the fleet to Alexandria to be put in the service of Muhammad Ali rather than run the risk of being controlled by the infidel Russians. As it was, the empire weathered this "Russian threat."

British and Ottoman pressures effectively halted the reformist and expansionist actions of the Egyptian ruler. Muhammad Ali retained his role as governor of Egypt and was given the right to hereditary rule, but he lost much in the bargain. He relinquished the Ottoman fleet, pulled out of Syria, reduced the size of the army from 130,000 men to 18,000, and accepted the 1838 Anglo-Ottoman Commercial Code. The 1838 Commercial Code enlarged the preferential treatment afforded to foreigners doing business in the Ottoman Empire and made state monopolies illegal. The aggressive economic policies of the preceding thirty years had changed the face of Egypt. Some ventures had been successful, but many operations were wasteful and inefficient. Although Egypt may not have been able to sustain these at such a pace, it was unquestionably shaking off its moribund status of the previous centuries. Acceptance of the 1838 Commercial Code both sealed the fate of Egypt's economic experiment and assured foreign control of most Egyptian commerce and industry.

The story behind the building of the Suez Canal under the direction of the remarkable Ferdinand de Lesseps illustrates European dominance in a spectacular fashion. The terms of the contract to build the canal (1854), the methods used to construct the canal, and subsequent European actions serve as a model of imperial deceit and connivance at its worst. Essentially, Egypt supplied all of the labor, about 20,000 men, and gave the shrewd de Lesseps free access to the Egyptian treasury through various contract provisions, bribes, and bullying. In return, Egypt retained seven-sixteenths ownership but surrendered most of its rights to the profits until the canal was completed (1869). Other smaller ventures proposed by Europeans and accepted by the weakened heirs to Muhammad Ali's governorship were similarly one-sided. The granting of concessions to Europeans ended in a financial crisis that opened the way to total European control.

The financial chaos that engulfed Egypt in the 1870s was not, however, due exclusively to European chicanery. The Civil War in the United States brought a tripling of cotton prices and also deprived English mills of cotton grown in the southern states. The Egyptian governor of this period, Ismail Pasha, in an attempt to Europeanize Egypt, constructed a large system of canals, railroads, bridges, harbors, and telegraph facilities, and brought over a million acres of land back into cultivation. He did much of this on the assumption that cotton prices would remain high. Many of the contracts with foreign construction firms were made on highly unfavorable terms, the Egyptian administration being very corrupt. The spending extravaganza, coupled with the end of the U.S. Civil War and the consequent dive of cotton prices, put Egypt in an impossible position. The external debt of Egypt had reached over £ 70 million by the time the Suez Canal opened, as opposed to about £ 3 million six years earlier. Thus, an increasing proportion of the government's revenue went directly to foreign debt repayment—about 60 percent in 1875. In that year the British government bought the Egyptian shares in the Canal for £ 4 million, in what amounted to a liquidation sale. Egypt was now bankrupt and faced with foreign ownership of the Suez Canal. By 1876 British and French officials were overseeing Egyptian and Ottoman finances in order to protect European interests.

To improve Egypt's finances, the puppet governor Tawfiq imposed an austere fiscal policy that led to an army rebellion in 1882. This gave the British ample excuse for drastic action to protect their investments. At the "official request" of Tawfiq, British forces invaded Egypt, crushed the rebellion, and settled in for the next seventy-five years. The official British position in Egypt was awkward, however. Although they had been invited to enter at the governor's request, they nevertheless owned the Suez Canal, which in turn was situated in a province of the Ottoman Empire. This ambiguous situation was to persist until Egypt was declared a British protectorate in 1914.

Britain had an excellent reason for wanting to control Egypt: The Suez Canal shortened the route between England and India by 4,000 miles. The occupation of Egypt, however, burdened the English with the usual geopolitical anxieties. The security of the Red Sea, and thereby the Arabian peninsula, became vital. The Levant and the Sudan also had to be dealt with if security was to be assured. The latter two problems were solved by convincing the Ottoman sultan to cede the Sinai peninsula to Egypt (1906) and by establishing a joint Anglo-Egyptian force to reimpose rule over the Sudan (1898). Britain entered the twentieth century with a firm foothold in Egypt.

THE LEVANT

Muhammad Ali's control of the Levant during the 1830s forms a watershed in the history of the area. The reforms introduced and the subsequent European penetration have been aptly called "the Opening of South Lebanon." In the decades before the Egyptian incursion, the population of the interior, if not the coast, looked eastward when they were looking outside their immediate area at all. European trade had been on the decline, and Europeans were treated with a xenophobic hostility when they did manage to gain access to the area. The area had a relatively sparse population (about 1,300,000), rapacious Ottoman governors, and a highly insecure hinterland. However, the urban population, about half of the total, had learned to live with the situation by developing a relatively closed system of production and distribution.

The modernized, Western-oriented Egyptian army radically altered this situation. Security of travel was greatly enhanced; life in the cities became more secure; and, most important, a wave of European commercial interests quickly entered and soon dominated economic life. By the time of the Egyptian withdrawal, Syria was looking to the West for trade; the indigenous craftsmen had to shoulder the brunt of the change because their nonstandardized, low-quality, high-priced goods could no longer find a local market. The process continued after the Egyptian departure.

Western ascendancy was given a further boost in 1858 when the **Maronites** created a crisis in Lebanon by declaring it a republic. Under Ottoman rule, the **Druze**, Sunni Muslims, and Maronite Christians had achieved an uneasy balance. The Tanzimat declaration of equality for all non-Muslims in the empire had already aroused Muslim antipathy. In 1860 the situation worsened and erupted into large-scale religious massacres. Because they had long-standing interests there, the French landed troops under the pretext of giving aid to the Ottomans, and they calmed the situation. An autonomous Lebanon, limited to the mountains and not including the coastal areas, was established. A Catholic Christian governor was to administer the area and maintain a local militia. The Ottomans maintained only titular control and effectively abandoned the area. Thus the French, and a host of Christian missionaries, gained a base of operations in the Middle East.

THE ARABIAN PENINSULA

In the history of the world's major religions, circumstances occasionally allow strong revivalist movements to form and flourish. The Middle East in the nineteenth century provided the right circumstances for Islam. The **Sanussi** movement in Libya, the rise of the Mahdists in the Sudan, and the Wahhabi movement in Arabia were three of the most important.

Muhammad ibn Abd-al-Wahhab (1691–1787) spread his message during the latter part of the eighteenth century. He was convinced that the strict, austere Hanbali law was superior to the other three sanctioned Sunni schools of law and that Islam had deviated from its true path. He criticized especially the Sufi (and pre-Islamic) custom of venerating saints by worshiping at their tombs, which he thought to be idolatry. Abd al-Wahhab spread his word throughout the **Najd** region of Arabia; in time he converted a powerful tribal ruler, Ibn Saud, who spread the doctrine and his rule over great stretches of Arabia.

The Ottomans had long controlled the coastal Hijaz and the holy cities of Mecca and Medina. From there, Ottoman rule arched out over what is now Jordan and extended south to the al-Hassa area of Arabia on the Persian Gulf. It is likely that the Wahhabis would have been left undisturbed in the great desert areas if their religious beliefs had allowed them to adhere to geopolitical boundaries. But this was not to be the case. They declared that those who practiced the idolatry of saint worship were infidels and, as such, deserved death. By 1803 the grandson of Ibn Saud controlled the Hijaz, including Mecca and Medina. The tombs were destroyed, and many worshipers were put to death. The Ottoman authorities, of course, could not tolerate a renegade force holding two of the most holy cities of Islam, but lacked the means to expel them. It was not until Muhammad Ali consolidated his strength in Egypt that an attempt was made to beat back the Wahhabi movement. The first Egyptian forces were dispatched to Arabia in 1811; however, the armies of Ibn Saud were not pushed deep into the interior until the Egyptian campaign of 1818–1820.

For the remainder of the century the interior of Arabia passed back and forth between the authority of the Ottoman-backed Rashids and the forces of the Saud family. It was only in 1902 that a small band of Saudi forces raided Riyadh, the seat of Rashid power, and began to assume control of most of what is now Saudi Arabia—with the exception of the Hijaz, which remained under Ottoman control. Saudi power was more or less consolidated by the beginning of World War I.

Nineteenth-century European interests in the Arabian peninsula centered on trade and communications; therefore they concentrated on securing the safety of the coastal areas. The British were seeking greater control in the area in order to defend India from possible encroachments by the French, Russians, and Germans.

Napoleon's invasion of Egypt in 1798 brought a swift reaction. In addition to Nelson's destruction of the French fleet off Alexandria, the British took Perim Island (1799), which lies between Africa and Arabia in the narrow southern inlet to the Red Sea. Because they lacked supplies, especially water, they were quickly forced to abandon the island and withdraw to Aden, a port area long known and used by the British in their East India dealings. The British reluctantly made Aden a permanent outpost as event after event dictated their presence; they would retain control of Aden until 1967.

What Westerners call the Persian Gulf (and the Arabs call the Arabian Gulf) came under British control with the taking of the Strait of Hormuz in 1622. (A glance at a map reveals that whoever controls the Strait of Hormuz controls all traffic in and out of the Gulf. Since a substantial percentage of the world's petroleum passes through the strait, the area is vital.) To the British in the seventeenth century, the security of the Strait of Hormuz and the ability to ensure safe passage through the Gulf were important because they needed a quick line of communications to India. The route around the Cape of Good Hope was long and risky, and the Red Sea was under uncertain Ottoman control until the British intervened in Egypt in 1882. The next best route from India to England was to sail to what is now Kuwait and then travel overland through Basra and Baghdad.

By the 1830s the British had largely suppressed piracy in the Persian Gulf through military forays and treaties with the coastal powers. Later in the century they thwarted other European trade schemes in the Middle East by entering into treaties with local rulers that prohibited trade or other dealings with any other foreigners without British approval. The most notable of these agreements was the one made with Kuwait in 1899.

In the nineteenth century, then, British Gulf policy changed from simply establishing a line of communications within the empire to defending it. British control of Egypt and the Suez Canal relieved them from having to penetrate the interior of Iraq in order to protect their communication lines. German influence in the Ottoman Empire gave them reason to go on the defensive. The Germans gained a concession in 1899 to build a railroad through Ottoman territories in the Middle East. By the beginning of World War I, the Constantinople–Baghdad portion of the line was complete. But by as early as 1900, the ruler of Kuwait, in accordance with the recent British treaty, had refused the Germans permission to build a terminal on the Gulf.

Events, however, finally forced the British to push into Iraq. In 1907 petroleum was discovered in the Abadan area of Iran, and there was some evidence that nearby Iraq would hold equally important fields. Another chapter of Middle Eastern history was beginning to unfold.

IRAN

Although all of the nation-states in this area are special cases in many ways, Iran stands apart. Because of its political, social, and cultural differences, and because of its geographical position, Iran's relationship with the Middle East proper has waxed and waned over the centuries.

During the eighteenth and nineteenth centuries, Persia was subject to less European influence than Egypt or the Levant. European commercial interest, of course, had become well established during the preceding centuries, but the full-scale economic, military, and philosophical thrusts of the West had not yet penetrated to the heart of the Persian system. Yet Persia's nationalist sentiments—generally reactions against foreign domination that are expressed in mass movements—in some ways presaged those in other parts of the Middle East. This seeming contradiction is not yet fully understood, but it is clear that important aspects of Persian society included such elements as official social classes, power relationships designed to increase insecurity and mistrust, and the central place of the Shia clergy.

From Sassanian times on, the social structure of Iran consisted, with some exceptions, of four major groups: (1) the royal family, (2) the political and military bureaucracy, (3) the religious establishment, and (4) the masses. Although some outstanding individual cases helped promote a popular belief in easy social mobility, shifts from one class to another were relatively infrequent. Widespread belief in the possibility of upward mobility, of course, enabled the ruling class to promise the less fortunate a chance to enjoy a better life. But in such a system, downward mobility is just as possible; favored positions were therefore jealously protected. Desirable posts were usually procured by some form of money payment, or bribe, indicating that accumulated wealth was generally a prerequisite for entering and retaining a high position. Since the accumulation of wealth depended on having a good position, the system not only reduced mobility but promoted class tensions. The bureaucracy also suffered, since considerations of individual merit were often set aside. The shah thus presided over a system that was full of class rivalry and predatory competition. The ruling class could move social inferiors about with relative ease and frequency, as if they were chess pieces, thereby limiting any individual's or group's power and influence.

Iran had long had a Shia majority. Traditionally, the Shia had opposed any secular authority because of their belief that the betrayal of Ali had given rise to a series of illegitimate rulers. While waiting for the return of the Hidden Imam, who would set the world on the correct path again, the Shia believed that the clergy had an obligation to examine all secular actions and make them consistent with Islamic thought. Since interpreting the correct path of state and religious affairs depended on specialized scholarly wisdom and knowledge, a loose hierarchy of clerical authority developed in Iran that was lacking in Sunni Islam. Since most secular authorities are unwilling to submit to higher authorities, an understandable tension developed between government officials and clergy. And since the clergy had the ear of the masses, any secular ruler had to be careful and restrained in dealings with the clergy.

Bazaar merchants have traditionally been important sources of discontent and have led opposition movements in the Middle East, but in Persia they were subject to the same insecurities that shackled the bureaucrats and the military. The clergy, through their spokesmen, the **mujtahids** (learned religious leaders with successful ministries), were the only group not under the shah's direct control.

The Qajar Dynasty

The Qajar dynasty (1779–1925) came to power about fifty years after the fall of the Safavid Empire. At first, the Qajars were extremely brutal in their attempts to consolidate power. Once they had established a reasonable degree of control over the various tribes, however, they then had to face the emerging threat from the West. By the 1850s, two major Western actors—England and Russia—had forced Persia into the arena of Western politics. The British feared that a Russian advance southward would ultimately threaten India. The Russians had long desired access to the Indian Ocean.

The Qajars seem to have seen the need for radical bureaucratic and military reforms, but their actions were no more than superficial palliatives. Shah Nasiruddin's rise to power (1848–1896) roughly marks the beginning of the reform movement; the Persian elite began to realize that the Western powers could not be banished but would have to be accommodated. The last half of the century saw numerous intrigues between the British, Russians, and occasionally the French, as they entered into agreements over their respective roles in Persia, broke the agreements, and then hammered out new ones. The shah, meanwhile, in order to maintain Persian independence, was attempting to play off one power against the other and create a stalemate between them.

To accomplish this, and to build up the treasury, the Qajar rulers during this period began to grant concessions to Europeans. In essence, a European adventurer–entrepreneur would pay a sum of money to obtain a monopoly in some sphere of economic activity. The concessionaire would then return home to sell shares in the new company to speculators and thereby turn a profit. The rulers granting these concessions welcomed European money because it absolved them from having to impose heavier taxes on an already restive population. They also hoped that they could check European power by granting concessions to individuals of different nationalities; that the Europeans would see the need for political security and stability in Persia so as to protect profits; and that they would introduce some industrial development to boot. To be successful, such a policy called for a finely tuned balance of forces. The concessionaires, however, often played fast and loose with contracts, and the ruling elite were increasingly concerned with shoring up royal revenues. The 1872 concession drawn up by the grand vizier for Baron Julius de Reuter, a British citizen, is a spectacular example of the sorry state of Qajar affairs. The concession gave de Reuter a monopoly over railways, mines (excepting precious metals and stones), irrigation construction, all future factories, telegraph lines, road construction, and, for twenty-five years, the proceeds of customs collections. In return, the royal purse was to be increased by a small flat payment and a share of the profits of the various ventures. In short, the country had been sold, and sold very cheaply. The reaction against this outrageous concession was swift in coming. Protests erupted from the Russians, members of the royal court, the clergy, and nationalistic groups. The combination of international pressure and internal discontent forced the shah to cancel the concession on a technicality.

This was not the end of concession granting, however. The British continued to make inroads, the most significant being the right to form a national bank, the right to navigate the Karun River, and the granting of a tobacco monopoly. The tobacco concession (1890), following on the heels of the bank and river navigation concessions, was to be complete—from the growing of the tobacco to export sales. Again, Russian reaction was strongly negative. Internal reactions led by a domestic coalition (which was to surface periodically throughout the twentieth century) signaled the beginnings of the drive for a constitution.

Under the inspiration of the remarkable Jemal al-Din al-**Afghani**, who was active all over the Middle East as a proponent of pan-Islamic policies, a coalition was formed of merchants, clergy, and intellectuals, many of the latter having a Western orientation. The intellectuals and mujtahids were able to set aside their fundamental disagreements in the face of their common hatred of what they viewed as the selling of Persia. The Russian government gave material and moral support to the coalition.

As the dissatisfaction grew into a countrywide protest—ironically coordinated through the use of the British telegraph system—and the country tottered on the brink of revolution, it became clear that the reaction against the tobacco concession was part of a larger hatred toward all foreign concessions and, thereby, the policies of the Qajar regime. Facing the prospect of revolution, the shah canceled the tobacco concession in 1892.

The "tobacco riots" and the cancellation of the tobacco concession had far-reaching implications for the subsequent history of Persia. For the first time, a nationwide protest against the policies of the regime, spearheaded by the relatively independent and very powerful clergy, had immobilized the government. After many years of quietude the clergy took an active role. The internal coalition formed the backbone of the movements that later resulted in the granting of the 1906 constitution and the overthrow of the Pahlevi dynasty in 1978–1979. More immediate effects included a decade of Russian ascendancy in Persia, the slowing of concession granting to foreigners, and the beginnings of the same kind of disastrous debt policy that had brought so many woes to Egypt and the Ottoman Empire in previous decades.

The shah was forced to pay a sizable compensation to the tobacco concessioners. Because he lacked requisite funds, the British provided a loan. The Russians, fearing a reassertion of British influence, also provided loans, thereby tightening the financial noose. In this respect, Persia was closing the gap between it and other Middle Eastern countries by the beginning of the twentieth century. On the other hand, it received little benefit from foreign intrusion because of the conditions of the intervention, the corrupt, obsolete government structure, and the relationship between the various social classes.

Further British inroads were made with the award of a petroleum concession in 1901, the discovery of petroleum in 1908, and the British government's purchase of most of the shares in the resulting oil company a few months before the beginning of World War I. The weakness of the Qajar dynasty, and growing fears of expansionist Germany, also led the British and Russians to formalize an often-breached agreement that divided Persia into spheres of influence: The Russians were to have the north and the British the south, with a neutral strip in between.

The Qajar dynasty limped along until the conclusion of World War I, but its power rested on a weak base. Riots in 1905–1906, led again by the mujtahids with the support of modernizers and merchants, forced the granting of a constitution (1906) and the formation of a consultative assembly, the Majlis. Although the assembly initiated a series of reforms, intrigues by the rulers and international powers, internal dissension in the Majlis, and economic recession militated against a full-blown democratic and modernizing movement.

During World War I the Allies viewed Persia as a vital conduit through which to supply materiel to Russia. Due to the success of the Russian Revolution of 1917, the Bolsheviks renounced the tsarist claims in the 1907 Anglo-Russian agreement. The British then moved northward and assumed almost total control of Persia. Shortly after this, they withdrew from the Caspian Sea area, and the Soviets invaded the port of Enzeli. The Iranian Soviet Socialist Republic of Gilan was formed in 1920, but the Soviet Union withdrew its support for it less than a year later and the republic failed. In this chaotic swirl of events, Reza Shah came to power.

Reza Shah led the Russian-trained Cossack Brigade, one of the few effective military units in the Persian army, if not the only one. He assumed power on February 26, 1921, named himself commander in chief of the military, and appointed an intellectual ally as prime minister. As Reza Shah gathered more power, he dismissed the prime minister in 1923. In 1925 he ascended to the throne and took the ancient and kingly Persian name of Pahlevi.

Reza Shah was an extraordinary modernizer and autocrat who faced the formidable tasks of establishing internal order, lessening foreign domination, and establishing Iran as a modern nation. The Majlis continued to function under his rule. Indeed, his taking of the Peacock Throne was confirmed by a vote of the Majlis and by an amendment to the constitution, but the Majlis failed to fulfill the hopes of those opposed to autocratic rule, in that it merely rubber-stamped Reza Shah's policies rather than evolving into an independent legislative body. The shah promoted divisiveness among those on the periphery of power. This created insecurity, fragmented the opposition, and convulsed the machinery of government. Acting along the lines of Muhammad Ali in Egypt a century earlier and his contemporary Ataturk, the shah developed a series of reforms to lessen the power of the clergy and increase his own. He also laid the foundation for a modern economy by constructing an improved communications network and instituting educational reforms.

Because of the shah's flirtation with Germany during the 1930s, culminating in his refusal to join the Allied cause at the outset of World War II, the 1907 Anglo-Russian accord was renewed, the British protecting their petroleum interests in the south and the Russians controlling the north. To save the throne, Reza Shah abdicated to his son, Mohammed Reza Pahlevi, in 1941.

CONCLUSION

Nineteenth-century Middle Eastern history was dominated by the tidal wave of European power that swamped and distorted every society it touched. Although the procedures and timing of European penetration differed in the specific countries, there were some common features.

First, most Western inroads were made with reference to European geopolitical rivalries. It was not until the twentieth century that the Europeans (and the United States) seriously considered the economic prizes to be gained from the Middle East. During the nineteenth century the various European powers generally tried to avoid the financial and political headaches associated with direct rule; rather, they sought to establish client relationships.

Second, the general process of Western dominance had a certain inevitability due to the technical superiority and advanced organizational structure of the West. The technical revolution had been largely institutionalized in the West after centuries of cultural and scientific preparation. Military might was the most obvious manifestation of this superiority, but it was perhaps no more important than the organizational and cultural modifications that supported the technical revolution.

Third, European involvement in Middle Eastern affairs dramatically disrupted the area's society and culture. Some countries attempted to adopt Western ways; others rejected all Western influence. All countries, though, generally recognized the technical superiority of the West and tried to avoid Western domination; however, they all failed. The peoples of the Middle East fought a rear-guard action; their policies and pronouncements tended to be protective, not affirmative. Much of the history of the Middle East in the twentieth century can be viewed as an unraveling of the consequences of nineteenth-century European domination.

CHAPTER FIVE

The Rise of the State System

1914–1950

The period after World War I saw the decline of Western political hegemony in the Middle East. However, many events during the preceding decades paved the way. For example, the defeat of the Russians by the Japanese in 1905 was greeted with much satisfaction in the non-European world. A Western power had been humiliated at last by an Asian power. The news of the Russian defeat, together with other events, provided a needed catalyst for action in the unsettled Middle East. In Persia, the revolts of 1905–1906 severely weakened the Qajar dynasty and resulted in the establishment of a consultative assembly. In Turkey, the Young Turk revolution of 1908 sealed the fate of the Ottoman rulers. In Egypt, an incident in 1906 sparked a nationalist movement.

Each change in Ottoman policy over the first decade of the century—from pan-Islam to pan-Turkism—had a strong impact on Arab lands. After 1908, the ethnic nationalism of the Turkish leaders became openly imperialistic. Under the millet system, an individual's nationality was not defined by geographic boundaries. An Ottoman Muslim could identify equally with all Muslims of the empire—members of his own millet. Ottoman Muslims did not consider themselves to be Turks, Iraqis, or Syrians: These words existed

as historical terms or identified administrative districts. As pan-Ottomanism and then pan-Turkism weakened identification with the empire, and as Western influences filtered into the Middle East, the Arabs of the provinces began to search for a new set of symbols on which to base their identity. The Ottoman Middle East, then, was in a state of political and intellectual flux at the onset of World War I.

The strong ties between Germany and the Ottoman Empire that had developed over the preceding quarter century led to an alliance in war. The Allies had good reason to fear Ottoman entry into the war: The Ottoman military forces were reasonably strong and the truncated Ottoman Empire still posed a considerable threat to what the Allies, especially the British, perceived as their national interests. The Suez Canal and the petroleum fields of Persia were of particular importance.

Egypt was still nominally part of the Ottoman Empire until the outbreak of the war, even though British forces had occupied the country since 1882. Egypt was made a British protectorate in 1914, after England declared war on the Ottoman Empire. There was little fear for the security of Egypt from the west and south. Libya (then

Tripolitania and Cyrenaica) had been invaded by the Italians in 1911 and declared a possession of Italy. However, the Italians faced continual tribal resistance, especially after their entry into the war on the Allied side prompted the Central Powers to aid the Libyan guerrillas. When members of the Sanussi, a largely rural religious movement, were beaten back after moving to attack Egypt, the fractious Libyan resistance became ineffective. The Sudan had been administered by the joint Anglo-Egyptian condominium since 1898–1899 and caused little concern.

The Arab lands of the Hijaz and (Greater) Syria posed the most significant threat to the security of Egypt and the Persian Gulf. Two basic concerns faced the Allies: the Ottoman military threat and the closely related, but distinct, question of the attitudes of the local Arab leaders.

The military concern was realized early on both the Egyptian and Persian Gulf fronts. By early 1915 Ottoman forces had reached the Suez Canal and Ottoman supporters had disrupted the flow of petroleum from Persia. There followed a long and bitter struggle by the British to beat back the enemy. After sustaining very heavy losses, the British entered Baghdad by March 1917. The British pushed through Palestine, taking Jerusalem in December 1917. An armistice was reached only in October 1918. By then the British had pushed toward Homs and Aleppo. The "sick man of Europe" had waged a brave and tenacious battle.

With the military balance in doubt until the end of the war, the Allies sought aid from every available quarter. This led to a series of secret agreements and overt pledges that helped swing the outcome in their favor; but these same pacts contained fundamental contradictions, some of which have not yet been resolved.

THE McMAHON–HUSEIN CORRESPONDENCE

At the onset of the war an immediate Allied concern was how the people in the Ottoman provinces would react to the coming call for a jihad by the sultan-caliph. Obviously, an Arab revolt against the Ottomans would aid the Allied war effort in the Middle Eastern front. There were reasons to suppose that conditions were ripe for such a re-volt. The key figure to be won over was Sherif Husein, sherif of Mecca and emir of the Hijaz. The British high commissioner in Egypt, Sir Arthur Henry McMahon, contacted Husein, hoping to persuade him to sever his already strained relationship with the Ottoman Empire.

The McMahon–Husein correspondence (July 14, 1915 to January 30, 1916) set the terms for an Arab revolt. In return for entering the war on the Allied side, Husein was assured that a large stretch of Ottoman–Arab territory would be made independent under his leadership at the conclusion of the war; it included the Hijaz and what now is Syria, Iraq, and Jordan. He had first demanded that other territories be included, but allowed his claims to lapse on what now is the non-Hijaz portion of Saudi Arabia, Lebanon, and areas extending northward into Turkey. The fate of Palestine was left somewhat ambiguous in the correspondence: After the war, the British seized on this ambiguity to press their claim that Palestine was not part of the agreement.

Husein's silence to the call for a jihad was transformed into a call for an Arab revolt. Although the revolt did not produce anything resembling a mass movement, it brought relief to the Allies. The crack Ottoman troops stationed in the Yemen were isolated in Medina and between the Hijaz and British-dominated Aden, and the people of Syria found cause to retaliate against the brutality of their Ottoman rulers.

The British also made an agreement with Ibn Saud, recognizing his rule in the non-Hijaz area of what is now Saudi Arabia; allowed for a formal recognition of Kuwait; and entered into agreements that essentially called for the Persian Gulf peoples to cooperate with the British without forcing them to take up arms in the actual conduct of the war.

The success of the British in promoting the Arab revolt by promises of independence did not prevent them from completing negotiations with the French and the Russians (who repudiated their claims after the 1917 revolution) that created a new division of Western influence in the Middle East. The Sykes–Picot Agreement (1915–1916) gave the French control of the Levant coastal area and the right to oversee the interior of Syria. The British were to receive what is now most of Iraq and Jordan. Palestine was to become an international zone. The terms of this agreement were revealed to Husein by the Russians during the war, but the British managed to calm his fears by minimizing the document's importance. However, this agreement formed the basis of the postwar division of British and French areas of domination. The Allies entered into other agreements that defined areas of influence or rule throughout the rest of the region. As with the Sykes–Picot Agreement, the Allies were able to dictate terms that would expand their influence after the war. These agreements were to cause much frustration and bitterness.

The Balfour Declaration

Although the disposition of Palestine was unclear under the McMahon–Husein Agreement, it seemed most likely that it would become an independent Arab state. The Sykes–Picot Agreement called for Palestine to become internationalized. After the British issued the famous Balfour Declaration on November 2, 1917, the fate of Palestine remained unclear. The declaration, sent by Lord Balfour to Lord Rothschild, must be quoted in full:

> I have much pleasure in conveying to you on behalf of His Majesty's Government the following declaration of sympathy with Jewish Zionist aspirations, which has been submitted and approved by the cabinet:
>
> His Majesty's Government view with favor the establishment in Palestine of a National Home for the Jewish People, and will use their best endeavors to facilitate the achievement of this object, it being clearly understood that nothing shall be done which may prejudice the civil and religious rights of existing non-Jewish communities in Palestine, or the rights and political status enjoyed by Jews in any other country.
>
> I should be grateful if you would bring this declaration to the knowledge of the Zionist Federation.

The carefully constructed ambiguity of the statement was designed to elicit Jewish support for the Allies without alienating the Arabs. It succeeded in the former but failed in the latter, and

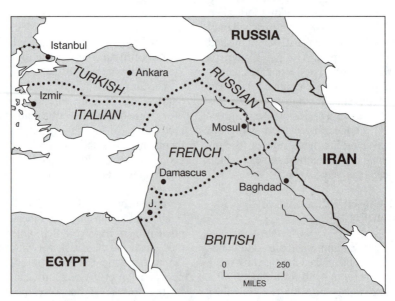

Secret Partition of Turkey and the Sykes–Picot Agreement, 1915–1917.
Source: Yahya Armajani, *Middle East Past and Present,* © 1970, p. 304. Reprinted by permission of Prentice Hall, Upper Saddle River, N.J.

thus added another layer of misunderstanding to the growing dilemma.

Palestine, the Holy Land of the Bible, had always had Jews among its population. But it was not until the last two decades of the nineteenth century that substantial numbers emigrated to Palestine from Europe. Many European Jews were motivated by the ethnic nationalism that had spread throughout Europe in the nineteenth century and was now beginning to take hold in other areas. But wherever they lived, the Jewish people were a small minority—a minority that had frequently endured extreme physical brutality and systematic social and economic discrimination. While their situation was not always desperate in Christian Europe, it was always insecure.

Whether or not the Jews could or should be assimilated into their European countries of residence, therefore, was a central question for Jewish leaders. Many of them began to believe that the Jews were entitled to self-determination. However, to enjoy this, the Jewish people would have to have their own political entity, a separate state. The trickle of Jews who settled in Palestine before the turn of the century came primarily from Russia and Poland (the great majority of Jewish émigrés from these countries fled to Western Europe and the United States). Those who emigrated to Palestine did so for many reasons—religious, secular, socialistic, and personal. All, however, sought a better life.

The World Zionist Organization

The idea of creating a special homeland for the Jewish people was popularized by Theodor Herzl (1860–1904). After covering the Dreyfus trial (1895) as a correspondent, Herzl became convinced that as long as they remained a minority people, Jews would always suffer periods of deprivation. His book, *The Jewish State* (1896), aroused enough interest to warrant calling the first World Zionist Congress, which was held in Basel, Switzerland, in 1897. The congress created the World Zionist Organization and called for the formation of a Jewish homeland in Palestine. The movement spread quickly throughout Europe. However, Palestine had not been a unified area

under the Ottomans; rather, it had been divided into two provinces, with the area around Jerusalem enjoying a special status.

During the nineteenth century, millions of Europeans were emigrating to new lands in various parts of the world; the Jewish call for a homeland in Palestine was therefore not unique in that regard. Zionist leaders, however, believed mistakenly that hardly any local people would be displaced since most of Palestine was relatively empty. Moreover, they believed that what people were there were of such a low culture that they could only benefit from contact with sophisticated Europeans.

The World Zionist Organization financed and organized a substantial wave of immigration to Palestine in the decade before World War I. By 1914, about 85,000 Jews were living in Palestine, three times the number thirty years earlier; however, they constituted less than 15 percent of the total population. Jews were still a small minority even in Palestine; but they were a highly organized and growing minority. A settler's life was often difficult, and a number of settlements failed because of lack of farming experience, harsh agricultural conditions, and a host of other reasons. But the settlements generally succeeded. It should be remembered that, however loosely it was controlled, Palestine was still part of the Ottoman Empire, and the settlers were subject to Ottoman law and administration. For example, Ottoman law did not always allow noncitizens to own land. A complex system of third-party land ownership had to be worked out. Also, Russian Jews were often singled out for harsh treatment because Russia was an Ottoman enemy.

With the beginning of World War I, the Ottomans imposed systematically harsh treatment on all Jews in Palestine. Wartime dislocations and a failed harvest compounded the woes of all residents—Muslim, Christian, and Jewish alike. By the time of the Balfour Declaration, the Jewish population had declined to about 55,000. Given these deteriorating conditions, Zionist leaders saw their vision of an independent Jewish state rapidly receding. The war posed difficult problems for them. Jewish leaders were not sure that supporting the Allied cause would improve the position of world Jewry or further the goal of creating a

Jewish homeland. Germany, in fact, had recently improved conditions for Jews and created a better environment for them than had any other country in Europe. Seeing that Jews would have a difficult time wherever they lived, and seeing widespread anti-Semitism in the Allied countries, the Zionist leaders gave the Allies only halfhearted support.

The Allied powers, however, were facing enormous difficulties during the war and needed support. Dr. Chaim Weizmann, a Manchester University chemist with connections to high-ranking officials in England (due to his war-related research) and a Zionist leader, pressed the Zionist cause with the British. Zionists in other Allied countries were doing the same. Finally an agreement was reached that culminated in the Balfour Declaration.

THE MANDATES

The Allies were well aware that the contradictory agreements made during World War I were going to be difficult to resolve. After the war, the Americans (with some British support) urged the formation of a commission to ascertain the wishes of the local populations. The French, however, rejected the idea and insisted that the Sykes–Picot Agreement be carried out. The British suspected the French of wanting to establish a firm foothold in the Middle East and tried to change the terms of the agreement. An understanding was reached in September 1919: Mosul would eventually be appended to Iraq rather than Syria, Palestine would come under British control, British troops would leave Syria, and the French would be compensated with a share of the Turkish Petroleum Company.

Syria and Lebanon

A son of Husein, Faisal, led the Arab revolt against the Ottomans and helped to capture Damascus near the end of the war. He correctly foresaw France's intentions in Syria, but underestimated the extent to which Palestinian nationalism had flowered during the war. He was more concerned with the French than with the Zionists. Consequently, he entered into negotiations with the Zionist leaders, seeking their aid in thwarting France; in return he accepted the legitimacy of Zionist aspirations. The French accord with the British placed Faisal in an impossible position. Since his agreement with the Zionists was conditional on the granting of Syrian independence, he repudiated the pact and was declared by the Arab Congress to be king of Syria and Palestine in March 1920. The French protected their claim to Syria by seizing on Faisal's failure to reply to an ultimatum calling for the acceptance of the mandate; the French brought in troops from Lebanon and routed Faisal. Faisal had, in fact, sent a telegram of capitulation to the French, but it did not stop the troops.

The Syrians of the interior were quite hostile to the French invasion; France responded with firm political and military action. To win over the Lebanese elite, France quadrupled the area of Lebanon. To fragment the anti-French nationalistic movement, Syria was split into separate autonomous administrative districts. Although Syrian administration was centralized after about a year, the French found that this cosmetic remedy did not solve their problems. The hostility of the Syrian population required France to maintain a military presence and suppress all political activity. Damascus was shelled on several occasions. Direct French rule was also imposed on Lebanon. Although there was considerable opposition in Lebanon, it did not rival that in Syria. However, the new, enlarged Lebanon now included areas dominated by Muslim Arabs; the delicate balance of political, ethnic, and religious groups was upset, and tensions between the various indigenous groups occasionally spilled over into violence.

Early in World War II, in 1941, British and Free French forces invaded Lebanon and Syria to wrest them away from Vichy France. When it appeared that the French would renege on their promises of independence at the end of the war, the British forced them to withdraw. Lebanon and Syria finally achieved political independence.

Iraq and Transjordan

The expulsion of Faisal from Syria in 1920 left the British in a particularly delicate position. The wartime promises made to Faisal's father, along

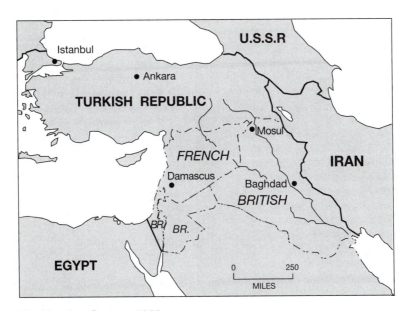

The Mandate System, 1920.
Source: Yahya Armajani, *Middle East Past and Present,* © 1970, p. 304. Reprinted by permission of Prentice Hall, Upper Saddle River, N.J.

with Faisal's widespread (albeit thin) popular support, spelled increased instability and a loss of British influence. The British responded by engineering the election of Faisal as king of Iraq and by creating another area, Transjordan, where they installed Faisal's brother, Abdullah, as emir. The government of British India had supplied troops and administrators to Iraq during World War I. When the League of Nations gave Britain a mandate over Iraq instead of granting independence, widespread insurrection broke out. After a particularly bloody campaign to restore order, the British sought to install a friendly ruler and selected Faisal in July 1921. In 1922 Iraq was given a special status, and in 1932 it was granted nominal independence, with a continuing British military and administrative presence. The British, however, retained their prominent position in Iraq for another quarter century.

Transjordan had been carved out of the new British mandate of Palestine. Abdullah had been made emir to mollify Husein and to keep Abdullah from invading Syria in revenge for his brother's defeat. By splitting the mandate, the British hoped to defuse Palestinian nationalism. In fact, British

policy won the enmity of both Arabs and Zionists who were seeking control of Palestine. Transjordan was an extremely poor and sparsely populated country and did not have a strong current of nationalism. It attained formal independence in 1946, but remained dependent on British and United States aid. It was, in short, a client state.

Generally, Britain's policy of indirect rule in Iraq and Transjordan better prepared those countries for independence than France's direct rule in Syria. This is not to imply that British policy was particularly farsighted; although they were swayed by Wilsonian notions of self-determination, the British were weary of war and no longer wished to continue the heavy financial burden of direct rule. But by staying in the background, the British allowed the area's indigenous people to educate themselves for self-government and to adapt to technological change. On the other hand, the French, ever fearful of increasing local power, kept their subjects politically and technologically ignorant.

A national consciousness determined by the boundaries drawn by Europeans began to form during the interwar years in Syria, Iraq, and Transjordan. The people who had for so long traveled between Baghdad, Damascus, and Amman with no sense of being in foreign cities were now beginning to observe the new international borders. However, passports were not the only things that kept Iraqis, Syrians, and Jordanians estranged from each other. Iraqis and Syrians learned different European languages, worked with incompatible technologies (the electrical system being a prime example), and started to perceive themselves as being of different nationalities.

EGYPT

The longtime (1883–1907) consul general of Egypt, Lord Cromer, brought financial order and economic progress to Egypt by establishing a highly effective administrative system and by major projects such as the first Aswan Dam. The nominal Egyptian rulers (and their even more nominal Ottoman rulers) were at the mercy of the British, but they had little reason to complain. Although the British controlled Egypt, they viewed their stay as temporary, brought order out of chaos, and prevented the nationalism of the urban intellectuals from gathering much steam. A 1906 incident in which British officers shot one villager and hanged three others touched off deep nationalist and anti-British feelings. The British then began to make very limited concessions to nationalist demands for political representation and participation. These all but stopped when Egypt became a British protectorate in 1914.

Immediately after World War I, Saad Zaghlul, a nationalist and a respected administrator, asked the British for permission to circulate a petition for Egyptian independence. After they refused, he organized an independence movement. The British arrested and deported him in 1919. Riots followed, and after a time the British began to relent on some issues. Because of the weakness of the official "puppet" government and the considerable size of Zaghlul's following, the British decided to negotiate with him personally. But their concessions did not satisfy him or the other nationalists. After negotiations broke down, the British tried to maintain civil order by unilaterally declaring Egypt to be independent on February 28, 1922. The decla-

ration contained, however, four "absolutely reserved" clauses in which the British retained control over areas they deemed vital to their interests: (1) the Sudan—and with it, the Nile River; (2) all foreigners and minorities in Egypt; (3) the communications system; and (4) Egyptian defense.

After returning from a second British-imposed exile, Zaghlul saw his Wafd party win a sweeping victory in September 1923 in a parliament that had been recently declared by the king. Zaghlul was then asked to form a new government. Because the British refused to back down on any of their four conditions, he saw no point in organizing a government. More riots followed. The assassination of a key British official, Sir Lee Stack, prompted fierce British reprisals, and the nationalist movement declined. By the late 1920s, the movement was in disarray. In 1936, the Egyptian government signed a treaty with Britain based on the 1922 declaration of independence and the revision of the four clauses: The British high commissioner would leave, British troops would be restricted to the Suez Canal Zone, and the capitulations (regarding the special status of foreigners) would eventually end. The 1936 agreement was prompted by British and Egyptian fears arising from Mussolini's invasion of Ethiopia (1935), the death of King Faud, the accession of King Farouk (a quiet and ambivalent nationalist sympathizer in those days), and the relatively quiescent state of the nationalist movement.

With the beginning of World War II, the British felt it necessary to reassert their control over Egypt. The country virtually became an Allied base for the duration of the war. Since many of the Egyptian political elite had pro-Axis leanings, the British intervened in Egyptian politics, especially in the selection of political leaders. The local Egyptian authorities were reluctant to take up arms against Britain's enemies: The British had humiliated the Egyptian nationalists, whereas the Germans and Italians had not. As at the conclusion of World War I, Egyptian nationalism entered the post–World War II era with renewed vigor.

The Egyptian political struggles since 1882 had been three-sided and unevenly matched. Basically, the aspirants to political power, the nationalists, were strong enough not to be ignored, but weak enough to be manipulated between the British and the monarchy. The position of the king was delicate. He supported the nationalist cause to some degree to convince the British that the ruling elite would maintain civil order if power devolved to it after independence; on the other hand, he opposed the nationalist cause when it seemed to be getting strong enough to threaten the monarchy. For their part, the British discouraged nationalist causes that the king advocated and approved the causes when the king seemed to be getting too much power. The nationalists made only modest gains, for several reasons: They advocated reform, not revolution; they were mostly members of the middle class; and various factions had been weakened by being played off against each other.

The first modern nationalist movement in Egypt had resulted in the 1882 British invasion. The nationalists had been jolted into action then by the financial collapse of the Egyptian government and the exploitative policies of Britain and France. Nationalists had gathered strength during the following decades, only to see their gains swept away by the British takeover during World War I. They again pressed their claims immediately after the war, gained some measure of self-rule, but then fell victim again to imperialist power. The trauma of World War II, another event that was basically a European affair, alerted the nationalists to the insufficiency of their past gains.

The Wafd Party and the Muslim Brotherhood

The nationalist groups in Egypt during the interwar period were of various persuasions, but they all saw the British as a common enemy. The two most important movements were the Wafd party and the Muslim Brotherhood. The popular Wafd party of Zaghlul was a secular reformist movement, one that basically accepted British ideas of representative government and, thereby, could accuse the British of perverting their own stated ideals. The Muslim Brotherhood, founded in 1928 by Hasan al-Bana, expressed its hatred of British domination by calling for a return to Islamic fundamentals, including the formation of an Islamic government. Estimates of its membership in the late 1930s ranged up to a million. The message of the Brotherhood was disarmingly clear: The

wretched condition of the masses, the venal behavior of the elite, and the general degradation of their common heritage were a result of the acceptance of Western ways. The solution to the situation was equally clear: Get rid of the Westerners and their puppets and establish an order that would make the Koran the constitution of the country.

Although the Wafd party had considerable influence with the middle-class voting population, the Brotherhood laid out a straightforward message that appealed to the masses. The Muslim Brotherhood's strident message was feared by the establishment. Because of this perceived threat, and because of occasional assassinations by zealots, it frequently had to operate in a clandestine way. An assassination attempt on Nasser in 1954 drove the group underground, and it was declared illegal. It remains a force, although the leadership of Egypt viewed it as a minor irritant until the assassination of President Sadat.

The Muslim Brotherhood represented an early twentieth-century attempt to establish a new Islamic identity after two centuries of Western exploitation. The economy of Egypt was mangled, divisions among social classes were widening, and secularism was on the rise. Many observers think that the Muslim Brotherhood is naively fighting a rear-guard action that it will ultimately lose. While these prognostications may yet prove true, it is now clear that the success of the Brotherhood in the 1930s helped similar political forces to coalesce in such far-flung countries as Syria, Libya, Iran, Pakistan, and Indonesia.

Egypt after World War II

After World War II, socialism gained widespread popularity in the Third World. Nationalists of all persuasions were quick to adopt current socialist slogans and formulate grandiose programs. Most socialist creeds were not based primarily on Marxism or any other intellectual system. Rather, they were more a reaction against the Western private enterprise system and commercial domination. Socialist programs called for an end to the gross income disparities in society. The misery of the masses was apparent enough, and the cause of their misery was held to be the selfishness of the local elites, who were allies of the imperialists. As young intellectuals and technical specialists absorbed these ideas, nationalist movements began to gather momentum. Broad-based nationalist parties then attempted to draw in the masses, especially those in cities, who were more sophisticated than those in rural areas.

The situation in Egypt after World War II reflected these trends. When the British resisted the Egyptian government's demands for a troop withdrawal and a renegotiation of the 1936 treaty, popular sentiment erupted into major riots in Cairo. The situation was complicated by the desperate economic conditions and the failure of the Egyptian army to prevent the formation of the state of Israel, which many Egyptians regarded as another outpost of Western imperialism. On January 26, 1952, a month after forty-three Egyptian policemen had been killed in a pitched battle with British troops in Ismailia, rampaging masses burned many Western-owned buildings in Cairo. Six months later, on July 23, 1952, a group of young army officers, including Gamal Abdel Nasser, Anwar Sadat, and Muhammud Neguib, staged an almost bloodless coup that forced King Farouk to abdicate and leave Egypt three days later. The monarchy was abolished the following June.

SAUDI ARABIA

After capturing the Rashid stronghold of Riyadh in 1902, Ibn Saud began to consolidate his rule over the interior of the Arabian peninsula. He defeated the last Rashid forces in 1921. The British were divided as to what to do about this growing tribe of religious zealots. During World War I, it had looked as if Husein would not be able to control the important Hijaz region against the hostile Wahhabi forces of Ibn Saud. The British decided to back both Husein and Ibn Saud on the condition that British financial support would be withdrawn from whatever side first attacked the other. The strategy worked through the war years but crumbled after the last Rashid power had been destroyed. For it was then that Ibn Saud could turn his attention to the birthplace of Islam.

By 1924 Husein was in a particularly vulnerable position, both at home because of poor administration and abroad because he unilaterally

declared himself caliph after Ataturk had abolished the title in Turkey in March 1924. Ibn Saud's forces struck and in short order forced Husein to abdicate in favor of his son Ali, and established a protectorate of sorts over the Hijaz. In 1926 Ibn Saud was proclaimed king of the Nejd, the central area of Arabia, and in 1932 of Saudi Arabia (incorporating the Hijaz). Thus, a small band of Wahhabis, led by the Saud family, had spent the whole of the nineteenth century warring for temporary power in an "inhospitable and unimportant" area and had now achieved statehood. Given the region's chronic instability and poverty, one can forgive the British and others for their inability to see Ibn Saud's potential as a leader or the significance of the nation he created.

Saudi Arabian political stability was achieved through a combination of centralization and wise leadership. Ibn Saud extended the traditional system of Bedouin rule to the nation by demanding that all significant power flow through him, by carefully adjudicating complaints, and by ensuring that those who came under his rule were treated with magnanimity. As power was consolidated and the flow of petroleum started to transform life in Saudi Arabia, an essentially ad hoc system of government evolved. Although the line separating national from local power is still ambiguous, the council of ministers that was established in 1953 clarified the areas of responsibility and took over some of the powers of the king. The system has undergone continuous revision and adjustment, with the king and royal family incrementally losing power.

The evolution of Saudi Arabia's administrative system, however interesting, pales in importance when compared with the history of its petroleum revenues. In the 1930s Ibn Saud used the first trickles of oil money to subsidize and calm tribes that were reluctant to stay within the nation and to strengthen the weak financial base of the kingdom. After a time, the trickle of oil revenues became a torrent. But the kingdom still had financial troubles because there was no system of accountability. By 1962 an alarmed council of ministers (and other powerful notables) had convinced the weak King Saud, son and successor to Ibn Saud (who died in 1953), to submit the country's finances to modern budgetary procedures. By this time, the activities of some members of the royal family seemed to be based more on the visions of grandeur in *The Thousand and One Nights* than on the strict tenets of Wahhabi fundamentalism. Prince Faisal became king in 1964 when King Saud was forced from power by family pressures. It is important to recognize that the term *king* is somewhat misleading when applied to the leader of Saudi Arabia. He is better described as a leader chosen from and by the core elites of the country.

TURKEY AND IRAN

The two large non-Arab countries of the Middle East, Iran and Turkey, emerged from World War I in chaos. In each country reforming autocrats came to power—Mustafa Kemal (later named Kemal Ataturk) in Turkey and Reza Shah (later Reza Shah Pahlevi) in Iran. Each gathered power and brought order to his respective country during the interwar period. Each instituted secular, nationalist, and developmental reforms. Each country became aligned with the West, especially the United States, after World War II. However, the two countries followed distinctively different paths: Turkey moved unsteadily and tentatively toward Western-style democracy, while Iran continued to be ruled by one family.

The policies of secularization—both substantive and symbolic—had definite political aims: to lessen the power of the religious establishment and create a new set of allegiances. In Turkey, the new allegiance was to be to the nation and democratic institutions. In Iran, the shah became the locus of power and the central symbol of the nation.

Turkey

Ataturk had a habit of ramming programs through the legislature and of not tolerating any significant opposition—a habit that conflicted with his populist ideal of involving the masses in political life. He encouraged opposition movements, but suppressed them as they gained strength. Since his reforms often involved "radical" secularization, they were sure to be opposed and cause populist ideals to be temporarily shelved. Indeed, Ataturk considered the policies of his party—which controlled the Grand National Assembly—to be the only correct and permissible ones.

However, Ataturk was far more than a simple autocrat. He had a considerable influence on the development of democracy in Turkey. He set up democratic institutions, broke the power of the old ruling elite, patched up Turkey's international relations, brought a sense of nationhood to the country, and laid the groundwork for positive economic gains. In short, he lived up to the name bestowed on him—Ataturk, "father of the Turks."

When Ataturk died in 1938, Ismet Inonu, a long-time ally, was the natural choice of the Grand National Assembly to be the second president of the republic. With the autocratic Ataturk gone, a pent-up desire for reform gushed forth. But the reformers had to bide their time as Inonu negotiated Turkey through the years of World War II, declaring war on Germany only in 1945, when it was quite clear that the threat of a German invasion was practically nil. Turkey emerged from the war in near economic collapse and under the threat of Soviet expansion southward. Under the Truman Doctrine of 1947 and other pacts, the United States gave Turkey (and Greece) significant military and economic aid in order to thwart perceived Soviet intentions. United States aid also put Turkey firmly in the Western camp.

The clamor for reform after a quarter century of rule by the same political party proved too great for Inonu to overcome. The 1950 elections resulted in a stunning upset when the opposition party gained a legislative majority. The election marked a turning point in Turkish politics; a change of government had come about by popular vote.

While the military had not intervened, it remained a formidable force in Turkish politics. Indeed, the internal financial troubles that had beset rapidly developing Turkey brought a military takeover in 1960. But the military leaders respected the role of political parties in Turkish life. Their stated goal, which they carried out within a year, was to return Turkey to civilian rule once a reasonable degree of social and economic order was established. The military staged another coup in 1971; again they promptly turned the reins of power back to the civilians once order was reestablished. As if running in ten-year cycles, the military reluctantly took power once more in

1980. Civilian rule was partially in place two years later.

Iran

The 1950 elections and the later military coups in Turkey contrast sharply with events in Iran. In 1951 the Iranian prime minister, Dr. Mohammed Mossadegh, a long-time nationalist, led an unsuccessful battle to nationalize the British-owned petroleum company. The Iranian legislature, the Majlis, was dominated largely by those interested in maintaining the status quo and had gained considerable political power in the previous decade. In 1941, the Allies had forced Reza Shah Pahlevi to abdicate because of his flirtation with Germany and his refusal to accept Allied demands to redivide Iran into British and Soviet spheres of influence. His young son, Mohammed Reza Shah Pahlevi, ascended to the Peacock Throne. During the 1940s the new shah had his hands full simply maintaining the throne as both internal rivalries and Allied actions sheared power away from him and transferred it to the Majlis. Dr. Mossadegh then convinced the members of the Majlis that it was in the national interest and their personal self-interest to vote for nationalization of the British-owned petroleum company.

Nationalization with due compensation was an established point of international law, but the Mossadegh-led Majlis met with British-led Western intransigence. The Western powers boycotted Iranian petroleum. World petroleum supplies were abundant enough to absorb the loss of Iranian production, especially since the region's other major producers did not support the Iranian nationalization and continued to sell their petroleum to the West. If they had cooperated, it is possible that Iran would have won the day and the course of Middle Eastern history would have been changed.

As it was, the economic toll of the boycott mounted and support from the Majlis dwindled; its members' nationalistic zeal fluctuated with the size of their purses. The Majlis's consequent rejection of Dr. Mossadegh's oil policy in the face of Western pressure reconciled it to the shah, for whom a nationalist victory would have meant a loss of power.

Dr. Mossadegh and his group of supporters became isolated. He could either capitulate or take his case to the streets. He chose the latter course and won a short-term victory; the outpouring of nationalization sentiment was strong enough to topple the throne. But in 1953, with the active support of the U.S. Central Intelligence Agency, the military intervened, arrested Mossadegh, and restored power to the shah and the equally conservative Majlis. A revised agreement with the petroleum company was then drawn up; this new agreement changed the terms of the previous agreement but allowed for continued Western ownership. Those pressing for economic independence—the clergy, the communists, and a growing group of reformers—had lost the battle.

Within a year Iran entered into a military pact with the United States and put itself firmly in the Western camp for the next quarter century. As Turkey struggled with a highly imperfect representative rule, Iran saw all its political and economic power become increasingly centered in the person of the shah.

By the early 1960s, the shah had promulgated the White Revolution, the goal of which was to hasten the industrialization of Iran and to better the lot of the peasants through a land reform program. It is no accident that the White Revolution shifted power away from the clergy and the restive urban technocrats and intellectuals. While it promoted economic growth, the White Revolution also promoted insecurity among the opposition and concentrated more power in the hands of the ruling elite.

As the growing petroleum revenues enabled the shah to transform the Iranian economy, they also made his continued tight control of all political processes increasingly problematic. The same social forces that had coalesced in the 1890 tobacco riots were again finding a common bond. There is some irony to the fact that the shah's decisive support of the quadrupling of petroleum prices in 1973–1974 accelerated this process. As the shah immediately spent the riches that poured in, he began to lose control over the flow of events. The careful balancing of interests demanded by the informal Iranian political system degenerated into an indiscriminate bludgeoning of the opposition, as the SAVAK (the Iranian secret police) and its network of informants struggled against widespread resentment. The system was running amok.

FROM PALESTINE TO ISRAEL

By 1920 the forces that were to create the dilemma of Palestine for the remainder of the century were in place. The basic issue was, and remains, which group has the right to control the area.

The British were aware of the potential difficulties even before they were granted the mandate for Palestine. The Zionists clung to the idea of a national homeland as proclaimed in the Balfour Declaration. The Arabs demanded the same self-determination that had been promised to those living in other contiguous Arab lands. Over the next twenty-five years, British responses to the situation clearly reflected the policy dilemma but did little to bring an acceptable resolution. The British issued periodic white papers that outlined the extremely low probability of a peacefully negotiated settlement, but formulated no coherent policy. They momentarily cooled the passions of first one side and then the other without resolving the source of the conflict.

Nationalism had infected both the Arabs of Palestine and the Zionists by the end of World War I. Self-determination was the goal of each group. The British military administration and the civilian mandate government allowed Jewish immigration on a limited scale and made it easier for Jews to acquire property. Arabs and Jews were involved in several incidents in 1920, and in 1921 Arabs had made several significant attacks on Jewish settlements. The British promptly suspended immigration for a month until tempers subsided and then put the old policy back into force, temporarily acceding to violence and then continuing business as usual. They ignored the King–Crane Commission of 1919, which was organized by Woodrow Wilson, and British committee reports that indicated that there was little room for compromise.

Winston Churchill, then colonial secretary, stated in 1922 that the phrase "national home" in the Balfour Declaration did not mean that all of Palestine was to become a Zionist nation, but that a national home for the Zionists could be created in Palestine. The British also separated Transjordan, first created in 1921, from the Palestinian mandate, thereby shutting off Jewish settlements there. The Zionists viewed these policies as attempts to thwart their movement and abrogate the Balfour Declaration. Arab leaders saw the policy as working within the confines of the Balfour Declaration in that it simply redefined the specifics, and they therefore rejected the "clarifications." Indeed, for the next two decades, Arab policy was based on the premise of the illegitimacy of the Balfour Declaration. They therefore could not acknowledge Britain's repeated attempts to modify the declaration. Indeed, the Arabs rejected Britain's attempts to have Arabs and Jews sit on a joint consultative body in Palestine for the same reason; to sit in the same chamber would give legitimacy to the Balfour Declaration and, thereby, to the Zionists.

Although the Zionist community was composed of several competing factions, its government was solidly organized and well structured, and it could depend on British support for its major concerns. The Arabs of Palestine stood in stark contrast: While most politically aware Palestinian Arabs wanted self-determination, they had no effective political organization. Their rejection of the Arab–Zionist consultative bodies had its logic, but it was politically unwise because it deprived them of a forum in which to air their grievances.

The Arab Executive, a committee formed by the Third Arab Congress in December 1920, was the most important Palestinian Arab organization during the first years of the 1920s. Since Syria had been occupied by the French earlier that year, the idea of Palestine becoming part of southern Syria had faded. The new Arab strategy was first to unify the Palestinians, second to protest British moves that facilitated Zionist settlement in Palestine, and third to prohibit the League of Nations from forming a mandate on terms unfavorable to the Arabs.

Although the Arab Executive managed to hold the various Palestinian Arab groups together for a couple of years, it split apart in 1923. In September of that year, the League of Nations finished drawing up the provisions of the mandate. Thus, one of the major forces for unity was lost.

The Arab Executive was divided over what strategy to use. Should it lodge official protests and try to negotiate and persuade, or should it simply not cooperate at all? Some advocated not paying taxes, but landowners feared that this would lead to property confiscations. At the same time, some elite families revived their long-standing feuds.

The Sixth Arab Congress (1923) was the last for five years. The Palestinian voice became muted. Official negotiations ceased, and the Jewish and Arab (Muslim Arab and Christian Arab) communities became more isolated from one another. The Zionists prohibited Arabs from leasing or even working on land purchased by the Jewish National Fund. And Histadrut, the General Federation of Jewish Labor, was insisting that Jewish-owned establishments hire only Jews. Outside of Jerusalem and Haifa, where Arabs and Jews lived side by side, the two peoples lived and worked apart in an atmosphere of growing hostility.

Arab fears went beyond the fear of becoming a numerical minority in their own land. Most Zionists, after all, were Europeans, and however separated they had become from the mainstream of European society, they nevertheless were steeped in Western ways. In 1930, over 90 percent of all Jewish males in Palestine were literate, as opposed to only 25 percent of all Arab males. About 75 percent of the Jews were urban residents, as opposed to 25 percent of the Arabs.

The relative calm that prevailed during the mid-1920s belied a growing sense of frustration and bitterness. The Jews made up about 10 percent of the total population of Palestine in 1922 (the remainder consisted of 10 percent Christians and 80 percent Muslims). Their numbers grew at a moderate rate through immigration except in 1925, when a relatively large number entered. Due to a harsh recession, more Jews left Palestine in 1927 than entered. It seemed to the Arabs that the Zionist cause had lost its appeal, and that the Arabs would remain a firm majority. But 1927 proved to be an anomaly. By 1930 Jews comprised about 16 percent of the population. It was clear that Zionism was alive and vigorous.

The Seventh Arab Congress convened in 1928. Encouraged by the 1927 decline in Zionist immigration, the congress sought to present a united front to press Arab claims. The new Arab coalition sought legislative representation as a first step toward self-determination. But events were to severely weaken the coalition and lead to its dissolution in 1934. A few months after the meeting of the Seventh Congress, Zionists demonstrated at the Wailing Wall by raising the Zionist flag and singing the Zionist anthem. There were clashes with Arabs. By August of 1929, full-scale rioting broke out, resulting in 740 deaths (472 Jews and 268 Arabs). The cautious, elite-dominated Arab Executive was losing its grip on its base of power. Arab politics in the 1930s was fragmented at the top and radicalized at the bottom.

The British sent an investigating team to Palestine after the Permanent Mandate Commission of the League of Nations, in response to the 1929 riots, issued a report outlining Arab–Jewish tensions. The subsequent British white paper recognized the seriousness of the situation and called for an immediate temporary end to immigration. Arab satisfaction at the position taken in the Passfield white paper was short-lived. In England, the Zionist reaction was quick and vehement. An open letter from the British prime minister to Chaim Weizmann, the highly influential British Zionist, repudiated the latest immigration policy. This "black letter," as the Arabs referred to it, indicated to some Arab leaders that they could not hope to negotiate with Britain for independence. Britain was henceforth to be regarded as an enemy. An Arab boycott followed.

Although they succeeded in having immigration reinstated, the Zionists were also troubled by British actions. While the British had acceded to Zionist pressures, it was quite clear that they had no clear commitment to the Zionists' ultimate goals. The British, then, were faced with hostility from both camps.

The rise of Nazi Germany in 1932 produced a steady stream of Jewish immigration to Palestine. The Jewish population of Palestine increased fourfold from 1933 to 1936; by 1936, Jews composed over 27 percent of the total population. The Zionist resolve to accommodate Jews fleeing the horror of Nazi Germany aroused intense Arab bitterness. In April 1936, terrorist violence broke out between the two communities. The Arab leadership, somewhat united by the crisis, called for a general strike. Within a month the strike became a civil war. The dispatch of 20,000 British troops and mass arrests halted the general strike and the civil war by the end of October.

Another British investigating commission arrived in Palestine in 1936. The British accepted the report of the commission and issued another white paper calling for the partition of Palestine into Jewish and Arab sections with an international corridor extending from Jaffa to Jerusalem and beyond. The plan was rejected by significant (but not all) factions of both sides, and fighting broke out again in September 1937. At one point the British had put several thousand Jews under arms to help quell Arab hostility. The arrangement broke down after the British hanged a convicted Jewish terrorist in June 1938, setting terrorist groups on a rampage of reprisals.

The adverse reaction to the 1936 white paper advocating partition prompted the appointment of a commission to reconsider the exact boundaries. Although the report of the commission, which was published in 1938, contained three potential partition plans, it also pointed out that the notion of partition was impractical.

A conference in London followed in 1939. The participants worked for a peaceful resolution, but they failed to gain acceptance from either side. The only interesting result was that the British government made the McMahon–Husein correspondence public for the first time. After the conference, the British decided unilaterally that within ten years a united Palestine would receive a constitution that would guarantee Arab representation and protect Arab land rights. Jewish immigration was first to be reduced and then to cease after five years. Jews demonstrated their anger by burning and sacking government offices in Palestine and by launching terrorist attacks on the British.

Eight thousand Arabs and 21,000 Jews from Palestine served in the British armed forces during World War II. Hostility to the British in Palestine, however, continued. The Jews were especially active because they considered the British policy to be a virtual death warrant for those fleeing the Holocaust. By 1946 the unofficial army of the Jewish Agency (to which the World Zionist Organization had changed its name in 1930), the

Haganah, numbered 60,000. Various terrorist groups, most notably the Irgun (of which the later prime minister Menachem Begin was the leader) and the smaller Stern Gang, complemented this force.

The Zionists had taken the initiative in attacking the Arabs and the British. The weaker but numerically dominant Arabs attacked the Jews and the British. The war-weary British attempted to quell the violence, which was now out of control. As more and more survivors of the Holocaust illegally entered Palestine, the British desperately grabbed for a solution. In 1946 an Anglo-American committee devised a variant of the partition proposal that again was rejected; a 1947 British proposal calling for a five-year British trusteeship met with a similar fate. The British were totally frustrated and angry over European and, especially, U.S. support of Zionism; the United States, however, had refused to allow mass Jewish immigration to its shores. The British washed their hands of the affair and turned the problem over to the fledgling United Nations.

A subsequent United Nations commission found what all previous commissions had noted: The demands of each side were understandable, inflexible, and irreconcilable. In November 1947 the United Nations called for the partition of Palestine. The mandate was to end on May 1, 1948, and the two states were to be established on July 1, 1948. The Arab states began to rally their forces in support of the now disorganized Palestinians who had rejected all aspects of the plan, but it was too little too late. A Zionist offensive resulted in victories as the British pulled out. On May 14, 1948, David Ben-Gurion announced the formation of the state of Israel. The Zionists had Palestine, or at least a portion of it. Subsequently, Egypt administered Gaza militarily, and Transjordan announced the annexation of the West Bank of the Jordan River not under Israeli control (1950).

However, the formation of Israel did not give the Zionists complete security. The Arab population that had remained in Palestine, along with the sizable number who fled as the fighting became particularly vicious, viewed Israel as illegitimate and the Zionists as a foreign power. Further, the Arab countries that had been defeated by the highly efficient Israeli army in the war following the declaration of independence suffered a deep humiliation. Although the Arab states surrounding Israel had a substantial numerical advantage, they were militarily weak. Their armies were ill-trained, badly equipped, and lacking in dynamic leadership.

According to the Arabs, Israel was just another outpost of Western hegemony. Various Arab leaders vowed that they would not rest until the state of Israel was destroyed. According to the Israelis, British vacillation, the Nazi Holocaust, and the refusal of the Western countries to accept large numbers of persecuted Jews proved Herzl's 1896 argument that only in their own sovereign state could Jews expect to be safe and secure. To the age-old Jewish dictum, "Next Year in Jerusalem," was added the cry "Never Again."

There was no ground for accommodation on the issue of Palestinian rule. Both sides were desperate and bitter: The struggle had been waged for a third of a century, and almost every long-time resident knew someone who had been killed or attacked. The "freedom fighters" of one side were considered to be brutal "terrorists" by the other.

CONCLUSION

Most countries of the Middle East had achieved political independence by 1950. Few, however, had achieved self-determination. The Western powers had substantial economic and strategic interests in the area that they were determined to protect.

The new alignment of Western powers into Soviet and American camps set the stage for renewed attempts to carve out spheres of influence. The American-led group sought to establish client relationships with the northern tier of nations— Turkey, Iraq, and Iran—in order to thwart Soviet aspirations. To the south the United States sought to protect Gulf oil and the Suez Canal. Since overt outside control of local political systems was quickly becoming a relic of the past, the great powers tried to maintain their influence by other means. They gave economic and technical assistance and military aid to muffle revolutionary impulses. The primary aim of the United States and

the Western powers was to stop Soviet expansion, not to develop independent economies and military forces. To strengthen Middle Eastern countries against revolution, the Western powers helped build a military and economic apparatus that was effective and resilient but still depended on Western support.

The postwar economic and military position of most Middle Eastern countries was extremely weak. The political elite of these countries generally wanted to avoid fundamental reforms. In this, they had much in common with the United States: They both sought political stability. The extent of military and economic dependency was the major point in question. However, the growing militant nationalism in the Middle East complicated the matter.

The need to achieve economic independence and strengthen the indigenous cultures began to be appreciated by those concerned with self-determination: Political independence would not suffice. Those who saw economic dependence as the major impediment to self-determination found socialism particularly attractive. It was, after all, Western private enterprise that had transfigured and dominated the economies of the Middle East. A restructuring of the local economies to meet local needs was going to be necessary, but this would be almost impossible in a system dominated by foreigners and serving foreign markets. Furthermore, if the foreign private enterprise system controlled the course of local economic events, it could also be blamed for the continuing misery of the masses. (Leaders of private enterprise systems seldom have been noted for placing at the top of their political agenda concerns for a more equitable distribution of income; socialists, on the other hand, generally do.) Not all modernizers shared these thoughts, nor were their ideas set out in a neatly framed system. Rather, the sentiments more often than not arose from a sense of dissatisfaction—a growing awareness that a fundamental reordering of society had to occur before full self-determination could be achieved, and that the restructuring could not take place as long as foreigners remained dominant.

Another source of dissatisfaction came to the surface during this period: It appeared that continued Western domination was stripping away the cultural fabric of Arab (and especially Islamic) society. Calls for an indigenous cultural renaissance had been made throughout the century, but the pulse of the movement, led by disaffected religious leaders, gained momentum in the postwar era. As with the secular modernizers, the clergy also called for an end to the current order. They sought a return to Islamic fundamentals rather than a culture heavily laden with Western values, whatever form of economic independence was achieved.

Middle Eastern political leaders thus faced a difficult choice. Accepting Western aid would enhance their economic and military strength and possibly mute some of the discontent caused by the "revolution of rising expectations." But this alliance would meet with resistance by those who perceived continued Western economic or cultural domination as a barrier to self-determination. The situation was complicated for several Arab countries because the American-led bloc supported Israel, a country that the Arabs generally thought of as a Western colonial settler state.

The Drive
for Self-Determination

1950–1990

Most of the major nations of the Middle East achieved independence by 1950. However, for some independence was neither permanent nor even meaningful. Superpower, regional, and internal struggles were still in the process of shaping and being shaped in all countries. While the postwar decline of direct European political control was bound to change Middle Eastern political relationships, it was an open question of whether those relationships and government institutions would be altered in a fundamental fashion. Amid this uncertainty came the growing recognition that attaining political independence was not the same as achieving self-determination. The latter was not likely to occur in a state if its economy was dependent on that of another, nor if the population looked to imperialist powers for cultural sustenance. Many false starts, program reversals, and policy contradictions occurred. There was no readily available blueprint for action, no clearly defined and agreed-upon analysis of the problems and solutions. All parties were feeling their way through a minefield of political dangers.

The very difficult task of building nations from states became more complicated after 1973. The petroleum price changes of the 1970s significantly changed many relationships between and within nations. The 1980s were dominated by another series of shocks: moral, societal, political, military, and economic. Finally, three fundamental events during 1988–1991 changed the very playing field on which the game was being contested. These changes—the intifadah, the breakup of the U.S.S.R., and the Iraqi invasion of Kuwait, along with equally fundamental changes occurring around the turn of the twentyfirst century—are the subject of the next chapter. This chapter sets the stage.

The major sections in this chapter deal, respectively, with the impact of an ideology, the effects of a change in economic well-being, and the analysis of a particular arena of conflict.

The first section deals with the role of Egypt generally, and Gamal Abdel Nasser particularly, with respect to self-determination and Arab unity. Although the complexity of internal and regional politics denies a neat encapsulation of events and trends, it is clear that the visions held by Nasser were widely shared, that there was universal difficulty in effecting solutions, and that there was widespread disagreement on what package of policies would best serve as a vehicle to meet the goal. It could be argued that there is a connection between the decline of Arab unity as a symbol and the rise of "Political Islam." As Arab unity was becoming ever-more-discredited through the years, especially after 1967, new paths were sought.

Gulf politics, including the general impact of petroleum prices, forms the basis for the second section. OPEC-initiated actions in 1973 and 1974 and 1979 and 1980 increased the nominal price of petroleum tenfold—to about $30 a barrel. In 1985 and 1986 prices crashed to $12. Prices soared to $40 in the immediate aftermath of Iraq's invasion of Kuwait and then settled back to $20 a few months later. By 1998 the real (inflation-adjusted) price of petroleum hovered around pre-OPEC (1973) levels. Prices rebounded substantially in 1999. The petroleum-exporting countries are in profoundly different places now than before the first wave of price increases. The resulting income disparities within and between countries are a potential source of instability. This rapid material change was accompanied by wars, the establishment of the Islamic Republic of Iran, and uneasy times for the monarchies of the Arabian peninsula as they struggled with citizen's calls for greater political participation.

The third and longest section is given to an analysis of Israel and Israeli-Palestinian-Arab state tensions. The reader should not infer from the length of this section that these issues dominate the Middle Eastern landscape. It is quite clear that they are only dimensions of the larger scene and that most of the fundamental issues of conflict and accommodation would remain in force if the antagonists in this arena settled their differences. There are three major reasons why an extended discussion is in order. First, Israel has a unique place in the Middle East. The heritage of its people and the origins of its statehood differ in significant ways from other nations of the region. Second, the Israeli/Palestinian/Arab state issues have had a high degree of international visibility that often has been translated into simplistic notions of "good guys and bad guys." While it is difficult not to get passionate when millions of lives hang in the balance, it would be foolhardy to ignore the complex reality and, thereby, throw reason to the wind. Third, this arena serves as an enduring example of the difficulties involved in conflict resolution.

ARAB NATIONALISM

The 1952 Free Officers' coup in Egypt is a good example of a transition in the Middle East. The leaders of the coup represented a new force in Egypt particularly and in the Middle East generally. Typically (but not exclusively) they were from non-elite families and had been among the first generation of their class allowed to rise in the ranks of the military. They viewed traditional regimes as preserving the status quo and maintaining the division between the haves and the have-nots. Their revolution was premised on the belief that a continuation of the existing political order would consign the majority of the population to permanent impoverishment. They also thought that widespread political corruption and indifference to national needs were responsible for Egypt's humiliating defeat by the Israelis in 1948. It is clear that the Free Officers had no clear plan for their new postrevolutionary society; rather, they saw the new society rising like a phoenix from the ashes of the old regime.

Gamal Abdel Nasser emerged in 1954 as the leader of the Revolutionary Command Council (RCC), the name adopted by the Free Officers after taking power. Three years after the revolution he wrote of his disillusionment with the notion that a new social order based on equality and justice would evolve naturally. It became clear to him that the various groups competing to influence the reordering of Egypt generally were concerned with enhancing their own well-being without much regard for truly national concerns. He perceived them as attempting to change the actors in the political and economic hierarchy without changing the structure. He believed, therefore, that Egypt needed a transition phase between the old order and the new; he called this transition "guided democracy," and the RCC was to be its guide. Nasser and his associates felt that individual competition had to be channeled if it was to result in positive change. In practice this meant that a just and democratic society could be attained only by temporarily limiting democratic action. With no clear definition of ultimate objectives and means, and given the day-to-day pressures of political life, Nasser and the RCC developed policy through experience and perceived necessity.

The Arab League was formed in 1945 in recognition of the power of collective action. The League did not provide much more than a forum for debate during the first decade of its existence, but events centering around Egypt during 1955–1956 highlighted the need for cooperative action and provided an impetus to engage in fresh efforts to attain it. The historic Bandung Conference of 1955 brought together for the first time a large group of Third World leaders who wished to develop a nonaligned status. They clearly expressed their desire to be free of United States and Soviet entanglements, the presumption being that the superpowers were unreliable allies who would manipulate Third World countries for their own interests. The superpowers generally discouraged notions of nonalignment and sought to exploit situations that would at least keep the nonaligned countries from being wooed by the other side. Nasser emerged from the conference as a leader of the movement. The United States was particularly alarmed by what it saw as Egypt's drift away from the Western bloc; it reasoned that if the Soviets vaulted the northern tier of U.S. allies—Turkey, Iraq, and Iran—its vital interests would be challenged.

The Suez Canal Crisis and the Israeli War (1956)

The United States decided to deny military assistance to Egypt on the grounds that such assistance would promote an arms race in the Middle East (irrespective of American arms sales to Israel). This decision provided the impetus for the decade-long Soviet ascendancy in Egypt. Nasser purchased arms from the Soviet bloc in 1954–1955 in return for promised future deliveries of Egyptian cotton. When the United States countered in 1956 by withdrawing proposed financial assistance for the construction of the massive Aswan High Dam, Nasser nationalized the Suez Canal. Egypt and Britain had negotiated an agreement in 1954 which called for the end of British military presence in the canal but allowed Britain to use the military installations in time of crisis. Nasser's nationalization action thereby weakened Britain's position. Nationalization itself was not contrary to international law as long as just compensation was paid to

the owners of the property. However, military actions took place before issues of compensation could be settled. About three months after the nationalization, Israel invaded and captured the Sinai peninsula and the Gaza Strip, stopping short of the Suez Canal. Israel claimed it needed to disrupt Egyptian-based guerrilla raids into Israel, that Egypt's blockade of the Straits of Tiran severely compromised its vital interests, and that a three-day-old Egyptian-Jordanian-Syrian defense pact, accompanied by verbal declarations to destroy Israel, constituted an immediate threat to its security. A couple of days after the Israeli invasion, British and French forces attempted to capture the Suez Canal. Their objective failed, a cease-fire was quickly arranged through the United Nations, and all three invaders subsequently quit Egyptian territory. United Nations troops were placed in Gaza and at the head of the Gulf of Aqaba. The Soviet Union then offered to provide financial assistance for the high dam at Aswan. The United States now had more reason than ever to believe that the Soviets were jumping the northern tier. However, Nasser's policy of nonalignment prevented Egypt from joining the Soviet camp.

Nasser emerged from the Suez crisis as an Arab hero, and Egypt's long history of leadership in the Arab world was reaffirmed. Along with the status accorded Nasser was a recognition that Arab unity could help meet major Arab goals, victory over Israel being high on the list. Nasser and the RCC had, of course, realized that it was worthwhile to cooperate with other "progressive" Arab states on some matters and with all Arab states against Israel, but Arab unity now began to assume a new meaning. Instead of an end in itself, it came to be seen as a means to Arab victory in Palestine. Events in Syria were to provide Egypt with its first opportunity to exercise leadership under the banner of pan-Arabism.

Syria

In contrast to the relative ethnic and religious homogeneity of Egypt, Syrian society is characterized by considerable heterogeneity. Sunni Muslims form a majority of the population and are in an economically preferred position. However, minorities play vital roles. Particularly important are large numbers of relatively prosperous Christian merchants and landholders, a large number of relatively poor Shia, and the Druze and the Alawites. The latter dominate the senior ranks of the military, partially due to the successful preindependence French policy of fragmenting power and the unwillingness of the Sunni elite to encourage their sons to enter the military as a career. Syria spent its first three years of independence, 1946–1949, under ineffective civilian rule; a coup in 1949 ushered in the first of many military governments.

In 1954 the Arab Socialist Resurrection Party, or **Baath**, gained considerable influence in the government, influence that it held through 1958 and that figured prominently in the 1958 drive to form a political union with Egypt. Baath ideology combines socialist thought with visions of past Arab unity. The Baathists argue that the unity of the Arab peoples will evolve naturally as the individual states move along a socialist path. Baathist influence in Syria in the 1950s, however, was far from being uncontested. From the right they faced the growing hostility of conservative elements who saw Baathist policies of income redistribution and nationalization as simple expropriation. On the left the relatively strong Communist party was seeking closer ties with the Soviet Union, a country which the Baathists considered to be imperialist. The threat of a communist takeover of Syria occurred at a time when the Baathists were suffering a loss of prestige and power; the Baathists felt compelled to act forcefully to lessen the chance of Syria falling under Soviet hegemony. Nasser's immense popularity as an anti-imperialist and his growing enchantment with broad socialist principles helped promote the union between Egypt and Syria. Such a union fit neatly into the Baathist ideology of Arab unity, while it offered the Baathists a hope of maintaining their own position in Syria.

The United Arab Republic

The United Arab Republic, UAR, was formed in 1958 following a relatively brief period of negotiation and a hasty working through of the mechanics of formal acceptance in each country. As opposed to Muhammad Ali's expansionist motives in the capture of Ottoman Syria in 1832, Nasser's aims were limited and were more a result of Syrian persuasion than of any enthusiasm within Egypt. While the union undercut communist influence in Syria, Egypt's growing control of the Syrian bureaucracy and its sometimes heavy-handed implementation of previously legislated but largely ignored income-leveling policies led to Syrian dissatisfaction with the union. Since the Baathists were the driving force behind the union, they suffered a corresponding loss of prestige. The experiment ended when the Syrian army forced the Egyptian high command to leave the country in September 1961. Nasser accepted the decision rather than engage Syrian forces. A nonsocialist government was formed in Syria, but it was ousted from power in early 1962. A military Baathist group staged a coup in 1963; the Baathists had managed to regain a share of power.

The next round of power shifts resulted from a split within the Baathist party into a moderate faction led by people with political experience in Syria and a progressive faction led by younger men, generally army officers, who represented the minorities. Animosities between the two groups culminated in a 1966 coup in which Alawite officers played a prominent part. In 1970 another coup took place and the Alawite position became more firmly established under the leadership of Hafez al-Assad. He has led Syria since. This long continuous rule was accomplished through the establishment of tight organizational control of the armed forces and bureaucracy and suppression of local opposition. Although there is little argument that the rule of Hafez al-Assad has brought a measure of domestic stability and prosperity to Syria, there is a question as to whether the transition to another leader will be smooth. Beyond instability that can be caused by "palace politics," the substantial heterogeneity of the population and the unevenness of power sharing must be considered. There have been times when elements of the population were restive. Especially noteworthy are the actions against civilian uprisings in Aleppo (1980) and Hamma (1982). It was necessary to dispatch regular forces to quell the disturbances. Much blood was spilled.

Syria assumed an ever-more-important role as regional powerbroker. Especially important was the role it played in Lebanon, a country that holds immense strategic value to Syria. Besides having troops in Lebanon since the mid-1970s, President Assad positioned Syria as the only national body that could guide, but certainly not direct, affairs in Lebanon.

Syria's role in Lebanon specifically and the Middle East generally was enhanced during and after their participation in the coalition which expelled Iraq from Kuwait. The Syrian economy suffered during the 1980s because of inefficient state-run enterprises, a cumbersome system of economic controls, heavy defense expenditures, an extended severe drought, and significant cutbacks in Soviet bloc military, economic, and educational aid. During the last couple of years of the 1980s, Syria worked hard at satisfying the major demands of the United States by being more supportive of private enterprise and free trade and more flexible toward convening a peace conference with Israel, and dealing with the nettlesome issue of "state-sponsored terrorism." Although they made some progress repairing relations with the United States, they were still in a very delicate position until the Iraqi invasion of Kuwait (1990–1991) and the subsequent need of the United States to build an alliance which included important Arab nations. Syria received substantial benefits from joining the alliance. They received tacit permission to rid Lebanon of (Christian) General Aoun who had rejected a peace formula for Lebanon agreed to by most other actors. Syria's intervention helped bring peace of sorts to Lebanon while enhancing Syrian power and prestige—some would say hegemony. Syria also received substantial financial aid from the Gulf States. Finally, increased U.S. pressure was put on Israel to join a peace conference.

Jordan, Lebanon, and Iraq

The 1958 formation of the United Arab Republic helped to trigger significant events in Jordan, Iraq, and Lebanon. Jordan and Iraq were still ruled under separate Hashemite kings who had been installed by the British after World War I. However, the monarch in each country, King Hussein in Jordan and King Faisal II in Iraq, was in considerable difficulty by the time the United Arab Republic was formed.

Jordan.   Jordan was a client state of Britain. It depended on Britain for military assistance and subsidies to prop up its weak economy. The nationalists of Jordan saw British aid in particular and Western actions in general as part of a new imperialism. For example, they viewed Britain's 1954 Suez agreement with Egypt as a dangerous compromise since it allowed for reoccupation whenever British national interests were at stake. In 1955 Britain formed the Baghdad Pact with Turkey, Pakistan, Iraq, and Iran. Jordan was pressed to join, but nationalist reactions led to rioting in January 1956. King Hussein, then twenty years old, responded to the crisis by expelling the British military command from the country, including General Glubb, who had been in Jordan for twenty-five years. This popular move brought temporary respite to the monarch, but elections in October brought a pro-Nasserist and socialist majority to parliament. The British-French-Israeli invasion of Egypt a month later led the Jordanian government to sever ties with Britain, thereby ending the subsidy. Hussein began to receive financial support from the United States in 1957, but he faced considerable political opposition even though he had suspended the parliament.

When Egypt and Syria formed the UAR, there was much local popular sentiment for Jordan to join. In order to counter this, and with advice from the United States, Jordan and Iraq hastily established an Arab Union. But in July 1958, a revolution in Iraq ended Hashemite rule there and brought an end to the short-lived Arab Union. Hussein then was granted his request for two thousand British troops to be stationed in Jordan to help save the throne. Military and economic aid was also given by the United States to help the young king. Contrary to the expectations of most informed observers, the dynasty survived not only that scrape but also several other crises through the decades. Indeed, King Hussein was regarded as a much stronger leader than most observers would have imagined possible only a few years earlier. For example, he made significant initiatives with respect to Israeli/Palestinian issues and partially patched up long-standing contentious relations with Iraq.

Lebanon. The rise of pan-Arab sentiments during the 1956–1958 period also had far-reaching consequences in Lebanon. The National Pact, an understanding rather than a formal document, went into effect in 1943 and guided Lebanese political life for a third of a century. The pact formally recognized the religious and cultural heterogeneity of Lebanon and divided the major governmental posts among the different groups who were to share power. It also stipulated that the Christians would not look to France for support, and that the other Lebanese Arabs would abandon their hopes of affiliation with Syria. The formula for political rule was based on the results of the 1932 census, which indicated that no single group constituted a majority of the population: Of the three largest groups, the Christian Maronites comprised 29 percent, the Sunnis 21 percent, and the Shia 18.5 percent. Since the Muslim birthrate exceeded the Christian, the Sunni-Shia Muslim population gained majority status in the ensuing decades, and the Shia became the largest group. However, because all parties doubted that a new pact could be worked out, the population ratios from 1932 remained in force; no subsequent census was taken in Lebanon. The story of Lebanon during the last half of the twentieth century is a case history for the need for careful analysis: For decades outsiders marveled over the Lebanese talent for political compromise. It seemed as though they were building a solid nation. But as was to become painfully apparent, many Lebanese held deeper loyalties to their ethnic/religious group.

The government that came to power in 1943 lasted until 1952 when the president, Bishara al-Khoury, became isolated by a coalition of disaffected politicians of different religious affiliations. The government fell when the army refused to follow a presidential order to break up a protest demonstration. This change of government, called the Rosewater Revolution, brought Camille Chamoun to power. The coalition that brought the government down and elected Chamoun, the Social National Front, started to split into factions as soon as its source of unity, opposition to the former government, was removed.

The carefully managed balance of religious forces tended to support the status quo; any fundamental reordering of the system ran the risk of upsetting the balance in unpredictable ways. The Christian leadership had an added incentive to resist change, for Christians held more economic power than non-Christian citizens. But there were also forces calling for significant changes. For example, the Druze leader Kamal Jumblatt supported a package of reforms aimed at liberalizing the political structure and equalizing the income distribution. The Muslim population saw Chamoun leaning toward France as pan-Arab sentiments swelled. When Chamoun did not take a forthright stand against the 1956 attack on Egypt, his image as a pro-European was reinforced. Discontent became more widespread and seemingly more dangerous for the Christian leadership as Muslims were swept into the pan-Arab movement.

By the time of his 1958 visit to Damascus in conjunction with the formation of the UAR, Nasser was more than a popular hero: To many people he symbolized the drive for Arab self-determination. Muslims from Lebanon flocked to Damascus to hear him speak. The event catalyzed Lebanese discontent. Many called for a new census to rid the country of its fictitious Christian majority; some suggested that Lebanon join Syria in the UAR. President Chamoun responded to this slow but inexorable wave of discontent by imposing piecemeal controls on political expression.

Lebanon was on the brink of civil war from May to October of 1958. A massive demonstration and general strike took place in May in response to overall conditions; it had been triggered by the assassination of a pan-Arab publicist. The pan-Arab Muslims were joined by a loosely organized group headed by the Druze leader Kamal Jumblatt and several prominent Christian leaders who saw Chamoun's policies leading to failure and, thus, a victory for the pan-Arab forces. In mid-July Hashemite rule in Iraq ended by revolution. As King Hussein of Jordan received British troops, President Chamoun called on the United States to send help under the Eisenhower Doctrine. Troops from the United States landed on the beaches of Lebanon before the end of the month. It is difficult to say what effect these troops had.

Their presence probably cooled passions sufficiently to allow the Lebanese to forge a compromise out of an intractable situation. Although Chamoun was replaced by the end of July, fighting along communal lines continued on a sporadic basis. A cabinet that would endure was pieced together in October; it contained equal numbers of Muslims and Christians, thereby partially recognizing the changed demography. United States troops left Lebanon by the end of the year.

Although the Lebanese managed to avoid full-scale civil disorder until 1975, maintaining the fragile peace became increasingly difficult. First, calls for Arab unity and later for pan-Islamic unity were met with sympathy by a significant portion of the Arab population, thereby putting the system under direct attack. Second, the Western bias of its free market economy put Lebanon out of step with most other Arab nations and drew corresponding criticism. Third, there were periodic incidents with Israel. Lebanon managed to avoid conflict with Israel during the 1956, 1967, and 1973 wars without being completely ostracized by the Arab community of nations. But border problems with Israel led to the civil war of 1975, the entry of Syrian troops into Lebanon, a deepening schism between the religious communities, and the Israeli invasion of 1982.

The Palestinians who were living in Lebanon did not pose a serious problem for the government until the mid-1960s. To be sure, having more than two hundred thousand Palestinians in loosely supervised camps administered by the United Nations caused much worry. But it was not until the rise in power and popularity of the Palestinian Liberation Organization (PLO) that the situation threatened to get out of hand. As Palestinian forces struck Israel, Lebanon suffered reprisal raids. The Lebanese government was in a difficult position. To suppress the PLO would anger the sizable and passionate anti-Israeli groups in the country and, most probably, lead to civil war. To allow the Palestinians to operate freely would result in further crippling reprisal raids.

By late 1969 an agreement between the Palestinian and Lebanese leaderships was reached with the help of President Nasser. Essentially it gave the Palestinians the right to rule the refugee camps and to move freely through the country in return for a promise of cooperation with the Lebanese government. After King Hussein of Jordan defeated a PLO army in Jordan in September 1970, the situation started to deteriorate; Lebanon became the only base from which the Palestinians could mount attacks on Israel. During the first few years of the 1970s, attacks on Israel increased and Israel responded with reprisal attacks.

Civil war broke out in April 1975. A peace was hastily constructed, but it fell apart in August and fighting raged again. The army of Lebanon intervened during the first few months of 1976, but some units joined the forces favoring the Palestinian position. Things had irrevocably fallen apart.

It would be inaccurate to characterize the Lebanese civil war as divided strictly along communal lines. While communal divisions were certainly present, many Christian Arabs supported the Palestinian cause. In any case, the Palestinians and their allies gained the upper hand and threatened the largely Christian strongholds. Israel announced that it would decisively counter the present danger. When the Syrian army then sent forces to Lebanon to bring some order to the situation, Syrian president Assad was put in an extremely delicate position. The overriding immediate aim of Syrian policy was to defuse an explosive situation. The Palestinians and their supporters had to be held in check, but this meant that the Syrians would have to support the Christians. The irony was made complete by the open secret that the Christians were also supported by Israel.

The tragic conflict, which eventually claimed at least 60,000 lives, gradually subsided as the Syrians stabilized the Christian areas. A coalition of Arab nations originally led by Saudi Arabia hammered out an agreement with the parties and installed an Arab Deterrent Force in Lebanon. The force was predominantly Syrian; it consisted of about 22,000 Syrian troops and about 5,000 from the other participating nations. Lebanon limped through the remainder of the 1970s with a largely powerless government, the Syrian army controlling the countryside, a growing Christian army, better armed private militias, a restive Palestinian population, the economy in shambles, and the future uncertain.

Understanding events in Lebanon always demanded an unusual attention to detail: The coalitions essential for order were based on intricate intersections of many forces. A change in the position of one group necessitated adjustments by all others if political coherence was to be maintained. While it is apparent that the (1975) civil war started the unraveling of the delicate political web that held the country together for one-third of a century, the aftermath of the 1982 Israeli invasion made it clear that a reconstruction of the old web was impossible. A new order had to be established.

On June 6, 1982, Israeli forces invaded Lebanon. Israel had been ever more frustrated by PLO actions. An assassination attempt on the Israeli ambassador to Britain served as the official reason for the invasion. Israel's stated goal was to establish a 40-kilometer *cordon sanitaire* so as to blunt terrorist attacks on northern Israel. Another primary goal, unstated at the time, was the destruction of the PLO. In rather short order, Israel destroyed the Syrian air force located in east-central Lebanon and had Syria accept a cease-fire. This allowed Israeli troops to move up the coast directly to Beirut to do battle against PLO forces concentrated in several large "camps." Aerial bombardment of the camps preceded the troops.

Two months later an arrangement was made whereby PLO forces in and around Beirut would quit Lebanon. The removal to several different locations was supervised by a multinational force that included a relatively large contingent of U.S. troops. The multinational force left Lebanon by September 10, shortly after the evacuation. In the midst of this Bashir Gemayel was elected president of Lebanon. He was assassinated one month later (September 14). Two days later Israeli forces allowed Christian militia to enter the Palestinian camps of Sabra and Shatila. During the next three days many hundreds of Palestinians were massacred. A few days later Amin Gemayel, brother of Bashir, was chosen to be president, and shortly thereafter the multinational force returned to Beirut. Amin Gemayel remained in office until his term expired in 1988. The presidency remained vacant until 1991.

By 1983, then, the situation in Lebanon had changed dramatically. Syrian forces remained in large parts of eastern Lebanon, the army of Israel occupied the western part of the country north to Beirut, and the PLO was in disarray due to the exit of 8,000 of its troops from Beirut. In addition, the superpowers moved ever closer to direct involvement. The Soviet Union poured a massive amount of military aid into Syria in order to replace and upgrade the equipment destroyed by Israel. Soviet technical advisers were on hand to assist the Syrians. United States marines, part of the multinational force, were in barracks at the Beirut airport. Their stated task was to assist the regular Lebanese army. Since no significant militia recognized the legitimacy of the government, the goal of U.S. forces lost meaning.

Internal security deteriorated markedly through the next two years. There were numerous battles between the various militias, and between the militias and the Israelis. U.S. forces and mountain-entrenched militia exchanged artillery fire. In addition, urban terrorism increased. It became somewhat commonplace to have a bomb-laden vehicle explode in this or that quarter of the city, killing scores at a time. Selected foreigners, especially Americans, were killed or kidnapped. The most spectacular action against Americans, who were generally perceived as allies of Israel and/or the Christian-dominated government, was the bombing of the airport barracks, killing 241 marines and prompting the United States to leave Lebanon shortly thereafter (February 1984). The bombing seems to have been a direct response to a U.S.-brokered (and subsequently forgotten) peace agreement (May 17, 1983) between Lebanon and Israel.

In late 1983, rejectionist PLO units forced a second evacuation of forces loyal to Yasir Arafat, this time from the northern port city of Tripoli. The rebel units, initially aided by Syria, acted because of their distaste for a conciliatory attitude Arafat was taking toward a proposal to establish a Palestinian "entity associated" with Jordan. Israel finally quit most of Lebanon in mid-1985, although its forces continued to indirectly control the southern portions of the country.

While the Christian leadership was unwilling to yield its position of preeminence, the Shia plurality was "awakened" and found political voice. This awakening of the Lebanese Shia is a complex social phenomenon. However, a few convenient benchmarks can be mentioned. First, the appearance, success, and (somewhat) mysterious disappearance of a prominent and charismatic religious leader, Musa al-Sadr, served as focal point. During the 1970s he organized the Shia of southern Lebanon and guided the formation of AMAL, a political and later military force that bypassed traditional Shia leadership. Second, the success of the Iranian revolution gave inspiration and material aid to many of these self-described "disinherited." Third, the successive dislocations of the local population of southern Lebanon by the Israeli-supported Christian militia, the Palestinians, and the Israeli army in the aftermath of the 1982 invasion increased the pressure to act.

AMAL advocated a Lebanon free of confessional politics, a policy that, not surprisingly, would strip power from the Christians in favor of the Shia. AMAL was not ideological in that it did not call for the complete overhaul of the organization of Lebanese society: It merely sought a larger share of the pie in a peaceful Lebanon. Thus, it was in substantial, if unstated, agreement with the apparent goal of Israel and Syria. The leadership of AMAL reflected this "reformist" attitude in that it was largely middle class.

AMAL, however, had to contend with another potential champion of the Shia, **Hizbollah** (Party of God). Hizbollah was led largely by clerics, financed by Iran, and strongly ideological in that it advocated the formation of an Islamic republic. It seems that grass-roots loyalties to each group were rather ephemeral, depending on particular and immediate material conditions rather than deep-seated ideological beliefs. Therefore, the popularity of Hizbollah has been linked to the desperate state of the Shia of Lebanon and the perceived inability of AMAL to effect a solution. The spectacular rash of hostage-taking in the 1980s often was alleged to have direct links to Hizbollah or some associated group.

The formal Lebanese government and its army were powerless as the various communities became more insular and desperate. Each of the major confessional groups, with the exception of the Druze, splintered into smaller factions and retreated into a vicious and fluid communal bloodletting. Lebanon was less a country than a tribal battlefield. Yet it continued to survive.

Amin Gemayel's presidential term was to end in September 1988. Efforts to find a new power-sharing arrangement and a new presidential candidate failed. The United States and Syria (generally in opposition to each other) were involved in the searches (and the vetos). The presidency fell vacant and Gemayel appointed (Christian) General Aoun to head a caretaker military government. General Aoun refused to recognize a proposed government headed by (Sunni) prime minister Hoss, and an Arab League attempt at compromise failed. General Aoun, supplied with weapons by an Iraq wanting to curb Syrian power, tried to wrest power through the ouster of Syria. Finally, an Arab-League-initiated effort resulted in the Taif accords (November 1989). The Lebanese parliament (elected in 1972) was convened in Taif, Saudi Arabia. They agreed to a new power-sharing agreement. The number of seats in the parliament was to be expanded (to 108), equally divided between Christians and Muslims (instead of the old 6:5 Christian majority). The powers of the (Christian) president were trimmed and those of the (Sunni) prime minister enhanced. Further, the Lebanese "special relationship" with Syria allowed Syrian troops to remain in Lebanon to help the government disarm the various militias. The clear winners were the Lebanese Sunni and the Syrians.

General Aoun rejected the government. He finally was removed from power in October 1990, under the fire of Syrian forces—and at a time when the United States needed Syrian participation in the coalition against Iraq and, therefore, gave a diplomatic "green light" to Syrian plans. As the new government assumed more control, and as the various militia were disarmed (of their large weapons), the average Lebanese citizen enjoyed more peace than in the preceding fifteen years.

Lebanon, however, remained in a difficult position. The Syrians held sway in large parts of the country. The Israelis and their Christian clients occupied the south. The Bekka valley had several thousand Iranian militia. The Palestinians remained. And the Lebanese themselves were still seeking common ground. That common ground seemed to be emerging during the 1990s as Lebanon continued its tentative march toward political and economic reconstruction. Still, the Israelis and Syrians continued to cast large shadows over Lebanon even though Israeli forces left Lebanon by 2000. It is highly probable that Lebanon will continue to have foreign forces on its soil until a peace agreement is reached between Syria and Israel.

Iraq. The July 1958 revolution in Iraq, led by General Abdul Karem Kassim, brought death to many of the country's traditional rulers, including King Faisal II and the veteran prime minister, Nuri al-Said. The coup was originally supported by an assortment of nationalist and leftist groups. The alliance, however, began to unravel soon after the revolution. The Iraqi Baathists urged joining the UAR, but unlike the Syrian Baathists, those in Iraq were not sufficiently powerful to force the decision. Rather, Kassim played off the pan-Arab Baathists against the communists. The nationalist group, the National Democrats, gained early favor with Kassim but lost most of their influence within a year. A highly turbulent five years followed; the communists tended to gain in power as a group but individuals had to remain vigilant because of Kassim's frequent purges of top government leaders. Kassim himself was killed in a 1963 coup. General Abdel Salam Aref came to power. Aref had been an original member of the 1958 group that destroyed the monarchy and himself had been purged in 1958. Aref brought Baathists into the government, but they were again purged within a year. When General Aref died in a helicopter accident in 1966, he was succeeded by his brother, Abdel Rahman Aref, the prime minister at the time, who held office until the 1968 coup, which brought General Ahmed Hassan al-Bakr to power. Again the Baathists returned to a position of prominence, but it was a Baathist party stripped of

its pro-Nasserist fervor. By 1968 the pro-Nasserist and communist elements were widely distrusted in Iraq. Part of the strength of General Hassan al-Bakr's rule stemmed from the fact that many of his associates came from the same area in Iraq (indeed, many came from the same village). When illness caused him to resign in 1979, Saddam Hussein took power. As vice-president for a decade, Saddam Hussein assumed an ever-greater proportion of strictly presidential roles for the aged and ailing al-Bakr.

The decade of the 1970s in Iraq can be characterized as one of economic growth, fueled by petroleum price increases, and political consolidation of power through brutal repression and genuine progress in forging broad-based alliances with some major Kurdish and Shia groups. The 1980s were dominated by the horrifically bloody war with Iran (1981–1988). It is important to note that Iraq was able to continue quick economic growth through loans and grants given by the Arab Gulf states as well as credits extended by a variety of Western creditors. Indeed, Baghdad had enough money to have about two million foreigners working in the economy as Iraqi men fought and died at the front. Although generally not mentioned, the war with Iran also had a potentially profound effect on the role of women. During the war they filled jobs heretofore reserved for males; and after almost a decade of employment in a wide variety of posts it was clear that the clock could not be turned back.

Iraq entered the 1990s with several pressing economic problems. First, the Gulf states stopped providing financial aid once the war with Iran was concluded, and the debt-servicing requirements of loans contracted during the decade were becoming a heavy burden. Second, petroleum prices were sagging. Third, Iraq's major port, Basra, was going to be closed for the indefinite future because the Shatt al-Arab, the waterway from the gulf to Basra, was filled with sunken ships and unexploded ordinance and had silted up. Beginning in the early months of 1990, official Baghdad articulated its grievances. They lost about one billion dollars per year for every $1 per barrel decrease in the price of petroleum. They claimed that certain members of OPEC, notably Kuwait, were exceeding their quota, thereby depriving Iraq of badly needed revenue. Kuwait's action was particularly galling since it had arguably the world's highest per capita income and was earning more from interest earnings on foreign investments than petroleum sales. Iraq also charged that Kuwait was cheating Iraq in that they were pumping more petroleum from a shared field than agreed to. Further, Kuwait would not discuss yielding to Iraq two islands which were vital to protect Umm Qasr, Iraq's only sizable port after the closure of Basra.

Iraq also realized that the winds of change were blowing in the conservative monarchies of Arabia. For example, Kuwaiti elections in April of 1990 were roundly criticized as a sham, and were effectively boycotted by groups of Kuwaitis calling for significant democratic reform. Finally, there did not seem to be a military counterforce in the area that would prevent an Iraqi takeover, and it was quite clear that most governments were not particularly sympathetic to Kuwait.

On a larger scale, the Iraqi leadership seems to have thought that it was poised to assume the mantle of leadership in the Arab world. One would have expected Iraq to be war weary in early 1990; it was not. Rather, it was aggressively proud that it had survived a war against an enemy with three times its population, that it had experienced economic growth through the period, and that the Kurds and especially the Shia did not heed Iran's calls to revolt. Words, actions, and visual symbols of the upbeat attitude abounded, one of the most startling being a billboard outside of partially reconstructed Babylon showing in profile Nebuchadnezzar and Saddam Hussein.

The invasion was the first in a series of Iraqi miscalculations. The United States quickly responded to a request from Saudi Arabia for protection. Iraq (10 percent) and Kuwait (10 percent) controlled about one-fifth of world petroleum exports. If Saudi Arabia is added, the figure exceeds 40 percent. After two months the U.S. buildup was revised to include an offensive capability, this after the United States gathered European and Arab (especially Egyptian and Syrian) nations into a coalition against Iraq. On the international diplomatic front, the United Nations passed a series of resolutions against Iraq, and the Arab League condemned the invasion while seeking an all-Arab solution.

Although the Iraqi position became increasingly hopeless, they did not move. Finally, the coalition forces attacked in January 1991, killed many thousands of Iraqis, perhaps greater than 100,000, devastated the infrastructure, and liberated Kuwait. Saddam Hussein remained in power as the coalition forces stopped short of a full-scale occupation. In the immediate aftermath of the defeat, the Shia and the Kurds were in open revolt. They were quickly crushed by the remnants of the army. United Nations postwar sanctions against Iraq proved to be troublesome. The Iraqis were not forthcoming with UN inspection teams charged with locating and destroying the nuclear, biological, and chemical military capabilities of Iraq. On the other side of the ledger, the sanctions brought suffering and death to thousands of average Iraqis who could not receive medicine, were denied spare parts to repair the water systems, and so on.

The difficulty of governing Iraq has been complicated by the pressure of communalism—the attempts of the various religious and ethnic communities to assert their power on the nation. Although Sunni Muslims are a minority, they have had a far greater hand in ruling the country than their numbers would indicate. The Shia Muslims in the southeast form the largest bloc of citizens, about 60 percent, but they had been largely excluded from power. It was with some concern, then, that official Baghdad viewed revolutionary Iran's calls to the Iraqi Shia to overthrow the government; their numbers were large and they had some basis for discontent. The other large minority, comprising nearly 20 percent of the population, is the Kurds. They are non-Arab Sunni Muslims with their own language and culture, and they have been extremely tenacious in their almost continuous struggle for autonomy against the governments where they are a sizable minority—Iraq, Syria, Turkey, and Iran.

Although the Treaty of Sèvres (1920) called for the establishment of an independent Kurdistan, this plan was not carried out. Kurdish leaders still seek an independent status, and the governments of Iraq, Iran, Syria, and Turkey have had long-standing difficulties trying to assimilate them. The Kurds have numbers large enough (maybe twenty-five million) to be a constant threat, but they are few enough in any one country so that they never have had enough power to break away.

Generally, Kurdish fortunes take dramatic turns during times of regional conflict as the major actors selectively lend support to Kurdish resistance groups in the country of the antagonist. Thus, the shah of Iran supported Iraqi Kurds in their battle against Baghdad until a 1975 Iran/Iraq agreement was reached. In the early years of postrevolutionary Iran, the Kurds of Iran were supported by Iraq. By the mid-1980s Iran had forged an alliance with some Iraqi Kurdish groups. The 1988 Iranian capture of a strategically important city in Iraq brought a particularly brutal Iraqi response: It dropped chemical weapons on the city, reportedly killing 5,000 (Iraqi) Kurdish noncombatants.

Although the fractious Kurdish resistance continued through the decades following World War I, partially due to aid delivered by one or more of the regional antagonists, the prospects for an independent Kurdish state remained dim because it was not in the interest of any nation to have the Kurdish movement become too successful. Indeed, regional cooperation on the issue started in 1984 when Iraq and Turkey agreed on joint action against Kurdish rebels. In 1987 Turkey and Syria agreed to "cooperate" on Kurdish security questions. After the 1988 cease-fire between Iraq and Iran, the Iraqi government launched a series of major attacks against the Kurds, driving many thousands to refugee camps in Turkey and Iran. On a more positive note, Turkey initiated a substantial economic development program in the Kurdish areas of Turkey in an attempt to woo Kurdish loyalties; however, Kurdish independence movements continued.

After the 1991 war, the prospects of the Kurds continued to follow this decades-long pattern, albeit in a more spectacular fashion. The Kurds captured the attention of the world for a couple of weeks following the end of the war as television crews recorded poignant scenes of hundreds of thousands of civilian refugees walking through snowy mountain passes to escape the advancing Iraqi army, only to be met by Turkish border guards refusing sanctuary. In contrast, Iran accepted more than one million Iraqi Kurds. Concerted coalition action led to an arrangement

where Iraqi troops would stay out of specified Kurdish areas. Major Kurdish leaders then entered into negotiations with Baghdad concerning the form and extent of Kurdish autonomy within Iraq. As the talks dragged on without conclusion, the international media became bored and the Kurds once more were forgotten by the larger world, except for an occasional blurb showing their desperate condition. And as the world stopped paying attention, the Iraqi military moved against the Kurds, only to be rebuffed by allied forces. The arrangement allowing the Kurds semiautonomous status continued, albeit with two long-standing Kurdish liberation parties and their respective armies dividing the area and engaging in bitter feuds. They did, however, claim a unity of purpose once the United States signaled that it would act to force a "regime change" in Iraq (in 2002). Although the Iraqi Kurds said that they wanted to remain part of Iraq after the regime change, most observers found it incredible that they would so suddenly abandon their goal of a Kurdish state.

IRAN, THE GULF STATES, AND PETROLEUM

A substantial percentage of world petroleum supplies come from the Gulf countries through the Straits of Hormuz or by pipelines in the Middle East. Since the industrial power of the West and Japan is critically dependent on Gulf petroleum exports, any threatened long-term disruption of supplies from the area invites intervention from the great powers and thereby runs the risk of starting a global conflict.

The Iran/Iraq war was a central concern through the 1980s. As each of the antagonists attempted to disrupt the petroleum-exporting capabilities of the other, the remaining Gulf nations and the great powers stood by nervously. The stakes were raised in 1987 when the United States responded to a Kuwaiti request for protection of vessels from Iranian attack by "reflagging"—having ships sail under the U.S. flag—and offering safe passage to these tankers plying the Gulf. Within a year there were several limited engagements between U.S. and Iranian naval units. There also were a couple of disastrous mistakes, including an Iraqi air attack against a U.S. Navy vessel, killing 37 personnel, and a U.S. ship-based missile attack on an Iranian civilian airliner that killed 290.

Iraq's invasion of Kuwait brought renewed concerns over Gulf shipping safety. Environmental concerns became much more important during this episode. Massive amounts of petroleum were dumped into the Gulf during the conflict. Besides potentially disastrous effects on the fragile environment of the shallow Gulf, the slicks for a time threatened to foul desalination plants in Saudi Arabia and ruin significant fisheries.

The Iranian Revolution

It is a somber irony that the Gulf's economic growth, which was made possible by the West's need for petroleum, generated instability. For example, the checks and balances that the shah of Iran employed to discourage any gathering of power outside of his control became ineffective with economic growth. By the middle of the 1970s the modified traditional Persian system of creating insecurity among the potentially powerful had broken down. The shah, especially through SAVAK, the large secret police organization, responded by applying more overtly repressive measures. It was as if the shah had traded his rapier for a meat axe. Much has been written about the heavy-handed role of SAVAK—originally trained and supervised by the CIA of the United States and Mossad of Israel—and how popular reactions against it helped to bring the downfall of the Pahlevi dynasty. However, it is also important to understand why those in power thought that these actions were necessary. As the old system of controls was breaking down under the weight of its own complexity, the shah was faced with the choice of accepting a loss of power or redoubling his efforts to stamp out opposition. He chose the latter course and lost the gamble.

The apparent inability of the U. S. government to interpret the danger signals emanating from Iran during the shah's decline was dramatically illustrated when President Carter toasted the shah on New Year's Eve, 1977, with the remark that Iran was "an island of stability." The view from the palace, however, was not the same as the one from

the streets of Tehran. By New Year's Eve of the following year, the U.S. government urged all of its citizens in Iran, some 40,000, to depart. The shah left Iran for a "vacation" on January 16, 1979. He was to die in an Egyptian military hospital a year and a half later, never having returned.

The young politically alienated urban technocrats joined the antigovernment movement in a manner surprisingly similar to the 1890–1892 tobacco riots. Again, it was the clergy who led the revolt. They had two deep sources of disagreement with the shah. First, the policies of "modernization" introduced by the shah were unabashedly secular in design. Second, some policies, land reform for example, were designed partly to woo peasant support away from the religious authorities and over to the shah. Ayatollah Ruhollah Khomeini had been in exile in Iraq from 1963 until 1978, when he was expelled as part of the Iraqi-Iranian attempts to patch up their contentious relations. Iraq also had its own reasons for wanting the powerful leader out of the country. Shia Muslims comprise a majority of the Iraqi population and are concentrated in the southeast of Iraq. The Kurds, who are Sunni Muslims but not Arabs, account for about 20 percent of the population and live in the north. The Sunni Arabs of central Iraq have controlled the government and have generally been in an economically advantageous position. For obvious reasons, the government of Iraq preferred not to harbor someone of Khomeini's stature and ideology. The banishment of Ayatollah Khomeini from Iraq did not lessen his influence against the shah. As the leaders of the tobacco riots used the telegraph to coordinate their actions, so Ayatollah Khomeini directed the Iranian revolution by telephone from Paris, until his return to Iran on February 1, 1979.

The streets of Tehran ran with blood during 1978 as demonstrations, many of them peaceful, were repeatedly met with brutal force. By December 1978, it was apparent to most observers that the shah's time was limited.

The Iranian Revolutionary Government

Khomeini's return to Iran brought a massive outpouring of popular approval. The last government appointed by the shah before he left Iran fell on

February 11, 1979. Revolutionary Iran appointed a government headed by Mehdi Bazargan, but the civilian government was subject to the dictates of the Revolutionary Council headed by Ayatollah Khomeini and found it extremely difficult to conduct day-to-day business. Prime Minister Bazargan tendered his resignation several times before it was accepted (November 6) by the Revolutionary Council. The Revolutionary Council ruled until the outlines of a new constitution could be drawn and a new president elected. Abolhassan Bani-Sadr was elected president in February 1980, and the new parliament, the Majlis, was elected in May 1980. The first Majlis of the new republic was dominated by the Islamic Republican Party—a group led by many of the country's most important religious leaders. The president, although closely aligned with this group when both were in opposition to the rule of the shah, was generally considered to have a more secular orientation than the clergy.

Although the particular twists and turns of events in postrevolutionary Iran were impossible to predict, the revolution followed a familiar pattern in that once the glue of common discontent toward the policies of the shah was removed, the fundamental differences between the various opposition groups surfaced. The enduring lessons are that successful revolutions are those which hold the important factions together once the old government has been removed, and that success or failure must be measured in terms of what has happened to the country some decades after the seizure of political power.

While the transition from one form of government to another is always problematic, Iran faced a very unusual set of circumstances. First, it was attempting to establish an Islamic republic in a form apparently quite different from other governments adopting that label. A particularly difficult initial point involved the conflicts of authority between the president and the religious leaders. During the early days of Bani-Sadr's presidency, Ayatollah Khomeini directed the government to reverse its decisions on several occasions. It would have been difficult for the government even in the easiest of circumstances to decide on the limits of religious authority in matters not strictly religious, but the charismatic power of Khomeini was such

that the issue was never in doubt: The government was forced to accede to his directives.

The crisis of authority deepened throughout the presidency of Bani-Sadr. In early June 1981, Ayatollah Khomeini stripped the president of his role as commander of the armed forces. The Majlis then declared Bani-Sadr politically incompetent, clearing the way for Ayatollah Khomeini to dismiss him as president on June 22. The role of president was to be filled by a three-person commission until a new president was elected. The three individuals, all members of the Islamic Republican Party, were the chief justice, the speaker of the Majlis, and the prime minister. Violence between the country's various political factions had been increasing in the months preceding the ouster of Bani-Sadr. The strife intensified, culminating in an explosion in Islamic Republican Party headquarters in Tehran, killing seventy-four, including the chief justice (Ayatollah Beheshti), several cabinet ministers and subministers, twenty members of the Majlis, and other party leaders. The course of the Iranian revolution became highly problematic: Bani-Sadr was in hiding and being sought by the government, the political leadership was in disarray, and groups again were taking to the streets. The crisis of political authority was but one of the major issues faced by the new government. There was considerable diversity of opinion concerning the economic role of the state, the proper extent of limitations to be placed on private enterprise, the ideologically correct nature of contracts, and so on.

The revolutionary government survived the near chaos of these years through a consolidation of formal political power by the clerics, systematic suppression of some important opposition forces such as the Tudeh (communist) Party, the reestablishment of a functioning bureaucracy, and so on. The new government also had pressing international problems, especially with respect to the United States. It was commonly believed that the U.S. Central Intelligence Agency had brought the shah back to power in 1952. Would the United States attempt to do it again? The leaders of the revolution knew that they were in a stronger position than the 1952 nationalists, but they also knew that thousands of SAVAK and military personnel loyal to the shah would take up arms at the bidding of the United States. Although the U.S. government tried to distance itself from the shah, its messages to Iran were mixed and were received with skepticism. As a positive step, the United States announced on October 5, 1979, that it would resume the shipment of some military replacement parts to Iran. Most of Iran's immense arsenal of military hardware had come from the United States, and the United States had been supplying parts roughly on an "as needed" basis. Without an adequate supply of spare parts, Iranian military capability would be at a disadvantage. The promised parts, however, were not to be shipped because of events during the next month.

On October 22, 1979 the deposed shah entered the United States to receive medical treatment for cancer. The U.S. government had been told repeatedly that the entry of the shah into the United States would only inflame Iranian passions, increase suspicions about the United States, and endanger U.S. citizens still in Iran. On November 4, the U.S. Embassy in Tehran was occupied by individuals identified only as "students." About sixty embassy personnel were taken as hostages. In the following weeks many furious words were hurled about without much action. However, some points seemed clear: Those holding the hostages were following the dictates of Ayatollah Khomeini, and the United States would refuse to meet Iranian demands to return the shah to Iran.

The government of the United States worked to bring diplomatic sanctions against Iran in the United Nations; it also imposed economic sanctions of its own and encouraged its allies to do the same. It used intermediaries not generally thought of as being in its camp to try to negotiate the release of the hostages. These U.S. actions did little to cool Iranian hostility. However, it is questionable what difference a conciliatory tone would have made, for Iran was full of conflict and contradiction. In April 1980, President Carter ordered military units to attempt a rescue of the hostages, but the mission was aborted when several problems made it impossible for the attack force to advance beyond a desert landing point south of Tehran. Given the apparent high odds against success, the fact that it was attempted at all indicates the president's overpowering need to end the crisis. As it was, the United States was forced to take

a more patient stance. The hostages were released in January 1981. But the war with Iraq had started a couple of months earlier.

The Iraq-Iran War: 1980–1988

The new republic faced the nettlesome problem of dealing with the minorities in Iran. The Kurds of the north, a Sunni group, had begun to agitate for independence. The Iraqi government supported Iranian Kurds in their efforts, just as the shah had supported Iraqi Kurds before a 1975 agreement with Baghdad. The government also faced challenges from the Baluchis of the southeast and the Azerbaijanis of the northwest. For its part, Iranian radio was exhorting the Iraqi Shia to overthrow their government. Other Gulf countries, all with sizable Shia populations, were understandably nervous. Even Saudi Arabia had cause for worry; its relatively small Shia population is located in the petroleum-rich northeast, and was receiving the same message that was being sent to its Iraqi counterparts.

Iraq revoked its 1975 agreement with Iran that had ended Iranian support of the Kurds in Iraq in return for the settlement of a long-disputed border in the Gulf area in Iran's favor. The agreement had set the border between the two countries along the Shatt al-Arab thalweg, Iraq's only major route to the Gulf and thus the only sea route for imports and exports from their port city of Basra. Iraq apparently wanted to regain control of the entire waterway—the pre-1975 (disputed) convention gave Iraq rights of the Shatt al-Arab to the Iranian shore. The initial Iraqi assaults were verbal and attempted to foment trouble among the substantial Arab population in Iran's petroleum-rich Khuzistan area. Open warfare broke out on September 22, 1980. Iraq scored initial victories by taking some Iranian territory along the Shatt al-Arab and by damaging the important port and refinery city of Abadan. Iran responded by bombing Baghdad on several occasions and by making a considerable effort to hold Abadan.

The war droned on. There were times of relative quiet, furious offensives, deliberate bombings of civilians, the use of poison gas (by Iraq), and attempts to widen the war. There was little movement toward resolution, militarily or diplomatically.

Indeed, official Tehran said on several occasions that there could not be peace as long as the government of Saddam Hussein held power. The war may have strengthened the power of the Iraqi government in ways it did not perceive when it initiated the conflict. For example, the government found it worthwhile to work to placate the country's Shia majority in order to counter messages from Iran calling for a Shia revolt. Also, the receipt of Gulf financial aid and the use of Jordanian transport routes served to strengthen ties with a couple of important Arab neighbors. Finally, at the close of 1984 the United States resumed diplomatic relations with Iraq, ending a seventeen-year break. The benefit to Iran was nil except for the possible internal unity gained from having such an active external threat.

A cease-fire was arranged in mid-1988. Earlier in the year each side had terrorized the population of the enemy's capital city by lobbing missiles into civilian areas—a phase of the conflict dubbed "the War of the Cities." Then Iraq scored a series of major battlefield victories. Both countries were war weary.

The very fact that Iran accepted a cease-fire pointed to changes in the course of the revolution. Early in the conflict Iranian leaders proclaimed that a theological imperative directed their efforts: Iran would not yield until the "infidel" government in Baghdad fell. The world stood by nervously during Iran's "moment of enthusiasm" in the immediate postcoup years. Calls for the export of the revolution gave pause to conservative governments of the area. While the cease-fire did not quiet all fears, it did signal that revolutionary fervor was lagging in an Iran increasingly ready to be guided in its internal and international affairs with the cold calculations of the pragmatist rather than the passion of the ideologue.

After Khomeini's death in 1989, the pragmatists strengthened their position. Khomeini was succeeded in the faqih-ship by Hojatoislami Ali Khamenei, a prominent cleric and ally of speaker Rafsanjani, the leader of the pragmatists. Rafsanjani was elected to an enhanced presidency later in 1989. Iran stood aloof from the Iraq-Kuwait affair in 1990–1991 and apparently was instrumental in the piecemeal freeing of all of the U.S. hostages held in Lebanon—the last being released in December 1991.

The subsequent elevation of title of Hojatoislami Ali Khamenei to Grand Ayatollah in 1991 signaled another vector of the power of the "pragmatists." Khamenei's new title met with substantial displeasure by more than 100 members of the Majlis. They stated that Khamenei did not have the theological background to assume the role of successor to Ayatollah Khomeini. The semiofficial conservative press summarily dismissed the complaints. It is also interesting that they did not champion Khomeini's son, Ahmad, as a worthy alternative. This further hints that the revolution was becoming institutionalized, and that dynastic succession was not to be the rule. Elections to the Majlis in 1992 further strengthened the hand of the pragmatists. This trend toward increasing pragmatism, however, moved rather slowly thereafter. One important consequence of the lack of a clear vision of the correct path to be taken was that the economy continued to perform poorly. This, in turn, led to further recriminations and yet more policy stasis. Further, Iran was not fully accepted in the international community and received differentially harsher treatment by the United States. Closer to home, the Gulf states continued to view Iran as a potential source of difficulty.

Saudi Arabia's Political Stability

On November 20, 1979, the day after "extremists," whose motivations initially were unclear to the outside world, took over the Grand Mosque in Mecca, the United States came under attack in widely scattered parts of the Islamic world. The attacks seem to have been sparked by a radio broadcast in which Khomeini implicated the United States in the Grand Mosque seizure. U.S. embassies were attacked in Calcutta, Dacca, Istanbul, Manila, Rawalpindi, and Lahore. The American embassy in Islamabad, Pakistan, was burned down; two Americans were killed and several others narrowly escaped death after waiting hours for the local authorities to intervene.

Until the attack on the Grand Mosque, Saudi Arabia's political stability had been shaken only slightly. When King Faisal was murdered by a nephew in 1975, there was some speculation that it was a political act, but the assassin seems to have been mentally unstable. Faisal was succeeded in orderly fashion by King Khalid. Partially because of his weak health, he was to yield many major state responsibilities to Prince Fahd. Fahd assumed the throne on the death of Khalid (1982). Since Saudi Arabia's massive petroleum output and low population had allowed it to accumulate enormous financial reserves, the West was particularly fearful of political instability in Saudi Arabia. Its petroleum was essential and it could severely disrupt world financial markets by moving its reserves from country to country. But the monarchy was politically cautious and conservative, and the Western countries viewed it as a moderate, "sensible" nation. Likewise, Saudi Arabia's adherence to strict Islamic ideals blunted criticisms of its monarchical form of government by most "progressive" Arab nations. Given this position and the desire to assume a greater leadership role in the Arab world, the Saudis promoted and developed a reputation as conciliators.

Saudi Arabia's public image of tranquility and stability, however, concealed as much as it revealed. Saudi society was undergoing massive and rapid change. Its per capita income was one of the highest in the world, it was one of the world's leading financial powers, and it had begun countless expensive construction projects. Only a few decades earlier, central Arabia had been one of the poorest areas of the world. Social change has not yet occurred on as dramatic a scale as the change in income. However, the tens of thousands of Saudis who have studied in the United States and Britain are not likely to completely accept their country's traditional political culture nor its Islamic austerities. The seizure of the Grand Mosque in Mecca may have been an isolated event, but it is possible that such disturbances will begin to occur more regularly as the popular desire for more political participation increases.

The Iraqi invasion of Kuwait, and the military action that followed, shook Saudi Arabia to its core. First, it was clear that the Saudi military could not stop Iraq if Iraq's ultimate intentions were to overrun them. The first question they had to answer was, should we take the chance that they will not cross the border? No, they decided. Then they had to determine the proper response. While the Arab world generally opposed the invasion, many called for an "Arab solution" to the prob-

lem. But, they were not ready to defend Saudi Arabia—at least not quickly—and time was not on the Saudi side. They knew that the West thought well of them, if for no other reason than that they supplied vital petroleum on a regular basis. But requesting the West, specifically the United States, to intervene would run counter to a host of important considerations: The Arab governments would not view Western intervention favorably; worldwide Muslim sentiment would not favor the keepers of the holy places of Mecca and Medina to allow infidels on their soil; and, finally, the influx of Western forces could upset the delicate interplay between religious austerity and material wealth. In the end, the Saudis had over one-half million allied forces in their country. Although they weathered the crisis, it is difficult to imagine that Saudi Arabians were not changed in the process. Indeed, one such manifestation was the 1992 announcement of the intent to form a consultative assembly (appointed).

The collapse of petroleum prices in the mid-1980s gave rise to a different set of tensions faced by the Saudi government. In the early 1980s, Saudi Arabia earned over $100 billion per year through petroleum sales. The figure fell to under $20 billion by the last years of the decade. At first the government ran deficits financed from previous earnings; then it was forced into the politically unpopular act of slashing expenditures.

Another potential cause of instability concerned the "awakening of the Shia." For example, in December 1981, Bahrain authorities arrested and subsequently convicted seventy-three individuals for plotting a coup. Bahrain charged that the coup was to be part of a larger effort, one that was to bring the fall of Saudi Arabia, and that the plotters had direct ties with Iran. During the Hajj of 1987 Saudi authorities clashed with demonstrating Iranian pilgrims in Mecca. More than 400 Iranians were killed. Shortly thereafter, the Saudi embassy in Tehran was overrun by Iranians. Relations between the two countries reached an all-time low, although diplomatic relations were quickly restored.

The Shia population in the Gulf is substantial. What is not indicated are the particulars of the population, which tend to give it potential influence beyond that predicted simply by the strength of numbers. For example, Shia in Saudi Arabia represent less than 10 percent of the population but are concentrated in the petroleum-rich northeastern part of the country. The Shia in Oman represent less than 5 percent of the population, but they are concentrated in specific businesses. Those of Bahrain are the poorest and least educated of that country. It also should be remembered that many of these Shia have ethnic tries to Iran. Therefore, the governments of the Gulf countries, all ruled by Sunni elites, have to be especially sensitive to this issue.

Yemen

North and South Yemen effected a surprisingly quick and smooth unification ratified in May 1990. As opposed to several ill-fated attempts at unification in the Arab world, there was a strong logic to this move. During the prior several decades North Yemen (actually, largely to the east of South Yemen) was evolving away from its thousand-year-old theocratic and xenophobic state. Meanwhile, South Yemen was losing its radical zeal.

The Peoples Democratic Republic of Yemen, generally called South Yemen, attained independence in 1967 when the British pulled out of Aden. In 1970 it became a Marxist state. As the only long-standing nonconservative government in the area, South Yemen was involved in many political battles in the Arabian Peninsula. It received aid from the Soviet Union, East Germany, and China. Although any state in this volatile region must be taken seriously, it was tempting to regard South Yemen as the neighborhood's bad boy. It was continually in somebody else's backyard, but when dealt with sternly was dissuaded from doing much damage. However, this analogy does not illustrate its potential importance in the region (Ethiopia, Djibouti, and Somalia are all in the strategically important Horn of Africa across the Gulf of Aden), its past involvement with rebels in Oman, and its support of Iraq during the Iraq/Kuwait war.

There were several impulses for unification, including a civil war in South Yemen in 1986, the collapse of the Soviet bloc, and the discovery of significant petroleum reserves in both countries.

The Gulf Cooperation Council

The Gulf Cooperation Council (GCC) was formed in 1981 by the conservative Gulf states—Saudi Arabia, Kuwait, Bahrain, Qatar, the United Arab Emirates, and Oman—partially in response to the perceived threat from revolutionary Iran and partially in recognition of some of the more obvious economies of scale to be garnered through cooperation. They proceeded slowly with respect to the establishment of joint security arrangements. They made somewhat more progress on the economic front. Customs duties were eliminated on a wide range of products manufactured or grown in the member countries, and skilled labor was allowed freedom to take employment in any of the states.

The GCC also tried to build a common educational system. The most ambitious of these was the establishment of the campus for the Gulf University in Bahrain. The campus, however, has no students. The squeeze on petroleum-based budgets in the late 1980s directly led to a forced fiscal austerity of the GCC.

Although the accomplishments of the GCC have been modest, it remains an important body in that it has provided a forum for collective political and economic ventures. This became obvious during the 1991 threat from Iraq. Cooperation and coordination was much smoother than it otherwise would have been. However, formidable problems remain; for example, a customs union first proposed to come to fruition around 2000 was formally delayed several years as the deadline approached.

ISRAEL

The Jews of Palestine were not able to bask in the glory of victory after the state of Israel was formed in 1948. Their turbulent history has been dominated by war and the threat of war. Indeed, it was not until President Anwar Sadat of Egypt set foot on Israeli soil in November 1977 that any Arab leader officially recognized that Israel was a permanent entity in the Middle East. Even then, President Sadat's act isolated Egypt in the Arab world for several years.

More than most nations of the world, much of Israel's daily life is directly, consciously, and openly affected by international events. It is no exaggeration to say that virtually every long-time citizen of Israel has known someone killed in war. The Israeli "siege mentality" has been born of experience and is firmly based in reality. Israel has been under siege since its inception. It has heard numerous calls for its destruction over the years, it has lost many of its sons and daughters in military action, and it has witnessed its enemies' tremendous growth in financial power and military capability. This is not to say that all Israelis agree on how to resolve Israel's almost continual crisis. On the contrary, Israeli public opinion on most vital issues reflects the considerable heterogeneity of Israeli society.

The Political Setting

Israel's prime minister is the *de facto* head of government: The position of president is largely ceremonial. Until 1996 the prime minister was chosen from the members of parliament, the Knesset, and instructed to put together a cabinet; since then, the prime minister faces direct election. Members of the Knesset are elected through countrywide proportional representation. The voters choose between "lists," each list representing a political party or coalition of parties. The 120 Knesset seats are divided between the lists according to the percentage of the national vote garnered; for example, a list gaining 10 percent of the vote receives twelve seats. Any single list must gain a minimum of 2 percent of the vote to be eligible for a seat. If the government is to function effectively, of course, it must maintain the support of a legislative majority on at least the key issues of the day. This point is essential for an understanding of Israeli politics; coalition politics has dominated the system because no single party has ever gained a clear legislative majority.

Although Israeli citizens have been presented with a wide range of lists in each general election, they generally select from three prominent groups: the labor-dominated left-center, the right-center, and the religious parties. The Labor list formed the governments from 1949 through 1977. The right-center put together the ninth and tenth Knessets (1977–1984). The religious parties generally have gained between 10 and 20 percent of the vote and have been the group that the other two have turned to in order to form a legislative majority. Therefore, they have had an influence beyond their voting strength. It also should be remembered that the very fact that Israel defines itself as a Jewish state gives the message of the religious parties a particularly strong resonance among the population.

The Labor list itself is a coalition of several distinct parties that unite for election purposes. Generally these parties have espoused a socialist ideal in domestic affairs. The most powerful Labor group, the Mapai, held the loyalties of many Israelis through its control of the Histradut, the pervasive Labor organization. Since the Mapai drew its leadership primarily from the Histradut, it has become identified by many as the group that in the past provided temporary relief to immigrants, helped them secure housing, and gave them employment. Other major Labor groups were more strident in their socialism, more willing to subsume nationalist aspirations and identify with the working classes of all nationalities. The Labor parties were able to garner a plurality of Knesset seats until 1977; they constructed their legislative majority by taking the religious parties into the fold. The religious parties, as the name suggests, are concerned primarily with religious issues—for example, the notion that Israeli Jews have the right to settle in all biblical lands irrespective of existing political boundaries.

The Labor alliance started to lose power during the 1960s, partially and ironically because of its past success. Because it could not manage to win a majority of Knesset seats, and because the Labor bloc itself was an amalgam of parties and viewpoints, it had to broaden its political position to accommodate more of the electorate. But in so doing, the political focus became blurred, and dissension within the bloc grew. A host of other factors contributed to its inability to gain a majority, including the changing profile of the voters (rural to urban, older to younger) and voter disillusion with incumbents who had failed to ensure peace and security.

The performance of governments based on coalitions is always problematic. The Labor bloc was large enough to prevent a quick succession of governments, but it had to depend on other parties and found it difficult to move away from the status quo. The status quo, however, meant insecure national borders and a large military budget.

Although there had been defections of important figures from Mapai during the 1960s, it was only after the 1973 war that the coalition began to face serious challenges to its premier position. The war resulted in heavy Israeli casualties, no military victory, and a psychological shock. In June 1974, the government of Prime Minister Golda Meir was forced to step down in favor of another set of Labor-bloc leaders headed by Itzhak Rabin. However, the new government also faced a rocky road. Israel was becoming more and more isolated internationally, the military budget grew larger and more burdensome, and the economy faced high rates of inflation. Since the Rabin government was forced to adopt the amorphous policies of its predecessors, it had difficulty in resolving vital issues. Finally, in 1977, a series of financial scandals involving Rabin and some cabinet ministers eliminated the government's remaining strength.

The Democratic Movement for Change (DMC) then emerged as an important new coalition party. It was a single-issue party that advocated changing Israeli electoral laws to rid the Knesset of debilitating factionalism. The leadership of the DMC was drawn from a wide ideological spectrum, although much of the platform resembled that of the Labor bloc. Their apparent aim was to gain enough seats in the Knesset to help form a majority in return for a promise of electoral reform. The results of the election dashed their hopes.

The Labor alignment had its number of Knesset seats reduced from fifty-one in 1973 to thirty-two in 1977. Since the National Religious Party, holding twelve seats in 1977, no longer desired to unite with the Labor alignment, it proved impossible for the alignment and the DMC (fifteen seats), along with the other smaller parties, to form a majority in the Knesset. The big winner in the 1977 elections was the Likud bloc, which emerged with a plurality of forty-three seats. After a month of negotiations, a government was formed (June 1977) that aligned the Likud bloc with two religious parties (and later with the DMC, which reserved the right to disagree on questions including religion and occupied territories). Menachem Begin, the leader of Likud, became the new prime minister. The new government was conservative in domestic issues and aggressive in foreign policy: It advocated a selective dismantling of socialist policies in favor of private enterprise, and the settlement of Israelis on land occupied since the 1967 war. Indeed, Prime Minister Begin referred to the occupied area as being "liberated." As the new government became established, it remained unclear whether the basic shift away from Labor-bloc positions would continue. Analysis of the 1977 election indicated that Israelis voted against the Labor alignment rather than for the Likud coalition.

The Likud coalition fell apart in early 1981. The results of the June 30, 1981 election gave Labor and Likud forty-nine seats each. The smaller parties generally lost seats but gained in bargaining power since both Labor and Likud eagerly sought their favor in hope of forming the needed sixty-one-seat majority. Likud finally patched together a fragile coalition and Begin continued as prime minister. The coalition fell apart in two and one-half years and another election was held in July 1984. Israel was in the midst of a particularly difficult set of circumstances. Especially important were the heavy psychological, financial, and human costs exacted by continued Israeli presence in Lebanon, which they had invaded in 1982. Contributing factors included domestic and international antagonisms generated by the accelerated pace of settlement in the West Bank, and an unusually harsh economic climate.

Prime Minister Begin dropped out of political life well before the election—he did not even campaign for or publicly endorse Likud candidates. Election results again yielded a stalemate (forty-four seats for Labor, forty-one for Likud). After prolonged negotiations, Likud and Labor joined forces to form a "National Unity Government." The Labor leader (Shimon Peres) was prime minister for the first two years, and the new Likud leader (Yitzhak Shamir) first filled the post of foreign minister and then switched with Peres. If nothing else, this unique arrangement of power sharing indicated the impossibility of either party to form a coalition government by bringing the increasingly contentious smaller parties into its fold.

Analyses of the election indicated that there was a hardening of attitudes among the voters, and that voting by ethnic blocs increased (Ashkenazi to Labor; Oriental to Likud).

The 1988 elections yielded the same sort of stalemate. However, both Labor (thirty-nine) and Likud (forty) won fewer seats than in the previous election. The religious parties gained seats, but both Labor and Likud were unwilling to adopt certain religious party issues in order to form a coalition. Therefore, Labor and Likud again formed a unity government. During the campaign both blocs had agreed that this cumbersome power sharing was to be avoided: Israel needed decisive action on several pressing issues, and a unity government essentially meant that any such action would be blocked by one of the blocs. But the postelection realities dictated another round of power sharing. The obvious debilitating results of an electoral system based on proportional representation were not ignored, and electoral reform became a serious issue again.

The coalition fell apart in March 1990, and a new government was formed in June. Labor failed to form a new government; Likud gathered the needed majority by hammering out an agreement with the religious and right-wing parties. In the interim, there was a rally of 100,000 in Tel Aviv calling for electoral reform. However, the call went unheeded.

The government fell apart again in January 1992, when two religious parties bolted from Likud. Israel had suffered through a tough year during 1991. It was forced to sit on the sidelines during the Gulf War, failed to settle Soviet immigrants in a coherent fashion, was rebuffed by the United States when it requested a $10B loan guarantee to aid in the process, initiated a socially disruptive furious pace of settlement on the West Bank, and was pressured into the beginnings of a peace conference. If nothing else, the Israeli political process points to the dangers of having an electoral system which rewards fringe parties in a setting of social heterogeneity when core values are at stake.

Likud suffered a stunning defeat in the June 1992 election, winning only thirty-two seats. Labor won forty-four seats and, more important,

the liberal lists gained enough seats to allow Labor to form a coalition with them without yielding to the demands of the ultranationalist and religious parties. Labor prime minister Rabin acted quickly to reinvigorate the peace process that had stalled under the Likud government.

Social Setting

The coming to power of a non-Labor government in 1977 was in many ways the political expression of the social change that had been occurring since 1948. The composition of the Israeli population in 1950 was markedly different from what it was two years earlier. Estimates (open to some question) made by the United Nations team that drew up the 1947 partition plan showed a total population of 1.8 million, two-thirds being Arabs. By the end of 1949, the Arab population had fallen to about 160,000 and represented one-eighth of the total; the Jewish population had roughly doubled to 1.2 million. The Arabs became a minority. Jewish immigration continued to be heavy through 1952. Thereafter, natural rates of increase and immigration contributed equally to the population growth. By 1990 the population of Israel was five million, 85 percent being Jewish. Also, by 1990, Israel was receiving large numbers of Jews immigrating from the Soviet Union (due to the general Soviet relaxation of restrictions). Israeli authorities were quick to embrace these people, but they faced the prospect of financing the absorption of up to one million new citizens within a couple of years, a daunting task.

Israeli society is a complex amalgam which nevertheless invites categorization and, thereby, oversimplification. Perhaps it is easiest to begin with a three-way ethnic breakdown: European Jews, Oriental Jews, and Arabs. The European (**Ashkenazi**) group also includes Jews who immigrated to Israel from North and South America and South Africa, but the major distinguishing factor is the common parental or cultural lineage with European Jewry. The great majority of Jews who came to Palestine during the five preindependence waves of immigration were from Europe; the first four were primarily from Russia and Eastern

Europe; the fifth wave included a considerable number of Jews fleeing the Holocaust. The leaders who emerged from the first four waves set the ideological tone for the young state, a blend of socialism and Zionism that emphasized the virtues of working the soil. The fifth wave came to Palestine largely out of desperation. These people faced death in Nazi Germany and had been denied adequate refuge in the Allied countries. Their motivation was survival, and not necessarily the socialist-Zionist pioneering spirit that had guided former immigrants. Although their impact on Israeli society should not be overemphasized, many of these immigrants were urban, middle class, skilled, and more closely in touch with Western European culture than those from Eastern Europe and Russia. Their numbers were large and their votes had to be counted. Nevertheless, immigrants of the first four waves headed every government save one—that of Rabin, a Sabra (native-born Israeli). The postindependence wave of Eastern European immigration was largely over by 1952.

In the first few years following independence, many Jews from Asia and Africa immigrated as Arab governments acted in increasingly unfriendly ways and as local populations sometimes vented their anger at Israel toward these people, who by and large had nothing to do with Israel. During the first twenty-five years of independence, Israel absorbed three-quarters of a million of these immigrants, the largest group, 255,000, coming from Morocco. The effect on the social structure of Israel has been profound. Jews of African-Asian origin, called imprecisely either **Sephardic** or Oriental Jews, came to Israel to escape hostility and did not share the Western values and orientations of the Ashkenazi Jews. Their shared Jewishness was all that bonded them with their fellow Israelis. Although there are notable exceptions, the Oriental Jews of Israel generally have a substantially lower than average per capita income, have had less education, hold less significant government posts, have less desirable housing, and are viewed in a somewhat disparaging light by many of their fellow citizens. They are the soft underbelly of the Jewish population of Israel. The most notable exceptions to these generalizations

are the Sephardic Jews who were longtime residents of Palestine. The Sephardic Jews of Palestine were totally conversant with local Arab culture and had an articulated social structure in place well before the Zionist movement started. This small Sephardic elite tended to view all Jewish immigrants with some disdain.

Although many Sephardic Jews found government posts under the British mandate, neither they nor the Oriental Jews of more recent arrival shared fully in Israeli political life after independence. Their numbers swelled during the first decade of statehood until they became the Jewish majority by the 1970s, and the Ashkenazi-controlled major political parties had to woo their votes. The scene was complicated by the rise in numbers of another identifiable Jewish group, one that cut across Ashkenazi and Oriental distinctions: Sabras, or native-born Israelis. Although generally associated with their parents' group and marrying within that group, Sabras started to form another social force and comprised over half the Jews in Israel by 1977, most of them of European parentage. The immigration of Soviet Jews further complicated the mix.

If the Oriental Jews are the underside of Israeli Jewish society, many Arabs are in the position of belonging to a different culture while being citizens of Israel. The flight of Arabs out of Palestine from 1947 to 1949 was motivated largely by a concern for personal safety, the same concern that brought many Jews to Palestine. Since the fighting in Palestine in 1947–1948 was largely between Jewish and local Arab forces, it is not surprising that various Jewish groups actively sought to rid the fragile state of the hostile Arab population. The most famous—or infamous—terrorist act of this early period was the massacre in the village of Deir Yasin, where 250 Arab men, women, and children were killed. While the political leaders of Israel officially opposed the act, they did not proceed in a forceful manner to end terrorism by the armed bands that cooperated with the military.

Arab migration from (and within) Israel destroyed any semblance of order and coherence in the remaining Arab population. The two sources of leadership, the urban professional elite and the traditional leaders of villages, generally had fled. Of the major cities of Israel, only Nazareth maintained a large Arab population; only a few thousand remained in the other urban centers. A wide-open and often bitter competition for power took place in many rural areas. There was no center around which the Palestinian Arabs could rally. They were further divided along religious lines: 70 percent were Muslim, 21 percent Christian, and 9 percent Druze and other religions. In the immediate postwar years, Palestinian Arabs had no political leadership and suffered extreme economic deprivation.

Neither Zionist theory nor past political policy gave the leaders of the new state a clear formula on how to deal with an Arab minority in a Zionist state. Indeed, some Israelis hoped for a time that the problem would solve itself—that the flight of the Arabs would continue until none were left. In any case, the fledgling state had other pressing problems to deal with in order to survive. The economy was in chaos, the machinery of government was incomplete, and thousands of indigent, relatively unskilled immigrants were flowing in. The *ad hoc* policy toward Palestinian Arabs was mainly concerned with the maintenance of state security.

The geographical concentration of the Arab population made administration somewhat simple. A few months after Israel was formed, the army units which had occupied Arab-populated areas were formally charged with administering them. Since most of the Palestinian Arabs lived in areas that were Arab under the UN partition plan, a military administration was logical in that Israel was an occupying force. However, the military administration was to continue until 1966, well after annexation of these areas. Regardless of its other policy measures, the emplacement of what essentially was an army of occupation defined the basic attitude of the state toward these "part-citizens." However, even within the Military Administration the principles of administrative action were not clearly spelled out; security remained the only articulated goal. Security would be enhanced if the Arab population was fragmented geographically and politically, if their economic power was limited but not desperately low, and if their emerging leadership was placed in a dependent situation and co-opted. Many of the Israeli government's poli-

cies can be connected to one or more of these aims. For instance, land use and land rights policies consistently had the effect of stripping land away from the Arab population, especially in those areas the government deemed necessary to place under full Jewish control. Travel restrictions made it difficult for Arabs to reestablish political unity, and other policies established tight control over the Arab labor force. Occasionally the policies of the military administration resulted in spectacular displays of violence. In October 1956, for example, forty-nine residents of the Arab village of Kfar Kassim were killed for disobeying a curfew order of which they were unaware. The growing tensions surrounding the 1956 war and the need for absolute control led to the tragedy. That the responsible officers were given relatively light sentences confirmed the Arab view of the Israeli government's attitude toward them.

By the mid-1970s the Arabs of Israel began to express a sense of nationalism, but it was not until the 1988 uprising in the occupied territories that they moved to build a unified political base with strictly Arab concerns at the forefront. Their formidable task was complicated, however, by the increasingly severe restrictions the government placed on their political activity.

Israel and the Border States

Following the May 14, 1948 declaration of statehood, Israel immediately was engaged in war by Egypt, Iraq, Lebanon, Syria, and Transjordan. The initial round of fighting lasted for a month and was followed by a month-long truce administered by the United Nations. Ten more days of fighting was followed by a second truce. Sporadic fighting and truce arrangements occurred throughout 1948. Finally the British government declared that it would act on the 1936 treaty with Egypt that allowed British troops to enter Egypt to protect vital British interests. This announcement, and pressures from the United States government on Israel, helped bring about a series of bilateral armistice agreements between Israel and its neighbors.

The war and the armistice agreements increased Israeli territory by more than 30 percent beyond what was allowed for in the partition plan.

The Israeli army, although outnumbered substantially, mounted a series of crisp and well-coordinated attacks on the various Arab armies. However, the Israeli success was due at least as much to the ineptitude of the Arab armies and the lack of coordination between them. While various Arab leaders charged that Israel won because of Western support, several Arab nationalist spokesmen expressed their dissatisfaction with the kind of leadership that resulted in such humiliation. Terrorist activities ripped through Egypt in the latter part of 1948 and throughout 1949; the Egyptian prime minister was assassinated. The winds of discontent in Egypt continued to blow until the Free Officers' revolution in 1952. Three coups occurred in Syria during 1949–1950; none of the leaders, however, engaged the public's imagination. King Abdullah of Jordan was assassinated in July 1951. The shame of the 1948 defeat resulted in more Arab reprisals against their own governments than against Israel. Their anger was well placed, but it would take another quarter century before Arab armies could begin to match Israeli forces.

The task of creating and maintaining stability in newly created states generally has proved to be a formidable task. Israeli leaders had their job complicated by continued hostile relations with Arab states and by Israel's special population and economic problems. The flood of Jews coming from Europe after the close of World War II and from Arab countries during the late 1940s and early 1950s put the new state under tremendous strain. Israel, after all, was to be the homeland for all Jews. Indeed, the Israeli declaration of independence implied, and subsequent legislation (the Law of Return) granted, this right. Therefore, all immigrants had to be accepted. On the other hand, the economic and social system was put under an enormous burden, so enormous that many feared Israel would collapse. In 1952 the Jewish Agency, the organizers and financiers of most of this immigration, in an attempt to ease the crisis, introduced certain financial criteria for immigration. However, the new criteria for immigration did not solve other pressing problems, including the fact that many immigrants did not adhere to the Zionist-socialist ideology on which the early settlers had founded Israeli society, and that the flight of Arab farmers and the cessation of agricultural trade with Arab states caused a food shortage that assumed crisis proportions.

Many immigrants had to be settled on the land, but most were not ideologically suited to life on a kibbutz (a form of collective farm developed by earlier settlers), nor in the cooperative agricultural villages, the moshav. The government placed many immigrants in farming villages under the supervision of instructors who gave technical information, executive direction, and ideological guidance. Ideally the villages were to be located behind the border settlements and evolve into autonomous cooperatives. This process was carried out by fits and starts, with successes and failures.

The first several years of statehood, then, were difficult. However, the population, food, shelter, and state security problems were adequately solved by the mid-1950s. A considerable amount of ingenuity and hard work had been required, but the job was eased a great deal by a large amount of foreign aid flowing into the country that made it possible for Israel to cope with the situation. Immediately after independence the ratio of the value of exports to imports was about 15 percent—that is, for every dollar spent on imports only fifteen cents was earned from exports. The ratio climbed to 60 percent in the 1970s, but the absolute value of the gap increased. The gap between international spending and earning was covered by international remittances—gifts and loans from governments and individuals. About 15 billion dollars was received during the new nation's first twenty-five years. Twenty-five percent came from Jewish Fund collections, 25 percent from German reparation and restitution payments, 9 percent from bond sales, 13 percent from direct, unilateral transfers (generally from individual to individual), 13 percent from U.S. government loans and gifts, 7 percent from direct private investment, and 8 percent from various short- and medium-term loans. Much of Israel's economic growth was due to these sources.

The economic successes of the first couple of decades of statehood were not to be sustained. Israel's international debt position deteriorated considerably. Per capita external debt ranked among the highest in the world by 1980, and debt service payments became increasingly onerous, averaging around 20 percent of the value of export earnings in the 1980s. Growth slowed, inflation sometimes topped 100 percent,[1] and the extensive social welfare state constructed in the first two decades did not allow for a flexible response by the government. Solutions to these problems required a strong government; as it was, Israel went through most of the 1980s and early 1990s with coalition governments unable to reach agreement on crucial policy issues.

The 1956 Arab-Israeli War

As Israel steadied its economy and settled its immigrants, the Arab nations limited their anti-Israeli activity. They generally did not have firm control over their own internal political situations and, therefore, shied away from full-scale conflict. However, Nasser's success in nationalizing the Suez Canal aroused Israeli fears of Arab unity. A few years earlier Israel had initiated its policy of severe military reprisals against any government from whose territory attacks on Israel were launched. The policy was designed to discourage further attacks by making the punishment exceed the transgression. Although Israel was censured by the United Nations on several occasions, it held firm to the policy. Israel and the West were deeply concerned with the pan-Arab sentiment which was growing under Nasser's leadership and Egypt's drift toward the Soviet bloc. Israel was also concerned with the increasing number of raids from Egyptian territory, and Egypt's refusal to allow Israeli ships through the Suez Canal and especially the Straits of Tiran.

Israel invaded Egypt on October 30, 1956. Within four days, Israel was in control of the Sinai and the Gaza Strip. One day after the start of the Israeli invasion, the British and French announced a joint expedition to seize the Suez Canal, an action that the United States opposed. When the fighting ended a few days later, the British and French held Port Said at the northern terminus of the canal. An eventual settlement called for the

removal of the invading forces from Egyptian soil and the stationing of UN troops along the Egyptian-Israeli borders (primarily the Gaza Strip and the important Straits of Tiran, through which Israeli shipping could reach the port of Aqaba and thereby avoid the Suez Canal).

The Arabs henceforth considered Nasser a hero. He had turned back Israel, France, and Britain, and had earlier rebuffed U.S. attempts to limit Egyptian military strength. Israel had scored an impressive military victory but found itself in a more delicate position than before as Nasser's influence and the pan-Arab movement gathered momentum. During the decade following the 1956 war, Nasser remained the undisputed leader of the Arab world, although he had to share some of his prestige with Ahmed ben Bella after the success of the Algerian revolution. Nasser was also concerned with the situation in Yemen and sent 70,000 troops to support the republicans against the Saudi-backed royalists.

The 1967 Arab-Israeli War

From 1956 to 1966 Israeli-Arab tensions remained just below the boiling point as a host of large and small issues—including important disputes over water rights in the Jordan River, changing relative military strength, and shifting Arab alliances—threatened to fan the conflict again.

For two years the Syrian government had permitted Al-Fatah, a military arm of the fledgling Palestine Liberation Organization (PLO), to use Syria as a base for raids into Israel. In May 1967, various Arab leaders became convinced that Israel was about to launch a massive reprisal attack against Syria. As a visible display of Egypt's willingness to go to war, Nasser had Egyptian troops march through Cairo on their way to the Suez Canal. This action sounded like a battle cry in the Arab world, which then called on Nasser to crush Israel. Since his popularity had begun to wane, Nasser needed to be firm and decisive if he was to remain the leader of the Arab world. Confrontation politics are always dangerous, but especially so when each side has developed a worst case scenario. On May 19, 1967, Egypt requested that UN troops be withdrawn from Egyptian territory. The United Nations complied promptly—too promptly

---

[1]It should be noted that the disruptive effects of the enormous rate of inflation are ameliorated considerably because the economy is indexed. That is, wages rise automatically with inflation, thereby lessening the usual kinds of redistribution of income generally associated with inflation.

to suit many observers. On May 24, Nasser announced that the Straits of Tiran were closed to Israeli ships.

The die was cast. The Six-Day War started in the morning of June 5; the Israeli air force destroyed most of the Egyptian air force while it was still on the ground. Quickly and efficiently Israel pressed the advantage it secured by air; within a week it had taken the Sinai and Gaza from Egypt, Jordanian territory west of the Jordan River, and the Golan area from Syria. In contrast to the postwar agreements of 1956, Israeli troops continued to occupy territory in which well over a million Arabs lived. The war was another crushing humiliation for the Arabs, and Nasser offered his resignation.

Israel gained a clear military victory and established three buffer areas it considered vital to its security. But it also had to control well over a million additional Arabs at a time when the Palestinian movement was gathering steam. Israel's occupation of Arab territories put it in a difficult position in the United Nations. The Security Council of the United Nations responded by adopting Resolution 242, which required Israel to withdraw its forces from occupied territory and Arab states to recognize Israel's right to exist, among other things.

The 1973 Arab-Israeli War

The end of the 1967 Arab-Israeli war did not bring peace. Israel continued to hold the occupied territories and even to build settlements on them. It faced a line of hostile Arab states, especially Egypt, and was burdened with an enormous defense budget.

By 1973 Egypt's president Anwar Sadat had had three years of experience in office. He had ceased to be viewed as a weak, sometimes comical, figure and had begun to assert his own brand of leadership. The 1967 war had been devastating to the Egyptian military and economy. Since the economy had already been extremely weak, partially due to the abrupt and untimely way in which Nasser nationalized many industries in the early 1960s, and the high population growth rate, the capacity of the average Egyptian to endure hardship was being severely strained. The Soviet Union was reluctant to give President Sadat the military

aid he needed, probably because of the possibility of upsetting the movement toward détente with the United States. In July 1972, President Sadat ordered the immediate departure of 40,000 Soviet military personnel and their dependents from Egypt. The oil-rich Arab states already were supplying Egypt with considerable aid but could not be expected to deliver military hardware. If Egypt had allowed the status quo to continue, the minimal demands of the military would have worsened the already dangerous economic situation. The government of Israel, seeing Egypt's plight, then set down more stringent conditions for peace, obviously hoping that President Sadat would accede. But acceptance of the Israeli position would have endangered Egypt's aid from the oil-rich states and possibly triggered a coup. President Sadat then embarked on a fruitless international diplomatic offensive as a last step short of war.

Because he saw no other way out of the stalemate, Sadat and President Assad of Syria then planned a joint attack on Israel for October 6, 1973. The war, called the Ramadan or Yom Kippur War, was launched on time. Carefully trained Egyptian forces managed to penetrate Israel's defenses for the objective of seizing a strip of the Sinai east of the canal. However, Israeli forces crossed the canal at another point and isolated the Egyptian army. A cease-fire, sponsored by the United Nations with the encouragement of the great powers, took effect on October 24. It took until the following May for terms to be worked out on the Syrian-Israeli front.

The Israeli army had again proved capable of meeting the Arab threat. It had recovered from the initial forays of the Egyptian army and mounted its own offensive; it also beat back Syrian attempts to regain the Golan Heights. But the results of this conflict were different from the earlier wars on at least a couple of counts. First, the cost of the effort in terms of money and men was staggering. It was obvious that neither side could afford many more such ventures. Second, the Egyptian army performed as a tough, skilled unit. Although it did not in any sense win the military battle, it was obvious to many that a limited Egyptian victory was well within the realm of possibility.

It seems that President Sadat's gamble in initiating the war had paid off. The Egyptians had mounted a successful limited strike and invited the great powers to help Egypt find a way to break the stalemate with Israel. It was a high-risk strategy, one which came dangerously close to forcing direct military involvement by the United States and the Soviet Union. But the stalemate was broken as the U.S. secretary of state, Henry Kissinger, took the lead in promoting a new settlement. In the months after the war, Dr. Kissinger and a number of other interested parties flew repeatedly from one capital to another in what was called "shuttle diplomacy." After a time, terms of peace were established between Egypt and Israel. President Sadat had put much stock in efforts of the United States to bring the needed settlement. The Syrians, still engaged in combat against the Israelis and unable to win back any territory, were understandably upset by Egypt's separate agreement with Israel. Sadat's actions were considered to be a form of appeasement, and Egypt became isolated in the Arab world. Syria's president Assad assumed the leadership of the front-line states.

Nevertheless, President Sadat continued his efforts to bring a lasting peace to Egypt. His most spectacular move was to go before the Israeli Knesset in November 1977. Although the major issues between Egypt and Israel were not resolved by this dramatic initiative, it did set the stage for further negotiations, the most important being the Camp David talks between Prime Minister Begin, President Sadat, and President Carter. These resulted in a formal peace treaty and diplomatic relations. Egypt and Israel continued their sometimes fractious negotiations through the remainder of the 1970s, resulting in a gradual Israeli withdrawal from the Sinai and a partial normalization of relations between Egypt and Israel. Israeli withdrawal was completed in April 1982.

Egypt's partial accommodation with Israel continued to alienate it from Syria and its supporters, and the Palestinians. It was charged that Egypt forgot the Palestinians in a selfish and short-sighted attempt to gain temporary security. Sadat's dismantling of Nasser's socialist economy was seen as further evidence of his Western bias. Syria, the new claimant to Arab leadership in the struggle against Israel, was caught in an ironic swirl of events. As noted earlier, Syria had found it necessary to place troops in Lebanon to control

Palestinian activities and avoid Israeli reprisal attacks. By 1982 Christian separatist forces controlled a sizable strip of southern Lebanon, with the help of Israeli materiel and military aid. Syria effectively controlled the rest of Lebanon (not including parts of Beirut and some mountainous areas), including the Palestinians.

The 1982 Invasion of Lebanon

The 1982 Israeli invasion of Lebanon profoundly changed the character of several key political relationships in the Middle East. It has been argued that the 1967 war resulted in an Arab moral crisis. It became clear that visions of Arab unity were pure illusion; Nasser's dream was dead. In the same light, the invasion of Lebanon marks a profound moral cleavage in the Israeli polity. Israeli opponents of the invasion tended to view it as brutal aggression that undermined Israel's moral foundations. Israeli peace groups gained new life; a protest demonstration in Tel Aviv drew several hundred thousand participants. Supporters of the government, of course, saw the action as necessary, arguing that the last PLO foothold had to be destroyed. Political divisions hardened.

The 1982 invasion of Lebanon, of course, did not occur without reference to Israeli security on other borders. Israel's separate peace with Egypt culminated with the April 1982 withdrawal of Israeli forces from Sinai. The process of withdrawal was aided by the presence of a multinational peacekeeping force. Included in the agreement were scheduled, and continually postponed, talks which were to lead to eventual autonomy in the Gaza Strip.

Withdrawal from the Sinai necessitated that Israelis be removed forcibly from their illegal settlements. This threatened the fragile domestic coalition that depended on the support of those members of the Knesset favoring virtually unlimited settlement in occupied territories. Prime Minister Begin weathered the storm, partially due to prior decisions on the rapid settlement of the West Bank and the extension of Israeli civilian law (December 1981) in the Golan Heights, an action which translated into *de facto* annexation.

In early May 1982, the Knesset formally supported Prime Minister Begin's statement that

Israeli settlements would not be dismantled as part of any peace negotiations, and that Israeli sovereignty over the West Bank would be established once the interim arrangements called for in the Camp David Accords had run their course. During the first several months of 1982 there was considerable unrest in Gaza and the West Bank.

Israel apparently thought that if the PLO were crushed in Lebanon, and if Syrian forces were neutralized, it could establish more secure borders to the north and east; the agreement with Egypt had provided breathing space to the south. The invasion and occupation of Lebanon (1982–1985) accomplished some objectives—the PLO in Lebanon was severely weakened, and time was afforded for the continued rapid settlement of the West Bank. But it carried substantial liabilities, including the weakening of Christian power in Lebanon, an ultimately more powerful Syrian presence, a rapprochement between the PLO, Egypt, and Jordan, and considerable domestic unrest.

These adverse conditions, however, were but surface manifestations of deeper seismic rumblings caused by the war. Of prime importance was the subsequent regrouping of the PLO, and its 1985 acceptance of the "Jordanian option." While it is dangerous to draw specific long-range implications, it is quite clear that there are straightforward connections between the 1982 invasion and the Palestinian uprising.

THE PALESTINIANS AND THE 1988 UPRISING

The Palestinian diaspora that resulted from the Israeli victory of 1948 was largely to Arab countries. In 1950 about 900,000 Palestinian refugees were in camps operated by the United Nations in Lebanon, Jordan (and the West Bank), Syria, and the Gaza Strip. The plight of these people was deplorable. The United Nations relief effort was minimal; the food ration was limited to 1,600 calories a day, and housing often consisted of scraps of material loosely thrown together to form primitive shelters. No national Palestinian leadership had arisen before the establishment of Israel, and refugees grouped together on a traditional village basis. Throughout the 1950s the outside world

heard little about the refugee camps, except for occasional news shorts showing their humiliating and stultifying living conditions. The rest of the world seemed to wish the Palestinians away; the Palestinians were unable to generate any coherent response to their plight. On the few occasions when they protested their conditions, they were suppressed by the host Arab governments, the most notable early example being Egypt's actions in the Gaza Strip in the 1950s.

Organized resistance eventually did develop, beginning with the formation of Al-Fatah in the late 1950s and the creation of the Palestine Liberation Organization in 1964 through an initiative of the Arab League. It was apparent to the various national leaders that the festering discontent in the refugee camps was being used to form effective paramilitary units dedicated to the overthrow of Israel. These groups took heart in the success of the Algerians in thwarting the best efforts of France through a combination of tight organization, urban guerrilla terrorist activity, and tenacity. Palestinians began to think that they too could bring a Western power to its knees. However, there were significant differences between the two situations, one being that the bulk of the Palestinians and the heart of the resistance movement were outside Israel. Israel's reprisals against any nation from which anti-Israeli actions originated, coupled with its military superiority, deterred the Arab League. The League thus decided to control the Palestinian activists. It thought that the PLO could serve as a Palestinian umbrella organization and at the same time be subject to the League's control. Al-Fatah, under the leadership of Yasir Arafat, however, remained active.

With the end of the 1967 war, Palestinian fortunes began to rise. For most of the 1960s Palestinian leaders had disagreed with Nasser's dictum "Unity Is the Road to Palestine," preferring instead "Palestine Is the Road to Unity." The outcome of the 1967 war made it clear to them that their hopes for nationhood would be dashed if they followed Nasser's proposition. The Palestinians believed that only they could and would act to defeat Israel. Therefore, they ignored Arab pleas for unity. The various "front-line" nations bordering Israel, however, faced the prospect of having independent armies in their territories, armies bent on destroying an enemy that the nations themselves were not prepared to attack. The PLO could no longer be expected to control the different Palestinian groups or obey the wishes of the Arab League. Each country therefore gave tacit support to a particular Palestinian organization, supported its growth, and tried to control its activity. Well over a dozen sizable groups and a bewildering array of splinter groups formed between 1967 and 1969. In 1969 Yasir Arafat of Al-Fatah became the head of the PLO. Apparently the thinking in Arab capitals was that Arafat's successful organization would be controlled more easily if he were given a new mantle of authority.

King Hussein of Jordan tended to view the Palestinians as potential citizens of Jordan rather than aspirants to a separate nation. Since the PLO had between thirty and fifty thousand troops in Jordan by 1970—forces better described as a conventional army than as guerrilla fighters—and since the fractious liberation movement was demanding more and more autonomy in Jordan, the king could either sit back and watch his country being dismantled or take decisive action. Black September is the name the Palestinian movement gave his response; in September 1970, Hussein ordered regular Jordanian troops against the PLO. Thousands of Palestinians were killed, and Palestinian power in Jordan was broken. The only remaining sanctuary close to the Palestinian homeland, Lebanon, absorbed large numbers of refugees and found itself traveling down a dangerous road. The Palestinians were in decline, but they remained a force to reckon with.

The PLO was not significantly involved in the 1973 Arab-Israeli war except for promoting strikes in the occupied West Bank. In November 1973 the Arab heads of state declared the PLO the sole legitimate representative of the Palestinian people. To Arab leaders, the move made sense for several reasons. Jordan's King Hussein had been discredited as a representative of Palestinian interests due to the events of Black September, it was necessary to include the PLO in any peace negotiations, and the PLO now seemed to be more flexible than before on many issues. In November 1974 Yasir Arafat addressed the United Nations and saw that body pass resolutions declaring the right of Palestinians to seek independence and granting

the PLO permanent observer status in the United Nations. The PLO had attained international legitimacy. But it was not recognized by Israel and, therefore, could not enter into direct negotiations. Nor was it accorded more independence of movement by the Arab nations.

Its fortunes took a turn for the worse during 1975 when Lebanon fell into civil disorder. The PLO had been hinting that it could accept the continued existence of Israel if Palestinians were granted an independent status on West Bank territory. Israel indicated that it could accept a Palestinian "entity" on the West Bank only as long as that entity was formally part of Jordan and as long as Israel was allowed to maintain defense forces in the area. While these positions were far apart, they at least allowed the participants room to negotiate and continue the slow process of finding a mutually acceptable solution. But the moderating forces in the PLO lost ground to the "rejectionists"—those who saw the elimination of Israel as the only possible foundation for a Palestinian state. Since the PLO could not control rejectionist activities during the collapse of Lebanon, its claim to preeminence was compromised.

Events following the evacuation of PLO forces from Lebanon in the aftermath of the Israeli invasion of 1982 point to a couple of facts. First, the PLO is a multinational organization; it did not collapse due to the evacuation. Rather, the organization simply changed the primary locus of activity away from that country. In addition, those evicted from Lebanon were afforded considerable prestige in parts of the Arab world because of the tenacity of their forces in the face of the clearly superior firepower of the Israelis, and they gained a more cordial relationship with several important Arab governments, especially Egypt and Jordan. The well-established organizational structure of the PLO, and the financing offered by several Arab governments (along with a Palestinian income tax), indicated that the PLO would be a force to reckon with for some time.

Second, Al-Fatah continued to be the most powerful group within the PLO, and Yasir Arafat maintained his position as head of both Al-Fatah and the PLO. Rejectionist forces and breakaway Al-Fatah groups failed in their attempts to wrest power away from this now clearly dominant group. The most prominent of these rejections of Arafat's leadership occurred after the first PLO evacuation from Beirut. Al-Fatah forces located close to Syrian positions in Lebanon took up arms against their brethren when the PLO was seen as entertaining notions of compromise that would have yielded considerable territory to Israel. The same group, with Syrian support, wrested control of large camps around Beirut from Al-Fatah.

Third, the PLO strategy for the struggle for Palestine allowed more accommodation. In the 1970s the PLO abandoned the notion that Israel needed to be destroyed if Palestine were to exist; that is, it moved from a military to a political strategy. By the 1980s it was giving strong indications that the establishment of a Palestinian "entity," which need not include all of the territory occupied by Israel, would be acceptable if assurances could be given for eventual independence. King Hussein of Jordan and Arafat held discussions on these matters a little more than a decade after Black September: Irreconcilable differences have a transient quality.

The First Intifadah

The widespread Western, and especially American, view of Israel as a beleaguered David struggling against an Arab Goliath was shattered in 1988. Television screens around the world showed confrontations between stone-throwing Palestinian youth of Gaza and the West Bank and the Israeli Defense Forces (IDF). Palestinian teenagers took on the persona of the stone-throwing David, while the Israeli crack troops with sophisticated weapons appeared as Goliath. Television cameras revealed instances of the inevitable excessive use of force by the IDF. As the 1982 invasion of Lebanon had thrown Israel into moral crisis, so the uprising intensified it and laid to rest notions of a beneficent military occupation.

An auto accident in Gaza in December 1987 provided the spark that ignited the uprising, popularly called **intifadah** by the Palestinians. Apparently all of the principals were surprised by the strength, depth, and spread of the initial stages of the rebellion. The PLO was among those surprised, and quickly scrambled to coordinate the

civil disorder. Although the auto accident provided the catalyst for the intifadah, the discontent had been growing for some time.

The 1967 war resulted in Israeli occupation of Gaza, the Sinai, the Golan, and the West Bank (including East Jerusalem). Each of the areas presented Israel with different opportunities and problems. The Sinai, of course, provided a massive buffer against Egypt. A decade later this land was traded for peace as part of the Camp David Accords. The Golan district was earmarked for permanent control almost immediately after the war's conclusion. Because Israel feared Syria more than any other belligerent neighboring Arab state, this strategic border area would not be relinquished. The task of maintaining control was eased because close to 90 percent of the prewar population had fled.

Gaza had been militarily administered by Egypt since 1949. Although it lost between 15 and 20 percent of its population due to the 1967 war, it still contained about a third of a million residents in a very small area. Furthermore, a large percentage of these families were refugees from the 1948 war, still openly hostile to Israel. Consequently, Israeli policy in Gaza was dominated by police action rather than settlement.

East Jerusalem was claimed as Israeli territory shortly after the war. It was a piece of property that Israeli politicians could not contemplate giving back. The West Bank was more problematic. Immediately after the cessation of hostilities in 1949, King Abdullah of Jordan hastily convened a conference of West Bank Palestinian notables who gave their blessings to the formal annexation of the West Bank by Jordan. The international community never accepted the result, but it did allow the *de facto* administration of the territory by Jordan. However, the majority of the Palestinian population never accepted Hashemite rule. The disputed status of the West Bank allowed each interested party to frame arguments and policies consistent with its most convenient premise. For instance, Israel held that it could negotiate only with the government of Jordan, while the PLO claimed that it alone represented the occupants of the occupied territories. After six months of the intifadah, and some forty years after the annexation announcement,

Jordan formally renounced any claim to the West Bank.

The West Bank lost about a quarter of its population in 1967. Especially important was the fact that over 90 percent of the population of the West Jordan Valley, located between the Jordan River and the western mountains of the rift, fled to the East Bank or other nearby places of rural refuge. Only 10,000 Palestinians remained.

Israeli's Allon Plan, although never formally accepted as official policy, provided the basic blueprint for Israeli action in the first decade of occupation. The plan called for settlement of (l) the Jordan Valley rift from the northern Israeli border to just north of the Dead Sea and (2) an area from Jerusalem south past Hebron to the border, and from Jerusalem to the Dead Sea in the east. This meant that the Palestinian area of the West Bank was divided into two parts, which the Israelis called Judea and Samaria. The northern enclave (Samaria) had a corridor that joined Jordan at the northern end of the Dead Sea. The areas marked for Israeli settlement (including a strip west of Samaria and one running along the Sinai border) were designed primarily with defense in mind.

While the Allon Plan served defense interests, it did not satisfy the increasingly popular goal of settling throughout the West Bank—including the religiously important and heavily Palestinian-populated central areas ignored by the Allon Plan. The Likud bloc victory of 1977 extended the settlement policy to include Judea and Samaria. In 1977 Prime Minister Begin declared that the "Green Line" (the 1967 borders) had "vanished." To the Labor government's security rationale for settlement, the Likud government added a theological imperative: The land had been promised to them by God. Although believing in the same God, the Palestinians did not receive the same message. Nevertheless, colonization proceeded apace.

By 1990 about 100,000 Israelis had settled in the occupied territories, mostly on the West Bank, mostly in bedroom suburbs of Jerusalem and Tel Aviv. The bulk of these settlers were not religious zealots but middle-class Israelis trading a crowded urban environment with scarce and expensive housing for newly constructed subsidized units only fifteen minutes from the city center. These units also served a military purpose. Called "fortress settlements," they generally are multi-story apartment complexes built on high ground, close to each other (or interlocking) so as to prevent enemy penetration, and with other defense-like features, such as narrow windows with metal shutters. Jerusalem is virtually surrounded by these fortress settlements. The 1991 acceleration of settlements guided by the Minister of Housing, Ariel Sharon, largely followed this policy by "thickening" the urban clusters.

A substantial number of settlers in the earlier years went to newly constructed towns throughout the West Bank. In order to build these settlements, land rights had to be secured, transport and power grids constructed, and water systems put in place. By 1988 half of the West Bank's land had been ceded to Israelis through the application of a wide range of measures. A road network was in place, connecting the cities, bypassing Arab towns, and preventing the development of ribbon settlement of Palestinians next to the roads. Access to water, especially for agricultural use, became increasingly difficult for Palestinians. Although the placement of some settlements was dictated by the desire to control a particularly important religious site, the overall pattern was designed to isolate the Palestinian towns.

Israelis opposed to the settlements complained about the expense of the program in times of economic hardship. They argued that annexation would undermine Israel's stature as a Jewish state if the Palestinians were given full citizenship rights, or destroy the democratic character of the state if they were denied citizenship. But colonization continued: *De facto* annexation took place.

Many of the refugee camps were forty years old at the time of the uprising. The tents of four decades ago had been replaced by concrete block structures that had rooms added to them as the camps took on more the character of permanent settlements than places of temporary refuge. Some camp residents owned autos, many homes sprouted television antennas, and an articulated economic order brought increases in material well-being. Some material conditions, however, remained appalling; for example, open sewers draining into disease-ridden, fetid pools of filth. Residents were reminded daily of their occupied status: Men of Gaza gathered every morning to get transport to Tel Aviv for regular jobs or day labor. Israel demanded that they return to the camps every night or have identity cards that permitted their stay in Israel.

The usual colonial pattern of discrimination in wages and types of jobs available prevailed. Over 100,000 Palestinians of the occupied territories worked in Israel. Economic dependence was not limited to the labor market or the camps. For example, agricultural produce and industrial output of the occupied territories were denied ready access to Israel when they would compete with Israeli-produced goods, licenses to produce goods in potential competition with Israel were denied, water rights were curtailed, and so on. The military plan for maintaining civil order was called the "Iron Fist": long-term detentions without charge or trial, collective punishment, deportations, and strict control of basic political expression. When this is placed in the context of a systematic loss of land rights and increased economic dependence, it is not surprising that the Palestinian population became more embittered and desperate.

The widespread nature of the rebellion meant that a decisive response by the IDF would result in unacceptable levels of carnage. As it was, the limited response still resulted in an average of a Palestinian death per day. As Israel groped for solutions, the revolt continued. In addition to some widely reported excesses of the military, several largely symbolic statements and actions by Israeli officials fanned the flames. Prime Minister Shamir at one point said that the troublemakers were mere "grasshoppers" and would be dealt with as such. Ariel Sharon, early architect of the settlement policy on the West Bank and of the 1982 invasion of Lebanon, moved his residence to the Muslim quarter of the old city of Jerusalem. Some members of the Knesset called for the forcible removal of all Palestinians from the West Bank. Substantive actions supported these symbolic acts. In April 1988, Abu Jihad, the supposed PLO coordinator of the uprising, was assassinated in Tunis by a team widely assumed to be associated with official Israel. Deportations, detentions, and other restrictive measures increased, but the rebellion continued. Israel was a few months away from elections and the Palestinian National Congress was preparing a declaration of independence.

It was no surprise that the 1988 election campaign in Israel was vicious. Israel's position in the occupied territories was increasingly precarious, and international opinion was increasingly sympathetic to the Palestinian position. The crisis of conscience brought to center stage by the 1982 invasion of Lebanon intensified. The Labor bloc advocated (with many provisos) the convening of an international conference that would trade land for peace. Likud was not so disposed. The always important religious parties hardened their positions.

The religious parties gained seats in the November 1988 election. Likud (forty seats) and Labor (thirty-nine seats) garnered about an equal number. A coalition was put together after six weeks of negotiations. Likud, which was called on to form a government, initially negotiated with the religious parties but finally found the positions of the religious bloc to be unacceptable. Particularly controversial was the policy proposed by religious conservatives of redefining the Law of Return so that the only converts to Judaism eligible for "return status" would be those converted by Orthodox rabbis. Many Jews outside Israel, especially in the United States, expressed deep shock and hinted that acceptance of this policy would change their attitude toward Israel. Also, after the election and before the formation of the new government, the Palestinian National Congress declared an independent Palestinian state (November 15, 1988), a move that received warm worldwide support. A month later Yasir Arafat addressed the United Nations. In the address, and in subsequent clarifying remarks in the next several days, the PLO stated its recognition of the state of Israel and renounced terrorism. A few days later, and after much diplomatic dancing, the United States opened official discussions with the PLO, something it had not done for thirteen years.

The new coalition in Israel again joined Likud and Labor in a marriage of inconvenience. Before the election, all parties agreed that the policy paralysis of the last such government should not be repeated. There were differences in the composition of the new government, the most important being that Likud would hold the posts of prime minister and foreign minister throughout the coalition (instead of the Labor-Likud split and midterm switching), but many of the debilitating aspects of power sharing remained. The major actors of the new government declared agreement on their unwillingness to talk to the PLO and the need to end the intifadah. They disagreed on most other important matters. As stated earlier, the coalition fell apart by 1990. The subsequent Likud-Religious Party government met a similar fate in 1992.

CONCLUSION

The nations of the industrialized world had many decades to develop their forms of government, economic structures, and cultural perspectives. Most countries of the Middle East have not had time to gently sift and winnow such weighty ideas. Rather, they have been thrown headlong into the race for "modernity" and are still in the process of defining their identity. We can expect to see many changes in the Middle East, although we can identify only the broad contours.

Many of the important issues in the Middle East are connected to the drive for self-determination. Although most of the countries had gained formal political independence by 1950, they still faced the tasks of establishing an effective government, charting an independent economic course, and settling on a coherent cultural identity. Their job was complicated by the acceleration of worldwide technological and organizational revolutions which acted to make the world more interdependent. Greater world interdependence meant that one nation's policy changes could easily conflict with the interests of other nations, and that they would have to make a greater number of decisions between mutually beneficial and harmful interdependencies. Statements of many Third World leaders still reflect the dilemma; they generally have been quick to point to the difficulties, but have not been able to arrive at affirmative policies. However, some guides to the future are identifiable from the decisions of the past.

First, none of the powerful countries of the world can feel sure of having this or that bloc of Middle Eastern nations in its camp. The nations of the Middle East are now able to act independently. It also seems likely that the various regional relationships will continue to be fluid. For example, Libya sought political union at times with Egypt and the Sudan, but has had hostile relations with these nations at other times. It also strongly backed the "progressive" government of Iraq during some periods and strongly opposed it at others. The rise of independent and majority Muslim republics in the southern reaches of the former Soviet Union in the early 1990s led Iran and Turkey to scramble into new regional alliances. The changing alliances and relationships reflect that the actors are still in the process of searching for fundamental common interests that will transcend transitory conflicts.

We also know that the Middle East's dominance of world petroleum markets will continue to have a major effect on regional and global politics. For example, Gulf tensions regularly bring statements of neutrality from Western governments along with warnings that the West will not tolerate actions that might close the petroleum spigot. Such pressures on the Middle East are certain to continue. Furthermore, the financial strength of the petroleum-rich countries will continue to alter regional relationships between have and have-not nations. Conflicting interests will also continue to surface between the have nations; for example, Iran, which has low petroleum reserves, can be expected to have an attitude toward petroleum pricing different from Saudi Arabia, which has large reserves.

Perhaps of greatest ultimate importance, Middle Eastern societies will continue to change at a rapid pace. Rapid change has stimulated a search for a new sense of identity that is bound to take different directions across countries and through time. The most arresting manifestation of this search has been the resurgence of Islam as a regional, national, and personal symbol of identity. It is difficult to know whether this resurgence will act as a vehicle through which social tensions will be played out, will serve as a causal agent itself, or create its own dynamic. In any case, the Islamic resurgence promises to continue to be a significant political force.

Turning Points

This chapter was originally written to explain the impact of three largely unpredicted events in the late 1980s and early 1990s that altered strategies of conflict avoidance and conflict resolution in the Middle East in a fundamental fashion: the Palestinian rebellion, the meltdown of the U.S.S.R., and the Gulf War of 1990–1991, separately and in combination, changed the already changing face of the political landscape.

A decade later another series of events led to more turning points.

September 11, 2001 has been described (with some hyperbole) as "the day the world changed." For the purposes of this work, there is little need to rehearse the full story of the suicide bombings of the World Trade Center and the Pentagon. Nor is it necessary to detail the U.S.-led coalition that intervened militarily in Afghanistan, pursuing Al-Qaeda and toppling the Taliban government. However, it is important to point out some of the Middle Eastern seeds of these events and the subsequent repercussions.

Fifteen of the nineteen individuals that hijacked the planes were Saudi nationals, reasonably well educated, and obviously highly motivated. What were their rationales? One rationale was that the United States was seen as the primary force supporting what they saw as corrupt regimes in the area, especially (but not exclusively) Saudi Arabia. They viewed the Saudi government as corrupt, profoundly undemocratic, traitors to Islam for (among other things) allowing U.S. forces to use Saudi soil for military actions, and so on. This rationale, and others, were cloaked with religious certainty, a profound belief that these actions were in defense of core values.

The events of September 11 impacted, directly and indirectly, the contours of U.S. antiterrorist policy in the Middle East. President Bush declared that the United States was determined to end the regime of Saddam Hussein in Iraq, declaring it (along with Iran and North Korea) to be an "axis of evil." The U.S. government drew up plans for an invasion of Iraq. European and Arab governments generally strongly advised against any such action, at least in public pronouncements. The United States submitted a resolution to the United Nations demanding a return of UN-mandated weapons inspectors to Iraq; they left Iraq in 1998 after being frustrated by Iraq's refusal to fully comply. The U.S. resolution also called for military action if Iraq did not accept the inspectors.

Important opinion makers in Washington widened the net in the summer of 2002 by painting the government of Saudi Arabia as a nation not to be trusted, a nation that needed to engage in serious reform if it was to remain a U.S. ally. The people attacking Saudi Arabia apparently were convinced that the Saudi government's well-known acquiescence to the religious authorities was at the root of much of the spread of "Islamic terrorism" in the world. The contention was that the government's financial largesse nurtured the proliferation of religious schools, especially in Pakistan, that led to the profoundly anti-American sentiments of the Taliban and Al-Qaeda, among others. Other observers noted the irony that the United States encouraged these developments in the 1980s as a countermeasure to the Soviet occupation of Afghanistan. Some found it to be more than coincidence that the attacks on Saudi Arabia heated up several weeks after Crown Prince Abdullah of Saudi Arabia presented a peace plan that, among other things, would have brought diplomatic recognition of Israel by all Arab states in return for a comprehensive settlement between the Israelis and the Palestinians.

Finally, the second Palestinian intifadah, which began in September 2000, took a horrific turn. During the first half of 2002, Palestinian suicide bombers targeted Israeli civilians, resulting in many hundreds of deaths. Israel responded with massive military force, occupying almost all key Palestinian Authority controlled areas in the West Bank. The Israeli military crushed the infrastructure of the Palestinian Authority, including surrounding the compound of Yasir Arafat, virtually holding him under house arrest. Many hundreds of casualties ensued, many thousands of Palestinians were arrested, and finally a lull in the suicide bombings took place. After the Israelis withdrew their forces, the bombings resumed. The Israelis returned, now for a longer stay. The political crisis forced the Palestinians to call for elections in early 2003. Shortly thereafter, the Israeli government collapsed and they also called for elections in early 2003.

So again three turning points affected the region and, thereby, the world. But the outlook in the early years of the new millennium was far bleaker than that of the "turning points" of a decade earlier. First, the earlier era witnessed the beginnings of a peace process between Israel and its neighbors. By 2002, the peace process was in shambles, and violence increased spectacularly.

Second, Iraq was put on center stage again. By November 2002, the United Nation passed a resolution demanding that Iraq accept UN inspectors looking for weapons of mass destruction (after a four-year hiatus) or face invasion. The inspectors returned, but the crisis remained. After a couple of months the United States complained that Iraq was not fully complying with the UN resolution. After failing to convince the United Nations that military action was needed, the United States (and Britain and a group of minor actors) geared up for war. Military action started mid-March. Within a month the war was finished and the Iraqi regime vanquished. The physical and political reconstruction of Iraq was fraught with danger. But the United States stated that its forces would remain until the tasks were completed.

Third, terrorist networks associated with Middle Eastern causes became global and were likely to remain global. U.S. forces remained in Afghanistan. Terrorist bombings of Westerners continued. Also, an unmanned U.S. aircraft killed suspected terrorists in Yemen in October 2002, marking the first time that U.S. forces directly conducted activities in the Middle East related to the war on terrorism.

The goal of this chapter is to link the turning points of 1990 to those of 2001. First, then, we present a brief description of the earlier turning points.

Palestinians in the territories occupied by Israel since 1967 rebelled in December 1987. The intifadah brought increasing domestic and international pressure on the Israeli government to finally resolve the "Palestinian issue." Israeli defense forces acted to suppress the rebellion, but to little avail, even though more than a Palestinian per day was killed for several years. By early 1996, Palestinians held elections that signaled the opening steps of the establishment of a Palestinian state. By early 2000, after a three-year hiatus, negotiations between Palestinians and Israelis addressed core issues. By 2003, many Palestinians came to see the promising turning point of the early 1990s come full circle. Occupation had been reasserted, the Palestinian Authority was woefully ineffectual, and the chances for true independence and peace were almost nil.

Second, the collapse of the U.S.S.R. as a superpower ushered in a series of dramatic changes in official ideology, demography, and international political alignments. Those states that received aid from the U.S.S.R., notably Syria, Iraq, and South Yemen, were cut adrift financially and militarily. During this period, the Soviets announced that they would allow the emigration of a large number of Jews—up to one million people. Israel faced the prospect of having its Jewish population increase by 20 percent in a couple of years, enhancing its position as a Jewish state but also presenting it with an immense financial and social burden. Also, the rise of nations with a majority Muslim population (the central Asian republics) from the ashes of the Soviet empire meant that westward-leaning Turkey, more religiously oriented Iran, conservative Saudi Arabia, and others scrambled to forge new alliances. The collapse of the U.S.S.R. presented the sole remaining superpower with unique challenges. One of the most prominent of these was the extent to which the United States was to posture itself as the leader of wide-ranging multinational coalitions, or essentially to define and execute policy in a more unilateral fashion. The Clinton administration leaned toward the multilateral approach. The second Bush administration favored unilateral action.

Third, the 1990 invasion of Kuwait by Iraq, and the subsequent war, shook the foundations of the area. Indeed, the combination of the collapse of the Soviet Union, the intifadah, and the Iraqi invasion signaled changes so deep-seated that they rivaled in importance the mandate system that gave the basic geopolitical boundaries to the region.

In the early morning of August 2, 1990, Iraqi forces invaded Kuwait, and within a couple of days were dug in at the Saudi border (with Kuwait) after having an easy time with the totally outmatched Kuwaiti defense forces. Six months later, an allied force, led by over one-half million U.S. troops, and supplied with a stunning display of high-tech weapons, liberated Kuwait and crippled the Iraqi military and economic infrastructure. The

military victory came with surprising ease: The campaign was over in about a month with very low allied losses. The effects of the invasion and war, however, will take decades to play out. In the immediate aftermath, Saddam Hussein was still in power, had crushed a Shia revolt in the south, and bargained an uneasy and unstable compromise with the Kurdish resistance in the north. Jordan, a nervous supporter of Iraq after the invasion, partially due to the domestic popularity of Saddam Hussein's postinvasion call for the liberation of Palestine as part of Iraq's comprehensive bid for a settlement, suffered a loss of Western and Gulf financial aid and had to deal with the burden of several hundred thousand Palestinians who had been expelled from Kuwait due to their "support" of Iraq. On the other side of the war front, about one million Egyptians returned home after Iraq expelled them due to Egyptian support of Iraq's enemies. Several hundred thousand Yemeni workers were evicted from Saudi Arabia because the Yemeni government "supported" Iraq. Syria, a crucial ally of the United States in the coalition against Iraq, gained the ability to reinforce their control over Lebanon. Israel suffered missile attacks from Iraq during the war, and faced increased pressure to settle with the Palestinians after the conflict. The Middle East had changed forever.

This chapter is confined to broad-brushed discussions of two important themes: the changing character of nationalism and the peace negotiations between Israel and its neighbors. The reader should be especially cautious in making simple and straightforward predictions about the potential future contours of the Middle East. The evolution of meaningful national independence in a setting of increasing global interdependence is not well understood in the best of cases: It is very muddled in the Middle East.

GLOBALIZATION

The rise of globalization and the demise of the bipolar world have complicated area studies in general, and the study of the Middle East in particular. This section gives a brief summary of these complications. The section begins with a discussion of globalization. It then turns to the related notion of why it may be wise to rethink ideas about what we mean by an "area." Unfortunately, this can become complicated rather quickly, but the complications are necessary. Since notions of "academic scribblers" lie behind many policy decisions, and since in this case radically different views of the coming shape of the world result from the adoption of different assumptions, it becomes vital that we examine some core issues.

Globalization usually refers to increasing economic, political, and cultural interdependence. There are significant arguments over the identification of the most important motive forces of globalization. For example, economic globalization many times is said to have been caused by the (putative) triumph of free markets in combination with the information revolution. While there is some merit to the argument that free markets enhance globalization, it seems overly restrictive to mark it as the most important cause of the phenomenon. In a similar vein, the rise of free markets generally is associated with democratic gains. This also has merit, but the lines of causation are not always clear or complete: Aspects of ideological cheerleading color many analyses.

While the root causes of this thing called "globalization" are not known with certainty, there is no doubt that the demise of the U.S.S.R. further muddied the analytical waters. The absence of a bipolar world has led a large number of analysts to venture hypotheses of the future nature of the international order. One highly contentious theme centers on what is meant by "an area," or indeed if the concept holds much meaning. Financial capital markets, for example, are so highly integrated that it makes precious little difference if you are trading in Hong Kong or Chicago. From this lens, analyses of financial markets in terms of geographic areas is of little use. Others argue that the notion of areas of the world will continue to hold central importance, albeit in a different fashion than that of the bipolar world. In one such version, the core commonalities of areas will no longer be based on political and economic ideologies (for example, free enterprise versus state control of the economy) but on core cultural, especially religious, values. This notion was first famously put forth by Professor Huntington in his provocatively

titled article "The Clash of Civilizations?" Specifically, he argues that the emerging Islamic civilization poses the greatest danger to the (Christian) West. Although he has nuanced the basic argument since the writing of the original article, the basic point remains: Islam and the West are and will continue to be at fundamental odds.

The emerging alternate views of what ought to be contained in the analysis of "areas" are not neatly defined but they offer valuable insights. There seem to be at least three key jumping-off points: (1) considering borders as "thick" rather than thin, (2) thinking of areas in ways that transcend a land-based geography, and (3) looking at processes rather than traits as being more useful for analysis.

Area studies began as a distinct subject of academic inquiry in the United States because of national security needs after the close of World War II. Lines were drawn on maps in order to block out areas of the world that presumably had enough in common so that coherent foreign policies could be established. The "Great Game" of the four decades after World War II largely involved the material and ideological battles of the U.S.S.R. and the United States. Although all serious analysts clearly recognized that the pencil point thin borders delineating areas, say the Middle East and South Asia, involved some fiction, it nevertheless was thought to be useful. For example, Iran generally is considered to be part of the Middle East, while Afghanistan and Pakistan are not. Yet even the most casual of analysts knows that there is much commonality.

The basic point is that geographical demarcation necessitates a degree of arbitrariness: A line has to be drawn somewhere. So perhaps an initial caution is that "areas" defined solely in terms of a sharply delineated geography do not carry as much intellectual heft as is usually thought. The meltdown of the U.S.S.R. further complicated the picture. Areas initially were defined with respect to national security needs. But now the rules had changed, so it seemed sensible to reexamine the notion of what was meant by an area. Globalization provided another motivation to engage in a fundamental rethinking. While Huntington provided one such new view, his concept did not go unchallenged.

The notion of using "thick" borders as an analytical device is not terribly controversial when standing alone; it is widely recognized that geographic fault lines neatly separating areas are not universally present and may shift with time. Examples are easy to cite. Turkey generally is considered to be part of the Middle East. In many ways this makes sense; after all, the Ottoman Empire ruled most of the area for centuries. On the other hand, the Turkey of today aspires to be a part of the new Europe; this also is credible, as witnessed by a 1999 European Union decision to make Turkey a candidate for membership. A line that puts Turkey firmly in the Middle East, with all of the important traits used to define the area (for example, Islamic) does not do justice to the rich diversity of beliefs and behavior. Perhaps it is better to think about civilizational or areal shadings rather than razor-thin lines.

A related argument deals with the efficacy of thinking of areas solely in terms of geographic space. The (usually implicit) defenders of "areas as geography" argue that the effect of the (undisputed) proliferation of international interdependencies on basic political, economic, and cultural groupings will be minimal. This group largely calls to mind the last third of the nineteenth century when significant revolutions in communications and transportation allowed for massive increases in the international movement of goods and people. A polar view prognosticates basic changes in human organizations and relations. The more radical interpretations see the weakening, some would say demise, of the nation in the offing: The argument is that important aspects of the current wave of globalization will encourage individuals to develop vectors of primary identity that will be stronger than loyalties to the nation. For example, immigration to the United States at the beginning of the twentieth century generally meant that individuals were by-and-large cut off from their place of birth. Transport and communication were relatively time consuming and expensive. Over time the migrants adopted the lifeways of their new home; they developed new sets of loyalties and attachments, the nation being of prime importance. By the end of the century the remarkable drop in travel and communication time and expense meant that many millions of migrants could stay connected through frequent air travel, telephones, and most recently the Internet. Will these groups to some significant degree retain old loyalties? Will they develop "hybrid" loyalties? Will nonmigrants also change because of this?

The growth in the number, size, and influence of nongovernmental organizations (NGOs) often is offered as partial evidence of this trend. For example, to what extent will the use of the Internet help environmentalists to band together in a fashion that significantly strengthens loyalties to the worldwide environmental community? Will the women's movement further transcend national borders? The foregoing considerations have led some analysts to believe that the notion of geographically defined areas, with each area having a set of distinguishable traits, is less valuable than commonly perceived. A geographic and trait-based definition views the Middle East as an Arab/Muslim world with undemocratic and/or unstable governments. The West has Christian and democratic traits. The detractors of this sort of classification argue that it runs the risk of overstating the differences in geographic locations in an age of increasing interdependence. Professor Appadurai prefers to think of "scapes" rather than areas. By this he wants to convey that the replication and mutation of civilizational affinities is not limited to geographic space. He further argues that the static notion of traits detracts attention from another, possibly more important concept. He prefers to think of "processes." This refers to the dynamics of world culture, politics, and economics. It places weight on the (dynamic) fashion in which people interact, solve problems, and change in a world of globalization.

Why is all of this a matter of serious contention? Remember that Professor Huntington contends that geographically based civilizational areas are likely to produce the next source of international conflict and that Islam poses the greatest threat to the West. The detractors claim that Huntington has constructed a false dichotomy, that the assigned traits are overdrawn and placed in a static framework. They contend that Huntington's conclusion of "Islam versus the West" does violence to reality, and that the ongoing globalization process will tend to show Huntington's argument ever less useful. Indeed, they further argue that an acceptance of the "clash of civilizations" argument will lead to wrongheaded and possibly tragic policies.

The rise to prominence of Al-Qaeda provided a straightforward example of the difficulty of sorting though these complications. It represented par excellence the dark side of the NGO phenomenon. Its members and operations were multinational, cloaked with both nationalist and Islamic motivations and rhetoric. Transcending the expected limits of national borders, Al-Qaeda allegedly operated in more than sixty countries, a truly global terrorist organization.

ARAB NATIONALISM

Almost every border in the Middle East initially was defined by European powers—by way of the Balfour Declaration, the mandate system, and various territorial realignments thereafter. Middle Eastern governments, almost without exception, railed orally, if not through policy, against the artificial nature of the imposed borders. This notion held special force for the Arab nations. Arab unity, they said, would be denied as long as the borders remained. However, these same governments actively sought to build and strengthen loyalties to the nation-states described by the hated European-imposed boundaries. They succeeded in these efforts to various degrees, but the ideologically convenient dream of Arab unity, albeit moribund after 1967, continued to be part of the required rhetoric of some leaders until the invasion of Kuwait by Iraq.

The invasion was universally condemned as an illegitimate exercise of state power. Several regional actors (Algeria, Libya, Jordan, the PLO, Sudan, and Yemen) contended that an "Arab solution" would be the only acceptable solution. The countries of the Gulf (except Yemen) disagreed; they called for Western military intervention. Egypt and Syria were persuaded to accept this view and, importantly, to contribute troops to defend Saudi soil (but not to invade Iraq). It is difficult to overstate the enormity of these actions. The invasion of Kuwait marked the first time that a modern Arab state engaged in a full-scale invasion of another. The Arab world was quick to point to the sanctity of the borders. Then the United States, a long-time staunch supporter of Israel, along with excolonists France and the United Kingdom (and others), were invited to Saudi soil to do battle.

The Arab allies in the war against Iraq consisted of the petroleum-rich and population-poor countries of Arabia (except Yemen), Egypt, Syria, and distant Morocco. It should be noted that Egypt essentially had laid to rest notions of pan-Arab unity a decade earlier in the Camp David Accords, when it reached a separate peace agreement with Israel, thereby ignoring the Israeli-occupied territories, except to the extent that reference was then made to vague and unworkable linkages concerning negotiations for the formation of Palestinian "autonomy." By 1990, Egypt was in a difficult economic situation—a situation eased, after its participation in the allied cause, by U.S. and Gulf economic aid and significant debt forgiveness. Syria also faced a long-standing malaise: a burdensome defense outlay in Lebanon, continued Israeli occupation (and settlement) of the Golan (Quneitra) territory, and cutbacks in aid from the Soviet bloc. It needed to repair relations with the United States; the crisis in Kuwait provided a convenient entrée.

Although the allied forces crippled Iraq quickly and easily, Saddam Hussein remained in power after the conflict. There are a couple of reasons why the allies did not press their advantage until he fell. First, although Iran generally watched the spectacle from the sidelines and had shown signs of considerable political moderation, neither the United States nor the Gulf states wanted to see the postwar Gulf dominated by Iran, an event that would be more likely if Iraq fell into prolonged chaos. The removal of Saddam Hussein likely would have assured such a case since his brutally repressive regime had decimated opponents and thereby rid the country of an identifiable alternative leadership. The communal nature of Iraq— the Shia of the south and the Kurds of the north—meant that it was likely that the country would crumble without a strong central authority. And without a center holding the country together, the allies, especially the United States, would have had to settle in for a long-term military occupation. This was rejected out of hand. As it was, the Shia and Kurds revolted against Baghdad anyway. The Shia were quickly and savagely repressed by Saddam Hussein as the allied forces sat less than fifty miles away. However, thousands of Shia continued the revolt despite increasingly energetic campaigns by the Iraqi military. By 2002, the Shia remained in a precarious position; they continued to be under the thumb of official Baghdad, experienced internal conflict, and suffered economically.

The Kurdish revolt in the north took longer to sort out, partially because of the long-standing organized Kurdish resistance forces, as well as the flight of millions of Kurds into Turkey and Iran. As has been the case since the 1920s, Kurdish resistance briefly gained the sympathy of the wider world. As before, the world soon grew bored with news clips of the Kurdish plight. And, as always, those countries with substantial Kurdish populations, most notably Iran and Turkey, were not particularly anxious to see the Kurdish independence movement succeed. The Kurds of Iraq were given some protection through the application of measures designed by the United Nations to keep Iraq's military from unleashing its full force on the Kurds. Official Iraq viewed the UN actions as violations of its national sovereignty. While Iraq pressed for greater access to the Kurdish areas, the Kurdish opposition supplied the world with documentation to support their claim that even before the war there was an Iraqi policy of the systematic extermination of the Kurds.

UN sanctions against Iraq, and Iraqi reluctance to meet the terms of the United Nations, kept tensions high. Iraqi citizens were suffering terrible consequences from the sanctions, but the government of Iraq did not change its position. A particularly bothersome sanction was the issue of UN inspection teams charged with finding and disarming Iraq's stockpile and production facilities for weapons of mass destruction. On several occasions the teams were denied access. As the years passed, Iraq engaged in a piecemeal compliance—yielding on one site to be inspected, calling for the end to sanctions, having these calls be rejected by the United Nations, and then relenting a bit more. And the common person continued to suffer. The sanctions worked in this sense, but it was not clear

how much they weakened the power of Saddam Hussein.

During 1995 and 1996 there were several indications that Iraq was increasingly ready to relent on some of the UN demands. First, the regime suffered a setback when two of Saddam's inner circle, indeed his sons-in-law, defected. They gave information on growing dissatisfaction in Iraq, as well as evidence that Iraq had not told the truth to UN authorities on compliance with UN resolutions. This meant that some European nations that had been urging a softer line, most notably France, were forced to distance themselves from that approach. Second, Jordan, a vital lifeline for supplies, had largely patched up its relations with the Gulf states, and Iraq had to wonder if Jordan's transport routes would continue to remain open. The hope of a possible "opening" of Iraq faded on two counts. First, and most important, the United Nations was dissatisfied with conditions the Iraqis wanted to impose on the investigations. The second reason for pause was a bit bizarre: The defected sons-in-law asked to return to Iraq. They were given assurances from official Baghdad that all was forgiven, they returned, and they were murdered two days later by members of their own extended family. The UN inspectors were withdrawn from Iraq in 1998.

The civilian population of Iraq suffered the horror of war from 1980 through 1988, and then again in 1991. Thereafter, their suffering continued; some would say it increased. Iraq suffered from rising rates of infant mortality, disease, and malnutrition. Iraq, the country with arguably the best balance of resources in the Middle East, had a precipitous and continual decline in real per capita income. Indeed, a UN study reported that child (under five years) mortality rates increased dramatically: They stood at 56 per 1,000 live births during 1984–1989 and increased to 131 during 1994–1999. The report concluded that Iraq ought to be given an expanded "food-for-oil" allotment.

The (northern) Kurdish regions of Iraq continued to be under the control of the United Nations, albeit with (different) local administrative authorities and associated militias in charge of day-to-day decisions. There the child mortality rate fell from 80 to 52 in the same time frame as the dramatic increase in the country as a whole. A major goal of the sanctions was to pressure the Iraqi government to comply with the UN inspection teams charged with ferreting out weapons of mass destruction. Since the teams destroyed many (but not all) weapons, and since they were excluded from working in Iraq through the whole of 1999, after the United States and Britain mounted a substantial air campaign, there was much argument that the sanctions should be scrapped or at least eased. Those in favor of continuing the sanctions replied that the increased child mortality rate and other horrors suffered by the common Iraqi had more to do with decisions of the government than the sanctions; they argued that an easing of sanctions would only help the inner circle of the regime. And the suffering continued. By the end of 1999, the United Nations was trying to shape a program that would end the sanctions if Iraq agreed to more inspections. These efforts failed. All along, the United States continued its "quiet" air war against the Iraqi military.

While the Kurds of Iraq experienced increased security, if not prosperity, under the protective UN umbrella, and despite violent squabbles among the major political blocs contending for Kurdish loyalties, the Kurds of Turkey had a different experience. The Turkish military destroyed over 3,000 Kurdish villages during the 1990s in an attempt to quash the Kurdish independence movement. The government regularly had about 50,000 troops in eastern Turkey and spent perhaps $8 million (U.S.) annually in these actions. In February 1999, Abdullal Ocalan, the long-time leader of the PKK, the Kurdistan Workers Party, and a sought terrorist, was captured, put on trial, and convicted of murder. Kurds throughout Europe expressed their outrage; the Turkish government breathed a sigh of relief. The Kurdish revolt quieted.

So, the Kurdish issue remained fundamentally the same as at the time of the mandates. The Kurds are divided among countries and among themselves, and they have only dim prospects of a more independent future.

Turkey's actions toward the Kurds were complicated by the desire to become full members of the European Union. The EU stated that a full consideration of Turkish membership would not be put on the table until (among other things) the Turkish government considerably improved its

human rights record with respect to the Kurds. This was brought to a head in the summer of 2002 in the midst of a political and economic crisis. The aging, infirm, and politically besieged prime minister apparently saw an advantage in supporting civil rights reforms for the Kurds in hopes of gaining the considerable popular support of joining the EU. The picture was further muddled when the U.S. government sought to weld together the various Iraqi forces opposed to the government of Saddam Hussein. This complicated matters for the Turks because of their fear that Kurdish success in Iraq would spill over into Turkey.

The long and severely deep economic recession in Turkey, coupled with political paralysis, led to national elections in November 2002. The results were stunning. An Islamic party rode to victory, and the party claiming roots to Ataturk was crushed. It was difficult, however, to interpret this as a rejection of secularism in Turkey. The victors in the election publicly endorsed the secular political traditions of Turkey. And it also seemed that the voters were sick of economic decline and massive corruption of the old order; they sought a fresh approach. The leadership of the Islamist party voiced the same opinion.

International Organizations

It is sometimes useful to distinguish between those international organizations under control of the constituent member states (for example, the United Nations and the International Monetary Fund [IMF]), and international nongovernmental organizations (for example, Amnesty International). Both groups face enormous challenges, and they often are in conflict with each other and with single governments.

It was apparent that the role of the United Nations in Iraq signaled something more than a straightforward consequence of the dissolution of the bipolar world. It was clear that the role of many nongovernmental organizations (NGOs) would become more important in the affairs of countries. However, it remains unclear how they will function; indeed, it is not clear if they will be effective in conflict resolution or if they will simply add more complications. The importance of the emerging role of NGOs goes far beyond the roles of watchdog and enforcer of international opinion that the United Nations took on in Iraq. For example, scores of NGOs pledged aid to the emerging state of Palestine. During the 1999 relief efforts in Kosovo, several Arab Gulf countries, led by local NGOs, provided significant (and, significantly, highly visible) aid to refugees.

It also seemed that regional alliances were assuming more importance. At the end of the 1991 war, a series of pronouncements called for a "new order" in the Middle East. The Gulf Cooperation Council (GCC) countries along with Egypt and Syria were to provide for regional military security on a cooperative basis, thus providing a vehicle for dissuading further invasions. However, the Gulf states apparently feared the brawn and long-term intentions of Egypt and Syria. Consequently, they immediately started to back away from the agreement. For their part, Egypt and Syria were not ready to engage in significant military expenditures and risk loss of life without receiving substantial compensation, a compensation not being offered by the Gulf states. The members of the GCC then significantly increased their defense spending; and they attempted, with limited success, to coordinate their defense forces.

After the war it was recognized that the extreme disparity in income and wealth between the haves and have-nots posed considerable danger to stability. Therefore, various actors dreamed up schemes that allowed petroleum-inspired Gulf charity to flow into the income-poor and population-rich countries. But the petroleum-rich countries would have difficulty in the best of times satisfying the appetites of Syria and, especially, Egypt, and these were not the best of times; the oil-rich states felt a considerable financial pinch as oil prices wobbled downward and defense expenditures increased. Also, some of the Gulf countries felt betrayed by the lack of support in quelling the Iraqi threat by Jordan, Yemen, and the PLO during the war. It would be quite extraordinary, then, if large-scale income distribution took place. The rich states probably will continue to write checks to pay for defense and otherwise defang the nettlesome desires of some neighbor. The basic schisms are likely to remain. And these schisms are likely to continue to excite resentments on the part of the poorer nations. After all, the extremely

high income of, say, Kuwait, resulted from being lucky; if vast amounts of petroleum had not been found under its patch of territory, Kuwait would be yet another small and poor country.

Although a study of the complicated international actions in the former Yugoslavia are beyond the scope of this book, there are some overarching points of interest. First, significant military actions were taken by NATO, the U.S.–European defense organization, not the United Nations. If nothing else, this indicates the complicated interactions of organizations controlled by member governments. Second, NATO actions in Kosovo were designed to protect ethnic Albanians against the politically dominant Serbs. Using a different set of descriptors, differences in "traits," the actions could be described as Western Christians defending a group of Muslims against Orthodox Christians. While this should not be seen as the centerpiece of the conflict, it does point to the complications encountered when the more simplistic formulations of the "Clash of Civilizations" argument are accepted. Richer explanations are called for. In the midst of the drama in Kosovo, scores of NGOs (among them, the Red Cross and the Red Crescent) scrambled to provide relief to the Muslim Albanians.

It may be that the above-mentioned calls for international cooperation, wealth sharing, and a greater role for NGOs will not be as important as the ability of individual governments in the region to engage their citizens in the process of nation building. As every student of politics knows, there is no simple and straightforward model or plan of action that will guarantee success. It involves a host of issues, including the construction of a set of meaningful symbols that convey attributes of the nation that are believable, and behavior of the government that reinforces the believability of the symbols. When significant economic and political reform are called for in order to meet the goal, the process gets more complicated.

ECONOMIC LIBERALIZATION

During the 1980s it became increasingly clear that many government policies were detrimental to the process of economic growth. The presumed need to intervene in the economy through the establishment of state-owned enterprises and various rules and regulations constraining private economic behavior have deep and complicated roots that often are tied to the structure of the colonial economy. The statist economic programs of several Middle East countries tended to lose favor during the 1980s. Indeed, privatization programs became a worldwide phenomenon, including such diverse countries as the United States, Ghana, India, Mexico, and Malaysia, along with many others. It is important to note that among the promoters of a scaling back of government involvement in the economy were major international institutions such as the International Monetary Fund and the World Bank.

The nub of the argument was, and is, that many government programs were grossly inefficient, stifled individual initiative in the bargain, and as a result guaranteed low economic growth and bureaucratic arrogance. While this view of the consequences of an "overly activist" government has considerable merits, we should recognize that the emphasis on economic efficiency does not speak (at least explicitly) to notions of distributive justice. So, while many a Middle Easterner could agree with the diagnosis of the sickness of their government, they had difficulty accepting the prescription; after all, unshackling businesses could be viewed as a policy of widening the income gap in a country.

But it is not only the fear of the "rich getting richer and the poor poorer" that accounts for resistance to the opening of markets. The time-tested notion of comparative advantage states that the opening of trade between countries will enhance the economic well-being of each due to each specializing in the production and sale of a good of which it is the relative low-cost producer. The theory is applicable to most real world situations that can be imagined. However, some potentially significant complications must be considered. First, although each country will benefit, there will be winners and losers in each country. Those owning the resources specialized in the good or service that faces competition from imports will lose. Those owners facing an expanded market through exports will gain (and wage earners/consumers may gain or lose depending on their consumption

pattern). Social and political conflict, therefore, should be expected.

Other questions buried in the comparative advantage argument are those of price trends, export earning volatility, and the potential for a country to lose its comparative advantage rather quickly. The price trend question is this: Are there forces that will drive the price of primary products (for example, cotton and petroleum) lower relative to imports (that is, manufactured goods)? If so, the country exporting primary products will have to export a greater volume each year simply to pay for the same volume of imports. Even if this is the case (and the results are mixed), there is the question of price volatility. It is obvious that wildly gyrating prices make planning more difficult.

Finally, there is the question of the length of time that a country will hold a comparative advantage in a product. Petroleum is a good example. The high petroleum prices of the 1970s prompted research for new sources of petroleum and for different energy sources. The world seeks a low-cost energy source to meet its needs, not simply more petroleum. So, as solar and other energy sources are developed, the cost advantage in the production of petroleum by, say, Saudi Arabia loses some significance: Why would people pay more to buy the cheapest petroleum if they could get energy from other sources (for example, solar,) at a lower price? The more that a country is dependent on a single product to provide export earnings, the more pressing these questions become.

It has been appreciated only recently that the process of reform can be exceedingly difficult. Although some issues are technical, a primary basic reason is rather straightforward: Significant groups prosper from the status quo, groups that would be harmed by reform. Likewise, the prospects for successful reform differ depending on what is going to be reformed and in what country; power relationships depend on complex political and economic relationships. It also is sometimes the case that a country in the midst of a liberalization program will experience economic downturns before the fruits of liberalization are realized. For example, some countries fix food prices below their free market level, but this tends to reduce the supply of food coming to market. Abolishing maximum prices for food, therefore, will increase food production. But this takes time; in the interim, the average consumer may see food prices increase without an increased supply. Thus, even right-minded reform can carry a high political cost.

In sum, economic liberalization has great appeal to most economists. However, the very process of moving to more open markets may be disruptive and expensive in political as well as economic terms.

By the late 1990s, some important international organizations largely controlled by the rich countries of the world, notably the International Monetary Fund and the World Bank, started to pay more attention to the "poorest of the poor." They argued that if the poor were not beneficiaries of economic development policies, there would be a greater probability of lower national growth and increased social instability. The onset of terror against the rich symbolized by the events of September 11, 2001 strengthened this view. It remains, however, an abstract aim.

Political Islam

Since thoroughgoing economic reform often involves the acceptance of a different role for the state in economic affairs, this can translate into questions regarding the nature of the "good" society. These issues tend to become explicit during periods of considerable flux; the argument of this chapter is that this is such a time in the Middle East due to the aftermath of the dramas of the past quarter century. These events, of course, did not occur in a vacuum; rather, they were placed in a context of rapid economic and social change in some countries, of stultifying stagnation in others, of some ideological frameworks becoming stale, others gaining in appeal, and sometimes of a profound distrust of those in charge of the mechanics of government.

Religious movements often provide the context in which these concerns are played out: This ought not to be surprising; after all, concern about "the good life" is central to religion. In Algeria, an Arab country generally not covered in this

book, civil order essentially broke down, with many thousands of lives lost, when the secularly oriented authorities repressed an Islamic political movement when it seemed assured of winning elections and fulfilling its promise to install an Islamic government. Islamists gained power in Sudan, and that desperately poor and war-racked country started to be viewed by the international community as a prime safe haven and training ground for terrorists, somewhat replacing an ideologically evolving Iran as the premier rogue nation in the area. Relations between Sudan and Egypt, never free of some contention, soured as official Egypt blamed Sudan for the increasingly popular, powerful, and disruptive groups of religiously based movements in Egypt.

There are indications that the leadership of some of the more prominent "extremist" organizations (for example, Turabi of Sudan) changed their tactics during the 1990s. Running the risk of oversimplification, during the 1980s the attitude of these groups was characterized by a total rejection of existing governments and a heavy reliance on displays of violence. Although this view and behavior did not disappear during the 1990s, there was a greater tendency for compromise and for use of the political arena to secure victories: Hizbollah participated in Lebanese elections (with surprising results), Hamas was persuaded not to boycott (1996) Palestinian elections, and an Islamic party gained more votes (December 1995) than any other party in supposedly secular Turkey. It is difficult to sort out the meaning of this. Some commentators believe that the softening of rhetoric and action was primarily due to the fact that the Islamists suffered significant failures through the decade, that the change of tactics grew out of failure, and that the age of "Political Islam" is over. This, indeed, may be the case, but another view must be considered: It may be that they are becoming woven into the political fabric and will gain strength in the coming decades.

Finally, it may simply be that the 1990s represented a lull. Indeed, wealthy disaffected Saudi resident Osama bin Laden gained prominence during the late 1990s by providing the financing and training of terrorists. The United States sent its warplanes to bomb his training site in Afghanistan and a chemical factory in Sudan that U.S. officials (on slim reeds of evidence, it seems) thought was producing biological weapons. This occurred after U.S. embassies in Kenya and Tanzania were bombed with considerable loss of life. The U.S. government reported that its attack on bin Laden was designed to prevent another round of attacks on U.S. facilities in scattered parts of the world. But the USS Cole was bombed in 2000 while at port in Yemen. Then came September 11, 2001. Globalization has many faces.

These conflicting currents were readily seen in Egypt during the 1990s. During the early years of the decade, various groups engaged in acts of violence against the Egyptian government, Egyptian secularists thought to be their enemies, and foreign tourists. They also acted within the law to harass their enemies; for example, bringing legal suits charging apostasy. The government acted by changing various laws so as to protect those being harassed and mainly with a thoroughgoing repression of the "religious extremists." During the middle years of the decade more than fifty individuals convicted of terrorist activities were sentenced to death, and thousands lingered in prison. Although it is understandable that the Egyptian government viewed the extremists solely as security threats, it also meant that this stance precluded an examination of the root causes of the desperation and despair.

The various radical groups—groups often with wildly different rationales—reacted in a variety of manners. In March 1993, a huge bomb ripped away part of New York City's World Trade Center. In rather short order, a group of individuals were arrested and subsequently convicted not only of that act but also of planning to blow up a number of important New York buildings and bridges, as well as planning for the assassinations of many prominent people. The leader of the group was an aged Egyptian cleric. He and his followers apparently believed that a series of strikes at the United States would further their aim of returning Egypt to Islamic traditionalism. In 1995, a suicide bomber crippled the Egyptian embassy in Pakistan. Islamic Jihad claimed responsibility for this attack, and they promised more. On the other side of the ledger, members of the Muslim Brotherhood, an organization barred from formal

political action, and the group that probably suffered most from the government crackdown, announced in 1996 the formation of a new party (the Center Party), and the leadership of the Muslim Brotherhood gave public assurances that they would not act outside the law. By 2002 there were indications that many of those in Egypt who had called for or tacitly supported violence had changed their thinking. Personal piety started to be favored over political action. Or so some people argued.

The conviction of a very prominent Egyptian (secular) civil rights activist led the U.S. government to openly criticize Egypt in mid-2002. The United States also indicated that they would withhold supplemental economic aid to Egypt because of the conviction. Before this time, U.S. criticism of the Egyptian civil rights record was muted and not placed on center stage.

Generally, people will struggle for significant changes in the ordering of government and society when they see no way to meet their goals through the present system. Many times they seek power in order to root out what they see as a growing cancer in the body politic. It is of some interest to speculate on a potential conflict between this call, or cacophony of calls, and the acceptance of many governments of a "liberalized" economic order.

It is difficult to predict any definite outcome to these various swirls of activity. Nations of the Middle East seem to have developed distinct, if sometimes fractious, identities. And they are striving to strengthen these identities. However, economic liberalization within countries and the growing interdependence between countries tend to constrain the actions of governments and weaken notions of national identity.

Political Legitimacy in the Gulf

The monarchies of the Gulf faced another set of difficulties regarding the proper extent of political participation. Officials could argue that their majlis-based tradition of consultation and consensus gave the average citizen a more meaningful voice in national policy than countries that professed democratic forms but did not actually allow opposition. But they still had to deal with the issue of formal political participation and power sharing.

It was obvious to all serious observers that the massive response against Iraq's invasion of Kuwait had more to do with protecting supplies of petroleum than preserving the Kuwaiti government. Iraq and Kuwait each supplied about 10 percent of the world's petroleum. Saudi Arabia supplied another 25 percent (and most of the Saudi supply came from the area bordering Kuwait). Since industrialized economies must have adequate supplies of petroleum to function, having Iraq control a large percentage of world output was unacceptable to the industrialized countries.

The war was enormously expensive for Saudi Arabia (maybe $60 billion directly, and the same total indirectly), but the Saudi leadership knew that the expenditure had to be made, given the alternative. But victory did not mean that the kingdom was free of trouble. Indeed, mobilization gave focus to some of the more problematic aspects of the state. The royal family came under attack from a number of sources. Some in the worldwide Muslim community wondered if the Saudis abrogated their function of guardian of the holy sites of Mecca and Medina by inviting over one-half million infidels into the country. Some saw the sprawling royal family as engaging in wasteful and sometimes corrupt policies. Saudis from the left and right wondered if the role of women in the society was properly defined. And some made calls for Western-style democratic reform.

Traditionally the royal family used the power of the purse to quiet dissent. But postwar Saudi Arabia faced a harsh budgetary reality: They had been spending beyond their means for more than a decade, drawing down their international financial reserves in the process. In 1994, the government announced a 20 percent cut in expenditures. They cut expenditures again the following year. The government also started to cut back on its lavish system of subsidies—education, gasoline, water, telephone services, electricity, and so on—in order to become financially sound. Unless the price of petroleum increases dramatically, the Saudis will have to continue to tighten their fiscal belt.

In 1993, the government created a sixty-one-member consultative council (Majlis al-Shura),

all appointed, in response to calls for more political voice. It also felt it necessary to arrest some dissidents, as well as make significant policy changes favored by senior members of the religious establishment. In November 1995, a car bomb exploded in a Riyadh military building where U.S. personnel were training Saudi military forces (five Americans died, and scores of individuals were injured). Official Saudi Arabia blamed the attack, generally received with skepticism, on foreigners. In January 1996, King Fahd, weakened by illness (probably a stroke), handed over responsibility for running the government to Prince Abdullah, Fahd's half-brother.

That the amount of Saudi discontent with the government increased markedly during the 1990s is not particularly surprising: After all, the war against Iraq was a major trauma, one that called many basic precepts of the society into question. It is not clear, however, how these pressures will be played out. It is important to remember that the legitimacy of the state has rested on the dual pillars of the royal family and the religious establishment. In the last quarter century, a third pillar grew, that of the professional middle class: businessmen, bureaucrats, and academics. Many of these people either were trained in Western universities or assimilated a range of Western values and lifeways. The government of Saudi Arabia responded with conciliation and repression, depending on the presumed offense and the source. While this is an understandable set of responses, the net result may not lead to a stable reordered system.

As stated earlier, it was not lost on many observers that the majority of the September 11 bombers were Saudi Arabian citizens. The U.S. government then began a process of distancing itself from Saudi Arabia, quietly and not-so-quietly calling for substantial reform, especially actions that would mute the public policy role of the clergy.

The other monarchies of the Gulf also had to deal with significant changes during the last decade of the century. Kuwait, of course, was torched and pillaged by Iraq. Not long after the invasion, Iraq announced that Kuwait was properly (historically speaking) part of Iraq. Since the Iraqis planned to stay in Kuwait, structural damage to buildings initially was limited; but anything movable was potential booty. The University of Kuwait lost its 700,000-book library and all of its computing facilities. Office buildings and hotels were systematically cleared of furniture, autos were stripped, the national museum was looted, medical supplies were taken, and so on.

After the war, the physical reconstruction of Kuwait City happened quickly: After all, the Kuwaitis had accumulated a fortune in international reserves to pay for whatever was needed. But there were tougher "reconstruction" projects with uncertain futures. First, more than a third of a million Palestinians living in preinvasion Kuwait had to leave; their perceived pro-Iraqi stance during the occupation deeply embittered the Kuwaitis. Along the same lines, Kuwait announced that it would reduce its prewar population (2.2 million) by one-half by placing limits on the number of foreign nationals allowed in the country; only then could Kuwaitis become a majority in their own country. Also, calls for increased political participation resumed. Finally, there were the Kuwaiti oil fields. Before the war the world had never seen more than five wells burning at the same time. The Iraqis torched 640 at the time of their retreat. The extent of the ecological damage probably will never be known. As with many such events, the worldwide media provided immediate footage of the spectacular fires. Then the coverage all but stopped; it became old news. To the surprise of all observers, the last burning well was doused in nine months (December 1991) instead of the originally estimated two to five years.

The other monarchies of the Gulf experienced serious political rumblings during the 1990s, albeit with short-run outcomes that favored a continuation of the status quo. A coup in Qatar resulted in a change of power within the ruling family; inner circle intrigue in Oman failed; the (Sunni) Bahraini leadership continued to worry about their Shia majority, including serious rioting; and the U.A.E. was forced to clamp down on expressions of opposition. A basic question, then, remains: Are the monarchies of the Gulf becoming increasingly anachronistic, or will they develop creative solutions so as to remain in power?

There was a change of leadership during 1999 in Bahrain (March), and in Morocco (July) with the death of long-standing King Hassan. In addition, the small Gulf country of Qatar continued to undergo significant change. In 1995, a son toppled his father in a bloodless palace coup. There was a failed countercoup in 1996, and the (1999) arrest of one of the putative designers of that coup. The new Qatari leadership significantly increased media freedom (especially if the host government was not the subject of media scrutiny), promised a democratically elected parliament sometime in the future, and generally attempted to "open" the country to significant political and social change, including a political role for females. The Qatari TV station Al-Jazeerah caused a significant stir, first in the Arab world and then worldwide. The proliferation of satellite TV reception meant that the wider Arab world was receiving news relatively free from government control. Several Arab governments complained when unfavorable news of their country was broadcast, but the Qataris held firm. Within a year, the station had established itself as an Arab version of CNN. Then it gained wider notice because it, virtually alone, reported and interviewed prominent leaders of the Taliban and Al-Qaeda.

Oman, Kuwait, and the U.A.E. also experienced rapid change in social relations, including open discussions of a role for females in political life. Although it is too early to be definitive, it may be that 2000 signaled the "beginning of the end" of the old monarchical ways of organizing political and social life in the Gulf kingdoms.

Although the international situation of Iran remained markedly different from that of Saudi Arabia, there were some broad commonalities on the domestic scene. Sanctions imposed by the United States (since 1979) constrained the ability of Iran to rebuild its infrastructure, military, and petroleum facilities, although Western European reluctance to follow the U.S. lead meant that Iran was not close to the dire situation faced by Iraq. In an apparent attempt at partial rapprochement, in 1995 the Iranian government awarded Conoco, a U.S.-based firm, a chance to invest in Iranian oil and gas production. The U.S. government forced Conoco to reject the offer. Whatever the reasons given by the United States, both the offer and the rejection point to a salient set of facts: It seems that the Iranian "pragmatists" were indeed reaching out to the wider international community, and the United States was not ready to accede. Another proposal for Western petroleum investment in Iran was made in 1999; this time the U.S. government implicitly signaled a change in attitude by being mute.

The government of Iran faced domestic discontent from a variety of sources. Although President Rafsanjani managed to stay in power, his range of domestic policy options remained quite limited due to his reluctance to alienate any of the major political blocs. The continued poor performance of the economy initially was blamed on international sanctions, but it became apparent over time that domestic policy shared the blame. Since the Iranian revolution promised a full renaissance of the country under the banner of a reinvigorated Islam, the discontent over economic failure was intimately tied to larger issues of faith—that is, of self-definition. Indeed, the revolution defined this religious renaissance as applying to the entire Muslim world, and many of the clerics close to the seat of government power saw Iran as the locus of the movement. However, there is evidence to suggest that the revolution also engendered a renewed pride in the Iranian nation, that religion did not provide the sole source of continued inspiration.

Mr. Khatami followed Mr. Rafsanjani to the post of president. The election was spirited, and the landslide victory seemed to signal the desire for political reform, especially in the softening of religious dicta on everyday life. But the transition, if indeed it was a transition, was not smooth. Many clerics opposed to reform used their considerable levers of power. An especially important battlefield concerns the proper extent of freedom of the press. During 1999, a conservative clerical court banned two progressive newspapers and arrested the editors. University students took to the streets and suffered fatalities. Then a reformist ministry of the government brought a lawsuit against three conservative newspapers. The conservatives returned the salvo by calling for the imprisonment (some called for the death) of two students who wrote a satirical play that the conservatives thought blasphemed Islam. We could view this series of events as a sideshow, but it can be profitably seen as the core of the struggle for reform.

If the conservative clerics-cum-politicians lose their struggle on being the sole definers of proper political expression, we could expect a different set of debates (and policies) than if they win. The struggle over fundamental political issues continues in Iran. In 2002, President Khatami directly called into question the authority of the clerical establishment to overturn legislative initiatives. He called for changes in the constitution that would weaken their right to summarily change the course of Iranian history to fit their vision of a just society.

The next chapter argues that many Western perceptions of the social customs of the Middle East are either wrong or need to be nuanced considerably. This is especially true of the role of women. However, the fact remains that most women in the Middle East have not been afforded the "public space" held by their sisters in most places of the world. Therefore, it may be notable that proposals of voting rights for women have been put forth by the leadership of several countries. The rates of female school attendance at all levels increased dramatically in the past two decades, especially so in Iran and the Gulf states. Education transforms lives. It may be that an ever-increasing cadre of coherent female voices will indeed lead to an opening of the public sphere to women.

FROM OSLO TO JERUSALEM

The 1999 election of Mr. Barak as prime minister of Israel was hailed by many as a turning point in the long process of creating a sustainable peace between Israel and the Palestinians. It, indeed, was a turning point; with bitter irony it marked the beginning of a downward spiral.

A 1993 accord signed by Yasir Arafat and Yitzhak Rabin seemed promising. And, although negotiations were very slow and fractious, there was some movement toward a resolution. Then, an assassin seemed to halt the process. On November 5, 1995 Israeli Prime Minister Rabin was assassinated by a lone Israeli Jew who objected to the hotly contested peace negotiations between Israel and the Palestinians. Shimon Peres inherited Labor bloc leadership and the office of prime minister. It was first feared that the peace negotiations would be derailed by the assassination. The road to peace started after the conclusion of the Gulf War. Many bumps and roadblocks had to be negotiated between that time and January 1996, when Palestinians held elections in Gaza and the West Bank, thereby presumably entering the final stage of their long battle for independence.

The implications of the Gulf War for Israel were secondary in the physical sense, but emotionally and politically they were profound. The intifadah was droning on at the time of the invasion, enervating all parties. After facing a universal diplomatic firestorm during the first week of the occupation of Kuwait, Saddam Hussein announced that Iraq would withdraw if Israel quit the occupied territories and if Syria withdrew from Lebanon. Despite Saddam Hussein's past indifference to the Palestinian cause, the PLO embraced him and the Palestinian people took heart. When faced with such threats in the past, Israel often responded with a preemptive strike. However, it was constrained this time; the allies needed Arab participation in the war effort, and it would not happen if Israel were to strike Iraq. Therefore, Israel was pressured to sit back—they even maintained this stance during the war when Iraq lobbed psychologically devastating and physically ineffective Scud missiles into Israel. Israelis went through the war donning their gas masks at every air raid warning: There was a fear (unrealized) that the Scuds would be armed with biological or chemical warheads. Palestinians "danced on the rooftops" as the Scuds sped toward their targets. Not surprisingly, Israeli attitudes toward the Palestinians hardened, and the already dispirited Israeli peace movement collapsed. Ironically, however, the June 1992 elections resulted in a government that was closer to meeting the goals of the peace movement than any government since the territories were occupied in 1967.

Israel was also affected by U.S. agreements with other members of the coalition. First, Syria was given a green light to root out Christian general Aoun from his fortified Beirut position. He had denied the implementation of a new power-sharing agreement since he saw it as bringing grief to the Christian population of Lebanon. Syria

quickly routed Aoun, saw the new government installed, had the new government request Syrian help in disarming the various militia, and signed a treaty ensuring a very strong Syrian voice in Lebanon. A united and Syrian-dominated Lebanon placed Israel in an awkward position: For more than a decade Israel controlled much of southern Lebanon directly or through a Christian militia proxy. Withdrawal would remove a buffer for the northern Israel border and weaken the Israeli position in the Golan. To remain meant that Israel would face increasing international pressure. Israel remained. The Syrians agreed to withdraw their forces from all of Lebanon except the Bekka valley. However, the Syrians ensured their prominent position in Lebanon through the engineering of a 1992 election in Lebanon that yielded a government friendly to Syrian interests. Israel finally quit Lebanon.

After the conclusion of the conflict, the United States placed considerable pressure on Israel to come to a peace conference. As the only remaining superpower, and with newly forged ties to important Arab governments, the United States was in a unique position. After a considerable amount of posturing, initial meetings between Israel, various Arab governments, and Palestinians (but not the PLO directly) were held (the "Madrid" meetings) in late 1991 and 1992. Over the next couple of years, the process continued, albeit at a frustratingly slow pace. Indeed, some observers thought that there would not be any further significant movement. This perspective was confounded by an announcement that the Israeli government and the PLO had been talking secretly in Oslo and had entered into an agreement (the Oslo Accords) that would bring the two parties into open direct negotiation for the first time. It is of some significance that the accords were brokered without the active engagement of the United States.

By 1993, Prime Minister Rabin and Yasir Arafat shook hands on the White House lawn, a rather startling scene symbolizing their agreement to work toward peace. In 1994, Jordan signed a peace treaty with Israel. Syria and Lebanon remained out of the fold, although intense negotiations brokered through the United States brought the parties ever closer.

It will take some years to unravel the details of the various negotiations. Several points, however, are rather obvious. First, the details of the peace arrangements between Israel and the Palestinians angered significant elements in each camp. For example, Hamas initially rejected the very idea of peace with Israel, they viewed it as a capitulation, and they promised resistance. But they were persuaded to change their views, probably because peace seemed ever more inevitable; but that view was not firmly rooted, as subsequent events showed. Hizbollah, a champion of the Shia of southern Lebanon (occupied by Israel) seemed to moderate their stance when it became clear that attacks on Israel by them would, as always, call forth massive Israeli retaliation—but now Hizbollah could not count on the support of the Palestinians. This is not to say that violence on the part of these groups and their comrades ceased; far from it.

The Palestinians did not have a monopoly on peace plan–inspired violence. Various groups, often settlers in the territories, took arms against Palestinians, the most spectacular display being a massacre in Hebron, when a settler killed more than twenty Palestinians praying in a mosque located in the Tomb of the Patriarchs. It was profoundly shocking that many of his fellow settlers considered him to be a hero and martyr. In January 1996, a Palestinian terrorist dubbed "the Engineer" because of his sophisticated use of bombs was assassinated in Gaza by persons unknown but widely believed to be associated with Israeli intelligence. Since "the Engineer" had been responsible for scores of deaths, the Israeli population would have liked to breathe a sigh of relief. But "the Engineer" had become a hero in Gaza, and over 100,000 marched in Gaza City the next day, calling for revenge. By this time, Israel had withdrawn its military forces from Gaza in favor of Palestinian Authority police. Palestinian critics of the peace plan pointed to the Israeli action as yet another reminder of the extremely limited extent of Palestinian freedom of action—another indication to them that the peace plan was a sham.

The November 5, 1995 assassination of Prime Minister Rabin—by a Jewish religious student who thought that God had directed his actions as a way of stopping the peace process—sent profound shock through Israel. There were deeply disturbing aspects of Rabin's death beyond that of clouding the prospects for peace. This was the first time in Israel that a politician had been assassinated. Israeli political debates have always been rather raucous, often punctuated by references to violence. During the whole of 1995, the level of bitterness and hate expressed by the enemies of the peace process increased, some of the most vicious attacks calling for the death of leaders who entered into such a peace. Some of the more radical combed religious texts for a justification of such violent acts. Some commentators asked if Israeli society had crossed a Rubicon, if more political violence could now be expected. A related matter, and one that required less speculation, was the fact that a small but significant portion of the Israeli population were dangers to the functioning of the state. They had to be controlled in some fashion, but at what price? One problem relates to the continuing need for coalition building to form a political majority in the Knesset; religious parties of one stripe or another often have provided the votes necessary for the party with a plurality to form a majority. The obvious implication is that control had to be accomplished without alienation.

The agreement touched the definition of Israel itself. Israel has always had two potentially conflicting notions of self-identity. First, it operates as a democratic and largely secular state by definition of basic political rights such as voting. But many other rights and relations to the government are defined through the dual notions of ethnic Jewishness and/or religious Judaism. For example, Israeli Arabs generally are not allowed to serve in the Israeli Defense Forces, and IDF service is a prerequisite for eligibility for a wide range of government subsidies and services. On a more fundamental level, the raison d'être of Israel is tied to religion in a more immediate sense than it is for most nations. However, loyalty to the nation and loyalty to religious precepts can come into conflict.

Israeli settlements on the West Bank and in Gaza provide an important example of the kinds of difficulties the peace negotiators faced. It was not possible for the Israeli government to consider the dismantling of the settlements; it was thought, with considerable evidence, that no government could survive such a policy. And the settlers had to be protected once control of the areas passed to Palestinian hands. Adequate protection demanded that safe transport to Israel proper had to be assured, water rights needed to be guaranteed, and so on. A number of Palestinians objected to the notion that the settlements would remain, and that Israel would have an effective veto power in other realms of activity. They contended that Palestinian independence in this context would be meaningless, that a subservient dependence would remain. On the other side of the ledger, some Israelis said that the plan in essence was an abandonment of the settlements and the settlers.

The status of Jerusalem was left to future negotiations. Both sides knew that this was the single issue on which neither side could compromise, at least for the moment. Therefore, Israel continued to regard Jerusalem as its capital; the Palestinians regarded it as their future capital. In this fashion, both Israeli and Palestinian negotiators could tell their respective constituencies that they held firm on the all-important issue of the status of Jerusalem. For example, the January 20, 1996, Palestinian elections included those voters in Jerusalem. But Israel stated that actually those votes were to be treated as absentee votes from another area. Each side ignored the call of the other. The Palestinians could elect representatives from Jerusalem, while the Israelis could say that those votes actually were for representatives of other areas (since Israel claimed all of Jerusalem). As it happened, the voter turnout in Jerusalem (and Hebron) was far lower than in the rest of the West Bank and Gaza.

The Palestinian elections of January 20, 1996, were for an interim eighty-eight-member legislative council. Although the Palestinians were in control of only patches of West Bank territory, the victorious Mr. Arafat was correct in stating that "this is the foundation stone for our Palestinian State." About 70 percent of the registered voters turned out—a strong indication that calls for a boycott from "rejectionist" elements were not heeded. Although the formation of the legislative council could be considered to be a foundation stone, plenty of work was needed before an independent state could be constructed on it. Israel needed to leave the rural areas of the West Bank

and urban Hebron, and the PLO had to reject its charter calling for the destruction of Israel, before the permanent-status talks scheduled for May 1996 could even begin. And there would be much hard bargaining in the talks.

Syrian-Israeli negotiations centered on the familiar problems of Israeli settlers, water rights questions, and border control. It was obvious that Syria needed to have the Quneitra District (the Golan), first captured by Israel in 1967, freed of Israeli settlers. Over time, the Israelis moved to accept this position—but they would only accept it if water rights would be guaranteed and Israeli towns bordering Syria would be safe from attack. In January 1996, the United States offered to station peacekeeping forces at the border, attempting to meet Israeli security needs and Syrian demands that they have full control of the use of their soil. An agreement with Syria was important to Israel beyond constructing peace with that particular neighbor; it was thought that formal relations with the Gulf states would follow if an agreement with Syria could be brokered. This would leave Lebanon as the only border state without a formal peace agreement with Israel—a Lebanon with Israelis in control of the southern part of the country, Iranian-supported groups in the south-central areas, and considerable Syrian influence throughout.

The proposed timetable for an Israeli/Syrian agreement became clouded in February 1996 when Prime Minister Peres called for elections in May 1996 instead of waiting the full term and having the elections take place in October. Apparently, Mr. Peres calculated that an election victory was more likely the closer the election was to the drama of Rabin's assassination. Indeed, he began to interpret the election as a vote for peace with Syria and continuing "normalization" with the Palestinians. But there also was the risk that the election might disrupt the fragile peace talks.

In February and March 1996, spectacular terrorist bomb attacks for which Hamas claimed responsibility threatened the Israeli-Palestinian peace talks. In the first large-scale terrorist action, one that broke a period of relative calm, bomb blasts killed twenty-five (twenty-two Israelis, the bomber, and two U.S. citizens). The nation was horrified and stunned. Peace talks were put on hold, the borders between Israel and the territories sealed, and the proponents of continued negotiations scrambled to avoid having the incident lead to a series of deadly reprisals. Indeed, Hamas said that the attacks were reprisals for the death of "the Engineer" several months earlier. During the following week the Israeli leadership of those opposed to the peace negotiations (as constituted) gained voice and public support for the first time since the death of Rabin. A week later (March 3) another bomb exploded in central Jerusalem, killing nineteen. Again, Hamas claimed responsibility. Both Peres and Arafat vowed to root out the terrorists. Vital security issues dominated the scene; negotiating for peace would be impossible without a set of acceptable assurances that terrorist actions had permanently ceased. Israeli public opinion markedly turned against peace with the Palestinians.

In the elections of May 1996, Benjamin Netanyahu was elected prime minister. After some time he cobbled together enough allies in the Knesset to form a government. The elections marked an overall slowing of the peace movement, although a dramatic peace initiative took place in August of 1998 (the Wye Accords) when President Clinton presided over a meeting between Mr. Netanyahu and Mr. Arafat. The meeting ended with a timetable for Israeli withdrawal from portions of the territories it occupied (and after cancer-ridden King Hussein made an appearance calling for peace). But the optimism of the day quickly faded. The language was familiar: Israel wanted the Palestinian Authority to do a better job controlling those Palestinians opposed to the peace process. The Palestinian Authority claimed to be doing all that was possible, and that the situation would be eased only after Israel fully complied with the withdrawals and other parts of the agreement. Negotiations with Syria ended. The peace process had ground to a halt.

Israel held another election in 1999. A relative political novice, Ehud Barak, defeated Mr. Netanyahu on the promise to speed the peace process. He also promised to bring any peace settlement to the vote of the electorate. As usual, it took time to cobble together a coalition government. Significantly, the Shas, an ultra-Orthodox (religious) party gained enough seats in the elec-

tion to become the third largest party in the Knesset. Prime Minister Barak gained his majority by including the Shas in the government (along with three ministerial posts). In turn, the Shas leadership agreed not to block peace negotiations.

By the end of the year, a series of steps had been taken that revived the moribund peace initiative. For the first time in three years Israel and Syria negotiated, and there were confidence-building measures taken by both the Israelis and the Palestinians. And, as always, the leadership of each side had to account for their constituents who were hostile to the process. So, for example, building permits on Israeli settlements continued apace and the Shas gained budgetary approval for their financially strapped school system. The leadership of all parties (Israel/Syria, Israel/Palestine) agreed that they would construct the framework for a final agreement by February 2000.

The Palestinian leadership viewed the Israeli/Syrian negotiations with some trepidation; they worried that an early Israeli/Syrian accord would isolate the Palestinians. And it seemed likely that this agreement could occur rather quickly, especially after Prime Minister Barak indicated that Israel was ready to relinquish most of the Golan, an area to which Israel does not have strong ideological claims (opposed to Gaza and the West Bank). The struggle between the Israelis and the Syrians was strategic, overwhelmed by issues of security. Once an agreement was reached it was very likely that Lebanon would follow. That would leave the Palestinians alone. In addition, Mr. Barak indicated that the several million Palestinians living in UN camps or in the wider diaspora would not be allowed to return. As always, the issue of Jerusalem was off the table.

All of these movements toward a peaceful settlement were dashed in rather short order. As seems to be habitual in the Middle East, events confound prediction. Yasir Arafat struggled to exact ever-greater gains out of the peace process while attempting to convince the Palestinians that the deal he was seeking was the best possible. On the other side, Prime Minister Barak's proposed concessions to the Palestinians severely eroded his support in the Knesset. Opposition groups on both sides acted to subvert the peace process. A visit by Ariel Sharon to the Muslim holy sites on the Temple Mount was the catalyst that sparked the unraveling of the peace process. The scenario was familiar enough: Palestinians rioted, Israel responded, deaths resulted, the voices of moderation were subdued, and the position of the "hard liners" in each camp strengthened. Finally, Barak was forced to call elections. Ariel Sharon became prime minister; and the Israeli position hardened. It was significant that Sharon was forced to accept Labor bloc members into his cabinet in order to form a majority in the Knesset.

The second Palestinian intifadah started in September 2000. Until the early months of 2002, militant Palestinian action focused primarily on the assets of official Israel, mostly in the occupied territories. But then tactics changed: A spate of suicide bombers entered the fray; their targets were Israeli civilians. After some time the Israeli military responded by invading most Palestinian cities, severely disrupting the infrastructures for water, transportation, and electricity, as well as crippling Palestinian Authority centers of control and command. Thousands of Palestinians were arrested. Many on each side died. The IDF withdrew, only to return a month later as suicide bombing resumed. In July 2002 the Israeli air force (using an F-16) dropped a 1,000-pound "smart bomb" into a crowded apartment complex in Gaza City. The attack was successful in that it killed the leader of the military wing of Hamas, an individual the Israelis claimed planned many of the suicide attacks. The bomb also killed 14 others and wounded over 100 people. A firestorm of international criticism followed. Over the years many in the international community had criticized other Israeli policies and actions deemed contrary to international law, such as collective punishment. This case was somewhat different. The Israelis had to know that a bomb of such size would kill innocent civilians. And they had to know that U.S. law prohibiting the use of U.S. weapons from knowingly targeting civilians was violated by such an action. They weathered the international criticism.

The bombing took place a day after the spiritual leader of Hamas had issued a statement that the suicide bombings could cease if the Israelis withdrew from Palestinian territory. The Israelis did not offer an explanation for the bombing in light of this apparent opening to the end of suicide attacks.

The Palestinian government and the population suffered in ways other than the loss of life and assorted indignities of occupation. The Palestinian Authority depended on Israel to hand over tax revenues collected by the Israelis. These transfers ended with the onset of the intifadah. The funds that the PA did have seemed to have been grossly mismanaged, with numerous agencies controlling funds, refusing to be accountable to the PA. By mid-2002 the PA started to assert its authority over its finances—a first step in assuring accountability.

Palestinian citizens also suffered physically. A 2002 study commissioned by the United States Agency for International Development (USAID) indicated that 30 percent of Palestinian children under age six suffered from chronic malnutrition, up from 7 percent two years earlier. About 50 percent of females of childbearing age were anemic. Fifty percent of the population depended on outside assistance for food, largely because the unemployment rates were well over 50 percent. The Israelis also stepped up their policy of collective punishment. For many years they destroyed homes of families who had a member thought to have engaged in terrorist activities. During 2002 the Israelis extended this punishment to include deportation.

Both leaders—Arafat and Sharon—scrambled to maintain internal support while weathering substantial international criticism. In late 2002 the Labor members of the coalition quit Sharon's government, eventually forcing him to call for early elections. Labor quit the coalition because they felt that the continual endorsement of settlements was self-defeating. Those members of the Knesset in support of the settlements refused to join Sharon's government because they perceived him as being too "soft" on the Palestinians.

CONCLUSION

It should be obvious to any serious observer that interpreting the past, to say nothing of predicting the future, is a dicey business. It is a necessarily subjective process, one of sorting through various "facts," picking the important ones, and fitting them into a conceptual pattern, a pattern that the analyst has chosen as most appropriate. Saying that, history ought to be more than "the latest fairy tale": History ought to inform and guide.

There is a strong temptation for the analyst to choose a single motive force underlying human action. For example, the Christian crusades in the Middle East originally were presented as an ideological cause—to regain control of the Holy Land. Then the crusades were given various materialistic explanations: the onset of Western imperialism in the search for greater power, the need to solve basic property rights issues in Europe, and so on. Then explanations again tended to include religious idealism. While we could appropriately argue that each variety of explanation yields insights into the past, the acceptance of any one view also helps to define the present and guide predictions of the future. Simple explanations usually are simplistic.

The failure of analysts to predict the tumult of the past couple of decades, the turning points, attests more to the enormous complexity of the world rather than to some fundamental analytical flaw in the ruminations of the experts. Will the Palestinians gain meaningful independence? Will peace between Israel and its Arab neighbors be stable? Will Iraq emerge from its long nightmare, and if so, in what form? Will the monarchies of the Gulf (and Jordan) survive in their present form? How will Turkey's Islamic leaders chart their country's political and economic course? Will Islam be employed as an increasingly powerful motivation for political change, or will it retreat from political life? The list could go on, but the point should be clear: More fundamental changes will occur in the character and behavior of the nations of the Middle East. The remaining chapters will detail some of the economic, cultural, and political contexts of these changes.

The Politics of Religion, Culture, and Social Life

In recent years the role of religion and culture in Middle Eastern politics has attracted increased attention. However, few aspects of Middle Eastern politics are so difficult to understand without introducing our own cultural biases and distortions. Try as we may to transcend ethnocentric prejudices and pursue a deeper insight, the goal remains elusive. In our introduction we cautioned against certain popular but misleading assumptions. These assumptions include the conception of non-Western cultures as inherently stagnant and of non-Western persons as unreflective and unimaginative with regard to the choices facing them. This is the sort of view reflected in some Western writers' condescending depiction of "the Arab" as "a child of tradition." Western journalists frequently portray a renewed commitment to Islam as an unthinking "return" to some irrelevant and regressive past, while Christian or Jewish renewal in the West tends to receive a more nuanced and tactful treatment and to be placed in a richer explanatory context.

We have also mentioned the limitations of the "modernization" theories popular from the 1950s to the 1980s, which attempted to explain social change in developing countries as the result of the adoption of a more rational cultural outlook.

According to this theoretical paradigm, people achieve modernity when they trade in their unthinking obedience to tradition for a set of attitudes more appropriate to life in a changing, cosmopolitan world. While each theorist had a slightly different list, these imputed traits tended to draw a distinction between "modern" and "traditional" people that was as self-congratulatory to the former as it was unflattering to the latter. "Modern" people are purportedly empathic, mentally flexible, ambitious, rational, democratic, egalitarian, open to change, punctual, hard-working, and so forth. Implicit in much writing about modernization was an unstated premise that "modern" equals "Western."

While some modernization theorists were more cautious and sensitive than others, this general approach had some inherent faults apart from its frequent descent into outright ethnocentrism. First, it tended to understate the diversity, the dynamism, and the critical awareness that can exist in "traditional" cultures. Second, by treating such a broad range of social transformations simply as the product of an attitude adjustment, this type of analysis ignored (among other things) the relations of political and economic inequality central to the colonial and postcolonial order, implicitly recasting colonialism as an educational outreach program. This politically self-serving interpretation, vestiges of which still survive in some social science literature, can cloud our understanding of the complex historical processes that have led to current political realities. This brings us to a third flaw in modernization theory, to which we shall return momentarily: its failure to shed much light on the resurgence of Middle Eastern religious and cultural values that have become so central to the contemporary scene.

The modernization theories were based on an element of truth: Certain ways of living and thinking have become more widespread, especially among people in urban-industrial settings and those whose social circles are the most cosmopolitan. In our introduction we characterized many of the emerging traits of contemporary life in terms of Marshall Hodgson's relatively value-neutral concept of "technicalization," a social trend in which the demands of specialized technical efficiency come to play a more central role than they did in preindustrial and precapitalist societies. Throughout this book we have used the terms *modern* and *modernizing* to refer to the complex set of changes that accompany the technicalizing trend. We do not mean to suggest that these developments are necessarily desirable or that they define the inevitable direction of social change; in fact, they have sometimes raised moral questions and provoked negative reactions in the West as in other parts of the world.

Any discussion of the politics of cross-cultural understanding, especially as regards the Middle East, should include some reference to the work of the prominent literary and cultural critic Edward Said. In *Orientalism* and other works, Said discusses the intricate web of assumptions by which Westerners characterize Muslims and Middle Easterners in terms of timeless, exotic essences.[1] Such depictions, Said argues, have more to do with the West's need to define itself by contrast with an imaginary "other" than with any genuine traits, interests, or motives of so-called "Oriental" people. In fact, Said maintains that the "Orientalist" (whether the classic colonial sort or the mod-

ern "expert") shows surprisingly little interest in how actual "Orientals" view themselves or what they have to say on their own behalf. In Said's view, loose generalizations about such things as "the Arab mind" provide all-too-convenient substitutes for a deeper look at the common human motives, historical developments, and specific concerns that motivate flesh-and-blood people.

While critiques of this sort may themselves be taken to ethnocentric extremes, the problem Said describes is very real. Some of these pitfalls may be unavoidable whenever different peoples try to understand one another—especially when doing so from a distance. But if we want to demystify the motives of Muslims and other Middle Easterners and to understand them in plausible human terms, it is in our interest to move beyond wholesale characterizations and to examine the maze of challenges, strategies, and interests that characterize the interactions of individuals and collectivities in the region. This is especially difficult when we turn to such emotionally charged issues as cultural identity, religion, and social values.

THE POLITICS OF CULTURE

It is often suggested in the Western press that Middle Easterners must either side with the forces of growth and progress (rashly equated with Westernization) or remain in the clutches of the dead hand of tradition. This view is based on a notion of non-Western cultures as static and unreflective, stifled by authoritarian doctrines and unchanging consensus on social, moral, and intellectual issues. The hand of tradition, however, turns out to be more animated (and more manipulated) than one might suppose. Even in the most stable societies, cultural consensus is partially offset by ambiguities within the traditions and by diverse strategies of interpretation.

Social theorists have come increasingly to view cultural tradition not so much as an inert body of rules and beliefs as a battleground of shifting, contested meanings. Tradition is a perpetually unfinished project; how people comprehend their traditions and apply them to practical situations is subject to constant negotiation. In complex situations such as that of the contemporary Middle

---

[1]Edward Said, *Orientalism* (New York: Pantheon Books, 1978).

East, the process of interpretation is complicated by conflicting—and often disguised—power interests at various levels ranging from the individual, communal, class, and ethnic to the international and intersocietal arenas. The range of acceptable cultural interpretations within any given community is defined as much by their relation to social forces as by any logical justification or compatibility. In keeping with our broad definition of politics as the conflict and accommodation of competing demands for control of limited resources, the struggle over authoritative definitions of cultural meaning can aptly be called a "politics of culture." In the arena of cultural politics, power interests assert competing claims to the labels, ideals, and symbols that a community holds in high esteem.

The Politics of Culture in Islamic History

We have seen that Islamic civilization was characterized from the start by a complex cultural and political dialogue. The ideal of a religiously inspired social order has always embroiled Islam in the politics of cultural belief and everyday social practice. To begin with, there was the question of how impeccable the religious credentials of the Umma's leadership must be, with the Shia insisting on leadership in the Prophet's genealogical line and the Sunnis more inclined to accept any overtly Islamic leadership able to govern effectively. Beneath this rift lies a deeper concern shared by Sunni and Shia alike: the danger of apostasy, of falling away from true Islamic guidance.

The time before the Prophet is viewed by Muslims as an age of great wickedness and barbarity (**jahiliyya**), but the original Muslim community under the Prophet's leadership (and in a different way, the great age of the caliphate) was a golden age, an exemplary time that later societies will never excel but can only hope to emulate. Since Muhammad was the Seal of the Prophets and his revelations completed God's message to humankind, there will be no future prophecies and no improvements on the rightly guided life of the Prophet's community. To turn away from that model is to renounce God and to slip backward into the darkness of jahiliyya. Innovation (**bida**), in the sense of forsaking the

essential elements revealed by Muhammad and practiced in the Islamic golden age, is the slippery slope to apostasy. The early Islamic period was also an era of unequaled cohesion and expansion, a fact which reinforces the association of political success with piety and political decline with apostasy.

Because Islam has been grafted onto a variety of local cultural traditions and has spanned long periods of social change, the question has often arisen as to how far everyday practices may depart from those of the Prophet's community without subverting Islam. To compound the problem further, there is plenty of room for disagreement as to just what is authentically Islamic and what is innovative. Ordinary people in past-oriented societies have tended to project their own practices back in time, so that any custom may appear to be validated by tradition and, in the case of Muslim societies, to merge with Islam itself. The high ulema have despaired of this tendency and sporadically denounced folk practices as innovations, even though they may not always agree on what deserves this sort of condemnation. Is the seclusion of women, for example, a tenet of Islam or is it really a folk custom that departs from the practices of the Prophet and the original Muslim community? Is the veneration of the Black Stone in Mecca a central part of Muslim worship as most Muslims believe, or is it, as some purists have claimed, an example of idolatry? Islamic civilization displays an inbuilt tension over such issues of social and cultural correctness, a tension that has energized and shaped much of its political dialogue. Over the whole of Muslim history we can see cyclical periods of sociocultural "decline" followed by zealous revitalizing movements, often led by charismatic warriors under the banner of a purified Islam. While these movements were deeply intertwined with the play of secular power factions, their capacity to mobilize support often depended on their claim to cultural, and ultimately religious, authenticity.

Colonialism and Cultural Politics

The confrontation with the West has added a profound dimension to cultural politics in the Muslim Middle East. Prior to the colonial career of the

West, Christian Europe represented an external military threat and a challenge to Islam's universality. But it also reinforced the Muslim perception of the unbeliever as uncivilized and insignificant. All this was to change radically with the rapid rise of European influence, a cultural and political explosion unequaled since the expansion of early Islam. It was not until the seventeenth and eighteenth centuries that Europe, which had previously lagged behind the Middle East, decisively surpassed it technologically. By the end of the nineteenth century, however, Europe had established its power throughout the Muslim Middle East. This came as a bitter blow to a civilization that, despite occasional setbacks, had remained the most powerful and cohesive force in world politics for more than a millennium.

The relation of colonialism to economic and formal political hegemony has been discussed in previous chapters, but it is also important to consider the profound cultural meanings that colonialism had for both the colonizers and the colonized. Whatever their material motives, the colonial powers generally thought of their efforts as part of an inexorable pattern of universal progress, in which culturally advanced peoples acted as benevolent protectors and teachers of the "backward" elements of humankind. From the colonial point of view, acquiescence seemed a small price to pay for the generous tutelage of a higher culture, and those who resisted seemed obtuse and ungrateful. In recent decades, Western influence has shifted from overt political rule to various modes of cultural and economic hegemony, supported less by a conscious ideology of domination than by a set of cultural assumptions that make Western preeminence seem a natural consequence of living rationally in the modern world. The latent ethnocentrism of this neocolonialist outlook, cloaked in the seemingly neutral language of reason and modernity, can be more seductive and threatening than was the older, cruder ideology of colonial subjugation.

In addition to the effects of domination, colonialism has brought about a special set of problems with regard to sociopolitical identity. The Middle East, particularly under the Ottoman Empire, was an intricate mosaic of linguistic, regional, and religious groupings, the balance among which was disturbed by colonial intervention and the ensuing political changes. The impulse to assert local identity raised such questions as "Who are we first and foremost? Are we citizens of the Ottoman Empire, or Arabs (Turks, Persians, and so on), or Egyptians (Iraqis, and so on), or Muslims (Christians, Jews, and so on), or Shia (Sunni)?" The problem of local identities was also compounded by the drawing of modern national boundaries, most of which reflected the concerns of colonial powers rather than those of the peoples contained within—or divided by—those boundaries.

The confrontation with Europe has also posed some philosophical problems for Muslims. As mentioned above, Islam has generally looked to the past—the Islam of the Prophet and the splendor of the caliphs—to define its ideals. The post-Enlightenment Western secular world view, by contrast, embraced the idea of unlimited human progress through reason. Although the presence of a progress-oriented ideology is neither a necessary nor a sufficient condition for actual improvement of the human condition, it lent Western ascendancy a philosophic dimension that challenged orthodox Muslim thought and invited some kind of response. Muslims had to find a way of linking profound social changes with their own cultural conceptions of a golden age.

THE CONTEMPORARY POLITICS OF ISLAM

One of the most dramatic shortfalls of classic "modernization" theory was, as we have suggested, its failure to anticipate the phenomenal resurgence from the 1970s through the 1990s of Islam as a political force. In order to understand the Islamic revival, it is not enough to place it within a simplistic dichotomy of reason versus tradition; we must relate it to the specific problems of Middle Eastern societies and the diverse tactics that have been employed to address them. We have already noted the internal dynamic of Islamic civilization as it struggled to maintain political and social viability over the centuries, and the important role that religious renewal has played in this internal process. In the modern global context,

Muslim civilization must not only contend with these perennial problems of internal cohesion and growth, but also with the threat of being overwhelmed by economic, political, and cultural forces from the outside. The response to these challenges since the beginning of the last century has embraced a wide range of possibilities. Some movements or leaders have tried to align the Middle East culturally with the modern world by the wholesale adoption of Western practices and values in many areas of social life. Others have used Western ideas more selectively, aggressively asserting national identities and goals at odds with some Western interests while embracing modernizing technical and social reforms that seem to further those objectives. Still others have supported a reassertion of Middle Eastern social and religious ideals, in some cases rejecting modern social values as inimical to Islam, or at other times claiming Islam to be compatible with (or even uniquely supportive of) such modern ideas. The past two centuries have seen these diverse strategies combined in various ways to form a rich internal dialogue in the Muslim Middle East, a dialogue in which cultural values and historical symbols—both local and imported—are interpreted in conflicting ways. The Islamic revival is a part of this discourse, and it must be understood in relation to the other parts.

The phenomenon to which we refer has been variously labeled Islamic resurgence, Islamic revival, Islamic renaissance, the Islamic revolution, Islamic fundamentalism and radical Islam, among other terms. We shall use *Islamism, Islamic revival,* or *resurgent Islam* to refer to the whole spectrum of movements whose aim is to strengthen Islamic influences in political, economic, and social life. The Islamic revival is real and pervasive and raises challenges to most forms of constituted authority, whether modern bureaucratic, charismatic, democratic, or authoritarian.

Not all Islamic revivalists share the same vision. The conservative revivalist wants to see the prevailing version of Islam taken more seriously but does not envision any radically new interpretations or any purging of accepted religious practices. The Islamic fundamentalist, on the other hand, advocates a return to what is perceived as a lost purity in religious practice. This may entail not only the reimposition of the Sharia law and Koranic education but also a rejection of many locally accepted traditions of belief and ritual that do not strictly agree with the vision of a pure and uncorrupted Islam. Fundamentalists often take a dim view of cultural values and social practices originating in the West, although they may be quite accepting of technical innovation. We will employ the term *Islamic extremists* when referring to those who would use violent or coercive means to implement a fundamentalist Islamic political agenda.

While the Western press has given considerable attention to the fundamentalists, who seem to exemplify Muslim fanaticism, it has less to say about another kind of Islamic revival. Islamic **modernism** is predicated on the belief that Islam can be adapted to the circumstances of modern life without losing sight of the fundamental truths of Muhammad's revelations. In opposition to the fundamentalists, who see the Koran as a strict, literal, and unvarying prescription for righteous behavior, modernists wish to preserve the spirit and intent of Islam in a modern social context. Modernists begin with some of the same premises as the fundamentalists, including the need to cleanse Islam of accumulated human innovations that depart from the original purity and intent of God's revelations. Unlike the fundamentalists, however, the modernists locate the core of Islamic truth in its liberal ideals of justice and reason, arguing that Islam is entirely compatible with modern life—or at least, with a version of modern life that steers away from the godlessness, hedonism, social injustice, and abuse of power that they see in many developed nations. While modernism and fundamentalism can at times lead to radically different positions, they may at other times be rather difficult to distinguish. We shall illustrate some of the differences and convergences of these two positions in our discussion of sexual politics later in this chapter.

One of the ironies concerning the modernist wing of the Islamic revival is that it achieved considerable visibility long before the recent wave of fundamentalism rose to prominence. Modernist arguments were articulated in the well-known writings of Jamal al-din al-Afghani (1838–1897), who traveled widely in the Muslim world, and by his pupil Muhammad Abdu (1849–1905), whose ideas contributed to social reforms in Egypt, Turkey, and elsewhere. Islamic modernism has had a considerable following among educated and liberal-minded Muslims and still has its influential advocates. But while this kind of moderation may prevail in the end, the mildness of the modernist position does not seem to make for good political drama and news headlines or, more important, to address forcefully enough the concerns of the average Muslim in times of social upheaval. We do not suggest that the Islamic revival is entirely dominated by fundamentalists. It would be rash to say that the majority of Muslims today are fundamentalists, much less Islamic political extremists. For various reasons, however, it is the most extreme variants of Islamic resurgence that achieve a disproportionate amount of local and international visibility.

The contemporary Islamic revival springs from a number of political and historical sources. First and foremost, the movement attempts to address the current predicament of the Umma: the subjection of Islam to foreign control; the apparent falling away from simple pious faith, particularly among the urban intelligentsia and ruling elites; the Western technological challenge to time-honored social conventions; the fall of Arab and Islamic influence to an all-time low. All this can be explained as the consequence of turning away from the true and uncorrupted revelation of Islam. Implicit in the movement, then, is the expectation that a return to Islamic purity will restore the Umma to its rightful place on earth and bring Allah's beneficence once again to his people.

Prior to the Iranian revolution, none of the successful Middle Eastern political movements of the twentieth century was driven primarily by the sort of religious concerns that had remained important to the average person. The leaders of the Egyptian revolution, for instance, first seized power and only later turned their attention to the articulation of their (largely secular) principles. Baathism, despite its origin among Levantine intellectuals, was at best ambivalent in its recognition of Islam as a guiding moral force. Similar observations could be made of the Shah's White Revolution in Iran or the Turkish revolution under Ataturk. They all subordinated Islam to a broader secular framework, excluding it from the specifics of their ideology and

policy. Thus they denied the connection of Islam with political practice, thereby failing to address some basic concerns of the pious masses and neglecting a powerful source of political legitimation.

Modernization in the Middle East in the 1960s and 1970s became increasingly a program of Westernization and technological development lacking any consistent social or moral vision responsive to public sentiments. For example, in the educational systems, religious schools were replaced by secular government-controlled institutions. From the perspective of its fundamentalist critics, Westernization brought increasingly immodest dress, permissive attitudes toward sex, the consumption of alcohol, and "corrupt" entertainment, including motion pictures, television, pornography, and rock music. The growing wealth of the cities enhanced this image; as the political and social elites consumed Western products more extravagantly, the pious folk became more and more estranged from the elites of their societies.

The growth of urban wealth, concentrated in the elites, has given rise to perceptions of a widening economic gulf between the rich and the poor. Such a gulf is particularly obnoxious to the pious Muslim who takes seriously the Koranic injunctions regarding charity. The failure of elites to support a more equitable distribution of national resources has become a rallying point of revivalist Muslim opposition demanding social justice. In this setting, the Islamic resurgence draws on the radical egalitarian and democratic impulse associated with Islam in its earliest forms. Thus, a particular interpretation of values rooted in the Islamic tradition has been used to express dissatisfaction with existing patterns of social relations, and with existing political authority.

The notion of the West as a source of moral degeneracy is in some respects a reaction to the humiliating colonial doctrines of Western cultural superiority, but it is also moved by specific opposition to certain Western-inspired social trends. The Islamic revival often calls for the rejection and expelling of Western influences depicted as "Satanic" in origin. During the Cold War many proponents of Islamic revival professed to see little difference between the social systems of capitalism and communism, a view adopted by some secular Middle Eastern leaders as well.

The existing tension between the worldviews of Muslim fundamentalists and Western modernists found a fine focus in the controversy that followed the 1988 publication in England of Salman Rushdie's *The Satanic Verses,* a novel that includes in its narrative a thinly disguised interpretation of Muhammad's revelation. The novel, although strongly critical of the moral decay and racism of colonialism and the modern Western societies, also contains material relating to Islam that many religious authorities, particularly in the Shia clergy, found overtly blasphemous. On this basis, Iran's Ayatollah Khomeini pronounced a sentence of death on Rushdie and announced a bounty of $5 million for whoever carried it out.

Western governments were initially incredulous at this and ultimately were outraged. Muted criticism of the decision was also heard from the less fundamentalist Sunni ulema, suggesting that the Islamic world did not universally share this judgment. Nonetheless, most other countries with substantial Muslim populations banned the book, if only to head off communal conflict (a major consideration in India's decision). The author condemned the censorship, expressing surprise over the reaction and protesting that he only wanted to present a "secular humanist view of the creation of a religion."

That such a view would be unacceptable to anyone believing in divine revelation seems obvious. But whatever the author's intent or readers' judgments, the controversy has expressed forcefully the divergent assumptions upon which we predicate our views of the world. Even within the Muslim world there has been evidence of differing views, and some Muslims have defended the author's freedom of expression despite the book's offensiveness to them. Nevertheless, many years after the publication of his controversial book, Rushdie has reentered public life, although cautiously.

Groups espousing an Islamic revival gained political power in Iran, Sudan, Libya, Afghanistan, Pakistan, and, arguably, Turkey. They contended for power in Lebanon, Morocco, and Algeria, and they figure in the politics of every Middle Eastern nation. They are actively, if irregularly, advocating the inclusion of Islam in government or even promoting an Islamic Republic in which the Sharia would be established as the law of the land. Their progress has been uneven to date, and the obstacles to their programs are serious. These experiences notwithstanding, such movements have gained in strength over the past three decades. At the same time, there are signs that the coming years may see a gradual revitalization of modernist Islam.

The phenomenon of Islamic revivalism cannot be treated in isolation from the larger dialogue of which it is part. This dialogue includes not only religious issues but also the problems of cultural identity, the challenge of serious moral, social, and economic problems, and the quest for collective self-esteem and self-direction. The resulting discourse brings up diverse and often conflicting perspectives from which to address the challenges of a changing world. The examples of Turkey, Egypt, Saudi Arabia, and Iran illustrate some of the complex forms this dialogue has taken.

TURKEY: RADICAL WESTERNIZATION AND THE DURABILITY OF ISLAM

Turkey's unique historical circumstances have placed it in an ambiguous position with regard to Western Europe. At the height of the Ottoman Empire, Turkey functioned as a frontier state that directly confronted, and at times threatened, the Christian West. Europe itself was regarded as a less-accomplished civilization, and Christian Europeans were among the subject peoples within the Empire. At the same time, Turkey's proximity and long commercial association with the West, its cultural distinctiveness from other Muslim peoples, and its political strength compared with other Middle Eastern nations in the colonial period, allowed for an exceptional policy toward the West. No other Muslim nation has so explicitly committed itself to the project of cultural Westernization, and Turkey's experience reveals the limits of a Westernizing strategy.

The Tanzimat reforms of 1839–1876 (see Chapter 4) were aimed not at fundamentally changing Turkish culture or society but at strengthening its military and government structures. Nevertheless, these reforms helped to shape the attitudes of a generation of middle-level government officials with strong sympathies toward Western humanitarian and libertarian ideals. The liberalizing trend found strong expression in the Young Ottoman movement of the 1860s. Far from leading to an acceptance of colonialism, liberal ideals were linked with the project of casting off foreign control and pursuing the sort of self-determination achieved by the European nation-states. Thus, the liberals viewed with extreme distrust the sort of Westernizing elites who collaborated in European domination. The liberal movement emphasized the potential contributions of Turkish national culture to modern life; for example, the florescent Turkish literature of the time emphasized a more colloquial language and democratic idiom than the classical forms, and expressed the ideals of the liberal intelligentsia. In this setting flourished a modernist interpretation of Islam that located the core of Islamic tradition in its liberal values. According to this interpretation, Islam's pure monotheism, its commitment to freedom and social justice, and its opposition to superstition make it the most rational of world religions and therefore the most compatible with modern life. Such an interpretation not only validated Islam, but it suggested that the reversal of fortunes lately suffered by the Muslim world might only be temporary. It gave a traditionalist mandate for rooting out, in the name of a purified (that is, rationalist) Islam, the "superstitions" and customary practices associated with Islam by the common folk and the conservative ulema.

During the period of 1876 to 1909, modernizing changes continued, not under the auspices of liberalism but under the authoritarian rule of Sultan Abdulhamit, who suspended the recently adopted constitution and ruled by means of a despotic police state. Abdulhamit's use of religious legitimation was different from that of the Young Ottomans. Initially appealing to the conservative ulema against the liberal modernists, he soon turned to a new brand of pan-Islamism, pressing his claim (contrary to existing Islamic interpretation) as "caliph," not in the restricted capacity of overseer of the Sharia and the Muslim community but as political ruler of an Islamic empire. Abdulhamit's project of building a Hijaz railway

to carry pilgrims to Mecca, symbolic of his attempt to unify the Umma, drew material support from Muslims the world over. Despite his restrictions on freedom of expression, he continued to develop modern schools, build literacy, and promote Western science and technicalization.

The Young Turks rebellion of 1908, which restored the constitution and eventually forced Abdulhamit from power, had to face anew the confusing question of Turkey's identity. Should Turks align themselves with the Muslim world or with Europe? Should they form a Turkish nation based on a common language and culture, or unite with other Muslims under the banner of pan-Islamism, or try to maintain control over a religiously diverse Ottoman realm, even as Christian and other fragments of that Empire seemed intent on going their own way? Military conflicts over territory gave the Young Turks little respite, and events connected with the First World War soon put an end to the Ottoman Empire and, very nearly, to Turkey itself. Turkey struggled for its very life, and Mustafa Kemal, who emerged in the 1920s as the hero of that struggle and "father" of the Turks ("Ataturk"), was in a uniquely powerful position to make sweeping changes in Turkish society.

Ataturk's vision of the Turkish nation was influenced by European nationalist romanticism by way of the Turkish social theorist Ziya Gok-Alp. Arguing against the pan-Islamic and pan-Ottoman ideologies popular at the beginning of the century, Gok-Alp had promulgated a vision of a strictly Turkish, Westernized nation-state. Humankind, he argued, is naturally divided into "nations," each marked by a distinctive language, culture, and folk "spirit." Thus, Turkey could adopt whatever outward forms of government and elite culture were most progressive at the time without compromising its immutable national character; the ascendant Western cultural forms could serve Turkish development as a world power in the twentieth century, just as the Persian-Arabic civilization had served the purpose centuries earlier. Gok-Alp adopted a liberal modernist view of Islam, arguing for its place in Turkish national culture but not in a capacity that would damage Turkey's aspirations as a modern Westernized state.

This vision of Turkey as a modern state in the Western mold was resolutely implemented by Ataturk. In a series of measures from the middle to the late 1920s, Islam was disestablished as a state religion: Sufi orders were officially abolished and their property seized by the government; the madrasah schools were closed and the state-sponsored training of the ulema came to an end; Sharia law was replaced in its official capacity by a slightly modified version of the Swiss personal law. The interplay of symbolic and pragmatic elements is dramatically evident in certain of Ataturk's policies. In 1928 he abolished the use of Arabic script, decreeing that Turkish must be written with occidental letters; this was not only a symbolic alignment with Western culture, but in practical terms it cut succeeding generations off from the literary heritage of Ottoman civilization. Similarly, the purging of Persian and Arabic elements from the Turkish language celebrated the language of the ordinary Turkish people at the expense of the classical Persian-Arabic high culture. (When non-Turkish roots were necessary, preference was often given to Latin and French.) The Muslim call to prayer, heard the world over in Arabic, was changed to Turkish.

Perhaps Ataturk's most deeply symbolic political gesture—and the one that prompted the most riots—was the 1925 ruling that adopted the Western brimmed hat and outlawed the fez and all other brimless headgear. The various hats, caps, and turbans had distinguished the many traditional ethnic groups, religious orders, and statuses within the Islamic community while serving the common practical function of allowing believers to touch forehead to ground during the performance of Muslim prayer. Thus, as Hodgson observes, Ataturk's policy

served . . . several functions at once. It symbolized the rejection of the Perso-Arabic and the adoption of the Western heritage (in itself the brimmed hat was not particularly modern—for instance, it was not particularly efficient—but it was very explicitly Occidental). More substantively, it [abolished] for the whole population the old distinctions of status which headdress had marked and which were incompatible with the interchangeable homogeneity which a modern nation-state presupposes; and it particularly re-

duced the visibility of those religious classes whose prestige and influence Kemal had to eliminate if the secular Republic were to survive. Finally, it served as a psychological coup. Even in language, "the hatted man" had meant a European, and "to put on a hat" had, as a phrase, meant "to Europeanize"—that is, "to desert Islam, or the state" (which came to the same). Kemal was demanding, in effect, that every Turkish man own himself a traitor to all that the Ottoman state had stood for. It was one of those blows which forces people to come to an inner decision: either they must resist now, or acknowledge defeat and henceforth hold their peace. Those most so minded did resist and were crushed; the rest now had overtly to admit Kemal's authority, if not his wisdom, and found themselves implicitly committed to whatever more might be implied in Westernization.

Ataturk's policies helped to strengthen Turkey's educational system and its industrial economy, as well as to promote economic and social reforms associated with modernizing societies. Turkey has moved toward a closer association with the West, but the movement has not been as all-encompassing as Ataturk might have envisioned. His policies themselves departed so radically from popular sentiments that he could ill afford to promote the kind of political freedoms that might have brought Turkey closer to the political ethos of the West. And despite his veneration of the common people, Ataturk's policies went against the current of popular religious commitments.

The Kemalists never intended to abolish Islam but rather to guide it toward a more personal, rationalized, Westernized form similar to Protestantism. To some degree, however, the closing of the madrasahs had the contrary effect of reducing the influence of educated (and modernist) ulema and promoting more folk-oriented versions of Islam. Despite the Kemalist ideas taught in the school systems, local imams continued to compete for the loyalty of most villagers. Sufism, far from being crippled by the dismantling of the tariqahs, was somewhat purified by it and flourished at the grass-roots level. The growth of

---

[2]Marshall G. S. Hodgson, *The Venture of Islam*, Vol. 3 (Chicago: University of Chicago Press, 1974), pp. 264–265.

religious freedom after the Second World War saw the return of formal religious training and of the tariqahs, and in this atmosphere some factions became openly dedicated to undoing Ataturk's policies.

Turkey today, while still officially adhering to the fundamentals of Kemalism, is characterized by a wide array of positions on Islam and Westernization, from secularism and Islamic modernism to fundamentalism aimed at reestablishing Sharia law. In the 1995 national elections the Islamist Refah ("welfare") party made significant gains, suggesting that, in some broad sense, the Islamists were in a position to move forward toward their goal of enhancing the influence of Islam in Turkish state politics and law. The reemergence of Islam in Turkish national politics stands as a testimony to the durability of Islam.

EGYPT: THE LABYRINTH OF POSSIBILITIES

Egypt's brush with French colonization at the beginning of the nineteenth century dramatized its need for an effective strategy of self-definition and self-determination. Its unique position in the Middle East suggested a number of particular qualities, needs, and possibilities. Egypt possessed an ancient pre-Islamic urban and agrarian heritage, and its long history of urban culture had helped it to become one of the premier centers of learning and culture in the Islamic world; al-Azhar in Cairo was the recognized center of Sharia scholarship. Located at the fringes of Ottoman control, Egypt was semi-independent and a ripe target for European colonization. During the nineteenth century the European powers, particularly Britain, established a strong social, political, and economic hegemony in Egypt that fell just short of outright colonial rule and that was to last until the middle of the twentieth century. At the same time, Egypt could and sometimes did define itself as a legitimately Western nation, pointing to its active role in the classical Greek and Roman world at a time when Western Europe was still at or beyond the periphery of Western civilization.

In the first half of the nineteenth century, Muhammad Ali tried to bring Egypt into the modern world on a basis of cultural and material strength. His program of selective assimilation stressed military technicalization, economic development, and modern forms of education and government. Even at this early date, rural Islamic-oriented resistance to these modernizing changes posed a significant challenge, leading Muhammad Ali to attempt control of the Sufi orders by manipulating and coopting their leadership.

Islam, however, was not simply a conservative force. The Persian scholar Jamal al-din al-Afghani (1838–1897) traveled throughout the Muslim world, including Egypt, promoting ideas foundational to much of twentieth-century pan-Islamic, Islamic nationalist, and Islamic modernist thought. Like other restorers of the faith, he held that Muslims should return to the example set by the first caliphs and the early Muslim community. At the core of al-Afghani's teaching was the natural affinity of Islam with science and reason, the unity of the Umma as against local and ethnic loyalties, and the need for a unifying political leadership modeled on the pious early caliphs.

His student Muhammad Abdu (1849–1905) became the chief religious authority of Egypt and a seminal spokesman for Islamic modernism as a model for Egyptian sociocultural development. Like al-Afghani, he rejected the wholesale adoption of Western ideas in principle, preferring instead to use the disciplined methods of reasoning developed by certain prestigious early Islamic scholars, and employing established ideas from Sharia interpretation such as the principle of *maslahah* (preservation of the public welfare). He saw reason as given by God to protect humankind from either excess or adulteration in religion. Abdu placed more emphasis than did the Persian al-Afghani on the glories of classical Arab civilization and on Egypt as an exemplar of Arab culture. But like al-Afghani, he saw Islam as providing a superior basis for social justice, moral cohesion, and intellectual progress—a vehicle for outdoing Europe even in the areas of its greatest strength, while at the same time retaining the moral-religious virtues of Islamic civilization and the full benefit of local cultural integrity.

Some of Abdu's scholarly disciples interpreted his ideas of *salafiyya,* or the true wisdom of the pious ancestors, in a manner sympathetic to the conservative Muwahhidun (Wahhabi) movement of Saudi Arabia. But for the majority of the urban middle and upper classes, a loose interpretation of Islamic modernism became a license to adopt secular and Western ideas at their convenience without the stigma of religious apostasy. This is not to say that Islamic modernism eliminated the role of Islam either as a personally meaningful element or as a symbol of Egyptian identity. Nor did it make conflicts over cultural identity any less troublesome. While foreign-sponsored schools taught European ideas in European languages, a native flowering of Arabic literature struggled to reconcile the vastly different worlds of classical Arabic language and literary forms, the local Arabic vernacular and popular literary culture of the Egyptians, and the foreign literary genres which expressed "modern" individualistic conceptions of the self. Meanwhile, the discovery of the tomb of King Tutankhamen in 1922 renewed a popular interest in the glories of pre-Islamic Egypt that coexisted uneasily with the sentiments of either Arabism or Islamic renewal. In short, Egyptians faced a bewildering smorgasbord of different, and partly incompatible, cultural symbols and identities.

The first half of this century saw a growth of specific social problems besides those of economic and political self-determination referred to in previous chapters. Social changes were creating new sources of discontent, including, for example, uncontrolled population growth, urban migration that greatly outstripped economic development and resulted in endemic unemployment, and a highly unequal distribution of land, capital, and other social resources. The effect of growing inequality was worsened by the breakup of communal village holdings and a weakening of familial and other networks of support for the destitute. These structural problems were accompanied by the growing prominence of films, popular songs, and sundry entertainments that, according to their critics, extolled individualism, romantic love, and other harbingers of hedonist immorality.

Although Gamal Adbel Nasser rose to power in 1952 by seizing a political opportunity, he became the first Egyptian leader in many decades to develop doctrines addressing a broad spectrum of his country's social problems. Eschewing the "borrowed ideologies" of the capitalist West and the communist bloc, he employed Islamic slogans and vocabulary in support of policies whose ultimate objectives were essentially secular. Nasser's ambition to bring the Arab world together under Egyptian leadership was based on a doctrine of Arab nationalism, which promoted the idea of a single Arab nation united by language, culture, and historical achievements. (Arab nationalism gained by its representation of Israel as a Western colonial settler state, and of the Palestinian cause as a symbolic rallying point for Arab resistance to foreign domination.) The pursuit of social equality in the form of "Arab Socialism," oriented toward state control of the means of production and redistribution of income and land holdings, was linked with Islamic concepts of equity, the care of the needy through zakat (alms), and the ideal of the unity and common good of the Umma. Nasser reformed the great mosque school of al-Azhar to resemble more closely a modern university, and he persuaded the high ulema to issue religious decrees, or fatwas, in support of such government policies as birth control. Islamic organizations and publications were organized and sponsored by the Nasser government to legitimize official policies at home and abroad. Although Nasser did much to reintroduce Islam into Egypt's political rhetoric, its use was selective and was essentially a means to other ends. By this time, however, a far more serious movement for the Islamic redemption of Egyptian society had been gathering strength at the grass roots.

The Muslim Brotherhood was founded in 1928 as a Muslim young men's association promoting personal piety, but by the 1940s it had become a radical, sometimes violent, political faction highly critical of Egyptian government, society, and culture. Drawing its membership largely from the ranks of educated and professional people—traders, teachers, engineers, and the like—it advocated the restoration of Islamic law and government as an antidote to the decadence it saw everywhere in Egyptian life. Sayyid Qutb, a modernist literary critic whose two years in America had helped to turn him against Western lifestyles and modes of thought, led the Brotherhood through some of its most radical years until his execution in 1966. At first sympathetic to Nasser and the Young Officers, the Brotherhood soon parted ways with the government on a variety of issues.

Like the modernists, the Muslim Brotherhood sought a return to the roots of Islam in order to create a more just and decent society, hoping to reopen the process of *ijtihad* (Sharia interpretation) and reapply the values of the past to the problems of the present. But the Brotherhood's vision of Islamic values drew on different traditions of Sharia interpretation, resulting in a fundamentalist ideology that contrasted starkly with the liberal-rationalist Islam of the modernists. They opposed Western-style democracy and Marxism alike as incompatible with Sharia rule, questioned the teaching of Western philosophy and modernist Islam in the schools, and opposed the formal separation of religion from government. They had less tolerance than the modernists for religious minorities, Sufism, or folk religious practices. They targeted for criticism a broad array of "anti-Islamic" values and decadent practices that they associated with modern life—from exploitation, domination, materialism, and bank interest to "entertainment," consumerism, romantic song lyrics, popular women singers, mixing of the sexes, and birth control. While they opposed Nasser's Arabism as an anti-Islamic attempt to draw distinctions within the Umma, they nevertheless criticized the lack of attention to classical Arabic—the language of the Koran and of high Islamic culture—in the schools and media. Where Abdu and the modernists had chided the ulema's hidebound conservatism, Qutb's Muslim Brotherhood attacked them for their timidity in defending Islamic traditions.

So vehement was the Muslim Brothers' opposition to the Nasser government that they considered resistance to it a higher cause than the struggle against Israel. In the political rhetoric of the Brotherhood, Nasser was equated with every enemy of Islam from Crusaders, Jews, and Mongols to Turkey's Kemal Ataturk. Almost from the beginning, the Brotherhood was divided between those (including Qutb) who shunned violence and those who were willing to use assassination and other forms of terror. The latter gave the government an excuse for suppressing the Brotherhood by force.

Both the Brotherhood and the establishment used symbols and concepts from Islamic history to revile one another. Qutb drew on the writings of a prestigious medieval Islamic thinker, Ibn Taymiyya, to press the argument that any Islamic leader who fails to apply a significant part of the Sharia has thereby abandoned Islam. The Brotherhood equated the state of Egyptian society with jahiliyya, the period of utter wickedness before the coming of Islam. The pro-Nasser faction, speaking through sympathetic ulema, countered that the concept of jahiliyya properly applies only to a specific historical time, and reversed the charges of apostasy by labeling the militants as *Kharijites* (the fanatical sect which, claiming "sinners" to be outside the Umma, assassinated the prophet's son-in-law Ali), thus contending that it was actually they who had left the Umma.

After Nasser's death the fundamentalists were at first encouraged by Anwar Sadat's apparent interest in Islam. Sadat began and ended his speeches with Muslim benedictions, he declared the Sharia as the basis of all legislation (a matter more of labeling than of substantive reform), and during the 1973 "Ramadan" war against Israel (code-named "Badr" after one of the Prophet's famous victories) he employed the Muslim battle cry "Allahu Akbar" ("God is great"). He encouraged Muslim student associations in order to combat residual Nasserite Arab socialism. But Sadat wanted it both ways, declaring the separation of religion and government and instituting in 1979 family laws that liberalized women's rights in divorce, alimony, and child custody. His assassination by Jihad, a militant army cell including some former members of the Muslim Brotherhood, was a sobering lesson for Sadat's successor Hosni Mubarak.

The Muslim Brothers were as much a factor in the 1990s as in Nasser's time. The 1980s saw the growth of widespread popular interest in various forms and degrees of Islamic revival. The vast majority of Egyptians in all walks of life continue to be devout Muslims, and the visible expressions of that faith became more evident during the decade following the Iranian revolution. Muslim student associations earnestly promoted Islamic morality, politicians debated whether Egyptian laws are in keeping with the Sharia, and television shifted away from such fare as *Dallas* toward a greater emphasis on religious programs. Attendance at mosques increased. Merchants and bureaucrats were more likely to interrupt official business for daily prayers. The government, responding to both international and domestic Muslim pressures, prohibited the sale or consumption of alcohol except to non-Muslim foreigners. A movement toward quasi-traditional forms of Islamic dress, especially for women, not only symbolized an interest in Muslim norms of sexual modesty but also asserted local resistance to Western fashions and subdued the display of differences in wealth and social status. Bearded men and veiled women were more often seen in the streets of Cairo. The label "imported ideas" became a common expression of disapproval, and rationalist interpretations of Islam were often stigmatized as irreligious innovations (*bida*). Despite recent signs of a liberal reaction, the symbols of Islamic resurgence mentioned above are no longer the exclusive province of radical fundamentalism but are often associated with popular, middle-of-the-road conservatism.

While the Muslim Brothers are still censured by the government, their influence and affiliation reach into the officially tolerated Islamist Center party on one end of the spectrum. At the other end of the political spectrum they may have connections with the radical fringe of extremist groups inclined toward violence against the Christian Copts, foreign tourists, and others seen as enemies of the faith. The Egyptian government has, in turn, singled these groups out for harshly repressive countermeasures that have drawn criticism from international human rights observers. It is not easy to predict with any confidence what path Egyptian society may find through this labyrinth of conflicting factions, visions, and possibilities.

A number of social forces have conspired to encourage cultural nativism and religious conservatism in modern Egypt: a succession of modernizing leaders who underestimated the importance of popular religious sentiments; the failure of modernizing secular policies to deal with internal social and economic problems; the humiliating defeat by Israel in the 1967 war, interpreted by some Muslims as a divine punishment;

the example of the 1979 Iranian Revolution; the long-standing presence of a minority Christian community; cultural strains caused by tourism; pressure from Saudi Arabia to adopt stricter laws as a condition for aid; the example of Sadat's assassination; the increasingly dangerous cauldron of Islamic political extremism in the Sudan; the critique by Third World intellectuals of Western cultural domination; perhaps even the West's own disaffection with some aspects of modern life.

Egypt illustrates many of the diverse cultural issues and possibilities facing modern Muslim nations. Although the interpretation of cultural tradition lends itself to manifold possibilities, it is no longer prudent for political leaders to ignore popular religious and cultural values on the assumption that they will soon fall before the juggernaut of secular Western ideas. Not surprisingly, President Mubarak's public policies and personal lifestyle show an appreciation of the importance of religious and cultural symbolism in contemporary Egypt.

SAUDI ARABIA: AN ISLAMIC CAMELOT?

It is hard to imagine a nation commanding more of the symbols of Islamic legitimacy than does Saudi Arabia. Its roots lie in an Islamic purification movement begun by Muhammad ibn Abd al-Wahhab in the mid-eighteenth century and carried forward by the Saudi family, which unified the present nation in 1932 under the leadership of Abdulaziz ibn Saud (1879–1953). Inspired by the strict Hanbali school of Sharia law, ibn Wahhab's teachings (whose adherents prefer the designation "Muwahhidun" [unitarian] over the popular term "Wahhabi") embraced a puritanical version of Islam that today forms the core of Saudi Arabia's religion, politics, society, and culture. Saudi Arabia is formally dedicated to the ideal of jihad, or struggle on behalf of the faith: Its flag displays the shahada (declaration of faith) and a sword.

Saudi Arabia had from the beginning what many Muslim fundamentalists elsewhere still struggle for: the Sharia as virtually the sole law of the land. When King Khalid ascended to the throne in 1975 he reaffirmed that "Islamic law is and will remain our standard, our source of inspiration, and our goal." (His homage to the Sharia was astute, since the consent of the ulema is needed for all transfers of power and was instrumental in the deposition of the dissolute King Saud in 1964.) Lawyers are scarce in Saudi Arabia, for Sharia religious courts decide all legal cases excepting certain commercial actions and suits against the state (the latter are adjudicated by appointees of the royal family). This stern interpretation of the Hanbali legal code, with its provisions for beheadings and amputations, has become for most Westerners (and for many non-Saudi fundamentalists) a vivid symbol of zealous Islamic justice.

American troops stationed in Saudi Arabia during the 1991 Persian Gulf conflict were surprised at the strictness of Saudi social norms. Saudi women wear full facial veils in public; non-Saudi and even non-Muslim foreign women may be publicly upbraided for failing to cover their hair. Men too must dress modestly and could never, for example, appear in public wearing tank-tops or shorts. The ubiquitous semiofficial "religious police" patrol the streets ready to rap the exposed ankles of immodestly dressed women, to ensure that shops are closed promptly at prayer times, to enforce the fast of Ramadan, and generally to scold or even detain persons behaving in a manner that strikes them as un-Islamic. Mingling of the sexes in public is considered inappropriate, schools and universities are segregated, and even foreigners caught in the company of women who are not their spouses may find themselves in trouble. Possession of alcohol is a serious criminal offense. American forces in Saudi Arabia during the Persian Gulf War were obliged to rename chaplains "spiritual advisors," avoid wearing their religious insignia, and go through the motions of concealing the nature of Christian and Jewish religious services (ironically, the "enemy" regime in Iraq not only tolerated but even subsidized Christian worship).

Saudi Arabia is unique among Muslim nations in being the birthplace of the Prophet and the site of Islam's holiest places. The Saudi royal family makes much of this; King Fahd has the official title "Guardian of the Two Holy Mosques" (Mecca and Medina). The government has gone to great lengths to provide facilities and services for pilgrims during the hajj, and the royal family may be seen participating in the yearly ritual cleansing of Mecca's holiest shrine, the Kaaba.

In many respects, then, Saudi Arabia might appear to be an Islamic fundamentalist's Camelot, confidently enforcing strict Islamic norms while occupying a place of privilege in Muslim ritual and history and wielding the power of a premier oil-producing state. But beneath this apparent self-assurance one detects a certain precariousness and insecurity in the position of the Saudi elites. So far, the regime has been reasonably successful at pursuing three potentially incompatible goals: (1) the maintenance of a credibly devout Islamicism safe from fundamentalist challenges, although the success of Al-Qaeda in recruiting Saudi nationals is disconcerting; (2) the pursuit of a permanent place in the modern global economy; and (3) the preservation of the Saudi monarchy. The third element, Saudi rule, is important not only from the viewpoint of elite self-interest but because it has so far tried to head off a direct collision between the first two aims. However, the strategies used so far to reconcile these diverse ideals could eventually shatter along the fault lines of inherent contradictions and double-edged political tactics.

The Prophet Muhammad is reported to have said, "The princes will corrupt the earth, so one of my people will be sent to bring back justice." In November of 1979, on the first day of the Muslim year 1400, several hundred followers of a man who claimed to be the Muslim deliverer, or Mahdi, produced weapons from under their cloaks and seized the Grand Mosque at Mecca. Securing the permission of the ulema, Saudi forces retook the mosque after many days of combat during which more than 200 soldiers, hostages, and rebels, along with their family members, lost their lives. Most of the rebels were Saudis, some of whom were driven by old political grievances with the government. But their stated complaints had to do with the erosion of religion and the breakdown of morals in the kingdom, as evidenced by working women, Western entertainments, the surreptitious consumption of alcohol, and so forth. At the root of their protest were issues of religious purity,

Western influence, and the alleged moral corruption of the Saudi rulers. While the Saudi populace and the Muslim world were appalled at the audacity of these rebels, their claims resulted in a number of symbolic gestures toward increased moral strictness. The incident dramatized before a world audience the vulnerability of Saudi prestige.

The Saudi public takes a certain pride in its royal family, for it symbolizes the lofty, independent spirit of a people who have never submitted to foreign rule, as well as the immense progress that the nation has made from the isolation and poverty of only a generation ago. At the same time, however, the notion of monarchy is not in strict accordance with Koranic ideals of equality before God, nor is it in keeping with the contemporary fundamentalist preference for rule by popularly chosen religious experts. Thus, the monarchy is at pains to show that its rule is dedicated not to its own aggrandizement but to the welfare of the Umma. However, the huge influx of oil wealth in the past few decades has enabled the royal family (which has thousands of recognized members) to lead lives of privilege and self-indulgence, provoking criticism throughout the Muslim world, especially among the poor and the devout. The display of privilege and materialism is not only unseemly, it is unjust and un-Islamic. On the other hand, the Saudi rulers make an important ritual gesture toward traditional modes of public access by holding royal audiences where the humblest citizens can bring their troubles to be adjudicated.

Not all the problems facing the house of Saud involve questions of lifestyle; some have to do with conflicting requirements of the society. For example, the Saudi government has declared that the Saudi educational system is, above all, Islamic in its intent. However, another important goal of the Saudi state is to establish an economy that can continue to develop and be self-sufficient without dependence on the single, exhaustible resource of petroleum exports. In doing so it must emphasize high-tech industry, communications, and international commerce, for which a religiously-oriented educational system is not particularly well suited. Thus the Saudi universities must place religious goals in the background if they are to compete with the best Western institutions (where many Saudi royalty are still educated), but to turn away from traditional educational goals is to incur the wrath of religious critics.

Saudis are sometimes led to inconvenient or inconsistent practices by the contradictions of a society that is highly technicalized in some ways but that hopes not to compromise moral norms developed in a very different social context. Because women are not allowed to drive, for example, a male professional might have to leave work and take his wife or child to the doctor (or entrust them to a chauffeur, who is usually a foreigner, and sometimes an infidel). While alcohol is legally forbidden, it is a mark of prestige and hospitality among certain affluent, cosmopolitan Saudis to offer a guest fine Scotch whiskey worth hundreds of dollars a bottle on the black market. This nation of great affluence and sophisticated information technology submits every imported videotape to rigid censorship; the Muppets do not qualify because one of the characters is a pig. Trivial enough in themselves, these examples point to the coexistence of very different social values within a single system. All societies involve significant contradictions; whether those in Saudi society will continue in their present form, or resolve themselves in some particular direction, only time will tell.

Saudi relations with the United States pose something of a dilemma for the Saudi leadership. Islamists of the past few decades have been adamant in their opposition to communism, but the United States is equally disliked in some circles, not only because of its power and its secular materialism but also for its role as Israel's closest ally. Saudi Arabia's educational, commercial, and military security needs—to say nothing of its prestige in the West—are well served by friendship with America. Yet the social policies required to promote one's image in the United States are sometimes the opposite of those needed for a nation aspiring to Islamic legitimacy, and any concessions to foreign influence are certain to arouse fundamentalist antagonism. Even as American troops went into battle in the Gulf War defending Saudi interests, religious fundamentalists abused Saudi women's rights advocates by calling them "American sympathizers." The latent cultural tensions that surfaced during the Gulf War may continue to complicate the Saudi government's difficult task of reconciling its American connections with Islamic legitimacy, a problem dramatized by a November 1995 attack by Saudi extremists on an American military training mission in Riyadh.

The issue of Saudi Arabia's image in the West was highlighted by its official opposition to the 1980 British-produced television documentary *The Death of a Princess*. Broadcast in the United States and Britain, the program dealt—somewhat loosely, its critics say—with the execution of an adulterous Saudi princess and her commoner lover. The program, which the Saudis tried to prevent from airing, outraged Saudi honor by making public the shame of the royal family and by going so far as to suggest that Saudi princesses cruised the desert in limousines looking for sex. Whatever its factual basis, the "documentary" reveled in Western stereotypes of Islamic justice and Saudi extremism. In the end, some stations chose not to air the show and others followed it with a panel discussion including Arab (but not Saudi) speakers. Although the program reached only a small audience, the incident suggests the degree to which even conservative Muslim nations are sensitive to the way they are perceived elsewhere in the modern global village.

Saudi prestige in the West took a substantial drop in the aftermath of the attack on the World Trade Center in New York in 2001. Saudi Arabia was criticized both for the large number of its citizens involved in the attack (fifteen of the nineteen involved) and for tolerating Islamic extremism among its ulema and religious institutions. The government responded with an ambitious public relations campaign designed to rehabilitate Saudi Arabia's public image in the West and the United States in particular.

There seems to be a growing worldwide consensus on human rights and essential freedoms (even though many nations prefer to make exceptions in their own cases), and international prestige and internal order appear to be increasingly linked to these criteria. However, the rights and freedoms widely accepted in the modern world may not always be compatible with the demands of the Muslim conservatives and fundamentalists whose opposition the Saudi government wishes to avoid.

For example, the country's Shia minority is economically and politically underprivileged—and ripe for agitation from Saudi's archrival, the revolutionary Islamic government of Iran. Several disturbances have already occurred, including one indirectly related to the Grand Mosque incident of 1979. But for the Saudi government to assuage Shia demands for improved rights and economic conditions would be to inflame Sunni fundamentalist sentiments of the sort that provoked the Mosque takeover. Indeed, any move toward equal rights for women and religious minorities, freedom of worship, or certain other rights recognized in the West and elsewhere is likely to incite radical Islamic opposition that could conceivably unseat the government. Having taken the road of Islamic legitimation, Saudi Arabia has not only tapped a powerful force in its favor, but it has also limited some of its political options.

Saudi Arabia's self-cultivated role of world Islamic leadership also poses serious challenges and problems that partially offset the rewards of prestige. While the guardianship of the holy places gives the Saudi regime a high religious standing, it also puts it under the burden of maintaining the ritual purity of Saudi soil; the presence of American troops during the Gulf conflict was seen by some purists as a desecration. And while the exposure of pilgrims to Saudi Islam may sometimes help promote it as the normative model for world Islam, interregional contact during the hajj also keeps alive the dialogue of diverse possibilities for Islamic culture. Saudi Arabia's sponsorship of countless international Islamic conferences has had a similar effect, bringing forth both liberal and ultrafundamentalist perspectives potentially critical of Saudi practices.

The Saudi Arabian ulema, like the royal family, are in a delicate position. While they enjoy exceptional power in government and the courts, their cooptation by the monarchy has led them to relinquish much of the oppositional function historically exercised by the ulema in Muslim society. Should they become too closely allied with the ruling elite, they could lose their credibility among the more stringent Muslim factions, and with it their usefulness to the monarchy. On the other hand, if they express too much opposition to government policies, they could find their influence in government diminished. Saudi monarchs have already shown a willingness to circumvent conservative ulema with rulings designed to win international credibility, as when King Faisal mollified President Kennedy by abolishing slavery and permitting television in private Saudi homes.

The Gulf War drew international attention to Saudi Arabia, its social and political order, its political restrictions, and its dissenters. In March of 1992, after years of lobbying from a coalition of Saudi liberals and religious conservatives, King Fahd announced the formation of a long-promised *Majlis Asshura,* or consultative council. Accompanying the announcement was a carefully worded decree spelling out the regime's doctrines of political legitimacy and answering a number of implicit questions about Saudi rule. It asserts that the announced changes are not innovations, but simply the continuation in a new form of religiously mandated practices that have always existed in the kingdom. The principle of "mutual consultation," which is mentioned in the Koran, is said to have been present all along in various arrangements for consultation with the ulema. The decree also pledges to "ensure the rights of individuals and their freedom and refrain from any action that will affect these rights and freedoms except within the limits stipulated in the laws and regulations." Protection of property and freedom from illegal search, arrest, or imprisonment are affirmed. Concerning the monarchy, the decree states that the Sharia "identifies the nature of the state, its goals and responsibilities, as well as the relationship between the ruler and the subjects." The king notes that this relationship is based on "fraternity, justice, mutual respect, and loyalty," and that "there is no difference between a ruler and a subject. All are equal before the divine laws of Allah." Above all, the decree declares unequivocally that the Sharia is the law of the Saudi state, and that "the Kingdom's constitution is the Holy Qur'an and the Sunnah (sayings) of the Prophet."

King Fahd's astute attempts to clarify the basis of Saudi political legitimacy show a keen understanding of political forces, but not everyone will be satisfied. Because the council is appointed by the ruling family rather than elected, and would therefore place no real limitations on royal authority, it falls short of the hopes of either the liberals or the conservatives. Each of these groups favors popular election and freedom of speech, but this apparent agreement of goals may conceal deeper divisions that could surface if the base of participation broadens. The recent experience of Algeria shows that religious extremists may envision democracy and freedom of speech as a means rather than an end, employing them to establish a strict reign of religious and cultural authoritarianism. An opening up of Saudi political processes may reveal a deep rift between the long-term objectives of the fundamentalist and the liberal wings of the opposition. The liberals, for example, might see reform as leading to greater rights for women and the Shia minorities, while religious conservatives might envision democracy as a process of installing pious ulema who would protect the community from just such changes.

By commanding Islamic symbols of legitimacy so effectively, Saudi Arabia's elites have managed to forestall many of the complex debates and issues that have troubled Egypt, Turkey, and most other Muslim nations. How long they can continue in this way is another question.

IRAN AND THE ISLAMIC REPUBLIC

Iran's Twelver Shiism is based on the premise that, until the reappearance of the Hidden Imam, no earthly government is truly legitimate. This philosophy is well suited to an oppositional role, but the rise of the Shia-based Safavid Empire in the fifteenth century prompted a modification of this theory: Although the Hidden Imam is the only true ruler, the Shia ulema can and should lead the people in his absence, and their guidance can legitimatize secular rule.

At the beginning of the present century, two factions were vying for control of the government: those advocating active guidance from the ulema according to the rationale stated above, and those pressing for a modern constitutional government. In 1906 these factions reached a compromise that provided for constitutional government, but with guarantees as to the Islamic nature of the government and a stipulation that all laws would conform to the Sharia. This compromise was set aside, however, with the ascendance of the Pahlevi dynasty in 1925. As he moved away from the representative government provided by the constitution, Reza Shah paid little attention to Islamic values and did much to suppress the visible manifestations of Islam. A split between secularizing and Islamic factions began to grow. With the forced abdication of Reza Shah and the partial return to democracy in the 1940s, a renaissance of Islam led to the reappearance of veiling, religious garb, and public ritual.

The young Mohammad Reza Shah was at first allied with the moderate religious establishment. During the 1950s, however, the United States colluded with him to eliminate the popular nationalist prime minister, Dr. Mohammed Mossadegh, and the shah moved steadily toward autocracy. Aided by American assistance and growing oil revenues, he launched a program of modernization that he dubbed the "White Revolution." His programs included much that was potentially beneficial, including land reform, industrialization, and the advancement of public health and education. However, he had little appreciation for the social and cultural context of these developments, forcing a pace of change that was self-defeating and that brought severe social upheavals.

Land reform stripped power from the clergy, and it moved faster than the ability of the people—including its peasant beneficiaries—to adapt to it. Ships loaded with goods arrived to find no docking facilities; thousands of cars and trucks sat idle without adequate roads or trained drivers; millions of dollars of oil revenues went for imported goods rather than the development of home manufacture, while urban migrants from the countryside looked for employment. The shah refused to listen to competent advisors, Muslim clergy, or popular sentiment, ruthlessly suppressing all dissent with brutal police state tactics. Despite important contributions to the material standard of living, the shah's policies resulted in a political condition that was more repressive and less promising than in 1906 when the first Iranian constitution had been adopted.

Perhaps looking for a source of legitimation that would not bind him to the authority of the Shia clergy, the shah turned to the political symbolism of the pre-Islamic Persian Empire. He was not the first to think of this; during the nineteenth century, certain critics had attributed the decline of Iran to the dilution of Persian culture by Arab and Turkish influences, and some even blamed Islam itself. Thus, they advocated turning away from these influences to a renaissance of Persian culture. The shah's regime chose this strain of nationalism: He dubbed himself the "Sun of the Aryans" and had his wife Farah crowned empress—the first since A.D. 632. Although the shah's "Peacock Throne" ideology did not renounce Islam, it dismantled a long-standing balance between nationalist and Islamic definitions of political authority and turned Islam from a potentially powerful source of legitimation into a lethal weapon for the opposition.

Although the opposition to the shah included a broad spectrum of religious, secular modernist, Marxist, and other viewpoints, the shah's brutal tyranny tended to unite them and to make their differences seem less significant. The opposition ideology derived much of its character from the negation of the shah's excesses—his denial of human rights and free speech, insensitivity to popular opinion, submissiveness to American interests, and so on. Whatever their diverse social ideals, the dissenters were brothers in oppression, and a bravely resisting figure such as the Ayatollah Ruhollah Khomeini seemed in some sense to speak for the common cause of the disaffected. In the case of the Iranian revolution—as in so many others—it proved easier to unite in opposition to evil than to join in a vision of the good. The Iranian Revolution of 1979 was followed by a reign of terror in which thousands were executed, beginning with the minions of the old regime and proceeding gradually to the leftists and other out-of-favor elements among the dissidents, and to social misfits and ethnic or religious minorities.

At the core of the revolutionary ideology was the total institutionalization of Islam in government. The revolutionary "Council of Experts" articulated a theory of government by "the jurist" (faqih), a religious figure chosen to represent Islam; Khomeini was, of course, the jurist. Ironically, the traditional Shia opposition to worldly rule has elements that can be used to legitimize forms of political-religious leadership that make Sunni political authority seem humble by comparison. The chiliastic concept of a Hidden

Imam who will eventually appear to redeem the world and punish the wicked (and who may send a deputy to rule in his name until his arrival) led many to see Khomeini as a divinely appointed spokesman for the Imam, or even as the Imam himself. (It should be noted that most of Iran's Shia clergy have opposed such extremes, and that many reject involvement in worldly politics both on theological and practical grounds.)

Postrevolutionary Iran was steeped in Islamic values and symbols. The educational system was aimed at purging Western influences and making people better Muslims, and college entrance examinations stressed religious education and attitudes. "Islamic dress" became the norm. The language of politics and the mass media was rich in religious symbolism. Chiliastic imagery and the Shia idealization of martyrdom figured prominently in patriotic rhetoric, and major political announcements were timed in accordance with auspicious dates in the Muslim calender. As a reaction against the shah's choice of cultural and historical symbols, "nationalist tendencies" were eschewed as contrary to Islam: Persian literature and poetry fell into disfavor, and it was even suggested that the Persian Gulf be renamed the "Islamic Gulf," at once symbolizing the unity of the Umma and rejecting the celebration of a pre-Islamic cultural identity. While some of these expressions of revolutionary Islamic zeal have mellowed, especially in the cosmopolitan circles of Tehran and other urban centers, the revolution has profoundly altered the nation's culture, society, and politics in a way that will be felt for generations to come.

The identification of the United States as "Number One Satan" expresses a number of themes in the revolution. To begin with, there is a secular political grievance: the United States supported the shah and helped to depose Mossadegh, a charismatic popular leader who might have changed Iranian history for the better. SAVAK, the shah's notoriously cruel secret police force, was organized and trained with the help of the FBI and CIA to search out "internal enemies." But the United States also functions in radical Iranian Shia thinking as a potent symbol of the powerful, antireligious, worldly oppressor—as against the oppressed, righteous, martyred victim who will

triumph with God's help in the end. The United States is associated in political rhetoric with the satanic figure of "Caliph Yazid," the historical caliph who martyred Ali's son Husayn. Thus, symbols of American or Western influence, such as clothing and entertainments, are excoriated as anti-Islamic. Any victory in the conflict with the Great Satan is claimed as evidence of God's favor, while a defeat may be seen in light of the perennial martyrdom of the righteous. Of course, it is not only Iran that uses common enemies to promote internal unity, and it is not only the United States that is demonized in Iranian political rhetoric—Iraq, for example, also symbolizes the irreligious oppressor. Furthermore, it should be kept in mind that not all factions in Iran are comfortable either with the extremism or the international isolation that this militant rhetoric entails.

Khomeini's political philosophy placed great emphasis on the conflict between the oppressor and the oppressed. The oppressors included both the West and the former communist bloc, as well as assorted local and internal villains. The regime has expressed its commitment to Iran's poor, favoring them for rationed goods and offering them government employment. It also endeavored to raise their condition through rural development and nationalization of private commercial assets.

The Islamic Republic

One way in which the revolutionary government of Iran has attempted to address "oppression" is by exporting its style of Islamic revolution to other Muslim countries. The direct appeal of Iran's strategy is greatest where there are substantial Shia populations, as in Iraq, Lebanon, and the Gulf states. But even non-Shia Muslim militants may be inspired by the success of the Iranian Revolution, and the decade following 1979 was one in which the whole Muslim world reverberated with the concept of "the Islamic Republic." Even though many in the Muslim world reacted with distaste to some of the excesses of the Iranian formula, Iran continues to enjoy a certain kind of prestige as the first modern Islamic Republic and the harbinger of a hoped-for age of Islamic ascendance.

The concept of an Islamic state has an understandable appeal for Muslim activists accustomed to being on the defensive. However, the Islamic Republic raises a new set of troublesome issues. While it is clear that the Koran regulates social life in a variety of ways, it makes no provision for government as such: Nothing is said about leadership, succession, or the structures and institutions that make up a system of government. Indeed, some Islamic modernists have argued that it was not the intent of God's revelations to establish any particular system of government, and that whatever their moral and religious responsibilities, governments are entirely human creations.

If one does accept the notion that the Koran requires an Islamic government, the exact form of that government must rest on elaborate, and potentially debatable, interpretations of the Koran and Sunna. The body of preexisting interpretation in the Sharia is concerned mostly with personal conduct in ritual, family, and business matters—and of course, it does not refer to uniquely modern situations and problems. While the Sharia cannot in principle be modified, its application to contemporary legal and political affairs would require considerable extrapolation. It could be argued that the extension of Islam and the Sharia into highly contested social and political applications might weaken it by tying its fortunes to the vagaries of politics. The same kind of issue arises with regard to the role of the ulema. Historically, participation of the ulema in government has tended to weaken their oppositional role (as in the Ottoman and Saudi cases) and thus potentially to diminish their status as an independent moral force. Furthermore, strong links with governing factions or structures can quickly become liabilities when the tide of politics turns against them. For these reasons, many ulema are wary of excessive direct involvement in politics.

The supporting ideology of the Islamic Republic parallels in many respects the doctrines of Third World liberation. For example, there is the emphasis on social justice, dignity and empowerment of the common people, rejection of foreign domination, and celebration of indigenous spiritual and cultural values. At the same time, the Islamic Republic is theoretically incompatible with one of the classic elements of most Third World movements, namely, nationalism. There is but one Umma and it includes all believers in Islam. Any less-inclusive Islamic republic that pursues its own national interests in opposition to the rest of the Umma can expect its status as an Islamic republic to be contested. The pursuit of a single, universal Islamic Republic offers little hope of success in the contemporary world scene, but the existence of competing Islamic Republics is a contradiction in terms.

Democracy also poses a problem for the Islamic Republic. As long as the will of the people is suppressed by a non-Islamic establishment, it is easy enough to use the demand for popular participation as a blanket concept for a variety of different and incompatible goals. Islam has a long history of populist thought that defines popular participation largely as participation by the ulema, insofar as they embody accepted religious ideas and apply the Sharia in a manner consistent with social justice and equality before God. This is quite different from the Western conception of democracy, and it raises urgent practical issues including the right of dissent, political rights of religious minorities, limits on suffrage and representational government, and constraints on legislation. The Islamic concept of unity, or **tawhid**, refers not only to the oneness of God but to "unity" in a variety of other meanings, including the political. While tawhid is part of the ideal Islamic state, it is difficult to reconcile tawhid with the actual plurality of ethnicity, political views, culture, and religion encompassed within any modern state. Although Islamic-based governments like Saudi Arabia and Iran have tried to equate the will of God with the will of all the People, it is inevitable that one or the other will be compromised to the detriment—in someone's eyes—of the regimes' legitimacy.

What is the future of the concept of an Islamic Republic? Has it already had its day, or will it continue as a serious option for Muslim states? High ideals can become tarnished—sometimes unfairly—when they are obliged to confront the complications, compromises, and intractable problems of the political arena. The problems of Middle Eastern nations are sobering enough, and the Islamic Republic raises some of its own. Some observers detect a strain of disillusionment within Iranian society, and the success of the moderate Rafsanjani faction in the elections of April 1992 signaled a move toward a more pragmatic and less ideologically ambitious definition of Islamic government. And the succeeding government of President Khatami also made headway in the moderation of social life and extension of political rights. All in all, the ideal of the Islamic Republic has not only demonstrated its durability in Iran for more than two decades, but it has also become the dominant political force in the Sudan, Libya, and Pakistan.

SEXUAL POLITICS

Throughout this book we have treated politics as a dynamic process of conflict and accommodation, a process that connects in complex ways with cultural, societal, religious, and economic factors. We have referred to arenas and levels of conflict and resolution that dip and swirl irregularly, so that issues on one level may have ramifications for others. More specifically, we have identified *cultural politics* as the arena of conflict that centers on conflicting definitions of cultural norms, categories, and symbols. Few problems better illustrate these kinds of conflict than male-female relations in the Middle East. These relations deserve to be termed *sexual politics,* not only because of their potential for conflict and resolution, but also because of their relevance to the struggle for power and authority in domestic, community, national, and international contexts, and their multifaceted relations with other political problems discussed in this book.

Sexual Equality in Islam: The Modernist Interpretation

Despite Western stereotypes to the contrary, there is a case to be made for Islam as a liberating and egalitarian influence in opposition to rigidly sexist traditions. This case has been made by a variety of Middle Eastern Muslims and outside apologists since the middle of the last century, in an attempt to free Islam of the taint of "backward" folk traditions and reconcile it with modernizing trends. The view that many of the standard, prevailing interpretations of Islam are actually un-Islamic, and that the true, original Islam is more compatible with "modernization" than those pseudo-Islamic social traditions is characteristic of "Muslim modernism." There is much in the historical record to support a modernist interpretation of Islam as regards sex roles. Few would deny that the Koran ended a number of abuses against women or that it established inheritance and property rights that were extremely liberal by the standards of the time; Muslim feminists sometimes refer to these provisions of the Koran as a "feminist bill of rights." Beginning with Muhammad's wife Khadija, the women of the early Muslim community were active in public life, even to the occasional extreme of serving as warriors or instructing men in religion. After a delegation of women converts questioned the Prophet about the male-oriented language of his earlier revelations, certain key Koranic verses used a "he or she" locution similar to that of modem "nonsexist" writing. As we noted in Chapter 2, the Koran seems relatively free of the intimations of spiritual and moral inequality that one may find in parts of the Christian Bible.

The modernists have rightly pointed out that many of the "Muslim" customs that outsiders criticize as sexist are not necessarily Islamic in origin. We have already noted that the veiling of women existed in pre-Muslim times as a symbol of social status. Koranic references to the veil are ambiguous at best, and can be read merely as prescribing modest dress in public. Similarly, many modernists deny that the Koran provides any general support for the custom of secluding women in the home. The exclusion of women (until recently) from public worship in the mosques is also said to be a reflection of folk tradition directly at variance with the practice of the Prophet and his early followers. The Prophet's admonition against a man taking a second wife if he doubts that he can treat them equally, together with his statement elsewhere as to the impossibility of equal treatment, is offered as evidence that Islam really meant to rule out polygamy. Besides, others have pointed out, polygamy is mentioned in the Koran only in connection with certain special and unusual circumstances and is nowhere endorsed as a general practice. The Koranic basis for the rule of evidence in Islamic courts, that a woman's testimony is worth only half that of a man's, is also noted as applying to certain (perhaps obsolete) social circumstances and not, the argument goes, intended to be universal. Modernist writers have also pointed out that some antifeminist sentiments commonly attributed to the Prophet are based not on the Koran but on the less-reliable hadiths.

Furthermore, the apologists point out, even unequal institutions may sometimes be better than they appear. Seclusion in the harem, for example, accustomed women to a considerable degree of freedom and achievement in a predominantly female world. Thus women physicians, for example, were (and are) surprisingly common in the Middle East, as are all-female work groups in the contemporary mass communications industry and elsewhere. Similarly, polygamy is sometimes said to have relieved the burden on the traditional wife while providing sororal companionship. The fact that the Koran allocates to women only one-half the man's share of inheritance must, it is said, be balanced against the recognition that men are required to provide for women but not vice versa, and that the dowry paid by the husband at marriage becomes the wife's personal property.

Perhaps the strongest point on behalf of the egalitarian interpretation, however, is that the main thrust of the Koran is the elimination of injustice and the protection of the weak from abuses by the strong. If one accepts this as the overriding message of Islam, even customs once considered as Muslim might be superseded in the name of this ultimate Islamic principle.

Sexual Inequality in Islamic Tradition

The above arguments notwithstanding, there are certain historical realities that even the most devoted modernist is obliged to recognize. To begin with, the social regulations of the Koran do portray a world in which public affairs were handled mainly by men, a world in which women usually moved in a domestic sphere circumscribed by male authority. The inequality recognized in the Koran is social rather than spiritual in nature, entailing a number of sexually asymmetrical regulations such as the difference in inheritance shares,

the fact that only men can take more than one spouse, and the exclusively male ability to obtain a divorce without publicly showing cause. Although the outlook of the Koran is probably no more male-oriented than that of Jewish and Christian scriptures, the Koran is explicit in its regulation of domestic life, and its detailed implementation in Sharia law leaves little latitude for interpretation.

There is no mistaking the trend in sex roles after the Prophet's death. Conservative views arising both from folk tradition and from the practice of the Persian and Byzantine upper classes led to consistently antifeminist interpretations of the Koran and the accumulation of antifeminist hadiths attributed to the Prophet. By the time Sharia law had taken its definitive form in the ninth century, these conservative interpretations had taken on the authority of divine command. For example, the Sharia gives legal force to the husband's right of unilateral divorce, but it leaves up to the man's judgment the fulfillment of the Koranic requirements that he have good cause and seek reconciliation. Similarly it gives legal status to the Prophet's permission to marry up to four wives, but it leaves up to the husband the fulfillment of the Koran's clearly stated precondition of equal treatment. The Sharia occasionally even sanctifies customs that cannot be documented in the Koran and seem at odds with the Prophet's attempts to strengthen the family. This particularly includes the custom of "triple divorce," in which a husband can divorce his wife simply by saying "I repudiate thee" three times in one sitting. In most schools of Muslim jurisprudence, this divorce is binding and cannot be rescinded even at the husband's will. Most ulema, while disapproving of the practice, must recognize its legality as an established part of the Sharia. It must be kept in mind that the Sharia, technically at least, is not subject to modification; thus its explicitly conservative interpretations of sex role issues pose an inconvenience to the modernists.

Equally problematic is the tendency of rank-and-file Muslims and even the ulema to imbue traditional practices and attitudes with the sanctity of Islam. Whether or not the Koran actually insists on traditional female subordination, ordinary people may feel that they are defending Islam whenever they resist innovative, especially Westernizing, influences in favor of their own traditions. There is even a basis for this in Islamic theology, since the Prophet is reported to have said that God will not let His people agree in an error. Hence, Muslim jurisprudence recognizes consensus (that is, the consensus of the ulema) as one criterion of religious truth. Thus, traditional attitudes about women and sexuality achieve a quasi-religious status despite their lack of any direct basis in scripture or theology.

Important among these attitudes is the notion that female unchastity is the most potent threat to family honor, and that women's sexuality threatens the social order. It is taken for granted that men will be possessive and protective of the women in their own families and opportunistic toward others. Women are thought of not as self-controlling but as being controlled by others; a good woman submits to the control of her father, brothers, and later her husband, while a bad one submits to the predatory stranger. Women are not to be trusted but rather contained—confined within the circle of male overseers, within the veil, and whenever possible, secluded and protected in the women's quarters of the household. Many Muslim men may see this private patriarchal domain as their last bastion of authority in a world otherwise dominated by exogenous forces. A sense of helplessness in the face of other changes might even lead to a retrenchment of this miniature polity within the home.

The Struggle for Reform

Much of the modernization of sex roles in the Middle East has stemmed indirectly from international politics. Turkey and Egypt, as the two main centers of Middle Eastern Muslim power in the early nineteenth century, were the first to feel the threat of the Western incursion. Their response in each case was a judicious attempt to modernize the military and other sectors of society that might help stave off foreign rule. These programs of modernization, implemented by Western-educated cadres, led to a general fascination with, and grudging respect for, Western culture. Colonialism was, of course, as much a cultural as a military

onslaught, and Middle Easterners were faced with a significant challenge in the West's claims of cultural superiority. It was in this context that the first Muslim modernists began their attempt to rediscover Islam, purified of its misguided "folk" interpretations, as the progressive religion par excellence. By the turn of the century the Egyptian modernist scholar Qasim Amin had produced such works as *The Emancipation of Women* and *The Modern Women*. Decades ahead of their time, these works set out such modernist arguments as those discussed above, for which they were publicly condemned as un-Islamic. Amin argued that full equality of the sexes was required by Islam and also that it was necessary for Egypt's national development.

Although such ideas were unpopular, they provided a basis for a more active wave of feminism. In 1923, educated Egyptian women formed the Feminist Union, publicly cast off their veils, and began to campaign for legal reform. The same year saw the establishment of the Republic of Turkey under the leadership of Kemal Ataturk, the ardent modernist reformer. Building not only on his role as founder of the modern Turkish state but also on nearly a century of reform in women's status and other social issues, Ataturk instituted sweeping reforms that eliminated legal distinctions between the sexes, abolished polygamy, and allowed women to vote and stand for office. Although he did not outlaw the veil and could take no direct action against the deeper attitudes that gave rise to it, he never missed an opportunity to dramatize publicly his support of sexual equality. Yet although he replaced the Sharia with the Swiss Civil Code, Ataturk claimed to be purifying Islam of its latter-day misinterpretations.

In 1956 Habib Bourgiba, after leading Tunisia to independence, initiated a process of reform that placed his country alongside Turkey and Egypt in the vanguard of sexual egalitarianism. Unlike Ataturk, who disestablished the Sharia as the law of the land, Bourgiba based his program on his own radically modernist reading of the Sharia. His reforms, generally similar to Turkey's, banned polygamy, required informed consent of a bride as a precondition of marriage, set a minimum age for marriage, gave the sexes equal rights in divorce and child custody, and provided equal educational opportunity. Justifying these changes in the name of purifying Islam and catching up with the West, Bourgiba even went so far as to provide free abortions to married or single women without the need of a husband's or guardian's permission. Like Ataturk, however, Bourgiba has left an unintended legacy of backlash against what is increasingly seen by Islamists in the post-Bourgiba era as a campaign against Islam.

If Ataturk's and Bourgiba's initial successes were due largely to their favorable political positions, reforms in some other countries have failed for equally political reasons. In Algeria and Morocco, for example, schooling for girls and other egalitarian reforms were sponsored by the hated French colonial regime and became associated with the taint of cultural imperialism. Despite the important role played by women in the war of independence, postcolonial Algeria and Morocco deliberately adopted a conservative interpretation of Muslim women's roles as part of the repudiation of Western culture. These sentiments, along with a fear that working women would add to the severe male unemployment, have led to policies aimed at keeping women in the home. In Saudi Arabia, where political legitimacy rests on Muwahhidun conservatism, the veiling and segregation of women are actively enforced and have encountered only weak opposition. An organized demonstration during the 1990 Gulf War, in which Saudi women defied the rule against driving automobiles, resulted in widespread denunciation not only of the women involved but also of the American influence on which the protest was blamed.

Most Middle Eastern countries, however, lie between these extremes and are characterized by a dialogue between the forces of conservatism and change. Modernizing economies, urbanization, a greater variety of role models, and women's education provide the foundation for fundamental, though often very slow, changes; in the meantime, legal reforms gradually accumulate.

Women in the Islamic Revival

Since the mid-1970s, the plodding pace of social and legal reforms in women's roles has been overshadowed by a more dramatic turn of events: a widespread popular movement devoted to a restoration of Islamic behavior and dress. If this movement were simple conservatism among the traditionally oriented rural population, it would hardly be surprising. It is understandable that even seventy-five years after Ataturk's reforms, rural Turkish villagers still continue in the patterns of marriage, dress, and sex roles that prevailed in the old days. Paradoxically, however, the most self-conscious reassertion of Islamic roles for women is found in those places where Westernization, social reform, and education have proceeded the farthest. Again ironically, the protest is often most evident among educated middle-class women, the daughters and granddaughters of the women who boldly emerged from their harems, cast away their veils, and campaigned for legal reforms. In Egypt, women university students have taken increasingly to wearing various forms of modest "Shari" dress, some go veiled in public, and a few have even elected to seclude themselves in their homes. In Tunisia, where reforms of family and divorce laws had gone particularly far, educated women clad in veils publicly confronted President Bourgiba to protest his liberalizing policies and reaffirm the value of traditional feminine roles. Today, Muslim women take part in lively discussions on the Internet, testifying to the liberating value of Islamic dress and Islamic concepts of womanhood. These events reflect more than mere inertia against change; they constitute a political phenomenon in their own right.

A comparison between the Middle East and China with regard to sex role changes might be instructive. In postrevolutionary China, the ideal for sex role change was clearly and unequivocally portrayed: The old patriarchal order was to be abolished and replaced by sexual equality. Of course, changes in behavior have not entirely lived up to the ideal, nor have they been painless. Nevertheless, the degree of change within only a generation or two has been remarkable, especially in comparison with the Middle East, when one considers the strength of patriarchal attitudes and institutions in Chinese tradition. Of course, the Middle East as a whole has not experienced anything like the upheaval of the Chinese Revolution, but there are other differences as well. The role of Islam in establishing the cultural and social forms of the Middle East, in placing it so centrally in world history, and in structuring a centuries-old competition with the Christian West, all contribute to the importance of Islam as a vehicle for the political response to Western domination. The Middle Easterners' struggle for self-determination, in other words, is expressed in the need to be Muslim. But Islam, as we have seen, is uniquely concerned with marriage and family life, and thus the domestic arena becomes, in a sense, a setting in which the drama of international domination and resistance is symbolized and is acted out.

Seen in this context, the West's vocal concern over the plight of Middle Eastern women is itself an example of cultural politics—another blow in the age-old rivalry over "who is more civilized than whom." Western feminists may add to this sense of rivalry by unconsciously equating Westernization with progress—a habit of thought that tends to muddle the issues and to divide those who could be united by deeper common interests. In this setting of cultural and political rivalry, departure from traditional family and sex-role patterns in favor of those prevailing in the West— even when sponsored by popular nationalist leaders or justified in the name of purified Islam—is widely seen as a capitulation to foreign domination.

The case of Iran aptly illustrates the interplay of sexual politics with the national and international arenas. Interest in greater opportunities for women began during the nineteenth century among the Western-oriented middle class, and by the early decades of this century women were involved in forceful public demonstrations in support of nationalist and democratic causes. In the 1920s, some educated women braved persecution in order to operate private schools for girls. The cause of sexual equality was, however, unwittingly sabotaged by the policies of the Pahlevi rulers. Reza Shah, who came to the throne in 1925, pursued a program of Westernization that included public schooling for girls, forced abolition of the veil, and other changes in family life. Reza Shah's high-handed methods fostered an ulema-led opposition which, after his abdication in 1941, led to a dramatic backlash against his policies. Legal reforms were reversed, and the ulema publicly called for a return to the veil.

During the 1960s and 1970s Mohammad Reza Shah attempted another program of legal changes including women's suffrage and the Family Protection Laws of 1967 and 1973, which modified in women's favor the prevailing practices regarding polygamy, divorce, child custody, and related matters. It seems, however, that the shah valued these changes more as symbols of "modernization" than as actual advances toward equality. In a much-publicized interview with an Italian journalist he scorned "Women's lib," pronounced women inferior to men in ability, and remarked that "women count only if they are beautiful and graceful. . . ."

Authoritarian in his methods and reliant on the United States for support, the shah came increasingly to be seen not only as an agent of cruel outside oppression but more specifically as a harbinger of Western-style profligacy whose "feminism" was really nothing more than an attempt to turn women into painted playthings. Through an ironic twist of politics, a strong ulema-led opposition to the shah's policy of women's suffrage became (for some, at least) an important rallying symbol of popular empowerment. The movement against the shah appealed to people's sense of social justice, personal freedom, national pride, and religious piety. The appeal was equally to women and to men, and both participated actively in the revolution. As often happens, the success of the revolution brought rude surprises for some. While perhaps many women had never aspired to a growing personal freedom or equality with men, others felt betrayed by the repeal of the Family Protection Laws and the attempt to return women to their traditional roles. Some women who had worn veils as symbols of protest against the shah felt differently when the new government began to require "Islamic" dress.

Beneath the apparent unity of Khomeini's Iran lies a great diversity of assumptions and opinions about the direction of progress. Iran's religious leaders claim that it is they who truly respect women's equality with men, while the chief threat to women is those who would plunge them into Western-style "immorality." While many women appear to accept this claim, others see it as a rationalization for reactionary, sexist policies that amount to a betrayal of their trust.

The changes in Iran, though dramatic, are not entirely unique. In Egypt, modest Islamic dress has been voluntarily adopted by a growing number of young women, often from the educated middle class. Liberal family and marriage laws championed by Mrs. Sadat were later repealed following repeated protests by veiled Egyptian women, and a leading Egyptian feminist and film director was pressured into self-exile by opponents who labeled her a "foreign agent" for her feminist views.

We have argued that these reversals against women's rights are in part a spinoff from the Islamic resistance to Western domination. This is aided by the inevitable tendency of any culture to form inaccurate and ethnocentric stereotypes about another—in this case, an exaggerated notion of promiscuity, materialism, and breakdown of family life in the West. It may be more difficult for the Westerner to see, however, that some elements of the "revival" may also stem from informed reflection, women's self-interest, and intelligent cultural criticism. Middle Eastern women directly familiar with Western culture have pointed out its flaws as a model for women's fulfillment: Accustomed to moving in a segregated women's world, they see Western women as obsessed with dating, pairing, and heterosexual attraction. While criticizing the traditional Middle Eastern domination of women within the domestic setting, they are shocked and repulsed by what they see as the tasteless public exploitation of women and femininity for hedonistic and commercial purposes. In this light, veiling and other forms of neo-Islamic dress take on still another meaning: Islamic dress is for many women an assertion of personal choice, a way of preserving their privacy and dignity in a public or work setting, and an affirmation of their cultural pride in the face of a smug and domineering West.

As the above example shows, it is not always easy to distinguish reactionary elements from modernizing ones. Although one might expect fundamentalist and modernist Islam to be irreconcilable opposites, the two may at times be almost indistinguishable. The writings of Ali Shariati (1933–1977) provide a case in point. Educated in sociology at the Sorbonne, Shariati endured two decades of imprisonment, surveillance, and exile from his native Iran because of his opinions. As an articulate defender of Islam and critic of Western society, Shariati became a spokesman for the anti-shah movement and a veritable saint of the Iranian revolution following his death, and his writings continue to provide guidance for Muslim revivalism in postrevolutionary Iran and elsewhere. Shariati, however, was an Islamic modernist in the tradition of Muhammad Abdu, Qasim Amin, and al-Afghani; while he defended Islam in the face of Western secular thought, he was equally eloquent in his attack on the traditionalists who "confuse being old-fashioned with being religious." He blamed tradition for depriving women of their rightful place in Muslim society, for excluding them from religious life, and for ranking them in social standing "at the level of a washing machine." To the discomfort of many Shiite ulema, Shariati flatly proclaimed the equality of the sexes and advocated their equal participation in social life. His ideal, however, was not the "superficial" modernity of the Western woman. Instead, he offered as his ideal woman the Prophet's daughter Fatima, the perfect wife and mother, exemplar of courage and social responsibility, and leader in the protest against the materialistic trends in the religion of her time. Was Shariati a modernist or a traditionalist? The very fact that this question is so difficult to answer may suggest that, in the end, the meaning of modernity must be defined within the terms of each society's historical experience.

CONCLUSION

We have defined politics as the process of conflict and resolution involved in the pursuit of limited good, and we have suggested that this good may include the privilege of defining the symbols and values by which people live. Political behavior everywhere shows patterns that, if not always strictly rational, display a more or less intelligible logic once the underlying premises are understood. Those premises, however, are invariably rooted in cultural values and symbolic relationships that cannot be reduced to pure rationality. This is not a situation that peoples and nations are likely to outgrow in the forseeable future; perhaps not ever. Religious and cultural symbols are both a defining source of social goals and a reflection of historical striving toward those goals. Thus in our discussion of the Islamic revival, for example, we have steered away from explanations that would reduce religion and its associated values to the status of mere political devices, or on the other extreme, make politics simply the tool of religious dogmas. History shows a dynamic, evolving relationship between social life and changing interpretations of religious and cultural heritage. To see one as a mere puppet of the other, or to reduce either to nonhistorical essences, is to pursue a comforting simplicity at the expense of genuine understanding.

CHAPTER NINE

Political Elites

The study of political and social elites has been extraordinarily rewarding to social scientists. Among the reasons for this is the fact that most complex societies have well-defined elites. These elites are prominent; they are easily identified and studied. Elites are intimately involved in the processes that produce and resolve group conflict over the allocation of resources; they exist in all of the arenas of conflict, whether they be local, regional, national, or international; and elites prompt or resist or reflect changes in the social, economic, and political processes.

In all but the most simple societies, certain people perform political functions; they make the binding decisions of the society. These people, the elite, can be distinguished from those who do not exercise substantial power, the public or the masses. In other words, at one level or another, and with varying degrees of effectiveness, an elite is composed of those people who decide "who gets what, when, and how." And since those decisions are going to both satisfy and disappoint members of that society, especially since allocations take place in an environment of relative scarcity, the activities of the elite both resolve and generate conflicts. For example, a decision to transfer land from traditional landowners to the

previous tenant farmers will satisfy the demands of the tenant farmers but will motivate the landlords to seek some form of compensation for their losses. Thus, the elite in its action creates new demands on the system as it attempts to reconcile existing conflicts.

Members of an elite tend to represent the interests of the group of society from which they spring. A member of an elite whose ancestors were small farmers can be expected to represent the interests of those with similar backgrounds, *to a predictable degree.* An elite member whose ancestors were landless peasants would be expected to represent a substantially different point of view, especially on those problems that directly involve the conflicting interests of landholders and tenant farmers.

If members of the elite represent their own groups of origin with some predictability, then the composition of the elite can reveal much about the state of politics in a given society. For example, the overrepresentation of one segment of society in the elite would imply that disproportionate shares of that society's produce were going to that group. And on the other hand, the absence of a potentially important elite group—the educated professional class, for example—would imply that the group was being disproportionately penalized by the actions of government. Thus, the composition of the elite is of great importance to the society attempting to modernize, for a modern society attempts to involve most or all of its citizenry in the pursuit of a new social and political consensus. Consensus is not built by excluding large or important groups from the political process or the elite. The general representativeness of the elite, therefore, is an important indicator for anyone attempting to understand the political process in a given country or region.

The analysis of the elite in a transitional society—and most of the systems under study here are in a transitional state between the traditional and the modern—will generally reveal an elite of changing composition. In particular, we should be alert to changes in the elite that indicate an expansion of the elements of society participating in political decisions and to evidence that indicates traditional opposition to that change. It is axiomatic that established elites will oppose such changes, since those changes involve a dilution of the elites' past influence. Conflict is implicit between those elements of the elite proposing and supporting technical modernization and those elements of the elite opposing such changes. In most of the countries of the Middle East, this process expresses itself in terms of religious elite opposition to the modernizing efforts of the bureaucracy, professional classes, and the military. Since World War II and the nominal political independence of the nations of the area, this conflict has occurred between the traditional religious elite of the Middle East—the ulema—and the government, usually dominated by the military bureaucracy.

Although we have discussed the peculiarities of the ulema in earlier chapters, it is important to recall some of its primary characteristics, particularly since it complicates our analysis. First and foremost, the ulema is unusually diffuse; it has no clear hierarchy, or rules of membership, or formal organization. Existing independent of the political order, it has nonetheless historically penetrated and influenced that order, reflecting the pervasiveness of Islam in general. The ulema is consequently difficult to pin down in sociographic terms. But there is no denying its existence and no denying its desire to maintain its authority de-

riving from sacred or religious sources. And it is the ulema's maintenance of sacred sources of authority and knowledge that brings it into conflict with the focus of modernization. For modernization, as it developed in the West, recognized the authority of man, not God.

Thus, the ulema, as the front-line bastion against secular authority, often finds itself in fundamental opposition to the secular values of Western-style modernizers. As we shall see, this opposition takes various forms in the political systems of the Middle East. Historically, the ulema has sought to influence and advise government rather than serve formally as officers of the state. They have further preferred to exercise moral vetoes over unacceptable policy. There are indications that this policy has changed in Iran, Saudi Arabia, Libya, the Sudan, Egypt, and the Gulf states; but historically, the political power of the ulema has been negative—oppositional power rather than the power of positive influence or accommodation.

A prominent exception to this situation involves the Shia community in Iran. Here the clergy, more formally organized than in Sunni-dominated areas, has taken direct control of the government for the purposes of implementing an Islamic republic. Although this experience is important, it is also important to remember that the Shia account for only approximately 10 percent of the world's Muslims. In most states, the ulema still keeps its distance from government, seeking to exert moral or oppositional influence in contrast to the direct exercise of political power. But there are growing numbers of ulema in many states anxious to take a direct role in the affairs of state.

The relatively recent spread of "political" Islam (the term is controversial) has involved the ulema in overt political activity in many Middle Eastern countries. Although in most situations the proportion of the ulema taking direct roles in political organizations and formal oppositions is relatively small, the consequences can be momentous. This is certainly the case in Algeria, where a determined and well-organized Islamic party confronts the government both politically and militarily; in the Sudan, where the ulema effectively directs the affairs of state; in Egypt, where ongoing Muslim opposition to the Mubarak government is apparent; in Turkey, where an Islamic party successfully challenged the dominance of both major secular parties, only to be removed from office by the military; in Saudi Arabia, where conservative ulema have increased their criticism of the royal family and its policies; and in Israel/Palestine, where Hamas is supported by a large number of politically committed ulema, many uncomfortable with the secular posture of the Palestinian Authority as well as Israel. It is difficult to identify patterns of behavior here that transcend local or particular political systems. Nonetheless, ulemic activism is one of the emerging realities in the Middle Eastern constellation of elites.

By contrast, the modernizing forces in the Middle East can be described as adopting the opposite of the political style of the ulema. The forces generally supporting technical modernization in the Middle East are the governmental entities that gained political power in the aftermath of independence. Although nominal power at that time was held by hereditary monarchs (such as Farouk in Egypt and the Hashemite monarchs of Jordan and Iraq), more actual political power was held by the bureaucrats and military officer corps of those governments. And as the political pressures of independence grew, the actual formal political power of these elites grew, ultimately displacing the hereditary traditional authorities in countries such as Egypt, Iraq, and Libya. In other countries, such as Saudi Arabia, Iran, Oman, and the U.A.E., a system of shared powers between the traditional and the bureaucratic-military elites developed.

It is not surprising that the technically modernizing elements in the political elites of the Middle East should so often come from the bureaucratic/military cadres, for the preceding colonial regimes tried to create a capable, modernized bureaucracy without an attendant modernized, independent political structure. Thus, at independence, those elements that had been most exposed to the logic and philosophy of secular modernity were the bureaucrats and the military.

Consequently, we expect to find the elite structures of these Middle Eastern political systems in a state of flux, reflecting the low level of consensus in the society as a whole. The historical traditional order preceding the transitional stage to modernization was characterized by relatively high levels of consensus and elite congruence, and presumably the emergent modern order will be as well. Just as predictably, the intermediate transitional state will reflect the growing conflict over the objectives and basis of sociopolitical organization.

One of the most interesting and pervasive changes in the elite environment has revolved around recent changes in communications technology. Satellite-based broadcasting has resulted in the exposure of new sources of information and world views for individuals and groups that could be characterized as "information poor" less than a decade ago. Computer-based communications systems, primarily the Internet and the World Wide Web, have allowed instantaneous communication among individuals and groups widely separated by space and culture. The result of this is that elites and counter-elites are in much wider and more intimate contact than was true only a decade ago. We can no longer think of elites as bound by state or nation. Quite the opposite is true.

The consequences of these new information flows is important for government. It is more difficult, for instance, for governments to "manage" news or information flows. The system is nearly anarchic in the sense that it resists management from the top. The result is a public with greater sources of information and with greater possibilities for coordination. Individuals and groups formerly isolated in diasporic living situations can now communicate and participate in conversations and exchanges literally half a world away. There will be consequences to these new realities, although they are unclear at this point in time. Higher levels of elite consensus could be possible than under previous conditions of information scarcity. And counter-elites may find it more easy to maintain relations with like-minded dissidents within and outside any particular country.

During those periods in a country's history when elite consensus and integration predominate, the leadership of the country can be indifferent or undistinguished without great cost, for the widespread agreement upon processes, institutions, goals, and the like will provide adequate direction to even the most unimaginative regimes. But when elite conflict and competition are evident, and consensus absent, the resources, imagination, and capability of the individual head of state become of great consequence. Since the Middle East finds itself in just such a transitional situation, we will spend some time in the next chapter analyzing the emergent styles of political leadership in the region. We will attempt to show the political and social consequences of varying political leadership styles, including styles that we shall call traditional, modern-bureaucratic, and charismatic.

TRADITIONAL, TRANSITIONAL, AND TECHNICALLY MODERNIZING ELITES

Figures 9–1, 9–2, and 9–3 present models of the elite structures of traditional, transitional, and modern Middle Eastern societies. Before discussing each of these elite categories, a few remarks on the diagrams themselves are in order.

In these models, we distinguish between three levels, or strata, of society: the elite, represented by the smallest group of circles in the center of each diagram; the ruling class, or those groups from whom the elite is regularly recruited; and the mass public, those members of society with considerably fewer resources and influence, who make up the majority of the society. The broken lines surrounding the ruling class vary in the three diagrams; they are intended to indicate the ease with which movement from the mass public to the ruling class can occur. If there is real opportunity for persons of demonstrated merit or capability to move from the mass public to the ruling class, we describe the society as having open, or permeable, boundaries; and if there is little possibility of an individual moving from one class to another, we label the society closed, or impermeable. The quality of permeability is of great importance to a society's ability to adjust to the changing demands of modernization.

Another feature of our model reflects the degree of cohesion, or consensus, in the elite. In this model, the closer the elite elements are, the higher the degree of consensus among them. You will notice that two of the identified elite models have

relatively high degrees of association, while the transitional model indicates a high degree of bifurcation and internal conflict. Finally, while these models describe national elites, they can also apply to regional and local elites as well. All countries in this area are, in effect, mosaics of elite structures.

The Traditional Elites

In many respects, we have already discussed the traditional elite structure in the preceding chapters dealing with classic Islamic social organization and the early stages of modernization. We need, however, to put that knowledge into the context of elite competition in the contemporary world. A short review of the main components of each elite is appropriate here, however, and we shall begin with the center of the traditional elite, the monarch (caliph, sultan, bey, or sheikh) and his immediate subordinates (traditionally, the *diwan*).

In most classic Islamic states, the ruler perpetuated his control largely on the basis of the elite's acceptance of his traditional right to rule. Particularly in Sunni political systems, a very high priority was placed on the maintenance of the established rule, with many theorists claiming that even tyrants should be obeyed until the very structure of the Islamic community itself was threatened. Shia communities were less disposed to accept established authority, but even in these communities, established authority had high credibility. In most traditional Islamic states, the head of state ruled on the basis of a widespread belief that such rule was correct and, moreover, divinely determined.

The bureaucratic apparatus that supported the monarch, however, was subject to greater vagaries. The diwan, drawn primarily from privileged families in the nobility and ruling class, were much more subject to being removed from office, not uncommonly at the caprice of the hereditary monarch. In some traditional systems, notably the Turkish Janissary corps and the Egyptian Mameluks, rulers and high ministers might come from slave origins, devoid of family connections. Such arrangements were designed to minimize family or clan-related court intrigues, but often succeeded only in substituting one form of intrigue for another.

The diwan, and their aides and staffs, administered the kingdom; they collected the taxes and maintained the appropriate records. The record keepers, the **katib**, provided the source from which many of the ministers of the diwan were recruited and exerted much influence on the matters of court. The caliph, diwan, and katib, combined with the caliph's favorites, constituted the bulk of the court in a traditional Islamic state.

Also of the elite, but not so regularly or intimately a part of courtly life, were the wealthy merchants of the capital city, large landowners, military officers, and the higher ulema. All of these elements had a restraining role on government: practically, in the merchants' and landowners' reaction to taxation; and morally, in the higher ulema's criticisms of policy. The ulema, in particular, limited the role of government by deciding which questions should be resolved by the caliphate and which questions were in the exclusive domain of the Islamic community, essentially the greater and lesser ulema. The relationship between caliphate and ulema was periodically rocky, and many a traditional authority defied the moral sanction of the ulema, formally and informally, successfully and unsuccessfully.

Many of the conflicts between caliph and higher ulema in Sunni states centered on religious opposition to efforts at modernization or changes in the social and political structure of the state. One major exception to this pattern has been the continually strained relationship between the monarchy and the Shia higher ulema in Iran. In this case, the Shia mistrust of political authority (see Chapter 3) has resulted in the higher ulema's espousing a strong form of constitutionalism as a basis for government. In this restrictive sense, the Iranian ulema has been among the forces striving for a more modern political system, fomenting conflict with the authoritarian aspirations of the Iranian shahs. This conflict has persisted down to the present day in Iran. However, in other areas of life, such as the liberalization of women's roles or

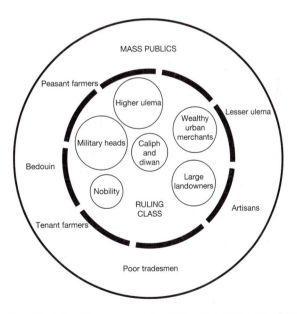

Elite Characteristics:
—Low permeability
—High elite consensus
—Small ruling class

Nation in Traditional Classification:
Kuwait

Figure 9–1   The Traditional Elite

secular education, the Iranian ulema's position is nearly indistinguishable from that of the Sunni ulema.

The military hierarchy has also been a persistent element in the ruling class and the elite of the Islamic state and of traditional political authority. There is no Islamic tradition separating military authority from political, social, or religious authority. Moreover, military life has traditionally been a means of social access and upward mobility. Particularly in linking outlying Bedouin military forces with the urban caliphate and elite, the military played an important role in the integration of the traditional elite. And as we shall see, the military is an important force in both the transitional and modernizing elites.

Generally, the traditional elite has a very low permeability—that is, the ruling class is very stable and outsiders move into it only with great difficulty. With the exception of the ulema (particularly the lesser ulema) and the military to some degree, social mobility was largely unknown in the traditional elite. Elite circulation was historically confined to the established ruling class and resulted in considerable unresolved tension. Indeed, many of the theorists of Islamic society, including the well-known Ibn Khaldun, attributed the decline and fall of the caliphates to the increasing restiveness of the mass publics (peasants and Bedouins), and the inability of the ruling class and elite to respond to them. The very cohesiveness of the traditional elite, its homogeneity and small size, contributed to its ultimate demise.

The weakness of the traditional state becomes most obvious when conflicts arise. In the traditional Middle East, political control, as a rule, declined proportionately to the distance from the political center. With the ruling class and elite centered primarily in the capital city, it was but a matter of time until the periphery suffered from neglect or exploitation. Common causes of provincial unrest came from such factors as deteriorating irrigation systems, increasingly exploitive taxes, and failure of the government to protect farmers and merchants from banditry and other forms of predation. As opportunists perceived the possibilities deriving from these growing demands, the power of the central authority dwindled to a point of crisis. If the traditional authority was lucky or aggressive, the threats might be laid to rest. If not, new elites and political structures, often drawn from restive elements within the ruling class and not from the mass publics, would be constituted and the whole process continued.

In the late nineteenth and early twentieth centuries, these traditional Middle Eastern political systems—notably the Ottomans and their client states—came under heavy pressure from the national systems of Europe. The traditional political elites found themselves hard pressed to respond adequately to superior European political, military, and economic power. At this time the only surviving traditional political system in the Middle East is in Kuwait, where the rulers have retreated from most of the initiatives at political reform that occurred before or in the immediate aftermath of the Gulf War. Other countries previously classified as having traditional elites—Oman, the U.A.E., and Qatar,—can now be classified as transitional. In each of these countries we can now recognize changes in the political system that have resulted in broader, more representative elites, and changes in governments allowing limited movement toward democratic institutions.

The Transitional Elites

The consequence of elite disagreement over the basic forms and derivations of authority produces a type of structure called *transitional*. The term is most often used to denote the stage between the disruption of traditional authority and the triumph of technical modernization; however, it might just as easily occur prior to an aggressive reassertion of traditional leadership, although this is unusual. It does seem to apply to the turmoil afflicting contemporary Iran and the rise of conservative Islamic political parties.

The transitional elite (see Figure 9–2) has a dotted line separating the elite and ruling class into two polarized and contending groups. Although the specific composition of the elite can vary from country to country, certain groups or elements are likely to have a prominent role. For instance, wealthy landowners who owe their prosperity to the support of the traditional leadership still participate in political decisions. The military,

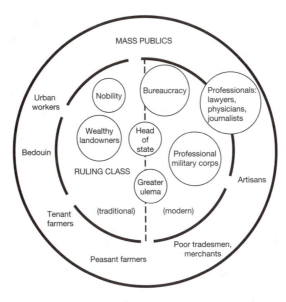

MASS PUBLICS

Urban workers

Nobility

Bureaucracy

Professionals: lawyers, physicians, journalists

Wealthy landowners

Head of state

Bedouin

Professional military corps

RULING CLASS

Artisans

Greater ulema

Tenant farmers

(traditional)   (modern)

Poor tradesmen, merchants

Peasant farmers

Elite Characteristics:
—Regular permeability
—Low elite consensus, internal elite conflict
—Growing ruling class, presence of
  "new" groups in ruling class

Nations in Transitional Classification:
Bahrain   Libya
Iran   Saudi Arabia
Jordan   Yemen
Oman   U.A.E.
Qatar

Figure 9–2   The Transitional Elite

often the first group to be systematically exposed to the influence of secular modernity by reason of their education, can usually be counted upon to support modernizing programs. The bureaucracy, trained in the science of public administration by a prior colonial administration, will also tend to support modernizing change. Those elements of the traditional elite with hereditary power can be counted on to cling to that power, by and large. And most of the greater and lesser ulema can also be counted upon to take sides in the issues at hand, although their decisions can frustrate both traditional and modernizing elements in the elite.

The transitional elite is generally composed of and represents more social groups than the traditional elite, in spite of the transitional elite's disagreement over the means and ends of political, social, and economic life. Internal conflict in the elite can produce irregular policy, wavering between the demands and desires of a fragmented society. This may often lead to frustrating incon-

sistencies that produce growing dissatisfaction from both traditional and modernizing elements. Thus, transitional societies are subject to growing internal pressures that demand resolution. Not uncommonly, these pressures build up to political violence—assassinations, demonstrations, and the like. On a more positive note, such behavior, short of violence, bespeaks a broader level of political participation and is one of the early signs that the pressures of change are building. The transitional society and its elite—as disorganized and chaotic as they sometimes seem—carry the seeds of a new social order based on greater participation and wider social consensus.

Oil has been a major factor affecting the prominence of transitional elites in the Middle East. Two relatively large and influential oil producers—Iran and Saudi Arabia—are transitional in character, as are the smaller Gulf states of Bahrain, Oman, Qatar, and the United Arab Emirates. In combination they account for the bulk of oil production and reserves in the Middle East, indeed, in the world. As a group, these countries also exhibit radically different political styles: modernizing monarchies, and two variants of the Islamic republic.

The transitional elites in the Middle East have provided the arenas for some of the most important political changes in the entire region. The fall of the shah of Iran in 1979 is, of course, the most dramatic of these changes and in some respects the most important. But the styles of politics and elite organization in Libya and Saudi Arabia have been equally as important and deserve some mention here.

Iran. The fall of the shah can be directly related to the strains placed on his political authority by a failure to accommodate new groups in the political elite and by a parallel failure to maintain the support of the more traditional groups in Iran. For example, the newly emergent professional middle class was largely uninfluential in the shah's autocracy. Since this group holds a near monopoly of modern technology and skill, it can be ignored only at the ruler's peril. Ironically, the ambitious technical modernization program of the shah simultaneously enhanced the size and potential power of the middle class at the same time as it alienated them. Thus, disaffected professionals found it advantageous to join with the forces of the traditional Muslim leadership against the shah. The opposition of the Shia ulema, again ironically, was based on the disruptive and secularizing influence of the shah's modernization program. The combination of traditional and modern opposition was too much for the shah's primarily military base of support, and he was forced to leave the country. The results of the change—particularly the attempt to establish an Islamic republic—are now clear. The theocratic regime in Iran appears to be fully in control of the country. Considerable institutionalization has occurred and there are indications that the relevant elite has expanded, reincorporating professional and middle-class elements that had previously been excluded in the early days of the revolution.

The initial political coalition that governed Iran during the transition from the shah's rule to the new republic can be characterized as a "temporary pluralism" dominated by the Shia clergy under Ayatollah Khomeini. Indeed, the new government organized by Mehdi Bazargan was heavily populated with ministers representing the urban professional and secular political groups that combined with the Shia opposition against the shah. As the design of the new republic became apparent, Bazargan's secular/professional government was replaced by a government under Bani-Sadr, a government dominated by nonclergy Shia leaders committed to the implementation of the Islamic Republic. Under Bani-Sadr's stewardship, and partially responsive to the strains of the U.S. hostage crisis, the Shia clergy began to play a growing political role in the government. By the early 1980s, after the fall of Bani-Sadr, the clergy had consolidated their power, assuming most of the important positions in the Islamic Republic.

The last months of the Iran-Iraq war placed the Iranian government and elite under terrific strain. As a consequence, Iran's governing elite was divided between the poles of the Iranian moderates, led by then-Speaker Rafsanjani, and more conservative groups committed to even greater levels of Islamization and further prosecution of the war. The stakes in the controversy included the right to nominate the successor to Ayatollah Khomeini as the "religious expert," the faqih of the Islamic Republic. Reports from Iran in late 1988 indicated the execution of a number of the members of the leadership of the most moderate factions of the ruling Islamic coalition, particularly among the followers of Ayatollah Montazeri. Commentators equated this action with the consolidation of power within the elite by the Rafsanjani faction, empowered by Khomeini's public stand in favor of ending the war. Ultimately this version proved to be true, with Rafsanjani and his followers consolidating their control over the Republic's institutions.

The complexity of Iranian politics was exemplified in the political ramifications of Khomeini's reaction to the novel *The Satanic Verses,* written by Salman Rushdie, an Indian citizen living in London. This novel, found blasphemous by many Shia mullahs, prompted Khomeini to sentence Rushdie to death and place a price on his head. Ayatollah Montazeri opposed this action, and in the process questioned the direction of government generally. Khomeini responded by demanding and receiving Montazeri's resignation as the faqih designate. In a related move, Khomeini attempted to kick Speaker Rafsanjani upstairs to a more ceremonial post as president of the republic. Other commentators have assumed that these actions indicated the increasing influence of the uncompromising conservative faction within the governing coalition.

Two other equally plausible explanations deserve consideration, however. First, this may be just one more example of a charismatic leader finding it difficult to relinquish power, a common phenomenon in the later stages of charismatic rule. Secondly, Khomeini may have been concerned that the revolution was losing ideological momentum and, like Mao Tse-Tung in the Great Cultural Revolution in China, sought to institutionalize the ideological/revolutionary fervor of his movement. In truth, all of these observations may be appropriate.

After the war with Iraq and Khomeini's death, the Rafsanjani faction consolidated its power. The elevation of Ayatollah Khamenei to the position of the faqih increased the moderates' influence, since Khamenei lacked the prestige of his predecessor. Under the leadership of President Rafsanjani, the government of Iran adopted relatively moderate foreign policies. Iran's neutral posture during the Iraqi invasion of Kuwait improved its prestige and positioned it as one of the influential states of the Gulf region. But the conservative factions were not totally excluded from power; and leftist revolutionary groups began modest terrorist operations against the government in the early 1990s. The government was unable to secure agreement to lifting the sentence imposed on Salman Rushdie, although considerable economic benefits were likely to follow from such a decision.

The politically active Shia clergy now dominates the Iranian elite, but there is new evidence that the urban professional classes and important ethnic and religious minorities are regaining some influence in the political process. The election of Muhammad Khatami as president of Iran in 1997 and his subsequent reelection revealed the political muscle of moderate opposition to conservative clerical rule. President Khatami has pursued a gentle relaxation of the most conservative domestic policies and pushed for better relations with the West and the United States. His administration is a bellwether of social and political change in contemporary Iran. Salman Rushdie has cautiously reemerged in the international literary community, a sure sign of the moderating trend in the Iranian polity.

Most surprising to many analysts have been apparent changes within the Iranian ulema, with moderate and even liberal leaders coming into public prominence, challenging the authority of the traditional mujtahids. One popular cleric of moderate disposition, Hojatoislami Nouri, has been a focus of conservative attempts to deny him public voice, convicting him of various offenses against the revolution and the religion. His experience is likely to set the tone for future conflicts within the Iranian ulema. The continuing conflict between Ayatollah Khamenei (the faqih of the Islamic Republic) and President Khatami suggests that the Iranian revolution is reaching a new stage of development, with broader representation and more tolerance of social and religious diversity possible.

Saudi Arabia.   By distinct contrast, the elite changes taking place in Saudi Arabia have been occurring more *within* the ruling family and its coalitions. King Fahd announced a broad reorganization of his cabinet in 1995, changing some key assignments. Early in 1996, failing physically, Fahd relinquished daily responsibility for the government to his brother, Prince Abdullah. Both changes came in the context of increasing criticism of the royal family and its policies by a coalition of conservative ulema and critics of the economic excesses and domination of the royal family. The flow of delegated power to the king's heirs has accelerated in the last days of the century, constituting a *de facto* political transition. In the early twenty-first century, the crown prince and other senior princes have taken increasingly visible roles as administrators and spokesmen for the kingdom.

As princes and retainers of the monarchy have received substantial educations in the elite institutions of the West—Oxford, Cambridge, M.I.T., Harvard, and the Sorbonne, for example—they have become increasingly aware of the need to adapt to the pressures and advantages of modern social organization. Indeed, the organization of OPEC has often been attributed directly to just such influences. The Saudi elite appears to be attempting to modernize the economic and technical facets of Saudi society without making corresponding changes in the political and social facets. This is a very difficult maneuver, for as the experience in Iran suggests, the educated and professional classes begin to desire power and influence. Ordinarily, analysts would be inclined to predict failure in this effort and disagree only on the timing of the ouster of the monarch and his ruling family. But the extraordinary wealth of Saudi Arabia, combined with its relatively small indigenous population, may allow for unusual and unanticipated developments. It is clear at this point, however, that the Saudi system has gone from traditional to transitional elite politics in a fairly short period of time, largely within the framework of the hugely extended royal family. The abdication of King Saud in favor of his more progressive brother, Faisal, and the publicly emerging differences of opinion between the royal princes under King Khalid provided evidence of both the changes and the relatively short time frame within which they occurred.

Rivalry within the royal family has come down recently to competition between three branches: the Sudairi, led by King Fahd, which includes many of the technically trained and sophisticated bureaucrats; the Jilwa, led by Prince Abdullah, head of the National Guard, which is the branch traditionally concerned with the cultivation of the tribal loyalties that have supported Saudi rule; and the religious branch of the family, the al-Baz, descendent from the Wahhabi reformers of the 19th century and the dominant force in the ulema. The death of King Khalid in 1982 and the resulting transfer of power to King Fahd consolidated the power of the Saudi modernist factions in the elite, but not completely at the expense of the opposition. Members and associates of the religious faction have become progressively dissatisfied with the social and religious policies under King Fahd. Several prominent members of the Saudi ulema were in fact placed under arrest in 1995 for advocating and petitioning for government reforms. The activities of Osama

bin Laden, a Saudi exile from a prominent family, accused of masterminding several terrorist plots against U.S. interests, has allegedly received financial and moral support from dissatisfied Saudi citizens. The attack on the World Trade Center on September 11, 2001, organized by bin Laden's terrorist organization, Al-Qaeda, strongly embarrassed the Saudi elite. Under enormous pressure from the United States, the government has been forced to take a closer look at the radical ulema preaching in the kingdom and make attempts to identify and detain members of Al-Qaeda and other radical groups. This fact suggests a higher level of internal elite dissatisfaction and conflict than conventional analyses would identify.

The Saudi elite has conceded extensive social power to the religious branch of the family, with the result that Saudi Arabia maintains one of the most conservative social atmospheres in the Middle East. The quasi-official religious police, the **mutawwa**, are responsive to leadership from the religious branch of the royal family. They are responsible for maintaining the codes of propriety in dress and worship. In the aftermath of Desert Storm, this branch of the royal family complained publicly about declining standards of personal conduct, demanding even more restrictive rules and punishments. At the same time, other elements in Saudi society encouraged the creation of a consultative assembly, and King Fahd did so, appointing both a national and other local assemblies (in Arabic, **as shura**). The importance of these assemblies has grown slowly over the decade, and in the long run may provide a small opening to more democratic participation in the kingdom. But many observers connect the demands for political liberalization and opposing demands for greater conservatism with the catalytic presence of foreign troops during the confrontation with Iraq. All in all, the political elite of Saudi Arabia found itself under considerable political strain.

Responding to increasing criticism of his government, King Fahd announced a broad reorganization of his cabinet in 1995, changing some key assignments, including the top management of the Saudi oil company. As discussed before, early in 1996, failing physically, Fahd relinquished daily responsibility for the government to his brother,

Prince Abdullah. Both changes came in the context of increasing criticism of the royal family and its policies by a coalition of conservative ulema and critics of the economic excesses and domination of the royal family.

Nonetheless, intrafamily adjustment to political realities continues to characterize Saudi rule. Saudi pragmatism, combined with its great wealth, should allow it more latitude for maneuver than most monarchical regimes under similar pressure.

It is clear in hindsight that the bombing of the Khobar Towers barracks, the bombing of a U.S. advisory mission in Riyadh late in 1995 (with considerable loss of life), and the 1998 attack on the U.S. embassies in Kenya and Tanzania signaled an important change in the strategy and tactics of the opposition to the monarchy. The Al-Qaeda attack on the New York World Trade Center involved a large percentage of Saudi citizens. The emergence of the exiled Saudi citizen Osama bin Laden as the chief architect of international terrorism against the United States and the West has embarrassed the Saudi elites. And bin Laden's continuing ability to garner financial resources from Saudi nationals suggest that visible public dissatisfaction with the regime is but the tip of the iceberg. Like the other states of the Gulf, Saudi Arabia finds itself increasingly under pressure to change, internally and internationally.

Kuwait. Developments in Kuwait in the early 1990s were traumatic and violent. The brutal, and largely unanticipated, invasion of Kuwait by Iraq in August of 1990 threatened to terminate Kuwait's long-standing monarchy. The diplomatic and military response to the occupation are discussed in detail in the following chapters. But from an elite perspective, the results of the events were significant.

Returned to power by an international coalition led by the United States, the Kuwaiti royal family was widely expected to institute long-awaited democratic reforms. Unfortunately, they did not materialize. Instead, the government of Kuwait embarked on a program of reestablishing the traditional government and increased "nativization," an attempt to ensure security by drastically reducing the guest population in Kuwait. Hundreds of thousands of foreign nationals—particularly, but not exclusively, Palestinians, Jordanians, and Iraqis—streamed out of Kuwait. Many held important positions in the government and in the professions. A series of public trials of those accused of collaboration with the Iraqi occupiers contributed to an already negative environment for foreign workers. Both collaborators and non-collaborators were expelled or fled. As a result, the political elite of Kuwait has actually narrowed in the years since Desert Storm. Democratic reforms have been considered but not implemented, and in late 1999 the Kuwaiti assembly vetoed a proposal to extend political rights to women.

Whether or not this reassertion of more traditional elite domination will work remains to be seen. It is not clear that there are enough native Kuwaitis willing or able to staff the offices of a complex modern bureaucracy. But like Saudi Arabia and the other Gulf monarchies, the vast oil wealth of Kuwait gives it more possibilities than less affluent regimes. There are no signs that the ruling family of Kuwait is interested in sharing power or expanding the scope of the Kuwaiti political elite. For these reasons, we have left Kuwait in the traditional elite category.

Bahrain. Changes are afoot in Bahrain, at least partially a product of a change in leadership. The death of Amir Issa in 1999 brought his son Hamad to power. Amir Hamad has taken his new position as an opportunity to engage in modest political reform, expanding the role of the consultative assembly and in 2002 conducting elections for a Bahraini parliament.

High unemployment has exacerbated Bahraini Shia anger at what is perceived as policies preferential toward the extended royal family, its retainers, and the Sunni minority. Street demonstrations, critical pamphlets, campus seminars, and the like have placed the issue squarely in public view. The government of Bahrain has conceded some of the points and promises to ameliorate the causes of discontent. A slow process of extending elite boundaries to include more of Bahrain's Shia in the government was under way.

Libya. The prevailing situation in Libya is in great contrast to that in Iran and Saudi Arabia. In Libya, the change from traditional to transitional status came with the elimination of the monarchy in 1969. In its place has developed a unique blend of Muslim puritanism and radical Arab nationalism, personified by Qadaffi, a charismatic leader. The Libyan regime is run largely by its military bureaucracy, within which are recognized competing factions. And there are some contributions from a small professional elite and an equally small traditional ulema. Libya, one of the major oil exporters of the region, is particularly uneven in its development. Thus, changes within the transitional elite structure of the country can be anticipated, although constrained by the erratic influence of Colonel Qadaffi. Qadaffi's attempts to replace regular bureaucratic organization with democratic peoples' delegations have confused the situation in Libya substantially, and he plays this confusion to his own benefit. Elite consequences are sure to follow from these innovations and strains, but their character and direction are uncertain.

In the past, Libya's substantive support of radical and terrorist groups, including the Palestinians, brought substantial benefit to these movements. However, the U.S. raid on Libya in April 1986 seems to have somewhat reduced Libyan predilections for international intrigue or the support of terrorist movements. Nonetheless, Libya continued to pay for its past sins. Early in 1992, Britain and the United States accused two Libyan diplomats of directing the bombing of Pan Am Flight 103 over Lockerbie, Scotland. Both countries demanded the extradition of the two, and, uncharacteristically, the Libyan government finally conditionally agreed to such surrender and allowed their trial to proceed. One of the alleged terrorists was convicted, the other acquitted.

All of this has resulted in growing legitimacy for Libya in Western Europe. For whatever reasons, internal or external, the Libyan elite seems more focused in the new millennium on its internal problems and less interested in staking out an international role.

Jordan.   The Jordanian political system has few tangible economic resources. It has also had the unenviable role of being a front-line state in the conflict with Israel and of being a neighbor of Iraq and Syria, both countries with a historical interest in regional dominance. During the Iraq-Kuwait war, it managed to alienate both sides in the conflict. But in spite of these negatives, Jordan has survived to transform itself into a relatively stable country with reasonable short-term prospects and a growing tradition of democratic government. At least part of the responsibility for this state of affairs could be attributed to the leadership of King Hussein and his ability to adroitly maneuver between contending powers. His death in 1999 brought his son Abdullah to power, displacing the crown prince in the line of succession. And with this change in leadership came another political opening.

Jordan's political system has many internal political fractures. Chief among them is the division between the Jordanian Bedouin populations and the large Palestinian population, both native and refugee. This fact led to the bloody confrontation between Palestinian guerrillas and the Royal Jordanian Army in 1970–1971. This confrontation, important for both the Palestinian and Jordanian elites, was caused by a growing recognition by both parties that political power was slipping increasingly into the hands of the Palestinian-dominated bureaucracy. Relying primarily on the Bedouin-dominated Arab Legion, King Hussein managed to expel the most militant of the Palestinians at that time, who fled to southern Lebanon and elsewhere.

It has long been recognized that one possible solution to the Palestinian problem—namely, the integration of the West Bank and Gaza Strip into Jordan, or some other form of federation—held great risks for the existing Jordanian elite, as great numbers of well-educated Palestinians unsympathetic to the Jordanian regime became politically active and legitimate. Moreover, the relationship between King Hussein and the PLO has been a turbulent one, oscillating between periods of cooperation and outright conflict. Nonetheless, King Hussein's announcement in July 1988, abdicating political and administrative responsibility for Gaza and the West Bank, surprised many observers, particularly in Israel and the United States, where fanciful hopes for a "Jordanian solution" had been kept alive. Hussein's action, while distressing to those seeking a "moderate" solution to the Palestinian problem, was probably of positive consequence to the Jordanian political elite, removing the major threat to its continued existence and eliminating many Jordanian-Palestinian officials from its ruling class.

In the new millennium, Jordan found itself in the unprecedented situation of having been a beneficiary of the Israeli-Arab relationship, with dramatic increases in trade, tourism, and investment, only to have these gains put at risk by the collapse of the Oslo Accords and the peace negotiations; and the presumptive, preemptive U.S. war against Iraq.

King Abdullah has attempted to maneuver between these hazards and to maintain Jordan's standing in both the region and with the United States. Balancing the Jordanian elite's comfort with the United States and the West in general with the sentiments of the Jordanian "street," with its strong sympathies for the Palestinians and resistance to a punitive war with Iraq, has prompted King Abdullah to retrench on some of the political liberalizations pursued by his father.

From 1988 to 1990, political liberalization appeared in Jordan. Elections to the legislature provided a substantial broadening of the political elite. Men and women from a variety of parties and professions gained office. The king and his counselors appeared willing to accept the practical limitations on monarchical power implicit in such changes. The future for democracy appeared much brighter. But events since 1990 prompted both King Hussein and King Abdullah to rein in the legislature, limiting its role and purging some of its membership.

Earlier gains were put at risk during the events of Desert Storm. Jordan, highly dependent on its trade with Iraq, attempted to maintain a neutral posture. Neither side would tolerate such diplomatic niceties, and as a result Jordan paid a high political price for its attempted independence. American and Gulf state aid virtually disappeared, and Jordan found itself diplomatically isolated and the subject of great suspicion. Street demonstrations in support of Saddam Hussein and Iraq did little to dignify King Hussein's argument that he was attempting to broker a negotiated settlement between the parties. During Desert Storm and its aftermath, Jordan became the terminus of a massive migration of its nationals from Iraq, Kuwait, and the Gulf states. A near doubling of the refugee

population in Jordan further strained the already inadequate resources of the state, while at the same time remittances from workers abroad declined.

Jordan's emerging democratic institutions and its changing elite were severely tested after King Hussein's rule. In the aftermath of the signing of the Israeli-Palestinian peace accords, King Hussein boldly placed Jordan as a proponent of regional peace. Israeli-Jordanian tourism became a major factor in Jordan's economy, and many joint ventures between Israeli capitalists and Jordanian businessmen were launched. Ironically, legislative dissatisfaction with the king's intimate relations with Israel kept the pressure on and the promising democratic reforms begun in 1988 slowed. Membership in the Jordanian elite depended to no small degree on an individual's stance vis-à-vis the Palestinian or Israeli question(s).

The Muslim Brotherhood opposed the Jordanian rapprochement with Israel and the government responded with limitations on press and political freedoms, particularly for the representatives of the Islamic conservatives and the ulema. Jordan had as much (or more) to gain as any state in the region from the solution of this long-standing problem, and it is ironic that closer economic and political ties with Israel and its Palestinian entity should result in increasing tension within the Jordanian political system.

The political transition from King Hussein to King Abdullah has alleviated some of these strains. The new king reinstated a number of key advisors to his father, isolated the extremist elements from the legislative system, and brought responsible elements of the Muslim Brotherhood into the government. Press freedoms were partially restored. Jordan's commitment to the peace process was reconfirmed. But all of these positive trends were put at risk by the collapse of the Palestinian-Israeli negotiations, the terrorist attack on the World Trade Center, and the U.S. efforts to accomplish "regime change" in Iraq.

Gulf Emirates. Positive change can also be recorded among the Gulf emirates: Bahrain, Oman, Qatar, and the U.A.E. In each of these countries, progress has been made toward the nativization of the national bureaucracies. And in each of these countries consultative assemblies were put in place and given wider responsibility in advising on government policies. In Oman and Qatar, the political leaders have publicly speculated on the desirability of eventual democratization. Qatar has allowed the establishment of an important Arab-language satellite channel, Al-Jazeerah, which has become noted for its independence and somewhat fearless coverage of global political issues. Qatar also is in the process of creating a set of basic laws that will provide the basis of an eventual Qatari constitution.

The oil and gas wealth of Qatar and the U.A.E. have allowed considerable investment in the education and development of the indigenous populations. As a result, the "emirization" of government positions has proceeded with great dispatch. And even in the Gulf countries with greater economic constraints—Bahrain and Oman—progress in elite modernization is apparent.

All of the transitional regimes of the Middle East are important to the region and to the larger world community. As indicated earlier in this chapter, these regimes are all in an incipient state of change. This incipient change is further magnified by elements in the new global system, facilitating communication through satellite links and the Internet, economic change contingent on the higher levels of international trade, and the unprecedented physical mobility of average people. It is unrealistic to think of traditional or transitional elites as necessarily naïve or placebound. And increasingly, the major differences between them lie in their preference or ambivalence toward democratic institutions. But, all of that understood, they thus constitute much of the kindling for the Middle Eastern tinderbox—and the general direction of their change will have profound implications all over the world.

The Modern Elites

In contrast to the transitional elites, the modern elite is one whose day has come. The traditional elite has been either excluded from rule completely or had its influence substantially reduced. Emergent groups who represent larger sections of the population now hold sway. These new groups find themselves in the heady but unaccustomed position of being able to exercise real political power. The political experimentation following the power consolidations of the modern elite may cause instability in policy at first, but eventually an equilibrium should be reached in which the decisions of the new elite will begin to have discernible effects on the society.

Figure 9–3 illustrates the composition of the modern elite. The central figures in the elite will generally be the head of state and his government ministers. It is likely, but not necessarily certain, that the head of state will have reached that position through a career in the bureaucracy or the military. A more unusual approach may be through the emergent party system, or even through the professional modern elites such as medicine, law, or related fields. Even less probable but still possible is advancement from the mass public, since the modern elite is characterized by greater permeability. The established officer corps and nonpolitical middle- and upper-level civil servants complete this rough outline of the modern elite. The ulema and the wealthy landowners still may be present, however. They continue to occupy positions of privilege in a modern society, but they have lost much or all of their political influence.

Several things distinguish modern elites from traditional and transitional elites. One of the greatest differences lies in the modern elites' worldview or philosophy. In contrast to the traditional and transitional elites, modern elites are much more likely to see the world as a place that can be radically changed by political, social, and economic policy. In other words, they see the social and political order as a consequence of man's activity and policy, rather than as the result of divine order or some asserted tradition. This point of view often, but not always, associates itself with a secular belief system—that is, a belief system centered on human rather than divine values. For this reason, the modern elite often finds itself in fundamental conflict with religious or sacred values. Some modernizing leaders—such as the former shah of Iran or the late Prime Minister Bhutto of Pakistan—have found religious opposition to their rule to be fierce and ultimately successful. Other modern Arab leaders—for example, Qadaffi of Libya—claim that a modern viewpoint can be supported by traditional Muslim authority and law.

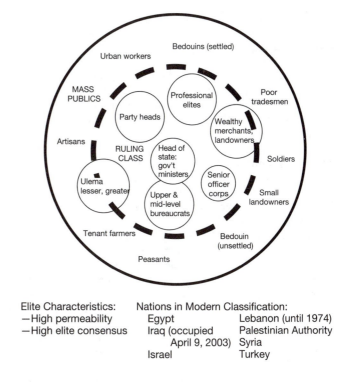

Figure 9–3 The Modern Elite

Elite Characteristics:
—High permeability
—High elite consensus

Nations in Modern Classification:
Egypt   Lebanon (until 1974)
Iraq (occupied   Palestinian Authority
April 9, 2003)   Syria
Israel   Turkey

The ulema itself is split over this problem, some inveighing against any semblance of human-centered values or policy and others adopting a more flexible viewpoint. And many political leaders now show increasing interest in Muslim sensibilities, balancing the demands of technical innovation with new concerns for the agenda of Muslim fundamentalists.

One of the most prominent features of contemporary Muslim politics is the growing interest in the possibility of establishing modern Islamic republics, states capable of modern control over both environment and policy without relinquishing the claims of Islam over social life generally. Islamic republics have been officially established in Pakistan, Libya, Sudan, and Iran; and many other countries are currently wrestling with the problematic relationship between Islam and political authority. Of those countries in the process of establishing an Islamic republic, Iran has made the most progress, but even here progress has been uneven and fraught with controversy. The specific design of the republic is

likely to inject substantial conflict into elite dynamics in most Middle Eastern countries. These experiments hold the seeds of substantial transformation of the policies in question and thus are of substantial contemporary and future significance.

The triumph of a modern elite does not in any way eliminate group conflict, or for that matter even minimize it. To the contrary, the composition of the modern elite includes more groups in the political process than do the traditional or transitional political systems. Moreover, the intensity of conflict may increase as well, particularly as more elements in society make stronger and stronger claims on social services and goods. For example, traditional and transitional societies generally have low levels of public literacy. As modern societies increase literacy, they also increase the social and political awareness of groups of their particular situations vis-à-vis other groups in the society. Thus the social good—literacy—carries with it the premise of higher political consciousness and hence more and greater political participation. The result is an increase in the scope of conflict and subsequent greater attention to conflict resolution. Issues and publics that are simply not relevant to the traditional regime are suddenly and irreversibly part and parcel of a geometrically expanding political process. Both mischief and progress attend this change.

International conflict can also affect these elite systems. The secular-modern regimes of Egypt, Syria, and Iraq have often found themselves individually in conflict with the transitional regimes of the Sudan and Iran, or the traditional regimes of Saudi Arabia (under Saud and Faisal) and Kuwait. Their respective beliefs are often seen as mutually exclusive and irreconcilable.

Our contemporary focus on the Arab-Israeli conflict in the Middle East often blinds us to the equally valid differences existing within the Arab and Muslim world. These differences are likely to play larger and larger roles in the immediate future, particularly as different elites make claims on the political loyalties and sensibilities of citizens in other countries. This level of conflict is difficult to resolve without resorting to widespread violence—violence that is all too capable of spilling over into other arenas of international conflict. The long and stubborn war between Iran and Iraq is a good example. The story of the events surrounding Iraq's occupation of Kuwait in 1990 is an even more forceful example.

Modern elite systems—Turkey, Egypt, Syria, Iraq, Lebanon, and Israel, and, very problematically, Palestine—while sharing the characteristics of a more open and competitive structure, are clearly a heterogeneous group of nations that have substantially different histories and cultures. The specific compositions of their elites are also different, although they tend to share similar outlooks on modernization.

Turkey.   Under the Ottoman sultans, Turkey was the model of a traditional elite. But it was the first Middle Eastern nation to throw off the mantle of the traditional past and embrace European modernization, perhaps because it alone straddles Europe and Asia. Although many political and economic changes occurred in Turkey under the sultanate, Turkey emerged as a modern political

system with the remarkable innovations of Mustafa Kemal Ataturk, who proclaimed a new, secular republic in 1923. Ataturk, supported by his political party, the Republican People's Party, mounted a strong and sustained attack on the traditional order. Reforms ranged from the general to the specific, but the major thrust was the secularization of political power, a corresponding reduction of the power of the Muslim hierarchy, and the virtual elimination of the institutions of traditional rule. Ataturk aimed at no less than the total transformation of Turkey from a weak, illiterate, agricultural nation to an industrial nation with all the attendant skills and attitudes that this implies. The very idea of a political party, even a single-party system, implied levels of public political participation undreamed of in the preceding regime.

From these revolutionary beginnings, Turkey has moved toward a complex, industrial, participatory system. The rudimentary forms of truly competitive political parties now exist in Turkey, although periods of military rule have occurred in 1960, 1971, and 1980–1981. Military-approved reforms in the early 1980s and later in the 1990s appear to have eliminated some of the fragmentary tendencies of the Turkish party system, and the system continues a slow move toward independent democratic institutions and greater representation of Muslim organizations and groups.

The Turkish political elite have made some progress toward their goals. The vision of Ataturk has yet to jell in the economic sector, and some traditional elements—particularly Muslim conservative groups and separatist Kurdish groups—have put considerable strain on the country's political institutions. And yet progress has been made. Turkey's politics are remarkably participant in comparison to those of the transitional countries, and freer than most other modern countries in the Middle East—no mean achievement for any country experimenting in the development of democratic institutions.

In 1995–1996, conservative Muslim parties emerged as a potent element within the Turkish electoral system. The Welfare Party (Islamic) received the largest percentage of votes in the December 1995 parliamentary elections, prompting the resignation of Prime Minister Ciller and subsequent negotiations between the two minority parties (True Path and Motherland) to organize the government. Clearly, Islamic democrats had become a force to be reckoned with in Turkey, with concomitant changes in the Turkish elite. And it was encouraging that the Welfare Party leadership was willing to negotiate within the arena that included secular as well as religious parties.

In a related vein, emergent demands for policy reform from Turkey's small Shia populations have been reported; and many Kurds, fleeing repression in Iran and Iraq, have entered the country, amplifying the demands addressed to the government. In a major setback for the Kurdish People's Party (PPK), the Turkish government apprehended the leader of the PPK, Abdullah Ocalan. His trial, conviction, and death sentence ratified the Turkish military's continued campaign against Kurdish separatism in western Anatolia.

Ultimately, the political successes of the Welfare Party drew attention from militant secularists in the military. In 1996 the military intervened, forcing the resignation of the Welfare government and reestablishing secular party rule. A decision of the Constitutional Court in 1998 forbade the participation of the Welfare Party in electoral politics and prohibited its key leaders from political participation for a period of five years. Suspicion of Islamist parties prompted the Turkish government to reject earthquake relief aid from international Islamic organizations and governments. Given the severity of the earthquakes and their damage to Turkish infrastructure, this decision was not taken lightly. This setback for Islamist groups in Turkey has not apparently dampened their mass appeal and the desire of some Turkish groups for a higher level of Islamization in Turkey.

Consequently, in the Turkish elections held in the fall of 2002, another Muslim party dominated the election. This party, the Justice and Development Party, went out of its way in the aftermath of the elections to emphasize its commitment to the secular constitution of Turkey. This electoral victory suggested a maturing of the Muslim elements in the Turkish political process and notably improves Turkey's chances for membership in the European Union, a highly significant objective for the new Turkish government.

As noted earlier, the achievement of a modern elite structure does *not* signify an end to internal political conflict but rather signals a change of arena and scope of conflict. In this regard, Turkey has shown itself capable of adjusting to serious political conflicts in recent history; and the future promises more and tougher challenges. The permeability and representativeness of the Turkish elite should be a considerable asset in meeting these tests.

Egypt. Unlike Turkey, Egypt had long been a victim of direct imperialist control and continued to be until comparatively recent times. The Egyptian revolution occurred in 1952 with the revolt of the Free Officers. This revolt, which expelled the corrupt and ineffective monarchy of King Farouk, brought to power in Egypt a junta of young army officers, most of them trained abroad. This group of officers was subsequently to demonstrate extraordinary cohesiveness, bringing a revolution of considerable scope to a faltering Egypt. Initially led by General M. Naguib, the group was ultimately headed by Colonel Gamal Abdel Nasser, one of the most remarkable leaders to grace the political landscape of the Middle East.

Under Nasser, attempts were made to create a party of national revolution. Several formulas were tried, and in 1962 the efforts jelled in the formation of the Arab Socialist Union. The union was conceived of as a party of national integration and ideology, bringing the masses into political contact and cooperation with the central regime. Under Nasser, the party took on some distinct characteristics that were to have profound effects both in Egypt and in the Middle East generally.

Nasser, a charismatic leader of the first order, tapped or created a reservoir of sentiment that is now called *Arab nationalism*. Essentially arguing that the Arab people were split unnecessarily and unwisely into a number of competing camps and nations, Nasser made an emotional appeal for a new Arab unity, one that would reclaim a prominent world role. Nasser's vision inspired many movements across the Middle East that were often viewed with suspicion outside of Egypt. Cynical observers were to see in Nasser's calls for Arab unity the distinct possibility of Egyptian political dominance. Others were disturbed by the coincidence of Nasser's Arab unity with his concept of Arab socialism and mass political participation. Nasser's forthright opposition to the traditional elites of Egypt did not endear him to the beleaguered traditional and transitional elites of other Middle Eastern countries.

Nasser had a particular vision of Arab socialism. This combination of politics and economics should not be viewed as socialism in any European or Marxist sense; rather, it was more a socialism of secular Islam. Its practical expression came in terms of the nationalization of basic industries, the elimination of foreign ownership, and the construction of hospitals, mosques, and schools in as many Egyptian villages as possible. There was no sophisticated understanding of socialist economics in Nasser's formula. There was, instead, an interest in the common man expressed in terms of daily needs and concerns—concerns like food, a place of worship, employment, and national ethnic pride.

The implementation of Nasser's socialism had benign political effects: mass public participation in the Arab Socialist Union, a very real improvement in Egypt's international prestige, and the integration of the professional and political classes with the military bureaucracy. But it nearly created an economic disaster: high inflation, low industrial productivity, high unemployment. As critical as we may justifiably be of Nasser's economic policies, however, we cannot deny his beneficial influence on Egyptian and Arab politics. His symbolic value to the emergence of an appropriate twentieth-century Arab identity is enormous.

Nasser's death and the consolidation of control under Anwar Sadat brought many substantial changes to Egypt and its elite. Under Sadat, the scope of the elite broadened as government policy became more tolerant of people and institutions in the private sector. In the mid-1970s, Sadat launched an ambitious program to create a parallel private economic structure; and he attempted to create competition between left, right, and center parties in the Arab Socialist Union. These efforts broadened the representativeness of the elite.

Sadat's rather bold changes to Nasser's political vision did not come cheaply or without opposition. Attempts in 1978 to raise the artificially low price of bread met with widespread and angry public demonstrations, forcing the government to back down. Nasser is still a potent symbol in the hearts and minds of the Egyptian peasantry and bureaucracy, and one is more likely to encounter his picture in a peasant home than that of Anwar Sadat. It is clear that much of the thrust of the Egyptian revolution under Nasser survives. It is also clear that Sadat made a mark on that revolution himself, as the Egyptian treaty with Israel (1978), the dramatic break with the U.S.S.R., and the wooing of Western industry to the Nile demonstrated.

Sadat's government, however, came under increasing domestic pressure from groups dissatisfied with these changes. Palestinian organizations placed a price on his head, as did Libya's volatile Colonel Qadaffi. The Muslim Brotherhood, violently repressed by Nasser in the early days of the revolution, showed signs of resurgence, encouraged by the Islamic revolutions in Libya, Iran, and Pakistan. And Arab nationalists, unhappy with Sadat's unilateral peace with Israel, began to oppose Sadat's rule. These factors ultimately coalesced in the fall of 1981 in the assassination of Anwar Sadat by members of a Muslim fundamentalist cell in the Egyptian army.

Sadat's successor, Hosni Mubarak, was more careful to avoid direct conflict with these alienated groups, and ample evidence documents a broadening of the ruling class under his rule. Mubarak allowed limited representation of conservative Muslim groups in the Egyptian political elite and has avoided the personal displays of consumption and irreverence that brought Sadat into disrepute with Egyptian fundamentalists. But at the same time, Mubarak moved forcefully to reduce fundamentalist influence in the Egyptian military and government bureaucracy. Some incremental and modest Islamization has occurred, particularly in the areas of family law. Muslim political groups have been allowed to contest for seats in the legislature. And the government appears to be at great pains to avoid antagonizing the fundamentalist ulema. The prospects seemed to suggest continued conflict between groups in the Egyptian elite, successfully moderated through existing Egyptian political institutions and modest electoral freedom. The Egyptian role in international affairs—particularly Desert Storm and the Oslo-era Mideast peace negotiations—increased the prestige of the government domestically, an asset it needed as domestic pressures on government capacity increased.

Contemporary Egypt is under enormous pressure from competing ideologies, population growth, economic stagnation, and religious extremism, at home and abroad. The elite structure of Egypt has apparently broadened and expanded in recent years. But the emergence of political terror in Egypt, particularly the occasional targeting of foreign tourists, Egyptian Copts, and governmental officials for assassination, including the attempt on President Mubarak's life in Ethiopia in late 1995, has led the government to retrench on its emphasis on democratization. The government has reacted firmly to attempts by politically extremist and even moderate Muslim organizations to take over important Egyptian unions and professional associations, and the government continues to manipulate election rules to effectively disenfranchise smaller or fringe Islamic parties. As a result there are growing political strains on the Egyptian political system and decreasing permeability to the Egyptian elite. Future domestic conflict is highly likely. The prestige of moderate Islamist groups in Egypt grows as the legitimacy of the Egyptian government declines. These factors hold the seeds of future political conflict as new generations of restive citizens attain political maturity.

Syria.   Syria shares many characteristics with Lebanon and the people of Palestine. One of the most economically viable of the Middle Eastern countries, Syria has considerable arable land, reasonable water resources, and a well-educated population. Syria has for many years exported its professional and commercial expertise, an indicator of its well developed and sophisticated elites. Syria's borders were the result of arbitrary decisions by the victorious European allies; it is also one of the front-line states in the Arab-Israeli conflict. Like Egypt and Lebanon, Syria carried much of the financial and personal burden of the confrontation.

Syrian politics have been dominated since the early 1950s by a combination of party ideology (the Baath party) and military opportunism. Currently, Syria is run by a military-bureaucratic elite whose power is periodically confirmed by national elections. Most influential positions, including that of the president, are currently held by Alawite Muslims, a small and obscure sect. There is substantial resentment in the Sunni and Shia communities over this inequity, a resentment leading at least in part to broad-scale uprisings in Aleppo (1980) and Hama (1982), forcefully put down by the government. Sunni and Shia participation in Syrian government since that time has been both cautious and deliberate.

Although the Baath party (in both Syria and Iraq) has a substantial ideology of nationalism and moderate socialism, pragmatism is a strong influence in contemporary Syrian policy. The collapse of the Soviet Union left Syria exposed diplomatically and militarily. As a consequence, since the late 1980s Syria has slowly moved toward the West and the United States. In the 1990s Syria abandoned many of the hallmarks of association with the Soviet alliance, pursuing modified market economics and improved diplomatic and trade relations with the West. The education of Syrian students in the West has increased dramatically, and English has eclipsed Russian and French as the second language of commerce and culture.

Syria gained a measure of political stability under Baathist military rule, a stability that stands in marked contrast to the highly unstable early days of its independence, when the coups d'état were literally too numerous to count reliably. A modicum of economic growth has been achieved, and internationally Syria has achieved a far greater influence in the Arab bloc than her size and power would indicate. The aftermath of the Israeli invasion of Lebanon led to a dramatic rise in Syrian prestige in the region, an opportunity carefully exploited in President Assad's diplomacy. And Syria's key role in the U.S.-led coalition against Iraq in 1990–1991 contributed greatly to its regional prestige. Syrian foreign policy in the last decade of the century centered on the recovery of the Golan, a related peace with Israel, and consolidation of its influence in Lebanon.

These international successes continue to be a domestic asset for the government. The expanded role taken by Syria in Lebanon since 1986 continues, and a Lebanese economic and political recovery reduces strain on Syrian political resources. A *de facto* annexation, once considered highly unlikely, is no longer out of the range of possibility. By the late 1990s Lebanon enjoyed uncharacteristic calm and political order. There are many strong ties between elements in the Lebanese and Syrian elites and some sentiment in favor of continuing this relationship on both sides.

Syria's role in Lebanon is one of the intangibles in the negotiations with Israel over the return of the Golan region. After the assassination of Prime Minister Rabin, succeeding Israeli governments (Netanyahu, Barak) linked a full Israeli withdrawal from Golan to effective Syrian guarantees of reduced Hizbollah guerrilla activity in southern Lebanon and the negotiation of a comprehensive peace treaty. This Israeli position would strengthen the Syrian position in Lebanon even further, but it may be predicated on a dubious assumption. The assumption in question is the degree to which Hizbollah and its allies are in fact controlled by Syria. Iran is certainly a factor in the constellation of support for Hizbollah and other movements in the region. At any rate, however, it is clear that a peace treaty between Israel and Syria, meeting both Syrian and Israeli needs, would constitute a formal expansion of the Syrian area of influence and require another extension of the Syrian political elite.

The Syrian political elite has become progressively more representative in the past decade, as national elections and the promulgation of a more or less democratic constitution demonstrate. Syria is one of the most socially progressive of the Middle Eastern nations—the status of women, for instance, is traditionally higher in Syria than in the rest of the Middle East. Syria, with adequate water and growing petroleum reserves, is potentially one of the economic bright spots outside the Gulf area.

Iraq.   Iraq, being both Baathist in ideology and a geographic neighbor of Syria, might be expected to share many of Syria's political characteristics. This, however, is not so. The Iraqi form of Baathism has been consistently more radical, and

political conflict in Iraq has been resolved at a much higher level of violence. Since the overthrow of the monarchy in 1958, Iraq has been ruled by a series of political juntas. Most elite conflict has taken place in the military, most often in the form of bloody coups. There is also the continuing problem with the Kurdish minority in the northern mountains of Iraq. Fiercely independent and stubborn, the Kurds have fought an on-and-off war of national independence since Iraq gained its independence, a war often costly to Iraq in terms of lives and political stability. The Kurdish revolt following the defeat of Iraq in Desert Storm clearly tested the resources of the staggering Iraqi regime. Turkish fears of an independent Kurdistan on its borders probably gave Iraq the breathing room it needed at the critical moment. The Kurds were abandoned once again.

This problem with the Kurdish minority is not, of course, restricted in any way to Iraq. The Kurds, the largest and most militant stateless minority in the Middle East, occupy the contiguous territory of Iraq, Iran, Syria and Turkey. All these countries have pursued policies at one time or another ranging from neglect to open hostility and even genocide. The Kurds currently find themselves treated as a "nongroup" in Turkey, are under military pressure to conform to the Islamic revolution in Iran, and have been subjected to a brutal resettlement strategy in Iraq, designed to move them away from the oil fields in the north and into the deserts of the south. They were the group least likely to benefit from government policy or economic development. Their circumstances changed dramatically after the 2003 removal of the Iraqi regime.

Exploited by both sides in the Iran-Iraq war, the Kurds have been subject to violent suppression by governments suspicious of their loyalties in the conflict. Whole villages of Kurds have been destroyed and at least one Kurdish village, Halabja, was gassed as it attempted to play Iran against Iraq. Others have been relocated to more secure regions. Other Kurds have moved in large numbers into neighboring countries, especially Turkey. Their numbers and influence in the Iraqi elite have declined from the admittedly marginal prewar levels.

The Shia populations in Iraq fared better at the hands of the government during the conflict. In fact, perhaps fearing Shia sympathies to Iran, the Iraqi government overtly courted Shia leaders, bringing many new faces into the Iraqi elite. Thus, while the war brought continued pressure against the Kurds, it can also be viewed as a rationale for the limited extension of the ruling class to the Shia leadership. Events after the Gulf War put an end to such elite expansion, however.

Government policy during this period notably emphasized the leadership of Saddam Hussein, to the point that critics of the regime characterized it as a "personality cult" of enormous proportions. In point of fact, the overrepresentation of officials with origins or connections to Saddam Hussein's hometown of Tikrit is clear. This clique of leaders related to each other by blood, experience, or faction was a dominant influence in Iraqi politics.

As the pressure of the war with Iran wound down in late 1988 and early 1989, Saddam Hussein reinstated many development projects that had been abandoned during the war with Iran. These projects had the potential to reinforce his popularity and stabilize the Iraqi elite. They were unfortunately squandered in the adventure with Kuwait in 1990 and the subsequent UN sanctions and U.S.-led air strikes against Iraq's military and economic infrastructure.

The Iraqi regime was implacably opposed to Israel and quick to blame Western diplomacy for the continued vitality of Israel. Consequently, the Iraqi elite sought closer ties with the Soviet Union and Eastern Europe and marketed a considerable percentage of its great crude oil production in those areas. Although Iraq was by no means a satellite of Soviet foreign policy, the Iraqi elite maintained closer ties with the Eastern bloc than did nearly any other Middle Eastern state.

The strong support of American allies for Iraq during the war with Iran led to many new opportunities for contact. Many Iraqi students studied in the West and many Western corporations bid on the reopened development projects. But although there were many signs of new relationships with the West, there were few signs that Iraq was changing its views on the subject of Israel. Thus, Iraqi policy continued to have its points of conflict with the West.

The Iraqi invasion of Kuwait in 1990 and the resulting military confrontation with the U.S.-led coalition in Desert Storm severely damaged the political, economic, and military capacity of Iraq. It is remarkable that the regime survived, but it did. The Kurdish problem was unresolved and the periodic interventions by the coalition on behalf of the Kurds did not result in fundamental improvement of their plight. The Shia rebellion in the south was crushed as well.

Many faces in the elite and ruling class have changed, but the basic equation, privileging Saddam Hussein and the Tikritis, changed only marginally.

The defection of two of Saddam's relatives to Jordan in 1995 raised hopes outside of Iraq that Saddam and his clique might be on the decline. But the regime weathered that storm without obvious consequences, and the two defectors returned voluntarily to Iraq six months later. They were subsequently killed in a shootout with their relatives. Western and moderate and conservative Arab regimes were extremely frustrated over Saddam's longevity. Covert efforts to destabilize the regime increased, and it seemed unlikely that the UN or other international agencies would soon allow the political or diplomatic rehabilitation of Iraq. The United States and its allies continued an almost daily bombing of Iraq, with few positive consequences.

Under increasing pressure from the Bush administration, Iraq became the object of U.S. attempts at regime change early in the millennium. Efforts were made to inspire antigovernment movements among the Kurds and Shia populations. United Nations resolutions brought weapons inspectors back to Iraq in late 2002. All of these pressures, sanctions, and attempted interventions only seemed to increase the rigidity of the regime. A potent or effective opposition to the established Iraqi ruling elite was not apparent.

In March of 2003, an exasperated United States launched Operation Iraqi Freedom, a unilateral invasion of Iraq to accomplish regime change. By April 9, the Baathist government under Saddam Hussein had been destroyed and the beginnings of an occupation administration initiated. Apparent conflicts among Sunni, Shia, Kurdish, and Turkoman communities were aggravated as the occupying power looked for a formula that would restore order, reestablish basic services, and facilitate a transition to an Iraqi regime, hopefully democratic in nature.

Lebanon. Until the spillover of the Arab-Israeli conflict literally tore it asunder, Lebanon was the most cosmopolitan country in the Middle East. Beirut, a city of charm and energy, was a center of commerce and finance; it had attracted a highly skilled and mobile international population. Blessed with considerable national resources, including a well-educated and ambitious population, Lebanon seemed to have a very bright future.

The Israeli invasion of Lebanon in 1978, primarily to eliminate Palestinian terrorist bases, put an effective end to the dream of the Lebanese. But in point of fact, the dream was fragile long before. Lebanon, another of those countries based on a series of unwise and shallow judgments made in Europe, was composed of at least three highly differentiated ethnic groups: Christians, Muslims, and Druze. Never integrated into a national political or economic unit, these groups lived in proximity but not intimacy. The National Pact or charter of Lebanon, promulgated at a time when the Muslim and Christian populations were nearly equal, parceled out political offices to particular ethnic groups. For example, the president was required to be a Maronite Christian while the prime minister had to be a Sunni Muslim and the speaker of the Assembly a Shia Muslim. These and other offices were apportioned on the basis of the supposed relative balance of religious-ethnic groups at the time of the National Pact. National censuses were forbidden for fear of upsetting the delicate balance between the groups.

The fiction of stable, counterbalancing religious groups served Lebanon well until it was forced, seemingly against its will, into the mainstream of the Arab-Israeli confrontation. After the invasion of Lebanon by Israeli units in 1978, Lebanon was plagued by a civil war that was aided and abetted by foreign intrigue. Links between Israel and right-wing Christian groups, formalized in the aftermath of the 1982 invasion, deteriorated in subsequent years. Syrian troops occupied much of Beirut and Lebanon, with little pretense of peacekeeping and with the open

intention of exercising political control. Thus, what remained of Lebanese independence was completely destroyed in the aftermath of the Israeli invasion of Lebanon in the summer of 1982, an invasion and occupation disastrous for nearly every actor concerned. The expulsion of the Arafat wing of the PLO created a vacuum of power in the elite, leading to the rise of the Shia militias (particularly the Amal and Hizbollah), Syrian-backed factions of the Palestinians, and the Syrians themselves. Lebanon was in a state of civil war.

There have been many efforts to "fix" the situation in Lebanon and most have failed. The Taif Accords, however, midwifed in 1989 by Saudi Arabia and Lebanese legislators, produced substantial progress. In effect, Syria became an active participant in stabilizing Lebanon, forcing substantial disarmament among the independent militias and establishing a governmental military presence. As a result, Lebanon by the early 1990s enjoyed a modicum of stability. Many of the Lebanese social, economic, and political elite that had fled to Jordan, the Gulf states, and Europe announced plans to return. For the first time in twenty years, there was real cause for optimism that Lebanon might resolve its civil war. The Lebanese elite appears to be broadening, with greater representation of the previously disenfranchised Shia. This bodes well for the establishment of effective government in this decade. And certainly the diplomatic aftereffects of Desert Storm reduced some of the international pressure on Lebanon, making it less attractive as an international battlefield. The release of all American hostages in Lebanon in late 1991 was apparently a joint venture of Lebanon, Syria, and Iran and the United Nations. The release certainly reduced the rhetorical conflict in the Middle East, to Lebanon's advantage.

As was noted in the preceding discussion, progress on the Israeli/Syrian peace negotiations appeared to strengthen the Syrian hand in Lebanese politics. The unexpected withdrawal of Israel's occupying forces from southern Lebanon reduced much of the pressure on the Lebanese government, with salutary effects. This appeared to contribute to the progress made in Lebanon in the last few years, continuing the trend toward development of an independent stable and effective government. A comprehensive peace settlement with Syria and Lebanon by Israel would go a long way to improving the political and economic outlook in Lebanon. This seemed increasingly unlikely as the Israeli-Palestinian conflict spiraled to higher and higher levels of violence and intransigence.

Israel. In some respects, the Israeli elite is the most modern of the Middle Eastern elites; and in other respects, it is among the most traditional. It is modern in that its members are highly educated and technically competent. There has been an important infusion of Russian émigrés into the elite in the past decade, permitting some elite expansion in size and experience. The Israeli elite has mastered the technological skills and values necessary for a modern society. For those who qualify for elite status—primarily on the basis of religious preference, technical competence, and social origin—the established political process is participatory and representative.

Recent political trends in Israel have enhanced (perhaps exaggerated) the presence of the religious Orthodox and Ultraorthodox elements in the Israeli elite. Their influence as the swing factions in the coalitions in the Knesset have given them influence out of proportion to their numbers. They now compete effectively with the previously dominant secular factions, and their presence in any government's ruling coalition is critical to its survival there. In fact, the withdrawal of support by two very small parties in January of 1992 forced general elections, and similar defections led to the demise of the Netanyahu government in 1999 and the Sharon government in 2002. Ultraorthodox parties continue to enjoy disproportional influence in government and the Israeli elite.

However, large groups of citizens are effectively disenfranchised in the Israeli system. First and most obvious are the Arabs, who number in the hundreds of thousands and who live in both Israel proper and the various occupied territories of Gaza, the Golan Heights, and the West Bank. From the government point of view, the Arabs constitute a serious security problem and as a consequence they are subject to a wide range of political, economic, and social controls. These controls greatly increased during the Palestinian intifadahs, indicating a growing government resolve to stamp out any vestige of sympathy for independence. The Palestinian intifadah eventually motivated civil disobedience and demonstrations among Israeli Arab citizens as well, leading to more problems for this poorly represented constituency. Ironically, the growing legitimacy of the Palestinian Authority in the West Bank and Gaza has resulted in higher levels of estrangement for Arabs living within Israel proper, citizens or not.

Disenfranchisement was not the fate only of the Arabs, however. Intra-Jewish conflict has been well documented in recent decades, demonstrating that certain Jewish groups have very little access to the ruling class. Tensions continue between the politically dominant European Jews (Ashkenazi) and the more recently arrived and less modern Oriental Jews (Sephardim) from Asia and Africa. Moreover, there are growing separations between recent immigrants from both the Ashkenazi and Sephardic communities and the native-born descendants of the founders, the Sabras. Hundreds of thousands of Jews from the former Soviet Union have emigrated to Israel. They are not well integrated into the Israeli political system and have not yet found their economic or social niche. Many African Jewish immigrants are living lives of unemployed marginality in hotels originally built for the tourist trade. Their isolation is palpable and begs for solution. The revelation in 1996 that thousands of units of blood donated by Ethiopian Jews (Falasha) had been destroyed for fear of "contamination" led to public demonstrations by this disadvantaged group. In point of fact, Israel has been swallowing considerably more immigrants than it can effectively integrate into its system, resulting in large numbers of European and African Jews living in political and economic limbo. Growing levels of inflation have exacerbated these problems.

The implementation of the Israeli-Palestinian peace accords placed new strains on both the Israeli and Palestinian political elites. The return of Gaza and Jericho to Palestinian control brought vehement opposition from fundamentalist Jewish groups, particularly the settler movements in the West Bank. Increasing tensions between the nonobservant Israeli leadership and the observant leadership became public and vitriolic. Further grants of responsibility to the new Palestinian Authority increased friction further. This situation led directly to the assassination of Prime Minister Yitzhak Rabin by a fundamentalist Jewish extremist in October of 1995.

Public and media reactions to the assassination, to the unseemly celebrations of the event among settler and American Jewish communities, and to the evidence that ultraconservative rabbis had at least indirectly approved of the murder led to a swing in public opinion toward continuation of the peace process and a decline of support for extremist groups in Israel. But a spate of terrorist bombings from a militant wing of Hamas in the winter of 1996 placed this momentum in jeopardy and allowed a reemergence of antipeace sentiment in political discourse. As Prime Minister Barak proceeded in the implementation of the peace accords in 1999, increasing tension between the settler groups and the government became apparent. Polarization between the Israeli left and right occurred.

The same period of time saw the formal emergence of a Palestinian political elite. The formalization of a Palestinian authority and the consequent empowerment of Palestinian police, administrative officials, teachers, principals, and other functionaries enriched and expanded this particular elite. Elections held in early 1996 further increased the level of Palestinian participation in their "government." Many of these newly constituted political elites have come from the Fatah faction of the PLO and have returned to Palestine from their former diaspora. Domestically, Arafat and his followers have pursued the marginalization of Hamas followers, while tolerating the emergence of a "loyal opposition" composed of prominent individuals like Dr. Haider al-'Shafi, former head of the Gaza Red Crescent Society, and Hannan Ashwari, a prominent spokesman for the anti-Arafat faction. This consolidation of Fatah influence in the Palestinian elite is likely to continue in the near future, as is the growing legitimacy of an internal opposition.

The result of the intermittent and uneven progress toward Israeli-Palestinian peace has resulted in the emergence of two political elites, Israeli and Palestinian, with a common stake in the success of the peace effort. The genie of Palestinian autonomy, even Palestinian independence, is out of the bottle. It cannot be contained again without wreaking havoc and destruction on both parties. Both elites have managed to weaken the radical fringes of their memberships. And both now see more to be gained in cautious cooperation than in formal and systematic hostilities. This is a fundamental change in the political equation in Israel, and in the Middle East as a whole.

CONCLUSION

It is clear that political, social, and economic pressures in the Middle East ultimately affect the elite structure of politics. The Middle East is unusual in having a wide variety of elites—traditional, transitional, and modern. It is also clear that changes in the composition of an elite can ultimately cause profound changes in the policies and world view of a political system. Unfortunately, these effects are not specifically predictable.

On the other hand, we can safely predict that these changes will produce new strains and demands upon the political system, and that these strains and demands will create new and often unexpected conflicts both domestic and international. We can thus with some confidence predict a continuation of the unsettled nature of contemporary Middle Eastern politics. And without doubt, we can predict that Islam, in its various forms, will be intimately involved in that process. These factors, combined with the commonplace but accurate observation that the world is growing smaller, suggest that the political implications of these changes in elite structure will influence all our hopes and lives.

Political Leadership in the Contemporary Middle East

Having discussed the ruling elites in the Middle East, we shall now focus on those individuals in the highest political offices: monarchs, generals, presidents, and so on. While effective leadership is important to the world's affluent and powerful societies, it is even more important to the disadvantaged and recently independent countries that are confronting serious internal and external challenges. Countries in which the institutions of governments are new, fragile, or discredited have a far greater need for effective leadership than those with long histories of political order and stability.

There are three basic styles of political leadership: traditional, modern technical bureaucratic, and charismatic.[1] We shall examine a leader representative of each style and show how his career exemplifies that style's essential nature. We shall then examine other contemporary Middle Eastern leaders and see how their styles of rule fit the pattern. Finally, we shall briefly examine how these leadership styles affect domestic and international politics.

[1] This leadership typology originated with Max Weber, the great German sociologist. Our use of it, however, differs substantially from his. See Hans Gerth and C. Wright Mills, eds., *From Max Weber* (New York: Oxford University Press, 1964).

The three basic leadership styles are necessarily broad and general and do not account for fine differences, nor do they accurately predict the political consequences of any one kind of leadership; they are only rough guides. To illustrate the three types, we shall focus on four prominent figures in twentieth-century Egyptian politics: King Farouk (traditional), Gamal Abdel Nasser (charismatic), and Anwar Sadat and Hosni Mubarak (modern bureaucratic).

TRADITIONAL LEADERSHIP

Traditional leaders base their claim to leadership on the assertion that they are the clear and logical successors to a line of leaders that stretches back in time and that is legitimized by practice. They are leaders because of historical forces, and they claim the right and obligation to continue. They often imply that their leadership is necessary to maintain the social order on the right course. Traditional political orders, while conservative, are not rigid or unyielding to change; but they may be slow to implement a schedule of changes or react to changing conditions. They expect change to occur over relatively extended periods of time. As Almond and Powell observe, a definite promise of performance is implied in the assertion of the right to rule:

> most traditional societies have some long-range performance expectations built into their norms of legitimacy; if crops fail, enemies invade, or floods destroy, then the emperor may lose the "mandate of heaven," as in Imperial China; or the chiefs their authority; or the feudal lords, their claim to the loyalty of their serfs.[2]

The traditional leader depends on the force of tradition, or his interpretation of it, to establish his legitimacy as a ruler. Legitimacy refers to the public perception of the ruler's right to his position of leadership, and is not restricted to traditional leaders alone. The willingness of the populace to accept a particular leadership structure as right and defensible legitimizes the political process as it exists. But it is no substitute for effective policy nor can it protect an ineffective ruler forever.

Some examples of traditional legitimization may clarify the problem. There is a logic to the use of tradition as a legitimizing symbol. The shah of Iran, for instance, often publicly argued that the Persian cultural tradition demanded monarchical leadership, that the Iranian political practice for thousands of years found its most effective and satisfying expression in a monarch. As monarch, Mohammed Reza Pahlevi was therefore performing an important service for the Iranian people. The rulers of Egypt made similar arguments.

That tradition may legitimize but not stifle change is also well demonstrated in Saudi Arabia. There is no gainsaying the importance of tradition in legitimizing the Saudi leadership. But tradition has not been a logical reason for continuing a weak leader in office. The transition from King Saud to King Faisal, based on decisions within the royal family itself, suggests that this traditional elite was responsive to contemporary difficulties. Tradition was mobilized to legitimize the change and the new leadership.

The right or legitimacy of traditional leaders is often bound up in the intersection of political and religious tradition: The king or sultan may also be the defender of the faith, for example; or the

sheikh may be patron of the ulema, as in the relationship of the Egyptian monarchy with the mosque university of Al-Azhar. These roles and symbols, given great weight by their persistence over time, are the most important factors in legitimizing the traditional regimes.

In the absence of competing claims, traditional leaders may find the invocation of ancient roles and symbols adequate to protect their base of power. Given the twentieth-century phenomenon of competing claims from charismatic or modern bureaucratic aspirants to office, traditional leaders have often been forced to attempt limited reforms within the recognized tradition. And so, traditional leaders have attempted to modernize their political, social, and economic systems without sacrificing their right to rule. The Tanzimat reforms in Ottoman Turkey can be interpreted in this light, as can the White Revolution of the shah of Iran. In both cases, the traditional leader attempted to come to terms with modern technology and administrative procedures without relinquishing his monopoly of political power. It is instructive that both efforts ultimately failed.

King Farouk of Egypt

Many characteristics of traditional political leaders are exhibited in the experience of King Farouk of Egypt, the last Egyptian monarch. Farouk's rule (1936–1952) embraced a period of time that saw a fundamental redrawing of the international political order, including the rise of Soviet and American power, the concomitant decline of European—especially British—influence in the Middle East, the emergence of mass political parties, and the political reassertion of Islam and Islamic groups. Farouk's response to these changes demonstrates both the essence of traditional leadership and its fundamental defects.

Born in 1920 into the royal lineage founded by the great Egyptian leader Muhammad Ali, Farouk was raised in a strong tradition of royal absolutism. The line of Muhammad Ali treated the whole of Egypt as its personal possession. King Farouk proved himself to be no stranger to this tradition.

The royal family, like most of the ruling houses of Egypt for the past 3,000 years, was not of Egyptian extraction. In the case of Farouk's family,

---

[2] Gabriel Almond and Bingham Powell, *Comparative Politics* (Boston: Little, Brown, 1978), pp. 31–32.

the line was founded by an Albanian adventurer, Muhammad Ali, with very tenuous ties of loyalty to the Ottoman Empire. Enormously successful at realizing the political, social, and economic potential of nineteenth-century Egypt, Muhammad Ali was frustrated by European, especially English, intervention. A large extended family buttressed by extensive retainers and officials saw Egypt as a private fief run for its own benefit. With few ties to the Egyptian masses, the royal family routinely assumed its right to absolute rule and consistently opposed the extension of political rights or influence to native Egyptians.

Farouk himself was educated and socialized in a conservative atmosphere; he was exposed to periodically rabid Anglophobia and persistently pro-Italian sympathies. Farouk's tutors included the most notable ulema of Al-Azhar University, who instilled in him a serious appreciation of his role as protector of the faith. King Fuad's death placed Farouk on the throne at age sixteen, still in his minority. A regency council was formed to advise and educate him in his responsibilities as ruler of Egypt.

Farouk's father, King Fuad, saw the emergence of the first legitimate mass political party in Egypt, the Wafd. Much of Fuad's political labors in later life were devoted to frustrating Wafd aspirations to power, a policy continued by the young king. The combination of mass political activity and growing nationalism had a disquieting effect on the royal house. By complex political maneuvers, Fuad and Farouk attempted to exclude the Wafd from power. Thus, they both demonstrated one of the chief characteristics of traditional political leadership: a great reluctance to *share* political power with anyone, particularly with mass or nationalist groups. This is not to imply that Farouk was bereft of policy or ambition—indeed, there is evidence to the contrary. The point is that these ambitions never included a broadening of the base of political power.

Farouk demonstrated his traditional orientation to political power in other ways. His fascination with ceremony, pomp, and circumstance reflected the concern of the traditional leader for rituals and rite that confirm the assertion and maintenance of traditional authority. Decked out in rich uniforms for every occasion, Farouk's movements around his kingdom were spectacles in themselves: elegant livery, scores of retainers and entertainers, international celebrities and sumptuous banquets in luxurious palaces or country estates. Grandeur was not only a perquisite of office, it was an obligation; and Farouk became increasingly enthusiastic about it.

In a similar vein, the royal house under Farouk became internationally noted for its hedonism. Drunkenness, particularly offensive to the emerging Muslim Brotherhood, sexual abandon (often reported graphically in the international press), and disturbingly regular accusations of official corruption involving minor members of the royal family were commonplace. Farouk's appreciation for attractive women became an international symbol of Egyptian royal decadence, set in the most luxurious spas of Mediterranean Europe.

There was a curious tension between Farouk's hedonism and his public attitude toward Islam. One could not call him personally pious, particularly in view of his devotion to Koranically prohibited pleasures: wine, women, and pornography. On the other hand, Farouk took his role as "defender of the faith" seriously; he made substantial contributions to the maintenance of Al-Azhar and welcomed a number of political exiles to Cairo. He also subsidized programs designed to maintain Egyptian prestige in the larger community of Muslim nations, which lacked any focus of authority since the abolition of the caliphate. These practices solidified his relationship to the higher ulema at the same time that his hedonism was coming under growing criticism by fundamentalist Muslim groups.

Despite these irritants to the prestige of the royal house, Farouk's rule and government enjoyed a legitimacy that demonstrates the strength of traditional leadership. Most analysts of the period assert that Farouk's government far outlasted its effectiveness. Aside from noting the population's predisposition to accept the traditional, little in the last ten years of Farouk's rule suggests that his political, social, or economic *performance* commanded popular support for the government.

The final blow to Farouk's rule in Egypt resulted from a combination of domestic and international forces. Farouk's pro-Italian sympathies quickly ran afoul of international events in World

War II, resolving in favor of his British enemies. In addition, the public became dissatisfied with his opposition to the Wafd party, and the increasingly militant fundamentalist Muslim Brotherhood was disillusioned by his personal licentiousness. Riots in Cairo involving the Wafd, extremist groups, the Muslim Brotherhood, and students became commonplace. The final blow came with the miserable performance of the Egyptian military in the war against Israel in 1948, although the full implications of the war were not to become clear to the public until the revolution of July 23, 1952. Charges of corruption and ineptitude gained widespread circulation and validity. The war became a focus of resentment against the low level to which Arab and Egyptian prestige had sunk. Farouk became increasingly unable to manipulate the forces of Egyptian politics, and instability and drift became the governmental norms.

Farouk's fall and abdication were a result of actions by the military, not the political forces that opposed him for so long. His final attempts to abrogate the Anglo-Eyptian treaty in 1951 produced a series of ugly confrontations between Egyptian and British forces, which in turn set off a series of antigovernment and antiforeign riots in the urban centers of Egypt. The army's inability to handle these incidents further inflamed the king's opponents, and British efforts to reinforce their garrisons added even more fuel to the fire. Finally, on July 23, 1952, a group of military officers known as the "Committee of Free Officers" overthrew the government and established the Revolutionary Command Council under the titular leadership of General Naguib. On July 26, the council requested the formal abdication of King Farouk. Farouk complied, abdicating in favor of his son, and promptly departed for Italy. Farouk never recovered his influence in Egypt. His abdication itself demonstrated his inability to come to terms with the emerging political order.

Towards the middle of the afternoon, it was announced in a broadcast from Cairo that "some very important news would be given at six o'clock." Everybody understood and prepared to listen.

All round the Ras El Tin palace and along the coast road to Alexandria an enormous crowd had gathered, tense with expectation and with mixed feelings of anguish and joy. Then came the prodigious sight: the royal exit in the rays of the setting sun, on to the sea which a hundred and fifty years earlier had brought, to the Egyptian shore, the Albanian soldier of fortune, Muhammad Ali, the great-great-grandfather of the sovereign who was now taking his leave.

At ten minutes to six . . . Farouk, in his splendid white uniform of *Admiral of the Fleet,* came slowly down the palace steps towards the sea. He was followed by Queen Narriman, carrying the new king, six months old. . . . While the royal flag was being fetched from the palace, a cruiser in the bay fired a twenty-one-gun salute.

General Naguib went aboard. . . . Farouk appeared to be touched, behind the screen of his dark glasses. "Take care of my army," he said. "It is now in good hands, sire," Naguib replied. The answer did not please Farouk, who said in a hard voice, "What you have done to me, I was getting ready to have done to you." Then, turning on his heel, he took leave of the conquerors.[3]

Farouk's final years became a mishmash of sybaritic excess in the most expensive and exclusive resorts of Europe. Throwing himself with abandon onto the gambling tables, onto the dining tables, and into the arms of many an attractive companion, Farouk ended his life as a corpulent playboy dedicated to things of the flesh and the moment—a sad ending in many respects, far removed from the promise of leadership in the sixteen-year-old youth who ascended the throne in 1936.

King Farouk, of course, is hardly the best example to use of a traditional ruler. He was weak and was unable to rise effectively to the challenges of his times. Indeed, he helps to maintain the myth of decadent Middle Eastern rulers. Compared to the historical importance of the shah of Iran or Ibn Saud of Saudi Arabia, Farouk is something of a footnote to contemporary history.

However, King Farouk's example is important for several reasons. First, the crises of leadership that have afflicted the decolonializing world have

---

[3] Jeanne and Simone Lacouture, *Egypt in Transition* (New York: Criterion Books, 1958), pp. 156–59.

often involved the reluctant departure of ineffective traditional leaders. To focus on strong leaders would distort our analysis. Second, the myth of decadence is not a myth. Absolute rulers, traditional and otherwise, have not shown themselves to be disinterested in pleasure or pomp or luxury. Indeed, much of the basis for their legitimacy comes from just such a claim to the perquisites of royalty. Finally, the influence of weak and ineffective leaders on world history is arguably as important as the impact of the few "great men" of our times.

We will return to the subject of traditional leadership at the end of this chapter. The crisis of confidence in traditional leadership, which undermined King Farouk just as it undermined many other Middle Eastern leaders in this century, leads to three possible alternatives:

1. Traditional political governance from a different political ruler, an apparently unlikely and short-term phenomenon.

2. Leadership based on the claims of the modern bureaucratic managers in the society, such as the military or a nascent political party.

3. Charismatic leaders who offer their transcendent leadership as a substitute for the claims of tradition or bureaucratic efficiency.

In the period after the fall of the Egyptian monarch, the third alternative materialized in the form of Gamal Abdel Nasser, a young officer in the movement that called for Farouk's abdication. Definitely a charismatic leader, Nasser was to have an important effect on Egypt and the Middle East.

CHARISMATIC LEADERSHIP

As defined by Max Weber, a charismatic leader possesses particular characteristics that set him apart from normal leaders. A charismatic leader is, in a word, unique. He possesses personal characteristics that are suited to a peculiarly intense leadership style, and he is capable of creating or participating in an intense, reciprocal psychological exchange with his followers. His actions and proposals are legitimized by reference to some transcendent source, either religious, historical, natural, or mystical. Recent world leaders recognized as charismatic include Adolph Hitler, Charles de Gaulle, Tito, Sukarno, and Gamal Abdel Nasser.[4]

Our definition and description of charismatic leadership is complicated by two factors. First, charismatic leadership is often erroneously equated with other leadership characteristics such as personal beauty, rhetorical skill, popularity, and the like. Thus, the use of the term in general circulation may distract us from the necessary distinguishing characteristics of the charismatic leader. Secondly, charismatic leadership appears to be idiosyncratic to the culture in which it occurs; thus the characteristics of a charismatic leader in Egypt would differ from those of a charismatic leader in, say, France or England. The chemistry of the relationship between leader and followers changes according to the particulars of the culture and historical circumstance. Despite these difficulties, the phenomenon of charismatic leadership is real and is important in any analysis of Middle Eastern politics. Charismatic leaders have had, and continue to have, enormous impact on the politics of the region. The Sudanese Mahdi, Gamal Abdel Nasser, Ayatollah Ruhollah Khomeini, and Colonel Muammar Qadaffi—all have had, or have, the potential to alter dramatically the course of political events.

In spite of the idiosyncratic qualities of charisma, we can make some general observations about the phenomenon. First, charismatic leadership almost always appears during a social or political crisis—particularly a crisis in which the prevailing institutions of government have been discredited or destroyed. Examples might include the ruinous inflation in Germany that preceded the rise of Hitler or the legislative-executive deadlocks that preceded de Gaulle's second entrance into French politics. Theoretically, the public in these situations is predisposed to seek a heroic leader to provide a substitute for discredited authority.

---

[4] For a broad treatment of charismatic leadership, see Ann Ruth Willner, *The Spellbinders: Charismatic Political Leadership* (New Haven, Conn.: Yale University Press, 1984).

Another expectation is that the charismatic leader will promulgate substantial and convincing images of a new order, perhaps ordained in heaven, that will raise the community to new levels of activity and accomplishment, or, in another variant, restore the community to its rightful place in the world. In giving substance to the visionary demands of a disillusioned populace, the charismatic leader provides them with psychological sustenance and heightened self-esteem.

Yet another characteristic of charismatic leaders is their resonant rhetorical gift—resonant in the sense that they can raise sympathetic responses from their followers. This rhetorical gift may vary dramatically in style. Compare, for instance, the dramatic histrionics of Adolph Hitler with the icy, Olympian quality of de Gaulle's pronouncements. Whatever the style, the successful charismatic leader has the ability to move a nation by the power of his rhetoric. Indeed, in many cases the rhetoric may be more politically important than the substance of the policies articulated.

Finally, the charismatic leader leads by example. Once again, this quality seems idiosyncratic to culture. The simple, introspective life of a Gandhi can be contrasted with the cheerful hedonism of Sukarno in Indonesia or Marcos in the Philippines. But in each case, the leader in his personal life sets a standard of personal behavior that strikes the populace as desirable and ennobling.

These characteristics provide the public with personal knowledge of the leader. He has a place in the collective psychology of the nation. The leader in turn gains a larger-than-life perspective on himself, thriving and growing on the demands and support of the followers. Thus, a powerful, reciprocal psychological exchange is established, which ultimately allows a single personality to substitute for a complex of institutions.

As powerful as this reciprocal dynamic can be, there is a critical defect in charismatic leadership. That defect is the mortality of the leader himself, upon whom the whole social transaction is based. Charismatic leaders, like ordinary mortals, die, and the transition from a charismatic leader to his successor is fraught with hazard. Charismatic leaders do not appear on demand. Thus, one cannot count on replacing one charismatic leader with another. Usually, charismatic leadership must give

way to either traditional rule or modern-bureaucratic leadership—so nature and the human condition dictate. Let us now turn to the charismatic leadership of Gamal Abdel Nasser.

Gamal Abdel Nasser

Nasser presents an interesting counterpoint to King Farouk. Born in Alexandria in 1918 into the family of a low-level civil servant, Nasser was ethnically Egyptian, as opposed to the Albanian origins of Farouk. Educated in the new modern schools of the time, Nasser entered the Egyptian military academy in 1936. Farouk's first military job was as chief of state at age sixteen. Where Farouk was elegant and pampered, Nasser was simple and ascetic.

Nasser's physical and personal qualities have inspired many writers to attempt to capture the factors that contributed to his commanding presence. The following passages by Jeanne and Simone Lacouture are representative:

> What first impresses you is his massive, thick set build, the dazzlingly white smile in his dark face. He is tall, tough, African. As he comes toward you on the steps of his small villa on the outskirts of the city, or strides across his huge office at the Presidency, he has the emphatic gait of some Covent Garden porter or some heavy, feline creature, while he stretches his brawny hand out with the wide gesture of a reaper, completely sure of himself. His eyes have an Asiatic slant and almost close as he laughs. His voice is metallic, brassy, full, the kind of voice that would be useful on maneuvers in the open country. . . .
>
> The impression of strength remains when he relaxes. He has an air of youthfulness, together with a certain timidity. He is gray at the temples but his hard face, that reminds you of a ploughshare, sometimes takes on an adolescent look.[5]

Nasser, in short, was heady tonic to a people accustomed to foreign rule and previously convinced that government was not an Egyptian aptitude. His personal presence, reflecting both real and potential power, combined with an electrifying rhetorical style, spoke directly to the powerlessness of

---

[5] Jeanne and Simone Lacouture, *Egypt in Transition,* p. 453.

the masses. Nasser, it seems, became the personal embodiment of the aspirations of the people. He in turn grew in response to their fervent commitment.

Nasser entered politics indirectly. His biographies indicate an early dissatisfaction with foreign rule and political corruption, but he originally intended to reform the Egyptian military. Nasser and his associates did not come to power in the revolution of July 23, 1952, with any plan for political rule. Instead, it appears that political power and responsibility were thrust upon the officers as they began to recognize the inability of Farouk and the Wafd to work cooperatively for reform.

Ideologically, Nasser's early political views can be summarized by the formula "Fight Against Imperialism, Monarchy, and Feudalism." Only later, as he matured in the office of president, did Nasser's political views develop. These views demonstrated the cosmological quality of Nasser's leadership. Particularly in his promotion of Arab socialism and pan-Arabism, Nasser demonstrated the charismatic leader's claim to some cosmological source of authority. In making regular symbolic reference in his speeches and writings to the greatness of the Arab past, the Egyptian past, and to Islam and the Umma, Nasser not only provided a cultural and historical identity to the Egyptian people, but he legitimized contemporary policy in non-Western terms. In many respects, this can be labeled a triumph of form over substance, for Nasser never specified the policy implications of his ideology consistently. Nevertheless, for the fragmented and uncertain Egyptian community of the 1950s and 1960s, the Nasser prescription was just what was needed.

Nasser's relationship to Islam reveals his lack of ideological precision. Although he recognized a direct relationship between Islam and Egypt's past and present, and although he appeared to be personally pious and upright, Nasser was nevertheless a secular political leader. Early on in the revolution the Free Officers came into conflict with traditional Islamic forces: the ulema, which was in league with the monarchy and was opposed to the revolution, and the Muslim Brotherhood, which did not recognize any distinction between politics and religion. In steering a course between these forces, Nasser and the Free Officers opted

for a view that derived inspiration from Islam and its writings but simultaneously honored the principle of separation of church and state. This separation was anathema to the leadership of the Brotherhood, and a nasty confrontation was inevitable.

Nasser's socialism was ambiguous and imprecise. Essentially a philosophy of equitable distribution, Nasser's socialism has been rightly criticized for economic naïveté and a devotion to publicly managed projects of dubious value. While these projects were politically palatable, their contribution to a coherent economic policy was negligible. The steel complex at Helwan is a case in point. The claims of this grandiose project could not be justified by even the most optimistic economic projections. The project was to supply most of Egypt's need for steel, employ large numbers of Egyptian workers, and ultimately to contribute to the balance of payments through export. Of these goals, only the employment of more and more Egyptians was accomplished.

Similarly, the revolution's effort to guarantee jobs to every college graduate created a swollen bureaucracy that operated on the principle of disguised unemployment. This policy often resulted in several people sharing a job that could be handled more effectively by one employee. Intolerable inefficiencies were thus built into state enterprises and made administration very difficult. Once again, the political gain outstripped the economic realities.

The differences between Nasser and Farouk are quite sharp. There is one point, however, in which their leadership styles converge. The personal presence and lifestyle of each leader supported his claim to political authority. Of course, their lifestyles differed dramatically. Farouk's love of pomp and ceremony contrasts sharply with Nasser's modest private life. Each to a great degree personally demonstrated in his private life the basis of his claim to power.

Finally, both leaders' careers came to abrupt ends. Farouk abdicated to a life of leisure one jump ahead of the executioner; Nasser died unexpectedly of a heart attack in 1970. Neither of them left office under "normal" circumstances—that is, as the result of regular or normal political processes. Of the two leaders, Nasser clearly left the greater impression on Egyptian politics. As Bruce Borthwick pointed out, in spite of the difficulties besetting the regime, "Nasser had . . . received the 'gift of grace' that endows charismatic leaders. He and the Egyptian people were one; his actions and his voice were theirs. They would not let him resign in June, 1967, and when he died suddenly on September 28, 1970, the masses poured out their emotions for him in a frenzy of grief."[6] To this day, portraits of Nasser occupy the place of honor in the simple homes of the Egyptian peasantry. The imprint of Farouk is a historical curiosity, and no more.

The ultimate consequences of Nasser's charismatic leadership are manifold. First and foremost, through his charismatic claim on political power, Nasser gave Egypt a focus of legitimate power. In a time when the existing institutions of power were discredited (such as the monarchy, nobility, and political parties), his exercise of charismatic power filled what would have been a dangerous vacuum. Moreover, the cosmological qualities of Nasser's leadership, such as his commitment to the Islamic Umma, Arab culture, and the Egyptian nation, provided a potent national identity for the Egyptian masses. His powerful rhetoric and commanding presence provided real evidence that his claims and goals were viable and realizable, if difficult to achieve.

However, Nasser's rule had its negative aspects. His economic policies were at best naïve. His international adventures, as in the case of his military intervention in Yemen, often strained Egyptian capabilities beyond their limit. And his persistent confrontations with Israel committed vast proportions of the Egyptian economy to wartime production. Finally, his flirtation with international communism (domestic communists were suppressed and jailed) could have generated yet another wave of foreign intervention in the Middle East.

All in all, however, Nasser's leadership was of great benefit to Egypt. Ultimately the force of his leadership spilled over to the new institutions that implemented the revolution and prepared the way for modern bureaucratic politics. Thus, Egypt moved from a political process dependent on a single, fragile personality to a political system characterized more by institutional stability and strength.

MODERN BUREAUCRATIC LEADERSHIP

Modern bureaucratic leadership is predicated on the promise of adequate short-term performance in government. Claiming technical and organizational superiority over the older, traditional means of governance, modern bureaucratic leaders promise to transform society through the application of management skills. In short, these leaders believe that contemporary problems can be solved, that man can purposively change his physical and social environment if only given the chance and the right organization, and that these changes can lead to several possible social, economic, and political outcomes.

Although all modern bureaucratic leaders base their right to rule on their ability to perform and solve problems, some rule within publicly accountable systems (democratic) and others within authoritarian systems. Publicly accountable modern bureaucratic leaders recognize the right of the public to evaluate periodically their performance and decide whether to retain them in office. Authoritarian, or Kemalist, modern bureaucratic leaders reject the regular review of their right to rule, arguing instead that no one has the ability to judge their leadership or its performance.[7] Authoritarian leaders often conceive of their political rule as a period of political trust and tutelage during which society learns and practices the skills and procedures that will lead to genuine publicly accountable politics. In most cases, authoritarian modern bureaucratic regimes are military in nature; publicly accountable regimes have usually emerged from a political party background. In the emerging countries, where modernization was

---

[6] Bruce Borthwick, *Comparative Politics of the Middle East: An Introduction* (Englewood Cliffs, N.J.: Prentice Hall, 1985), p. 182.

[7] Kemalist refers to the modernizing authoritarian rule of Kemal Ataturk in Turkey that was aimed ultimately at the creation of a democratic process.

first achieved among the military, it is not surprising that Kemalist regimes predominate.

Anwar Sadat and Hosni Mubarak

The immediate successor to Nasser in Egypt was another member of the original Free Officers, Anwar Sadat. Original predictions suggested a relatively short tenure in office for Sadat, seeing him presiding over a period of transition during which more capable leaders would contest for the mantle of power. (Similar predictions had been made for the institutions of governance that had developed during Nasser's rule, particularly the Arab Socialist Union and the People's Assembly.) Both Sadat and those institutions proved much more durable than anticipated. By 1981, the Sadat regime had been in office for over ten years and had made a number of substantial changes in political emphasis and direction. Far from being a caretaker or transitional leader, Sadat proved himself to be a legitimate and strong leader in his own right.

Sadat's personal history was not unlike that of Nasser. Like Nasser, Sadat was born into a peasant family and benefited from a liberalization in education policy. Like Nasser, Sadat entered the Egyptian military academy during the time when the regime was trying to develop an Egyptian officer corps. And like Nasser, Sadat participated in the Free Officer movement that led to the coup of 1952. It is surprising, then, that there should be so few similarities in the leadership styles and political views of these two men.

Anwar Sadat was not a charismatic leader. His claims to the loyalty of the government and the public were based on his performance. He hoped for a low-keyed, coherent managed solution to Egypt's problems of the 1970s. Indeed, to compare Sadat's political thought to Nasser's is to compare the thought of a technician to that of a dreamer. Moreover, Sadat's rhetorical style bore little or no similarity to Nasser's impassioned, moving speeches.

Sadat's personal style contrasted sharply with those of Nasser and Farouk. Comfortable in Western dress, Sadat often appeared in a conventional Western suit and tie, as opposed to Nasser's simple tunics and Farouk's elaborate uniforms.

Sadat lived in an impressive villa, although it hardly compared with Farouk's palaces. Mrs. Sadat wore the latest Paris fashions and moved in the highest international social circles. Sadat was comfortable with modern political leaders around the world. He cultivated an image of international sophistication in dress, language, and personal manner.

Nothing underscores the difference between Sadat and Nasser more than their respective treatment in the American press. Where Nasser was often presented in uncomplimentary terms with thinly veiled suggestions that he was a communist or radical, Sadat was presented as a leader of quiet authority and dignity. As regular guests on American talk and interview shows in the 1970s, Mr. and Mrs. Sadat personally raised Egypt's national image by their humane, warm, and comfortable styles. Such democratic sophistication would not have occurred to a Farouk nor have been tolerated by the mercurial Nasser. Sadat was definitely a different kind of political animal.

Sadat reversed Nasser's economic policies, particularly those toward private industry. He openly sought foreign private investment in Egypt, strengthened ties with the United States and Western Europe, and pursued a political solution to the Israeli question and Palestinian demands. Domestically, he permitted new political parties to develop, although they were carefully controlled. He subtly tried, and failed, to demythologize Nasser.

Sadat believed that his reforms had relieved much of Egypt's economic and military burdens, and to some degree he has been proven correct. The Sinai had been recovered, and commercially exploitable oil resources expanded. The West gave military and technological support, but foreign investors were reluctant to enter the mixed Egyptian economy. Ultimately the failure of the Egyptian-Israeli peace talks over the question of Palestinian autonomy gave ammunition to his enemies in and out of Egypt. As a result, Sadat retrenched on many of his political reforms, the secret police became more active, and a number of political opponents were placed under house arrest.

Some of Sadat's reforms met with widespread resistance. In 1977 he attempted to raise the price of bread, which had been subsidized at artificially low prices since the revolution; there were riots in Cairo in which mobs burned luxury hotels and nightclubs catering to foreigners and chanted "Sadat-Bey, Sadat-Bey," equating Sadat with the hated Ottoman rulers of an earlier age. Foreign corporations attempting to enter the Egyptian economy reported that in spite of sympathy at high government levels, mid-level and low-level bureaucrats did not share this enthusiasm and made life miserable for Western business managers.

In governing Egypt, Sadat had certain advantages that were not available to either Nasser or Farouk. He had a tested set of bureaucratic and technocratic institutions upon which he relied for counsel and for implementation of policy. These institutions were less efficient than many of their counterparts outside Egypt, but they were a distinct improvement over the administrative vacuum that attended Egyptian political crises earlier in the century.

Anwar Sadat's rule ended on October 6, 1981, with his assassination while viewing a military parade. The assassins were members of a fundamentalist Muslim group within the Egyptian military and reportedly had strong ties to other fundamentalist groups active in Egypt. The transition of rule was remarkably smooth, and Sadat's vice president, Hosni Mubarak, was elevated to the presidency. The orderly transfer of power and the quiescent acceptance of the events by the Egyptian masses evidence the remarkable progress toward institutionalization of government since Nasser.

Under Mubarak's rule, Egypt recovered much of the prestige lost in the Arab world as a consequence of Sadat's peacemaking with Israel. Mubarak has been able to capitalize on Sadat's close relationship with the United States, the economic gains stemming from the military disengagement with Israel, and the aftermath of the disastrous Israeli invasion and occupation of south Lebanon. Mubarak's key role in the U.S.-led coalition that confronted Iraq in 1991 also contributed greatly to his domestic and international prestige. His leadership style has proven to be relatively low-key and accommodative, with the result that many of the Egyptian groups dissatisfied with Sadat's policies or personal style now find themselves cooperating with the government. This is

not to suggest that political conflict or tension has somehow been eliminated from Egyptian politics, and it is clear that the government has strenuously suppressed extremist Islamist opposition groups, but it is to suggest that there has been substantial improvement since Sadat's death and that the scope of political participation in Egypt has modestly widened. Since the political equation in Egypt is of critical importance to the larger political equations of the Middle East, stability and progress there generally benefit the larger system. Mubarak must continue to deal with the problems of economic growth, population explosion, Muslim fundamentalism, and international conflict that bedeviled his predecessors. But he can do so with a significantly stronger set of political institutions than any of his twentieth-century predecessors.

The aftermath of 9/11 placed Mubarak in a difficult position with his American allies. The "green light" perceived by Israel's leadership relative to its suppression of the Palestinian movements prompted uncharacteristic criticism of both Israel and the United States for its repression of the Palestinians. And Mubarak has proved to be a vocal critic of U.S. ambitions for a preemptive war against Iraq, another conflict that places Egypt in a difficult squeeze.

CONSEQUENCES OF LEADERSHIP STYLES

The contemporary Middle East presents a melange of leadership styles. Traditional and modern technicalist bureaucratic leaders predominate numerically (see Table 10-1), but charismatic leaders like Ayatollah Khomeini and Colonel Qadaffi have had disproportionate influence. Many of the international strains and tensions in the Middle East are partially a result of divergences between leadership styles.

Traditional leaders make up the largest group in the Middle East. Historically, these leaders tended to oppose modernization or modernize in only strictly technological ways; they all resisted any substantial sharing of powers. But in recent times, some traditional leaders have looked toward political reform, advocating changes that would result ultimately in a diminution of traditional

Table 10-1 Contemporary Leadership Styles in the Middle East

Traditional	Modern Bureaucratic	Charismatic
Bahrain	Egypt (K)[*]	Egypt under Nasser
Egypt under Farouk	Iran	Iran under Khomeini
Iran (Pahlevis)	Iraq (K) under U.S. occupation, April 9, 2003	Libya under Qadaffi
Jordan	Israel (for Jewish citizens)	
Kuwait	Lebanon	
Oman	Syria (K)	
Qatar	Turkey	
Saudi Arabia	Yemen (K)	
United Arab Emirates	Palestinian Authority	

[*]K = Kemalist Modern Bureaucratic

authority in favor of more democratically constituted future rule. But all traditional leaders, including those with modernization on their minds, depend greatly on formal assertions of their traditional right to rule, undergirding these claims with the performance of traditional rituals and the maintenance of complex interpersonal relationships with other leaders.

TRADITIONAL STATES

The enormous oil revenues of Saudi Arabia, Oman, the U.A.E., Qatar, and Kuwait permit them to manage their economies and give them some political breathing time. For those traditional leaders in poor countries—King Abdullah of Jordan, for example, or Emir Hamad of Bahrain—the maneuvering time is considerably reduced. In the case of Jordan, Bahrain, and Yemen, foreign subsidies have been crucial in maintaining the existing political authority, a compromise with independence distasteful to all leaders. However, recent discoveries of exploitable petroleum reserves in Yemen may ultimately produce major changes there.

Serious challenges to existing authority have emerged in all of the countries under traditional leadership. The fall of the shah of Iran is a likely harbinger of things to come. In Kuwait a traditional ruling class traumatized by the Iraqi occupation in 1990–1991 searched for security by expelling most of the Palestinian and Jordanian guest workers that manned their institutions, substituting guest workers from more distant and less

politically risky origins. Promises of greater democratization have not materialized and the as-Sabah family seems content with maintaining its traditional political authority even as small groups of Kuwaiti citizens petition for greater democratization.

In Jordan, a new king must deal with the domestic and international tensions that nearly toppled his father, King Hussein, a number of times. Early indicators suggest that King Abdullah will aggressively confront political issues in Jordan and has succeeded in working out practical compromises with Islamist factions in the Jordanian legislature. He has also continued his father's participation in the Israeli-Arab negotiations, forcefully insisting that both sides negotiate fairly and implement agreements in a timely fashion. He has been willing to support and criticize both sides in the conflict. On the other hand, the king has scaled back the commitment to developing democratic institutions, disbanding the legislature and postponing scheduled elections. King Abdullah also appears willing and able to take a publicly visible role in the political life of Jordan. U.S. and Israeli pressures on Jordan to take stronger, pro-Western positions on the Israeli occupation and the suppression of Iraq have put the king in a difficult position, particularly given strong public opinion in favor of the Palestinian resistance and public sentiment against a war with Iraq. Jordan was hard pressed by the United States to take an active role in the 2003 war with Iraq, a pressure largely resisted by the king. King Abdullah has largely lamented the plight of the Palestinians (rhetorical support) and refused to allow Jordan to be the base for U.S. troops attacking Iraq.

Oman, increasingly important in the international politics of the Persian Gulf, is bordered by Yemen to the west, conservative Arab states to the northwest, and an unpredictable Iran across the straits. Sultan Qabus has established close military relations with the United States, a relationship exercised during Desert Storm. But like most of the current rulers in the Gulf, he has refused to allow Omani bases to be used in a U.S. war against Iraq.

The eventual and inevitable end of Qabus's rule (he has no heirs) apparently precipitated an in-government coup attempt in 1995, one that resulted in the removal and arrest of a number of important Omani officials and influentials. But the situation in Oman is unclear at best, and even the sultan himself has publicly speculated on the form of governmental transition and the eventual emergence of democratic institutions. Omani economic conditions have improved, and educational programs have produced a capable, growing native elite quite capable of handling a transition to a new government or system in the coming future. Planning for a future transition continues.

The collective leadership in the United Arab Emirates have made similar arrangements, as have the leaders of Bahrain and Qatar, all pursuing policies of "nativization" and modest political reforms, including consultative assemblies. They all seem aware of the necessity of future changes in the form and structure of governance. The new leadership in Bahrain under Sheikh Hamad al-Khalifa has allowed the development of new institutions of representation and elections have been scheduled. The restive Shia population of Bahrain have been the focus of economic and social reforms and apparently are responding positively to them. Bahrain, like its other Gulf neighbors, has responded negatively to U.S. attempts to use Bahraini bases in the wars against Iraq.

Perhaps the most dramatic changes in the Gulf states have occurred in the small state of Qatar under the leadership of Sheikh Hamad al-Thani. Qatar's experiment with modern communication, the independent Arab news service Al-Jazeerah, has injected a new element of mass communication into the Middle East generally. Its broadcasts

of communiqués from Osama bin Laden and his lieutenants have incited furious negative reactions from other Middle-Eastern and Western states. And Qatar has allowed the United States to develop a large military facility as an alternative to similar facilities in Saudi Arabia and other Gulf states. Qatar was the only Gulf state to publicly support the proposed U.S. assault against Iraq. Modest democratic reforms at the municipal level are also under way.

All the Gulf states have serious security problems occasioned by their small size and the attractiveness of their oil reserves. As many observers remark, these small states live in a "bad neighborhood" with strong and aggressive neighbors. They all rely increasingly on the coordination of their foreign policies through the Gulf Cooperation Council, seeking a measure of security in collective defense relationships. Recent calls for a GCC organized trade and customs union have been positively received, suggesting a growing role for this important regional actor.

Saudi Arabia is the dominant political actor among the traditional states of the region and plays a key role in the larger Middle Eastern system. The Saudi decision to invite U.S. troops onto Saudi soil to defend against Iraq clearly had a high risk/reward ratio. The aftermath of Desert Storm placed the Saudi royal family under new pressures, from both the left and right. Both groups have been energized by what they observed during the coalition presence in Saudi Arabia. Groups interested in increasing democratization and social liberalization petitioned the leadership for a consultative assembly and a liberalization of the strict Saudi social rules. The religious right called for increased emphasis on conservative social values, opposing the liberalization espoused by the left. The royal family cannot satisfy both camps, and an increasing level of domestic political conflict results.

In the spring of 1992 King Fahd announced the creation of a national consultative assembly and a number of local consultative bodies. These assemblies are constituted with no power other than the persuasive quality of their advice. Nonetheless, they are widely interpreted as a first, although cautious, move by the royal family in the direction of democratization. In another significant move, the royal family agreed to broaden the pool of future candidates for king, a move that could substantially increase the size of the ruling class in Saudi Arabia when such an eventuality occurs.

Rising internal pressures associated with economic strains and increasing polarization between conservative and liberalizing factions, punctuated by the terrorist bombing of an American military facility in Riyadh in 1995, led to a number of political and administrative changes in the Saudi leadership in 1995 and 1996. King Fahd rearranged the cabinet and replaced a number of senior bureaucrats. And, in early 1996, he delegated day-to-day political responsibilities to the crown prince, Prince Abdullah. King Fahd's personal health appeared to play a decisive role in these actions, but it is also probable that demands for reform within and outside the royal family also helped to precipitate these changes. At any rate, the vaunted stability of the Saudi leadership is under challenge, and subsequent changes are likely.

The events of 9/11 have had important effects for the Saudi government. More than any other state in the region, the Saudi relationship with the United States, its principal ally and guarantor, was strained by the attack on the World Trade Center. What appears to have been an intentional al-Qaeda strategy of using mostly Saudi nationals in the attack has created great stress for the Saudi government, as an orchestrated public relations attack on the Saudi government followed in the wake of the disaster.

What may be a low point in the U.S.-Saudi relationship occurred in late 2002 as an advisory board to the U.S. defense department heard a research report labeling the Saudis as unworthy allies and basic enemies of the United States. And, in fact, Saudi prestige plummeted dramatically in the United States under a withering public relations campaign against it. Although the official organs of the U.S. government (president, state department, defense department) deny holding such opinions and assert the strength of the relationship, it is also clear that Saudi opposition to a unilateral U.S. attack on Iraq has strained the alliance. The relationship has also been strained by U.S. insistence that the Saudi leadership dismantle much of the Islamist/fundamentalist infra-

structure in the kingdom, citing the strident anti-Western rhetoric of many Saudi ulema, and the devastating bombings of residential compounds in Riyadh in May of 2003. Saudi leaders have agreed to some of the "suggestions" coming from the West but are not ready to completely abandon their religious commitments or their highly valued independence. It is clear that U.S./Saudi relations are evolving.

In short, the traditional states of the Middle East, rich and poor alike, appear to be subject to increasing domestic and international pressure for change. Some of these traditional polities are fighting a rearguard action (Kuwait, Saudi Arabia). Others have been embracing moderate democratic change (Bahrain, Oman, Qatar, the U.A.E.). The inevitable transition to constitutional/democratic monarchies, modern bureaucratic, or charismatic rule will be quite stressful to these traditional leaders and to those nations dependent on their petroleum and natural gas exports.

MODERN BUREAUCRATIC STATES

The second largest group of political systems in the Middle East is governed by some kind of modern bureaucratic leadership. Four of these states—Egypt, Iraq, Yemen, and Syria—are ruled by Kemalist regimes. The military or civilian leaders in Syria and Iraq professed adherence to Baathist ideology, although the two countries are ruled in quite different ways. While Mubarak apparently believes in the principal of public accountability of leaders, he has not yet entrusted substantial political authority to the parties or legislature. The Arab Socialist Union and the National Assembly, while influential, are still subject to his veto.

Egypt, Syria, and Yemen seem unlikely to face serious internal challenges in the immediate future. In Syria, the transition of power from Hafez el-Asad to his son Bashar appears to have proceeded with little opposition or difficulty. In Yemen, the government is challenged by an increasingly vigorous Islamist minority, but there does not appear to be a serious challenge to the legitimacy of that government.

The government of Iraq, however, was under serious political pressure internally and externally.

Although it was plagued for some time by feuding within the ruling Baathist military group, by the late 1980s Iraq appeared to be emerging as a stable and competent political regime. Encouraged by its growing petroleum revenues, in the mid-1970s Iraq had embarked on an ambitious program of economic and social investment. Simultaneously, the leadership's anti-Western posture softened, and growing numbers of Iraqi students had enrolled in European and American universities, particularly in management and technology programs. A growing disenchantment with communist influence in the Iraqi army led to a number of executions and imprisonments and explorations with non-Soviet European governments regarding trade and technology.

The long war with Iran accelerated these tendencies, as Iraq became increasingly dependent on the European West and the moderate Arab states for financial and military support. U.S. aid to Iraq was channeled mainly through other governments. The war was extraordinarily expensive to both Iran and Iraq, in terms of money, military and civilian casualties, and deferred public projects. Both countries, however, managed to avoid widespread domestic discontent, an indication of effective leadership and progress in political institutionalization. Saddam Hussein, during the darkest periods of the Iran-Iraq war, appeared to initiate a "cult of personality" to offset public dissatisfaction with the conduct of the war. In fact, his personal presence rose dramatically, through use of techniques often associated with charismatic leadership. The lack of a charismatic public response, however, was equally obvious, leaving us with the impression of Saddam Hussein as an aspiring charismatic leader in search of a constituency. That said, the reins of power seemed firmly in his hands.

All apparent progress in Iraq was put at risk by Saddam Hussein's decision to invade Kuwait in 1990. This invasion, and the subsequent ejection of Iraq from Kuwait by a U.S.-led coalition of Western, Arab, and other Third World states, changed the trajectory of development for Iraq. Saddam Hussein's inept military leadership resulted in the deaths of tens of thousands of his countrymen and the rekindling of two serious revolts by the Kurds in the north and the Shia in the south. Iraq was placed under onerous economic embargo and political isolation by the UN Security Council. UN inspection teams roamed Iraq in search of Iraq's programs to produce "weapons of mass destruction." All in all, Iraq and its government received heavy punishment for its transgressions in Kuwait.

Saddam Hussein's survival of this humiliation amazed commentators everywhere. Although his removal was not an official objective of the Desert Storm coalition, the rhetoric of the conflict left little doubt that this was an unarticulated goal. It was believed that the military humiliation of Iraq and attendant economic and social disruptions would lead the Iraqi elite to remove him from office. This did not occur and Saddam Hussein remained in power years after the war. The survival of his key military establishment—the Republican Guards—gave him the breathing space necessary to suppress the Kurdish and Shia revolts. And given the highly integrated nature of Iraq's political elite, he was able to forestall political opposition among his influential rivals in government. External opponents of the Saddam government were cheered in 1995, when several key members of Saddam's ruling clique defected and sought refuge in Jordan. The cheering was short-lived, however, when the dissidents returned to Iraq months later to face death at the hands of their own families for "treason." The whole affair did little to change the internal political equation in Iraq. It appeared to many observers that Saddam Hussein was grooming his son, Uday, as a probable successor to his rule.

U.S. and Western opposition to Saddam Hussein has been implacable. Efforts by the Clinton administration to oust Hussein ranged from large-scale air campaigns, to an ongoing "airwar of attrition" launched during the Kosovo crisis, to renewed emphasis on support for opposition groups and espionage. All failed to push Saddam Hussein from his perch or generate substantial opposition to his rule. The biggest losers in the conflict appeared to be the children of Iraq, damaged in nearly unprecedented ways by a combination of repeated attacks on crucial infrastructure and the embargo of critical medical supplies and foodstuffs.

In the aftermath of 9/11, the Bush administration pushed the removal of Saddam Hussein toward the top of the U.S. international agenda, superseding even the war against terrorism and al-Qaeda. In a speech that stupefied many scholars of the region, President Bush pronounced the existence of an "axis of evil" constituted of Iraq, Iran, and North Korea, the logic of which is not immediately evident. This notion quickly evolved into the idea of "regime change" and "preemptive war." World and regional opinions notwithstanding, the United States proceeded on a course designed to remove Saddam Hussein from power and replace the regime with a more acceptable leadership and democratic institutions. The regime of Saddam Hussein officially collapsed on April 9, 2003, the victim of U.S. unilateral military invasion and occupation of Iraq. The construction of a new Iraqi political regime commenced.

Of the two non-Kemalist modern bureaucratic regimes, one country, Turkey, has a recent history of relatively free and open review of its leadership. Only occasionally has the military felt it necessary to intervene and suspend the political processes, and then only to back off after a period of adjustment. The military rule established in 1980 was progressively withdrawn in favor of a civilian government. To date, the Turkish military has taken steps to minimize the number of parties allowed to contest elections, in the hopes of avoiding the legislative stalemates characteristic of the prior multiparty government, and allowed an extensive experiment in free-market economics begun by President Turgut Ozal. The apparent success of the reforms, and the ability of the existing leadership to deal effectively with restive political minorities, have resulted in a continued reduction of the military role in Turkish politics. And Turkey's aggressive pursuit of full membership in the European Community would appear to support a continued trend in this democratic direction.

The viability of Turkey's democratic system was tested in 1992 when the party coalition supporting President Turgut Ozal lost its majority in the parliament. The election of Suleiman Demirel to the prime minister's position brought an old political enemy to an important position in the government. Both Ozal and Demirel subsequently demonstrated their ability to work together, an important improvement in institutional legitimacy and pragmatic political leadership. The Turkish government was also able to effect an orderly transition in its leadership after the death of President Ozal to a new leader, Prime Minister Tansu Ciller.

The success of an Islamist political party in 1995 brought committed Muslim leaders to power in a coalition government. Uneasy with the religious implications of this change, the military intervened again in the Turkish political process, dislodging the Welfare Party and its Prime Minister Erbakan in favor of secular leadership. The Welfare Party was dissolved and its leadership banned from political elections for a period of years. Turkey is ruled now by a coalition government of secular parties, led by Prime Minister Bulent Ecevit.

In the late fall of 2002, another moderate Islamist party won the national elections. The Justice and Development Party (AKP) celebrated its electoral victory with great modesty, as its leadership asked its followers to omit cries of "Allahu Akhbar" after the election and went well out of its way to endorse the secular assumptions of Turkish government. Initial indicators suggest that this form of very moderate Muslim political activity will not trigger a Turkish military intervention. The success of the venture, that is, an electorally and governmentally successful moderate Muslim political initiative, will likely provide a useful example to other states in the region. It will improve Turkey's chances for membership in the European Union, a long-time high-priority goal of Turkish foreign policy.

Lebanon, in a state of civil war and occupied by Syrian, UN, and, Israeli forces, all of whom share power with private Christian, Muslim, Palestinian, and independent armies, is proof of just how bad things can get when domestic and international forces combine to challenge or undermine existing political authority. The pre-1976 government of Lebanon, predicated on the fiction of relatively equal and stable Muslim, Christian, and Druze populations, functioned in an effective and publicly accountable way. It was, in many respects, something of a showplace for democracy in difficult circumstances. The enormous contrast between then and now suggests that when all pretense of political civility disappears, the potential for political and social disorganization is great.

The disastrous invasion and occupation of Lebanon by Israel (1982–1985) did succeed in removing the Arafat elements of the PLO in and south of Beirut, but it did not succeed in removing other Palestinian groups or their military bases. The occupation also failed to tip the equation of forces in Lebanon in favor of the Christian militias, and apparently stimulated the political and military growth of the Shia organizations, particularly the AMAL and Hizbollah. The result was the government of Lebanon ruling less and less of East Beirut while political and military groups with ties to major international actors (Syria, Iran, Iraq, Israel, Libya, the PLO, and the United States) jockeyed for position.

Frustration with this situation led eventually to a regional conference in Taif, Saudi Arabia in 1989. In the adopted accords, Syria assumed a major role in disarming the competing militias and supporting a nonsectarian parliamentary government. Key events included the disarmament of General Aoun's army in 1990 and the systematic reestablishment of the regular Lebanese army under governmental direction. By 1992 it was clear that this initiative had dramatically changed the political equation in Lebanon, allowing the potential emergence of genuine national political leadership and the establishment of a second republic. Clearly, some progress has been made in this regard, although Syria still plays a major role in domestic Lebanese politics.

Israel's withdrawal from southern Lebanon in 1999 surprised nearly everyone. Dispirited by the incremental loss of military personnel to Hizbollah attacks in the zone of occupation, Prime Minister Barak decided to cut Israel's losses in Lebanon and concentrate on its dealings with the Palestinians. This event allowed a considerable reprieve for Lebanon and the short-run effects have been lugubrious. By late 2002, the government of Lebanon had made substantial strides toward institutionalization of its government and legitimization of government in general. Syria still wields considerable influence in domestic Lebanese politics. But for the first time since the 1982 invasion, internal developments in Lebanon have been positive.

The leadership situation in Israel certainly deserves discussion. Our categorization of the regime as certainly modern bureaucratic but uncertainly democratic or Kemalist depended on whether one was focused on Israeli citizens within the normal confines of Israel (pre-1967 boundaries) or the administered Arab populations of the West Bank, Gaza Strip, and Golan Heights. The problem would not be so great were the populations involved not so large. We must distinguish, then, between the democratically responsible leadership of conventional Israel and its authoritarian rule over what remains as the occupied territories.

The apparent progress of the Israeli-Palestinian peace negotiations changed with the initiation of Intifadah 2, the Palestinian reaction to a visit by Israeli extremist Ariel Sharon to the Haram al Sharif/Temple Mount in August of 2000. Sharon's electoral victory over Barak in the ensuing elections changed everything, as the Israeli government changed the assumptions of the peace process from "land for peace" to "peace for security," a formula that called for Palestinian destruction of internal Palestinian resistance to the occupation. The result was to set the Israeli-Palestinian relationship on a track of reciprocal violence to a point unprecedented since the return of the PLO to Israel over a decade earlier.

Sharon's conduct of repression in the West Bank and Gaza have initiated unprecedented levels of "asymmetric war," the application of full military coercion against a nongovernmental foe. For its part, the Palestinian Authority replied with a series of escalating violence against the Israeli military and more significantly against Israel's civilian population. The increase of suicide bombings from desperate Palestinians precipitated increasingly deadly reprisals from the Israeli military in a spiral of violence that brought a series of brutal military "incursions" into the occupied territories. Neither side seems willing to back down and the result is an increasingly horrific war with large numbers of civilian casualties. All in all, this presented a nightmare conclusion to the Oslo Peace Accords, initialed so hopefully a decade earlier, and abrogated in 2002 by the Sharon government.

The brutality of the confrontation plunged Israel into its deepest political divisions since the 1973 Yom Kippur/Ramadan war. Public opinion has become highly polarized, and Sharon's government has been weakened by defections from the moderate parties that initially supported him. The parties of the left, mostly Labor or Labor affiliated, continued their opposition to the policies advocated by the Likud government. To the Israeli right, Sharon was embraced as a genuine hero of Israel's expansion, its settlements and continued control of the occupied territories, and its hard-line response to Palestinian resistance. His periodic attempts to embarrass, dismiss, or injure Yasir Arafat played to rave reviews in the Israeli right. To the left he became the apotheosis of violence and repression, an embarrassment to historical Israeli values. Internal divisions grew deeper and more vituperative.

The legitimacy of Arafat's leadership increased substantially among the Palestinian public. It is difficult to envision a scenario in which the Israeli government could remove him from the political system, in spite of Sharon's and Bush's dismissal of him as "irrelevant." As Israel systematically demolished the physical and social infrastructure of the Palestinian Authority in the summer and fall of 2002 and periodically laid siege to Arafat's government headquarters in Ramallah, Palestinian resistance stiffened and the prospects for a moderate Palestinian leadership also dimmed. Things at the end of 2002 looked as black as in any period in the preceding fifty years of Palestinian-Israeli conflict, personified in the head-to-head conflict of two irreconcilable enemies: Ariel Sharon and Yasir Arafat.

Ariel Sharon and Yasir Arafat present disconcertingly similar leadership history and styles to their constituencies. Both leaders have played important roles in their countries' political travails over the last fifty years. Both are admired within their own constituencies, and just as equally vilified and demonized in the opposing constituencies. Both have significant blood on their hands contingent on their roles and responsibilities over the past decades. Both are widely considered to be war criminals and terrorists, both within and outside their respective political systems. Finally, each despises the other. The result is a sort of mirror image of the current Israeli and Palestinian leaders. This personal symmetry complicates the negotiations between the two entities dramatically. Many analysts think that the Palestinian-Israeli

issue will not make dramatic progress until both of these aging antagonists are out of power. In the spring of 2003, yielding to wide-ranging and insistent pressure from the international community and Israel, Arafat appointed Mahmoud Abbas (also known as Abu Mazen) as the prime minister of the Palestinian Authority, ceding substantial administrative authority to the new minister. An immediate consequence of this appointment was the acceptance in principle (with reservations) of the road map to Middle Eastern peace proposed by the Quartet (United Nations, European Union, Russia, and the United States), promising an independent Palestinian state by 2005.

On the other hand, Israel has proven many times over its ability to change leadership within the structure of public accountability. Prime Minister Menachem Begin represented a conservative religious coalition, the Likud bloc, which came to power in May 1977 and broke the dominance of the Labor bloc, which had been in power since 1948. Begin's responses to Arab demands and terrorist raids were much harsher than his predecessors'; in addition he encouraged Israeli settlements in the West Bank. (We shall deal with this policy in greater detail in subsequent chapters.) However, the formal inclusion of the West Bank and Gaza Strip into the state of Israel was sufficient to classify Begin's regime as Kemalist authoritarian, since it was unwilling to extend full political rights to the resident Arab populations.

The 1982 Israeli invasion of Lebanon proved to be abortive politically, both in Lebanon and Israel. The domestic consequences of the invasion included the opening of substantial cleavage in the Israeli polity over the appropriate treatment of the Palestinians. The official government inquiry into the atrocities at the Sabra and Shatila refugee camps did not clear the leadership of the Israeli Defense Force or General Sharon of a cloud of suspicion. An active Israeli peace movement, advocating dialogue and bargaining with the Arabs, emerged to question Likud's policies. The occupation of Lebanon also proved to be economically very expensive. In 1984, a dispirited Menachem Begin resigned his position in favor of Foreign Minister Yitzhak Shamir. The resultant elections were inconclusive, leading to a "coalition" government between Labor and Likud. Neither Prime

Minister Peres or Prime Minister-to-be Shamir appeared able to exercise the decisive leadership characteristic of Golda Meir or Menachem Begin in his prime.

The fall 1988 elections did little to resolve the stalemate between the Labor and Likud blocs, resulting in yet another round of coalition government, an alliance of unlikely bedfellows motivated by the unexpected initiatives of the PLO in the fall of 1988 and the U.S. agreement to begin a dialogue with the PLO. In order to present a united Israeli front to these unsettling developments, Likud and Labor (Shamir and Peres, respectively) ceased their courtship of the conservative religious parties and continued their uneasy coalition. One unintended consequence of this decision was to defer, for the moment, continued consideration of legal regulation limiting commerce and entertainment on the Sabbath and further limiting the definition of Jew along lines acceptable to the Orthodox and Ultraorthodox leadership. Such restraint eventually became a casualty of partisan politics. Elections were held and the Likud, under the leadership of Yitzhak Shamir, openly sought the support of the minority religious parties to establish a legislative majority in the Knesset. Under Shamir's leadership, Israeli policy toward the PLO and the intifadah became increasingly rigid and repressive.

Government reaction to the Palestinian intifadah became extremely brutal, further polarizing the Israeli polity. Military repression of Israeli Arab demonstrations occurred late in 1988 and posed an ominous portent to Israel as a pluralistic democracy. The December 1988 declaration of Palestinian independence brought a diplomatic problem to the Israeli leadership, particularly given the PLO acceptance of UN Resolution 242. The Israeli leadership found itself confronting an increasingly domestic conflict for which there were no easy or palatable remedies. A large leftist peace coalition attempted to offset the growing influence of settlers, religious extremists, and the proponents of Palestinian "transfer" within the ruling coalition.

The Iraqi invasion of Kuwait changed the internal political equation in Israel. Palestinian sympathies for Iraq undermined the legitimacy of the peace movement in Israel. The government responded by increasingly repressive measures in Gaza and the West Bank and by implementing an aggressive settlement policy in Gaza, the West Bank, and annexed Jerusalem. In so doing, the Shamir government ignored settlement in the relatively underpopulated regions of the Galilee and Negev, in favor of displacing settled Palestinians and ensuring a Jewish majority in "Eretz Israel." This policy polarized international opinion and eventually led to a crisis between Israel and its primary supporter, the United States. The elections of 1992 were clearly fought on the arena defined by this emerging conflict between an Israeli government determined to annex its biblical geography and an American administration committed to a formula of "land for peace."

The elections of 1992 ended fifteen years of Likud rule and effected the transfer of power from Prime Minister Shamir to Yitzhak Rabin. Rabin was able to craft a coalition composed of only three parties, thus avoiding a coalition subject to minority party veto. Prime Minister Rabin thus inherited a political situation with a greater latitude of action than his predecessor.

Rabin used this latitude of action to initiate the negotiations with the Palestinians for political autonomy. The result was the beginning of a reconstitution of the Israeli-Palestinian conflict—and ultimately, of course, Rabin's assassination in October of 1995 at the hands of an extremist Jewish fundamentalist. Rabin's death precipitated a transfer of power to his successor, Shimon Peres, also of the Labor Party and a key actor in the developing peace negotiations. Peres was able to maintain or even increase the momentum toward peace during the first months of his new administration. The subsequent elections held in May of 1996 constituted something of a watershed for Israeli politics.

The Israeli elections of May 1996 produced a number of changes, not the least of which was the election of Binyamin Netanyahu as prime minister, elected for the first time independent of the Knesset elections held simultaneously. Netanyahu was able to craft a ruling coalition between the Likud bloc and the ultraconservative religious parties in the Knesset, unseating Shimon Peres and the Labor government. These results were certainly momentous.

Prime Minister Netanyahu brought many personal strengths to his position. An accomplished master of television and other electronic media of communication, Netanyahu was able to appeal to two distinct and important groups in the Israeli electorate: moderate Israelis nervous about the security implications of the peace process and right-wing religious groups and settler groups implacably opposed to nearly all of the peace objectives embraced by the previous government and embodied in Israel's treaty obligations.

Netanyahu's early actions as prime minister reassured his most conservative constituents, as he reestablished, many of the most repressive features of the pre-Oslo policies, including stringent curfews, reductions in Palestinian work permits, administrative detention, and the doctrine of collective punishment for anti-Israeli activity. Settlement activities were increased, annexations of Palestinian land around Jerusalem accelerated, and the government opened a symbolically important "tourist" tunnel in the Old City of Jerusalem, over loud and alarmed Palestinian opposition. Deadlines for withdrawal and redeployment from West Bank cities and areas were repeatedly postponed in order to assure the most security to the Israeli public.

Most of Netanyahu's conservative supporters took great heart at these actions, and the moderate to liberal opposition viewed the policies with alarm. Thus, it was a surprise to both groups when, early in 1997, Netanyahu bowed to his treaty obligations and to enormous international pressure and agreed to an Israeli withdrawal from 80 percent of Hebron, the symbolically most emotionally charged of the Israeli settlements on the West Bank.

In embracing the peace process, however reluctantly, and in honoring the treaty obligations of his successors, and in to some degree suppressing his personal ambivalence or dislike for Yasir Arafat and his Palestinian followers, Netanyahu demonstrated the modern/bureaucratic nature of Israel's political institutions. He eventually paid a high political price for these acts of desperate principal, but his acceptance of the political costs for these

actions suggests that Israel's institutions are stronger than the incumbents that inhabit them. And that is a defining quality of "modern" government as we currently understand it.

Netanyahu's successor as prime minister, Ehud Barak of the Labor Party, brought his own strengths to the leadership of Israel. A decorated war hero, Barak brought new optimism to the public and to the negotiators working on the elusive peace between Israel and the Palestinians. Expectations ran high among Israeli moderates and the Israeli left, and among the Palestinian leadership. The Clinton administration also welcomed the change, expecting breakthroughs in the peace process.

While Barak quickly proved himself to be a different type of prime minister than his predecessor, there was more of Prime Minister Rabin in his style than of Prime Minister Peres, his two Labor predecessors. Thus, while reengaging the peace negotiations, Barak simultaneously increased settlement activity and launched punitive air raids against Lebanon, as far north as Beirut and the Bekaa Valley. This combination of velvet glove–iron glove produced modest gains, but the settlement activity eventually derailed the final status negotiation timetable that Barak had publicly endorsed. The result shortly after his election: marginal progress on implementation of the Wye Accords and increasing friction with his U.S. allies, who were pushing hard for a breakthrough on the talks.

Prime Minister Barak also faced an intensification of Israel's own internal self-appraisal. Years of work among revisionist historians in Israel brought many of the internal contradictions of the Israeli experience to the forefront. Questions involving the treatment of Arabs during the Israeli war of independence were raised, forcing government acknowledgment of atrocities and brutalities. The question "Who is a Jew?" gained renewed weight, particularly as orthodox, ultraorthodox, liberal, and reform Jewish communities jockeyed for influence and status in the system. Looked at from an external view, these new controversies revealed a dynamic and appropriate reappraisal of many of the basic assumptions about the nature of the Israeli state: religious or secular; Jewish or pluralist; democratic or clerical. Seen from the inside, the questions raised fears of factionalism and serious internal divisions. Like it or not, Barak was forced to confront many of these issues during his tenure as prime minister.

One such confrontation occurred in late December of 1999, just weeks before the resumption of Israeli-Syrian discussions over the Golan. In this instance, the Shas Party, one of the key coalition members, threatened to bolt the coalition if the government refused to increase appropriations to the health and education ministries that it controlled. Shas' departure from the coalition would have seriously damaged Barak's ability to deliver enough votes to confirm any agreement with Syria or Lebanon, not to mention the Palestinian Authority. The issue was resolved by the government's backing down on its intended reduction of budget, securing Shas' continued participation in the governing coalition. Such encounters are a constant challenge to the prime minister and his leadership.

Ehud Barak's loss of the prime ministership to Ariel Sharon in 2000 occurred in the context of established Israeli electoral processes. For all of our criticism of Sharon's policies toward the occupied territories and the brutality of his military responses to Palestinian resistance, his leadership is still firmly embedded in the institutional and legal structure of the state of Israel. He is by no means an authoritarian leader in the conventional sense of the term. This is an important point to make, even as Sharon's leadership leads to increasing polarization within the Israeli polity. The conventional modern bureaucratic nature of the regime holds the prospects for democratic resolutions of the conflict at hand. We can only hope for such a process to work its weal.

In late November of 2002, Sharon and his coalition lost a key vote of confidence in the Knesset, necessitating yet another round of elections. In the Likud primary elections, Sharon was able to beat back a vigorous attempt by former prime minister Netanyahu, who attempted to displace Sharon as the leader of the Likud bloc. Netanyahu's leadership of the Likud would likely have moved the bloc even further to the political right than Sharon has already accomplished. Elections in January of 2003 reconfirmed Sharon and his strategy for dealing with the Palestinians.

All of this suggests that Israeli leadership is certainly conventional in its base of authority. Begin, Peres, Rabin, Shamir, Netanyahu, Barak, and Sharon can all be described as modern bureaucratic leaders. Their survival in power is directly dependent on the consequences of their policy choices, not their charismatic or traditional appeal. We should also point out that the political leadership of Israel is aging. Many Israeli leaders, including Sharon and Peres, are in their seventies and facing the end of their long careers as party and government leaders. A new generation of Israeli leaders waits in the wings. As Israel faces a range of difficult problems—economic, political, racial, international, ethical—the quality of her leadership will be of great importance. The leadership that emerges from the uncertainties of the 1990s to deal with the new global realities of the twenty-first century will have its work cut out for it.

CHARISMATIC RULE

Two Middle Eastern countries, Iran and Libya, were under charismatic rule throughout the 1980s. Both rulers can be described as irregular, unpredictable, and dramatic; but their governments and ideologies were inherently different.

Ayatollah Ruhollah Khomeini

Ascetic and gaunt, Ayatollah Ruhollah Khomeini appeared to confirm the trite Western stereotypes of Muslim fanaticism. This predisposition to judge harshly was exacerbated by the outrage generated by the Iranian militants' seizure of U.S. diplomats and embassy employees in November 1979. Thus, it is hard to find a publicly sanctioned, dispassionate description and analysis of Khomeini and his beliefs.

Khomeini was clearly a charismatic leader. He believed that his ultimate authority was derived from Allah, an indisputably cosmological referent. His speech was laced with hyperbole and jeremiads against the West, the shah, the devil, and all corruption and debasement. His followers responded with strong outpourings of emotion. His branch of Islam, Iranian Shiism, is mystical and chiliastic. He used the Shia tenets of Islam as the basis of a new, revolutionary economic, social, and political organization.

Khomeini's opposition to the shah's regime and to Western influence in Iran was partly based on his personal history. Khomeini's father was allegedly murdered by a landlord closely allied with Shah Reza Pahlevi. Raised as an orphan, Khomeini was passed from relative to relative largely out of charitable obligation. His training, exclusively in traditional religious schools and subjects, was exactly opposite to the modern education promoted by the Pahlevis. As an adult, Khomeini was often in trouble with the regime, which restricted his movements and preaching and finally exiled him. His promotion to the rank of ayatollah was prompted, it is claimed, by other Muslim clergymen's attempts to protect him from the shah's courts and certain imprisonment or execution. Long periods of exile awaited the ayatollah, during which his son was murdered, allegedly by SAVAK. Thus, Ayatollah Khomeini had a long history of personal and religious opposition to the Pahlevi regime.

Khomeini's political behavior bewildered most Western correspondents. Two Shia traditions may explain some of it. First, the Shia community in Iran has long practiced the right of **taqiyyah**, or dissimulation. If the defense of the faith requires it, the faithful may say or do anything that would allow them to pursue the true way, including the denial of adherence or membership. In the darkest days of SAVAK's repression, many Iranians protected themselves by exercising this right. Thus, public political statements were often contradictory or misleading. It is indicative of Khomeini's moral status with the Shia faithful that he was able to dictate the abandonment of taqiyyah during the last stages of the fight against the shah, and from a position of exile at that.

The second tradition is the low status of political officialdom in Shia Islam. Therefore Ayatollah Khomeini instinctively avoided the regular, continual exercise of political power characteristic of the "normal politician." Khomeini apparently wished instead to correct or direct politicians by exercising a moral veto when they deviated from the divine will. Khomeini's exercise of power was thus irregular and intermittent, a fact of life that

confounded and confused the Western observer accustomed to administrative regularity and continuity. Khomeini's role as faqih in the Islamic Republic also confused Western observers, particularly those who simply did not comprehend institutions of mixed sovereignty—in this case, of God and man.

One also needs to understand something of the political and religious history of Iran. The doctrine of taqiyyah, for example, developed in response to the persecution of the Shia faithful by established Iranian political authority. Dissimulation, when necessary, advanced the interests of the good community. It was not a simple or universal justification for lying. The Ayatollah's symbolically rich speech similarly derived from the long Persian tradition of complex, poetic language. Much of it is impossible to translate accurately into English. An example of the difficulty is the *heech* controversy of 1979.

Heech is an Iranian word of some subtlety. It can mean "nothing" in both a literal and/or an ironic sense. Upon returning to Iran from exile in Iraq and France, Khomeini was asked by Western newsmen how it felt to return to Iran after all those years in exile. Khomeini expressed his contempt for such a superficial question with the observation, "Heech." The newsmen interpreted his response to mean that he had no feelings, emotional or otherwise, about his return and concluded that he was coldly self-controlled. Khomeini intended to convey his disgust at being asked such an obvious and superficial question. Unfortunately, Khomeini's efforts were rewarded with misunderstanding. Khomeini's behavior and justifications remain valid for Iran and largely misunderstood in the world arenas.

Khomeini's charismatic power was not restricted to Iran; it also operated among Shia minorities along the Persian Gulf and in Jordan, Syria, Iraq, and Lebanon. In addition, many fundamentalist Sunni Muslim groups recognized Khomeini's impact and wished to emulate his success without adopting the Shia disciplines. Finally, Khomeini's rabid anti-Western attitude taps a venerable tradition of opposition that dates back to the maturation of European imperial power in the area. As a successful leader, attempting the radical de-Westernization of Iran based on the tenets of Islam, Khomeini was a living example of the political potential of Islamic revival.

In the late 1980s, as Khomeini aged and his health deteriorated, he was frequently absent from the seat of government. Nonetheless, as the Iran-Iraq war degenerated into a human sacrifice of epic proportion, Khomeini was able to provide moral support to the faction in government seeking a settlement. Without his influence, it is likely that a greater protraction of the controversy would have occurred. It should be noted that Khomeini backed the settlement at great risk to his own political reputation, potentially sullied by "backing down" to Iraq and Saddam Hussein.

Khomeini's political maneuvering in the aftermath of the war gives good insight into some of the difficulties of exercising charismatic power and ensuring an appropriate succession to the charismatic leader. The publication and reaction in the Muslim world to the book *The Satanic Verses* provided Khomeini with an opportunity to exercise the moral dimensions of his leadership to disadvantage his political opponents. His pronouncement of a death sentence and bounty for the author of the book prompted criticism by Ayatollah Montazeri, Khomeini's designated successor as faqih of the republic. This reaction, and earlier statements by Montazeri critical of the policy directions of the regime, gave Khomeini the opening he desired. He demanded Montazeri's resignation, arguing that in opposing his actions Montazeri had demonstrated his unfitness to interpret God's will. Montazeri resigned, and no prominent successor of his public status was nominated to succeed Khomeini. Speaker Rafsanjani, who might have benefited from Montazeri's fall, was unable to capitalize on the situation until much later. And, in fact, the most conservative factions of the ruling coalitions were empowered in the short term by this sequence of events. Ali Khamenei ultimately succeeded Khomeini as faqih, but his less-prestigious reputation signaled a de facto decrease in the institution's role.

This question almost asks itself: Why did Khomeini impeach his personally designated successor? The answer may reside in the very character of charismatic leadership, qualities in the leader that militate against the sharing of power. And it just as well may offer evidence of the implicit conflict between charismatic leadership and the institutional/bureaucratic leadership it eventually spawns. Whatever the reason, these actions appeared to make the inevitable transition of power from Khomeini to a successor more problematic and difficult than ever, a prospect that did not augur well for stability within the regime or the revolution. That the transition from Khomeini's charismatic rule to the more pragmatic bureaucratic rule of Rafsanjani and Khamenei occurred without great public disorder is a monument to the progress in political institutionalization that developed in the later years of the Iranian revolution.

Under the divided leadership of Ayatollah Khamenei and President Khatami, Iran has clearly moved in a moderating direction, both in the domestic and international arenas. Broad public support for the loosening of Islamic dress and behavior has resulted in the reemergence of a middle class less interested in a revolutionary religious life and more interested in life in the larger, global sense. This progress is noted in public life, where Iranian nationals feel freer to express their political opinions; and in the public behavior of women, many of whom have put off the chador in favor of conventional, nontraditional dress.

Iran's clerical leaders have by and large resisted these trends to liberalization, resulting in a series of fits and starts. But the overall trend of modest liberalization is definitely occurring, and this trend is certainly enhanced by the moderating influence of President Khatami.

Colonel Muammar Qadaffi

No less an enigma is Colonel Muammar Qadaffi, the unofficial head of state of Libya, a country with few people and considerable oil wealth, located next to Egypt on the Mediterranean coast of Africa. Qadaffi has held power since the Revolutionary Command Council (RCC) removed King Idris from power in 1969. Since that time Qadaffi has consolidated and expanded his political power. His position is currently secure as head of the military group ruling Libya.

Qadaffi's power is also indisputably charismatic, although it differs substantially from

Khomeini's. Qadaffi is a radical, modernizing charismatic leader who has based his policy on unique, innovative interpretations of the Koran. Personally pious and reputedly ascetic, Qadaffi rejected the authority of the hadith and sunnah, preferring instead his own reading of the Koran as the sole authority. His personal philosophy is detailed in the Green Book, the handbook of the Libyan revolution. Qadaffi thus finds himself in opposition to the conservative ulema, whereas Khomeini's power derived from it. Although both men were anti-Western and anti-imperialist, Qadaffi is enthralled by Western technology and science.

Qadaffi and Khomeini also differed markedly in physical appearance. Khomeini appeared dour, dark, and sober, with downcast eyes, and dressed in the traditional garb of the mullah; Qadaffi is quick to flash a bright, toothy smile, dresses in flattering quasi-military tunics. Where Khomeini's rhetoric was apocalyptic, Qadaffi's is more persuasive and personal.

Like Khomeini and Nasser, Qadaffi aspires to leadership in the larger Muslim community. Qadaffi has openly espoused the causes of numerous revolutionary and terrorist groups around the world, and offered hospitality to their leaders. Qadaffi's influence has spread to the Philippines, where Libya has supported the Moro National Liberation Front. It has also spread to Uganda, and to Egypt and the Sudan, where Libya had been openly hostile toward the modern bureaucratic regimes of Sadat and Numeiri. In 1981, Libya intervened in the civil war in Chad, ostensibly to aid the Muslim groups in their consolidation of power. The government in Chad backed away from a proposed formal union, however, and the extent of Libyan control or influence there is problematical.

One of the staunchest of anti-Israeli Muslim leaders, Qadaffi has in the past provided aid, comfort, and a base for operations to diverse groups in the Palestinian nationalist coalition. These causes, and his personal claim to a universally valid view of Muslim revolutionary government, have not been well received in the conservative or secular governments of the Middle East. The disappearance of Imam Musa'Sadr in Libya in 1977 increased Qadaffi's distance from the Shia community. And increasingly visible Libyan assassination squads targeted against Qadaffi's political opposition in exile in England and Italy further blackened Libya's international image. Libya, moreover, tilted decidedly toward the U.S.S.R. in its foreign policy, although the relationship was not sufficiently strong to prevent the 1986 U.S. air raid against its capital.

The sudden transformation of the international system has resulted in the growing isolation of Libya and Qadaffi. The collapse of the Soviet Union deprived Libya of its major international protector. The stabilization of petroleum prices reduced Libya's discretionary income. And the emergence of a moderate to conservative Arab alliance in the region has effectively eliminated Libya as a major player in international events. The international support received by Britain and the United States in 1991–1992 as they demanded the surrender of two Libyan diplomats allegedly involved in the bombing of Pan Am Flight 103 is a strong indicator of Qadaffi's rapidly declining international prestige. Qadaffi's surrender of the two Lockerbie suspects to a UN court in Amsterdam was a dramatic departure for Qadaffi from his previous policies. The conviction of one of the bombers and the acquittal of the other has allowed Libya to seek new economic and political relationships, particularly with Mediterranean Europe.

Nonetheless, Qadaffi keeps Libya on a revolutionary course. Based on his philosophy as expressed in the Green Book, Qadaffi has continued on a course of radical democratization in the context of the original Islamic revelation. Detractors are quick to point out that Qadaffi may in fact be confusing his own role with that of the prophet. Nevertheless, Qadaffi seems quite intent on working through a system of "people's power" committees, unions, and boards. Ultimately these peoples' committees are intended to replace the RCC, although the RCC and Qadaffi still appear to be in control of the Libyan political process. The rising role of Muslim fundamentalist movements in the Maghreb have occurred without any direct Libyan involvement. This fact alone suggests that the international consequences of Qadaffi's charismatic leadership have declined. Qadaffi's charismatic leadership is more and more a domestic fact and not an international one.

CONCLUSION

The contemporary Middle East presents a mosaic of leadership styles with definite implications for conflict and conflict accommodation. The traditional Muslim leaders of the Middle East are conservative. Fighting a rearguard action against increasing demands for a larger share of political power, traditional leaders are coming under increasing domestic and international political pressure. Although traditional leaders of rich or potentially rich states may be able to buy time politically, in the long run, their right to power will be undermined by the social effects of such wealth.

Most traditional regimes will be replaced eventually by modernizing bureaucratic regimes, either democratic or authoritarian in nature. We see confirmation of this point of view and these trends in the reforms enacted in the countries of the Gulf. These regimes will try to mobilize mass political sentiment but keep it under strict control. Technological and economic progress are likely under these regimes, but they are not guaranteed. They will come increasingly under the pressure of fundamentalist Islamic groups seeking to establish Islamic republics that derive their form and mandate from the Koran and Islamic tradition. And they will retain their vulnerability to mischief from other groups and countries.

This assault on the secular aspects of the modern bureaucratic regime may lead to instability and internal conflict, with predictable negative consequences for the systems. Modern bureaucratic leaders like Mubarak of Egypt and Assad of Syria, basing their claim to power on demonstrated policy results, will find themselves more and more challenged by credible alternative concepts of the public good and public order. These concepts, arising from a mixture of religious, political, and foreign influences, will produce potent claims for future performance, finding root in increasingly sophisticated political publics.

It is impossible to predict when charismatic leaders will appear or what the consequences of their regimes will be. They are capable of creating emotional political storms that float over the frag-

ile boundaries of nation-states. Nasser, Khomeini, and Qadaffi, all of whom enjoyed at one time substantial support outside their own countries, challenged the authority of both traditional monarchs and modern bureaucratic leaders. Their potential for destabilization and mischief or political good were great. Currently Ayatollah Khomeini's sermons reportedly enjoy a wide circulation in the Fertile Crescent, and now in the independent republics of central Asia, inspiring many active organizations. Colonel Qadaffi attempted to oust Sadat from Egypt and succeeded in ousting Numeiri from the Sudan in an attempt to extend his leadership into new areas. The recent decline of his influence does not negate the possibility of other charismatic leaders emerging. And it does not take a political soothsayer to predict the probable consequences of charismatic rule in, say, Saudi Arabia with its petroleum wealth or in Egypt with its large population and critical geopolitical position. And, on a much more abstract level, we must recognize the potential for charismatic leadership in the Muslim Umma generally, a leadership capable of transcending familiar national entities. Such leadership would have worldwide impact. Islamic tradition is certainly predisposed in this direction.

Finally, we must note that the American "war on terror" has placed all Middle Eastern leaders in a difficult position, particularly as the United States identified organizations as terrorists that other leaders understand as "freedom fighters" or part of a legitimate resistance to oppressive rule. Clearly Hamas and Hizbollah present those leaders with just such a problem. And the U.S. enthusiasm for war with Iraq is not shared by most political leaders or their followers throughout the region. The U.S. assertion that states are either "with us or against us" in both areas placed all of these leaders in a difficult political situation, torn between cooperating with Washington and also staying true to the beliefs of their respective publics. How this resolves remains to be seen. But common sense in and out of the Middle East crucible maintains and expects serious political consequences for Middle Eastern leaders, from both policy questions.

The Economic Setting

The Middle East presents a remarkably wide spectrum of economic circumstances. It includes some of the richest and poorest nations in the world and some of the most fertile and most barren land. Some of these nations have been cosmopolitan for a millennium or more, while others only recently peeked beyond their boundaries. Some mix religion and politics in puritanical systems, and others advocate secular socialism. The Middle East's unusual diversity of conditions generally is not appreciated.

Some cautions should be mentioned at the outset. Nations are complex and most short statements about them tend to be incomplete. This is understandable: The interplay of cultural, economic, and political forces is difficult to understand in the most straightforward of circumstances. When the forces are rapidly changing character in a context of a quest for meaningful political independence, growing economic interdependence, and sometimes spectacular instances of instability, the task becomes daunting. Many works—from Baedekers to sophisticated technical analyses—deal with the economic conditions of the individual countries under study. Our approach will be to deal with central themes of conflict and resolution rather than geographic or national entities.

The reader also should realize that the precision implied by statistics is often illusory. Indeed, some of the available statistics purporting to describe the Middle East are in gross error due either to faulty measurement or to bias. Numbers have political uses, of course. Petroleum production figures must be viewed with caution due to the frequent, and frequently acknowledged, tendency of members of OPEC to cheat on their production quotas. Migrant labor statistics are suspect for a variety of reasons. Sometimes all parties agree to ignore a changing reality. For example, the government of Lebanon consistently lacked data on the measurable economic and social characteristics of its Muslim and Christian populations. The always precarious balance between the groups could have been thrown into disarray through political action premised on such information.

The economy of Israel has many problems common to the various Arab states, but it differs considerably in other respects. As contrasted to its Arab neighbors, its labor force is more highly educated and from a different cultural setting, its agriculture is more capital-intensive, its industry contributes relatively more to national income, and it has received greater amounts of international aid. Common problems include significant migration, serious water management problems, and the need for a large and expensive military sector.

The second column of Table 11-1 reports the Human Development Index (HDI) ranking constructed by the United Nations Development Program. This index bases the relative rank of a country on more than per capita income; specifically it attempts to factor in educational attainment and health. The argument for a more comprehensive index is straightforward: Income levels do not tell the whole story about the well-being of the populace. So, while Kuwait has a per capita income substantially larger than Israel, Israel has a higher HDI. While the rankings contain a large dose of subjective choices, they do tend to offer a richer view of the relative status of the citizens of a country. For example, relatively low levels of female literacy in most of the Middle East lead to lower rankings than a per capita income measure.

Table 11-1 also indicates the per capita income levels of various Middle Eastern economies. Although these figures are sufficiently reliable to provide a general idea of the level of economic

activity, they are far from exact. For example, the poorer countries of the region have a per capita income substantially different than indicated in Table 11-1 when income levels are calculated in a different fashion. All the countries listed have experienced some increase in per capita income, although there have been tremendous variations. In the early 1960s, Israel was clearly the leader (excepting Kuwait), having a level of per capita Gross Domestic Product ($939 U.S. in 1960), about double that of Lebanon and four to seven times that of the other adjoining countries. By the end of the century the situation had changed dramatically: The measured lead of Israel increased over its oil-poor neighbors but suffered substantially relative to some of the petroleum-exporting states. The remarkable differences in per capita income are a potential source of conflict, especially when it is realized that the high-income countries generally have relatively small populations and suspect defense systems.

Per capita income figures do not show what each citizen has available to spend; they indicate how much of the national income each individual would have if the income were evenly distributed.

Table 11-1 Income and Human Development Indicators

Country	HDI Rank 2000	Real per Capita Income 2000 U. S. $ (PPP)*	Average Annual per Capita Real GDP Growth 1975–2000	1990–2000	Real per Capita GDP Rank Minus HDI Rank
Israel	22	20,131	2.0	2.2	1
Kuwait	45	15,799	−0.9	−1.4	−10
Bahrain	40	15,084	0.9	0.7	−2
Qatar	48	—	—	—	−25
U.A.E.	45	17,935	−3.7	−1.6	−19
Libya	59	—	—	—	−2
Lebanon	65	4,308		4.2	20
Saudi Arabia	68	11,367	−2.2	−1.2	−26
Turkey	82	6,994	2.1	2.1	−18
Oman	71		2.8	0.3	−38
Jordan	88	3,966	0.4	3.3	−1
Iran	90	5,884	−0.7	1.9	−22
Syria	97	3,556	1	2.8	−2
Egypt	105	3,635	2.9	2.5	−10
Yemen	133	893		2.3	14
Sudan	138	1,797	0.6	5.6	−7

*Purchasing power parity.

Source: From *Human Development Report 2002* by United Nations Development Programme, copyright © 2002 by the United Nations Development Programme. Used by permission of Oxford University Press, Inc.

The enormous gulf between the rich and the poor found in some of the states is thus ignored, as are military expenditures. The fact that Egypt has devoted about one-quarter of its GNP to military needs while, say, the U.A.E. has spent a much smaller percentage means that the gap between the two countries is much larger than indicated.

Per capita income figures for the small-population petroleum-rich countries can vary substantially from year to year. Income earned in these economies closely follows petroleum export earnings. For example, the measured per capita income in Saudi Arabia in 1983 ($12,230) fell almost 45 percent by 1986 (to $6,950), reflecting the substantial fall in petroleum prices beginning in late 1985. This does not mean that the average Saudi citizen experienced a 45 percent loss of income. To cushion the decrease in income earned, the government spent reserves accumulated in earlier years. But even the fabled Saudi wealth has finite limits. By the 1990s the government was forced to adopt a more modest budget; continued weak petroleum prices, along with enormous expenditures related to the 1991 war against Iraq, meant that relative budget austerity continued through the 1990s. Kuwait was more insulated from petroleum price shocks: Indeed, interest earnings from international investments exceeded revenue from petroleum sales during the 1985–1990 period. These earning also financed the massive reconstruction project after Iraq was pushed out of Kuwait in 1991. Those countries (for example, Jordan, Egypt, and Yemen) that export labor to the petroleum-exporting countries also must worry about petroleum prices; remittances of migrant workers to the home country constitute a substantial percentage of foreign exchange earnings.

The negative growth in per capita income in Kuwait deserves some comment. The figure reflects the fact that Kuwait, along with the other low-population, high-income petroleum exporters, had huge increases in population in the preceding three decades. Many of the immigrants worked in low-paying occupations for Kuwaitis. Hence, per capita income decreased as Kuwait became rich!

The growth record, whether viewed from the simplicity of Table 11-1 or from a more sophisticated framework, was reasonably satisfactory during the 1960s if one ignores Egypt and impoverished Yemen. Petroleum price increases in the 1970s assured the phenomenal growth of some countries and put the countries without petroleum under ever-greater strain, especially those countries that had established an industrial base and needed oil.

The decade of the 1980s was not good for most Middle Eastern economies. Wars (for example, Iran-Iraq), virtual anarchy (Lebanon), insurrection (Palestine-Israel), wildly fluctuating petroleum prices, continued high rates of population growth (adding over one million per year to Egypt alone), significant droughts, and clumsy government intervention in economic life all contributed to the record. By the end of the decade a number of countries (Egypt, Israel, Iraq) had significant debt-servicing problems, and others (for example, Syria) saw their sources of economic and military aid dry up because of the sudden collapse of the Soviet system. The 1990s were characterized by continued modest growth in some countries, negative growth in others, mainly due to wildly fluctuating petroleum prices and a move toward more private enterprise in several of the countries.

In 2002 the UNDP issued the first Arab Human Development Report, a study (by Arab analysts) of the roots of economic and social stagnation in the Arab world. The conclusion was that three basic causes explain why the growth of real per capita income was a dismal 0.5 percent per year in the two decades preceding 2000. The first was autocratic governments that supported incompetent and sometimes venal civil administrations, despite the outward trappings of elections and seemingly open civil codes. This lessens the chances for growth-inducing economic action. The second identified shortcoming was the low quality of education. The third was the inferior status of females, even though female literacy rates increased almost threefold in the last two decades of the twentieth century.

The last column of Table 11-1 deserves some comment. It takes the rank of a country's per capita GDP and subtracts the broader-based Human Development Index rank. As is apparent from the figures, only Israel and Yemen posted positive numbers. The meaning of a negative number is straightforward: The overall well-being of the population lags per capita income. This is understandable for those countries that experienced rapid rates of income growth due to petroleum. The health and educational systems, especially with respect to women, did not have time to respond. It indicates that these countries have a long road ahead before wider measures of human development are on a par with per capita income.

THE ECONOMIC RECORD

Three overriding phenomena have shaped the economic record of the Middle East in the past half-century: the above-mentioned failures of government; war, or the threat of war; and the changing nature of the petroleum industry. On a more general level, the major long-run economic issue is that of resource imbalances. High rates of population increase, when placed in the context of a limited supply of water and arable land, is the most obvious set of problems.

Likewise, petroleum is a nonrenewable resource; supplies are exhaustible. Economic growth in these circumstances may not be sustainable. Additionally, growing resource imbalances increase the probability of conflict within and between nations.

The Persian (Arabian) Gulf and Israel have been the foci of most major military conflicts. Israel and the countries bordering it have consumed a substantial chunk of their resources for military strength in the past half-century, resources that could have been directed toward economic growth. Wars have deleterious economic effects beyond the pure waste of committing resources to nonproductive uses; the occasional outbreaks of war and the constant possibility of war disrupt plans and projects, discourage investment, and divert attention from nonmilitary objectives. The disruptive effects are greater in the less-developed countries than in their richer counterparts, for the less-developed economies are far more fragile than the developed ones. A poor country is poor, in part, because it does not have the physical infrastructure—networks of communication, transportation, education, and electrical power—the right variety and amounts of economic resources, and the social and political complements necessary for sustained growth. These countries experience significant setbacks when they have to absorb shocks to their economies. This is exactly what happens when the local military machine is obliged to garner resources that otherwise could be used to build a stronger national economic foundation.

Local circumstances, however, dictate that this statement needs to be tempered. Although the long (1980–1988) war between Iran and Iraq was enormously expensive in terms of material and human life, the effect on Iraq was ameliorated substantially by the receipt of tens of billions of dollars of grants and loans, especially from the petroleum-rich Gulf states. By the time of the cease-fire, Iraq had in their workforce upwards of two million foreigners, almost all Arab, the majority being Egyptian. Their externally financed presence meant that the Iraqi economy was able to grow throughout the conflict.

However, by 1990, Iraq was facing a set of stringent economic conditions that represented an important cluster of motivations for their invasion of Kuwait. Gulf grants had ended and debt servicing was burdensome. OPEC production exceeded agreed limits, lowering the price and thereby depriving Iraq of foreign exchange earnings (Iraq lost about $1 billion per year for every dollar drop in the price of petroleum); and the port city of Basra would be closed indefinitely because the Shatt al-Arab was clogged with mines, sunken ships, and silt.

If war generally is very expensive, so is the establishment of peace. The Camp David Accords between Egypt and Israel provide a useful case history to keep in mind as the more comprehensive peace process involving Israel is contemplated. An essential element of the Camp David Accords was Israeli withdrawal from the Egyptian Sinai territory captured in 1967. This meant that Israel was asked to relinquish a formidable natural buffer between it and Egypt. Neither Israel nor Egypt had the financial resources necessary to construct and maintain an "electronic fence" to serve as a substitute for the buffer of the desert. Neither side could afford peace. It was necessary for the United States to foot the bill.

Negotiations of "land for peace" in the 1990s involved the same sort of financial bind. All parties face severe water problems, and Israel receives a substantial percentage of its supply from the territories it occupies. It must be assured of secure water supplies. One way to accomplish this is through the construction of (very expensive) desalination plants. The only other way is through detailed negotiations that allow for both an equitable system of water sharing and ironclad guarantees that water supplies will not be interrupted.

Egypt engaged in four wars with Israel, had a consequential involvement in a civil war in Yemen and several confrontations with Libya, and participated (with compensation) in the 1991 effort against Iraq. In the best of circumstances the task of creating an economy capable of sustained growth is difficult; the need to be in an almost constant state of military readiness has greatly compounded the problem. Jordan has had to contend with a tremendous influx of Palestinians on several occasions, Syria has been engaged with Israel, the delicate balance in Lebanon unraveled, and so on. Israel, of course, has felt particularly beleaguered, being constantly under threat, although massive international aid for many years buffered the problem. Given these conditions, the countries under study have experienced more rapid growth than one would expect. But the prospects for sustained rapid growth were dim until 1974.

One of the most remarkable transfers of wealth the world has ever seen was ushered center stage by changes in the petroleum industry. The members of OPEC roughly quadrupled (to $12) the price of petroleum between October 1973 and January 1974, not so much by acting as a cartel but by taking advantage of worldwide changes in supply/demand conditions. The price doubled (from $15 to $30) in 1979–1980, largely in response to the disruption of petroleum supplies caused by the outbreak of the war between Iraq and Iran. Saudi Arabia, the leader, had accumulated more financial reserves than most other countries of the world by 1980. The other petroleum producers in the area, most notably Iraq and Iran, along with some of the small Gulf states, also had spectacular increases in revenue. The results of this accumulation of financial power were felt, in greater or lesser degree, throughout the world.

For example, the Middle East became a more important trading partner for Japan (as measured by the value of trade) than the European Community. The petroleum-producing countries had the financial wherewithal to promote economic development; their allies benefited through various direct and indirect measures, and their enemies suffered. Much of the Middle East changed forever; and because of this, the world changed. But the situation was not to last. High prices invited substantial exploration and a subsequent increase in worldwide supplies coming to the market. Weak petroleum prices through most of the 1990s severely restricted the ability of the petroleum-exporting countries to continue the spending spree they engaged in during the previous two decades. Indeed, the real price of petroleum wobbled around pre-1973 levels toward the end of the 1990s. At the end of the decade OPEC used its power over production as worldwide demand increased: Petroleum prices increased substantially.

ORGANIZATION OF ECONOMIC ACTIVITY

The three major economic goals of most countries are growth, stability, and an equitable distribution of income. There is much debate as to which of these is the most important and how the goals are best pursued once a reasonable consensus is reached on the "correct" mix. Indeed, governments and universities resound with arguments that champion a range of solutions from private enterprise to socialism. The issues have importance beyond scholarly debate; the choices are real and the stakes are high.

Several countries have been proponents of "Arab socialism," while others have monarchies that directly influence much of the "private" enterprise of any note. Others have taken a more eclectic stance, and a few are attempting to give coherence to the phrase "Islamic economics." There seems to be little consensus about the specific contours of Arab socialism, a concept that receives ever-less support as the years pass. The lack of a clearly defined and consistent ideology is due to several factors, including disagreements across national boundaries and espousals of an idea without any particular plan of action. What is clear is that most Middle Eastern "socialist" governments came to power with a definite desire to provide greater economic growth, stability, and a more equitable distribution of income and wealth. In order to meet these goals, the leaders initiated land reforms, froze prices, and nationalized major industries. But these measures are better described as nationalistic than socialistic, especially when they are designed to lessen foreign influences in the economy.

During the 1980s a pronounced shift occurred in the ideological stance of many of the proponents of Arab socialism. Indeed, there was a generalized worldwide shift away from government involvement in economic life in favor of private markets. During the preceding decades most academics and policymakers favored large-scale government involvement. Their preference was rooted in various notions of the development process, from Marxist to neoclassical renditions of the failures of the marketplace in the specialized settings of low-income countries. National leaders often adopted one or another of these moorings, either from intellectual conviction or as a convenient excuse to pursue another goal. However, by the 1980s the blame for the miserable economic performance in many of these countries was placed on government, the very agent that was seen as the driving force of development only a few years earlier. It was claimed, with a considerable number of case studies at hand, that government action stunted growth. At the same time, the U.S.S.R. was falling apart.

It is probable that some countries professed socialism because it was a convenient way for their political leaders to eliminate business opposition, or to strike an appropriate international posture; the professed ideals often faded as circumstances warranted. In 1973, three years after the death of Gamal Abdel Nasser, clearly the leading proponent of Arab socialism in the region, Anwar Sadat declared an Egyptian "open-door policy" to foreign investment. A little more than a decade earlier Nasser had severely restricted not only foreign business operations but also private domestic investments. Nasser's relationship to the business class probably had something to do with his decisions. The abrupt change in Egyptian policy may

have been based on Sadat's desire to curry favor with conservative King Faisal (died 1975) of Saudi Arabia. Ideologies may shift dramatically with the political climate.

Iraq, considered a radical state in the 1970s, reacted strongly against the post-Nasser economic drift in Egypt. A few months after the open-door policy was announced in Egypt, and after the 1973 Arab-Israeli war, Iraq proposed that the Western supporters of Israel should be punished through a boycott of petroleum sales. By adopting this policy it proved its radical mettle to the world at large. Of course, the world at large may not have known that Iraq was selling its petroleum to the U.S.S.R., which in turn sold petroleum to Western Europe. Without impugning Iraq's motives, it is fair to say that it was able to maintain its international reputation as a "hard-line" state without having to suffer significant revenue losses from decreased petroleum sales.

Through the 1980s Syria depended on the Soviet bloc for the bulk of its economic and military aid. Especially noteworthy is that much of the aid (especially educational) was given by the respective communist parties to the Syrian Baath party. But then the Soviet bloc crumbled. The consequent almost total shutoff of the aid spigot coincided with a series of drought years in Syria, which had an agricultural system particularly sensitive to rainfall. It also became increasingly apparent that the extensive system of government ownership of industry and rigid price-fixing was becoming ever more burdensome. The Syrian government responded to their economic crisis by drawing closer to the remaining great power, the United States. They adopted a series of measures designed to "liberalize" the economy, along with an attempt to make some of their political policies more acceptable to the United States. The 1990 U.S. call for Arab participation in the coalition against Iraq presented Syria with a unique opportunity.

After the war Syria continued to change its orientation in several ways. Among the changes was an official reinterpretation of Baathist notions of the "Arab Nation" and the role of the government in the economy. Although always in foggy and dreamlike terms, the keepers of Baathist ideology had spoken of some future time when there would be a pan-Arab nation free of boundaries imposed by Western powers. By 1991 they were speaking of the "Arab Nation" in the same tones as the members of the European Community were speaking of a united Europe—a closely cooperating group of nations, each with its sovereignty. Likewise the past record of heavy government involvement in the economy was explained as a phase necessary to fit the objective conditions of the 1970s and 1980s; the "new objective conditions" dictated that it was time for the private sector to take a greater role. The widely reported weak health of President Assad fueled speculation as to the future direction of the Syrian economy. Although one of his sons (the first potential claimant, Basil, died in an accident) assumed power after the death of his father near the close of the 1990s, it was not certain that this potential economic liberalizer would have enough political power to bring about significant changes in the organization of economic life. If not, would the mantle of leadership pass to long-established politicians who had a hidebound devotion to Baathist notions of the organization of the economy?

The same kinds of observations concerning ideologically flexible pronouncements and policies can be made about the growing list of countries that profess to follow private enterprise as an operating principle. In a few countries, most significant ventures initiated by the private sector are tied directly to the government, either through formal public participation or through the intervention of well-placed individuals in the government. The Iranian royal family, for example, gained ownership shares in many significant industrial ventures in that country. The royal family participated both because it desired wealth and because it perceived a need to exert control over industrialists and the growing industrial sector.

In many cases this kind of intervention has had a profound effect on the functioning of the marketplace. Competitive private enterprise markets in the Western world tend to be impersonal, ideally excluding all considerations except for those of price and performance. The highly personalized industrial ventures in Iran under the shah or in Saudi Arabia, for example, should not be expected to yield the same results. It is difficult to know what to call such systems: Perhaps etatism will suffice. In any case, they are not private enterprise systems as generally thought of in the West.

Islamic Economics

The study of Islamic economics became a growth industry after the success of OPEC and the increased interest in the formation of an Islamic state. Before this, first-rate work was relatively rare and/or obscure. The term *Islamic economics* covers a wide variety of issues and problems, although Western attention has focused almost exclusively on the Koranic proscription on the taking of interest and the consequent need to redesign the financial system. Since the range of inquiry is so comprehensive and the analyses so recent, many questions remain—but there are many points of agreement.

The fundamental starting point of mainstream (Western, neoclassical) economic analysis is extreme: "Well-offness," utility, is maximized by an individual solely with reference to material goods (and services). Further, the theory usually posits that I make myself better off by ignoring the well-being of others. That is, it adopts an extreme individualistic and materialistic stance. While Western economists generally agree that this narrow definition defies reality, they argue that it is a most useful starting point, and that the analysis can be adjusted further down the line. However, a group of Muslim theorists feels that this abstraction from reality is not warranted: The Koranic concern for the well-being of the Umma is so central that the "complications" need to be introduced at the outset. Consequently, some Muslim theorists have grappled with the very complex issue of modeling individual utility functions that jettison extreme individualism and materialism. This meant that thorny issues of the "proper" distribution of income and wealth (including the assignment of property rights) were brought center stage at the outset.

Many other issues hold the attention of those concerned with Islamic economics. For example, specific Koranic guidelines deal with the scope of inheritance, the proper system of taxation (including zakat), the nature of government expenditures, and, more generally, the proper role of government in meeting the wider material and ethical concerns of the Umma. On some matters basic principles are quite clear, but the mechanisms for goal achievement are not. The principle of the obligation of zakat is straightforward; the manner in which it is to be levied, and by whom, is not clear. On a more general level, the Koran does not express explicit hostility toward private enterprise, but its egalitarian concerns for the Umma leave open some basic questions relating to the proper extent of property rights, limits on the accumulation of wealth, and other fundamental issues.

The Koranic proscription against the taking of interest has captured most Western attention concerning Islamic economics. Most Muslim theorists are convinced that the taking of interest is indeed forbidden—after all, the Koran seems to be quite clear on the issue. However, we should realize that although the Koran specifically declares that interest is forbidden *(haram),* straightforward acceptance of even this involves a theological position. Some theorists argue that the words of the Koran reflect a prohibition against usury—"exploitatively high" interest rates—rather than interest per se. A strict literalist position, one that takes the Word as immutable through time and not subject to interpretation, renders the modernist view as heretical. In any case, there now is rather widespread agreement on the need to develop an interest-free banking system.

As with any price, the price for the use of money, the interest rate, balances supply and demand forces. In general, individuals need to be compensated for deferring consumption (saving). That is, Western banks pay interest in order to encourage a flow of loanable funds. Borrowers create the demand. They are willing to pay interest because the rate of return they expect from investing the borrowed money, say, building a factory, is greater than the interest payment they are obligated to pay the bank. The bank serves the function of making this market, of bringing together people who gain from deferring consumption and those who gain from investing. Notice that the equilibrium interest rate, that which yields the same quantity demanded as the quantity supplied, also serves the economy as a whole by matching the community's desire to forgo present consumption with future rewards; that is, it helps determine the upper limit of growth.

How, then, can an interest-free system operate efficiently? How does a financial institution encourage deposits and choose among potential borrowers? Islamic institutions provide an answer: a profit/loss share system. The banks compete for deposits by indicating that the depositor gains shares, claims on potential bank profits—and they advertise what they have paid out per share in past years. Depositors in an Islamic bank do not have the contractual guarantee of a return promised by a Western bank, but they do have some knowledge of the track record of the bank and can earn more if the bank has a particularly good year. This method of gathering loanable funds is in place in several countries, including Iran and Pakistan, and seems to work well—there is no fundamental difference from interest banking.

The lending decisions of the bank follow the same share principle. Instead of a firm borrowing money and having a fixed repayment schedule, the bank essentially buys shares in the activity of the borrowing company, with the provision that the firm has the ability to repurchase the shares (as well as an obligation to share profits). Since the banks are competing for the funds of potential savers, they must endeavor to deliver the highest share of profits. This, in turn, forces them to lend to those who have the highest probable rate of return. As in the interest system, competition enforces efficiency on the market.

While zero-interest banking can mirror an interest-paying system with respect to efficiency, there are several important differences that reflect Koranic concerns for equity. General Koranic ethical norms state that it is not acceptable to profit from an individual in dire straits. The share system satisfies this norm. The borrower is not obligated to make repayments to the financial institution if the investment goes sour. For example, the farmer who faces a crop loss due to bad weather is not obligated to make a payment to the bank in the same period. Rather, the bank, as partner, shares the burden. In the same fashion, the bank is not obligated to pay a return to depositors if the bank has a bad year. Both gains and misfortunes are shared.

The Islamic system of zero-interest banking, then, provides for the usual efficiency conditions of interest banking, and it fits Koranic ethical norms. Actually, the system is far more complex, and some of the details of operation and policy implications are not fully understood. However, it is clear that the system is economically rational and managerially feasible.

Economic Liberalization

The three large-population countries in the Middle East—Egypt, Iran, and Turkey—changed their economic orientation markedly during the last three decades of the twentieth century. The 1973 pronouncement (legislated in 1974) by Sadat of a policy of *infitah* ("opening up") of the Egyptian economy to private foreign and domestic investment was a clear political statement rejecting Nasser's policies. The movement was to be toward building "market socialism" and away from the Soviet-type material balances approach. This meant that many prices were to be market determined rather than set by a planning agency. It also meant that the private sector would be strengthened. Although the Egyptian economy grew at a robust pace for the next decade, about 8 percent per annum, the proximate causes of the growth cannot be attributed to the new policy. Rather, a surge in foreign exchange earnings emanating from forces largely out of the control of Egypt seem to have been responsible. The four major items were petroleum exports, receipts from the (newly reopened) Suez Canal, remittances from Egyptians working in the petroleum-rich states, and substantial international aid programs. During the 1980s and 1990s President Mubarak slowly nudged Egypt toward more private enterprise.

A host of domestic forces consigned Egyptian policy makers to a very narrow range of options. It seems as though a policy stasis emerged. The fundamental problems of a high rate of population growth, an urban and industrial bias, and a troublesome income distribution were not matters given priority. While the root causes of this policy stasis are not fully understood, it seems that one significant factor was the emergence of a new amalgam of social forces. The technocratic class gained members and prominence under Nasser. Many of this class were members of the bloated government, and Sadat's emphasis on the private sector was a clear threat to their power. As a result,

the usually cumbersome bureaucratic apparatus seemed to cease to function altogether when private investors sought government approval for some aspect of their operations. The agricultural sector was another source of resistance to Sadat's policy shift. Those peasants who rose toward the top of the agricultural ladder through the Nasser-initiated land reform policies would lose if there was a significant change in the system. The best off of those in agriculture stood to lose since they received substantial subsidies (and important exemptions from regulations). In counterpoint to the technocrats and new agricultural elite, the old elite class came to the surface under Sadat after many years of quietude under Nasser. They pressed for promised favors for the private sector.

The debt crisis of the 1870s led to a reordering of Egypt. One hundred years later Egypt again was in the middle of a nervous game in the international marketplace. The opening of the Egyptian economy removed some gross inefficiencies. However, its foreign exchange earnings were subject to the volatile petroleum market (for petroleum sales and migrant worker remittances to Egypt), and the equally uncertain political environment (Suez Canal earnings and international aid). The basic issues of population and income distribution were largely ignored. It is of consequence that the U.S. government forgave Egypt $7 billion in loans after Egyptian participation in the 1991 war against Iraq; the Egyptian economy was carrying a very heavy debt burden.

The process of economic liberalization in Egypt took root, and there were decent gains until the regional slowdown of the late 1980s due to the fall of petroleum prices in 1986. Egypt suffered again during the early 1990s, and then showed a substantial recovery. A good deal of the recovery has been attributed to the opening of international trade coupled with international investors' increased confidence that Egypt would stay the course. On the other side of the ledger, the service sector and government bureaucracy remain very inefficient. It is very difficult to quickly dismantle decades of inefficiency.

The Turkish solution to a faltering economy mirrored Egypt in that the economy was opened to foreign trade, but it differed in other basic aspects. While the primary reason for the 1980 military takeover in Turkey was to curb the alarming amount of politically motivated violence (about 180 deaths per month by mid-1980), it was clear that a grossly inefficient economy also was of concern.

The military leaders of the 1980 coup thoroughly reformed the Turkish political system by (1) disbanding all political parties and confiscating their property, (2) barring political activity (for ten years) for all of those who at the time of the takeover were in leadership positions or in the Grand National Assembly (for five years), and (3) initiating and guiding to passage a new constitution (in November 1982). One important set of provisions in the new constitution dealt with electoral reform. In particular, proportional representation was ended and national parties needed to receive at least 10 percent of the national vote in order to have a candidate seated. This blunted the efforts of many small parties and made it easier for the largest party to govern without being saddled by debilitating coalitions.

The election of 1982 brought a technocrat, Turgot Ozal, to power and gave his Motherland Party a majority in the Grand National Assembly, a majority that increased substantially in the 1987 elections. This cleared the way for Ozal to act decisively to bring order in the streets and coherence in the economy in order to meet the constitutional provision which stated that the economy was to be based on private enterprise. He initiated a set of "liberalizing" policies—policies designed to strengthen the free market, such as tariff reduction, foreign investment promotion, a wholesale dismantling of state-owned enterprises, a bid to join the European Economic Community, and (after the breakup of the U.S.S.R.) the formation of a Black Sea economic cooperation group of nations. Although the Motherland Party lost its legislative majority in 1991, the die had been cast; the majority in the legislature differed from Ozal in many ways, but they framed their differences within the basic market-liberalizing blueprint laid down in the 1980s. As with Egypt, involved Western actors, from governments to private creditors, worried over the seeming inability of Turkey to service its debt, assisted in the effort. And, as with Egypt, the Turkish economy seemed to be more vibrant during the last decade of the century

as economic reforms, albeit highly incomplete, took root. However, the vibrancy was lost by 2000, and the Turkish economy went into a deep and serious depression. An election in 2002 toppled the old ruling alliances. A party that claimed to be Islamic took power in a stunning victory. They stated that their main goal was not to infuse religion into the center of Turkish political life; rather, they claimed that the goal was to end decades of corruption in order to restore economic growth.

During the 1980s, the International Monetary Fund, the major international organization capable of providing financing to beleaguered governments, joined the academic world in their disillusionment with extensive government control of the economy. Countries seeking financial assistance always had to meet "conditionality" clauses if their requests were to be met. By the 1980s these clauses more explicitly argued for economic "liberalization," the strengthening of the private sector. The financial weakness of the country often meant that they had little choice but to accept the conditions. However, economic liberalization often meant that policies had to be initiated that made things worse before they got better. This was an increasingly bitter pill to swallow for those countries already in deep trouble. It also seemed unfair to those countries that arrived at their poor status because of wild gyrations in the international marketplace rather than internally generated failings.

For example, in 1989 Jordan completed negotiations with the International Monetary Fund that allowed it to borrow from the IMF on the condition that prices of key basic commodities in Jordan be increased to reflect economic costs. This is the usual procedure for the IMF; it will approve loans only if the country institutes a program that will correct fundamental imbalances. The case of Jordan clearly illustrates why many countries object to this "conditionality." Substantial increases in food and fuel prices designed to limit imports were met by civil unrest among those elements of the population thought to be the most loyal to the government. In response to the unrest, Jordan's prime minister was forced to resign and the king promised more political participation. The political costs of economic adjustment can be high.

Through the 1990s, the International Monetary Fund (and major international lending countries) came under increasing pressure to temper their conditionality clauses through a recognition of volatile political realities.

Iran, the other large-population country of the Middle East, took a different course. Its revolutionary government rejected moves toward a more globally interdependent economy, whether under the market socialism of Egypt under Sadat or the free market goal of Turkey. Although there was considerable debate in Iran about the economic role of the state and private enterprise, there also was rather widespread agreement that there would be no infitah in Iran. If anything, the goal would be that of removing foreign influence from the internal economy. Twenty years after the revolution, Iran was still fitfully moderating its position on foreign investment. Iran also had to deal with Western, especially U.S., obstacles to foreign investment. For example, in 1995 the U.S. government prohibited Conoco, a large U.S. petroleum company, from entering into a multibillion-dollar contract with Iran. However, liberalizing forces in Iran continued to make gains, almost always hotly contested, through the 1990s.

LIBERALIZATION AND GLOBALIZATION

The difficulties of the transition to a greater reliance on the free market generally were not well appreciated during the 1980s; painful experiences in the 1990s brought the lesson home. Free markets do not exist in a vacuum; to function properly, private enterprise must have a set of institutions that support it. There must be a legal system that can dispose of contract disputes in a fair and timely manner. There must be an administrative network that translates law into action. The financial system must be reasonably competitive and free of undue restrictions. The list could go on, but the point has been made. The putative triumph of free markets over statist systems makes sense from some perspectives, but free markets will not provide an answer to economic malaise without an institutional environment that supports the functioning of the market. In many cases, that environment was incomplete in the liberalizing countries of the Middle East. By the

close of the century, the IMF seemed to recognize that it was essential that governmental institutions needed to be reformed if economic liberalization was to succeed. They also paid much more attention to the plight of the poorest of the poor; the IMF argued that the poor needed to be directly involved and gain from economic development schemes. Their previous, albeit implicit, assumption that benefits would quickly "trickle down" to the poor was quietly shelved.

Liberalization was further complicated by globalization; the opening of economies can be painful to some segments of the society as markets are lost to global competitors and income within the country is redistributed as a result. Free capital markets allow foreign investment to flow into the country; but, as several Asian countries found out in the mid-1990s, that freedom also means that there can be quick and massive capital flight.

To further complicate the picture, the increasingly worldwide reach of the Internet, sometimes called "the death of distance," probably will have a profound effect on local companies everywhere. The local manufacturer, say, used to having firms within its geographic space buy from it, will increasingly find their customers surfing the net for the best worldwide buy. And since transportation costs have been decreasing, the advantage of buying locally is further eroded. The upshot is that global competition will seep into very local geographic spaces: the death of distance.

Although the ideological stance of the various nations may be important, we must look beyond surface pronouncements and deeds. The remaining sections of this chapter will analyze how different circumstances lead to different policy measures, and why the same policy measures may lead to different results.

LAND POLICIES

Table 11-2 gives the geographical area of the various Middle Eastern countries. Saudi Arabia is the twelfth largest country in the world; Iran ranks fifteenth, being about one-half the size of India; Sudan and Algeria are the two largest countries in Africa. In comparison, Kuwait, Bahrain, Qatar, the U.A.E., Israel, and Lebanon are very small indeed.

Table 11-2 Land and Urbanization

Country	Surface Area (1,000 km)	Arable Land per Capita (hectares)	Urban Population as a Percent of Total Population		
			1975	1997	2015
Israel21	0.06	86.6	90.9	92.6	
Kuwait	18	0	83.8	97.3	98.2
Bahrain	0.7		79.2	91.2	95
Qatar	11		82.9	91.8	94.2
U.A.E.	83.6		65.4	84.8	88.8
Libya	1,759.50		60.9	86.4	90.3
Lebanon	10		67	88.5	92.6
Saudi Arabia	2,150	0.2	58.4	84.1	89.7
Turkey	775	0.4	41.6	71.9	84.5
Oman			19.6	79.5	92.8
Jordan	89	0.08	55.3	72.6	79.8
Iran	1,633	0.3	45.8	60	68.8
Syria	185	0.33	45.1	53.1	62.1
Egypt	1,001	0.05	43.5	45.1	53.5
Iraq	438.3		61.4	75.5	81.6
Sudan	2505.8		18.9	33.3	48.7
Yemen	528	0.09	16.4	35.3	49.2

Source: From *Human Development Report 1999* by United Nations Development Programme, copyright © 1999 by the United Nations Development Programme. Used by permission of Oxford University Press, Inc.

A great percentage of the land in the Middle East is either not arable or only marginally so. With a few minor exceptions, all of the arable land in Egypt runs along the Nile; that of Libya is contained in a narrow band of land along the Mediterranean. The Arabian Peninsula has significant arable land only in parts of Oman, Yemen, and the Hijaz region of Saudi Arabia. Much of the Iranian steppe and the mountainous terrain of Turkey is unsuitable for high-yield agriculture. The vast deserts of the Middle East often have been compared to a sea; while they have an unrelenting, harsh, and beautiful power, they are difficult to control. These formidable deserts are both barriers and vast havens. However, their power to promote insularity has eroded considerably in the twentieth century. The finances necessary to overcome the power of the deserts—to cross them with roads, build airports, purchase transportation systems, dam rivers, and build radio transmitters—were generated in some countries by colonial administrations and in others by nationalist modernizing forces, by means of taxes and oil revenues. Whatever the source, the deserts are slowly

being changed. They will, however, continue to present severe constraints on life in the Middle East.

Agricultural land distribution and ownership patterns are generally considered to affect productivity. Obviously, they are also indices of economic justice and power. All of the countries in this survey have seen significant changes in the pattern of land ownership in the twentieth century. There have been formal agrarian reform programs in six of the countries—Egypt, Iran, Iraq, Syria, Libya, and (South) Yemen. There have been no reform programs in Jordan, Lebanon, the U.A.E., or Saudi Arabia. Land ownership and use patterns have changed considerably in Israel, but it is best to consider Israel apart since the circumstances of these changes have been unique.

Various land ownership patterns exist in the Middle East, but three types are most common. The first is **mulk**, or private ownership. The second is **miri sirf**, land owned by the state, generally with very strong *usufruct* rights (right of use without ownership) granted to the tenant. In practice, this is often little different than mulk. The third is waqf, a uniquely Islamic institution. One type of waqf allows for title to the land to be given to some officially recognized religious or social institution, sometimes with the condition that the family and heirs of the donor are to receive some share of the proceeds from the land either until the family line no longer exists or for some specified period of time. Another form is strictly private. A rough Western equivalent is trust funds. And as with trust funds, a waqf may be established and administered with the most honorable of intentions, or simply to protect individual assets from the tax collector. In any case, modifications of waqf status can involve massive changes in the distribution of wealth and political power.

The following thumbnail reports on some countries' experiences with land and agricultural policy illustrate several points beyond the gleaning of country-specific information. First, policies often have unintended results. Second, there is a wide range of ideological flexibility in the adoption of programs. Third, there can be serious international consequences to internal actions. Fourth, some policies can be very wasteful. Fifth, agricultural policies are intertwined with population and water issues. And, finally, profound political tremors can be triggered by changes in policy.

Turkey

Turkey put itself on the path of modernization with the thoroughgoing Westernizing revolution of Kemal Ataturk. Years of Ottoman neglect of agriculture, except as a tax base, were quickly reversed. At least four distinct periods stand out in Turkish agricultural history since the formation of the republic in 1923. First, during the years of Ataturk (1923–1938), the oppressive tax structure was reformed and a host of infrastructure projects were developed. The second era began after the close of World War II. The government engaged in a considerable effort to improve storage and marketing facilities as well as to introduce mechanization. Up to 1960, agricultural output expanded tremendously. Wheat production nearly doubled between 1948 and 1953, allowing Turkey to become a net exporter of this grain for a short time.

A great deal of this expansion came about by extending the area under cultivation as opposed to increasing the yields per hectare. This resulted in two deleterious effects that slowed the agricultural growth rate after 1960, the third phase. Because most of the new lands were marginal, they lost whatever productivity they had during each period of drought, since there was relatively little irrigation. Second, the methods used to expand the area under cultivation resulted in a loss of soil fertility and a greater runoff of water. The fourth phase has been characterized by an extensive series of irrigation projects made possible by the construction of dams, especially on the Euphrates. This has caused intense concern in Syria and Iraq, the other countries that depend heavily on the flow of Euphrates waters.

Egypt

The 1952 revolution in Egypt ushered in a substantial program of land reform and redistribution that proceeded by fits and starts for the next two decades. In 1952 about 1.2 percent of the largest holdings encompassed 45 percent of the agricultural land. In contrast, the smallest 72 percent of the holdings accounted for 13 percent of the land, an average of about one feddan (1.06 acres) per holding. Because of population pressures and a lack of alternative employment, the rental rates charged by the mostly absentee owners of the large estates were very high.

The first lands to be expropriated were those of the royal family. These lands, plus the waqf lands in their possession, accounted for 5.5 percent of the total agricultural land. Land reforms also lowered the maximum feddans which an individual could hold from 200 in 1952, to 100 in 1961, and finally to 50 in 1969. At first, the larger landowning families simply split their holdings among various family members and thereby avoided being severely affected. The law, however, was gradually tightened, and by 1970 the government had redistributed 18.6 percent of all agricultural land. In 1981 the laws were modified in order to stimulate settlement on what otherwise was desert. Small-holders were allowed to own up to 300 feddan, and agribusinesses could own up to 50,000 feddan. The record indicates that the large agribusinesses have been more successful than the small-holders, partially because of their ability to move the creaky Egyptian civil service.

Syria

The process of land reform followed the same general pattern in Syria. However, due to the extreme variability in land productivity, the redistribution was based on estimated incomes to be derived from the land; therefore, larger parcels were given to those on low-productivity land. As with many countries, the redistribution effort proved far more difficult than the promulgation of laws restricting maximum size. In Syria as in Egypt, the class of large landholders was more tenacious than anticipated. The reforms quickened in pace only as the political power base of this group diminished. However, a new group of agriculturists-cum-capitalists took the place of the traditional landholding elite and complicated issues of government control.

Libya and Iraq

In Libya and Iraq large landholders were rather suddenly shut out of the political decision-making process, although the situation in each country was somewhat different. Libyan agricultural landholdings were of two polar types: a small number of large estates located on relatively good and well-irrigated land, mostly owned by Italian nationals, and vast stretches of marginal land, partially (about one-third in 1960) owned on a tribal basis. The 1969 overthrow of the monarchy led to the expropriation of the Italian farms in 1970. The Libyan agricultural reform methods fit both the ideology of the socialist government and the agricultural situation. A mere redistribution of the poor lands would not accomplish much, if any, gain in productivity. Likewise, the average yields of the large productive farms probably could not have been retained if the farms were split up. These large units, therefore, were transformed into state farms. The redistribution of marginal lands was tied to an ambitious scheme to invest some of the country's considerable oil revenues in order to raise agricultural productivity; wells, roads, and

marketing facilities were included in this effort. Attempts also have been made to strongly discourage, if not eliminate, absentee ownership of arable land.

In Iraq, local sheikhs—generally better described as political dignitaries rather than religious leaders—were transformed into landholders in the twentieth century largely because the British attempted to transform the communal tribal ownership patterns into those of private ownership. The 1958 revolution left the sheikhs without a political power base, and the carving up of their holdings was assured. State lands, the miri sirf, also provided a base for redistribution. But the state of Iraqi agriculture and the country's political instability led to highly uneven results for this potentially highly productive nation.

Most agricultural land in Iraq is dependent on irrigation to support even reasonable levels of productivity; declines in agricultural productivity occur when the central authority neglects its responsibilities in this area. The neglect lasted for over one thousand years. The relative political stability and petroleum-generated wealth of the 1970s and 1980s reversed the process at long last. But the process stopped due to the ravages of war and the UN-imposed sanctions.

Large-scale land reform started in Iran in 1962, and without the impetus of a true revolution. The shah redistributed some royal lands in the 1950s, but the White Revolution, promulgated in January 1963, promised for the first time a set of sweeping changes throughout the economy, including substantial land reform (the "revolution" was called "White" because it was to be peaceful). Before the redistribution, absentee landlords controlled much of the fertile lands in Iran; the peasants generally had no tenancy rights. The landowners often owned huge tracts of land that encompassed many villages. To minimize evasion of the law, redistribution was stated in terms of villages rather than area. Legislation in 1965 closed some loopholes in the law, transferred waqf land administration to the central government, and presented the landholders not affected by the 1962 legislation with five basic choices: (1) lease the land, (2) sell the land, (3) divide the land between themselves and the peasants on the basis of old sharecropping agreements, (4) form a cooperative with the peasants, or (5) purchase peasant rights to the land and continue farming. This wide range of choices clearly reflected the triangle of tensions then present between landlords, peasants, and the shah. The shah needed to reduce the landowners' power, or at least give the appearance of doing so, but it was so great that an attempt at outright expropriation seemed inadvisable.

The results of this land reform can be analyzed fairly accurately by examining what happened in a particular village.[1] Before redistribution, about half the land in this village was in (public) waqf status, the other half being owned by a single individual. The peasants farming the waqf lands secured tenancy rights through the government. The landlord chose to split his property in half (the basis of the old sharecropping agreement), keeping, as might be expected, the most fertile land under his control. The peasants who worked this land, therefore, were excluded from redistribution policies. Other similar results followed: The largest and most fertile parcels lying outside the new domain of the landlord were worked by the family and friends of the village headman, who up till then had been the manager of the lands. On gaining property rights, almost half of these village elites rented their land to the headman and became absentee landlords themselves. Also, the custom of drawing lots every three to five years to ensure that particular peasants would not be permanently consigned to the least fertile land ended, of course, when title was assigned. This meant that some of the landed peasants were put in a permanently disadvantageous position.

It is very difficult to assess the effects of these events on agricultural productivity. However, the peasants became increasingly stratified socially and economically, a new class of absentee landlords developed, and the de facto changes in power relationships with the central bureaucracy were different than stated. Especially important in this respect was the shearing away of clerical power in rural areas. Quite obviously, some of the goals of the program were achieved—many peasants gained ownership or secured tenancy rights to the land. But in a country plagued with low produc-

tivity in the best of times, the new sets of problems generated from the reforms did much to blunt the overall positive effect.

Issues of land reform also vexed the revolutionary government. There was widespread appeal for fundamental land reform, an appeal that had been given voice by prominent members of the new government and Ayatollah Khomeini well before the revolution. But there was no clearly defined program. In the year following the fall of the shah a confused picture emerged.

In some areas villagers seized large estates and farmed them on a communal basis; in other seizures estates were broken into private plots; and in some areas disgruntled tribal leaders recaptured their feudal lord status, which had been stripped away by prerevolutionary reform. Since provincial courts and administrators gave contradictory rulings, the issue was brought to the Majlis for resolution. The attitude of members of the Majlis toward private property varied considerably and much haggling ensued. As somewhat more "progressive" members consolidated power, proposals were brought forth that severely restricted landowning. However, several prominent clergy gave opinions that indicated that the proposed legislation was at variance with Islamic principles. On another ideological level, arguments were made that raised questions about the power of Islamic jurists on this matter. Although legislation finally passed, a number of fundamental land-related issues remain unsettled.

AGRICULTURAL POLICIES

Most countries of the world prefer to be self-sufficient in agricultural production. Indeed, most have made considerable efforts to achieve this goal, and most have failed. The countries of the Middle East are no exception. Although all of the Middle Eastern countries are unlikely to meet the goal of self-sufficiency in the foreseeable future, the region could make considerable strides in this direction.

Total agricultural output can be increased in two general ways: an increase in the yield per unit of existing agricultural land, and an increase in the number of units cultivated. The post–World War II record of the countries under consideration

---

[1] D. Craig, "The Impact of Land Reform on an Iranian Village," *Middle East Journal,* Vol. X (Spring 1978), 141–154.

is mixed. Yields for the important foodstuffs grown in Egypt (wheat, rice, and barley) increased substantially and compare favorably on a world-wide basis. This was accomplished through labor-intensive cultivation and without much aid from the high technology of Western (and some Israeli) agriculture. The record of Iraq, although not as good as that of Egypt, and suffering through two decades of war and sanctions, shows the same general trend. These are the two countries that have access to long stretches of major rivers. The record of the remaining countries, except for Israel, is mixed. Both Syria and Iran have shown increases in the yields of some crops and decreases in others. The yields of wheat, for example, have decreased in Syria because marginal land has been brought under cultivation. Such poor yields, however, are not necessarily due to the chemical composition of the soil. Water is the scarce resource; its availability could markedly change the situation. Underground water deposits in Jordan, Libya, and Syria, for example, could call forth relatively high yields per unit if they could be brought into the production process at a reasonable cost. Another potential bright spot is that, except for Israel, the gains thus far have been made without heavy capital expenditures nor a relatively heavy reliance on fertilizers or pesticides by individual farmers.

A Saudi experience illustrates that increased agricultural output can waste resources. In the early 1980s, the Saudi government decided that it could make the desert bloom—with wheat—through the application of a system of generous subsidies to farmers. Land, water, seeds, fertilizers, and so on were provided well below cost. Within a few years Saudi Arabia had become an exporter of wheat. It also became painfully aware of the cost of this "success" when the exported wheat was sold at the world price of $3 a bushel. The cost of production was about $18 per bushel, meaning that the Saudis were using their resources to subsidize world wheat consumption. When the government announced that the system of subsidies had to stop, considerable opposition was voiced by the wheat growers, who had invested on the assumption that the subsidies were to remain in place. While the Saudi Arabian government was in the enviable position of being able to compen-

sate the farmers in order to stop this wasteful use of resources, most countries are not so blessed.

It is difficult to project these production trends into the future because the ecological balance is particularly sensitive in the Middle East; the productivity gains have not resulted primarily from a wholesale transfer of Western technology, nor have they simply appeared as manna from heaven. The successful innovations have been those that have considered the particular needs of the area. Whether or not enough of these successful innovations will continue to occur is a highly problematic and important question. It is problematic because of our inability to identify the forces that lead to sustained innovation and growth. It is important because of the area's very high rate of population growth and relative scarcity of water.

WATER

By 1990 it was apparent to most Middle East policy makers and analysts that water shortages were becoming ever more acute in most of the area. Indeed, some observers were predicting that the age of "oil wars" would be supplanted by "water wars." They may be correct; the looming water crisis is staggering.

Water is the scarcest resource in the Middle East. There are only a few significant rivers in the area. Egypt has the Nile. The Tigris and Euphrates both start in mountainous Turkey and wind through Iraq, the Euphrates also cutting across Syria. The most fertile areas of the Middle East lie in the valleys of these great rivers and the Levant. Other agricultural areas generally must depend on rainfall.

The Nile is the lifeline of Egypt. At Aswan, the width of productive land is only a few hundred meters on each bank. The productive valley widens as one travels north, fanning out into the great Delta north of Cairo. For thousands of years the annual flooding, occurring with great regularity, provided a natural replenishment of necessary soil nutrients, as well as drainage. The Delta was long viewed as the breadbasket of the region and later as the source of cotton for English textile mills. Harnessing the great power of the Nile would give farmers a dependable source of water year round, increase the yields from a single planting, enhance the region's ability to double-crop, and meet the nation's demand for electricity. The building of the massive Aswan Dam and the filling of Lake Nasser behind it was hailed, therefore, as a project that would alter the face of Egypt. The financing, however, was beyond the government's ability. In the mid-1950s the United States negotiated with Egypt to provide financing and technical assistance to the then-young government headed by Gamal Abdel Nasser. The Egyptian government was groping for a positive course; it was trying to end the corrupt and inefficient rule of the royal family that was overthrown in 1952.

As part of the move toward a nonaligned status, and because it needed to be ready for war with Israel, the Egyptian government shopped in the world arms market for military goods. Rebuffed by the United States, it signed an arms agreement with Czechoslovakia in 1955. This prompted the United States to withdraw its support for the Aswan Dam project and implicitly invited Soviet sponsorship and a consequent ascendancy of Soviet influence in Egypt. Consonant with its history, Egypt became a focal point for world politics. This time, however, Egyptian nationalism provided a check on the benefits to be gained by world powers.

The building of the Aswan Dam necessitated a massive movement of people from villages located where Lake Nasser would form. The Nubian villagers, well out of the mainstream of modernizing influences and culturally more akin to the citizens of Khartoum to the south than those of Cairo, were uprooted in a wholesale fashion and relocated in parts of existing towns or in newly formed villages. Since the rhythm of the river was the heartbeat of the local culture and economy, the relocation amounted to radical surgery. These people were thus forced to rely on the central government much more than previously. They had to abide by new rules, as compensation was calculated, rents and land rights were established, and a new social order was set in place.

The dam had different consequences for the fellahin to the north because the river level was now constant. The water table began to rise, and as it did so, the soil became saturated with salt. By the mid-1970s, the centuries-old high productivity of certain parts of the Delta had decreased dramatically. The decrease was especially marked in cotton production; cotton is particularly sensitive to the level of salinity in the soil. Keeping the Delta region productive by lowering the water table required two basic strategies: control over water use and improved drainage. Each of these efforts required the government to impose regulations and spend considerable sums of money. The government had to control the operation tightly because individual economic incentives worked against actions that corrected the problem. Ironically, the increased availability of water led to tighter water controls.

While the government controls the amount of water flowing into many irrigated areas, it cannot easily control how it is shared, a difficulty that has caused hostility between neighboring farmers. The allocation of water for individual farm use was complicated by the introduction of machine-driven pumps, and by the land reforms that significantly reduced average farm acreage and thereby increased the number of farm units to be controlled. The provision of adequate drainage presents similar difficulties. Substantial capital expenditures are needed for drainage, but an individual landholder will not significantly improve productivity acting alone. Likewise, if all of the farmer's neighbors spend their precious capital for adequate drainage, the lone party who resists will share in the benefits as the water table recedes. The government, therefore, must finance and control drainage in a systematic fashion.

Therefore, the boon to agricultural productivity, which was the raison d'être of the Aswan Dam, has been offset by important negative side effects that have strained the scarce financial and administrative resources of the government. Indeed, some estimates placed the cost of the Deltawide drainage expenditures as greater than the cost of the dam. Many of these side effects were anticipated before the building of the dam. However, the need to feed a quickly growing population and provide adequate electricity was thought to be more important.

Both the Tigris and Euphrates rivers originate in the Armenian highlands of Turkey, are fed by melting snow, and flow into the Persian Gulf. But the rivers are dissimilar in some important ways and present different kinds of opportunities and problems. The Euphrates cuts across Syria and Iraq on its journey. It has only a few major tributaries and, therefore, is rather slow moving and has a regular flow. The Tigris passes directly from Turkey into Iraq and has many tributaries. It is liable to heavy flooding, has a swift current, and carries a large volume of water. Irrigation from the Tigris is complicated by the timing of the floods and the irregular level of the river. Flooding usually occurs in the spring, in about the middle of the growing season for most crops (except rice and barley). The land cannot simply be inundated as in Egypt. A system of catchment areas must be employed so the water can be released at the appropriate times. And here too, provision has to be made for adequate drainage to prevent excess soil salinity.

These problems were faced a thousand years ago by the Abbasid caliphate. They exploited the fact that the Euphrates, a western neighbor of the Tigris around Baghdad, has a higher elevation than the Tigris. A canal system was built between the two rivers that allowed for catchment, irrigation, and drainage. Regular maintenance was required, as the Euphrates carried a substantial amount of silt. If the Tigris flooded, a considerable additional effort was needed to clear the irrigation system. Relatively large and continuous infusions of capital were necessary to keep the system running. Since the irrigated lands were owned by many different parties, and the benefits of maintenance and repair were spread unevenly among them, the absence of a well-defined and enforced set of rules discouraged private investment in the canal system. An effective and stable government was needed to maintain agricultural productivity on the irrigated lands. Once the Abbasids passed their zenith, the system fell into decay for a millennium.

This situation contrasts markedly with that of Egypt. Government actions maintaining adequate drainage certainly have affected agricultural productivity in Egypt, but short-term neglect did not lead to a total failure of the system—at least not until the Aswan Dam was built.

The Euphrates cuts across Syria and Iraq before emptying into the Gulf. The construction of dams in Turkey, especially the massive GAP project, has caused considerable anxiety in both Syria and Iraq. Although officials from the three countries have held regular meetings on the principles and details of water sharing, considerable tension remains. The problem is further complicated by the fact that a large percentage of the farmers of Syria and Iraq who are heavy Euphrates water users have been troublesome to the central government in the best of times. So when the Syrians cut back on downstream flows in order to fill the lake behind their huge dam, it was Shia farmers of southern Iraq who suffered.

Israeli water demands may serve as a significant roadblock to any proposed peace settlement. Israel garners a large percentage of its water from the territories occupied since the 1967 war. Especially relevant is Israeli control of the Golan, an area generally described by Israel as a military stronghold necessary to avert attacks from Syria. While this argument does not hold much water, the Golan does. The Israelis are taking water from this source (largely via the Sea of Galilee), securing a sizable percentage of its national water needs (through the National Water Carrier). South of the lake, the Jordan River has been reduced to a small polluted stream. This causes obvious water shortage problems for the kingdom of Jordan. The Israeli presence in southern Lebanon had a water security dimension; the Litani River is located there and flows largely unimpeded to the sea. Israel also pumps water from the (largely rain-fed) aquifers in the West Bank for the use of settlers there as well as for general Israeli water use. By the early 1990s they were pumping water out at an unsustainable rate; the water table was so low that substantial salt water infiltration became a problem. Substantial Soviet Jewish immigration heightened the problem. Rainfall, of course, helps ease the situation, but there is a significant drought in this region every four years or so. We cannot expect Israel to leave the West Bank (and Gaza) without ironclad assurances of a secure water supply. Desalination plants are one potential answer, but these plants are very expensive.

Saudi Arabia faces its own water problems. First, there was great fear during the worst days of the war against Iraq that the desalination plants in the Gulf would become clogged with millions of barrels of petroleum that were floating down from Kuwait. Fortunately, that crisis was averted. The ecology of the Gulf is very fragile; the massive amount of petroleum transported through it poses a continual danger. Since the Gulf is an international waterway, this points to the need for international agreements on the protection of these waters. Second, several studies have indicated that the Saudis are rapidly depleting their (nonrenewable) aquifers in the central regions of the country.

This suggests that comprehensive water management programs should be employed, and that research programs such as the United Nations–affiliated International Center for Agricultural Research in the Semi-Arid Areas be funded adequately, especially since agriculture accounts for over three-quarters of the annual water consumption in most areas. The research aim is to increase agricultural yields without an increase in water usage.

When water sources become overburdened in the face of ever more densely packed populations, human disease flourishes (schistomiases, malaria), property rights need to be redefined, the role of government water policies becomes critical, and, more generally, social conflicts increase in number and severity. As it is, rivers and renewable underground sources account for about half of the water in the entire region. This translates into severe water shortages in many areas of the Middle East. With the prospect of increased populations, annoying shortages will become crises in the near future.

POPULATION

Although the population of the Middle East has been increasing for at least a century, the post–World War II growth rate acceleration and subsequent decline is of particular interest. It is one of the ironies of history that local, national, and international efforts to prolong life have led, albeit indirectly, to more suffering. Increasing the population base without increasing the food supply results in less food per person. The average annual rates of population increase in the Middle East have ranged between 2 and 3 percent in the last couple of decades; at these rates, the population doubles every quarter century.

Rates of population increase are expected to fall during the coming decade. This deserves some explanation. During the last quarter of the century infant mortality fell and the average age of death increased substantially, as indicated in Table 11-3. These changes will not be repeated during the next quarter century; there is not the same "room" to lower infant mortality nor increase the average age of death. This means that the major sources of population growth during the last decades of the twentieth century will be absent; rates of population increase will decline. Also, during the last decade of the century fertility rates unexpectedly fell worldwide, including the Arab world. As shown in Table 11-3, every country experienced a pronounced decline. However, Arab countries still had higher fertility rates than most other areas of the world.

Despite the decrease in fertility rates, the mathematics of demography means that populations will continue to increase rapidly in the next couple of decades. As a result, an enormous number of young people will continue to put pressure on the beleaguered educational systems. It also means that large numbers of young people will enter the workforce in economies that have not been creating jobs. This could be a potent force causing social discontent.

Migration

A significant portion of the population increases of a few countries have come about through massive movements of people rather than natural increases in the indigenous population. The exodus of Palestinians in 1948 markedly altered conditions in Israel and Jordan. Indeed, the event has dominated much of what has happened in Jordan since independence. At independence Jordan was an extremely poor country and had few natural resources. The flood of Palestinians into Jordan following the formation of Israel more than trebled the population. Already impoverished, Jordan faced seemingly insurmountable problems, since the majority of the refugees were destitute. The addition of the West Bank to Jordanian territory added only 7 percent to the total land area but 30 percent to the total arable land. However, these benefits did not come close to compensating for the massive influx of humanity.

During the 1950s almost all expert opinion was pessimistic on the ability of the Jordanian

Table 11-3 Population and Fertility

	Growth Rate		Total Fertility Rate		Life Expectancy at Birth	
	1975–2000	*2000–2015*	*1970–1975*	*1995–2000*	*1970–1975*	*1995–2000*
Israel	2.3	1.6	3.8	2.9	71.6	78.3
Kuwait	2.6	2.5	6.9	2.9	67.2	75.9
Bahrain	3.4	1.4	5.9	2.6	63.5	72.9
Qatar	4.8	1.4	6.8	3.7	62.6	68.9
U.A.E.	6.6	1.4	6.4	3.2	62.5	74.6
Libya	3.1	1.9	2.6	1.3	52.9	70.0
Lebanon	0.9	1.9	4.9	2.3	65.0	72.6
Saudi Arabia	4.1	3.1	7.3	6.2	53.9	70.9
Turkey	2.0	1.1	5.2	2.7	51.4	65.4
Oman	4.2	3.2	6.0	3.6	49	70.5
Jordan	3.7	2.5	7.8	4.7	56.6	69.7
Iran	3.0	1.4	6.4	3.2	53.9	68.0
Syria	3.1	2.4	7.7	4.0	57.0	70.5
Egypt	2.2	1.5	5.5	3.4	52.1	66.3
Sudan	2.5	2.1	6.7	4.9	43.7	55.0
Yemen	3.9	3.9	6.4	3.8	42.1	59.4
ARAB STATES	2.7	2.0	6.5	4.1	51.9	65.9
ALL DEV. CO.	1.9	1.4	5.4	3.1	55.6	64.1
HIGH INCOME	0.7	0.4	2.1	1.7	72.0	77.8

Source: From *Human Development Report 2002* by United Nations Development Programme, copyright © 2002 by United Nations Development Programme. Used by permission of Oxford University Press, Inc.

economy to function in a reasonably coherent and growth-inducing fashion. Throughout that period Jordan received a substantial amount of international aid. Although it remained a very poor country, during the 1960s signs of positive movement started to appear. Many Palestinian refugees were highly skilled and experienced in commerce and industry. This "imported" skilled labor, along with considerable Jordanian efforts to improve education, especially at the postsecondary level, began to increase the country's productivity.

The 1967 Israeli occupation of the West Bank and the success of OPEC since 1973 complicated Jordan's problems. The occupation, of course, meant that a good portion of Jordan's arable land was lost and that a new wave of refugees entered the country, thus putting an even greater strain on the system.

The mobilization of PLO forces in Jordan and the consequent pressure that these forces put on Israel, coupled with the Israeli policy of retaliation, led to King Hussein's decision to have Jordanian troops do battle against the armed Palestinians in September 1970. This brought home in stark and tragic relief the fact that many of the residents of Jordan held another national allegiance. The East Bank, an area showing progress amidst the abject poverty of the refugee camps, was not fully under the control of the Jordanian government.

The success of OPEC signaled another wave of population movement as Jordanians rushed to fill positions in petroleum-rich countries. From 1975 forward, about 40 percent of the Jordanian workforce (a large percentage being Palestinian) were abroad. Remittances from these workers assumed rather staggering proportions by 1981, measured as a percentage of GNP (27.8 percent), imports (39.0 percent), or exports (168.2 percent). Some difficulties are associated with this influx of foreign exchange. One is the obvious heavy dependence of the Jordanian economy on the continued flow of remittances. Also, a major asset of Jordan, human capital, was depleted to the point that skilled positions within Jordan were understaffed. It is probable that several other labor-exporting countries faced selective labor shortages due to migration; the Egyptian construction industry, for example, seems to have suffered substantially. Jordan fell on hard times in the last years of the 1980s. Remittances (private and official) fell, the current account deficit increased, and international financial reserves were depleted. In addition, in 1991, Jordan had to accommodate several hundred thousand Palestinians fleeing Kuwait (and generally without their hard-currency savings) and had Gulf aid dry up because of its support of Iraq.

The small-population, petroleum-producing countries have been the major importers of skilled labor. They include Saudi Arabia, Bahrain, Kuwait, Libya, Qatar, and the United Arab Emirates. Iraq also imported labor during the 1980s during their war with Iran. Egypt, Yemen, and Jordan were the major suppliers from the area. Indigenous entrants to the labor force in the rich countries often have been absorbed in government service as a matter of policy rather than need. Although this policy tends to keep measured unemployment lower than otherwise and serves to pacify potentially disgruntled members of the workforce, it also results in a considerable amount of disguised unemployment since the measured productivity of these workers is often nil. Apparently notions of economic efficiency have taken a back seat to political and social issues.

The extent of labor migration has been dramatic. In 1975 about one-quarter of the population of these countries were migrants; by 1985 it was close to 40 percent. Indeed, nationals are a minority in some countries. Since most of the migrants do not bring their families, the percentage of foreigners in the workforce is more dramatic. This, of course, significantly influences foreign and domestic policies. For example, in Kuwait, about one-quarter of the expatriates (one in every five workers) were classified as coming from Jordan, a high percentage of them being Palestinians. The government of Kuwait found itself in a rather delicate position whenever Arab states had to stand up and be counted on Palestinian issues. The generally conservative government had to guard against a reaction from the Palestinian expatriates if it took the wrong stance.

The most dramatic change in the composition of the migrant labor force was the increase in the number of Asians—mainly Indians, Pakistanis, and Koreans—working in the Gulf states in the 1970s and 1980s. There are several complementary reasons why the increased demand for labor was not met exclusively by Arabs. First, the major suppliers already had substantial percentages of their workforce abroad. Second, skilled and semi-skilled workers were in particularly short supply in the Arab supplier nations. Third, the Asian labor market was well organized, Asian labor was relatively cheap, and the labor force was sometimes tied to construction projects awarded to Asian firms. Fourth, they tended to be less politically troublesome. By 1985 the percentage of total migrants to Middle Eastern labor importing countries who came from India (8.6 percent), Pakistan (13.1 percent), and Southeast Asia (10.9 percent) was substantial. About 150,000 of the migrants were Korean. In total, about one-half of the migrants were not Arab.

The 1991 war against Iraq displaced millions of people. Several hundred thousand Kurds fled to Turkey, and over a million went to Iran in order to escape Iraqi forces attempting to reestablish control after the war. Tens of thousands of Shia in the south fled either to Iraq or the fabled Iraqi marshlands after their postwar resistance was crushed. Before the war Iraq had more than one million Egyptian guest workers. All of these, and others, were expelled. Between 350,000 and 400,000 Palestinians were forced out of Kuwait, and several hundred thousand Yemeni guest workers had to leave Saudi Arabia after their government tilted toward Iraq.

The perceived consequences of having too many foreigners in a country was faced squarely by Saudi Arabia a decade before the 1991 war; they slowed the implementation of their development plans partially because of a fear that the cultural influences of the foreigners would erode important traditional Saudi values. The U.A.E. (especially Dubai and Abu Dhabi) provide a living illustration of Saudi concerns; the overwhelming majority of the population is foreign. It is clear to the most casual observer that much of traditional emirate culture is being swept away by a tidal wave of international commerce.

Kuwait decided to lower the foreign share of the population in a different fashion than Saudi Arabia. It had a preinvasion population of about 2.2 million; only 600,000 were Kuwaiti citizens. After the war with Iraq it decided to stabilize the population at 1.1 million—the notion being that Kuwaitis needed to be a majority in their own country. Since the infrastructure of Kuwait needed more than 1.1 million people to function smoothly, the goal had to be modified. However, almost all Palestinians were forced to leave and many other guest workers, mainly from Asia, were restricted in number. The government also changed the terms of (nonprofessional) guest worker employment. No longer were they allowed to bring their families with them, and the work permits were to expire after three years, more or less assuring that the foreign population would not develop roots in the country, as in the U.A.E. However, by 2002 the population of Kuwait had climbed back to 2.3 million, with foreigners accounting for about the same percentage of the population as before the war and about 80 percent of the workforce. Indeed, expatriates accounted for over one-half of the workforce in every Gulf state, ranging from about 55 percent in Saudi Arabia to an astounding 90 percent in Qatar.

Israel had a different sort of population influx during the last decades of the century: Jews immigrating from the former Soviet Union. It absorbed about 350,000 people from the beginning of the influx in the late 1980s through 1991, and more than that number waited—although limits of Israeli absorptive capacity and the breakup of the U.S.S.R. stemmed the flow. This potential massive influx, a 20 percent addition to the population, was greeted with much fanfare in Israel; after all, the raison d'etre of the state was the ingathering of world Jewry. The timing also seemed propitious: The Israeli psyche was in a moral quandary—large numbers of its citizens felt that the continued occupation of the territories was tragically misguided. The influx also eased the fears of some Israelis who thought that the higher Arab birthrate was leading to some future point at which the Jews would be a minority in the Jewish state. It is, therefore, not surprising that the Israeli government worked hard to assure that Jews could leave the Soviet Union and that Israel was the only haven.

But the massive influx also carried significant problems. The immigrants had to be housed, fed, and otherwise assimilated into the society. The government budget was not up to the task, so they asked the U.S. government to guarantee up to $10 billion in loans they had to raise. But the United States balked—mainly because Israel was at the same time quickening the settlement of Jews in the occupied territories, a policy against international law. Many of the Soviet Jews took over jobs otherwise given to Palestinians, thereby worsening the economic condition of these people. And over time they became a significant force in Israeli political life. During the last half of the 1990s Israel thought it proper to limit the number of work permits issued to Palestinians in the West Bank and Gaza. The shortfall in the (largely) unskilled labor force was made up by allowing Asian migrants to come to Israel for relatively short-term stays. The second intifadah brought a new group of immigrants to Israel—mostly from Eastern Europe, Romania, the Philippines, and Thailand—as the restrictions on Palestinian labor tightened. By 2002 migrants constituted close to 10 percent of the workforce.

Urbanization

There are different sources and consequences of population problems, the overarching being one of resource imbalances. Population increases and rapid urbanization are related in an integral fashion to many of the cultural, economic, political, and social problems many Middle Eastern nations are struggling with. But it is politically dangerous to attack the population issue squarely; indeed, it is the rare politician who opts to champion a policy of population control. After all, the issue strikes at the very core of family life. More often, governments simply do not enter public discussion of the issue. Some governments, notably Iraq, provide explicit economic incentives and public applause to those with large families. On the other hand, by the late 1990s Iran had established a formidable family planning program.

Egypt provides a classic and sad case of an overpopulated country. Its population doubled in less than thirty years, exceeding 68 million in 2002. Virtually all of the jump is attributable to natural increases. Since almost all of the arable land in Egypt is along the Nile River and the Delta, this narrow strip is one of the most densely populated areas in the world. Because the amount of arable land, although increasing somewhat through irrigation, is close to being constant, there has been ever-increasing pressure on the land to produce more. But the additional labor could do little to add to production since the methods employed already were highly labor-intensive. This combination of population increases and a constant amount of land to be worked is close to fitting the Malthusian dilemma of population increases resulting in permanent subsistence living. Egypt has avoided taking the dreary course predicted by Malthus through the application of modest technological advances, a reorganization of landholding patterns, greater availability of water from the Aswan Dam, and the shifting of crops from cotton to food. Egypt still has to import food, however. The race between productivity and population has been close. A sanguine outcome is not assured, partially because the continuing high rate of population increase has led to urban sprawl that is covering prime agricultural land. Further, land reclamation has proved to be ever more difficult, and water shortages have been felt.

Cairo holds about 20 percent of the population of Egypt. Although some of the increase in the past half century, from 2 million in 1950 to 13 million in 2000, can be attributed to flight from the war-torn cities of the Suez Canal area, most of it has been due to people leaving the farms. Once in the cities, the rural people have not been assimilated easily or quickly. Indeed, they often form pockets of essentially rural culture and lifestyles that are surprisingly resistant to change. The Middle Eastern urban populations in 2000 included four cities exceeding ten million: Cairo (13), Tehran (11), Istanbul (11), and Baghdad (11).

It is quite clear that the movement of people from rural to urban settings upsets traditional patterns, but it is not clear whether or not these changes should be considered beneficial or dysfunctional. Generally the rural migrants do not have skills useful in the urban environment. Further, there is considerable worldwide evidence that at least for the first several years in an urban setting individuals are apt to be alienated from the urban society and have considerable difficulties adapting to the regimen of factory life, if they are lucky enough to land a job in the first place.

Tardiness, absenteeism, and quit rates generally are quite high. The factory, it seems, is a particularly difficult place to adjust to. At the same time, evidence (from areas other than the Middle East) indicates that the factory is the single most effective source from which to accumulate that set of attitudes that are considered "modern."

A rapid increase in the population of major cities also can lead to the breakdown of city services. Transportation becomes a nightmare as thousands of vehicles are jammed into what is essentially a pre-twentieth-century road network; electrical supply capacity is strained; the telephone system becomes virtually unworkable. On the other hand, it is easy to generate arguments to indicate that if the migrants stayed in a rural setting, per capita income and possibly agricultural production would fall. Besides having one less mouth to feed, the farmer often receives remittances from the family member in the city; this can finance technical change. Since government actions, fiscal and otherwise, have pronounced effects on the flow of labor to urban areas, we must also consider how those flows will change when particular measures are being considered. For instance, will an attempt to improve urban conditions merely lead to an increased flow into the cities and thus thwart the original effort and disrupt agricultural planning? A related urban bias problem is that usually one city is favored. For example, Damascus garners many more resources than Aleppo, but the resource base of the country is closer to Aleppo than Damascus.

Employment

Most countries profess full employment as a primary goal. A brief account of a government's problems in attempting to meet this goal may give the reader a sense of the complexity of designing a coherent employment scheme. The first job is to figure out what percentage of the population is to be counted as part of the labor force. Dependency ratios are good shorthand indicators of the issue. This is simply the ratio of those defined as being out of the labor force (under age fifteen and over age sixty-five), people dependent on others to produce goods and services (the numerator), to those of working force age (fifteen to sixty-five, the denominator). The figure for most high-income Western countries is about 0.5. In a rough way this means that two workers are available to help support one person not in the labor force. In the Middle East it approached 1.0. As indicated in Table 11-3, this figure is expected to decrease markedly in the coming decades. The very high ratios of the earlier period are due to the rapid increase in population due to the decrease in infant mortality rates and increase in the average age of death. These will not change as much in the coming decades, but as earlier noted, female fertility rates have decreased, thereby decreasing the dependency ratio (relatively fewer children to support).

Defining potential members of the labor force involves questions concerning the role of women and the minimum acceptable age of entry into the labor force, issues that are not easily resolved. The task of the planner and analyst of the labor force is further complicated by the obvious fact that individuals are not interchangeable parts—the illiterate construction worker cannot be placed in a job for a materials engineer. An economy may have labor shortages in some areas and surpluses in others. Correcting the perceived imbalances is not an easy task, especially considering that many of the high-skill positions demand relatively advanced formal education. It is not clear, for example, to what extent the goal should be that of universal primary education, the strengthening of the secondary school environment, or expanded opportunities for higher education. Several governments adopted policies that virtually guaranteed employment to indigenous workers of a certain level of educational attainment. These policies are not limited to petroleum-rich states. For example, for many years Egypt guaranteed government employment to all college graduates. The combination of limited employment opportunities and heavy government subsidization of university education resulted in a bloated bureaucracy. Studies, including one commissioned by the government, indicated that in Cairo alone about one-quarter million government employees had no function except to receive their salary. While this policy lowers the measured level of unemployment, there are obvious gross inefficiencies.

When education is provided and employment opportunities are lacking, bitterness and social unrest can result. Palestinian earnings and unemployment in the West Bank and Gaza changed markedly after the 1980s. Before 1972 there were no institutions in the area that granted postsecondary school degrees. By 1986 there were twenty (funded largely by outside sources). The flood of Palestinians with higher education resulted in a large decrease in the wage difference between skilled and unskilled labor; that is, the rate of return to education fell dramatically. Also, unemployment among the more highly educated increased significantly. One reason for this is simply the rather remarkable increase in supply. But another portion was due to living in conditions of occupation. Israeli policies often acted to limit employment potential. Youth unemployment is high in all of the countries, including Israel. It is obvious that continued long stretches of unemployment lead to frustration and bitterness. It forms a fertile ground for recruitment into organizations opposed to the current order.

The labor force participation rate of women in the Middle East is much lower than that of men. Indeed, it is much lower than most other areas of the world. In short, Middle Eastern growth is lower than it otherwise would be because of the low female participation rate. We could argue that placing the productive power of women in the labor force runs against long-standing cultural norms. However, it cannot be denied that the disparity has enormous consequences. On the other hand, the rates of increase in female literacy and average number of years of schooling relative to men were substantial during the last decades of the twentieth century (Table 11-4). This is likely to have a positive impact on health and productivity even if females continue to be consigned to household chores. An overwhelming amount of evidence collected worldwide indicates that when females are literate it follows that infant mortality, low birth weights, wasting, and child stunting all decrease. More generally, the rather breathless pace of social and economic change in the Middle East in the past several decades has led to substantial change in the role of women and substantial confusion with respect to what could and ought to follow. For example, it seems that many

Table 11-4 Selected Female Demographics

Country	Total Female Literacy Rate	Female Literacy as Percent of Male		Female Secondary Rates as Percent of Male		Tertiary Rates as Percent of Male
	1997	*1970*	*1997*	*1997*	*1985 = 100*	*1997*
Israel	93.4	—	96	—		—
Kuwait	77.5	65	93	100	74	134
Bahrain	80.7	—	90	108	93	—
Qatar	81.2	—	102	97	90	531
U.A.E.	76.8	—	104	105	153	608
Libya	62.9	22	71	100	122	—
Lebanon	78.3	73	86	—	—	—
Saudi Arabia	62.5	13	77	82	127	—
Turkey	73.9	49	80	72	134	—
Oman	55	—	72	96	319	97
Jordan	81.8	45	89	—	—	96
Iran	65.5	43	81	88	168	60
Syria	56.5	33	65	87	79	—
Egypt	40.5	40	63	88	158	64
Iraq	—	36	—	—	—	—
Sudan	41.3	—	63	—	—	—
Yemen	21	15	32	—	—	14

Source: From *Human Development Report 1999* by United Nations Development Programme, copyright © 1999 by United Nations Development Programme. Used by permission of Oxford University Press, Inc.

Saudi women now use the Internet not only to shop but to run businesses. Without this technological change, Saudi restrictions on the activity of women in public places all but ruled out significant business ventures of women.

Most observers would agree that there are significant labor problems in the agricultural sector of most less-developed countries. Typically, however, one does not find much open unemployment in agriculture; rather the problem is one of underemployment. Underemployment can be described as a situation where at least some of the labor force is not working to full capacity. The usual implication is that these "surplus" workers could be freed from agricultural work with little or no decrease in output. But this conclusion is not necessarily the correct one and is, in any case, too simplistic. For instance, there is a tremendous seasonal fluctuation in the demand for agricultural labor in most of the Middle East. Labor must be available on a standby basis to perform essential tasks. Another qualification is that the labor force in agriculture is not homogeneous; custom dictates that women and children are to perform some tasks and men others. Since the household (ex-

tended or nuclear) is the basis of most small farms in the Middle East, it becomes difficult to sort out the work patterns of the various types of labor. Generally, it seems that the cycle of seasonal work for men, although substantial, is less pronounced than that for women and children.

Equity considerations and efficiency also may clash when we consider rural land use and labor deployment policies. It seems that large plots require less seasonal labor than small plots. Although the reasons for this tend to be specific to the area under study, generally we can assume that the cultivator of the larger plot has greater access to capital inputs (chemical fertilizers, pesticides, tractors). A policy of creating larger plots, therefore, would free underemployed labor and make it available for other productive uses. But several conflicts are involved in this approach; a move toward larger plots is not easily accomplished. Considerations of equity have led a large number of countries to legislate land reform programs designed to result in smaller-sized holdings. If seasonal laborers could be released from the land, one must then determine where they would be employed. Industrial growth on a substantial scale is needed to absorb this labor, and that growth has not been forthcoming in most of the countries under consideration. Also, since women and children are most apt to be seasonal workers, it presumably would be they who would be freed for alternative employment. Obviously, there would be considerable resistance to any such move.

Another problem in evaluating the labor force is that urban unemployment is open and obvious as contrasted to that in the agricultural sector. Therefore, the planner may begin with a bias and develop plans that commit more resources to urban areas than are warranted by strict economic criteria. This tendency is buttressed both because of the politically volatile nature of the urban population and because most notions of modernity, both naïve and sophisticated, are linked to industrialization and industry is linked to urbanization.

INDUSTRY

Because of OPEC's success, industry in the Middle East has grown dramatically. There are several prerequisites for large-scale, sustained industrial growth. Systems of communication, power, transportation, and education are needed if a modern industrial structure is to emerge and prosper. The history of all of the industrialized countries of the world indicates that this process takes a long time, that it generally proceeds by fits and starts, and that "economic miracles" have their roots in earlier centuries, not decades. But because of OPEC, several oil-rich economies are being transformed at an unprecedented rate.

Until the spectacular increase in the price of petroleum, Egypt, Turkey, and Iran were the focus of most speculation about the course of industrialization in the Middle East. They have large populations, thus providing the potential for domestic markets, as well as a longer history of significant industrial activity than the other countries of the region. Industrialization in Egypt received its first substantial impetus under Muhammad Ali in the 1820s. This ambitious attempt ground to a halt after a couple of decades and was largely moribund until the 1920s, when Egypt received a measure of independence. Industrialization in Egypt moved slowly for the next thirty years; it finally

began to receive close attention in the 1950s under Nasser. The 1960s in Egypt saw the large-scale nationalization (and weak industrial performance) of major industries; during the post-Nasser period there was a selective encouragement of private enterprise. A series of reforms during the 1980s and 1990s encouraged foreigners to invest in Egyptian manufacturing. Direct foreign investment in Egypt increased from $400 million in 1995 to over $1.2 billion in 1997; about one-half was in manufacturing and 30 percent in banking. It should be noted that foreign investors in manufacturing were not solely responding to liberalizing economic policies; they also began to sense that the reforms had "staying power" and that there was a commitment to strengthen the institutional framework that supports private enterprise.

Iran began to industrialize more than a century later than Egypt. The years between World War II and 1960 were spent laying a foundation upon which industrialization could occur. Fueled by petroleum revenues, the growth process accelerated. By the middle of the 1970s, per capita income in Iran was about five times that of Egypt, up from less than double in 1960. In any discussion of the future of industrialization in the two countries, most observers favored Iran. Petroleum sales provided the money to purchase capital goods and to quickly train a modern labor force. (In 1978 one out of every nine international students studying in the United States was Iranian.) However, the Iranian revolution and the war with Iraq (1980–1989) seriously disrupted economic activity in Iran and made the predictions of sustained industrial growth questionable. The decade of the 1990s provided some breathing space for the leaders of the government to sort through economic policies, including significant overtures to fully rejoin the international economic community. But there was serious opposition, and with the revolution more than two decades old, Iran remained tentative and the United States continued to press, albeit less forcefully than earlier, for continued restrictions on trade and investment in Iran.

Lebanon and Kuwait provide another set of contrasts. Lebanon has a long history of commercial and industrial development. Its relatively mature economy, its geographic position, and its tradition as the financial hub of the Middle East allowed some impressive industrial growth during the 1960s and the first half of the 1970s. Since most of the industrial establishments were centered in and around Beirut, however, the devastation of that city beginning in 1976 halted Lebanon's industrial and financial activity. It wasn't until the mid-1990s that sustained significant investment in Beirut resumed. Kuwait, long an earner of substantial amounts of foreign exchange through petroleum sales, attempted to diversify its industry and not rely exclusively on petroleum-related production. The Iraqi invasion of 1991, of course, put that process on hold. Indeed, most of the oil-producing Gulf states sought economic diversification, especially after petroleum prices took a long downward slide during most of the 1990s.

Bahrain has a different set of problems. The Shia of Bahrain constitute a majority of the population but are in a decidedly disadvantageous economic and social position. Since many of the Bahraini Shia have close cultural and ethnic ties to Iran, the Sunni leadership has evinced considerable concern. But Bahrain does not produce enough petroleum to finance large-scale employment-generating industry. It is no surprise, therefore, that Bahrain has been in the forefront of GCC members calling for closer economic cooperation in ways that would ameliorate unemployment.

PETROLEUM

Oil has been called black gold—and for good reason. Petroleum was the focus of many a country's national and international affairs during the twentieth century. Indeed, petroleum has been so important to everyday life that this has been dubbed the Age of Hydrocarbon Man.

The vital need to secure adequate supplies has been complicated by the fact that it has been exceedingly difficult to predict when supplies will run dry or be multiplied by the development of a new field. It is only with mild hyperbole, then, that European control of Middle Eastern petroleum at the onset of World War I prompted Britain's Lord Curzon to remark that "the Allies floated to victory on a wave of oil." About a half a century later, some were predicting that the rise in petroleum prices would create a new Arab Golden Age. The clearest recent example of the

worldwide importance of steady petroleum supplies is shown by the Western response to Iraq's 1991 invasion of Kuwait. Petroleum is the dominant economic influence in the Middle East, and Middle Eastern petroleum is vital to the economies of the world. Finally, petroleum has been responsible for one of the most rapid transfers of wealth in world history—a true revolution.

The Early Years

The half-century preceding World War I was a time of rapid change in the Middle East. The Ottoman Empire was in disarray and decaying despite sporadic bursts of energy and direction. Turkey and Egypt accumulated very heavy public debts; one-third of Turkey's government expenditures and one-half of Egypt's were applied to debt servicing. Turkey was declared bankrupt in 1875 and Egypt in 1876. European interests in the area were becoming more pervasive and were setting the stage for twentieth-century events.

By the turn of the century, most major investments in the Middle East were European in origin and ownership. European domination, of course, did not begin with these investments. Western influence was substantial well before Napoleon occupied Egypt in 1798, as commerce between the two areas grew. European investments in dams, canals, railroads, and electrical systems built up gradually as the Middle East became more secure. But the surge of nationalism in the Middle East around the beginning of the twentieth century forced Europeans to relinquish direct control of some of their investments.

In the two centuries preceding the opening of the Suez Canal, Britain gained control of the Persian Gulf through a series of military maneuvers and treaties with local sheikhs. The route from India through the Persian Gulf, up through Basra and Baghdad, and then to Mediterranean ports provided a vital communications link for the empire until the opening of the Suez Canal. The area was again central to British interests in the 1890s because Britain wished to thwart German influences and because of the discovery of substantial amounts of petroleum in Iran.

After securing control of the Suez Canal, the British had been content to control commerce on the Persian Gulf and not travel inland; but the discovery of a large petroleum field in Iran in 1907 changed their intentions. The industrial revolution, although first fueled by coal, was becoming increasingly dependent on oil and other petroleum products. Petroleum products also were becoming increasingly valuable for military uses. Therefore, large consumers sought a steady and dependable supply. By 1900 the United States and Russia produced 90 percent of the world's petroleum. When the Iranian field east of Abadan was discovered, the British moved to assure their control over the area. Although the British had concessions for Iranian petroleum as early as 1872 (and then in 1889 and 1901), the rights were not considered particularly valuable. In 1908 the Anglo-Persian Oil Company (later changed to Anglo-Iranian) was founded. As tensions in Europe heightened, British needs for a dependable source of petroleum increased, partially because the British navy was converting its fleet from coal to oil. In May 1914, about one week before European hostilities broke into widespread conflict, the British government acquired a 50 percent interest in the venture.

The finds in Iran stimulated exploration for petroleum in southern Iraq. The results of negotiations completed in 1912 allowed for the formation of the Turkish Petroleum Company (TPC). The TPC was reorganized in 1914 and again in 1920, when German interests were removed and France and the United States moved in. The participation of U.S. firms was accomplished through vigorous diplomatic activity. In 1920 there was widespread fear of an impending oil shortage in the United States. Indeed, the U.S. government even considered direct government participation instead of relying on private enterprise, but decided against it.

The agreement that formed the TPC, later renamed the Iraqi Petroleum Company (IPC), contained a proviso that limited the seeking of concessions to the area within the Ottoman Empire, which was shown by a red line drawn on a map. The Red Line Agreement stated that the individual companies in the IPC would not act in a fashion that would upset the balance of company power within the red line. They were not to operate any other fields in the area and thereby gain relative power.

Although British interests had the only concessions in Arabia, there was no production until 1934. In 1930 Standard Oil of California (SoCal) had gained an option from a British syndicate for Bahrain. Petroleum was found in 1932, and exports started to flow two years later. In 1933 SoCal gained the concession for the al-Hasa province of Saudi Arabia. Petroleum was found a few years later. In 1934 Gulf Oil and British Petroleum (BP) entered Kuwait.

The entry of U.S. firms into Saudi Arabia, and the subsequent development of the huge oil fields found there, threatened the dominance of the IPC, especially after SoCal joined with Texaco in 1936 to form the Arabian-American Oil Company (ARAMCO) in order to take advantage of the Far Eastern marketing network of Texaco.

The fear of a petroleum shortage immediately after World War I sparked a flurry of exploration during the next two decades. World supply had increased markedly by 1930 through various major fields coming into production, most notably in the Far East, Middle East, Venezuela, and the United States. With the increased world supply and more oil firms in the market, the "majors" maneuvered futilely to retain control of the world petroleum market.

Petroleum was in abundant supply during the worldwide depression of the 1930s. As machines were turned off due to the depression, so also was the demand for petroleum products: The fears of an oil shortage turned into fears of a large and continuing glut. The sustained depression, especially in the United States, caused changes in the structure of the petroleum industry. Weak firms, especially those that were not vertically integrated, generally failed.

World War II to 1970

By the beginning of World War II, it was apparent that Middle Eastern petroleum would be vital to the world oil market. The United States, although supplying much of the petroleum products needed by the Allies during World War II, feared that its postwar position would be weak. Again there was talk of the need for direct government participation and for protecting the United States position in the Middle East. Saudi Arabia provided the United States with a major foothold in the Middle East. In efforts to keep the support of the Saudis, lend-lease agreements were put into force whereby the British actually extended the aid since Saudi Arabia was not eligible. It should be remembered that Saudi Arabia was still a very poor country and received only modest revenues from the petroleum industry. The Saudis needed aid. Largely because the United States feared that the British would use their influence as intermediaries to curry Saudi favor, Saudi Arabia was made eligible for direct lend-lease aid in 1944. But there was another problem; the Saudi government wanted to increase production in order to increase its revenue. The U.S. government wanted to assure an adequate supply, but ARAMCO did not have the financial resources necessary to substantially expand Saudi production. The U.S. government first planned to buy directly into ARAMCO and then to build a pipeline to the Mediterranean in return for preferential prices and guaranteed strategic reserves. Both plans failed to come to fruition, and the U.S. government finally, in 1948, arranged with the financially stronger Standard Oil of New Jersey (later named Exxon) and Mobil, both IPC members, to buy into ARAMCO (30 percent and 10 percent, respectively). The entry of these IPC members signaled the end of the Red Line Agreement.

By 1948 seven Western companies controlled Middle Eastern oil: Four were based in the United States—Standard Oil of New Jersey, Mobil, SoCal, and Texaco; one was British—British Petroleum; and one was a joint British-Dutch venture—Royal Dutch-Shell.

The selling price of any product, of course, is determined by the interaction of supply and demand. Although the record of the petroleum industry after World War II is too complex to be forced into a couple of equations, it is nevertheless instructive to highlight these two basic forces. The tremendous worldwide economic expansion that occurred in the decades following World War II increased the demand for petroleum products considerably. In addition, the Western nations and Japan were building energy-intensive societies and shifting ever-greater percentages of their energy sources from coal to oil. The combination of these

forces meant that the demand for petroleum was doubling every six and a half years.

The steady price of petroleum throughout the 1950s and most of the 1960s indicates that the supply of petroleum was increasing at about the same pace as the demand. The character of the industry, however, was changing in substantial ways. New independent firms were entering the petroleum industry, and the producing countries themselves began to feel new strength. The entry of more firms into the industry meant, quite simply, that the seven firms that controlled Middle Eastern petroleum production were slowly losing their influence in the market. Governments demanding greater revenues from petroleum exploitation were thus in a better position to bargain. For example, because of its very heavy reliance on Libyan production, Occidental Oil was more likely to respect Libyan demands for increased monies than if it had widely diversified holdings. In contrast, the Iranian attempts at nationalization of the petroleum producers in 1951 failed in large part because of the relatively plentiful and more diversified world supply. During the 1950s and 1960s, the Middle East also was becoming relatively more important with respect to production and proven reserves. During the 1960s, it became clear to close observers of the scene that there had been a fundamental change in the market. A greater percentage of world supply originated in the Middle East, petroleum supplies started to lag behind demand in the latter part of the decade, and an upward pressure on prices began to be felt.

The OPEC Revolution

The Organization of Petroleum Exporting Countries (OPEC) did not have any significant power in the first decade of its existence (1960–1970). The organization of the industry and the plentiful and diversified supply of oil blunted any thoughts about manipulating the market. However, the situation had changed markedly by 1970. During that year the postrevolution government of Libya started negotiations for substantially increased payments from the petroleum companies. Algeria and Iran had gained better concessions in 1969. Although these actions represented a breakthrough for the producing countries, they were also viewed as special cases. Revolutionary Libya, strongly backed by "radical" Algeria and Iraq, called for much greater revenue increases than previously sought and threatened outright expropriation if its demands were not met. Libya succeeded for various reasons. World supply and demand conditions, aggravated by the 1967 closure of the Suez Canal, caused prices to rise; the Occidental Oil Company was vulnerable because almost all of the petroleum for its European operations came from Libya; the companies operating in the Middle East were unable to form a common front; the home governments of the oil companies could not bring any unified pressure to bear on the producing countries; and OPEC was presenting a relatively united front. Prices were increased further after President Nixon's August 1971 announcement of a proposed devaluation of the U.S. dollar (which meant that the dollar earnings of the petroleum-exporting countries would lose purchasing power). They also rose because of a continuing decline in U.S. petroleum production, worldwide inflation, and unabated increases in petroleum demand. Upward pressure on prices and calls for increased participation, partial ownership, and outright expropriation continued through 1973.

Intense negotiations between OPEC and the oil companies through the first ten months of 1973 resulted in substantially higher posted prices. These increases came without direct reference to the Arab-Israeli situation. Members of OPEC, Arab and non-Arab, were simply exploiting worldwide market conditions; they were seeking to get as much revenue as possible before their precious natural resource was depleted. The decline in the value of the U.S. dollar was eroding the purchasing power of petrodollar earnings, giving more reason to increase prices.

The 1973 Arab-Israeli war provided the catalyst that permitted the Arab members of OPEC an opportunity to flex some economic muscle and to see petroleum prices (roughly) quadruple in less than a year. Any such dramatic OPEC action needed the support of the largest producing nation, Saudi Arabia. King Faisal needed to be convinced that this bold and dangerous move was the proper policy: Saudi conservatism and substantial Saudi ties to the United States dictated against a precipitous break with past policy. However, Western, and particularly U.S., support for Israel during and immediately after the 1973 war convinced the Saudi leadership that a dramatic increase in the price of petroleum and a selective boycott by the Arab members of OPEC was necessary to change Western policy.

The boycott was lifted in March 1974. The higher prices remained. The industrial world struggled through the next couple of years attempting to adjust to the change. Of particular importance were the massive balance-of-payments problems that resulted from the price increase and the related—but not necessarily causally determined—inflation that continued to plague them. A simple example will clarify what was happening. Assume that the United States was producing the same amount of goods each year. Now suppose that the price of imported oil increased and the United States continued to import the same number of barrels. More dollars were flowing out of the United States and less were being spent by U.S. consumers on U.S. goods. Now suppose that the exporting country spent all of those earned dollars on U.S. goods. With the same total amount of money being spent on the same total amount of goods, the straightforward result is that the oil producer had more goods and the United States had less. The only way out of this situation was to eliminate spending on imports by conserving energy and developing internal sources.

The U.S. government, however, failed to respond with a clearly defined program. Attempts to develop comprehensive energy programs floundered throughout the decade. Instead, individual actors, aided by a pliant government, attempted to recoup their losses by spending more. In terms of our simple scenario, they pumped more money into the system. More money chasing the same amount of goods results in inflation. And inflation meant that members of OPEC could purchase less with each petrodollar earned. OPEC, therefore, raised prices in order to recoup its position. The 1970s inflation in the United States was not caused primarily by OPEC actions; rather, continued U.S. inflation virtually guaranteed further rounds of OPEC price increases. Since the United

States remained the most powerful economy in the industrialized world, it transmitted these problems to other countries.

Although the situation was far more complicated than the foregoing description suggests—especially important were the complications that arose from the exporting countries not spending all of the petrodollars they earned—it represents the nub of the issue. The members of OPEC had control of a large enough percentage of world petroleum supplies to call the tune. They had become a full-fledged cartel that controlled the supply in the supply-demand equations. Most petroleum companies clearly understood these shifting power relationships by the late 1960s. At least one went so far as to launch an advertising campaign calling for a more sympathetic view of the Arab cause with respect to Israel. Others sent similar messages to official Washington. They knew that they were engaged in a rearguard action and were attempting to forestall the inevitable. The U.S. public had another point of view. Most people saw the situation as resulting from a U.S. government blunder or from oil company actions. Conspiracy theories abounded. It was as if the public could not quite believe that a group of Third World countries could have the power to foment such disorder and then get away with it. Indeed, it was the first time that a group of Third World countries had secured such a position.

The Third World countries that had begun to industrialize but had no oil could not fully share in the jubilation. Instead, they suffered. They were not economically strong enough to adopt the Western attitude of considering the price increases to be an unfortunate irritant that caused problems but nevertheless could be lived with. The major Arab members of OPEC responded to the plight of the poorer countries by stepping up their aid programs. The Western nations had surrendered their grip on the political systems of the Third World during the preceding years of the century. Was the success of OPEC the first major victory of a future economic trend?

None of the foregoing should suggest that the OPEC members all agree on the extent of the price increases. The position of any individual country depends on its particular economic needs. The countries aiming for very high prices generally had economies that could absorb all of the goods that petrodollars could buy; they had reasonably solid industrial bases and/or large populations. Iran and Iraq were the Middle Eastern members of OPEC that most readily fit this pattern. The price moderates, led by Saudi Arabia, generally were countries with large petroleum reserves, small populations, and less-developed economies. At least in the early years of OPEC success, they did not have the ability (or the desire) to spend all of the petroleum earnings to strengthen their economies.

Another round of significant petroleum price increases was initiated by OPEC in 1979–1980 and aided by the onset of the Iran-Iraq war—this time the price was roughly doubled (from $15 to $30 a barrel). Worldwide inflation since the first (1973) round of increases eroded the purchasing power of their earnings considerably. However, several objective conditions affecting the petroleum market had changed markedly since the first round of price increases. First, there were more significant non-OPEC sources of petroleum that came on-line in the intervening period, the Mexican and North Sea fields being two prominent examples. Second, many heavy petroleum-using countries had adopted some conservation measures. Third, the industrialized world suffered a rather deep recession during 1980–1982. These increases in supplies and decreases in demand put downward pressure on prices. It should be remembered that reduction in individual supplier output is the mechanism through which price increases can be made effective. But several members of OPEC felt that they could not reduce supplies and, therefore, their foreign exchange earnings without causing harm to their economies. There were significant defections from the posted price and output goals, Nigeria being the most important.

During the first half of the 1980s, OPEC managed to hold together through a series of complex technical maneuvers and price rollbacks. The organization was aided in its efforts through a reduction of Iranian and Iraqi output caused by the war, and a strong U.S. dollar. Most petroleum sales are denominated in U.S. dollars. When the U.S.

economy began in 1982 to grow at a robust rate with lower inflation and high real interest rates, the value of the dollar increased relative to the currencies of most of its trading partners. This meant, for example, that the petrodollars could buy more deutsch marks than before and, thus, more German goods. Thus, a constant dollar petroleum price translated into increased purchasing power.

Petroleum prices started a remarkable downward slide in late 1985. By the end of the first quarter of 1986, petroleum prices were close to the 1974 level (about $12 per barrel). There were several reasons for the decline, including larger worldwide supplies from new fields and a decision by Saudi Arabia to increase its output. The Saudi decision deserves some comment.

Saudi Arabia is the largest producer in OPEC. Furthermore, it acted as the "swing" producer. It was Saudi Arabia more than any other country that changed its supplies so as to have the supply-demand equations yield the agreed price. As more non-OPEC petroleum entered the world market, the Saudis decreased production. Because of a complex of unfavorable worldwide economic conditions, many OPEC producers found themselves financially strapped by the early 1980s. They responded by increasing production beyond the limit they agreed to as members of OPEC. Saudi Arabia was in an increasingly tenuous situation. Finally, by late 1985, it felt that it had to increase production. It doubled production in the following months—and at that was producing only one-half of its capacity.

The slide of petroleum prices would have occurred without Saudi action; its decision, however, made the decline steep and rapid. Those petroleum exporters with massive debt problems (for example, Mexico, Nigeria, Indonesia) were dealt a harsh blow. So was Iran. Petroleum accounted for the overwhelming majority of the foreign exchange earnings of Iran. It is not by chance that Iran initiated a vigorous offensive against Iraq in early 1986 and threatened to widen the war to the Gulf states if the Saudis insisted on driving the price of petroleum down by producing more and by continuing to provide Iraq with financial aid for the war effort.

OPEC reached another agreement in 1988: The price of petroleum was to increase several dollars (to $18) through a complicated rearrangement of production quotas. It was impossible to increase the price to previous peaks due to increased world supplies. However, some action was needed to ease national budgetary burdens. For example, despite massive war-related aid from Saudi Arabia and Kuwait, Iraq had accumulated a staggering debt burden. Even the Saudis felt the pinch: Their petroleum revenues fell to about $20 billion in 1988 from a peak exceeding $100 billion in the early 1980s. Although the price of petroleum went up to $40 after the invasion of Kuwait, increased Saudi supplies quickly brought it back to about $18. The real (purchasing power) price of petroleum in 1996 was lower than in the mid-1960s.

Many analysts interpreted the weakened position of OPEC as the long-predicted demise of the cartel. While the spectacular successes of OPEC during the 1970s and early 1980s are not likely to be repeated, the Middle Eastern members of OPEC still hold the lion's share of world petroleum reserves, and they have the ability to influence the market substantially again, albeit only on a short-run basis. Petroleum prices fell and then increased rather dramatically during the late 1990s. Some of the decrease is attributable to a unique set of circumstances. El Niño was causing an unusually warm winter in much of the northern hemisphere. The Asian economic meltdown and consequent fall in demand was another force. And, as the economies of OPEC countries felt the pinch, there was more cheating on agreed-upon quotas, increasing the supply of petroleum. It seems likely that the incentive structures embedded in the price system will continue to depress petroleum prices over the longer run. First, relatively high prices call forth alternate sources of petroleum supply. Second, substitution takes place; people demand energy, not petroleum per se. Research geared to develop nonpetroleum sources of energy at competitive prices, say, solar energy, intensify. Third, and probably not as important, high prices call forth conservation efforts, reducing demand. This, of course, has been recognized by the leading petroleum producers of the Middle East; several times during the late 1990s real (inflation-adjusted) petroleum prices dipped to pre-1973 levels. This is one reason that several Gulf producers scrambled to establish themselves as the regional finance centers; they know that economic diversification is essential for long-term growth. But the widely agreed-upon demise of OPEC as a major player in the petroleum market could be premature. As world demand for petroleum increased in 1998 and 1999, OPEC, led again by Saudi Arabia, cut supplies and sent prices from $10 to levels not seen since the 1980s (about $25 per barrel).

The future of OPEC is uncertain. Its history is remarkable. The powerful industrialized countries of the world are dependent on OPEC supplies. Being dependent, these countries have had to reorder their policies toward the Middle East, especially their attitudes and actions toward Arab-Israeli hostilities. Petroleum became a political tool of the first order after 1973; alliances had to be altered and new approaches to conflict resolution developed.

CONCLUSION

Economic growth depends on a complex array of factors beyond the technical blending of labor, natural resources, and physical capital. There must be a coherent set of institutions and policies properly related to both the institutions and the purely economic resources if there is to be sustained growth.

Increasing resource imbalances led by rapid population growth have a distinct tendency to accelerate a degradation of the quality of life without necessarily triggering self-corrective mechanisms. Gently put, the growing resource disparities in the Middle East are straining the capabilities of the political system. Bluntly, conflicts are bound to multiply as the system spins out of control. A major challenge, then, exists. One nettlesome dimension is that a forward-looking policy often demands the imposition of painful short-run measures (such as placing a price on water use) that will yield noticeable benefits only in the long run, and that the majority of political leaders have a short time to satisfy the demands of their populations. They have powerful political incentives to ignore fundamental problems until they cannot be avoided; that is, until there is a crisis. Lives hang in the balance.

Of course, not all instances of a degraded quality of life result from the long accretion of pressures and ignored long-term remedies: War quickly can undo decades or even centuries of change. The 1991 deliberate torching of 640 of Kuwait's petroleum wells by retreating Iraqi forces is the most spectacular case in point. Although the last of the fires was snuffed out much quicker than anticipated (by December 1991, instead of a few years later), the manifold effects will take decades to understand, even partially. The Kuwaiti desert, the air, the Gulf water, of course, experienced immediate trauma. But more subtle effects were at work. Bahrain, some 200 miles to the south, experienced its coldest summer in a millennium; oil-soaked rain fell thousands of miles away; and it is anybody's guess as to what happened to the geological structure of the fields.

The coalition's destruction of the Iraqi infrastructure brought another set of shocks. For example, Iraqi infant mortality quadrupled in the year following the end of the war. The UN-imposed sanctions on imports to Iraq had another set of consequences. Many more thousands died for want of medicine and hundreds of thousands suffered malnutrition, a condition that has profound lifelong implications for the young. Massive epidemics became highly probable. The sanctions imposed by the UN, along with a quietly sustained U.S.-led bombing campaign through the 1990s, meant that the misery of the average Iraqi continued.

The sudden and spectacular loss of life caused by war sometimes blinds observers to the relatively gradual and potentially more pernicious effects of high rates of population growth in a setting where complementary resources are growing more slowly. The following simple linear causal chain illustrates one aspect of the problem: Population growth increases the demand for food, which calls for more irrigated land, which strains water resources and leads to contaminated water supplies, which spreads disease, which decreases human productivity, which leads to lower real income. The issues, of course, are far more complicated: Property rights conflicts surface, the health care system becomes overburdened, the educational system falls into crisis, and social conflicts generally increase.

It is the prudent analyst who shuns the opportunity to predict the specific path and shape of future Middle Eastern economic realities and ideologies. One of the central lessons of chaos theory is that the course of complex systems is impossible to predict. A related maxim from that body of theory is that there are complex causal links and feedback mechanisms between variables usually thought to be unrelated—folk culture, economics, the physical environment, the arts, and notions of the "good life" are part of the same cloth.

At the same time, humans organize themselves for purposive ends; the behavior of purposive actors counts. Because of the obvious resource imbalances in the Middle East, thoughtful policies must be devised and tinkered with as conditions change.

International Relations in the Contemporary Middle East

1945–1990

One of the predictable characteristics of all international orders has been the concentration of power in a small number of states. Thus, at any moment in time, one can identify a short list of international actors with power and influence well beyond the capacities of most other states. It is inevitable that these states, at some point, will come into conflict with one another. And it is equally plausible that they will externalize those conflicts into their relations with other states. Earlier chapters in this book, for example, have described the role played by the great powers of Europe in the establishment of the contemporary state system in the Middle East. And in this chapter and the succeeding two chapters we will place great emphasis on the architectonic effect of the bipolar conflict between the United States and the Soviet Union. Until very recently, the very late 1980s, in fact, the way in which most of us looked at the world was determined by this contest for global hegemony.

Although one can define international relations strictly in terms of the contests between great powers for relative advantage over the others (the "Great Game," as it has been called), to restrict the analysis to these actors would eliminate much that is of importance. The effect of this competi-tion on weaker states is important as well, particularly to those weaker states themselves. It would also be inappropriate to assume that because the so-called great powers were economically and militarily powerful, their diplomacy and decision making were somehow more rational or insightful than the diplomacy of other states. Finally, we would caution against the assumption that great-power status is somehow immune to the laws of nature or physics. In fact, the inevitability of the decline of great powers is a well-known fact.[1] The dissolution of the Soviet Union in 1991 and U.S. attempts to orchestrate world events from a position of relative decline are just the latest demonstration of this process.

The international system has many features not found in national political orders. The most important of these features is the lack of a legitimate sovereign power, or even of some entity with a viable claim to the exercise of sovereign power. In comparison to the average national system, the international system is nearly anarchic—political power is at once broadly diffused among its actors

[1] See, for example, Paul Kennedy, *The Rise and Fall of the Great Powers: Economic Change and Military Conflict from 1500–2000* (New York: Random House, 1987).

and yet enormously concentrated among a few. Furthermore, international power is transitory and difficult to assess comparatively.

The actors that comprise the international order have a power base that can be broken down into three areas: *economic power,* or the power to produce or acquire material goods; *political power,* or the power to coerce or influence their own populations or the populations of other states; and *military power,* the ability to gain goals through the direct application of organized coercive force. These capabilities are not distributed evenly among the actors in the international system. Saudi Arabia, for instance, possesses enormous economic power based on its extensive oil reserves, but it has a population insufficient in size and technical sophistication to maintain a truly international military capability. Egypt, by contrast, has a large population sufficiently skilled to maintain a large military machine, but lacks the economic base to develop it without foreign aid. The relative international power of Saudi Arabia and Egypt, then, must be calculated on different bases, quantitative and qualitative. This enormously complicates the calculations involved in international politics, particularly since one actor's analysis of the capability of another is a core determinant of its foreign policy.

The relationships between international actors embrace a wide field of human activity. International relations occur at many levels and in many functional arenas. For example, no state can isolate itself from international trade, for to do so it would have to greatly reduce its economic activity. Thus, any nation finds it necessary and desirable to allow the movements of goods and services into its territory as varying amounts of goods and services flow out. Most states, then, are involved in some level of international economic exchange that requires cooperation with both friendly and potentially unfriendly powers. It is instructive to note that at the nadir of Iranian-American relations, Iranian oil was still being imported by the United States at the rate of some 80,000 barrels per day—a fact as politically unpalatable to President Carter as to Ayatollah Khomeini. International relations, then, possess a logic that is to some degree independent of the best wishes or intentions of their actors—or, to put it another way, international politics and economics make strange bedfellows.

Actors in the international system pursue a combination of specific and general goals that can be lumped together under the term *national interest.* The national interest presumably directs the foreign policy of a nation, at least at the strategic level. For instance, the national interest of the Soviet Union (now the C.I.S.) has long required a safe, warm-water port, while the contemporary U.S. national interest requires regular delivery of petroleum from its Middle Eastern sources. Needless to say, these two national interest goals have a potential for conflict in the area of the Persian Gulf.

The problem in analyzing international relations strictly from the national interest viewpoint can be summarized briefly. First, nations may in fact not clearly perceive their true national interests: American involvement in Vietnam in the 1960s is a case in point. Second, power—the base of implementation of national interest—is an enormously complex entity. Miscalculations of one's own power or of the reputed power of another actor inject a quality of uncertainty into international relations. An example is Nasser's miscalculation of Israeli responses to his mobilization in 1967. Finally, international relations are only rarely dyadic—that is, involving only two nations. Although for analytic purposes we often discuss foreign policy in dyadic terms, most international exchanges involve the interests of secondary and tertiary actors. These complex intersections of national interests—both primary and secondary, immediate and long-term—create the Gordian knots of the international process. All too often the solution to these problems is war, with its attendant human miseries and material losses.

Finally, it should be noted that in viewing the international system from the perspective of decades and centuries, we perceive dramatic changes taking place. Nations, even entire civilizations, change their positions in the relative power hierarchies of the international system, rising and falling for reasons that are often idiosyncratic or obscure. It is even possible, as was the case with the nineteenth-century Ottoman Empire, for a country to improve its absolute power—to have more financial, military, and human resources—and still decline relative to its competitors (in this case, the emerging national powers of Western Europe and Russia). As intellectually disconcerting as this may be to students of the international system, we live in a time in which just such changes are occurring. The transformation of the U.S.S.R. into a Commonwealth of Independent States (C.I.S.), the newfound political independence of Eastern Europe, the political integration of Western Europe, the dispersal of economic power to new centers, dramatic change in policy directions in China, quantum increases in the sophistication and utilization of conventional and chemical weapons, and dramatic and unlikely diplomatic initiatives (such as the Palestinian declaration of statehood in December of 1988) force a reevaluation of basic premises upon which foreign policy is predicated.

None of the preceding should be interpreted as denying order or process in international relations. The Middle East, in particular, has seen the rise and fall of many separate international systems. The region witnessed the development of an international theocratic movement during the early days of Islamic expansion, in which the world was seen as a contrast between the *Dar al Islam* (world of peace) and the *Dar al Harb* (world of war); centralized bureaucratic empires based successively in Damascus, Baghdad, and Cairo; loose relationships between competing centers of power, as peripheral kingdoms arose in the Maghreb, Spain, Europe, Central Asia, Persia, and India; the consolidation of power in the decentralized millet system of the Ottoman Empire; the intrusion of European imperial power, predicated on a classic balance of power in Europe; after World War II, the bipolar conflict between the United States and the U.S.S.R. At the dawn of the new millennium, yet another international order presents itself, with concomitant challenges and changes in the international environment.

The origins of the contemporary international order can be found in the deterioration of the system that emerged just after World War II and prevailed until the early 1970s. This first order, the bipolar international system, was produced by an unusual concentration of military and economic power in two rival political systems, the United States and the Soviet Union, that saw each other as threats to their own national interest as well as to the larger political order. In this situation, the alliances surrounding these two superpowers grew rigid and confrontational. The term *Cold War,* which applied to the early period following World War II, suggests a confrontation between the two blocs just short of overt military hostilities. During this time, the two superpowers enjoyed a nuclear monopoly and rapidly growing economies. Stymied in their confrontation in Europe, the United States and the U.S.S.R. turned to the nations of the Third World—Africa, Asia, Latin America, and the Middle East—for potential alliance partners in their crusade against international communism and international capitalism respectively.

From the point of view of international actors in the Middle East, this transition was frustrating. Neither the United States nor the Soviet Union had well-established bases in the area. European power, while on the wane and definitely inferior to that of either superpower, was nonetheless still something to contend with. Finally, the ideological claims of both capitalism and communism did not find fertile intellectual soil in the Middle East.

Regional factors also injected themselves into the emerging international order. Primary among them was the creation of Israel in 1948 and its subsequent protection by the United States. This issue, transcending such questions as Arab unity, water resources, economic growth and development, or Islamic resurgence, provided the mechanism for the entrance of bipolar politics in the area. The unevenness of American policy toward the Arab states, combined with U.S. unwillingness to hedge on the question of Israeli security, provided the Soviet Union with an entree, particularly to Egypt, Syria, and Iraq, the major powers confronting the Israeli state. But in spite of great Egyptian, Syrian, and Iraqi dependence on Eastern-bloc sources for weapons and expertise, the U.S.S.R. was unable to capitalize on its advantages domestically in these countries. The United States, for its part, confused the desire for independence in these countries with a drift toward communism and reacted hostilely to Soviet gains there. Thus, the bipolar alliance system did not extend completely into the Middle East, and both Soviet and American policy goals were frustrated.

The 1960s saw the gradual erosion of the "eyeball-to-eyeball" confrontation between Soviet and American global power. The age of détente ushered in a period in which Soviet and American ability to control their alliances and dictate policy declined. The emergence of competing centers of economic and political power—Japan, Western Europe, and China—ultimately produced an international system in which the great powers of the United States and the U.S.S.R. were reduced by the growing economic powers of their allies and by the loss of their nuclear monopoly. The resulting international system, maturing in the late 1980s and ultimately transformed by the dissolution of the U.S.S.R. and the creation of the C.I.S., can best be described as an emerging set of relatively independent power centers orbiting loosely and often erratically around the United States as the last surviving superpower. Moreover, additional sources of international power appeared to be maturing, based on the growing economic and political systems of Asia, Africa, the Middle East, and Latin America. These centers of power were more and more inclined to define national interest in their own terms. All of this contributed to the complexity and potential instability of the international order. Many saw in all of this the emergence of a new international order, a topic that we will take up specifically in Chapter 14.

Let us now examine the implications of these changes for the international system that is the Middle East. Our method will be to move from macroanalysis in Chapter 12; to regional analysis in Chapter 13; and finally to consideration of dyadic relations involving the foreign policies of Egypt, Saudi Arabia, Iran, Iraq, Syria, and Israel. In each of these chapters, we will discuss four phases of international relations in the Middle East. Phase I, 1945–1948, embraces the immediate postwar period; Phase II, 1948–1974, includes the period of transition from tight bipolar confrontation to loose bipolar competition; Phase III covers the period from the 1973 Arab-Israeli war and the Arab oil embargo to 1990. Phase IV, from 1991 to the present, and including the dramatic changes occasioned by the collapse of Soviet power, the causes and consequences of Desert Storm, and the prospects for negotiated peace between Israel and the Arabs, will be discussed in full in the final chapters.

THE GREAT-POWER SYSTEM AND THE MIDDLE EAST

In the relatively short span of forty years, actors in the Middle East have gone from a system in which their policies were largely reactive to the policy goals of the United States and the U.S.S.R., through a period in which international power appeared to disperse toward other industrial states of the temperate zones, to an international system in which many Middle Eastern nations can realistically view themselves as capable of originating international exchange, politically, economically, and militarily. Some Middle Eastern actors—most notably Saudi Arabia, Egypt, Iraq, Syria, and Iran—see themselves as major actors in the international arena. Decisions reached in Riyadh, Cairo, and Tehran now have repercussions in Moscow, Washington, and Tokyo.

The current system contains a number of international power centers that have substantially altered the relative influence of the United States and the U.S.S.R (C.I.S.). This is not to say that the power and national interests of these two megapowers are unimportant. On the contrary, their pursuit of their national interests is in many ways more important and more dangerous today given the greater number of probable actors. The primary effects of policy shifts may be predictable, but the secondary and tertiary effects, involving other actors indirectly, are rarely predictable or controllable. For example, as the United States reduced its dependence on Iranian oil imports in the late 1970s (a primary policy decision), Japan and other United States allies simultaneously increased their imports of Iranian crude (a secondary effect), which in effect increased their vulnerability to pressure from Soviet intervention in the Persian Gulf. Of the two great superpowers, the United States held the more enviable position of power in the Middle East. European (specifically British and French) power in the area was generally replaced by American power. The United States was historically removed from the abuses of colonial policy in the area, and many Arab leaders looked

Table 12-1 Foreign Policy Priorities in the Middle East, 1945–Present

Phase	United States	Soviet Union (C.I.S. after 1990)	Europe (England, France, Germany, EC)
I (1945–1948)	1. Extension of influence. 2. Exploitation and protection of promising petroleum production in Saudi Arabia and Iran.	1. Extension of influence into Mediterranean, Turkey, and Iran. 2. Frustration of U.S. power and prestige in M.E. 3. Support of Jewish community in Palestine.	1. Reestablishment of prewar influence. 2. Exploitation and protection of petroleum production and trade relations in M.E. 3. Limited support of Jewish migration to Palestine.
II (1948–1974)	1. Support and protection of Israel. 2. Maintenance of influence and prestige against Soviet invasion; Baghdad Pact. 3. Exploitation and protection of petroleum production in Saudi Arabia and U.A.E.	1. Extension of military influence into M.E. via anti-Israeli governments in Syria, Egypt, and Iraq. 2. Frustration of U.S. power and prestige in M.E.	1. Maintenance and expansion of petroleum production and trade relations. 2. Maintenance of prestige and influence in M.E. 3. Support of Israel.
III (1974–1990)	1. Support and protection of Israel. 2. Maintenance of influence and prestige. 3. Exploitation and protection of petroleum production in Saudi Arabia and U.A.E.	1. Maintenance of influence in Syria and Iraq. 2. Frustration of U.S. power and prestige in M.E.; support of national liberation movements in Yemen and Oman, PLO. 3. Access to M.E. petroleum and warm-water ports.	1. Maintenance and expansion of petroleum production and trade relations. 2. Compete with U.S.–U.S.S.R. efforts in M.E.
IV (1990–present)	1. Ensure stability of region; maintenance of Desert Storm Coalition. 2. Protect petroleum production in Persian Gulf. 3. Solution of Arab-Israel conflict. 4. Support for Israel.	1. Commonwealth of Independent States seeks new diplomatic relations, trade relations.	1. Protect petroleum production, establish European Community trade relations. 2. Solution of Arab-Israeli conflict. 3. Support of Israel.

with affection toward the United States. Thus, the period after World War II saw an extension and expansion of U.S. power in the Middle East, oriented toward an alliance system aimed at frustrating Soviet moves, particularly in Turkey and Iran.

Table 12-1 simplifies the foreign policy objectives of the great powers in the Middle East from the end of World War II to the present. The table suggests some sharp changes in policy over that relatively brief period of time.

U.S. FOREIGN POLICY

Phase I

United States policy toward the Middle East was not coherent or logical during Phase I. Indeed, after World War II, the United States' concern for the Middle East grew directly as it recognized that its allies (Britain and France) were unable to play their traditional roles.

The United States also feared that the Soviet Union, the other principal winner in World War II, would attempt to exploit the political uncertainties in Greece, Turkey, and Iran. This concern led to the Truman Doctrine, a statement of real opposition to Soviet imperialism in the area, which committed the United States to direct military and economic support for the threatened areas.

As in other areas of the world, the United States found itself moving into unfamiliar political seas in order to fill what was generally recognized as an incipient power vacuum. The exploitation and importation of crude petroleum was clearly of a secondary nature in its foreign policy priorities. Critically, moreover, the United States, in honoring its commitments to the governments and policies of its allies, set itself squarely in the camp of Middle Eastern conservatism. This early commitment, as we will see, ultimately played havoc with U.S. credibility and prestige in the area.

Phase II

During Phase II, U.S. policy and presence in the Middle East were inextricably linked with Israel. Truman's hurried recognition of Israel, combined with U.S. influence in the United Nations, placed the United States squarely in the role of protector of the Israeli state. This, coupled with intractable Arab opposition to Israel, provided the Soviet Union with its first major successes in Middle Eastern policy. From 1958 to 1975, the U.S.S.R. was able to exploit the situation resulting from U.S. support for Israel by supplying arms and advisors to Egypt, Syria, and Iraq. Thus, the United States attempted to maintain a preeminent power position while the Soviet Union attempted to exploit potential weaknesses in the U.S. posture. It may be a tribute to the diplomacy of Middle Eastern nations that neither power managed to envelop the area within its alliance systems or to systematically dictate policy in the area.

This period in international relations saw a determined American effort to extend the tight bipolar alliance system into the Middle East and to link NATO in Europe with the SEATO alliance in Asia. The Baghdad Pact (1955) represented the greatest success of the United States in this regard. It was seen in the United States as a logical response to Soviet aggression; many Middle Eastern leaders, however, saw themselves in danger of being pulled headlong into the ideological confrontation between the United States and the U.S.S.R. Nasser succeeded in popularizing the concept of nonalignment in the area; and the pact, lacking full support by the signatories after Iraq's withdrawal in 1958, was replaced by direct aid to Iran. Full support of the shah by the United States was implemented by means of a bilateral mutual assistance treaty in 1959.

During this period, Middle Eastern petroleum production was a relatively low order of priority: The U.S. oil fields until the early 1960s were more than capable of supplying most domestic petroleum needs. Thus, the maintenance of its influence, the protection of Israel, and the frustration of Soviet ambitions provided the motivation for U.S. policy. Until the late 1960s, the United States was able to accomplish all of its objectives simultaneously. The emergence of the Palestine independence organizations, however, coupled with growing international recognition of their rights and legitimacy, made the support of Israel very costly to U.S. influence and prestige. The Soviet Union capitalized on this situation by breaking relations with Israel and providing arms and aid to

Egypt, Syria, and Iraq. U.S. decision makers assumed the worst, that Soviet aid meant Soviet control; and a period of very tense, even hostile, relations between the United States and these nations ensued.

In short, during Phase II, the United States was able to consolidate its alliance positions with the "northern tier" states—Turkey, Iran, and Pakistan—while its relations with the core states of Syria, Egypt, and Iraq deteriorated. Strains even appeared between the United States and its client states Jordan and Saudi Arabia, at once pro-American and increasingly anti-Israeli. The maintenance of any alliance in which conflicting goals are present is extraordinarily difficult. Consequently the United States was called upon many times to put out "brush fires" in the area. The attempted nationalization of Iranian oil in 1953, the Suez Crisis of 1956, and the crisis in Lebanon in 1958 are examples. Ultimately, these foreign policy objectives were to become more clearly and forcefully contradictory. Particularly clear by 1974 was the incompatibility of maintaining and expanding the Middle East's petroleum flow to the West and the unyielding support of Israel.

Interventions in Iran. During the early Phase II diplomacy, the United States was forced to intervene directly in the Middle East. The first of these interventions was prompted by developments in Iran from 1951 to 1953, a period in which Iranian politics were dominated by the leadership of Premier Mohammed Mossadegh. Mossadegh effectively challenged the Anglo-Iranian oil agreements and moved to nationalize the company's holdings. Simultaneously, Mossadegh virtually isolated the young shah from political power, taking control of the army and moving to abolish the representative assembly, all with strong support from the Iranian public. American and British interests responded with a carefully orchestrated policy of intrigue that ultimately brought Mossadegh's downfall and the return of the shah.

The shah's power, based on his increasingly effective control of the military, waxed from that period on. The petroleum production of Iran was finally organized on a consortium basis in which American and European corporations shared the profits on a fifty-fifty basis with the Iranian National Oil Company. From this time onward, and particularly during the White Revolution, the shah enjoyed generous support from the United States, which perceived Iran as playing a "policeman's role" in the important Persian Gulf. Resentment over U.S. support for the shah became an important factor in Iranian politics after the successful revolution of 1979. The United States labored unsuccessfully to escape the consequences of its support for that repressive regime.

The Suez War. The second major U.S. involvement in the Middle East also had long-term consequences for U.S. interests in the area. From 1948 onward, Egypt and Israel were periodically at some level of armed hostility, ranging from small guerrilla raids to larger punitive expeditions. Egypt sought American arms, the better to engage the superior capabilities of the Israeli armed forces. The successful Israeli raid on the Gaza Strip in February 1955 led Colonel Nasser to request arms sales from the United States and Great Britain. These requests were emphatically rejected.

Rebuffed by the Americans and the British, Nasser turned to the Eastern bloc for relief, concluding a barter deal (cotton for arms) with Czechoslovakia. U.S. reactions were abrupt, resulting in the July 1956 cancellation of U.S. support for the construction of the high dam at Aswan. The connection between this refusal and Nasser's independent pursuit of Soviet arms through Czechoslovakia was made clear by the United States. Moreover, in backing out of its commitment to the dam, the United States threatened the very heart of Nasser's development plan for Egypt. Relations between Egypt and the United States deteriorated rapidly from this point.

Nasser reacted to this great-power action by nationalizing the Suez Canal Company in July 1956. The canal, of great importance to Europe as a trade route and defense link, had heretofore been operated by a corporation dominated by Britain and France. Their immediate response was to oppose the nationalization, freeze Egyptian funds in their respective banks, and seek a UN solution to the problem. U.S. interest in the proceedings was indirect until Nasser made it clear that Israeli shipping would continue to be denied access to the canal. Britain and France became increasingly restive about the failure of the United States to condemn Egypt. This frustration was to lead ultimately to the Suez War of 1956.

The events of the Suez War suggest collusion between Israel, France, and Great Britain. The war began with Israeli occupation of Gaza and penetration and control of the Sinai up to the canal. France and Britain demanded that the belligerents (Egypt and Israel) withdraw to positions ten miles on either side of the canal. Egypt's rejection of this ultimatum prompted the invasion of the canal zone by British and French paratroops and the occupation of Port Said.

After a period of intense collective and unilateral diplomacy by the United States, UN troops (UNEF) were placed between the belligerents, and they were exhorted to withdraw from the territory. In point of fact, the United States placed heavy pressure on its allies, particularly Israel, to withdraw. French and British troops quit the area by December 1956. Finally, in March of 1957, an agreement was reached for Israeli withdrawal from the Sinai.

The resolution of the Suez War found the United States opposing the actions of its strongest allies—Israel, France, and Great Britain. This pro-Arab action led to considerable strains in the Western alliance but did little to persuade Nasser that U.S. policy was ultimately benevolent.

The Lebanon Crisis of 1958. The third U.S. intervention in Middle Eastern affairs was generated by the Lebanon crisis of 1958, an intervention that saw the movement of U.S. marines into Beirut on July 15. The details of the Lebanese situation that produced the American intervention were complex, involuted, and confusing. The Lebanese political situation was becoming increasingly unstable, and the delicate balance between Muslim, Christian, and Druze interests was deteriorating. This deterioration had attracted the attention of Egypt, which directly intervened in the struggle on behalf of the Sunni Muslims. The successful revolution in Iraq, on July 14, heightened the feeling of tension. At the request for aid by President Chamoun, the U.S. Sixth Fleet moved 3,600 marines into Beirut to stabilize the situation. This tactic, combined with intense behind-the-scenes negotiations, brought some order into the Leban-

ese conflict and helped to forestall a civil war. The action was successful, and the Lebanese regime survived until the civil war in 1975 and the Israeli-Syrian interventions from 1976 onward. Nonetheless, this event revealed the willingness of the United States to intervene directly in Middle Eastern affairs if it felt its national interest was at stake—a right it steadfastly denied to its allies and adversaries alike.

Phase III

The United States—indeed, all of the recognized powers and superpowers—had clearly entered a period in which international political power was shared, a dramatic change from the era of unilateral intervention that preceded it. U.S. foreign policy in the Phase III era was conceived and executed by "postmodern" presidents, beginning with President Carter. As Richard Rose succinctly puts it:

> A postmodern President no longer enjoys isolation from other nations. The White House retains the attributes of the modern presidency, but in a changing world these resources are no longer adequate. A postmodern President cannot secure success simply by influencing Congress and public opinion; the President must also influence leaders of other nations and events in the international system.[2]

During Phase III of its Middle East policy, U.S. commitments to Israel were strained by its need for regular supplies of Middle East petroleum. The seven-month Arab oil embargo of 1973–1974 was initiated in direct retaliation for U.S. support for Israel in the war of October 1973. This war, initiated by a surprise attack by Egyptian forces, was ultimately concluded by means of intervention via the United Nations. As a result, the United States, by shipping arms to Israel, first prevented the collapse of the Israeli military, and then, through its diplomatic activity in the United Nations, rescued Egypt from probable defeat.

From the October war of 1973 until the 1991 Gulf War, the United States' attempts to play both sides of the Arab-Israeli conflict were unsuccess-

---

[2] Richard Rose, *The Post-Modern Presidency,* 2nd ed. (Chatham, N.J.: Chatham House, 1991), p. 25.

ful in rescuing its prestige in the area. Indeed, U.S. policy seems to have alienated both sides in the conflict. Israeli complaints about U.S. waffling on aid became more frequent in the 1980s, characterized by the public complaints of Prime Minister Menachem Begin and his successor Yitzhak Shamir. The Arab "rejectionist" states were not satisfied or mollified by U.S. economic support for Egypt or increasing U.S. arms sales to Egypt and Saudi Arabia. More and more, the United States was pressured to consider the Arab view in the Arab-Israeli conflict. The diplomacy of the Carter administration, in particular the Camp David Accords, which led to bilateral negotiations between Egypt and Israel, was most probably the United States' only realistic option.

The Camp David agreements resulted in the cessation of diplomatic hostilities, the return of most Sinai territory to Egypt, and the opening of genuine diplomatic and trade relations between the two countries. The negotiations, however, did not engage the most basic questions regarding Palestinian autonomy in the West Bank and Gaza. The problem of Jerusalem, claimed by Israel as its historic capital and an important religious site for Christianity and Islam as well, also proves to be difficult. However, since Egypt bore the brunt of past military confrontations with Israel, an outbreak of war became unlikely.

The early foreign policy of the Reagan administration did not hold the promise of substantial change in U.S. Middle Eastern policy. Early administration decisions to accede to Saudi requests for longer-range and more sophisticated fighter-bombers were balanced by promises to increase military aid to Israel. As in the preceding administration's foreign policy, neither side was ecstatic about the U.S. effort to play both sides.

Reagan administration efforts to organize an anti-Soviet alliance in the Middle East were gently but firmly rebuffed in the early months of 1981. Administration concern for Saudi security prompted its approval of the sale of sophisticated radar planes (AWAC) to Saudi Arabia, a decision that produced considerable pro-Israeli objections in the U.S. Congress. The June 1981 Israeli air raid on the Iraqi nuclear facility near Baghdad prompted the administration to suspend shipment of four F-16s to Israel, which also strained rela-

tions. It is instructive that the UN resolution condemning the Israeli raid and calling for compensation was a joint product of American and Iraqi diplomats at the United Nations. Such a collaboration would have been unthinkable a decade earlier, and certainly became unthinkable a decade later. All of these examples underscore the difficulty of maintaining traditional U.S. policy priorities in the decade of the 1980s. No less an authority on U.S.-Israeli relations than former president Jimmy Carter has observed that on many fundamental issues, the interests of Israel and the United States diverge.

The issue of Palestinian rights led the Reagan administration to offer "the Reagan Plan." The plan, which was based on the creation of a "Palestinian entity" nominally attached to Jordan, was rejected by Israel and alternately rejected and accepted by other Middle Eastern actors, never simultaneously and never with enough consensus to get the proposals a serious hearing. Israeli objections, interestingly, centered on Prime Minister Begin's flat refusal to consider in any way the return of areas considered part of historical Israel, particularly Judea and Samaria. This, in effect, announced a *de facto* annexation of the West Bank, a point of policy firmly opposed by the United States. Prime Minister Shamir continued this emphasis under his administration, with just as much rigidity and energy.

These growing disagreements were minor when compared with the difficulties engendered for the United States by the massive Israeli invasion of Lebanon in June 1982. What was announced initially as a limited-objective foray against Palestinian bases in south Lebanon quickly became a drive to Beirut. Indeed, Israeli Defense Forces stopped only just short of a complete occupation of Beirut and all of southern Lebanon. The United States was apparently caught unprepared by the scope of this military action and hastily created a U.S. military presence in Beirut, ostensibly to police the withdrawal of Palestinian troops from the area.

Shortly thereafter, U.S. marines were reintroduced into the Beirut area in the role of guarantor of the Bashir Gemayel government and tutor for the government's new army, composed primarily of Maronite Christian militia. The United States thus took a position opposing Israeli attempts to elevate other Christian groups, primarily the Army of South Lebanon, led by Major Saad Haddad. Both the United States and Israel failed to achieve their objectives. The formal U.S. presence in Beirut was demoralized by a terrorist bombing of the U.S. marine barracks with great loss of life; and ultimately by a similar attack on the U.S. embassy annex. The U.S. hope for an effective national government based on the Gemayel administration deteriorated as other groups and countries controlled more and more Lebanese territory. What hopes Israel had countenanced for the creation of a neutral or pro-Israel government dissipated in the anarchy created by the sudden removal of the Palestinians from the military-political equation in Lebanon. The primary gains from the invasion of Lebanon appeared to accrue to the Syrians, now the arbiter of political relations in Lebanon and consequently enjoying a substantial rise in diplomatic prestige, and the Shia groups, particularly AMAL and Hizbollah, who rose to oppose first the government, then the Palestinians, and finally the Israelis.

U.S. policy at this time appeared to be more reactive than active. The events in Lebanon proved a major setback to U.S. efforts to promote a negotiated settlement between the Israelis and their Arab neighbors, and resulted in a dramatic decline in U.S. prestige in the area—a decline underscored by the Lebanese hostage crisis of June 1985. U.S. losses in Lebanon were slightly offset by the maintenance of close, even intimate, relations with Egypt and by a substantive but informal supportive relationship with Iraq. Neither policy vector was well received in Israel, and thus U.S. policy in the Middle East, yoked as it was to unqualified support for Israel, retained the internal inconsistencies apparent since World War II.

Two dramatic sets of events transformed Reagan administration policy from reactive to active. The first involved direct U.S. involvement in the Iran-Iraq war, initially in an effort to secure the release of U.S. hostages, and later as an attempt to maintain open sea-lanes in the Persian Gulf. The second involved the remarkable events of the Palestinian intifadah and the subsequent efforts of the PLO to gain multilateral support for direct negotiations toward the creation of a Palestinian state under UN Resolutions 242 and 338. Each of these events needs separate discussion.

Direct U.S. intervention in the Iran-Iraq conflict occurred first during 1985–1986 as a covert effort to gain Iran's cooperation and intervention in the release of U.S. hostages held by various groups in Lebanon. The effort was directed in secrecy by an office in the National Security Council and eventually involved the U.S. government in a bizarre arrangement linking arms sales to Iran to support for covert Contra (anticommunist) operations in Nicaragua. The details of the initiative are still unclear, but the effects of the policy are known: The sale of key weapon systems and badly needed spare parts to Iran (particularly antiaircraft and antitank missiles) neutralized much of Iraq's qualitative advantage in military equipment and put the Iraqi military in a dangerous corner. With its back against the wall, Iraq responded with missile attacks on key Iranian cities and the utilization of chemical weapons, chiefly gases, against Iranian troops and its domestic Kurdish opposition, who were sympathetic toward Iran. Simultaneously, Iraq and Iran both extended their attacks on domestic shipping in the Persian Gulf, each attempting to damage the other's ability to earn foreign currency to continue prosecution of the war. These attacks, particularly against noncombatant Persian Gulf states, brought a U.S. naval presence into the Gulf.

The United States, prompted by Kuwait's threats to invite a Soviet naval force into the area, eventually moved a large naval task force into the Gulf, ostensibly to protect all shipping, regardless of source. Kuwaiti tankers were reflagged as American tankers. (In practical effect, this meant action against Iran.) The task force included most of the paraphernalia of modern superpower technology, including AWACs radar surveillance, AEGIS guided-missile cruisers, destroyers, minesweepers, helicopters, and smaller vessels. The Iranians deployed more mines and utilized small, high-speed boats for grenade and small-caliber attacks on slow-moving tankers. The Iraqis relied most heavily on air-launched missiles. The result of all this military activity was an increase in the complexity of traffic in the Gulf region, an area already congested in its sea and air lanes. This compression of traffic and activity increased the levels of uncertainty in the area, a fact that led to the May 1987 attack on the U.S.S. *Stark* by an Iraqi Exocet missile, with substantial loss of American lives. This incident was resolved by an Iraqi apology and payment of damages.

The U.S. response to this attack was to beef up its presence in the Gulf. Higher states of alert were required and more ships deployed. Petroleum continued to flow from the Gulf, protected by the U.S. Navy. U.S. encounters with Iranian attacks and mines led to limited action against Iranian bases, particularly converted oil platforms. But the Iran-Iraq war ground on with appalling levels of casualties, military and civilian, culminating in the accidental shooting down of an Iranian jetliner in July 1988 by the U.S.S. *Vincennes,* a sophisticated AEGIS class cruiser. This attack, and the almost universal diplomatic indifference to it, contributed to the Iranian acceptance of a negotiated end to the conflict, through the auspices of the United Nations. A distraught Ayatollah Khomeini supported the decision to end the war, against his personal sentiments. A war that began badly, with some U.S. covert involvement at its inception, ended similarly, with U.S. covert and overt actions affecting the course and conduct of the war.

There are lessons to be learned from this protracted conflict and the U.S. role in it. The U.S. role in the world, while important, was no longer definitive. At the same time, it was clear that policy decisions in Washington did have effects, sometimes intended, as is the case in the Persian Gulf intervention; sometimes unintended, as the hostage–arms sales relationship with Iran demonstrated, for it was clearly not in the interest of the United States to tip the balance of power in that conflict toward Iran; and yet in the short run, that was the clear impact of our policy. Some critics of U.S. policy in the Gulf conflict suggested a lack of clarity in U.S. objectives; others have pointed out the essentially reactive U.S. role there. Still others have suggested that a greater multilateral presence in the Gulf would have proven useful to U.S. purposes, sharing costs and blame more equally among those benefiting from the petroleum flow. Once again, these criticisms and suggestions reinforce our previous observations about the changing nature of the international system

and the U.S. role in it. (These commonplace criticisms of U.S. decision making in the Iran-Iraq war have an almost eerie resonance in the criticisms of U.S. shortsightedness in the Gulf War with Iraq in 1991.) But, in any case, the United States was now just one of many important actors in the arena. This reality became extremely clear through the remarkable events in Israel's occupied territories.

In December 1987, Palestinians on the West Bank and in Gaza began a civil insurrection against Israeli occupation. Most of those participating in this intifadah were Arab youths not directly affiliated with the PLO or other mainstream organizations professing Palestinian rights. Many analysts have concluded that this insurrection was sparked by the sense of alienation that many young Palestinians, bereft of a meaningful future, had come to experience. Israeli protestations to the contrary, there is little evidence to suggest that the early stages of the protests were conceived, organized, or executed by formal groups outside of Israel, including the PLO. In other words, this insurrection was indigenous to the occupied territories and sparked by a generalized sense of despair and frustration, particularly among third- and fourth-generation Palestinians in the refugee camps of Gaza and the West Bank.

The Shamir administration responded to these demonstrations and riots with ever-increasing firmness. The policy of the "Iron Fist," predicated on group responsibility for individual acts of resistance or rebellion, produced daily incidents of beatings, arrests, expulsions, jailing without charge, broken bones, and many deaths, mainly among Palestinian teenagers. That these protests could continue on a very protracted basis suggests the depth of the feelings motivating both sides in the conflict. And clearly, like it or not, the Palestinian intifadah quickly became an element in the international equation in the Middle East, as the PLO attempted to control the rebellion for its own ends, Israel tried to contain it as a domestic dispute, and growing numbers of the international community perceived the events as a major human rights problem.

The attempt by the PLO to benefit from this uprising led to many strains within its ruling coalition. In November 1988, the Palestinian National

Council, in a move that surprised many of its friends and foes alike, declared an independent Palestinian state and asked for diplomatic recognition. The specific resolution implied recognition of Israel, but stopped short of the unambiguous statement required by the supporters of Israel. The Israeli government reaction was strongly negative, although growing minority sentiment in Israel favored a "land-for-peace" trade. The U.S. official position at this time echoed formal Israeli policy.

Later in 1988, Yasir Arafat announced plans to speak before the UN General Assembly in New York, for the purpose of presenting new proposals on the Arab-Israeli conflict. In a surprising move, Secretary of State Shultz refused Arafat a visa, on the grounds that he represented a terrorist organization. Earlier congressionally mandated efforts to close the information offices of the PLO set the stage for this development, but even so, Shultz's refusal shocked many in the international arena, and charges were made that the action violated the U.S. contract with the United Nations. After repeated efforts to change the State Department's decision failed, the meetings were moved at great expense to Geneva, Switzerland, where, in December 1988, Arafat addressed the General Assembly.

The content of Arafat's speech was astounding to all participants in the long-standing conflict. Arafat acceded to U.S. demands for unequivocal PLO positions on three points: the right of Israel to exist in peace within secure boundaries; acceptance of UN Resolutions 242 and 338; and a specific renunciation of terrorism generally, and of the use of terrorism as a political tool. Arafat ultimately accepted the explicit language required by the United States, as defined in multilateral discussions in Sweden, and the United States immediately moved to begin direct diplomatic discussions with the PLO in Tunisia. Supporters of Israel in the United States were hard put to explain the sudden change in American policy, and the Israeli government formally expressed its "disappointment" with the American decision. The most likely explanation for this substantive change in direction is to be found in Secretary Shultz's earlier attempts late in the Reagan administration

to revive the peace process. U.S. attempts were rebuffed by a recalcitrant Israeli government, a fact that angered the administration and began the erosion of administration support.

This sudden shift in U.S. policy energized the peace process in many ways—primarily in eliminating the last practical barrier to an international consensus (minus Israel) favoring multilateral discussions of the Palestinian question. The PLO proposals for the convening of a multilateral conference in Geneva ultimately provoked an Israeli response preferring U.S.-U.S.S.R.–mediated discussions of the problem. While there was no obvious solution to the problems immediately at hand, international diplomacy seemed at this juncture to be taking a more active role in bringing the conflict to some conclusion. Just what kind of "autonomy" or "independence" awaited the Palestinian people had yet to be determined. But there was little doubt that the dramatic change in U.S. policy toward the PLO created more possibilities and probabilities for change than previously existed. And the tacit approval of the Bush administration, during the presidential transition in the United States, further suggested continuity in U.S. policy for the next few years. Indeed, such prospects were realized in the U.S.-led peace negotiations that began in the fall of 1991, bringing multilateral diplomacy to bear on this difficult problem. The specifics of this process are discussed in greater detail in the following chapter.

In spite of the special relationship between the United States and Israel, and in spite of the presence of a highly visible and effective Israeli lobby in the United States, the realities of different interests ultimately expressed themselves. Optimistically, we can hope for a more mature relationship between Israel and the United States in the near future, one that facilitates growth and development for all states in this long-lasting conflict.

SOVIET FOREIGN POLICY

Initially, Soviet foreign policy toward the Middle East was opportunistic and reactive. It was opportunistic in that the Soviet Union attempted to exploit the postwar difficulties of Greece, Turkey, and Iran in its historic attempt to secure a year-round warm-water port. It was reactive in that it attempted to exploit the consequences of U.S. policy in the Arab-Israeli conflict.

In Phase I of its Middle Eastern policy, the Soviet Union attempted a combination of subversion and guerrilla intervention in the northern tier nations. Soviet diplomatic pressure on Turkey was intense, particularly with regard to its navigation rights in the Bosporus Straits and the redefinition of the Thracian border in favor of Bulgaria. This, combined with more direct military adventures in Iran, prompted President Truman to declare the Truman Doctrine and unilaterally commit the United States to the defense of these states. Soviet ambitions in these areas were frustrated, and Soviet policy in the Middle East became more reactive to U.S. policy.

In Phase II, the Soviet Union seemed primarily interested in exploiting the difficulties raised by the U.S. commitment to Israel. Thus, in order to find a way to move its growing military capability into the Mediterranean, the Soviet Union began courting the most rabidly anti-Israel states. The first major opportunity came in Egypt, hard on the heels of the Israeli raid on Gaza, the French-British-Israeli attack on the Suez Canal, and the U.S. cancellation of support for the Aswan Dam. The Soviet Union abandoned its initial support for Israel, moved into the arms race in a major way, and ultimately committed itself to the construction of the high dam in Egypt. Soviet arms aid was supplemented by a vigorous economic aid and trade policy that succeeded after 1958 in orienting the trade relations of Egypt, Syria, Yemen, and Iraq toward the Eastern bloc. Extensive cultural programs were also implemented, many involving educational opportunities for Arabs in Eastern Europe and the U.S.S.R. These programs, combined with its support of nonalignment movements worldwide, succeeded in raising Soviet prestige and influence at the expense of the United States. Until the events of the 1990s reversed the trend, Soviet-trained academics dominated the university systems of Syria, Iraq, and Yemen and remained influential in Egypt.

The Soviet Union was able to turn some of these gains into tangible results. It was given the use of military facilities in Egypt, most notably an extensive naval base at Alexandria, and communication and airfield facilities at Luxor. At one point, Soviet technical and military experts in Egypt numbered close to 20,000. Similar gains were scored in Syria and Iraq, although not on such a grand scale. Its support for the front-line states against Israel and later for the Palestinian guerrilla movements, some of which received technical aid and support from Soviet allies, also contributed to the heightening of Soviet prestige in the area.

Most of the Soviet Union's overt political gains during Phase II were nonetheless intangible. Soviet attempts to influence directly the governments of Nasser and Sadat in Egypt were frustrated. The Egyptians seemed adept at taking gifts from the Russian bear while simultaneously avoiding its hug. To a lesser degree, similar events transpired in Syria and Iraq, where allegedly communist-inspired coups were detected and crushed, accompanied by army and university purges. When Sadat ordered the Soviets out of Egypt in 1972, American influence and prestige enjoyed something of a recovery. Syria and Iraq, in recent years, slowly reoriented themselves toward a more positive, but wary, relationship with the United States.

Phase III of Soviet foreign policy initially paralleled U.S. policy shifts. The Soviet Union aggressively supported wars of national liberation in the area. Frustrated in its attempts to consolidate its advantages in the Fertile Crescent, the Soviet Union turned to overt military aid and surrogate (Cuban) intervention, most notably in Yemen and Ethiopia, where it became involved in the Eritrean dispute. Its invasion of Afghanistan raised warning signs all over the Middle East, particularly among those states formally committed to Islamic rule. Its occupation of Afghanistan lowered its prestige and influence in the region and heightened Middle Eastern awareness of its poor treatment of Soviet Muslim groups. Afghani resistance to Soviet control continued to plague the Soviet and Afghan government troops, leading many commentators to regard this venture as "the Soviet Union's Vietnam." This probably overstates the case, but the fact is that the Afghani fighters (mujahedin) refused to go away and attracted greater external support. As the U.S.S.R. escalated its presence, Muslim governments throughout the area became more suspicious. A case in point is Iraq, where after considerable waffling, the Soviet Union offered substantial support for the war against Iran. In spite of this, Iraq continued its pro-Western tilt. Soviet support for Syria, particularly during the Israeli invasion of Lebanon, raised Syrian prestige and indirectly improved Soviet prestige. But Syria is determinedly independent, and it is hard to imagine a less tractable or more unpredictable alliance partner in the Middle East. The 1988 decision to withdraw from the Afghan imbroglio eliminated one of the Soviet Union's negatives in dealing with the states of the Middle East, but this did not in and of itself raise Soviet prestige in the area.

From a geopolitical perspective, the turmoil in the Persian Gulf presented the Soviet Union with some opportunities and risks. Intervention in Iran could conceivably have produced both a warm-water port and increased access to foreign petroleum. A successful venture in Oman could have placed the Soviet Union in a position of influence at the very opening to the Persian Gulf. And success in the northern tier, bordering as it does on the Soviet Union itself, could have been exploited militarily and politically. On the other hand, the United States' response to such success was hard to envision. The movement of Iran into the Soviet orbit, for example, could upset the international balance to such a degree that the United States would resort to military action. The Soviet Union had avoided such a direct confrontation with its nuclear adversary since the Cuban Missile Crisis of 1962. Soviet diplomacy during the worst days of the Iran-Iraq conflict was cautious and appropriate. Its attempts to improve relations with Israel reflected its growing interest in a greater diplomatic role in the region. And finally, its apparent withdrawal of overt support for wars of national liberation improved its standing in the international community.

The Soviet Union made other international moves that were astounding in view of past policies. Under Gorbachev great efforts at internal reform were attempted, and it became clear that the Soviet regime equated declining international tension with an opportunity to put its own social and economic house in order. The 1988 nuclear disarmament treaty with the United States evidenced new assumptions in Soviet foreign policy, and the very real decision to implement a phased withdrawal from Afghanistan suggested a new realism in Moscow. Of great interest and importance to regional actors in the Middle East were new expressions of political activity taking place in Soviet Central Asia, particularly in Azerbaijan, where a regional dispute with the Armenian Republic flared into substantial communal violence. Reliable reports circulated of Soviet Muslim demonstrators carrying placards of Ayatollah Khomeini. Soviet policy toward these marginal elements was an important indicator of the true intent and character of Soviet reforms. And with the benefit of hindsight, it now seems clear that the attraction of the republics of Azerbaijan, Kazakhstan, Uzbekistan, and Turkmenistan toward Turkey and Iran in the early 1990s suggests that Islam was in fact an important social and religious fact of life of those former Soviet republics.

The consensus after 1988 conceding the U.S.S.R. a role in mediating the Israeli-Palestinian conflict was further evidence of the maturation of the Soviet role in the politics of the Middle East. A joint U.S.-U.S.S.R. initiative was understood to have considerable weight on both sides of the political divide and enhanced prospects for eventual solutions to existing problems. Again, the events of the 1990s demonstrated the viability of this model, as the United States and the Commonwealth of Independent States (C.I.S.) jointly sponsored negotiations between Israel and the Arab states.

There is a substantial irony to this state of affairs. Many Middle Eastern intellectuals have long believed that the United States and the U.S.S.R. were basically identical—that they were both interested only in maintaining and extending their political and military power. For these two adversaries, accustomed to seeing each other in absolute, polarized terms, such a conclusion must have seemed outrageously inaccurate. Of course, the collapse of Soviet international power in 1990 and the dissolution of the Soviet Union in 1991 put an end to the bipolar structure of international relations and made the whole argument moot. And both states now recognize a fundamental convergence of their basic interests in international stability and relative peace.

BRITAIN AND FRANCE

As indicated in this chapter, the postwar international scene saw a substantial reduction of British and French power. Both nations emerged from World War II victorious but exhausted. Even with the direct help of the United States, these two countries were hard pressed to reassert their authority over their former colonies. Both reluctantly began a series of retrenchments.

Of the two, Britain's withdrawal from strategic power was the more graceful, the less disruptive. While the French confronted two divisive and difficult wars of national liberation in Vietnam and in Algeria, the British planted supposedly independent, pro-British regimes in their former colonies. When things got out of hand, as they did in Iran in 1952–1953, Britain participated in intrigues designed to bring a friendly face to the throne—in this case the return of the shah from exile.

Both countries attempted to use World War I and World War II diplomacy to extend and develop their influence in the Middle East. Pursuing a course of naked self-interest, the British and the French promised, at one time or another, everything to everybody. In the end, the Middle Eastern state system, a pastiche of kings, emirs, presidents, and sheikhs presiding over geographic entities drawn by committees in Europe, emerged. In this emergence, the power of the British and the French paled in comparison with that of the United States and the U.S.S.R. Thus, in the Phase I period, they contented themselves with attempting to perpetuate their cultural and economic influence in the area under American military protection. Israel received enormous support in return for taking in the great numbers of displaced European Jews. Extensive oil resources were being developed in Iraq, Iran, Kuwait, and Saudi Arabia.

In Phase II the British and French turned their attention primarily to trade relations. The abortive Suez War in 1956 effectively ended what predisposition they had for an overt military role in the area. After that time the orientation of the European powers became essentially commercial and focused on the exploitation of the increasingly important petroleum reserves. During this time, it also became evident that support of Israel had become secondary to other objectives. French and British arms were sold indiscriminately in the Middle East, to the anguish of both the United States and Israel. These sales demonstrated the growing inability of the United States to control its alliances.

In Phase III of their Middle Eastern policy, the U.S. allies grew even less dependent on American initiatives and policy direction. Britain, France, and West Germany have, since 1974, sold increasingly sophisticated weapons and technology to assorted Middle Eastern governments. Even nuclear technology, over specific, energetic U.S. opposition, has been made available to such Middle Eastern governments as Iraq, Egypt, Libya, Algeria, and Iran. All of these countries have the combination of financial, physical, and intellectual resources necessary for the construction of nuclear devices. At some point in time it seems likely that one or more of this aspirant group will succeed in building nuclear weapons. This, combined with the nuclear arsenal in Israel, raises the specter of nuclear confrontation in some unspecified future. This recognition certainly prompted the 1981 Israeli air raid on the Osirak reactor near Baghdad, a raid launched without regard to anticipated diplomatic fallout. Iraq's president Saddam Hussein subsequently called for aid from "peace-loving" nations to help in the development of Arab-controlled nuclear weapons, for the specific purpose of countering Israeli nuclear devices.

Following the 1988 cease-fire, many European businesses reentered Iran, Iraq, and the threatened Gulf nations. A more unified, vital, and active Europe expanded its economic and political presence in the Middle East, yet another proof of the changes taking place in the international system. European states and businesses also continued to sell sophisticated technical equipment in the area. It is now clear that by 1990 Iraq had made substantial progress toward its goal of nuclear weapons, its success only incidentally put at risk by its ill-advised invasion of Kuwait and the subsequent coalition response.

Significantly, many European leaders have expressed dismay at U.S. hostility toward Libya, opinions representative of emerging differences in basic policy between Europe and the United States. During this period, the governments of Europe became even more dependent on Middle Eastern petroleum. France, Germany, Italy, Belgium, and Holland must import much of their petroleum from the Middle East. They hastily separated themselves from the United States during the Arab oil embargo. By 1980, all of the major governments of Western Europe enjoyed privileged status in trade relations in the area, exchanging trade and technology for petroleum.

European relations with Israel have generally paralleled world opinion. Israel has found most European countries hostile toward its policies on Palestine and Jerusalem. In the United Nations, they have joined the majority in opposing Israeli aggression and imperialism and have been vocal in their insistence that Israel accept Resolution 242 (1967), which calls for a return to the prewar boundaries. Not surprisingly, then, the states of Europe were supportive and encouraging of the PLO initiative toward multilateral consideration of the Palestinian question. Israel found itself increasingly isolated in the court of European public opinion and under mounting pressure to enter into a dialogue with the PLO.

Western Europe, during Phase III, began to act as though it were just one of a number of centers of world power. In 1980 and 1981, the European Common Market called for new peace talks in the Middle East that would exclude the Soviet Union and the United States. As the contemporary international system matures, we can expect to see more independent European and Japanese policy initiatives. And as we have emphasized previously, the economic interdependence of Europe and the Middle East continued to grow throughout the 1980s. The fate of Turkey's application for full membership in the European Community should provide an indication of the future of the relationship. Should Turkey finally manage to gain entry, the levels of exchange between the two regions should grow even faster.

CHINA AND JAPAN

The foreign policies of China and Japan toward the Middle East have become important in the last decade. During Phase I, both China and Japan deferred completely to the policy dictates of the U.S.S.R. and the United States. In the 1960s, during Phase II, both countries turned their attention toward the Middle East, but not in the intense or manipulative way of the superpowers or the European powers. China has historically supported Arab movements toward nonalignment and occasionally offered minimal support to wars of national liberation in Southern Arabia. Its interest in frustrating the growth of Soviet power has led China to supply military replacement parts to Egypt after the Soviet Union cut them off. Japan, during this period, became a progressively larger consumer of Middle Eastern oil, on which it is almost totally reliant to fuel its industry. Japan has thus placed a high premium on innocuous, positive diplomatic relations in the area.

In Phase III, China became more directly active in its attempts to frustrate Soviet gains in the area. Overt Chinese support for anti-Soviet elements in Afghanistan was instrumental in frustrating the U.S.S.R. there. The Chinese also opposed Soviet interests in the horn of Africa. China appeared to be interested in a worldwide alliance designed to frustrate Soviet "hegemonism." The coordination of U.S.-Chinese policy in this regard has been minimal and of little importance to the contemporary Middle East, save for Afghanistan and Pakistan. As indicated earlier, Japan has seen its dependence on Middle Eastern (particularly Iranian) oil grow to critical proportions. Japan thus has had its latitude of action severely restricted and has resorted to a low profile in its international policy in the area. This dependence certainly characterized Japan's diplomatic posture during the entire Iran-Iraq conflict, a period in which Japanese imports of Iranian oil grew unabated. For the Japanese, with few natural energy resources of their own, the need for regular and predictable supplies of Middle Eastern petroleum continued to militate against taking any position of risk or exposure in the area—a point underscored by the domestic controversy over its financial support of the coalition in Desert Storm. Japanese economic activity and trade in the area continues to grow, keeping Japan ahead of Europe in its total trade activity in the region.

Chinese domestic politics turned in an authoritarian direction after the horrifying suppression of dissidents in Tiananmen Square. Many of the progressive gains made in the decade preceding were dismantled. And there was a reflection of these changes in China's foreign policy. China has become something of an indiscriminate supplier of arms, including middling quality nuclear technology and Chinese-built Scud missiles. Middle Eastern states, including Iran and Syria, have been heavy buyers of these replacements for Soviet armaments. China is not the only non-European source of missile technology, but clearly its participation in this type of international trade was and is potentially destabilizing. For its part, China seems more inclined to independence in its foreign policy than in the decade of the 1980s, less inclined to accept the strictures placed on it by the industrial West. It would seem inevitable that fundamental interests of China and Japan would eventually come into salient conflict.

CONCLUSION

In summation, all great and near-great power actors have recently found the Middle East a difficult area in which to implement policy. Changes in the very structure of the international system have frustrated Soviet and American policy initiatives in the area. The growth of economic power

centers outside the bipolar axis increased the number of players in the game; and the collapse of Soviet power further accelerated the trend. And Middle Eastern leaders have shown themselves to be surprisingly adept practitioners of classic diplomacy in this emergent balance-of-power system.

Many of these factors and actors came into play in the immediate aftermath of the Likud electoral victory in May 1996. Prime Minister Netanyahu's efforts to renegotiate details of the Oslo agreements led to a truly international effort to keep the process on course. Near nonstop mediation by the United States, using special envoys and its diplomatic representation in Israel, was critical in keeping the Israeli government and the Palestinian authority negotiating. Periodic public exhortations by Egypt's President Mubarak and King Hussein of Jordan also proved important, and King Hussein's personal intervention in Israel in early 1997 was critically important at a moment when both sides were ready to break off negotiations. Other important players in this scenario included the Commission of the European Union, Prime Minister Chirac of France, Chancellor Schroeder of Germany, and the Islamic Conference, all of which contributed to the chorus calling for continued negotiation and implementation of the Oslo agreements. It is clear that events in this area of the world are considered of great importance in other regions and a legitimate arena within which to exercise the prerogatives and responsibilities of power.

International Relations in the Contemporary Middle East

1945–1990

The Regional Actors

The international politics of the Middle East have been, in the current period, highly conditioned by the realities of great-power competition. The classic balance-of-power system that prevailed in Europe from the late eighteenth century through the early twentieth century put the region at the center of wars, intrigues, and maneuvers pitting variously England, France, Germany, and Russia against one another for influence and control. Thus, regional actors found it necessary to define their policies largely in reaction to initiatives from the outside. And calculated reaction was complicated by the realities of spying, intrigue, subtle maneuver, double-dealing, and the sheer ignorance of many of the great-power decision makers.[1] Informed rationality was only occasionally important in the exercise of international relations in the region. Decision makers on all sides harbored appallingly inaccurate and inappropriate images of the "others."

Similar realities appeared in the heyday of the bipolar system, as both the United States and the U.S.S.R., ill-prepared for the role of international arbiters, blundered their way into and through the politics of the region. U.S. belief that Nasser's Egypt had become a Soviet satellite poisoned relations with that important state for many years. And the Soviet Union's casual disregard for Muslim sensibilities led it into a political morass in Afghanistan, a policy that carried Soviet prestige to new lows regionally.

For newly independent states of the Middle East, foreign policy was a continuing challenge, combining their highest aspirations for independence with the overwhelming reality of their relative weakness. Contemporary regional international relations can be partially understood as the attempt by regional actors to acquire the capabilities (political, economic, social) that support their independence in the international system.

The Middle East is an area seemingly designed for intensive regional activity. As noted elsewhere in the text, the region's nations have many physical similarities: aridity, uneven population distributions, oil reserves, sophisticated communications systems, and trade centers. Moreover, they share many ethnic and cultural similarities: large

[1] The notion that the great powers conducted their international diplomacy with high-minded rationality was certainly destroyed by David Fromkin, *A Peace to End All Peace: The Fall of the Ottoman Empire and the Creation of the Modern Middle East* (New York: Avon Books, 1989).

contiguous blocs of Arabs, Turks, and Persians; the predominance of the Arabic language; and the pervasive influence of Islam. Thus, there are many physical, ethnic, and cultural bridges across the national boundaries of the state system. Accordingly, there have been many attempts—public and private—to exploit these similarities.

The oldest of the regional associations in the Middle East is the Arab League. Founded in Cairo in 1945, the League initially was composed of Egypt, Iraq, Saudi Arabia, Syria, Transjordan, Lebanon, and Yemen. Although there were serious internal divisions within the League from the outset, it accomplished some positive action. Critical histories of the League invariably stress its early difficulties in coordinating the war against Israel in 1948. In this war the mutual suspicions between the Hashemites, Saudis, and Egyptians severely split the Arab forces. In the Phase II period, the League was successful primarily in nonpolitical areas—for example, in social and economic cooperation. It has never been able to resolve the fractious politics of its Arab constituency and has survived by avoiding those difficult problems for the most part. More effective efforts at Arab unity have been pursued from the base of national power, as in Nasser's pan-Arab movement, the Baath party, and OAPEC. In Phase III, the League has been an important sounding board for diverse Arab interests.

During Phase II (Table 12-1), there were two notable attempts to achieve Arab political unity. The first was the pan-Arab movement launched by Nasser in 1958; the second was the formation of the Baath party, which was based on the philosophy of Michel Aflaq and found its most receptive constituency in Syria and Iraq. These two movements (pan-Arabism and Baathism) have often been at odds, supporters of each accusing the other of simply advancing the national interests of its leaders.

Nasser's pan-Arab objectives were couched largely in terms of national union. Based on a loosely articulated ideal of Arab unity and cooperation, Nasser's movement was considerably more pragmatic than the ideological basis of the Baath movement. Where the Baath party depended on loyal cadres to spread its ideology and raise it to power, Nasser pursued the constitutional union of Egypt with a variety of potential partners. At one time or another, Egypt has proposed unification with Syria, Iraq, Yemen, Libya, and the Sudan.

Nasser's pan-Arab strategy produced some tangible results. The 1958 union of Egypt and Syria, the United Arab Republic, survived until 1961, when the federation succumbed to a Syrian army coup. Some critics argue that a failure of the union was prompted by Nasser's efforts in 1959 to effect a true economic, political, and military union—one that would to some degree extinguish remaining Syrian political identity. Others argue that Syrian nationalism simply proved too potent an obstacle for union. Nasser's attempts at federation with Yemen (1958) were much looser and much less ambitious. A proposed union with Iraq in the 1960s was frustrated by a military coup and the subsequent entrenchment of Baathist regimes in both Syria and Iraq. In spite of these frustrations and failures, Nasser maintained his commitment to Arab unity via political union. Most countries of the Middle East counted among their populations groups strongly supportive of Nasser's dream. These groups were in the main not strong enough to implement his vision of unity, although they were strong enough to continually worry their governments. These governments continued throughout Nasser's presidency to suspect his motives, question his actions, and frustrate his international ventures.

Baathism is at once a political party and a political philosophy. It is one of the very few indigenous political party movements in the Middle East. Based in the work and writings of Michel Aflaq and Salal al-Din al-Bitar, it was founded in 1943 and is committed to the ultimate goal of Arab unity through nationalism, socialism, and pan-Arabism. The Baath (Resurrection) Party specifically aims to recover past Arab greatness. Baathism found its normal constituency among the intellectuals and military of Syria, Lebanon, Jordan, and Iraq. Since 1963, it has successfully maintained itself in power in Syria and until recently in Iraq. It should be noted that in Syria, Baathist support came largely from the civilian sector; in Iraq, Baathist power resided mainly in the military, many of whom had earlier supported union with Nasser's Egypt.

The Baathist regimes in Syria and Iraq have been in the forefront of the assault on Israel. Between 1965 and 1975, Iraq openly supported Palestinian separatist and terrorist organizations. Iraqi troops were moved into position during the 1967 and 1973 wars with Israel, although they were for the most part noncombatant.

Syrian policy during Phase II moved closer and closer to the Soviet Union, particularly after dissolution of the union with Egypt. Syria was frigid in its relations with Israel and the United States, cool with the traditional Middle Eastern states (Saudi Arabia, Iran), and increasingly friendly with Libya and Algeria. Substantial economic and cultural ties with the Soviet Union and the Eastern bloc were maintained.

The dramatic expansion of Syrian influence following the Israeli invasion of Lebanon (1982) moved Syria into the forefront of diplomatic activity in the area. It seemed possible that this elevated role would lead Syria into the role of a strategic "broker" in regional conflicts. And in fact, Syrian influence in the region has waxed steadily since that time.

Nonetheless, the Baathist regimes of Syria and Iraq were often at loggerheads, in spite of their ostensible commitment to Arab unity. Both countries have relatively long and potent histories of nationalist feeling, and it is possible that these factors have been a determinant in their foreign policy. Thus, they have only given lip service to regional unity movements. For example, Iraq and Syria split forcefully during the Iran-Iraq conflict, with Syria taking a publicly pro-Iranian position, in spite of considerable pressure from other regional players backing Iraq. This position put the Syrians and the Israelis in common cause, since Israel viewed the Iraqi regime as much more dangerous than any probable Iranian government.

The end of the Iran-Iraq conflict did not ameliorate relations between Damascus and Baghdad, and as Iraq sought ever-closer ties with the United States, Western Europe, and the moderate bloc of Arab states (Egypt, Saudi Arabia, Jordan), Syria burnished its already well-established ties with the Soviet Union and cautiously pursued improved relations with the United States. The events of 1991 occasioned by the Iraqi invasion of Kuwait, of course, stood this relationship on its head. Syria aligned itself with the U.S.-led coalition against Iraq and after the war moved aggressively to improve relations with the United States. But Syria and Iraq still remained at loggerheads, in spite of the dramatic changes in alliance politics.

A digression on the role of Islam in the regional politics of the area is necessary here. During Phase II, Nasser's pan-Arabism, Baathist ideology, and the traditional systems of the day all stressed the importance of Islam as a common source of tradition and identity. In nearly all of the participating states, however, Islam was conceived of in politically secular terms. It was fashionable to recognize the existence of Muslim society (a society composed primarily of Muslims) as a desirable reality, while simultaneously rejecting the idea of an Islamic state (a state based on the Koran and Islamic tradition). While there were exceptions to this professed secularism—the Muslim Brotherhood, mainly, and a number of Sufi orders—there were no effective challenges to the political orthodoxy of the day. Arab socialism in particular depended on Islamic sources for inspiration, but few economists were willing to suggest that modern economies could be based on the principles contained in the Koran, the hadith, or their subsequent commentaries and codifications. This complacency regarding the role of Islam in politics, economics, and social life was strongly challenged from the 1970s onward (see, for instance, the discussion of Islamic economics in Chapter 11), and it would be foolish to dismiss the emergent role of Islam in the international relations of the region. Important political, intellectual, economic, and cultural links complement the established religious connections.

Islam was, is, and is likely to remain one of the major facts of international life in the Middle East. Reports of fundamentalist sympathies among Sunni groups in Egypt, Turkey, Jordan, Algeria, Morocco, the Gulf states, Saudi Arabia, and the occupied territories of the West Bank and (especially) Gaza indicate that Islamic fundamentalism has emerged as a potent force in previously secular political systems. Although these groups do not seem as radical in their views as their Shia counterparts in Iran and Lebanon, it does appear that Islam will be a growing element in the regional politics of the Middle East.

Growing fundamentalist influence in Algeria early in 1992 resulted in massive electoral victories. Unwilling to accept the prospects of a potential Islamic republic, the incumbent government and the military abrogated the elections and instituted emergency rule. The conflict in Algeria between fundamentalist Muslims and secular bureaucrats is representative of the tensions emerging in many Middle Eastern states. And the international implications of these movements emerge as other governments support or oppose restrictions imposed on fundamentalist parties, and as these groups communicate and support each other across increasingly permeable state boundaries. For Middle Eastern states as well as their Western counterparts, the distinction between domestic and international politics becomes increasingly difficult to ascertain.

One of the most promising and important regional developments was the organization of the Gulf Cooperation Council (GCC). Founded in 1980, the Gulf Cooperation Council was based on the realization that only cooperative economic policies and collective security arrangements could ensure the continued independence of the small states and sheikhdoms ranged along the south side of the Persian Gulf. These states—the United Arab Emirates, Qatar, Oman, Bahrain, and Kuwait—joined with Saudi Arabia, their larger but still vulnerable neighbor, to form an organization that would coordinate the defense policies of the region. Among the early successes of the GCC was the standardization of key defense systems. For instance, the GCC members all committed themselves to the purchase of compatible French and British fighters and bombers. Compatible and integrated communication, command, and control systems were installed. Saudi AWAC planes provided a platform for coordinated early warning and air traffic control. A Rapid Deployment Force was organized to meet unexpected threats. A high level of military cooperation and co-ordination was established. Politically, the GCC was seen as a necessary response to the attempts of Iraq and Iran to establish dominance in the Gulf. The long-running war between those two states provided continual incentive to keep the development of the GCC as a high priority among member states. The rising tide of Muslim, and especially Shia, fundamentalism also kept pressure on the Gulf states.

Saudi Arabia, by geographic size and population, was destined to play a dominant role in the GCC. In fact, the GCC became the primary instrument of Saudi policy in the Gulf. In keeping with the established principles of Saudi diplomacy, the GCC attempted to keep at arm's length from entangling relationships with the superpowers or other regional powers. On this basis Saudi Arabia criticized Oman for its participation with the United States in military maneuvers in 1981.

In point of fact, the diplomacy of the GCC states adopted much of the content and style of traditional Saudi diplomacy. For instance, although the GCC states formally aligned with Iraq in the Iran-Iraq war, the constituent states still kept formal diplomatic relations with Iran. "Burn no bridges, make no enemies" could easily be the diplomatic slogan of the GCC.

Political and economic cooperation slowly followed the military/diplomatic success of the GCC. Left to its own devices, the GCC would likely have moved slowly toward regional integration. With the added goad of the Iraqi invasion of Kuwait and the ensuing war, the immediate future of the Gulf Cooperation Council seems brighter. The small, and mostly rich, states of the Gulf still live in a "bad neighborhood" with untrustworthy and unfriendly neighbors. Further integration appears to be the most likely avenue of political survival.

GCC relations with the United States have paralleled Saudi relations with the United States. That means that the GCC has often expressed reservations about the desirability of accepting the U.S. security umbrella. Historical American preferences for Israel and the astonishing U.S. attempts to trade hostages for arms with Iran during the Iran-Iraq war (the Iran-Contra affair) make the GCC states wary of publicly visible linkages with the United States. The Iraqi invasion of Kuwait changed most of those reservations, and the GCC currently allows a high level of integration with the U.S. military. Linkages tested in Desert Storm remained in place afterward, and the U.S.-GCC strategic alliance is one of the new facts of Middle Eastern international relations.

PALESTINIAN INTERNATIONAL ACTION

It is unfortunate, but in much of the world terrorism is equated with the Palestinians. It is unfortunate in the sense that the Palestinian people are for the most part no more engaged in the activities of international terror than are the members of any other nation. Nonetheless, the peculiar status of the Palestinians as a large, concentrated but stateless people struggling for some form of independence makes them particularly vulnerable to the kind of stereotyping that victimizes and dehumanizes them. That they struggle for independence against a government with a "special relationship" with the United States also makes objective analysis difficult. For the reality is that although most Palestinians are normal people who simply want to work and live their lives, terrorism has been a necessary strategy for those Palestinians organizing their drive for independence. To a people without a state, a police force, an army, or a capital, terror is the only available instrument of revolt against established state power.

Any discussion of political terrorism, regardless of how dispassionate or neutral, will inevitably raise emotional objections from those who initiate it or suffer from it. In these objections, the motives of either side in the equation of terror are reduced to the most simple and limited perspective. "Terrorists are simply bloodthirsty animals," say the objects of terrorist attacks. "No, we are freedom fighters attempting to overthrow a pitiless, merciless, repressive regime," respond the attackers, "and we must fight these monsters to the death with whatever means are at our disposal." Thus, in the final analysis, one person's terrorist is another person's freedom fighter. This fact, coupled with the widespread use of terror and political violence in our modern world, makes analysis difficult.

And yet, there are dispassionate and insightful observations that one may make about terrorists and their objectives, counterterrorists and theirs. Above all, terrorists seek the creation of a psychological mood. Terror works best in the glare of intense publicity and coverage by the mass media. This coverage can cause a small-scale and apparently random act to translate into a gnawing sense of anxiety in the target population. We know of

no government overthrown simply by the cumulation of terrorist acts. Thus, terror tactics, although morally reprehensible, can best be perceived as a sort of harassment or irritant, an activity that can claim the attention of government but rarely topple it. Reprisals against terrorists can, ironically, result in losses to the afflicted government, especially if the reprisal is not cleanly and clearly focused against the terrorists themselves. Thus, government attempts in Northern Ireland to suppress terrorism have generally created a fund of ill will among those nonterrorists who are nonetheless disadvantaged or hurt by the governmental policies. Policies of restraint are generally the most profitable in the long run, while policies of overreaction may in fact have negative consequences in the climate of world public opinion.

All of this has direct applicability to the situation in the Middle East, particularly as regards the Arab-Israeli conflict. Only the most studiously isolated individual is unaware of the wide-scale use of terror by the Palestinian groups confronting Israel. And Israel, particularly under the guidance of Prime Ministers Begin and Shamir, has made no secret of its intention to repay terrorist activity in kind, following the biblical injunction of "an eye for an eye, a tooth for a tooth." In keeping with the contemporary cry of "Never again," the government of Israel has invoked powerful symbols in its decision to utilize a counterterror strategy in its dealings with the Palestinian Arabs.

What follows in the next few pages is an attempt to place this pattern of violence and reprisal into the flow of contemporary international relations. It is not an attempt to draw moral lessons from either side's utilization of terror or violence, but simply to identify the consequences of those actions. Moreover, our effort here is not to catalogue those activities, but rather to emphasize those events that had the most symbolic importance in defining and redefining adversary roles in the conflict.

Totally frustrated in their efforts to obtain relief before 1967, Palestinians began to express their frustrations by violent means. Lacking a national base or homeland, the Palestinians were a genuinely regional group, moving from country to country as the patience and tempers of their hosts wore thin. Of the many organizations they formed, the two major ones were the umbrella Palestine Liberation Organization (PLO) and its most powerful constituent organization, the Harakat al-Tahriral-Falastini (Al-Fatah). Both of these organizations, between 1965 and 1975, accomplished a most dramatic change of status. From the image of bumbling PLO bureaucrats or of ragtag, terrorist revolutionaries (Al-Fatah) furtively slinking across the Middle East landscape, they became accepted internationally as the government in exile of the Palestinian nation and are welcomed in many of the capitals of the world and in the United Nations.

This transformation was not accomplished without difficulty and pain. Dispersed across the Middle East, substantial groups of Palestinians inhabited dehumanizing refugee camps in Lebanon, Syria, Jordan, Gaza, and the West Bank. Others, more fortunate, occupied expatriate positions in the economies of nearly all the nations of the Middle East; they have become a valued resource, given their high level of education. Leaders of this fractured community could with good reason suggest that the Arab states had little interest in solving the Palestinian question, since to do so would reduce the pressure on Israel. Thus, it was not until the 1967 Arab-Israeli war that the Palestinian organizations found the tide of events moving, although sluggishly, in their direction.

Ironically, it was the Arab losses and the Israeli victory in 1967 that gave the PLO and Al-Fatah the needed impetus. The movement of Israel into the West Bank created a new flood of dispossessed Palestinians, many of whom found the claims of the PLO and Al-Fatah attractive. Simultaneously, the defeat of the Arab armies undermined the prestige of the Arab states and their leaders, creating something of a power vacuum, at least where the confrontation with Israel was concerned. At any rate, the two Palestinian organizations suddenly found themselves in positions of preeminence in the Palestinian diaspora.

Al-Fatah, under the leadership of Yasir Arafat, became the most successful group in terms of violent operations against Israel and in providing organized social services to its constituents. Operating initially out of bases in Jordan, Al-Fatah launched a number of attacks against Israel, attacks that ultimately prompted an Israeli retalia-

tory raid on a Jordanian staging area. The Israeli raid, although successful, encountered stiff Palestinian resistance, which was perceived by many young Arabs as an effective action, bringing increased attention and more volunteers to the organization.

Between 1968 and 1970, Al-Fatah and other, smaller Palestinian groups engaged in increasingly violent guerrilla and terrorist activities, culminating in the hijacking of a number of jets—a Swissair DC-8, a TWA 707, a Pan American 747, and a BOAC VC-10. These audacious actions captured the attention of the international mass media, inevitably bringing the Palestinian organizations into public prominence. With this public prominence came discussion of Palestinian grievances. Ultimately, the PLO was granted observer status in the General Assembly by the United Nations.

The year 1970 marks a watershed for the Palestinian movements. The event known as Black September, the expulsion of the Palestinian guerrillas from Jordan, proved to be a serious setback to the movement. Moving to Lebanon, from 1970 to 1972, groups of Palestinians accelerated their military and terrorist activities, leading the Lebanese government to repressive measures. Palestinian units began to operate openly in southern Lebanon, in defiance of the government.

The growing role of the Palestinians in Lebanon was formalized in 1969 in a document midwifed by the Arab League and signed by the government and the PLO. Specific rights and areas of governmental competence were given to the PLO, supporting the war of attrition from southern Lebanon. Palestinian influence and position in Lebanon steadily improved until the PLO was generally recognized as one of the most potent political and military groups in the country. The Israeli invasion of Lebanon in 1982 radically altered this situation. The Israeli sweep placed the PLO between at least four dangerous enemies: the nascent Shia militias; the Syrian army; Syrian-backed factions of Palestinians opposed to Fatah; and the assortment of Christian family armies centered in Beirut and the adjacent mountains. The withdrawal of Arafat and his fighters, under U.S. protection, transformed the loyal PLO groups from military to diplomatic actors, with the PLO headquartered in Tunisia. Other Palestinian groups quickly emerged to continue the military and terrorist pressure on Israel.

Conflict between the various factions of Palestinians often turned violent, producing what has been called the "war of the camps." Of some international importance is the fact that the PLO itself became the focus of terror, during the Israeli invasion and occupation. The horrifying massacres in the Palestinian refugee camps in 1982—carried out by Christian Lebanese militia while the Israeli army sealed off exit from the camps and provided logistical support—created substantial international sympathy for the beleaguered PLO. Yasir Arafat has shown himself more than able to exploit this drift of sympathy, and now realigned with his former foes in Jordan and Egypt, enjoys wide recognition as the only credible national leader of the Palestinian people.

The departure of the Arafat factions of the PLO did not result in a net reduction of terrorist activity in Lebanon. If anything, the scope of terrorism expanded, including not just Israel, but other targets as well. Many of the terrorist actions were attributed to a shadowy organization called Islamic Jihad. This may in fact be a convenient clearinghouse for a variety of organizations. What is clear is that terrorism is widely considered an appropriate vehicle for political action. It is a fact of life, and not just in the contemporary Middle East.

Two events of 1985 and 1986—the hijacking of the cruise ship *Achille Lauro* and the coordinated attacks on the passenger lounges at the Vienna and Rome airports—demonstrate the complexity of dealing with terrorist action. In each case, initial assumptions about the origin and affiliations of the terrorists proved to be either wrong or oversimplifications. For instance, the centrality of the Libyan role in these actions was initially assumed to be clear and incontrovertible but in the long run was shown to be problematic, with facts, motives, and organizational structure proving to be murky and diffuse. The identity of the terrorist organizations also proved to be difficult, and accountability hard to establish.

A final resolution of who was responsible for the bombing of Pan Am Flight 103 over Lockerbie, Scotland, may never be accomplished. But the string of credible accusations again demonstrated the difficulty of affixing responsibility. U.S. and British authorities initially charged the Abu Nidal faction of the Palestinian movement with responsibility. Syrian involvement was eventually added, and at other times it was claimed that Iran had contracted for the bombing, in an act of revenge for its passenger liner shot down over the Gulf by a U.S. warship. Ultimately, the responsibility was pinned on Libya, and U.S. and British spokesmen demanded the extradition of the Libyan diplomats charged in the bombing. Syria, Iran, and the Palestinians, by 1991, had all been exonerated in the bombing. But political pressures and realities may yet reverse even that finding. Accountability for terrorist activity is as difficult to determine today as it was when it began in earnest in the 1970s.

Phase III Palestinian activity benefited from a growing world recognition of the fact that Jewish relief had resulted in Palestinian injustice. It also benefited from growing financial support from OAPEC members, including Kuwait, Saudi Arabia, the U.A.E., and Khomeini's Iran; from the United States' growing inability to ignore Arab wishes in regard to the Palestinian question; and finally, and not insignificantly, from what was perceived as Israeli tendencies to overreact to terrorist raids on its territory. The West Bank settlement policies of Israel, in particular, convinced many governments of Israeli intransigence toward negotiated Palestinian autonomy on the West Bank.

The Palestinian intifadah beginning in late 1987 prompted Israeli reprisals and Draconian attempts to suppress this insurrection. The televised images of public beatings, tear-gassings, shootings, deportations, destruction of housing, and the like by the Israeli army did much to change international public opinion, particularly in the United States, where many Jewish political action organizations professed public distaste for the violence in Israel. American television networks and news wires began carrying information revealing Israeli repression, further contributing to a change in public opinion in the United States. Most important, protest emerged within Israel itself, further polarizing the Israeli polity and influencing the elections in the fall of 1988.

For this and other reasons, the PLO decided that the fall of 1988 was the right time for a "peace offensive" of major proportions, including a public disavowal of terrorism. Arafat's difficulties in enforcing such a line among the very complex set of organizations that make up the Palestinian diaspora was dramatized in the December bombing of Pan Am 103, en route from Frankfurt to New York, with large loss of life and attendant publicity. Although the PLO was ultimately found innocent in the bombing, it was nonetheless embarrassing to Arafat and was greeted by a chorus of "I told you so's" from Israeli leaders. Nonetheless, the transformation of the PLO into a legitimate governmental organization that speaks for Palestinian interests was under way.

OPEC AND ISLAM

Regional Arab relations in Phase III were dominated by two emergent trends: first, the effect of OPEC petroleum pricing on the incomes of Saudi Arabia, Iran, Libya, Kuwait, Iraq, the U.A.E., and others; second, the emergence of Islamic fundamentalism as a potent force in Arab politics. These two trends were in fact intertwined.

With the exception of Iraq, the major petroleum-producing countries in this region were also religiously conservative: Saudi Arabia is dominated by the severe Wahhabi school of Islam; Iran is governed by fundamentalist Shia revolutionaries led by the ulema; Kuwait and the U.A.E. are ruled by traditional leaders who rely on the support of the ulema; and Libya is currently dominated by a unique Islamic fundamentalism developed by Muammar Qadaffi. These countries have utilized their substantial oil revenues to support religious goals. Kuwait and Saudi Arabia have tied loans and investments to specific Islamic reforms in Egypt and the Sudan. Iran and Libya have supported a variety of anti-Israel, anti-Western movements across the Middle East, both Sunni and Shia. Fundamentalist movements have gained ground in Syria, Lebanon, Iraq, Jordan, Egypt, Turkey, and Algeria, all working toward the establishment of an Islamic state—a government based specifically and exclusively on the precepts of Islam. The Muslim Brotherhood, long proscribed in Egypt since its conflict with Nasser early in the revolution, found new bases of support in Egypt and the Fertile Crescent. These

movements, fragmented across many lines, nonetheless posed a singular threat to the prevailing secularism of the earlier international order.

Coordination of policy and collective action have tended to increase in the area in recent years. The early success of OPEC, and of its Arab subgroup OAPEC, led to a number of international development projects funded out of the growing revenues of the petroleum-rich states. Some of these projects had at the minimum a semblance of collective control. Joint economic ventures between OAPEC members, such as the huge drydock facility in Bahrain, were also examples of collective action. The successful pursuit of Palestinian rights in the United Nations has been mentioned earlier, and Arab members have occasionally coordinated the freezing of deposits for World Bank projects seen as hostile to the Palestinian cause.

Islam itself has spawned a large number of international conferences and organizations, as a growing Islamic international community searches for ways to implement Islamic principles in banking, commerce, and social and political organization. A group of forty-two Islamic nations met in 1980 to consider and protest the Soviet action in Afghanistan, and a small number of them actually broke off relations with the U.S.S.R. as a result. A similar meeting was held in Taif, Saudi Arabia, early in 1981. This meeting affirmed the earlier position taken on Afghanistan and additionally took a very dim view of the Iran-Iraq war, which was perceived as damaging to the Umma. The conference was persistent, although unsuccessful, in its efforts to mediate the Iran-Iraq conflict.

Nuclear Arms and Regional Politics

Finally, nuclear politics appear to have taken on a regional flavor. The Israeli nuclear arsenal has long been recognized as a major factor in any major Middle Eastern confrontation, although the specifics of those nuclear weapons are carefully guarded secrets. Arab responses to the Israeli nuclear capability have included regional support for the development of nuclear weapons, often described as the "Islamic bomb." Documented reports of cooperation between Iran, Pakistan, and

Libya have circulated. The Israeli preemptive strike against Iraq's nuclear reactor was thus set against a backdrop of a changing nuclear world. Complicating matters was the fact that nuclear technology was no longer the dark secret that it once was: The technology was now available for purchase, and many Middle Eastern states had sufficient financial resources to do so. The aftermath of the collapse of the Soviet Union put many sophisticated Soviet nuclear scientists on the world market.

In the aftermath of Desert Storm it was all too clear that Iraq had made substantial progress in its drive for nuclear capability, utilizing a combination of domestic and international human and technical resources. All of this suggests an enormously more complicated international system, one capable of taking the world to the edge of nuclear catastrophe from a regional level of conflict. If these trends work out as it appears they may, we will have to abandon our metaphor about the "tinderbox" Middle East and replace it with more apocalyptic imagery.

Nuclear weapons were not the only area of armament concern. In the last stages of the Iran-Iraq war, Iraq and Iran fought with chemical weapons and with independently modified ballistic missiles. The lack of effective international condemnation of these uses apparently spurred production in Iraq and in many other countries as well. In 1988, U.S. accusations that Libya was building a chemical weapons facility in the guise of a pharmaceutical plant led to a confrontation between U.S. and Libyan aircraft, resulting in the shooting down of two Libyan Mig-23s over international water. President Reagan, in the waning days of his administration, publicly speculated on the desirability of a "surgical strike" to eliminate the Libyan facility. Once again, intentions and facts are difficult to pin down, since facilities that can produce fertilizers, soaps, or pharmaceuticals can easily be transformed to produce gases, explosives, and other chemical weapons. Again, the evidence from Iraq confirmed the hypothesis that chemical and biological weapons of mass destruction were technically and economically feasible in Third World countries. This, combined with the fact that a consortium of Third World nations now produce missile delivery systems independent of great-power technology, suggests that the world is becoming a more dangerous place. The Middle East is, of course, a case in point.

THE FOREIGN POLICIES OF EGYPT, SAUDI ARABIA, IRAN, AND ISRAEL

In this section, we will discuss the respective foreign policies of Egypt, Saudi Arabia, Iran, and Israel. Collectively or independently, these nations have been responsible for most of the international initiatives and exchanges in the region.

Egyptian Foreign Policy

In the post-1948 Middle East, Egyptian foreign policy concerned itself with the following major issues: opposition to colonialism-imperialism, opposition to Israel, Arab unity, and, after the revolution, opposition to conservative Arab regimes.

For some 2,000 years Egypt had been the prime example of a colonized state. In that long span of time, rarely had the Egyptians been ruled by anything faintly resembling an Egyptian ruling class. The rejection received by Napoleon when he proposed self-rule to the Egyptian ulema was characteristic of the relationship between Egypt and her rulers: Egyptians were intrinsically suspicious of outside powers. All of this was to end after World War II, when Egypt struggled to free itself of European domination. Farouk's foreign policy consisted of attempts to play one set of European powers (England and France) off against another (Germany and Italy). With the Egyptian revolution and the rise of Nasser, however, the concept of anti-imperialism took on greater depth and meaning, until it meant to many the complete removal of foreign influence from Egypt. This rejection of foreign influence, moreover, was an issue with domestic origins and consequences—an issue to which the Egyptian masses would respond wholeheartedly. Opposition to colonialism-imperialism became as important to domestic policy as it did to foreign policy.

Nationalism and anti-imperialism are very often delicately intertwined, producing a complex fabric of action and reaction. The question is in some final sense unresolvable: Does an anti-imperialistic movement create nationalism, or is anti-imperialism itself created by emergent nationalistic feeling? The resolution of this question must await further study. At this point, and especially in the case of Egypt, we must note the existence of a symbiotic relationship between the two forces—a relationship that has enormously complicated Egypt's pursuit of a consistent foreign policy.

Although Egypt was nominally independent of direct foreign control before Nasser's rise to power, many postcolonial problems needed resolution. These problems dominated Egyptian foreign policy in early Phase II. Among them were the relationship between Egypt and the Sudan, both former British dependencies (political union was one of the early ideological goals of the revolutionary movement); British rights to control and defend the Suez Canal; and a pattern of mutual defense agreements negotiated before and during World War II. The range of possible solutions was limited because these issues evoked powerful emotions in the Egyptian public, particularly in Cairo, where any agreement with a foreign power would be seen as suspect. The great powers insisted that these problems were only a subset of the larger bipolar confrontation of East and West.

The question of the Sudan's relationship to Egypt was resolved peacefully, but not in a way that was consistent with Egypt's initial objectives. A series of elections led the Sudan ultimately to opt for independence rather than union. The other problems were more complicated and led to international tensions. The sensitive problem of Egypt's relations with the West and the problem of its security goals, conflicting as they did with Egypt's difficulties with Israel, resulted in the Suez crisis and the frustrations over the Aswan High Dam detailed earlier in this book.

The Suez crisis and the Aswan High Dam controversy confirmed Nasser's belief that relations with the Western alliance were going to be uneven. The United States' and Europe's response to Egypt's negotiations for Eastern bloc arms was hostile and proved that promised economic and technical aid had clearly visible political strings. Accordingly, Nasser moved more and more to a posture of nonalignment and began to play an important role in that world movement.

Egypt took a leadership role at the first major nonalignment conference in Bandung, Indonesia (April 1955). Spurred on by his distaste for the Baghdad Pact and the extension of the bipolar conflict into the Middle East, Nasser subsequently hosted many of the major meetings of the nonaligned powers and forcefully argued for nonaligned foreign policy in the region. Nasser attempted to coordinate his nonaligned foreign policy with such neutralist leaders as Nehru of India, Tito of Yugoslavia, and Sukarno of Indonesia. He attacked the Eisenhower Doctrine of 1957, and continued his unrelenting opposition to European imperialism.

In the 1960s, Egypt's opposition to Western imperialism and to Israel necessitated closer military relations with the Soviet Union, on which it was now solely dependent for arms. This, combined with the growing number of Soviet technicians assigned to the Aswan High Dam project, confirmed many Western judgments that Egypt, along with Syria and Iraq, had slipped irretrievably into the orbit of the Eastern bloc. These reactions were premature, and underestimated Nasser's ability to take aid and maintain his own independence of action. The Soviet Union, for its part, was never able to consolidate its gains in Egypt, and in 1972 it departed on Sadat's orders.

Egypt's relationship with Israel has been paradoxical; Egypt has lost every military encounter with Israel but has won much more in the peace settlements. Israel's obviously superior military forces defeated Egyptian armies in 1948, 1956, 1967, and 1973; Israel also intervened with small tactical units in neighboring Arab nations at will during the same period. Each victory became more expensive to Israel and Egypt alike, requiring extensive and speedy military rearmament. Egyptian losses in these encounters far outstripped the losses of its allies, leading to the widespread observation that other Arab states were willing to fight the Israelis "to the last Egyptian."

Despite these consistent military losses, Egyptian prestige in the Arab world was enhanced by these defeats. World public opinion turned gradually in a pro-Egyptian direction, and Israeli interests in the United Nations began to wane. In both Egypt and the wider world, the struggle against imperialism and colonialism came increasingly to be seen as continuous with the struggle against Israel.

The political results of the 1967 Arab-Israeli war illustrate Nasser's gift at turning liabilities into assets. The war itself began as a result of Nasser's miscalculation. Increasingly irritated by the presence of UNEF forces on Egypt's territory but not on Israel's, Nasser ordered the removal of the UN barrier troops. Shortly thereafter, he announced his intention to blockade Israeli shipping at the Straits of Tiran. Since Nasser was at the time involved in a costly and frustrating venture in Yemen, it is doubtful that he expected the Israeli attack that occurred on June 5, 1967. At the end of the brief war the Israeli army occupied all of the Sinai, had taken the Golan Heights from Syria, had destroyed most of the Iraqi air force on the ground, and had occupied Jerusalem and the West Bank of the Jordan River. These losses were traumatic to Nasser and the Arab states. UN intervention once again brought a cease-fire and an end to the fighting. On June 9, Nasser submitted his resignation as president, citing his failure in the war. The Cairo masses refused the resignation with an outpouring of support, prompting Nasser to rescind his resignation and resume his leadership role. What in military terms could be described as a rout became a reaffirmation of Nasser's leadership.

UN involvement did not stop with the cease-fire. Most important was the passage of UN Resolution 242 on November 22, 1967. This resolution called for the removal of Israeli armed forces from territories gained in the 1967 war, and called upon all the nations of the region to recognize each other's rights to "live in peace within secure and recognized boundaries free from threats or acts of force." This resolution was greeted with mixed emotions by Egypt and its allies. While they approved of the return of the conquered territory, they were not pleased with the second point of the resolution, which would permanently recognize Israel's right to exist in peace. Events in the 1970s found the Arab states anxious to accept the resolution and Israel reluctant to surrender the territory. In the final analysis, Arab support of Resolution 242 became a key item in the Arab propaganda conflict with Israel. The support for the resolution was an important factor in the shift of world opinion toward the Arab and Palestinian cause.

Egypt's venture in Yemen was also frustrating. The Egyptian army was largely removed from Yemen on an emergency basis to shore up defenses after the 1967 war. From 1962 to 1967, the Egyptians had intervened substantially in the Yemeni civil war on the side of the republican forces. During this period Egyptian troop strength rose to around 80,000 in Yemen. They were opposed by Saudi Arabia, which provided logistical and communication support to the ousted imam, and by tribesmen in the Yemeni hill country. As with the 1967 war, there was no clear solution to this conflict in sight. The expenditure of many lives and dollars resulted in a coalition government, with the royalists and the republicans sharing power. The Egyptian goal, the establishment of a pan-Arab revolutionary regime, was frustrated. The Saudi goal of rescuing a traditional system from revolutionary pressure was also frustrated. The conflict between the modernizing pan-Arabs led by Nasser and the conservative traditional leaders led by Saudi Arabia was not resolved: Saudi and Egyptian relations reached a low point.

From the 1967 war until his death in 1970, Nasser pursued a political solution to the Arab-Israeli conflict. This political strategy necessitated regional cooperation, both formal and informal. Egypt's encouragement of the PLO and Al-Fatah during this period is an example of its informal diplomacy. At the time of his death, Nasser was presiding over a pan-Arab conference in Cairo designed to resolve the Black September conflict between the Palestinian fedayeen and the Jordanian army. This exemplified his formal diplomacy in the post-1967 period.

Egyptian relations with Libya, its western neighbor, were relatively uneventful prior to the emergence in 1969 of Colonel Muammar Qadaffi as the Libyan ruler. A charismatic leader, Qadaffi possessed a sense of mission and saw himself as Nasser's heir apparent as head of the pan-Arab movement. The tension between the leadership styles of Sadat and Qadaffi soon became quite apparent, although Sadat acquiesced in a proposed Egyptian-Libyan union in 1972–1973. Sadat's reluctance was probably based equally on his misgivings about the great differences between the two countries demographically and economically and his appraisal of Qadaffi's erratic and radicalizing leadership. The union never got off the ground, and it brought the two leaders into open confrontation. In 1974, the Egyptians claimed they had discovered a Libyan plot against Sadat's government.

Since that time, relations between the two states have been cold, occasionally erupting into overt conflict. Libya's support of terrorist movements and its leadership role in the anti-Israeli rejectionist bloc have set it at formal diplomatic odds with Egypt. Libya took the severest stand against Sadat for his bilateral negotiations with the Israelis, and reputedly placed a price on his head. As the promise of the Camp David Accords dimmed, Libya's pressure on the Egyptian leader took on more international weight. Egypt thus found itself, in Phase III, increasingly estranged from the Arab states that it once sought to lead. Egyptian diplomatic efforts during the Iran-Iraq war were largely ignored in the Arab states, confirming Egyptian isolation. For its part, Iraq accepted limited Egyptian military aid during its conflict with Iran.

Egyptian Foreign Policy Under Sadat and Mubarak. The foreign policy of Anwar Sadat constituted a dramatic shift in emphasis from that of Nasser. Under Nasser, Egypt had pursued a policy of Arab unity through revolutionary action and development. Sadat sought friendly relations with all Arab states, regardless of their revolutionary status. The hostility that previously marked Egyptian relations with Saudi Arabia and Jordan, for instance, declined markedly. Sadat put great emphasis on the political resolution of the Israeli question, building on Nasser's belated conversion to this policy. Sadat's personal gifts allowed a public-relations offensive to be launched in the West, particularly in the United States, where he showed himself to be very adept at talk shows and news interviews.

Soviet influence also declined under Sadat's leadership. Soviet involvement in the attempted coup against Sadat in 1971, and its hesitance to supply sophisticated new weaponry to the Egyptian army, eventually resulted in its abrupt expulsion from the country in July 1972. Since that time, U.S. influence and arms have gradually replaced the Soviet presence.

Sadat's commitment to a political solution to the Arab-Israeli conflict did not prevent him from initiating the war of October 6, 1973—the Ramadan, or Yom Kippur, War. Sadat's attack on the Israeli Bar-Lev line met with short-term success but incurred heavy armaments losses on both sides; Egypt and Israel called for immediate arms deliveries. The United States responded with airlifts to Israel, which the Israeli army was quick to exploit. The Israeli army was able shortly thereafter to reverse the Egyptian gains and reestablish its positions along part of the Suez Canal. The Egyptian Third Army was effectively surrounded when the Israelis crossed the canal. The threat of the annihilation of the Egyptian force brought a threat of intervention from the Soviet Union.

At this point, the Arab states proclaimed an oil embargo against the United States and its Western allies. This embargo caused the United States to exercise its influence more evenly; as a result of U.S. pressure, the Israeli army did not follow up on its advantages in the Sinai, and the Egyptian Third Army was extricated from the cul-de-sac into which it had been thrown. Subsequent "shuttle diplomacy" conducted largely by U.S. Secretary of State Henry Kissinger and his assistant Joseph Sisco resulted in a cease-fire and the initiation of many rounds of diplomacy between the United States, Israel, and Egypt. Once again, having lost the war, Egypt may be said to have won the peace.

These diplomatic exchanges, referred to collectively as Sinai I and Sinai II, resulted in the following: the withdrawal of Israeli forces back to the Mitla and Gidi Passes; the monitoring of the neutral zone between the passes and the canal by U.S. electronic surveillance; recovery by Egypt of the oil fields in the western Sinai; and the reopening of the Suez Canal with its attendant revenues. But most of all, the United States had been drawn into the Arab-Israeli confrontation in a more balanced manner. From this time on, Sadat sought closer relations with the United States and attempted to use these relations to bring increased diplomatic pressure to bear on Israel. Thus, the stage was set for Egyptian foreign policy in Phase III.

Sadat's postwar diplomatic offensive reached its zenith in his dramatic November 1977 address to the Israeli Knesset. The visit of an Arab head of state to Israel was an enormous symbolic and substantive act. His speech effectively broke the diplomatic deadlock. From that point on, Egypt engaged in bilateral negotiations with Israel, a policy bitterly opposed by the Arab rejectionists—Syria, Iraq, Libya, South Yemen, Algeria, and the PLO. These negotiations unfortunately produced little or no tangible results. They did, however, prepare the way for the remarkable events associated with the Camp David Accords, reached in September 1978.

The Camp David Accords have been described as a triumph of personal diplomacy for President Carter. During eleven days of face-to-face negotiation at Camp David, Maryland, Carter convinced Sadat and Begin to agree to a set of accords that would create a "framework for peace" in the Arab-Israeli conflict. The accords can be divided into two sections. The first accord dealt with the bilateral relations between Egypt and Israel. It involved the return, by stages, of Egyptian territory in the Sinai, and the normalization of relations, including the eventual exchange of ambassadors. By 1980 large numbers of Israelis were touring in Egypt, at least one Jewish temple was reopened in Cairo, and reports of the opening of kosher restaurants circulated in the Western press. To protect Egypt from the potential criticism of the rejectionist states, however, the first accord was linked in principle to a second accord dealing with the West Bank and the Gaza Strip. The second accord directly addressed the problem of the occupied territories and the future of the Palestinian people. The Palestinians, in the loosely worded agreement, were to be granted "autonomy" on the West Bank, although the implications of this term were not spelled out.

The negotiations that followed between Egypt and Israel proceeded fairly smoothly where the disengagement of their forces and the return of Sinai territory were concerned. Simultaneous negotiations on the second accord, however, immediately began to stall on the question of the West Bank. Ultimately, while the first part of the accords was fully implemented, resulting in a near normalization of relations between Israel and Egypt, no discernible progress was made on the subject of Palestinian autonomy. In fact, shortly after the Camp David Accords were announced, the Begin government began to increase the number of Jewish settlements on the West Bank; and late in 1980, it announced that henceforth Jerusalem would become the indivisible capital of Israel by action of the Knesset. Apparently, Israel's leaders did not share Egypt's concepts of autonomy.

Predictably, Egypt came under intense Arab criticism for backsliding on the confrontation with Israel. Even the more conservative states of Saudi Arabia and Kuwait joined in the condemnation of Egypt. Radical groups announced the formation of assassination teams aimed at Sadat. Egypt, for its part, gained economically and socially in the bilateral agreement with Israel, but at the cost of its leadership position in the Arab world. Israel gained a secure border that was guaranteed by its most dependable international ally, the United States. The Palestinians, as usual, lost another chance for self-determination and independence.

As Egypt came more into confrontation with its Arab neighbors, it became more dependent on American aid and support. Cooperation between the two nations occurred in the economic, political, and military areas. Nasser's cherished nonalignment policy became a casualty of Sadat's pragmatism.

Ultimately, Sadat himself became a casualty of his domestic and international policies. Egyptian foreign policy under Sadat's successor, Hosni Mubarak, recaptured much of the prestige and status that had eroded in the Arab world since Camp David. Mubarak successfully sought the restoration of relations with the Arab states and cooled his relations with Israel to a diplomatically "correct" temperature, particularly after the invasion of Lebanon. Mubarak's relationship with Washington also remained strong, and growing U.S. economic and military aid to Egypt indicates that Washington perceived Cairo as a trustworthy ally. The two countries have in recent years conducted joint military exercises (Operation Bright Star) predicated on joint operations. All in all, Mubarak has been able to substantially improve his relations with his Arab neighbors (including Arafat's PLO) without threatening the close Egyptian-U.S. relationship. Egypt provided much of the venue for U.S. support of Iraq during the war with Iran, a posture palatable to all of the major Middle Eastern actors except Libya, Syria, and, of course, Iran. Mubarak engaged in "personal diplomacy" in his ongoing attempts to facilitate political "conversations" between the PLO, Jordan, the United States, and, ultimately, Israel. In this sense, he continued the broad reconciliation policy initiated by Sadat.

Egyptian-Israeli relations were greatly strained by the Israeli effort to control the intifadah in the occupied territories. One result of the cooling in relations was strong pressure by Egypt on Arafat and the PLO for an initiative that would bring some movement on the Palestinian question. As Arafat acquiesced to pressure from Egypt and other moderate Arab states, and from the United States and the Soviet Union alike, the prestige of Egypt increased. This growing prestige was given a great boost from Egypt's early participation in the coalition formed against Iraq after its invasion of Kuwait. Egyptian prestige grew again as the U.S. pressed forward with an attempt to solve the Palestinian question through Arab-Israeli negotiations. At one point, facing destructive public rhetoric from Yitzhak Shamir and Hafez al-Assad, Mubarak threatened to make public their earlier "private" meetings and conversations. Egypt is clearly one of the premier international actors in the region. And the election of an Egyptian, Boutros Boutros-Ghali, in 1992 as secretary-general of the United Nations further increased Egypt's international visibility and prestige. On the negative side, Mubarak's growing international prestige as a regional "moderate" may result in growing friction with the fundamentalists gaining political strength in Egypt.

The special relationship between Egypt and the United States has remained intact since the Camp David Accords and strengthened during and after the Iraq-Kuwait crisis, assuring Egypt a generous flow of American aid and the forgiveness of $6 billion in debt. One should not overestimate the influence that this aid garners the United States in Cairo, but there is clearly a relationship of mutual respect between the two countries that translates into specific policy gains for both parties.

Saudi Arabian Foreign Policy

Saudi Arabia is the one Arab country that immediately after World War II could point to a long-standing relationship with the United States. This relationship began in the 1930s as American oil companies began to appreciate and exploit the enormous petroleum reserves of this recently consolidated kingdom. In fact, the earliest relationships between Saudi Arabia and the West were exclusively the product of the oil companies' initiatives. King Ibn Saud, in desperate financial straits in 1933, required a loan of £30,000 in gold sovereigns as part of the original oil concession agreements. This loan, put up not by the U.S. government but rather by the participating oil companies, came at a critical time for the king, allowing him to maintain the loyalties of key elements in his new tribal coalition. The American government was at this time relatively uninvolved in the affairs of this remote region. The loan apparently produced enormous goodwill toward the oil companies in particular and toward the United States in general. From that point on, in spite of cordial relations with Britain and concerted efforts by the Germans and Japanese just before World War II, Ibn Saud expressed his preference for America. He was to pursue this preference during World War II, in spite of his experts' counsel to the contrary and in spite of lost potential oil revenues from sales to the Axis powers. His loyalty proved to be an enormous asset to the United States during the war and immediately thereafter.

The emerging relationship between the United States and Saudi Arabia just after World War II can be fairly characterized as special, a term connoting an unusual mutuality of interests and policy between the two states. U.S. interest in Saudi oil was complemented by its interest in maintaining and expanding its air base at Dharan, a base that linked Western interests in India with the Mediterranean, as part of the larger Western attempt to contain possible Soviet expansion. U.S. payments to Saudi Arabia, both governmental and corporate, began to rise annually. The new-found wealth prompted the initiation of a number of ambitious development projects from 1947 on, which in turn necessitated the movement of a large number of American technicians and advisors to the kingdom. The development projects, which ran the gamut from communications, transportation, and electrification to public health and public education, significantly raised Saudi prestige in the Middle East. Ibn Saud's ministers fully entered into the international relations of the region. From this time, Saudi Arabia was to be one of the major actors in the Middle Eastern international order.

One of King Ibn Saud's first international ventures in the postwar period concerned the future of the Palestinians. Relying on the special relationship he had had with President Roosevelt, King Ibn Saud sought and received assurances that no decisions affecting the future of the Palestinians and Jerusalem would be made without consideration of Arab wishes. Ibn Saud's public espousal of the Palestinian cause heightened his prestige among the Arab states. It also made for his first major disappointment in U.S. policy, as President Truman virtually ignored Roosevelt's promise of consultation in his hasty recognition of Israel in 1948.

Saudi Arabian prestige and power were clearly on the rise at the time of King Ibn Saud's death in 1953. He was succeeded in power by his son Saud ibn Abdulaziz. Simultaneously, the new king's younger brother Faisal was named crown prince. The new King Saud was a far less effective monarch than his father.

King Saud, from 1953 onward, changed the basic thrust of Saudi foreign policy. Where his father had pursued a policy of close alignment with the United States, Saud moved into a closer alliance with revolutionary Egypt, accepting the principles of nonalignment put forward by Nasser. Simultaneously, Saudi Arabia opposed the Hashemite kingdoms of Jordan and Iraq. The Hashemite family, long influential in the tribal politics of the Arabian peninsula, had been among the final obstacles to Ibn Saud's consolidation of his kingdom. Fear of possible Hashemite reprisals from bases in Jordan and Iraq motivated much of Saudi international policy.

Ibn Saud had protected himself against potential Hashemite intrigue by allying himself with England, the major international guarantor of the Hashemite house. King Saud approached this problem by formally adopting in 1955 the Egyptian revolutionary policy toward Jordan and Iraq. This policy essentially involved a continuing attempt to isolate the two countries diplomatically and to actively support antimonarchical movements there. However, although Egypt and Saudi Arabia had common interests, including opposition to Israel, it was becoming increasingly clear to the Saudi elite that Saudi Arabian interests would ultimately conflict with Egypt's.

Growing dissatisfaction over King Saud's conduct of policy, domestic and foreign, led to efforts within the royal family to limit his power and to enhance the power of Crown Prince Faisal, acting as prime minister. These efforts bore fruit in 1958. The emergence of Faisal as the primary decision maker signaled what was to become an important shift in the foreign policy posture of Saudi Arabia. Under Faisal's influence, King Saud became increasingly cool toward Cairo and increasingly cordial toward Iraq and Jordan. Encouraged by the United States, which feared growing Soviet influence in the area, Saudi Arabia ceased its attempted destabilization of Jordan and Iraq. This is the same period in which the Eisenhower Doctrine was pronounced, offering and guaranteeing necessary aid to any Middle Eastern state suffering foreign aggression. King Saud endorsed this declaration after a state visit to the United States.

Crown Prince Faisal proved to be an effective leader. His domestic reforms quickly restored fiscal stability to the kingdom. His foreign policy was more finely balanced and moderate, a foreign policy informed more by Saudi self-interest than by international alliance politics. Substantial domestic policy gains were scored, all of which contributed to a recovery of Saudi prestige in the Middle East. Relations with Cairo became formal and correct, but not warm. Soon, the two countries would enter into protracted hostilities in Yemen.

Faisal's initial period of rule was challenged by dissident elements in the ruling family. These elements persuaded King Saud to place certain policy demands on Faisal that he was unwilling to accept. Faisal resigned and was replaced by a candidate from the dissident ranks. The new prime minister, Prince Talal, fell victim to jealous intrigues himself, some eight months after his rise to power. From 1962 to 1964, Crown Prince Faisal gradually reacquired his lost power and gained more, until he became the virtual ruler and Saud became a figurehead. This situation was finally resolved in November 1964 when Saud was deposed by royal family consensus and Faisal made king. Saud died in 1969.

King Faisal continued the close relationship between the United States and Saudi Arabia, but the relationship changed substantially between 1964 and 1975. Faisal became increasingly bewildered and irritated by the United States' unconditional support of Israel. This developing tension between the two countries did not suffice to reorient Saudi policy toward the revolutionary Arab states or the Soviet Union, but it was undoubtedly instrumental in Faisal's decision to participate in the Arab oil embargo immediately after the 1973 Arab-Israeli war. That embargo, which shook the American economy, was indicative of a new Saudi attitude toward the United States and the U.S.S.R.—an attitude that emphasized the growing independence of Saudi Arabia in foreign policy. Saudi Arabia thus moved into Phase III of its foreign policy. In this phase, relations were based more and more on the grounds of pragmatism and national interest, a new posture at least partially facilitated by the increasing income generated by its petroleum sales. Thus, although Saudi Arabia participated fully in the 1973 oil embargo against the United States, it continued to maintain close economic and military relations with the United States. And Saudi Arabia, under Faisal and his successor, Khalid, attempted to substantially improve its independent military strength through the purchase of sophisticated armaments and training from the United States and elsewhere. In 1980–1981, the Saudis sought to significantly upgrade their tactical air capabilities and to purchase sophisticated U.S. radar planes (AWACs). Israeli opposition to such transfers was vehement.

The assassination of Faisal in March 1975 by a minor and mentally unstable member of the royal family ended the administration of this remarkable leader. He was succeeded in office by King Khalid. The transition was smooth and involved minimal administrative disruption. Of some importance from an elite perspective was the continued influence of Prince Fahd, whose influence on Saudi government continued unabated from the reign of King Faisal through the reign of King Khalid. Under Khalid, Fahd would assume even more direct control over the conduct of foreign policy.

Between 1978 and 1980, Saudi Arabia became even more disillusioned with U.S. policy in the Middle East. Saudi spokesmen such as Prince Fahd and Sheikh Yamani (minister of petroleum) were openly critical of U.S. policy. In their view, a quid pro quo between the United States and Saudi Arabia developed shortly after the 1973 oil embargo. This agreement required Saudi Arabia to increase its oil production and oppose extreme price increases by the militant members of OPEC and OAPEC. In return, the United States committed itself to an evenhanded Middle Eastern policy; it agreed to sell sophisticated military technology to Saudi Arabia and Egypt, and to pressure Israel to return the occupied territories and settle the Palestinian question. In the Saudi view, they were faithful to their part of the bargain, while the U.S. dragged its heels on armament sales and failed to force the Begin government to implement the Camp David Accords regarding Palestinian autonomy. In the immediate aftermath of Desert Storm, in 1992, the Saudis reluctantly joined in the multilateral peace conference organized by the Bush administration, demonstrating their continuing reservations about U.S. policy.

King Khalid's death in 1982 brought Prince Fahd to the throne. Fahd's stewardship of Saudi foreign policy continued a modest activism, culminating in the presentation of a comprehensive peace plan for the Middle East. Like other Saudi efforts, it was predicated on the United States taking a more active role in constraining and influencing Israeli policy. And like other efforts, the initiatives failed to bear fruit. The Saudis continued to place much of the responsibility on the United States for its reluctance to "play tough" with Israel. Another constraint on Saudi foreign policy was declining petroleum revenues, forcing harder domestic and international choices. Both of these factors were important influences in the

Saudi decision to strongly commit its leadership and resources to the Gulf Cooperation Council, an organization that Saudi Arabia dominates and that demonstrated its importance as a diplomatic and military coordinating body during the Iraqi invasion of Kuwait.

The Saudi complaints about the U.S. policy inconsistencies have substance, but in fairness the Saudi elite probably overestimates the independence of the American president in the conduct of foreign policy. Israeli influence in Congress and in presidential elections has been strong enough historically to make a pro-Arab stance a severe political liability. On the other hand, the United States and Saudi Arabia continue to maintain a strong military and economic relationship. Saudi and U.S. interests, at base, are predicated on a number of similar assumptions: primarily, that the political status quo is preferable to revolutionary change.

It is also clear that in the past twenty years Saudi Arabia changed from being an uncritical ally of the United States to a country pursuing its self-interest based on its growing financial and economic power. More and more, the elites of Saudi Arabia have turned away from dependent international alliances and toward independent national pragmatism. The Islamic revolution and attendant events in Iran did much to undermine Saudi confidence in the ability of the United States to unilaterally protect the Saudi monarchy and Saudi territory; and the danger to Saudi Arabia during the Iraqi invasion of Kuwait made this realization even more tangible and manifest. Saudi Arabia can be expected to pursue an even more independent foreign policy in the coming years—years that will see growing internal pressure on the Saudi elite. These internal pressures, combined with the potent forces of revolutionary Islam in the contemporary Middle East, could thrust Saudi Arabia into new domestic and international conflicts.

Saudi Arabia's increasingly paternalistic posture toward its Gulf neighbors, the U.A.E., Qatar, Bahrain, Kuwait, and Oman, is also an indication of its growing international independence and regional influence. Its commitment to the coordination of regional defense and economic policy was implemented in the organization of the Gulf Cooperation Council. Saudi Arabia saw these states as part of its defense perimeter and thus sought closer relationships. For the most part, these efforts proved successful. All of the Gulf states exist in the shadow of two much larger neighbors, Iran and Iraq, both of which have been determined to achieve military and political dominance in the area. Both have actively courted the Shia populations of the GCC states and thus constantly raise the suspicions of those governments.

Oman became a primary focus of U.S. attempts to improve its position on the Gulf and the Strait of Hormuz after the Iranian revolution; this focus also indirectly improved the scope and quality of U.S. relations with Saudi Arabia, allowing the coordination of defense planning through the GCC without unwelcome visibility. Yemen is another sensitive area of concern. Saudi Arabia has intervened in Yemen whenever necessary since 1962, and there are no signs that this concern for Yemeni stability will abate, especially given the recent unification of Yemen. Yemen is now a potentially stronger neighbor than before, with a dramatically different worldview. Saudi Arabia expelled many Yemeni guest workers during and after Desert Storm, perceiving Yemeni sympathies for Iraq as potentially dangerous. Tensions remain high along their mutual border.

Saudi Arabia has taken the initiative in all of these relationships. As Saudi Arabia seeks a greater degree of partnership with the United States, as opposed to a more dependent relationship, it stands to reason that it will become even more aggressive diplomatically. These issues will be discussed in greater detail in the following chapter.

The precipitous decline in petroleum prices in the mid-1980s reduced Saudi Arabia's ability to accomplish its diplomatic agenda strictly with grants-in-aid or other payments. Relatively speaking, the moderation in petroleum prices and the declining rate of increase in demand during the period strained Saudi Arabia's ability to complete its ambitious development programs on schedule. Although the country still enjoyed considerable revenue from petroleum exports, less and less of the revenue could be considered "excess" and available for diplomatic purposes. One consequence of this situation has been greater Saudi involvement in the efforts to reinvigorate OPEC and reestablish a sounder relationship between petroleum supply and demand. Iran and Iraq, desperate to improve their economic conditions, were loath to accept production restrictions, as were other non–Middle Eastern producers, Nigeria especially. Dramatically increased Saudi production, put in place as a retaliatory measure to punish those states unwilling to join in production limits, was implemented, with the effect of falling prices for petroleum worldwide. Given Saudi Arabia's growing levels of proven petroleum reserves, a factor that differentiates this country from many other producers, this policy promises to remain a centerpiece of Saudi foreign policy.

During the events of the Iraq-Kuwait conflict in 1991 and 1992, Saudi Arabia dramatically increased its petroleum production to offset losses in Iraq and Kuwait. In the recovery following, Saudi Arabia was positioned as even more of a dominant influence in the pricing and marketing of petroleum internationally. Saudi Arabia has continued to support moderate prices that stimulate continued demand for the product without instigating a search for viable alternatives.

Events in Afghanistan in 1979–1980 brought a heightened awareness of Soviet power in western Asia. This new awareness produced some cooperation between old adversaries. Iran and Saudi Arabia, for example, tried to frustrate the Soviet-sponsored war of national liberation that was launched against Oman from South Yemen, and Iraq and Saudi Arabia agreed finally during the Iran-Iraq war to divide the "neutral zone" between them, a long-standing source of conflict. Healthy fear of Soviet penetration in the area had produced "discussions" between the conservative states of the Middle East and all but the most radical revolutionary states. Saudi Arabia was deeply involved in these developments. But the dramatic events that first occasioned the collapse of Soviet international power and then precipitated the dissolution of the union itself in 1991 changed the equation completely. The Soviet Union (now the C.I.S.) was completely out of Afghanistan; and even more important, it was no longer an influential international actor in a bipolar world. This fact changed the face of international relations in the Middle East. Saudi Arabia reacted to those changes by seeking diplomatic relationships with countries it had shunned earlier, particularly Syria and Iran.

Because of its security concerns in the emerging international order in the Middle East and because of its unique role in Islam as the custodian of Mecca and Medina, Saudi Arabia has become a center of pan-Islamic activity. Many conferences have been held in the past decade in Saudi Arabia that embrace a variety of questions confronting the Islamic world. Conferences on Islamic banking and finance, Islamic law, and economic development have been held in Riyadh, Mecca, Taif, and Dharan. In these conferences, the weight and prestige of the Saudi government have been prominent. The emergence of revivalist Islam as a potent force in the Middle East may have presented the Saudi elite with a counterstrategy against the revolutionary secular governments of the region. Prestige politics of this kind are not without some hazards, it should be noted. Iranian attempts to exploit the hajj for propaganda purposes have disrupted the pilgrimage on more than one occasion and prompted Saudi police action against the demonstrators. Thus, while Saudi Arabia obviously benefits as custodian of the holiest shrines of Islam, its stewardship also raises envy and provides opportunities for embarrassment. To some degree the fundamentalist movements in Islam exacerbate this problem, a topic discussed in more detail in other chapters in this book.

Iranian Foreign Policy

Iran's geopolitical position in the Middle East has always assured it of a central role in the international relations of the region and the world. Unfortunately, this has not always worked to its advantage. It has frequently been involved in the ambitious plans of stronger nations. In the nineteenth and twentieth centuries, Russia attempted to extend its influence in Iran or gain control over Iranian territory. Britain, the Ottoman Empire, and Germany tried to frustrate Russian gains. These international pressures were compounded by the complicated domestic makeup of Iran, composed of many diverse cultures and nations. The Persian-Shia core of Iran is surrounded by large concentrations of Kurds, Azeris, Baluchis, Turks, and Arabs, all of whom nurtured dreams of relative autonomy or independence at one time or another. And although Iran is predominantly Shia, there are substantial populations of Sunnis and Bahais. This makes for a political system of great complexity and potential conflict, inviting foreign intervention.

The rise to power of Shah Mohammed Reza Pahlevi in 1941 indicates the degree to which Iranian domestic politics have been influenced by international relations. The shah came to power after his father, Reza Shah, was forced to abdicate by a combination of Soviet and British pressure. In deference to the pro-German sympathies of Iran's ruling class, Reza Shah had tried to keep Iran neutral in World War II. Soviet and British leaders would have none of this, of course, and demanded his abdication. The reorientation of Iran from neutrality to alliance with the West was accomplished during the war. A definite policy of pro-Western and anti-Soviet international relations was pursued deliberately by the shah from that time on, often causing domestic opposition to the policy. The period of stress and disorder from 1951 to 1953, engendered by Premier Mossadegh's attempts to nationalize British oil holdings, is an example of the domestic opposition to the shah's foreign policy.

From the immediate postwar period through the 1970s, the shah of Iran pursued a foreign policy predicated on close, even intimate, relations with the United States, rabid anticommunism, and the systematic expansion of Iranian military power. The shah envisioned Iran as the dominant political and military force in the Middle East policing an area of growing economic and strategic importance. Associated with these goals were the recovery of Persian greatness and the transformation of Iran into a modern industrial complex ruled by a benevolent monarchy. The petroleum reserves of Iran made such grandiose ambitions distinctly possible. Iran's sharing of a boundary with an increasingly powerful Soviet Union added the necessary note of urgency.

Iranian relations with the United States were not a one-way street. The United States played an important role in the shah's return to Iran in 1953. Subsequent American aid under the Eisenhower administration—aid denied to Premier Mossadegh during his brief stay in power—helped stabilize the shah's power. Shortly after this consolidation, American oil companies successfully negotiated entry to the Iranian oil concessions. The "love affair" between the shah and the United States was definitely reciprocal. A charter member of the Baghdad Pact, Iran was a major success in American strategy among the northern tier nations. Substantial aid and trade followed. Relations with the Soviet Union, already cool, cooled further.

The 1958 revolution in Iraq signaled the onset of strained relations between Iraq and Iran. The border became the scene of tension and frequent armed hostilities. The Kurdish minorities were exploited by each side in their attempts to embarrass or occupy the attention of the other. As the revolution in Iraq moved into its Baathist phase in 1963, relations became even more strained. Conflicting claims over territory at the Shatt al-Arab of the Persian Gulf aggravated an already unfriendly relationship, as did concern over the safety of Iranian pilgrims in southern Iraq. Both sides viewed each other's military growth with alarm. With the Soviet Union supplying arms and material to Iraq, and the United States fulfilling a similar role for Iran, the bipolar confrontation manifested itself in the regional politics of the Middle East.

Iranian relations with the United States were not unduly complicated by the Arab-Israeli conflict, at least not to the degree seen in the foreign policies of Egypt and Saudi Arabia. As a Persian rather than Arab nation, Iran did not share the rabid anti-Israel sentiments of its neighbors, particularly Syria and Iraq. In fact, during most of the shah's reign, Iranian relations with Israel were cordial and constructive, with Iranian oil fueling the Israeli economy. Cooperation also existed in other spheres, with both countries exchanging intelligence, espionage, and police technology. Iran, alone among Middle Eastern oil producers, declined to participate in the Arab oil embargo of 1973–1974 and continued to sell oil to the United States and Israel.

During Phase II, the shah committed Iran to a series of major reforms that he called the White Revolution (1963). These reforms were in part prompted by the international course charted earlier. Growing Iranian military and economic power necessitated a skilled population capable of managing the complicated machines of war and production. Predictably, the changes attendant on the White Revolution produced strains and tensions in Iran. These tensions, which included the growing alienation of the landed gentry from the shah, the outrage of the Shia ulema over the secular thrust of the reforms, and the political frustrations of groups wanting social and economic modernization, prompted increased political repression. The instrument of this political repression was SAVAK, the Iranian secret police.

SAVAK became a nightmarish fact of life in Iran, presiding over a pervasive network of spies and informants, utilizing the latest in surveillance and interrogation techniques. Widely recognized in Iran as a client of the U.S. Central Intelligence Agency and the Israeli Mossad, SAVAK killed tens of thousands of Iranians and tortured and mutilated many, many more. SAVAK became increasingly linked in the public mind with the shah and the United States. These factors combined with other political forces to bring on the revolution of 1978. Before the final act was played out, however, the shah managed to acquire one of the largest military machines in the world.

It would be simplistic and incorrect to portray the shah of Iran as a mere puppet of U.S. interests. Toward the end of his rule, particularly after the success of OPEC greatly increased Iran's oil revenues, the shah pursued policies sometimes at odds with the United States. This is particularly evident where oil pricing was concerned. In this policy area the shah pursued a course best described as militant, arguing for massive increases in the royalties paid the producing countries. The shah was very aware of the limited nature of Iran's petroleum reserves and wished to use the remaining production to build a postpetroleum economy. Needless to say, the dramatic increases in petroleum prices he advocated were not perceived as in the U.S. interest, or in the interests of its European and Japanese allies. The shah pursued the price increases vigorously, in spite of American discomfort and pressure. In point of fact, the shah was one of the earliest supporters of OPEC and thus played a key role in ushering in

the third phase of post–World War II international relations in the Middle East. The shah, even given the most conservative assumptions about his rule, contributed greatly to the changing face of Middle Eastern politics.

In Phase III diplomacy, the foreign policy of Iran was increasingly influenced by domestic politics. After 1975, rising domestic opposition to the shah's regime and to SAVAK repression prompted the shah to pursue even more drastic measures to control his opposition. Many of the opposition were exiled or fled to Iraq, whose government lent support and a podium for verbal attacks. The success of these attacks contributed materially to the ultimate decline of the shah's national prestige.

In this phase of its foreign policy, Iran became even more involved in the politics of the states neighboring the Persian Gulf. Iran sought close and amicable relationships with the smaller states of the Gulf as well as with Saudi Arabia. In spite of this policy, Iranian troops occupied three small islands near the Straits of Hormuz in 1971, thus achieving potential control over traffic in and out of the Gulf. When a Marxist-backed rebellion threatened the security of Sultan Qabus of Oman, Iranian troops were dispatched to Oman to help suppress it. All in all, from 1972 to 1978, Iran enjoyed something approaching military hegemony in the Persian Gulf. This was the high point of Iran's international power and influence under the shah.

The year 1978 saw the effective consolidation of the shah's opposition, leading to a virtual state of anarchy in Iran's cities. On January 16, 1979, the shah left Iran with his family. He would not return. Iran, under its revolutionary Islamic leaders, would enter a new age of Iranian diplomacy and foreign policy.

The Foreign Policy of the Iranian Revolution. Iranian foreign policy under Ayatollah Khomeini was nearly diametrically opposed to that of the shah. The United States, instead of being seen as a steady and respected ally, became the personification of imperialism and decadence, rivaled only by the Soviet Union. The foreign policy of Iran was to be based on the principles of Shia Islam, not on the interests of Persian nationalism. Iranian ideology reflected an imperfect combination of

Islamic social and political thought with the drives for political independence and nonalignment characteristic of Phase III developments in the region. Compounded by the irregular and intermittent leadership of Ayatollah Khomeini, it was no surprise that Iranian foreign policy would appear to its detractors as a mishmash of contradictory impulses and goals.

A low point in U.S.-Iranian relations occurred with the seizure of the U.S. embassy and the taking of its employees as hostages on November 4, 1979. The degree of complicity between the government and the students who seized the embassy was unknown, but the seizure was triggered when the United States admitted the shah for medical treatment. Many in Iran believed that the United States, so instrumental in returning him to power once before, would attempt to do so again. The seizure of the embassy was seen by these groups as one way to forestall such an effort.

The seizure and continued holding of the hostages was contrary to international law in both its symbolic and pragmatic dimensions. Negotiation proved fruitless, especially since the Iranian regime connected the future of the hostages with the return of the shah by the United States for trial. Traditional U.S. contacts with the Iranian elite had been obliterated by the revolution. In April 1980 the United States attempted a military rescue of the hostages, but it failed. More and more, the situation began to resemble a classic no-win situation for both sides. The international prestige and patience of the United States were severely tested by the seizure. Iran suffered from the U.S.-imposed and inspired economic sanctions initiated in early 1980.

The resolution of the conflict came in January 1981, on the day of the inauguration of President Reagan, and some fifteen months after the hostages had been seized. Although both sides attempted to portray the outcome as a great victory, more sober judgments prevailed. As ABC correspondent Pierre Salinger concluded after his exhaustive analysis of the negotiations, it may have been a victory for the human spirit of the hostages themselves; it was not a victory for the United States. Nor was it a victory for Iran. Both sides lost considerable prestige and influence in the exchange.

Subsequent events later in the decade provided more opportunities for pain and embarrassment. The Iran-Contra initiative was revealed as a bungled American attempt to free hostages in Lebanon by selling badly needed arms to Iran at the very moment that the United States was attempting to organize an international boycott of weapons sales to Iran. And the accidental shooting down of an Iranian domestic airliner over the Persian Gulf demonstrated Iranian weakness in the face of U.S. power while it simultaneously embarrassed the United States in revealing the operational weaknesses of its high-technology warfare.

Iranian relations with the United States continued to be cold and antagonistic. Although the hostage situation held the spotlight for most of 1980, other shifts in Iranian foreign policy could be observed. First, Iran became one of the rejectionist states in the Arab-Israeli conflict. Yasir Arafat met with Khomeini shortly after the latter's return to Iran in 1979, and the two pledged to work together for the liberation of the occupied territories and for Palestinian independence. The Israeli mission was turned over to the PLO. Iranian proxy groups in Lebanon carried on much of the terrorist initiative against Israel—particularly Hizbollah, a Shia fundamentalist group in southern and central Lebanon. Iranian opposition to Israel became a major premise of Iranian foreign policy.

The Soviet Union, while obviously enjoying the United States' predicament in Iran, was unable to capitalize on the Iranian revolution. Virulently anticommunist, the Iranian revolutionary elite was in domestic conflict with pro-Soviet elements, particularly in the cities and the oil fields near Abadan. As a consequence, Iran did little to reverse the shah's anti-Soviet foreign policy. The Soviet Union, with large populations of Muslims bordering on Iran, contemplated the disorder in Iran with apprehension. The Soviet invasion of Afghanistan, in 1980, brought Soviet-Iranian relations to their lowest point. Soviet withdrawal from Afghanistan did not in itself notably improve Soviet-Iranian relations. And Soviet willingness to reflag Kuwaiti tankers to protect them from Iranian attacks during the last stages of the Iran-Iraq war removed any vestige of the idea that the U.S.S.R. might be neutral in that conflict. Soviet diplomacy in the area reassured no one and renewed suspicions about the underlying motives of great-power diplomacy in the region. Iranian foreign policy continued to identify both the United States and the Soviet Union through 1991 as unwelcome interlopers.

Iranian relations with Iraq, always troublesome, turned violent following Iraq's seizure of disputed territory in the Shatt-al-Arab on the Persian Gulf. For eight years Iran and Iraq engaged in a war of varying intensity: periods of relative quiescence followed by short bursts of vicious fighting. The conflict quickly spilled over into the Gulf region, with both sides attacking tankers headed to enemy ports. Both Iraq and Iran suffered substantial declines in petroleum revenues and horrifying casualties.

With its larger population base and substantial economic infrastructure, Iran was probably best situated for a protracted conflict. Iraq, given this reality, was the recipient of substantial foreign military aid. Conservative and moderate Arab states—notably Egypt and Saudi Arabia—provided money and arms to keep Iraq from defeat. Egypt channeled European and American arms to Iraq. Syria, Libya, and Israel independently aided Iran, obviously for different reasons.

The end of hostilities in the Iran-Iraq conflict was a bitter pill for the government of Iran. The prosecution of the war exacted very high costs, both financially and in human terms. Reportedly, Ayatollah Khomeini concluded reluctantly that further prosecution of the war would be disastrous; and with great pain he endorsed Speaker Rafsanjani's plan to accept UN mediation to end the conflict. The result prompted something of a hiatus in Iran's role as fomenter of radical change in the area—a turning inward toward domestic conflicts and problems. The diplomatic isolation of Iran, very apparent in the muted world reaction to the shooting down of its airliner over the Gulf, continued.

Iran's regional influence and international prestige received a great boost in the early 1990s, benefiting from the confluence of events in Europe and the Middle East. Specifically, the collapse of Soviet power and the reorganization of the now-independent republics (C.I.S.) created an area of fluid potential in the region. And the miscalculations in Iraq that led to Desert Storm pitted two of Iran's bitterest enemies against each other. By taking a relatively neutral position, Iran became one of the most immediate beneficiaries of Desert Storm.

Iran was able to gain politically and economically in this scenario. It has used revenue from its increasing petroleum sales to shop for arms, reportedly spending nearly $20 billion in 1992 to reequip its armed forces. One of the possible applications of this new power just might be in Central Asia, where Iran supports movements of fundamentalist Muslims intent on establishing an Islamic republic. Much of the military materiel, ironically, came from the former Soviet Union.

Simultaneously, the Rafsanjani government embarked on efforts to improve Iran's relationship with the Western powers. Relations improved slightly, going from cold to chilly, and the United States allowed the release of some of the funds seized during the hostage crisis of more than a decade earlier. Iran reportedly paid millions of dollars to the Lebanese groups holding American hostages, with resulting releases in late 1991 of all American hostages held there. Similar advances were made in Europe, although some problems continued to beset Iran's efforts. The death sentence imposed on novelist Salman Rushdie for the publication of *The Satanic Verses,* a novel widely regarded as blasphemous by fundamentalist Muslims, still rankled Great Britain; and Iranian terrorist reprisals in other European states also prevented the development of "normal" diplomatic relations.

Iranian influence in the foreign relations of the Middle East is still best thought of in moral and symbolic terms, although circumstances could change quickly. The Islamic revolution in Iran, with its Islamic constitution and its stress on Islamic sources of social, economic, and political policy, is still a dramatic demonstration of the revolutionary potential of Islam in the contemporary world. Coming, as it did, during widespread disenchantment with the politics of bipolar confrontation, the Iranian revolution spoke to the ability of peoples in the Middle East to organize domestic and international politics on their own terms, in their own way. And now, with the bipolar system a memory of history, peoples and movements in the region are even less constrained by external influences on their political life. Iranian influence is indirectly evident in the fundamentalist political movements in Jordan, Egypt, the Sudan, Algeria, and Morocco. These movements ultimately may have momentous consequences for the international system.

Israeli Foreign Policy

More than any other Middle Eastern state, Israel was formed in the crucible of international relations. The difficulties that afflicted the Jewish community in Europe in the late nineteenth and early twentieth centuries produced the international Zionist movement. This diverse group of Europeans was able, against heavy odds, to establish a Jewish state in the Middle East. In the Zionists' view, this state symbolized a return to the historical site of their religion and civilization. In the view of the Palestinians living there at the time, the state symbolized an aggressive invasion of their homeland by European colonists. Neither side perceived a middle ground between these two positions. Consequently, Israel's foreign policy is also its domestic policy. Domestic security in Israel has always been a function of its international situation.

During Phase I of Middle Eastern diplomacy, the leaders of Israel were concerned with the physical establishment of the state. To accomplish this, they resorted to a variety of international efforts, legal and illegal. Above all they sought international approval for their efforts, both unilaterally and bilaterally. In this they were successful, much more so than their Arab opponents. Unanimous great-power recognition of the state of Israel came virtually upon the announcement of sovereignty. The fledgling United Nations provided the necessary diplomatic midwifery. All of this, of course, occurred in the immediate context of Arab diplomatic and military opposition.

Support in the United States for the young Israeli state was widespread. In addition to formal U.S. aid, Israel received great infusions of financial and political aid from the American Jewish community. This private aid proved to be critical for Israel. Support for Israel assumed a mantle of inviolability in the United States, particularly in election years. Opposition to support for Israel

was characterized as anti-Semitic or baldly fascistic. To say the least, Arab prestige was not high.

During Phase II, Israeli foreign policy was linked tightly to its domestic policy. Domestic development depended on safe and secure boundaries; domestic development would help provide those same boundaries. In this stage of Israeli policy, successive governments of Israel sought to capitalize on their diplomatic advantages over their Arab neighbors. Thus, Israel moved enthusiastically and fully into the bipolar alliance structure of the postwar period. American arms and aid flowed freely into Israel from its founding until Phase III diplomacy necessitated an American reappraisal of the relationship.

In its relations with its Arab neighbors, Israel pursued a carrot-and-stick policy. The carrot in the relationship was the supposed benefit of bilateral negotiations with Israel—the carrot ultimately nibbled by Sadat at Camp David. The stick was Israel's undisputed military superiority. The statement that the best defense is a good offense was put into practice by Israel in the Suez War of 1956 and the 1967 war. In both instances, Israeli first strikes initiated armed conflict.

Although the Israeli military actions were impressive for both their speed and their effectiveness, the price was high. During this period, military superiority and preparedness began to take a higher and higher toll on the Israeli economy. This toll was reflected both in increasing levels of inflation and in the economic losses connected with the full mobilization of the Israeli military. Israel, with a small population, found it more and more difficult to sustain full military mobilization and a thriving economy simultaneously.

Repeated confrontations with superior Israeli military forces made the Arab states reluctant to do battle with Israel. Instead, the Arab states chose a strategy of diplomatic confrontation and isolation, a strategy that began to pay off first in the United Nations. The 1967 conflict, in which Israel occupied the West Bank, Gaza, and the Golan Heights, prompted UN Resolution 242, calling for the full restoration of those areas. Israel found itself increasingly isolated in the United Nations and relied more and more on friendly vetoes from the United States. World public opinion began to turn, resulting in a repolarization of attitudes toward Israel.

This period of Middle Eastern history also saw the beginning of Palestinian diplomatic and military activity against Israel. This activity was not confined to Israeli territory; it included many harassment actions such as the hijacking of commercial airliners, and horrifying acts such as the seizure and murder of Israeli athletes at the Munich Olympics in 1972. Israeli reprisals included assassination squads sent into Beirut, the imposition of punitive curfews and penalties for political agitation, the shooting down of a Libyan commercial airliner that strayed over Israeli air space, an air strike in 1985 on PLO headquarters in Tunisia, and multiple routine air strikes on PLO staging areas throughout Lebanon.

By the mid-1970s world opinion had shifted markedly in a pro-Palestinian, anti-Israeli direction. In 1975, the UN General Assembly adopted a resolution condemning Zionism as a form of racism. Semiofficial "observer" status was extended to the PLO at the United Nations. Israel's treatment of imprisoned Palestinian Arabs was condemned by Amnesty International, and a similarly critical U.S. State Department report surfaced in the mass media. Israeli prestige, initially created and supported by the larger world community and the United Nations, was now on the defensive in the same forums.

The same set of circumstances that ushered in Phase III diplomacy and resulted in a heightening of Arab prestige also signaled the growing diplomatic isolation of Israel. During this period, Israel became more and more protective of its special relationship with the United States. At the same time, the Nixon, Ford, and Carter administrations became more evenhanded toward the Middle East. The result was an inevitable and growing political strain between Washington and Tel Aviv. The United States, more and more dependent on Middle Eastern petroleum production, found unyielding support for Israel increasingly expensive.

The Camp David agreements of 1978 demonstrate one dramatic attempt to reconcile the security needs of Israel with the economic problems confronting the United States. The first section of the agreements, implementing a bilateral disengagement between Egypt and Israel, proceeded smoothly; section two, which would have established Palestinian "autonomy" on the West Bank and Gaza, made little progress. Prime Minister Begin, after the implementation of section one of the accords, began a policy of new Jewish settlement in the "occupied territories." Israel was determined to maintain an effective presence in the West Bank, regardless of what Palestinian autonomy entailed.

The inability of Egypt and Israel to make progress on section two of the accords was aggravated symbolically by the Knesset's decision in 1980 to make Jerusalem the undivided capital of Israel. Arab reaction to this was predictably strong. As we have seen, King Khalid of Saudi Arabia called for jihad to bring East Jerusalem back under Arab control. Coming as it did from a leader who had cultivated an image of restraint and control, such a call was indeed a sign of the growing Arab irritation over the expansionist policies of the Begin government. The Palestine Liberation Organization fueled these flames of discontent by increasing its raids against Israel. Israel responded with air strikes, commando raids, and a tightening of security precautions, all of which served to heighten the sense of urgency among the Arab states.

The Israeli elections of June 1981 injected yet another note of uncertainty into Middle Eastern politics. The elections were called after the Begin government found it increasingly difficult to control its parliamentary coalition. At the onset of the campaign, the Labor bloc enjoyed a healthy lead, at least as reported in national polls, but by the end of the campaign the Labor and Likud blocs were in a virtual dead heat. This turn of events was at least partially attributable to the prevailing atmosphere of international confrontation.

Two major conflicts dominated the period prior to the elections. The first involved Israeli expansion of its role and activity in Lebanon, including stepped-up counter-Palestinian raids in southern Lebanon, air surveillance of virtually all of Lebanon, and strong financial and military support for right-wing Christian paramilitary groups. Syrian action involved increased pressure on the Christian units, particularly to the east of Beirut, and the introduction of a large number of Soviet-supplied SAM antiaircraft missiles into eastern

Lebanon and especially in the Bekaa Valley. Prime Minister Begin vowed to remove the missiles by force if Syria failed to withdraw them. A nasty diplomatic confrontation between Syria and Israel emerged. It is difficult and perhaps meaningless to try to determine the sequence of events that led to this confrontation. What is important is to recognize the seriousness of both sides in the conflict and its potential for widening the Arab-Israeli conflict. U.S. shuttle diplomacy, utilizing the talents of retired State Department official Philip Habib, focused on keeping the confrontation contained, using international diplomatic pressure. In this, Habib was at least partially successful.

The second, and much more dramatic, international action involved the Israeli raid on Iraq's nuclear reactor complex (Osirak) near Baghdad. The raid, using American-built F-15 and F-16 fighters, succeeded in knocking out the reactor in what must be described as a flawlessly executed exercise. World opinion nearly unanimously condemned the raid, and the United Nations formally condemned Israel for the raid and asked for compensation to Iraq. Significantly, the UN resolution condemning Israel was a joint product of the U.S. and Iraqi delegations to the United Nations, a collaboration unthinkable a decade earlier. Many saw in this reaction an increasing international isolation of Israel and growing resolve of Prime Minister Begin to go it alone, regardless of the consequences. For his part, Prime Minister Begin characterized the attack as defensive in nature, given the reactor's ability to produce weapons-grade plutonium, and argued that the raid was a moral imperative to avoid another Holocaust.

Controversy over these two actions—the confrontation with Syria and the raid on Iraq—polarized Israeli politics more than at any previous time in its political history. Many backed Begin for his firm handling of the Arab danger, and as many criticized him for unnecessary reliance on military action where diplomacy might have been successful. The virtual dead heat between Labor and Likud doubtless found much of its cause in this internal division.

Instead of caution, the confused internal politics of Israel resulted in a more aggressive foreign policy. Moves toward the annexation of the West Bank and the Golan Heights were initiated. And in the spring of 1982, the Israeli army began an invasion of Lebanon, ostensibly to remove Palestinian terrorists from bases adjacent to the Israeli border.

What was initially presented as a limited action was instead, it was soon apparent, a full-scale invasion. Israeli troops quickly seized the southern cities of Sidon and Tyre and commenced a fast-paced move up to and into Beirut itself. The professed goal of the invasion changed to the elimination of the PLO presence in Lebanon, not simply the removal of bases near the Litani River. It appears that the architects of the invasion hoped not only for the removal of the Palestinians, but also to tip the political equation in Lebanon in favor of conservative Christian groups with whom they could negotiate a favorable peace treaty. None of these goals were achieved. In fact, it is difficult to identify any positive short-term results attendant on the invasion.

From the perspective of international and regional relations, the invasion introduced serious strains between Israel and the United States, strains increased by revelations of systematic Israeli spying on U.S. intelligence agencies; led to a substantial enhancement of Syria's power and prestige; failed to eliminate Palestinian terrorist groups in Lebanon, although the Arafat factions of the PLO were forced to leave; further reinforced images of Israel as intransigent and militaristic; created circumstances that led to the politicization of hitherto quiescent Shia groups, particularly AMAL and Hizbollah; and ultimately failed to create a sympathetic government in Beirut.

Domestically, the invasion produced substantial internal political division over the wisdom of the invasion and its moral consequences. The Kahan Commission investigating the massacres at the Palestinian refugee camps was very critical of the Israeli Defense Forces (IDF) officer corps, and a public discussion of Shin Bet executions of Palestinian terrorists damaged governmental secrecy while simultaneously polarizing public opinion. The growing number of Israeli casualties during the three-year occupation disheartened many families. And the Israeli economy went into a tailspin, at least in part a function of the costs of invasion and occupation. Politically, the invasion was a major factor in the resignation and withdrawal from politics of Prime Minister Begin, and the progenitor of the odd sequential coalition between the Likud and Labor blocs in the face of a divisive and yet indeterminate election.

The aftermath of the Israeli withdrawal from Lebanon in the summer of 1985 saw the Arab-Israeli conflict taking on new coloration. The U.S. role in the area was visibly reduced and Israel's self-confidence in its moral rectitude challenged. The Palestinians had more faces than ever, and the prospects for a negotiated settlement appeared dim. Courageous leadership, of the type exhibited by Sadat during his trip to Jerusalem, seemed a scarcer commodity than ever. Both Arab and Jew have paid a high price for the privilege of settling disputes through violence.

The assassination of President Sadat on October 6, 1981, served to emphasize the degree to which the United States and Israel had predicated their policies on the particulars of Egyptian policy. They, most of all, found themselves in the process of agonizing reappraisal of their foreign policies. In the main, these reappraisals centered on the question of whether or not the policies of Sadat would survive his administration or would fall victim to the new political realities likely to follow.

The continuity in Egyptian foreign policy under Mubarak placed Egypt in a position of high prestige with nearly all of the international actors in the region. Mubarak complied with the letter of the Camp David Accords, reclaiming the Sinai territory lost in previous conflicts. Egypt did not repudiate the treaty even after the Israeli invasion of Lebanon, an act repugnant to most Egyptians. Egypt provided a warm welcome to the exiled Arafat and recovered a measure of its revolutionary bona fides in the process.

The relative calm of U.S.-Israeli relations was jarred when the Palestinian revolt prompted renewed U.S. efforts to promote a settlement. Secretary of State George Shultz personally engaged in an extensive round of regional diplomacy, alternately needling and wheedling the respective players for substantive action. Israeli leaders were successful in ignoring these pressures until the fall of 1988, when the actions of the PLO reenergized the U.S. effort. Other powers entered the discussions, and even England, long stalwart in its refusal to talk with PLO representatives, relented and opened lines of communication. This effectively left Israel very isolated and with a diminishing set of possibilities. Israeli diplomatic maneuvers centered on discrediting the PLO for continuing terrorist activity and attempting to define a different set of Palestinian leaders with whom to negotiate. International pressure in favor of some form of "autonomy" for the occupied territories was building, and the Israeli government, fragile coalition that it was, was hard pressed to find palatable and practical policies. Short-run solutions to the problem seemed unlikely, but it also seemed that a process had begun that *could* in time lead to an amelioration of the plight facing the Palestinians under Israeli control.

Public opinion in the United States, reacting to the brutal suppression of the intifadah and Israeli unwillingness to enter into substantive dialogue with a changing PLO, reflected declining support for Israel—particularly among the American Jewish community, long noted for its unwavering support but now disconcerted by the repressive policies of the Israeli government in the West Bank and Gaza. These changes presented a serious challenge for Israeli leadership, particularly given the importance of U.S. aid in maintaining the security and economic vitality of the country. Thus, as is so often the case, clear linkages between domestic and international policy existed, complicating already complex calculations.

The collapse of the coalition government in 1988 brought the Likud back to power and ushered in another Shamir administration. The foreign policy of the Shamir government was predicated on a hard line toward Palestinian independence, increased Jewish settlement in the occupied territories, and a willingness to accept deteriorating relations with the Bush administration as the price for this set of policies. This initially resulted in growing tensions between Washington and Tel Aviv and increasing rhetorical conflict between Israel and its Arab neighbors. The continuing Israeli response to the Palestinian intifadah added to this declining prestige.

Israel also found its foreign policies affected by the emergence of a new world order. The decline of the bipolar system devalued Israel's purely military value to the United States. And the changes in the Soviet Union allowed dramatic increases in Soviet emigration to Israel, straining the economy with dramatically growing resettlement and housing expenses.

Iraq's invasion of Kuwait proved both a blessing and a problem for Israel. Excluded from the formal coalition, Israel was not a front-line state in Desert Storm, and its losses were confined to a few Scud attacks with little loss of life or property. Palestinian sympathy for Iraq increased the latitude of the government in its attempts to control the Palestinians. Onerous curfews, the closing of schools and other institutions, deportations, and increased settlement activity placed even greater pressure on the Palestinian community. It is clear that Israel's officially low-profile role in the conflict gave it the opportunity to increase the pressure on its Palestinian population.

On the debit side of the ledger, the aftermath of Desert Storm found the Bush administration pushing hard for multilateral talks aimed at settling the Palestinian question. Implicit in the effort was a "land for peace" formula that the right wing of Israeli politics found absolutely unpalatable. Kicking and screaming, the Shamir government was forced to the conference table in late 1991 and 1992 by a combination of "carrots and sticks." Israel's detention of Palestinian staff traveling to the peace conference and its military operations in southern Lebanon in the winter of 1992 contributed further to the existing strains. The domestic political consequences of entering into these discussions prompted two religious parties to drop out of the Likud coalition in the Knesset, necessitating new elections in the summer of 1992.

The international events of the early 1990s damaged the prestige and reputation of Israel and brought it into increased confrontation with the United States. Major changes in the structure and dynamics of the new emerging international order present serious challenges to the Israeli government today. And as high-technology weaponry suffuses the area, bringing even relatively small states substantial increases in military capability, simple and direct military action becomes ever more destabilizing and less likely to produce the desired effects. Perhaps the events of the turn of the millennium herald the beginning of more pragmatic initiatives from all parties to the conflict. In this political mare's nest, we dare not hope for less.

CONCLUSION

In the years since the end of World War II, the Middle East has been the scene of intense international exchange. The forces of great-power interests, emerging national self-interest, international economic interdependence, and secular and Islamic revolutions have changed the international relations of the Middle East. No longer reacting primarily to the bipolar strategies of the United States and the Soviet Union, the Middle Eastern states themselves now initiate international moves to which other powers must respond. Pragmatic self-interest pervaded the policy atmosphere of Phase III diplomacy. This attitudinal change, together with the real financial power of the petroleum-rich Arab states, signaled the emergence of the Middle East as one of the several independent power centers that make up the multipolar world.

It is clear that thinking about the world as a bipolar system yielded powerful insights from 1948 right up through the 1980s. But in the midst of that last decade the explanatory power of the model declined, and the behavior of states seemed to be less and less conditioned and constrained by bipolar considerations. We now see the end of that system and the emergence of a new, multipolar world. This change is sufficiently significant that we have added another chapter to this book, examining the possible consequences of this New World Order for the domestic and international politics of the Middle East. In particular, the following chapter examines the dimensions of the newly emergent international system; the effect of Desert Storm on that system; and the prospects for real peace between the Arabs and Israelis.

CHAPTER FOURTEEN

The Middle East and the Changing International Order

1991–2001

By the end of the 1980s it was clear to most observers that the prevailing international system was in the process of change. But few foresaw the rapidity and implications of that change. Processes that were assumed to be stable deteriorated in a matter of years, even months. The result was the disruption of the old order before the dimensions of the new order were clear. Many statesmen spoke glibly of the "New International Order," but few were clear about the contours and details of the new system. As is so often the case in this new age, changes occurred faster than the ability of governments to perceive or understand them.

Reviewing the signal events occurring between 1988 and 1991 gives us some idea of the early direction of change. Events began with uncharacteristic agreement on nuclear weapons treaties between the United States and the U.S.S.R. With hindsight, it appears that both protagonists in the great Cold War were economically exhausted by the competition. These agreements were closely followed by Soviet retrenchment throughout the world, including its withdrawal from Afghanistan and drastic reductions in its support for its allies elsewhere.

These emerging trends assumed the proportions of an avalanche by early 1990, and in short

order the Soviet Union abandoned its political and military role in Eastern Europe. "Velvet revolutions" occurred in Poland, Czechoslovakia, and Hungary. The Berlin wall fell and German reunification was permitted and then quickly implemented. The Warsaw Pact was dissolved and many of its members, including the Soviet Union, unsuccessfully petitioned for membership in NATO. The "eye-ball to eye-ball nuclear confrontation" of some forty years duration took less than forty months to evaporate. The bipolar world order was defunct.

Emboldened, perhaps, by the events in Eastern Europe, the Baltic states of the Soviet Union increased their demands for independence. And once again, events outpaced the expectations of statesmen and scholars. In fairly short order, Lithuania, Latvia, and Estonia gained a measure of independence from the Soviet center. These changes precipitated others until the chain of events eventually challenged the Soviet government itself. Decades of pent-up regional and nationalist sentiments were released. As republic after republic in the Soviet Union declared its independence, the authority of the communist party and the central government progressively declined. The reform movement headed by Mikhail

Gorbachev lost momentum to the forces of revolutionary change, increasingly symbolized in the leadership of Boris Yeltsin and the political and economic centrality of the Russian Republic.

The forces of radical change were energized again in August of 1991 when threatened members of the old Soviet elite attempted a coup against Gorbachev and his government. The failure of the coup resulted in the formal dissolution of the communist party and the progressive transfer of power from the Gorbachev government to the governments of the republics. In December of 1991 a majority of the republics of the old Soviet Union ratified a new Commonwealth of Independent States. This entity of confederation—a system of relative autonomy and cooperation between ethnically and historically defined regions—formally replaced the Soviet Union of old and finally and practically signified the last gasp of the old communist order.

Even the names of the players changed, and most probably not for the last time. For although the Soviet Union has been reconstituted as the Commonwealth of Independent States (C.I.S., for short), events ocurring after January 1992 reduced the vitality of the new C.I.S. and demonstrated the emergence of a newer and more intense Russian nationalism. The mixed success of the Yeltsin government in 1995, 1996, and again in 1999–2000 to suppress the attempted secession of Chechnaya is a case in point. Attempts to negotiate a settlement failed and periodic violence from each side appeared to strengthen the resolve of the other. Similar observations regarding resurgent nationalism, separatism, Christian and Islamic religious extremism, and basic political uncertainty characterize many Russian provinces (Chechen Republic, Dagestan, Ingushetsia, for example) and many of the new states of central Asia. These include notably Azerbaijan, Georgia, Turkmenistan, Kyrgyzistan, and Armenia, and the fragmenting components of the former Yugoslavia, particularly in Bosnia and Kosovo—all, we should emphasize, within or bordering on the nominal cultural and political region we understand as the Middle East.

But it is in the emerging relationship between Israel and the Palestinians that the immediacy of the changing world order finds its most dramatic evidence. After decades of intransigence, two old and battle-scarred combatants—Itzhak Rabin and Yasir Arafat—warily exchanged handshakes in Washington in September of 1993, under the beaming countenance of President Clinton. This, and the subsequent encounters between Israeli and Palestinian officials, began the process of negotiation that would lead eventually to real transfers of power to the Palestinian National Authority, under the elected leadership of Yasir Arafat. This image, of Yasir Arafat and the PLO exercising real administrative power in Gaza and the West Bank, of armed Palestinian police officers patrolling in cities and villages, is one that would have been inconceivable a decade earlier.

Also inconceivable would have been the cast of characters active in the process that led to such change. For it was secret diplomacy exercised by the government of Norway, not the United States or any of the so-called "great powers," that broke the deadlocks between Arafat and Rabin in 1993 and 1995. And it was King Hussein of Jordan that, by his presence and his remarks, contributed to the healing of Israel after the assassination of Prime Minister Rabin, and who literally left his hospital bed to restart stalled Palestinian-Israeli negotiations at Wye Plantation in Maryland in 1998. In point of fact, regional and world actors acting in good faith for idealistic reasons have been of great importance in bringing the Palestinian-Israeli relationship to its current state and condition.

There is no doubt that the old international bipolar system is gone. But the system replacing it is an act in progress, not a finished product. Change, and its handmaiden of uncertainty, is in the air and on the land. Consider the collaborators in the decision to intervene in Bosnia in 1995 and Kosovo in 1999. Who would have predicted only a year or two earlier that NATO, under the nominal direction of the UN, would put troops on the ground in an area far removed from its normal theater of operations? And who would have predicted broad support for the reintroduction of German troops into the Balkans? And who would have predicted the combination of U.S. and Russian troops working together to establish a peaceful climate in which a government born of negotiations in Dayton, Ohio could come to fruition? We truly live in a dramatically changing world. And yet, there are trends and developments that suggest the outlines of a new international order.

DIMENSIONS OF THE EMERGING INTERNATIONAL ORDER

Although it is very early to specify the full dimensions of the emerging world system, some trends are apparent. In order of importance we would note the following:

1. The new world order is *not* unipolar. In other words, the collapse of the Soviet Union did not automatically elevate the United States to the level of a hegemonic power. In fact, the very pressures that caused the collapse of Soviet power appear to constrain U.S. power as well. Both are counting on reductions in military appropriations to reinvigorate their lagging economies. And so are the other principal world powers. Finally, we should emphasize that the new C.I.S. is a nuclear power of great importance even in the chaotic situations attending its formation.

2. The emerging world order *is* apparently *multipolar,* a world system in which military, economic, and political power is more widely dispersed than in the previous bipolar system. And it is also likely that few countries in this system will have across-the-board capability. In other words, the new order will be characterized by the economic and military power of one actor combining with the military and political power of others, in a relatively free-floating set of international combinations.

3. The movement toward *regional integration* will continue. Economic regional integration will proceed in Western Europe, North America, Eastern Europe, Southeast Asia, East Asia, North Africa, and the Persian Gulf. There are potentials for increased integration in Latin America and sub-Saharan Africa as well. These new institutions will eventually constitute power centers with consequences for the conduct of international affairs. At the minimum, their existence implies a system of shared powers and responsibilities, a system quite unlike the one it replaces.

4. In this environment, *international organizations* will become increasingly important. Multinational organizations like the UN and NATO will perform important coordinating roles in the international order. And nongovernmental international actors will also take on an increasingly important role in international affairs, organizations like Médecins Sans Frontières or the International Red Cross/Red Crescent.

5. Global political, social, and economic *interdependence* (globalization, as this process is often identified) will continue to accelerate, considerably reducing the independence of governments and their actions. Resource scarcity (water, fuels) and global pollution (ozone depletion, ground water contamination) and population control will require international cooperation for solutions. Nearly instantaneous international communication will keep us all aware of the human costs of disease, famine, war, and natural disaster; national politics will be ever more visible to attentive publics on the outside. Technology will continue to diffuse independently of the attempts of governments to restrict it.

6. *Regional conflicts* will become more active and numerous as the restraining effect of the bipolar competition fades. War and conflict will not disappear because of the changing international system, but the size and consequences of conflict will change. The arenas of conflict are being redefined by the changes at the system level. The great powers of the world will face increasing levels of regional and local risk as the dangers of global nuclear threat recede. Smaller conflicts and more of them are likely occurrences in the brave new world we all now face. The civil war in Yugoslavia is a good example of this, and the plight of the Kurds, spanning the boundaries of Turkey, Iran, Iraq, and Syria is another.

7. The *north-south conflict* is likely to intensify. As the previous system of ideological competition fades, conflict between economically and socially defined groups is likely. Demand for more equitable sharing of the world's resources is a likely nuance of the emerging world order. Global conflict between rich and poor is likely to become a political and moral, if not military, fact.

8. Finally, and in many ways most important, a blurring of the distinction between domestic and international policy confronts all major nations. The domestication of the international and the internationalization of the domestic make coherent policy making difficult. As Robert Pranger has observed, "Because the demands placed on national interests by international and domestic environments differ in ends and means, foreign policy . . . is more complicated than domestic policy . . . and requires areas of expertise not normally available in any abundance to leaders whose legitimacy usually depends on domestic political authority."[1]

THE MIDDLE EAST IN THE EMERGING INTERNATIONAL ORDER

These profound changes in the international system have resonant effects in the international relations of the Middle East. Many corollaries and consequences of the change had begun to emerge in the late 1980s, maturing in the mid-1990s. Chief among these were a new caution in Soviet relations with the area and visible changes in the U.S. posture toward the area as the Soviet threat retreated. The Soviet retrenchment in Afghanistan was but the most visible of what became a general withdrawal of the U.S.S.R. from the region's conflicts. Allied states such as Syria, Iraq, and South Yemen received smaller amounts of foreign and military aid and less encouragement in the support of wars of national liberation. The PLO sensed these changes and sought dialogue with the West, attempting awkwardly to adjust to the new realities. All in all, a sense of uncertainty and change pervaded the area.

Analysts could also see changes in U.S. policy as a result of the reduced Soviet role in the region. The end-game of the Reagan administration began and ended with reinvigorated attempts to solve the ongoing Israeli-Arab conflict, including the previously unheard-of dialogue with the PLO. And the first year of the Bush administration began and

ended with attempts to restart negotiations between Israel, her Arab neighbors, and the PLO.

In spite of unsuccessful attempts to jump-start the peace process in the Middle East, early 1990 was a time of international optimism. The cumulative effects of the transition from the old order to the new put statesmen in a mellow mood. Many dangerous maneuvers in Eastern Europe and the former Soviet Union had been accomplished without disaster. A "peace dividend" appeared near at hand, providing some economic and political relief to states that had been strained in capacity for some four prior decades. The Iran-Iraq war had sputtered to a halt. The world appeared to be in for a period of relative progress and prosperity.

So the news in August of 1990 that Iraq had invaded its neighbor Kuwait was received in the halls of government with anger and frustration. This act and its subsequent denouement demonstrated many of the points emphasized earlier in this chapter. Depending on one's point of view, the crisis constituted the last response of the old order or represented the first response of the new. In any event, Iraq's invasion of Kuwait and the world community's response to it constituted the primary international event of the early 1990s. Other regional events—the continuation of the intifadah, the release of hostages, or attempts to begin peace negotiations between Israel and the Arabs—were overshadowed by this single event. Thus the conflict was certainly architectonic to the conduct of international relations in the Middle East, and, at the minimum, evidence of the new international politics. It must be looked at and analyzed with care if we are to draw appropriate inferences.

The Iraq-Kuwait Crisis

The background to the Iraqi invasion of Kuwait in August of 1990 is complex. There is a long history of conflict between the two states, and this was not the first time that Iraqi troops had rolled down the Basra highway toward Kuwait. There are claims and counterclaims. Iraq has long claimed Kuwait as its own, an area severed from it by the arbitrary act of the previous colonial power; by contrast, the al-Sabah family claims to the region are old and long-standing. But in point of fact,

---

[1] Robert Pranger, "Foreign Policy Capacity in the Middle East," in Judith Kipper and Harold Saunders, eds., *The Middle East in Global Perspective* (Boulder, Colo.: American Enterprise Institute, Westview Press, 1991), pp. 20–21.

both Kuwait and Iraq were only recently defined as independent nations, emerging from the interaction of two colonial administrations, Ottoman and English.

And there was much geographic uncertainty and strain as well. Due to the nature of the desert terrain, the borders between Kuwait and her neighbors have never been clear or well defined. Areas of disputed ownership predate this conflict and the presence of petroleum in some of the disputed areas has resulted in areas of joint exploitation and/or administration. Nomadic herders crossed these porous borders with impunity for decades, further complicating the problems of national definition. Kuwaiti control of key areas at the top of the Gulf frustrated Iraq, whose access to the Gulf through the Shatt al-Arab was all but destroyed by the war with Iran. The effect was to virtually land-lock Iraq and make import and export difficult. Kuwait evinced little concern over these Iraqi difficulties.

These historical and geographic conflicts were exacerbated by the long-running war between Iraq and Iran. As one of the states backing Iraq in that war, Kuwait had extended loans and credits to Iraq. Now, as the war ended, Iraq sought further help and the forgiveness of the loans. Kuwait responded by demanding payment. Iraq was outraged and this outrage was further fueled by its belief that Kuwait had pumped unfair amounts of petroleum from the Rumeilah oil fields, fields that dip slightly into Kuwait but whose bulk lies in Iraq. Moreover, Kuwait played a key role in OPEC decisions in the summer of 1990 not to raise the price for petroleum. Iraq, counting on a substantial increase in price to offset the costs of the war with Iran, felt that it had been "whip-sawed" by Kuwait, which both opposed price increases and deliberately exceeded its production quotas.

These charges of unfair profiteering were given some credence by the reputation of Kuwaitis prior to the invasion. It is no exaggeration to suggest that Kuwaiti prestige was fairly low in the Middle East at the time, particularly in those countries without substantial petroleum resources. Wealthy Kuwaitis vacationing in London, Cairo, Damascus, and Baghdad did for the Kuwaiti public image what earlier generations of ugly Americans, ugly Germans, and ugly Japanese had done for their own countries' reputations. Public sympathy for the plight of the wealthy Kuwaiti minority was relatively scarce outside of Saudi Arabia, the Gulf states, and the European west.

U.S. restraint on Iraq evaporated shortly before the invasion of Kuwait. In a much-publicized conversation with Saddam Hussein, the American ambassador in Baghdad, April Glaspie, observed to the Iraqi leader that the United States had no mutual defense treaty with Kuwait. The interpretation of this remark was apparently critical to Saddam Hussein's appraisal of probable U.S. reaction to his planned invasion. Inadvertent or not, a green light of sorts was presented to Iraq in the prosecution of its dispute with Kuwait. The Soviet Union, long a supporter of Iraq, was not a major partner in these discussions.

The Iraqi invasion was swift, brutal, and massive when it occurred. Well over 150,000 heavily armored Iraqi troops flooded into Kuwait. In a matter of twenty-four hours the nominal defenders of Kuwait were routed, and less than a day later Iraqi troops were digging in on the borders with Saudi Arabia. Iraqi troops took up reinforced positions along the Saudi Arabian border, a presence that prompted fear in that country and in its customers for petroleum. Indeed, the concentration of Iraqi forces on the border went far beyond that needed for the mere defense of the captured territory, raising speculation about the ultimate intentions of Iraq. At the peak, Iraqi forces in the Kuwaiti theater numbered well over 250,000 (during the hostilities these force numbers were greatly exaggerated in the coalition press and briefings). The ambiguity raised by such great concentrations of Iraqi power quickly forced reaction from interested parties, particularly Saudi Arabia, the Gulf states, the United States, and Western Europe. Within a week an initial force of U.S. and Gulf area troops took up positions on the Saudi side of the Kuwaiti border and Desert Shield/Desert Storm began.[2]

Events within occupied Kuwait did little to reassure Iraq's neighbors. As many as one-third of Kuwait's native population fled, including most of

[2] Desert Shield was the name of the defensive phase of the operation. It was succeeded by Desert Storm as the coalition forces went on the offensive.

the government and armed forces; those that remained behind were subjected to repressive occupation. Hundreds of thousands of guest workers from Jordan, Egypt, India, Bangladesh, and the Philippines also fled the area, becoming instant refugees and straining neighboring states' ability to provide for them.

A puppet regime was quickly established by Iraq, and the reorganization of Kuwait proceeded. As the occupation continued, reports of torture, rape, murder, and looting became regular features in the outside press. Sensationalism and exaggeration make objective appraisal of the occupation difficult, even long after the events in question. But it is clear that the occupation was brutal, if uneven in its administration and effect.

Iraqi objectives in this invasion were unclear, as mentioned. If Iraq's ultimate aim was the limited one of embarrassing Kuwait, securing the Rumeilah fields, and opening a water route to the Gulf, then Iraq overcommitted in its efforts and prompted a stronger response from the international community than was necessary. On the other hand, if Iraq's ultimate objectives included the annexation of Kuwait or even the seizure of the major Saudi oil fields in its eastern province, then its decision to take up defensive positions along the Saudi border signaled either a strategic miscalculation or a failure of nerve. Either way, the levels of force involved in the Iraqi invasion of Kuwait convinced the major world powers that Iraq was involved in a dangerous game that demanded a full and effective response.

The response to the invasion was not long in coming. Economic embargoes against Iraq were quickly put in place by the United States, the European Economic Community, and Japan. On August 6, the UN Security Council ordered a worldwide embargo on trade with Iraq. These actions were initially symbolic, since economic processes are relatively slow to respond to changes in rules. But in the long run the economic punishment of Iraq took a great toll, particularly on the nonmilitary populations. And by August 9, one week after Iraq's invasion, troops from the United States and other Saudi allies began to materialize on the border with Kuwait.

The United States took the leading role in confronting the Iraqi threat. President Bush, working chiefly through the United Nations, orchestrated a multinational response. The number of foreign troops in Saudi Arabia rose steadily in the fall of 1990, until they could in fact credibly contain an Iraqi attack. Desert Shield, as the exercise was named, built quickly, reaching a level of roughly one-half million men by December of 1990. By the time of the offensive against Iraq their number had grown to in excess of 715,000 troops. Approximately one-half of the troops were from U.S. forces, with the remainder drawn from Saudi Arabia, the U.A.E., Britain, France, Egypt, Syria, Italy, Morocco, Bangladesh, and a symbolically important contingent of Kuwaiti troops in exile.

Iraq, during this period, continued to reinforce its positions along the Kuwaiti and Saudi borders, substantially hardening its placements with extensive earthworks, minefields, and modern trench facilities. The elite Republican Guards were placed to the north, along the Iraqi-Kuwaiti border, in position to maneuver against invading forces. Diplomatic initiatives from a variety of sources, including France and the Soviet Union, failed to persuade Saddam Hussein of the seriousness of the coalition facing him, and as the new year dawned, "Desert Shield" changed into "Desert Storm."

The coalition facing Iraq broke new ground in Middle Eastern coalition building. Working under the legitimizing mandate of a series of UN resolutions, President Bush assembled a group of most unlikely partners. Indeed, any political coalition including Syria and the conservative monarchies of the region would have previously been considered unthinkable. For that matter, for the United States and Syria to be working partners would have stretched credibility even further, given persistent efforts by the United States to brand Syria a "terrorist state" and Syria's ongoing attempts to portray the United States as a "colonialist-Zionist" state.

For all of these states to work harmoniously with Egypt, Algeria, and Turkey further stretched political credibility. And for these former colonial states to consider military cooperation with France, Great Britain, and Italy against another Arab-Muslim state also seemed farfetched. But such a coalition was indeed assembled and did indeed endure—for no nation in that coalition was prepared to countenance Saddam Hussein's Iraq

Table 14-1   Coalition Members with Forces Committed at the Start of Desert Storm

United States	Bangladesh
Britain	Morocco
France	Oman
Saudi Arabia	Niger
Egypt	Pakistan
Syria	Qatar
Kuwait	Senegal
Bahrain	United Arab Emirates

as the dominant military and economic power of the region. Ultimately, sixteen nations contributed ground forces to the war (see Table 14-1).

The absence of Israel from the U.S.-led coalition was crucial to its stability. The Bush administration recognized from the start the symbolic importance of Israeli nonparticipation in this unprecedented coalition. This necessitated a diplomatic high-wire act as the United States moved to reassure both Israel and its enemies simultaneously. This was done with mixed success, particularly within Israel, where calls for direct action against Iraq increased geometrically with each SCUD missile launched against Israel. Although the SCUDs did little actual damage, the psychological impact was great. The government of Israel paid a relatively high price domestically for its perceived passivity in this conflict.

Multinational Actors in the Conflict

As alluded to earlier in this discussion, international organizations were major actors in the confrontation. The United Nations, acting under the guidance of the Security Council, took an active role in confronting Iraq's hostile action. And the United States, careful to assure that its actions were either anticipated or approved by UN resolution, clearly legitimized its military and diplomatic response to Iraq.

Among the key UN initiatives were the following resolutions:

660 (August 2, 1990): calls upon Iraq to immediately withdraw from Kuwait.

661 (August 6, 1990): reminds all member states of their obligation to deny financial or economic resources to Iraq (embargo).

662 (August 9, 1990): rejects Iraq's annexation of Kuwait as illegal.

665 (August 25, 1990): invites member states to implement embargo and engage in necessary military action using Military Staff Committee of the United Nations.

These resolutions and the others that followed internationally legitimized the coalition response to Iraq's aggression. But other international organizations also provided legitimation and support to the effort. NATO provided key logistical and political support, although informally, from the opening days of the crisis.[3] Other organizations joined in the chorus of condemnation: the Organization of African Unity, August 3; Gulf Cooperation Council, August 3; Organization of the Islamic Conference, August 5; League of Arab States, August 10. These organizations, representing the opinions of variously Arab, Muslim, and Third World states, contributed immeasurably to the legitimacy of the U.S.-led opposition and greatly reduced the value of Iraq's invocations of Muslim and Arab unity.[4] Finally, the United States and the Soviet Union proclaimed joint resolutions condemning the attack, demonstrating a commonality of purpose among the world's two superpowers. The Soviet government followed these statements with diplomatic missions to Baghdad attempting to dissuade Iraq from staying in Kuwait. The government of Iraq rejected numerous efforts to arrange a nonviolent withdrawal from Kuwait.

Iraq was able to muster formal support only from Libya and the PLO. Jordan, caught in the middle between its two most important economic partners, attempted to play the role of mediator and failed in this attempt. Branded a collaborator by the coalition leadership, Jordan paid an extremely high economic and political price for its attempted neutrality. Iran, officially opposed to the annexation of Kuwait, waited to take

---

[3] It is unlikely that U.S. forces could have moved into the region in such a short time without the logistical support of NATO, or without NATO's willingness to allow great reductions in its forces and supplies in Europe.

[4] For example, Saddam Hussein's repeated attempts to invoke jihad were blunted by the refusal of other Islamic authorities to recognize the legitimacy of his claim.

advantage of the coming storm. The isolation of Iraq was complete.

Desert Storm

The coalition against Iraq went on the offensive in January of 1991. Under the UN resolutions, the allies were justified in forcibly ejecting Iraq from Kuwait and restoring the previous government. They were even required to do so. Hostilities began with an air campaign on January 16, 1991, utilizing the latest technologies in "smart" weaponry and some of the heaviest concentrations of "dumb" technology since World War II. Air supremacy was quickly established over Iraq, and what followed was a "turkey shoot" of unprecedented intensity. In the first week of the air war, over 10,000 sorties were flown, punishing Iraq day and night. Well over 80,000 tons of munitions were dropped.

The air war was covered from Baghdad by the surviving staffs of U.S. news networks, most notably CNN. This time the world was privy to war from the perspective of the pilot and his targets. The viewing public was shown the thorough destruction of Iraqi infrastructure, particularly in communication and transportation. Careful censorship in the coalition staging areas kept the official images technical and clinical, while the images streaming from Baghdad and other media sources supplemented this with endless footage of death and destruction.

As the air assaults continued and Iraqi antiaircraft capability was suppressed, B-52 raids were initiated, targeted against major economic and military targets, including power plants and suspected military production facilities, and increasingly against the dug-in troops on the Saudi border. The unknowns regarding Iraq's rumored chemical, biological, and nuclear programs prompted an ever-broadening range of targets. The result, as inevitable as it was distasteful, was increasing loss of life among the civilians in Iraq. The totals of noncombatant losses in the air war will probably never be known, but certainly number in the tens of thousands. When combined with those who died in the coming land war, and from the effects of the war on water, food, and sanitation facilities, total Iraqi losses may have been as high as 200,000.

The duration and savagery of the five-and-one-half-week air campaign was conditioned by expectations that the following air-land battle would be long and bloody. Many analysts expected the land war to run for weeks and to generate high casualties on both sides. The Iraqi army, supposedly seasoned by a decade of high-intensity war with Iran, was considered a formidable adversary, particularly the elite Republic Guards held in the theater rear. Another factor for caution was based on Iraq's previous use of chemical weapons in the war with Iran. Iraq also possessed a large number of tanks and impressive numbers of long-range artillery, along with sophisticated munitions for both of these systems. Further pause was given by Iraq's mining of most of the Kuwaiti oil fields and wellheads and its progressive firing of those charges as attack became imminent.

Given these expectations, the land phase of the battle for Kuwait was something of a disappointment. Begun on February 24, coalition forces were able in short order to breach the vaunted Iraqi defenses. The heavily dug-in Iraqi forces were not able to maneuver and were systematically destroyed by highly mobile forces using more sophisticated technology. In fact, most U.S. losses in the land phase of the battle came from "friendly fire." At any rate, the Iraqi forces were quickly surrounded and a major rout of the Iraqi army ensued. Within only four days of battle, Kuwait was rid of its occupying army and was in the process of restoring its government and civil services. Iraqi troops streamed north, using whatever transport was available. The slaughter along the highway north was so complete that it was called a "turkey shoot" by knowledgeable military analysts. The Iraqi army in Kuwait was in danger of annihilation.

With the southern quarter of Iraq occupied, a cease-fire was negotiated permitting the withdrawal of the defeated Iraqi troops. Desert Storm had succeeded in expelling Iraq from Kuwait and in reestablishing Kuwait's legal government. There was great optimism in the West and considerable chaos and despair in Baghdad. Kurdish rebels in the north of Iraq and Shia groups in the south began secessionist struggles. Informed opinion awaited the inevitable coup deposing Saddam Hussein and the establishment of a government that would attempt to negotiate with the coalition leadership.

The end-game of Desert Storm was disappointing to those who expected and wanted a thoroughgoing destruction of both Iraq's military establishment and the leadership of Saddam Hussein. But in fact, the expulsion of Iraq from Kuwait and the reestablishment of the as-Sabah government satisfied the letter of the UN resolutions. The coalition itself had not defined its role further and it is not clear that the political will existed for the final action against Iraq. What was a clear and signal military victory eventually transformed itself into a typical political quagmire.

The Middle East at the End of Desert Storm

As Desert Storm blew itself out over the deserts of the Middle East, the political, economic, and military contours of the region had changed. Iraq was no longer the dominant military power in the region, although its military plant had by no means been eliminated. But Iraq, still ruled by Saddam Hussein and the Baath Party, had been profoundly damaged in the conflict. Disease and famine began to take its toll of the weakest in the country, mostly the children and elderly across all group and ethnic spectrums. As many as 100,000 Iraqis may have died from the war and its direct and indirect effects. Reliable figures will probably never be known.

Economically, both Iraq and Kuwait were exhausted. Neither was pumping significant amounts of oil, and in Kuwait over 700 burning oil wells created a nightmarish ecological disaster. The long-term effects on the atmosphere are unknown, as is the long-term effect of the intentional oil spill on the northern Gulf. But the short-term effects were obvious: Life in Kuwait was a bronchial nightmare for the first six months following the war. If the prevailing winds did not clear the air, Kuwait was darkened at noon, with a reddish sun barely able to penetrate the rising plumes of smoke and gas. Great lakes of pooling oil and petroleum byproducts dotted the landscape. Fires ringed the capital city, stretching out to the horizon. Kuwaiti nationals returned to a country transformed by the events of the war, changed from a center of leisure and luxury to a country where the basic necessities could not be guaranteed. As many as 10,000 Kuwaitis may have died in the war, of both direct and indirect effects. A good number had been tortured and executed in a short but brutal occupation.

Political life in Iraq at the end of the war was dogged by uncertainties. The cease-fire agreement did not incorporate domestic political changes into its terms. Air and land surveillance by the coalition and by the United Nations proceeded in fits and starts, with agreements often negotiated on the scene on an ad hoc basis. The search for Iraq's "weapons of mass destruction" turned up development programs of impressive size and complexity. As the government of Iraq attempted to implement a "shell game," hiding basic facilities from the inspectors, coalition leaders threatened the renewal of hostilities unless a measure of cooperation was extended. Coalition forces were forced to offer support and supplies to the Kurdish refugees fleeing in the north of Iraq and through narrow mountain passes into Iran and Turkey. Iran and Saudi Arabia were forced to give similar support to the Shia rebels in the south. In the long run, it would appear, the coalition allies had little stomach for the creation of independent Kurdish or Shia states on their own borders. In this situation, the plight of many refugees became desperate.

In summary, an elegantly executed military confrontation against a clear danger succeeded, only to produce an outcome of great ambiguity and frustration. Many of these factors were embedded in the very nature of the new international order.

Desert Storm as Indicator of New International Realities

To what degree did the Iraq-Kuwait crisis demonstrate the emergence of a new international system? Let us apply our observations from earlier in this discussion.

First, did the event show the disappearance of the old bipolar order and the emergence of a multipolar world? Certainly it did in the absence of an influential role for the former Soviet Union. The U.S.S.R. clearly responded to the initiatives of the United States and its coalition partners. Soviet military power was not engaged in the conflict and never became an important factor in the strategic or tactical implementation of Desert Storm. The minimum standards of bipolar interest or confrontation were not demonstrated in the diplomacy or the military phase of the conflict. Only in the waning months of the century did Russia speak again in favor of its old ally, Iraq, calling for an end to economic sanctions and an end to the UN-sponsored inspections of its military facilities. This support, while significant, and augmented by European concerns for the future of Iraq, did nothing to change the overall situation facing the Iraqis.

Second, the multipolar nature of international power was demonstrated. States from a variety of alliances and regions were involved directly and indirectly in Desert Storm. The U.S. leadership found it both expedient and desirable to maintain a coalition of disparate members. It would be a distortion to call the operation a "U.S. effort." Members of the coalition demonstrated political independence during the crisis, often at the displeasure of the United States. The role of France, Germany, and the U.S.S.R. in last-minute attempts to persuade a peaceful Iraqi withdrawal are cases in point.

By 1998, the United States was joined only by Great Britain in its efforts to penalize Iraq for expelling the UN weapons inspectors (Operation Desert Fox, December 1998). And in point of fact, from 1998 on, the United States engaged in a lonely war of attrition against Iraq with daily flyovers and weekly limited bombing of Iraqi facilities: a quiet war of attrition against Iraq with declining international support and even less international visibility.

Third, the role of international organizations in Desert Storm was of critical importance. The UN played an indispensable role in legitimizing the use of force against Iraq. Without UN sanctions, the presence of U.S., British, French, and Italian troops in the Middle East would have precipitated powerful denunciations of neocolonial imperialism. The domestic consequences of participation for the Egyptian, Syrian, and North African gov-

ernments might have been disastrous. As it developed, however, their participation in the coalition did not result in widespread or effective domestic opposition.

In a different way, NATO played a key role. It is unlikely that the United States could have managed the concentration of troops and materials in the Gulf in such a short time on its own. Although it acted unofficially, NATO not only released large quantities of munitions and supplies from storage, but coordinated the transportation of these supplies to the region. NATO staffers worked hard to identify the location of key technical equipment (chemical "sniffer" tanks, for instance) and make them available to U.S. procurement officers.

NATO was supportive in other ways as well. NATO staff provided much-needed intelligence to the coalition forces. And NATO command, communication, and control procedures were used to coordinate the naval blockade of Iraq and Jordan and the tremendous complexity of the air campaign, allowing fighters and bombers of six nations to fly in and out of Iraqi air space without mishap as many as 2,000 times (sorties) a day. Nato's indirect experiences in the Iraqi campaign were important precursors of NATO's subsequent interventions in Bosnia (1996) and Kosovo (1999), both under the legitimizing umbrella of the United Nations.

Other international organizations were important to the effort. The Islamic Conference was an important element in keeping the confrontation secular and in discrediting Saddam Hussein's efforts to link the conflict to religious issues. The Organization of African Unity was important in defusing the charge of yet another neocolonial intrusion into the area. And the Arab League effectively kept the issue of Arab unity out of the conflict. From the start of the conflict, international organizations were fully in play. And it is very clear that their activities were responsible for much of the color and texture of Desert Shield–Desert Storm.

Regional actors also were important factors in the crisis. The response of the Gulf Cooperation Council to the Iraqi invasion was key in catalyzing the initial response to Iraq's invasion. The GCC forces sent to the Saudi border were important beyond the significance of the troops. It also signaled the marshaling of very significant international financial resources in the conflict, resources that underwrote U.S. expenses and promised political and economic support to Egypt and Syria. The crisis tested the commitment of the U.A.E., Bahrain, Qatar, and Oman to the GCC and in the final result raised it to a new level of importance in political and economic coordination of these states. The GCC has expanded its role subsequent to Desert Storm, embracing solutions for regional disputes among its neighbors and beginning the first steps toward economic integration, particularly in the establishment of a GCC customs union.

The European Community was important in its early boycott against Iraq, and in its tacit approval of NATO's informal but key role in logistical support for the coalition. Proposals for a European-led rapid deployment force within NATO got a real head of steam from the crisis and the European Union is now engaged in the development of a multilateral military force. This will contribute substantially to the political independence of this new regional international actor.

Nor should U.S.-Canadian regional integration be overlooked. Working largely through its NATO force commitments, Canada was shoulder to shoulder with the coalition in the crisis, particularly politically and in the naval blockade. Cooperation between Canada and the United States is nothing new, but the vitality of this regional integration deserves some emphasis, particularly as Mexico moves into alignment with the two. At any rate, regional actors were conspicuous in the crisis.

Nongovernmental international actors were also present and involved. The International Red Cross–Red Crescent worked both sides in the conflict, handling international relief efforts and the exchange of hostages and military captives. Amnesty International documented the outrages committed in the occupation of Kuwait. American Friends of the Middle East provided emergency relief to refugees occasioned by the war and to the endangered public in Iraq at the end of the war. Nongovernmental international agencies have proliferated in the last two decades of the century. They are increasingly relied on by governments for back-door channels to opposing powers. And

they may in fact be more capable of providing relief to endangered populations than their own governments. Certainly, the Kurds have received as much help in their plight from these nongovernmental actors as from their own governments. Many analysts see these institutions as key actors in the future we all face.

Global interdependence was demonstrated in the Gulf crisis in a number of ways. First and foremost, the vulnerability of the world to disruption in petroleum supplies was obvious. To many analysts, the crisis was simply another manifestation of the world's dependence on a shrinking supply of petroleum. Second, the environmental effects of the war on the atmosphere and on the Gulf itself suggest our interdependence and vulnerability. The long-term effects of the environmental damage will not be known for some time, although it seems clear enough that the predictions of environmental catastrophe at the global level did not occur. On the other hand, global environmental systems are complex and poorly understood. It is likely that some effect was occasioned by the burning of many billions of barrels of oil and cubic feet of gas, and there was real damage to the fisheries of the Gulf.

The type and quality of weaponry on both sides demonstrate the inexorable diffusion of technology around the world. The acquisition of "weapons of mass destruction" has somehow been democratized. No longer must a nation be a superpower to pretend to chemical, biological, nuclear, or high-tech weaponry. The postwar documentation of Iraq's nuclear development program showed efforts of great sophistication—"world class physics," in the words of one UN inspector. Iraq was possibly less than a year or two away from the assembly of a workable atomic weapon. And Iraq had a credible armory of other high-tech weapons, including cluster bombs and fuel-air bombs. It had independently modified the primitive Soviet SCUD missiles for longer-range and larger warheads. It is a mystery of the war why these weapons were not deployed or used to better effect. But in the larger sense of things, Iraq's armory suggests that technological diffusion is one of the prominent realities of the new world order. And only multilateral international initiatives have the muscle to deal with them.

The UN-sanctioned boycott against Iraqi oil sales and ongoing UN investigations of Iraqi efforts to acquire weapons of mass destruction kept Iraq and its regime on the defensive many years after Desert Storm. Although some neighboring Gulf states have supported a reduction in the sanctions on humanitarian grounds, joined by Russia, France, and China, Iraq continues to be a subject of multinational international intervention. Combined with the UN roles in Haiti, Bosnia, and Kosovo. it would be difficult to argue that multinational influence in world politics has declined.

The crisis certainly demonstrated the phenomenon of instantaneous international communication. Saddam Hussein and President Bush were able to engage in an international game of name-calling in "real time." Negotiations in Geneva were presented to the world as they occurred (and failed). And the conduct of the war itself was presented in the most complete detail, in spite of the efforts of both sides to control and censor the flow of information. Charges of treason against CNN for its continuing coverage of events from Iraq only demonstrate the significance of that coverage. *Time Magazine* anointed CNN founder Ted Turner as its "1991 Man of the Year" in recognition of these new realities. Consider also the emergence of Middle East Broadcasting Center, a new non-national cable news organization that is broadcasting all over the Arab world. Known to its viewers as MBC, and owned principally by Saudi investors, the service seeks to imitate the success of U.S. networks in providing relatively unbiased news coverage. It now broadcasts to over 300 million potential Arab viewers without government censorship or control. And Al-Jazeerah, a satellite service based in Qatar, has set new standards for independent journalism in the Arab world.

Many alternative news sources and technologies (specialized news services utilizing satellite transmission, fax, phone, VCR, audio cassettes, even print) exist now. The images they produce, whether of the whimsy of a smart bomb pursuing a fleeing truck into its garage or of the horror of men, women, and children incinerated together in a concrete shelter, all affect our worldview. It is conceivable that without the goad of international televised reports of their difficulties, the coalition partners would not have come to the aid of the Kurds or the Shia, or, for that matter, Bosnians or Kosovars. As many governments have found, it is difficult to prosecute war in the light of television cameras. Russian attempts to limit or control coverage of the suppression of the Chechen rebels in 1995 and 2000 are a case in point, and Russia lost an element of independence from the widespread knowledge of what was transpiring in Grozny. A state can assume the luxury of privacy in fewer and fewer places.

Regional conflicts did not go away as a consequence of Desert Storm. There are still points of conflict between many of the coalition partners. Syria and Turkey have problems along their mutual borders that include both people (Kurds, again) and resources (water, in particular). Turkey and Iran continue to compete for economic and political advantage in the Muslim republics of central Asia. Saudi Arabia is still engaged in a hostile relationship with Yemen. Bahrain claims evidence of Iranian encouragement of its domestic dissidents. The U.A.E. has lost two small islands in the Gulf to Iranian seizure. Qatar continued in its efforts to change its borders with Bahrain and Saudi Arabia. Egypt was outraged over the 1995 attempt by Sudanese extremists to assassinate President Mubarak on a trip to Ethiopia. Most Arab states still find themselves in disagreement with Israel over the future of Jerusalem and the meaning of "autonomy" for the Palestinians.

Regional conflicts have in fact been exaggerated in the wake of the 1991 Gulf crisis, as Iraq was taken out of the regional military equation. At any rate, although we may see new axes of regional conflict, conflict itself has not declined. The world is still a dangerous place. In 2000 more than thirty "small" wars smoldered on around the world.

The conflict of rich against poor is also not solved in the region. In many ways, the conflict may have been intensified. The oil-rich states of the Gulf are under continued pressure to share their wealth with their poorer and more populous neighbors. One can make a point that the political stability of Egypt, Syria, and Jordan, all with few natural resources and fast-growing populations, can only be assured with substantial subsidies from the rich and developed nations. Failure to provide this aid will most likely result in increasing demands for a more equitable world order. The recovery of international petroleum prices at the turn of the century has done much to aggravate the sense of distance between the haves and have-nots of the region.

Finally, is there an apparent "domestication of the international" apparent in the postcrisis Middle East? Whether new or not, all governments seem to have international policies complicated by domestic concerns. Can a Muslim political leader sign an accord that will leave Jerusalem in Israeli hands? Can any government of Israel surrender most of the West Bank to Palestinian control, evacuate Jewish settlers from Hebron, or return the Golan to Syria without consequence? Can the successors of Prime Minister Rabin avoid continued domestic violence? Can the United States, for any reason, countenance a dramatic reduction in the supply of Middle East petroleum to the Western industrial system? Can any country in the region countenance the surrender of its water resources to an international or regional water authority, no matter how independent or scrupulously fair it might be? The answer, superficially at least, is a resounding "no." Domestic opposition would be fierce in any of these cases.

And yet there are examples of leaders and governments ignoring these consequences and plunging ahead. Foreign policy may be severely constrained by domestic considerations, and vice versa. But the stakes are too high to allow such simplification. Leaders must live with these constraints and work around them as well. The Gulf crisis resolved the question of Iraq's attempted annexation of Kuwait. But it left most other regional conflicts alive and kicking. How they are dealt with will be a crucial indicator of the real direction of life in the changing international system.

This rough survey suggests that events are moving in the direction of a new world order and increased global interdependence as we have loosely defined it. If this is true, these new realities should have manifested themselves in the most intractable of Middle East conflicts: the five-decade-old dispute between Israel and the Arabs. And in fact, it has.

THE ARABS AND THE ISRAELIS

One of the most telling criticisms of the U.S.-led coalition in Desert Storm was its inability or unwillingness to spell out its ultimate objectives. One analyst of the crisis catalogued no less than fifteen major reasons for the effort, as articulated by President Bush. These justifications ranged from ensuring international oil supplies through the protection of American jobs to the "definition of the Bush presidency." Ultimately, of course, the coalition limited its objectives to the rather narrow goals of ejecting Iraq from Kuwait and reestablishing the al-Sabah government. This, of course, left many regional questions unanswered.

Chief of these questions concerned Israel and its occupation of Gaza, the West Bank, southern Lebanon, and the Golan Heights; and the very human question of the future of the Palestinians in Israel and in diaspora. Saddam Hussein, early in the conflict, attempted to link his action to the liberation of the Palestinians. Although the linkage was enthusiastically accepted by the PLO, it was universally rejected by the governments of the coalition. Nonetheless, a widespread public expectation existed in the area that the same principles that invalidated Iraq's annexation of Kuwait also applied to Israel. In other words, many in the Arab publics expected the coalition to apply similar pressure and energy to the solution of the Israeli-Palestinian question. To do less would be to publicly endorse a double standard, one for Arab states, the other for Israel.

Analysts have long considered the Arab-Israeli conflict to be primary in the Middle Eastern system. No other important issues could be settled without or before progress on this issue. And, in fact, the issue has been remarkably persistent and pervasive. For this reason, it was deemed very important when President Bush in his March 1991 address to Congress included "justice for the Palestinian people" in his list of objectives for the postcrisis Middle East.

President Bush soon acted on this new initiative, sending Secretary of State Baker to the

Middle East to enlist the coalition partners in a new effort to resolve the Arab-Israeli conflict. Between April and October, Secretary Baker formally visited the region at least eight times, shuttling patiently between Israel, Syria, Jordan, and Egypt. Ultimately, Syria and Israel proved to be the most intransigent of the principals involved; and, of course, the shadow of the PLO hovered over most of these discussions and negotiations.

President Bush eventually prevailed in his efforts to convene a multilateral Middle Eastern Peace Conference. The first session of the conference was held in Madrid in November of 1991. And the mere convening of such a conference indicated international diplomacy of a high and intensive nature. How was the United States able to bring these adversaries to the table, in spite of their bitter history and long memories?

It is clear in retrospect that President Bush interpreted the success of Desert Storm as a mandate to go further in solving Middle Eastern problems. Bush and Baker took advantage of this postwar environment by embarking on a series of very high-level diplomatic conversations, conversations so private that even the upper-level bureaucrats of the foreign policy establishments were in the dark as to what was agreed upon. One meeting between Secretary Baker and President Assad reportedly continued for eight hours with no breaks for relief or refreshment. At the end of the marathon, letters were exchanged between Baker and Assad, the contents and assurances therein known only to their most loyal and intimate advisors. In this way, domestic reaction to the negotiated points was minimized.

The most serious problem—the unwillingness of Israel to sit at any table populated in any way by the PLO—was overcome by a two-track approach. On one level, Jordan agreed to include a Palestinian component in its delegation to the conference. This met historical Israeli preferences. On the other track, the United States identified and encouraged the creation of an indigenous Palestinian leadership independent of the PLO. Although in fact such an indigenous elite already existed in the occupied territories, they were for the most part contaminated in Israeli eyes by their association with Arafat and the PLO. The fiction of an independent Palestinian negotiating team was accomplished by the expedient of selecting Palestinians of high educational and humanitarian accomplishments. The head of the Palestinian segment of the Jordanian delegation, for example, was the distinguished and long-term head of the Gaza Red Cross–Red Crescent, Dr. Haider abdul-Shafi. One by one, a delegation acceptable to even the most hard-line Israeli official was assembled. It is also clear that the legitimacy of the delegation in the Palestinian community in the occupied territories was based on their support of the intifadah, a revolution that occurred beyond the direct control of the PLO.

We should not minimize the significance of this accomplishment. Much of the sympathy in Israel for the plight of the Palestinians had evaporated as Palestinian support for Iraq became apparent. Palestinians cheering the SCUDS from their rooftops effectively destroyed the Israeli peace movement. And the Gulf crisis also provided the government of Israel with a pretext to clamp down tightly on the Palestinian community with a brutal six-week curfew. Both of these actions greatly increased the tension and distrust between the Israeli and Palestinian communities.

It is also clear in hindsight that the United States was willing to use both the carrot and the stick in motivating conference participants. Syria was exonerated in the bombing of Pan Am Flight 103, a boost to Syrian prestige, and financial incentives flowed from the Gulf states to Damascus. Israel received compensation for SCUD damage received in the war and an increased flow of U.S. weapons to the IDF. The Soviet Union extended formal diplomatic relations to Israel, improving the prospects of emigration for many Soviet Jews. These carrots were important in Israeli and Syrian calculations.

Among the sticks applied were these. For Syria, there would be no postwar subsidies if it failed to come to the table and the end of a warming relationship with Washington. In the case of Israel, the Bush administration successfully withheld U.S. loans in the amount of $10 billion, dedicated to the settlement and housing of Soviet refugees in Israel, subject to Israeli participation in a peace conference. The Israeli lobby in the United States raised a furious objection to this linkage, but the Bush administration held firm and prevailed. In the opinion of many analysts,[5] this was the first and only example of an American president since 1948 successfully standing up to the Israeli lobby.

Another important carrot presented to Israel was the possible revocation of UN Assembly Resolution 3379 (1975), which equated Zionism with racism. This resolution had long poisoned Israel's relationship with the United Nations, and its promised removal would constitute a considerable gain in prestige for the government of Israel, both at home and abroad. After Israeli participation in two early phases of the peace conference, in Madrid and Washington, the resolution was indeed revoked under U.S. leadership. And although most Middle Eastern and Muslim governments voted against revocation, the motion passed easily. Although the measure in both instances was largely symbolic, the symbolism was important. The aggressive role of the United States in its revocation was an important article of faith between the United States and Israel at a time when many other issues divided them.

It is also important to realize that certain positions were not abandoned. Israel, for instance, not only refused to slow down or cease its settlement policy in the West Bank and Gaza, but it seemed to time the announcement of new settlements to coincide with Secretary Baker's visits. Prime Minister Shamir, moreover, never retrenched on his refusal to concede the "land for peace" formula that implicitly undergirded the conference premise and refused in any way to discuss the future status of Jerusalem or to countenance any withdrawal from the Golan. Syria, for its part, insisted that Israeli withdrawal from the Golan was a prerequisite to peace and continued its support of Palestinian movements independent of and opposed to the PLO. It also continued to press its case that Yitzhak Shamir was himself a terrorist, involved in the assassination of UN peacekeeping officials and the murder of Palestinian noncombatants in the 1948 war. For the Palestinians, the intifadah did not end, although its intensity was reduced. And the independent Palestinian delegation publicly voiced its sympathy for the PLO as

the appropriate representative of the Palestinian nation. By and large, these reservations and obstructions were ignored by U.S. diplomats. Even a small number of gratuitous acts of terror by Israeli and Palestinian extremists failed to derail the opening session in Madrid.

In fact, U.S. hopes for the conference were both practical and visionary. In the most practical sense, U.S. decision makers placed great hope in the process of negotiation, in and of itself. The momentum of the conference itself, undergirded by the privately assured carrots and sticks, would be hard to overcome. Thus, once the principals came to the table they would find it increasingly difficult to leave. International pressure, domestic public opinion, and the hopes of finding real solutions to intractable problems would also provide incentive to stay with the process.

In terms of idealism and vision, the conference structure suggested coming to terms with a wide variety of regional issues. While highly ceremonial conferences on the big issues of peace and war took place, lower-level bilateral discussions and negotiations between Israel and Lebanon, Syria, Jordan, and the Palestinians, respectively, were to consider many important specific questions. Among them were regional arms control, nuclear proliferation and reduction, the return of occupied territories for guarantees of peace, land and autonomy for the Palestinians, water rights and distribution, regional environmental problems (of which there are many), and possible economic cooperation.

There was a frustrating aspect to these "successful" postwar peace conferences. In particular, this frustration was based on the realization that successful negotiations would be played out over a long period of time. Months, even years, would denominate the success of the effort. Moreover, early agreements often turned out to be difficult to implement. Consider the widely heralded Camp David accords of 1978. By the late 1980s it was widely conceded that the accords had produced a "cold peace," a reduction of conflict but not the hoped-for developments economically, culturally, or politically. For in the compressed and critical space that is the Middle East, finding common solutions to long-standing problems involves the development of common trust. This rarely comes

---

[5] See, for example, the article by Tom Friedman, *New York Times,* October 6, 1991, p. E3.

quickly, and sometimes not at all. History is full of failed peace efforts.

On a more positive note, it is almost always better to talk than to make war. If an emergent consensus on the desirability of peace in the Middle East is one of the factors in the emerging international order, then the nations, international organizations, nongovernmental organizations, and information media will continue to keep pressure on the principals in the conflict. And progress may in fact occur. It is important to note that the progress made through 1992 would have been in fact unthinkable in the depths of the preceding bipolar world order. So some optimism was in fact justified. In the fits and starts of discussions between old enemies, there was some room for hope. A report of the United States Institute of Peace put the situation succinctly:

> Arab and Israeli leaders will finally sign if and when they become persuaded that they have more to lose if agreement slips away. They then demand a panoply of extra "side" benefits to help justify to their domestic constituencies the concessions they have made. Only a major power, in fact only the United States can now meet this need, which helps to explain why the United States remains uniquely acceptable as the essential third-party mediator for the Arab-Israeli conflict.[6]

In fact, the authors of the preceding quote got it both right and wrong. The Israelis and Palestinians did subsequently begin a process of substantive negotiations. But, in fact, the United States was less a player in this process than the authors anticipated.

From Jerusalem to Oslo

The dramatic signing of the peace accords in Washington in 1993 was less a confirmation of U.S. international influence and more a testimony to the growing influence of smaller states and nongovernmental organizations, and a graphic demonstration of the changing international system. Frustration with the idea of the United States as an

[6] Kenneth W. Stein and Samuel W. Lewis, with Sheryl J. Brown, *Making Peace Among Arabs and Israelis* (Washington, D.C.: U.S. Institute of Peace, 1991), p. 31.

honest broker between the parties led Itzhak Rabin and Yasir Arafat to engage in secret negotiations in Oslo, Norway, in the spring of 1993. In retrospect, it appears that a common recognition between the antagonists that the United States could not be counted on to provide the incentives for an even-handed solution led the leadership to accept previously unacceptable.

For Prime Minister Rabin, the unacceptable meant face-to-face meetings with the PLO and its leadership, with the notion of some measure of autonomy for the Palestinian people. For the Palestinian leadership and Chairman Arafat, the unthinkable was the end of military resistance toward Israel, the elimination of the goal of the destruction of Israel from the Palestinian National Charter, and the acceptance of a status considerably removed from independent statehood. Facing a situation threatening the survival of Israel as a Jewish state and the possible elimination of any future state for the people of Palestine, two hardened players in the toughest international game glared at each other across the negotiating table. The master of the game, the dealer so to speak, was not the United States of America but tiny Norway, a Scandinavian state with little direct interest in the Middle East. In this effort, Norway was assisted by representatives of a large number of international nongovernmental organizations and other peace-committed groups. The negotiations came as quite a surprise to the great powers of the world.

The product of the first Oslo negotiations (Oslo 1, 1993) and a second set of negotiations in 1995 (Oslo 2) was a set of fuzzy objectives accompanied by broad timetables for their completion. In fact, few of the objectives were implemented as originally conceived; and only a few met the original deadlines. That said, in a general way the objectives agreed on in Oslo and symbolically ratified in Washington have been implemented. Chairman Arafat and his government in exile did return to Gaza and Jericho. Palestinian policemen, trained in Jordan and subsidized by great-power donors, deployed progressively over about 30 percent of the West Bank and Gaza. Palestinian principals took over the management of schools, Palestinian doctors took responsibility for Palestinian health care. And Israeli and Palestinian extremists did their best to undermine the implementation of the agreements.

Some actions carried more symbolic weight than others. Bus bombings and political murders combined with public demonstrations and political resistance to polarize the polities of both Israel and Palestine. Two events merit mention, since they both had the potential to set the process back considerably. The first was the assassination of Prime Minister Rabin in November of 1995, by a young Jewish extremist. The subsequent investigation of the murder revealed the extent to which this murder occurred in a context of political extremism, including secret and violent organizations among Israel's settler groups. And it demonstrated the implacable opposition of some groups in Israel to the very idea of returning land for peace, the key formula in the Oslo agreements.

Many observers of these events expected this to slow the peace process as Israel sorted out the political implications of the event. In effect, the peace process seems to have gained momentum in the aftermath, as Shimon Peres succeeded to Rabin's position and used the opportunity to confirm the integrity of the peace process. Public opinion polls showed a considerable change in Israeli public opinion, in favor of continuing the process. There was also evident a deepening cleavage between those supporting the process and those opposing it. Unseemly celebrations of Rabin's assassination by extremist settlers and American Zionist radicals contributed to this polarization. Most significantly, Palestinian elections, previously scheduled for January of 1996, went forward.

The Palestinian elections of 1996 elected eighty-eight members of a new Palestinian National Council and ratified Yasir Arafat as president of the Palestinian National Authority. The election, monitored closely by representatives from interested foreign governments and international nongovernmental organizations (ex-President Jimmy Carter, for example), was an important step in the transformation of Arafat and the PLO into something other than a simple opponent of Israel. It conferred not only a small measure of real political power on the new institutions of Palestinian governance, but more important, it symbolically placed Arafat and the other Palestinian leaders in the role of government of-ficials, a reality not assumed in the original accords.

Any hopes that the Israeli election of May 1996 would provide more impetus to the evolving peace process were dashed with the narrow election of Binyamin Netanyahu as the prime minister and an even narrower victory for the Likud bloc in the Knesset. Netanyahu ran on a platform calling for greater Israeli security assurances in a dramatically slowed peace process and on a private reputation embedded in many speeches and articles expressing an uncompromising opposition to the return of any land for peace: The election of Netanyahu energized the domestic opposition to the peace process and greatly exaggerated the importance of the religious right in the Israeli government.

In the early days of his administration, Netanyahu reimposed many of the most oppressive of his predecessors' restrictions on the Palestinians in the West Bank and Gaza. Moreover, the government took many steps that seem in retrospect intentional efforts to marginalize the Palestinian leadership. The most controversial of these acts involved the opening of a tunnel beneath the ancient walls of the Temple Mount, bringing Israeli tourists within meters of the Al Aqsa Mosque and the Dome of the Rock. Prime Minister Rabin had declined to open this tunnel on the grounds that it would be extremely provocative to do so. The decision did turn out to be provocative and in fact became symbolic of a number of similar affronts to the Palestinians particularly and the peace process in general. Deadline after deadline, all agreed on in international treaties by previous Israeli governments, was postponed.

To most of those involved in the conflict, both inside and outside of Israel, the question of Hebron and the scheduled Israeli withdrawal from it was the most controversial issue. Hebron, claimed by both Jews and Palestinians as the burial place of their patriarch, Abraham (or Ibrahim), carries great symbolism for both sides. Both sides have experienced ethnic violence there; and both sides see it as a historically important place in the development of their respective ethnic and religious identities. Neither side, whether Palestinian Arab or Jewish settler, wants to see the site fall into the other's hands. This is particularly true of the 400-odd Jewish settlers living in the heart of Hebron, with the intention of reclaiming the city as Jewish. These settlers, among the most rigid and intransigent of Israel's radical religious right, became the living symbols of those Israelis rejecting the basic formula of "land for peace."

Hebron, and Israel's treaty obligations there, became the focus for intense domestic and international politics. The intersection of the domestic political system with the international system is clearly evident in the Hebron crises of 1996 and 1997. As such, the crises serve as evidence of the changing nature of the international system and the prospects and dangers these changes bring.

Nine months after the beginning of the new government, Israeli troops began a "redeployment," turning over 80 percent of Hebron to the control of the Palestinian Authority. Israel retained security responsibility for the area of the city containing its settler compounds and the Tomb of the Patriarchs. Numerous amendments to the original accords were agreed upon, most of which increased the rights of the Israeli government in the West Bank. But these gains were offset somewhat by Israel's agreements to a more definite schedule of withdrawal from other areas. Both sides claimed victory in the negotiations, and both sides still had failed to satisfy their most vehement domestic critics.

In agreeing to the substance of these renegotiations, Prime Minister Netanyahu bowed to a number of international realities. First and foremost, he bowed to the pressure of the great powers (particularly the United States) insistent on the continuation of the peace process and the observance of treaty obligations. He also bowed to the domestic security needs of Israel's nominal allies in the region, most notably Egypt and Jordan, whose domestic politics would not have received news of a peace collapse well. And finally, the prime minister bowed to the interests of his own political center, a large bloc of Israeli voters concerned both for increased security and for the continuation of the peace process.

President Arafat of the Palestinian Authority also bowed to many international realities. In accepting a deferred schedule of Israeli withdrawals from the West Bank, he compromised his legiti-

mate legal position in the interests of accommodation with his long-time enemies in Israel. In many ways, he has allowed the second-class status of his government to be ratified in international agreements. And he has made little or no formal progress toward recognition as an independent Palestine. For this, and for other reasons, he will continue to reap a harvest of invective and opposition from his own domestic opposition, most of whom accuse him of settling for too little in his negotiations with Israel.

Somewhat ironically, he shared with Prime Minister Netanyahu the dubious honor of becoming the focus of anger among his right-wing religious constituencies. If there is one thing that ties Hamas to Gush Emunim, it is their mutual hatred for the peace process and accommodation between Israeli and Palestinian.

The peace process had transformed the conflict between Israel and Palestine. It had in effect been institutionalized and transferred to the physical arena of Israel itself. Critics of the process, on both sides, pointed to large unanswered questions. For example, it was still left to decide whether independent statehood was the ultimate status for the Palestinians, or whether Israel would insist on some dependent autonomous condition. The important question of the right of return for Palestinians in the diaspora must be dealt with, a question of great importance to the some six million Palestinians living outside of Palestine. And the status of Jerusalem, a city holy to nearly two billion religious faithful of Jewish, Christian, and Islamic belief, has yet to be clarified.

The Israeli opposition to the peace process declared the surrender of land to the Palestinians a price too high to pay. The Palestinian opposition accused Arafat of taking a bad deal, one that continued Israeli domination of Palestine and penalized the Palestinian people. Arafat and Peres had the unenviable task of creating a silk purse.

The May 1999 Israeli elections swept Netanyahu and the Likud from power. In their stead, a Labor-led coalition brought former IDF General Ehud Barak to power as prime minister. Barak moved quickly to reassure his constituencies of his intention to reinvigorate the peace negotiations with the Palestinians, as well as his willingness to reengage Syria over the question of the Golan and the ultimate withdrawal of Israeli forces from the "security zone" established in Southern Lebanon. And in point of fact, Prime Minister Barak made uneven progress on all fronts in the first year of his administration.

During Barak's first year as prime minister, Israel completed most of the military withdrawals agreed upon in the Wye Plantation Accords of 1998 and suspended by the Netanyahu government. Some of the withdrawals were subject to continuing negotiations and maneuvers, but all in all, the large print in the accords was honored. Moreover, the Barak government began, in early 2000, face-to-face negotiations with the government of Syria over the status of the Golan region seized from Syria during the 1967 war. Like the West Bank, the Golan negotiations are complicated by the strategic importance of the Golan Heights, with its commanding view of western Syria; by the presence of nearly 20,000 Israeli settlers in the province; and by the importance of the region as a source of fresh water for both Israel and Syria. A land for peace formula will be very difficult to negotiate on the ground and still honor the security needs of both states. The United States is seen by both the Israeli and Syrian governments as a necessary presence in the negotiations, particularly since the final security arrangements will undoubtedly involve the presence of multilateral or U.S. forces on the site.

Barak, from the early days of his administration, attempted to move quickly toward the "final status" negotiations envisaged in Oslo and Wye. Here the questions of the status of Jerusalem, the right of return for Palestinian refugees, and the right of the Palestinians to declare a state on the West Bank and in Gaza would have to be engaged. These are sticky questions and only the most foolhardy analyst would predict the contours of a "final" peace accord between the Israelis and the Palestinians.

SUPERPOWERS AND GREAT POWERS

As we have previously noted, recent events have radically changed the configuration of the international system. Nowhere is that more noticeable than in the change of status among the superpowers. Neither the Commonwealth of Independent States nor Russia itself brings to bear on international events the power and/or prestige of its predecessor, the Soviet Union. That leaves the United States in a position as the only surviving superpower at the end of the bipolar era.

But that position is less than enviable because the United States now confronts a world in which unknown risk replaces the known threat. To be successful as a global power, the United States will have to make prudent judgments about just when and where its fundamental national interest is at risk. To do otherwise, to jump about the globe from crisis to crisis and conflict to conflict irrespective of their importance invites a fate similar to being bitten to death by ducks: a slow, inexorable, and painful decline.

U.S. policy, as defined originally by the Bush administration and continued by the Clinton administration, saw the world system as one in which decisive U.S. action, augmented and legitimized by multinational agreements and the actions of international organizations, could defend both U.S. national interests and the larger system interests as well. In the Middle East this apparently translated into a policy of a continued U.S. role in its regional conflicts.

In a less-abstract formulation, this meant that the United States must try to have its cake and eat it too, finding and supporting solutions that would both satisfy the security needs of its allies in the region and protect real U.S. interests. Those needs, as understood in the U.S. view, included continued security for Israel, restraint of Iraqi power and influence, the containment of Iran, and the continued stability of the oil-producing states in the Gulf. Added to this was the unknown potential of Islamic extremism, raising the possibility of internal instability in such important allies as Egypt, Saudi Arabia, and Turkey.

Internationally, Desert Storm provided an opportunity for the United States to strengthen its political and economic and military relationships with the states of the Gulf. New U.S. bases were established, forward supply depots were organized, and a steady flow of new weapons systems increased the capability of the Gulf military. These augmented previously established military relationships with Egypt and Oman. Economic cooperation, particularly with Saudi Arabia and

Kuwait, is intimate and reciprocal. The Saudi decision to purchase Boeing airliners for its national airlines is a multi-billion-dollar example of the connections between the United States and its ally. In short, the United States is now the full guarantor of the peace in the region of the Gulf. U.S. planes and warships regularly monitor activity in and around the Gulf; joint maneuvers are common; and the United States has demonstrated its ability to reinforce Kuwait when a threat from enfeebled Iraq seems possible.

The United States now presides over a grand alliance in the Middle East, composed of formerly hostile factions from the Arab system. It is anchored in the Gulf by the conservative states of Saudi Arabia, the U.A.E., Bahrain, Oman, Qatar, and Kuwait. It is buttressed on the west by Egypt, the largest of the Arab states and the most influential politically, and it includes Syria in the Levant, now one of the strongest Arab military powers. Jordan has been rehabilitated, rewarded for its quick signing of a "warm" peace agreement with Israel, no longer doing penance for its unwillingness to join in the coalition against Iraq. Each of these states at one time or another has been at loggerheads with another state in the alliance. Thus the alliance brings previously hostile nations together in a pragmatic relationship. Israel is also part of this grand alliance, based on its special relationship with the United States. Given the fundamental differences between members of the alliance, and the historical strains between them, it will take a good deal of energy and diplomacy to keep the alliance intact.

There are, however, good reasons for doing so. The United States and the Western industrial states are still highly dependent on a regular and reasonably priced flow of petroleum from the area. Military interventions have proven very costly, even when costs are shared by the beneficiaries, as in the Gulf crisis. And the steady proliferation of weapons of mass destruction argue for a logic of mutual defense rather than going it alone. Finally, intangible benefits accrue from reducing international stress and conflict.

Middle Eastern countries outside the alliance are for the most part objects of U.S. concern. Iraq, Iran, and Libya are all to an important degree iso-

lated by the alliance. The strategic importance of Yemen also keeps it an object of U.S. attention. The Islamic government of the Sudan, strongly motivated by the desire to export political Islam, also has worried U.S. decision makers, particularly after the terrorist attacks on U.S. embassies in Kenya and Tanzania and the U.S. belief that the Sudan was a base and haven for its "terrorist de jour," Osama bin Laden.

Iraq, greatly weakened by the Gulf War, nonetheless showed signs of life. U.S. policy continued to try to keep Iraq from a major recovery, economically, politically, or militarily. The removal of Saddam Hussein and the Baath Party from power would continue to be a U.S. priority, and the relaxation of economic sanctions would probably not occur as long as the Baathist regime stayed in power. The alliance was fraying over the question of Iraq, and the European components of the alliance showed increasing signs of distress at U.S. insistence on maintaining the economic sanctions against Iraq, and against Libya, as well.

Iran, now in the maturity of its revolution, was still viewed by the United States as a dangerous state. Even the release in late 1991 of all of the remaining U.S. hostages in Lebanon failed to completely erase U.S. suspicions. And Iranian purchases of military equipment from Russia (submarines and nuclear technology) and China (missile components, for example) were also alarming. But the U.S. effort to discipline Iran by forbidding Conoco from contracting to produce oil in Iran was offset by the actions of U.S. allies allowing such contracts.

Extremist Islamic political movements drawing moral support and encouragement from Iran still exist in Egypt, Jordan, Syria, Turkey, Algeria, and Morocco. And tiny Bahrain complains that Iran has helped foment public discontent in that island state. As the independent republics of the former Soviet Union establish new relationships with the central Asian states of Turkey, Iran, and Afghanistan, the United States will most likely recognize growing priorities there as well. The United States will continue to place a high priority on frustrating the export of Iran's Islamic revolution to the rest of the Middle East. Efforts of the Khatami government to improve relations with the

West are still embryonic, complicated by conservative opposition to normalization of such relations. But analysts agree that there is a real possibility of a warming relationship between Iran and the United States if domestic trends toward liberalization continue to develop there.

U.S. relations with Libya took a nose dive in 1991 as investigators finally placed the blame on Libyan diplomats for the 1988 bombing of a Pan Am 747 over Scotland. U.S. demands for the extradition of two Libyan officials were rebuffed. Surprising many in the United States, Qadaffi in 1999 agreed to the extradition of the two officials to the International Court of Justice, presided over by a Scottish judge. Many U.S. allies, including the European Union, are now pushing for a wholesale rehabilitation of Libya and scrambling for lucrative contracts and trade agreements. U.S. resistance to this trend is unlikely to be effective in the long run.

Western Europe's relations with the Middle East are increasingly conditioned by its movement toward economic and political integration. The European Union is currently in the process of defining its common economic relationship with other world regions. Turkey, now approved for applicant status in the European Union, is unlikely to gain that status anytime soon, in spite of its European geography and millions of guest workers in Germany and Belgium. The states of North Africa (Morocco, Algeria, and Tunisia, mainly) have been given privileged access to the EU as a consequence of their previous colonial experience. They also have many guest workers, particularly in France and Belgium. And Gulf Cooperation Council states are also engaged in discussions with the EU. If these three relationships are indicative of future agreements, we can look forward to EU special relationships with other Middle Eastern states, including Iraq and Iran, currently enjoying rising sympathy and prestige in Europe.

EU political relationships with the region are changing. The European Union is now a much more tangible political entity, particularly following the successful introduction of the common currency, the euro, and the successful prosecution of the international intervention in Bosnia and Kosovo. EU efforts to define and implement a common foreign policy are beginning to bear fruit. And the fruit is clearly not simply a clone of U.S. policy preferences, as the EU efforts to establish political and economic relations with Libya, Iraq, and Iran demonstrated. EU interest in dropping or decreasing the severity of the existing sanctions against Iraq and support for new and different elements in Iraqi inspection teams produced strong U.S. objections. As the U.S. occupation of Iraq proceeded in 2003, the European actors actively positioned themselves for a role in the new Iraq and continued their efforts to increase economic and political relations with Libya and Iran.

Japan, as a dominant financial and industrial world power, continues to place strong emphasis on ensuring a regular supply of petroleum from the area. As in the past, Japan protects regular supply relationships with the Gulf states Saudi Arabia and Iran. Japan will likely continue its mutual trade relationships with the richest of the Middle Eastern states. It is unlikely that any dramatic increase in Japan's military capability will occur. Slow economic growth has been a fact of Japanese life in the last decade of the twentieth century and will likely constrain any significant growth in Japanese commitments in the region. Japan will most likely continue to pursue the politics of prestige in the region. Nationally, Japan must contend regionally with a rapidly growing Chinese economy and political influence. Given that reality, it is likely that Japan will seek stronger political and economic ties with individual Middle Eastern states. As noted, Saudi Arabia and Iran are probable targets of Japanese initiative.

MIDDLE EASTERN STATES

Egypt

Egypt emerged from the period with enhanced prestige. Its early commitment to the coalition confronting Iraq was of immense importance to U.S. efforts, providing both Arab and Muslim legitimacy. And Egypt's long tradition of anticolonialism further legitimized the effort. It was able to quickly commit substantial numbers of well-trained troops to the Saudi theater. Its history of military cooperation with the United States, particularly its joint exercises in the 1980s and the 1990s and its adoption of the NATO munition and command and control standards, gave it the ability to coordinate command, control, and communication with the United States. By any measure, the Egyptian military contribution to the coalition was the most substantial of any Arab state.

Egypt remained close to the United States in the aftermath of the Gulf War. It became an important player in the convening of the Arab-Israeli peace conference, particularly in reassuring (and pressuring) Syria and Israel. And Egypt was a critical voice when either the Israelis or the Palestinians threatened to withdraw from or slow the peace process. As a result, Egyptian prestige experienced yet another increase and the flow of U.S. military and economic aid also increased, as did the flow of aid from Saudi Arabia, Kuwait and the U.A.E. The election of Egyptian statesman Boutros Boutros-Ghali as Secretary General of the United Nations also enhanced Egyptian international prestige and reflected continued great-power approval of the Egyptian regime.

But the road has not been completely smooth. Egypt has experienced increasing tension with the Sudan, its neighbor to the south. An attempt to assassinate Mubarak during a state visit to Ethiopia in 1995 was reputedly linked to a Sudanese political organization. Islamist opposition to the regime resulted in a series of attacks against tourists and Coptic communities in Upper Egypt and attendant strains on revenue from Egypt's important tourist industry. The increases in prestige and continued foreign aid notwithstanding, Egypt still faces a bleak economic and political scenario. A very high birthrate, declining revenues from overseas workers, and a relatively stagnant economy continue to put great strains on its political system. Efforts at regional economic cooperation and integration and accelerated foreign investment appear to be likely Egyptian strategies in the new century.

Saudi Arabia

Saudi Arabia took great risks in inviting the U.S. response to Iraq's invasion of Kuwait. No Arab state can routinely invite a foreign military pres-

ence, given the sensitivity in the region to its colonial and postcolonial past. And Saudi Arabia, as custodian of the holiest of the shrines of Islam, has a special obligation to protect the purity of its land. The prospect of non-Muslim Western men and women tramping casually across the holy land of Arabia was distasteful to many people inside and outside of Saudi Arabia, but particularly to the religious elites and the most conservative elements in the political elite.

Saudi Arabia risked the exposure of its citizenry to the different social and political values of its guests. A country in which the most conservative of values prevail socially—including the public veiling of women, requirements of modest dress, and the prohibition of alcohol—could theoretically be scandalized or destabilized by the presence of large numbers of tank-topped, beer-swilling, Christ-worshiping foreign soldiers. Or at least so the argument went. The point was made by a rigorous segregation of foreign troops, even to the point of entertaining them on cruise ships anchored in the Gulf. And in the postwar environment, the Saudi government reasserted its emphasis on its traditional social and political values.

In spite of these efforts, the religious establishment in Saudi Arabia issued a number of public warnings to the Saudi government, indicating its dissatisfaction with the state of public morals and the policies of the government. The announcement by King Fahd in early 1992 that a consultative assembly would be formed was clearly a response to increasing domestic pressure from its important religious allies. But such a concession failed to satisfy the conservative critics of the regime. Tensions increased in 1995–1996, punctuated by the bombing of an American training mission, evidence that the stakes in the internal conflicts in Saudi Arabia were rising. Osama bin Laden, a famous terrorist mastermind and former Saudi citizen, enjoys significant support in some Saudi circles and reputedly still harvests substantial financial support from sympathetic parties. This is a source of embarrassment to the Saudi government.

Before and after the Gulf War, Saudi priorities remained basically the same. With a small native population spread out over a large and mainly uninhabited expanse, security concerns remain paramount, both externally and internally.

Saudi economic, political, and military relationships with the United States were enhanced by Desert Shield–Desert Storm. Saudi Arabia expanded its petroleum production to levels that ensured moderate prices globally. And its distribution presence in the United States market was allowed to expand, giving it a higher stake in the United States domestic economy. New discoveries of petroleum were acknowledged, increasing the Saudi percentage of known world petroleum reserves. Military cooperation with the United States reached new heights, and there is little doubt as to the mutual assurances and guarantees existing between them. Dramatic increases in Saudi military capability were achieved, with the majority of the new systems coming from the United States. "Nativization" of the military and related security agencies was emphasized as well.

Regional relationships also intensified. The success of the GCC in coming to terms with the Iraqi crisis enhanced its attractiveness, and the GCC developed into a substantial tool for military and economic coordination among its member Gulf states. Saudi commitment to the GCC is tangible and growing. Military and political cooperation are understood as a high priority for countries with small populations and relatively modest military capacity. Saudi Arabia and the Gulf states have finally abandoned their longstanding policy against recognition of Israel and have attended the Arab-Israeli peace conferences as observers, further solidifying their joint relationships with the United States.

Saudi pragmatism continues to manifest itself internationally. It played a critical formal and informal role in the attempts to settle the political questions in Lebanon, an initiative that brought it into intimate discussions and relationships with Syria. It continues diplomatic relations with Iran, exchanging visits between state ministers and the military, in spite of Saudi reservations about the regime in place there. It continues modest financial support to Lebanon and Jordan. The Saudis played a visible role in the relief efforts in Bosnia and Kosovo, both areas out of the traditional orbit of Saudi foreign policy. And Saudi private invest-

ments in the new territories under Palestinian control continue and are likely to accelerate as Palestinian independence takes on more substance.

Saudi Arabia and its Gulf neighbors continue to live in a "bad neighborhood." Both Iran and Iraq are clearly perceived as potential threats. Bahrain continues to fear outside agitation of its restive Shia majority. Yemen has unresolved border disputes with Saudi Arabia and Oman. And the deterioration of political and economic life in the nearby Horn of Africa (Somalia, the Sudan, Ethiopia) presents potential threats as well. The introduction of nuclear capability into the India-Pakistan conflict in 1999 brings nuclear weapons closer to the neighborhood. Thus, fluid and creative alliance politics will likely continue to be a major priority of the Saudi government and its Gulf allies for the indefinite future. And the politics of prestige will continue to be a high priority, as Saudi Arabia continues to use its unique role in the history of Islam in its self-defense.

Other Gulf States

The foreign policies of the U.A.E., Bahrain, Qatar, Kuwait, and Oman generally bear great similarities. The coordinating role of the Gulf Cooperation Council is particularly important for these small states. By and large, their foreign policies seek security through mutual cooperation and by extension of their military and economic relationships with the United States and their economic and political relationships with the EU and in the surrounding region. Bahrain, Oman, and Kuwait have been the most aggressive in approving U.S. basing agreements and the prepositioning of military supplies. Bahrain continues to extend port facilities to the U.S. Navy as it patrols the Gulf, and U.S. sailors and aviators are common on the streets of Abu Dhabi and Dubai, even as the government continues to resist a formal defense arrangement with the United States. Like Saudi Arabia, the richer of these states—principally the U.A.E, Qatar, and Kuwait—seek an additional measure of security by providing generous subsidies to the poorer neighboring states.

Kuwait has particular problems, occasioned by Iraq's invasion and occupation. Rebuilding has been a daunting task, although many of the earliest estimates of damage costs proved to be excessive. For example, the extinguishing of some 700 oil well fires was accomplished in less than nine months, instead of the two to three years some experts had suggested. And the damage to the Kuwaiti physical plant was very selective, also minimizing reconstruction costs. But even then, billions of dollars were needed. Fortunately, Kuwaiti oil production recovered faster than imagined, and Kuwait's very substantial foreign investments provided income that was used in the reconstruction.

Kuwait wanted to reduce its population to roughly half of its prewar level, eliminating many of the foreign guest workers who dominated its economic and professional life and eliminating that point of vulnerability in its security. A "nativized" and expanded military is also progressing. These programs dispossessed permanently many foreign workers, particularly Palestinian, Jordanian, and Egyptian workers. This has exacerbated social pressure in Jordan and the West Bank. Grants in aid somewhat offset these effects in Egypt. Kuwait is not alone in reducing the number of Middle Eastern foreign workers—all of the neighboring Gulf states have pursued similar programs. The expatriate communities in these states now have higher proportions of Indian, Pakistani, Sri Lankan, and Philippine nationals, workers less politically engaged or significant than their Arab counterparts.

One measure of the changing realities for the Gulf states is apparent in Qatar, which is positioned to surpass the Sultanate of Brunei as the richest country in the world. Qatar, with a new leader and an expanding elite, is clearly working to settle most of the border disputes it has had with Bahrain and Saudi Arabia. It is positioning itself, along with the U.A.E. and Oman, as a long-term supplier of liquified natural gas to its traditional customers, and to the Indian subcontinent as well. Qatar is clearly a country in the midst of substantial change, both domestically and in its relationships with the international system. Qatar's enthusiastic participation in the 2003 war with Iraq, including its hosting of the U.S. Central Command Headquarters in Doha, has confirmed its close relationship with the United States and, to a degree, distanced itself from its other Gulf neighbors.

Syria

Of all the states in the Middle East, Syria has made the biggest changes in its foreign policy. For years Syria was a close ally of the U.S.S.R., enjoying a wide range of subsidies and support. Syria's foreign policies opposing imperialism, Israel, the United States, and monarchism were supported in the main by Soviet economic and military subsidies. Its support for wars of national liberation (particularly in Israel by the Palestinians), pan-Arabism, Iran in its war with Iraq, and international socialism enjoyed similar advantage. But with the collapse of Soviet power, new international realities impinged on Syria's formula. As a result, Syria has changed many of its foreign policies to adjust to the emerging new world.

Syria's cooperation with the 1991 coalition forces against Iraq signaled a watershed in its foreign policy. Alignment with the United States, Saudi Arabia, Great Britain, and France against another Arab power would have been unthinkable in the Syria of the 1970s and 1980s. Even more unthinkable would be the current Syrian bilateral negotiations with Israel over the Golan. Syria earlier insisted on a comprehensive multilateral set of negotiations. That particular objective was undermined by direct Israeli-Palestinian negotiations, and Syria signaled its willingness to engage in direct negotiations with Israel in late 1999 and early 2000. These negotiations are important in the ultimate resolution of the Israeli-Arab conflict, and ultimately they reflect a change in worldview among Syrian leaders.

Recovery of the Golan region and Israeli withdrawal from southern Lebanon are high priorities for Syria. Fully normalized relations are a high priority for Israel, which still seeks to escape its relative isolation in the region. President Assad previously considered Israeli withdrawal a precondition for negotiations, just as Israel considered a formal peace treaty a prerequisite to its withdrawal from the Golan. But both countries have backed down from these preconditions and

Syria and Israel have entered reluctantly into serious negotiations.

Syria for its part has not abandoned all of its prior international agenda. Forces for pan-Arabism are still influential in its politics. Syria has not abandoned its dislike for monarchical regimes and remains committed to their replacement with democratic institutions. Its competition with Egypt for leadership of the Arab world continues. Syrian relations with Iran remain warm, introducing a note of disquiet into its new relations with the West. Syria shares a long common border with Turkey, and the water resources that flow across it will be an important concern for Syria. In fact, water policy generally is a high priority for Syrian decision makers and is the subject most likely to lead Syria into regional compacts and cooperation.

Syria still pursues military parity with Israel, albeit with fewer resources. Noting these apparent contradictions in its foreign policy, analysts suggest that Syrian policy is in the process of evolving. And, given Syria's history, it would be foolhardy to predict its final contours.

Lebanon

Lebanon made progress toward reestablishing governmental legitimacy after the Taif Accords of 1989, only to relinquish that authority to growing Syrian influence. Syrian troops and administrators played key roles in suppressing the factional warfare that was the hallmark of the Lebanese civil war over the past decades. Lebanon's recent economic revitalization and relative political stability provide evidence that Lebanon is emerging from the worst of its difficulties.

Lebanese foreign policy priorities have largely revolved around recovering the "buffer zone" seized by Israel during its 1982 invasion. The zone, which also contains the watershed of the Litani River, is important to the Lebanese government both symbolically and substantively. This area, and the Bekaa Valley north of it, are the homeground of Hizbollah, Israel's most implacable foreign enemy and a considerable problem for the government of Lebanon.

The improvement of civil life in Lebanon is sufficient to have attracted real estate investment back to Beirut. But clearly, the importance of establishing stable, representative government inclusive of the major factions and religious groups is still a pressing priority. Until that is accomplished, Lebanese foreign policy is destined to be at the bottom of the Lebanese priorities. A timely resolution of the Syrian-Israeli peace negotiations could have a very profound effect on the substance and content of Lebanese foreign policy.

Iran

Iran gained much in the new politics of the Middle East. It was an interested bystander in the Gulf crisis, skillfully exploiting the difficulties of its old adversary, Iraq, without entangling itself in the actual conflict. Iraqi planes fled to sanctuary in Iran, only to find the planes first impounded and eventually integrated into the Iranian air force. The revolt of the Shia in southern Iraq clearly benefited Iranian interests, but again Iran seemed content to reap such rewards indirectly. Iran did not move quickly to the establishment of an independent Shia state in the south of Iraq, although Iranian public opinion would probably have supported such a move. The Rafsanjani regime played its cards conservatively and cautiously during the crisis.

Iran emerged in retrospect as one of the primary beneficiaries of Desert Storm. Clearly, the destruction of Iraqi military power directly increased the relative power of Iran. And in concrete terms, Iran has used much of its increased oil revenues to substantially increase its armaments. Thus, Iran emerged from the Gulf crisis with enhanced military power. Its purchases of Russian submarines and nuclear equipment and Chinese missile components and other military equipment suggest that it has not abandoned its quest for military-based regional influence.

Iran has moved in recent years from a domestic climate of revolutionary intensity to a more moderate political climate. Under the leadership of President Khatami, moderate influences in Iran have competed successfully with the more conservative clerical groups, moving Iran toward a moderating domestic and international set of policies. Iran has moved to improve relations with its Gulf area neighbors and seeks improved economic relations with Europe and the United States. As noted in previous chapters, U.S. allies have been anxious to capitalize on new trade relations with Iran, often to the express dissatisfaction of the U.S. administration.

Iran has reached out to the West in other ways. Cultural delegations have been welcomed to Iran in the waning days of the century and into the new. Iran has sought opportunities to engage in wide-ranging discussions with Saudi Arabia, Oman, and the U.A.E. And Iranian leaders publicly call for improvement in the climate of its relationship with the West and the United States in particular. Finally, Iran's defusing of its targeting of author Salman Rushdie has reduced some of its tensions with the European states, particularly Great Britain. Iran seemed poised, at the turn of the century, to reclaim some of its earlier international influence.

Regionally, Iran appears concerned about establishing good relations with the new independent republics of central Asia. Iran competes with Turkey in this process and both countries have invested economically in the resource-rich Muslim republics, particularly Kazakhstan, Uzbekistan, and Azerbaijan. By 1996 Iran had established diplomatic relations with most of the twelve republics, including the Russian Federation. Relations with Turkey remained cool, although both Turkey and Iran have a common interest in suppressing independence movements among the Kurds. Water resources are a recurring problem, as Turkey disrupts the flow of water into the Tigris and Euphrates systems to fill the dams and reservoirs of its Grand Anatolia Project. Given all of these factors, it seems clear that Iran will continue to play a large role in the international politics of the region over the next decades.

Turkey

Turkey is an important member in the coalition suppression of Iraq, and it continues to play a key role in the efforts to punish Iraq for its refusal to accept UN weapons inspectors. U.S. and British aircraft continued to fly from Turkish bases in their periodic overflights of Iraq's "no-fly" zones. Turkey continues to be an important member of NATO and to pursue full membership in the European Union.

Turkish foreign policy is closely linked to the United States. In the waning days of the century,

with the decided encouragement of the United States, Turkey engaged in a series of military training exercises with U.S. and Israeli defense forces. Unencumbered by Arab sentiment, Turkey accepted a de facto military alliance with the United States and Israel that greatly disconcerted its neighbors in Syria, Iraq, and Iran. But such a policy posture fits neatly with Turkish notions of its place on the globe.

As a nation astride the continents of Europe and Asia, Turkey has often identified itself with Europe. This has been evident in its attempts to achieve membership or associate status with the EU. In order to qualify for membership, Turkey moved substantially in the direction of free market economics, accepting the economic and social costs of the attendant destabilization. Millions of Turkish workers continue to labor in Europe, and the Turkish army is the largest in NATO (except for the United States). In spite of these political, economic, and military policies, Turkey has been excluded from membership in the EU, although now Turkey has been admitted to candidacy for membership. EU membership will most likely continue as an important goal of any Turkish government; that is, if the Turkish domestic political equation stays constant.

Like Iran, Turkey saw opportunity in the dissolution of the U.S.S.R. and the emergence of independent states in Soviet central Asia. Turkey moved quickly to establish diplomatic relations with the Muslim and neighbor republics; foreign investments in communications, transportation, and resource development have taken place in Azerbaijan, Kazakhstan, Uzbekistan, and Turkmenistan. Turkey would like to be seen as a democratic role model for the emerging republics, a logical alternative to the Islamic republic model in Iran.

Relations with the Kurdish minorities continue to be problematic for both Turkey and Iran, and both have had to contend militarily with independence movements in the area. Turkey's forceful attack on the Kurdish independence guerrillas in western Anatolia in 1995 was strongly supported by the United States, but it was roundly condemned in other quarters. All of this changed quickly when Turkey was able to capture the leader of the Kurdish independence movement (Abdullah Ocalan) and bring him to trial.

Turkish relations with Greece, Bulgaria, and Cyprus continue to smolder. A satisfactory resolution of its dispute over Aegean islands with Greece, its border problems with Bulgaria, and the continued Turkish occupation of half of Cyprus will have to precede any Turkish entry into the EU.

Bulgaria forcibly expelled many Turkish nationals from its territory in 1991, creating great ill will between the two states and many refugees in European Turkey. Relations with both of these countries remain frigid. The civil war in Bosnia and Kosovo also raised concerns among the Turkish leadership, but NATO's successful intervention in both of these conflicts seems to have met Turkish concerns for the Muslim populations of this region.

Algeria, Morocco, and Tunisia

Algeria, Morocco and Tunisia share some of the key difficulties facing Turkey. Like Turkey, they have been at pains to establish a working relationship with the EU. And unlike Turkey, they have been somewhat successful at establishing regional cooperation, particularly in the Saharan regions where boundaries are particularly permeable. Their governments in the main cooperated with the U.S.-led coalition against Iraq in the Gulf War. All in all, these states have enjoyed improving relations with the United States and the EU.

Domestically, however, they all face a growing tide of Islamic extremist dissatisfaction with their secular regimes. In Algeria and Tunisia, these actions have resulted in Islamic extremist success at the ballot box. The invalidation of the Algerian election by the losing government precipitated widespread, violent opposition. The military government of Algeria entered into negotiations with the Islamic opposition in 1995 and 1996, but no formal resolution of the dispute has been accomplished. The Islamist opposition in Algeria has initiated a horrifyingly brutal campaign against the government and its allies. As a result, Algeria is increasingly isolated internationally.

An organized Islamic opposition to the monarchy continues to grow slowly in Morocco. We can conclude that all three states face a rising tide of organized Islamic activism and political extremism. This tide threatens to change the political face of the Maghreb. Once again, the long-run implications of fundamentalist extremist rule are not clear, but most likely their policy preferences would run counter to those of the United States and the EU.

Libya

Libya, since the U.S. raid in 1986, has adopted a fairly low profile internationally. The U.S.-Great Britain determination that Libyan diplomats orchestrated the Pan Am Flight 103 bombing reinvigorated Western demands for more punitive action against Libya. Libya's surprising decision to surrender the accused for trial in Europe appears to be part of a concerted effort to gain political rehabilitation with the West. The EU seems anxious to seize this opportunity, much to the chagrin of the United States, which would prefer to maintain the program of sanctions and embargoes against Libya.

Muammar Qadaffi appears to have chosen a course designed to minimize the rationales for punitive action. As such, the foreign policy of Libya has become relatively conservative and quiet, seeking an economically based rapprochement with the European west. The earlier decline in world petroleum prices had also deprived Libya of the financial resources necessary for an expansive and aggressive foreign policy. Libya's current overtures toward the West demonstrate an economic and political pragmatism likely to find fertile ground in the emerging world system.

Israel

The emergence of the new world order has been especially important to Israel, which finds both positive and negative implications. On the one hand, the collapse of the Soviet Union and the emergence of the Russian Federation allowed the continued emigration of Eastern European Jews to Israel. On the other hand, the collapse of the Soviet threat removed one of the key rationales for the privileged "special relationship" between Israel and the United States. The United States simply does not now need the Israeli military in the way it did during the dangerous confrontations of the bipolar Cold War. This new fact was made very clear during Desert Storm, when the United States formally kept Israel from participating in the coalition attacks on Iraq, going so far as to deny key communication codes to the Israeli air force. It seems clear that the nature of the relationship between Israel and the United States changed dramatically under the Bush administration.

As indicated earlier in this chapter, Israel was more or less goaded into participation in the Arab-Israeli Peace Conference begun in 1991. The Shamir administration was unenthusiastic about multilateral negotiations under any circumstances, and it was ideologically committed to a policy of "no return of land" to the Palestinians under any circumstances. The very nature of the coalition supporting the Likud government made any major deviation from this proposition unlikely, even in the improbable event that the government would see the negotiations in a positive light. These two attitudes put Israel on a collision course with the Bush administration, which saw the surrender of occupied territory in exchange for security guarantees as the most appropriate formula for settling the long-standing dispute.

Israeli policy after Desert Storm thus exhibited some fundamental inconsistencies. These inconsistencies have plagued Israel, the United States, and the Palestinians in the ensuing decade of negotiations and agreements, from Madrid, through Oslo I and II, through the Wye Plantation Accords in 1998, and up to and including Israeli-Palestinian negotiations in and around Washington. A series of Israeli governments (Shamir, Rabin, Peres, Netanyahu, and Barak) found themselves both dependent on and resistant to the guarantees and influence of the American administrations of George H.W. Bush, Bill Clinton, and George W. Bush. Unwilling to totally alienate a U.S. administration, the Israeli governments allowed themselves to be bullied into participation in the peace talks. They found themselves agreeing to concessions that would have been politically impossible without U.S. pressure or security guarantees. The result has been a peace process proceeding in fits and starts, with high risks and rewards for participants on both sides.

Israeli extremist groups and Palestinian extremists in and outside of Israel did their best to disrupt these negotiations. Israeli settlers, armed to the teeth and espousing the most nationalist of Zionist philosophy, established settlements illegally, seized Arab housing forcibly, even beat and murdered Palestinians. Palestinians outside the coalition involved in the peace talks also attempted to disrupt events. The complexity of the situation was underscored in one attack by Palestinian guerrillas on a bus transporting settlers, killing two. The Palestinians, attempting to disrupt the peace process, killed two settlers on their way to a rally to oppose the peace negotiations. Both Israel and their Palestinian counterparts had to walk a very narrow ledge.

We have previously described and discussed the events that transformed Israel's relationship with the PLO. Although clearly an act in progress, the partial resolution of the conflict has changed the style and focus of Israel's relations with her neighbors, and with the United States and the other powers. Most of these changes have been previously mentioned in other contexts. But given their importance, they bear review once again.

The conclusion of substantive peace agreements with its Palestinian foes has reaped some real, concrete rewards for Israel. Relations with the Clinton administration continued on a positive note and U.S. formal economic and military support for Israel has continued unabated. Israel's European relations have also been enhanced, particularly with Great Britain, France, and Germany, all of whom had been encouraging a rapprochement with the PLO. All of these sets of relationships are warmer in the twenty-first century than in the twentieth.

This is not to suggest that tensions between Israel and the Palestinians have been eliminated, for they have not. Final status negotiations have yet to settle the question of settlements, the right of return for Palestinian refugees, the creation of a Palestinian state, or the final status of Jerusalem for both governments.

Relations with the United States also have their problems. Arafat has frequently called on the United States to pressure Israel to honor its agreements, leading to difficult conversations between the American presidents and the Israeli prime ministers. Both prime ministers Netanyahu and Barak publicly called on the United States to become a silent partner in peace negotiations, to no particular effect. And the repeated requests by Israeli prime ministers for the release of convicted Israeli spy Jonathan Pollard have done little to improve the tone of U.S.-Israeli conversations. Sometimes, disagreements between friends are the most troublesome. But nothing here should suggest any substantive decline in the U.S. preference for Israel in these foreign relations.

Relations within the Middle East have also improved. Israel's relationships with Jordan have become positively hot. Tourists pour across the Allenby bridge, seeking Petra and Jerasch and Salt. Palestinians from Jordan visit their families in Israel with fewer obstacles and hindrances at the border. More important, Israeli and Jordanian businessmen search for investment opportunities. Foreign investors tour Amman in increasing numbers, looking for the pots of gold that follow in the wake of peace and the normalization of relations. Israeli progressives hope for a similar awakening in its relations with Egypt and Syria.

And there are signs that the tense relations between the Gulf monarchies and Israel are also getting better. Symbolically, Gulf diplomats have ceased referring to Israel as "the Zionist entity," a phraseology emphasizing the lack of legitimacy of the state of Israel. Israel is now referred to as Israel. For its part, Israel supported Oman's appointment to the UN Security Council in 1995, an act unheard of in the earlier age. Trade with Israel now comes from the ports and trading centers of the Persian Gulf and the Red Sea. Ambitious plans that combine Palestinian labor and real estate with Israeli technology and Arab capital continue to float across the desert. And legions of nongovernmental organizations continue to provide relief and support for those unfortunates not yet swept up in the changes taking place. These are the surface signs of change, and many of them are encouraging. But difficult problems remain to be solved.

CONCLUSION

Questions abound. Is the old world order gone? Definitely. Is the new world order here? Maybe. Do we know the details and implications of this new system? Not yet. Does this new order complicate our understanding of and relations with the Middle East? Definitely. To what can we look forward?

If our description of the emerging international system is correct, we can look forward to a rapidly changing Middle East. We can confidently predict that the changes there will have an impact on much of the world. The industrialized world is still dependent on a regular flow of petroleum from the region to fuel its industrial economies. The concentration of financial resources in the hands of the petroleum producers will continue to make them important friends or foes in the world economy. That much has not changed. But the way in which we respond to risk and threat seems to have changed, both within and without the region.

It seems likely that the trend toward multinational responses to conflict will continue. The UN, in particular, seems destined to play a critical role in the conflicts that emerge in the region in the near future. And the European Community, using whatever military and diplomatic resources it creates in the coming years, will also likely play an important role. The influence of independent nations seems destined to relative decline, although the action of powers like the United States, EU, Japan, and Russia will continue to be important.

Within the region, alliance realignment and new concentrations of power seem likely. Desert Storm clearly increased the relative regional influence of Iran, Syria, and Egypt. But here, too, regional multinational organizations seem destined to play larger roles than in the past. The Arab League, the Gulf Cooperation Council, the Islamic Conference, and the U.S.-led coalitions have many substantive problems to address. Among them are arms control and the management of new arms technologies, particularly "instruments of mass destruction," the disposition of refugees, and the regional management of water resources.

Many of the problems confronting the region are only manageable with international cooperation. The problem of declining water resources is one obvious problem. But the problems of environmental degradation, dramatic increases in refugees, Palestinian and Kurdish aspirations for independence, population growth and attendant health and disease questions, and open access to religious sites are also complicated and persistent. In point of fact, there is no shortage of serious problems for these organizations to attack.

There is also the phenomenon of the rising tide of religious extremism, in and out of the region. No states in the Middle East are immune to the dynamics of religious extremism. The process unleashed in Iran has resonance throughout the Islamic and Christian world. The critique of government that nourishes Islamic activism, and, in some instances, political extremism, is based squarely on the public perception of policy failures by secular or monarchical government. Social justice, the principles of compassion and fairness that inspire the pious folk of Islam, has not been widely achieved, even as the technology of modern communication brings that failure to the attention of greater numbers in the public. The increasing gap between rich and poor nations, and between the rich and poor within nations; the failure of governments to articulate a future other than the simple imitation of the industrial West; the obvious materialism and hedonism of many officials and businessmen—all these fuel the fires of politics and extremism.

Governments inside and outside the Middle East are still "lagging participants" in the politics of this new age. They are still deeply mired in the assumptions, conflicts, and constraints of the old order.

The View from 2000

All in all, as the new millennium opened in 2000 C.E., there were reasonable grounds for cautious optimism. A new American president, George Walker Bush, proclaimed an era of "humbler" American foreign policy, a policy less confrontational and less insistent on imposing American values abroad. Prime Minister Barak's administration in Israel removed Israeli troops from Lebanon and actively engaged the Palestinian Authority in peace negotiations, supported by an administration interested in an evenhanded role in the dispute. President Bush publicly endorsed the idea of an independent Palestinian state, living peacefully with its Israeli neighbor. Only later in the summer of 2000 would Israeli-Palestinian relations descend into Intifadah II, as General Ariel Sharon outmaneuvered Prime Minister Barak, regaining the government for Likud and initiating a bloody conflict that by late 2002 had taken over 1,500 Palestinian lives and over 500 Israeli lives.

Oil supplies and prices appeared headed for relative stability. Nascent democratic institutions were emerging cautiously, even in the oil monarchies of the Gulf, long the most resistant to change. The region seemed on the cusp of important new relationships.

All of that optimism was to disappear in little less than an hour on September 11, 2001, as two hijacked airliners piloted by Islamist terrorists plunged into the World Trade Center in New York, initiating a new and frightening era in international relations. It is important to gain a systemic perspective on that event and the policy changes that followed it. We will turn to this discussion in the next chapter.

Did 9/11 Change Everything?

There is no doubt that the events of September 11, 2001—specifically, the horrific terrorist attack on the World Trade Center in New York and the Pentagon in Washington, D.C.—resulted in major, important changes in the conduct of foreign policy by the United States. That is clear enough in the abrupt changes in rhetoric and policies that flowed from the attack. President George W. Bush, in the immediate aftermath of the attacks, found a new voice in his denunciation of the terrorists themselves, the states that supported them, directly and indirectly, and even those who sympathized in any way with them.

Departing from a foreign policy position that called for a "humbler" and more sensitive foreign policy, one respectful of the differences in beliefs and systems that existed around the world, President Bush headed in a new direction, calling for a war on terror and all its allies. Proclaiming a "line in the sand," pursuing Osama bin Laden and Al-Qaeda "dead or alive," declaring that states must choose to actively support the U.S. effort or embrace its enmity, the president loudly declared that the states of the world are either "with us or against us in this war." There was no room for moderation or indecision.

Within months of the attack, the administration put words into action, launching a major attack against Al-Qaeda in its camps, compounds, and caves in Afghanistan. In doing so, the administration took on the destruction of the Taliban, the extreme Islamist movement governing Afghanistan since 1996. In a series of asymmetric attacks against Taliban troops and installations, making effective use of U.S. special forces capabilities, the administration ran the Taliban out of power and pursued and killed many of its supporters.

Deprived of governmental support and patronage, the Al-Qaeda moved into the valleys and mountains of rural Afghanistan, dug in, and attempted to resist the U.S. forces pursuing them. The United States, its Afghan allies, and a small smattering of troops from Great Britain, Canada, and Australia began a slow and dogged pursuit of Al-Qaeda groups and operatives in some of the most remote regions of Afghanistan. Some of the Al-Qaeda fighters stayed to make a fight of it; others melted into the ill-defined border areas between Afghanistan and Pakistan, Iran, Uzbekistan, and other nearby countries. Osama bin Laden himself disappeared and no one was sure whether he was "dead or alive."

A similar fate befell some of the other members of the Al-Qaeda "coalition." In the Philippines, U.S. special forces aided the Philippine military in attacking and destroying one of the guerrilla groups of Abu Sayyaf, on Basilan Island and in Northern Mindanao. Other successful raids were conducted in the Sudan and Yemen, and U.S. special forces teams were based in Djibouti and Eritrea. All in all, from a military point of view, the United States seemed to be successful in its initial attempts at suppressing the terrorist organizations attacking the United States and its allies.

By the spring of 2002, the Taliban and Al-Qaeda were effectively suppressed in Afghanistan and a friendly government was established under the leadership of Mohammad Karzai. International promises of support for the new government led to high expectations that the Karzai government might garner the resources necessary to project its power out of Kabul and into the Afghani interior, creating the basis for a legitimate Afghan state with real pretensions to sovereignty. But only a small percentage of the pledged support materialized, and by the summer of 2002 it was apparent that the struggle for effective government in Afghanistan would be a long-term project.

THE REEMERGENCE OF IRAQ

The Bush foreign policy at that moment, the spring and summer of 2002, took a sudden change in direction. In one of President Bush's oratorical excesses during his 2002 State of the Union message, he had proclaimed the existence of an "axis of evil," composed of Iraq, Iran, and North Korea. All three states were conflated in this famous equation as states that broadly and infamously supported terrorists and their organizations. Despite scholars' and pundits' protests against this particular grouping of states, two of them longstanding mortal enemies themselves (Iran and Iraq), the administration decided to pursue the suppression of Iraq, moving the focus of U.S. policy away from Al-Qaeda and onto perpetual opponent and villain Saddam Hussein.

The administration argument on Iraq presumed the existence of Iraqi weapons of mass destruction and the intent of Iraq to eventually use them

against the United States, Israel, or Iraq's neighbors. Additionally, it accused Iraq of suppressing its own citizens, primarily Kurds and Shia, and of supporting Al-Qaeda and other terrorist groups. Evidence supporting the terrorist assertions was insubstantial and unpersuasive, particularly assertions that "secret evidence" documented an alliance of convenience between Saddam Hussein and Osama bin Laden, both understood conventionally as mortal enemies.

In the face of near-universal lack of international support for "regime change" in Iraq, in the summer of 2002 the United States threatened to "go it alone" if necessary and launch a unilateral attack on Iraq. U.S. forces in the region were beefed up and nominal U.S. allies in the region were pressured to cooperate with them. In the end, only Great Britain and Israel were enthusiastic supporters of an American unilateral attack on Iraq; almost all of the 1991 Gulf War coalition partners refused to support or provide legitimacy for such an attack.

The lack of support for the war overseas, and growing domestic opposition to the war, was given some momentum by the assertion that the United States had the right to launch a "preemptive" war against Iraq, that is, a war that would begin with a U.S. attack on Iraq with no presumptive *causus belli*. Such a war would in fact entail acceptance of a doctrine that has been anathema in most of American history, particularly since the sneak attack on Pearl Harbor by Japan in 1941, a "day that will live in infamy." Opposition and cultural antipathy toward such ideas aside, the administration pursued and promulgated a war-fighting doctrine that reserves the right of preemptive attacks and the use of chemical, biological, and nuclear "weapons of mass destruction."

Reactions within the U.S. polity and within the administration itself were divided. In spite of the loud and confrontational rhetoric emanating periodically from the White House, it became apparent that the administration itself was divided over the question of whether or not the United States would be well served by a diversion of its attention from Al-Qaeda to Iraq, and whether or not such an intervention could or should be attempted unilaterally. This largely boiled down to the question of whether the United States should seek UN approval for its proposed intervention, disarmament, and regime change in Iraq or simply proceed alone on a unilateral basis.

As is often the case, these questions and conflicts resulted in the appearance of personalities and personality conflicts. In this case, the internal White House divide was personalized in the leadership of Colin Powell, Secretary of State, former U.S. Army Chief of Staff and an architect of the 1991 Gulf War, and Vice President Richard Cheney, former White House Chief of Staff and Secretary of Defense. In this case, Powell led those administration and professional military elements that emphasized a need for broad domestic support for the venture, a broadly based international coalition in support, and clear United Nations support for any military intervention—in short, a multilateral foreign policy strategy.

Vice President Cheney, joined by National Security Advisor Condoleeza Rice and Secretary of Defense Donald Rumsfeld, argued in favor of a muscular unilateralism, wherein the United States would exercise its military superiority without concern for the breadth of the international support or public reaction to it. The sooner the United States began its regime change in Iraq the better, to this coalition within the administration.

The drums of war were pounding so hard by August of 2002 that most U.S. and foreign observers expected the United States to go to war with Iraq unilaterally in the fall. Material published by Robert Woodward (*Bush at War*) indicated that the administration was in fact deeply divided about the prospects of a unilateral war and was internally vacillating between the two policies. Ultimately, the administration decided to go to the United Nations to make its case against Iraq. But even at the very last minute, as reflected in the two dozen revisions of President Bush's speech, the administration was not clear about whether to simply present the U.S. case and then initiate hostilities (the Cheney position); or to pressure the UN, more specifically the Security Council, for a resolution demanding the destruction of Iraq's weapons of mass destruction and invoking drastic penalties if it did not (the Powell multilateral strategy).

The Powell position prevailed and President Bush announced, before the United Nations, his intention to obtain a Security Council resolution on Iraq, specifying the demands and consequences for noncompliance. After tortured diplomacy within the Security Council, the UN complied and produced a resolution (SCR 1441) demanding the admission of UN weapons inspectors with unfettered access to Iraqi sites, programs, and personnel; and language threatening the strongest of responses if Iraq should fail to comply with the intent of the resolution. The final resolutions were remarkable in the breadth of support received, suggesting that the support for multilateral interventions was very much more palatable internationally than the muscular unilateralism of the world's remaining superpower.

As 2002 stumbled to a close, the world found the United States poised and prepared for an attack on Iraq, given a "material breach" of the UN resolutions. Saddam Hussein and his government met several key deadlines, including the acceptance of the UN Security Council resolution; and they delivered thousands of pages of documents to the UN detailing their weapons programs or lack of them. Teams of UN weapons inspectors doggedly pursued biological, chemical, and nuclear weapons of mass destruction across Iraq. Unimpeded access to Iraqi sites was allowed, including the vaunted "palaces" of Saddam Hussein. And in the ultimate irony, Saddam Hussein counseled the Iraqi public to cooperate with the UN inspectors as a way of refuting the U.S. claims about Iraq. In spite of its cooperation with the UN inspections regime, Iraq, for the most part, was isolated politically, economically, and militarily.

The ongoing U.S. preparations for war with Iraq inevitably detracted from the administration's pursuit of Al-Qaeda. Some critics of the administration's turn to the Iraqi front pointed out that the suppression of Al-Qaeda was incomplete and that the organization would reconstitute itself if the pressure were not continued on them. And the appearance of a controversial audiotape purporting to be the voice of Osama bin Laden himself in late November of 2002 added fuel to that fire.

More than the purported bin Laden tape, however, a series of attacks during the same period seemed to confirm the continued vitality of Al-Qaeda. Terrorist attacks on a tourist nightclub on the island of Bali, an Israeli-owned resort hotel in

Table 15–1 Two U.S.-Led Coalitions: 1990 and 2003

Country in 1990–1991 Coalition	Favors 2002 Unilateral U.S. Action	Favors Multilateral UN Action
United States	Yes	Yes
Britain	Yes	Yes
France	No	Yes
Saudi Arabia	No	Yes
Egypt	No	Yes
Syria	No	Yes
Kuwait	Yes	Yes
Bahrain	No	Yes
Bangladesh	No	Yes
Morocco	No	Yes
Oman	No	Yes
Pakistan	No	Yes
Qatar	Yes	Yes
U.A.E.	No	Yes
Turkey	No	Yes
Noncombatant states		
Russia	No	Yes
Germany	No	Yes
China	No	Uncertain
Japan	No	Yes
Israel	Yes	Yes
International organizations		
United Nations	No	Yes
NATO	Uncertain	Yes

Positions declared publicly by December 2002

Mombasa, Kenya, and a French oil tanker off the coast of the Arabian peninsula, and the assassination of an American aid official in Amman, Jordan, combined to remind the world that organized terror with a worldwide reach still existed and still required strenuous efforts to identify their supporters and root them out of the sixty-plus countries in which Al-Qaeda is believed to work.

Another irony of American foreign policy in this period is that while there was apparent opposition to a unilateral U.S. attack on Iraq, substantial enthusiasm existed for the U.S. "war on terror." It was far easier to garner international support for coalition attacks against presumptive Al-Qaeda targets around the world than for a coalition of forces to punish Saddam Hussein.

TWO COALITIONS

It is instructive to compare the positions of those key states and international organizations that supported the U.S.-led Gulf War in 1990–1991 and their positions on the Iraq question in 2002.

The prevailing international sentiment in favor of a program of inspections followed by a multilateral intervention if necessary seemed very clear and unlikely to change. From this we argued that a U.S. insistence on a more-or-less unilateral attack without explicit Security Council approval would harm U.S. reputation and interests internationally. The "blowback" from the attack could be substantial and damage American international interests for some time, particularly in the Middle East.

For these and other reasons, the UN Security Council in the winter of 2002 refused to endorse an attack on Iraq, preferring to continue the regime of inspections that was in place. For American diplomats, French, German, and Russian opposition to the war, and Chinese ambivalence to it, reduced the UN and the Security Council to "irrelevance." French and Russian threats to exercise their veto infuriated the U.S. administration and resulted in U.S. efforts to coordinate a "coalition of the willing" outside the UN, relying mostly on the support of Great Britain, Spain, Italy, and Australia to legitimize a U.S. preemptive strike on Iraq. Ultimately, the United States was able to marshal over 40 states in its "coalition of the willing"—although the coalition lacked most of the international actors that could be described as influential or powerful.

This situation, moreover, raised many related questions. Among them are: Why did the coalition put together by the Bush administration in 1991 fail to support another Bush administration coalition in 2002? Are different issues in play at the international level? Can regional and local changes account for this dramatic shift? The answer(s) is problematically "yes," necessitating an examination of levels and points in the international system, a system that has certainly changed in the intervening years. Let us turn to a more detailed examination of the bases of support and opposition for U.S. unilateral action against Iraq.

THE MIDDLE EAST QUARTET

Although the United States is arguably the only remaining world superpower, that does not suggest that the United States should or could act unilaterally on the world stage without consequences. Other powers may not be as strong individually as the United States but, taken collectively in various constellations, they are capable of mustering enough military, economic, political, or social power to frustrate or punish the United States for simple-minded and/or nakedly self-interested independent actions.

To many international actors, Iraq is simply not the architectonic issue that must be solved before progress can be made on other issues. The ongoing conflict between Israel and the Palestinians, they argue, is a much more compelling issue, one more in need of solution than the come-again, go-again policies of Iraq. And so also for the war on terror, which threatens most states and shows no signs of going away. This point of view is true for many states active on the international scene and for a number of transnational international organizations.

One combination of states and organizations with a strong focus on the Israeli-Palestinian question is the so-called Middle East Quartet, a grouping of Russia, the European Union, the United Nations, and the United States. The United States has hoped that this group could provide some leadership on the Palestinian question. And in fact the group has advocated more aggressive efforts to settle the ongoing conflict.

The United States stands alone in this potent group of international players in its insistence that the situation in Iraq deserves a higher priority than the Israeli-Palestinian conflict. All members of the group are critical of the U.S. administration's largely one-sided support for Israel as the conflict slides into higher and higher levels of violence and intransigence. In fact, European Union diplomats played key roles in the protection of President Arafat on the several occasions in which his office was surrounded by Israeli soldiers and tanks, camping out in the few square feet of office space left after the deliberate destruction of the Palestinian Authority headquarters in Ramallah.

As the European Union moves slowly toward a unified foreign policy for its members, the EU leadership has found consensus on its call for more balanced and fair negotiations between Israel and the Palestinians. It is one of the few issues where the various EU populations share the perception that the Palestinians are the victims of a brutal occupation and repression, support the creation of a Palestinian state, and call for Israel to recognize and implement the key standing resolutions of the UN Security Council.

While the European Union continues to see the Israeli-Palestinian conflict as important and architectonic to Middle East politics, it also resisted the U.S. pressure for a military incursion in Iraq. The issue of U.S. policy was important in recent elections in both Germany and France and both Chancellor Schröder and President Chirac campaigned on a platform strongly critical of the Bush administration's Mideast policy. In some forums in Germany, U.S. foreign policy was compared to Hitler's. And in others, the United States was accused of nurturing imperialist aspirations. Neither of these allegations would have been raised a decade ago in public settings.

In another significant arena, the European Union began negotiations with Iran to normalize and expand trade relations with the union. These discussions, in the context of World Trade Organization rules and regulations, reflected another significant difference in policy between the EU and the United States. European enthusiasm for improved relations with Iran go contrary to the U.S. "dual containment" policy and vitiate the U.S. categorization of Iran as a "problem" state.

In Russia, President Vladimir Putin, in spite of a close working relationship with the United States and with President Bush personally, opposed the U.S. plans for military intervention in Iraq. Russia and Iraq have a long history of mutually beneficial economic and military relations, which has left Iraq with considerable debt to Russia, a debt that very well might be repudiated by a new government in Baghdad. Russia can ill afford to write off substantial foreign assets in a time of domestic economic stress. It thus opposed the U.S.-sponsored regime change in Iraq.

The final member of the Quartet, the United Nations, was also reluctant to see the U.S.-Iraq conflict go directly to war. Secretary General Kofi Annan skillfully worked to bring a new, vigorous inspections regime to Iraq, and he was important in the diplomatic maneuvers in the Security Council as the new resolution demanding Iraqi compliance and disarmament was hammered out. Consistent with the organization's charter, the UN was organizationally and principally committed to the peaceful resolution of disputes where possible. And in the eventuality of a clear and public Iraqi material breach of the UN Security Council Resolution 1441, there was little doubt that the UN would provide the legal rationale for military action against Iraq. In the meantime, however, it was preferable from the UN viewpoint to talk and talk and talk, and inspect, inspect, inspect, rather than to go immediately to war.

REGIONAL ACTORS

States within the Middle East were also suspicious of the proposed U.S. preemptive war against Iraq. In many cases, this reservation was predicated on fears of destabilization and disruption of the existing international system. This was particularly true of states immediately bordering on Iraq (Turkey, Iran, Syria, Jordan, Saudi Arabia, and Kuwait), and Egypt, Libya, Morocco, and Lebanon. Of these regionally situated actors, only Israel professed genuine public enthusiasm for a U.S. preemptive attack on Iraq, "the sooner the better," say Israeli leaders. But outside of Israel there is also a widespread belief that the military intervention has distracted the United States from its leadership role in the resolution of the Israeli-Palestinian conflict, a conflict with particular emotional power on the urban streets of the region. Should Israel, for whatever reason, engage in the "transfer" of Palestinians from the West Bank and Gaza, or expel or even assassinate Yasir Arafat, the resultant anger in the Arab street could threaten many governments in the area. It is clear that opposition or support for the U.S. policy has local, practical implications and ramifications.

Turkey had much at risk if the United States pursued its military agenda against Iraq. Turkey not only shares a long and porous border with Iraq, it also shares the two largest populations of Kurds, long a restless minority in both countries and historically bent on gaining a country of their own. Although U.S. officials insisted that the United States would not sanction or encourage the creation of an independent Kurdish state in Iraq, on the borders of Turkey, the Turks were not sure that the United States could indeed dictate this particular outcome. Under the best of circumstances, an independent Kurdish state would create expectations among Turkish Kurds and nourish their own dreams for independence. This would endanger the ambitious development schemes that Turkey had begun in eastern Anatolia. And it could subtly or indirectly interfere with Turkish membership prospects in the European Union, the single highest foreign policy priority for the Turkish state.

The electoral victory of an Islamic political party in the fall 2002 Turkish elections also complicated the equation. It was clear that the new government of Turkey was more concerned with its prestige in the Muslim Middle East than the preceding government. It was less anxious for open conflict with other Muslim states. A compromise of sorts was produced. The result was Turkish willingness to allow key air force bases to be used in the U.S. effort, but an unwillingness to allow the stationing of U.S. troops in Turkey on the Iraqi border, as U.S. diplomats urged. Longstanding intimate relations with the United States notwithstanding, Turkey moved from uncritical support toward modest support for the U.S. policy.

Syria has long been at odds with Iraq, in spite of their geographical proximity, common ideological history (Baath Party), foreign policy alignments with the Soviet Union, and similar demographic characteristics. Syria did not hesitate to back Iran in the Iran-Iraq war in the 1980s and joined the U.S.-led coalition in 1991 to expel Iraq from Kuwait. It also voted in the fall of 2002, as a nonpermanent member of the UN Security Council, in favor of Resolution 1441. In addition, Syria cooperated in the hunt for terrorist organizations and was helpful in the search for Al-Qaeda links and allies.

In spite of this, Syria still ranked high on the U.S. list of "problem" states, states that encourage and support terrorism. In this case, the problem was the definition of "terror." Syria saw some organizations that the U.S. classifies as "terrorist" as political resistance organizations. This explained Syrian support for Hizbollah and Hamas (two organizations fighting Israeli occupation in Gaza, the West Bank, the Golan Heights, and, until recently, in Lebanon). The Israeli classification of the groups was simply as "terrorist." In truth, there was more of a distinction here than was embraced in the simplistic rhetoric of "lines in the sand" and so on. For the reasons already enumerated, Syria was unlikely to reap any direct benefits from its support for the inspection regime in Iraq. In this case, the Israeli tail clearly wagged the U.S. dog.

One can also classify Iran as one of the major Middle Eastern states unsympathetic to Iraq. The Iran-Iraq war was a major drain on the Iranian economy and the cause of millions of Iranian deaths. Iran's political system, as an Islamic republic, is theoretically and operationally opposed to the secular republican notions of Iraqi Baathism. Nonetheless, Iran is reluctant to endorse even UN-mandated intervention as a dangerous precedent for the region. As the number two country on Israel's "hit list" of terror-sponsoring states, this home of Hizbollah and supporter of Hamas is not interested in legitimizing the intrusion of Western or European superpowers into the area.

Jordan was one of the few regional states that did not join the coalition in 1991. Jordan and Yemen, for different reasons, declined to contribute troops to the suppression of Iraq. For Yemen, the choice was mostly ideological. For Jordan, the problem was more complex, particularly since Jordan was one of the major trading partners of pre- and postwar Iraq, and since the Palestinian populations of Jordan to a large degree conflated their support of Palestinian independence with the Iraqi situation. Fear of anger on the street prompted a cautious reluctance in King Hussein.

Hussein's successor harbored fewer of these reservations and generally supported the multilateral approach to dealing with Iraq. And King Abdullah allowed joint military training exercises to take place with U.S. special forces. But Jordan was still reluctant to allow military operations to operate from its border facilities and air bases. The domestic political consequences were clearly just too high.

Egypt was a prominent member of the 1991 coalition against Iraq, providing a substantial number of troops and important intelligence to the coalition. Its presence to a large degree legitimized the operation and provided symbolic cover to the United States in much of the Arab world. By 2002, Egypt was less enthusiastic about the U.S. proposals for regime change and disarmament. Domestic critics of the war saw a resurgence of classic colonial politics in the U.S. attack on Iraq. Thus, the role of Egypt in the coalition fast became a domestic political issue that put serious pressure on President Mubarak and his government.

It can be argued that Saudi Arabia found itself in the most ironic circumstances of the original coalition members. One of the earliest supporters of the 1991 Gulf War, Saudi Arabia allowed its bases to be used by U.S. forces; contributed troops, material, and energy to the effort; and paid a large percentage of the costs of the war. It considered itself a loyal ally of the United States, in a mutually beneficial relationship based on perceived common interests: U.S. need for a regular and reasonably priced supply of petroleum and the Saudi need for military and political security in a dangerous neighborhood. This deal, they thought, was in good shape and standing. The attack on the World Trade Center brought these assumptions into question.

The first problem for the Saudi government was the embarrassment of discovering that fifteen of the nineteen hijackers in the attack were Saudi citizens. In retrospect, this is not surprising, given the Al-Qaeda strategy of recruiting members from the mujahedeen soldiers of the Afghan war. Many of these men, supported then by the governments of Saudi Arabia and the United States in their efforts to drive the U.S.S.R. out of Afghanistan, had been socialized into a radical understanding of Islam and Islamic jihad. Moreover, bin Laden and his family had enjoyed a privileged life in Saudi Arabia, creating more opportunities for the recruitment of Saudi nationals into Al-Qaeda. Given these circumstances, it is not surprising that a substantial element of Al-Qaeda's membership would be Saudi by national origin.

The decision by Al-Qaeda's leadership to employ a disproportionate number of Saudis in the attack can also be explained. After the retreat of the U.S.S.R. from Afghanistan, Al-Qaeda turned to new projects, including the destruction of what they perceived as corrupt political regimes. Saudi Arabia topped that list, particularly given the important religious sites of Mecca and Medina in the country. And the United States, perceived by Al-Qaeda as the "great satan," was also high on the list of desirable targets. By using predominantly Saudi nationals in an attack on the World Trade Center, Al-Qaeda accomplished a twofold success: a demoralizing attack on the United States and the presumption of Saudi complicity.

Saudi Arabia's enemies in the United States, long angered by the privileged status of Saudi Arabia in U.S. foreign policy, launched a vigorous public relations attack against Saudi Arabia, accusing that state of being more of an enemy than a friend, of being a sponsor of the virulent variety of Islam that promoted international terrorism, and blaming a corrupt Saudi state for tolerating extremist religious leadership in exchange for their domestic political support. This attack was well coordinated and even resulted in public hearings conducted by Defense Department advisory panels.

The anti-Saudi argument gained momentum in the United States as the Saudi government rejected U.S. requests to use Saudi air bases in a future war against Iraq. Saudi Arabia refused in essence to recognize the U.S. raison d'être for a unilateral attack on Iraq. Ultimately, the Saudi government agreed that the bases could probably be used in the event of a UN-sanctioned attack on Iraq. But in the U.S. public and governmental view, this was less than satisfactory, and the United States turned to develop alternative sites for the war. Saudi prestige in the United States plunged to an unprecedented low and was unlikely to recover quickly. The relationship at the official level was still positive, but stress between the two governments was growing as the prospects of war with Iraq loomed larger.

If Saudi Arabia was a reluctant partner in the U.S. policy toward Iraq, the tiny state of Qatar expressed no such reluctance. Qatar enthusiastically endorsed the U.S. position on Iraq and permitted the construction of a large air base and command center on the Qatar peninsula that could easily serve as the nerve center of a U.S. attack on Iraq. Joint military exercises in December 2002 included the movement of material and personnel from the U.S. Central Command in Tampa, Florida, to the base in Qatar. All in all, an intimate relationship developed between Qatar and the United States.

This relationship was uncharacteristic of the other Gulf states. Bahrain, a host port for the U.S. naval forces in the Gulf, refused to endorse the U.S. unilateral attack, as did the governments of the United Arab Emirates and Oman. This reduced regional support for a unilateral U.S. attack on Iraq to Israel, Kuwait, and Qatar. All three of these states have prepositioned U.S. military supplies on their territories, have cooperated with the United States in joint military maneuvers and exercises, and have accepted the U.S. reasoning behind its proposed military suppression of Iraq. Taken collectively, they represent a very small subset of the region and a marginal percent of the Arab world. This suggested that regional and world opinion had formed against the U.S. war on Iraq.

The proposed war on Iraq was enthusiastically endorsed by Israel. In fact, governmental and public opinion in Israel was and is supportive of a series of U.S. interventions, not only against Iraq, but against Iran, Syria, and Libya as well. Israel has publicly vowed to use its weapons of mass destruction, including its nuclear arsenal, against Iraq should Iraq venture an attack against it. It was unlikely in the event of actual war between Iraq and the United States that Israel would be noncombatant. The 1991 precedent, which kept Israel out of the conflict, was apparently over and the United States actively developed basing sites and coordinated strategies with the Israel Defense Forces. It seemed likely that in the event of a more or less unilateral U.S. attack on Iraq, Israel would take a key role. This was not well received in the rest of the Middle East.

Israel also assumed a green light from Washington in its dealing with the Palestinian intifadah. The Israeli reprisals to Palestinian attacks became larger in scale and intensity. Renewed emphasis on the destruction of Palestinian infrastructure, collective punishment, administrative detention, long-term general curfews, assassinations, and the construction of new settlements brought the conflict to new heights of violence, as increasing numbers of Israeli and Palestinian citizens died in the conflict.

Palestinian groups (Hamas and Hizbollah among them) responded with suicide bombings, ambushes, and attacks against settlements and military posts. As the conflict continued to spiral upward, Israeli politicians publicly contemplated the desirability of a mass expulsion of Palestinians (transfer), the exile or assassination of Yasir Arafat, and the final annexation of all of the occupied territories.

All of this convinced world public opinion that a major peace initiative, with the United States in the lead, was past due. This opinion did not prevail in the United States, however, and it was unlikely that the United States would make any new attempt at an evenhanded resolution of the conflict.

WORLD PUBLIC OPINION

Domestic critics of the proposed war with Iraq often pointed to a deteriorating public regard for the United States abroad. In late 2002 and early 2003, a number of polls confirmed this belief. U.S. prestige, high and robust after the World Trade Center attack and during the U.S. pursuit of Al-Qaeda and the Taliban, plummeted as the United States turned its attention from terrorism to Iraq.

Moreover, the deterioration in public regard for the United States proceeded not only among the usual suspects, countries traditionally suspicious or at odds with the United States, but among the populations of states long considered to be friendly and alliance partners. Decline in public support for the United States in Great Britain, France, Germany, and Canada was clear. In these states, the United States appeared to be viewed as increasingly arrogant, self-centered, and intransigent. In a world characterized by increasing complexity, the simple rhetorical flourishes of the U.S. government did not find a receptive international ear.

As the *International Herald Tribune* reported in December of 2002:

> While majorities in nearly every country supported the U.S.-led war on terrorism, U.S. threats of war against Iraq appear to have heightened concerns, recorded in earlier surveys, about an American foreign policy seen as overly aggressive and insufficiently concerned with the interests of friends and allies.[1]

Is world public opinion important? Does it matter whether EU citizens develop a low regard for the United States and its citizens? Does our ability to travel as welcome guests weigh heavily in

---

[1]Brian Knowlton, "A Global Image on the Way Down." *International Herald Tribune,* December 5, 2002.

the equations of modern ideas of the good life? Should public opinion, at some important level, drive the foreign policies of states? Should governments be attentive to public opinion abroad in the same way they emphasize it at home?

In the short run, world public opinion can be discounted as an immediate concern for policy makers. Polls often register volatile results, and in the short run analysts and politicians can discount the variation. But in the long run, as trends and data consolidate, public opinion polling can register a reality that impinges on decision makers and political relationships. Were the United States to squander the decades of goodwill it generated as a positive force in the world by engaging in self-centered and muscular unilateralism, were it simply to see the world in terms of its own naked self-interest, then the tide of opinion could swell to a proportion that complicates U.S. foreign policy and leads to increasing isolation in its "fortress." If U.S. troops are unwelcome, if its diplomats are put at risk, if business leaders encounter boycotts of their goods and services, if travelers cannot presume their safety and a friendly welcome, then the world will be a more difficult place in which to live.

The world now presents a series of difficult and complicated choices. The choice between muscular unilateralism and international multilateralism is one such choice. If the United States insists on going it alone and ignores the wishes and policies of international organizations, there will be consequences. If the United States insists on a rule of law but seeks exemptions for its own officials in the new international criminal courts, there will be consequences.

WAR

In early March of 2003 it became very clear that the United States had reached the limit of its patience with the UN and Security Council procedures. On March 17, in a televised address to the nation and the world, President Bush announced the end of diplomacy and the beginning of direct action against the Iraqi regime. After a general review of Iraq's previous violations of a series of UN resolutions and agreements, President Bush gave Saddam Hussein and his sons forty-eight hours to leave Baghdad for exile abroad. Precisely at the end of forty-eight hours, U.S. and British forces began a military campaign against Iraq, moving from bases in Kuwait into southern Iraq. Shortly after, air strikes began against Iraqi targets. The long-predicted war against Iraq had begun.

Substantial opposition to the war was apparent in the United States and overseas. U.S. efforts to characterize the war as the effort of a broad-based coalition were greeted with skepticism at home and abroad. The war was essentially a U.S. unilateral intervention, with approximately 200,000 U.S. troops joined by less than 30,000 troops from the "coalition" states. Muscular unilateralism prevailed over multilateralism and international consensus. The long-term consequences of the decision will mature over the coming decades.

In the short run, the U.S. war of "Shock and Awe," designed to demoralize the Iraqi opposition and decapitate the Iraqi government, worked well. Within two weeks of the invasion, U.S. and British forces had secured southern Iraq, including the major city of Basra, and were converging on the outskirts of Baghdad, over 200 miles north of the Kuwait staging areas. Within three short weeks the "Battle for Baghdad" had begun. All along the axis of conflict, Iraqi military formations collapsed and offered at the most token resistance. Superior U.S. airpower and land-based maneuvers destroyed Republican Guard divisions in their positions. No classic tank or infantry battle worthy of the name materialized and formal Iraqi military opposition literally melted away.

Such resistance to the U.S. advance as did materialize did so as the action of irregular Iraqi paramilitary troops (for example, the Fedayeen Saddam) engaged in guerrilla ambush tactics. While actions like this did distract and slow the relentless U.S. movement to Baghdad, it did less to hinder U.S. forces than did two to three days of intense sand storms in the Iraqi deserts.

The much-anticipated battle for Baghdad never materialized. The occupation of Baghdad was characterized mostly by the destruction of regime assets and Saddam Hussein iconography (statues, murals, palaces), and an orgy of looting set off by the sudden absence of police and other agents of political authority. The war in the north of Iraq progressed easily as well, as long-established Kurdish militias (Pesh Murgah, for example) came down from the hills and occupied important urban sites, cities like Erbil, Dohuk, Kirkuk, and Mosul. The invasion of Tikrit, Saddam Hussein's birthplace and hometown, likewise turned out to be a non-event militarily. The expected "last stand" of Hussein loyalists never happened, allowing U.S. troops to move in without material opposition.

The war, by any American military expectation, went extraordinarily well. But this is not to suggest that the war was conducted without damage to Iraqi military personnel, Iraqi infrastructure, and Iraqi citizens. It seems clear that U.S. military ordinance was measurably more precise and deadly than the ordinance used only a decade before in the first Gulf War. The use of precision-guided munitions allowed the U.S. military to more precisely target its objectives. Deep-drilling "bunker buster" bombs were used to target the Iraqi command and control facilities and to attempt the destruction of Saddam Hussein himself and his leadership elite.

No military action, no war, can yet be characterized as "surgical" or "precise." During this war some munitions failed to reach their intended targets, others were improperly targeted (mistakes were made) and "collateral damage" ensued. The phrase *collateral damage* is one of the most objectionable linguistic misrepresentations of modern war. When it occurs, civilians die but linguistically their deaths are sanitized and dismissed.

One of the most interesting aspects of the war was the incorporation of journalists from varying nationalities and organizations into the front line military units. Called journalistic *embedding*, journalists were trained to join combat units during the exercise of their missions. There were, of course, stringent limitations on what those embedded journalists could report, both as a consequence of security concerns and of the public relations concerns of the administration.

For example, embedded journalists were forbidden to broadcast the location of the troops with which they were operating. And it was considered a matter of policy not to broadcast images or descriptions of U.S. or British casualties or those killed in action. The resulting coverage offered 24/7 imagery of the war in progress, sanitized to a considerable degree and enthusiastic about the soldiers themselves.

And there were real casualties among the journalists so embedded. A few were killed by enemy fire, a smaller number killed by friendly fire or unfortunate health problems, as in the death of NBC reporter David Bloom. Peter Arnett, a veteran journalist stationed in Baghdad and reporting for MSNBC and the National Geographic Channel, was fired for giving to Iraqi national television an interview critical of the war's progress. Other independent journalists found themselves detained and removed from the area by both Iraqi and coalition forces. Journalistic objectivity, always a difficult standard to judge reportage by, apparently suffered at the gain in unprecedented images of the military operations in Operation Iraqi Freedom.

As American media, embedded with troops and otherwise, decided for one reason or another not to publicize or recognize the deaths of civilians in the conflict, the true costs of the conflict do not enter our public space. During the press coverage of this war, U.S. media decided not to carry graphic images of dead soldiers or civilians. As a result, American media consumers saw a different surgical war than did their counterparts in Europe, Asia, and the Middle East, where media outlets carried explicit (and often horrifying) images of maimed and mangled soldiers and civilians and of the physical damage to buildings and historical sites. What resulted from such a difference in perspective led to a fundamental divergence in public opinion about the war. American public opinion coalesced in favor of the war (roughly 70 percent support) while public opinion abroad generally moved in the opposite direction (70 to 80 percent opposed). As might be expected, public opinion in neighboring Arab states achieved even higher levels of opposition.

Casualty figures for the war are imprecise, particularly on the Iraqi side of the equation. The figures that follow are for the most part estimates and should be taken as such. At any rate, by the end of the military campaign, four weeks into the war, U.S. and allied casualties totaled just less than 150. Of this figure, roughly half were the result of accidents or "friendly fire" incidents. In manpower terms, the invasion of Iraq was accomplished with very low levels of military casualties.

The same cannot be said of Iraq. The total number of Iraqi casualties may never be known, and it was not in the interests of either the coalition or the emerging Iraqi administration to emphasize them. Extrapolating from the number of military units that the coalition troops destroyed, one can easily project Iraqi military casualties to the tens of thousands and civilian noncombatant casualties in the thousands, from 3,000 to 4,000. There were no reliable estimates of civilian deaths due to environmental effects or infrastructure damage, such as water and electrical grids. And there are no reliable estimates of the extent of physical damage to Iraqi infrastructure such as roads, airports, buildings, hospitals, schools, and museums. Second-hand reports and anecdotes suggest substantial physical damage requiring extensive reconstruction efforts. The overall costs are likely to be in the tens of billions of dollars. The coalition victors were quick to proclaim that Iraqi oil fields in the north and south were liberated without significant damage, leading to the conclusion that Iraq could afford to pay at least for part of the damage inflicted during the conflict.

There were other bothersome ambiguities in the early successes of the coalition. Saddam Hussein himself was still unaccounted for, his whereabouts unknown. Without a captured or killed Saddam, the war lacked a symbolic final moment. The destruction of numerous statues, murals, and representations of Saddam Hussein substituted for proof of his death. And a final symbolic moment of sorts was reached as American generals took over Saddam's largest Baghdad palace and smoked celebratory cigars in the dictator's own home.

Advocates of the war expected a joyous Iraqi welcome for the liberating troops. In fact, U.S. and British soldiers were met with a range of reactions and welcomes, including cheers, jeers, rocks, and rifle fire.

It is important to note one critical and unanticipated consequence of the war. Apparently, the invading forces underestimated the social disorder that would accompany the destruction of the Baathist regime. As a consequence, incalculable damage was done to Iraqi and world history as priceless artifacts in the Iraqi National Museum and other historical sites were broken or stolen. Artifacts as old as 7,000 years appeared for sale on the international art markets shortly after the looting. The losses are incalculable. Much of the evidence of the earliest days of human civilization is simply gone.

Coalition leaders denied responsibility for the looting and for failing to protect the artifacts, pleading military and security priorities. But critics outside those official circles were vociferous, leading to severe criticisms of the United States. For example, British journalist Robert Fisk filed this report from Baghdad in *The Independent:*

> U.S. troops have sat back and allowed mobs to wreck and then burn the Ministry of Planning, the Ministry of Education, the Ministry of Foreign Affairs, the Ministry of Culture and the Ministry of Information. They did nothing to prevent looters from destroying priceless treasures of Iraq's history in the Baghdad Archaeological Museum and in the museum in the northern city of Mosul, or from looting three hospitals.[2]

Fisk goes on to report with considerable indignation that U.S. troops did manage to protect two Iraqi ministries: Interior and Oil, both of which were apparently more important, in his estimation, than the others.

The looting and public disorder that followed the close of military hostilities did raise a significant issue, that of the transition from military intervention to occupation and administration. Having destroyed the regime of Saddam Hussein, the United States and its allies were now faced with the necessity of providing an alternative.

Within a week of the end of military operations, a U.S. management team, led by retired Lt. General Jay Garner, entered Iraq and began planning for an interim administration. Such an administration would, presumably, put basic services back on line while the Iraqi public and its leaders prepared for independence and a democratic form of government. A parallel administration, composed

[2]Robert Fisk, "Americans Defend Two Untouchable Ministries from the Hordes of Looters." *The Independent,* April 14, 2002.

of senior coalition bureaucrats, would monitor and mentor a cadre of Iraqi managers, until Iraq was ready to resume independent governance.

The managers and designers of the new Iraqi government had to deal with numerous problems beyond the military damage to the country's infrastructure. Primary among the problems was the balance of power between the country's major ethnic and religious groups, primarily the majority Shia, the Arab Sunnis, and the Kurds. A number of Shia religious leaders presumed that the government would automatically reflect the majority status of the Shia community, and one Ayatollah announced his unelected mayorship of an eastern Iraqi city. In the north of Iraq, Kurds coming from the mountains clashed with the Sunni Arab administrators of important northern cities, and U.S. troops were pushed into uncomfortable mediation between the two groups. And at one point, U.S. soldiers opened fire on Iraqi demonstrators armed with stones and epithets. Upwards of a dozen Iraqi civilians were killed and scores wounded.

The pure fact of the situation is that the military destruction of Iraq was easy compared to the project of restoring public order and creating effective and legitimate government. There are no manuals and readily applicable paradigms for the transition from a brutal personal dictatorship (Saddam Hussein's government) to a Western-modeled electoral democracy. Such a project will likely be measured in years and months, not weeks and days.

One cannot deny the overwhelming military victory of the United States and its allies in Iraq. But the world was watching carefully how the United States implemented the postwar regime. In taking on the physical and political reconstruction of Iraq, the United States had the opportunity to show the world that its intervention was truly predicated on the greatest good to the Iraqi nation and to the international community, and not simply a self-interested grab for power, petroleum, and influence in a crucial region of the world. A quick transition to effective Iraqi government, accompanied by a quick departure of U.S. troops, would reassure many critics of the United States around the world.

Similarly, an extended occupation, with the certainty of Iraqi resistance, accompanied by the self-serving exploitation of Iraq's petroleum resources by U.S. and British corporations, would bring the United States under increased suspicion and ultimately generate more political hostility. Great global stakes hinged on the ultimate perception of the war and its objectives. Particularly troublesome were those critics who saw in the war an assault on Islam.

Perceptions

The war and its aftermath are perceived differently in different parts of the world. In the United States, as the war ended, roughly 70 percent of the public supported the war. In coalition ally Great Britain, slightly less than 50 percent of the public supported the action. In Spain, another coalition state, nearly 90 percent of the public opposed the war. Why were there such different perceptions of the event?

One reason is the ubiquitous presence of the mass media, present as both embedded media and more politically independent media from both U.S. and non-U.S. sources. The ways in which these different media framed images and issues in the war go a long way to explaining U.S. public support for the effort and wide-ranging opposition outside of the United States.

Take, for example, the following widely circulated description of an incident. During the drive to Baghdad, U.S. forces encountered quasi-guerrilla attacks and suicide bombers. Both of these left U.S. troops edgy and fearful. In this context, an Iraqi van approached a U.S. checkpoint and failed to heed orders to stop. U.S. troops opened fire on the vehicle. After the shooting stopped, it was determined that the occupants of the van were Iraqi women and children fleeing the conflict.

U.S. and foreign media framed the event differently. American media, while acknowledging the loss of innocent life, chose to focus on the tearful reactions of the U.S. soldier who had opened fire on the vehicle. The soldier's reaction showed the personal agony that accompanied his decision. Moral soldier, amoral warfare. Many foreign media chose to focus on a surviving woman in the van, cradling her dead children in her arms and weeping inconsolably. In this case, an innocent parent was victimized by amoral warfare.

The two images, derived from the same event, prompted different reactions. Americans could take pride in their soldier, a man clearly bothered by the consequences of his caution and action. Others could feel indignation over the deaths of Iraqi children, an act accomplishing nothing for the conduct of the war or the suppression of Saddam Hussein. "Collateral damage," indeed.

Other observers differed over the advisability of appointing General Jay Garner, retired, as the U.S. administrator for postwar Iraq. Americans saw in General Garner a seasoned military official and administrator clearly capable of dealing with the postwar damage to Iraq and its infrastructure. They also saw in him an individual able to deal with the postwar militias and warlords likely to emerge in the ashes of the Baath regime, seasoned by his experience in the Kurdish north.

Observers in the Middle East and in Western Europe had different reactions to General Garner's appointment. They saw in this appointment the empowerment of an American general close to Prime Minister Ariel Sharon, a man publicly sympathetic to Israel and unsympathetic to the Palestinians. General Garner was well known for advocating a "get tough" policy for the West Bank and Gaza, an indicator of a repressive administration in Iraq.

General Garner was replaced within a month of his assignment by L. Paul Bremer, a highly regarded U.S. diplomat. This change reduced the most virulent criticisms of the post-war administration in Iraq.

Although public opinion moderated in a pro-American direction after the termination of the military phase of the conflict, overall majority public opinion abroad was generally critical of the United States and its deeper motives for the war. Certainly, the differing framing of the conflict complicated differences in perception of the war by a globally empowered media and its consumers.

Governmental opinion in the region also coalesced against a long-term role for the United States in Iraq. Shortly after the fourth week of the war, eight neighbors of Iraq met in Saudi Arabia to consult on a postwar Iraq. Representatives of Turkey, Iran, Jordan, Kuwait, Saudi Arabia, and Syria were joined by Egypt and Bahrain. The parties all agreed that an immediate withdrawal of U.S. troops and the involvement of the UN in the management and reconstruction of postwar Iraq would best serve the interests of the region. Needless to say, U.S. officials did not concur. Nor did they concur with the conference sentiment that U.S. political pressure on Syria, prominent as the war wound down, should be moderated.

Clearly, differences of opinion, globally distributed, accompanied the U.S. war against Iraq.

A Clash of Civilizations?

There are political theorists who have predicted a clash of civilizations as the likely successor to the Cold War between the U.S.S.R. and the West. Samuel Huntington describes the relationship between the West and the Islamic world in these terms:

> The underlying problem for the West is not Islamic fundamentalism. It is Islam; a different civilization whose people are convinced of the superiority of their culture. . . . The problem for Islam is not the CIA or the U.S. Department of Defense. It is the West, a different civilization whose people are convinced of the universality of their culture.[3]

Although Huntington does not insist on the inevitability of civilizational war, he does insist on the probability of the same. In this, religious and political leaders in both the Western and Islamic worlds, who apparently wish to hasten the conflict to a higher, more-violent level, join him.

Prominent religious spokesmen in the United States have spoken out against Islam, in what has appeared to be a coordinated attack on the religion, widely reported in both the Western and non-Western press. Reverend Jerry Falwell, for instance, pronounced the Prophet Muhammad a "terrorist." Reverend Franklin Graham denounced Islam as an "evil" and "wicked" religion. Reverend Jimmy Swaggart called for the expulsion of all Muslim foreign students from the United States, and a similar fate for those Muslim citizens who protested it. The Reverend Pat

---

[3]Samuel Huntington, *The Clash of Civilizations: The Remaking of World Order* (*New York:* Simon & Schuster, 1996), pp. 217–218.

Robertson publicly criticized President Bush for his kind words on Islam on the occasion of Eid al-Fitr, the conclusion of the Islamic holiday of Ramadan, suggesting that he leave theology to the theologians.

These tirades against Islam are registered and remembered in the Islamic world. And they are echoed by the Islamic equivalent of this demagogic quartet, mullahs and imams who use their privileged place in the madrasahs and mosques of the Islamic world to rail against the "heresy," materialism, hedonism, and excessive individualism of Christianity and the West in general. Collectively, they would increase the divide between East and West, between Christianity and Islam, to serve their own personal and religious needs.

These religious extremists appear to be in the minority in their respective countries. But the public appeal of apocalyptic imagery is strong: simple-minded charges of evil and wickedness are credible to a zealous religious community. In their zeal to bring about the "end times" of the apocalyptic prophesy, both Christian and Islamic extremists add fuel to the fire of international conflict.

Nothing in the individual theologies of Judaism, Christianity, and Islam necessitates such militant conflict between the faiths. They are, in fact, all Abrahamic religions, recognizing a common point of origin for all three faiths. And the faiths are all insistently monotheistic, a belief sanctioned by a series of prophets recognized by all three faiths. But history is nonetheless replete with horrifying examples of religious wars and conflicts: the Crusades, the Thirty-Years War, the persecution of the Huguenots, the Holocaust; the list can go on and on. So although there is no theological requirement of religious strife, there is every evidence of the probability of it.

CONCLUSION

The conflation of religion and politics adds measurably to the volatility of international politics. When one stirs into the mix extreme religious views, the sort associated with Islamic jihadists, Christian Zionists intent on hastening the apocalypse, Christian Identity organizations that racialize religion, modern Jewish zealots intent on building a new temple on the site of the Haram al-Sharif or recreating the "Promised Land" between the Euphrates and the Nile, then the brew becomes particularly unstable and amenable to the tactics of terrorism.

In their recent study of international terror, Daniel Benjamin and Steven Simon make the following observation:

> Time, as we have seen, is compressed for those in the thrall of apocalyptic ideas. Ancient dramas replay themselves in modern circumstances, and when the believer acts forcefully enough, a reversal in history occurs, wrongs are righted, and injustices avenged.[4]

If this view of sacred terror is accurate, the best corrective is a global system that takes the suffering of people seriously and attempts to ameliorate it. A "Fortress America" mentality or a "Europe First" mentality will only aggravate a growing trend augmented by demographic change. It is time for a major, coordinated assault on the causes of misery and pain in the world. Who is better prepared and positioned for such an effort than the only remaining superpower, the United States of America, aided by its allies?

[4]Daniel Benjamin and Steven Simon, *The Age of Sacred Terror* (New York: Random House, 2002), p. 445.

Internet Resources

One of the most obvious and important of the new forces for globalization is the Internet and the related World Wide Web. The penetration of this network, and the range of information available on it now, have prompted us to substitute this modest list of Web sites for the "Country Profiles" of previous editions. This is, however, a decision not to be taken lightly. You should take care when using various Web sites to determine the identity and nature of the organization sponsoring and maintaining the site. Most Web sites have a clear point of view driving their selection and presentation of data. Moreover, not all Web sites are created equal. Some are scrupulous in their efforts to ensure the accuracy of the information they contain. Others are nearly anarchic in character, using a "caveat emptor" approach to data quality and interpretation. Still others are clearly advocates for a particular point of view or movement.

This is not to suggest that such sites are useless—but a student or scholar seeking objective and verifiable information should be careful in selecting and using Web-based data. It is also true that Internet-based data should be integrated with traditional research materials: journal articles, books, periodicals, newspapers, and other more traditionally presented resources. We live in an information-rich world; but we must maintain great vigilance to stay in control of relevant information. Vigilance is necessary even when using high-prestige sources: For example, a recent dispatch in the *New York Times,* widely conceded to be a newspaper of high quality, placed Muscat, the capital of Oman, in the United Arab Emirates—and not just once, but twice in the same article.

A list of appropriate suggested Web sites follows. This list is suggestive only and not a comprehensive listing. Moreover, the Web is a very dynamic system: Some Web sites may be nonexistent by the time this book is published; other sites publish or update sporadically. Caution is again advised.

USEFUL WEB SITES

For general information about the political and social systems of the Middle East, the following Web pages and Internet sites are good starting points. All of the states of the area are covered in two or more of these sites:

Arab Countries WWW Sites: http://www.liii.com/
Arab Net: http://www.arab.net/

CIA Factbook: http://www.cia.gov/cia/publications/factbook

Library of Congress, U.S.: Country Studies: http://lcweb2.loc.gov/frd/csiqtocl.html

Middle East Links: http://www.mees.com/dotcom/mecountries/index/html

The Middle East Network Information Center: http://linic:lanic.utexas.edu/menic/

Middle East Studies Association: http://w3fp.arizona.edu/mesassoc/

The National Council on U.S./Arab Relations: http://www.nacusar.org

Netscape: Political Resources. Net: http://www.politicalresources.net/m_east.htm

Organization of Petroleum Exporting Countries: http://www.opec.org/

United Nations: http://www.un.org/

U.S. State Department: http://www.state.gov

U. of Utah: http://wizard.ucr.edu/~skiastap/menet.htm.

Most newspapers, wire services, magazines and other widely distributed sources of information and opinion have pages dedicated to the Middle East. We have found the following to be consistently useful:

Arab News: http://www.arabnews.com/arabnews/welcome

Associated Press: http://www.ap.org

Beirut Times: http://www.beiruttimes.com/

Cairo Press Review: http://www.sis.gov.eg/pressrev/html/indexfrm.htm

Chicago Tribune: http://chicagotribune.com/

Christian Science Monitor: http://www.csmonitor.com/

Gulfwire: http://www.arabialink.com

Ha'aretz (Israel): www.haaretzdaily.com

International Herald Tribune: http://www.int.com/

Jerusalem Post (Israel): www.jpost.com/

The Jordan Star: http://star.arabia.com/

New York Times: http://www.nytimes.com

Reuters Wire Service, at Yahoo: http://dailynews.yahoo.com

Washington Post: http://www.washingtonpost.com

There are topically focused Web pages, dealing with contemporary events, military affairs, terrorism, peace efforts, economic affairs, ad infinitum. Most of these sites have a definite and apparent bias. You are cautioned to pay close attention to the organizations responsible for the sites. If you are confused about the sponsor of a Web page please talk to your instructor.

Some useful examples:

American Near East Refugee Aid: http://www.anera.org/

Birzeit University: http://www.birzeit.edu/

Fateh Online: http://www.fateh.org/

Golan Heights Information Server: http://www.golan.org.il/

Hadassah: http://www.hadassah.org

Islamic Association for Palestine: http://www.iap.org/

Islamic Texts and Resources: http://wing.buffalo.edu/sa/muslim/isl.html

Israel Defense Forces: http://www.idf.il/

Israeli Government Press Office: http://www.gpo.gov.il

Israeli Knesset: http://www.knesset.gov.il

Janes Information Group: http://www.janes.com/

Palestinian Assoc. for the Protection of Human Rights and Environment: law@lawsociety.org

Middle East Realities (publishing erratically): http://www.middleast.org/

Palestinian Authority: http://www.pna.org/

Peace Now: http://www.peace-now.org/

World Zionist Organization: http://www.wzo.org.il

Glossary

Abbasids An important Hashemite Arab family descended from Abbas, which founded the Abbasid caliphate at Baghdad in 750. This dynasty saw the highest development of the caliphate during what is recognized as the golden age of Islam.

Afghani Jemal al-Din al-Afghani. A nineteenth-century Egyptian schoolteacher who became one of the first modern nationalist writers and spokesmen. He traveled widely and was important in inspiring Middle Eastern opposition to European colonialism.

Alawites A nonorthodox sect of Islam, found primarily in Lebanon and Syria. The Alawites dominate the Syrian government under President Assad, causing considerable internal resentment and tension among the Sunni majority.

AMAL (or Amal) Acronym for a Lebanese faction favoring pragmatic, secular political strategies. They are often in conflict with Hizbollah for the loyalities of the Lebanese Shia.

Ashkenazim The term generally used to describe Jews of European origin, specifically from northcentral Europe.

As shura A consultative assembly appointed by the king or emir.

Baath The Arab Socialist Resurrection party, a political party dedicated to Arab nationalism and socialism. Founded in Lebanon in the 1940s, the Baath party controls Syria and controlled Iraq until the ouster of the Saddam Hussein government.

Bedouin Refers generally to Arabic-speaking camel-herding nomads in the Middle East and especially in the Arabian peninsula.

Bida Un-Islamic innovations or deviations from tradition.

Caliph The title given to the successors of Muhammad as leaders of the Umma.

Diwan Originally, a record listing those fighting for the Umma, used to determine shares of conquered booty; later it became the rudimentary bureaucracy of the early Muslim state.

Djimmi A religious community given special recognition in Islam, particularly Jews and Christians, the "People of the Book." Such communities enjoyed immunity from forced conversion but had to pay higher taxes than the Muslims. Also included, eventually, were Zoroastrians and Hindus.

Druze Mystical, nonorthodox Muslim sect, located in Lebanon and Syria.

Fellahin (singular, fellah) Peasants, or occasionally, manual laborers in an urban work force.

Fiqh Islamic jurisprudence. Literally, an "understanding" of Sharia law. Different schools of fiqh were founded during the first centuries of Islam, most prominently the Shafi, Hanafi, Hanbali, and Maliki.

Ghazi Defender of the faith, usually as a soldier.

Hadith The collected reports about the life of the Prophet, which, along with the Koran, constitute the major authoritative sources of Islamic thought.

Hajj The pilgrimage to Mecca, one of the five pillars of Islam and the once-in-a-lifetime obligation of the faithful, given adequate health and finances to undertake the journey. A successful pilgrim becomes known as **"hajji"** and enjoys significant prestige.

Hashemite The family of the Quraish tribe to which Muhammad belonged, and which subsequently became influential in Muslim affairs. Traditionally powerful in the Hijaz region of the Arabian peninsula, Hashemites were established in power in Iraq and Transjordan following World War I.

Hijaz A mountainous region of the Arabian peninsula adjacent to the Red Sea coast, including the cities of Mecca and Medina; the region in which Islam originated.

Hijira The migration of those faithful to Muhammad's preaching, from Mecca to Medina (then called Yathrib), in 622. At Medina the full fruition of the political and social aspects of Muhammad's revelation took place.

Hizbollah An Iranian-supported radical Shia group in Lebanon, often associated with terrorist activities; rival of the more moderate AMAL.

Imam A religious teacher. Most often, the term refers to a leader of services in the mosque. In Shiism the term also refers to the leader of the Shia community.

Intifadah The uprising of Palestinians against Israeli occupation and rule in the Gaza Strip and the West Bank. The rebellion began in December 1987.

Ismailis The followers of Ismail, the seventh imam of the Shia tradition. The sect is marked by a more esoteric and mystical emphasis than other branches of Shiism and includes the Qarmatians.

Jahiliyya The "time of wickedness" before Muhammad; also used by some fundamentalists to refer to the contemporary loss of Islamic moral guidance.

Janissaries The slave-soldiers who eventually became the core of the Ottoman bureaucracy. Highly trained in special schools, in the early years they were denied the right to have children, thus eliminating hereditary claims to administrative office.

Jihad "Striving" on behalf of Islam. Sometimes called the "Holy War," jihad refers to the obligation of the faithful to extend the Umma and protect it from its enemies, either by actual warfare or by spiritual struggle.

Kaaba A shrine dedicated to Allah, of great historical importance in Arabian history. Although of pre-Muslim origin, it was incorporated by Muhammad into the Islamic faith and associated with the prophet Abraham. Located in the Grand Mosque of Mecca, the Kaaba is the ultimate destination of the pilgrim (hajji). Maintenance of the Kaaba is very important to the wider Islamic community and to the government of Saudi Arabia in particular.

Katib The scribes, or record keepers, employed by the traditional governments, especially under the caliphate.

Kharijite An early puritanical movement in Islam; initially allied with Ali, this radically democratic group eventually turned against him and assassinated him in 661.

Koran The written word of Allah as revealed through his Prophet, Muhammad.

Madrasah Schools of religion, sometimes independently supported by waqf endowments; often associated with a prominent urban mosque.

Mahdi The messiah or redeemer in Islam, expected to come to earth in the final days to lead the faithful in their war against the infidel.

Mameluks The slave dynasty of Circassians who ruled Egypt from 1250 to 1798. From 1517 until their destruction, they alone ruled Egypt, giving only nominal allegiance to the Ottoman sultan.

Maronites A Monophysite Christian sect located primarily in Lebanon and Syria.

Millets The religious groups given official status in the Ottoman Empire. In matters of civil conflict among members of the same millet, the conflict would be resolved by the traditional authorities and processes of the respective millet. Thus, a Christian was governed by Christian laws in his dealings with Christians, regardless of his physical location in the Ottoman Empire.

Miri sirf State ownership of land with specified rights to the tenant farmer.

Modernism (Islamic modernism) An interpretation of Islam that stresses its abstract spiritual values, rationality, and commitment to social justice rather than the accumulated details of Sharia law, and that argues that these basic Islamic ideas are compatible with modern social life. Modernist interpretations of Islam have been set forth by various Islamic scholars in the nineteenth and twentieth centuries.

Mosque An Islamic house of worship.

Muhammad Ali (also **Mehemet Ali**) Ruler of Egypt from 1805 to 1849. He initiated major reforms in Egypt, many of which were blunted by a combination of European and Ottoman strategies. The economic and military power of Egypt was greatly increased by Muhammad Ali, who was also the first of the great modernizers in the Arab world.

Muharram A month of the lunar year, dedicated in the Islamic community to commemorating Hussein's martyrdom. The commemoration is a very emotional event for the Shia faithful.

Mujtahid Religious leader, preacher, and scholar, the equivalent of the Sunni ulema.

Mulk Private ownership of land.

Mutawwa Semiofficial "religious police" in Saudi Arabia.

Muwahhidun "Unitarians"; the preferred designation for the fundamentalist sect that prevails in Saudi Arabia, founded in the eighteenth century by Abd al-Wahhab and popularly referred to as "Wahhabi."

Najd The extremely arid north-central region of the Arabian peninsula.

Ottomans (Ottoman Empire) Founded by the Turkish leader Osman, the Ottoman state gave rise to the last great Islamic caliphate. Centered in Anatolia, the empire lasted from its founding in the thirteenth century to the second decade of the twentieth century.

Pir A recognized master in a sufi tariqah or order.

Qarmatians A long-lived communal movement within the Ismaili sect of Shiism.

Quraish An important and powerful Arab tribe, which controlled Mecca at the time of Muhammad. As descendants of the Prophet's tribe, the Quraish have always been accorded a special respect in Islam.

Ramadan One of the lunar months of the Muslim calendar. Fasting during the daylight hours of Ramadan is one of the five pillars or ritual obligations of Islam.

Riddah The Wars of Apostasy, fought soon after the death of Muhammad, forcing rebellious Arab tribes to continue their allegiance to Islam.

Sadaqa In Islam, a voluntary charitable contribution, bringing religious merit to the donor.

Sanussi A Sufi order that became very influential in North Africa.

Sephardim Generally, the "Oriental" Jews of Spanish, African, Asian, or Middle Eastern origin. Specifically, the term refers to Jews from Spain.

Shahada The declaration of faith in Islam: "There is no God but Allah, and Muhammad is His prophet."

Sharia The Muslim legal code, founded on the Koran and hadith (traditions of the Prophet) and codified by various systems of interpretation or fiqh.

Sheikh A term that can apply to high-level political, local, communal, or religious leaders.

Shia Muslims following Caliph Ali and his successors, differing on various points of doctrine from the orthodox Sunni majority. Shiism, concentrated largely in Iraq and Iran, is divided into several different sects. Most Shia prefer this designation to the commonly used term, "Shiite."

Sufism A movement pervasive in Islam, based on mystical experience. The diverse Sufi orders, each with its own tradition of mystical teachings, have cultivated the inner, ecstatic aspect of Islam, and their appeal has greatly aided the spread of Islam in some parts of the world.

Sunni The largest, "orthodox" division of Islam.

Suq Bazaar; a place for commerce, composed of a number of merchants selling a limited variety of wares. An important setting for social interaction as well as commercial exchange.

Sura Chapter in the Koran.

Tanzimat Generally, a series of attempted reforms in the Ottoman Empire from 1839 to 1876; at least partially a response to growing European dominance at that time.

Taqiyyah Dissimulation, or the disguise of one's true religious feelings in order to avoid persecution. Widely used among the Shia in response to the many attempts to control or persecute the Shia community.

Tariqahs Specific orders of Sufism, with specified secret paths to mystical ecstasy. After the decline of the caliphate, tariqah lodges often filled many local social needs as well.

Tawhid The undivided unity of God and His authority over humankind; also refers to other, derivative concepts of unity, including social or political unity.

Ulema Muslim scholars who function as religious leaders in Islam. Unlike Christian priests, the ulema are not organized into a clergy and claim no special powers of sanctity beyond their study of the documents of Islam.

Umayyad One of the most powerful and important of the Arabic families at the time of Muhammad. The Umayyad caliphate was founded at Damascus by Muawiya after his conflict of succession with Ali.

Umma The worldwide community of Islam, which ideally commands a Muslim's loyalty above all considerations of race, kinship, or nationality.

Wahhabi Another, less preferred, term for Muwahhidun.

Wajh Group honor, "face," a concept of great importance in the maintenance of group and individual prestige.

Waqf Religious endowments, usually made in perpetuity, that support a specific institution devoted to good works, such as a madrasah, a home for orphans, or a religious building. The institution of waqf sometimes became a device for avoiding taxation.

Zakat One of the five pillars of the Islamic faith, obligating the faithful to support the unfortunate and the needy.

Index

The Cambridge Companion to Percussion

Percussion music is both the oldest and most recent of musical genres and exists in diverse forms throughout the world. This *Companion* explores percussion and rhythm from the perspectives of performers, composers, conductors, instrument builders, scholars, and cognitive scientists. Topics covered include percussion in symphony orchestras from the nineteenth century to today and the development of percussion instruments in chapters on the marimba revolution, the percussion industry, drum machines, and the effect of acoustics. The chapters also investigate drum set playing and the influences of world music on Western percussion, and outline the roles of percussionists as composers, conductors, soloists, chamber musicians, and theatrical performers. Developments in scientific research are explored in chapters on the perception of sound and the evolution of musical rhythm. This book will be a valuable resource for students, percussionists, and all those who want a deeper understanding of percussion music and rhythm.

RUSSELL HARTENBERGER is Professor at the University of Toronto and has been a member of both Nexus and Steve Reich and Musicians since 1971. With Nexus, he created the sound track for the Academy Award-winning Documentary Feature *The Man Who Skied Down Everest*. With Steve Reich and Musicians he has recorded for ECM, DGG, and Nonesuch Records and performed on the Grammy Award-winning recording of *Music for 18 Musicians*. His awards include the Toronto Arts Award, Banff Centre for the Arts National Award, a Juno nomination, and induction into the Percussive Arts Society Hall of Fame.

Cambridge Companions to Music

The Cambridge Companion to Monteverdi
Edited by John Whenham and Richard Wistreich

The Cambridge Companion to Mozart
Edited by Simon P. Keefe

The Cambridge Companion to Arvo Pärt
Edited by Andrew Shenton

The Cambridge Companion to Ravel
Edited by Deborah Mawer

The Cambridge Companion to Rossini
Edited by Emanuele Senici

The Cambridge Companion to Schoenberg
Edited by Jennifer Shaw and Joseph Auner

The Cambridge Companion to Schubert
Edited by Christopher Gibbs

The Cambridge Companion to Schumann
Edited by Beate Perrey

The Cambridge Companion to Shostakovich
Edited by Pauline Fairclough and David Fanning

The Cambridge Companion to Sibelius
Edited by Daniel M. Grimley

The Cambridge Companion to Richard Strauss
Edited by Charles Youmans

The Cambridge Companion to Michael Tippett
Edited by Kenneth Gloag and Nicholas Jones

The Cambridge Companion to Vaughan Williams
Edited by Alain Frogley and Aiden J. Thomson

The Cambridge Companion to Verdi
Edited by Scott L. Balthazar

Instruments

The Cambridge Companion to Brass Instruments
Edited by Trevor Herbert and John Wallace

The Cambridge Companion to the Cello
Edited by Robin Stowell

The Cambridge Companion to the Clarinet
Edited by Colin Lawson

The Cambridge Companion to the Guitar
Edited by Victor Coelho

The Cambridge Companion to the Organ
Edited by Nicholas Thistlethwaite and Geoffrey Webber

The Cambridge Companion to the Piano
Edited by David Rowland

The Cambridge Companion to the Recorder
Edited by John Mansfield Thomson

The Cambridge Companion to the Saxophone
Edited by Richard Ingham

The Cambridge Companion to Singing
Edited by John Potter

The Cambridge Companion to the Violin
Edited by Robin Stowell

The Cambridge Companion to

PERCUSSION

....

EDITED BY

Russell Hartenberger

CAMBRIDGE
UNIVERSITY PRESS

University Printing House, Cambridge CB2 8BS, United Kingdom

One Liberty Plaza, 20th Floor, New York, NY 10006, USA

477 Williamstown Road, Port Melbourne, VIC 3207, Australia

4843/24, 2nd Floor, Ansari Road, Daryaganj, Delhi - 110002, India

79 Anson Road, #06-04/06, Singapore 079906

Cambridge University Press is part of the University of Cambridge.

It furthers the University's mission by disseminating knowledge in the pursuit of
education, learning and research at the highest international levels of excellence.

www.cambridge.org
Information on this title: www.cambridge.org/9781107472433

© Cambridge University Press 2016

First published 2016

A catalogue record for this publication is available from the British Library

Library of Congress Cataloging in Publication data
Hartenberger, Russell.
The Cambridge companion to percussion / edited By Russell Hartenberger.
Cambridge : Cambridge University Press, 2016. | Includes
bibliographical references and index.
LCCN 2015036057 | ISBN 9781107472433
LCSH: Percussion instruments.
LCC ML1030 .C26 2016 | DDC 786.8–dc23
LC record available at http://lccn.loc.gov/2015036057

ISBN 978-1-107-09345-4 Hardback
ISBN 978-1-107-47243-3 Paperback

Contents

Figures

Music examples

Contributors

Michael B. Bakan is Professor of Ethnomusicology and Head of World Music at Florida State University, where he directs the Balinese gamelan and the Omnimusica intercultural ensemble. He is the author of the books *World Music: Traditions and Transformations* and *Music of Death and New Creation: Experiences in the World of Balinese Gamelan Beleganjur*, as well as of more than fifty publications on topics ranging from world percussion and rhythmic systems to the ethnomusicology of autism. He has performed as a percussionist with the Toronto Symphony, Music at Marlboro, championship gamelans in Bali, and leading jazz and world music artists.

Bob Becker's performing experience spans nearly all of the musical disciplines where percussion is found. As an artist with the Malletech company, he has created signature instruments and mallets, and published over fifty compositions and arrangements. An endorser and designer for the Sabian cymbal company, he was honored with a Lifetime Achievement Award in 2005. In 2006, he was recognized as a "Master Drummer" by the International Association of Traditional Drummers. In 1999, as a founding member of the percussion group Nexus, he was inducted into the Percussive Arts Society Hall of Fame.

Thomas Brett is a musician who holds a PhD in ethnomusicology from New York University. He has written articles on fandom, creativity, and the music of Autechre for the journal *Popular Music & Society*, and on therapeutic soundscape app listening for the forthcoming *Oxford Handbook of Music and Virtuality*, and is currently working on a book about music performance, perception, and memory. He has also released several collections of electronic music, including music for singing bowls. Since 1997, Thomas has played percussion on Broadway and blogs about music, sound, and culture at brettworks.com.

William L. (Bill) Cahn is a co-founder of the Nexus percussion group (1971–). He was Associate Professor of Percussion at the Eastman School of Music (2006–2015) and a visiting artist at the Showa Academy in Kawasaki, Japan (1998–2014). Bill was the principal percussionist in the Rochester Philharmonic Orchestra (1968–1995), on the RPO Board of Directors (1995–2004), and on the RPO Honorary Board (1995–). He has conducted and composed for symphony orchestras, and his compositions for percussion are widely performed. Bill's fourth book is *Creative Music Making* (2005). He received a Grammy Award (2006) with the Paul Winter Consort.

Colin Currie is a hugely esteemed figure in the world of solo percussion and contemporary music. As a concerto artist, he has given over two dozen such premieres and performed with over 150 orchestras worldwide. Composers who have written for him include Elliott Carter, Louis Andriessen, James MacMillan, and Einojuhani Rautavaara. He is also an avid solo recitalist and collaborator, while his ensemble, the Colin Currie Group, tours internationally every season

performing the music of Steve Reich to great acclaim. As a committed educationalist, he regularly gives master classes and adds educational/outreach events to his concert giving.

Peter Erskine is known for his versatility and love of working in different contexts. He appears on 600 albums and film scores, and has won two Grammy Awards and an honorary doctorate. He has played with Stan Kenton, Maynard Ferguson, Weather Report, Steps Ahead, Joni Mitchell, Steely Dan, Diana Krall, et al., and has been a soloist with major orchestras worldwide. Peter was designated "Best Jazz Drummer" ten times by *Modern Drummer* magazine. He attended the Interlochen Arts Academy and Indiana University. Peter is an author of several books; his latest is the autobiography *No Beethoven*. He is currently a professor at the University of Southern California.

Russell Hartenberger is Professor and former Dean of the Faculty of Music at the University of Toronto. He has been a member of both Nexus and Steve Reich and Musicians since 1971. His compositions are published by Keyboard Percussion Publications and the CD *Persian Songs*, released in 2015, includes his arrangements of music by Moondog and of Persian classical music, featuring Iranian vocalist, Sepideh Raissadat. His articles appear in *Percussive Notes* and *The Ashgate Research Companion to Minimalist and Postminimalist Music*, and his book *Performance Practice in the Music of Steve Reich* is forthcoming from Cambridge University Press.

Aiyun Huang enjoys a musical life as soloist, chamber musician, researcher, and teacher. She was the winner of the First Prize and the Audience Award at the Geneva International Music Competition in 2002. A champion of new music, Aiyun has premiered over 100 works over the last two decades internationally. Born in Taiwan, Aiyun holds a DMA degree from the University of California, San Diego. She is a researcher at the Centre for Interdisciplinary Research in Music Media and Technology, and holds the position of William Dawson Scholar at McGill University, Montreal, Canada.

John R. Iversen is a cognitive neuroscientist studying the connections between music and the brain. As a research scientist at UC San Diego, he studies the brain mechanisms of perception and production of rhythm in music and language, the role of culture in rhythm perception, and whether rhythm perception is uniquely human. John draws from a lifelong interest in percussion, currently expressed through Japanese *taiko* drum performance with San Diego Taiko, which he cofounded in 2004. He has degrees in Biophysics at Harvard, History and Philosophy of Science at Cambridge, and a PhD in Speech and Hearing Science from MIT.

Garry Kvistad, founder and CEO of Woodstock Chimes˚, has been a member of Steve Reich and Musicians since 1979 and is one of eighteen to win a Grammy Award for the recording of Reich's *Music for 18 Musicians*. He has been a member of the acclaimed Nexus percussion group since 2002. Garry earned his BM from the Oberlin Conservatory and MM from Northern Illinois University. Formerly on the faculties of Northern Illinois University and the University of Cincinnati College Conservatory as a member of the Blackearth Percussion Group, he is currently on the faculty of the Bard College Conservatory.

Rick Mattingly is Senior Publications Editor for the Percussive Arts Society and former Senior Editor for *Modern Drummer* magazine. His articles have appeared in *Percussive Notes, Rhythm! Scene, Modern Drummer, Modern Percussionist, Drum!, Down Beat,* and *Jazziz* magazines, and *The New Grove Dictionary of Jazz*. He is author of the books *All About Drums, The Drummer's Time,* and *Creative Timekeeping,* and coauthor (with Rod Morgenstein) of *The Drumset Musician* and (with Blake Neely) *FastTrack Drums,* vols. 1 and 2, all published by Hal Leonard Corporation. His arrangements for percussion ensemble are published by Hal Leonard and Alfred Music.

William Moersch is Professor and Chair of Percussion Studies at the University of Illinois, Urbana-Champaign. Internationally renowned as a marimba virtuoso, chamber and symphonic percussionist, recording artist, and educator, he has appeared as soloist with orchestras and in recital throughout North and South America, Europe, the Far East, and Australia. Moersch has performed on more than seventy recordings and is perhaps best known for commissioning much of the prominent modern repertoire for marimba. Currently, he is Principal Timpanist of Sinfonia da Camera and the Champaign-Urbana Symphony Orchestra, and Artistic Director of New Music Marimba.

Jeff Packman holds a PhD from the University of California, Berkeley, and is an ethnomusicologist whose research focuses on professional music-making and cultural politics. A former freelance drummer, he is completing a book on local working musicians in Salvador da Bahia, Brazil. Since 2007, Jeff has also been part of a collaborative fieldwork project investigating various manifestations of *samba de roda,* an Afrodiasporic music and dance practice from rural Bahia. His writing on these topics has appeared in edited collections and journals including *Black MusicResearch Journal, Ethnomusicology, Latin American Music Review,* and *Ethnomusicology Forum.* He currently teaches at the University of Toronto.

Steven F. Pond, Associate Professor and Chair of Cornell University's music department, works on jazz and musics of the African diaspora generally. His first book, *Herbie Hancock's Head Hunters: The Making of Jazz's First Platinum Album,* received the International Association for the Study of Popular Music's Woody Guthrie Prize for best monograph in popular music studies. His current book project centers on jazz historiography of the 1960s, particularly in regard to the politics of genre classification. Pond is active as a percussionist and drummer, and is director of Cornell's Brazilian music group Deixa Sambar.

Steve Reich has been called "our greatest living composer" (*The New York Times*) and "the most original musical thinker of our time" (*The New Yorker*). His compositions embrace not only aspects of Western classical music, but the structures, harmonies, and rhythms of non-Western and American vernacular music, particularly jazz. Reich was awarded the Pulitzer Prize in Music for his composition *Double Sextet.* Among his other numerous awards are the Preamium Imperial Award from Japan and the Polar Prize from the Royal Swedish Academy of Music. His compositions *Music for 18 Musicians* and *Different Trains* have each won a Grammy Award.

Steven Schick is a percussionist, conductor, and author who has commissioned more than 150 works, many of which are standard repertoire for percussionists. Schick founded the percussion group red fish blue fish – now celebrating its twentieth anniversary – and was the original percussionist of the Bang on a Can All-Stars. He is currently music director of the La Jolla Symphony and Chorus and artistic director of the San Francisco Contemporary Music Players. Steven Schick is Distinguished Professor of Music at the University of California, San Diego, and holds the Reed Family Presidential Chair in performance. He lives in La Jolla with his wife Brenda.

Michael Schutz is Associate Professor of Music Cognition/Percussion at McMaster University, where he directs the MAPLE (Music Acoustics Perception & LEarning) Lab. He previously spent five years as Director of Percussion Studies at Longwood University, performing frequently with the Roanoke and Lynchburg Symphonies and serving as principal percussionist with Opera on the James. He currently conducts the McMaster Percussion Ensemble, has performed at multiple PASICs, and is featured on Judith Shatin's album *Time to Burn* (Innova Recordings). Michael holds percussion degrees from Penn State (BMA) and Northwestern (MM), in addition to a PhD in Psychology. For more information visit www.michaelschutz.net.

Adam Sliwinski is a member of the quartet Sō Percussion, a group dedicated to expanding percussion music. With them, he has toured throughout the world and worked with some of today's most exciting composers. Adam is a lecturer and performer-in-residence at Princeton University and leads the percussion department at the Bard College Conservatory of Music. In addition to playing percussion, Adam has performed multiple world premieres as a conductor with the International Contemporary Ensemble, and is releasing a solo piano album in 2015 with Dan Trueman's *Nostalgic Synchronic* etudes. Adam earned his doctorate at Yale University and writes regularly about music on his blog.

Jason Treuting is a percussionist, composer, and improviser. As a member of Sō Percussion, he has performed internationally at venues such as Carnegie Hall and the Barbican Centre and has worked with a variety of artists including composer Steve Reich, maestro Gustavo Dudamel, *tabla* virtuoso Zakir Hussain, and indie rock gurus The National. As a composer, he has written most prominently for his own ensembles, contributing substantially to Sō Percussion's *Imaginary City* and *Where (we) Live*. His large-scale work *Amid the Noise* has been performed by ensembles worldwide. In 2013, Treuting was named a Princeton Arts Fellow and remains there as a performer-in-residence.

B. Michael Williams, Distinguished Professor of Percussion at Winthrop University in Rock Hill, South Carolina, holds degrees from Furman University, Northwestern University, and Michigan State University. His *Four Solos for Frame Drums* was among the first published compositions for the medium. Williams's book, *Learning Mbira*, for the Zimbabwean *mbira dzaVadzimu*, has been acclaimed as an effective tutorial method for the instrument. The supplemental four-volume set of *mbira* transcriptions, *MbiraTab*, continues the series. His CD recording, *BataMbira*, has been featured on National Public Radio, the Voice of America, and other broadcasts worldwide. Williams serves as Associate Editor for *Percussive Notes* magazine.

Acknowledgments

Many friends and fellow musicians have provided substantial assistance in preparing this volume. In particular, I would like to thank Kate Brett, Fleur Jones, and Vicki Cooper from Cambridge University Press for their assistance and advice throughout the project. I offer special thanks to Jeff Packman and Danielle Robinson, who were my guides through the initial stages of this undertaking. Many of my colleagues on the faculty and in the library at the University of Toronto have assisted me in countless ways; in particular, I want to thank Gregory Johnston, James Kippen, and Mary Ann Parker, who are paragons of scholarly integrity as well as valued confidantes. Finally, I would like to thank my wife, Bonnie Sheckter, who was really an equal partner in preparing this book. She contributed her expertise in the complexities of computer programs, jpegs, tiffs, photoshop, cover design, and other technical matters. But most importantly, she provided me with her personal support and encouragement throughout the entire project.

Other contributors would also like to express their thanks to individuals who assisted them in preparing their chapters.

From Michael Schutz:

Many colleagues provided feedback on earlier versions of this draft. In particular I would like to thank John Beck, John Brownell, Rob Dillon, Will James, Kris Keeton, Michael Overman, and Danny Tones for lending their perspective on this material. Additionally, I am grateful to Mary Broughton, Sofia Dahl, Fiona Manning, Jessica Phillips-Silver, Chia-Jung Tsay, and Johanna Vuoskoski for clarifying and improving my summaries of their work. I am also grateful for financial support from the Natural Sciences and Engineering Council (NSERC), the Social Sciences and Humanities Research Council (SSHRC), and the Canadian Foundation for Innovation (CFI). This enabled my team's research and the writing of the chapter. Support from the Ontario Early Researcher Award, Petro Canada Young Innovator Award, and McMaster Arts Research Board was also essential for the completion of this project.

From Adam Sliwinski:

I would like to thank Cristina, Eric, Josh, Jason, Russell Hartenberger, Laura Kuhn and Emy Martin, Jonathan Hiam, Gene Capriglio and C. F. Peters, B. Michael Williams, Michael Rosen, and Robert van Sice.

Introduction

RUSSELL HARTENBERGER

The *Cambridge Companion to Percussion* is a collection of articles that discuss issues relating to percussion and rhythm from the perspectives of performers, composers, conductors, instrument builders, scholars, and cognitive scientists. It is intended to be a companion to percussionists in their study and performance and an accompaniment to those who want a deeper understanding of percussion music and the rhythmic aspects that are embodied within it.

The *Companion* is not a historical documentation of percussion or an encyclopedia of instruments, terms, or usages. There are several excellent books and a growing number of journal articles and dissertations in these areas. It is also not a book on percussion technique, although the authors, all notable percussionists and percussionist/scholars, provide enlightened perspectives on performance issues. However, it is a valuable resource for students, amateurs, or professionals who seek insight into topics related to rhythm and percussion from experts in the field.

The percussion sphere is vast and worthy of a separate *Companion* in any of its areas. Consequently, for this volume I have chosen topics that will, hopefully, have wide interest and appeal and are from the points of view of Western-trained percussionists. The chapters are all written by percussionists whose backgrounds represent the range of interests commensurate with the breadth of the world of percussion.

The book is organized in broad areas, although there are overlaps throughout. Chapters 1 and 2 discuss the traditions of orchestral timpani and percussion from a historical perspective and also with a view to the future. Chapter 1 traces some of the "schools" of timpani playing that originated in European cities and have had an impact on percussion practice throughout the world. In Chapter 2, William L. Cahn, long-serving principal percussionist in the Rochester Philharmonic and later a member of its Board of Directors, cites issues that confront orchestral percussionists in the twenty-first century and possible solutions for them to consider.

Chapters 3–6 examine the development of percussion instruments and literature. In Chapter 3, marimba soloist and historian William Moersch writes about the rapid growth of interest in marimba and other mallet percussion instruments. The compositions, performers, and composers

listed in this chapter provide an extraordinary overview of the evolution of mallet instrument repertoire. In Chapter 4, percussionist and instrument builder Garry Kvistad analyzes the acoustical properties of percussion instruments and explains the value of this knowledge for percussionists. In Chapter 5, Rick Mattingly, Senior Publications Editor of the journal, *Percussive Notes*, provides insight into the percussion industry and the cross-over between manufacturers and performers. And in Chapter 6, scholar, composer, and Broadway percussionist Thomas Brett documents the history of drum machines and their effects on percussion and music in general.

Chapters 7–10 discuss percussion in performance areas that have emerged in the late twentieth and early twenty-first centuries. In Chapter 7, Adam Sliwinski, a member of Sō Percussion, looks at the percussion ensemble repertoire as chamber music from the early works of John Cage through the influential compositions of Steve Reich. Solo percussion performance is a relatively new phenomenon, and in Chapter 8, acclaimed soloist Colin Currie describes the solo and concerto repertoire for percussion while providing insight into the role of the percussion soloist. There is drama in the act of percussion performance, and in Chapter 9, Aiyun Huang, winner of First Prize and the Audience Award in the Geneva International Music Competition in 2002, describes the formalization of percussion theater through recent compositions. Percussionists often find themselves in the role of conductor, either formally or informally, and in Chapter 10, esteemed percussion soloist Steven Schick describes the challenges he faced in undergoing the transformation from professional percussionist to orchestral conductor.

In Chapters 11–13, three percussionist/composers describe their individual approaches to writing music for percussion and the concerns and issues that they have confronted in writing music in this idiom. Chapters 11 and 12 provide insight into the compositional styles of Bob Becker and Jason Treuting, two of the leading percussionist/composers of our time. There are many references throughout this book to the music and influence of composer/percussionist, Steve Reich. Chapter 13 is a collection of thoughts on percussion and rhythmic usage in Reich's music by the composer himself.

Three views of drum set playing are discussed in Chapters 14–16. In Chapter 14, legendary drummer Peter Erskine explains the elusive term "groove" and how drum set players achieve this feeling. In Chapter 15, Steven F. Pond, author of the award-winning book, *Headhunters, the Making of Jazz's First Platinum Album*, examines funk drumming through the frequently sampled drum break of Clyde Stubblefield. Drum set player and scholar Jeff Packman, in Chapter 16, describes technological

developments in the drum set itself, and the impact these changes have had on jazz and popular music.

Music played on percussion instruments is both the oldest and youngest of musical genres. The tradition of percussion exists in most countries in the world and has been a part of musical culture for as long as we know. The merger of these instruments and musical ideas has had a significant impact on contemporary Western percussion performance and is examined in Chapters 17–19. Chapter 17 is a conversation with the great *mrdangam* virtuoso from South India, Trichy Sankaran, and his daughter Suba Sankaran, both of whom have found ways to combine Indian and Western musical traditions. In Chapter 18, *mbira* player and African percussion pedagogue B. Michael William provides an overview of the influence of music from the African diaspora on many forms of music in the Western Hemisphere. In Chapter 19, percussionist/scholar Michael B. Bakan looks at the connections between percussion ensemble and Balinese gamelan and provides insight into a style of gamelan that uses only percussion instruments.

The perception of rhythm by humans is a relatively recent area of research by cognitive scientists. In Chapters 20 and 21, two percussionist/scientists look at some of the laboratory work that affects the way percussionists play their instruments and think about rhythms. In Chapter 20, Michael Schutz discusses the research on movement relevant to percussionists and focuses on those gestures that lack acoustical consequences. Chapter 21 concludes *The Cambridge Companion to Percussion* by bringing us back to the beginning of our relationship with rhythm in a discussion by John R. Iversen on the evolutionary origins of musical rhythm in humans.

My hope in presenting this volume is that it is representative of the growing significance of percussion and rhythm in Western music. Using the mantra of my first percussion teacher, Alan Abel, who instructed me to "follow the line" of the music, I encourage all readers who are inspired by the articles in this book to follow the many lines of percussion that lead to innovations in instrument development, composition, performance techniques, rhythmic ideas, and scientific research into future worlds heretofore unimagined.

Orchestral percussion

1 Timpani traditions and beyond

RUSSELL HARTENBERGER

One whose insight is the same as his teacher's lacks half of his teacher's power. Only one whose insight surpasses his teacher's is worthy to be his heir.[1]   LINJI YIXUAN (D. 866)

Timpani, or kettledrums, were the first percussion instruments to be included in the classical symphony orchestra, and the musicians who were called upon to play them were often string players, wind players, or, on occasion, singers. As composers wrote more complex parts for timpani, these newly minted timpanists began to create individual techniques based on their instruments, orchestra, repertoire, conductor, concert hall, and sociocultural environment. The players adapted to all these factors in creating individual approaches to sound production and musicality, and in doing so, became progenitors of the first schools of percussion. Orchestras in European cities spawned lineages of timpani players that, in some cases, still maintain links to their early timpanists through continuous teacher–student associations.

The first orchestral timpanists had no historical precedent for their playing techniques; the interpretation of their parts was based on their innate musicality combined with their imagination. As these musicians began to teach others the art of timpani playing, the techniques they developed became codified and, as time went on, even ossified as young players attempted to replicate the styles of their teachers. The timpanists who became the most influential were the ones who honored their teacher's precepts but responded to the changing musical environment by incorporating new ideas into their fundamental techniques. And as evolving generations of timpanists migrated beyond Europe creating family trees with branches extending in many directions, a cross-fertilization began to take place that enriched the use of percussion in Western musical traditions.

At the beginning of the twentieth century, orchestras were forming in major North American cities, and musicians from Europe were hired to fill many of the principal positions. The timpanists who arrived brought their traditions to their new orchestras but gradually modified them to accommodate orchestras with amalgamated groups of musicians playing in venues with different acoustics from the great concert halls in Europe. As percussion instruments gradually became

more commonly used in orchestras, the focus of timpani schools, in both Europe and North America, expanded to include snare drum, xylophone, glockenspiel, cymbals, and percussion accessories such as tambourine and triangle. Then, with the advent of recordings, theater orchestras, jazz and other forms of popular music, and later, compositions for solo percussion instruments and percussion/chamber ensembles, percussionists had career options beyond symphony orchestras. As a consequence, timpani became but one of many areas of focus for young players. Timpani styles began to merge as generations of percussionists moved from place to place and as creative players adapted to concert halls, new instrument designs, and diverse repertoire. However, the basic approaches to making a musical sound and interpreting a phrase that began with European timpanists continued to be valid and are still used by timpanists and percussionists today. One of the most intriguing stories of a European timpani tradition that found its way to North America and propagated an extended timpani and percussion lineage began in Leipzig, Germany.

Ernst Pfundt

Ernst Gotthold Benjamin Pfundt (1806–1871) had some training on a variety of instruments, including timpani, in his youth, but he was a choral director, tenor soloist, and piano teacher when, in 1836, he was called upon to play timpani in the Leipzig Gewandhaus Orchestra. According to timpani scholar Edmund A. Bowles, the orchestra's conductor, Felix Mendelssohn, "became dissatisfied with the timpanist, Friedrich August Grenser (who doubled on second violin, a common practice in those days). During a rehearsal, Grenser had so badly bungled the drum and piano solo in the concluding moments of Beethoven's 'Emperor' Concerto that Mendelssohn ... immediately hired Pfundt as a temporary replacement, who then performed so well that he earned Mendelssohn's everlasting gratitude." Pfundt became "arguably the most famous kettledrummer of his generation," and "wrote one of the very first instruction manuals for the instrument, thus establishing one of the first 'schools' of timpani playing."[2] Pfundt seems to have been a consummate musician from a musical background; he was the son of a singer, and nephew to Friederich Wieck, the father of Clara (later Schumann).[3] We can only speculate that, when Grenser "bungled" the timpani part to the Emperor Concerto, Pfundt was able to transfer his musical sensibility from singing and playing other instruments to timpani.

Figure 1.1 Drawing of Ernst Pfundt by Carl Reimers.

Alfred Friese; Saul Goodman

The legacy of Pfundt and the school of timpanists in the Leipzig Gewandhaus Orchestra that followed him extends to some of the early timpani players in orchestras in North America. Alfred Friese was a violist in the Gewandhaus Orchestra who became interested in timpani and studied with Hermann Gustav Schmidt (1857–1926), the Leipzig timpanist from 1893–1923.[4] Friese earned a position as timpanist in the Winderstein Orchestra in Leipzig and later moved to the United States where he was

timpanist in the Philadelphia Orchestra, Pittsburgh Symphony, and the New York Philharmonic. It was in New York that Friese taught Saul Goodman, who eventually succeeded him as timpanist in the New York Philharmonic and played there from 1926 to 1972.[5] Even though Goodman studied with the Leipzig-trained Friese, he credits a German from Dresden, Oscar Schwar, with giving him important advice about timpani playing.

> I owe a debt of gratitude to my dear friend and mentor, Oscar Schwar, the celebrated and unique timpanist of the Philadelphia Orchestra who died in 1945. Back in the late 1920s, I used to meet him every time the Philadelphia Orchestra came to New York City. Schwar had the most beautiful tone of any timpanist I have ever heard. With the encouragement and cooperation of Leopold Stokowski, he achieved tone colors from the timpani never heard before. He knew how to care for the instrument and how to keep it up to the highest state of perfection in order to produce the best results. In my many conversations with him, especially over a glass of beer, I learned much about these details that are so important for the timpanist.[6]

Goodman developed his own style of playing through his lessons and advice from Friese and Schwar, and also by playing from a position on stage at Carnegie Hall that Alan Abel describes as a "hot spot."[7] From this acoustically live site, his sound projected into the hall with clarity and authority. Anthony J. Cirone, who studied with Goodman at the Juilliard School, says Goodman "constantly reminded his students about three important considerations when performing: precision, sensitivity, and musicality."[8] Students of the "Goodman school," sometimes referred to as the "New York school," occupy numerous timpani and percussion positions in orchestras throughout the world, and the legacy of Goodman's teaching still echoes from his "hot spot."

Oscar Schwar; Cloyd Duff

Oscar Schwar, who Goodman acknowledges as a mentor, studied violin as a boy in Bautzen, Saxony, and entered the Royal Conservatory of Dresden as a violinist. He switched to timpani and studied with Herr Heinemann, timpanist at the Dresden Royal Opera. After finishing his schooling, Schwar served as timpanist in orchestras in Finland and Russia before moving to the United States where he was timpanist in the Philadelphia Orchestra from 1903 until his death in 1946. He was the first percussion teacher at the newly created Curtis Institute of Music when it opened in 1924. One of Schwar's students at Curtis was Cloyd Duff, who became timpanist in the Cleveland Orchestra in 1942 and played there until his

retirement in 1981. In an interview with Andrew Simco, Duff said of Schwar, "He was the most highly regarded player of his time. Even Saul Goodman studied with him." In describing what Schwar was like as a teacher, Duff explained,

> First of all, he scared the daylights out of me! He was a charming gentleman, but also a good, tough teacher. At that time I did not have a symphonic background but I gradually grew into his demands! I knew what he wanted, and he was always conscious of *tone* and *balance* ... As Schwar taught mainly timpani, you had to know your percussion. Having been a rudimental drummer was good for me, as he was very much concerned with precision, as were most musicians of a German background.[9] [Emphases in the original]

Duff continued the Schwar legacy through his teaching at the Cleveland Institute of Music and the Oberlin Conservatory of Music where he trained generations of timpanists in the "Duff school," or "Cleveland school," of playing based on Schwar's concepts of "tone and balance."

George Lawrence Stone

Even though Schwar taught mainly timpani, his concern for precision that Duff described carried over into other areas of percussion playing as the Dresden–Schwar school of timpani began to diversify with future generations of percussionists in North America. George Lawrence Stone (1886–1967) studied timpani with Schwar but followed a different path from orchestral playing. Stone was introduced to various percussion instruments at a young age by his father, who was a drummer, drum teacher, and drum manufacturer. After his father's death in 1917, Stone became principal of the Stone Drum and Xylophone School in Boston. Stone started his musical life as a drummer, but he still felt the influence of a non-percussion instrument. In 1935, he published *Stick Control for the Snare Drummer*,[10] a book that is often referred to as the "drummers' bible."[11] It was patterned after the *Arban Trumpet Method* (1864), likewise known as "the Bible of trumpet players,"[12] and written by Jean-Baptiste Arban, a virtuoso French cornet player who studied and was later on the faculty at the Paris Conservatoire. Stone often used the *Arban Method* with his xylophone students,[13] and in 1949, published *Mallet Control*, a book in which he used some of the same pedagogical ideas that he outlined in *Stick Control*.

With the publication of *Stick Control*, Stone became much in demand as a teacher. His students included jazz drummers Gene Krupa, Sid Catlett, George Wettling, Lionel Hampton, Ted Reed, Joe Morello, as well as Vic Firth,[14] timpanist in the Boston Symphony from 1952 to 2001.[15] Firth said this about Stone:

He was probably one of the first technique builders of the teachers, and he felt it was terribly important to make music. His theory was that you can be a sculptor by virtue of owning a hammer and chisel, but you don't really sculpt anything until you have the technique to do it. Likewise, before you can do anything "shapely" in music, you've got to have the hands to do it with.[16]

One of Stone's students who certainly had "the hands to do it with" was Joe Morello, drummer with the Dave Brubeck Quartet (and another drummer who began his musical career on another instrument – in his case, the violin). In 1961, Stone published a sequel to *Stick Control* titled *Accents and Rebounds*, a book that incorporated some of Joe Morello's ideas about adding accents to the *Stick Control* exercises.[17]

Stone and his *Stick Control* book can also be credited with having an impact on the compositions of Steve Reich. Reich was introduced to the Stone book when he was a teenager taking drum lessons from Roland Kohloff, a young drummer in New York City at the time who attended Juilliard where he studied timpani with Saul Goodman.[18] The repeated patterns of the *Stick Control* exercises along with the effect created by the varied distribution of right and left hand in these patterns planted a seed in Reich's subconscious that would later surface in many of his works.[19]

William Street; Fred D. Hinger

A contemporary of Stone's, and one of the most influential teachers of his generation, was William G. Street, timpanist in the Rochester Philharmonic and percussion teacher at the Eastman School of Music from 1927 to 1967. Street was a Canadian-born, self-taught musician who developed his own "school" of playing that utilized an upstroke concept.[20] John Beck, a student of Street's and his successor as percussion teacher at Eastman, wrote,

> [Street] always stressed quality of sound regardless of the instrument being played or the volume. His idea of producing quality sound was through lifting the mallet, stick, or beater from the instrument. He would tell us never to hit into the instrument. "Play to the ceiling – not the floor . . . you must be aggressive to play percussion, but not offensive." He also stressed relaxation as a major point in producing sound. Musical phrasing was always paramount in his teaching and playing. He believed that snare drum, timpani, and marimba were all capable of producing a musical line.[21]

One of Street's students at Eastman was Fred D. Hinger (1920–2001), a musician who combined musical ideas from string players, wind players, as well as percussionists in developing his unique approach to timpani. Hinger was timpanist in the Philadelphia Orchestra from 1951 to 1967

Figure 1.2 William G. Street (1895–1973), oil on canvas (2004) by Sari Gaby.

and in the Metropolitan Opera Orchestra from 1967 to 1983. After gra-
duation from Eastman and a stint in the US Navy Band as percussionist
and xylophone soloist, Hinger joined the Philadelphia Orchestra in 1948 as
principal percussionist. Oscar Schwar, having died only two years earlier,
was still a legend among conductors and fellow musicians in the orchestra,
and Hinger absorbed as much information from them as he could about
Schwar's timpani style. When Hinger was appointed to the timpani position in 1951, he combined Schwar's style of playing with his own ideas
about sound and musicianship.

Hinger was a throwback to the nineteenth-century German timpanists
who also played other instruments. At Eastman, he minored on violin in
his music education degree program. He later adapted bowing techniques
to hand patterning on percussion instruments, devising a system of arm

Figure 1.3 Fred D. Hinger, portrait (1966) by Shirley Hinger Corbett.

movement he called "time in motion." While in the Philadelphia Orchestra, Hinger studied the ideas of phrasing and musicianship from two of his colleagues, principal flutist William Kincaid and principal oboist Marcel Tabuteau, and transferred these concepts to timpani.

Kincaid and Tabuteau were both products of French woodwind players. Kincaid was a student of Georges Barrère at the Institute of Musical Art (the original name of the Juilliard School) in New York City. Barrère, who was born in Bordeaux, attended the Paris Conservatoire before becoming the principal flutist in the New York Philharmonic. Tabuteau, born in Compiègne, France, was a protégé of Georges Gillet at the Paris Conservatoire before moving to the United States to play oboe in the New York Symphony Orchestra and later with the Philadelphia Orchestra. Both Kincaid and Tabuteau taught at Curtis and are credited not only with populating North American orchestras with their students but with helping to develop a sound in these orchestras that differed from that of European orchestras and became known as the American orchestral sound.[22]

Kincaid's teaching techniques and words of wisdom were assembled by one of his students, William Krell, in a book titled *Kincaidiana*. Some of the aphorisms attributed to Kincaid in this book are similar to advice Hinger gave to me when I was a student of his at Curtis from 1962 to 1966:

You never really learn anything until you can forget it.

Articulation is the pronunciation of musical sound.

Swirls [of notes] will sound faster if the notes are evenly distributed rather than faked through as a smear of sound.

Thoughtful repetition is the key to facility.

Music ... is sound in motion and is immediately involved with the progression of time.

The important consideration is not having the *right* plan, but having *a* plan.

Happily, there is no *one definitive* solution to a phrasing problem; rather, there are *several definitive* solutions with the validity of each depending upon the personal frame of reference and the conviction with which it is executed.[23]
[Emphases in the original]

Tabuteau became well known for his woodwind class at Curtis in which he discussed his ideas of phrasing and musicianship. The class was open to other musicians and Hinger took advantage of this opportunity to attend some of them. One of Tabuteau's pedagogical techniques was a number system used to teach the principles of phrasing. Laila Storch, a student of Tabuteau's at Curtis, described his number system this way in her diary entry of April 1, 1943:

[Tabuteau] was explaining something about this new, original system of his – says it would revolutionize the whole foundation and conception of music and that it is what makes his playing sound *different*– that everyone imitates him, but they don't know the secret so they don't sound the same. It is all based on numbers and when you know that, you can actually hear it when he plays. You can hear 1, 1–2, 2–3, 3–4 as plain as day. Every note is placed exactly at a certain spot as if on a micrometer. It seems to me it would take almost a superhuman accuracy and perfection to play like that and you'd think anything so calculated and mathematical would sound cold and dry, but it certainly doesn't the way he does it. He'll have me play five notes over and over to get just the right impulses ... I think his system of thinking of notes by numbers ... would put a very solid foundation under everything you do and would keep your playing from sounding aimless and pointless.[24]
[Emphasis in the original]

One of the categories of Tabuteau's numbering system as listed by David McGill in his book, *Sound in Motion*, is what he calls "Motion Numbers," and is Tabuteau's best-known use of numbers. A sequence of four sixteenth-note groups without using Tabuteau's phrasing would be counted 1234 1234 1234 1234.

The same grouping of four sixteenth-notes with Tabuteau's phrasing and number system would be counted 1,123 4, 123 4, 123 4, 123 4.[25]

Hinger adapted Tabuteau's number system to percussion playing, and used stickings to create shadings of phrase. He may have begun thinking about the relation of stickings to phrasing when he was a student of Street's

Example 1.1 Four sixteenth-note groups without Tabuteau phrasing.

1 - 2 - 3 - 4,   1 - 2 - 3 - 4,   1 - 2 - 3 - 4,   1 - 2 - 3 - 4,   1

Example 1.2 Tabuteau motion numbers to demonstrate forward motion.

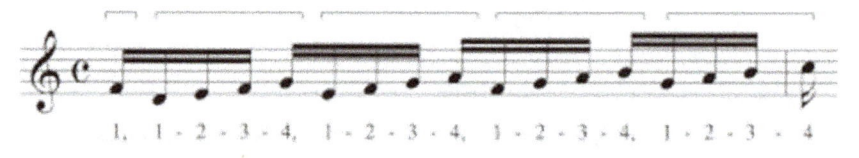

1,   1 - 2 - 3 - 4,   1 - 2 - 3 - 4,   1 - 2 - 3 - 4,   1 - 2 - 3 - 4

at Eastman. According to Bob Becker, who also studied with Street, one of Street's mantras was, "Stickings are the music of the snare drum."[26] At the core of Hinger's approach to sticking and phrasing was that an audible difference existed between two notes played by alternating hands and two notes played by the same hand. Hinger described the difference this way: "Because of the varying strengths and weaknesses of either hand, each hand holding a stick actually plays a different pitch or timbre. It can be difficult to match these pitches. The differences, though, however slight, can be used for phrasing."[27]

He also felt that if a repeated attack in a rhythmic pattern was played by the same hand, the time-space between the two attacks would be ever so slightly larger than the time-space between two attacks that were played by alternating hands. In order to create the separation between attacks indicated by repeated numbers, Hinger used "doublings," or consecutive attacks played by either the right or left hand. He used a doubling as a way to lead into ends of phrases, to begin phrases with impetus, and to create space while moving from drum to drum in certain musical excerpts. Hinger advocated experimentation with doublings when playing consecutive note groupings. His theory was that a doubling anywhere in a consecutive note group would break up the back-and-forth feeling of alternating strokes and add life to the phrase. Tabuteau's numbering indication of four sixteenth-notes followed by a downbeat would be 1123 4. Hinger's doubling for the same example would be RRLR L. Using this doubling principle, a doubling with the right or left hand creates a separation, whereas alternating strokes give a sense of forward motion.

Hinger's inquisitiveness led him in many different directions as he experimented with techniques and ideas that could be applied to timpani playing. After discovering the book *Zen in the Art of Archery*, by Eugen

Herrigel, he took up archery to better understand the philosophy of Zen. Hinger compared the act and art of striking a timpani head to a Zen archer's relationship with his target as described in the introduction to the Herrigel book by Zen Buddhist philosopher D. T. Suzuki:

> In the case of archery, the hitter and the hit are no longer two opposing objects, but are one reality. The archer ceases to be conscious of himself as the one who is engaged in hitting the bull's-eye which confronts him. This state of unconscious is realized only when, completely empty and rid of the self, he becomes one with the perfecting of his technical skill, though there is in it something of a quite different order which cannot be attained by any progressive study of the art.[28]

In adapting this concept to timpani, Hinger developed his theory of "resistance." In his book *Technique for the Virtuoso Timpanist*, he described it this way:

> Over the years of my professional life, I have been striving for a system of playing that compliments [*sic*] the methods used by other instrumentalists and have come to the conclusion that all players are faced with a common problem, one of resistance. Resistance is provided partially by the instrument and partially by the performer himself. It can be quite obvious that each instrument provides a physical resistance, but the resistance that the performer provides is a very personal one and requires a great deal of analysis.
>
> The percussion instruments are the only ones not in contact with the player before the instruments are vibrated. Therefore, it can be difficult to relate the resistance of the instrument to the resistance of the player. There *must* be a balance between the resistances, or, the mental–aural picture that the player must "presuppose" will emerge distorted and the resultant sound will be uncontrolled. A very definite theorem must be correlated at this point concerning desired sound. *"The kind of sound that is desired by the player is determined by the length of time the mallet is on the vibrating body."* This "self-resistance" allows for musical control . . . [29] [Hinger's emphases]

Hinger was aware of his percussion predecessors, and frequently spoke of the American rudimental drummer Sanford A. "Gus" Moeller (1886–1960), who was a contemporary of George L. Stone. Moeller is another example of a percussionist who began on another instrument, in his case the piano. He wrote a well-known book titled *The Moeller Book: The Art of Snare Drumming*, in which he considered drummers to be students of eurhythmics. Hinger studied eurhythmics at Eastman and often made reference to this pedagogical method in his teaching in order to demonstrate his "time in motion" ideas.

In addition to using some of the eurhythmic techniques of rhythm and movement espoused by Moeller with his students, Hinger required them to read a page in the Moeller snare drum method titled "Confidence." Part of

the reason for this requirement was to emphasize to students that no single way of playing percussion or no single teacher could lead the way to success, and that it was up to each individual student to explore and draw from as many sources as possible. In his essay, Moeller states,

> No success can be obtained without confidence. This holds good in drumming . . . . a drummer needs confidence in his ability and schooling to accept a prominent position . . . He may go to some drummer more or less known and throw himself on his mercy, give him money and follow his teachings minutely and still be found fault with. Sooner or later he will become aware that no one drummer knows it all or has invented any new system that all bow to. He will seek the truth from all sources until he has that confidence in himself that criticisms run off like the water from the duck's back . . . .Soon his reputation will precede him and he is the censor and not the censored.[30]

Like many of the other teachers who generated schools of playing, Hinger was a strong advocate of students finding their own way of playing. Both he and Moeller would certainly have endorsed the saying from Linji Yixuan at the beginning of this chapter.

Conclusion

The transition from Leipzig, Dresden, and other European timpani traditions to the twenty-first-century view of percussion could be summarized by a quote from *New York Times* critic Allan Kozinn: "If you think about it, drums are the new violins."[31] The influence of violins and other instruments on percussion has come full circle from the days when Pfundt was plucked from his position as choral director at the Leipzig City Theater to perform the Emperor Concerto timpani part with the Gewandhaus Orchestra. Percussion is the focal point for much contemporary music, and percussionists now have successful careers as soloists, chamber musicians, composers, and conductors. However, the musicianship that began with the early timpani schools, and the principles of "tone and balance," "precision, sensitivity, and musicality," creating a musical line, and performing with confidence are still cornerstones of the timpanist's art.

Timpani, more than any other orchestral percussion instruments, are firmly entrenched in the canon of Western classical music, and the traditions of timpani playing that originated in Leipzig, Dresden, Vienna, Amsterdam, Paris, London, and other European cities established the foundation of timpani sound and technique. This association that timpani playing has with the historical while residing in a progressive age makes it imperative that contemporary timpanists use

their imaginations in interpretation of their parts. David Kent, long-serving timpanist in the Toronto Symphony Orchestra, wrote in his book *Timpani Playing in the 21st Century*, "In the end ... the determining factor in anything related to playing music should be the way in which it actually sounds."[32] My North Indian *tabla* teacher, Sharda Sahai, who came from a long tradition in the Benares *gharana* of *tabla*, expressed a similar sentiment when I questioned him about the accompaniment patterns I should and should not play on *tabla*. He admonished me by saying, "You can do anything as long as it's beautiful." The same can be said to aspiring young timpanists. It is important to honor tradition, but equally important to embark on new adventures in music-making as long as you have an understanding of what makes music sound beautiful. Ernst Pfundt used that approach in 1836, and it is still an appropriate attitude today.

Notes

1. R. F. Sasaki, *The Record of Linji*, T. Y. Kirchner (ed.) (University of Hawai'i Press, 2009), p. 328.

2. E. A. Bowles, "Mendelssohn, Schumann, and Ernst Pfundt: A Pivotal Relationship between Two Composers and a Timpanist," *Journal of the American Musical Instrument Society*, vol. 24 (1998), 7–9. Pfundt's instruction manual is *Die Pauken* (Leipzig: Breitkopf und Härtel, 1849).

3. *Ibid.*, p. 7.

4. According to Tom Greenleaves, one of the current principal timpanists with the Gewandhaus Orchestra, there is no record of Schmidt having studied with Pfundt; however, Schmidt did augment Pfundt's timpani method with a snare drum tutor in 1894. So it is very likely that Schmidt played timpani in much the style of Ernst Pfundt. (Greenleaves, email communication, November 12, 2013).

5. F. D. Fairchild, "PAS Hall of Fame: Alfred Friese," *Percussive Notes*, vol. 17, no. 2 (Winter 1979), 28.

6. S. Goodman, "Timpani Talk," *Percussionist*, vol. 17, no. 3 (June 1997), 103–4.

7. A. Abel, personal interview (Philadelphia, PA, October 16, 2012).

8. A. J. Cirone, "Portraits in Rhythm Newsletter," N1, www.anthonyjcirone.com.

9. A. Simco, "An Interview with Cloyd Duff," *Percussive Notes*, vol. 31, no. 3 (February 1993), 56–7.

10. G. L. Stone, *Stick Control for the Snare Drummer* (Boston: George B. Stone & Son, Inc., 1935).

11. R. Mattingly, "George Lawrence Stone," *Percussive Notes*, vol. 35, no. 6 (December 1997), 10–11.

12. B. Chidester, "Arban Trumpet Method – What Is It?" *The Trumpet Blog* (October 7, 2013). Arban, in turn, was supposedly influenced by the virtuosic technique of violinist Niccolò Paganini.

13. Mattingly, "G. L. Stone," 10.

14. Vic Firth was another timpanist who began his musical studies on instruments other than percussion and who generated his own school of timpani playing. He first studied cornet with his father, a successful trumpet and cornet player, then studied trombone, clarinet, piano, and percussion. In addition to holding the principal timpani position in the Boston Symphony for forty-nine years and founding his own percussion products company, he has been on the faculty of the New England Conservatory since 1950. J. Strain, "Hall of Fame: Vic Firth," *Percussive Notes*, vol. 33, no. 4 (August 1995).

15. Mattingly, "G. L. Stone," 11.

16. *Ibid.*, p. 11.

17. *Ibid.*, p. 11.

18. Roland Kohloff was timpanist in the San Francisco Symphony from 1956 to 1973. He then succeeded Saul Goodman as timpanist in the New York Philharmonic where he played from 1973 until his retirement in 2004.

19. S. Reich, personal interview (New York City, December 18, 2003).

20. According to John Beck, Street developed this technique after hearing a

xylophone recital by Japanese soloist, Yoichi Hiraoka. Personal communication (Rochester, NY, May 4, 2012).

21. J. Beck, "William G. Street," unpublished pamphlet distributed at "Genesis Percussion Teachers" panel discussion at PASIC (Indianapolis, IN, November 15, 2013).

22. J. Krell, *Kincaidiana: A Flute Player's Notebook* (Culver City, CA: Trio Associates, 1973), p. vii.

23. *Ibid.*, pp. 3, 17, 23, 25, 30, 45, 47.

24. L. Storch, *Marcel Tabuteau: How Do You Expect to Play the Oboe If You Can't Peel a Mushroom?* (Indiana University Press, 2008), pp. 235–6.

25. D. McGill, *Sound in Motion* (Indiana University Press, 2007), p. 73.

26. B. Becker, *Rudimental Arithmetic: A Drummer's Study of Pattern and Rhythm* (Asbury Park, NJ: Keyboard Percussion Publications, 2008), p. 54.

27. F. D. Hinger, *Time & Motion: The Musical Snare Drum* (New Haven: Cornucopia Music, 1991), p. 16.

28. E. Herrigel, *Zen in the Art of Archery* (New York: Vintage Books, 1989), p. viii.

29. F. D. Hinger, *Technique for the Virtuoso Timpanist* (Hackensack, NJ: Jerona Music, 1975), pp. 5–6.

30. S. A. Moeller, *The Moeller Book: The Art of Snare Drumming* (Chicago: Ludwig Music Publishing Co., 1982), p. 3.

31. A. Kozinn, "Percussionists Go From Background to Podium," *New York Times* (December 27, 2009).

32. D. Kent, *Timpani Playing in the 21st Century* (Asbury Park, NJ: Keyboard Percussion Publications, 2014), p. 8.

2 Orchestral percussion in the twenty-first century
Concerns and solutions

WILLIAM L. CAHN

Introduction

A professional percussionist in a symphony orchestra occupies one of the special areas of human endeavor capable of providing a lifetime of fulfill- ment. It is truly wonderful to have the opportunity to engage on a regular basis with music created by some of the greatest minds of Western civilization (and increasingly of Eastern civilization as well). It can also be highly fulfilling to be regularly immersed in the glorious sound of an orchestra and to have acquired the ability to listen deeply and be touched by orchestral music. For those percussionists who have a "love" of orches- tral music, it can be as much of a privilege to sit quietly through three movements of a symphony in order to play the one (and only) cymbal sound in the middle of the fourth movement as it is to play a challenging xylophone solo passage in a contemporary piece that requires many lonely hours of practice.

There are a number of attractive aspects to playing in an orchestra that are unique to percussionists. There is a certain directness and visceral clarity for audiences in connecting the physical motion of a percussionist striking an instrument with the immediacy of the sound produced. Except for the conductor, the percussionists are the most visually accessible performers seen by audiences due to their physical movement around instruments within the percussion section. In addition, percussionists, perhaps more so than other instrumentalists, have a considerable degree of freedom in the selection of sounds to be produced for any particular passage in the music. To non-percussionists a triangle is a triangle, but to percussionists the term "triangle" implies a fairly wide spectrum of instrument possibilities from a small triangle with a high clear-pitched sound to a larger triangle with a lower-pitched sound that is rich in overtones. It is in the selection of sounds that each percussionist displays an individual musical voice, and only rarely will a conductor ever challenge a percussionist's choice.

Of course, to become a professional orchestral percussionist, one must first make a significant commitment to learn to play a variety of percussion instruments at the highest technical level, and then to learn the standard orchestral repertoire in order to become acquainted with the generally

accepted performance practices. However, while playing on percussion instruments can in itself be a reliable source of enjoyment for the player, that pleasure alone may not be enough to sustain a sense of fulfillment throughout a career. In the long run, the decision to devote one's professional life to orchestral music will likely be most fulfilling when motivated as much by the enjoyment of listening to orchestral music as by playing it. That being said, the question becomes, "what kinds of concerns will percussionists face in the years ahead?"

Constant improvements in the standard orchestral percussion instruments

There has been a steady growth in the variety of traditional orchestral percussion instruments available in the marketplace worldwide. Percussionists in the twenty-first century have easy access to dozens of triangle manufacturers, and the same is true for tambourines, snare drums, and virtually every kind of percussion instrument. The number of varieties will only continue to grow. At the same time, as the number of instrument options is increasing, there will also be regular innovations in design, construction, and materials used for the standard orchestral percussion instruments. It would not be unreasonable for percussionists in the future to see timpani with built-in automatic electronic tuning mechanisms, snare drums with devices to automatically turn snares off and on, new materials for drumheads, or various extended-range keyboard percussion instruments with bars made from new materials.

This virtual explosion of instrument options and innovation has already had an impact. For example, until the late 1950s, the only option available for timpani heads was calfskin. But since then, as new materials have become available and as the skills of tanners gradually went the way of the blacksmiths – they were no longer needed – the generally accepted timpani sound quickly shifted to various types of synthetic plastic heads. Of course, there will continue to be die-hard advocates for calfskin heads because of their distinctive sound characteristics. These players must be willing to endure the added efforts needed to maintain them in performance-ready condition in differing indoor and outdoor environments.

Most orchestras own a standard set of four timpani, but it is not unusual for timpanists, especially in the larger-budget orchestras, to own one or more personal sets. The acceptable standard for timpani has gradually shifted, especially in North America, to the Dresden style (with ratchet or hydraulic tuning pedals and all mechanics placed outside of the suspended copper bowl) from the American style (with spring

counterbalanced pedals and some of the mechanics placed inside the bowl). The timpanist also has options for the shape of the copper bowls, which has an effect on the "brightness" (presence of overtones) or "darkness" (absence of overtones) of the sound.

Snare drums have also undergone an evolution. Percussionists are normally required to provide their own snare drums, and they have dozens of manufacturers and style options from which to choose. Along with this steady growth of options comes the need to remain informed and current. For each piece in the orchestra repertoire, snare drummers have the freedom to determine which type of snare drum and sound they will use; among their options are shell depth, thickness and material of the shell, number and type of tension lugs, calfskin or plastic heads, amount of tension on the heads, completely open or partially muted, single snare type or multiple-material snares, and so on.

Percussionists have a similar field of options and the same expanding degrees of freedom with bass drums, although along with these options comes a responsibility to constantly maintain the instrument in performance condition. As with the timpanist, this responsibility regularly requires some extra time in advance of rehearsals and performances. For this reason, some orchestras designate one of the section players to be the regular bass drummer who must be committed to clearing and tuning the bass drum heads as well as removing the regularly occurring unwanted rattles and noises from the drum's hardware or suspension cradle. Normally, bass drums are owned by the orchestra, but it is not unusual, especially in the case of designated bass drummers, for percussionists to have personal instruments. The accepted standard for bass drums has also evolved from large-diameter, Turkish-style (head diameter greater than shell depth) drums with calfskin heads, to smaller diameter, Scottish-style (shell depth equal to or greater than head diameter), ribbed-plastic bass drums. Some European orchestras prefer to use a "gong" bass drum – single headed and highly tensioned.

Usually, it is the orchestra percussionist's responsibility to provide most of the standard small percussion instruments – cymbals, triangles, tambourines, wood blocks, castanets, and more. Some of the widely used books on orchestration define cymbals and triangles as non-pitched percussion instruments. Actually, that description is only half true. Both instruments, and in fact most percussion instruments, do have a fundamental pitch. In the case of cymbals and triangles, the fundamental pitch, which is mostly audible only after the overtones have faded away, is ignored in favor of the characteristic strike sound, which is rich in overtones that mask the fundamental pitch. As composers gradually become aware of the pitch aspect of percussion

instrument sounds, it is likely their writing will be affected in the same way that using a double-bass bow to produce sustained sounds on cymbals and triangles has become ubiquitous over the last few decades. There are compositions already in existence that require percussionists to produce certain specific pitches when bowing a cymbal. Obviously, this also requires that the percussionist obtain a cymbal with an overtone array capable of producing the specific pitch.

Another standard orchestral percussion instrument, the tambourine, has witnessed the development in recent years of a variety of nontraditional performance techniques influenced by frame drumming practices common to non-Western music genres. Composers have also explored the use of multiple tambourines having jingles with relative pitch differences – high, medium, low. As implied above, it is even possible to compose for specific pitches of a tambourine's jingles. Of course, such a requirement would necessitate that percussionists seek out and obtain the instruments that are appropriate to the part, an effort made considerably easier with the resources of the Internet.

Most woodblocks, temple blocks, and even castanets are clearly pitched, although as with most writing for percussion instruments, the pitch of the instruments is not normally considered. Rather, the interest is focused on their "tone color" quality. Innovations in design, materials, and production have made it possible for percussionists to select from a variety of available instruments, either traditionally wooden or newly synthetic, in order to meet the requirements of the music.

In some of the orchestral repertoire the terms, "gong" and "tam-tam" are used interchangeably, when actually these two instruments, which may appear to be similar visually, are different in their characteristic sound. The term "gong" technically refers to a metallic (bronze) disc or pan that is shaped by casting and/or hammering to produce a specific pitch, with relatively little overtone presence in the overall sound. A "tam-tam" is a metallic disc too, but technically, its sound is characterized by a strike tone having a rich spectrum of overtones, including some "white noise" (virtually all overtones within a portion of the frequency spectrum). Tam-tams do have a fundamental pitch, but as with cymbals, that aspect of their sound is generally irrelevant for most of the orchestra repertoire. Tam-tams are normally owned by the orchestra although they, as well as pitched gongs, are frequently obtained from percussion instrument rental services for specific pieces. The principal percussionist is usually responsible for locating any needed instruments, while the orchestra covers the rental charges.

In contrast to the performance skills required of percussionists in the past century, orchestras now require that all members of the percussion section,

not just one or two dedicated members, have a high level of skill on the standard keyboard percussion instruments, the xylophone and glockenspiel. Contrary to the relatively short passages for these instruments that exist in most of the repertoire composed prior to the 1960s, it is not unusual for these instruments to have extended and highly technical parts in contemporary compositions. In addition, the standard ranges of both of these instruments have expanded from 3.5-octaves to 4-octaves for xylophones and from 2.5-octaves to 3-octaves for glockenspiels. While in most instances orchestras own these instruments, percussionists may also choose to use their personal instruments, especially if their instrument is a highly regarded vintage xylophone (e.g., Deagan Artists Special) or glockenspiel (e.g., Deagan Parsifal Bells).

Another consideration for the keyboard percussion instruments is the tuning of the bars. In recent years, it has been an acceptable practice for xylophones and glockenspiels to be tuned slightly higher (A=442) than the standard orchestra tuning (A=440). Some players prefer that only the upper octave of the instrument be tuned high, but when instruments need to be retuned, it is almost always the principal percussionist who determines the tuning. Percussionists should also take into account that while xylophones in North America and Japan are usually quint-tuned (with a predominant second-harmonic overtone – an octave and a fifth above the fundamental pitch of each bar), European xylophones are commonly octave-tuned (with a predominant third-harmonic overtone – two octaves above the funda-mental). This can be a significant factor for orchestra percussionists to consider when touring, because there is a noticeable difference in the sound quality between these two tuning systems.

In recent years, there has been a rapid expansion of the technical requirements for performance on two other keyboard percussion instru-ments, the marimba and the vibraphone. While the xylophone and glock-enspiel have essentially been limited to orchestra repertoire that is playable with two-mallet techniques, the marimba and vibraphone have both had a renaissance due to the worldwide interest among percussionists and com-posers in four-mallet techniques, particularly the performance capabilities made possible using the mallet grip (with two mallets in each hand) developed by Leigh Howard Stevens in the 1970s.

Gaining access to new generations of acoustic and electronic percussion instruments

The expansion of orchestral repertoire, including not only symphonic music but also opera, pops, and other non-symphonic genres, increasingly requires

that members of the percussion section perform on nontraditional instruments and produce novel or unusual sounds. Global communications, travel, and trade have made it possible for composers to write for instruments from non-Western cultures. As the world's percussion instruments become more widely known and obtainable, composers are writing for increasingly large percussion sections. At the same time, percussionists and inventors are continually creating new kinds of percussion instruments and sounds. In addition, electronic instruments that generate, modify, and amplify sounds are finding creative applications in both standard and recently composed orchestral works. It is increasingly important that orchestra percussionists know how and where to find the instruments required by the repertoire.

The problem of gaining access to unusual percussion instruments is now addressed by companies that offer instrument rental services. These companies are usually located in major metropolitan areas and they serve as a central resource, where percussion instruments can be obtained, transported, stored, and maintained in good playing condition. These tasks, because of the expense and time involved with the ever-increasing array of percussion instruments, have become too costly for many percussionists to do on their own. Companies that rent percussion instruments can be located easily on the Internet.

Another source of percussion instruments that has seen growth in recent years is catalog sales. Along with the simultaneous growth of Internet-marketing, instruments which in the past might have taken weeks of effort to locate can now be found and purchased with a few strokes on a computer keyboard or other digital device. As orchestra budgets continue to tighten, the responsibility to purchase instruments needed for any particular piece could fall on the orchestra's percussionists themselves. It should be noted that pre-owned/used instruments can frequently be found on the Internet at prices much lower than in catalogs or from retailers. Orchestras that are located near music schools and universities may have access to high-quality instruments on a loan basis.

Embracing new performance techniques, styles, and technologies

Having obtained the required instruments, orchestra percussionists may on occasion need to develop their own individual techniques in order to obtain acceptable sounds on unfamiliar instruments. This might mean performing on standard orchestral percussion instruments in nontraditional ways, for example, by playing specific pitches on a bowed cymbal or by scraping a drumhead for a specific sound. It might mean learning some

traditional techniques used by non-Western percussionists on instruments associated with African, Asian, Brazilian, Indian, or other non-Western music. And, it might mean developing an understanding of ways to use electronic instruments in a performance environment such as placement of microphones and speakers, sampling techniques, and electronic sound modification techniques. Fortunately, there are a growing number of opportunities to obtain information through the Internet, from colleagues (one's network), and more deeply through workshops, seminars, and evening or summer courses offered by music schools and universities.

Staying current with new developments, particularly regarding rapid advances in digital technologies, will certainly continue to present challenges to the percussionist's workload. Advances in digital sound production will continue to improve the ease with which any sound can be electronically reproduced in real-time performance, with the performer/ percussionist having virtually as much control over the sound as with any acoustic instrument. The devices that make this possible will continue to become more responsive to real-time spontaneity in performance thanks to newer generations of software that allow the performer to be intuitive and flexible. For percussionists, the entire spectrum of sound effects – natural acoustic sounds, electronic sounds, or any combination of sounds that can be imagined – will be only a keystroke away in performance.

Digital technologies and the Internet will also continue to improve the ease with which percussionists can gain access to orchestra scores, printed parts, recordings and performance practices; the value of these resources to musicians is immeasurable. The Internet also makes it possible for percussionists to obtain information easily through blogs, chat rooms, and direct contact with other percussionists worldwide.

Preparation of percussion parts

One of the biggest challenges facing percussionists in contemporary music, especially in contemporary music scored for a large percussion section, is dealing with page turns in parts that are frequently in score form, with all of the percussion parts lumped together. In this scenario, a single page may contain only a few bars, requiring frequent and virtually impossible page turns. Unlike solo pianists, percussionists cannot expect to have dedicated page turners, though it might be possible on rare occasions for one percussionist who is momentarily available to turn another percussionist's page. Sometimes cloned parts are required simply to avoid the need for a percussionist to pick up a part to carry it to another location within the percussion section, and occasionally it is necessary to enlarge a cloned part

so that it can be read by a percussionist on a distant instrument. Generally, it will be the principal percussionist's responsibility to insure that all of the players in the percussion section receive individual parts that clearly indicate which instruments and passages they must play. However, the individual players still have the ultimate responsibility to see that their own part is in order. The parts must have reasonable page turns and be "cleared" of any unwanted markings from previous performances. Even in situations where parts are used from previous performances by the same orchestra, the number of players in the percussion section may be different, requiring a reassignment of instruments or passages. Generally, the principal percussionist will work with the orchestra librarian to address such problems.

Fortunately, the technological advances in photocopying and scanning have enabled easy duplication of printed materials so that each player can have a dedicated clone part that can be yellow-highlighted to clearly indicate that player's assignments. Another option, when appropriate, would be to make clone copies of parts that can then be cut-and-pasted for each individual player. On rare occasions, it may even be necessary for a percussionist to hand-copy or type out on a computer and print a specific percussion part. The use of tablet computers and digital screens in place of printed parts has already been done effectively, and such uses will likely continue and expand.

Embracing the increasing influence of digital music

It has become possible for anyone anywhere in the world to access free websites such as YouTube on the Internet and to view performances that were originally video-recorded in virtually every video technology since video-recording became possible. In addition, the potential exists for the Internet ultimately to provide easy access to almost every audio recording that has ever been made and preserved. Newer digital technologies are certain to be developed in the future that will enable continual improvements in the quality of sounds and images. For music students and professionals at all levels, this development will prove to be a valuable resource for the study of performance practices in the same way that early audio recordings were in the early twentieth century. At the same time, having easy access to an ever-higher quality of audio and video-recorded performances may very well prove to be an attractive alternative to attending live performances, luring listeners away from live concerts.

To address these developments, orchestras and their musicians will have to find innovative ways to attract audiences by emphasizing the

strengths of live performance over recorded performances, while at the same time rethinking some of the formal aspects of the traditional concert model – format, content, dress, concert length, pre- and post-concert talks, visual enhancements, and so on. To some extent, the Metropolitan Opera has already demonstrated some success with its live broadcasts that are digitally streamed to local theaters throughout the world. Orchestras will have to find ways to connect with younger audiences digitally in response to the worldwide expansion of social networking. Methods will have to be found for orchestras to use digital media cost-effectively in order to get their messages distributed and heard regularly.

Solving problems

As in the past, percussionists, orchestral and otherwise, will continue to be problem solvers as they have always been, taking advantage of available resources. They will surely continue to be challenged to invent the means necessary to satisfy the requirements of the music in varying performance scenarios, through creative substitutions of instruments, self-directed playing techniques, or creative ways of suspending, positioning, and striking percussion instruments.

A serious problem exists today in rethinking what the job of an orchestra musician actually entails in an evolving digital environment with shifting social values. It has been said that it takes musicians just as many hours to prepare a Beethoven symphony today as it did in Beethoven's time. That is true, but today's environment also requires that in addition, orchestra musicians, especially in the smaller orchestras, need to have a "big picture" understanding of the forces that make orchestras viable – for example, social values, markets, economics, and finances.

Acquiring "big picture" skills

In order to sustain orchestras financially and to maintain the relevance of orchestras within their communities, it will become increasingly important for musicians, especially professional symphony orchestra musicians, to become as well informed as possible about virtually every aspect of their orchestra's business by acquiring (or at the very least, by understanding) certain basic business skills in addition to the high level of performance skills that they are normally required to maintain. Among the basic skills

that would prove to be of significant value to orchestra musicians in sustaining their careers and their orchestras are the following:

Leadership Skills	presenting a positive and supportive attitude to others, including colleagues, audiences, business associates (orchestra staff), and media *This is managing.*
Listening Skills	accurately assessing the effects of one's actions on others, including colleagues, audiences, and supporters, by asking the right questions and listening to the responses *This is marketing.*
Advocacy Skills	developing writing and public speaking skills in order to help others to better understand and appreciate the value of the music *This is promotion.*
Financial Skills	understanding and using budgets, accounting, and financial analysis *This is financial management.*
Funding Skills	understanding successful strategies to obtain financial support *This is development.*

These additional skills can be acquired by means of regularly scheduled professional development workshops and seminars presented by local or national business and arts professionals, managers, financial officers, publicists, marketers, and so on. In an ideal world, such workshops would be structured as paid services for orchestra musicians. Business understanding and skills might also be acquired through self-directed reading and study or through formal courses offered by schools and colleges.

Embracing alternative orchestra models

The ongoing struggle of the major symphony orchestras in trying to preserve their traditional models of presenting full seasons of formal concerts of Western symphonic music performed by a full-time staff of professional musicians will continue. But an increasing number of orchestras, especially those with shorter seasons and smaller budgets, will have to embrace new models in serving their communities in conjunction with the need to remain financially viable. The ever-increasing financial squeeze, especially for orchestras in communities outside major population centers, will necessitate a rethinking of the nineteenth- and twentieth-century orchestra model as orchestras try to remain relevant within their communities through expanded pops and educational programming. If costs

continue to rise faster than revenues, more orchestras may be forced to move toward a "pay-per-service" model (a number of orchestras have already done so), thereby eliminating fringe benefits and reducing the job security of their professional musicians. This model would also increase the necessity for musicians to acquire the broader sets of performance and business skills described above in order to preserve their financial viability.

In a pay-per-service orchestra model, percussionists may be required to take on responsibilities such as providing, transporting, maintaining, and storing percussion instruments, assigning and/or preparing their own individual parts, organizing their own percussion setups, keeping more detailed personal financial records, and more. In essence, each pay-per-service percussionist would be taking on the role of operating his/her own small business just as freelance musicians already do. Except for this new relationship with its musicians, under a pay-per-service model, the "orchestra" as an institution could continue to operate in virtually the same way as in the traditional model with a professional administrative staff to raise funds, schedule events, enter into contracts with guest artists, and so on. In an extreme scenario, the musicians themselves might have to take on the responsibility for these operations, too.

Another alternative model, a "music central" model, would be one in which an orchestra might simply exist as an association of independent musicians in all musical genres, serving as a central organization to provide the entire spectrum of live music services to a community from classical and pops concerts to chamber music, school and community programs, music education services, Broadway shows, jazz, world music, and possibly even community social events. In some small communities, forms of this model already exist, mainly in university music departments, which provide virtually all of their community's live music services. Such orchestras may be semi-professional or even amateur/volunteer. Here again the orchestra percussionist may also have to occasionally take on the role of impresario, manager, educator, publicist, accountant, or more. To the extent that percussionists have the ability to perform in a wide range of styles (symphonic, chamber, solo, jazz, world) and to share their knowledge (music classes, lessons, lectures, workshops, public occasions), they will be better equipped to sustain their careers in music while also remaining financially viable.

Various forms of part-time community orchestras, comprised of amateur, volunteer, or semi-professional musicians, can provide satisfying opportunities for those who want to perform in an orchestra, but who also have found employment elsewhere in jobs that produce a higher level of financial security, for example, as doctors, lawyers, technical engineers,

or administrators. In this scenario, it may not be as crucial for these musicians to have achieved the highest level of performance skills, though having such skills could certainly increase the satisfaction derived from performing.

Generating supplemental income

Except for percussionists who are fortunate enough to have positions in full-time symphony orchestras that can provide the income and benefits necessary to sustain a family of four in a middle-class lifestyle, most percussionists elsewhere will find it desirable to have supplemental sources of income. Some of the same skills that freelance musicians routinely have to use – maintaining business relationships (networking), having basic business skills (described above), being reliable in fulfilling obligations, showing up on time, treating associates and clients with respect, and of course, doing the job well – are crucial.

Orchestra musicians have traditionally generated supplemental income by teaching their instruments either in conjunction with music schools or in their own private studios. There are a variety of teaching styles in the twenty-first century, but many teachers in their private studios have embraced a soft style in which each student is treated individually, rather than having every student conform to a strict pedagogy. This style of teaching requires the teacher to observe thoughtfully each student's performance and then to respond in a positive manner to address specific problems while providing some degree of inspiration in order to motivate the student to continue to make progress. To some degree, this skill is acquired through a process of trial and error, and experience is usually the primary means by which a teacher continually improves effectiveness with this teaching style.

Presenting workshops, seminars, and guest residencies can also be a professionally satisfying way to generate supplemental income. To be most effective, these kinds of services can require a significant amount of advance planning to develop a database of potential presenters, to make individualized contacts, and to target the program content toward specific age groups or areas of interest. Preparing and maintaining repertoire for solo recital/performance opportunities, possibly in conjunction with the workshop and seminar presentations, would certainly be an added option, though it could also require an additional investment of preparation time. Another related source of supplemental income could be preparing and performing chamber music repertoire, or even forming and managing an ad hoc chamber ensemble with colleagues.

Acquiring the performance skills necessary to become an orchestral percussionist

Having considered some of the issues faced by percussionists when they are already in a symphony orchestra, attention will now turn to general steps that can be taken to help an aspiring orchestral percussionist win a position in an orchestra's percussion section. The most important decision for anyone who wants to pursue a career as an orchestra musician is selecting, as soon as possible, the right teacher, the teacher who provides the necessary support and inspiration through the lengthy process of acquiring technical skills while remaining healthy emotionally. It will obviously be most helpful if the teacher has a strong background in orchestral music, primarily as a performer, but also as an educator and advocate. A useful rule of thumb is to find a teacher who is doing exactly what it is that the student ultimately wants to do. In other words, the person who decides to be an orchestra musician will be best served by finding a teacher who is already performing in an orchestra, and preferably in as high-ranking an orchestra as possible. However, it is important to bear in mind that a great performer is not necessarily a great teacher, so if a supportive and inspiring atmosphere is missing, the student should consider looking elsewhere for a teacher.

The second important decision is to determine which specific environment – conservatory, music school, university, or alternative – would be the best one in which to assimilate and nurture the skills necessary for success in a career as an orchestra musician. A conservatory that has faculty members who are closely connected with a professional orchestra would generally be the best choice. Other factors such as the city in which the institution is located and the availability of access to regular performances by high-level orchestras should be considered. The leading conservatories will also generally have very gifted students on all instruments who can provide "lateral learning" – the additional support and inspiration that students provide for each other.

For anyone really serious about playing professionally in an orchestra, attending graduate school may merely postpone the process of preparing for auditions and proactively spending the time necessary to seek an orchestra position. By the time one graduates from a music school or conservatory, the technical skills needed to win an audition for a full-time professional orchestra position should already be in place. If a deep familiarity with the standard orchestra repertoire is also in place, so much the better. A more proactive alternative for the person who is disciplined enough to do so would be to use the resources of time and money that would otherwise have been spent on graduate school to instead prepare

audition materials and to listen to the repertoire in order to learn the music as a whole and not just the specific parts. Time could also be devoted to arranging periodic personal coaching sessions with one or more actively performing orchestra musicians, preferably with ones in major orchestras. This could be an effective way to insert one's self into the network of professional orchestra musicians. Additionally, it would be wise to attend as many concerts by orchestras as possible to observe the percussion performance practices and to deepen an understanding of the repertoire through active listening. Follow up by making every attempt to meet with the orchestra's percussionists after each concert to solicit their perspectives on the performance.

Networking

The late Charles Owen, who was the principal percussionist in the Philadelphia Orchestra from 1954 to 1972, regularly offered the following observation: "It's not who you know that counts, it's who knows you." Networking – building a web of relationships with others who have the potential to be helpful in achieving desired outcomes – has always been important, and it will certainly continue to be so. For anyone who is serious about becoming a percussionist in a professional orchestra, a useful strategy is to be proactive in networking; make contact with current orchestra percussionists and arrange to meet with them for a lesson, lunch, or coffee. Ask if they know of any openings or opportunities, not just for full-time positions, but also for extra players, and be sure to leave a calling card. If travel costs are a concern, start close to home and gradually expand further.

Planning for percussion auditions

Auditions for symphony orchestras are highly competitive with ever-increasing numbers of exceptionally fine players seeking available positions. In this environment, it has become extremely challenging to stand out in an audition. At the most basic level, auditions are simply about the notes – playing what's on the page. Mistakes and missed notes, especially on the keyboard percussion instruments, and incorrect rhythms must be fully addressed early in the process of preparing for an audition. But beyond these basics, in order to stand out in an audition, the preparation needs to be very deep. Cramming usually won't work, so it is best to have a detailed plan for preparation over a minimum of two months prior to an

audition. Having mini-goals for each day of preparation and having mile-markers to assess progress should be part of the plan. Ideally, having a long-term plan will build confidence, which can also be enhanced by regularly playing the audition repertoire for others who are following along with a score or by recording one's self and listening to the playback with a score. The primary goal in preparing for an orchestra audition is to know the required repertoire in depth. Possessing a deep knowledge of the music, including all of the parts, not just the percussion parts, will provide a significant advantage over other auditionees who have not gone to the trouble to do so. Really liking the music is even better. Fully knowing the music, having a big-picture sense not only of the music's details but also of its structure and emotional force, will also be helpful in dealing with ancillary issues in an audition: reading alternate print versions of the parts, playing along with a conductor, being asked to count out loud, making variations in tempi, and so on.

The plan of preparation can also include efforts to become familiar with as many versions/editions of the parts as possible, including all of the percussion parts in the audition repertoire, even the parts on instruments other than the ones specified on the audition list. Excerpt books can be very helpful, but it is best to become familiar with the regular published editions that are actually used by orchestras.

As technical performance standards on all instruments continue to increase, orchestra auditions require that solo repertoire be performed, even by non-principal players. On keyboard percussion instruments, a secure technique in performing four-mallet solo marimba and vibraphone repertoire has become an expectation in orchestra auditions.

An important detail for timpanists is to know in advance of an audition which specific instruments will be available, and then to find ways to practice on similar, if not identical, timpani in order to be familiar with the operation of the pedals and the overall sound quality. It would be ideal if an auditionee could provide his/her own timpani, but the added commitment of time and expense would have to be considered in each situation.

There are upfront costs in any business enterprise, and seeking a new position as a professional orchestra musician is no exception. It is critical for success to have a plan that takes into account the costs of traveling to and from auditions, researching potential openings, and communicating with orchestra administrations, not to mention the regular day-to-day living expenses while in the process of preparation for the next audition. It is wise to plan for it to take from five to ten years of auditioning to finally win an audition, though with a bit of luck it could happen sooner. It is also wise to plan to take as many auditions as possible, including openings for

part-time positions. A part-time position, along with some private teaching, can provide enough income to cover living expenses and also to bolster a résumé. But regardless of what kind of employment may be needed, care will have to be taken to find the daily preparation time necessary for future auditions with higher levels of orchestras.

Percussion auditions

To the extent possible, it is helpful for percussionists to bring their own instruments to an audition, simply because auditionees will then be that much more familiar with obtaining desired sound qualities. Small instruments such as tambourines, triangles, cymbals, and even snare drums are relatively easy to bring along. Any of these instruments that would be provided by the orchestra are likely to be unfamiliar, which will just add another layer of potential problems in a situation that is already stressful. Larger instruments such as bass drums and keyboard instruments are usually provided by the orchestra, and auditionees should be prepared with appropriate sticks and mallets, especially for bass drums of differing sizes.

It is wise to have thought about ways to ensure that there will be rapid accessibility to any personal instruments and sticks during an audition. The object is to avoid wasting precious time trying to find mallets or to set up instruments during the audition. One solution is to view the audition space in advance in order to determine where personal instruments and sticks can be placed in that area, taking into account ease of access as well as minimal disruption to other auditionees. Two stick bags can be preset specifically for the audition repertoire. One stick bag that can easily be carried along by the player from instrument to instrument would contain only mallets used for the specific instruments to be played, for example, one pair each of xylophone, glockenspiel, vibraphone, snare drum, bass drum, and suspended cymbal mallets. The second stick bag would be placed in the preselected spot within the audition area, and it would include one set each of harder and softer mallets for each instrument in the event that the audition committee or conductor requests a change of mallets or sound.

Maintaining a healthy (positive) attitude

Above all, it will continue to be enormously useful to constantly remind one's self of whatever it was about making music that provided the

inspiration and motivation in the first place to pursue a career as a symphony orchestra musician.

General concerns regarding economic and social pressures affecting symphony orchestras

It will be generally helpful to foster some sense of the current economic and social conditions in which symphony orchestras find themselves. Symphony orchestras in Europe that were entirely supported by aristocratic patrons through the eighteenth and nineteenth centuries have more recently been financed by national and local governments in keeping with long-standing values associated with national identity. However, the steady influence of globalized economics and communications has placed new financial pressures on governments in Europe, causing them to gradually pull back on their support for orchestras. To a lesser extent, governments and symphony orchestras in Canada, Latin America, and Australia are also feeling the same global financial pressures, while orchestras throughout Asia are experiencing exactly the opposite – a rapidly growing interest in orchestral music associated with newly gained wealth coupled with a strong sense of national identity and a desire for international prestige. As Asian economies continue to grow, symphony orchestras and Western classical music should fare very well there, with steadily increasing support not only from their national and local governments, but also from newly wealthy individuals and businesses.

The same global financial pressures on governments and arts organizations have been present for years in North America, though a few orchestras in a handful of major cities have been able to accumulate endowments that are large enough to provide some insulation from these pressures and to enable them to sustain themselves, at least in the short term. But in the early years of the twenty-first century, many symphony orchestras in communities outside of the major metropolitan areas find themselves under severe financial stress, resulting from steady decreases in attendance and reductions in government and corporate arts funding.

One significant factor in North America affecting both attendance and giving by individual donors and businesses is that there has been a long-term decline in the study of classical music, not only in grade school music education classes, but also in teacher training, in favor of an increasing focus on more popular musical forms (Broadway show music, popular "Idol" television shows, etc.). The effect on the general public has been a diminishing appreciation for orchestral music and a decrease of interest in

public support for symphony orchestras. This shift has occurred in an environment of increased competition for the available leisure time by a growing number of performing arts and fine arts institutions, as well as from mass-market media – live and digital – and from the increasing influence of digital devices.

Music has become ubiquitous in the environment. It can be heard electronically virtually everywhere throughout the day – waking up to an alarm clock/radio, viewing morning television programs, riding in an automobile, in elevators, in offices and retail settings, while walking on city sidewalks, while exercising, when sitting in a movie theater, when connected to the Internet, when cell phones ring, and so on. The net effect of this constant barrage of environmental music on the ears is to diminish the sense of music's preciousness. The challenge for orchestras and their musicians is to preserve and share the sense of preciousness in their music, not only through their performances, but also through education and advocacy.

Yet another major factor affecting symphony orchestras is the flooding of the world's orchestral marketplace with ever-larger numbers of instrumentalists who have achieved very high performance levels. Not only has the pressure of greater competition for available positions in professional orchestras been raised, but even after winning a position, the value of that position, in terms of the winner's income, is ultimately going to be affected by the laws of supply and demand – the greater the supply of highly qualified applicants, the lower the income potential for winning applicants. These trends will likely continue to have an effect on symphony orchestras in varying degrees for some time to come, regardless of where any particular orchestra exists on the spectrum of government support – from little or none to total – and there is no turnaround in sight. In fact, these trends are accelerating, and they will have to be taken into account by anyone considering a career as an orchestral musician, even for musicians in those orchestras fortunate enough to have some measure of insulation from global market forces.

Valuing school and community educational programs

In many places, especially in North America, it cannot be assumed that public education, and even the formal education of music teachers, will provide an in-depth appreciation of Western classical music or of orchestral music in particular. It will become increasingly important for symphony orchestra musicians to recognize that virtually every time they perform, they are educators as well as performers. Musicians who are

comfortable with public speaking and writing will be better equipped to help audiences, especially new audiences, to better appreciate the music that is being performed. It would also be useful for performers to be able to assess their audiences in order to tailor the specific information and delivery style to each particular audience. The goal is not to "dumb down" the experience, but rather to help inexperienced listeners to better appreciate the music they hear.

However, there is some encouraging news. The music presented to audiences by symphony orchestras has long been ranked among the most inspirational in the world with much of it being the product of some of the greatest minds of Western civilization, past and present. It is likely that this genre of music will continue to be valued by a significant segment of the world's population, albeit with an intrinsic bias toward older, more educated, and more affluent demographics. Additionally and out of necessity, although with some push-back from traditionalists, orchestras everywhere are broadening the scope of their offerings in order to attract and engage wider audiences through thematic programming, pops concerts, educational concerts, collaborations with dance and theatrical companies, and experimentation with video and digital media in live performances.

One thing is certain – as satisfying as it can be to hear a performance of any of the great music from the orchestral repertoire, there can scarcely be an experience anywhere to compare with the satisfaction to be had in performing the snare drum part to Rimsky-Korsakov's *Scheherazade* or the bass drum part to Stravinsky's *Le Sacre du Printemps* with a professional symphony orchestra.

The development of percussion instruments

3 Marimba revolution

Mallet instruments, repertoire, and technique
in the twenty-first century

WILLIAM MOERSCH

The antecedents of modern mallet instruments may be the oldest known melodic instruments, with some artifacts believed to date as far back as the Neolithic Period, between 5,000 and 9,000 years ago.[1] Glockenspiels and xylophones eventually entered European orchestra usage in a variety of forms: individual bars, simply used as needed; keyboard activated, as in the celesta and keyboard glockenspiel; and the mallet-played configurations of the four-row xylophone and the chromatic keyboard. The marimba evolved from Africa, through Central America, and into North America, introduced in modern form by early twentieth-century manufacturers in the United States, primarily J. C. Deagan and the Leedy Drum Company. Various instruments offered by Deagan in 1910 included Roundtop and Parsifal glockenspiels, and hybrid marimba–xylophones in ranges of up to six octaves (E2–E8).[2] The vibraphone developed in the late 1920s through the innovations of Leedy and Deagan in the United States and the Premier Drum Company in England.

The history and application of the various mallet percussion instruments also influenced their development. Glockenspiels were primarily used in orchestral music and changed little over the years. Xylophone, although part of the orchestral tradition, became the first solo mallet instrument in the low-fidelity days of acoustic recording and later radio, reaching a high standard in the Deagan "Artist Special" and Leedy "Solo-Tone Green Bros. Special" instruments of the 1920s and 1930s. The marimba was primarily an ensemble instrument, whether in the marimba bands of Guatemala, with one or two instruments shared by several players, or in the marimba orchestras of Clair Omar Musser of the 1930s, with many instruments in a variety of ranges, each played by a single player. Thus, the famous Deagan World's Fair marimbas of three-and-a-half or four-and-a-half octaves (C3–F7) and King George marimbas of four octaves were accompanied by separate bass marimbas of one-and-a-half or two octaves. When the marimba finally began to develop as a solo instrument in the 1940s and 1950s, the state-of-the-art instrument was the four-and-a-third-octave (A2–C7) Musser Canterbury.

By the 1960s, instruments manufactured by Deagan and Musser in the United States, Premier in England, and Bergerault in France dominated the market, with standardized ranges of two-and-a-half-octave glockenspiels, three-and-a-half-octave xylophones, three-octave vibraphones, and four- or four-and-a-third-octave marimbas. However, in the 1970s, ranges began increasing. In Japan, Keiko Abe worked with Yamaha to extend the bass of their then current four-octave marimba, first to four-and-a-half octaves (F2–C7) in 1973 and later to five octaves (C2–C7) during 1981–1984.[3] Michiko Takahashi requested a custom marimba from Saburo Mizuno that resulted, in 1979, in an instrument of seven octaves (C1–C8): a five-and-a-half-octave Korogi marimba (C2–G7), with a half-octave extension on the top and an octave bass extension on the bottom.[4] In Europe, five-octave marimbas were introduced by Studio 49 in Germany and Bergerault in France during the late 1970s. In the 1980s, Japanese Korogi marimbas were marketed in the Netherlands as "Concorde" and in the United States as "Kori," including a four-and-a-half-octave instrument (F2–C7). American-made marimbas also gradually increased in range during the 1980s and 1990s until the five-octave marimba became the worldwide standard, available now from an assortment of manufacturers, including Adams, Bergerault/Dynasty, Coe Percussion, DeMorrow, Korogi, Majestic, Malletech, Marimba One, Ludwig Musser, and Yamaha. Recent developments include continued refinements in intonation, production models of five-and-a-half octaves (C2–G7), and prototype pedal damper systems for marimbas.

Vibraphones followed a similar path in development: Deagan introduced a four-octave instrument in 1976, followed by Bergerault and, more recently, by Yamaha, three-and-a-half and four-octave models. Ludwig Musser added new frame designs by Gary Burton and John Mark Piper. Various forms of amplification pickups and MIDI capability have been introduced, and radically new instrument designs from Malletech and VanderPlas are now entering the market. Xylophones, glockenspiels, and chimes have all seen similar development in recent years in both range and quality, and the Aluphone, a keyboard composed of spun aluminum bowls, is the latest member of the mallet percussion family.

The mallets themselves have undergone as many changes. By the 1960s, mallets were commonly unwound brass, plastic, wood or rubber, and yarn- or cord-wound rubber, in two to four gradations of hardness and with rattan handles. Among the few "signature" mallet lines were Terry Gibbs and Lionel Hampton cord-wound vibraphone mallets, Red Norvo "slap" mallets, and Jose Bethancourt raw-rubber-wound, Guatemalan-style marimba mallets. In 1968, Keiko Abe needed a new type of mallet for some of her repertoire: a single mallet that could be both soft and hard. In response,

Hidehiko Sato developed the "two-tone" mallet and the first of several editions of an Abe signature line from Yamaha soon followed in the 1970s.[5] In the United States, Bill Dreiman (aka "Bill Marimba") founded the short-lived Good Vibes Malletworks and produced exceptionally fine mallets, primarily signature mallets for prominent vibraphonists including Gary Burton, David Friedman, Bobby Hutcherson, Mike Mainieri, Dave Pike, and David Samuels. Good Vibes Malletworks was quickly acquired by Ludwig Musser. Influenced by the stiff hardwood handles of Guatemalan-style marimba mallets, Leigh Howard Stevens (LHS) began experimenting with birch handles and softer yarn; his signature mallet line was first offered by Vic Firth. Additional mallet-specialty companies soon followed, including Balter, Deschler, Hyer, Encore, Malletech, and Innovative, and each year now brings new signature mallet lines. The latest, Innovative's Pedro Carneiro series, changes the concept from the now-standard "two-tone" into "multi-zone," heightening the contrast of different faces of the mallet head to produce varied timbres as the players raise their wrists.

The trajectory, if you will, of the solo repertoire for the mallet percussion instruments began as a small light in the darkness, slowly gaining momentum and altitude, cresting and then bursting forth in a chrysanthemum display of fireworks. A sequence common to the introduction of any new instrument transpired: first featured primarily as a novelty, then seeking legitimacy through the performance of transcriptions of accepted music originally written for other instruments, and finally developing a unique and original repertoire. Also particular to the keyboard percussion instruments has been the transition from producing purely percussive effects, to emulating the sound and phrasing of single-line instruments, that is, strings, brass, winds, or voice, to modeling on polyphonic instruments, primarily piano. Each instrument has followed this path through a series of advocates and innovators, including, for the xylophone: George Hamilton Green, Red Norvo, Eiichi Asabuki, and Yoichi Hiraoka; the vibraphone: Lionel Hampton, Norvo, Milt Jackson, and Burton; and the marimba: Musser, Vida Chenoweth, Abe, and Stevens. A closer examination of the evolution of concert repertoire for mallet percussion will help to illustrate this point.

1940–1960

The first pieces of concert repertoire for solo marimba were written in the 1940s and 1950s: the concertos of Paul Creston, Darius Milhaud, James Basta, Robert Kurka, Benigno Cruz, Jorge Sarmientos, and Ernst Mahle;

and the solo works of Musser, Eloise Matthies Niwa, Alfred Fissinger, Emma Lou Diemer, Harald Mommsen, Eugene Ulrich, Bernard Rogers, and Lorraine Goodrich Irvin, most of them championed by Chenoweth. Many of these pieces feature single-line melodies or block chord chorales, although a few, for example, those of Milhaud, Kurka, Sarmientos, and Fissinger, include more contrapuntal writing. The vibraphone, although known primarily as a jazz instrument during the same period, gained some notice in Milhaud's *Concerto for Marimba and Vibraphone* (1947) mentioned above and through its increasing use in chamber music, including Pierre Boulez's *Le marteau sans maître* (1955) and Karlheinz Stockhausen's *Refrain Nr. 11* (1959). The xylophone, after its heyday in the era of acoustic recording, ragtime, vaudeville, and radio, was in decline, having been replaced in popular favor by the mellower vibraphone and marimba and was largely still limited to playing transcriptions.

1960–1980

In 1962, Vida Chenoweth performed her second and final Town Hall recital in New York and released a recording, *Vida Chenoweth: Classic Marimbist*, each featuring a combination of original repertoire and transcriptions. The xylophone gained two major concertos, *Fantasy on Japanese Woodprints* (1965), by Armenian-American Alan Hovhaness, and *Concertino for Xylophone* (1965), by Toshiro Mayuzumi of Japan, both written for Yoichi Hiraoka. George Crumb's *Madrigals, Book I* (1965), for soprano, vibraphone, and contrabass, cataloged a growing number of "extended" vibraphone techniques, including dead strokes, harmonics, damper bar clusters, finger dampening, and "pitch-bending," which was first popularized by Gary Burton, but credited by him to Emil Richards.[6] Burton's own *Solo* (1966) and *Four Mallet Studies* (1968) were the first publications to document his more pianistic, four-mallet approach to vibraphone. Equally significant for the marimba were Keiko Abe's Tokyo recitals of 1968, 1969, and 1971, which introduced a large body of new Japanese solo, chamber, and concerto repertoire, including *Conversation Suite* (1962), *Torse III* (1965), and *Concerto for Marimba and String Ensemble* (1969) by Akira Miyoshi, *Two Movements for Marimba* (1968) by Toshimitsu Tanaka, *Time for Marimba* (1968) and *Concerto for Marimba and Orchestra* (1969) by Minoru Miki, *Divertimento for Marimba and Alto Saxophone* (1968) by Akira Yuyama, *Quintet for Marimba, 3 Flutes, and Contrabass, "Mattinata"* (1968) by Teruyuki Noda, and *Mirage for Marimba* (1971) by Yasuo Sueyoshi.[7] Many of the Japanese pieces utilized the marimba in a more demanding role in terms of

technique, dynamic contrast, and musical context, than previously existing repertoire. Yuyama's *Divertimento* was one of the first pieces calling for six mallets.

The 1970s brought more international recognition to marimba. Paul Sifler's *Marimba Suite* (1971) was written for Karen Ervin Pershing, who placed second in the *Concours Internationale d'Execution Musicale* in Geneva. Abe, who began teaching marimba at Tokyo's Toho Gakuen School of Music in 1970, was featured on an international recording, *Contemporary Music from Japan: Vol. I: Music for Marimba*, containing some of the music from her recitals. When the record came out in the United States, it had an immediate impact on many developing American marimbists.[8] Japanese marimbist Michiko Takahashi commissioned Dutch composer Ton de Leeuw's *Midare* (1972) and won first prize in the Gaudeamus Foundation Interpreters of Contemporary Music Competition in 1973. Toru Takemitsu's *Gitimalya* (1974), for marimba and orchestra, and Hans Werner Henze's *Five Scenes from the Snow Country* (1978) were also written for Takahashi.

The Percussive Arts Society (PAS), founded in 1961, held its first Percussive Arts Society International Convention (PASIC) in 1976, which introduced marimbists Leigh Howard Stevens (LHS) and Gordon Stout. Stevens, a student of Chenoweth, had developed a new marimba technique and was commissioning pieces to utilize it, including Raymond Helble's *Preludes for Marimba* (1971–1973, 1974) and *Toccata Fantasy* (1979), David Maslanka's *Variations on Lost Love* (1977), and John Serry's *Rhapsody for Marimba, "Night Rhapsody"* (1979). Stout, who has become one of the most significant of marimbist/composers, made an immediate impact with his *Two Mexican Dances* (1974) and *Etudes for Marimba* (1973–1976). The following year, Abe (see Figure 3.1) made her PASIC and New York debuts, allowing North American audiences to experience her and the Yamaha YM-5000 marimba live for the first time. The repertoire on this tour included several of the solo pieces mentioned above, plus Katsuhiro Tsubonoh's *Meniscus for Marimba* (1971) and Tokohide Niimi's *For Marimba I* (1975). As a result of Abe's recitals in North America, many marimbists began traveling to Japan to study with her at Toho Gakuen. Abe also began her long and fruitful contribution as a composer with *Michi* (1978).

The xylophone enjoyed considerable benefit in the 1970s from the efforts of Bob Becker, William Cahn, and the other members of Nexus in reviving the music of xylophonist George Hamilton Green through both their concerts and a direct-to-disc recording, *Nexus Ragtime Concert* (1976).

Other significant composers writing for mallet percussion were Steve Reich, in *Drumming* (1971), and much of his other music to date; Luciano

Figure 3.1 Keiko Abe.

Berio, with *Linea* (1973) for two pianos, marimba, and vibraphone; Peter Maxwell Davies, with *Ave Maris Stella* (1975), written for his chamber sextet, The Fires of London, and featuring a prominent solo cadenza for marimba; and Charles Wuorinen, in *Percussion Duo* (1979), for marimba, vibraphone, and piano, written for Steven Schick and James Avery. Two pieces by German composer Tilo Medek, *Konzert für Marimbaphon und Orchester* (1976) and *Zur Unzeit Erblühtes* (1977), may well be the first published for five-octave marimba. Other marimba concertos by Werner Thärichen, Akira Ifukube, Jiri Valek, Raymond Helble, and Rand Steiger were among the more than thirty written during this period in Europe, Japan, and the Americas.

1980–2000

If an explosion was yet to come, the fuse was lit in the 1980s, as Stevens followed the publication of his *Method of Movement for Marimba* (1979) by founding the annual LHS Summer Marimba Seminar, Stout accepted a position at Ithaca College, and many prominent composers were enticed to write for the marimba. William Moersch, after commissioning Irwin Bazelon's *Suite for Marimba* (1980), Richard Rodney Bennett's *After Syrinx II* (1984), and Andrew Thomas' *Merlin* (1985), partnered with Stevens, Stout, and PAS to commission Jacob Druckman's *Reflections on*

the Nature of Water (1986), Roger Reynolds' *Islands from Archipelago II: Autumn Island* (1986), and Joseph Schwantner's *Velocities* (1990), with funding from the National Endowment for the Arts. Moersch founded New Music Marimba (NMM) in 1986, and their subsequent commissions include Bennett's *Concerto for Marimba* (1988), Thomas' *Loving Mad Tom*, for marimba and orchestra (1990), and Libby Larsen's *After Hampton: Concerto for Marimba* (1992). Eric Ewazen's *Northern Lights* (1989) was also commissioned by Moersch, but ultimately premiered by and dedicated to Stout.[9] The 1990s saw the introduction of marimba degree programs at institutions in the United States; Moersch created graduate marimba degree programs at Rutgers University and Peabody Conservatory, and later moved to the University of Illinois.

Abe returned to the United States in 1981, as soloist in Ifukube's *Lauda Concertata for Orchestra and Marimba* (1976) in her Carnegie Hall debut and also to perform at PASIC. She brought with her a prototype Yamaha five-octave marimba. For her next PASIC appearance in 1984, Abe introduced the Yamaha YM-6000 marimba and Miki's *Marimba Spiritual* (1984).

South African composer Peter Klatzow's *Figures in a Landscape* (1984), *Concerto for Marimba and String Orchestra* (1985), *Dances of Earth and Fire* (1988), and *Concerto for Flute, Marimba, and Strings* (1993) were all written for American Robert van Sice, one of many who traveled to Japan to study with Abe. Stout's *Sedimental Structures* (1998) was also written for van Sice, who taught at the Rotterdams Conservatorium in the Netherlands from 1988 to 1997, and then returned to the United States, teaching at Yale and Peabody Conservatory.

Robert Aldridge's *Combo Platter* (1983), written for Nancy Zeltsman, inspired the founding of her marimba and violin duo, Marimolin (1985–1996). Marimolin, in turn, inspired the creation of many new pieces, including Thomas Oboe Lee's *Marimolin* (1986), Robert Aldridge's *threedance* [sic] (1987), Lyle Mays' *Somewhere in Maine* (1988), Gunther Schuller's *Phantasmata* (1989), and Paul Lansky's *Hop* (1993). Zeltsman also partnered with Moersch, van Sice, NMM, and PAS to commission Steven Mackey's *See ya Thursday* (1993), Eugene O'Brien's *Rhyme and Reason* (1993), and Schuller's *Marimbology* (1993), with funding from Meet the Composer/Reader's Digest. In 1993, Zeltsman began teaching at both the Boston Conservatory and Berklee College of Music.

Dame Evelyn Glennie, in the United Kingdom, was another visiting student of Abe's. Kenneth Dempster's *Concerto Palindromos* for marimba, vibraphone, and orchestra (1985) was the first of her many commissions. Others for mallet percussion include David Gow's *Marimba Concerto* (1992), Rory Boyle's *Marimba Concerto* (1993), Thea Musgrave's *Journey*

through a Japanese Landscape (1994), and Ney Rosauro's *Concerto for Vibraphone* (1996).

The marimba gradually began to gain recognition in the classical music world. The New York-based recital competitions Concert Artists Guild, Young Concert Artists, Affiliate Artists, and East West Artists, each previously largely uninterested in either percussion or contemporary music, began recognizing rising marimba talent: Douglas Walter (1984), William Moersch (1988), Joseph Gramley (1993), Makoto Nakura (1994), and Nanae Mimura (1998) were all winners of prizes. Then, in 1995, both the LHS International Marimba Competition (Eric Sammut, first prize) and the International Percussion (Marimba) Competition Luxembourg (Momoko Kamiya and Katarzyna Mycka, first prizes) were held, beginning an ever-growing roster of marimba-specific international competitions. Subsequent incarnations included the World Marimba Competition Stuttgart (1996 and 1999), a second LHS International Marimba Competition (1998), and the World Marimba Competition Okaya (1999).

Prominent orchestras also began to recognize the marimba through commissions. The Boston Symphony Orchestra commissioned a concerto for marimba and orchestra, Maurice Wright's *Concertpiece* (1993), to feature orchestra member Will Hudgins, and the Oregon Symphony commissioned Tomas Svoboda's *Concerto for Marimba and Orchestra* (1995), for Niel DePonte. Other prominent marimba concertos of the more than 113 written during these two decades include those of Marta Ptaszynska (1985), Rosauro (1986), Frank Nuyts (1987), Serry (1987), Maslanka (1989), Miguel Franco (1991), Klatzow (1993), Alejandro Viñao (1993), Abe (1995), Anders Koppel (1995), Kevin Puts (1997), and Ewazen (1999).[10] Of particular note for marimba in chamber music are Elliott Carter's *Esprit rude/esprit doux II* (1994), for marimba, flute, and clarinet, written in honor of Pierre Boulez's seventieth birthday, David Kechley's *Valencia* (1998) for marimba and saxophone quartet, and Kenji Bunch's *Paraphraseology* (1999) for marimba and violin.

Composers also began featuring the marimba in combination with electronic sounds, at first prerecorded and then progressively interactive. Some of the more notable examples of this period are Gary Kulesha's *Angels* (1983), Martin Wesley-Smith's *For Marimba and Tape* (1983), Nigel Westlake's *Fabian Theory* (1987), Daniel McCarthy's *Rimbasly* (1989), and Christos Hatzis' *Fertility Rites* (1997).[11]

As the North American version of the marimba gained in international recognition, so did greater awareness of its Central American predecessor, largely through the efforts of Chenoweth and Laurence Kaptain. Special mention should be made of Maestro Zeferino Nandayapa, the patriarch of

Marimba Nandayapa. Federico Alvarez del Toro's *Sinfonia "El Espiritu de la Tierra"* (1984) was written for Nandayapa and the First International Festival of the Marimba, for the African and Central American versions only, was held in Mexico City in 1991.

Concert repertoire for vibraphone also expanded significantly during these two decades, evidenced by Takemitsu's *Rain Tree* (1981), François-Bernard Mâche's *Phénix* (1981), Christopher Deane's *Mourning Dove Sonnet* (1983), expanding on "extended techniques," Rodney Sharman's *Apollo's Touch* (1992), and Emmanuel Séjourné's *Concerto for Vibraphone* (1999).

2000–present

Advances in communication technology have long spurred both the dissemination of information and collaboration in creative activity. Mallet percussion has been a beneficiary of these developments, from the xylophone's advantage in acoustic recording, to the debut of the vibraphone in electric recording. The advent of the digital age has profoundly affected both society and music. The development of desktop publishing allowed for exponential growth in composition, with Stout, Zivkovic, Rosauro, and Pius Cheung, among the more notable of a torrent of marimbist/composers.

While the 1980s and 1990s were marked by the commissioning of major composers, funded by grants and consortia of arts organizations, the twenty-first century has seen the advent of private consortia on an international scale, funded by smaller, individual contributions and the growth of online "crowd funding" for a variety of projects. Commissioned marimba repertoire resulting from such new funding models includes Akemi Naito's *Memory of the Woods* (2000), Viñao's *Khan Variations* (2001), David Lang's *String of Pearls* (2006), Lansky's *Idle Fancies* (2008), Serry's *Groundlines* (2009), Wuorinen's *Marimba Variations* (2009), James Wood's *Secret Dialogues* (2014), and Lukas Ligeti's *Thinking Songs* (2015). In a similar manner, Zeltsman's ZMF New Music project produced the *Intermediate Masterworks for Marimba* (2009) by twenty-four composers including Louis Andriessen, Carla Bley, Chen Yi, Mackey, Mays, Paul Simon, Schuller, Steven Stucky, and Chinary Ung. Zeltsman's efforts were echoed in turn by Samuel Solomon's compilation, *The MassChap 2010 Xylophone Collection*, featuring short works from fifty composers. Other compilations for mallet percussion include *Marimba Concert* (2000) and *Summit: Compositions for Unaccompanied Orchestra Bells* (2007), both edited by Sylvia Smith.

Several of the previous examples are also indicative of increasing attention being given to mallet percussion pedagogy. G. H. Green's mail-order

subscription *Instruction Course for the Xylophone* (1924–1926) and Morris Goldenberg's *Modern School for Xylophone, Marimba, and Vibraphone* (1950), long standard teaching materials in the field, were supplemented by Stevens' *Method of Movement for Marimba* (1979), Gary Cook's *Teaching Percussion* (1988), and Stout's *Ideo-Kinetics* (1993). Significant recent additions include Zeltsman's *Four-Mallet Marimba Playing* (2003) and Cheung's *Colors* (2011). College and university percussion positions, largely held in the previous generation by orchestral percussionists or music educators, are now filled by an ever-increasing number of mallet percussion artists. However, the heralded rise of mallet specialists in the 1980s and 1990s appears to have resulted in a subsequent generation of more broadly skilled generalists, as many percussion students absorb once-innovative techniques and repertoire as a matter of course.

The path of development from novelty to single-voiced melody to contrapuntal use is increasingly evidenced, perhaps none more so than by Cheung, from his performances and recording of the complete *J. S. Bach: Goldberg Variations,* to his own compositions, including *Symphonic Poem* (2007), *Poetic Fantasy* (2009), *Poem of Water* (2012), and *Princess Chang Ping: Concerto for Marimba* (2012). In turn, the last two pieces were written to feature the six-mallet abilities of Pei-Ching Wu. Six-mallet technique evolved through the efforts of several marimbists and vibraphonists including Abe, Chenoweth, and Nandayapa; Ludwig Albert, Séjourné, and Kai Stensgaard; and Dean Gronemeier, Robert Paterson, and Karol Szymanowski. Other marimba repertoire featuring six mallets includes Gronemeier's *2HT2HDL* (1996), Andrew Thomas' *Wind* (1999), Evan Hause's *Circe* (2000), Paterson's *Komodo* (2004), and Joe Porter's *Concerto for Six-Mallet Marimba* (2012).[12] Albert has taken multiple-mallet technique a step (or two) further with his eight-mallet technique, as has Jane Boxall with her performances of "Marimba from Zero to Eight Mallets," featuring compositions for each of the various increments.

Of note for vibraphone repertoire in recent years are Philippe Hurel's *Loops II* (2002), Stockhausen's *Vibra Elufa* (2003), Erik Lund's *Blessed B* (2006), Halim El-Dabh's *Sailing Wind* (2009), and Elliot Cole's *Postludes* (2012), for one vibraphone and four players with two bows each. Technological advances have also led to increased opportunities in electronic music, particularly for vibraphone and interactive live electronics. Some representative examples include Karlheinz Essl's *Sequitur XI* (2009), Baljinder Sekhon's *Vibraphone+Electronics* (2013), and Steven Snowden's *Long Distance* (2013).

The full flowering of the arcing trajectory has at last arrived: multiple international marimba festivals and competitions occur each year in North

and South America, Europe, Australia, China, and Japan. Slovenia hosted the "first ever" International Marimba Concerto Competition in 2005, chaired by Zivkovic.[13] Since 2000, over eighty marimba concertos have been introduced by composers including Frangis Ali-Sade (2001), Martin Blazevich (2005, 2007), Anders Koppel (2001, 2002, 2004, 2006), Mackey (2005), Kurt Schwertsik (2008), Bright Sheng (2004), Christopher Theofanidis (2013), and Erki-Sven Tüür (2002).[14]

The PAS maintains the invaluable online bibliographic indexes, the *Siwe Guide to Solo and Ensemble Percussion Literature* and the *Fujii Database of Japanese Marimba Works*. As of this writing, the *Siwe Guide* lists 3,100 compositions for solo mallet instruments: 1,842 compositions for marimba, 741 for vibraphone, 248 for "mallets" (unspecified, or in any combination, for one player), 217 for xylophone, forty-four for glockenspiels or orchestra bells, and eight for chimes. These include concertos with band, orchestra, or chamber ensemble, sonatas for mallet percussion and piano, unaccompanied solos, and works for solo mallet percussion in combination with other instruments, voice, or electronics. The *Fujii Database* lists 724 compositions for marimba, whether solo, chamber ensemble, or concerto.[15] The author's own *New Music Marimba Concerto List* now has entries for 250 concertos for marimba with orchestra or wind ensemble. While there is some unavoidable degree of duplication between these various references, these numbers signify truly exponential development.

Vida Chenoweth's eloquent plea for the future of the marimba, "I would like to see the dedication of Stradivari on behalf of marimba construction. I would like to see the dedication of Beethoven on behalf of marimba composition. I would like to see the dedication of Wanda Landowska on behalf of marimba performance,"[16] has indeed been fulfilled.

Notes

1. "Stone-Age 'Marimba' Is Discovered in Vietnam," *New York Times* (March 18, 1954), p. 3.

2. M. Wheeler, "J.C. Deagan Percussion Instruments," *Percussive Notes*, vol. 31, no. 2 (1992), 61–4.

3. R. Kite, *Keiko Abe: A Virtuosic Life* (Leesburg, VA: GP Percussion, 2007), pp. 208–9.

4. M. Takahashi, Interviewed by W. Moersch (New York, October 30, 1991).

5. Kite, *Keiko Abe*, p. 52.

6. G. Burton, *Learning to Listen: The Jazz Journey of Gary Burton* (Boston, MA: Berklee Press, 2013), p. 269.

7. Kite, *Keiko Abe*, pp. 57–60.

8. *Ibid.*, pp. 84–5.

9. In a similar fashion, M. Harris' *Potpourri* (1996) and R. Aldridge's *From My Little Island* (1988) were commissioned by S. Stevens (no relation), written for L. H. Stevens, and premiered by Moersch and Zeltsman, respectively.

10. W. Moersch, *New Music Marimba Concerto List* (Champaign, IL: New Music Marimba, 2015), pp. 3–11.

11. Y. Chen, "A Catalog of Solo Works for Marimba with Electronics and an Examination and Performance Guide of *Flux* for Marimba and Electronic Tape by Mei-Fang Lin," unpublished DMA thesis, Arizona State University (2011).

12. P. Wu, "Extended Multiple Mallet Performance in Keyboard Percussion

through the Study of Performing Techniques of *Flame Dance* and *Water Fairies* by Wan-Jen-Huang," unpublished DMA thesis, West Virginia University (2005), and J. Porter, "A New Six-Mallet Technique and its Pedagogical Approach," unpublished MM thesis, University of Lethbridge (2011).

13. N. Sakimura, "International Marimba Concerto Competition 2005," *Marimba.org*, February 12, 2005.
14. Moersch, *NMM Concerto List*, pp. 11–6.
15. www.pas.org.
16. L. H. Stevens, "An Interview with Vida Chenoweth," *Percussive Notes*, vol. 15, no. 3 (1977), 22–4.

4 Instrumental ingredients

GARRY KVISTAD

Percussionists and designers of percussion instruments have traditionally looked for ways to improve the quality of their instruments and designs by making innovations to existing instruments or by developing entirely new ones. For these innovators, and for percussionists who want to improve the quality of sound they produce on their instruments, it is advantageous to study the science of sound, specifically the acoustics of percussion instruments.

My interest in percussion instrument design and acoustics began at Oberlin Conservatory in 1967 at one of my first timpani lessons with Cloyd Duff. He showed me the cartwheel-style timpani sticks he used in producing his mellifluous sound on timpani, and I wanted a pair. I couldn't afford to buy them, so I took a pair of Vic Firth wooden sticks with a round ball on the end that I already owned and went to Building and Grounds. I asked them to put the stick on a lathe and flatten the top and the underneath part of the ball, making it into a cartwheel shape. Duff had just showed me how to re-felt his cartwheel sticks, so I put the felt on these newly lathed sticks and brought them to my next lesson. Duff asked, "You made these from Vic Firth wooden sticks?" I said, "Yeah, I adapted them," and he responded, "You're getting an 'A' this semester!" With Duff's encouragement, I began to explore other ways to improve and adapt percussion instruments. In fact, as I began playing the music of John Cage and other composers that required the percussionist to find unusual instruments for the parts, I found that I was (almost) more interested in selecting the instruments than practicing the parts.

After graduating from Oberlin, I moved to Northern Illinois University in DeKalb, IL, where my newly formed percussion group, Blackearth, was appointed ensemble in residence. At Northern Illinois, I had more time to devote to making instruments and I decided I wanted to make a melodic percussion instrument. I had been reading Harry Partch's *Genesis of a Music*[1] for a couple of years trying to absorb it all. Partch made many melodic percussion instruments; however, his book was really obscure and pedantic, and I was just beginning to understand his theories.

Partch created a tuning system based on a scale of forty-three pitches to the octave, but he didn't use all forty-three pitches like Schoenberg would have done. Instead, he would select five or so pitches, but the right five

pitches to play specific scales. Partch discussed scales from ancient cultures in his book, including a five-tone Greek scale devised by Olympos, a Phrygian flutist and lyre player from the seventh century BCE. I was curious to hear this scale, but of course there is no extant music from that long ago. In order to hear the scale, I would have to build a melodic percussion instrument that could realize it.

My situation at Northern Illinois was a fortuitous one. Right next to the music department was the art department with a great wood shop and metal shop. Then I discovered that one of the professors in the physics department was acoustician Thomas Rossing, author of *Science of Percussion Instruments*.[2] As a faculty member, I was allowed to take a couple of courses a semester, so I enrolled in metalworking, woodworking, and physics classes. From Rossing, I learned how percussion instruments vibrate and how to affect their tuning. I also discovered that in order to hear the scale of Olympos, I would have to learn about the natural harmonic overtone series – the system on which this scale was constructed.

Natural harmonic overtone series

The "just intonation" tuning system[3] used in Greek and other ancient cultures is based on the natural harmonic overtone series and is very different from the "equal temperament" tuning system that I had heard all my life on piano, marimba, or almost any other instrument used in Western music. To help me understand the terminology used in the natural harmonic overtone series, I wrote out the following definitions:

Natural harmonic overtone series – A series of frequencies that are related by whole real number integers.

Equal temperament – A method of tuning based on equal distances between each pitch of the scale.

Just intonation – A method of tuning based on the natural harmonic overtone series.

Fundamental – The first partial of a sound in the natural harmonic overtone series.

Principle frequency – The strongest vibrational mode of a sound (which is not always the fundamental tone) that determines the musical pitch.

Overtones – All the components of a given sound *except* the fundamental.

Partials – All the components of a given sound *including* the fundamental.

Harmonics – All the components of a given sound *including* the fundamental whose frequencies *are related* by whole real number integers.

Harmonic overtones – All the components of a given sound *except* the fundamental whose frequencies *are related* by whole real number integers.

> *Nonharmonic overtones* – All the components of a given sound *except* the fundamental whose frequencies *are not related* by whole real number integers.
>
> *Node* – Location on a vibrating body that has minimum vibration.
>
> *Antinode* – Location on a vibrating body that has maximum vibration.

With an understanding of these basic terms, I was ready to tackle the acoustical world that was introduced to me by Rossing, including the natural harmonic overtone series and modes of vibrations.

Fundamental and overtones

All sounds are the result of complex modes of vibration that include a fundamental tone and overtones. The relationship of the fundamental to its overtones determines the timbre of the sound. The purest sounds contain relationships that are related mathematically by low number integers (1, 2, 3, 4, etc.). This means that the fundamental tone (f1) vibrates at a given frequency while its overtones vibrate twice as fast, three times as fast, four times as fast, and so on (f2, f3, f4...). When these relationships exist, the overtones are considered to be harmonic and belong to the natural harmonic overtone series.

Modes of vibration

Modes of vibration can be most easily understood by examining the vibration of a string. When a string is plucked, it vibrates in literally hundreds of different modes simultaneously; the whole string goes up and down, pivoting from both ends hundreds of times a second, creating the fundamental tone that we recognize as the pitch of the string. At the same time, the string is vibrating from various nodal points throughout the length of the string. These vibrations are in a mathematical relationship to each other as described above. The first overtone, an octave above the fundamental pitch, is vibrating twice as fast, and so it is in the relationship of 2:1. The second overtone, an octave and a fifth above the fundamental pitch, is vibrating three times as fast as the fundamental and is in the relationship of 3:1. This phenomenon continues infinitely with each new harmonic vibrating at an increasing ratio to the fundamental. A vibrating string creates all the harmonic overtones in the harmonic overtone series, thus giving string instruments a pure sound.

Scale of Olympos

With this basic understanding of acoustics in relation to musical instruments, I embarked on my quest to hear the scale of Olympos. I am not a scientist, and I certainly am not a physicist. However, in my studies with Rossing, I was able to absorb the information I needed (and not much more) in order to create an instrument to replicate the ancient Greek scale of Olympos. I began my odyssey by cutting up aluminum tubes from old lawn chairs I found in the dump – they were a free source of material. I first tuned the tubes using an oscilloscope, then I discovered that Motorola made a tuner called a Scalatron that could produce 1,024 pitches to the octave. The Scalatron allowed me to tune the aluminum tubes precisely, and I created the scale of Olympos.

According to Partch, the ratios of the scale of Olympos were 1/1, 9/8, 6/5, 3/2, 8/5, and 2/1. These ratios form a pentatonic scale plus an octave, and since it has two minor seconds, it is called a minor pentatonic – a scale that is unusual in Western music. While we don't know the exact frequency of each pitch that Olympos used, we do know the relationship between each pitch. Partch had a tuning fork tuned to G 392.01 hertz (Hz), or number of cycles per second, and used this as the basis (1/1) of his 43 tone scale. If you multiply each of these ratios by 392.01, you obtain the frequencies of each pitch relative to the frequency of G.

Scale of Olympos in hertz based on just intonation relative to the frequency of G:

$$1/1 \times 392.01 = 392.01$$
$$9/8 \times 392.01 = 441.01$$
$$6/5 \times 392.01 = 470.41$$
$$3/2 \times 392.01 = 588.01$$
$$8/5 \times 392.01 = 627.22$$

When you compare the scale of Olympos expressed in just intonation with the same relative scale in equal temperament, you can get a sense of the difference in pitch relationships. In equal temperament, the distance of each of the twelve intervals in an octave is expressed by the twelfth root of two, an irrational number that equals approximately 1.05946309435929526456182529494219. If you multiply the frequency of any musical pitch by that (approximate) number, you get the frequency of the next higher pitch. While some of these frequencies are close to those tuned in the pure system of just intonation, the human ear is capable of hearing the deviation of even a fraction of a hertz and can detect this difference.

Scale of Olympos in hertz based on equal temperament relative to the frequency of G:

G = 392.01
A = 440
Bb = 466.16
D = 587.33
Eb = 622.25

I assembled the aluminum tubes, tuned to the scale of Olympos, in a row creating a metallophone, and I was finally able to hear how this ancient scale sounded. It was fantastic, and I knew other people would love to hear the sound. However, I realized that few people other than percussionists would play a metallophone, so I tried to think of a way the scale could be self-activated. I had used various kinds of wind chimes in percussion setups, but they were essentially noise-makers and didn't have specific tunings. It occurred to me that I could tune a wind chime to the scale of Olympos and anyone could hear the sound.

Wind chimes

I constructed a wind chime just as basically as possible – a wooden top, a circle of tubes, a clapper, and a wind catcher. I knew that in order to get the best sound from the fundamental pitch, I had to suspend the tubes and drill holes at the nodal points where there is the minimum amount of vibration. I also knew that I had to have the clapper hit somewhere around the middle of each tube. Since the tubes were fastened at the top, there would be different nodal placements depending on how long the tube was. I determined that twenty-one inches of tubing (for tubes of a one-inch outside diameter) was the longest tube I could practically use, and that length tube created a D a ninth above middle C (D5), so I constructed my scale with the just equivalent of D5 as the lowest pitch.

I couldn't simply drill all of the tubes at the same place. Instead, I drilled each of them at its individual nodal point, which is 22.4 percent from the end of any bar, rod, or tube that is free on both ends. I then put the clapper near the middle, but not exactly on the middle because that would bring out the third partial and would give the tube a zonky sound since the overtones of a tube are not harmonic. So I positioned the clapper in a way that would maximize the fundamental sound and provide the longest ring-time it could possibly have with as little resistance as possible. I discovered that the wood for the clapper had to be the right density. If it was too hard, like teak, it would be clangy, and if it was too soft, like pine, it would not be heard. I found that a wood like cherry or ash worked best for the clapper.

The weight of the wind catcher was also important. I experimented with all that and came up with something that I liked: a musical instrument that was played randomly by wind.

After my initial experiment with aluminum tubes that I salvaged from old lawn chairs, I went to a hardware store and bought shower curtain rods and flag pole material – one-inch aluminum tubing. I made three Chimes of Olympos and put them in my wife's craft show booth in Cincinnati – they sold immediately. I priced them at $27 and soon realized that should have been the wholesale price; that was my market research and also the beginning of my understanding of how business works. I decided to make wind chimes on a large scale, so in 1979, I moved to Woodstock, NY, and started producing them. My desire to hear an ancient Greek scale eventually led to a full-scale business enterprise called Woodstock Percussion, Inc.; it also gave me insight into the acoustics of percussion instruments.

Now that I had achieved my goal of creating an instrument to hear Olympos' scale, I began to look at the acoustics of the percussion instruments I had been playing all my life to see how this knowledge could improve the instruments or even affect my approach to playing the instruments. Percussion instruments have a full range of overtones from harmonic overtones on the marimba and xylophone to nonharmonic overtones on instruments like drums, cymbals, gongs, and tam-tams. Because of the variety of materials used to make these instruments, the acoustical properties were different from strings and even from the aluminum tubes I had used to make wind chimes.

Marimba and xylophone

Marimba and xylophone bars vibrate in a similar way to strings; however, with marimbas and xylophones, the overtones are determined mostly by carving the underside of the bars. In fact, the only harmonic overtones that exist in these bars are the ones carved into them by the tuner. Most of the early development of xylophones and marimbas was done by the J. C. Deagan company in Chicago. In early Deagan instruments, the fundamental was the only partial tuned – no overtones were tuned. In 1927, Deagan began tuning overtones on marimbas and xylophone bars, and today, most North American and Japanese manufacturers tune their xylophones and marimbas in the ways described below. These tuning systems, however, have not become a universal standard.

Most marimba bars are carved so that the first audible overtone is a harmonic overtone two octaves above the fundamental. Many marimba manufacturers tune the bars to include a few harmonics such as the fourth

harmonic (two octaves above or four times the fundamental frequency). In addition to that, on the lower bars, a major third overtone above the fundamental is also tuned (three octaves and a third above or ten times the fundamental frequency). Therefore the predominant partials tuned on the lower marimba bars are the first, fourth, and tenth harmonic partials. Other harmonics are generally not tuned and currently do not exist on most marimba bars. This tuning gives the marimba its distinctive timbre; it also reinforces the tone so that the bars sound a lot clearer and the low octave can be heard more easily.

Some of the most remarkable things about the sound of a marimba bar are the various modes of vibration – longitudinal, torsional, lateral, and transverse – all of which make up the timbre of the instrument. With longitudinal vibration, the bar gets longer and shorter – it's unbelievable to think it's doing that. This vibration creates a really high pitch that we are probably not hearing. With the torsional mode, the bar is actually twisting side to side, like wringing out a face cloth back and forth. Another mode of vibration is the lateral mode that is a side-to-side vibration that sometimes interferes with the first overtone in the lower range. In order to lessen the effect of this latitudinal vibration, a V cut is often made on the underside of the marimba bar. This prevents the vibrating bar from interfering with the first overtone and allows the bar to ring more. The transverse mode is the main mode of vibration, and it determines the fundamental and harmonics that are tuned into the bars.

In a xylophone, the bars are carved in a method known as quint tuning. The first overtone that is tuned is an octave and a fifth above the fundamental (f3) or three times the frequency of the fundamental. A strong fifth is heard giving the xylophone a different timbre from the marimba. In addition, the fundamental (f1) and fifth (f3) are odd-numbered harmonics, and these odd-numbered harmonics are amplified by the resonator that is under each bar. The resonators underneath marimba and xylophone bars are closed at one end creating an acoustical phenomenon that amplifies the odd-numbered harmonics. In a marimba bar, the first overtone that is tuned is two octaves above the fundamental (f4) – an even-numbered overtone. This amplification by the resonator on the marimba gives it a more pure sound than the xylophone. Ironically, while making the sound of both the marimba and the xylophone louder, the resonators shorten the ring-time of the bars a little as they steal energy from them through entropy.

With some basic information about the acoustical properties of a marimba or xylophone, you can make adjustments in your playing technique to achieve a desired sound. For example, if you want to get a very flat, pure sound on the low part of a marimba, you use really big, soft mallets and

strike the bar just off center, so you are getting mostly the fundamental sound; that makes the sound blend more. But if you want the sound to stick out of the texture, you use not quite as big a mallet and strike the bar a little closer to the nodal point of the fundamental in order to bring out the harmonic overtone – the first overtone, which is two octaves above the fundamental. On the low bars of the marimba where the tenth harmonic partial is tuned, you play in the center for more harmonic content, but you have to play with a smaller mallet in order to bring out the partial that has the third of the scale in it. We all know that mallets make a difference, and the reason is because they change the timbre of the instrument. A bigger mallet mutes the overtones, and a harder mallet brings out less of the fundamental, emphasizing the overtones.

In addition to using a variety of mallets, you can also experiment with the place you strike the bar in order to bring out different overtones. In playing a piece with a pedal point, like the first movement of the Bach *Suite for Unaccompanied Cello* in G, if you play the pedal tone in the middle of the bar and play near the nodal points on the upper notes, you will bring out a bass line that contrasts with the other notes. In any piece you play, there might be some lines in which you want to bring out the overtone and other lines in which you want the timbre to be flat. These kinds of adjustments can make a huge difference in the sound of the piece.

Glockenspiel and chimes

The bars of glockenspiels produce such high frequencies that overtones are presently not tuned due to the fact that most of the overtones are out of the range of human hearing and do not play an important part in its timbre or sound quality.

Tubular chimes are a very special case in that the sound is known to have a quality called a "missing fundamental." The actual sound of the note of a tubular chime is not vibrating in the air but is rather a result of our ears combining the overtones closely related to harmonic partials which creates a virtual fundamental. The pitch we hear on a chime is the principle tone. The fundamental of the chime is an octave lower than the principle tone and does not have enough energy to be heard. Partials two, three, and four are close enough to being harmonic that they create the principle tone in our ear that is perceived by our brain as the musical pitch that we hear.

I was convinced that this was the case in a laboratory experiment when a chime tube was struck and the spectrum was shown on an oscilloscope screen along with the sound of an electronic tone generator matching the same fundamental pitch of the chime tube. The fundamental and its

partials were represented on the oscilloscope screen until the tone generator was turned off. The fundamental disappeared from the screen while the fundamental of the chime was still heard.

Tam-tams, gongs, and cymbals

Tam-tams and cymbals yield many nonharmonic overtones and are considered non-pitched due to the multitude of modes of vibration, many of which have similar amplitudes (volume). Gongs, with the raised boss in the middle, emit a strong fundamental pitch and are considered a tuned percussion instrument.

Tam-tams, gongs, and cymbals vibrate similarly to a string, but the vibrations are like thousands of strings in a circle with the middle of the circle going back and forth while the edge of the instrument is pivoting. In addition, the modes of vibration break up into pie shapes in which four segments vibrate alternately, then eight segments, sixteen segments, and so on. In tam-tams, gongs, cymbals, and even drums, there are also circular sections of vibration in which the instrument is vibrating back and forth as one big circle and simultaneously in concentric circles.

Drums

All kinds of drumheads, like tam-tams and cymbals, have multiple types of vibrations, both circular and radial. The center of a drumhead is the antinode for the lowest frequency. It is a place we do not usually play because it creates a low thud causing the sound to die out quickly. On a timpani head, that low thud is actually the fundamental pitch, a sixth below the pitch that we hear as the true pitch of the drum. When a timpani head is struck on the normal beating spot, the overtone that is heard is the principle tone, not the fundamental of the head. Rossing found that the bowl of the timpani helps diminish the fundamental; it kills that vibration so you hear mainly the principle tone. The fifth of the musical scale is also a prominent overtone in timpani. The timpani head sounds most in tune when the principle tone and the overtone a fifth above the principle tone are heard clearly.

Mallet Phase

My latest experiment in designing instruments with just intonation is an instrument I built for a new arrangement of Steve Reich's *Piano Phase*, called *Mallet Phase* (see Figure 4.1). I have played this piece many times in

Figure 4.1 Garry Kvistad with *Mallet Phase* instruments and Olympos wind chimes.

the *Marimba Phase* version, but I wanted to hear what it would sound like in just intonation and on different materials.

For the first section of the piece, I built an *amadinda*[4]-style xylophone out of five pieces of cherry wood that are between 17 and 26 inches long, 3.25 inches wide, and 2 inches thick. I tuned the bars to the just intonation equivalent of the five pitches in this section of the piece: E, F#, B, C#, and D, beginning a third above middle C. The second partial was tuned an octave and a fifth above the fundamental as in the Western xylophone (quint tuning). I built a stand for the bars and mounted PVC resonators tuned to the pitch of each bar. To play the bars, I used large wooden dowels made from a Chinese soft wood and struck the bars on the ends at a forty-five degree angle (as one would normally play on an *amadinda*). As with all percussion instruments, the beaters had to be softer than the bars to keep from chipping them.

For the second section of the piece, I tuned aluminum tubes in just intonation to the required pitches: E, F#, A, B, C#, D, and E, beginning a third above middle C. The tubes are between 24 and 35 inches long, with 0.25-inch thick walls, and an outside dimension of 1.75 inches. Again, I built a separate stand for the tubes with built-in PVC resonators tuned to the pitch of each bar, and the tubes were played on their ends with the wooden dowel sticks as well.

My original idea for the third section of *Piano Phase* was to use slap tubes, pieces of PVC tubes tuned in just intonation and played with foam paddles on the top of each tube. I tuned these slap tubes to the required pitches for the last section: A, B, D, E, starting a sixth above middle C.

I recorded *Mallet Phase* with Russell Hartenberger in a studio in Toronto. We sent a copy of the recording to Steve Reich who liked the piece, but felt the third section with the slap tubes was a much weaker sound than the *amadinda* bar and aluminum tube sections. We agreed with Reich's comment, so I made additional *amadinda* bars in order to play the last part of the piece on the wooden bars, giving it a stronger feel. To create a different timbre from the first section of the piece, we played the *amadinda* bars with large, yarn marimba mallets, not on the ends, but on the top of the bars as one would strike a marimba bar. Since resonators amplify the odd-numbered overtones of quint tuning, the wooden bars were amplified even more, and the psychoacoustics of the instrument were enhanced by the brilliance of the overtone.

Pulse to pitch

The sonic phenomena in *Mallet Phase* are quite beautiful, and the rhythmic complexity of the music relates to my interest in acoustics in yet another way – the connections of pulse to pitch and polyrhythms to intervals. When you play a steady pulse, you are actually playing a very low pitch. For example, if you play a pulse at m.m. = 120 and double the speed five times, you create a pitch that is 28 cents lower than C2, two octaves below middle C. Polyrhythms are slow intervals. When you play a polyrhythm, you're playing two pulses and, depending on what the relationship is, you're playing a musical interval of some sort.

In the natural overtone series, when you hear the fundamental (f1), you also hear the second partial (f2) vibrating, and you also hear the third partial (f3) vibrating. When you play f2 and f3 together, you create the interval of a fifth. So the relationship musically speaking of a fifth is three pulses to two pulses: 300 vibrations per second is one pitch and 200 vibrations per second is another pitch, and together they create an interval of a fifth. Every interval that we know has a ratio that goes with it, and they are identical to polyrhythms.

When I was studying acoustics, I understood this principle conceptually, but I actually wanted to hear a polyrhythm become an interval. In order to prove this theory, I took two temple blocks tuned to different pitches so I could hear the difference and played three against two on them at a steady tempo for about forty-five minutes. I recorded it on a tape deck at the slow speed of 3¾ inches per second (ips) and played it back at the higher speed of 7½ ips. This tape transference immediately doubled the speed and brought it up an octave, but it still sounded like a polyrhythm. So I dubbed it onto another tape deck at 3¾ ips and kept bouncing it back

between the two speeds until I transferred it seven times. At the end of that process, I had about five seconds of sound, but I could hear that it created a perfect fifth. That was a real "aha moment" for me, and I had my proof. A few years later, I commissioned someone to write a computer program that allows me to tap a polyrhythm on the keyboard and speed it up many times until an interval is created.

Conclusion

My study of the science of sound has led me in directions I never imagined when I began my journey to hear an ancient Greek scale. It has taken me from repurposed timpani sticks and salvaged pieces of aluminum to wind chimes and the creation of an instrument to reimagine a work by one of the great composers of percussion music. My basic knowledge of the acoustics of percussion instruments has given me insight into the sounds that I can produce on percussion instruments, and as a result has enhanced my entire approach to both listening and music-making.

Notes

1. H. Partch, *Genesis of a Music* (New York: Da Capo, 1974).
2. T. Rossing, *Science of Percussion Instruments* (Singapore: World Scientific, 2005). For additional information on percussion acoustics, see: *The Science of Sound* (Boston, MA: Addison-Wesley, 1990); and T. D. Rossing, J. Yoo, and A. Morrison, "Acoustics of Percussion Instruments: an Update," *Acoustical Science and Technology* vol. 25 (2004), 406–12.
3. For additional information about just intonation, see: D. B. Doty, *The Just Intonation Primer: An Introduction to the Theory and Practice of Just Intonation* (San Francisco, CA: Just Intonation Network, 1993); and K. Gann, "Just Intonation Explained," www.kylegann.com/tuning.html.
4. For a detailed description of the *amadinda*, see: G. Kubik, "The Phenomenon of Inherent Rhythms in East and Central African Instrumental Music," *African Music Society Journal*, vol. 3, no. 1 (1962), 33–42; and Kubik, *Theory of African Music*, 2 vols. (University of Chicago Press, 1994).

5 The percussion industry

RICK MATTINGLY

Although the drum is considered the oldest musical instrument (aside from the human voice), much of the equipment used by modern drummers and percussionists is of relatively recent design, compared to such instruments as trumpets, violins, or clarinets, which have remained largely unchanged for well over a century. Percussion instruments, however, have continued to evolve, not only in terms of materials and manufacturing processes that have resulted in more consistent and durable instruments, but also in regard to innovations that have affected how and what musicians play. The result is a sizable percussion industry that ranges from large corporations that make a wide range of instruments to cottage industries that specialize in just a few products, or even a single product. While the manufacturers have often been the pioneers in terms of materials and workmanship, innovations in the instruments themselves and in the development of new instruments have largely been driven by the players.

Drum set innovations

One of the first inventions that had a significant effect on how drummers played was the bass drum pedal. Prior to the early twentieth century, bands typically had two drummers: a snare drummer and a bass drummer. When bands played inside in smaller areas, and as bands started playing in pits for vaudeville shows and silent movies, space became an issue and ways were sought to get by with fewer musicians. Various drummers rigged up mechanical bass drum beaters that could be operated with a foot pedal. The most successful design was patented by William F. and Theobald Ludwig in 1909 and remains the basis of modern bass drum pedals. The brothers started the Ludwig and Ludwig company to market their pedal, and that business grew to encompass a full range of drums and percussion instruments.

In light of later history, if a strong musicians' union had existed in those days, use of a bass drum pedal would likely have been banned, as it effectively put half the drummers out of work. But it led to the development of the modern drum set, which allowed a single, seated drummer to play a collection of drums and cymbals, along with various sound effects. The hi-hat pedal evolved from various predecessors that allowed

drummers to play a pair of cymbals with a foot pedal, and after drummers started hanging crash cymbals around their kits and "riding" on them to maintain a pulse, rather than using press rolls on the snare drum, cymbal companies began making larger and thinner cymbals that better suited the new style that was developing. That style became the basis of the drumming that drives popular music genres including jazz, blues, rock and roll, funk, and country music.

Most of the innovations in the development of the modern drum set came from drummers. In the late 1940s, after World War II, Fred Gretsch Jr., president of the Gretsch Drum Company, called a meeting to discuss the future of the company. Former Gretsch employee Duke Kramer recalled that meeting in a 1984 *Modern Drummer* article: "We all decided that we wanted to develop Gretsch into a major line. After the meeting we split up into two-man teams. We covered every major nightspot in New York that we could find and asked the drummers what they wanted in a drum."[1] Among the drummers' requests were smaller drums that could be carried around more easily, and hardware that was easier to set up and take down. That led to Gretsch being the first to offer twenty-inch bass drums and the invention of shell-mounted tom-tom holders and cymbal arms, as well as disappearing spurs.

One of the people at the Gretsch meeting was Phil Grant, who had been a drummer with the Pittsburgh Symphony and the Edwin Franko Goldman band. He was also an avid jazz fan who frequented New York nightclubs and knew many of the drummers. "Fred [Gretsch] was a very nice man, but he was not a musician," recalled big-band drummer Louis Bellson. "He was a businessman – a very smart one and a very good one. Whenever I went to Brooklyn [where the Gretsch factory and offices were located], Fred would always ask, 'Do you have any problems?' If he didn't understand something, he would turn to Phil Grant and say, 'Well, Phil, this is your department. If you think it is right, go ahead and do it.'"[2]

Among the products that Gretsch developed based on drummers' ideas was an adjustable bass drum tone control, which came from Jimmie Pratt, and single-headed tom-toms, which was requested by jazz drummer Chico Hamilton in the 1950s, long before rock drummers of the 1960s began to favor them. One of Bellson's requests was for a kit with two bass drums. While promoting the use of two bass drums would seem to have been a great marketing ploy for a drum manufacturer, several drum companies Bellson had previously approached were not interested. "Phil looked at my design," Bellson recalled, "and said, 'That's pretty wild, but I don't see why it can't work.' So they built the first one for me."[3]

Despite Bellson's prestige, double-bass drums were considered a novelty for many years, with very few drummers incorporating a second bass drum

into their setups. But in the 1960s, double-bass setups became more common after such popular rock drummers as Cream's Ginger Baker and The Who's Keith Moon used double-bass kits. The use of two bass drums allowed drummers to play patterns that would have been impossible with one drum. But, as with the invention of the original bass drum pedal and the request from jazz drummers for smaller bass drums, space became the motivation for another invention: the double-bass drum pedal. Some drummers wanted to play the double-bass patterns that were becoming popular, but they didn't have room for two bass drums (or didn't want to haul or couldn't afford another bass drum). Some drummers tried putting two bass drum pedals on a single drum, but because of the curvature of the bass drum rim and the awkwardness of having both of the player's legs next to each other, that proved impractical. Finally, in the early 1970s, the Zalmar company marketed a double pedal on which the beaters were side by side, but one pedal was in the normal position and the other pedal was a couple of feet to the left, where it could be placed next to the hi-hat pedal so a drummer could easily move his left foot from one to the other. This was another example of drummers creating a demand for a product that previously did not exist. Soon, most major drum companies were marketing double pedals, and more drummers started playing patterns that would have been impossible with a single pedal.

In the 1950s, jazz drummer Art Blakey – perhaps inspired by his trip to Africa, where many instruments are fitted with appendages that make them buzz or rattle – started hanging his key ring from the wing nut of his ride cymbal stand so that after the cymbal was struck, the keys would continue to vibrate against the cymbal to extend the shimmering sound. Other drummers experimented with similar ways to create that effect, with one of the most popular being to hang a beaded metal chain (the type commonly used to hold bathtub stoppers) from the wing nut. Some drummers went as far as to drill holes in their cymbals and insert nails that would buzz when the cymbal was struck. Soon, all the major cymbal companies were manufacturing "sizzle" cymbals that had rivets inserted in holes. Sizzle cymbals enabled drummers to get a more legato sound from ride cymbals and increase the sustain of a crash cymbal.

Latin percussion instruments

Martin Cohen, founder of Latin Percussion, was not a musician, but he loved Latin music and spent a lot of time at Cuban dance halls in New York. He was particularly impressed by bongo player Jose Mangual, so he decided to acquire a set of bongos, but, "The U.S. had initiated an embargo of Cuba, and that's where the good bongos, congas, and cowbells had

always come from," Cohen said in a 1989 *Modern Drummer* article. "So I decided to make my own."[4] Cohen did not own the necessary equipment to make the bongos himself, but with his degree in engineering, he was able to design them and hired a wood turner to machine the instruments, which he ended up selling. "By doing that I initiated a business," he recalled. "I started putting bongos in stores on consignment. I was getting a lot of satisfaction from serving the needs of the Latin percussionists."[5]

The Latin music scene was small in the early 1960s when Cohen began making bongos, and although a few jazz artists used Latin rhythms on occasion, the instruments had not found their way to rock and roll, so Cohen's customer base was limited. But CBS studio musician Specs Powell asked Cohen to make him a pair of bongos, and he wanted them mounted on a stand – which was unheard of in the Latin music community. "But he was so insistent that I devised a bongo mounting bracket that we sell to this day,"[6] Cohen said.

That small innovation led Cohen to a much bigger development when Powell introduced him to another prominent studio drummer, Bobby Rosengarden, who challenged Cohen to make a jawbone that didn't break. Cohen had never seen a jawbone used as a musical instrument, but he found out that a jawbone "was an animal skull that you would strike, and the sound would come from the teeth rattling," Cohen said. "So I took that concept and invented the Vibraslap."[7]

Rosengarden then asked for a cabasa that wouldn't break. At the time, cabasas were typically made of gourds with shells or beads wrapped around them with wire. They were very fragile, and the wire often broke. Cohen wrapped bead chain around the kind of textured metal he had seen on the walls of elevators, and his Afuché/Cabasa became his most successful patent in terms of sales.[8]

Some of Cohen's products were originally greeted with suspicion by the Latin community, such as fiberglass conga drums and the Jam Block – essentially a woodblock made of plastic. But the quality and sound of the products made believers out of the doubters, and the availability and affordability of Cohen's products led musicians in other genres to start coloring their music with instruments that had previously been impractical due to their scarcity (e.g., a jawbone), their fragility (cabasa), or their lack of volume (woodblocks and wooden congas).

Plastic drumheads

Similarly, it's hard to imagine how rock drummers of the 1960s and beyond could have done what they did without the development of the

plastic drumhead in the 1950s. The problem that the primary developers of the plastic head sought to solve was that calfskin heads constantly had to be tuned because humidity made them stretch and dry weather made them shrink (and often split). Plastic heads were not affected by weather, but drummers discovered that they were stronger, too. As rock and roll got louder in the 1960s, drummers found that they could hit plastic heads harder. Pretty soon, though, they were even breaking plastic heads, so companies like Remo and Evans developed double-ply heads for added strength. After drum corps started tensioning heads as tightly as possible to get an extremely dry, high-pitched sound (and breaking them), the drum-head companies began making heads from Kevlar – the material used in bulletproof vests. Those heads could be tensioned so tightly that drum shells and tension casings started breaking, so the drum companies built stronger drums to accommodate the new heads. Meanwhile, as kit drum-mers experimented with various types of muffling (e.g., tape on tom heads, pillows inside bass drums), the companies responded by developing heads that produced the sounds drummers were looking for without having to use external muffling devices.

So it was a back-and-forth relationship between the companies and the musicians. Drummers did not specifically ask for plastic heads, and many drummers rejected them at first. But after Remo and Evans began making them, drummers found that not only did they solve the problems created by humidity (or lack thereof), but since the drums could be tuned with more precision and tensioned more tightly, drummers could hit harder and use techniques that were not practical with calfskin heads, such as modern rudimental players incorporating "buzz roll" effects on their high-tension heads.

Xylophones, marimbas

Likewise, makers of xylophones and marimbas started experimenting with synthetic bars in the 1970s. One reason was that the rosewood favored for those instruments was becoming harder to get and more expensive. Also, like calfskin drumheads, rosewood was relatively fragile and had to be protected from the weather. So around the same time in the 1970s, the Musser and Deagan companies developed synthetic bars for xylophones and marimbas. At first, many players complained that the synthetic bars lacked the rich tone that rosewood produced. But synthetic bars allowed for less-expensive instruments, and they were much sturdier, so those instruments became popular in schools and enabled more students to afford a personal instrument. And because synthetic bars were unaffected

by weather, marching bands and drum corps started taking them outside, lining them up on the edge of football fields, and incorporating keyboard percussion into their marching shows, leading to the development of the marching percussion "pit."

Sticks, mallets

Some of today's large-scale percussion manufacturers started out with percussionists just making products for their own use. Vic Firth began by making his own timpani sticks to use with the Boston Symphony. When some of his students asked if they could buy some of his sticks, he made a few more, then added orchestral snare drum sticks. A couple of specialized drum shops offered to sell them, the business grew, and today Vic Firth is one of the world's largest manufacturers of sticks and mallets.

When Leigh Howard Stevens was in college, he didn't like rattan marimba mallets and he also wanted longer mallet shafts to accommodate the grip he was using. He bought some dowel rods and began making mallets in his college dorm room, with no desire whatsoever to go into business. But, as with Firth, a few people asked Stevens if they could buy some of his mallets, and he gradually built a mallet and stick business that today includes the manufacture of marimbas, xylophones, and vibes, as well as the publication of method books and music.

Percussion manufacturers

The percussion industry has changed over the years, much like other industries. In the 1980s, one could attend a music trade show and speak directly with some of the people whose names were on their products: Remo Belli at the Remo drumhead company; Armand Zildjian at the Zildjian cymbal company; Bob Zildjian at the Sabian cymbal company (named after his children SA-lly, BI-lly, and AN-dy); William F. Ludwig Jr. and III at Ludwig Drum Company; Joe Calato at Calato drumsticks; Vic Firth at Vic Firth drumsticks; and Robert and Toomas Paiste at Paiste cymbals. You could also talk to Martin Cohen at Latin Percussion, who didn't name his company after himself, but put his name on his products' logo badges. "I had seen David Brown's name on the label of an Aston Martin car," Cohen said, "and that told me that someone named David Brown had designed that car, and that he had put his name on it to be accountable. So I put my name on the LP labels for the same reason – so that somebody would always know who to complain to if the product failed."[9]

Even if the founders of the companies were no longer around, many of the leading products and companies bore the name of individuals: Clair Musser; J. C. Deagan; Bud Slingerland; Fred Gretsch. But in the 1970s, products began emerging with names like Pearl, Yamaha, and Tama, which were brand names owned by companies that often made other instruments besides drum and percussion gear. That wasn't necessarily unprecedented or bad; Gretsch was as highly regarded for its guitars as for its drums, and larger companies often had more resources that led to higher manufacturing quality.

There are still privately owned drum and percussion companies run by the individuals who started them, such as Marimba Productions/Malletech run by Leigh Howard Stevens, Drum Workshop (DW) run by Don Lombardi, Marimba One run by Ron Samuels, and Aquarian Accessories run by Roy Burns, among others. In addition, some of the original owners are still involved with their companies (as of 2015) to varying degrees, such as Remo Belli and Martin Cohen. In other cases, the founders' descendants are heading the companies: Armand Zildjian's daughters run Zildjian; Robert Zildjian's son runs Sabian; and a nephew of Fred Gretsch runs Gretsch. But more and more small companies are being absorbed into larger ones, larger companies are merging, and more decisions are being made by business people than by musicians.

According to John DeChristopher, vice-president, Artist Relations and Event Marketing Worldwide at Zildjian from 1989 to 2014,

> There has to be some involvement by drummers. At one point, it was mostly drummers at the major drum and cymbal companies making the important decisions about products. These days there are more business people involved. But there have to be some players in the mix, because this is a very unique business. It's not like selling vacuum cleaners. Some people might assume that you can apply one set of business standards to another business and it will be fine, but we've all seen examples of those kinds of mistakes. A lot of companies today are being run by non-musicians, and things are heading in a corporate direction. But it's very important for companies to not lose sight of the fact that musicians are very unique in what they like and think and feel. Drummers have a very tribal type of relationship with each other, and you can't put a corporate spin on something and think that drummers are going to buy it.[10]

The story of the Rogers Drum Company illustrates what can happen when business and marketing people run companies and don't listen to the musicians. Rogers was started in 1849 by an Irish immigrant named Joseph Rogers. In 1953, after he died, the company was sold to Henry Grossman, who, with designer Joe Thompson and marketing manager Ben Strauss, elevated Rogers to one of the major drum companies by the mid-1960s by virtue of innovative products like the Dyna-Sonic snare drum and Swiv-o-

Matic pedals and hardware. In 1966, the company was bought by CBS, who also acquired Fender guitars and Rhodes electric pianos.

Drummer Roy Burns was involved with the company as an endorser, clinician, and employee. Today, Burns heads Aquarian Accessories, which manufactures drumheads and other percussion products. "One of the things I realized that made me go in business for myself was that you have to have a musician in a position of power in a company," he said. "He doesn't have to run everything, but he has to have influence on the products. If the marketing guys or the factory guys or the R&D guys get control, the product ends up suffering because there is no one to say 'No, that's not good enough.'"[11]

Burns cites the Rogers bass drum pedal as an example: "Rogers had the best bass drum pedal on the market. Buddy Rich was a Ludwig endorser, but he used a Rogers bass drum pedal any time Bill Ludwig wasn't in the room. Well, after CBS bought Rogers, they decided to replace the needle bearings in the bass drum pedal with nylon bearings. They said no one would be able to feel the difference." In fact, the nylon bearings changed the feel entirely, giving the pedal less range of motion and less smoothness. Dealers started returning pedals "by the barrelful," as Burns put it, and the word got out that Rogers' pedals were no good any more. "It killed the product," Burns said, "and they were never able to revive it. They changed the bearings to save money, but they were making a profit on the pedal; they didn't need to save money."[12]

Burns said another situation that led to the company's downfall was that the Rogers accountant insisted that the company not order materials until they had orders for products. "When Rogers introduced an 8-ply shell, that was a wonderful product and no one else had anything like it," Burns says. "They announced it in October, orders poured in, but by December they still hadn't shipped any drums, so the orders got cancelled."[13]

Burns cites Henry Grossman as the one responsible for the innovations that originally put Rogers on the map. "He was a real visionary, and he let his people develop creative ideas. He told me one time, 'Roy, always stick with quality and you'll end up better off in the long run.' I took that very much to heart, and Aquarian has been in business for thirty-five years. I tell people I'm the 'safety net' of the company. If I don't like it, we keep working on it until we get it right."[14]

Artist endorsements

Although many companies are not headed by musicians or have many musicians as employees, most companies have artists who endorse their

products, and those players often participate in new product development and refinements of older products. "Endorsement deals are unique for some artists while generic for most," says jazz drummer Peter Erskine. "By 'generic,' I mean that the 'usual' norms will apply: a music company enlists the name, image and reputation of an artist and, in return, supplies that artist with equipment. The benefits are obvious: the artist receives equipment and musical instrument support, plus marketing promotion in the form of advertising, prestige by affiliation with the company and their other artists, plus logistical support while traveling. The one disadvantage to having an endorsement deal," Erskine adds, "is that the artist is more or less locked into playing that brand of instrument. Non-endorsed musicians can play whatever they want – total freedom! But freedom comes at a price – in this case, the cost of purchasing that instrument. There are no free lunches in this world. But that's okay."[15]

In the early stages of an artist's career, an endorsement can be more beneficial to the artist than to the manufacturer, as an up-and-coming artist will not be giving the company's products a whole lot of exposure. But the artist will be getting free or discounted equipment, as well as the "cred" that comes from having an endorsement deal (or two or three). Indeed, while the idea is that an artist endorses a product, young drummers will often put on their resumes that they are "endorsed by" a certain company.

Artists looking for credibility will often seek deals with the manufacturers whose artist rosters include some of the biggest names in drumming and percussion, but some prefer to sign with smaller companies who will give them more attention. That can often pay off in terms of the small company featuring the artist in ads or with clinic support. It can also result in exposure at large festivals, such as the Percussive Arts Society International Convention (PASIC) and the *Modern Drummer* Festival Weekend (no longer held). As *Modern Drummer* vice-president Kevin Kearns explains, "When selecting artists for a festival-type show, the producer of the show must balance the artists, the musical styles desired, and the companies the artists endorse, because when the producer is relying on endorsing companies for support, the producer cannot have one instrument manufacturer significantly represented over its competitors."[16]

While prominent artists typically have several endorsements (e.g., a drum company, stick company, cymbal company, and drumhead company), those who appear in multiple ads in magazines also endorsing cases, microphones, various electronic devices, auxiliary percussion instruments, and so on can earn the label "professional endorser" from their peers. That label can also be applied to once-prominent musicians whose playing

careers have faded but who are more prominent than ever in equipment ads, often with smaller companies.

Musicians can also be criticized for switching endorsements. What is one to think if a player sings the praises of a particular instrument company for several years and then suddenly (so it seems) switches to another brand? In some cases, a change in company management can result in certain artists being "let go," just as when prominent artists lose record deals. Peter Erskine offers some other reasons that artists may feel compelled to switch companies:

> I started out playing a Gretsch kit as a kid, switched to Ludwig in high school, and began playing Slingerland drums while a member of Stan Kenton's Orchestra in 1973. By 1981, I was a Yamaha artist. Twenty-five years later, I switched to Drum Workshop. Eleven years after that I changed to Tama. Why? Here's where the endorsement equation gets interesting. Endorsement relationships involve more than just free gear, clinic support, advertising, logistical assistance, and the like. The quality of communication and personal relationships between artists and their companies are often the most vital and important components of successful endorsement relationships. And these relationships often falter, more often than not due to a lack of good communication between the artist and the company. Artists are, by their very nature, thoroughbreds, vain stallions, pains-in-the-neck, and invaluable resources to any company. The artist-relations manager at any company has a crucial role in maintaining a healthy ecosystem between the artists and the company. Easier said than done in many cases, as my jumps from one drum company to another may attest.
>
> All of that said, my quest has been centered upon finding the instrument I truly want to play: the instrument that responds the best to my touch and that excites and inspires me to play my possible best – the very same qualities that every musician is looking for when he or she walks up to any instrument and begins to play it. Ultimately, it's all about the music.[17]

Endorsement deals can have a significant effect on a musician's finances. For drummers who break a lot of sticks and/or drumheads, endorsements with drumstick and drumhead manufacturers can help ensure that the drummer always has plenty of sticks and heads on hand. Even if the company will only provide a certain amount of free gear per year, endorsers can typically purchase additional items from the company at less cost than the price they would pay at a music store. As another example, musicians who frequently perform in other countries can rarely afford to ship their equipment around the world for tours of one-nighters. So they typically sign with companies that can provide equipment in a wide variety of locations.

It has been rumored for years that in addition to providing gear and clinic support, some artists have been paid to endorse a particular brand of

instrument. Mel Lewis insisted that during the 1950s and 1960s, no one was ever paid by Gretsch. "They gave you drums and cymbals, and you could always stop by the factory if you needed sticks or brushes," he said. "But they didn't give you unlimited equipment; in fact, when you got a new drum set you had to turn in your old one. Gretsch never even paid anyone to play their drums. They even preferred that you already owned a set of Gretsch before they offered you an advertising deal. Fred [Gretsch] wanted to know that you played the drums because you liked them. The only contract you had with Gretsch was that, in return for a set of drums, they were allowed to use your name and picture in their advertising." [18]

Peter Erskine says he is not aware of any music company that pays an artist to play its instruments, although he heard rumors that Buddy Rich was paid at one time. "The most significant financial arrangement that I'm aware of between some drummers and their sponsoring companies involves the companies providing healthcare coverage to those drummers, much the same as what those companies offer to full-time employees," Erskine says. "Anyone who thinks that drummers play a particular brand simply for the money – or for money at all, because that is a complete myth – is misinformed, and their opinion is as valid as someone who denies climate change or thinks that the earth is flat. Whatever mythology drummers-at-large wish to believe regarding endorsement deals, there's one simple fact that seems to get overlooked: all drummers, whether endorsed or not, are fans of the instrument. And, so, most decisions regarding instrument endorsement deals are driven by that youthful, innocent passion and excitement that a great instrument generates."[19]

According to John DeChristopher, "I've heard rumors about people being paid to endorse products, but I can't confirm that any particular person is getting paid today. There were people in the 1980s and '90s who were getting paid, but the business has changed a lot since then, and I think even the big companies can't afford to pay artists to endorse their products."[20]

One aspect of some endorsement deals is clinic support. Some drummers augment their careers by giving educational clinics at local drum shops as well as at music conventions such as those hosted by the Percussive Arts Society (PAS), the National Association of Music Merchants (NAMM), the Jazz Education Network (JEN), and the Music Educators National Conference (MENC). Depending on the situation, the manufacturer will pay all or some of the endorser's fees (including travel) and may also take care of all the details of a clinic tour so that the artists' only responsibilities are to show up and give the clinic. During such clinics, the endorsee is generally expected to sing the praises of the equipment manufactured by whoever is sponsoring the tour. "Contrary to some

perceptions," says Peter Erskine, "the amount of support for these presentations is generally modest."[21]

For drummers who have ideas for new products, or variations of existing products, endorsement deals allow direct access to company executives and designers. The companies, in turn, have a direct connection to influential drummers who can advise them on new products and test prototypes. According to John DeChristopher, many new products are a combination of artists' requests and the company looking to expand its product line by offering new models. "There is no shortage of artists giving their input and ideas," DeChristopher says. "As an artist relations person, one of my jobs was to make sure there wasn't an overlap or redundancy in the things artists wanted versus things the company already had that the artists weren't aware of or that were in development."[22]

DeChristopher cites Zildjian's K Constantinople line as an example of how the artists and the company worked together. After the American Avedis Zildjian cymbal company (see Figure 5.1) bought the rights to the K. Zildjian name and trademarks, the American company sought to recreate the sounds of the "old K's" that had been made in Turkey. "A number of artists had been playing K Zildjians from Turkey, and they were always looking for that 'old K' sound," DeChristopher said. "Zildjian was trying to make cymbals like that, there was some trial and error, and some products came out pretty good, like the Pre-aged K Light Ride. The way the K Constantinoples came about was that Armand Zildjian wanted to improve the orchestral cymbals and made it a top priority. At the same time [Boston Symphony Orchestra percussionist] Frank Epstein was looking for a sound like the old Turkish K hand cymbals, and was involved in testing prototypes. Armand, Lennie DiMuzio, and Paul Francis (whom Armand apprenticed), painstakingly did the R&D, and Lennie sent prototypes to other orchestral cymbal players. The process that was used in developing those cymbals was then transferred to the development of drum set cymbals, and drummers like Jeff Hamilton, Peter Erskine, Adam Nussbaum, Bill Stewart, Steve Smith, and Elvin Jones tested prototypes and helped shape those early K Constantinople cymbals. Since then, Paul Francis has evolved into one of the great cymbal makers and has taken the K Constantinoples to a whole new level."[23] According to Erskine, "A dynamic endorsement relationship will involve plenty of back-and-forth between the artist and company in terms of product betterment and development. Sometimes this will result in a 'signature' product – an instrument or accessory that generates royalty revenue for the artist."[24]

For many years, the primary signature products were sticks and mallets. It seemed that the majority of prominent players had their name on a

Figure 5.1 Avedis Zildjian III in front of old Zildjian factory.

drumstick, marimba mallet, or timpani stick. At first, most of the signature drumsticks were simply the standard models, to which the names of the drummers who favored them were added. But gradually players began asking for modifications to standard models – a heavier shaft, a different bead, harder or softer heads on keyboard and timpani mallets, even a different color – and those models became those artists' signature sticks and mallets. Signature products have expanded into almost all areas of the percussion industry (and the music industry in general), and now there are signature snare drums, cymbals, marimbas, conga drums, stick bags, and so on. It is common for companies to charge extra for signature products, and for the artists to receive royalties. Judging by the increasing number of signature items, customers must be willing to pay extra for them.

Conclusion

While the main goal of a manufacturer is to make money by selling products, the percussion industry is notable for its long-time support of music education. Granted, it's not pure charity, as the manufacturers realize that teaching more people to play results in a bigger pool of potential customers. Nevertheless, the percussion industry's support of the PAS has no parallel in any other instrument family.

"PAS receives tremendous support from the drum and percussion industry in various ways without which PAS could not exist," says PAS executive director Jeff Hartsough. "This includes, but is not limited to, artist support, exhibiting, and providing door prizes at PASIC and state chapter Days of Percussion, advertising, donated instruments for Rhythm! Discovery Center [the PAS percussion instrument museum in Indianapolis], and much more. And, despite the fact that many of the companies are competitors, there can be a surprising level of cooperation between all of them when it comes to supporting PAS and promoting the drum and percussion community at large."[25]

Many of the manufacturers joined together in the 1990s to create the Percussion Marketing Council, which sponsors International Drum Month – an event designed to promote percussion education in cooperation with local music stores. Manufacturers have also sponsored clinicians at such events as MENC conventions, various KoSA events, the Modern Drummer Festival, and at local music stores around the world.

Although some people complain that the modern percussion industry – and the musical products industry in general – is now run more by "suits" (i.e., business people) than by musicians, which is true in some cases, musicians still run a number of companies that produce quality and innovative products, and just about every company is getting feedback and new product ideas from its musician endorsers. As long as product development is driven by the people who use those products, the industry and the players should both benefit.

Notes

1. R. Egart, "Inside Gretsch," *Modern Drummer*, vol. 8, no. 5 (1984), 20.
2. *Ibid.*, p. 20.
3. *Ibid.*, p. 20.
4. R. Mattingly and A. Budofsky, "Latin Percussion's Martin Cohen," *Modern Drummer*, vol. 13, no. 9 (1989), 32.
5. *Ibid.*, p. 33.
6. *Ibid.*, p. 33.
7. *Ibid.*, p. 33.
8. *Ibid.*, p. 34.
9. *Ibid.*, p. 97.
10. Phone interview with J. DeChristopher (October 22, 2014).
11. Phone interview with R. Burns (September 12, 2014).
12. *Ibid.*

13. *Ibid.*

14. *Ibid.*

15. Email correspondence with P. Erskine (December 8, 2014).

16. Email correspondence with K. Kerns (August 3, 2014).

17. Erskine (2014).

18. Egart, "Inside Gretsch," 76.

19. Erskine (2014).

20. DeChristopher (2014).

21. Erskine (2014).

22. DeChristopher (2014).

23. *Ibid.*

24. Erskine (2014).

25. Email correspondence with J. Hartsough (January 11, 2015).

6 Virtual drumming

A history of electronic percussion

THOMAS BRETT

Introduction

One of the notable stories about music in the twentieth century was the emergence of electronic percussion technologies. Rhythm boxes, drum machines, percussion controllers, and software shifted drumming away from acoustic instruments, inspired techniques that shaped the sound of popular music, and foregrounded the aesthetics of groove. This essay traces a social history of electronic percussion instruments from the 1930s to the present by examining their designs, reception, and musical applications.[1] The first section examines early rhythm boxes, influential drum machines from the 1960s, 1970s, and 1980s, and concludes with a consideration of drum pad controllers and software. The second section explores the perceptual and creative changes brought about by these instruments to suggest that the mechanical, quantized sound of drum machines led to a discourse about human versus machine timing. The section also argues that programming techniques enabled musicians to make rhythmic textures unencumbered by the limitations of the drumming body. Finally, the last section considers the legacies of electronic percussion, from performance practices and recent hardware design to the rise of digital percussion apps. In sum, electronic percussion has made significant contributions to the practices and sounds of contemporary music. By offering new approaches for creating rhythms, the technologies redefined what it means to drum and thereby led musicians to think about what is human in music.

A history of electronic percussion

The story of electronic percussion begins in the early 1930s, when the American composer Henry Cowell sought a machine that could generate complex polyrhythms. In 1931, Cowell commissioned the Russian inventor Léon Theremin to build him a device that would assign rhythms to pitches. Theremin created the Rhythmicon (see Figure 6.1), a mechanized optoelectronic instrument with a one-octave keyboard and speaker

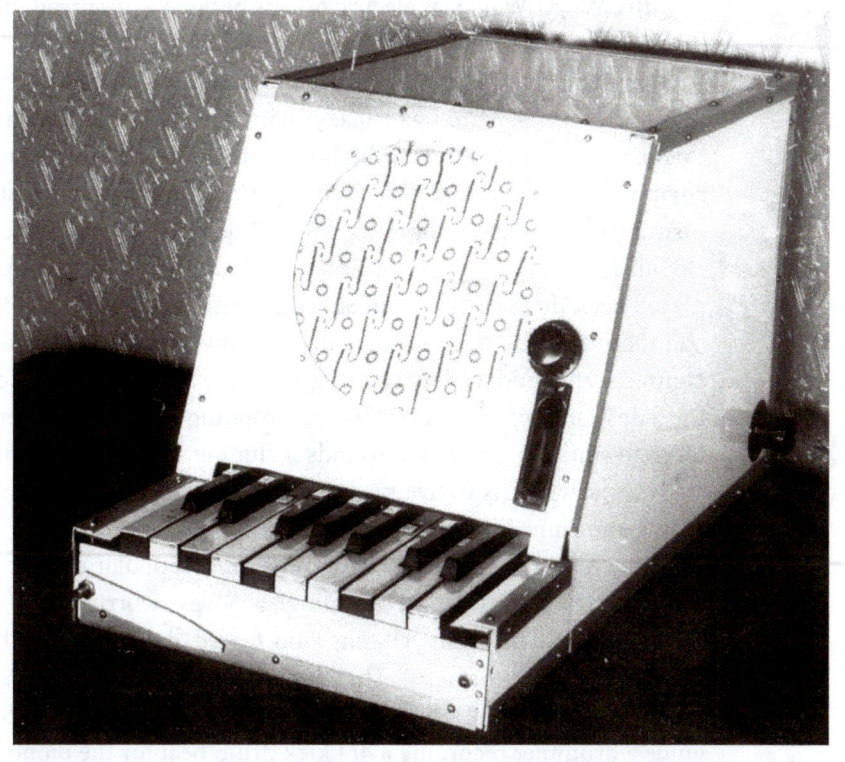

Figure 6.1 Rhythmicon built at the Acoustical Laboratory at Moscow Conservatory in the mid-1960s as part of Léon Theremin's research project. It is in working condition and in the collection of Andrey Smirnov.

housed in a large wooden box. When pressed, each key produced a pitched tone that repeated in a steady pulsation. Cowell hoped to use the Rhythmicon in his music to play multiple rhythms simultaneously and thus transcend the limits of human musicianship, believing that "further rhythmic development . . . needed the application of mechanical aid."[2] Critics who heard the Rhythmicon's debut demonstration at The New School in 1932 noticed the potential and limitations of mechanical rhythm. For Homer Henly, the "rhythmic control possible in playing and imparting exactitudes in cross rhythms [was] bewildering to contemplate."[3] Marc Blitzstein anticipated future debates about drum machine timing, noting how the musician "is constrained . . . without deviation from the regular beat."[4] And Alexander Fried considered the instrument a poor substitute for the natural imperfections of human timekeeping. "Hand-made music will always be the real music," he said, while "mechanical music at most will be of subsidiary use."[5] The Rhythmicon – of which only three were made – was soon abandoned by Cowell, yet the experimental device had sparked discussion about issues of performance, rhythmic control, and musical time.

After World War II, as electric organs became widespread in American homes, manufacturers offered features such as one-touch chords and rhythm presets to facilitate playing one-man band arrangements of popular songs. In 1949, an organ-maker named Harry Chamberlin addressed this market with his Chamberlin Rhythmate, the first sample-based rhythm machine. Designed to accompany organ players, this stand-alone instrument used tape loop recordings of acoustic drums playing various rhythms that could be sounded individually or blended together and played back through a built-in speaker. Within ten years, the Rhythmate had motivated the American organ company Wurlitzer to create the first commercially produced rhythm machine, the Side Man. Released in 1959, the Side Man used tube circuitry and a rotating metal disc rather than tape loops to simulate percussion sounds including snare drum, temple blocks, and claves, while its twelve preset rhythm patterns included the beguine, tango, and rumba. Marketed as a "full rhythm section at your side!" that could serve as accompaniment for Wurlitzer's popular electric piano, the Side Man and its tinny-sounding grooves worried the American Federation of Musicians' Union, who feared that it "would be used to displace a live performer."[6] That almost came to pass in 1975 when the Italian producer Giorgio Moroder used a Side Man as a metronome to guide a drummer recording a 4/4 kick drum beat for the pioneering disco song, "Love to Love You Baby."[7]

Inspired by the functionality of the Side Man, the pace of electronic percussion innovation accelerated in Japan, as the founders of a company that would become Korg Electronics, Tsutomu Katoh and Tadashi Osanai, collaborated on their Donca Matic series of rhythm machines. Released in 1966, the Donca Matic DE-20 resembled the Side Man but used solid-state electronics to create more realistic sounds intended "not just as accompaniment for home organists and light entertainers."[8] Korg's Stageman and Mini Pops series soon followed, instruments touted as having "natural metallic percussion" sounds and incorporating controls for drum "breaks and fill-ins."[9] Alongside Korg's early innovations, a Japanese engineer named Ikutaro Kakehashi founded Ace Electronics in 1960. Kakehashi also aimed to improve on the Side Man, releasing the solid-state Ace Electronics R 1 Rhythm Ace in 1964 and the FR 1 in 1967. Like the Korg's Mini Pops, preset rhythms on these units could be combined and, on the FR 1, further modified via mute buttons that silenced various sounds within the patterns to provide the musician with basic programming options.[10] These early Ace Electronics and Korg instruments would soon find their way onto popular music recordings. Robin Gibb allegedly used the FR 1's slow rock 12/8 rhythm preset on his 1969 pop ballad, "Saved by the Bell," and Jean Michel Jarre used a Mini Pops on his 1976

electronic instrumental music album, *Oxygène*. To create the beat for "Oxygène IV," Jarre pressed two rhythm presets simultaneously and then added filtering effects to the drum sounds "in a very subtle way to give life inside the patterns."[11]

By the late 1960s and early 1970s, numerous music technology companies had introduced rhythm machines similar to those of Korg and Ace. One of these units was used by a Miami lounge musician named Timmy Thomas on his austere 1972 R&B song, "Why Can't We Live Together," a sparse arrangement for a preset bossa nova beat, organ chords, and vocal.[12] Two rhythm machines became especially significant due to their adoption by prominent musicians of the era. The Percussion King rhythm machine, released in 1967 by the Vox amplifier company, was used by the pioneering German electronic music group Kraftwerk on their twenty-two minute 1974 piece, "Autobahn." Kraftwerk's music, made from drum machines, synthesizers, and sequencers, had a robotic and repetitive sound that would influence the direction of electronic popular musical styles for decades to come. Another unit, Maestro's Rhythm King MRK-2 that was released in 1970, offered eighteen rhythm presets, among them a disco beat. Sly and the Family Stone used a Maestro on their 1971 album, *There's a Riot Goin' On.* Predating Jarre's use of the Korg Mini Pops and Kraftwerk's repetitive beats, Stone manipulated what he called his "funk box" by overdubbing presets to make multipart grooves "in place of live drums."[13] It was around this time that the British psychedelic rock musician Arthur Brown presciently described drum machine technology as freeing "the whole scope of rhythm and [letting] you get into patterns of rhythm that you just can't get with a drum kit."[14]

In 1972, Kakehashi left Ace Electronics to found Roland, a musical electronics company whose first products were several rhythm machines such as the TR-66 and TR-77 models, which, following the accompaniment tradition established by Harry Chamberlin and Wurlitzer, were designed for using with home organs. In 1978, Roland released the more sophisticated CR-78 CompuRhythm, the first microprocessor-based unit with thirty-four rhythm presets, controls for accents and muting, and significantly, a memory for storing programmed drum patterns. Unlike Roland's earlier models, the CR-78 caught on with musicians. For example, it was used to lay the pulse for Blondie's "Heart of Glass," a Kraftwerk-influenced song from 1979 that generated controversy by combining a disco preset rhythm with a rock backbeat. As Blondie's singer Deborah Harry explained the public reaction to her group's drum machine experiment, "it was very unusual for a guitar band to be using computerized sound. People got nervous and angry about us bringing different influences into rock."[15] Phil Collins also used the CR-78 on his 1981 song, "In the Air

Tonight." Like Sly Stone and Blondie, Collins sought a backing rhythm track over which to layer his acoustic drumming. He recalled that the genesis of the song was "a pattern that I took off that CR-78 … I programmed a bass drum part into it, but basically the rest of it was already on there."[16] Collaborating with their drum machines even while perhaps not yet trusting them entirely, musicians were beginning to recognize how the technology could propel their songs by providing steady dance grooves "on which chords and melodies could sit comfortably."[17]

In the early 1980s, the arrival of digital sampling ushered electronic percussion to a new level of influence and acceptance. In 1980, an American guitarist and inventor named Roger Linn created the first digital drum machine with sampled sounds, the LM-1 Drum Computer, a 5,000 dollar unit that combined twelve percussion samples stored on memory chips with a step sequencer. With a print ad that provocatively juxtaposed the phrase "Real Drums" atop a photo of Linn's black box, the LM-1 and its realistic sounds gained notoriety. Linn recalled how musicians who heard it for the first time "couldn't believe the ghost in the machine that sounded like real drums."[18] In addition to its use of samples, the LM-1 was the first drum machine to feature timing subtleties by way of adjustable quantization and shuffle settings. In the LM-1's instruction manual, Linn described quantization as "auto-correct," a feature that corrected for "timing errors made while programming rhythm patterns." The LM-1's swing feel or "shuffle" setting softened quantization by shifting "drum entries on to time slots that make the part "feel" more human."[19] Shuffle added feel by delaying the playback of every second sixteenth-note subdivision by various amounts to alter the degree of swing,[20] an idea Linn would later credit to his work with the pianist Leon Russell, who taught him "about why certain recordings feel right and others don't."[21]

The LM-1's successor, the somewhat more affordable LinnDrum, was released in 1982 and became an essential instrument for pop music session drummers who – thanks in part to the influence of the LM-1 – were increasingly asked to program rather than play their parts. Drummer and drum programmer Jimmy Bralower describes the paradox facing drummers upon the LinnDrum's arrival: "It was like [producers] wanted the real guy to sound like a machine and they wanted the machine to sound like a drummer."[22] Recalling Wurlitzer's Side Man that had once worried the American Federation of Musicians, the digital drum machine was now a legitimate musical threat; the drummer Jeff Porcaro even advised "to get [a LinnDrum] and immediately learn it and know it, because the future of that is real heavy."[23] Indeed, as Bob Doerschuk observed at the time in *Keyboard* magazine, numerous so-called

"synthesizer rock" bands were turning to drum machines because they allowed "for unvarying sequences of identical percussion sounds and eliminate any possibilities of trance-breaking irregularities in the less dependable hands of human drummers."[24] With their dependability, convincing samples, programmability, and timing nuances, the LM-1 and the LinnDrum inspired the development of other digital drum machines and shaped the sound of 1980s pop through iconic songs such as The Human League's "Don't You Want Me" and Prince's "When Doves Cry."

A few months after the release of Linn's LM-1, Roland unveiled its TR-808 Rhythm Composer in 1980. Intended as a composing and accompaniment tool for songwriters, the unit had twelve synthesized percussion sounds and, like Linn's machines, step-programming capability. At the time, Roland's founder, Kakehashi, had envisioned that this programming feature would allow musicians to "slow the tempo down, enter your rhythm events, and then speed it up and hear the realistic rhythm pattern that you had just created."[25] But despite Kakehashi's suggestion to sequence "realistic" rhythms, musicians were finding other ways to use the 808. For example, in 1982 Marvin Gaye programmed it to play an unusual beat with nine parts on his R&B hit, "Sexual Healing." And the instrument's defining moment arguably occurred that same year at the inception of electro-funk music. DJ Afrika Bambaataa and producer Arthur Baker used an 808 on "Planet Rock," a track that mimicked the melody and beat of two Kraftwerk songs. Baker notes that when he and Bambaataa used drum machines they "didn't try to make them sound like real instruments' but rather embraced them for their futuristic aesthetic."[26] Using a springy 808 beat that defined the sci-fi sound of electro as a "response to people's mechanized, postindustrial landscapes," "Planet Rock" sparked an array of electronic dance music styles, including hip hop, Miami bass, and techno.[27]

By the early 1980s, Roland ceased production of the 808 because the unit had found little commercial success among songwriters; the synthetic tones of the 808 and its successor, the similarly short-lived TR-909, could not compete with the realism of Linn's digital samples. Roland's drum machines thus "ended up in pawn shops and second-hand musical instrument stores" where they were soon rediscovered by pioneering techno and house musicians searching for affordable electronic gear.[28] In Detroit, the techno musician Juan Atkins mixed 808 patterns into his DJ sets. Atkins' Cybotron, a duo influenced by funk, Kraftwerk, and disco, also used the 808 on its 1982 track, "Clear." Emphasizing the 808's booming sine tone kick drum and white noise snare drum and hi-hat sounds, "Clear" showed how a single electronic percussion instrument could provide a foundation

for electronic dance music. By the end of the decade, the sounds of the 808 and 909 were established as they propelled techno and acid house music such as A Guy Called Gerald's 1988 track, "Voodoo Ray" and 808 State's 1989 track, "Pacific State." In the mechanized idiom of electronic dance music, the synthetic timbres of Roland's drum machines had found a home and empowered musicians to sound cosmopolitan. As Graham Massey of 808 State puts it, "the technology enabled us to speak a more international language."[29]

While the Roland 808 and 909 were adopted for making electronic dance beats, Roger Linn collaborated with another Japanese company, Akai, on the MPC60 MIDI Production Center, a combined sampler, sequencer, and drum machine. Released in 1988, the MPC was the first electronic percussion unit to have a timing resolution of ninety-six parts per quarter note, sophisticated sampling capabilities, and sixteen small rubber drum pads. In the MPC's user manual, Linn framed the machine as a bona fide, playable instrument with its own criteria of virtuosity. "In the same way a violinist's style is identified by his or her vibrato and phrasing," he wrote, "your MPC60 virtuosity is identified by your particular swing settings..."[30] Hip hop musicians who used samples as the basis of their work embraced Linn's notion of the MPC as an instrument and all-in-one production tool. For example, in the 1990s, A Tribe Called Quest, De La Soul, Dr. Dre, and The Wu Tang Clan used the MPC60 and its successor models to make their landmark recordings. In 1996, the American hip hop producer Joshua Davis, aka DJ Shadow, used an MPC to create his sample-based instrumental album, *Endtroducing*. Working exclusively with sounds from old records, Davis referred to the MPC in terms of virtuosity by calling it "the instrument I took seriously in terms of becoming the best at it, or one of the best."[31] Davis and other producers learned to play the MPC, finger drumming on its pads to trigger samples and assemble entire songs.

As musicians adopted drum machines, electronic musical instrument companies began producing stand-alone percussion controllers equipped with touch-sensitive surfaces with sensors to trigger drum sounds. The first commercially available electronic drum was Pollard's Syndrum. Under the caption "percussion will never be the same," the company's 1978 magazine ad suggested that it "is the concept of dynamics and control that distinguishes Syndrum as a musical instrument."[32] Another pioneering controller was Simmons Electronic Drums. Founded in 1978, Simmons manufactured kits with hexagonal plastic pads that produced synthesized and sampled drum sounds. Image-conscious synth pop musicians in the 1980s such as Spandau Ballet and Duran Duran were drawn to the Simmons futuristic design, featuring the brightly colored electronic kits

in their music videos. Simmons also captured the interest of experimentalists in search of novel percussion timbres. Bill Bruford, a drummer who used Simmons pads for his "melody drumming" with the progressive rock group King Crimson,[33] described his interest in an electronic kit that was more than "a facsimile of a drum kit... We wanted a new instrument altogether."[34]

In the 1990s and 2000s, the sound and playability of electronic percussion controllers improved as companies such as Roland and Korg refined their technologies in pursuit of more than mere facsimiles of acoustic instruments. Roland developed its Compact Drum Systems and later V-Drums, an electronic drum set with tensioned drumheads. Korg released its Wavedrum, a slim hand-drum type controller that earned accolades for its drumhead and rim that reacted in a realistic way to a musician's touch. However, despite their tactile sensitivity and increasingly lifelike sounds, electronic percussion controllers over the past thirty years – from the Syndrum to the Wavedrum – have so far proved less influential than drum machines. Perhaps this is because no matter how sensitive their triggering surfaces and nuanced their samples, emulations of the feel and sound of acoustic percussion remain imperfect. Another possible factor is that as drum machines have enculturated musicians with the idea of programming rather than playing drum parts, drumming no longer requires either a drummer or a percussion controller per se. Nevertheless, some musicians use controllers instead of, or in conjunction with, acoustic drums in order to perform with electronic sounds.

Finally, in addition to controllers, electronic percussion since the mid-1990s has taken the form of computer software. Widely used digital audio and MIDI recording programs such as Live, Logic, and Reason present endless ways for creating beats through virtual drum machines, step sequencing, and sound design. In addition to these programs, dedicated software percussion instruments feature customizable drum kits, percussion sound modules with thousands of samples, and drum loop players. Improving upon the quantization and swing settings of drum machines, these software instruments can convincingly simulate the sound of live performers through randomized rhythmic nuances. For example, Spectrasonics' *Stylus RMX* software has a "chaos" feature that adds micro-variations in timing, dynamics, and pattern so that percussion loops resemble the varied performance flow of a human drummer. In its tweakability and sonic realism, software has irrevocably broadened the reach of electronic percussion to a point where it is difficult to discern between acoustically performed and electronically programmed drumming.

Perceptual changes brought about by electronic percussion: thinking about musical time and programming post-human beats

By the late twentieth century, electronic percussion technologies had made their presence felt in two main ways. First, their uses led musicians to think about musical time. In the instruments of Roland, Korg, Linn, and other companies, musicians encountered technologies that did not resemble real drummers timing-wise, and so adapted themselves to new machine-oriented musical aesthetics. Through this encounter, the groove or rhythmic feel of human drummers came to be referred to as natural and micro-varied, while the groove of machine timing described as unnatural and rigid. Second, electronic percussion technologies offered musicians opportunities to create rhythmic textures that moved beyond simulating real drummers toward a robotic complexity that "suited the mechanized music they were making."[35]

In the early 1980s, the timing of drum machines like the LinnDrum and the Roland TR-808 sparked a discourse about the aesthetics of rhythmic feel and its importance in making music with emotional power. Specifically, it was the rigid, quantized quality of drum machines that was considered lacking in expression and a constraint preventing musicians from adequately humanizing their music. Articles appeared in music trade magazines such as *Modern Drummer* and *Electronic Musician* about the dichotomy of the mechanical feel of the drum machine versus the organic feel of a human drummer. As *Modern Drummer* editor Rick Mattingly framed the issue in 1982, which feel – machine or human – is more musical?[36] The subject of these articles was how to negotiate quantization through techniques for programming realistic-sounding rhythms.[37] The subtext of these discussions was consistent: how rhythmic feel signifies the human element in music. By the late 1980s and 1990s, the discourse on how to humanize drum machines could also be found in articles in which authors discussed how to practice with and program them in order to mimic the sound of acoustic music ensembles.[38]

Along with inspiring discussions about musical time, electronic percussion made possible dense and complex rhythmic textures otherwise unplayable by a human drummer, freeing "the programmer to avoid the tried and tested conventions that the body unthinkingly repeats."[39] As session musician Jimmy Bralower described his approach to programming during the LinnDrum era: "What would a drummer do if he had three hands?"[40] Moreover, with the rise of synth pop, hip hop, techno, and other electronic dance music styles in the 1980s and 1990s, musicians increasingly used electronic percussion in ways not imagined by its developers.

Roger Linn observed as much when he noted that even though he had designed the LinnDrum to sound realistic, he was surprised to find that musicians deliberately made it "sound as inhuman and rigid as possible."[41] Similarly, the critic Simon Reynolds remarked that programmed percussion's "multi-tiered" rhythms could be "body-baffling and discombobulating."[42]

Linn and Reynolds' terminology – "inhuman," "rigid," "body-baffling" – evokes how the rhythms made possible by electronic percussion technologies from the 1980s onwards had begun to reframe what drumming could be and what it could sound like. To take one often-cited example, the 1983 synth pop song "Blue Monday" by New Order is built upon a bass drum pattern refrain consisting of a rapid sequence of sixteenth notes programmed on an Oberheim DMX drum machine. Described by vocalist Bernard Sumner as "an experiment in technology," the song illustrates the capabilities of drum machines to produce patterns idiomatically unlike anything a real drummer might play.[43] By the 1990s, electronic musicians were using samplers and software to design percussion parts far more intricate than the "Blue Monday" bass drum refrain. For example, producers of drum and bass music manipulated funk drumming "breakbeat" samples such as the "Amen" break from the Winston's 1969 song, "Amen, Brother." On tracks such as Roni Size's "Matter Of Fact" (1997), breakbeats are sped up and rearranged into stuttering, "hyper-syncopated" permutations.[44] As Rick Moody explains this move toward ever more abstract percussion programming, "it's the drums that really changed with digital editing."[45]

Legacies of electronic percussion: contemporary practices

In his book *More Brilliant Than the Sun*, a study of the aesthetics of sample-based electronic music, Kodwo Eshun notes that not only did drum machines and other forms of electronic percussion never sound like real drums; they also changed how we think about rhythm:

> There are no drums in [drum machines]. . . You'd listen and they'd sound *utterly* different from drums. The movement from funk to drum machines is an extremely incredible one: people's whole rhythmic perception changed overnight.[46]

In describing the "movement from funk to drum machines," Eshun describes a shift from rhythm as a body dexterity of the percussionist to rhythm as produced by the technology of an electronic device or computer software. Moreover, rhythm's electrification and virtualization brought about a change in the relationship between the musician and rhythm

patterns. Acoustic drumming joins gesture and rhythm whereby a "techno-physical, or bio-mechanical, relationship develops between the kit and the drummer's body, between the instrument and the playing techniques."[47] But virtual drumming – for example, pressing buttons on a drum machine, or programming software to sequence a pattern – involves a set of actions that for the most part decouples gesture and rhythm. It is in this regard that the story of electronic percussion is fundamentally about the reconfiguration of the interaction between musician and musical instrument by disconnecting rhythm patterns and sounding from the movements of drumming. Eshun suggests the notion of a "posthuman rhythmatics" to describe this automatization of rhythm and how drumming no longer requires a musician's motor patterns to produce it.[48] Unbound by the drumming body, beats today are as often *made* rather than *played* in any traditional sense.

This disconnect leads to two main legacies of electronic percussion. First, its uses have directed attention to the significance and subtleties of microrhythm in contemporary groove-based popular musics.[49] While the grooves of Sly Stone, Kraftwerk, Michel Jarre, and Afrika Bambaataa grew out of the limitations of early drum machines, the sound of twenty-first century popular music has largely embraced this mechanized aesthetic. As Jeremy Gilbert and Ewan Pearson note, what "were formerly prescriptions or restrictions have become active choices: while technology has enabled musicians to "loosen up" the beat, many chose not to."[50] Yet some musicians do loosen up the beat, resisting the perfect timing so easily produced by drum machines and software. For example, the experimental electronic musician Flying Lotus programs grooves using samples that are loose with micro-timing discrepancies; similarly, the late hip hop producer J. Dilla was admired for finger drumming his beats on an MPC without using quantization.[51] Moreover, musical instrument manufacturers have incorporated rhythmic subtleties into their technologies to counter the default of quantized perfection: Ableton Live software includes a series of groove templates that emulate the quirky timing of classic drum machines, and its Push hardware controller takes a cue from Roger Linn's shuffle algorithm by including a knob for adding swing feel by percentage. In these ways, electronic percussion technologies can produce rhythms that range from robotic to humanly swinging, or anywhere in between. A second legacy of electronic percussion is in hardware and software design. Resembling the design of Linn's original MPC, grids of small rubber drum pads are now a standard feature on most percussion hardware controllers so that musicians can finger drum on them.[52] Finally, there is now a plethora of electronic percussion music apps that range from simulations of acoustic instruments and drum machines to more experimental interfaces.

Electronic percussion has traveled far from early rhythm machines like the Rhythmicon, Rhythmate, and the Side Man. Since the 1970s, the technologies have substantially shaped the sounds and grooves of numerous electronic musical styles by inspiring musicians to innovate techniques while negotiating the constraints of the mechanized aesthetic and the challenge of how to program beats that sound like they were played by a real drummer. At the same time, electronic percussion introduced ways of making unusual rhythms, thereby extending the capabilities of musicians, and prompted theorizing about the nature of rhythmic feel and how it signifies the human element in music. In sum, the ongoing history of electronic percussion is a story about building upon traditional understandings of the conventions and limitations of the musical body in order to innovate new practices of virtual drumming and creating rhythm using machines.

Notes

1. Videos of all the instruments discussed in this article are available on YouTube.
2. L. Smith, "Henry Cowell's Rhythmicana," *Anuario Interamericano de Investigacion Musical*, vol. 9 (1973), 135.
3. H. Henly, "Music: New Futures for Rhythms," *Argonaut*, CX/2846 (May 20, 1932), 10.
4. R. Mead, *Henry Cowell's New Music: 1925–1936* (Ann Arbor, MI: UMI Research Press, 1981), p. 190.
5. A. Fried, "Mechanical Instrument Issue Raised," in M. L. Manion (ed.), *Writings about Henry Cowell* (Institute for Studies in American Music, Brooklyn College of the City University of New York, 1982), p. 204.
6. B. Saydlowski, "The A.F.M," *Modern Drummer*, February/March (1982), 20.
7. P. Shapiro, *Turn the Beat Around: The Secret History of Disco* (New York: Macmillan, 2006), p. 100.
8. M. Brend, *Strange Sounds: Offbeat Instruments and Sonic Experiments in Pop* (San Francisco, CA: Backbeat Books, 2005), p. 63.
9. Ad copy for Korg drum machines available at retrosynthads.blogspot.com.
10. Brend, *Strange Sounds*, p. 64.
11. T. Flint, "Jean Michel Jarre: 30 Years of Oxygène," *Sound On Sound* (February 2008) (www.soundonsound.com/sos/feb08/articles/jmjarre.htm).
12. Shapiro, *Turn the Beat Around*, p. 98.
13. M. M. Lewis, *Sly and the Family Stone's There's a Riot Goin' On* (New York: Bloomsbury Academic, 2006), p. 74.

14. S. Angliss, "Mimics, Menaces, or New Musical Horizons? Musicians' Attitudes Toward the First Commercial Drum Machines and Samplers," in F. Weium and T. Boon (eds.), *Material Culture and Electronic Sound* (Washington, DC: Smithsonian Institution Scholarly Press, 2013), p. 107.
15. D. Simpson, "How We Made: Heart of Glass," *The Guardian* (April 29, 2013) (www.theguardian.com/music/2013/apr/29/how-we-made-heart-of-glass).
16. R. Flans, "Classic Tracks: Phil Collins' 'In the Air Tonight,'" *Mix* (May 1, 2005) (http://mixonline.com/mag/audio_phil_collins_air/).
17. Brend, *Strange Sounds*, p. 69.
18. P. White, "Designer Drums: The Return of Roger Linn," *Sound On Sound* (June 2002) (www.soundonsound.com/sos/jun02/articles/rogerlinn.asp).
19. R. Linn, "LM-1 Drum Computer Instruction Manual" (1980), pp. 5–6 (www.ticklemusichire.com/support_pdf/linn1.pdf).
20. G. Scarth and R. Linn, "Roger Linn on Swing, Groove & The Magic of the MPC's Timing," (2013) (www.attackmagazine.com/features/roger-linn-swing-groove-magic-mpc-timing/).
21. P. Kirn (ed.), *Keyboard Presents the Evolution of Electronic Dance Music* (San Francisco, CA: Backbeat Books, 2011), p. 93.
22. B. Amendola, "Jimmy Bralower: Web Exclusive" (2010) (www.moderndrummer.com/site/2010/12/jimmy-bralower/#_).
23. R. Flans, "Forum on the Linn Drum Machine," *Modern Drummer* (February/March 1982), 19.

PART THREE

24. B. Doerschuk, "The New Synthesizer Rock: Stripped-Down Dance Music for an Electronic World," *Keyboard* (June 1982), 12.

25. M. Vail, *Electro Shock! Groundbreakers of Synth Music* (San Francisco, CA: Backbeat Books, 1999), p. 96.

26. R. Bushkin, "Afrika Bambaataa & The Soulsonic Force: 'Planet Rock,'" *Sound On Sound*, (November 2008) (www.soundon sound.com/sos/nov08/articles/classic tracks_1108.htm).

27. Angliss, "Mimics, Menaces," 96.

28. A. H. Tjora, "The Groove in the Box: a Technologically Mediated Inspiration in Electronic Dance Music," *Popular Music*, vol. 28, no. 2 (2009), 165.

29. R. Buskin, "808 State 'Pacific State,'" *Sound On Sound* (April 2014) (www.soundonsound .com/sos/apr14/articles/classic-tracks-0414 .htm).

30. R. Linn and D. Battino, "MPC60 Software Version 3.1 Operator's Manual, 2002," (1995), p. 2 (www.rogerlinndesign.com/downloads/ mpc60/docs/MPC60_V310_Manual.pdf).

31. J. David, "DJ Shadow on Sampling as a 'Collage of Mistakes'" (November 17, 2012) (www.npr.org/2012/11/17/165145271/dj-sha dow-on-sampling-as-a-collage-of-mistakes).

32. Syndrum ad, *Modern Drummer* (January 1978), 9.

33. S. K. Fish, "Bill Bruford," *Modern Drummer* (July 1983), 9.

34. B. Bruford, "Electronic Bill" (2009) (www.billbruford.com/downloads/interviews _2009_on_electronic_drums.pdf).

35. Angliss, "Mimics, Menaces," p. 124.

36. R. Mattingly, "The Drum Computer: Friend or Foe?" *Modern Drummer* (February/ March 1982), 12–21, 96–7, 100.

37. M. Stewart, "The Feel Factor: Music with Soul," *Electronic Musician* (October 1987), 57–65; D. Crigger, "Making the Groove," *Electronic Musician* (August 1990), 30–41; M. McFall, "Make Your Drum Machine Swing," *Electronic Musician*, (May 1992), 48, 52–5, 57–9; and D. Parisi, "The Search for the Perfect Beat," *Electronic Musician* (August 1990), 48–56.

38. R. Mattingly, "Tricking Your Drum Machine," *Modern Drummer* (April 1986), 46; S. Goodwin, "Living with The Machine," *Modern Drummer* (November 1986), 56, 62; M. Hurley, "Soloing with The Machine," *Modern Drummer* (March 1988), 66–7; C. Anderton, "Sequencing for Humans," *EQ*, 5, No. 2 (1994), 2, 20, 30; and N. Rowland, "Effective Drum Programming, Part 1," *Sound On Sound* (February 1998)

(www.soundonsound.com/sos/feb98/articles/ rythm.html). This discourse on programming continues in articles appearing every so often. See, for example, J. Buchanan, "A Guide to Drum Programming" (2013) (www.residentadvisor .net/feature.aspx?1748).

39. A. Goodwin, "Drumming and Memory: Scholarship, Technology and Music-making," in T. Swiss, J. Sloop, and A. Herman (eds.), *Mapping the Beat: Popular Music and Contemporary Theory* (Malden, MA: Blackwell, 1998), p. 125.

40. Amendola, "Jimmy Bralower."

41. R. Bencina, "The Interview: A Conversation with Roger Linn," *Audio Technology*, 90 (2012), 30 (issuu.com/ alchemedia/docs/at90).

42. S. Reynolds, *Generation Ecstasy: into the World of Techno and Rave Culture* (New York: Routledge, 1999), p. 254.

43. C. Ott, "New Order: Retro," *Pitchfork*, 23 (January 2003) (m.pitchfork.com/reviews/ albums/5766-retro-box-set/).

44. E. Davis, "Roots and Wires: Polyrhythmic Cyberspace and the Black Electronic" (1996) (http://www.levity.com/figment/cyberconf .html).

45. R. Moody, "Europe, Forsake Your Drum Machines!: A Genealogy," in *On Celestial Music and Other Adventures in Listening* (New York: Back Bay Books, 2012), p. 411.

46. K. Eshun, *More Brilliant Than the Sun: Adventures in Sonic Fiction* (London: Quartet Books, 1999), p. 186.

47. P. Avanti, "Black Musics, Technology, and Modernity: Exhibit A, the Drum Kit," *Popular Music and Society*, vol. 36, no. 4 (2013), 483.

48. Eshun, *More Brilliant*, p. 79.

49. For a survey of how technological mediation has influenced microrhythmical design in groove-based popular musics, see A. Danielsen (ed.), *Musical Rhythm in the Age of Digital Reproduction* (Surrey: Ashgate, 2010).

50. J. Gilbert and E. Pearson, *Discographies: Dance Music, Culture and the Politics of Sound* (London: Routledge, 1999), pp. 123–24.

51. For example, listen to the beat for Flying Lotus's "Getting There" (2012). On Dilla's track "Lazer Gunne Funke" (2009), the occasional backbeat pushes ahead or pulls back enough to deepen the song's groove.

52. These machines include Ableton's Push, Dave Smith and Roger Linn's Tempest, Elektron's Analog Rytm, and Native Instruments' Maschine.

Percussion in performance

7 Lost and found

Percussion chamber music and the modern age

ADAM SLIWINSKI

> Percussion music is a contemporary transition from keyboard-influenced music to the all-sound music of the future. Any sound is acceptable to the composer of percussion music; he explores the academically forbidden "non-musical" field of sound insofar as is manually possible.[1] JOHN CAGE, 1937

> A third concept . . . is to eliminate sounds of determined pitch from music. Or, in other words, to write pieces for percussion instruments alone. This idea seems to have been propagated mostly in this country, the U.S.A.; in fact, I have seen whole programmes made up only of percussion music. However interesting the use of rhythmic and other devices, I think it is nevertheless a rather monotonous experience for the listener to sit through a programme made up exclusively of percussion music. This is my feeling despite my high personal interest in the exploitation of percussion instruments in various new ways.[2] BÉLA BARTÓK, 1943

Noise

These conflicting statements by two major composers of the twentieth century highlight one of the great rifts in contemporary discussions about music: what do we do about noise? "Noise" in this case refers not only to sounds that are loud or irritating, but more broadly to any that do not correspond with a tone on the piano keyboard (A, Bb, etc.). The history of how we arrived at tuning those keyboard tones is fascinating: they are compromised tunings, designed to create a symmetrical and flexible instrument that can modulate to different keys. Since Johann Sebastian Bach's time, our musical discourse has revolved almost entirely around how to use them.

The role of the percussionist in Western music has long been to provide punctuation, color, and rhythmic drive. Within certain bounds of taste, composers employed noise to enhance their ambitious works. But it was taken for granted that for any piece of music to have real legitimacy and substance, it must consist of melodies and harmonies derived from the keyboard tones.

When, in the early twentieth century, Arnold Schoenberg took the seemingly radical step of systematizing the way the twelve tones were used in modern composition and breaking away from the traditional harmonic framework, he left this assumption of tone-based thinking completely intact. It was John Cage, a student of his in California, who took the most assertive step toward an all-encompassing world of "organized sound,"[3] an approach to composition that embraced the world's chaos and stillness all together.

[97]

As happens with most artistic breakthroughs, this idea was already in the air. The Italian Futurists glorified the grinding cacophony of the industrial age decades earlier, and Edgard Varèse imagined music as massive sound objects colliding with each other, attracting and repulsing like celestial bodies.[4] In 1931, Varèse premiered *Ionisation,* an elegantly assembled but raucous collection of sirens, drums, rattles, and bells, and the most important early work for percussion ensemble. *Ionisation* articulated a new insight that Bartók casually dismissed: percussion was not only an extension of colors and exotic flavors that comprised a new niche group of instruments. It represented, as Cage famously claimed, an artistic revolution.

Along with my colleagues in Sō Percussion, a quartet that I have performed in since 2002, I teach a course at Princeton University to PhD composition students on writing for percussion. We always begin the semester by examining Cage's *Third Construction* from 1941, a work written for a fantastic variety of percussion sounds that, in my opinion, is his greatest feat of craftsmanship. We do this because some composers have not yet tried their hand at building a piece of music without using tones as the primary organizing element. Cage's work is so dazzlingly brilliant that it is hard to deny that he has created something more than a novelty out of purely rhythmic and coloristic elements.

Cage achieves this in an ingenious way: instead of taking a tiny kernel motive and expanding its possibilities outward (Beethoven's duh-duh-duh-duuuuuuuh from his *Fifth Symphony* is an iconic example), he starts composing by deciding upon an outer shell: twenty-four sections of music consisting of twenty-four measures each (which creates a kind of square-root or fractal pattern). By determining this sturdy structure, he can add noise into the composition without each sound needing to justify its own existence as a cause or effect of other sounds; it can be just sound, and the piece will still hold together.

For instance, a shaker can be composed inside the shell structure to provide a nervous layer of noise for eight measures, pulsating on each bar, without justifying what the purpose of its existence might be for the goal of the piece. The shaker sound takes up time and space, making noise, and that is its justification for being in the scheme. But we can be assured that it will not go on shaking forever, because the larger section will have sixteen more measures no matter what. I don't want to leave the impression that *Third Construction* is static and does not build or climax – it does in the most spectacular way. However, it owes its existence more to a carefully planned subdivision of sections and rhythmic ideas than would any tonal piece (which relies on harmonic resolution for structure, not time).

Cage is most famous for his provocative 1952 "silent piece," most commonly referred to by the duration of the premiere performance: four minutes and thirty-three seconds. His great insight in composing 4'33" was that the one indispensable element of music was not melody, harmony, or even necessarily rhythm, but duration. Sound must exist during a span of time, and that is all. The duration of the piece is also its structure, much like the 24×24 measure structure of *Third Construction*.

In 4'33", the performer indicates the beginning of the piece, and then does not make any intentional sound, incorporating only a few more visual gestures (like the opening of a piano lid) to indicate sectional divisions of the work. Of course, no performance space is completely silent, and so diverse combinations of sound permeate the space of the work (audience coughing or snickering, air conditioner vents, outdoor sounds).

Third Construction was composed eleven years earlier, so it is not quite as radical (Cage's output seems only to get more daring and abstract over the years). Its noises are more controlled and intentional. Of course, there is still a lot of variation between different interpretations of what rattle or shaker should be used, but at least the noises are composed on paper in measures and beats, which makes them easier to compare to other music from the notated past.

Echo chamber

Example 7.1 shows a page from *Third Construction*. Cage's great aesthetic revolution aside, it looks very much like a page out of a classical string quartet. In fact, the means by which these lines dart in and out of each other's orbits resemble the interplay of a Haydn quartet. When our Princeton composition students hear us perform *Third Construction*, they see that resemblance immediately: we are in constant communication, cueing each other's entrances and listening with as much concentration as would any string quartet. Note that in this score, although there are no keyboard-matching tones, the notation does indicate higher and lower sounds so that it still looks like a traditional score.

As a percussion quartet, we owe an enormous debt to the string quartet tradition. Its transformation from the trio sonatas of Corelli and Telemann into the extraordinarily complex interactions of the string quartets of Mozart, Beethoven, and Bartók mirrors our own push from the back of the orchestra section to the front of the stage. Cage provides the fresh perspective that allows all-percussion music to begin, but earlier composers provide ballast, depth, and an ideal that inspires us to move forward.

Example 7.1 *Third Construction*, second half of letter S, mm. 469–480. Dense counterpoint and interplay.

One salient aspect of the string quartet to our evolution is that it was an engine of innovation in its own time, although it is often cast today as a staid, conservative genre. This has always baffled me, because much of the music written for string quartet – think of Bartók's cascading *glissandi* in his *String Quartet No. 4*, or Beethoven's Byzantine *Grosse Fuge* – is quite eccentric. The Western tradition of chamber music is so well absorbed and ingrained into our culture that we have become inured to its volatility. That is a shame, because it encourages us to see the old and new as so unlike each other, when in fact there is much to celebrate in common.

What is "chamber music"? What perhaps comes to mind first is the obvious connection: music fit for a chamber or salon. This suggests smaller forces, and compositions that function more like intimate conversations than universal statements or emblems of public religious observance. In fact, an important early usage of the term is in the *sonata da camera* (chamber sonata) of seventeenth-century Italy. The significance of the word *camera* was to clarify that the music was not meant for church (*sonata da chiesa*), which dictated some aspects of the style of the music. In general, "chamber" music tended to consist of multiple dance-derived movements (presumably for a small and select audience), while "church" music matched the solemnity of religious observance with abstract contrapuntal pieces (think of Bach's famous Toccata and Fugue in D minor as a descendent of the "church" style). Gradually these genre practices started to blur and overlap, but chamber music retained a tendency toward multi-movement dance forms, as well as a sense of intimacy.[5]

Of course, many different kinds of music were performed in the *camera*, but "chamber music" came to signify instrumental music. In the hands of composers like Corelli, and later Haydn and others, these evolved from pleasant little pieces into fully cohesive dialogues, conceived with internal musical logic and a more or less equal participation of all of the parts. Eventually the sonata style of composition provided an engine for generating longer works without text. Importantly, as musical forces expanded in the nineteenth century and the role of the modern conductor was invented to manage them, chamber music came more and more to be distinguished by the fact that the individual musicians could still navigate the music without his mediation. In current usage, this tends to distinguish "chamber" from "orchestra"-type ensembles.

Many aspects of contemporary percussion playing do not fit our image of the eighteenth-century aristocratic salon. But it is these deeper qualities found in the long history of chamber sonatas and string quartets that inspire us to identify pieces like *Third Construction* as chamber music. A lot of percussion ensembles in modern culture emphasize the power and virtuosity of uniformity among massive forces: observe a drum corps line, with ten razor-sharp snare drummers executing in perfect unison, or the physical power of Japan's Kodo *taiko* drummers. This is an effective use of percussion, but chamber music seeks to preserve the autonomy and quirky individuality of parts that can also be found in Haydn or Beethoven. In Cage's *Third Construction*, each player busily carves out a unique role in the texture of the music. As if to make this very point himself, Cage *never once* has the members of the ensemble all playing the same type of instrument at the same time.

Otherworldly

John Cage's meticulous inventory of percussion instruments from 1940, shown in Figure 7.1, lists the various instruments and beaters he had been collecting for several years. The west coast of the United States at this time was a bustling multicultural hive, and Cage was fascinated by all of the different knick-knacks that could be found in its immigrant quarters. At one point, he even held an instrument-purchasing fundraiser to which the famous author John Steinbeck contributed generously![6] A glance over this inventory reveals a collector's dream: instruments from China, Japan, Turkey, Native American tribes, Mexico, and a number of ordinary objects that are logged in as instruments (hand saw, forks, chopsticks). The list reveals a trend that would become manifest in Cage's own music as well as

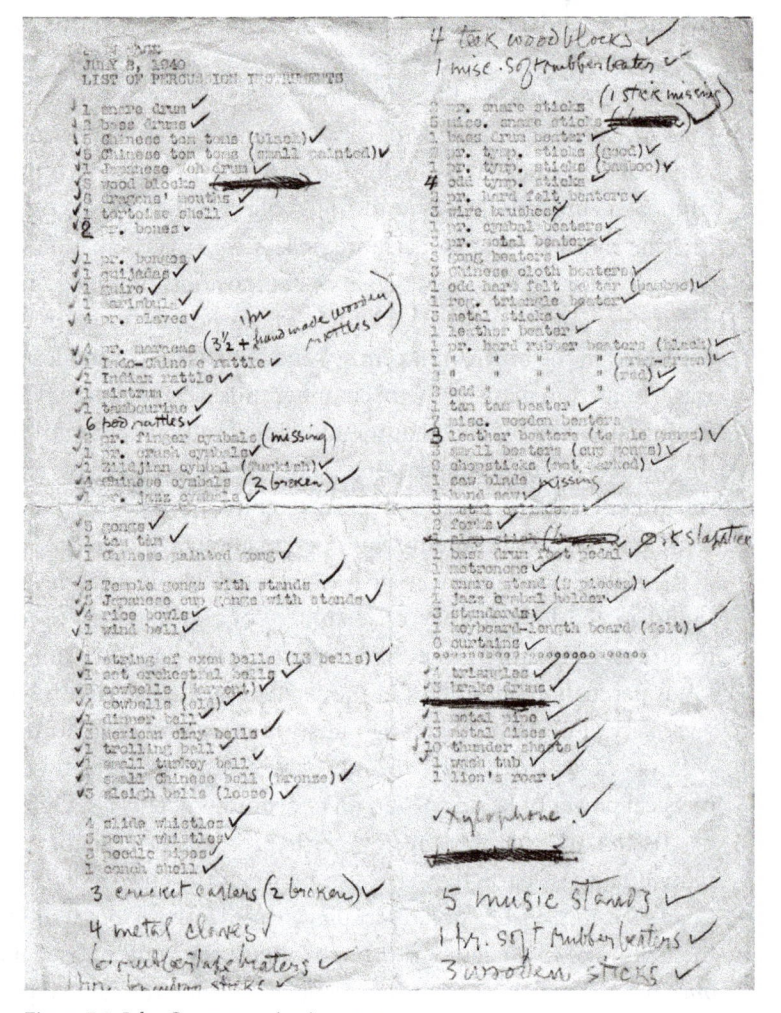

Figure 7.1 John Cage percussion inventory.

that of many other composers: the instruments were being collected, repurposed, and recombined for their sound qualities, not used in their original cultural context, if they even possessed one.

Despite the depth and richness of the history of orchestral percussion playing, European high culture has had a strangely antagonistic relationship with drums and percussion instruments. Nearly every other culture one can think of – Indian, Japanese, West African, South American, Native American, Indonesian – has a percussion orchestra at the center of its artistic life. It is true that the kettledrum player had an elevated status in medieval musical ceremony, heralding the arrival of royalty along with trumpets (though that instrument itself was adopted from the Middle East).[7] But the percussionist's position in the back of the symphony orchestra not only is a matter of acoustics, but also represents a way of keeping the potential violence and chaos of our sounds at arm's length.

Innovative composers like Berlioz, with his eight timpanists in the *Requiem*, or Beethoven, with his Turkish military references in the *Ninth Symphony*, found very impactful opportunities to deploy percussion. Even so, they understood fully that these moments were transgressive, exotic, or terrifying. It would never have occurred to them to generate entire pieces from only these effects (and let us not forget that timpani are tonal instruments anyway).

Western musicians became increasingly fascinated throughout the twentieth century with instruments and practices from around the world. The story of the ways in which these influences collided with Western culture is complicated, and sometimes very sad; it is important to acknowledge that this history is a difficult one. A dramatic example is found in the invention of the steel drums in Trinidad, where in the nineteenth century, British colonial authorities forbade the use of drums after carnival celebrations turned into antipolice riots. Stripped of the instruments that connected them with their African cultural roots, the Trinidadians began to invent new ones out of what was lying around: first bamboo, but eventually also car brake drums, biscuit tins, and discarded oil drums.[8] Over time, they fashioned these empty oil containers into gorgeous resonant metal drums. Today, that instrument is a treasure of Trinidad's culture, but it was born out of the unmistakable legacy of oppression.

In Cage's capable hands, instruments from other musical societies were appropriated in ways that deftly sidestepped the cultural complications that might arise. Since his new world of noise allowed for potentially any sound to exist on equal terms, instruments were happily adopted for their colors and characteristics. For instance, when he

wrote for tom-toms in the beginning of *Third Construction,* he indicated for them to be played delicately with fingers, avoiding a clichéd
tom-tom beat that would mimic Native American drumming (although
he did this knowingly in *Credo in US,* his eclectic pastiche of American
bourgeois conventions).[9] No other outlet in Western classical music
offers the richness of possibility for cross-cultural exploration that
percussion does. As an openly defined medium, it provided Cage
with the same encompassing container for diversity that his 24×24
structure allowed for the use of noise.

Lost and found

Among Cage's inventory, as well as in the score to *Third Construction,* we
see instruments that are not directly borrowed from any other culture: saw
blades, tin cans, thunder sheets, a wash tub. At first glance, they do not
appear to be instruments at all. Like the Trinidadians – though under
vastly different social and political circumstances – Cage gathered ordinary
objects that he thought might have musical value. When we consider the
precious and elevated status of instruments in classical music at the time –
Stradivarius, Guarneri, Steinway – we see that Cage and his contemporaries were opening up yet another challenge to convention by including so
much junk in their compositions. It was junk reimagined, but still junk; I
would be no more distraught to lose my washtub than any other piece of
trash I have. We call these "found" sounds, and they usually fall into the
domain of the percussionist. The musicians who collected and utilized
these sounds owed a great debt to artists such as Marcel Duchamp, whose
"ready-mades" turned the idea of the exalted art object completely upside
down.

One of Cage's most notable found instruments in *Third Construction* is
the tin can. He did not just casually write for a can here or there, but gave it
a prominent place in the composition: there are five tin cans in each
player's setup, playing mostly melodic lines. Example 7.2 shows an exciting
tin can moment in the piece, the crashing climax before the blown conch
shell propels the piece on to its accelerating finish (cans are in players two
and four).

A tin can is not only a vivid and complex sound, but also an elegant
solution to some of the philosophical and aesthetic questions that thoughtful composers faced in the twentieth century. First, it is noisy not only in
the strict sense that it does not articulate one of the twelve tones, but also in
the more familiar and associative sense: it makes a lot of noise! In 1987,
David Lang, Julia Wolfe, and Michael Gordon started a new music

Example 7.2 *Third Construction*, second half of letter "O," mm. 373–384. Tin can climax.

collective and festival in New York with the intention of conveying a sense of freshness, playful iconoclasm, and social inclusiveness around the world of avant-garde music. It is no accident that they chose to name their new organization "Bang on a Can," for the image and gesture of Cage's noisy tin cans perfectly conveys an anarchic yet loving break from the past. (Figure 7.2 shows John Cage with some of his instrument collection.)

Second, as I wrote in the previous section, the repurposing of instruments from other cultures does have its baggage. Unfortunately, European

Figure 7.2 John Cage with lion's roar, tin cans, wash tub, flower pots, and Chinese tom-tom.

and North American history is rife with insulting references to the customs and practices of other cultures. This legacy can be overcome by well-meaning artists, but junk is the solution that comes out of our own industrialized culture: it is uncomplicated by reference to anything outside our own backyards. The tin can is both a miracle of modern engineering and a blight on Mother Nature. For better and for worse, it is our own sound. If we embrace it, we understand ourselves better.

For composers living in bustling New York City or San Francisco of a hundred years ago, it was very difficult to ignore the fact that these were noisy places. Musical temples with flawless acoustics such as Carnegie Hall were built to idealize nature in all its abstract forms, but the society around them was everywhere bending nature to its will (Andrew Carnegie more than most). At the heart of the collision between the Romantic and modern sensibilities lay the question of whether to resist or embrace what we were actually doing to the world. Cage's tin can is the most perfect musical utterance of Walt Whitman's "barbaric yawp," an iconic expression of aesthetic industrial modernity.

Decisions, decisions . . .

Rather than specialist-performers, percussionists are more like curators of sound. We are utilized not just for our skills at playing particular instruments (though that's part of the job), but also for our *willingness* to cope with new instruments, ideas, techniques, and aesthetic purposes. My favorite example of this is the question of who should honk the car horns called for in George Gershwin's rambunctious orchestral work *An American in Paris*. Would an orchestra manager ever hand them to the horn section? Of course not! It would be the percussionists, as any police whistle would also be sent to the back and not to the piccolo section.

This is where our identity as chamber musicians runs into its greatest dissonance: some of the intimacy of chamber music is driven by the relationship that musicians have with their instruments, sometimes going on for many years. For a percussion quartet, quite literally every piece of music is likely to have different instrumentation. That issue of instrumentation – *what shall we play* – animates a large part of the act of making percussion music. Sounds can be endlessly combined and reimagined, using tools and resources that were completely outside of the experience of any of the great composers from the past. Each contemporary composer, rather than belonging to a single cohesive culture, is adrift in a sea of possibilities, both exhilarating and terrifying.

Let us return to Cage's *Third Construction* to see an interpretive situation that diverges mightily from what a string quartet would face. Example 7.3 shows part of the instrument key for the piece.

In many ways, it seems quite specific; there are a lot of instruments to gather based on just this partial list. But Cage leaves many questions of instrument selection unanswered. For instance, each player is instructed to play "3 graduated drums" and "5 graduated tin cans." Strictly speaking, this means that each player must have exactly that number of those instruments, and that the instruments should ascend or descend in perceived pitch (even if they don't fit into Bach's twelve tones, highness and lowness are distinctly audible). What the score does not say is how high or low these instruments might be set overall or exactly what characteristics the drums will have. With the string quartet, an infinite number of possibilities exist for interpretation, but that never includes the question of what instrument will be played. We would not compare two interpretations of Beethoven by noting how one ensemble chooses to play the top line on the cello, while another uses a violin (extremely similar instruments that play in different registers).

Another excellent example involves the claves (small cylinders of wood that form the backbone of much Afro-Caribbean and South American music). Example 7.4 shows an exquisitely intricate clave trio. Each pair of

Example 7.3 *Third Construction*, instrument key, players one and two.

ORCHESTRA

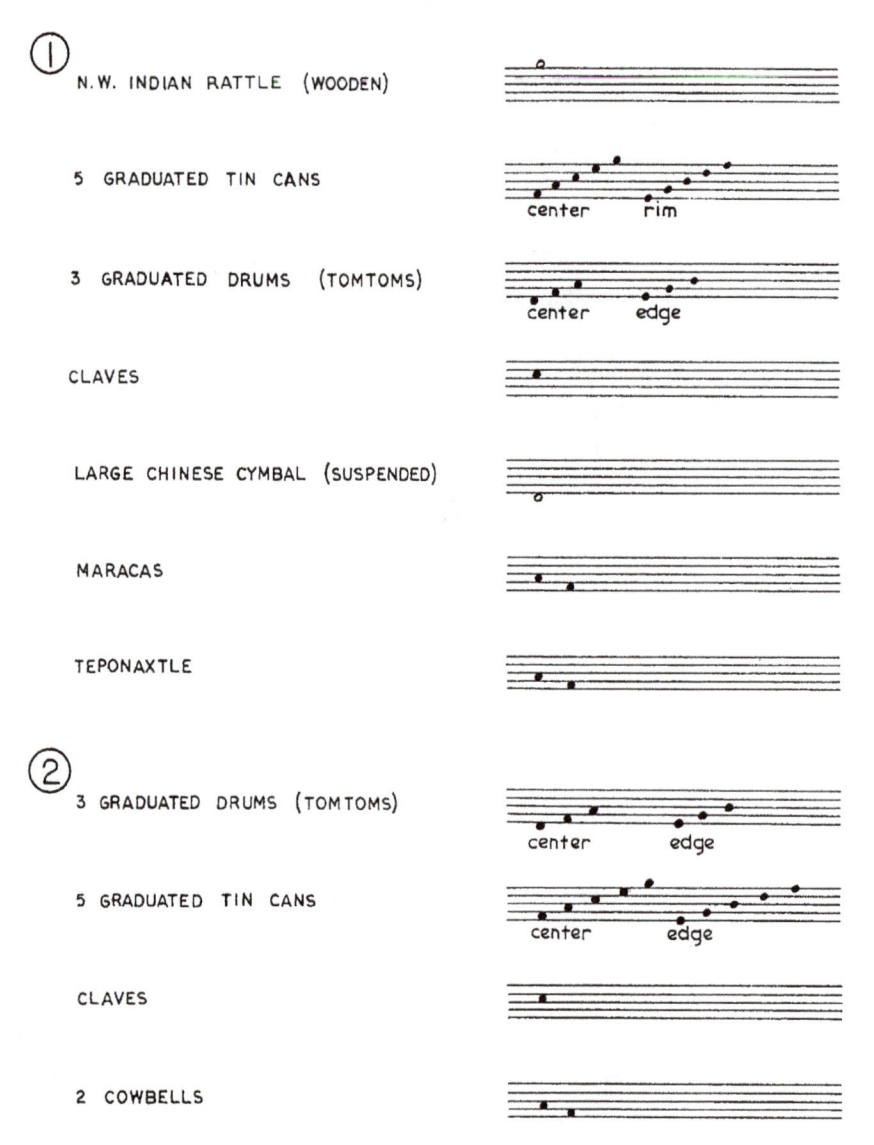

claves has a slightly different pitch, and depending on who plays which instruments, the melodic contour of this section could vary widely, as the interlocking, or hocketing, rhythms dance up and down. Leaving this kind of compositional decision to the chance element of the performers' instrument choices is not a common characteristic of most classical music. Notice that in Cage's score the claves (appearing in parts 1, 3, and 4) are notated on the same line, but are almost guaranteed not to be the same pitch.

Example 7.4 *Third Construction*, second half of letter "G." Clave trio.

Do it yourself

Professional percussionists in 1941 had never seen anything like *Third Construction*, and percussion chamber music was simply not a viable genre at that time. But this did not deter Cage, who simply gathered friends together and made do. His original ensemble consisted of the great dancer and choreographer Merce Cunningham (his longtime collaborator and later companion), his wife Xenia, and sometimes even the bookbinders that worked in the shop underneath Cage's apartment. Cage mentions that

there is a specific reason why they did not perform pieces with rolls, the continuous and rapid alternation of strokes used to produce a smooth legato: nobody in his ensemble could play them![10] In the absence of a skilled force of musicians to tackle his fresh ideas, Cage forged ahead with his own "do it yourself" (DIY) solutions.

On December 9, 1938, Cage's group presented the first full concert of percussion music in the United States at the Cornish School in Seattle.[11] This program consisted of works by William Russell, Ray Green, Gerald Strang, and Cage. In subsequent concerts, the group drew greater attention, attracting more players as well as compositions by Henry Cowell, Lou Harrison, Amadeo Roldán, and others. In May 1941, *Third Construction* premiered in San Francisco in a program of music by Cage and Lou Harrison. The original performers were Xenia Cage, Doris Dennison, Margaret Jansen, and Lou Harrison, with Cage conducting.[12]

One of my most cherished experiences was having dinner with Merce Cunningham and my Sō Percussion colleagues in the loft that he had shared with Cage in Manhattan. This was in the last few years of his life, and although he was confined to a wheelchair, his dance company was running strong and he was churning out new work every day. We pressed him to recount details of the days when their motley crew of artists, dancers, and musicians would travel around presenting their unusual work. It is all too easy to enshrine great talents like this in a glorious past – here was a man sitting with me who had danced Aaron Copland's original *Appalachian Spring* with Martha Graham! But the stories he most wanted to tell were about the freewheeling and chaotic nature of going on the road with his friends, stories that bore a striking and touching resemblance to the life we ourselves were living in Sō Percussion. Cunningham talked of throwing instruments in the back of a VW bus, lashing a few of Robert Rauschenberg's sets and paintings to the roof because there was no other space for them, and setting off down the highway, looking for places to present their work. The major difference between his trips and ours is that Cage insisted on getting off at the rest stop to forage for mushrooms and other plants, while we grudgingly but willingly will hit the Burger King when needed.

After Cage's prolific period of 1935–1943, he wrote much less music for percussion group, and for decades *Third Construction* lay unplayed. Then, in 1968, percussionist Jan Williams, a creative associate in Lukas Foss' new music group at the State University of New York in Buffalo, formed the New Percussion Quartet (NPQ) and, working with Cage directly, began performing his percussion music again. In 1975, *Third Construction* became available from C. F. Peters Publishing Co., and Williams'

Figure 7.3 Nexus playing *Third Construction*. Clockwise from left: Garry Kvistad, Bill Cahn, Russell Hartenberger, Bob Becker.

percussion quartet performed it in Buffalo and later in New York City. Garry Kvistad and Allen Otte, founding members of the Blackearth Percussion Group, heard one of these performances and began to include it on Blackearth's concerts. Members of the Canadian percussion group, Nexus, which had formed in 1971, heard a recording of a Blackearth performance of *Third Construction* and also began playing it regularly on their concerts (Figure 7.3). A performance by Nexus at the Percussive Arts Society International Convention in Knoxville, TN, in 1977 brought international attention to the piece. Other professional percussion groups, including Synergy Percussion (created in Sydney, Australia, in 1975), Kroumata (founded in Stockholm, Sweden, in 1978), and Amadinda (formed in Budapest, Hungary, in 1984), soon followed with performances of *Third Construction*, and it is now a centerpiece of the percussion ensemble repertoire.[13]

In addition, *Third Construction* and other works by John Cage are regularly included in university percussion ensemble programs. Paul Price established the first accredited percussion ensemble at the University of Illinois in the early 1950s. When he moved to New York to teach at the Manhattan School of Music in 1957, he again created a percussion ensemble as part of the curriculum. Percussion ensembles are now established programs in universities throughout the world. The Oberlin Percussion Group, formed in 1972 by Michael Rosen at the Oberlin Conservatory, and in which I performed as a student, is an

example of an ongoing university ensemble that regularly includes music by Cage and other composers of percussion music in its repertoire.

Often the spark that lights the future is to be found in obscure places. Although Cage's percussion compositions garnered plenty of attention in their days, it seems that Bartók's view was the prevailing one: however novel or worthwhile these explorations were, they were not thought to amount to much in the long run. As time passed though, Cage's vision of a noise-and-rhythm-enriched future came to be, and that's the world we are happy to live in now.

Present and future

We are all going in different directions.[14]   JOHN CAGE

Something very strange and wonderful happened near the end of the twentieth century: the idea of percussion-only chamber music, which Bartók was wary of and which Cage championed full throttle, seemed to take hold in a new way. This was no accident. In North America, the music of Steve Reich, particularly *Drumming* and *Music for 18 Musicians,* using percussion as the dominant voice in chamber ensembles that included strings, winds, and voices, reinvigorated percussion chamber music and inspired new groups to form. In Europe, composers like Iannis Xenakis and Karlheinz Stockhausen saved their most fascinating and radical experiments for the percussion ensemble. Xenakis' *Pleiades* (written for Les Percussions de Strasbourg, one of the first European ensembles) in particular calls for an entirely new type of metal instrument to be built just for the piece! The stature that these composers enjoyed in the broader music world drew more and more attention to percussion chamber music.

Sō Percussion was one of these groups and the beginning of our ensemble exemplifies the way percussion has continued in the development of new repertoire and approaches to performance. Founded as students in 1999 at the Yale School of Music, we came together to study with Robert van Sice, who from his own experiences in Europe and North America believed that the time was right for this music to have a wider audience. When Sō Percussion first started out, the operation felt just as "DIY" as it had for John Cage and his friends. We rented a space in nearby Hamden, CT, rehearsing most days from 7 to 9 in the morning so that everybody could go off to other jobs and schooling during the day. There was no heat, and many of those frigid Connecticut mornings were spent hashing out David Lang's new piece *the so-called laws of nature* with bulky winter gloves on.

We played a few concerts around campus, including an all-Steve Reich program that the composer attended, and started booking shows at art galleries and other alternative spaces. Audiences responded enthusiastically to our performances, but it seemed to me that there were other forces at work. Some kind of cultural maturity had accumulated in which the work of these great pioneers and the ensembles that championed them stoked the imaginations of several generations of listeners. The listeners tended to be a smallish group of die-hard fans of experimental art and music, but they existed nonetheless.

There was a combination of awareness and hunger for new ideas. Reich's *Drumming*, lasting more than an hour, was a cultural phenomenon in the 1970s, appealing enormously to the baby boomer generation who loved its meditative plateaus. Many who were fascinated by *Drumming* also embraced our work. But to honor the spirit of composers like Reich was not only to consolidate their music into a new classical canon, but also to forge ahead with our own new experiments. As stunning as *Third Construction* is, it is still only ten minutes of music – hardly enough to anchor even half of a concert program. When we attended concerts of the Tokyo String Quartet at Yale, we noticed that a large work by a master such as Beethoven or Shostakovich always anchored the second half of the program – thirty minutes of music at least.

Sō Percussion set out to commission as much bold new music as possible from the composers of our time, hoping especially to generate works that dared to contend with the old masters in scope and ambition. The veteran groups that we emulated like Nexus, the Amadinda Percussion Group, and Kroumata provided prolific models for this kind of activity. The first major piece that came out of the process was the previously mentioned work by David Lang entitled *the so-called laws of nature*. Lang's piece, a three movement, thirty-six minute journey, was a direct response to the grand statement of Reich's *Drumming*. It consists of extremely vivid and novel textures, notably flower pots (very delicate, tuned to specific pitches), teacups, tuned metal pipes, and car brake drums. The length of the work meant that it could stand alone on the second half of a concert as a unified statement. This was helpful not only artistically, but also because moving all those instruments around on stage was a huge pain in the neck!

One aspect of Lang's piece that differs from Cage's is that he uses tones, happily and freely, as primary resources in composing the piece. This is actually one of the greatest aspects of Cage's legacy as I see it: although he and other composers like Varèse had to tear a hole in the fabric of tone-thinking that ruled their age, we now have their example to emulate, and we need not stick exclusively to either only noise or tone-based sounds. In

the *so-called laws of nature*, tones introduce themselves in a way that derives from the thinking of minimalists like Reich. Instead of proceeding toward final goals as with traditional tonality (the final C Major chord in a C Major symphony), they resemble abstract mathematical patterns and cycles which collide with each other in unpredictable ways. Most of the tone-bearing instruments in Lang's piece fall into the "found" category that I mentioned above: hand-cut metal pipes and flower pots.

Many ambitious percussion groups find themselves in a position where they simply need more music to play – as I mentioned, even a great masterpiece like *Third Construction* lay dormant for many decades. It feels risky to generate a whole new repertoire, as we compete for audiences with classical groups who have winnowed the most exceptional pieces out of hundreds of years of practice. As a result, many classical listeners' expectations are conditioned by the fact that they are used to hearing fifteen of the most astonishing composers from the last 500 years over and over again. Percussionists are constantly orienting audiences to new ideas, infusing a sense of fun and exploration as we push forward in Cage's "different directions."

Since David Lang's piece, Sō Percussion, like many other percussion groups around the world, has continued commissioning composers and has also branched out in many other ways: composing, improvising, and collaborating with different kinds of other artists. My hope is that we've reached a tipping point, where diverse and innovative music like Cage's will no longer lie fallow while we wait for curious musicians to pick it up. The trend I see right now is toward percussion groups finding a new voice and niche for themselves, not rushing to artistically imitate other successful groups. We have common repertoire, but most ensembles work to find their own place among the explosion of new activity. My greatest wish for this field appears to be coming true, which is that we would rip the seams off of our limited perception of what truly new music might sound like. Following Cage's model, the goal of percussion chamber groups has not been to replace the old with the new, but to expand the vistas of possibility beyond what the old offered. Luckily for a percussionist, that doesn't have to mean taking Beethoven's bust off the mantle and shattering it. We only need to slip out the door and see what new sounds might be waiting for us in the world.

Notes

1. J. Cage, *Silence: Lectures and Writings* (Wesleyan University Press, 1961), p. 5.
2. B. Bartók, *Essays*, Benjamin Suchoff (ed.) (New York: St. Martin's Press, 1976), pp. 356–57.
3. J. Cage, *Silence*, p. 5.
4. E. Varèse, "New Instruments and New Music," in C. Cox and D. Warner (eds.), *Audio Culture: Readings in Modern Music* (New York: The Continuum International Publishing Group, 2004), pp. 17–8.

5. R. Taruskin, "The Italian Concerto Style and the Rise of Tonality-driven Form," in *The Oxford History of Western Music* (Oxford University Press) Kindle eBook.

6. P. Cox, "Percussion: The Future of Music: Credo," liner notes, "John Cage Bootlegs," Sō Percussion (2012), p. 7.

7. P. Titcomb, "Baroque Court and Military Trumpets and Kettledrums: Technique and Music," *The Galpin Society Journal*, 9 (June 1956), 56–7.

8. S. Dudley, *Music from Behind the Bridge* (Oxford University Press, 2007), pp. 4–5.

9. P. Cox, "Percussion," pp. 9–10.

10. B. M. Williams, "The Early Percussion Music of John Cage 1935–1943," unpublished PhD thesis, Michigan State University, (1990), p. 13.

11. B. M. Williams, "Percussion Music," p. 11.

12. *Ibid.*, p. 128.

13. R. Hartenberger, email correspondence (January 31, 2015).

14. J. Cage, "Introduction to Themes and Variations," in C. Cox and D. Warner (eds.), *Audio Culture* (New York: Bloomsbury Publishing, 2004).

8 Taking center stage

Percussionist as soloist

COLIN CURRIE

When approached about writing a chapter on the subject of solo percussion, I was delighted to accept and wondered how I should begin proceedings. Perhaps, with some forthright claims for the art form itself – that percussionists continually innovate and gather repertoire at such a commendable rate, that the visibility of the art form continues to claim new ground and command accolades. More people play solo percussion than ever before, at a higher level, and to a wider audience. Opportunities abound and acceptance of the art is worldwide – or words to that effect. However, looking back at just the intervening months alone since the proposal would make even such lofty claims appear too modest and guarded. The exhilarating fact is that the art of solo percussion is already a story of triumph, and one that prevails on a sturdy momentum. Furthermore, as an example of instrumental emancipation, it is one that has a fascinating short history and a brilliant future. Above all, I will present the flourishing breadth of repertoire, which for me has been the key to our castle of credibility. I will share my own personal adventures too, the challenges, thrills, and demands of being a percussion soloist, and where I believe all this could be heading.

Early percussion works

What has been achieved has certainly been done so on the shoulders of giants. I continue to cite four works that remain relevant to anyone wishing to understand contextually how these instruments came to gain the dignity and flexibility associated with art music of relevance and integrity. Those works, beacons shining from various points of the twentieth century, would be Edgard Varèse's *Ionisation*, Béla Bartók's *Sonata for Two Pianos and Percussion*, Karlheinz Stockhausen's *Kontakte*, and perhaps, let's say, your Xenakis-work-of-choice (in my case, *Komboi* for percussion and harpsichord). In each instance, we hear remarkable developments from composers of great genius who were able to ignite our sound world within edifying works of enduring influence. Although none of these maestri wrote concerti for percussion, they, alongside Stravinsky, Britten,

Messiaen, Berio, and Ligeti, would push percussion writing to a place ripe for the role of the soloist. The percussion virtuoso crystallized via these writers as players found themselves having to handle increasingly challenging passages in increasingly central roles, certainly now quite equal to demands made of their fellow instrumentalists. Such would be their influence that by the end of these composers' lifetimes, it would be too difficult to make an exhaustive list of percussion-composer-innovators; no matter how you compiled it, and I did try, it would invite omission.

The first works for solo percussion in the absolute sense are most likely creditable to John Cage, Morton Feldman, and indeed, once again, Karlheinz Stockhausen. Many pieces of chamber music would provide considerable innovation too, notably those of Steve Reich who would place the percussion family firmly at the center of his entire oeuvre, currently spanning six decades. The first recognized percussion concerto dates way back to 1929–1930, Darius Milhaud's hauntingly noir *Concerto pour Batterie et Petit Orchestre*. This would be followed by the same writer's amazingly dexterous marimba and vibraphone concerto from the 1940s and Paul Creston's sprightly marimba concertino, also from the 1940s. By the 1980s, a number of key performer-innovators became visible, and in tandem with their own contemporary composers, the cult of the percussion concerto gained firm ground. These works, being presented by symphony orchestras, would go on to give solo percussion arguably its widest, or certainly biggest, audience. From the 1990s, I would say that three works in particular consolidated the movement, thanks to their incontestable success with audiences and the hundreds of

Figure 8.1 Colin Currie.

performances they would continue to enjoy. These works are James MacMillan's *Veni, Veni, Emmanuel,* Joseph Schwantner's *Percussion Concerto,* and Christopher Rouse's *Der Gerettete Alberich.*

Personal background

My own encounters with the very concept of solo percussion began early in my life and, being as I am born in 1976, these might serve also as a laudable timeline for the accelerated rate of change in the art. My own studies began aged five at the piano and aged six at "the drums," and my earliest ambition was to become some kind of multi-instrumentalist. I was incredibly fortunate to hear Buddy Rich live on his final European tour in Edinburgh in October 1984, and this is worth mentioning because whatever one's feelings about his performance style, he was in his own way a landmark percussion virtuoso. A child or even baby prodigy, "Traps the Drum Wonder" was already performing professionally aged only eighteen months in the year 1919, making him a pioneer nonpareil. He would go on to command musical shock and awe via his epically driven big band, prowess matched only, and famously, in a drum battle with Animal from the Muppet Show. As an eight-year-old scatter-gun drummer/percussionist, my encounter with this "Super Drummer" (the words in Superman 3-D font proudly emblazoned across the central spread of the program booklet) was monumentally catalytic.

In 1989, another local encounter would have a huge impact on my own developing tastes for new music and the avant-garde, indicating to me for the first time also the direction and possibility of a classical percussion soloist. This was Danish percussionist Gert Mortensen's solo recital at the Edinburgh Festival, a brilliant and disturbing event that was packed with landmark music for the solo percussionist. Here, I heard for the first time Per Norgaard's *I Ching,* Iannis Xenakis' *Psappha,* and Askell Masson's *Prim.* Together these pieces represented a serious, considered, and moving sweep of music that fundamentally transformed my notion of what the instruments could collectively achieve – in the hands of the right kind of performer. In a lateral move from this concert, I also discovered a record by Japanese maverick, Stomu Yamashta, whose body of works by Hans Werner Henze, Peter Maxwell Davies, and Toru Takemitsu, all in fantastically eccentric form, would make for yet another glittering and baffling encounter. This album, dating amazingly enough from 1971, is another backbone of percussion's modernity and maturity.

Scottish composer John McLeod gave me some of my first musical training, introducing me to recordings of orchestras and giving me my first music theory lessons. He would go on to collaborate very significantly with

Scottish soloist, Evelyn Glennie, writing two of her key early works, both of which I attended in performance subsequent to their premieres. These are his arresting *Percussion Concerto* (1987) and *The Song of Dionysius* for percussion and piano which was given a fabulous first outing at Glennie's landmark solo percussion recital at the BBC Proms (London) in 1989. Glennie's formidable energy as a performer and her strive to overcome severe deafness over an astounding career would mark her out as heroine to a huge public, and her inspiration transcends the purview of this chapter.

Meanwhile, stateside, a generation of virtuosi, and indeed entrepreneurs in the field of solo marimba, were taking hold and changing not only the quality of performance, but the techniques and equipment used. Vida Chenoweth (a delightful polymath whom I met in Oklahoma City in 2013) and Clair Omar Musser were early key figures. Robert van Sice was the first marimba specialist I became aware of, and his recording of concerti by Alan Hovhaness, Peter Klatzow, and Frank Nuyts remains an important document of the progression of the instrument. The marimba world would indeed bloom magnificently and become peppered with an amazing variety of fantastically committed personalities with incredible diversity of approach to the instrument. Whether through the velvety rich-toned allure of Nancy Zeltsman or the more clattering wooden cascades of marimba doyenne Keiko Abe – presently still performing at the redoubtable age of 77 – there will forever be an approach to float your rosewood boat. Several companies would emerge specializing in the manufacture of marimbas, often with highly experienced players to publicly endorse their products via clinics, courses, residences, and recitals, to share the latest developments. In addition to the burgeoning marimba community, the United States also boasted its own commanding and erudite percussion soloist in the form of Steven Schick, whose manifold achievements extend well beyond commissioning and solo performing, into chamber music, conducting, research, teaching, recording, and writing magnificently on the art for which he is such a beautiful spokesperson.

Percussion chamber ensembles

Scarcely ancillary to the raising of the overall level of percussion playing have been the chamber ensembles and percussion groups that grew up in the 1970s, many of which continue to thrive and inspire to this day. I believe that the strong foundations laid by ensembles such as France's Les Percussions de Strasbourg, Canada's Nexus, Australia's Synergy, Hungary's Amadinda, and Sweden's Kroumata did a huge amount to

raise awareness and diversify the repertoire. Of particular personal import was the miraculous Safri Duo from Denmark. I encountered Morten Friis and Uffe Savery during their first foreign tours in the early 1990s and was captivated by their exuberant, feisty virtuosity and extravagant showmanship. Their collective sound really filled a room while their approach to the mallet instruments in particular, and the zest with which they engaged with them, was a revelation. This was a powerful unit, deeply expressive, with a gorgeously seamless sense of ensemble that was a sea change for percussion. They were also extremely encouraging and inclusive, informal, friendly types that naturally extended to the surrounding and succeeding generation. I recall a highly convivial post-concert dinner in London's Chinatown with them in 1999, for example, full of the japes and jokes that were part of their refreshingly generous spirit.

Percussion concerti

This backdrop of both great talent and innovation is the broad story of percussion playing in the last few decades. It is the community I grew up in and the one that continues to energize me. I will now retell some of my first forays as a soloist, as I am continually asked how it came to be that I could establish myself as such. My own experience began aged fifteen with a performance of Andrzej Panufnik's *Concertino* for timpani, percussion, and strings, courtesy of the London Symphony Orchestra's Shell-sponsored music scholarship, and performances of Ney Rosauro's *Concerto for Marimba and Orchestra* in the same year (1992). I then began an investigation of recital pieces, still particularly limited at the time, and would premiere my first concerto, by Errollyn Wallen, in 1994 at London's Barbican Centre. This work, commissioned by the BBC, was to mark the occasion of the BBC Young Musician of the Year accepting percussion candidates into their fold, alongside the more familiar categories of strings, wind, brass, and keyboard. The move was not without controversy, nor without success, but suffice to say that it was a major step for the visibility of the art form. The competition retains percussion candidacy and Adrian Spillett would win the competition outright in 1998. I then began largely orchestral studies at London's Royal Academy of Music, making time on my own clock for the emerging opportunities coming my way to perform as a soloist. These would often be in recital in and around London, at music clubs and in schools concerts. I would highly advocate a similar approach for anyone starting out – any gig is a great gig, and one's reservoir of experience is not venue-fussy, nor should it ever be.

In 1996, the Royal Scottish National Orchestra gave me an outstanding opportunity – to perform the still very fresh *Veni, Veni, Emmanuel* by James MacMillan. This should be recorded as it shows one of the moments when a work would command sufficient respect and notoriety to pass into the repertoire of a range of soloists. Since then, it has been my primary aspiration to establish as full a body of work as conceivable for soloists joining the scene and for percussive posterity in general. The MacMillan was an incredibly challenging learn for me aged nineteen, and I also pushed myself to perform it from memory in these first performances, adding further challenges to practical concerns regarding setup and integration with the ensemble. When I came to the initial rehearsal, it was for the very first time that I would be able to amass all the instruments needed for the work, and simply arranging the instruments at the right angle to be sure I could see the conductor and have proper connection to the wind, brass, and timpani were among the first teething lessons of this endeavor. Since then, I have always worked with the conductor placed considerably downstage to assure a solid visual connection and placed instruments/setups at a slight angle to allow connectivity with colleagues in the orchestra. Blend, balance, and awareness remain the fundamental ingredients of performing percussion solos with orchestra. Inevitably, *Veni, Veni, Emmanuel* remains a kernel of the concerto repertoire. Not only with its vast number of performances accrued to date (counted by the hundred-load) but for its ability to bring music of both dissonance and rhythmic complexity to mass appeal. My experience with the work, nigh on two decades worth now, is one in which the emotional content of the music cannot help but flow in every single performance. Largely, and impressively, it is also a concerto that concentrates on the un-pitched instruments, managing to integrate these sounds thematically and melodically into the musical argument. As such, it addresses a key question still raised by composer and lay-listener alike: how to write soloistically for the instruments of un-fixed pitch. Solutions here include giving them characterful, sustained lines to play and support them skillfully in the orchestration, varying this element to refract the different qualities of the instruments in question. These concerns surrounding the un-pitched instruments encountered another and vivid solution in one of my first major premieres, the large and ambitious *Rapture* by Michael Torke, in which every single un-pitched element would be doubled up, as a matter of the strictest principle, by a section of the orchestra. In the best performances of this work, a balance would be achieved in this scenario, turning my drum setup into a giant symphonic trigger system or perhaps some kind of vice versa arrangement. Whatever the solution, my strongest impressions to date are from the concertos that make these instruments take on some kind of new life in context, taking flight within the colors of the ensemble.

The strongest advice to anyone starting out as a soloist is to build your own repertoire. This is the likeliest route to achieving the notoriety needed to be on the radar of an ever-increasing circle, and the path with the famously twinned properties of both highest risk and rate of return. A stroke of luck for me was my proximity to two peers in particular with whom I developed in tandem and amassed a large number of pieces tailor-made for my sensibilities. I met Joe Duddell and Dave Maric in the melting pot of the Steve Martland Band which I joined in 1995, and the idea of forging a collaboration over a number of works with them quickly took hold of me. Of great personal import and vital to the repertoire as a whole are Duddell's two sublime concerti, the supple, keening *Snowblind*, for tuned percussion and strings, and *Ruby*, for solo percussion and symphony orchestra. *Ruby*, especially, was a huge turning point – a haunting work that harnessed a deep poignancy from the instruments, a concerto that was as introspective as it was outgoing. The mellifluous spell of the piece cloaks certain strands of pop music in a curious bi-tonality, reaching a timeless conclusion in the slow movement that kept thousands of people at the Albert Hall premiere frozen to the spot. For me, such moments would begin to point toward a growing maturity in the repertoire – more angsty lyricism than flying circus. This direction of repertoire could, I felt, earn the percussion concerto its long-awaited parity, something denied to it only by music waiting to happen.

Dave Maric's extensive percussion catalogue stems from his highly individual and instinctive feel for the instruments. I commissioned *Trilogy* in 2000 for my first full-length solo recital program, which toured in the United Kingdom, the United States, and Japan that season. A highly agile work, it has become a widespread multi-percussion classic, with attendant and sundry versions duly uploaded to the Internet. Following that work, others were commissioned from Maric, eventually pooled together onto the recital disc *Borrowed Time*, whose title track was written for tuned percussion and the organ of Westminster Abbey. Crucial in this case, too, was the composer's approach to the astonishing acoustic of this hallowed place, whose resonance allowed for the most remarkable kaleidoscope of chorales and sustain to emerge from the percussion instruments. With more than ten percussion-led world premieres from Maric, including a fabulous concerto largely for timbales, he remains a key part of the repertoire's diversification. At the time of writing, a new work mirroring the above-mentioned Bartók Sonata, scored for two pianos and two percussion, awaits imminent premiere.

In autumn 2005, two extremely exciting American works passed through my hands in premiere, namely Steve Mackey's *Time Release* and

Jennifer Higdon's *Percussion Concerto*. Mackey's work is a concerto for "marimba-plus," that is, surrounding the marimba-command we encounter numerous un-pitched instruments, all within easy reach. Supported by a Haydn-sized chamber orchestra, the work concentrates on a colorful and charmed interplay between soloist and ensemble. Dance-like, delightful, and maximizing the musical dividends of advanced technical demands, this is another work that added a stripe of maturity to the sleeve of the percussion soloist. When playing this concerto, one can really assume the role of a quintessentially classical concerto persona, expressive, intimate, and leading the emotional content of the music. Higdon's concerto, which had a wondrous brace of premieres – seven initial performances with the Philadelphia Orchestra including a Carnegie Hall concert – got off to an amazing start and has continued on an energetic arc ever since. I have played the work on average nearly once a month following its initiation, and the work has been taken up by countless others at many differing stages of development and study. Its ebullient orchestral palette, structural precision, and scope for an improvised cadenza give this piece exceptional appeal, and it is a joy to perform.

Two wonderful collaborations then ensued with composers of an older generation, as I began to consider what would result from approaching writers of a significantly advanced vantage point and with strong ties to the now receded twentieth century. Turning up in Helsinki simply to meet the great man, Einojuhani Rautavaara would shock me with a piano play-through of the concerto which he had already written for me in good faith, having listened to some of my recordings. The work was duly commissioned by four institutions, Philharmonics of London and Rotterdam, and the Baltimore and Tampere Symphony Orchestras. This work's orthodox structure and romantic sweep make its use of the percussion instruments sound all the more radical, for the bold statement of contemporary percussion used as lead voice in what is essentially a romantic concerto. A paradox well resolved, and a conceit also addressed by Kurt Schwertsik in his mercurial neo-classical marimba concerto *Now you hear me, now you don't*. Written for marimba and chamber-ensemble sized string section, this piece has a concerto grosso feel, Baroque, and robust with an acidic dose of Hindemith in the mischievous mix of harmonies.

The perfect foil to these two works was the arrival of a completely unclassifiable one, Simon Holt's anti-concerto *a table of noises*. Behaving like no other, this piece sought to pare down the use of the instruments to those placeable on a small, simple tabletop, plus a modest xylophone and glockenspiel. The mood of the music would be brittle and breakable, the soloist's vulnerable side exposed with somber grace, reaching a bleak, funereal conclusion. Containing some writing of almost loopy virtuosity,

this piece is also a great example of progressive collaboration with a composer. Not only did I select all the un-pitched instruments with Holt in person (careful never to break his rule of not using more than three sounds at any one time), but I also helped make important changes to the percussion parts. In this area of editing, it is paramount to pursue the music's original goals, with most writers keen to make any alterations necessary to maintain, for example, a challenging tempo. While many composers overestimate how quickly their music needs to be played to actually sound quick, it is nonetheless true that passages can often be resolved easily by note-swapping or removal to allow for a preferred velocity. Formerly, I would stick too tenaciously to a composer's first drafts, as a matter of obdurate principle, but I would like to think I have learned to occasionally let some notes go or be renegotiated in some manner. I certainly advise such a candid approach and hope that we will all leave scores and parts behind for posterity that will challenge but never needlessly. This is an essential part of the soloist's responsibility, and after each premiere I am now careful to "close" each score – signing off note changes, improvements to the notation, or, very crucially, updating tempo-markings.

Chamber music

Vital to my work as a soloist has been the constant feed of collaboration through chamber music and the giving of recitals. I believe strongly that the next generation of soloists will also do well to broaden our development by exploring idiosyncratic combinations of instruments and by making their own ensembles. Joyfully, percussion lends itself to this, as we can break musical bread with just about anyone. Of central fascination to me has been my work with string quartets and my duo with Swedish trumpet soloist, Håkan Hardenberger. I have learned more about my own instruments in their company than in any other setting. The attendant camaraderie of such projects is also very uplifting, and any soloist will agree that having companions both musical and social makes for an invigorating change. I am curious to see what the next pairings may be in the field and entrust this philosophy confidently to my musical nexts of kin.

Solo percussion recitals

Of a more unresolved nature remains the percussionist's solo recital, by which I mean genuinely solo, and unaccompanied by any other instruments. Despite widespread activity in this category, relatively few of its

works have bedded down as acceptable in the musical world outside of the percussion community. Percussion recitals presented in major venues to the general public remain relatively rare and full-length concerts of solo percussion music difficult to devise. Challenges include how to have enough variety of both sound and style in a program of prudent cohesion and how to build a set-list that does not necessitate a different batterie for every single piece, rendering the project impractical. Audiences tire of the dreaded "stage-change," yet finding a way to make a program that can go from one piece to the next without undue delay can be tough. These appraisals can feel counterintuitive, as the requisite skill level has long-since been attained and is shared by a vast number of players worldwide. I feel that this repertoire is the one most in need of more convincing representation, more premieres, and more champions. I would particularly like to throw this challenge at the solo marimba literature, which, although containing highly notable exceptions, is still in need of more masterpieces. One can tire of encountering the familiarly glum faces of a handful of works time after time in the master class setting, or even more galling, a dreaded transcription. As outspoken as this may be, it is only in the hope of inspiring activity by sharing any of my minor concerns regarding the mission as a whole. My own recent *Realismos Magicos* by Rolf Wallin will, l hope, enter this discussion, and I am presently planning increased recital activity in future seasons in an effort to address this imbalance.

New repertoire

The second decade of this century welcomed another wave of sensational new concertos into the repertoire, several pieces that would immediately become established through widespread repeat performances and commanding much excitement in the press. Stylistic diversity was another theme, as witnessed on one day in 2010 when I met Julia Wolfe in the morning to discuss her hip-hop inspired body-percussion concerto, and Elliott Carter in the afternoon to discuss percussion phrasing, sonority, and articulation surrounding his new double concerto for piano and percussion. It was delightful to consider this meeting of uptown and downtown aesthetics, in a Venn diagram with percussion at the center. Reviewers went on to universally herald the beauty of Elliott Carter's *Two Controversies and a Conversation*, a masterpiece, and *The Financial Times* would judge it the right time to devote an article to the "new wave" of percussion music and performers. Kalevi Aho added what can hardly be described as anything less than a symphony for percussion and orchestra, his much-performed *Sieidi,* which swaggers through a turbulent and

riveting thirty-six minutes. James MacMillan showed that once around the block was certainly not enough, and delivered a wonderfully contrasting *Percussion Concerto No. 2*, which also featured an entirely new instrument, the sonorous aluphone. Louis Andriessen showed his lugubrious side with a percussion-led threnody with the perversely upbeat title of *Tapdance*, a ghostly Horace Silver tune, *Señor Blues*, tormenting this murky piece throughout. HK Gruber's *Into the open*, a work I premiered in July of 2015, will become the largest-scale concerto in the repertoire in terms of its colossal instrumentarium, furthermore with all the traditionally un-tuned instruments such as the numerous drums, cowbells, and blocks, assigned definite pitches. Mark-Anthony Turnage meanwhile has added a concerto for marimba and vibes to his armory, already stocked with a double concerto and a superb concerto for drum set written for Peter Erskine.

Conclusion

What I hope to have shared through this in-depth discussion of the repertoire is my own sense of a genre being enriched and emboldened. Symphony orchestras now, when presenting a soloist beyond the established triumvirate of piano–violin–cello, are as likely to present a percussionist as anything else. The conundrum of how to present new music to this audience, largely attuned to classics of the nineteenth century, is also given a canny resolution with the physical appeal of live percussion spread over alluring setups, a great gateway to a potentially foreboding language. I am often told that my music "must be very appealing to a young audience," and while it is, I have received even further encouragement from more seasoned concert-goers who have had their perceptions challenged then changed by their unexpected percussion adventure. The hallmark of this new wave of concerto repertoire has been its power to engage and enliven the audience, with aspects of novelty and superficiality being steadily eroded by works of gravitas, wit, splendor, and delight. Particularly encouraging is the rate of repeat performances for works passing through world premiere, in my case with one-off performances of new works being vanishingly rare. This is a crucial point, because yet again it would suggest a convincing library of pieces for which there is a compelling demand.

What happens now is of great excitement. Both London's Southbank Centre and Rotterdam's De Doelen Hall are currently running percussion festivals to celebrate this repertoire,[1] and a major US orchestra has just appointed a percussion soloist as a resident Artist-in-Association. The pedagogy is in immaculate condition and countless international solo

competitions continue to showcase the incoming creativity, the playing standard reaching almost baffling levels. Solo percussion is solidly established, with works of convincing maturity, courtesy of several composer and player-led paradigm shifts. It certainly needs upkeep, fresh music, and an ever-evolving instinct for its cultivation by the next generation of practitioners. This will have to include new leading spokespeople who can perform, discuss, and represent it in the broadest public sphere and who can continue to entice new listeners to our beloved sound world. Of limitless variety in color and combination, and being stylistically completely unfettered, the solo percussion movement is one of music's most enchanting stories, and one that is just beginning.

Notes

1. Complete repertoire list for London's "Metal Wood Skin" and Rotterdam's "Frappez Toujours" Percussion Festivals, 2014–2015:

Kalevi Aho, *Sieidi*, Concerto for Percussion and Orchestra
Fredrik Andersson, *The Loneliness of Santa Claus*
Louis Andriessen, *Tapdance*
Béla Bartók, *Sonata for Two Pianos and Percussion*
Harrison Birtwistle, *The Axe Manual*
Anna Clyne, *Secret Garden*
Elliott Carter, *Figment V; Tintinnabulation*
Toshio Hosokawa, *Reminiscence*
James MacMillan, *Percussion Concerto No. 2*

Bruno Mantovani, *Moi, jeu...*
Dave Maric, *Trilogy; Trophic Cascades*
Steve Martland, *Horses of Instruction; Starry Night*
Per Norgaard, *Fire over Water* from *I Ching*
Joseph Pereira, *Mallet Quartet*
Steve Reich, *Clapping Music; Drumming, Part 1; Mallet Quartet; Music for a Large Ensemble; Music for Pieces of Wood; Quartet; Sextet*
Edgard Varèse, *Ionisation*
Kevin Volans, *Chakra*
Rolf Wallin, *Stonewave*
Julia Wolfe, *riSE and fLY*, Concerto for Percussion

9 Percussion theater

The drama of performance

AIYUN HUANG

> ... the true state of the percussionist is that physical action. Corporeal sensibility is essentially the most definitive instrument.[1] STEVEN SCHICK

The most definitive percussion instrument is that of the performing body. The approach to physical action and the awareness of body defines who we are as players; it gives us character and empowers our performance. The physical action of playing, whether it is timpani in an orchestra, marimba in a solo recital, or tin cans in percussion ensemble, can equally demonstrate musicianship and deliver musical expression. Awareness of the performing body enables us to connect physical actions and turn them into meaningful sounds and musical communication.

In this chapter, I discuss repertoire that illuminates the *seeing* aspect of percussion performance through works which cultivate, dissect, and expand on the special relationship between *seeing* and *hearing*. I present two approaches to the incorporation of theater from the performer's perspective. First, the action of playing percussion is, in itself, theater; we learn to become aware of our actions and then amplify them so they become an indispensable part of our musical expression. By leveraging our theatrical potential through the lens of gesture, we are enabling percussion performance to become theater by activating the multisensory experience.

Second, in theater works, we are asked to extend our skills through the incorporation of text, singing, dancing, or a combination of these. In this approach, the members of the French percussion group *Trio le Cercle* – Willy Coquillat, Jean-Pierre Drouet, and Gaston Sylvestre – were the first generation of performers to create a repertoire of theater pieces through their collaborations with a group of composers that includes Mauricio Kagel, Georges Aperghis, and Vinko Globokar. With their boundless imagination and fearless attitude, *Trio le Cercle* was influential in incorporating theater into their roles as percussionists. In addition to performing, one member of the group, Jean-Pierre Drouet, was also an important composer of percussion theater works.

The term percussion theater is used here to refer to works in which the *seeing* aspect is crucial to the understanding of the work. Other terms have been proposed previously and used to refer to overlapping bodies of works.

These terms include *instrumental theater*, often used to refer to the works of Kagel; *thèâtre musicale* commonly used to refer to the French school including the compositional works by Aperghis, Globokar, and Drouet; and *composed theater*, a term put forward by Rebstock et al. to describe composers such as Arnold Schoenberg, John Cage, Kagel, and Aperghis who "approach the theatrical stage and its means of expression as *musical material*."[2]

All percussion works are inherently theatrical because of the visceral nature of percussive gesture and corporeal sensibility required of the performer. In this chapter, I focus on repertoire that requires in-depth examination by the percussionist in the use of gesture, movement, voice, and dance in the forming of an interpretation and performance. I contextualize the chapter through investigations of the ways technology, perception, composition, and performance practice have shaped the creation of percussion theater.

Technology

Before the arrival of the gramophone, music was experienced live. When people attended concerts, the audience, for the most part, watched and listened to the musicians performing. Technological advancements in the last century enabled us to experience music in alternative modes through radio, sound recordings, movies, and as background music. These developments offered the audience the opportunity to compartmentalize their senses in experiencing music. As a result, new technology has at times encouraged us to experience music through our listening sense alone. In fact, as technology advanced, new types of listening emerged to couple with new technology. For example, when high fidelity arrived, many people preferred to stay at home and listen to recordings through their speakers rather than attend concerts; they argued that recordings sounded better than live music in halls with poor acoustics. When people began to use headphones, they developed a new intimacy with the music and its performers because of the proximity of the sound source to the ear.

There is no doubt that technology changed the habit of music consumption and listening experience. It also caused changes in performance standards, altered musical communication channels between performer and audience, and forced performers to shift priorities in music-making to adapt to new contexts. First, through editing, fewer mistakes are heard on discs. Over time, what we heard on recordings became the new standard for live performance. Second, performers could not always rely on the convention of a live concert to provide the multisensory communication

available to them when performing. Third, technology pushed performers to adapt to new contexts and to come up with different strategies depending on the situation. For example, the strategy used in recording a piece of music can be quite different from the strategy used in performing it (e.g., use of metronome, recording out of order). The issue of technology is relevant in this discussion because of its implication on the performer and audience relationship and its influence on the performer's approach in forming an interpretation.

Perception

So much of musical communication is expressed through bodily gestures. There are two major types of distinguishable gestures in playing: instrumental and ancillary (also termed expressive) gesture. Instrumental gestures are the movements required for sound production while ancillary gestures are not required for sound production, but play a crucial role in the understanding of musical intention. Musicians use ancillary gestures intuitively and/or consciously to form an inherent relationship with the music.[3]

Ancillary gestures are essential and crucial in musical expression both from the performer to the audience in music-sharing and among musicians in music-making.[4] For example, ancillary gestures may include gestures to signal structural points to help audiences anticipate and participate in the drama of music. Ancillary gestures are essential in chamber music playing as the bodily gestures can greatly affect synchronicity. Seeing the music helps the audience comprehend a deeper dimension of communication that hearing alone cannot always convey.

Michael Schutz and Scott Lipscomb used a professional marimbist, Michael Burritt, as a subject to test audience perception of long notes versus short notes.[5] The study recorded video and audio (separately) of Burritt playing long and short notes on three registers (high, middle, low) of the marimba. In addition, dampened strokes were recorded and used for audio only. The audio and the visual recordings were separated to create different pairings (e.g., short note visual with long note audio), and these examples were then tested on subjects (Northwestern University non-percussion music students). The study found that, first, there is no audible difference between the stroke types – the decay of the short stroke is indistinguishable from that of the long stroke. Second, the subjects determined the length of the stroke primarily through the visual representation of the stroke length rather than through the length of the sound. Last, while unable to create notes that were acoustically long and short, Burritt created

long and short *sounding* notes through gestural conditioning in the audience's perception. The sensory integration communicated the musical idea and covered up the acoustical shortcoming of the marimba.[6] More recent studies by Vines et al. examined nonverbal communication through "expressive body movement and musical sound, and found that musical expressive intention had the greatest impact when the music was seen"[7] (rather than heard or heard and seen at the same time).

These studies affirm thoughts in my own musical experience as a listener and performer. First, a multisensory experience is the preferred way to experience music-making. By omitting visual information, both the performer and the audience are "robbed" of true musical communication. Second, percussionists have long used their intuition to "act out" what their instruments cannot naturally do. Furthermore, the short history of contemporary percussion has allowed percussionists to be explorers without following established performance traditions. This helps explain why percussionists are willing to accept, and furthermore to embrace, challenges when asked to extend their performing bodies to incorporate other elements.

Compositional development

Many composers have taken special interest in the gestures of percussion playing and have made the specifics of percussive gestures (e.g., preparatory, sounding, or silent) essential musical material in their compositions. Cage's approach to theater in the 1950s and Kagel's instrumental theater are perhaps the most influential departure points.

In his 1937 "The Future of Music: Credo,"[8] Cage put forward the notion that music is the organization of sound (including noise and silence), and "percussion music is a contemporary transition from keyboard-influenced music to the all-sound music of the future."[9] Cage taught us to appreciate noise not as "the other" but as an integral part of music. With this belief, Cage wrote his first percussion ensemble works between the late 1930s and early 1940s, putting himself, historically and intellectually, in line with Edgard Varèse and his composition *Ionisation*. In the 1950s, Cage put forward two ideas that formed his approach to theater: give up control of material as a creator and solicit an active role in the listeners. His approach to theater was fundamentally a philosophical one – if we transform our perspectives by embracing our surroundings and listening to them with a fresh sensibility we elevate everyday chaos onto the platform of theater. Our mundane world could suddenly become theater by the sheer perceptual change in how we sense and engage with the environment. Cage's *4'33"* (1952) is as much a

Example 9.1 *Dressur*, "chair" instructions, mm. 5–8.

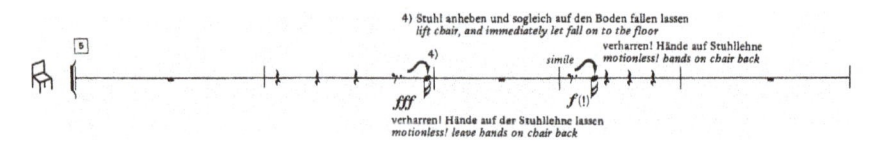

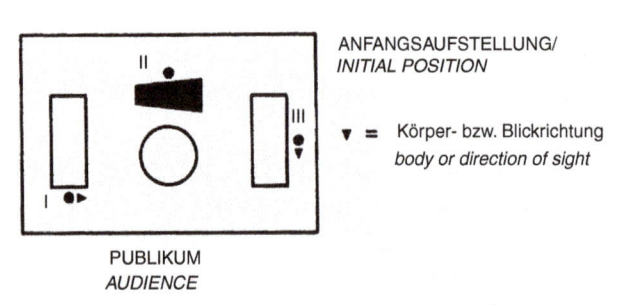

ANFANGSAUFSTELLUNG/
INITIAL POSITION

▼ = Körper- bzw. Blickrichtung
body or direction of sight

PUBLIKUM
AUDIENCE

Figure 9.1 *Dressur*, opening stage direction.

theatrical work as a musical composition. By allowing ourselves to sit and listen to the sounds of a space and then watch how the people behave and interact with others and with the space, we enter a theatrical temple with our shift in perception. *4′33″* is a musical composition; it has a published score and is performed in three movements. However, the experience of *4′33″* is largely a theatrical one for both the audience and the performer. Cage said, "Where do we go from here? Towards theater. That art more than music resembles nature. We have eyes as well as ears, and it is our business while we are alive to use them."[10]

Kagel's exploration into theater came shortly after Cage's. His *instrumental theater* works are built on a different set of principles, full of rigor and systematically researched in all aspects, and no doubt the most influential pieces of his creative output. Kagel composed his music with meticulous precision. He asserted absolute control over musical material and instructions for performing his works. Figure 9.1 is from *Dressur* (1976–1977) composed for *Trio le Cercle*.

This stage diagram shows the opening position of the three players with the specific instruction on the body direction each player should face (indicated with a triangle).

In Example 9.1, Kagel describes exactly when and how to put a chair onto the floor. He asks for the player to first "lift the chair and immediately let fall on to the floor," and then "motionless! Leave hands on chair back." The first time is marked *fff* and the second time is marked *f* (!).

The beginning of the score contains five pages of annotation on the specific instruments used in the piece. At the end of the instrumental annotation, the instruction reads:

Actions

Such musical events as occur within the context of a scenic "plot" require rigour and concentration. One must renounce to every kind of facial expressions and gestures which might be misunderstood as means of putting across a particular "content."[11]

At first reading, this instruction seems to go against my argument of using gesture to amplify musical intention. A closer look will give a different reading. Kagel never expected or wanted musicians to become actors. In fact, he discouraged acting in musicians as he felt that musicians are best at playing their instruments. The thought of acting will only distract musicians from playing their instruments. By asking the players to "renounce to every kind of facial expressions and gestures" and keep to the score, Kagel has in fact brilliantly designed a way to amplify his own prescribed gestures and theatrical expressions by discouraging others. By following this action direction, the performers in *Dressur* can naturally amplify all musical gestures in the piece to deliver a successful theatrical performance.

?Corporel (1985) by Vinko Globokar (b. 1934)

?Corporel was written as part of *Laboratorium* (1973–1985), a large collection of solo and chamber works for an ensemble of ten players including two percussionists. In *Laboratorium,* Globokar wrote one piece for ten players, two pieces for nine players, three pieces for eight players, and so on, including two percussion solos: *Toucher* (1973) for Jean-Pierre Drouet and *?Corporel* (1985) for Gaston Sylvestre. In *Laboratorium,* Globokar studied and focused on a single issue in each piece, and in *?Corporel*, he examined the issue of sound by using the body as the instrument. Original sound sources were mapped out using a male body. Globokar speaks about how he found his sound sources:

I first determined the different ways to produce the sound: finger, fist, flat hand, hitting, caressing, sliding, etc. I then explored the places on the body where to produce the sounds, considering areas where the bones are just under the skin like in the head, or if there are muscles separating bones and skin like in the stomach or thigh. Later, I added vocal sounds with the idea to imitate percussion sounds produced on the body using the voice. Finally I introduced a spoken verse written by the French Poet René Char.[12]

The opening instruction says "in canvas trousers, bare-chested, barefoot. Seated on the ground, facing the audience. Stage lighting. Amplification."[13] Although Globokar does not specify exactly how to light the stage, he states that stage lighting will help draw the audience's attention to amplify the presence of the performing body and, by extension, amplify the physical

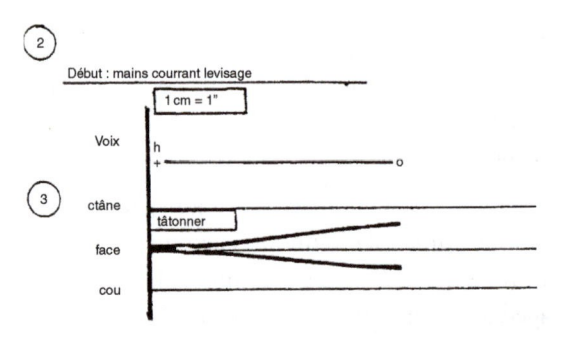

Figure 9.2 *?Corporel,* opening.

gestures. By the simple lighting request, Globokar changes a concert space into a theater, thereby asking the audience to pay extra attention to the movements and listen with their eyes open. By using amplification, he allows the audience to hear soft sounds presented in this work that can easily disappear in a large space. With these instructions, Globokar contextualizes the body as a musical instrument.

In Figure 9.2, there are four lines in the score: the top line represents the voice; the second line represents the head; the third line represents the face; and the bottom line represents the neck. On the very top, the phrase translates as "beginning, hands cover the face." In the middle, it says to "grope." In addition, one centimeter on the page is equal to one second in time on an original size score.

The voice produces the sound "h" from the position of mouth closed (+) to the position of mouth open (o). In the process of producing the sound from a closed position to an open position, there is a natural crescendo that comes with the gradual opening of the mouth. In this case, the mouth acts as an amplifier to project the sound "h" into space. Using the vocal sound as a guide, the hands become the visual representation of the voice in this opening line to "act out" the crescendo with an increasing speed of the gesture. Using the French word *tâtonner* (grope) as the metaphor, the hands can feel the skin on the face as to pull open the mouth to let the sound out.

It is fascinating for a player to discover what sounds a body can make. By combining these sounds into lines and then layering the lines, the player creates polyphony. However, in order to have all sounds heard, I use the strategy of "gesture as volume control" to amplify the perception of sound, and to further create cohesion between movement and voice.

Figure 9.3 uses the actions of scratching and pressing in order to produce two musical lines. The solid line in the shape of a rainbow represents one

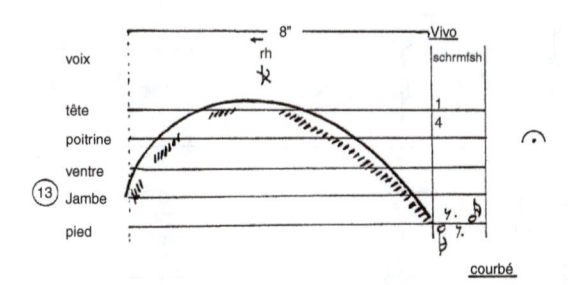

Figure 9.3 *?Corporel*, m. 13.

hand pressing onto the body while the second line – underneath the solid line and marked with slashes – means to scratch. The notation instructs the player to start at the leg (*jambe*) pressing with one hand while scratching with the other, and continue the motion while going up the torso until reaching the head. When the hands reach the top of the head, say "ah," and then come down the torso pressing and scratching all the way to the foot. Scratching is a universal human expression; both the performer and audience have the memory of scratching based on past experience. As a performer scratches him/herself in performance, the memory of scratching is triggered in the audience. By using gesture as volume control to amplify the present and trigger the past, the performance of *?Corporel* becomes an interwoven musical experience between the present (sounds heard in the space) and the past (sound stored in the audience's memory). It is possible that the listener does not hear the performer scratching his/her skin from the back of the hall. However, when the listener sees the performer scratching, the memory of the sound of scratching is activated in the listener and a musical communication is established.

Aphasia (2010) by Mark Applebaum (b. 1967)

In a more recent work, *Aphasia* by American composer Mark Applebaum, the composer takes the idea of musical gesture to a different level through an ingeniously designed and annotated set of hand gestures to a prerecorded soundtrack. Applebaum originally wrote the piece for baritone Nicholas Isherwood, but the piece has been adopted into the percussion repertoire. Why does the percussionist feel compelled to take on a piece in which no percussive sounds are made and all the player does is to wave his/her hands? It certainly does not require the specific training of a percussionist to execute such a work! It is an increasingly popular piece with percussionists, evidenced by its widespread use by performers on recital

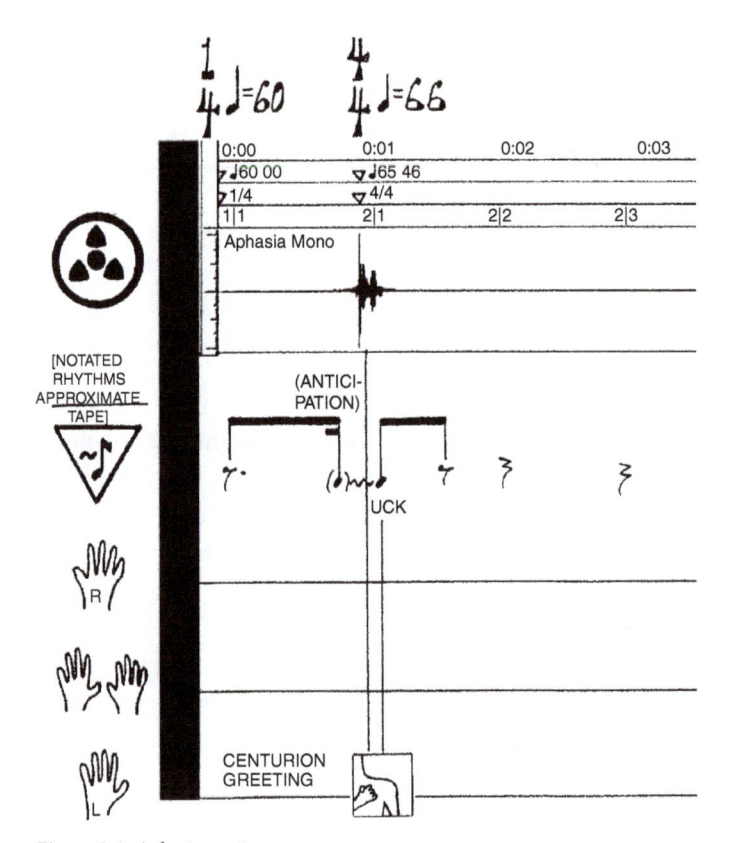

Figure 9.4 *Aphasia*, m. 1.

programs. What is significant about this piece that teaches us about being a percussionist?

Figure 9.4 is an excerpt from the score of *Aphasia* that shows a prerecorded soundtrack with a detailed notation of what is on it and what the performer is supposed to do and when. In fact, learning *Aphasia* is an extension of learning *?Corporel*, but in *Aphasia*, the performer is left to interpret the timing delivery of the imaginary sounding gestures, but not the sounds themselves. It is only natural for us to gravitate toward physical gestures as a form of musical communication. Think about how Burritt's legato notes were understood through the gestures. This is why percussionists eagerly adopted *Aphasia* into their repertoire. Each gesture is precisely drawn as a pictogram to mark the arrival timing of a gesture on the score. The performer is seated using the reach of his/her arms to create the illusion of a frame and perform various gestures forming a contemporary *tableau vivant*. While there is tactile information missing in the performance of *Aphasia*, the piece trains the performer to use a similar reflex and apply the rigor of precise timing as if one is performing a multi-percussion solo.

Les Pointes - The Fingertips

Par un mouvement d'élévation du poignet, seule l'extrêmité des doigts ten-
dus frappe la surface de la table.
La main en complète extension, en L par rapport à l'avant-bras.
*By raising and mowering the wrist, just the fingertips strike the table. The bend
at the wrist should make an L with the forearm.*

Figure 9.5 *Musique de Table*, instructions.

Musique de Table (1987) by Thierry de Mey (b. 1956)

Thierry de Mey teases out the relationship between gesture and sound through the lens of composer, choreographer, and cinematographer. In his work *Musique de Table*,[14] he choreographed three pairs of hands acting as ballerinas and drummers through sounding movements of dancing, tapping, sliding, and hitting, all performed on three pieces of wood (amplified through contact microphones). The composer asks the performer to be immobile except for his/her hands. Lighting focuses on the hands and excludes the face. The notation is specific in terms of hand movements. In Figure 9.5, de Mey depicts the use of fingertips on the board like *les pointes* – a ballet move with the tip of the toes.

Les Guetteurs de Sons (1981) by Georges Aperghis (b. 1945)

Trio le Cercle premiered *Les Guetteurs de Sons*[15] by Aperghis in Festival de Saint-Denis in1982.[16] It is performed with specific lighting designs involving three circles – each corresponds to one of the drum pairs and a player. Prior to *Les Guetteurs de Sons*, Aperghis wrote *Le Corps à Corps* for Jean-Pierre Drouet, in which Drouet used traditional Persian *tombak* techniques to create the musical material in the storytelling of a motorcycle race. In *Les Guetteurs de Sons*, Aperghis uses gesture, vocal sounds, and text to construct an abstract narrative of three lives from the stage of infancy through old age. He dissects basic percussion gestures in order to create drama and tension. The basic movement of drumming can be described as the arm moving down toward the skin and moving up away from it. Aperghis divided this movement into two parts: "up" and "down" as two separate musical actions and notated them separated with arrows pointing up and down.

Example 9.2 shows the notation for player one from measure 24 to measure 30. Measure 24 indicates the right arm moving down (with a downward arrow) toward the drumhead on the downbeat and moving up

Example 9.2 *Les Guetteurs de Sons, mm. 24–30.*

(with an upward arrow) on the second thirty-second note with silent strokes (marked with white note heads). Measure 26 shows skillful finger drumming combined with pitch modulation. Pitch modulation on a drum can be produced by applying pressure to the center of the drum or isolating vibration from part of the skin.

Aperghis uses two types of vocal sounds in this work: nonsense syllables and text. There are two goals in the use of the nonsense syllables – first is to imitate the drum sounds and second is to create the player's own drumming language through each of the three separate and distinctive musical characters that are established. The performers are free to design syllables corresponding to drum notes in certain passages, for example, the vocal line in measure 26 in Example 9.2. The composer does not indicate which syllables to use in this passage; the decisions are left to the performer. Once the syllables are chosen, the relationship between the syllables and notation is fixed with exact correspondence through the piece.

The second type of vocal sound is text. The original text is in French, and understanding the text is important in this work, in particular the phrase, "*Je dirai presque que le bruit est nécessaire parce qu'il éviter de trop penser*" ("I would almost say that noise is necessary because it prevents one from thinking too much"). Aperghis has summarized his underlying philosophy toward the work in this phrase. He encourages the translation of the French text into the performer's native language and/or to the language of the audience. This translation of the text into another language is crucial in forming the interpretation because most performers can produce stronger and more convincing delivery in their native language.

In Example 9.3, four short fragments "*Le silence, J'entends, Le bourdonnement, Il y a, J'ai l'impression de, Je ne sais pas*" ("The silence, I hear, the humming, there is, I have the impression of, I do not know") are used to create a blanket of textual noise. The text is notated with precise rhythm. By using a language, but not always following its natural syntax and rhythmic flow, Aperghis creates a situation to allow other interpretations

Example 9.3 *Les Guetteurs de Sons*, m. 187.

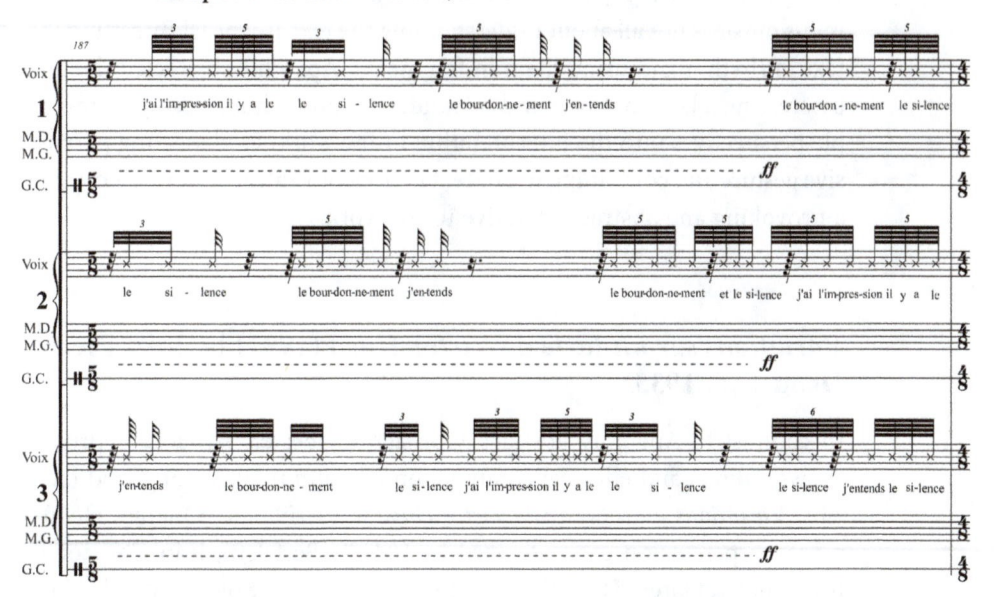

Figure 9.6 Aiyun Huang in performance.

and experiences using the same set of words. Perhaps, the goal of using text in his music is not all about understanding the text as words! By setting the text in rhythm and using them in fragments, Aperghis abstracted the text by creating a layer of noise and misunderstanding, thus offering us multiple perspectives into the interpretation of the work. By dissecting percussive gesture and combining use of text in nonconventional ways, he created a provoking and abstract narrative to the work.

Variations sur un texte de Victor Hugo (1991) by Jean-Pierre Drouet (b. 1935)

In contrast to Aperghis' abstract approach to theater, Drouet's approach shows a direct and effective combination of drumming, singing, and dancing. *Variations sur un texte de Victor Hugo* was written for Quatuor Hêlios, a French percussion group formed by Isabelle Berteletti, Jean-Christophe Feldhandler, Florent Haladjian, and Lê Quan Ninh. The piece is divided into three sections: drums with voice, dance with voice, and finally marimba with voice. Since the piece was a commission, the dance was designed to fit the genders of the group, one female (player one) and three male players.

   In this piece, Drouet expresses a critical view of the world through extending the performers' skills to include singing and dancing as well as through the use of instruments, setups, and staging. First, Drouet articulates the dichotomy between the façade that we live in and the reality that we deny. To achieve this dichotomy in the piece, the players use the floor-tom facing the audience (as a façade) and a tray of voice-matching instruments facing the back (as a denied reality). When the performers play the tom-toms, the expressive markings are usually calm and pleasant. On the other hand, the notation for the rear-facing musicians calls upon them to use various noisemakers in imitation of specified voice sounds. These consist of animal sounds – such as a snorting pig, and other nasal, ugly voices (see Example 9.4).

   Second, Drouet uses an excerpt from Victor Hugo's *Les Miserables* (1862) to make a comparison between Hugo's time and our time – to

Example 9.4 *Victor Hugo,* animal sounds.

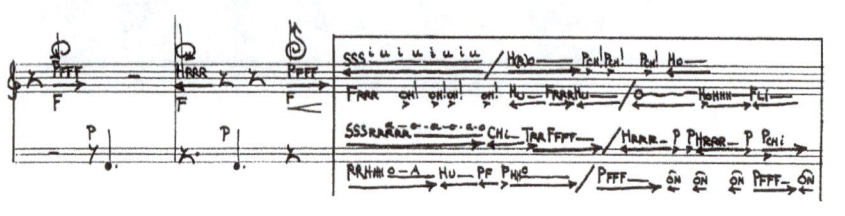

Example 9.5 *Victor Hugo,* text.

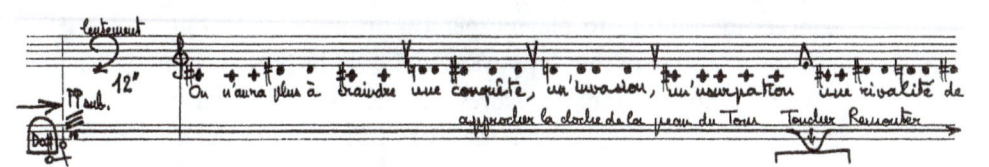

Example 9.6 *Victor Hugo,* dance movements.

demonstrate that Hugo's predictions about the future did not come true (see Example 9.5). In *Les Miserables,* Hugo expressed his expectations that in the twentieth century people would live in an ideal society where there would be no fear. It is clear that we still struggle with some of the same issues in different manifestations from Hugo's time.

Third, Drouet uses dance to express the peak of his frustration with the world (see Example 9.6). During the press conference for the performance of *Variations sur un texte de Victor Hugo* on March 18, 1998, in Taipei, a reporter asked Drouet "why is there dance in the piece?" Drouet replied by relating his feelings that he could no longer express what he wanted to say through music and text; therefore, dance was a natural choice of expressive medium for the climax of the piece. The dance in this piece is very percussive, employing techniques derived from tap-dance and flamenco. The extended skills in this work require the players to step outside of their usual roles in order to successfully perform their tasks. Some dance and voice coaching is recommended in order to play the piece with conviction.

Conclusion

In *Dressur,* the performers are encouraged to renounce all extra gestures in order to highlight the ones indicated in the score. *?Corporel* uses gesture to amplify sound as a visual volume control to form a coherent musical interpretation between sound and movement while in *Aphasia,* gestures are used to create visual tableaux with precise timing similar to performing multi-percussion. In *Musique de table,* the hands are the ballerina-drummer performing a compositional choreography. In *Les Guetteurs de Sons,* three musical characters are formed through the dissection and expansion on percussive gesture, voice, and text. The percussionists in

Variations sur un texte de Victor Hugo are asked to become singers and dancers in addition to playing percussion in order to fully express the musical intention of the composer. All the works presented in this chapter have fully notated musical scores sharing the following: first, the score gives stage directions; second, the score asks for stage lighting; and third, the notation is very specific to include not only pitch and rhythm, but also a set of instructions in order to perform the exact actions through space in time. All the compositions ask the performers to empower their theatrical potential through the embracing of their performing bodies. They demonstrate that the percussionist can approach theater through the simple shift in perception as Cage has suggested, through leveraging the impact of performance gestures so that they become more readable, through understanding how to use the voice as an extension of the performing body, and finally through the learning of other skills that allow the player to step into roles other than traditional percussion performance.

Notes

1. F. J. Oteri, "Steven Schick: Ready for Anything" (April 1, 2004) (www.newmusicbox .org).

2. M. Rebstock and D. Roesner (eds.), *Composed Theatre: Aesthetics, Practices, Processes* (University of Chicago Press, 2012), p. 9.

3. M. Nusseck and M. M. Wanderley, "Music and Motion – How Music-related Ancillary Body Movements Contribute to the Experience of Music," *Music Perception*, vol. 26, no. 4 (2009), 335–53.

4. C. Palmer, "Music Performance: Movement and Coordination," in Diana Deutsch (ed.), *The Psychology of Music*, 3rd ed. (Amsterdam: Elsevier Press, 2013), pp. 405–22.

5. For woodwind, brass, and string instruments, long notes are generally produced through continuous movement of breath or bowing. For percussion, long notes are produced either through roll (combining many short tones together to create the illusion of long tone), pedal (vibraphone), or gesture.

6. M. Schutz and S. Lipscomb, "Hearing Gestures, Seeing Music: Vision Influences Perceived Tone Duration," *Perception*, 36 (2007), 888–97. For more detailed information, see Michael Schutz's article, "Lessons from the laboratory," Chapter 20.

7. B. W. Vines, C. L. Krumhansl, M. M. Wanderley, I. M. Dalca, and D. J. Levitin, "Music to My Eyes: Cross-modal Interactions in the Perception of Emotions in Musical Performance," *Cognition*, 118 (2011), 157–70.

8. J. Cage, *Silence* (Wesleyan University Press, 2010), pp. 3–6.

9. *Ibid.*, p. 5.

10. *Ibid.*, p. 12.

11. M. Kagel, *Dressur* (Frankfurt: Henry Litolff's Verlag/C.F. Peters, 1983).

12. F. V. Kumor, Interpreting the Relationship Between Movement and Music in Selected Twentieth Century Percussion Music, unpublished DMA thesis, Kentucky (2002), p. 49.

13. V. Globokar, *?Corporel* (New York: C. F. Peters, 1989).

14. T. de Mey, *Musique de Table* (Tienen, Belgium: PM Europe Publications, 1987).

15. Drouet plays part one, Coquillat part two, and Sylvestre part three.

16. The score of *Les Guetteurs de Sons* was published by Edition Salabert, but the score is currently out of print. A PDF copy is available for download from the composer's website (http://aperghis.com).

10 Three convergences

A percussionist learns to conduct

STEVEN SCHICK

If it's true what they say that tragedy plus time equals comedy, I might just be ready to laugh at my first rehearsals as an orchestral conductor. I can smile a little now, but every one of those early rehearsals was an exercise in humility, if not humiliation.

Let me say in my defense that I never planned to be a conductor. I never trained for it; never conducted along with records, or imagined myself on the podium communing with Mahler or late Beethoven. To the contrary, my path as a contemporary percussionist led me away from the refinements of classical music. I was more at home in the wind-swept xeriscape of Xenakis than in the pruned garden of Mozart. But then one day eight years ago, I sat in on a meeting at the University of California, San Diego with the administration of the La Jolla Symphony and Chorus. I was there as a courtesy, a faculty member representing the department's Executive Committee. The conductor of the La Jolla Symphony had just stepped down and the search was on for guest conductors. Their question floated in the room: as they planned a formal search for a new music director, did we know anyone who could conduct a concert on relatively short notice? In a kind of out-of-body experience, I saw myself raise my hand and suggest that I could lead a concert. The chair of my department looked at me with incredulity. "But, you don't know how to conduct!" "True," I answered. "But, how hard could it be?"

At the beginning, it was more than simply hard; it was truly painful. Several times, I forgot to wait for the tuning note and simply started rehearsing. Once trying to solve a sight-line problem, I moved one of the string players more and more to her right until she finally exclaimed, "But I'm a violist!" Uncomfortable questions pelted me like freezing rain. Should a certain bowing be hooked? What kind of mute should a trombonist use? Where on the bow should a passage be played? And, God forbid I'd have to sight-read a chord involving horns, alto flute, and E-flat clarinet. The transpositions alone were killing me! In response, I did blank stares the way Meryl Streep does accents: more often than you'd like and usually at the worst moments.

Little by little I made headway. And, in the end that first concert was pretty OK. Actually, it was more than OK; it was invigorating! Even

choosing the program was fascinating. Since I thought that I was going to conduct precisely one orchestral concert in my life, programming was an exercise in option anxiety. I was coming from a discipline that had perhaps twenty good pieces, and suddenly found myself with a choice of hundreds. Eventually, I selected a short overture by my friend David Lang, *International Business Machine*, and the *Crouching Tiger Concerto* by Tan Dun featuring another friend, the wonderful cellist Wendy Sutter, who had been a band-mate in the Bang on a Can All-Stars. Finally, I opted for a total indulgence for a neophyte: the suite from the 1911 version of Stravinsky's *Firebird*. It was so much fun! I fell in love with the music and with the orchestra. The La Jolla Symphony was (and still is) a very fine amateur ensemble, full of dedicated musicians most of whom make their livings outside of music. Add some UC San Diego students and local professionals looking for an orchestral outlet, and you have a group that can really play and who come to each rehearsal with passion and good will. I might not immediately have known how rare that was, but the positive experience of my first concert convinced me to put my name into the running for the music director position. And – really, this came as a surprise to all of us – I won the job.

Now with the job actually in hand, my need to move beyond "not-bad-for-someone-who-doesn't-conduct" required serious analysis and lots of work. One of my biggest problems was that I didn't know what it meant to "learn a score" as a conductor. As a percussionist, the task of learning a piece of music was very clear: you have learned it when you can execute it reliably and repeatably at a level sufficiently high for concert presentation. If you satisfy these criteria, you know the piece, if not, go back to the practice room. However, the metrics of learning an orchestral score seemed murkier to me. Did I know a score when I had understood and analyzed the piece? Or was it when I was able to conduct a first rehearsal? Or, did I know a piece once I had actually conducted it in performance? Or, frighteningly, perhaps I would never truly know a piece, since as conductor, I make no sounds and play no instruments.

Conducting is externalizing a system of organization

At first it seemed that my experiences as a percussionist – those tens of thousands of hours of practice and performance – might not help me become a competent conductor. Then in a realization that has made all the difference, I discovered a convergence, an area of significant overlap between my old life as an experienced percussionist and my new life as a novice conductor. I realized that being an instrumentalist, in the traditional

sense, means internalizing a language of organization. But as an experimental percussionist – and, importantly, also as a conductor – the ability to externalize a system of organization was paramount.

A system that internalizes is easy to understand. You hear performers say something like this all the time: "I want to be one with my instrument." That essentially means reimagining a foreign object – the instrument you're playing – as an extension of your body. The most successful players so thoroughly anthropomorphize their instruments that there seems to be no difference between them. The cello is no longer a wooden box; it is a torso. The tuba is not a hunk of metal, but a kind of lung. In the hands of the best performers, the instrument becomes not just an extension of the body, but the body itself.

In this sense, percussionists are sometimes "internalists." Marimbists, timpanists, or vibists, like other traditional instrumentalists, seek to meld with their instruments to create a meta-body – a hybridized creature that is part human and part instrument. But this model does not always work in the percussion family. While objects like the marimba, vibraphone, and timpani *are* instruments in the traditional sense, many other objects a percussionist uses – a brake drum, a thunder-sheet, or a tin can – are not. Is it actually possible to anthropomorphize a foam-mounted railroad spike? And what psychic dangers await a percussionist who seeks to become one with a tuned saw blade?

For performers of these nontraditional instruments, a more useful system is external. An external system of organization reverses the paradigm: while an internal system redefines a foreign object as an extension of the body, with external organization the body is an extension of the object. In short, when I play a percussion piece with noninstrumental sounding objects (read, "pieces of junk"), I become the junk; the junk does not become me.

What does this mean in practical terms? When I play Iannis Xenakis' *Psappha*, a work replete in my version with objects of junk, from a frying pan to short steel pipes to hunks of u-shaped steel and planks of hard wood, my mind and manner become attuned to the world of junk, not the reverse. My movements in performance become spiky; my mental models are industrial and utilitarian, not organic and anthropological. Even the rhythmic language changes, divorcing itself from the *bel canto* model, which dictates that musical phrases are timed to the breath. In a *bel canto* world (the ultimate internal system since nothing is more inside of us than our voices), antecedent and consequent musical phrases resemble inhalation and exhalation. So common is this model that we no longer question it. However, listen to Mozart played by a flutist who can circular breathe and you will know how foreign traditional phrases can sound

when they do not conform to the need to breathe. My installations of junk function more like machines than bodies. Therefore, musical phrases are governed by the rules of the machine, not the body, and are subject in length only to the need for routine maintenance and the skill of the operator. Melodic moments can extend far beyond the length of a breath, and the instrumental color palette does not seek to blend, as in an organic model, but often is highly differentiated. The dynamic range from soft to loud is extreme.

This is what can happen to percussion playing when viewed through an external model. As a beginning conductor, I also learned to view the orchestra through the lens of an external system. Again, I become it; it does not become me. One important consequence of external orientation is that physical space becomes an important arena of expression. With internal systems, the goal is to reduce the distance between instrument and body, therefore rendering space moot as an agent of expression. Space becomes nearly meaningless as a signifier. But viewed the other way around, it becomes, well, huge. In a small example, I have developed the ability to track a phrase that moves from violins to upper woodwinds not only as the change of pitch over time, but also as a change of the position of a sound in space. (This feels very much like playing Stockhausen's *Zyklus,* when at a given moment the snare drum is clearly to my right and the gong to my left, in such a way that their interplay creates a spatially rich melody.) At the time of this writing, I am preparing for three performances of Hector Berlioz's *Requiem.* In many moments of this mighty work, little else is happening than a single chord diffused in space. In these Gabrielli-like passages, the orchestral sound saturates the space. Accordingly the ear of the auditor, at least metaphorically, expands to the size of the hall itself.

An important implication of sounds moving in space leads to gesture, a core concern of any conductor. In the La Jolla Symphony, the high strings are to my left and the low ones to my right. Accordingly, this means that harmonic changes based on root movements emanate from my right and migrate across the space to my left. The low strings frequently play slower music and speak less incisively than their higher partners. As a result, my physical language has evolved so that, in very general terms, my right hand gives larger and less incisive cues than does my left. My body reacts to the demands of the orchestra and not the reverse. Again, I have become it, not it me.

In a way, reversing the organizational paradigm to embrace an out-ward-looking rather than inward-looking model was its own reward. This eversion of basic premises was an invitation to reverse course in many other areas. I started by revisiting my commitment to performing from memory, a practice I have engaged in with dozens of pieces in a thousand

or more solo percussion concerts over more than forty years. My mantra has always been, first memorize, then master, then perform. Playing from memory is not really playing without a score; it is the act of rewriting the score on the muscles and mind of a player. Literally, internalizing it. But as a conductor, I have explicitly sought to externalize my method of learning a score by consciously avoiding memorizing.

As a percussionist, I never mark my scores. After all, the true score is the body. As a conductor, thinking externally, I mark liberally. I draw carefully, using a straight edge and well-sharpened pencils in several colors to create a document, which will serve simultaneously as a performance score and a kind of journal. I highlight harmonic changes in blue; formal points of arrival in green; tempo changes, dynamics, and cues in red. I use lead pencil (the indispensable Blackfeet Indian Pencil, to which my friend John Luther Adams introduced me) to sketch precise lines that connect one melodic idea to another. (My score of Arnold Schoenberg's *Five Pieces* looks like a map of the London Underground, thanks to the large number of interpenetrated and contrapuntal melodic lines.) I make copious notes in the margins about interpretative strategies, to-do lists for rehearsals, even notes about where I am traveling or what I am reading. For large and complex works, I also draw models on graph paper, showing the event horizon for sections or even entire pieces. I once made such an event map for an entire concert of the chamber music of Edgard Varèse at the scale of one minute to one inch. It became a twelve foot long, multicolor chart of musical "zones of intensity," to use Varèse's own term.

My goal in all of this has been to take what had become a comfortable internal process as a percussionist and invert it. Recently, after playing a solo percussion concert in Paris at the Centre Pompidou, Renzo Piano, and Richard Rogers's spectacular building at the Beaubourg, which has all of the internal guts of plumbing, air ducts, and stairways on the outside, I realized I was looking at an effective model for my approach to conducting. Just as the inner workings of the building are on the outside, so are the mechanics of conducting. The goal for a conductor is to translate thought to gesture, taking, therefore, what is on the inside, visible to no one, and placing it on the outside visible to everyone. At the most expressive moments of a performance, a conductor completely transports the internal world of musical idea and interpretative impulse to an external mode of physical expression. When that happens, he or she is empty, ready to be buoyed by the waves of sound and moved in any direction the power of the music dictates. The body ceases to have the singular function of expression on behalf of the one and turns to the evident and difficult task of expression on behalf of the many. And this all happens through a small repertoire of fairly banal gestures.

Figure 10.1 Steven Schick.

Conducting is gesturing

I estimate that it takes approximately thirty minutes to learn how to conduct. And most of that is learning how to handle cut-offs and fermatas. The rest can be summed up more or less by the phrase, "beat one goes down." Everything else about becoming a good conductor – and yes there is a lot – falls under the category of becoming a good musician. Nevertheless, the language of conducting is gesture, so perhaps it does warrant a moment of reflection.

In conducting, like percussion, serious misunderstandings arise in reducing the gestural language to the simple vectors of up and down. It's true that beat one goes down, just as it's true that a stroke on the snare drum goes down. But in both cases, the active mechanics of the stroke and its expressive potential are encoded not in the downstroke but in the upstroke – in the preparation.

Recently, the eminent composer Chou Wen-chung and I were discussing a new work he plans to write for the San Francisco Contemporary Music Players, of which I am artistic director. Wen-chung's idea is to translate the art of Chinese calligraphy to a musical score. In particular, he is interested in the way the meaning of a calligraphic character is collected in the tip of the brush at the height of its arc of preparation, just before it descends to the paper. "You must have the entire character – both its shape and its meaning in mind – before you lower the brush to paper," he told me. "Calligraphy is not expression in a western sense," he continued, "where meaning is pieced together, post facto, by assembling the sense of a phrase from a sequence of letters. Everything must be present together in pre-existing unity before any motion is made."

Yes.

But that means giving up a lot of control. Through a preparatory stroke, a conductor can prepare an ensemble to play by showing them when to play, just as a percussionist can prepare a sound by raising a stick, but the actual making of the sound cannot be controlled. The drumstick drops; the breath is expelled; the bow is lowered to the string. In each case, this is the natural consequence of the preparation. By the time the baton starts its downward motion to the downbeat, it's too late to change anything. The moment of agency, when a message may be imparted, exists only in the preparation. Therefore, the trick to executing a basic conducting pattern like 4/4 is to see each affirmative stroke not as a certain beat, but as the preparation for the beat that comes next. The downbeat, including the little rebound at the bottom of the stroke, is a preparatory movement that tells us where the second beat will fall. The second beat is the preparation for the third, and so on. So a typical conducting pattern then is simply a sequence of preparations, each stroke loading a musical moment with potential energy. The release of that energy is the province of the players, not the conductor. And in parallel fashion, each stroke on a percussion instrument creates a natural rebound that will provide the preparatory stroke for the following attack, again a succession of potentialities realized primarily by means of gravity rather than any action by the player.

It is a psychic arena that takes a little getting used to. The common image of both conductor and percussionist is a person (usually a man) of action. A drummer or conductor is epitomized by sweat, grim determination, and above all intense physicality. The realization that the task is nothing but a sequence of intentions, of inhalations, of preparations never to be realized, can seem ironic and deflating. Knowing and being able to control the qualities of a preparatory stroke but having no control over the qualities of its realization evokes Heisenberg and his theory on the limits of precision when applied to pairs of variables – the so-called principle of uncertainty. We have to get used to the idea of being able to control one without controlling the other and, even beyond that, we must embrace the idea that the more firmly one controls a given variable the less control one has over its corollary partner.

Since we have established that expression resides in the upward movement, culminating at the brief moment of stillness before the downward stroke begins, it makes sense to practice the upstroke and not the downstroke. The mechanics of lift, speed, acceleration, as well as the qualities of the pivot point at the top of the stroke are remarkably similar between conducting and percussion playing. I have spent a lifetime amassing a catalogue of percussion upstrokes. With conducting, my taxonomy is still under construction. Remarkably, the questions are nearly identical. Do

you move in a single fluid stroke, or do you break the upward stroke into subdivisions? Is there acceleration in the upward stroke? How long and with what quality of weightlessness does one pause at the top? In other words, what precisely is your relationship with gravity as you raise your hand? The answers to these questions differentiate resonant drums strokes and lyrical conductorly moments from sharply articulated cymbal rhythms or the sense of *scherzo* in a Beethoven symphony. Sometimes, the preparatory stroke is not on the vertical axis. Imagine playing a hanging gong, or starting on beat three after a fermata. Nevertheless, gravity must be imagined, and the sense of resisting it imposed even when it is absent.

In both conducting and percussion, the gestural plane of movement away from and toward your own body activates another set of mechanical and expressive possibilities. In a "multiple percussion setup" (one in which several instruments are arranged as a larger "meta-instrument"), a move closer to the instruments invites greater manipulation of sounds. When you are close enough to touch the instruments you can mute, dampen, or otherwise modify their sounds. A move away from the instruments – necessitated when a setup is very large and a player leans away from some instruments to play others – results in breaking contact with the setup. Here, a shift of the center of gravity of a player produces changes in sound quality. In the case of conducting, moving forward and back does similar things. Leaning forward can strengthen contact with a given section of the orchestra, but necessarily at the expense of another group whom you are leaning away from. Shifting back on the podium offers the chance to embrace the entirety of the ensemble, but at the expense of a slightly destabilized center of gravity. An error I made repeatedly in my first concerts was to lean forward toward the orchestra at moments when I wanted to take control or excite passion. I thought that if I could just reach out far enough to touch the performers I could incite them to greater heights. But as in nearly every social encounter, moving into someone else's space has the effect of making that person lean back. In the case of an orchestra, this makes for less not more intense playing. In recent years, I have gotten much better results from giving a cue to raise the emotional energy of a passage and then letting the orchestra come to me. In some cases, barely moving at all brings out the most impassioned playing. This is the same way a relaxed and powerful stroke on a bass drum or tam-tam produces more sound than one that is tense and overcontrolled.

Classical percussionists and conductors also have this in common: neither actually touches an instrument that produces sound. Of course non-Western percussion traditions are replete with hand-drummers, gamelan performers, and *congeros*: musicians who hold, cradle, mute, or otherwise touch their instruments. But as a contemporary classical percussionist, I

nearly always use sticks, mallets, brushes, or bows as physical intermediaries. I don't touch the instruments; I touch something that touches the instruments. Therefore, the percussionist spends his or her life in a deeply problematized relationship with "the instrument." Since we don't hold or touch them, we only hear them through our ears. Most other instrumentalists hear their instruments through both their ears and via direct contact with bones and muscles. (I can only imagine what a clarinetist, violinist, or a singer feels and hears while performing.) Add to this that we often play on unfamiliar instruments. (I know some percussionists who always travel with personal instruments. However, at least for me, in a country as large as the United States, it's a rare concert on tour when I am not playing borrowed or rented instruments.) We hold our instruments – literally and metaphorically – at a distance. But, with distance, we gain independence from the control exerted by a "governing object." With distance we gain freedom.

To unpack this, let's start with the idea that musical gesture is always in response to an object (even if this object is the larynx). The shape and use of an object govern the gestures required to activate it. But every object will control the gestures it prompts to a different degree. For example, in the extra-musical world, the very particular shape and function of a golf club means that to a considerable extent this object controls the gestures employed in its usage. Anyone picking up a golf club for the purposes of playing golf will move very much like anyone else who does the same thing. A flat plate of metal, however, exerts far less control over its functionality and therefore the gestures engaged in its activation. You can eat off a metal plate, skip it across a still pond, play it with a triangle beater, or prop open a door. All of these are legitimate uses of a metal plate, and as a result produce a great variety of possible gestures. Now let's substitute the governing object, replacing golf club with "cello" or "xylophone," and you see that the amount of gestural variety elicited is, likewise, limited and highly determined. Using a cello requires cello-like gestures; a xylophone, xylophone-like gestures. But the percussion world is full of objects just like a metal plate (in fact, it is full of metal plates) that evoke a varied and largely undetermined vocabulary of gestures. Consider also that a percussionist does not engage just one object, but in fact many hundreds, and you can begin to see the extraordinary diversity (and therefore, liberty) of gesture involved in the performance of percussion.

The conductor extends this argument further. Since a conductor neither touches an instrument nor makes any sound while conducting, the gestural world is even less controlled by a "governing object," and therefore even more free and varied. In addition to the rudimentary

gestures of beat patterns, a conductor's primary job is to give preparatory gestures that are readable to a diverse group of instrumentalists. An upbeat has to prompt simultaneous mechanisms of preparation from piccolo players to tubaists; from violinists to contrabass players; bassoonists to woodblock players. Since a single gesture triggers a dozen or more unique gestures of performance, the gestural mechanics of conducting cannot be too strongly attuned to any single instrument. A truly violin-oriented upbeat wouldn't work with a large wind instrument and might cause a trombonist, for example, to enter late. Likewise, the immediacy of attack with percussion is very unlike the relatively slow onset of a low string. A conductor must make a gesture that is legible to each. The solution is to use a nonmimetic gestural language, one that resembles only itself. In other words, the upbeat to a unison entry by winds and strings should not itself look like an inhalation or up-bow stroke. The conductor relies on the minds of the players to translate the general, nonmimetic gesture of an upbeat to the intake of breath or the lifting of a bow arm. In short, if a conducting gesture is nonrepresentational and therefore does not *mean* anything, its functionality is extrinsic, not intrinsic. Gestural meaning must be assigned. It must be learned. This is a premise any conductor realizes when working with performers who have not learned the system of gestural cueing. Try to conduct a noninstrumentalist – an electronics operator or audience member or amateur percussionist. It doesn't work. Even if you show a very clear upbeat, such a person is likely to play at the first sign of movement and will, almost always, be early.

Conducting is teaching

It is the communal and mutually reinforcing acts of teaching and learning – not the lofty goal of interpretation, not the questionable goal of being a *maestro*, nor the venal one of control and power over a group – that is the conductor's most important task. It's simple: conducting is teaching. Your job is to learn the score and teach it to people who do not know it. This very basic realization allowed me to return to a paradigm of teaching and learning that I had honed over decades as a percussionist and percussion teacher and apply it to conducting. The process of intake, refinement, and testing that I use in learning percussion music is the same one by which one can master anything from a symphony of Beethoven to tying a double-Windsor knot or making the perfect peach cobbler. The process is therefore not specific to the task at hand and should work with nearly anything.

Take an initial amount of material – roughly what you can digest in fifteen minutes or so. We'll call this a chunk. The chunk must be small

enough to be learned *in toto* (if you have to subdivide the chunk into subsections then that is the size of the chunk), but large enough to be meaningful. Then "embody" the chunk, that is to say transfer the information to yourself in the form of a physical skill (in the case of learning a percussion piece) or an ability to view and fully imagine a section of a piece (in the case of conducting). Inevitably, there will be flaws as you transfer the skills to your body. Repeat those areas of weakness, practicing to make them stronger. Then test them to make sure that the chunk has been learned intact and accurately. Go on to the next chunk and repeat the process. You will need to return to previously learned chunks regularly to keep them from decaying.

I love the beautiful tedium of this kind of work. For me, the slow construction of the mental/physical architecture creates the internal scaffolding that is a necessary counterbalance to the emotionally destabilizing act of performance. In fact, reconnecting with the deeply meditative process of learning was the most valuable thing conducting has done for me. In the first two years of my tenure with the La Jolla Symphony, I awoke most nights with a deep fear that I was incapable of delivering as a conductor on a level anywhere near that which I had attained as a percussionist. In part, the fears were social. Will my friends and colleagues be disappointed in me? Or worse, will they think I am foolish? The fears were also personal. By taking on a new and challenging occupation in my late middle age, I sought to avoid the pitfall of simply reproducing the acquired expertise of percussion playing. That was very positive. But was I dedicating an enormous part of my available energy, in what was arguably the last big creative phase of my life, to a quixotic and potentially unwise goal? Who cares what anyone else thinks: do I think I am being foolish? I'll leave these questions unanswered for the moment.

The process of learning might be remarkably similar across disciplines, but the way it manifests itself in any given discipline is unique. With conducting, the teaching/learning continuum coalesces around several issues: (1) gestures and their nuances, leveraged to produce an interpretation; (2) the score and corresponding questions of authenticity; and (3) cultivating collective wisdom in an orchestra; in other words, harnessing interpretative energy that supersedes the will of any individual. We have spent some time with the issue of gesture, though of course much more could be said. The latter two points are connected to each other and to one of the principal axes of contention in contemporary music since World War II: authorial supremacy.

It is not my intention here, nor is it within my expertise, to address issues surrounding the inviolability of the score or questions about interpretive indulgence on the part of this conductor or that one. There have

been plentiful occasions to react to Gunther Schuller's jeremiad, "The Compleat Conductor," or on the other side of the divide to extoll a particularly brilliant and personal interpretation by, say, Leonard Bernstein. I am not interested in this because the question itself is flawed. "Shall a conductor honor the score in all of its detail?" Such a question is rooted in the belief that a musical score is in fact an adequate representation of a composer's wishes. Whether one ultimately argues for a "pure and unadulterated" version, as Schuller would, or sees the score as a malleable means to an end, as Bernstein or even Mahler might, there is basic agreement on the question of the "firmness" of the score. Both sides acknowledge that a score exists and that the principal interpretative question rests in how one uses it. Very Old Testament.

Such a point of view makes no sense to this contemporary percussionist, who understands how limited a tool a score really is. I am thinking of a short cymbal phrase in Helmut Lachenmann's wonderful solo work *Intérieur*, though I could have chosen a hundred other examples in any of a dozen pieces. The passage involves a rolled crescendo on a large suspended cymbal from *pianissimo* to *mezzo forte*. It should take about one second to execute. This would seem to be a very straightforward indication. A realization of this single event could be analyzed along the same axis as the long-standing arguments about conducting interpretations: Should one execute it as indicated or change it for the purposes of personal expression? But a closer examination reveals that the score is not at all clear and firm. For starters, what is a large cymbal? Should it be a Turkish cymbal of modern construction (light and bright in the harmonic spectrum) or should it be darker with a more robust fundamental? And what if, because of the thickness of the metal or the way it is hammered, a smaller cymbal makes a deeper sound? Should a percussionist use the bigger cymbal anyway because of the indication "large?" And what about the fact that the crescendo to *mezzo forte* is designed to create an envelope of sound in which several small sounds that follow can resonate in an acoustical bed of the cymbal sound? Isn't *mezzo forte* then less an indication of dynamic volume and more of sustaining power or even harmonic richness? And what of those small elements that follow, the triangle and cowbell notes? If their brightness is to match the cymbal then perhaps a crescendo beyond *mezzo forte* to *forte* is in order since this will activate the upper partials of the cymbal and provide a matching harmonic spectrum. The result might be a sense of kinship between the *sostenuto* and articulate elements in the passage. Or perhaps, if *mezzo forte* is the right dynamic, a change in the basic tempo of the phrase needs to be made so that the sonic structure retains its integrity. Ah, which to choose? The correct sound, the correct dynamic, or the correct tempo? And we have not even begun to talk

about how a given sonic solution might respond in varying acoustical environments or with different mallets. And all of this ambiguity comes from the very simple indication of large suspended cymbal at *mezzo forte*.

As a result of hundreds if not thousands of similar situations in the contemporary percussion repertoire, I have stopped looking at a musical score as a compendium of answers, but rather as a map of musical relationships, what I think of as a "weather system." Perhaps, an interpreter becomes a kind of meteorologist, in which linked relationships in the musical weather system are explored. Such an understanding refutes the view of the score as the truth inscribed on sacred tablets. In a musical score, everything is important, but nothing is sacred. Conversely, nothing is insular; everything is interconnected. Changing the marked tempo at the beginning of Iannis Xenakis' *Rebonds* is intrinsically neither a good nor a bad move. But it will have profound effects on the way the forces of rhythmic and textural evolution are metabolized over the course of the composition. Likewise, changing mallets frequently in Karlheinz Stockhausen's *Zyklus* is neither good nor bad, unless an interpreter is unaware of what such a strategy may do to the linked questions of tempo and pacing.

This was the mindset that I brought to learning and conducting the classical repertoire for orchestra. Early in my conducting life, another conductor asked me whether or not I preferred to intone the upbeat or the downbeat in a passage at the beginning of Brahms' *Second Symphony*. I didn't have an opinion and was immediately stricken with a nauseating wave of self-criticism. How could I not know the answer to such a seemingly basic question? I looked to the score, sure that the answer was there. It was not. The score does not tell you how to answer this question, or another Brahmsian question about whether or not to shorten the notes at the ends of phrases, or a myriad of other concerns. The score, however, is the tool to evaluate the chain of significance that will ensue by choosing one option over another. Eventually, I decided not to place much emphasis on the downbeats at the beginning of Brahms #2, not because the voice of Brahms spoke to me through the score, but because the metric ambiguity that naturally ensued was a valuable tool to have as the piece progressed. By withholding the answer to the most basic metric question, "where's the downbeat?" in the early stages of the piece, the greater metrical firmness of the later music, culminating in an ultimate and incontrovertible assertion in the fourth movement, had greater power. When the score is a weather system, making a decision opens up possibilities in one direction and closes them off in another. Therefore, an interpretation is not only a set of correct choices, a catalogue of affirmative actions. It is also a compendium of loss, a listing of those many viable pathways that were not taken. The enemy of art is not a bad choice; it is the certainty that one has found the correct one.

Suspending the quest for authority means inevitably that there will be multiple authors. I marvel at the catalytic moment in a rehearsal cycle when the orchestra suddenly and collectively simply knows what to do. It is as though wisdom – nearly always the province of an individual – is suddenly transferred to a group. The collective ownership of musical authority is that moment when 40, 80, or 300 people suddenly hear a phrase in the same way, or manage an awkward tempo change in unison, or lift before a final fermata. No rehearsal cycle is long enough to perfect these moments via conductorly control – and recordings that purport highly defined interpretations often sound sterile as a result – so the sudden untutored appearance of a communal thought is a small gift. The collective intelligence of the orchestra, the group impulse that supersedes the will of any individual, is the rejection of the academic, the insular, and the dispassionate in favor of the real, the communal.

After that poetic sentiment, it's a good time for something more commonplace: a disclaimer. Even after conducting nearly 250 pieces, including almost all of the Beethoven Symphonies, the *Missa Solemnis*, Benjamin Britten's *War Requiem*, much of Mahler and Brahms, and large swaths of several contemporary composers including James Dillon, Pierre Boulez, Iannis Xenakis, and Edgard Varèse, I state with certainty (and even a little pride) that I am still a novice conductor. And to the extent that being a novice means retaining a beginner's mind, I hope I will always be a novice. My goal with these words is not to stake a claim as a professional conductor, but to aerate my thoughts on a practice that has become an important part of my life. In fact, staking a professional claim seems like a small and sad thing for an aging novice to do. The goal in conducting is the same as it has always been in percussion playing: to find a meaningful problem, and through miniscule steps toward mastery, occasionally find yourself in a state of grace through sound. Doubtless this is an overly grand formulation, but I wager that every practicing musician knows what I mean.

These moments of grace feel different to me as a conductor than they do as a percussionist. As a percussionist, there is a bodily sense that is marked, again and again, by the sweet kink of contact with an instrument. It is simultaneously a dance and, because of the physical realities of the instruments, a kind of practice. For me, at its best it feels like yoga. But everyone will have his or her own simile. The act of conducting, however, is less animal, less the surmounting of corporeal obstacles since there are none, and more a solitary act of exhortation to those who are doing the surmounting. Yet at times, the two roles feel remarkably similar. What they have in common – these two people, the expert percussionist and the novice conductor – is the need to look outside of himself/herself for sense, to retrain the inward gaze outward as a way of connecting to the

lives and thoughts of others. The expert percussionist and the novice conductor both rely on a language of gestures and the uncommon emotional freight involved in moving in order to be moved. Finally, both the expert percussionist and the novice conductor are pilgrims in a land of new noises; the goal for each is to find the right noise for the moment. And in the end there is the realization – this is so lovely – that expert and novice are not so very far apart.

Composing music for percussion instruments

11 Finding a voice

BOB BECKER

In his 1994 article *Composer or arranger: Is there a difference?*,[1] the distinguished Canadian composer Bruce Mather asked a loaded question: "What is composition?" In the article, he expressed dismay that many composers appeared to be rewriting music of the past. Mather wrote provocatively of "musical amnesia" to describe what he viewed as an aesthetic crisis: "The work of [certain contemporary composers] might be more worthy of esteem only if Bartók, Hindemith, Schoenberg and Stravinsky had never existed." He went on to analyze what he felt distinguishes composers and arrangers: "the distinction between composer and arranger is not exactly one of originality. Composers who develop a very personal language . . . are very rare. The distinction has more to do with the qualities of invention, the distinctiveness of materials, and the freshness of expression." I recall a comment by the late Japanese composer Toru Takemitsu that, at a given moment, any country in the world can have at most only one composer with a distinctive voice.

In relation to modern percussion music, we could update Mather's list of esteem-worthy composers to include names such as Cage, Partch, and Reich. John Cage, even late in his life, described himself as a "percussion composer," an expression that differs from "percussionist-composer" by more than a hyphen. Cage, at least early in his career, was forced to be a composer-percussionist. Although he had no formal technical training, he and a few similarly handicapped colleagues were obliged to play the instruments in his early percussion works simply out of necessity – there were no professional percussion ensembles in existence during the 1940s. Harry Partch became an accomplished performer on his own percussion instruments because, in order to realize music in a 43-tone-to-the-octave system, he was compelled to design and construct them all himself. At first, no one else could play a Diamond Marimba or Quadrangularis Reversum. Partch explained, "I am not an instrument-builder, but a philosophic music-man seduced into carpentry."[2] Steve Reich has stated, "I first decided that despite my limitations as a performer I had to play in all my compositions. It seemed clear that a healthy musical situation would only result when the functions of composer and performer were united."[3]

What exactly is the "function" of a composer, and can it, in fact, be united or combined in some way with that of a performer? When asked to

differentiate between composers and performers, I often draw an analogy with explorers and adventurers. A composer is an explorer – someone who goes off alone to remote, difficult, sometimes dangerous places, and takes risks to bring back something new and amazing to show everyone back home. One doesn't set out on expeditions like this without the proper training and equipment, and, for any genuine explorer, the objective is the discovery of unknown territory. A performer is more of an adventurer or tour guide – someone who scouts the terrain, gets all of the necessary gear organized, and then leads a party of people through exciting and spectacular scenery. The aim for everyone, including the guide, is to witness something extraordinary.

In more concrete terms, a composer's function is to create an account of his or her own imagination in a comprehensible form – that is, in an explicit notation or medium. It is a straightforward undertaking to learn and develop the skills necessary to notate musical sounds and rhythms accurately; however, it is a serious challenge to discover a unique method for encoding the abstraction of a subjective mental landscape. I think Mather means to apply the term "arranger" to composers who can't resist the seductive pull of a preexisting successful musical language, and "musical amnesia" is a kind of blindness to the entire proceeding. A great film composer like John Williams is an arranger by this definition, but surely one whose appropriation of musical styles is done with complete intention. In his article, Mather is rather less forgiving in selecting his list of contemporary arrangers. Stravinsky's famous quip, "lesser artists borrow; great artists steal,"[4] points to a line between referencing the past by actually developing and expanding on older forms and techniques in an original way and simply adopting a style – between deconstruction and reconstruction, between assimilation and appropriation. This line can be fuzzy, but anyone who wants to write music needs to choose a place to stand. Stravinsky himself seemed to find a unique position, straddling the line and planting one foot on either side.

The two roles – explorer and adventurer – certainly can overlap, and it's not difficult to imagine situations where the functions of composer and performer intersect. One obvious arena is improvisation, which may be viewed as a kind of spontaneous composition. A number of well-known percussionist-composers have remarked that they always begin, and often complete, a composition by extemporaneously playing on the instrument(s) chosen for the orchestration. Those who specialize in writing for solo marimba are particularly prone to this approach, and improvisation based on technical patterns is often the primary method for finding and developing the material used in a piece. On the positive side, an accomplished performer working in this way can produce

characteristic and technically assured music – much in the manner of pianist-composers like Carl Czerny, however, rarely with the authority of composer-pianists such as Rachmaninoff or Chopin.

The piano and its solo repertoire occupy a privileged position in Western classical music, and the marimba currently aspires to a similarly special place in percussion music. During the last two decades of the twentieth century, the marimba began to compete with (and displace) the snare drum as the fundamental source for technical training and conceptual development in percussion performance and pedagogy, particularly at North American universities. The 1970s saw the introduction and refinement of radically new approaches to marimba technique, along with renewed efforts to expand the range and enhance the quality of the instrument itself. Comprehensive training methods, complete with extensive progressive exercises and countless etudes, currently offer percussion teachers an instant syllabus. As a result, the marimba is beginning to take its place in college curricula as an instrument of serious specialization, and degrees with a marimba major not connected with the general percussion studio are already available from some institutions in the United States and Japan.

During the past forty years, percussionist-composers created a tremendous amount of repertoire for themselves and their colleagues through appropriating techniques developed by prominent composers and incorporating musical approaches popularized by jazz and "world" artists. It was an understandable, if less than inspiring, response to the near void of serious solo and ensemble music composed for percussion instruments during the twenty-eight years between Cage's *Third Construction* (1943) and Reich's *Drumming* (1971), a period Steven Schick refers to as "the big chill,"[5] Carter[6] and Wuorinen[7] notwithstanding. Although marimba repertoire does include some important music from this era by composers such as Creston,[8] Kurka,[9] Miki,[10] Miyoshi,[11] and Tanaka,[12] marimbists found themselves staring into a similar vacuum. The response by two virtuosos on opposite sides of the globe – Leigh Howard Stevens and Keiko Abe – was to push for the creation of new and original solo works by major composers. Their efforts during the 1970s resulted in a critical body of new music for the instrument, but consequently one that has almost drowned in a sea of imitative and nearly indistinguishable pieces written by marimbist-composers around the world.[13]

It is interesting to consider whether the endeavor of studying and playing percussion instruments, including the marimba, creates some sort of pressure to compose, as in Mather's "distinctiveness of materials." Is there a compositional imperative to be found in the great variety of styles and techniques that need to be assimilated by a contemporary

percussionist? The current inclusion of multiple disciplines in percussion training – orchestral, baroque (via the marimba), modern avant-garde classical, theater, jazz, military (marching lines/drum corps), and "ethnic" (everything else in the world) – may have led to an embarrassment of riches. The already extensive demands made on students will continue to proliferate as changes in the professional music environment accelerate, and a glance through any recent orchestration book confirms how difficult it can be for composers to keep up. Lacking suitable repertoire, it is a natural reaction for percussionists to attempt to incorporate all of their instruments and technical abilities into music they write for themselves. Unfortunately, an abundance of percussive skill does not ensure the ability to approach the rigors of creating a compositional voice of any originality or significance, at least not of the variety suggested in Mather's article.

Finding a conceptual basis for writing music, and then developing and honing it, is a gamble. There is no guarantee that a seminal idea will pay dividends in either the short or long term until it is tried and explored. My experience in this regard was a bit like winning a lottery because at first I was unable to judge the longevity of the basic methodology I elected to use in my work. A composer is the traveler in the folk paradox, "How can you choose a road to someplace when you don't know where you are going?" On the other hand, the corollary, "If you don't know where a road leads, it definitely will take you there," may not necessarily hold up. For composers, there are a lot of very short roads with abrupt endings. Still, not knowing where the road leads is the great adventure of composition, and the dialectic resolution "wherever you go, there you are" is undeniable.

For me, discovering my own compositional language felt something like a revelation, but it was nonetheless the result of a cumulative life experience. My earliest childhood encounters with music involved an intense emotional response to harmony. I can remember the physical feeling in my stomach and an awareness of "mood" for the first time. I responded to melody and rhythm too, but those aspects of music felt somehow more tangible. I could recreate them silently in my imagination, or audibly by humming or tapping. Harmony, on the other hand, has remained throughout my life something mysterious in its power to affect me. Studying music theory during high school and college neither changed nor illuminated the impact harmonic progressions produced or the feelings they could evoke.

Somewhat later in my life I encountered Hindustani music and had the opportunity first to study, and then practice and perform it, over a period of more than twenty years. As is well known, classical Indian music reaches astonishing levels of rhythmic and melodic sophistication, but has no functional harmony (as associated with Western tonal music) whatsoever.

Vertical pitch relationships only occur in the interval ratios between individual melodic tones and the ubiquitous drone heard throughout any performance. Although Indian modal scales, or *raga*s, are conceived to have a primary note (called *vadi*) and a secondary note (called *samvadi*), they do not contain dominant and subdominant tones as found in traditional Western scales and modes. The *vadi* and *samvadi* can be any two notes, depending on the particular *raga*'s construction. Indeed, a *raga* may contain as few as five scale degrees, and there may be no interval of a fifth in the mode at all. The exquisitely ornamented and melismatic melodic phrases of Indian music imply no harmonic direction and hold no cadential tension to be resolved by real or implied triadic progression. That is the view among Indian musicians and Indian audiences; however, my experience was quite different.

For someone born and raised in a culture saturated with music based on chord progressions, it is probably inevitable that the mind will supply imagined harmonies when hearing monophonic or heterophonic melodies; yet, in the context of listening within a new and exotic musical atmosphere it was an unexpected subliminal perception for me. The results were not unpleasant, and on occasion I was surprised by the particular harmony my mind proposed, apparently without any specific intent from my conscious awareness. Even so, it was a while before I understood how the process occurring inside my own mind could form a foundation for just the personal language I needed in my composition work.

Modern Hindustani music theory catalogues upwards of 100 distinct *raga*s, of which several dozen are currently in vogue. I found the modes with relatively few tones presented the most ambiguous harmonic implications, and some – for example, the pentatonic *chandrakauns* and *malkauns* – evoked particularly intriguing sensations. The scale of *rag chandrakauns* (which has traditional associations with the full moon and late night hours) happens to have no fifth degree: tonic, minor third, perfect fourth, minor sixth, major seventh. Working with these intervals immediately resulted in sonorities that sounded new to me, but it wasn't until I applied more complex procedures to the material that I began to understand its potential. I was able to derive some surprisingly elaborate structures, including the matrix of four nine-tone scales currently employed in my music. Finally, I determined a set of principles that gives a comprehensive, consistent, and personal methodology for handling both melodic and harmonic construction. While these conditions allow for some flexibility, they make definite constraints on what pitches may be used simultaneously at any point in the music. Composing in this systematic way, every note is *accounted for* horizontally, and all vertical relationships are *accountable to* the established rules. I can say I created the system, or that I discovered it, but more properly

it grew out of my personal musical trajectory: thoughts and feelings I experienced while listening to sounds; practical training I received on musical instruments; instruction I was given in analyzing and understanding musical form and structure; and probably most important for me, the impact of performing together with other musicians in a variety of stylistic and cultural contexts. A kind of psychological cross-referencing always seems to occur when one strong cultural expression encounters another. Twenty years ago, I wrote that, in my opinion, this perceptual phenomenon would be the defining issue for all of the arts and politics in the twenty-first century.[14] Today I feel even more convinced about it.

At this stage in my life I'm certain I am no longer "arranging," but a question remains: Am I a percussionist-composer or a composer-percussionist? Although I still may be in transition from the former, the principles and rules I need to function as the latter are firmly in place in my work. They arose from the exploration of a personal cognitive insight – informed by my own background and studies, and situated at a specific historical and technological moment. I have been told that in order to be successful, a composer needs to be prolific. By that rule, I will never succeed as a professional composer. However, I measure my success in this avocation not by quantity or variety, and not by financial gain or public approbation, but primarily by my own experience of discovery and growth, and secondarily by whether I feel the work has continuity and *significance*. For me, the measure of significance is not concerned with judging the relative "greatness" (however that may be defined) of musical works. It has far more to do with satisfying Mather's demand for a "personal language," and is what really differentiates the categories of arranger and composer, percussively modified or not. At least by this qualification, I can view my work as having some significance, both in a general musical sense and in relation to the continuum of the development of percussion repertoire. If percussionists recognize me to be a composer, and composers consider me to be a percussionist, perhaps that is the best of both worlds.

Notes

1. B. Mather, "Composer or arranger: Is there a difference?" Sound *Notes* (Spring/Summer 1994).

2. H. Partch, "Photographs of Instruments Built by Harry Partch and Heard in His Recorded Music," LP record insert (CA: Gate 5 Records, 1962).

3. S. Reich, *Writings on Music, 1965–2000* (Oxford University Press, 2002), p. 78.

4. Although this remark, or something very similar, is also attributed to others from Pablo Picasso to Steve Jobs, its implications regarding imitation would be difficult to express more succinctly.

5. S. Schick, *The Percussionist's Art* (University of Rochester Press, 2006), p. 65.

6. The first six of Elliott Carter's *Eight Pieces for Four Timpani* were composed in 1950, and the final two in 1966.

7. C. Wuorinen's *Janissary Music* (for solo percussionist) was published in 1966.

8. P. Creston's *Concertino for Marimba* was published in 1940.

9. R. Kurka's *Concerto for Marimba and Orchestra* was published in 1956.

10. M. Miki's *Time for Marimba* was composed circa 1968, and his *Concerto* (for marimba and orchestra) in 1969.

11. A. Miyoshi's *Conversation* (Suite for marimba) was composed circa 1962.

12. T. Tanaka's *Two Movements for Marimba* was composed in 1965.

13. A significant exception is Gordon Stout who, almost from the beginning of his composition work in 1973 with *Etudes for Marimba* and *Diptych No. 1*, established a distinctive approach to writing for the instrument. Even now, it is difficult to know whether to describe him as a marimbist-composer or composer-marimbist.

14. Program notes for *The Bob Becker Ensemble*, 1994.

12 Flexibility as a defining factor

I consider myself a performer/composer because I feel that my approach as a performer has heavily influenced the way I write music and the basic principles I value as a composer. When I perform music by other composers, I want to believe I am a needed component in the process, not merely a cog in the machine. I want to know there is room for my thoughts about the music.

Many times I have this experience because the music I perform is written specifically for me. When this happens, I work closely in collaboration with the composer so I can feel how my unique skill set and overall commitment impact the process and the outcome. Sometimes I perform music by composers I have never met, usually because the music was written before I was alive. In these cases, I am drawn to a piece because I feel a shared aesthetic approach with the composer and because something in the music convinces me that my contribution is valuable. Maybe there is a skill I have that not every classically trained percussionist has, and that would add something to the music; or maybe there is something about the rhythmic sensibility of the music that I can put my stamp on. Many times, it is just something ingrained in the piece itself, a flexibility that gives each performer room for choices which will substantially alter the way the piece sounds. Morton Feldman's *King of Denmark*, John Cage's *Third Construction* and Iannis Xenakis' *Psappha* are all examples of works I am drawn to for these reasons, and the approach each composer took has affected the way I compose.

Here's another way I have begun to look at this. As a member of the quartet Sō Percussion, I have the chance to travel around the world and talk with students and interested audience members about what we do. If someone knows I play in a percussion quartet, but has never heard us, I ask them to close their eyes and imagine what the stage will look like for our show. This is a wonderful exercise because it touches on one of the most basic qualities of our field. The Western classical percussion ensemble lineage is still in its infancy and that makes it a very open place to explore – there is no objective standard. If you close your eyes and picture a Western classical string quartet, inevitably you are thinking of two violins, a viola, and a cello. If you picture a percussion quartet, one person might see keyboard instruments on one side of the stage and drums filling the other.

Another will think of the "found" sound traditions of John Cage, Lou Harrison, and others. Some will think of drum sets and vibraphones and others will imagine orchestral instruments. There might be no instruments on stage at all and the audience could still enjoy a percussion quartet performance when the performers clap, slap, or rub their bodies, or use drumsticks on the floor.

In many ways, one might think that when writing for percussion, the composer's most basic decision would be to choose which instruments will be used for the piece. But still, many influential composers of the twentieth and twenty-first centuries allow the performers a great deal of leeway to decide what their music will sound like by allowing them to choose their instruments. Categories like skin, wood, and metal can be used as guiding principles, or an instruction like "five tin cans" will lead the performer in a direction with some specificity but allow for much variation within that. When the melodies of a piece are performed on five tin cans of the player's choosing, that player has great influence on the result. As a composer, I find this incredibly inspiring: those other composers must have had great confidence in the underlying structure of their music. As a performer, I find it rewarding to be able to make choices that will profoundly affect the way a listener hears a piece.

Composers can do this in other ways, too; for example, sometimes the performer is involved in the way the piece unfolds over time. Compositions like Terry Riley's *In C* or Steve Reich's *Drumming* allow performers to choose how long each event happens. Other composers write pieces for flexible instrumentation. An example of this is Louis Andriessen's *Workers Union,* written for any number of players. Andriessen writes specific rhythms to be performed in unison, but the pitched material is left open to the performers by asking them to follow the contour of the melodic line. Both of these approaches allow for a wonderful compromise of control between the composer and the performers.

I don't think all music needs to be made like this, and I don't write music like this all of the time. But the approaches outlined above have inspired me in a core way as a composer. They have made me a performer/composer. The first music I wrote was twelve pieces set to short videos called *amid the noise*. I wrote many of the pieces for myself and recorded them in layers. Later, they developed into pieces for Sō Percussion (the quartet I play in and write the bulk of my compositions for). Since the pieces were written for me and my musical family, the notation stayed in skeletal form for a long time. It was many years before any of the pieces were written down in a way that others could understand, and each piece was only codified in this way when another group offered to perform it. This process of composition to notation spanned ten years in some cases,

and that distance allowed me time to really think about how I wanted this communication to play out. What information did I need to pass on to the performers to ensure that the performances would represent my thoughts and, on the other hand, what information could I leave open to the performers?

The result is different for each of the twelve pieces that makes up the set. Sometimes I used notation that could be considered standard in the Western classical music sense, but more often I created bits of notation that use a staff and note-heads along with explanations in paragraph form and instructions on how to build the pieces from the ground up. My thought was, and continues to be, that if the performers learn the methods behind these structures, they will be able to convey them through their own interpretive lenses in a stronger way. The process has two ramifications: it is more time consuming to learn yet lends itself to unique interpretation. This is a trade-off I am happy with.

Let me give you a bit of background on these pieces. As I mentioned above, this set of music was written to be performed with video. A few of the pieces were originally part of a film score for *Invitations and Ultimatums*, a documentary film that my sister, Jenise Treuting, made. I wrote the music along with another composer, and we decided to try to find a method to make sure our contributions would fit together. I told him I had been experimenting with compositions that translated text into music using patterns found in the text. For example, I would create large structures using the series of numbers derived from the lengths of the words in the quotation. I would often use smaller patterns to structure a rhythmic layer, like taking alternating vowels and consonants and translating them to rhythmic patterns. We settled on a quote of Martin Luther King, Jr.'s that made sense with the subject of the film and, through experimentation, found ways to work together with this method.

For one example with a bit more depth, let's look at *June* from *amid the noise*. As with most of the works in this set, *June* was conceived in three core layers: drone, harmony, and noise/rhythm. Some of the other pieces in the set add a fourth melody layer as well. In this case, the drone is a C that continues throughout. For the harmony layer, there are six possible chords for the performer to choose from, and the order and how they move is largely up to the performer. The timing of these chords is prescribed, at least relatively. The length of the words in the Martin Luther King text guides the duration of each chord. The noise/rhythm layer is derived from the order of consonants and vowels in each word – this layer is the most flexible. Sō Percussion recorded this layer as fluttery hi-hats, but many other possibilities exist for each interpretation: sometimes more ambient

Example 12.1 Score to *June*.

june

Our scientific power has outrun our spiritual power;
We have guided missiles and misguided men. -MLK, Jr.

<u>Instrumentation:</u> Rhythmic   noise   element;   sustaining   chord
element; optional ambient or chance noise element; drone.

<u>Harmony/Melody:</u> Sustaining instrument performs the chords, using
the length of each word in the quote as a guide for length of
sustain. Each letter represents 1", so that the first chord will
sustain for 3" (our), the second 10" (scientific), etc. The
first group of 4 chords must be used exclusively for the first
line of text (Our...power). The second group of 2 chords may be
mixed in for the second line (We...men). Chords may be chosen
freely, **but only the top or bottom voice may change from one to
the next, not both.**

<u>Drone:</u> C natural above middle C. It can be smooth or active.

<u>Noise:</u> (optional   element)   Radio   broadcast,   ambient   noise,
crinkling paper, etc.

<u>Rhythm:</u> More than one rhythmic element performs a combination of
binary   elements   without   coordinating   with   each   other   (for
percussionists, R and L hand sequences). Using the quote, vowels
= one element (R), consonants = the other (L). A fast enough
sequence is preferred so that the parts go in and out of sync,
creating   a   noisy   chatter.   These   sequences   loop   until   the
sustaining instrument changes to a new chord.   The sustaining
instrument and the rhythmic element will follow the form of the
quote together.

For a percussionist, the first line of the score might read as
follows:

```
Our    scientific    power    has    outrun    our    spiritual    power
RRL    LLRRLLRLRLR    LRLRL    LRL    RRLLRL    RRL    LLRLRLRRL    LRLRL
```

<u>Form:</u> Proceed through the quote any number of times. Duration of
each letter can exceed 1" if desired.

noises are used and sometimes solid rhythms ground it. Example 12.1 is
the one-page score to *June*, which separates these elements.

In the end, I determined that with *June*, as with many of these pieces,
the composition relies on a core structure that cannot be modified. Most
often, this structure relies on harmony (and occasionally melody) and in
this way, the approach could be considered traditional. The accompanying

rhythms and noise elements are most often extremely flexible. And, like many of the pieces mentioned earlier, the orchestration is completely flexible.

As I write this down and distill my ideas in written form, I see that my approach seems anything but radical. As a performer, I find that many composers in today's musical climate rely more on specificity than flexibility, often with excellent results. But as a composer, I feel that allowing flexibility in the compositional structure as well as input from the performers can yield unique music-making. I am interested in continuing this exploration as a performer/composer in the vital percussion community in which I am lucky enough to belong.

13 Thoughts on percussion and rhythm

STEVE REICH

This chapter is a compilation of the thoughts of Steve Reich on percussion and rhythm taken from interviews with Russell Hartenberger in 2003 and 2012, and revised with additional thoughts by Steve Reich in 2015.

Early percussion training and influences

My interest in rhythm probably began when I was born in some gene in my body that you and I and a whole lot of other people share, and that people will probably find out about fairly soon. I took piano lessons when I was a kid – John Thompson simplified classics type thing – and it had very little impact on me. I heard what I call middle-class favorites when I was young: Beethoven Fifth, Schubert *Unfinished Symphony,* Overture to *Meistersinger,* Broadway shows, Bing Crosby. I never heard any music before 1750 or any music after Wagner or any jazz until 1950 at the age of 14 – it was a revelation. I had a friend who played me a recording of the *Rite of Spring*; I could not believe such a thing existed! It made an *enormous* impression and the seeds for me becoming a composer were planted that day. Later, that same friend played me a recording of the Bach *Fifth Brandenburg Concerto.* A bit later, through another friend, I heard recordings of Charlie Parker, Miles Davis, and the drummer Kenny Clarke, and this music absolutely grabbed my ear. The friend who played me the jazz records was a pianist with some jazz training. We wanted to start a band and I said, "I'm the drummer." So I started studying with Roland Kohloff, who in those days was known as "Butch." It was Butch Kohloff who played all the Gene Krupa solos with glow-in-the-dark sticks at the local movie theater. Of course, at the same time, he was studying with Saul Goodman and eventually took Goodman's place as timpanist with the New York Philharmonic. For my lessons, Kohloff gave me the Haskell Harr snare drum books, and the *Stick Control* book by George Lawrence Stone. He stressed the *Stick Control* exercises and I found them really interesting. Basically, the book is just continuous eighth-notes while constantly changing the hand alternation. I don't know why, but I thought "hmm, that's interesting," and it stuck in my head. I think that was one of the first things that pointed me in a direction that would really prove relevant later on in my compositions.

At the time, I used to go down to Birdland – I had to sit where they didn't serve drinks – and I remember seeing my idol, Kenny Clarke. The

Figure 13.1 Steve Reich at Brooklyn Bridge.

reason he was my idol was that he had this almost magical sense of time though he just played ride cymbal and a few kick drum (bass drum in those days) accents. What was magical about him was not his technique but the actual feeling of his playing the time, floating Miles Davis and the whole band on his ride cymbal. This was a unique quality, and I wanted to be like Kenny Clarke – but of course you always end up being yourself.

Max Roach was a much greater technician. He could play more stuff, and did play more stuff, and certainly was an inventive musician. But he never had the feeling of "magic time" or whatever you want to call it, that Kenny Clarke had with this incredible *ting ting-a-ting ting-a-ting* on his ride cymbal. Of course, it might have helped that he was playing with Percy Heath and Horace Silver, which seemed like the ultimate rhythm section to me. But it was that simplicity and the *quality* of him playing ride cymbal. Nobody could play it the way he did.

Time feel in music

That feeling of time and time sense is getting it "right" which might show up on an oscilloscope as "slightly wrong." A lot of very good players lack that magic because they are very concentrated on being right. What I'm talking about happens in music in general when you know something so well that you're not reading it, you're playing it after a long period of time and it's sunk into you. I think you have to get to a very high level of

competence, even if it's a little *ting ting-a-ting*. But it has to be an automatic, un-thought-about level, which means lots of rehearsals and performances have to happen before you get there. And then, some people have that quality of magic in their playing and others just don't. Maybe if people put electrodes on their heads and all over their bodies they will find why some people have it and some don't – but you know it when you hear it.

African music

I went to Ghana in 1970. At that time, the reigning musical aesthetic in the new music world was called "live electronics." Stockhausen was operating with banks of equipment in real time; that means he was in the concert hall twisting dials. John Cage was doing the same thing with David Tudor, making electronic pieces happen in front of an audience by manipulating this, that, and the other thing. I think it was Varèse who said something like "percussion led to electronics." This was the idea that non-pitched percussion led to the use of noise, and I kept thinking, "It's going to come out the other end; the progression is going to keep on going – electronics will lead back to percussion."

My trip to Ghana confirmed a number of things for me. First, the idea of phasing that I had before I went to Ghana was not something that the Africans do. And the rhythmic techniques used in African drumming are not what I do, but they are related to what I do. The important thing is that there is a tradition of *rhythmic* counterpoint in Africa (and also in Bali). Second, percussion is the dominant voice in African music, as opposed to the Western orchestra where strings are the dominant voice. So, the message to me was there's a tradition for repeating percussion patterns, you're not all by yourself; go, both in terms of the contrapuntal structure of the music and the instrumentation of the music. This is a solid well-trodden path. There's a past and that means there's a future.

African rhythm

In the Ewe pieces like *Agbadza* or *Atsiagbekor,* the ostinato pattern played on the *gankogui* double iron bell in a twelve-beat cycle is compelling because it is so ambiguous; and it is especially ambiguous when the players get going. They stop playing the low bell, which is struck once per cycle and gives a downbeat to the rhythmic pattern, and they ring out on the high bell

only. It's like a ride cymbal. "Where's one? I don't know." After a while, you don't know. All you know is that the music is powerfully moving forward without a clear downbeat to weigh it down. Everybody talks about twelve-tone music, well twelve is really a magic number rhythmically. The basic ambiguity is whether it's 1 2 3, 1 2 3, 1 2 3, 1 2 3, or 1 2 3 4, 1 2 3 4, 1 2 3 4. It could be twos, it could be sixes, it could be fives and sevens. It divides up and lends itself to subdivision more than any other meter. That's why it's hard to know how to write it out – 3/2 equals 6/4 equals 12/8, because they are all possibly present.

Balinese music

Balinese music, which I studied in Seattle and Berkeley in 1973–1974, is much simpler than African music rhythmically; it's basically subdivisions. One person is playing sixteenths, another person is playing eighths, still another is playing quarters, and so on, and one person plays the big gong every sixty-four beats – and that's great. I guess what interested me mostly were these interlocking patterns, the *kotekkan*, where one player plays against another player. This was certainly *not* how I used interlocking patterns. I did the same thing but canonically, with a pattern against itself. And it is different from African music; African drumming is basically the interlocking of *different* patterns. In *kotekkan*, you get something where one person is filling in rests, or overlapping. It's not what I do – it's not *canonic*. Another thing that interested me about Balinese music is how the drummers in the *Semar Pegulingan* control the tempo as *playing conductors*. That definitely influenced me, along with the master drummer *signaling* changing patterns in West African music – hence the idea of the vibraphone in *Music for 18 Musicians*.

Indian music

I have always admired Indian music, but it's basically a soloist with accompaniment. It's fabulous, but I wasn't much of a soloist. When Ransom Wilson and Richard Stoltzman approached me for solo pieces, instead I gave them *Vermont Counterpoint* and *New York Counterpoint* for multiple flutes or clarinets where they play one part and are in counterpoint with the live or prerecorded others; and that's worked out really well.

Rhythm in composition

At the beginning, basically my idea was that every change in my music was going to be rhythmic; there weren't going to be any changes of pitch or timbre. But then I wrote *Piano Phase,* which has changes in the lengths of pattern (first a twelve-note phrase, then an eight-note phrase, and finally a four-note phrase), *and* changes of *notes* in each pattern. But clearly the piece really develops primarily through *rhythmic means* in the changing unison canons or phases. *Violin Phase* has only one pattern and one timbre, but introduced resulting patterns – patterns which result from the interlocking of two, three, or four voice unison canons. In *Four Organs,* the notes and timbre stay the same but the durations gradually grow to enormous lengths. After that came the idea of the build-ups in *Drumming,* of substituting beats for rests or rests for beats in a repeating pattern to gradually create or gradually change a repeating pattern. *Drumming* takes one single rhythmic pattern, puts that pattern in constantly shifting unison canons, and then changes the pitches *and* the timbre from tuned drums to marimbas to glockenspiels to all of them together. *Drumming* was the last of the phase pieces and the end of that way of thinking. *Music for 18 Musicians,* for the first time, uses a harmonic ground plan to structure the whole piece, and of course that changed everything. Nevertheless, in the hour-long *Music for 18 Musicians,* the meter stays in that basic 3/2 = 6/4 = 12/8. Finally, in *Tehillim,* for the first time, the text spontaneously suggested constantly changing meters.

Overall, these rhythmic means have become kind of a vocabulary. I'll switch between 3/2 movements and constantly changing meter movements in many pieces like *The Desert Music, Sextet, You Are (Variations), Double Sextet, Radio Rewrite,* and others. Most importantly, I've spent a lot more time thinking about organizing the pieces harmonically.

Drumming

When I was a student at Juilliard back around 1959, there was a drummer by the name of Bobby Thomas. We had these lunchtime concerts, and at one of these concerts he played a percussion piece in which he had stand-mounted bongos he played with sticks. I don't remember what he played, but I remember the sticks on the bongos – WOW! So pitched, so loud, so clear! I thought, I'd like to do something like that, then I just completely forgot about it. Then more than ten years later, around 1970, I got the idea of doing *Drumming* with tuned drums and started thinking about how I could do it with bongos, stand-mounted and played with sticks.

As for the origin of the *Drumming* rhythm, I knew the African bell pattern, so it might have been related to that. I remember being on the

phone on speaker and drumming my fingers and it happened. It might have had something to do with the way the hands interlock in *Piano Phase*; I don't remember working it out. I remember working out the notes as it goes along, for sure. But the rhythm itself, I think, was one of those things that just *happened*. The symmetry of it was very attractive, and also the fact that the right hand was so completely divorced rhythmically from the left hand. Therefore, by using the appropriate notes in the right hand it would emerge, as it does, over and over again as a counter-rhythm.

When I was selecting the pitches for the bongos I wanted to make them as low as possible, but I began to realize that, just practically, on the lower drum of the bongos, if you went much lower than G# below middle C it was going to make a flabby drum sound and it wasn't going to stay in tune. So, it was a practical consideration about how deep you can make it and still count on a clear consistent pitch. As you know, bongos are usually tuned hard as a rock. So, with *Drumming,* the lowest note is the G# below middle C. It then came to me quickly that the other notes, A#, B, and C#, would be either G# Dorian, or finally, F# major. And once I established that tuning, then the range of the three-octave student marimbas was fine for the transition from bongos to marimbas. It also meant that the low point in the piece was going to be the bottom bongo, and that maintained itself.

I don't even know exactly when the light bulb went on for the marimbas, except I thought the piece ought to continue and marimba was the obvious choice. When I was playing the marimbas I heard the voices, I hallucinated the voices. Which meant that playing repeating patterns on marimba continuously produced acoustic by-products that sounded like women singing those notes. Soon, I invited Joan La Barbara, Jay Clayton, and Judith Sherman to try and sing and imitate those marimba melodies and it worked perfectly. As the piece grew, it finally required nine players to fill in all the patterns going up to the top of the three marimbas. Then, I realized that what was interesting was removing the lower notes and becoming harmonically more ambiguous by ending up on the upper part of the instrument, and that was the end of the marimba section. I then started thinking, "how high can you go?" And that's when I got the idea, "I might as well take this thing all the way up," – and that meant glockenspiels. Once I had this clarity, then I had the confidence to book the concerts in New York City at the Museum of Modern Art, Brooklyn Academy of Music, and Town Hall.

I began to realize that the key to this piece was *that one rhythmic pattern* which changed *notes* and changed *timbre.* I clearly remember that when I got into the glockenspiel section I realized I was left with these three *timbres,* and I began thinking, "I'm going to have to write a *finale,* an old style Western *finale.* I've got all these instruments in front of me, and I

invited all these people to dinner, and now I've got to serve dinner!" So, at the end it was very much a realization of a particularly Western obligation to put together these ingredients that I had dealt with independently. And I think, in a way, that moving forward from *Drumming* is really the beginning of moving back toward more traditional Western thinking.

The musical material in *Drumming* is so easy that you can pick it up very quickly. When I auditioned people to play in *Drumming,* I would try phasing with them. I could tell right away if they would work out or not. Even to this day, I find with pianists or percussionists who do *Piano Phase* or *Marimba Phase,* if they can perform the gradual phasing, everything else will work out.

We Americans are very pragmatic people. I think that's one of our great strengths as opposed to those interminable theoretical questions others get bogged down with. They think there's something hidden in the music: a coded philosophical message; fate knocking on the door. But, there's nothing hidden! What you hear is what you get. What you hear *is* the story, and that wordless story can be very deep.

Teaching *Drumming* by rote to members of my ensemble was the easiest way to get the music across rather than writing it out. The score came later, but first *ding a ding ding, ding a ding ding.* Then, as a very good player and a sensitive player, since playing the notes wasn't a challenge, you got into the feel of it. Then we would try playing it as a duet in canon. I discuss this a lot with people who ask about musicians in the ensemble and their backgrounds. I'm talking about you and Bob Becker in particular, but it holds for a lot of people in the group, a generation that more or less grew up at the same time. People like you and Bob had the qualifications, went to the right schools, achieved a very high level of excellence in Western percussion, and were ready to go into a major symphony orchestra. You could have had those jobs but chose instead to do advanced degrees in South and North Indian music and go in other directions.

Drumming and electronics[1]
Drumming is at the opposite extreme from electronics. (Unless you're playing an electronic drum set!) There seems to be a question of how deeply one can react to the sound of a machine. I used to think that the sound was the sound and that was that, and in a sense I still feel that way. But more and more as time passes, I feel that there is a limit as to how seriously I can take sounds made only by a machine. They may be something glorious, but there is something dubious about that glory. It doesn't have the emotional depth that instrumental sound has – and that may be why some formerly all electronic bands are reaching back to add acoustic instruments. But clearly, a drum is at the extreme end of the scale. It

represents the most primitive of musical instruments. The next step is simply to tune the drum and make it out of wood and one has a marimba or xylophone or make it out of metal and one has a bell or vibraphone or glockenspiel.

Music for Pieces of Wood

In composing *Music for Pieces of Wood,* I used the rhythmic pattern in *Clapping Music* and the next most primitive instruments – just tuned pieces of wood – tuned claves. I was composing exclusively with "build-ups" or substituting beats for rests. One of my rules of thumb was to try to avoid putting in the downbeat until near the end of the build-up, or actually at the end. That way the ambiguity would be heightened and then the next player would build up still another conflicting rhythm. Basically, the way I was working then was by overdubbing on tape. (That way of working is still the case today but now with the computer; I now play back using MIDI.) The basic pattern would be recorded and then I would add the next clave. What I would try to determine is: "What is the rhythmic distance between the voices? Is it one eighth away, is it two eighths away?" Certain things would recur; for example, three eighths away was frequently an interesting place to end up. Once I had established that rhythmic distance, I would decide on the most interesting note in the pattern to start the build-up and then the next note, and so on.

Six Pianos

Six Pianos began by just improvising at the piano and coming up with an alternating hand pattern. As I said, there was a long period of time when a lot of my pieces were in this all-purpose 3/2 = 6/4 = 12/8. And *Six Pianos,* spontaneously, because of the hand-alternation patterning that I came up with, was a 4/4 piece which I always thought was kind of a no-no. "Watch out, that's the meter that's going to really get bogged down." Because of the fact that it really worked, I felt particularly good about *Six Pianos.* It worked well even though it was in 4/4.

Tehillim

Tehillim is a *new rhythmic discovery. Tehillim* opens up a new chapter rhythmically, and one that was totally unforeseen. *Tehillim* is the Hebrew word for Psalms and means "Praises." It comes from the same root, *hey, lamed, lamed* as Hallelujah. When I set the first text "*hasha mayim* . . . The heavens declare the glory of G-d," I began to hear, as composers do, a melody in my head. This kind of association of music to words has probably been happening since people have been on the planet. When I said the opening line of *Tehillim,* a melody came to my mind, but at the

same time came, 1 2, 1 2 3, 1 2, 1 2 3, 1 2, 1 2 3. And I said, "what's that?" Well what that was, in terms of my personal background, was the Bulgarian rhythms in changing meters of Bartók and the changing meters of Stravinsky. These are the two composers that I heard who used rapidly changing meters. If I hadn't heard the music of Bartók and Stravinsky so many years earlier, I may not have heard those rhythms in my head. Nevertheless, for me it was a whole new rhythmic language and I assumed that it was the nature of Biblical Hebrew that was forcing me into this rhythmic feel. I thought, this is great, this is a whole different rhythmic approach. Instead of $3/2 = 6/4 = 12/8$, there was a constantly shifting group of twos and threes that might work out to a phrase like 7/8, 5/8, 6/8, 2/4, 5/8. Every bar was a new meter. Unfortunately, since *Tehillim* was my first piece using this rhythmic language, I wrote some very long bars with many groups of twos and threes because I got involved in trying to notate it in the way the melody actually went. Musically right, but difficult for conductors and string players who have to sit there counting threes and twos, but for a percussionist it's easy. The singers and woodwinds also seem to enjoy it since it spells out the melodic phrasing.

Speech rhythms

The use of speech rhythms in *Different Trains* was something new. *Different Trains* for the strings, on the one hand, goes back to my teenage drum studies. The locomotive was represented by paradiddles which came right out of the simplest hand-alternation pattern from way back in my first drumming books. But what was really new and interesting in *Different Trains*, of course, is the fact that the tempos are tied to speech samples. This produces music that constantly changes to an unrelated tempo, and this is something I had never done before. The way to solve that problem with live musicians was simply to have the prerecorded quartets make the tempo changes while the live players paused and then joined in when the new tempo was established. *Different Trains* is for three string quartets, one of which is live and the other two are prerecorded. The prerecorded quartets make the sudden changes in tempo, then the live quartet hears the new tempo and joins in.

In a still more difficult context, that is what happens in *The Cave* because there's less time spent with each speech fragment and more frequent changes of tempo. The idea of imitating the speaking voice with musical instruments is a totally different kind of rhythmic usage for me. It surely came out of my earlier tape pieces, *It's Gonna Rain* (1965) and *Come Out* (1966) where both pieces were made exclusively out of repeating loops

of prerecorded speech. The idea that tempo would change suddenly to an unrelated tempo is something that I never would have come up with if it hadn't been for my interest in using the speech samples. I felt that because of the things the people in *Different Trains* and *The Cave* were talking about – the holocaust and religious convictions – I couldn't just sit at my computer and change their tempos. I had to be the faithful scribe and go *with them,* because the speech is consciously a homage to *them.* I believe it really worked in those pieces. *The Cave* is a piece that *definitely* presaged a new kind of musical theater. I had been asked to do operas and I said, "thank you very much, but no." Finally, here was a way to go, and it came out of the idea of following speech melody. I was working in audio tape, but then I thought, what if it was video tape and you could see the interviewees and live musicians sitting right next to them? So, I approached the video artist Beryl Korot and she thought it might be interesting too. We made some tests, really liked them, and for the next three years or so we were off on field trips to Israel, the West Bank, Austin, TX, and then back to New York to record Israeli Jews, Palestinian Muslims, and Americans of all sorts answering our constant questions: "Who for you is Abraham, Sarah, Hagar, Ishmael, and Isaac?"

In *Three Tales,* I said, "let's put the music first. Now let's set the tempo and make the voices fit the music because the subject matter here allows that." Beryl wanted to use one screen instead of five because the technology had progressed so far allowing many images on one screen. Both decisions to keep the tempo constant and to use a single screen made *Three Tales* much more practical to stage and to make a DVD possible – and that is exactly what happened.

Musical intuition

All my compositional decisions are finally based on musical intuition. In the early days, I certainly had clear and firm ideas about making musical changes only through rhythm/duration, and *Piano Phase* and *Four Organs* are excellent examples of that. But in *Piano Phase*, there are three different sections set off by changes of duration – and notes! What are the new notes? Well, here comes a harmonic/melodic decision. In *Four Organs*, the pitches do not ever change in the E dominant eleventh chord, but the tones get longer and longer in duration in this strict musical process. Now, which tones, when, and how much longer in each bar? Musical intuition takes over to work out the exact details of the musical process.

Nobody can have enough technique or enough education, and everybody composes at whatever level they are on. But musical intuition seems

to me to be the real source, and that's just something that people are born with, although it certainly can develop. That's at the root of what I do; I don't think I'm really aware of it. After a while I just understand, "Aha, that's what I need to do."

Compositional style

I believe, although some people may argue, that there's a *huge* difference between pieces like *Piano Phase* and a piece like *Tehillim,* or between a piece like *Clapping Music* and a piece like *Proverb,* and so on. I have very often wanted to do something different because I get bored with what I'm doing, or a text will push me in some new direction, and I like that. I also realize that I may start working on a piece with pulsing pianos, and then, as a result of doing that, something new happens. Before beginning *You Are (Variations)*, I told myself, "let's just do something that's a pleasure and easy to do and see where it goes." As a result, it didn't go where any of my earlier pieces went at all. It started out sounding like other pieces and suddenly there was a big change. So you might say, "there's nothing new under the sun, but the combinations are endless."

Note

1. This paragraph on electronics is from Steve Reich's personal notebook housed at the Paul Sacher Stiftung in Basel, Switzerland, Sketchbook 4, (6/22/71), [p. 33].

Drum sets and drumming

14 In the pocket
How a drum set player grooves

PETER ERSKINE

The drummer's job in any ensemble boils down to providing rhythmic information to the band and listener while making the music feel good. *Groove* is a suitable one-word distillation of this job description. And while some players come upon the ability to groove naturally, most drummers must make a study of combining a number of skill sets to render music that is considered danceable, no matter the style. *The Oxford Dictionary* offers the following two definitions for the noun groove:

– an established routine or habit: *his thoughts were slipping into a familiar groove*
– a rhythmic pattern in popular or jazz music: *the groove laid down by the drummer and bassist is tough and funky*

and these two examples for groove as a verb:

– dance or listen to popular or jazz music, especially that with an insistent rhythm: *they were grooving to Motown*
– play popular music in an accomplished and stylish manner: *the rhythm section grooves in the true Basie manner.*

I'll admit to being more comfortable with "the Basie manner" versus "tough and funky," but you get the idea.

So a groove can be generated by a single musician, such as a drummer playing a beat, or by two or more musicians playing harmoniously in rhythm, for example, in a rhythm section. Let's look at the components of a *beat*. A drum beat is a succession of notes played in steady rhythm, or within a rhythmic framework, that generally form a pattern often repetitive in construct or nature. A beat works best within any given piece of music when the style of that beat is concordant with the genre, arrangement, or musical orientation of the band for any given song. The best musical results usually occur when a *bossa-nova* tune is given a *bossa-nova* beat, a funk tune is played with a funk beat, 4/4 swing with a jazz ride cymbal pattern, and so on. Genres can be mixed as well as matched, a concept I will explore later in this chapter.

The question, then, is: What defines a particular style? Any and every style of music is determined by the quality of the rhythmic subdivisions that occur within the primary pulses or meter of a piece of music. For example, most pop music employs a straight-eighth

subdivision, while funk utilizes the sixteenth-note subdivision as part of its feel. 4/4 jazz has a primary pulse of four quarter-notes to the bar, and each quarter-note pulse has a swung eighth-note subdivision. This is generally described as a triplet or bounce feel ... but this is where things get interesting.

By way of demonstration, imagine or sing a typical bebop melody or solo line to yourself. The Charlie Parker tune "Billie's Bounce" serves our purpose well (See Example 14.1).

Example 14.1 "Billie's Bounce."

Example 14.2 "Billie's Bounce," eighth-notes notated as dotted-eighth/sixteenth-note combinations.

Example 14.3 "Billie's Bounce," swung eighths notated as triplets.

Example 14.4 "Billie's Bounce," *legato* phrasing.

Are the written eighth-notes played or performed as dotted-eighth/ sixteenth-note combinations? (See Example 14.2).

. . . or triplets? (See Example 14.3).

or as straight eighth-notes (i.e., as written in Example 14.1)? . . .

OR as straight eighth-notes but played in a *legato* manner with (off-beat) accents? (See Example 14.4).

I submit that the most swinging or grooving rendering of the melody is achieved by employing this last approach. And when that more or less

Example 14.5 Ride cymbal triplet notation.

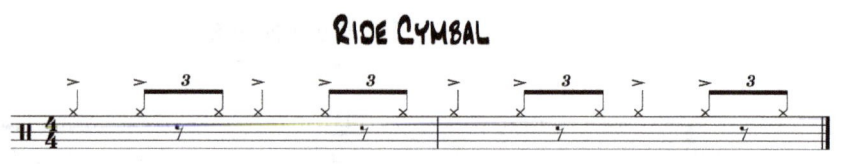

Example 14.6 Ride cymbal, tied quintuplet groupings.

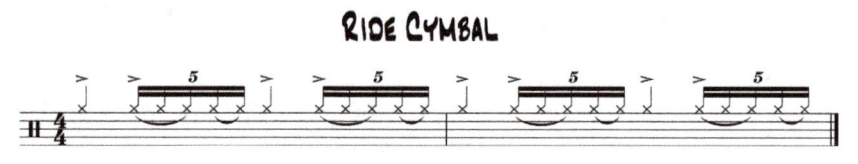

Example 14.7 Swing feel explanation.

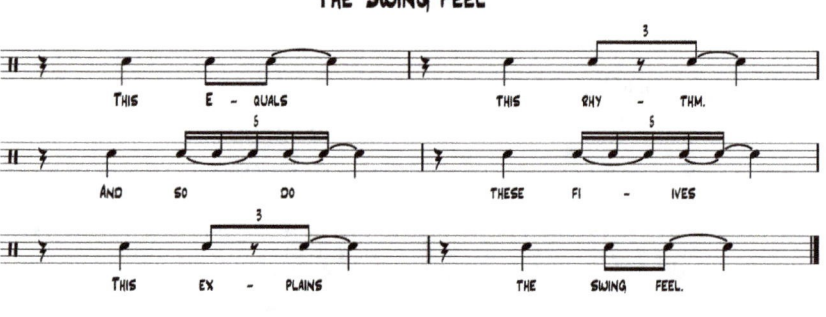

"straight" eighth-note feel is coupled with a drummer's triplet-feel ride cymbal pattern (see Example 14.5), ... the inherent tension and release creates an irresistible propulsion. It swings. "Groove," in other words.

Ah! But is the ride cymbal pattern *really* a triplet? This question has different answers, often depending on the tempo of a piece of 4/4 swing jazz, but for musicological purposes, let's notate this rhythm as accurately as possible (see Example 14.6).

Show me a drummer who visualizes their ride pattern in this manner and I'll show you a Vinnie Colaiuta. But even a rhythmic mastermind like Vinnie does not conceptualize or think of his ride cymbal pattern in so complex a fashion. The illustration is instructive, however. Successful musicians are guided by instinct more than anything else. *Feel.* A good drummer intuits whether or not a beat works for any particular piece of music, factoring in tempo and levels of density, dynamics, texture (i.e., what parts of the kit he or she is playing), and so on (See Example 14.7).

The rhythmic subdivision expressed by a musician is as revealing as a fingerprint left at the scene of a crime. It doesn't matter if the drummer is actually playing or articulating the subdivisions of any given style or genre of music – think of Jimmy Cobb's drumming on the Miles Davis album, *Kind of Blue*, where maestro Cobb plays a mostly quarter-note pulse during much of the material – as long as the drummer is thinking of the subdivisions to that music. This *singing to oneself* of the subdivisions actually makes the stark quarter-notes swing and groove, much more than if the drummer (or drum machine! More on that soon …) merely approached the quarter-note beat as, well, just quarter-notes. Subdivision awareness not only carves out the proper amount of space between each pulse, it also provides *intent*. Intention is a key element of swing or groove, pocket, or feel. We can't merely wish for the music to feel good; drummers must approach any piece of music in rhythmic context in order to groove.

By way of contrast, I submit that so-called disco or machine-made (computer-generated) music does *not* groove. Why? Because there is not enough air, or imagination, or craft, that is, humanity, or what we like to call *soul*. Repetition or consistency alone does not guarantee the best results, but subdivision awareness will.

Humans are not machines. But we do well not to *cheat the beat* when playing any piece of music, that is, rushing the open or empty spaces between the notes that are played. One secret to playing an R&B or pop groove is to sing or think of the backbeat as a *long* note, carrying all the way over to the next primary pulse; in other words, the backbeat is not a short or staccato sixteenth-note, but a lo-o-ong note. Try it!

Some of my personal favorite examples of groove are listed below, in no specific order:

> Steve Gadd "The Jealous Kind," from Joe Cocker's *Stingray* album
> Sonny Payne or Harold Jones with the Count Basie Band
> Papa Jo Jones with the Basie Band
> Sam Woodyard with the Ellington Orchestra
> Ed Thigpen with Oscar Peterson
> Fred Astaire or Gene Kelly dancing
> Mel Lewis with the Bill Holman, Gerry Mulligan or Marty Paich bands
> Motown recordings
> James Brown recordings

Most of these grooves are simple in nature, but they all share an important ingredient: the kinetic element. What is that? Power, and the power of surprise … all the more so because of the contrast to the relatively simple beat being played in good conscience and with focused intent. Complexity is fun, and I love Elvin Jones' drumming more than anything

else on earth when it comes to music, but the best grooves are a result of dedicated patience and crafted intensity: focused; surrendering to and serving the song; and simple. They are also all quite elegant. *Groove is the iron fist in the velvet glove.*

Historically, the drums provided a strong pulse in tandem with the band sprinkled by occasional syncopation occurring on the kit. This held true for early New Orleans jazz through swing-era drumming; any accents occurred within four- or eight-bar phrases for the most part. When bebop came along, pioneers such as Kenny Clarke began playing over-the-barline and *dropping bombs* (heavy accents) outside of the usual four- or eight-bar phrase, ending a fill on beat "two" of the new phrase, for example. All of this grooved, but it hinted at things to come. Post-bop drumming began involving more and more complex polyrhythmic devices, for example, Elvin Jones' and Tony Williams' drumming. Meanwhile, R&B and funk drumming began similarly to early jazz in which the drums maintained a steady groove without too much deviation or distraction. Ultimately, these types of music benefitted from the evolution of sophisticated additions to the beat, all of which, in both jazz and funk, began to beg the question, "What grooves the best?"

Intuition and common sense suggest that the best groove for any piece of music will occur when all of the musicians are thinking and feeling the rhythmic subdivisions alike, similar to a well-oiled machine where every component is in perfect synchronization. But music, like all art, depends upon counterpoint and the dynamics of tension and release to really flower or shine. And so it goes with some of the most interesting approaches to timekeeping.

As stated earlier in this essay, bebop lines are vertically constructed, generally with lots of eighth-note lines, but played or swung best in a horizontal, *legato*, manner. These eighth-notes are played in more of a duple manner than ternary or triplet feel, with emphases on the off-beat eighth-note. This, in itself, swings quite nicely, but there's an added element of kinetic energy when the drummer plays the ride pattern with a triplet feel. This "two-against-three" rub lies at the heart of jazz and all music that is derived from African drumming and rhythmic schemata.

Likewise, a swing beat that is played alongside or in conjunction with a Brazilian music style, like *samba* or *bossa-nova*, can groove as much as a purely derived Brazilian beat. This is the same with funk or pop, although it is an exception to the rule – and is certainly not to everyone's taste – but it is possible. The key element to sell any beat or rhythmic approach is that the drummer must take ownership of what he or she plays. Intent, along with authority, is very important in terms of groove. Tentative does not groove, in life or in music. So, while much of this music is improvised, and

Figure 14.1 Peter Erskine.

is thus in a constant state of spontaneous composition, there is an element of absolutism that is necessary for an ensemble to settle into or ride on top of a drummer's beat.

Key elements

Timekeeping, or grooving, is not a static thing. Improvisation is a key opportunity as well as an obligation for any drummer who wishes to contribute to the musical well-being of any enterprise. This accompaniment, used primarily while playing along with soloists but also during the melody of the tune, is known as *comping*. When an arrangement calls for tutti section setups or preparation, that is, *fills*, the drummer's role is normally more pronounced than when playing time, but ideally it all should groove.

Improvisatory play while timekeeping is best informed by the drummer being well versed in the vocabulary of any given style of music. Obvious examples include the quoting or calling upon of playing devices and choices made by such drummers as Sonny Payne or Harold Jones when performing a Count Basie big band chart. Or how better to play a James Brown tune than by quoting or emulating the drumming of Clyde Stubblefield or John "Jabo" Starks? The language of modern jazz drumming was developed by such bop-era drummers as Kenny Clarke, Max Roach,

Art Blakey, Philly Joe Jones, Jimmy Cobb, and Roy Haynes. Drummers *must* know much of this vocabulary if they want to play contemporary jazz.

The technical requirements to do this – beyond listening to the source of any style of music to be attempted – are simple enough for any drummer, but daunting to a non-drummer, as the simultaneous utilization of all four limbs in synchronous motion yet independent in terms of their specific or rhythmic chores can be found in few professions; playing the pipe organ in church or flying a helicopter readily comes to mind. Commonly referred to as *independence*, such four-limbed coordination is a staple of modern drumming. The first and most basic playing challenge is for drummers to be able to play the kit with any combination of their limbs in absolute rhythmic unison. This is simple enough when dealing with two limbs but can prove increasingly difficult as voices are added to a pattern or free-flowing expression of ideas while playing time, comping, or filling, that is, setting up an ensemble figure. Since drummers develop playing habits over time, it takes quite a bit of practice to overcome the tendency to play just what the hands and feet know. So, whether the goal is to keep a steady pattern going or to extemporize a rhythmic punctuation, drummers should be able to play what the music calls for or what they hear in their musical imagination. Next, then, is the ability to execute either linear expressions of rhythm or totally disparate rhythmic ideas that create good musical tension. If tension/release is recognized as the motor that keeps improvised music interesting, relevant, and fresh (and all contemporary music should involve improvisation whether soloing or not), then the intelligent use of contrapuntal rhythmic elements is desirable. Off-beat accents, counterpoint, and so on, in the style of the music while maintaining a good beat, are the hallmarks of creative drumming.

Such rhythmic devices can be played within the grain of the music, or *across the grain*. An example of playing within the grain of music is the following Sam Woodyard cross-stick pattern played while the ride cymbal and hi-hat (plus bass drum if the drummer is *feathering* the quarter-note pulse) maintain the beat (See Example 14.8).

Meanwhile, utilizing the same device but adding an across-the-grain rhythm in the style of Philly Joe Jones results in an irresistible bit of propulsion and adds a tremendous amount of fun to the beat (See Example 14.9).

Example 14.8 Sam Woodyard cross-stick pattern.

Example 14.9 Philly Joe Jones off-beat triplet.

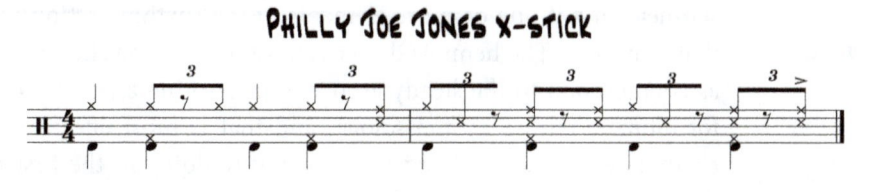

The release of the rhythmic tension springs the music forward. While not being quite the same as "the best thing about hitting my head against the wall is how good it feels when I stop," the effect is similar . . .!

Clarity is a key factor in all of this. Clarity is not just about sonic transparency. Clarity has much to do with *specificity*. A good, or grooving, drummer does not add such rhythmic clutter randomly. The grooving drummer is always listening to the music and interjects his or her comments in much the same manner as a well-placed "Uh-huh," "I see," or "You don't say?!" in a conversation. Imagine the musical equivalent to "I want to sue you!" while discussing the weather and you can easily imagine how many drum interjections can go tragically wrong when it comes to music.

Another key component to making all of this sound and feel good is the matter of balance. Drums are, by their very nature, instruments capable of producing a tremendous amount of sound – which is terrific on a battlefield or a football field, but not always so great in a piano trio on a concert hall stage. It is important that the drummer play in such a manner so that every instrument can be heard onstage as well as by everyone in the audience. Such ensemble balance is nearly impossible to achieve if the drum set is not in balance with itself, that is, if the bass drum is too loud or the drummer is always playing the snare drum with rim/head accents (more common than most drummers realize!). This takes a bit of touch, but it is all determined easily enough if the drummer truly listens to what is going on around him or her. There will be plenty of moments when the drums should stand out, but the majority of our playing time should be concerned with achieving a good blend with the other instruments or vocalist(s) in the ensemble.

Lest one think that all of drumming involves *playing well with others*, there are situations when it is best that drummer *not* play with others, at least in terms of imitative ideas. Jumping onto a soloist's motivic statements by replicating them in unison with the *other* is not always the best creative solution while accompanying them. By way of example: when a soloist begins to play an across-the-grain rhythm such as a hemiola, say, a series of dotted-quarter notes, he or she is most likely doing that because of

the steady groove or pulse being maintained by the rhythm section. It is self-defeating if one or more elements of the rhythm section jump onto that same idea. The hemiola device is most likely being chosen to function as counterpoint to the steady groove, thus creating a nice bit of tension-for-ultimate-release by the soloist, and that is most effective when the rhythm section keeps doing what they were doing in the first place. To illustrate this, I relate an experience I had while listening to the playback of the Weather Report album, *8:30 Live*.

> Meanwhile, here I am every night getting ready to play a duo with Wayne Shorter. Mind blowing! What am I doing up here playing with Wayne Shorter? Enjoying it, that's for sure. But I had a lot to learn. For example, Wayne would launch into a rhythmic figure while soloing, and I would hear it and then play it in unison with him. This occurs on the *8:30 Live* album that we made, and while mixing the album, it was just Joe Zawinul and me in the studio with the engineer listening. Joe is standing by these big speakers, I'm standing next to him and we're listening to the track. Wayne and I are playing on the tape and Joe turns to me and says, "Sounds good." I feel proud. Then, just at that moment, Wayne did this whole sequential ascending pattern thing, and I caught it. Zawinul hears that on the tape turns to me with a really sour look and said, "Uhm! Too bad you had to do that . . ."
>
> Later, during a rehearsal, Wayne stopped playing when I did the same thing again, and he said, "Don't do that." I began to understand that the role of the rhythm section is not to play in unison, but to provide the constant as well as the contrast, or counterpoint. So if the soloist starts playing syncopations, maybe you can do counter-syncopations as long as they don't get too busy. Or just keep doing what you're doing, because the soloist is cutting across the grain: that's what makes it cool. Imagine, the rhythm section is a bright blue background and the soloist cuts a brilliant red diagonal stripe across it, it makes no sense for us to turn red. Drumming for me is all about balance. You're balancing dynamically, but you're providing a counterweight to things, and if something is happening in the band, you're either providing a steady pulse or coming up with rhythmic counterpoint that makes the stuff dance.[1]

Another example of *advanced* grooving is when the drums maintain a steady rhythm but one or more of the musicians in the rhythm section change tempo. Sure, everyone can change tempo on a dime and that is fun and musically effective, but imagine the rhythmic tension when the bass begins to push or pull at the fabric of the time (tempo) while the drums maintain the steady tempo, or vice versa. This is a device with which bassist Marc Johnson and I liked to experiment, most notably in the trio we shared with guitarist John Abercrombie, or with Marc's band Bass Desires, with guitarists John Scofield and Bill Frisell; it's, admittedly, a "don't try this at home, kids" musical solution to an as yet unidentified musical problem.

Drum fills

What is a fill?[2]

A drum fill is a short solo that

1. is played in time
2. carries the music forward
   a. this could be while keeping time during a song
   b. playing *behind* (accompanying) a soloist
   c. playing between the band's written figures in an arrangement
3. is played in the style of the music
4. provides a musical groove
5. can provide excitement . . . plus the unexpected!

Drum fills can be simple or they can be complicated. Fills must be played in time with the rest of the music. The best drum fills provide enough rhythmic information to the rest of the band so that the other musicians can continue playing their best without getting nervous or wondering where the beat is. Fills are timekeeping deluxe. In short, drum fills are musical moments where the drummers can express their own personalities.

A drum fill will most always have a target or destination point. Getting there can be simple. The drummer may also play the sort of fill that is complex or completely unexpected. Which fills sound good or work the best? This is up to you, the drummer. The best way to know is to listen to enough music and drummers so you can decide what you would like to play.

Drum fills do not exist in a vacuum. An effective or good-sounding fill takes the music from where it has been to where it is going. We can practice fills on their own in order to work out and perfect the required stickings, hand, arm, and foot movements. But it's best to play fills in a musical context. It is within this context that you will best figure out what to play where. Whatever style of music you are playing, you can construct fills in one of the following three ways:

1. Play something you have heard another drummer play (and this is okay!).
2. Play something new.
3. Choose *not* to play a fill, and focus purely on the *time* for the moment.

Listening can teach us the most when it comes to (re)creating and playing fills. Some musical styles seem naturally to invite particular fills at a particular moment – so, whether your inspiration comes from Philly Joe Jones or Jeff Porcaro, the chances are great that their drumming ideas will serve you well.

Some timekeeping fills are like conversational chance takers. The drummer might not be sure how much space they have in which to

Example 14.10 Famous drum fills.

FAMOUS DRUM FILLS (SOLO BREAKS)

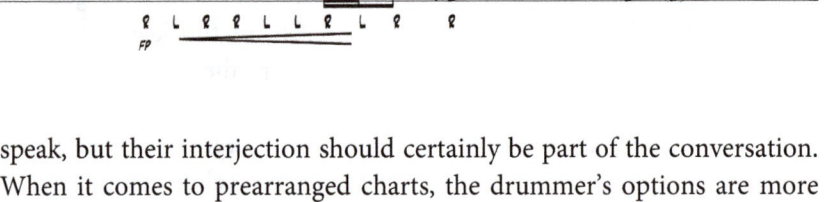

speak, but their interjection should certainly be part of the conversation. When it comes to prearranged charts, the drummer's options are more clear-cut: we can either play up until the next tutti entrance, for example, the downbeat or *target*, or the drummer can play through the figure, or over the bar line.

Here is a Top 4 list of famous drum fills – highly recommended listening (see Example 14.10 for notation of these fills):

1. Shadow Wilson's fill on the Count Basie recording *Queer Street*. Buddy Rich said of this fill: "This is the most perfect drum break ever recorded."
2. Buddy Rich's heart-stopping break on *Love for Sale* ("Big Swing Face," 1966); super-human single strokes for three bars, and then one second of silence.
3. Tony Williams' fills on *Seven Steps to Heaven* (from Miles Davis' "live" album, *Four & More*); bebop vocabulary turned upside down and inside-out.
4. The signature Motown drum fill; perfect for the song, every time.

Four Questions

1. Should we also be aware of the relative dynamics of the music when we play a fill? Should the fill be played loud or soft?
2. Is there a difference between the type of fill that occurs during or between an ensemble's musical phrases and a fill that occurs all on its own without any other instruments playing? What's the difference between a *fill* and a *solo*?
3. What kind of inner dynamics can we utilize in a fill? In other words, how many accents should we add to a rhythm, and where?
4. When playing time, how often should we fill?

Four Answers

1. If we are truly listening to the music we are playing, then we are aware of the relative dynamics, and we would honor and observe these dynamics. I call it *meeting the energy of the style of music* that we are playing. The use of loud or soft can have a musically dramatic effect, and contrast can be a good idea. Short answer: Use your ears.

2. Short answer: Everything is timekeeping, and it is all music! Longer answer: A fill is much like the next step you take when walking, while a solo is more like doing a tap dance. Whether you choose to add the juggling of flaming bowling pins to the routine is up to you.

3. Notes without accents are like syllables or words without inflection (or like food without spice). In other words, boring. Accents bring music to life and give shape to musical phrases. Just like all of the other drumming decisions you will be making when you play, listening and experience will be your best guides. Personally, getting the *flavor* just right has become the most interesting thing about drumming. Your fills will just keep getting better, trust me.

4. A few years ago, I asked Brazilian pianist Eliane Elias to provide a quote for my first instructional book. Her contribution was "Don't play a fill every two bars." Good advice!

Please remember: as far as other musicians are concerned, timekeeping is the most important part of drumming. Always play in such a way that will make the other musicians sound better. Your fills should help create a comfortable *and* exciting musical zone, as there will be times when you will need to bring in players who have been waiting to play (e.g., during a long solo section). Because their instruments might be cold or their attention level not at 100 percent, this would not be a good time to play a lead-in figure that is confusing.

Fills can be played in-between ensemble figures as stand-alone statements. This type of filling is commonly referred to as *playing the holes*. Embellishments can add some nice color and shape to a fill. Practice makes perfect. Better than preplanning which hand to place where on the kit (e.g., when to play a double-stroke in order to easily move from one part of the kit to another), you will want to create your own stickings on the fly.

Groove as melody

Speaking of stickings, a groove can be a melody played on the drum(s). One of the biggest challenges in playing a groove, that is, a flowing musical statement, can be when the cymbals are more or less removed from the game and the drummer is left to his or her own devices on, let's say, a snare drum. Short of changing the tension of the drumhead (like a timpani), how do we play or best infer melody *and* groove?

Example 14.11 "Billie's Bounce," w/stickings.

The answer is in using dynamics and creative stickings. Dynamics imply melodic shape, while stickings help to create and promote a sense of flow not possible with alternate right–left–right, and so on, sticking alone. By way of example, I conclude this chapter by bringing "Billie's Bounce" back into the discussion. Please note the stickings: the top note of each phrase is played by the dominant hand (in this case, assuming the drummer's right hand) and accented accordingly, much in the same way a horn player will naturally emphasize the top note of a phrase. Such stickings, employing the use of well-placed doubles here and there and creating *diddles*, allow for a *legato*, swinging and grooving bit of music-making (See Example 14.11).

Whether playing a beat, a fill, or a solo, the musical and musically valuable drummer will strive to groove in all matters musical ... play in the style of the music ... know the subdivisions ... speak the language and use the vocabulary ... own the tempo. All of this has to do with grooving. It's a good way to go through life.

Groovy, baby.

Notes

1. This story is taken from: P. Erskine, *No Beethoven: Autobiography & Chronicle of Weather Report*, R. Mattingly (ed.) (Emeryville, CA: Alfred Music, 2013).

2. The description of drum fills is adapted from: P. Erskine, *Essential Drum Fills* (Van Nuys, CA: Alfred Music, 2008).

15 The "Funky Drummer" break
Ghost notes, timbre, and popular music drumming

STEVEN F. POND

"Eighty percent of what the audience hears should be the bass drum and the [snare drum] backbeats on 2 and 4," advises longtime funk drummer and educator Jim Payne. "The softer ghost notes should be added without disrupting the basic groove. When you can do that, you've got it right."[1] Instruction manuals, recordings, and online lessons on funk drumming often offer pointed guidance on incorporating "ghost notes" into the mix. Barry Kernfeld broadly defines a ghost note as "a weak note, sometimes barely audible, or a note that is implied rather than sounded."[2] In the hands of an expert funk drummer, like the influential James Brown alumni Clyde Stubblefield and John "Jabo" Starks, session drummers Bernard Purdie and Steve Gadd, David Garibaldi of Tower of Power, or Mike Clark of The Headhunters, ghost notes become key expressive elements in establishing and propelling a groove.[3] Although one can think of them, simply, as faintly heard notes, primarily on the snare drum, as contrasted with main accented hits, ghost notes also function in two important ways: they add appoggiatura-like articulations that inflect an accented note in a groove, thereby adding musical emphasis to the accented note; and they fill sonic space, in interaction with the other instruments within the drum kit and the other instruments in the band, adding to the overall emotional punch of the music.

Funk drummers are also attentive to their instruments' timbral possibilities. These include drum tuning techniques that incorporate both tone and resonance, choices of cymbals for a variety of noise effects, stick techniques that add a wide variety of sounds, and drum tuning techniques attentive to both tone and resonance, for example, Stubblefield's attraction to a high-pitched snare drum "pop."[4] Mark Katz muses, "Imagine the 'Funky Drummer' break played with brushes instead of sticks. Or plucked on a harp. Not so funky anymore."[5] Katz's provocative thought experiment calls attention not merely to Clyde Stubblefield's (syncopated) rhythm, but also to the *sound* of one of funk's most emblematic (and most sampled) breaks, an eight-measure segment from James Brown's 1970 single, "The Funky Drummer."[6]

Using the "Funky Drummer" break to illustrate, this essay, although brief, addresses two entwined interests: the ways that drummers use

"ghost notes" and the ways they exploit the drum kit's available timbres. Together, ghost notes and timbral play add texture and, in the process, contribute vibrantly toward an affective setting.[7] What is it about ghost notes that help to propel a groove, break, or fill?[8] What is it about the *sound* of the drums that conveys excitement or nostalgia or awe? How does the interaction of the drums' sounds in funk (and rock),[9] and their reproduction for recordings or their setting in live performance, affect the sound of the whole, and how do these sounds drive emotional meanings in the song?

The "Funky Drummer" break and funk aesthetics

One of the many bloggers who extol the "Funky Drummer" break, SameOldSean retells the story of Brown setting it up with Stubblefield on the spur of the moment. "You don't have to do no soloing, brother. Just keep what you got," Brown exclaims on the recording. "And 45 seconds later, Stubblefield does just that. Everyone drops out, and perhaps the most famous eight bars in the history of funk begin."[10]

Why the instruction to do no soloing? David Garibaldi, outlining twelve key aesthetic considerations for funk drummers, emphasizes that "the dynamic of the jazz tradition is improvisation and the dynamic of the funk tradition is orchestration" and that for a funk groove "everybody has a defined role"; the crucial element is how it "all locks together."[11] A basic funk tenet is stability; nothing should be allowed to interrupt or confuse the rhythmic flow. Garibaldi's desideratum for funk drummers is to play "no fills. Zero. None. Have the discipline to lay one groove for the length of the song while resisting the temptation to 'make it better' by playing a fill. It's unnecessary."[12] His admonition echoes comments about playing behind James Brown by "Jabo" Starks, interviewed with Stubblefield: "We never used the toms. Never, for nothing. And it's amazing. I kept wondering why we had these drums up here."[13]

Yet, without intruding on the dance rhythm, by the five-minute mark of "The Funky Drummer" Stubblefield's ostinato has morphed from the much simpler version at the beginning of the song. That groove features closed hi-hat clicks on every sixteenth-note and shifts the expected kick drum hits on beats *one* and *three* by an eighth-note (thereby recasting them as anacrusis notes, setting up beats *two* and *four*). On snare drum, Stubblefield doubles the accented staccato horn hits in beats *two* and *four* (2-*ee*-rest-*ah*).[14] Over the course of three minutes, Stubblefield's groove adds a ghost note here, a crushed left-handed roll there, fueling a barely discernable, rising tension – a tension not fully grasped until a brief

digression by the band to B-flat brings back the introductory tag to reset the song in C, the horn riff now a negative image of the opening one, focusing attention on the *one* beat (3:12): ah-*one*-and. But now, with space granted by the more sparse horn hits, the drum pattern becomes more complicated,[15] soon settling into the pattern that will become the break at 5:22. Stubblefield's break pattern respects but extends the contours of his groove at the song's beginning: the missing *one* landing is now solidly supplied by the kick drum, the hi-hat cymbals are opened at the second sixteenth of beat *two* to create a *shhhT* response to the snare drum's rim-shot call; and ghost notes, both faint single strokes and left-hand crush rolls, fill the spaces primarily in beats *three* and *four*.[16] Those "ghost" notes, small *sotto voce* articulations between the accented notes, do two jobs at once: they interact with the hi-hat's *shhhT* and the kick drum notes to form a groove matrix. At the same time, they interact with the accented snare "pops" – a self-contained call-and-response cycle.

The break, then, as an elaboration of the earlier basic groove, evolves so subtly over several minutes as to seem unchanged. The incremental additions keep the important, accented notes at the forefront, the ghost notes and open hi-hat hits filling any sonic vacuum. Boiling underneath the rest of the band, the effect is as if it were a protracted, minutes-long crescendo – although the overall volume has not changed – and the sudden falling away of all distractions to the drum pattern as the break begins lends a sense of arrival, a move which should resolve the building tension. Yet, the break doubles down on the groove's rhythmic intensity.

Sounding funky

The rhythmic intensity in the "Funky Drummer" break would drive its adoption by hip hop DJs and producers as the can't-miss command to dance. The break's rhythmic intensity barely masks an underlying sexual tension.[17] Andrew Ward articulates the perhaps unnecessary point that "dance itself is not just a means to sex … it is or can be a form of sexual expression in itself." Beyond the notes themselves, the enveloping *presence* of the drums adds to the rhythmic urgency of the moment. Brown intones, "Ain't it funky? Ain't it funky?" but he might just as well be saying, "Ain't it sexy?" The "Funky Drummer" break's sound encompasses several elements – a "dry," tight click of the hi-hat, an equally dry thud of the kick drum interacting with the tautly tuned snare drum, that drum's sound itself suffused with a significant wash of ambient reverberation (reverb). As a whole, the isolated drum break, embellished only by Brown's vocal interjections and a close-miked,

barely audible whisper by one of the band members, possesses great power to get dancers sweaty on the floor.

The reverb sound, mapped onto the played notes, leads the listening-dancer into a subliminal, visceral setting, a combination of intimacy and spectacle.[18] The drum sounds' mixture of the "dry" and resonant offers a subliminal clue. Whether tied directly to space, as in the distance implied in an echo seeming to traverse a certain distance or as psychic distance such as memory – figuratively an echo of the past – any of these contexts will add emotional weight to a sound.

Peter Doyle has written about the mental pictures we construct with echo and reverb effects, the connotations of "place" and "space," whether physical space or an abstraction of "disordered" space.[19] To hear a recording – especially as an audio experience, without the visual cues that a video or "live" performance would offer – is to place oneself within an imagined environment. That reverb helps us imagine a sizeable room, a hall, even if the other elements of the sound – the dry hi-hat clicks, the nonresonating thud of the kick drum – give us a conflicting message. The overall effect places the listener and the drummer in a good-sized hall, the listener sitting (or dancing) in intimate, privileged, proximity to the action. Beyond the image of "real" – that is, imagined – space, Doyle points to record production's and cinema's use of reverb to signal interiority, of voices' "magicality and potency rather than that of their placement within a putative literal field."[20] In the case of the "Funky Drummer" break, the "voice" becomes the reverberant sound of the snare drum.

Along with space, echo and reverb connote time, in two related ways. In one sense, the subliminal calculation of space mentioned above joins with a similar calculation of time. If, say, the entire drum groove had been awash with a uniform echo, my mental image might place me in the same hall, but farther away from the drums, my brain calculating the distance by means of the time it takes between the initial hit and the echoed one, and the duration of its continued reverberation. The emotional weight of my position in this imaginary space might be analogous to being in a cavernous baroque cathedral pew and hearing a chord played on an organ. I may be impressed, even awed, by the grandeur of the cathedral setting and my relative insignificance to the whole, but not by its intimacy.[21] Moreover, other modes of entertainment exert influence: the cinematic convention of using echoes to convey dreamlike states, transitions to flashbacks and the like has trained listeners to associate the device with a certain gravitas.[22]

A drummer who has played on a practice pad knows the slightly frustrating sensation of hitting the pad – even full force – and receiving the sound of a quiet "click" in response. The tradeoff between gaining the reliable feedback about note placement from a stream of clicks (Are the

individual notes discernable and accurately timed?) and getting very little feedback about dynamics and tone makes practicing with a pad excellent for mastering certain rudimentary figures and nearly useless for developing subtleties of sound production. To return to Mark Katz's thought experiment, imagine the "Funky Drummer" break played on the same hi-hat and kick drum – and a practice pad. Not so funky anymore. The snare drum's reverberation implies physical space but also conveys emotional authority. With his crisply played hi-hat, kick drum, and snare drum pattern – pointedly with the intricately placed ghost notes – Stubblefield's affective target is not grandeur, but control, a space between display and intimacy, a space to lose oneself in the erotics of dance.

Offered a solo moment, Stubblefield constructs the drum pattern to fill the sonic (as well as the physical and emotional) space. Or rather, he does so pointillistically, placing a note on every sixteenth-note within each four-beat measure. We require the snare drum's reverberation to gauge the imaginary hall; but with no visual cues before us – the arc of his arm moving to the cymbal or drumhead, the force of his strike – how will we tell how loudly Stubblefield is playing? Hip hop deejays and producers sampling the break have sought to make the drum sound unambiguously hefty.

Low-end theory after "The Funky Drummer"

The "Funky Drummer" break has become one of the most sampled drum patterns in hip hop, appearing hundreds, and maybe thousands, of times on record (to say nothing of its use on the dance floor by live DJs).[23] Stubblefield joined James Brown's band in 1965; "The Funky Drummer," recorded in 1969 and released in 1970, reflects Brown's proto-funk of the late 1960s, even as it points to the JBs band that would be formed a few months hence. This was at the tail-end of a period in which AM car-radio airplay could be assumed to be point of delivery for funk or any other style of popular music.

The recent availability of mainstream high-fidelity home stereo components, and FM radio airplay playable on the new systems, was causing large-scale changes in pop music aesthetics.[24] Speakers capable of handling a much wider range of low to high frequencies, previously targeted exclusively to high-priced "high-fidelity" aesthetes, had hit the market in the early 1960s, and by now young consumers found the bookshelf-scaled components affordable.[25] By mid-decade, *Billboard* included a regular feature on "Audio Retailing" that tracked new products and sales trends.[26] Where routine studio practice before had called for a final mix to be done using cheap speakers as a reference for home record players and car AM

radios, now the end-user for records gradually could be assumed to listen on a much fuller range stereo.

At roughly the same time, Ringo Starr (aided considerably by recording engineer Geoff Emerick)[27] began to make significant, and highly influential, changes to the sound of his drum kit[28] tuning his tom-toms lower, with looser heads, and choosing cymbals with dark, slow-developing sounds. Recording practices now emphasized the lower frequencies,[29] starting a trend by Starr toward a lower sound, especially on kick drum and tom-toms. These alterations accompanied changes in his playing style, now with much sparer fills, and the combination sent aesthetic ripples through the ranks of drummers everywhere.

In his earlier groove style, Steven Baur points out, Starr would play a sixteenth-note ride pattern on hi-hat cymbals slightly opened to create a "shrill, pulsating" wash of sound approximating the wall of screams from the group's fans – the sound of frenzy. Now, both in grooves and in fills at the ends of phrases, Starr would allow plenty of space for the sound of the low tom-tom notes, and the dark cymbals, to develop and blossom, while also leaving room for the increasingly busy production additives (horns, orchestras, effects, and all).[30] The Beatles' massive popularity, and the groundbreaking approach to record production, especially from *Revolver* onward, guaranteed that drummers would be aware of the new sound, and a domino-effect movement toward deeper and deeper sounding bass drums and tom-toms ensued, coincident with more responsive home stereos to play them on, over the next several decades. To me, the aesthetics of *Revolver* and "The Funky Drummer" coincide at the point of their attentiveness to sound and to sound's affective possibilities. The two drummers focus their playing styles to fill (or contrariwise, to leave spare) sonic space, and their recordings reflect, in their final mixes, changes in how they would be heard by their assumed audiences; the aggregation of these strategies helps to drive the songs' emotional impact.

"The Funky Drummer" was used so often in the 1980s and 1990s, the "golden age" of sample-based hip hop, that it became symbolic, a historical reference to that age as well as to its original moment, and is no longer used "straight."[31] And yet, funky as it is, the "Funky Drummer" break, even at the height of its use in hip hop sampling, hasn't been used in isolation, left to stand on its own. Instead, latter-day hip hop producers who adapt the break have paid special attention to fattening the bass drum sound, layering additional, deeper pitches over the tenor-sounding bass drum played by Stubblefield, while retaining the clipped hi-hat and high-pitched snare drum sound largely intact.[32]

From its earliest days, hip hop deejays and producers have fixated on the emotional power and impact of low-end frequencies. DJ Kool Herc,

one of the progenitors of hip hop, made his name on the power of his sound system's ability to pump out more bass volume than his competition, an imperative he absorbed as a teenaged fan of massive "sound systems" in Jamaica's reggae scene. Similarly, the mid-1980s rise of the Miami Bass style conjoined America's car culture and bass fetishes: the "cars that go boom."[33] The bass – especially bass guitar and bass (or kick) drum – holds a key place in hip hop aesthetics.[34]

Yet, Stubblefield's kick drum is tuned relatively high, and the recording makes no gesture toward favoring the low end. His "busy" playing on the "Funky Drummer" break – amid the snare drum's reverberation on the recording – fills the sonic void and adds crucially to the break's excitement, but also provides a perhaps inadvertent opportunity for hip hop producers to adapt the break to their own ends.

This can be heard, for example, in "The Funky Drummer" as it appears in Public Enemy's landmark "golden age" hit, "Rebel Without a Pause." Here, the Bomb Squad (the production team of Hank and Keith Shocklee, Chuck D, Eric "Vietnam" Sadler, and Gary G-Wiz) use the "Funky Drummer" break as a basic ostinato, but with two prominent enhancements: a much deeper, louder kick drum sound overlaying Stubblefield's original notes, and an electronic "science fiction" keening glissando sound, very high pitched, and prominent in the mix.[35] By contrast, now the "Funky Drummer" break is somewhat folded into the overall sound, reinforced by a deep, booming kick drum and a distinct echo in the rapping voice. Now we have a purchase on the volume – and the urgent emotion – of the piece, regardless of the volume knob on our playback device.

The deep, conspicuous bass frequency – often matched with a high-pitched sound – asserts physical, but also economic, power. From hip hop's earliest days, it was important to be LOUD. DJ Kool Herc famously had the loudest sound system around and would roundly out-volume his competition. Much of that volume came from his massive bass speakers. Simply put, the stuff was both overwhelming and expensive – it conferred emotional power even as it displayed the financial and technical wherewithal to acquire it.

Conclusion

The world of popular music has become filled with a dizzying proliferation of genres, subgenres, and hybrids, adherents often stridently distinguishing each from the other. (How many variants of Techno are there? Of Ambient? Of Hardcore? Of Hip Hop?) Yet, a few overarching aesthetic approaches stretch across wide variations of tempo, groove, harmony,

lyric, vocality, and associated dance styles, regardless of the actual notes played (or, given the dominance of the synthesizer and sampler, "played"). All are discernable through Stubblefield's ghost-note-laden drumming on "Funky Drummer," his snare drum's reverberant sound, and the break's further appropriation by others: an attraction to filling sonic space, to using loud/soft articulations to convey space and time, to plumbing ambient sounds for their physical and emotive associations, and to pushing the limits of frequency ranges especially at the low end, all in the service of maximum aural – and affective – impact.

Notes

1. J. Payne, "Advanced Funk Drumming in Depth, Part 1: Four Types of Ghost Notes," *Modern Drummer* (December 2009), 76.

2. B. Kernfeld, "Ghost Note," in B. Kernfeld (ed.), *The New Grove Dictionary of Jazz*, 2nd ed., Grove Music Online/Oxford Music Online (Oxford University Press).

3. For ghost note techniques as extensions of snare drum rudiments, see instruction videos by S. Gadd, for example: "Steve Gadd: The Fills in 'AJA' – Ratamaques [sic]." See also J. Wald, "The 'Gadd Flutter Lick' – The Classic Steve Gadd Ghost Note Drum Lick - Recorded with Zoom Q4."

4. Stubblefield's high-pitched snare drum sound is also prized by David Garibaldi, who considers his own version of it to be fundamental to his sound. For Garibaldi's snare drum tuning techniques, see "David Garibaldi's 12 Funk Drumming Tips: The Tower of Power Legend Leads a Masterclass in Making It Funky," *Rhythm Magazine*, 23 (July 2012).

5. M. Katz, *Groove Music: The Art and Culture of the Hip-Hop DJ* (Oxford University Press, 2012), p. 25.

6. Recorded November 20, 1969 and released March 1970 under the King label. Reissued on *James Brown: 1970's Funk Classics*, Universal/Collectibles 8412, (2004).

7. I use "affective" in the sense of expressing emotion. This is not to claim that ghost notes and timbre are the sole components of funk drumming. For an additional discussion of funk drumming style, see S. F. Pond, "Laying Down a Funk Groove," in *Head Hunters: The Making of Jazz's First Platinum Album* (University of Michigan Press, (2010 [2005]), pp. 66–78. For dancers' feedback as funk authentication, and as improvisatory participants with the groove, see Pond, "'Chameleon' Meets *Soul Train*: Herbie, James,

Michael, Damita Jo, and Jazz- Funk," *American Studies*, vol. 52, no. 4 (2013), 125–40.

8. I deploy these terms to clarify the kind of pattern being discussed at any given time, rather than to attempt to define them categorically. "Groove" in particular defies consensus in the literature. In this essay, "groove" refers to a regular ostinato pattern underlying much, if not all, of a song. A groove may be distributed among several instruments – and in the case of the drum kit, across several tonal ranges and timbres – in what I have called a "'groove matrix" (Pond 2010), 66–78. A "fill" is a quasi-soloistic figure, often bridging the end of a phrase with the arrival of the next, but it can also be played to thicken the overall sonic texture or to fill a momentary sonic opening. A "break" often hits a mid-point: the drummer plays alone for an extended moment (usually several measures), but generally – as opposed to a fill – keeps to a stable pattern, albeit a more openly virtuosic one than the groove.

9. I am using these terms broadly, to encompass many styles of rock, hip hop, and electronic dance music (EDM), all of which sample, adapt, or recreate the approach to timbre and sonic space I investigate here.

10. SameOldSean, 'These Are the Breaks' – The History of the Backbeat," blog entry, 11 (February 2014)

11. Garibaldi (2012).

12. *Ibid.*

13. Starks and Stubblefield with Lawrence, *ibid.* More generally in the context of James Brown's funk music of the time, Clyde Stubblefield discusses the genesis of his approach to groove in a demonstration-interview with Marly Marl: "Clyde Stubblefield/Funky Drummer" (2008).

14. The groove saunters along in a stable C tonality, although the bass gestures to the subdominant F on beat *four* with a cadential

arrival on the tonic C at the next downbeat; the gesture reinforces the simultaneous sense of stability and arrival at each new measure.

15. For a brief discussion of funk groove as analogous to the two-part construction of clave (one half featuring rhythmic clash, the other resolution), see Pond (2010), 72.

16. For a transcription of the break – which, however, does not distinguish between accented notes and ghost notes – see SameOldSean, *ibid.* For an excellent tutorial on playing the break, with attention to ghost notes, see Sacha K, "How to Play the Funky Drummer Beat (James Brown)," SchoolofMusicOnline.com (June 30, 2012).

17. A. H. Ward, "Dancing in the Dark: Rationalism and the Neglect of Social Dance," in H. Thomas (ed.), *Dance, Gender and Culture* (New York, St. Martin's Press, 1993), p. 22. Ward echoes Curt Sachs, who argues that sexuality "can never really be extricated from dance, since the sex act itself may be considered as the ultimate form of dance," C. Sachs, *World History of the Dance*. B. Schonberg (trans.), (1937), cited in M. H. Nadel and D. Kutschall, "Dance and Sexuality," in V. L. Bullough and B. Bullough (eds.), *Human Sexuality: An Encyclopedia* (New York: Routledge, 2013 [1994]), p. 161.

18. "Musical experience forces an encounter between mind and body, clearing a liminal space that is simultaneously charged with affect and fraught with tension," D. R. DeChaine, "Affect and Embodied Understanding in Musical Performance," *Text and Performance Quarterly*, vol. 22, no. 2 (April 2002), 81.

19. P. Doyle, *Echo and Reverb: Fabricating Space in Popular Music Recording, 1900–1960* (Middletown, CT: Wesleyan University Press, 2005), p. 2.

20. *Ibid.*, pp. 113–14.

21. Doyle explores how the baroque cathedral's "long reverberations echo the workings of political power, spiritual authority, human sociality and individual transcendence all at once." *Ibid.*, p. 45.

22. Doyle points to these, but in exclusively spatial terms, even when "space" is construed as a psychic space. To me, the evocation of time is also significant, as I have suggested here, although a full discussion is not possible in this essay.

23. For excellent discussions of groove construction, hip hop aesthetics, and rhetoric, see J. G. Schloss, *Making Beats: The Art of Sample-Based Hip-Hop* (Wesleyan University Press, 2004); R. Walser, "Rhythm, Rhyme and Rhetoric in the Music of Public Enemy,"

Ethnomusicology, vol. 39, no. 2 (1995), 193–217.

24. For a discussion of the importance of FM "free form" radio in the late 1960s and 1970s, see Pond (2010), pp. 173–74.

25. Prominent among these were three-way "bookshelf" speakers manufactured by Acoustic Research. "Acoustic Research Posts Peak Year," *Boston Globe*, (December 18, 1965), p. 21. The term "three-way" indicates the number of speakers in each cabinet: woofer (bass), mid-range, and tweeter (high).

26. See, for example, "Scanning the News" *Billboard*, 78–9, 54: "The electronic home entertainment industry will hold its first national exhibition for the trade in 1967 and annually thereafter."

27. The Beatles, *Rubber Soul*, Capitol B 1970702 (CD reissue, 2014 [1965]. The Beatles, *Revolver*, Capitol B 1970902 (CD reissue, 2014 [1966]). Emerick became (at nineteen) the Beatles' lead recording engineer with *Revolver*.

28. Ringo Starr's contribution to the sound of the Beatles was fundamental and important, but remains largely unexamined in popular music scholarship. One excellent exception is S. Baur, "Ringo Round *Revolver*: Rhythm, Timbre, and Tempo in Rock Drumming," in R. Reising (ed.), *"Every Sound There Is:" The Beatles' 'Revolver' and the Transformation of Rock and Roll* (Aldershot: Ashgate, 2002), p. 82. Additionally, there exist several discussions of Starr's style on the Internet. See, for example, R. Pagano, "How to Drum Like Ringo Starr – Later Years" (October 23, 2012).

29. Emerick retrospectively demonstrates his approach to the new drum sound – and other sounds in the studio – as he works with The Fab Faux to recreate the Beatles' "And Your Bird Can Sing." R. Pagano adds discussion on Starr's drum tuning. See "The Fab Faux Take a Lesson from Geoff Emerick" (January 17, 2008), www.youtube.com/watch?v=Z6Kyf9wjZc4, esp. 1:38 – 2:25, 3:20 – 4:02.

30. Baur's excellent article goes into more detail than is possible here (174–75).

31. Stubblefield's drum break has become iconic, to the point where no producer today would venture to use the sample without a highly creative approach to altering it, Signifyin(g) on the original as well as its historical uses and contemporary competing versions. See Schloss, p. 36. For Signifyin(g) as a rhetorical strategy, see H. L. Gates, Jr., *The Signifying Monkey: A Theory of African-American Literary Criticism* (Oxford University Press, 1988).

32. *It Takes a Nation of Millions To Hold Us Back*, Def Jam, 1127298 (2014 [1987]).

33. The car-bass connection is captured in L'Trimm's 1988 hit, "The Cars That Go Boom," www.youtube.com/watch?v=okg3UN-GH51.

34. Several scholars have commented on this. For example, Tricia Rose connects the low register with core affective aesthetics: "Rap music centers on the quality and the nature of rhythm and sound, the lowest, 'fattest beats' being the most significant and emotionally charged." T. Rose, *Black Noise: Rap Music and Black Culture in Contemporary America* (Wesleyan University Press, 1994), pp. 64–65. William Jelani Cobb joins the Bronx-based early hip hop aesthetic with the "pavement rattling Miami Bass sound," as "hail[ing from] early days of the music in that the MC's lyricism was purely secondary to the intensity that the deejay/producer was putting down." W. J. Cobb, *To the Break of Dawn: A Freestyle on the Hip Hop Aesthetic* (New York University Press, 2007), p. 53.

35. Hip hop recordings of the time routinely included a high-pitched sound. In addition to its potential affective load, a very high-pitched note, whine, or ting gave the ear a means to calibrate the contrast between high and low, adding even more emotional weight to each end of the frequency spectrum.

16 Way beyond wood and skin
Drum sets, drumming, and technology

JEFF PACKMAN

It is not unusual to hear drums discussed and even disparaged in terms that evoke the fundamental and even primitive in music.[1] They seem ubiquitous across time and cultures and are based on what appears to be a simple concept – a resonant body is struck to produce a sound, no electronics or much else seems to be needed. Closer consideration, however, paints a different picture. As drum historian Matt Dean notes, preparing a membrane and securing it to a resonating body with enough tension to produce a pleasing sound when struck but without damaging the skin, the resonator, or the striking implement is no simple matter at all. Rather, it requires a great deal of applied knowledge about design, materials, construction, and playing technique: in other words, technology.

Technology is an especially salient matter with respect to the drum set, which, although sharing similarities with instruments that have been played for thousands of years, is the result of innovations that emerged in the twentieth century and continue today. While some aspects of the look, sounds, and playing techniques associated with the drum set in 2015 would likely be familiar to the instrument's pioneers in the early 1900s and other drummers long before, much of what is seen and heard now would be unimaginable to them.

This chapter is about the drum set and the manner in which drummers play it, both of which are and have always been inseparable from multiple types of technology. While this assertion can be made about any musical instrument, several factors make the drum set an especially interesting case of the complex entanglements between human music makers and technological knowledge. Not the least of these is the drum set's relatively short history and its emergence alongside the rise of sound recording, rapid changes in mass media, and widespread industrialization. Also entangled in this web of people, things, and ideas are new musical genres as well as movements of people, culture, and capital, all of which continue to inform the morphology, sound, and performance techniques of the drum set.

The current state of drum set affairs is in many ways defined by an unprecedented range of options. Yet, this abundance of choice is implicated in changes to drumming practice that can be both exciting as remarkable new expressions of virtuosity and musicality and concerning

for their impact on longstanding musical sensibilities and professional opportunities. At the center of these shifts and debates are the myriad ways that people interact with an array of objects, knowledge, sounds, and each other through drumming practices; and at stake are the sounds and meanings of music, drums, and drumming for those who call themselves drummers, those who work with them, and those who listen to their sonic production.

Drumming and the collective

Music has long been studied as social practice – activity that involves many different people doing different things. Indeed, ethnomusicology is predicated on this very conceptualization. Widening possibilities for understanding music in this way, sociologist Howard Becker and musicologist Christopher Small have asserted the importance of people whose involvement in the production of expressive culture might seem minimal, for example, those who make the tools of the trade.[2] More recently, ethnomusicologist Eliot Bates has drawn on the work of Bruno Latour to argue convincingly for the study of "the social life of musical instruments," in which the "agency" of the instrument, its capacity to inform musical action, is taken just as seriously as that of human musicians.[3]

Without digressing into a critique of Latour's and Bates' provocative ideas, I instead draw on their main premise and note that the many materials with which drummers interact can and do shape the manner, results, and meanings of drum set performance. Evidence supporting this is readily available in, for instance, the numerous discussions of equipment in online forums and interviews with noted drummers. Perhaps the traction of this seemingly simple idea – that the instrument one plays matters – is even better exemplified by a recent advertisement featuring contemporary drumming master Vinnie Colaiuta, who states that, thanks to his new drums, "I finally feel like I don't have to 'fight' the instrument anymore!"[4]

This ad and the beliefs about drumming that it conveys suggest a clear resonance with a most basic tenet of Latour's ideas, which are commonly glossed as actor-network theory, or ANT, that humans do not act independently of each other or nonhumans. To this end, Latour posits the idea of the actor-network in which an actor is anything that is made to act by "a vast array of entities swarming toward it."[5] Applied to music-making, this implies that music is what it is, sounds how it sounds, and means what it means because of relationships between people, ideas, and things in various and changing combinations.[6] While this might seem obvious, it is a

long way from taking for granted that, for example, a drum set is a drum set or a song is a song and that any artistry (or lack of it) is solely or even primarily the doing of the musician him/herself. This is not to deny the importance of the individual drummer, a key point to which I will return. But it is an important step toward understanding what drummers do as interweaved with the circulation of musical performances, particular ideas about music and the role of drums in it, and the physical instrument itself. This network, then, brings us back to questions of technology, its many forms, and the ways it shapes and is shaped by drumming practice.

The instrument(s)

Several written histories of the drum set take an approach that fits comfortably with Latour's conceptualization.[7] Drum historians typically link key changes in the morphology of the drum set with influential performers, their stylistic innovations, and related emergent musical genres. For example, perhaps the most fundamental technology for making the "modern" drum set what it is, the bass drum pedal, was the result of a confluence of issues and, in Latour's language, actors. In the early 1900s, the economic, spatial, and sonic needs of theater bands prompted the rise of "double drumming," which involved one musician playing the bass drum and snare drum parts normally played by two (or more) people in a marching band. Yet, double drumming also imposed constraints, especially with respect to snare drum technique since practitioners needed to use one hand on the bass drum and thus could not play intricate or even constant snare patterns.

The comparatively simpler role of the bass drum made finding a way to play it with the foot a logical solution; and that is what took place. Various approaches to the problem were pursued, but the pedal designed, patented, and mass produced by William F. Ludwig, Sr. is generally agreed to be the foundation for the device drummers use to play their bass drums even today.[8] After Ludwig's design set the standard, further experimentation has continually led to slight variations, major modifications, and a few radical innovations. Bass drum pedals and technique today, then, in some ways remain close to their early twentieth-century antecedents and in other ways depart dramatically from them.

The other technological innovation that effectively defines the contemporary drum set, the hi-hat, follows a trajectory similar to that of the bass drum pedal. Not coincidentally, the hi-hat also has a foot pedal, and it continues to be a focus of experimentation and innovation both in terms of material design and playing techniques. According to most accounts,

various attempts had been made to devise a foot-operated device for striking two cymbals together and several early devices, snowshoes and then low-boys, were capable of doing just that – and only that. Since these pieces of hardware positioned the cymbals just above the pedal, they could not be struck easily with a stick and were thus limited to providing a "chick" or crash sound via foot movement. However, the story goes, Jo Jones, drummer for Count Basie from 1934 to 1948, elevated the low-boy so that he could play the cymbal pair with his sticks. He also mastered using foot pressure on the pedal to coax different sounds out of the cymbals as he struck them, enriching the hi-hat's utility as a primary voice for ride rhythms. This paved the way for early forms of "coordinated-independence"– playing an ostinato on a cymbal with one hand and accents on other set components with the remaining hand and feet – which is the norm in (jazz) drumming today.[9] Like the bass drum pedal, numerous experiments, refinements, and innovations have engendered even more uses of the hi-hat by many different drummers.

In discussing these key early technological developments, my goal is not to recount a complete drum set history but rather to raise an important point. Despite the variety of drum set configurations used by drummers today and in the past, bass drums, snare drums, and hi-hats (or more generally, cymbals) remain core components around which many of the most significant technological changes and related technique shifts have revolved.

This is not to say that these "core" instruments are the only sites of dramatic change. For example, the development of specialized brushes (as opposed to actual fly swatters) provided new sounds and approaches to timekeeping that would become central to jazz drummers' vocabularies. More recently, in search of different sounds and also the feel of a stick at a lower volume, several makers created dowel bundles that are stiff enough to rebound adequately but flexible enough to attenuate volume. Even the humble drumstick is now available in a countless variety of sizes, shapes, and materials, allowing drummers to choose the tool that best suits them and their particular musical situations.

Numerous other technologies have opened new avenues of possibility for drummers. As noted drummer and teacher Ed Soph remarked, tunable tom-toms (as opposed to those with tacked on and, therefore, non-adjustable heads) fostered new techniques since the sounds and pitches of these instruments could now be precisely and consistently adjusted.[10] This point is echoed by Dean, who associates this development with Gene Krupa, Benny Goodman's drummer in the 1930s, who is widely recognized for bringing the drums into the spotlight with his soloing in songs such as "Sing, Sing, Sing" that feature his tom work.[11] For Soph, Max Roach's

highly influential "melodic approach" was very much facilitated by the availability of toms with tunable heads.

Then there are the heads themselves, which until the mid-twentieth century were made out of calfskin. As noted by Soph, drummers such as Buddy Rich, Louis Bellson, and many others had certainly mastered a particular touch – not to mention impressive speed, control, and when needed, power – while playing on a surface that could become slack because of weather changes. However, post-World War II developments in synthetics made drumheads made of polyester (Mylar) film possible and profitable. Drum historians tend to agree that this not only changed the sound of drums, but also paved the way for rock by allowing much harder playing without fear of breakage. As plastic heads caught on for drummers in nearly all genres, the warmth and sustain of calf gave way to the brightness and attack of plastic, meaning that individual notes could be heard more clearly at high volume and rapid speed.

Over time, experiments with heads continued, exemplified by the 1970s vogue for the sharp attack and quick decay of single-headed toms, the use of two plies of Mylar (and even a layer of oil between them), adhesive rings and center dots as a means to control overtones, variations in film thickness, and coatings to provide particular sounds and feels. Notably, all of these options in head configuration involve certain trade-offs. For example, longer sustain comes at the expense of articulation clarity, while more damped sound can sacrifice sensitivity, volume, and rebound. Nevertheless, head experimentation yielded choices that continue to inform the sound of particular drummers and even genres of music.

Drum sets, drummers, music

Los Angeles studio drummer and drum educator Ralph Humphrey told me that the most significant changes he had witnessed in drum set technique took place in relation to the music – "what it calls for and what it (or those in charge of it) will allow."[12] Humphrey's insight points to yet another factor in the dynamic actor-network of the drum set – it is used primarily in popular music genres. While certainly not absent in contemporary popular music, limitations related to authority (who decides what the music calls for and what it allows) are generally less formalized, institutionally reified, or historically entrenched than, for example, Western (and many other forms of) art music and even many "folk" practices. For example, much popular music that features a drum set often benefits from the input of many people including songwriters,

producers, engineers, and musicians of all kinds including drummers themselves rather than drawing on a tradition of privileging the intentions of an often absent composer and a written score.[13] Further, as Keith Negus notes, change within the context of existing popular music genres is a vital space for creativity and, at times, the emergence of new genres.[14] In many instances, these genre bending and breaking innovations happen from behind the drum set – as was the case with Jo Jones' hi-hat time-keeping, which established the convention for swing; or Kenny Clarke's shift to playing time on the ride cymbal and bass drum "bombs" as defining aspects of bebop; or Hal Blaine's single-headed "concert" toms as a signature sound of 1970s LA pop; or the straight eighth-note, backbeat feel of most rock; or the steady hi-hat sixteenths of disco; and numerous other examples. In a very real sense, drums and drummers help establish what the music calls for and what it will allow.

It is notable that in many instances when the drum set and drum set players serve as agents of musical change, their impact is often amplified (literally) via media technology of various kinds. Arguably, this is best exemplified by yet another moment of radical transformation that was mentioned by both Humphrey and drum set educator Dom Famularo when we spoke: Tony Williams' recordings as bandleader following his departure from Miles Davis' group.[15] Williams combined the technical skill, musical sensitivity, and interaction he nurtured with Davis with the power and sonic palette of 1960s era rock to create recorded performances that would influence countless drummers to follow. Of course Williams' forward-looking fusions were solidly rooted in techniques that earlier jazz, rock, and R&B drummers had been developing for over half a century, many of which were disseminated on recordings.

Influence, education, inspiration, imitation

Musicologist Scott DeVeaux has rightly asserted that jazz history is inseparable from recordings.[16] Much the same could be said about rock, funk, and numerous other popular music practices from around the world.[17] Owing to the drum set's emergence in the twentieth century, its centrality to jazz, and its prominence in popular music more broadly, it could well be argued that the history of this instrument is also inseparable from recordings.

This does not mean that recordings should be taken as inert documents of drum set performance. As numerous scholars writing about sound recording note, the way the music is recorded also affects what it sounds like and how it is played.[18] Music and technology scholar Paul Théberge

has noted that in multitrack recording sessions drummers often record their parts first with limited information about the tracks to follow.[19] One result of this is that drum parts are often kept simple to avoid clashing with later additions. Another aspect of contemporary recording practice that dramatically affects how the drums are played is the use of click tracks and sequencers – both of which demand an unwavering time feel since their digital precision can spotlight inconsistencies. Cognizant of this, one of the drummers interviewed by Simon Zagorski-Thomas mentioned that he altered his hi-hat technique for studio work, striking the edge of the cymbal pair rather than the bow of the top cymbal, to make his groove sound more in time.[20] Studio veteran Humphrey noted that at times he "plays" with the click when recording – for instance, playing on top of or behind it – according to the feel he aims to bring to the music.[21]

Humphrey's example in particular also illustrates the honing of a new ability in relation to what some might see as a constraint imposed by typical studio techniques. Along these lines, Soph noted that studio conditions allow him to play as he wishes with less concern for volume. As a result, he is freer to experiment, take chances, and focus on other aspects of his performance, which can lead to new and exciting results.

While the ways technological intervention informs drumming technique in the studio itself might be subtle, the impact of the sounds recorded cannot be overstated. This is because, as noted by Gareth Dylan Smith, the most common way drummers learn to play is by listening to recorded performances.[22] Interviews with famous drummers are full of references to hearing inspirational performances, playing along with favorite recordings, and in many instances transcribing them. Certain trends in recorded drum sound also catch on, for example, Blaine's concert toms and the dry (and precise) sound of Steve Gadd's drum sets. Notably, the influential sounds that are circulated are also the result of significant electronic mediation beginning with microphones and extending to gates, triggers, samples, edits, and more. Drum parts in many genres are also performed in part or completely by machines yielding, among other things, a highly quantized and dynamically even time feel. This aesthetic has informed the live playing of several drummers such as Jojo Mayer, who both Humphrey and Famularo noted for his remarkable ability to sound machine- like.

With the increased availability of high-quality, low-cost recording devices, the ability to self-record has also had an important impact on drummers and their technique. In his first interview with *Modern Drummer Magazine*, Dave Weckl described recording himself and critiquing his performances as a means to develop a more mature approach.[23] Self-recording was also the way that he discovered his much copied technique of beat displacement. After listening back to a performance

that he and keyboardist Jay Oliver knew was somehow off, he realized that they had felt the downbeat in different places. By analyzing the recording, Weckl was able to reproduce and continue to develop the "error" into a technique.

The increased circulation of "world music," further, has made it possible to hear, study, and incorporate sounds and rhythms from diverse drumming and percussion traditions from around the world. On the other hand, drum set techniques developed in North America and Europe have shaped "world" drumming. For example, upon attending a drum clinic in Salvador, Brazil, a local drummer friend and I noted that a prominent Rio-based drummer played samba in a manner akin to stylized jazz samba as might be heard in the United States. Moreover, several drummers I met in Salvador spoke to me about the influence of non-Brazilian musicians such as Weckl, Colaiuta, Neil Peart, and John Bonham.

Recordings are by no means the only way that media technology informs drum set technique. Printed information figures prominently as well. As noted by Famularo, however, for quite some time, Jim Chapin's *Advanced Techniques for the Modern Drummer* was one, if not the only, instructional book written specifically for drum set.[24] Thus, while countless drummers struggled with the exercises in this highly influential publication, many devised creative ways of interpreting and applying books written for snare drum or as rhythmic studies to the drum set.[25] As instructional books for drum set became more common, a number of authors combined text and recording, providing audio demonstrations of the written exercises and, in many cases, "play-along tracks" for applying the techniques in an ensemble context. More recently, magazines and now the Internet have made notated information about playing drums and play-along recordings even more readily available.

Especially significant today is the proliferation of drum videos. In 1983, the release of *Steve Gadd Up Close* inspired a wave of didactic material that capitalized on increasingly affordable home video equipment to give new insights into the techniques of well-known drummers to people who might never have had such access.[26] Countless drummers today have released videos, which can include demonstrations, lessons on an endless variety of topics, solos, ensemble performances, interviews, and more. Now students can see how to play what in the past could only be heard – that is if it could, in fact, be heard. In many instances, video viewers also get detailed explanations of not only how to execute grooves, fills, and solos, but also the underlying concepts, in some cases conveyed in an accompanying booklet. Affordable video cameras with respectable audio capability and Internet video file sharing has further stimulated the production and distribution of drum videos of all kinds, ranging from

polished, informative lessons to flashy demonstrations of skill to amateurish displays of problematic information. A number of established teachers, including Famularo, have also embraced giving online lessons. Thus, videos and the Internet have had a dramatic impact on the playing of drummers who might not otherwise receive formal instruction. Indeed, all of the drummers in Brazil who mentioned the influence of international drum stars had studied their playing on video.

Drum set actor-networks – some issues

The conditions of possibility for today's drummers are as rich as they have ever been. Inspiration is ample as is information about how to achieve the level of performance showcased on recordings, videos, and concert stages. Equipment improvements and innovations facilitate this by providing efficient, stable, and good sounding tools with which to work. Yet at the same time, as noted by each of the drummers I interviewed, there are also areas of concern especially with regard to the influence of media technology. By way of conclusion, I will address a few more fertile areas of creation arising in the wide network of drummers and technology as well as several problematic issues that were pointed out to me by Soph, Famularo, and Humphrey.

Earlier, I suggested that bass drum and hi-hat pedals are two definitive inventions for the drum set and how it is played and that creative adaptations of these instruments are central to key changes in drum set playing. For example, following Kenny Clarke's use of the bass drum for playing accents, and through books such as Jim Chapin's *Advanced Techniques* and Ted Reed's *Syncopation*, drummers have continued to extend their use of the bass drum. Gadd's first video famously illustrates a heel-toe technique that allows him to play a stream of notes with one foot, and other videos demonstrate techniques such as sliding and pivoting the foot for increasing bass drum speed. Louis Bellson's work with two bass drums in the 1940s also inspired many others to follow suit and move beyond his accomplishments. Famularo, for example, is well known for applying techniques originally intended for the hands (e.g., George Lawrence Stone's *Stick Control*) and applying them to his double bass drum playing. The results of this kind of innovation are evident in the playing of many drummers today who perform double-stroke rolls, flams, and other rudiments as well as intricate rhythms at blinding speed and remarkable precision with their feet or in hand and foot combinations. Their accomplishments were likely facilitated by the increased efficiency and adjustability of pedal mechanisms and then by the innovation of the double

pedal, which is dramatically cheaper and more convenient than two bass drums and two pedals. More recently, extended footboards provide increased leverage and facilitate, for some, the use of heel-toe and sliding techniques on double pedals, thus making even greater speed and power possible. In some instances, velocity and clarity are also facilitated by the use of newly developed bass drum heads with built in dampening rings (or other dampening systems) that help control resonance and change the feel of the playing surface. And of course, recordings, books, and videos have made inspiration and explanation related to emerging bass drum techniques available on a worldwide scale.

While the more dramatic aspects of the drum set's actor-network might be the core instruments I mentioned earlier and various forms of media, the importance of the bass drum pedal and hi-hat stand points out that often drum *hardware* (rather than drums, cymbals, or information about how to play them) is also of tremendous importance. Stands that allow drummers to position drums and cymbals securely and exactly where they want them allow for the customization of the instruments to suit individual bodies and objectives. There are numerous examples of this but boom stands for use with multi-tom and multi-cymbal setups and hi-hat stands with two legs or swiveling tripods that allow for tight positioning next to the auxiliary footboard of a double pedal are certainly significant for their ergonomic implications. The combination of the boom stand concept with the high hat, the "x-hat," means that this key component can now be placed nearly anywhere on a set, a point noted by Soph. This facilitates, among other things, complex two-handed hi-hat patterns and the playing of a closed hi-hat in conjunction with double bass drums. Pushing this idea further, "remote hi-hats" allow for a fully functional cymbal pair to be placed in nonconventional locations thereby opening up new technical and musical possibilities.

Much as hi-hat technique has benefited from hardware that allows more flexible positioning, the technology at the heart of the double bass drum pedal, the universal joint, has made it possible to play "remote" bass drums. Now, drummers such as Terry Bozzio and Thomas Lange use multiple bass drums and pedals to create intricate combination patterns that Famularo likened to organ pedal work. Such pedal configurations often include remote hi-hats as well as pedals that strike instruments such as cowbells, (synthetic) "wood" blocks, and more. Here, sonic inspiration, mechanical development, and hard work engender complex coordination that moves well beyond the then radical changes disseminated by Chapin's *Advanced Techniques* and recordings of bebop drummers.

As might be expected, much of this innovation has been supported by didactic videos and publications. For example, Gary Chester's *New Breed*

extends the idea of coordinated-independence while incorporating the use of new technologies such as supplementary hi-hats and especially the click track.[27] This book has had significant impact on contemporary playing in part because one of its early champions was Dave Weckl, who shook the drum world with, among other things, his Chester-inspired grooves and creative use of a second hi-hat.

Part of Weckl's appeal was also his drum sound: a dry, focused sound traceable to one of his key influences, Steve Gadd. A number of techno-logical factors contribute to this sound – head choice, miking, shell material, bearing edge shape, and more – and while more resonance is once again the norm in most drum mixes, it is typically complemented with a focused attack and reduced overtones that increase clarity and the articulation of individual notes. As Famularo told me, this sound helps drummers play with more control and precision. On the other hand, certain music such as acoustic jazz still emphasizes a more open, ringy tone. The importance of this is suggested by something I saw at a drum clinic in the late 1980s in Los Angeles. A drummer widely acclaimed for his fast, articulate, and precise playing was asked to demonstrate his jazz playing. He qualified his demon-stration by stating that the set he was playing – one with more dampened toms and bass drum – was not conducive to creating a convincing jazz feel, a time sensibility that Humphrey described to me as "elastic" when discuss-ing highly influential jazz drummer Elvin Jones.

Even with the typically more open sound of drums in the 1940s, 1950s, and 1960s and the related elasticity of time feel played by many of the drummers working in those eras (and many performing in more tradi-tional jazz styles today), it would be a mistake to suggest that such playing is not fast and precise in its own way. Yet, many drummers today have taken speed and precision to new and very different places with their exceptionally clean playing that often involves linear combinations of the hands and feet. Striking examples of this have been disseminated globally in the various videos of so-called "Gospel Chops" drummers, launching several of the featured musicians to high-profile gigs and drum hero status.[28]

As inspirational as these and other similar performances are, their availability and popularity are also at the heart of concerns expressed by the drummers with whom I spoke about the state of current drum set playing. While all were enthusiastic about what is happening, they also expressed certain reservations about the overabundance of unfiltered information available and lack of critical engagement with it. Famularo thus noted how important it remains for students to find someone who can help them sift through mountains of book and video possibilities on the market.[29] Soph, on the other hand, spoke more directly to questions of use,

noting that far too many drummers treat videos purely as "entertainment." Not discounting the importance of entertainment or inspiration, he mentioned that he sees many aspiring drummers who clearly pay little or no attention to anything but drummers playing fast and flashy. To this, he added that the very drummers who showcase their exceptional chops on video (including several of his former students) also play great time with appropriate restraint when called for.

Importantly, as noted specifically by Humphrey, not all drummers learn and apply information in the same way. All three teachers also mentioned that no method is perfect and effectiveness is contingent on the quality of the material, its application, and often employing a balance of approaches. For example, Humphrey, Famularo, Soph, and countless other drummers stress the importance of listening. Interviews with drumming greats are full of references to how hearing a particular musician opened up new avenues of performance and often how transcription was a vital tool to unlock what they had done.[30] Yet, Soph also discussed what he called the "myth" of transcription – that many drummers can either place too much faith in the process or, more commonly, focus on certain details of a drummer's performance rather than gaining a more well-rounded perspective of how it relates to its musical context.

Soph's critical perspective on transcription translated to his views about books. Again, never doubting their usefulness, he expressed concern that too many drummers get locked into book learning and fail to get beyond what is on the page. Adding to the risk of misapplication or overfocusing and raising the stakes for guidance through the overwhelming number of available books is Humphrey's concern about what exactly has been written. He noted that no one book does it all when it comes to drum set. That is, there is not, in his view, a comprehensive guide for the instrument, making careful selection and application of what is available all the more important. Famularo's perspective lines up well with those of Soph and Humphrey with the added caveat that there is a tremendous amount of crossover and redundancy, even plagiarism, within the literature. He noted that, in the rush to make material available (for the sake of income, publicity, or even with an earnest pedagogical aim), many drummers recycle ideas or only slightly vary what others have already done.

None of these educators suggested that technology including new types of equipment, better versions of old equipment, videos, recordings, and method books are not vitally important to the many significant developments in drum set performance that continue to take place. Yet, each of them advocated both balance and a critical approach to using the ever-increasing amount of material available. Again, the idea of considering what music calls for and what "it" will allow is key. The challenge, then, is

to develop a sense of this changing set of constraints and possibilities and find ways to work toward it.

Concluding thoughts

The question of musical constraint and possibility is no small one if for no other reason than there are more niches for drum set performance than ever before. Where drums might be viewed by some as primarily accompaniment instruments, the proliferation of drum clinics, videos, and now contests (many of which are circulated on video or YouTube) has created a space that encourages and even requires drummers to stand out, often through speed and flash. Playing a great groove in these contexts generally will not satisfy the judges (or many audience members). At the same time, the ability to keep time musically and tastefully accompany a band does not go out of style, and drummers noted for their sense of groove tend to keep working. On the other hand, with the circulation of music from all over the world, increasing studio savvy, instrumental skills, and a related continual push on genre boundaries, a great deal of music calls for and will allow new drumming approaches. This is in no small measure due to recent changes in the music industry such as an explosion of self-production and distribution. In this sense, many constraints that might have been imposed by producers, A&R people, or label executives have been eased greatly. At the same time, however, as Humphrey stressed, it has become more difficult to make a living playing drums despite the fact that it is arguably easier to make one's drumming audible. He further lamented that the LA studio scene has experienced a significant decrease in the amount of work available since so much drumming is now programmed. In yet another irony, however, he told me that where in the past he was commonly required to play very strictly orchestrated and precisely notated parts, machines now provide that function. As a result, he is more frequently asked to lend his vision to more loosely conceived parts, thus upping the stakes for his personalized style, feel, and sense of what the music calls for.

Music and the music business have seen radical and constant change during the entire lifespan of the drum set. Accordingly, the instrument and the way it is played have never stopped changing. As each of the musicians with whom I spoke asserted, the human contribution to the state of drumming – regardless of, or perhaps in spite of technological actors and the importance of actor-networks – is undeniable. On the other hand, few drummers would likely state that technology of various kinds does not inform what they do in profound ways. Even if it does not cause better playing, somehow seeing or hearing

a great performance, live or recorded, rarely fails to make a drummer want to play better. New drum books or new approaches to old ones *do* make many drummers want to practice. And sitting behind a great sounding, great feeling drum set is nearly always a surefire way to make a drummer want to drum.

Notes

1. Peter Avanti relates the apparent timelessness and ubiquity of the drum set to his assertion that percussion instruments, though not drums specifically, "were the first musical technologies after the human voice and body." P. Avanti, "Black Musics, Technology, and Modernity: Exhibit A, the Drum Kit," *Popular Music and Society*, vol. 36, no. 4 (2013), 481.

2. H. S. Becker, *Art Worlds* (University of California Press, 1982); C. Small, *Musicking: The Meanings of Performing and Listening* (Hannover: The University Press of New England, 1998).

3. E. Bates, "The Social Life of Musical Instruments," *Ethnomusicology*, vol. 56, no. 3 (2012), 363–94. This notion of object agency is elaborated in B. Latour, *Reassembling the Social: An Introduction to Actor-Network Theory* (Oxford University Press, 2007). As Bates notes, this aspect of Latour's work has been a focus of his critics.

4. "Welcome home Vinnie Colaiuta," www.ludwig-drums.com/features/vc/

5. Latour, *Reassembling*, p. 46.

6. See B. Piekut, "Actor-networks in Music History: Clarifications and Critiques," *Twentieth-century Music*, vol. 11, no. 2 (2014), 193.

7. For example, Avanti, "Exhibit A"; Bob Breithaupt, "The Drum Set," in John Beck (ed.), *Encyclopedia of Percussion*, 2nd ed. (New York: Routledge, 2007); M. Dean, *Drum: A History* (Toronto: Scarecrow Press, 2012).

8. See Avanti, "Exhibit A," 483–89 for a concise, detailed discussion of early bass drum pedals.

9. Breithaupt, "Drum set."

10. E. Soph, Telephone interview (December 12, 2014).

11. Dean, *Drum*, p. 201.

12. R. Humphrey, Telephone interview (December 28, 2014).

13. See P. Kivy, "Live Performances and Dead Composers: On the Ethics of Musical Interpretation," in *The Fine Art of Repetition: Essays in the Philosophy of Music* (Cambridge University Press, 1993).

14. K. Negus, *Music Genres and Corporate Cultures* (New York: Routledge, 1999).

15. D. Famularo, Skype interview (December 19, 2014).

16. DeVeaux also advocates for understanding jazz recordings as complex materials to be analyzed critically rather than as transparent artifacts of history. S. DeVeaux, *The Birth of Bebop: A Social and Musical History* (University of California Press, 1997), pp. 40, 365–66.

17. See P. Manual, *Popular Musics of the Non-western World: An Introductory Survey* (Oxford University Press, 1988), pp. 3–4.

18. For example, R. Philip, *Performing Music in the Age of Recording* (Yale University Press, 2004) and M. Katz, *Capturing Sound: How Technology has Changed Music* (University of California Press, 2004).

19. P. Théberge, "The 'Sound' of Music: Technological Rationalization and the Production of Popular Music," *New Formations*, 8 (1989), 99–111.

20. S. Zagorski-Thomas, "Real and Unreal Performances: The Interaction of Recording Technology and Drum Set Performance," in A. Danielsen (ed.), *Musical Rhythm in the Age of Digital Reproduction* (Surrey: Ashgate, 2010).

21. Humphrey (2014).

22. G. D. Smith, *I Drum, Therefore I Am: Being and Becoming a Drummer* (Surrey: Ashgate, 2013).

23. J. Potter, "Dave Weckl," *Modern Drummer*, 10 (October 1986), 16–21, 48–61.

24. J. Chapin, *Advanced Techniques for the Modern Drummer* Vol. 1: *Coordinated Independence as Applied to Jazz and Bebop* (Emeryville, CA: Alfred Music [1948] 2002).

25. The two most notable books of this type that were mentioned by Soph, Humphrey, and Famularo are G. L. Stone, *Stick Control for the Snare Drummer* (Emeryville, CA: Alfred Music [1935] 2009) and T. Reed, *Progressive Steps to Syncopation for the Modern Drummer* (Emeryville, CA: Alfred Music [1958] 1997).

26. S. Gadd, R. Wallis, and P. Seigel, *Steve Gadd Up Close* (New York: DCI Music Video, 1983).

27. G. Chester, *The New Breed* (Cedar Grove, NJ: Modern Drummer, 1985).

28. For example, *Shed Sessionz, Vol. 1* (Gospel Chops.com, 2006). For a scholarly study of gospel drumming, see D. Stadnicki, "Enjoying Gospel Drumming: An Investigation of Post-racial Appropriation, Consumption, and Idealization in Contemporary Black Musicianship," unpublished MA thesis, Carleton University.

29. See K. Miller, *Playing Along: Digital Games, YouTube, and Virtual Performance* (Oxford University Press, 2012).

30. See, for example, Potter, "Weckl." Various technologies have long been available to aid transcription.

World percussion

17 Speaking of rhythm

RUSSELL HARTENBERGER

The list of Western musicians who have been influenced by the music of India is lengthy, and the ways they have incorporated elements of Indian music in their own styles is wide ranging. From John Coltrane, George Harrison, Yehudi Menuhin, and John McLaughlin to Olivier Messiaen, La Monte Young, Terry Riley, and Philip Glass, performers and composers in the West have sought ways to use Indian musical ideas in their art forms. One of the most innovative groups to combine Indian and Western musical styles is Autorickshaw, a Toronto-based ensemble featuring South Indian/jazz vocalist, Suba Sankaran. Suba's background is unusual in that she has extensive training in Karnatak[1] music of South India, Western classical music, and jazz. In Autorickshaw, Suba is joined by *tabla* player, Ed Hanley, and multi-instrumentalist, Dylan Bell, in combining elements of both South and North Indian music with jazz and other contemporary music genres.

Suba's father, Trichy Sankaran, is one of the most highly esteemed musicians in India. Sankaran[2] is a disciple of the legendary *mrdangam* master, Sri Palani Subramania Pillai, and, in 2011, was awarded the prestigious title *Sangitha Kalanidhi* for his contributions to the world of Karnatak music as performer, scholar, and composer. In addition to his performances with all the leading musicians of South India, Sankaran has collaborated with Nexus, Glen Velez, Ghanaian drummer Abraham Adzenyah, *tabla* master Sharda Sahai, Evergreen Club Contemporary Gamelan, John Wyre's World Drum Ensemble, and many musicians from the worlds of jazz and contemporary music. Sankaran is a composer, Professor Emeritus of Music at York University in Toronto, and the author of the books, *The Rhythmic Principles and Practice of South Indian Drumming* and *Konnakol (Solkattu): Spoken Rhythms of South Indian Music.*

The background and experience of both father and daughter give them legitimacy in their performances as well as insight into the pedagogical, theoretical, and cultural issues that emanate from their fusion of Indian music with Western musical traditions. In August 2014, I met with Sankaran and Suba and asked them about the influence of Indian music on Western music and the issues that arise from combining elements of both, including questions of authenticity and cultural appropriation. In the

[229]

Figure 17.1 Suba Sankaran and Trichy Sankaran.

following conversation, we discuss these issues as well as the difference in
the approach to the study of rhythm in India and the West.

RH: Suba, tell me about your training in both Indian and Western music.

SUBA: I was born and raised in Toronto, but with a master drummer for a
     father, so my South Indian music training commenced quite early on.
     Basically when I learned to speak, I also began singing, starting with
     some of the short songs called *gitam*. I took piano lessons at the age of
     six and started choral singing about that same age. I went through the
     Royal Conservatory of Music piano program, and there I learned a lot
     about theory, harmony, counterpoint, and analysis. I attended an art
     school in high school, starting as a piano major, but eventually moved
     into the vocal program. That's when I started conducting, directing
     choirs, creating my own choirs, making arrangements, and compos-
     ing. After high school, I enrolled in York University to do a Bachelor of
     Fine Arts and then a Master's in Ethnomusicology. Off and on I still
     studied South Indian singing and sometimes drumming as well. Even
     though I began doing jazz in high school, I only really got into it and
     more contemporary improvisational styles in university. That's where
     I discovered that I had a real knack for improvisation and rhythm that
     is inherent in a lot of that music. Ever since, I've been straddling the
     worlds of East and West, but eating, sleeping, and breathing music all
     the while as composer, arranger, performer, producer, and singer.

RH: In relation to your Indian music training, did you take singing lessons
     with your father or someone else?

SUBA: I mostly took singing lessons from my father, although my mother also did some singing – not professionally, but there is always such a background just from the cultural perspective. We also had a lot of visiting artists from India come to our home. It's the tradition and obligation of the senior artists to pass the torch and impart their knowledge to the younger people, so I studied with many of the musicians who came through our home in my early, formative years.

RH: You must have learned about rhythm and drumming from your father. Was that around the same period of time?

SUBA: I started on the drums when I was six or seven. I played a little bit of *mrdangam*, mostly the basic lessons. My father also introduced me to the *kanjira*. It was a smaller instrument and I had small hands at the time and the drums were quite large. *Solkattu*[3] was something I really took to, and that's something that became kind of a game when I was younger. Other families played "name that tune," but we played "name that *nadai*."[4] That's what we did around the kitchen table.

SANKARAN: I also trained Suba in learning to keep *tala*.[5] I don't normally use a metronome because my training is different, so I would test her to see if she could keep *tala* to some of the more intricate patterns.

RH: Sankaran, what kind of education did you have in Western music, or did you have any in India?

SANKARAN: In India, none; it was all Karnatak. When I arrived here, it was all quite new to me, but I gradually absorbed and adapted myself to Western music and methods of teaching. I was able to read Western notation slowly and write slowly, but the rhythm was no problem for me. All these whole-notes, half-notes, quarter-notes were easy for me, but to understand the key signatures and so forth took me extra time.

In 1980, I taught part-time at San Diego State University and shared an office with a professor who had a piano. Since I had more time there, I enrolled in the basic Western classical musicianship course and practiced the piano. Later on, when I began composing, this came in very handy. Learning Western music was an essential part in translating many of the *korvais*[6] into Western notation. I realized how important it was for anyone to have some basic education on the piano, and to be able to read and write Western notation.

To take it further, I got involved with gamelan music in 1984 when my first composition, *Swaralaya*, was performed by the Evergreen Club Contemporary Gamelan Ensemble. In preparing a score for the ensemble, we debated about the cipher notation of gamelan – Javanese music goes one way and Balinese music goes the other way with the numbering. Finally we decided it was better to go with Western notation, so I prepared a Western score for *Swaralaya*.

RH: One of the things I am interested in is the learning process with notation and without notation since both of you have learned each way.

SUBA: Having started with South Indian music and learning everything by rote, learning aurally, I've always relied on my ears rather than my

sight for music. I didn't know this when I was very young, but I have perfect pitch. For me, sight-reading took me longer to do, because my ears always wanted to take me somewhere else. While I was sight-reading some Bach, I sort of made up the rest of the harmony. So in a way, I ended up improvising. It was fascinating for me, but frustrating for my teachers. I spent a lot of time in my middle school and high school years working on that. I read piano scores, almost eliminating the ear factor, and figured out how to sight-read, and also how to sight-read multiple parts.

When it came to learning music later, I found that it was quite easy to memorize everything, and I think that was from my South Indian training. In university when I sang interesting rhythmic passages in pop songs, for example, sixteenth-note passages with a lot of accents, I used *solkattu* to dissect what was going on so I could get a sense of what I was really supposed to be feeling in my body. I translated it into *solkattu* and then brought it back again. I found it very interesting to go between this idea of making music with my eyes and making music with my ears. More often than not I rely on the South Indian way of learning than the Western way; I superimpose South Indian on the Western more often than the other way around.

RH: Sankaran, you came from the Karnatak tradition and had to learn the Western way of dealing with music. What was that like?

SANKARAN: I come from a tradition where the music is memorized and learned at the feet of the teacher in the *gurukala* system. At the time that I studied, it was up to the teacher when he would be in the mood to teach, so the student should always be prepared. This teaches you patience; you have got to be really patient to learn from the teacher. And then, no questions could be asked. You can't ask, "why is this, why is that?" No. One time he says *kita taka thom*, another time he says *tere kita thom*. So you want to ask, "why are you saying *kita taka* one time, and another time you are saying *tere kita*?" No, you cannot ask. Later on, in my own teaching and research, I found answers to these which I have included in my *solkattu* book.

The old *gurukala* system is really to prepare you for *self-discovery*. You have got to discover yourself how *korvais* or *moras*[7] work in the *tala*. It is great training for the brain. I cannot overemphasize the importance of this oral tradition method by which we retain many of the intricate patterns all in our memory. Another advantage of the Indian system of training is getting up in the early morning and trying to practice. Practicing in the morning is advisable for good memory and for practice in all fields whether it is *mrdangam*, vocal, instrumental . . . anything.

Memory is something really amazing, and I try to point this out to Western music students. When they are so engrossed in reading the music, they are not really able to hear themselves. If I may say, I think notation closes off some venues for expression. Western students are

so involved in reading they are not able to feel a triplet happening somewhere in the music. Whereas in the Indian system, you really learn to master and to feel – *feel the rhythm*. That intensifies your training and you are able to handle rhythm in a better way.

RH: When you say, "feel rhythm," what is it that you are actually feeling?

SANKARAN: Perhaps I can explain by discussing the term, *layam* or *laya*. *Layam* is really fundamental and has two important meanings. People generally relate it to the rate of events: *vilamba laya, madhya laya, drutha laya*, or slow speed, medium speed, and fast speed. It also has a special meaning: the interval between two events. The interval – that is really the *layam*; in other words, duration. The duration is fundamental in realizing rhythms. *Laya* is also equated with yoga or meditation. So when we say we have to relax, we have to find external factors when we are dealing with intricate or complicated rhythms. You cannot do it in a rush or when you are in a hurry. But what it means is, we have to calm down; we have got to focus. Whenever I talk about *laya*, I say it has a melodic perspective, a rhythmic perspective, and a spiritual perspective. It is the spiritual perspective of *laya* where you learn to feel and experience time. Essentially, *laya* is the consciousness of time – being tuned in to time.

SUBA: I think of that idea of feeling the interval between two spaces when I am telling my students about South Indian singing. The microtonal inflections between certain notes I often call the universe within two notes. I tell students to feel what that universe is rather than thinking in terms of whole-tones or semi-tones. Think of what it is to be inside the music and to swim in this ocean that we don't quite understand yet. I also think there is a melodic equivalent to *laya*. It's much more obvious in South Indian music, but in jazz, when you're scat singing over something, or when you're improvising, there has to be an undercurrent of rhythm that is internalized so that you can float on top in a way that is meaningful. And it should have certain points of contact with the rhythmic grid so you are able to dance freely within it. In jazz, we often call it the "groove" or being "in the pocket"; really feeling the beat. But when we talk about *laya*, it's a much deeper concept of flow and fluidity. This also occurs in classical music, but it is something we don't often think about. For example, the architecture you find in Bach's music – there's so much rhythm in there. There's flow inside it, so many counter melodies, and so much subdividing that happens on melodic, harmonic, and rhythmic levels.

RH: This brings me to the topic of *tala*. Sankaran, we have talked before about how you always have the *tala* going on in your head when you're playing music, whether it's South Indian or other music. Even when you play Western music you have a sense of *tala*. Can you explain how that works?

SANKARAN: *Tala* is the external manifestation that gives us the cycle of eight beats, fourteen beats, and so on. *Tala* is something that you use to organize

rhythm in a certain way. *Laya* is the real rhythm. How accurate you are is what is really important. This kind of feel stays with me all the time. So yes, I do translate the Western bars into a *tala* in my head when I perform with Western/contemporary musicians.

Another interesting feature is the concept of *downbeat*, especially the first beat in a *tala* cycle we call *sam*. An enlightening experience occurred when I was featured in a performance with the African drummer, Abraham Adzenyah. During our solo section I was looking for *sam* in African drumming, but there is no such thing as *sam* in their music. At one point I said to myself, "forget *sam* and go with the flow." That is what really triumphed in that performance.

RH: Suba, how about you in relation to *tala*? One part of your life is in *tala* and the other part is not in *tala*. It must make you schizophrenic.

SUBA: Either way, I think the *tala* is always in the back of my head. In Chopin, you have these really interesting bars of, say, fifteen over four. I always had to translate it in terms of *solkattu* so I could understand it, rather than having it feel like a bunch of notes that fell within this time period. When I'm mixing different styles of music, let's say I'm taking a jazz standard but I'm giving it a little dose of Bollywood, I might have the rhythmic part be extremely South Indian versus the jazz scat singing that goes on top of it. I find that *tala* motivates a lot of my decisions in terms of how I arrange music as a sort of hybrid music or Indo-fusion, whatever that fusion may be.

From a choral perspective, I often think of conducting as a larger version of *tala*. So where we have one-two-three when we are conducting, it's similar to *rupaka tala*.[8] Keeping *tala* is a much more condensed version of conducting, and it is very much an external feature of the rhythms that we feel.

RH: You have worked in both Indian and Western music. What are the cultural issues to consider?

SUBA: I'm constantly thinking about that when I'm arranging for Autorickshaw or composing in multiple styles. I often like to say that I try to be sensitive to the cultures that I am borrowing from and to be sensible about how I bring those pieces together. In Bollywood music, for example, you see only the surface level aspect of Western music. They know what they know when it comes to Indian music, but the Western orchestration or harmonies that are superimposed can be quite tenuous and very simple.

When I'm approaching arranging or composing, especially for a group like Autorickshaw, I think about what's going to make the most sense. An example is my version of "Bird on a Wire," by Leonard Cohen. I found that it could really work well in a slow seven-beat *tala*. Then, the bass player at the time, Rich Brown, created a bass line that was a little bit outside of the original and ended up being in the Lydian mode. We have an equivalent in South Indian music, the *kalyani raga*, so I thought, "oh I could actually just keep the melody intact."

I didn't want to mess with it too much; it's beautiful poetry and it's a lovely melody. I could have created something completely different, but I ended up just deviating from it. It doesn't sound anything like the original unless you put it under the microscope. The melody is the same except for that one note, but there are all these microtonal inflections in it because I chose to look at it as the *kalyani raga*.

So I'm constantly thinking about what might work and what might not, what's a good balance between the different styles. Is it meant to sit more on, say, the jazz spectrum or the Indian spectrum? It's on a case-by-case or song-by-song basis that I make these decisions. There is such a treasure when it comes to melodies and rhythms in Indian music, so I find that's the place where I'll often go. But when it comes to harmony or counterpoint or orchestration, it will be on the Western side just because that's where the wealth is.

RH: You have legitimate training in both areas, so people can't accuse you of not treating both traditions with honesty and integrity. In a way, that's an advantage for you.

SUBA: I think so, too. I would feel pretty sheepish if I didn't understand what I was borrowing from.

RH: Sankaran, your experience is in both composing and performing, since you have performed with Nexus and World Drums, and also composed for Western groups.

SANKARAN: My experience has been different from Suba's. One thing is that I feel I have the responsibility of carrying on the thoughts of my guru, Subramania Pillai. I have an obligation to maintain and preserve that tradition. My advice to others is to be strong in your own tradition whether it is jazz, classical, or whatever. Don't try to deviate at such an early stage. At the same time, I feel I can take the material of my guru and show different dimensions to establish my own style. The masters also believed in that. "You follow my path, but you should be your own person." That's what I have tried to establish, and people really understand that.

My compositions dealing with Western classical music, gamelan, and other types have given me some unique experiences in combining music and learning to orchestrate and structure the music. For example, Steve Reich's composition, *Music for Pieces of Wood*, prompted me to write my piece, *Catch 21*. I was influenced by the way he introduced rhythmic fragments and how I could develop them into making a *tala*. Some of the African rhythms have influenced me, too, and I have learned how to convert those into the Indian way. I may take an African bell pattern such as the one used in *Atsiagbekor*, and play it in *tisra*,[9] in a pulse of three instead of four. Some people may recognize the connection and some people may not.

In my scholarly writings, or in my presentations at conferences, I never fail to point out to my own audience, "Don't think that

sankirnam is exclusive to Indian tradition. *Sankirnam* is nine. Have you heard Turkish music?" I really like taking something from other places and bringing it back to India. Of course, I have taken many things from India. This kind of give and take I really like, otherwise we live in our own world and think we are the greatest on the earth. There are equally great people in other cultures, and we have to acknowledge that.

RH: Suba, have you played in India with Autorickshaw?

SUBA: Yes, but not for the classical audience. We have played in rock venues, folk festivals, a jazz festival, but not classical.

SANKARAN: I wonder if Autorickshaw would be welcomed by the Madras Music Academy. One thing is that the members of the Academy may not understand what Autorickshaw is doing. Come to think of it, we really need traditional societies like those represented by classical Indian music. What if everybody changed? There would be no charm in it. That's why I think we should maintain traditions as they are, and for what we are.

SUBA: I was just thinking, to add to this idea of how we approach fusion, something you said about the conversion from African to Indian, cultural conversion. The other side of that perspective is what I like to call the "connecting of the cultural dots." When I'm creating some sort of hybrid, I'll think of the salient elements of that particular culture's music, and see if there are any connections. For me, the most obvious one is Indian music and jazz, especially due to the scope of each for improvisation. Then you go a little deeper and you've got three-time tags in jazz and you've got *moras* in South Indian music. Go even deeper than that and you have what we call the *pallavi* line or the repeated line. In popular music we call it a chorus or refrain, or the head in jazz. For me it was really fascinating when I started examining this, I thought, "Oh, these are basically the same thing." Growing up in a culture straddling East and West, to me everything is what we call "same thing, but different." It's just a different way of looking at it. A different name you put on the same thing. For me, that connecting of the cultural dots was really important when it came to fusing different styles of music.

SANKARAN: When we talk about the influence of Indian drumming on Western percussion, something that is very fascinating is the study of *solkattu*, which used to be only a part of our *mrdangam* learning. Those who specialized in it were called *konnakol* performers, and that art is mostly gone now, for one reason or the other. One of my interests is to revive the art of speaking *solkattu*, and that has worked out beautifully in the academic situation. The students learn rhythms and develop their rhythmic skills without having to learn drum technique. That is the advantage of this approach: anybody can learn *solkattu*. Now *solkattu* is a part of many ensembles. If you look at the film industry in India, they use

solkattu, for example, to depict a fight between father-in-law and son-in-law.

Solkattu can be taken as an entertaining art. It can be used for developing rhythmic skills like I did in developing rhythmic pedagogy and as a part of compositions. It can also be compared to scat singing in jazz or even beat-boxing. Now we have students who are researching the history and development of *solkattu* because it is the study of a whole different language: drummer's language.

RH: You have been talking about the advantages of *solkattu* in pedagogy. Can you both talk about ways you think the study of Indian rhythm could be utilized in Western music education?

SUBA: I think there are some disconnects in the Western upbringing. You have children doing their hand-clapping games that teach them to multi-task and divide their attention between clapping and speaking rhythms, but they are not taught to maintain this ability in their music education unless they learn Orff or Kodaly or something like that. So as they get older, they lose that ability, and then later it is imposed on them in a way that isn't really friendly. What I mean by that is the way they learn to speak certain rhythms by saying *ta ta, ti ti* is not actually ergonomically friendly inside the mouth. Whereas *solkattu* is actual instructions for a drummer in how to play, and it is ergonomically friendly in the mouth so that you can become fluent in this new language. Also you can build up the speed so it almost sounds like a stutter. When I work with school music teachers, and my father has done this as well, and introduce them to Indian *solkattu*, they abandon the old way they teach their rhythms in favor of *solkattu* because it's just the obvious choice.

One of the percussionists my father and I have worked with, Glen Velez, has incorporated frame drumming and walking patterns and his own hybrid version of *solkattu*. I have also taken *solkattu* exercises and added walking patterns. I eliminate the frame drum aspect of it so that it is just body, hands, and voice so the rhythms are really internalized. For example, I will do a slo-mo version of say, *rupaka tala*, with just *ta ki ta* exercise using the principle of doubling and isolating it so you get three-against-two and four-against-three. Then I do a forward and back simple walking pattern so that people can feel exactly when their body is centered. Then they can get a sense of how the rhythm floats on top of what their body is doing – bringing back that idea of divided attention. I never really understood what undivided attention meant when my kindergarten teacher said, "I want your undivided attention." It was only when I learned how to do the divided attention of the *solkattu* exercises or South Indian singing or improvising, that I realized, "Oh, that's what they meant!" That's the example that I use when I explain dividing attention or multi-tasking.

SANKARAN: To develop that further, *solkattu* is useful from simple counting to remembering the most complex compositions. When they used to say *one e and a, two e and a* in Western music, now they are saying *ta ka di mi, ta ka di mi*. Because these are simple percussive syllables, they don't mean anything else in terms of language, just a drummer's language. They don't have any other meaning, these *ta ka di mis, ta di gi na thoms*, and *ta ki tas*, so anybody can use it, once they develop it. Of course, having said that, it's not that easy to develop the fluency of doing *solkattu*, but gradually they can improve. Counting is so important in Western tradition, so you really need to have a useful system. If you believe in the system and experience it in your mouth and body, it will really help you.

I also compare *solkattu* to the North Indian system of *bols* – both are beautiful. Again, they come from a different language. The North Indian Hindi language uses more aspirated sounds, more like Sanskrit – like *dha din din na, tha din din na*. Also the Hindi approach to speaking rhythms is slightly different from the Karnatak style. The North Indian *bols* can elongate a syllable, and they are more lyrical. The South Indian syllables have a strong attack quality, so you can experience more precision with *solkattu*.

RH: Are *solkattu* based on Tamil?

SANKARAN: Yes, Tamil, not Sanskrit. But we have borrowed some sounds from Sanskrit: *ta dit ta jem*. Those syllables are really decorative syllables, and they come from Sanskrit. Those who want to go deeper into *solkattu* can also get into language technique; there is so much scope.

RH: Suba, in Autorickshaw, Ed Hanley plays *tabla*. How does this work for you combining music from North and South Indian music with jazz?

SUBA: The genesis of the idea or the core concept usually comes from Ed, then I will get him to teach me the North Indian syllables. But for me to learn them, I will sometimes do a South Indian translation just so I can internalize it in my body and my hands and my mouth. And then I'll learn the North Indian syllables which I find a little more difficult because they are not my first language, and they have a slightly different flow. Ed has studied with my father, so he is very conscious of the differences between North Indian and South Indian rhythms and the syllabic languages. He has also translated some of the South Indian compositions for *tabla*. It's very different sounding from the *mrdangam* even though there are similarities in the two. Or I'll compose something and I'll say, okay this is more like a *ta di gi na thom* kind of phrase, and he'll say, "well we don't really have that on the *tabla*." It doesn't have quite the same sound when you say it with North Indian *bols*; similar, but not the same. Also, Dylan does beat-boxing, very standard issue Western style beat-boxing, emulating the drum set. So we'll sometimes have a three-way percussion battle of the bands where I will recite in *solkattu*, Ed will imitate my rhythms on the *tabla*, and Dylan will respond by beat-boxing, or as he calls it "drumming with his face."

SANKARAN: So it's really a question of adaptation. I have students who are adapting *kanjira* and *mrdangam* compositions to drum set. The challenge is that you can't really emulate the sound of the *mrdangam* on the drum set, so you are going more for the rhythmic values. And yet, for the sake of fluency and the way you want to play a *ta ka di na thom*, you have to distribute your strokes, whether you put it on a high-hat or tom-tom, or bass drum; you have to create your own legend. These are the challenging things when it comes to adaptation. So you take rhythmic values as a compositional element without attempting to imitate *mrdangam* sounds exactly.

RH: I just have one more question. Did you have any reservations when Suba decided to pursue Western music? Did you have hopes that she might become a professional performer of Karnatak music?

SANKARAN: Honestly, deeply rooted in my tradition I would really have wanted one of my children to take to this music very seriously; but of course she has taken it seriously. At the same time I think what we have developed is world music happening in our home. I don't know how we did that but we have an open mind to learn and appreciate other music and not just dwell in our own culture saying, "Well, we are the greatest." So we are very happy that she is doing Western music. Still my wish is that she shows more interest in Karnatak music. Her forte is more into jazz fusion, but my doors are always open. That wish is always there, but I'm really happy and proud of what she is doing. There's no regret at all.

RH: She's gone in new directions and is definitely "her own person."

SANKARAN: I'm sure Suba realizes that it takes extra effort to specialize in one thing, and I know she could have done it if she wanted. Maybe just to get a little bit philosophical, I think the general trend now is overall education – a broader education – not just specializing in one thing. And this holistic approach to learning and to teaching is so important. From that respect, I think she is doing really well and, to some extent, me, too. I should also thank my wife, Lalitha, for taking care of the basic education of my daughters, an education that really started at home. I'm thankful to god to have a family like this.

Notes

1. Karnatak is often spelled Carnatic.

2. In this chapter, I will follow Indian tradition and refer to Trichy Sankaran by his last name, Sankaran. Trichy is the name of the town in southern India where Sankaran was born.

3. *Solkattu* (*sol* = syllable, *kattu* = bunch, group) is the system of South Indian rhythmic solfege. "Syllabic concept is the foundation for all musical concepts and precepts in the Indian musical system. *Akshara* (syllable) is the basic unit of thought and perception. Musical ideas are conceived and expressed in terms of syllabic structures, memorized by an indigenous system of solmization. These become the encoded form, word-formulas for the metric-syllabic

structures." T. Sankaran, *The Art of Konnakol (Solkattu)* (Toronto: Lalith, 2010), p. 1.

4. *Nadai* in Sanskrit, or *gati* in Tamil. "Flow; the number of subdivisions per *akshara* (see note 3) or beat." These subdivisions are generally 3, 4, 5, 7, or 9 (see note 9). Sankaran, *The Art of Konnakol (Solkattu)*, p. 119.

5. *Tala* is "a rhythmic cycle consisting of a certain number of beats, shown through codified hand gestures, according to traditional practices." Sankaran, *The Art of Konnakol (Solkattu)*, p. 120.

6. *Korvai*: "Literally, 'strung together.' A cadential form in which different phrase-patterns are strung together." *Mora*: "A cadential form which is marked by repeating a phrase or pattern three times." T. Sankaran, *The Rhythmic Principles of South Indian Drumming* (Toronto: Lalith, 1994), p. 162–63.

7. *Mora*: see note 6.

8. *Rupaka tala* is a rhythmic cycle of three beats (sometimes viewed as six beats).

9. *Tisra* is one of five *jatis* that represent five basic lengths of rhythmic units:

> *Tisra jati* – 3; *Chatusra jati* – 4; *Khanda jati* –5; *Misra jati* – 7; *Sankirna jati* – 9. Sankaran, *Rhythmic Principles*, pp. 20–1.

18 African influences on Western percussion performance and pedagogy

B. MICHAEL WILLIAMS

Introduction

As a percussionist, I am usually in the back of the orchestra playing instruments such as the snare drum, bass drum, cymbals, tambourine, triangle, timpani, or xylophone. Many years ago, I realized that nearly all these instruments in some way have their origins on the African continent. This realization led me on a quest to discover more about our percussive connection with Africa. What I found was a thread running throughout recorded history (and indeed beyond), an African continuum that is as much a part of every percussionist's heritage as the twenty-six standard rudiments of drumming. Prototypes of the earliest percussion instruments made their way into the European orchestra through the Turkish Janissary tradition (quite possibly via Arabic trade routes into North and West Africa long before recorded history), becoming standard instruments of the ensembles during the later years of the eighteenth century. Initially utilized to add color or an exotic flavor to the orchestral sound palette, percussion music found a creative foothold with the introduction of the percussion ensemble in the early twentieth century. Inventive composers such as Edgard Varèse and Amadeo Roldán, followed by Henry Cowell, John Cage, Lou Harrison, and other members of the "West Coast School," used conventional, ethnic, and "found" percussion instruments to greatly expand the possibilities of creativity in the era of early avant-garde experimentalism. These composers not only began to employ the instruments of African and other cultures, but utilized some characteristics of those cultures' rhythmic and tonal languages as well. As percussionists and composers sought direct contact with African musical sources, awareness of specific African musical elements (such as polyrhythm, call and response, and interlocking voices) made their way into compositions for percussion, exemplified particularly by the works of Steve Reich and other "minimalist" composers.

Roughly concurrent with the development of the Western orchestral percussion section and its eventual expansion into the modern percussion ensemble, the African diaspora was influencing the musical development of the New World in Cuba, Brazil, and the United States.

These diasporic influences would develop into genres such as rumba in Cuba, samba in Brazil, and jazz in the United States. Virtually every popular musical expression draws from African musical sensibilities and influences.

There are connections between the rudimental drumming tradition in North America (via Europe through the Janissary traditions) and the vocabulary of patterns employed in African drumming improvisations. Certain Africanisms such as groove, style, feel, voice, inherent pattern awareness, and "three-dimensional listening" can make a case for the study of traditional African music as a part of standard percussion pedagogy as we encourage our students to learn to "hear with African ears."

Orchestral origins

Antecedents of modern orchestral percussion instruments abound in Africa. The Moroccan *bendir*, with its single snare running across the underside of the head, is quite possibly an ancestor of the medieval *tabor*, which developed into the modern snare drum. In Ghana, the Dagbamba play a snared bass drum called *gungon* (see Figure 18.1),

Figure 18.1 *Gungon.*

with a curved stick in one hand and other hand bare. The main rhythms are executed with the stick hand, while the bare hand fills in gaps with embellishments at the top edge of the drum skin. In 1555, Pierre Belon described a similar technique of a Turkish Janissary musician playing a large drum called *davul*: " ... the right hand, holding a curved stick, plays accented beats while the left, holding (a thin switch), plays more rapidly."[1] Most scholars agree that the kettledrum originated from the Arabic *naqqarah* or *nakers*, although there are several examples of kettle-shaped drums throughout Africa. The medieval triangle developed from the ancient Ethiopian *sistrum*[2] with its trapezoidal shape and jangling iron rings attached to the lower rung.[3] Similarly, the modern tambourine has its ancestry in the Egyptian *riqq* and other prototypes from North Africa.[4] The marimba and other instruments of the xylophone family originated in Africa as well, although some scholars have hypothesized an Indonesian influence.[5]

Much of this discussion is purely conjectural, as most scholars have agreed that the Janissary instruments that eventually made their way into the European orchestra had Saracen (Muslim) origins or came from the East and that Islamic music had a particular influence on West African instruments and musical expression.[6] It is entirely possible that the musical influences traveled both ways by ancient trade routes from Africa through the Near and Middle East, as written accounts from European travelers on African soil did not occur until the European Renaissance was well underway.

No one knows what the original Janissary music sounded like, and descriptions of musical instruments are sketchy until 1588 when Thoinot Arbeau published his manual on drumming and dance titled *Orchésographie*.[7] James Blades lists the full complement of percussion instruments employed by the Janissary as consisting of "numerous pairs of cymbals, small kettledrums, triangles, tambourines and one or more Turkish crescents (*chapeau chinois*)."[8] Two famous early examples of the implementation of Janissary percussion in the orchestra are Haydn's *"Military" Symphony No. 100* (1794) and Beethoven's *Symphony No. 9* (1823), both scored for bass drum (in Haydn's case with both stick and switch), cymbals, and triangle.[9] What these composers sought in these new sounds was added color, along with a touch of the exotic. Steven Schick explains:

> In his Ninth Symphony, Beethoven doubled the advantage of percussion. He used it to create a vivid dance-like variation of the famous melody in the last movement. And further, by borrowing the perfumed percussion sounds of the cymbals, triangle, and bass drum from exotic Turkey, he managed to spice up an otherwise straightforward orchestration. Beethoven, not above dressing up yesterday's ideas with a splash of color, was a composer who knew how to accessorize.[10]

Advent of the percussion ensemble

The twentieth century ushered in a wealth of new sounds and rhythmic settings with the arrival of the percussion ensemble. The two earliest works for percussion ensemble, Roldán's *Ritmicas V and VI* (1930) and Varèse's *Ionisation* (1931), opened the door for a new generation of composers waiting in the wings and eager to develop the new genre with the inclusion of noises and indigenous instruments from a variety of cultures. Roldán's work, scored for a variety of traditional Afro-Cuban percussion instruments, reflected the African folk roots and rhythms of his native Cuba.[11] Varèse's composition presented an explosion of new sounds and noise aggregates to inspire the new generation.[12] Both of these seminal works inspired a group of composers, dubbed the "West Coast School," who revolved around the guidance of Henry Cowell. These composers (including Cowell, John Cage, Lou Harrison, Gerald Strang, Ray Green, and William Russell) began exploring music for modern dance inspired by their "interest in combining elements of non-Western music with modern Western compositional techniques."[13] Cowell's New Music Society began publishing scores in the quarterly *New Music*, which first appeared in 1927. In 1933, Cowell published Russell's *Fugue for Eight Percussion Instruments* and Varèse's *Ionisation*. In 1936, he issued six more works.[14] Cowell had categorized his growing collection of percussion compositions chronologically into four "schools," one of which arose from "direct experience with primitive percussion rhythms," particularly citing the works of modern Cuban composers such as Roldán and José Ardévol, who were "in close contact with the native Afro-Cuban music."[15]

Cowell introduced both Cage and Harrison to music of various world cultures through his course, "Music of the World's Peoples." Cowell's book, *New Musical Resources*, influenced Cage to enter the field of music. "That was important to me," Cage said, "to hear through him music from all the various cultures; and they sounded different. Sound became important to me – and noise is so rich in terms of sound."[16] Cameroonian musician and writer, Francis Bebey, expressed a similar sentiment to Cage's in describing music from Africa:

> There is still a lingering notion that noise and music are incompatible. . . .
> The African musician does not merely attempt to imitate nature by means of
> musical instruments; he reverses the procedure by taking natural sounds
> and incorporating them into his music.[17]

Although Cage and Bebey are discussing two different cultural expressions, both points of view agree. What Cage and the other composers of the West Coast School sought to achieve was a redefinition of what was acceptable

as music in the twentieth century. Noise and sounds of other cultures inter-twined in the earliest manifestations of the percussion ensemble. Cage and his West Coast cohorts experimented with found sounds such as automobile brake drums and thunder sheets, but they also employed indigenous instruments from various world cultures in order to make noise available for use as a musical resource. According to Schick,

> Finally, after more than a hundred years of development, percussionists were standing near the front of the line for acknowledgement and respectability. Then Cage, Edgard Varèse, and Henry Cowell came along with their revolution and greeted this newfound respectability with a brick to the head. . . . Early works for percussion ensembles were much more than just music; they were also social phenomena rising from a growing fluidity of cultural boundaries and new models of immigration in the New World. . . . Cage and his fellow revolutionaries were voicing concerns that we think of today as globalism, futurism, and individualism in the guise of polycultural noise constructions as early as the 1930s.[18]

Steve Reich and *Drumming*

During the 1960s, in reaction to the rigidity of serialism, a number of composers began paring down musical resources and borrowing certain elements (including rhythm, harmony, and in some cases instrumentation) from simpler popular genres as a kind of dialogue between "culti-vated" and "vernacular" expressions.[19] Steve Reich was at the forefront of this movement, along with such notables as Terry Riley and Philip Glass. The repetitive rhythms and simpler, cyclic chord progressions reminiscent to some degree of blues, jazz, and early rock music provided some of the flavorful seeds for what became known as minimalism or process music. Reich had been attracted to popular songs, jazz, and bebop styles as a teenager and his early musical language drew to some extent from this African-American infused music.[20] The next generation of minimalists (or "post-minimalists"), including such composers as David Lang, Julia Wolfe, Evan Ziporyn, and Michael Gordon, continues to follow Reich's and other minimalists' lead in blurring the lines of demarcation between art music and popular expressions.

Reich's work stands out for a number of reasons. He studied drumming as a teenager and was familiar with the rudiments of drumming, so his compositions had a percussive quality about them without the familiarities of the earlier percussion ensemble music of the West Coast School. He had heard recordings of African drumming and read A. M. Jones' book, *Studies in African Music*, in the early 1960s while a student at Mills College and those

experiences influenced his earliest works for tape loops. Later, in 1970, Reich traveled to Ghana to study Ewe drumming. *Drumming* incorporates the interlocking patterns derived in some ways from African drumming and combines them with the technique of phasing multiple unison canons with different rhythmic positions taken from his earliest tape works.[21] He was able to accomplish this in live performance because he surrounded himself with highly accomplished professional musicians (in contrast to the unschooled percussionists who realized Cage's earliest works) who shared his affinity for rhythm, groove, and what might be termed "pop," or at least "non-academic" sensibilities.[22] Concerning the African influence on *Drumming*, Reich wrote,

> The effect of my visit [to Ghana] was basically *confirmation*: that writing for acoustic instruments playing repeating patterns of a percussive nature was a viable means of making music, and had an ancient history. Thus, my visit to Africa did not directly influence my piece *Drumming*. That piece was mostly the result of my having studied drumming when I was 14 with Roland Kohloff. My studies of Western drumming as a teenager together with my undying attraction for percussion and my discoveries of phase shifting with short repeating patterns led to the composition of *Drumming* in 1971. The influence of African music on my composition really had happened much earlier in 1963 and '64, and from that point, as an influence, it diminished.[23]

What Reich valued most was finding his own voice within a somewhat African-derived structure of polyrhythmic interlocking patterns. Out of respect for African musical tradition, he rejected early the notion of employing authentic African instruments in his work.[24] While Reich clearly downplays direct African influence on *Drumming* and other works using similar procedures, the resultant patterns that emerge from the coincidence of multiple unison canons are strikingly similar to the inherent patterns of interlocking *mbira* voices in the Shona music of Zimbabwe and the Ugandan *amadinda* xylophone tradition. Still, the voice of *Drumming* clearly belongs to Reich.

The African diaspora

The African diaspora runs deep in the music of the Americas. African musical expressions are preserved and transcended in the forms of samba and bossa nova in Brazil; rumba and salsa in Cuba; reggae in Jamaica; calypso in Trinidad; blues, jazz, rhythm and blues, and rock music in the United States, and so many others throughout the New World. African customs, myths, and music came to the Americas by way of the slave trade of 1619–1808. African slaves from Cameroon, Ivory Coast, Guinea, and Senegal were brought to New Orleans, while those from Angola, Congo,

Nigeria, and Ghana landed in Brazil. Other natives from Nigeria, Ghana, and Ivory Coast arrived in Cuba and Martinique, "bringing with them the African calls, variegated songs, and dance music that would sow, in a new land, the seeds that would blossom into an ever-unfolding extension and elaboration of their progenitors' culture." [25]

Having charted and analyzed over 2,500 songs from 233 indigenous African cultures, Alan Lomax notes a remarkable homogeneity of musical style on the African continent. He describes African singing styles as relaxed, cohesive, repetitious, overlapped, antiphonal, and polyrhythmic in accompaniment. "It dominates African song from the Cape of Good Hope to the Straits of Gibraltar and west into the American colonies, and is the source of African cultural homogeneity."[26] The common stylistic thread that unites all African music, concludes Lomax, "is repetitious, cohesive, overlapping or interlocked, multi-leveled, and hot."[27]

The foundational elements of African-American music include calls, cries, and hollers, call-and-response devices, additive rhythms and poly-rhythms, heterophony, blue notes, bent notes, and elisions. Vocables and other rhythmic-oral declamations, interjections, and punctuations dominate singing expressions. Many of these vocal devices were incorporated into instrumental music. Offbeat melodic phrasings and repetition of rhythmic and melodic figures developed into riffs and vamps in jazz. In addition, timbral distortions of various kinds (both vocal and instrumental) and a metronomic sense underlie all African-American music.[28]

Africans throughout the New World attempted to continue their native religious practices involving drumming, dancing, and spirit possession ceremonies in neo-African cults. Cuba, Brazil, and other New World colonies eventually accepted and even embraced these activities and their accompanying drums, rattles, and bells. It was a different story in the United States, as John Storm Roberts relates:

> The varying degrees of tolerance or hostility directed against neo-African cults had a direct effect on the black music of the New World. The African elements in U.S. music are far more transmuted than those of other parts, and there is no neo-African music such as found in the Caribbean and parts of South America. One reason, no doubt, is that contact with Africa was broken earlier, and another is that – compared at least with some parts of the Caribbean – the black population is smaller. Moreover, it is probable that the main African influence on the United States was from a tradition that could blend well with white styles. But the banning of drums in many parts of the country was certainly a factor, especially in the disappearance of the cults. ... When the drums were silent, the old gods came no more.[29]

The southern plantations in America yielded the field hollers and ring-shouts that incorporated call and response into early spirituals. These vocal

styles merged into instrumental music and mixed with indigenous rhythms of drumming, as Floyd explains:

> The banjo, flute, triangle, drum, quills, and sticks (bones) were ubiquitous in slave culture. It is not surprising to find that this combination of instruments is perfectly suited to the realization of the heterogeneous sound ideal. The combination of these sounds creates a contrasting, not a blending, conglomerate, resulting in a sound that is ideally suited to the rhythmic, polyphonic, and tonal stratifications of African and African-American music. . . . The ideal sound played a critical role in determining the nature of blues, ragtime, jazz, gospel, R&B, and all the other African-American musical genres, and it also influenced mightily the unique sound of American popular music in general.[30]

There is probably not a single popular musical form or style that is not somehow touched by African music. As the diaspora continued to unfold, instruments were adopted and adapted: from fiddles (both African and European) to the banjo (a distinctly African instrument), even in the hands of Appalachian "hillbilly" musicians.[31] In similar fashion, the drum set developed from the marching funeral bands of New Orleans following the Civil War in the gestation period of early jazz.[32]

Pedagogical considerations

With such an abundance of African influences on current Western culture, it is incumbent on today's percussion educators to address matters of African musical pedagogy with our students. I have always been a firm advocate of teaching all first-year students, no matter how advanced or experienced, the twenty-six standard drum rudiments. I explain to my students that these patterns are not only an excellent way to develop a solid percussion technique; musically speaking, they are part of every drummer's ancestral heritage. I believe we owe it to our students to expose them to African music for the same reasons. The onomatopoeic verbalizations of standard patterns such as "flam," "ruff," "paradiddle," and "ratamacue" mirror the various verbalized rhythms of African drumming and extemporized vocables in African singing styles. The earliest rudimental fife and drum pieces consist of similar kinds of "constant repetition of rhythmic and melodic figures and phrases" referred to by Floyd as foundational elements in African-American music.[33] Peggy Sexton makes a compelling case that the syncopated "flamacue" may have developed from an African origin. Othar Turner's Mississippi Fife and Drum Band is a wonderful example of the synthesis of European-derived military music with African drumming roots, in which drummers employ improvisations filled with flamacue-derived rhythms bearing a distinctly Senegambian flavor.[34]

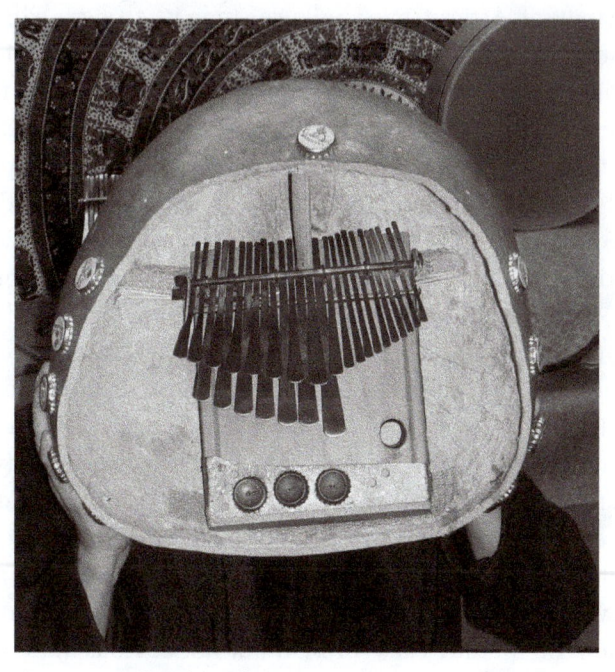

Figure 18.2 *Mbira dzaVadzimu.*

As is commonly prescribed by drum set pedagogues, I encourage my students to transcribe African rhythms from recordings as a way to "get inside" a particular soloist's tone, feel, groove, phrasing, and improvisational style.[35] I also encourage them to *sing*, as there is no better way to internalize African concepts of pitch and phrasing. Of course, it is vitally important to bring in African teachers and authentic culture-bearers to add the richness of social contact and context to the learning experience whenever possible.

In addition to African *djembe* drumming of the Mande tradition of Guinea and Mali, many of my students also study the Zimbabwean *mbira* (see Figure 18.2). The study of this elegant and powerful instrument, a "cousin" of the marimba,[36] brings a completely new realm of listening experience to the entire percussion curriculum. Melody, implied harmonies, inherent rhythms or resultant patterns, polyrhythm, modality, cyclic recursion, and singing are all available through the study of this single instrument. I have found that studying *mbira* can change the way students hear the more conventional works they play on marimba, timpani, multiple percussion, drum set, and any of the standard instruments of the percussion section. Contemporary compositions abound with musical Africanisms, whether or not intended by the composer, simply because they have become part of our contemporary musical language.

The study of African music allows students to hear with "African ears," to become aware that, as Berliner has related, "The music becomes 'kaleidophonic.'" [37] In a typical forty-eight-pulse cycle of a traditional *mbira* tune may be found dozens of inherent patterns that often overlap and intersect, facilitating the discovery of a fascinating depth to this seemingly repetitive music. These patterns are also polyrhythmic, and their effects are multiplied when two or more players perform together in interlocking *kushaura* (leading) and *kutsinhira* (following or complementary) parts. I compare the sensation of hearing and discovering these inherent patterns to the effect of viewing a sculpture in comparison with a painting. The music can be perceived as three dimensional. There is no starting and ending point to this circular, repetitive music, and yet it is anything but monotonous. Once a student has grasped this listening concept, these perceptions can enrich the aural experience, adding depth of understanding to any musical expression. Not unlike the music of Steve Reich, *mbira* music requires clarity of focus and heightened perceptive awareness on the part of the listener in order to bring attention to what Dumisani Maraire calls "present but not obvious lines" created by the combination of interlocking patterns, cross harmonies, overtones, or the interweaving of other, unintended sounds.[38] Such musical economy of means makes for a satisfying aesthetic experience using only the barest of musical resources, opening our perceptions to the exquisite ambiguity of African music, reflective of the mystery of life itself. One can discover in this music the seeds of ancient musical genres that continue to develop in the twenty-first century.

Understanding the shared cultural heritage of percussionists worldwide is vitally important to our overall pedagogy. We need to know where our music comes from in order to grasp where it is going. At the very least, we can honor our musical ancestors by fostering in our students an awareness of the "long shadow of black ancestral traditions" through which artistic expressions are culturally reworked "in the jaws of modern experience."[39] There is a rhythm from Mali called "Madan." It is a harvest rhythm played on the *djembe* for the cultivation of fields. The rhythm employs the three characteristic sounds of the *djembe*: bass (b), tone (t), and slap (s) as follows:

|| : b.tt.bs. : ||

I call this rhythm "the Ringo beat," the pattern Ringo Starr plays on the Beatles' tune "Twist and Shout" and countless other early rock tunes. It is over 800 years old. I first heard it in 1964 and it made me want to become a drummer. I did not know at the time that this

simple, catchy rhythm would lead me back to my musical ancestors, and I am grateful to Ringo for bringing it to my attention. This simple rhythm connects us to Africa, and Africa is a powerful nexus of the percussive arts, a continuum that has indeed been with us all along embedded within a very deep heritage.

Notes

1. H. Powley, "Janissary Music," in J. H. Beck (ed.), *Encyclopedia of Percussion* (New York: Garland Publishing, 1995), p. 196.
2. G. B. Peters, *The Drummer: Man* (Wilmette, IL: Kemper-Peters, 1975), p. 75.
3. J. Montagu, *Timpani and Percussion* (Yale University Press, 2002), p. 20.
4. *Ibid.*, p. 25; J. Blades, *Percussion Instruments and Their History* (London: Faber and Faber, 2002), p. 158.
5. B. M. Williams, "Mbira/Timbila, Marimba/Karimba: A Look at Some Relationships Between African Mbira and Marimba," *Percussive Notes*, vol. 40, no. 1 (2002), 33, 39.
6. C. Sachs, *The History of Musical Instruments* (New York: W. W. Norton, 1940); J. H. K. Nketia, *The Music of Africa* (New York: W.W.Norton, 1974), p. 260; Blades, *Percussion Instruments*, pp. 183–6; Peters, *The Drummer: Man*, p. 17. Also see: Montagu, *Timpani*, p. 16; E. Charry, *Mande Music* (University of Chicago Press, 2000), p. 45; 17; J. Blacking, *Music, Culture, and Experience* (University of Chicago Press, 1995), p. 138.
7. Montagu, *Timpani and Percussion*, p. 24.
8. Blades, *Percussion Instruments*, p. 265.
9. *Ibid.*, p. 260.
10. S. Schick, *The Percussionist's Art* (University of Rochester Press, 2006), p. 14.
11. R. K. LeVan, "African Musical Influence in Selected Art Music Works for Percussion Ensemble, 1930–1984," unpublished PhD thesis, University of Pittsburgh (1991), pp. 207–54.
12. Schick, *The Percussionist's Art*, p. 14.
13. LeVan, "African Musical Influence," p. 61.
14. L. Miller, "The Art of Noise: John Cage, Lou Harrison, and the West Coast Percussion Ensemble," in M. Saffle (ed.) *Perspectives on American Music, 1900–1950* (New York: Garland Publishing, 2000), 215–63.
15. *Ibid.*, p. 215.
16. B. M. Williams, "The Early Percussion Music of John Cage, 1935–1943," unpublished PhD thesis, Michigan State University (1990), p. 187.
17. F. Bebey, *African Music: A People's Art* (Brooklyn, NY: Lawrence Hill, 1975), p. 2.
18. Schick, *The Percussionist's Art*, p. 2.

19. K. Potter, *Four Musical Minimalists* (Cambridge University Press, 2000), p. 18.
20. S. Reich, *Writings on Music, 1965–2000* (Oxford University Press, 2002), p. 7.
21. For a complete description of the structural processes applied in *Drumming*, see Reich, pp. 63–7 and Schick, pp. 234–42.
22. Reich, *Writings on Music*, pp. 156–57.
23. *Ibid.*, p. 106.
24. *Ibid.*
25. S. A. Floyd, *The Power of Black Music: Interpreting Its History from Africa to the United States* (Oxford University Press, 1995), p. 38.
26. A. Lomax, "Africanisms in New World Music" in V. Rubin and R. P. Schaedel (eds.), *The Haitian Potential* (New York: Teachers College Press, 1975), p. 46.
27. *Ibid.*, p. 48.
28. Floyd, *Black Music*, p. 6.
29. J. S. Roberts, *Black Music of Two Worlds* (New York: Praeger, 1972), pp. 38–9.
30. Floyd, *Black Music*, p. 56.
31. E. Wald, *The Blues: A Very Short Introduction* (Oxford University Press, 2010), p. 97.
32. R. B. Breithaupt, "The Drum Set: A History," in J. H. Beck (ed.), *Encyclopedia of Percussion* (New York: Garland Publishing, 1995), pp. 173–85; T. D. Brown and R. B. Breithaupt, "The Evolution of Early Jazz Drumming," *Percussionist*, vol. 7, no. 2 (1969), 39.
33. Floyd, *Black Music*, p. 6.
34. P. Sexton, "Desperately Seeking 'Juba': Some Explorations into the Origin of the Flamacue, Part 1," *Percussive Notes*, vol. 45, no. 6 (2007), 20–4; Part II, *Percussive Notes*, vol. 46, no. 1 (2008), 30; J. Clark, *Connecticut's Fife and Drum Tradition* (Wesleyan University Press, 2011), p. 10; R. Damm, "Sharde Thomas and Mississippi Fife and Drum Band," *Percussive Notes*, vol. 51, no. 1 (2013), 22–4.
35. See Williams, "Mamady Keita's 'Kassa,'"*Percussive Notes*, vol. 35, no. 2 (1997), 36–43; "Getting Started with Mbira dzaVadzimu," *Percussive Notes*, vol. 35, no. 4 (1997), 38–47; "Mamady Keita's 'Mendiani,'" *Percussive Notes*, vol. 37, no. 4 (1999), 56–61; "Mamady Keita's 'Kuku,'" *Percussive Notes*, vol. 40, no. 4 (2002), 26–31.

36. Williams, "Mbira/Timbila, Marimba/Karimba," 32–9.

37. P. Berliner, *The Soul of Mbira: Music and Traditions of the Shona People of Zimbabwe* (University of California Press, 1994), p. 111.

38. Williams, "Mbira dzaVadzimu," 47.

39. V. Erlmann, "Communities of Style: Musical Figures of Black Diasporic Identity," in Ingrid Monson (ed.), *The African Diaspora: A Musical Perspective* (New York: Routledge, 2003), 98.

19 The gamelan beleganjur as Balinese percussion ensemble

MICHAEL B. BAKAN

When my son and daughter were little, I took them to hear their first live performance by an orchestra: a dress rehearsal reading of Mussourgsky's *Pictures at an Exhibition* played by the Florida State University Symphony. My daughter Leah, three at the time, was very excited by the experience and wanted to tell her grandfather all about it. She grabbed the phone from me while I was speaking to him that evening. "Guess what we did today, Grandpa?" she gushed. "We went to hear an American gamelan!" And as far as Leah was concerned, that is precisely what we had done. Her percussionist/ethnomusicologist father, after all, was a Balinese gamelan director at the University. She had heard plenty of gamelan concerts in her young life, but nothing like this. Gamelan music was familiar; it was normal. The orchestra? Now *that* was something different.

Gamelan orchestras?

Most readers of this chapter probably do not think of an orchestra as a type of gamelan, but it is likely that many do think of a gamelan as a type of orchestra. Indeed, we in the West have been routinely referring to gamelans as "Javanese orchestras" or "Balinese orchestras" for well over a century now, at least since the days when Claude Debussy famously alighted at the spectacle of Indonesian gamelan music performed at the 1889 Paris World's Fair.[1]

It makes no more sense to call an orchestra a gamelan than it does to call a gamelan an orchestra, but it makes no less sense either, and as I will endeavor to illustrate in this chapter, such cross-cultural frames of reference, shot through with egregious inaccuracies and essentialisms as they may be, offer gateways to rich and enlightening understandings of both the disparate musical traditions they enframe and the dialectical relationships that exist between those traditions. Analyzing orchestral repertoire through the use of concepts and procedures normally reserved for gamelan music analysis, for example, can reveal unique music-theoretical perspectives and insights, as is demonstrated in Michael Tenzer's gamelan-informed analyses of symphonic works by Lutoslawski and Ives.[2] In a different vein, the Javanese musicologist Sumarsam has theorized on how "exposure to Western modes of

thinking caused gamelan theories to develop along particular lines," especially in relation to the ascription by Dutch colonial officials of "high culture" status to Central Javanese court gamelan musics in the nineteenth and twentieth centuries, that is, to a status category normally reserved for European symphonic music and the like.[3]

The conceptual fluidity of scholars like Tenzer and Sumarsam – their willingness to stretch beyond the conventional boundaries of relativistic propriety for the sake of drawing parallels between ostensibly unrelated musical and cultural traditions – largely accounts for the creative richness of their work and the instructiveness of its findings. It inspires new ways of thinking not just about gamelans and orchestras, but about the products and processes of musical experience most broadly conceived.

My purpose in this chapter is to achieve something similar, though from a very different point of view. It is to make gamelan music make sense in terms of Western musical and cultural sensibilities rather than in opposition to them and, moreover, to accomplish such sense-making with a majority target readership of Western percussionists in mind. Toward this end, I limit the scope of both the investigation and its project of cross-cultural analogizing in two related ways. First, the discussion focuses on a single type of gamelan, the Balinese *gamelan beleganjur* (see Figure 19.1), a processional ensemble that is comprised exclusively of

Figure 19.1 The *gamelan beleganjur*.

gongs, melodic gong-chimes, drums, and cymbals. Second, I avoid generically analogizing gamelans and orchestras, favoring instead an alternate mode of analogy that is both more specific and more accurate: the gamelan beleganjur as percussion ensemble.

Whatever else the gamelan beleganjur may be – an emblem of Balinese cultural identity, an integral component of Hindu-Balinese ritual life, a forum for inter- and intra-village competition – it is indisputably a percussion ensemble as well. It lacks the string and wind instruments that are featured in many other forms of Javanese and Balinese gamelan and is thus an entirely appropriate medium for engagement in pure percussion ensemble terms. Adopting such an approach in the context of a volume like this one, geared as it is to percussionists and the percussively inclined, provides a rare and special opportunity to bridge the gaps of foreignness, exoticism, and esotericism that too often impede intercultural awareness, understanding, and empathy among and between the denizens of seemingly distant musical worlds.

The gamelan beleganjur as percussion ensemble

If the gamelan beleganjur is a percussion ensemble, this begs the question of precisely what kind of percussion ensemble it is. To answer that question, we must consider the ensemble in terms of its material, musical, performative, and cultural elements, and also in terms of key functional roles, contextual settings, and aesthetic priorities with which it is associated in Bali.

Instrumentation

The standard instrumentation of the gamelan beleganjur consists of two *kendang* (drums); eight pairs of crash cymbals (*cengceng*); two tempo-marking, hand-held kettle gongs called *kajar* (or *kempli*) and *kempluk*; another pair of hand-held kettle gongs called *ponggang* that furnishes the music's *pokok* (lit. "trunk" or "root"), or core melody; four smaller hand-held kettle gongs called *reyong* (or *bonang*), on which are played rapid interlocking figures that ornament the pokok; a medium-sized, flat-bossed gong, the *bendé*, which has a clangy timbre and plays syncopated figures; and two very large hanging gongs, the *gong ageng*, which together with the kajar, the kempluk, and a medium-sized hanging gong called the *kempur*, provide the music's foundational *gongan*, or gong cycle (colotomic) structure.

All of the instruments other than the crash cymbals are played with either padded beaters or yarn-wound mallets. The female (*wadon*) and male (*lanang*) gong ageng (lit. great gong) are typically played by a single performer, but there is a separate player for every other instrument in the ensemble:

one drummer each for the male (lanang) and female (wadon) kendang, eight cymbal players for the eight pairs of cengceng, four reyong players for the four reyong "pots," and one player each for the two ponggang kettles, plus the kajar, kempluk, kempur, and bendé players. Traditionally, beleganjur musicians were always male (the majority being teenagers and young men), though beginning in the 1990s some women's groups were established as well.[4]

As noted, the gamelan beleganjur is a processional ensemble, a Balinese-style drum line in essence. The processional order of instrumentalists may vary, but is always headed up by the two drummers. They are typically followed by two lines of cymbal players, one line of reyong players, and a fifth line of musicians playing the ponggang, kajar, and kempluk parts. Shoring up the rear is the gong section, with the bendé and kempur players on either side of the *gong* player.

The kendang are slung around the drummers' necks on straps and played lengthwise with a mallet on the right-hand head and open palm strokes on the left. The reyong, ponggang, kajar, and kempluk are held in the players' left hands and struck with mallets held in the right. The hanging gongs are suspended from thick wooden poles and usually transported on shoulder by nonplaying gong carriers. They are struck with very large padded mallets, except for the bendé, which is played with a thick, curved wooden beater.

Fundamental aspects of form and structure in traditional beleganjur music

Compared to most every other type of Balinese gamelan, the gamelan beleganjur is conspicuously limited in its melodic range and resources. The entire melodic dimension of the music is confined to the two-toned ostinato core melody of the ponggang and the interlocking melodic elaborations of the reyong an octave above. Rhythm, tempo, cyclicity, and energy (*gaya*), rather than melodic development per se, are what primarily define the musical character and functional efficacy of traditional beleganjur music, that is, *beleganjur kuno*.

The core foundation of all beleganjur music is an eight-beat gong cycle (gongan) called either *gilak* or *tabuh gilak*. Each of the eight beats is marked by the steady "quarter-note" pulses of the kajar part, which are reinforced on every other note by the kempluk (if present – this is an optional beleganjur instrument). The first and fifth beats are marked alternately by the female and male gongs, with beats six and eight punctuated by the kempur. The clangy bendé fills in the rhythmic spaces with a syncopated ostinato rhythmic figure, usually the following one (- = rest; / = stroke):

```
1   2   3   4   5   6   7   8
-  //  -  //  -  //  -/  -/
```

The ponggang's core melody, the pokok, is also one eight-beat cycle in length. Beleganjur uses a four-note *pelog*-type scale consisting of the Balinese pitches *dong, deng, dung*, and *dang*, which are represented as pitches 2, 3, 5, and 6 in Balinese cipher notation, and which usually correspond roughly to the Western pitches D, E, G#, and A. The two ponggang are tuned to *dang* (A) and *dung* (G#) and perform the following melodic pattern repeatedly, in conjunction with the gong cycle:

1	2	3	4	5	6	7	8
dang	-	dung	dang	dung	dang	-	dung

All of the other instruments – kendang, reyong, and cengceng – typically play together at the music's highest level of rhythmic density – sixteenth-notes to the kajar's quarter-note beat in most cases. Their continuous streams of sixteenth-note rhythmic motion are rendered by sets of interlocking patterns between the individual players. Sometimes these interlocks are created by straight on-beat/off-beat alternation of notes between two or more parts – basic hocketing, as it were. More often, however, the melodic/rhythmic figures that contribute to interlocking textures (known generically in Balinese gamelan music as *kotekan*, though alternate terminologies are used in different contexts) are more complex in structure.

In the case of the cengceng part, a set of three interlocked rhythms, the *kilitan telu*, are divided among the eight cymbal players. The basic rhythm of the set is called *megbeg* ‖: / - / / - / / - :‖. The two other rhythms are identical to megbeg but rhythmically displaced, with the one, *nyandet*, anticipating megbeg by a sixteenth-note
(/)‖: - / / - / / - / :‖ and the other, *ngilit*, following megbeg by a sixteenth-note
‖: - / - / / - / / :‖. These three rhythms together create a continuous stream of sixteenth-note rhythmic motion:

Kajar	‖: x - - - x - - - :‖
Megbeg	‖: / - / / - / / - :‖
Nyandet	‖: - / / - / / - / :‖
Ngilit	‖: - / - / / - / / :‖
Composite	‖: / / / / / / / / :‖

The same principle – and indeed the same types of syncopated rhythms – defines the structure of the majority of interlocking kendang and reyong parts as well. Thus, for example, a standard gilak interlock between the male and female drums would have the female (kendang wadon) playing ‖: / - / - / / - / - / - / - / / - :‖ while the male (kendang lanang) plays the "same" rhythm starting a sixteenth-note earlier:

(/) ||: - / - / / - / - / - / - / / - / :||. Again, the resulting composite pattern fills in all the rhythmic space, yielding continuous sixteenth-note rhythmic motion:

Kajar ||: x - - - x- - - x- - - x - - -:||
Kendang wadon ||: / - / - / / - / - / - / - / / - :||
Kendang lanang ||: - / - / / - / - / - / - / / - / :||
Composite ||: / / / / / / / / / / / / / / / / :||

The reyong parts work in essentially the same way, but with the added complexity of integrating a melodic element into the interlocking texture. In the example below, note how each time pitch 6 (dang, or "A") is struck, pitch 2 (dong, or "D") is played as well, creating a Balinese harmonized sonority of *empat* (lit. "four"). The notes that fall between these syncopated dyads alternate between pitch 5 (dung, or "G#") and pitch 3 (deng, or "E").

Kajar || x   x   x   x   x   x   x   x
Reyong ||: 6 5 6 3 5 6 3 6 5 3 6 5 3 5 6 3 5 6 5 3 6 5 3 6 5 3 6 5 3 6 5 3 :||
       ||: 2   2   2   2   2   2   2   2   2   2   2   :||

Beleganjur kuno in the context of ritual cremation processions

The gamelan beleganjur acts as a quintessentially functional ensemble in Hindu-Balinese ritual processions. Its designated purpose is to serve the ritual needs of the occasion rather than to satisfy any explicitly artistic or aesthetic objectives. One of the two drummers, usually the player of the male (lanang) drum, is the ensemble leader. It is his job to regulate the pace and energy of the procession by translating processional needs into percussive sounds, into music that facilitates the meeting of key ritual requirements and aspirations.

Of all the processional ritual contexts in which beleganjur music is performed, the one with which it is most closely identified is the *ngaben*, or Hindu-Balinese cremation, procession. Performing cremations for its members is the principal responsibility of every Balinese *banjar*, the village wards or neighborhood organizations that form the bedrock of Balinese society. Ngaben processions may include multiple – sometimes dozens – of deceased individuals, or they may involve just one. The following discussion focuses on the latter type.

During ngaben processions, the gamelan beleganjur is typically situated immediately behind the *wadah*, the tall cremation tower that bears the body or exhumed remains of the deceased. Its music serves several

important functions. First, it is believed by the Balinese to have the power to frighten and literally deflect *bhuta* and *leyak* evil spirits, whose nefarious endeavors include attempts to capture the *atma*, or soul of the deceased, and drag it down to the dreaded Lower World of the Balinese cosmos. The battles of human ngaben participants against their evil spirit adversaries enlist beleganjur sound as both weapon and shield: on the one hand, the music is used to startle and "strike" the bhutas and leyaks, fostering fear and inflicting injuries that deter them in their malicious pursuits; on the other, it forms a protective shield around the tower and the precious atma, a sonic force field that should ideally prove impenetrable.

This may not be enough, however, so additional measures are taken to ensure ritual success in the desired liberation of the atma from its earthly bonds and its ascent to the Upper World of gods and deified ancestors to await reincarnation. Bhutas and leyaks are believed to congregate in greatest abundance at crossroads along the procession route. These crossroads are, therefore, the most dangerous locations for soul loss, necessitating extra vigilance and strategic effort on the part of the atma's human allies. The tower is spun around a minimum of three times at every crossroad. This is done in order to confuse the evil spirits who gather there, since they are thought to have the ability to travel in straight lines only. Concomitant with the ritual spinning of the tower is an abrupt change in the beleganjur's musical style at these points. The lead drummer cues a dramatic rise in tempo as the cymbal players switch from their kilitan telu interlocking sixteenth-note patterns to a more driving rhythmic texture called *malpal*. The malpal rhythm features half of the cymbal section performing on-beat quarter notes while the other half answers with off-beat eighth-notes. This simpler interlock generates a steady, propulsive stream of eighth-notes rather than sixteenth-notes, and it is played as loudly as possible. The use of malpal at crossroads serves several interconnected purposes, energizing and strengthening the carriers of the heavy tower to spin the wadah quickly and decisively, heightening the capacity of the music's sound to terrify and ward off the swarming bhutas and leyaks, and emboldening the atma to be courageous even in the face of impending danger.

This last function of the beleganjur ensemble, both at crossroads and elsewhere along the procession route, is of crucial importance. The very same beleganjur sonic force that wreaks havoc on the meddlesome efforts of bhutas and leyaks is also thought to imbue the departing atma with the courage and strength needed to commence and successfully pursue its perilous afterlife journey. The beleganjur must do its part, for if the atma succumbs to fear, it is likely to try to escape from the tower and return to the native banjar as an unliberated soul. There, frustrated and in perpetual limbo, it will haunt and taunt the villagers ad infinitum for failing in their

ngaben efforts, potentially bringing about a host of serious problems, from illness and disease to drought and famine.

Finally, it is the responsibility of the gamelan beleganjur to establish, modulate, and maintain the proper mood and energy of the procession overall. Cremation processions can quickly devolve into anxious events since so much is at stake. An elusive balance of buoyancy and restraint on the part of the individual ritual participants and the collective super-organism they together form in this decisive moment of communitas must be achieved to ensure that all goes according to plan, leading to the desired outcome of the atma's ultimate safe passage to the Upper World. The beleganjur-dominated soundscape becomes like a ritualistic energy valve, the lead drummer its chief engineer. He must open and close the valve just the right amount at just the right times by shifting the tempo, dynamic level, mood, and texture of the music in alternately subtle and dramatic ways. There are times for the drums and cymbals to enter and times for them to exit (the gongs, by contrast, are played continuously from start to finish), precise moments to transition into and out of the kilitan telu and malpal passages, points at which the tempo and energy of the music must be eased back to counteract growing feelings of tension and anxiety, and others at which they must be ratcheted up to combat encroaching lethargy or complacency.

A purely music-analytic assessment of a beleganjur kuno performance will not reveal all that much in the way of formal or structural musical complexity, let alone innovation. With rare exception, the gong cycle is always gilak, the core melody always the same pokok, and the interlocking figures of reyong, cengceng, and kendang quite uniform. Textural contrast is mainly limited to sections of the performance when the drums and cymbals are played and those where they are not, and between the rela-tively relaxed *jejalanan* musical styles played during most of the procession and the more intense malpal style of the crossroads.

This predictable uniformity of style accounts for the quality of mal-leability that is so essential to beleganjur's functional value as a music of ritual procession. It allows for the performance to be continually shaped and crafted to the exact requirements of the ever-emerging moment, rather than being confined to the inflexible structural and formal demands of a predetermined composition and arrangement. Indeed, one of the main complaints levied against many beleganjur groups today is that they have forsaken the traditional kuno style of old in favor of the flashy newer styles of *kreasi beleganjur*, even in ngaben and other ritual contexts where the kreasi style is patently inappropriate. It is to this very different contemporary style that we now turn our attention.

The contest style: kreasi beleganjur

Beleganjur has always been a music of battle: spiritual battles between human beings and their evil spirit adversaries in ritual contexts like the ngaben; beleganjur-accompanied earthly battles fought by the royal armies of warring Balinese kingdoms in olden times; and, for the past three decades, the symbolic battles of *lomba beleganjur*, or beleganjur contests, in which rival groups compete before panels of judges and large audiences for trophies, money, prestige, and bragging rights.

The lomba beleganjur has roots in both the beleganjur kuno tradition and a series of intercultural musical developments dating back to 1979, the year of the inaugural Bali Arts Festival (Pesta Kesenian Bali) in Bali's capital city, Denpasar. The festival opened with a grand parade through the streets of the city. The music, that year and for the next four, was provided by large, Western-style marching bands.

In 1984, I Made Bandem suggested that a "genuine Balinese marching band" of some type would be more appropriate for the parade. This resulted in the formation of a giant *drumban* (drum band) called Adi Merdangga, Sanskrit for "Number One Drum." It employed a hundred musicians and twenty dancers. The instrumentation included sixty kendang of all sizes, dozens of hanging and melodic gongs, and a huge cengceng section. The music drew liberally upon many different styles of Balinese gamelan, as well as from Western marching band music, but its musical foundation was resolutely beleganjur.

Two years later, in 1986, a weeklong ceremony commemorating the eightieth anniversary of the Puputan Badung was held in Denpasar, the present-day location of the former royal palace of the Badung kingdom. The Puputan Badung took place on September 20, 1906. It was on that day that the kingdom fell to Dutch colonial forces. Rather than surrender, the king, his family, and thousands of loyal subjects committed puputan ("death before surrender"), taking their own lives with sacred daggers or marching directly into the line of enemy fire in enacting a "heroic and distressing mass ritual suicide."[5]

The 1986 ceremony was to commemorate the heroic martyrdom of the fallen and to conflate the heroic, *kepahlawanan* spirit of the puputan with the modern, patriotic ideals of the Indonesian nation. A committee including the great Balinese composer I Ketut Gedé Asnawa was formed to plan the commemoration. They decided that a grand music contest should be the capstone event, and, inspired by the popularity of Adi Merdangga and the long militaristic past of beleganjur itself, determined that a contest featuring modernized beleganjur music performed by groups hailing from banjars throughout the Denpasar/Badung region would be the perfect fit.

Asnawa was assigned the role of primary architect of the beleganjur contest event and the exciting new style of beleganjur music that it would showcase. He fashioned a formal set of criteria for evaluating contest performances that essentially prescribed the invention of a neo-traditional genre: kreasi beleganjur – "creative beleganjur" or "new creation beleganjur." This was to be a music built upon the same foundations as its traditional, beleganjur kuno counterpart: the eight-beat gilak gong cycle, kilitan telu cymbal rhythms, ostinato core melody of the ponggang, and characteristic patterns of kendang and reyong interlocking. Beyond adhering to these shared root elements, however, kreasi beleganjur took off in an entirely new direction right from the start. Displays of breathtaking ensemble virtuosity and technical brilliance replaced functional purpose and efficacy as the music's *raison d'être*. Elaborate choreographic sequences performed by the musicians as they played, *gerak*, became central to an aesthetic of showmanship and bravura. Colorful, matching costumes replaced the customarily drab attire of ceremonial beleganjur groups. The compositions and arrangements were formally complex and highly sophisticated, with a standard fast–slow–fast, three movement formal plan replacing the relatively simple with-drums-and-cymbals versus without-drums-and-cymbals alternating textures of kuno styles.

Within movements, too, works unfolded through a series of markedly contrasting *pukulan*, or variations, highlighting the various instrumental sections of the beleganjur ensemble in sequence and grafting source materials from myriad Balinese musical genres – as well as from other popular Indonesian styles such as West Javanese (Sundanese) *jaipongan* and even Western genres like funk and hip-hop – onto the music's core gilak base. This was music that prized novelty and innovation, flash and panache, wit and whimsy, and it was music created and performed with one guiding set of motivations in mind: to impress the judges, excite and enthrall the audience, and win the top prize.

Kreasi beleganjur was also a restless music that refused to sit still. Taking its cue from the well-established competitive traditions of the *kreasi baru* (new creation) repertoire of the *gamelan gong kebyar*, it became a cauldron of perpetual change and one-upmanship as rival groups tried to outdo one another year after year. By the early 2000s, some groups were straying so far from the original musical style and its associated cultural values that pioneers like Asnawa were inclined to essentially disown the genre, at least in its most radicalized incarnations.

As composers, arrangers, and ensembles looking for a competitive edge – or just excited by the music's open-ended possibilities – experimented with new gong cycles, breakneck tempos, stunning displays of interlocking complexity, radical textural variety (e.g., having the gong cycle

drop out for entire formal sections), pop music borrowings, odd meters, and satirical and sometimes subversive gerak routines, kreasi beleganjur became at once an explosive domain of artistic invention and a polarizing emblem of contemporary Balinese cultural expression.

Conclusion

The world of the gamelan beleganjur offers a revealing lens through which to view the myriad complexities and paradoxes of Balinese musicultural life, as well as its profuse vitality and resilience. I define ethnomusicology as "the study of how people make and experience music, and of why it matters to them that they do."[6] Exploring beleganjur as the musically unique and culturally situated percussion ensemble tradition I have endeavored to evince here offers rich opportunities to engage in ethnomusicological inquiry so defined.

Many questions and issues related to those addressed in the foregoing discussion extend beyond the scope of this chapter: What accounted for the surprising emergence and quick decline of women's beleganjur in the 1990s?[7] What can we learn from the experimental adaptations of beleganjur music into genres as diverse as Balinese avant-garde music,[8] jazz (e.g., I Wayan Balawan), and heavy metal (e.g., Mr. Botax)? To what factors might we attribute the growing popularity of beleganjur among North American, East Asian, and European gamelans in recent years? How might ethnomusicological ways of thinking about beleganjur open our ears and attune our minds to new ways of conceptualizing other types of percussion ensemble music, whether of drum lines and new music groups or taiko ensembles and steelbands?

Such questions take us outward from the core of the Balinese beleganjur tradition per se, but we might just as productively move inward toward deeper structure interpretations. By way of conclusion, I venture a small step in that direction.

When I was working toward the completion of my first book, *Music of Death and New Creation: Experiences in the World of Balinese Gamelan Beleganjur*, I happened upon an unfamiliar word in my Balinese-English Dictionary: *dihi*. Two definitions were provided. One defined dihi as "the main strip of material in basket-weaving, the main thread in weaving cloth"; the other as "self, [or] person ... [or as] one person (of two)."[9]

My unanticipated encounter with this intriguing word, dihi, brought a flash of insight that sent tingles up my spine. It seemed to capture, in its polysemy and metaphorical reach, a poignant answer to the question of why so many of the Balinese musicians I had known and played music with made

music as they did, as well as why it was so important and meaningful for them to do so. For them, I surmised in my new light of dihi awareness, the experience of making music in the intricately interactive and interlocked ways that Balinese gamelan performance requires was to embody an experience of becoming that main thread in the weaving of a cloth, that main strip in the weaving of a basket. It was to realize one's self by dissolving into the larger fabric of a communal musical/social ideal, to become whole by becoming an indistinguishable yet integral part *of* the whole.

As for evidence in support of my hypothesis, I need look no farther than the perfectly wrought web of interlocking rhythms that comprise the kilitan telu, through which a single rhythm, made manifest in three tightly bound variants separated from each other by the minute imitative distance of a single sixteenth-note, could be transformed into a sonic cascade of perpetual rhythmic motion. This was an infinitely strong sonic fabric whose threads were all in the right places, indeed, to the point that one did not perceive those threads individually at all anymore.

To conceptualize the kilitan telu as a manifestation of dihi – the self, the main thread – is, I think, to cut to the core of what makes a great beleganjur performance groove so hard, contain so much power, and make such good community. It extends from there to other realms of Javanese and Balinese gamelan music and much further as well, suggesting a quality of experience that I would contend defines the essence of ensemble music-making at its sublime best regardless of genre, culture, or context. Viewed from such a perspective, the notion of listening to a gamelan as an orchestra, or an orchestra as a gamelan, seems not only plausible, but positively enticing.

Notes

1. A. Fauser, *Musical Encounters at the 1889 Paris World's Fair* (University of Rochester Press, 2005), pp. 198–9.

2. M. Tenzer, *Gamelan Gong Kebyar: The Art of Twentieth-Century Balinese Music* (University of Chicago Press, 2000), pp. 426–32.

3. Sumarsam, *Gamelan: Cultural Interaction and Musical Development in Central Java* (University of Chicago Press, 1995), pp. 104, 241.

4. M. B. Bakan, *Music of Death and New Creation: Experiences in the World of Balinese Gamelan Beleganjur* (University of Chicago Press, 1999), pp. 241–76.

5. M. Hobart, U. Ramseyer, and A. Leeman, *The Peoples of Bali* (Oxford: Blackwell Publishers, 1996), p. 202.

6. M. B. Bakan, "'Don't Go Changing to Try and Please Me': Combating Essentialism through Ethnography in the Ethnomusicology of Autism," *Ethnomusicology*, vol. 59, no. 1 (2015), 117.

7. Bakan, *Music of Death*, pp. 241–76.

8. A. C. McGraw, *Radical Traditions: Reimagining Culture in Balinese Contemporary Music* (Oxford University Press, 2013).

9. C. C. Barber, *A Balinese-English Dictionary*, 2 vols. (Occasional Publications No. 2. Aberdeen University Library, 1979), p. 110.

Percussion and rhythm

20 Lessons from the laboratory

The musical translation of scientific research on movement

MICHAEL SCHUTZ

From our first lessons focusing on the direct relationship between movement and sound quality to explorations of gestures' theatrical possibilities, physical movements have long fascinated percussionists. Scientific study of the topic has recently shed light onto the psychological underpinnings' of movement's musical uses. Although I now recognize this research's clear practical value, in my student days I mistakenly viewed "music research" as largely disconnected from my goals as a percussionist. My initial experiences in graduate school did little to challenge this perspective, with mandatory courses on library usage and lengthy written exams covering topics seemingly removed from my interests as a performer. However, a project focused on the perceptual implications of marimbists' physical movements challenged my perspective, dramatically changing my performing, teaching, and even thinking about music. Consequently, I began striving to balance my time between research and performance, finding that my efforts in one area informed and improved my work in the other.

Throughout this chapter, I will discuss scientific research on musical movement – with a particular focus on movements lacking acoustic consequences. While these studies vary in the immediacy of their application, all ultimately provide valuable insight. In this sense, the study of music cognition is analogous to that of music history: although some aspects are less immediately applicable, a broad understanding is helpful in becoming a well-rounded musician.[1] My specific aims in writing this chapter are twofold: first to emphasize technical scientific studies' practical value for performing musicians, and second to encourage musicians to think about new research questions and topics growing organically out of their personal experiences. As powerful research tools become increasingly widespread, the potential for harnessing their use grows dramatically. Consequently, there has never been a better time for curious musicians to begin exploring the psychological basis of our art.

Music and body movement

As percussionists, we regularly face the importance of understanding physical movement. Renowned timpanist Fred Hinger's emphasis on the relationship between physical movement and sound quality[2] continues to influence many of today's leading percussionists. In addition to small movements of fingers and wrists, larger motions are required when playing drum set, marimba, timpani, and multiple percussion – not to mention merely arriving at the proper instrument in complex setups! Some composers have elevated physical movement to an art in its own right. Jennifer Stassack explores silent movements in her marimba solo *Six Elegies Dancing* (1987), and Thierry de Mey employs them to great artistic effect in *Musique de Table/Table Music* (1988). This issue is far from "new" – John Cage's *Living Room Music* (1940) touches on these issues to some extent by encouraging performers to creatively employ a variety of movements for reasons extending beyond their acoustic consequences. However, recent interest in "theatrical percussion" takes this relationship to a new level and is discussed at length in Aiyun Huang's article, "*Percussion* theater; the drama of performance" (Chapter 9 in this volume). My chapter supplements growing musical interest in this topic by exploring its scientific roots – *how and why* silent movements shape the musical experience. I am focusing on silent movements in particular as their role is counterintuitive, and also as acoustically consequential movements have understandably received more previous attention.[3]

Although rarely discussed in scientific terms, performers have long intuitively recognized movement's importance independent of its acoustic consequences. Steven Schick noted aptly that "physicality and gesture in percussion music are powerful tools of communication" and that "anyone who has ever attended a percussion concert can tell you that the experience of percussion music involves the eyes as well as the ears."[4] Although percussionists perhaps deal most directly with the consequences of extra-acoustic gestures, we are not alone in this matter. Composer Robert Schumann once famously remarked of a well-known pianist that "he must be heard – and also seen; for if Liszt played behind the screen, a great deal of poetry would be lost."[5]

Here I will summarize the latest scientific research on musical movement in two distinct sections. The first focuses on implications of *feeling our own* movements with respect to our perception of timing. The second explores the results of *seeing others' movements* when evaluating performances. Together, I hope this discussion will provide insights for composers, teachers, and performers. Although my focus is primarily on work relevant to percussionists, many of these issues apply equally as well to other musicians.

Feeling movement: moving to the beat affects timing perception

When I first joined the percussion faculty at Longwood University in rural Farmville, VA, I frequently found myself coaching students through challenging repertoire by demonstrating the movements I would use to perform certain passages. Initially intended merely to provide a demonstration, dialogue about why I used certain movements led to some interesting introspection. On more than one occasion, I found myself unconsciously using gestures that were not strictly "necessary" for sound production. These movements were spontaneous, and although they "seemed helpful" I began wondering if this were actually the case – after all, at one point using a death grip to ensure my mallets didn't slip "seemed helpful." Many musicians move to the beat while playing or even listening – are such non-sound-producing movements musically useful? Musicians have recognized links between movement and rhythm for generations, and scientists have recently begun explaining the psychological and neurological bases for this connection.

One study presented participants with a six-beat sequence of snare drum and slapstick notes. Lacking accents, the sequence was created to be metrically ambiguous and could be interpreted as being in either 3/4 or 6/8 time. While listening, participants mimicked the bouncing motions of an experimenter moving either two or three times per grouping. When bouncing three times, participants were essentially moving in 3/4; when bouncing twice, they were moving in 6/8. Subsequent evaluations with acoustic accents added on every second or third note sounded more similar to the ambiguous rhythm when it *aligned with their previous movements*. In other words, moving while listening altered their understanding of the sequence's structure.[6] Although movement's effect could in theory reflect culture-specific associations, a parallel study using seven-month-old infants suggests it is innate.[7] Head movement, rather than movement of other body parts, is the essential driving force.[8]

This documentation of links between movement and timing perception complements parallel explorations of brain structure. Neural areas tasked primarily with motor control respond when listening to rhythms – even when the listener is not moving.[9] While neuroanatomy is "compartmentalized" with certain areas more active in some tasks than others, the degree of cross talk between distinct areas is significant. It is no more possible to ignore the feel of one's movement when listening than to read the letters D-O-G without recognizing they refer to man's best friend. Movement's effects on our perception of ambiguous stimuli raises intriguing questions as to whether we can use such findings strategically. Although body movement *changes* our interpretation, can it *improve* our listening abilities?

Movement improves timing perception

To explore whether movement can be "helpful," researchers created a series of simple metronome-like sequences lacking metrical context (i.e., a stream of quarter notes with no rhythmic variation). They then removed certain notes to make the underlying pulse ambiguous. All participants moved their fingers while listening to this ambiguous sequence, but half were asked to tap their feet prior to this finger movement (the others listened without first tapping their feet). Foot tapping aided extraction of the underlying pulse, presumably by clarifying the tapper's perception of the beat within ambiguous sequences.[10] This suggests that movement may be helpful when extracting pulse from rhythmically complex passages. It also raises an intriguing question – beyond assisting with a subjective task such as beat extraction, can body movement *objectively improve* our listening abilities?

To explore this question, Fiona Manning (one of my graduate students) is working with a paradigm designed to quantitatively measure movement's effect on perception. Our approach uses customized software producing MIDI sequences while simultaneously recording participants' tapping on electronic drum pads. The task involves listening to a simple five-measure pattern with three measures of quarter notes in 4/4 time followed by a measure of silence. Participants then hear a *probe tone* on the downbeat of the fifth measure, "probing" their perception of the downbeat. The probe tone occurs at the correct time (i.e., right on the beat) on half of the trials and is off by a slight amount on the other half – roughly a sixteenth note or thirty-second note early/late. Participants indicate whether this tone is correct and tap on half of the trials. We ask them to listen without moving for the rest. Participants are better at detecting the probe tone's timing when tapping along as opposed to listening without movement.[11] This demonstrates that movement can objectively improve rhythm perception. Although intriguing, we then began wondering whether it is the movement itself that improves rhythm perception or instead the *acoustic results* of the movement (i.e., hearing one's own taps).

Pinpointing the exact source of movement's improvement required separating the feel of tapping from its acoustic consequences. However, as anyone who has attempted to silently pick up/set down a tambourine during quiet passages recognizes, silent movements are not always feasible! Unable to make the taps "silent," we masked their sound using white noise – the static heard when tuning a radio between stations. Additionally, participants wore foam earplugs inside their headphones, blocking the sound of their tapping without obfuscating the MIDI wood-block sequence. Although they performed better when hearing as well as feeling their taps, the movement benefit persisted even when the taps were

masked.[12] This shows that movement alone can improve rhythm perception, an insight useful when performing and/or listening to rhythmically intricate percussion music. The effects of movement documented in these studies were found in participants who were not selected for musical training, consistent with the idea that auditory-motor connections are innate or "hardwired." Nonetheless, the role of training is an important one to consider, and it consequently compelled a series of studies involving percussionists.

Our interest in training's effect arose in part from the opportunity to work with the percussion ensemble TorQ in preparation for the 2012 McMaster University *Neuromusic Conference*. As the event alternated between discussions of my team's research and TorQ's energetic performances, we tested the ensemble prior to the concert and showed their results as part of the event. Unsurprisingly, they were excellent tappers! Their performance in the experiment raised questions regarding the role of percussion training in auditory-motor interactions, and consequently Manning brought a team of students to the University of Toronto and University of Western Ontario to test their percussion studios. Additionally, through a partnership with the PAS Scholarly Research Committee and with funding from the Petro Canada *Young Innovator Award*, we were able to bring the MAPLE Lab to PASIC in 2013 and 2014, testing over one hundred percussionists in a series of experiments. These studies revealed that percussionists benefit more from movement than those without musical training.[13] To some extent, this reflects that percussionists are (predictably) good tappers. Curiously, however, percussionists did not outperform non-percussionists in the *absence of movement* – a surprising finding whose potential implications are currently being explored.

Seeing movement: silent movements affect musical evaluations

In addition to listeners' movements affecting their own perception, the movements seen by audiences can affect their hearing of the music – even when acoustically irrelevant. Scholars formally exploring performers' movements distinguish between two broad categories of gestures: *effective* and *ancillary*. Effective gestures are required for sound production – such as the downward motion used in striking a drum. Their acoustic relevance distinguishes them from ancillary gestures – movements more excessive than acoustically required. Elaborate sweeps of the arm after striking an instrument, head movements assisting with timekeeping in complex passages, and even rhythmic breathing are, in an acoustic sense,

"unnecessary."[14] Yet, they are regularly employed in performances, often to great effect.

Research on musical movement has blossomed in recent years, to the point where it is possible to synthesize multiple findings through a technique known as a "meta-analysis." This approach aggregates disparate results to summarize a large body of work. A meta-analysis including fifteen studies exploring visual influences on ratings of "overall quality," "liking," and "overall impression for performance evaluation" found that watching a performer's body movements had a consistent influence on ratings of their performances.[15] This formal quantification complements other reviews of the many ways in which vision affects evaluations of musical expressiveness,[16] which range from high-level attributes such as "performance quality" down to low-level properties such as timbre, pitch relationships, and volume.[17]

One challenge inherent in understanding the psychological basis for ancillary gestures' effects is designing studies capturing the full complexity of musical performances while yielding strong conclusions. One of music's endearing qualities is its complexity and variation, and no two performances are exactly the same. Although this variation makes music interesting, it poses unfortunate challenges for reproducibility and control – factors crucial for scientific progress. Simplifications of musical material can be helpful in designing experiments affording strong conclusions. However, this approach can make it challenging to determine whether conclusions drawn from such passages apply to realistic musical material. Therefore, a full understanding of performers' ancillary gestures requires a range of studies employing multiple approaches. In some cases, experiments conducted in realistic circumstances provide provocative suggestions, even if they defy clear conclusions. Alternatively, studies using constrained excerpts can be helpful as they offer convincing demonstrations of particular phenomena. Personally, I have found both approaches helpful in clarifying my understanding of how music "works." And in fact, it was through discussion of this kind of issue that I began my own journey into exploring music's psychological basis.

Hearing gestures, seeing music

During one of my lessons as a graduate student at Northwestern University, Professor Michael Burritt suggested I use more demonstrative motions in order to "shape the audience's listening experience." I naively protested that such movements were not part of the "true music" as they play no role in audio recordings. (I had not yet learned about research on ancillary gestures!) After all, this use of acoustically inconsequential motions seemed curious given our typical fixation on economizing

motion. Upon further reflection, I began wondering if certain movements could be musically relevant despite lacking acoustic consequences. After all, "unnecessary" movements are pervasive. In fact, videos of my own playing documented that I myself frequently employed such gestures – despite my protests at the time as to their musical relevance! To clarify, I began a "controlled" project based on recordings of attempts to create marimba notes differing in duration. While single-note excerpts are a far cry from most recitals, this constrained scenario afforded exploration of a long-running musical debate: whether it is possible to create "long" and "short" notes on the marimba.

This experiment featured renowned marimbist Michael Burritt, who employed both "long" and "short" striking motions. His long gestures featured a flowing movement with a graceful "bounce" after impact, whereas short gestures ended abruptly.[18] My colleagues and I then asked musically trained participants to judge the durations of the resulting notes. Our key manipulation was switching the notes in half of the videos, pairing the long striking motion with the sound produced by the short motion, and vice versa. Despite instructions to judge the duration of the sound alone, visible gesture length significantly altered duration ratings. Furthermore, when judged in the absence of the gestures, evaluations of the notes produced by long and short gestures were indistinguishable. This documents that although long and short gestures do not affect the sound of notes produced on the marimba, they do affect *the way these notes sound* within the mind of the listener.[19] Subsequent studies demonstrate that it is specifically the post-impact motion that controls an audiences' perception of musical note duration[20] and that this illusion is similar even in those without musical training.[21] I described the psychological processes giving rise to this illusion in my first *Percussive Notes* article on this project[22] and the specifics of the motions involved in my second.[23] Videos from these experiments are also available freely in a review published in *Music Theory Online*.[24]

I chose a "controlled" approach to exploring the role of gestures in order to arrive at strong conclusions regarding vision's influence on music perception. While this approach holds many benefits, it is admittedly based on simplified musical material – a single note! Therefore, I see it as complementing other approaches using recordings of complete compositions or at least prolonged passages. One such study used silent videos of a percussionist playing Goldenberg's *Melodic Study in Sixteenths*[25] – aptly identified by researchers as "neutral in emotional nature." The marimbist attempted to convey four different emotional intentions: anger, happiness, sadness, and fear. Participants watching silent videos depicting the movements without sound were able to consistently discern the performer's

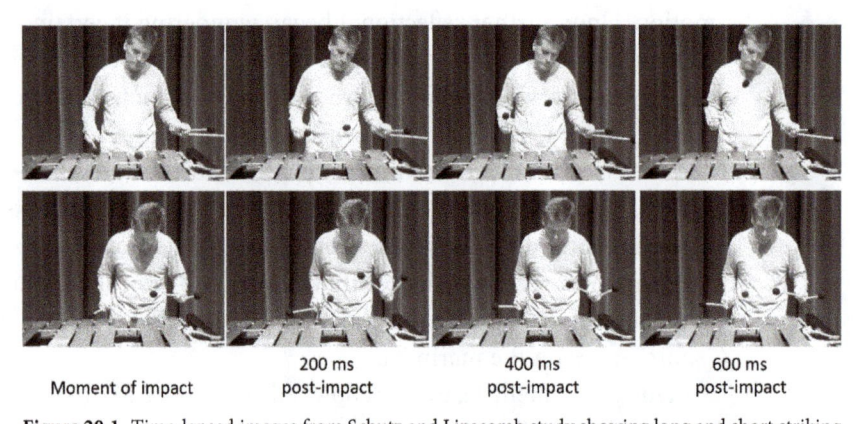

Moment of impact	200 ms post-impact	400 ms post-impact	600 ms post-impact

Figure 20.1 Time-lapsed images from Schutz and Lipscomb study showing long and short striking motions. Captured 200 milliseconds apart, the images show that acclaimed percussion soloist Michael Burritt's striking mallet (held in his right hand) continues moving for longer after impact when using a "long" flowing gesture (top) than a "short" choppy gesture (bottom). This difference in post-impact motion changes our *perception* of the tone's duration, even though it does not affect the tone's *acoustic* duration. To see an animated version of this figure (and download demonstrations for personal/educational use), please visit www.maplelap.net/illusion.

emotional intentions. Manipulations using only portions of the video (i.e., removing the hands, showing only the head) were generally also sufficient. However, removing head movements reduced recognition of the performer's emotional intentions.[26] Although this approach establishes that vision is capable of *conveying meaningful information*, it does not comment on whether this information *affects auditory evaluations*. However, this kind of question has been explored by percussionist/psychologist Dr. Mary Broughton.

Broughton is a professional percussionist who also earned a PhD in Experimental Psychology and now draws on this dual background to formally study marimbists' body movements. One of her investigations involved asking participants to rate their level of interest and the level of "expressivity" exhibited in excerpts of popular solos such as *Marimba Dances* (Edwards), *Suite for Marimba* (Yoshioka), *Nancy* (Séjourné), and *Merlin* (Thomas). Broughton recorded these excerpts in two styles – either "expressive" (similar to an actual performance) or "deadpan" (with expressive aspects kept to a minimum). Participants rated these performances after hearing either audio-visual or audio-alone versions. They were in fact adept at detecting the expressive versus deadpan performance styles – however, only when watching as well as listening.[27]

This type of approach involving multiple performances of basic repertoire offers a "realistic" exploration of performance practices. Furthermore, it shows that differences in intention are both visible and can affect ratings of audio-visual performances.[28] As such, this design

provides insight into ancillary gestures' effects on musical evaluations. At the same time, it does not afford disambiguation of the different performance intentions' visual and acoustic consequences. The expressive and deadpan conditions differ with respect to both body movements and the acoustic results of these movements (i.e., both effective and ancillary gestures). Consequently, other studies using tightly constrained excerpts provide an important complement to these approaches as they afford stronger conclusions.

One such investigation explores whether vocalists' facial expressions affect audience perception of their singing. Here, participants rated silent videos of a professional vocalist singing intervals ranging from a minor second to an octave. Participants were able to correctly recognize the relative sizes of the sung intervals from merely watching these soundless excerpts.[29] Subsequent studies built on this result by including an auditory component, pairing the facial expressions with different pairs of sung notes – either major or minor thirds. Here, rather than interval size, participants judged their emotional quality, building on differences in the emotional connotations of major and minor thirds in Western music. Singers' facial expressions changed evaluations of their sung intervals, providing strong evidence that they not only convey musically relevant information, but this information *affects evaluations* of sound.[30]

This work involving pairs of sung notes bears similarity to my own involving single marimba notes – both use constrained musical examples and tightly controlled procedures to arrive at strong conclusions. As musical performances generally involve more complex material, other approaches using longer excerpts hold certain advantages. Yet, the complexity of using "realistic" videos simultaneously precludes the manipulations of auditory and visual components required to reach unambiguous outcomes. Eliminating sound entirely allows for the use of more involved examples,[31] but introduces different challenges with respect to practical applications. Fortunately, methodological diversity is a bedrock principle of scientific exploration, as examination from multiple points of view helps in triangulating truth. And curiously, recent technological developments build on and affirm both approaches by using alternative representations of human movement affording new explorations.

Threading the needle: new approaches to balancing realism and control
Humans are adept at recognizing complex movements from surprisingly sparse representations. White dots tracking key locations (i.e., shoulder, elbow, hand, foot) against black backgrounds are effective at modeling many complex movements. In fact, movies such as *Avatar* use this approach to create compelling models of human motion. These models

appear curiously "realistic" given that they portray fictitious creatures never previously seen! In addition to their use in entertainment, these displays have a long history of aiding movement research,[32] including explorations of music[33] and dance.[34] I used a variation of this technique to create a "virtual marimbist," which served as an eerily accurate surrogate for an actual performer in some of my previous work.[35]

New extensions to this well-established technique offer powerful opportunities for balancing realism and control, as the sparse nature of point light representations affords manipulations preserving natural appearances. For example, "time warping" involves subtle changes in movements, allowing for rendering different versions of human avatars that remain realistic in appearance. In one intriguing approach, pianists played Chopin's *Prelude in E minor* with different degrees of expression – including "deadpan" (i.e., reduced expressivity), "normal" (i.e., typical expressive), and "exaggerated" (i.e., maximum possible expressivity). Pairing each time-warped movement sequence with each audio recording created visually identical but acoustically distinct (as well as acoustically identical but visually distinct) audio-visual performances.[36] Experiments using these hybrid audio-visual excerpts demonstrated a clear visual influence on performance evaluations of musical expressivity.[37] Because these animations used acoustically identical passages paired with different motions, they provide strong evidence that ancillary aspects of gestures can *alter evaluations* of concurrent acoustic information.

In an approach equally relevant to performing musicians, a different study explored the degree to which body movements provide insight into the winners of prestigious musical competitions. Six-second videos of finalists' performances were presented as either audio-visual, video-alone, or audio-alone clips. These excerpts showed violinists and pianists performing in high-stakes venues such as the Van Cliburn International Piano Competition and the International Tchaikovsky Competition. The overall level of playing was extremely high, and participants in the audio-alone and audio-visual conditions failed to perform better than chance at identifying competition winners. Curiously, only those watching *silent videos* performed better than chance! These results were robust across different assessments, and replicated even when using highly trained musicians as evaluators.[38]

Although many visual clues were available in videos, follow-up studies suggest that gross body movements played a crucial role. Silhouettes obfuscating facial features and smaller movements while preserving larger gestures again afforded predictions of the ultimate winners; however, still images did not.[39] Extensions of this paradigm involving ensemble performances in the Saint Paul String Quartet Competition and Fischoff

Competition suggest this phenomenon is not limited to solo performances.[40] Although further research is needed to determine the precise aspects of the performers' gestures contributing to this outcome (i.e., ancillary vs. effective), the use of material from important competitions means these results hold significant practical implications.

Concluding thoughts and future opportunities

I have summarized a variety of movement studies pertinent to our work as musicians. My hope is that this knowledge will not only help performers, teachers, and composers, but that it might also encourage musicians to propose and pursue new research questions. Given the growth in tools and training programs, there is now tremendous potential for curious musicians to make important discoveries. Personally, I have found insights from this research not only fascinating, but also musically useful. When students in my percussion ensemble are struggling with certain rhythmically intricate passages, I am able to explain to them that moving while performing can help their efforts to keep time. Additionally, arranging setups so that my students can see one another often helps them to better align their performances. When puzzling through transcribing or simply listening to complex rhythms, I now tap along, improving my ability to extract the beat and recognize rhythms.

Knowledge of how performers can shape an audience's listening experience through the proper use of ancillary gestures is invaluable in striving to ensure they contribute toward our musical goals. Such movements can be helpful communicative tools in recitals and competitions, unscreened orchestral auditions, and live performances in a variety of ensembles – as audiences' attention is often disproportionately drawn to the percussion section (and for good reason!). I also find knowledge of gestures' perceptual effects helpful in explaining to students that effective performance is less about technical flash and faster tempos than the communication happening between performer and audience.

Scientific studies of musical communication can be pursued in a variety of different manners. After completing my Master of Music in Percussion Performance, I took the somewhat unusual step of pursuing a PhD in Experimental Psychology rather than the more typical path of enrolling in a Doctor of Musical Arts program. This decision helped me to develop the skills required for running my own research laboratory – which now allows me to explore a variety of musical issues. However, this is not the only way to become involved in scientific research on music, as scientists are often eager to collaborate on projects of mutual interest.

For example, Roger Chaffin's group at the University of Connecticut has pursued novel explorations of practice and memorization techniques employed by professional pianist Gabriela Imreh.[41] This partnership proved quite fruitful, and he subsequently studied issues of memory in realistic practice and performance scenarios through partnerships with cellist Tânia Lisboa[42] and vocalist Jane Ginsborg.[43] Both Lisboa and Ginsborg now blend performance and research activities as part of their professional portfolios. Therefore, collaborations hold great potential for enhancing dialogue between the artistic and scientific communities and represent the epitome of interdisciplinary research trumpeted by universities. Musicians interested in exploring such opportunities may wish to consult the Society for Music Perception and Cognition map of researchers and facilities at http://musicperception.org/smpc-resources.html.

In conclusion, there are many ways in which psychological research can inform and inspire musical activities. I believe the importance of understanding music cognition parallels the importance of understanding more traditional subjects included in music curricula, such as musical harmony. A firm understanding of basic principles of music theory as presented in undergraduate textbooks provides useful insight into the structure of actual symphonies and solos – even though in practice "rules" are not always followed as cleanly as in the classroom. Similarly, controlled studies can be helpful in probing the general principles employed in processing more complex musical material. Although it is possible to recognize "moving to the beat" helps timekeeping without knowledge of the cognitive basis for this insight or that ancillary gestures on stage affect performance evaluations without an understanding of cross talk between neural areas processing sight and sound, understanding the cognitive basis for these phenomena only improves our understanding of music – and the musicians giving it life. Sound only becomes music within the mind of the listener, and consequently understanding music's psychological basis provides significant benefits for all who perform, teach, compose, and enjoy this important human endeavor.

As the field of music cognition grows, I am excited about the possibility of experimental psychology's powerful techniques to explore musically motivated questions, complementing music cognition's traditional focus on using music to explore psychologically motivated questions. As musicians, we possess finely tuned intuitions cultivated from a wide array of musical experiences, which hold the potential to lead organically to exciting new research questions. Such interdisciplinary explorations hold significant and far-reaching benefits, helping us inch closer to a fuller understanding of the surprising ways movement can be used to create more effective musical performances.

Notes

1. Those interested in the brain's processing of music are encouraged to read John Iversen's article on the neural processing of rhythm, Chapter 21 in this volume.

2. F. Hinger, *Technique for the Virtuoso Timpanist* (Hackensack, NJ: Jerona Music, 1981).

3. S. Dahl, "Striking Movements: A Survey of Motion Analysis of Percussionists," *Acoustical Science and Technology*, 32 (2011), 168–73.

4. S. Schick, *The Percussionist's Art: Same Bed, Different Dreams* (University of Rochester Press, 2006).

5. S. Morgenstern, *Composers on Music* (London: Faber & Faber, 1958), p. 156.

6. J. Phillips-Silver and L. J. Trainor, "Hearing What the Body Feels: Auditory Encoding of Rhythmic Movement," *Cognition*, 105 (2007), 533–46.

7. Phillips-Silver and Trainor, "Feeling the Beat: Movement Influences Infant Rhythm Perception," *Science*, 308 (2005), 1430.

8. Phillips-Silver and Trainor, "Vestibular Influence on Auditory Metrical Interpretation," *Brain and Cognition*, 67 (2008), 94–102.

9. J. A. Grahn and M. Brett, "Rhythm and Beat Perception in Motor Areas of the Brain," *Journal of Cognitive Neuroscience*, 19 (2007), 893–906.

10. Y. H. Su and E. Pöppel, "Body Movement Enhances the Extraction of Temporal Structures in Auditory Sequences," *Psychological Research*, 76 (2012), 373–82.

11. F. Manning and M. Schutz, "'Moving to the Beat' Improves Timing Perception," *Psychonomic Bulletin & Review*, 20 (2013), 1133–39.

12. Manning and Schutz, "Movement Enhances Perceived Timing in the Absence of Auditory Feedback," *Timing & Time Perception*, 3 (2015), 3–12.

13. Manning and Schutz, "Trained to Keep a Beat: Movement-related Enhancements to Timing Perception in Percussionists and Non-percussionists," *Psychological Research* (in press), 1–22.

14. M. Nusseck, M. and M. M. Wanderley, "Music and Motion – How Music-related Ancillary Body Movements Contribute to the Experience of Music," *Music Perception: An Interdisciplinary Journal*, 26 (2009), 335–53; Wanderley, B. W. Vines, N. Middleton, C. McKay, and W. Hatch, "The Musical Significance of Clarinetists' Ancillary Gestures: An Exploration of the Field," *Journal of New Music Research*, 34 (2005), 97–113.

15. F. Platz and R. Kopiez, "When the Eye Listens: A Meta-analysis of how Audio-visual Presentation Enhances the Appreciation of Music Performance," *Music Perception: An Interdisciplinary Journal*, 30 (2012), 71–83.

16. W. F. Thompson, P. Graham, and F. A. Russo, "Seeing Music Performance: Visual Influences on Perception and Experience," *Semiotica* 156 (2005), 203–27.

17. Schutz, "Seeing Music? What Musicians Need to Know about Vision," *Empirical Musicology Review*, 3 (2008), 83–108.

18. Samples of these videos are available online at www.maplelab.net/illusion.

19. Schutz and S. Lipscomb, "Hearing Gestures, Seeing Music: Vision Influences Perceived Tone Duration," *Perception*, 36 (2007), 888–97.

20. J. A. Armontrout, Schutz, and M. Kubovy, "Visual Determinants of a Cross-modal Illusion," *Attention, Perception, & Psychophysics*, 71 (2009), 1618–27.

21. Schutz and Kubovy, "Causality and Cross-modal Integration," *Journal of Experimental Psychology: Human Perception and Performance*, 35 (2009), 1791–1810.

22. Schutz, "The Mind of the Listener: Acoustics, Perception, and the Musical Experience," *Percussive Notes* vol. 47 (2009), 22–8.

23. Schutz and Manning, "Effectively using Affective Festures: What Percussionists Need to Know about Movement and Perception," *Percussive Notes* vol. 51, no. 2 (2013), 26–31.

24. Schutz and Manning, "Looking Beyond the Score: The Musical Role of Percussionists' Ancillary Gestures," *Music Theory Online*, 18 (2012), 1–14.

25. M. Goldenberg, *Modern School for Xylophone, Marimba, Vibraphone* (New York: Chapell, 1950).

26. Dahl and A. Friberg, "Visual Perception of Expressiveness in Musicians' Body Movements," *Music Perception: An Interdisciplinary Journal*, 24 (2007), 433–54.

27. M. Broughton and C. Stevens, "Music, Movement and Marimba: An Investigation of the Role of Movement and Gesture in Communicating Musical Expression to an Audience," *Psychology of Music*, 37 (2009), 137–53.

28. Subsequent investigations explore formal coding and analysis of movement types using the Laban movement system [Broughton and Stevens,"Analyzing Expressive Qualities in Movement and Stillness: Effort-shape Analyses of Solo Marimbists' Bodily Expression," *Music Perception*, 29 (2012), 339–57] and examine

individual differences in their detection [Broughton and J. W. Davidson, "Action and Familiarity Effects on Self and other Expert Musicians' Laban Effort-shape Analyses of Expressive Bodily Behaviors in Instrumental Music Performance: a Case Study Approach," *Frontiers in Psychology*, 5 (2014), 1201].

29. Thompson and Russo, "Facing the Music," *Psychological Science*, 18 (2007), 756–57.

30. Thompson, Russo, and L. Quinto, (2008), "Audio-visual Integration of Emotional Cues in Song," *Cognition and Emotion*, 22 (2008), 1457–70.

31. Dahl and Friberg, "Visual Perception," 433–54.

32. G. Johansson, "Visual Perception of Biological Motion and a Model for its Analysis," *Perception & Psychophysics*, 14 (1973), 201–11.

33. Davidson, "Visual Perception of Performance Manner in the Movements of Solo Musicians," *Psychology of Music*, 21 (1993), 103–13.

34. P. Toiviainen, G. Luck, and Thompson, "Embodied Meter: Hierarchical Eigenmodes in Music-induced Movement," *Music Perception: An Interdisciplinary Journal*, 28 (2010), 59–70.

35. Schutz and Kubovy, "Deconstructing a Musical Illusion: Point-light Representations Capture Salient Properties of Impact Motions," *Canadian Acoustics*, 37 (2009), 23–8.

36. These approaches built upon earlier work examining the body movements of pianists as they relate to desired manipulations of expression by Thompson and Luck, "Exploring Relationships Between Pianists' Body Movements, their Expressive Intentions, and Structural Elements of the Music," *Musicae Scientiae*, 16 (2012), 19–40.

37. J. K. Vuoskoski, Thompson, E. F. Clarke, and C. Spence, "Crossmodal Interactions in the Perception of Expressivity in Musical Performance," *Attention, Perception, & Psychophysics*, 76 (2014), 591–604.

38. C.-J. Tsay, "Sight over Sound in the Judgment of Music Performance," *Proceedings of the National Academy of Sciences of the United States of America*, 110 (2013), 14580–5.

39. *Ibid.*

40. Tsay, "The Vision Heuristic: Judging Music Ensembles by Sight Alone," *Organizational Behavior and Human Decision Processes*, 124 (2014), 24–33.

41. R. Chaffin and G. Imreh, "'Pulling Teeth and Torture:' Musical Memory and Problem Solving," *Thinking & Reasoning*, 3 (1997), 315–36.

42. Chaffin, T. Lisboa, T. Logan, T., and K. T. Begosh, "Preparing for Memorized Cello Performance: The Role of Performance Cues," *Psychology of Music*, 1 (2010), 3–30.

43. J. Ginsborg, and Chaffin, "Preparation and Spontaneity in Performance: A Singer's Thoughts while Singing Schoenberg," *Psychomusicology: Music, Mind & Brain*, 21 (2011), 137–58.

21 In the beginning was the beat

Evolutionary origins of musical rhythm in humans

JOHN R. IVERSEN

Every known culture has music with a sense of pulse, or beat, that organizes time, enlivens our bodies, and can enable groups of people to move in time in dance, music-making, or work.[1] There can be a sheer joy in coordinated action with others, and pulse in music is one vehicle for achieving this. While the basic idea of being able to perceive and move in time with the pulse of music may seem simple, this simplicity belies a rich complexity of central interest not only to musicians, but also to scientists of many stripes. The underlying neural mechanisms are fascinatingly complex, providing insights into how the brain shapes our reality and connects sensation with movement, while its evolutionary origins are matter of vigorous speculation and ongoing debate.

So, when and how did the beat begin? The universe is full of repeating patterns of light and dark, ebb and flow, swinging to and fro, and this is the milieu for all life. For organisms to be able to track *and predict*, for example, the coming of day or night has adaptive value, and synchronization with the light/dark circadian cycle is observed throughout nature. Most organisms create other rhythms of their own, of locomotion, breath, and heartbeat.

Despite the pervasiveness of oscillation and entrainment in the world, the ability to synchronize motor output to auditory input as humans do when dancing, performing, or just tapping a foot along with music turns out to be extremely rare in other animals, something Fitch has called the "paradox of rhythm."[2] There are at least two levels to this rareness: the first is basic, and often noted, that the presence of a neural link by which auditory pattern perception can influence motor pattern generation is necessary for synchronization with sound, but this link appears not to be present in most animals. It enables basic sensory motor synchronization (SMS), but this does not encompass human rhythmic capacities. It is thought that in humans this auditory/motor link is bidirectional, opening rich possibilities for an internal sense of beat to affect not just how we respond to the world of rhythm, but how we actively perceive it.[3] We will call this capacity rich beat perception and synchronization, or rich BPS, which we suggest is a second key development responsible for our rhythmic abilities. Highlighting the distinction between basic SMS and rich BPS

is important for understanding the origins of human musical rhythm, for it emphasizes that multiple steps were likely involved. The distinction between these is not always made clear in the literature, and the majority of comparative and evolutionary accounts have focused on basic SMS, while rich BPS has not yet been demonstrated in any other animal to our knowledge.

In this chapter, we will focus on a deeper origin question, asking what are the forces that shaped our ancestors to have these capacities? Frankly, it's an odd thing, to link sound and movement as we do. Adding a deep interest, remarkably, synchronized action often leads to deep feelings of bonding and oneness between individuals. Did the beat evolve because it had survival value for our distant ancestors? Is it a by-product of our complex emotional and social brains or an invented technology for pushing our minds in pleasurable or even useful ways? We cannot know for certain. Our tangible view of the past is quite limited, with the earliest musical instruments, bone flutes, found dating from only 40,000 years ago, indicating that tonal music at least was well under way in our Paleolithic ancestors.[4] Nonetheless, there is a wide range of other evidence to draw from in creating theories of the origin of musical rhythm, including behavioral and neuroscientific studies of rhythm perception and production in humans, a comparative look at other animals to see what aspects of rhythmic behavior they may share with us, and why, and studies of other cultures as a way to peel back our technological and cultural developments to glimpse how music and dance may have played a role in societies of the past.

Rich beat perception and synchronization: a view from cognitive neuroscience

First, what are we actually trying to explain? Here is a cognitive scientist's perspective, which may seem basic and familiar to a percussionist but with some differences in terminology and formulation. It can be boiled down to this: rhythmic patterns of sound are "out there" in the world; the beat is entirely "in here," a creation of our minds. Temporal patterns of acoustic energy exist in the world. Our brains are able to find regularity and thereby form predictions about the future of these patterns, predictions that influence our perception and action. Sound patterns become rhythms *only* through an interaction with our brains: what can be predicted from a given signal is a property of the perceiver, not the signal. Just as different frequencies of light become colors only by interacting with an eye and brain – the colors we see are very different from that of a bee – so it is with

rhythms: their periodicity is something we must be able to engage with. Consequently, much of our work in the cognitive science of rhythm is aimed at explaining our capacities for prediction in terms of internal mechanisms.

Beat-based perception

It has long been known that for humans when temporal patterns have, at least loosely, certain temporal properties, such has having note durations related to each other by simple ratios, or having some degree of periodicity or repetition, they can induce in us a pulse that enables a special form of temporal perception, beat-based perception.[5] This central human mode of rhythmic engagement involves the induction, from rhythmic input, of a continuous sense of periodicity or *pulse* (termed "beat" when reinforced by a periodic train of sonic events). A pulse can exist at multiple hierarchical levels, and all levels need not be isochronous (evenly timed), though often at least one is. The pulse tempo need not be metronomic, but can have a certain elasticity, although different levels often track each other (except, e. g., in music built incorporating multiple tempos phase slipping across each other – something that has not been much examined by science). While we can use the pulse hierarchy to organize the timing of our movements, the pulse also plays a central role in perception: one might say that the musical sense of rhythmic pulse forms a recurrent scaffold upon which time perception is organized. The timing of events is perceived relative to our internal pulse. In this way, an acoustically identical note can be perceived in very different ways: upbeat, downbeat, offbeat, afterbeat make no sense except in relation to an internal pulse through which they gain different perceptual identities and different performance realizations. Beat-relative perception also aids memory for patterns. Critically, the pulse is not slavishly determined by sound, but is something we can, to varying degrees, control: when we listen to highly syncopated rhythms, we can still "find" and tap our toes to the pulse of the music despite the complex sequence of note durations, many not beginning "on the beat." Conversely, we can generate highly syncopated rhythms on an internal pulse. When the internal pulse is shared among a group of performers, they can coordinate their perception and production of rhythm. We will present below a conceptual cataloging of increasingly complex features that comprise rich BPS and distinguish it from mere SMS, keeping track of which features have and have not been demonstrated in other animals.

Basic sensory motor synchronization

Modern scientific studies of rhythm perception and production have been under way for well over a century.[6] The most basic level and the

canonical paradigm for most of our work so far is 1:1 SMS with isochronous sounds, where people move once for each sound. Most humans, even without any explicit musical training, are extremely good at this in the sense of matching the average tempo of their movement (often finger tapping) with a metronome within a few percent. Two observations point to the *existence of an internal pulse*. First, synchronization is not a reactive process, but instead a predictive and anticipatory one – synchronized movements often precede a metronome, and the movement initially synchronized to a metronome can continue when the metronome is removed.

Even simple synchronization with others has a strongly emotional and social component that develops very early. It is prosocial, meaning synchronized partners feel more positively inclined toward each other. Children are more likely to help out an adult with whom they are synchronized.[7] Basic synchronization generally develops around age four;[8] prior to that children are generally animated and moving in response to music, but not in synchrony.[9] Underscoring the importance of social interaction if modeling an adult, even two-and-a-half-year-olds can synchronize.[10]

Animal evidence for basic synchronization
This basic form of 1:1 SMS has attracted the majority of attention in comparative studies and has been described in a number of animals including several species of insects and frogs which create "synchronous choruses."[11] These findings have inspired a number of evolutionary accounts explaining group synchronization because of the benefit synchronized chorusing has for increased spatial reach calls in order to attract mates or defend territory, the so-called "beacon effect."[12] Nonhuman primates have been shown to have only very limited aspects of basic synchronization. Macaques, after training, can match the tempo of auditory and visual metronomes but are unable to match the phase, always tapping after the metronome. This is in contrast to humans who can tap on or even before the metronome. This result suggests that macaques do not have the same degree of prediction, although they are able to make some predictive use of the regularity because their reaction time is shorter to regularly timed sounds than randomly occurring ones.[13] (For comparison, budgerigars have similarly been trained with similar results.)[14] Chimpanzees can be trained to alternately tap keys on a keyboard, and their spontaneous tapping is weakly affected by a metronome, but only at tempos close to the original spontaneous tapping rate.[15] It is not known if they can be trained to synchronize. Comparative results have informed a number of theories, including the vocal learning hypothesis (discussed below) as well as the "gradual audiomotor evolution hypothesis," which proposes that

our primate relatives might resemble earlier stages in the gradual emergence of BPS.[16]

Tempo and subdivision

Compared to animals, humans have considerable flexibility even for basic SMS: (1) they are able to synchronize across a broad range of tempi, from roughly 30 to 300 bpm,[17] and can predictively follow tempo changes. (2) Humans can generally change the mode of synchronization from one movement per metronome tick to subdivisions and multiples, tapping, for example, twice per tick, or every two ticks, which we could call *m:n* synchronization. This is one way of establishing metrical hierarchy. Binary subdivisions and multiples are generally the easiest for nonmusicians,[18] but the system can accomplish more complex divisions, meters, and polyrhythms.[19] The latter implies the existence of some distance between input and output into which pulses can be selected and manipulated, such that the output need not slavishly follow the input.

Complex temporal patterns, hierarchy

A second type of elaboration concerns the complexity of input and output patterns that can be represented and produced. Synchronizing with complex multipart music is an example of the former, while playing a complex drum pattern to a click track is an example of the latter. Of course, complex sounds can also lead to complex movements, and this is indeed the most common configuration. Key, however, is the existence of an internal pulse to tie it together. Basic auditory perception processes such as grouping of sounds, separation of different sources, and measuring event rate appear widespread in animals and are present in human newborns.[20] These processes are not necessary components of SMS, but rather enrichers of it, providing a wider variety of sound representations with which to synchronize.[21] A fully hierarchical, metrical, system of beats may further require brain regions that in humans are essential to language, which have been hypothesized to more generally implement nested hierarchies of action,[22] as well as require associated development of motor system complexity.[23] In animals, synchronization with actual music, with its multiple temporal scales, has been demonstrated to date in only cockatoos,[24] parrots,[25] and California sea lions,[26] with only cockatoos so far displaying hierarchical movement patterns – moving different parts of its body (head, trunk, feet) in sync with different metrical levels, as in human dance.[27]

Active perception

A third elaboration which we believe to be critical for the fuller set of behaviors associated with rich BPS is for the motor pulse to influence

auditory perception, even in the absence of movement. In support of this blurring of the distinctions between hearing and moving, it has frequently been observed that during the perception of strongly pulse-inducing rhythms, motor planning regions are activated even in absence of movement,[28] suggesting they may play a role in generating an internal pulse. By studying multiple metrical interpretations of a single ambiguous rhythm, we have demonstrated that the pulse can influence auditory responses.[29] We have proposed the action simulation for auditory prediction (ASAP) hypothesis to formalize the idea that the motor system plays a causal role in perception through reciprocal transformations of auditory and motor pulses via the parietal cortex and that one explanation for human abilities is the presence of robust bidirectional connections in this network.[30] The active influence of pulse on auditory perception has not been demonstrated in any other animals to date though it has only been tested in a few species.[31]

Human expertise and training

Though all of the foregoing mechanisms exist in humans, they may have varying levels of efficacy in different individuals and be dependent on implicit experience or training to be fully functional. For example, while synchronization with a metronome, simple subdivisions, or simple, strongly metrical patterns is easy for most nonmusicians, for many, synchronization with more highly syncopated patterns is more challenging.[32] Similarly, more complex $m{:}n$ polyrhythmic synchronization ratios generally have to be learned. Active perception, by which our internal pulse shapes how we hear rhythm, is often challenged when we hear unfamiliar music from a different culture; only through experience can we begin to understand intended pulse structures.[33] Many first time salsa or West African dancers are acutely aware of this and face the need to learn, usually through the body, how to hear the pulse of these rhythms. Musicianship demonstrates the human ability to build, maintain, and assert an internal sense of pulse even based on audiovisual input streams with complex, shifting temporal relationships to a central but not directly expressed or reinforced pulse.

There are other levels of elaboration that we will not deal with in this short treatment, including the involvement of short- and long-term memory, the potential for complex syntactic structures of nested rhythmic patterns within patterns, and the connection of these more mechanistic aspects of rhythm perception and production with goals, motivations, and emotions. Notably, these higher levels are what strike us as most musical, and it is these that are often accounted for most directly in evolutionary accounts of the origin of human musical rhythm.

Accounts of the origin of beat perception and synchronization

The first question is if musical behaviors evolved at all. Have we evolved to be rhythmic because of some fitness or survival benefit conferred to our distant ancestors that enabled those with the rhythmic skills outlined above to better survive to pass on their genes to the next generation? Alternatively, if rhythm is thought to confer no survival value, it cannot have been shaped by natural selection. In this case, is BPS merely a by-product of other adaptations which we have learned to use for musical purposes?

Nonadaptation views

Most famous of the nonadaptation views is Pinker's[34] argument that music is "auditory cheesecake" in the sense that it was invented in order to stimulate existing auditory sensitivities (to vocal emotion, language, auditory scene analysis, etc.) in much the same way cheesecake was invented to titillate our (presumably evolved) desires for foods high in fats and sugars. In his view, music is a mere "pleasure technology" with no biological utility, a statement that proved surprisingly offensive to many, perhaps because it appeared to trivialize one of humanities dearest attributes. Pinker was criticized for a view too rooted in our modern, Western relationship to music where listening to recorded music predominates: indeed superficially, being deprived of one's iTunes, Spotify, or music videos should have no effect on an individual's survival. This is debatable, given pervasive uses of music for motivation and emotional regulation which surely impact our well-being and worldly and reproductive success. Music as pleasure technology seems even less tenable in a world prior to on-demand recorded music or in other cultures in which music and dance performance still play a more central and participatory role in daily life.

A related view is Patel's[35] suggestion that while music is nonadaptive, it is biologically useful in the life of an individual. Music is not a mere pleasure technology, but a "transformative technology of the mind" (TTM) that has impacts on more general cognitive functions like attention and language and provokes emotions by exploiting existing reward mechanisms, such as the reward for correct temporal predictions. Its universality is explained by analogy to another human technology, the control of fire. With regard to rhythm, Patel's "vocal learning hypothesis" accounts for the emergence of BPS as a by-product of adaptations for vocal learning, which is assumed to require strong connections between auditory

and motor systems to enable the tuning of motor acts to match the acoustics of sounds to be imitated.[36] If such circuitry extended to the whole body, not just vocal musculature, Patel suggested it could be a foundation for BPS. The hypothesis predicts that only vocal learning species, among them parrots and dolphins, should be capable of BPS. This excludes other primates who are not vocal learners. The hypothesis was initially confirmed by the discovery of the first nonhuman animal that could synchronize with a musical beat, a sulfur-crested cockatoo named Snowball, that was able to intermittently synchronize head-bobs to music of different tempos, demonstrating the ability to abstract a pulse from music and couple it to movement.[37] Subsequent support came from a survey of public videos that showed the only animals that quantitatively synchronized with music were cockatoos, parrots, and an elephant, all vocal learners.[38] The relative inability of nonhuman primates to synchronize is likewise consistent with the hypothesis. Similar abilities were demonstrated in a California sea lion, not a known vocal learner,[39] possibly contradicting the vocal learning hypothesis, although there remains some controversy on this point given its close relation to walruses and harbor seals, which are known vocal learners.[40]

Nonadaptation views, perhaps surprisingly, are in the minority. For one thing, they do not accord particularly well with the use of music in small-scale cultures, where ritual aspects predominate, and if music was invented for its cognitive benefits, it seems a rather roundabout way of transforming the mind. Beyond this, other thinkers, for better or worse, seem unable to resist the sense that music must be an adaptation, with distinct survival or reproductive advantages, given the universality of music in human culture, and the fact that music is, at least in some sense, unique to humans, that aspects of it appear innate and are deeply linked to emotion and groups. We will turn to these accounts next.

A brief introduction to evolution

Natural selection was defined by Darwin as the principle "by which each slight variation, if useful, is preserved."[41] "Useful" in this case means a variation in a trait that enhances an individual's chance of surviving long enough to create progeny. This concept was proposed in the context that there is naturally occurring variation between individuals and there is considerable struggle for existence – because of geometric increases in population, many individuals will not survive. Over time, traits consistent with survival in the current environment will become enriched in the population. (The use of "natural" was

chosen in contrast to artificial selection by man, as in selective breeding.) Traits compatible with survival are often called *adaptations* and discussed as being *selected* by the environment, though both these terms are arguably too active to describe the phenomenon and should be understood without their usual sense of agency and goal direction. The beauty of this simple principle is that it can amplify traits at any level (so long as they can be inherited).

Darwin next defined *sexual selection* as a "less rigorous" form of selection not in terms of life or death, but an individual's chance of securing mates, which then impacts their ability to create offspring. Sexually selected traits tend to differ in males and females and include those involved in direct competition within a sex (such as the size of a stag's horns) and those involved in attracting the opposite sex, the canonical example of which is a peacock's plumage. Two additional forms of selection are often discussed but are more controversial: *kin selection* as a way of explaining traits that give benefit to one's relatives, though at the expense of oneself; and *group selection* as a way to explain traits that benefit the larger group, even though they may not directly benefit the individual. Group selection is controversial as it implies that groups are the units of selection, mutation, and reproduction (i.e., groups generate new groups). We'll sidestep this interesting argument. I think the most helpful view is that traits can have effects at multiple scales: to recognize that humans are inexorably bound up in groups, and thus may have some traits that enhance their ability to be in a group; and that if these traits have overall positive impacts on their individual fitness, then this is all that matters in the end as humans are individuals that reproduce and mutate. Indeed Darwin noted in the context of natural selection that "In social animals [natural selection] will adapt the structure of each individual for the benefit of the community; if each in consequence profits by the selected change."[42] That will do just fine for our purposes in understanding social aspects of rhythm.

Adaptational theories focused on the individual

Sexual selection

Darwin predates Pinker's skepticism: "As neither the enjoyment nor the capacity of producing musical notes are faculties of the least direct use to man in reference to his ordinary habits of life, they must be ranked amongst the most mysterious with which he is endowed."[43] He solved the mystery by suggesting, by analogy with bird song, that music must have played a role in our ancestors' courtship, but colorfully suggests that

cultural developments have eliminated any original sexual dimorphism in the trait.

More recently, Miller[44] renewed the argument stating, "Music is what happens when a smart, group-living, anthropoid ape stumbles into the evolutionary wonderland of runaway sexual selection for complex acoustic displays." Music is thus like Darwin's famous example of selection, the peacock tail. Miller amusingly applies a common trope that rock and rollers have lots of sex, but don't always live so long (so, music may actually be maladaptive for survival). Extrapolating to a time prior to birth control, he suggests this would have been a powerful means of enhancing reproductive success. Musical performance is an indicator of mate quality (though working through "preexisting perceptual and cognitive preferences" shaped by evolution). Musical expertise and prowess advertise stamina, physical coordination, and creative ability (a serious concern in novelty-craving species).

Others have rejected sexual selection accounts, perhaps too strictly, based on the fact that both sexes are musical (while most sexually selected traits are seen only in one sex). As we saw above, this is not a serious problem, as the differences could have been erased historically, or mate selection could be in both directions. Sexual selection may appear at odds with the group role of music in many small-scale societies, so sexual selection proponents tend to hark back to a time when music was more of a solo activity, which seems to be their major flaw. However, this seems not a critical objection, as who can doubt the ability of music and dance to introduce us to an individual intimately, whether they are alone or in a group, and play a role in attraction? For a social animal, part of attractiveness could well be the ability to stand out in a group while simultaneously displaying one's ability to cooperate with others in a group. Group music-making could have developed as a more efficient way of finding mates in larger groups, compared to one-on-one interactions.

Natural selection: adaptation for survival

One of the first of the recent writers to speculate on the survival value of music, Roederer[45] identified music as a kind of acoustical-emotional pattern perception training tool that would enable the mother–child dyad to tune up the infant's brain for the complex auditory pattern perception needed for speech perception as well as in emotional relationships. Infants and mothers deficient in necessary skills would be at a disadvantage in the social world. This view does not deal with rhythm or synchronization explicitly, but, as emotionally laden elements of music, accounts for a suggested role in maintaining group cohesion by

establishing ways to equalize or synchronize emotions. This view bears a striking similarity to Patel's transformative technology of the mind.

Theories rooted in bipedalism

A number of accounts have identified the special development of bipedalism as a reason for the emergence of rhythmic synchronization. Bipedalism had numerous survival advantages, including freeing up the hands and arms for tasks other than supporting the body. Unlike quadrupedal locomotion, the energetically most efficient gaits for bipeds are all isochronous, with strict left/right alternation.[46] Thus, all humans would have endless experience with producing and hearing isochronous rhythms, as well as have the ability to smoothly modulate tempo. This could explain the motoric substrates for synchronization, as well as explain the human preference for walking-tempo isochrony,[47] but it does not immediately explain synchronization of movement to sound.

One suggestion, by Riggle,[48] explains the emergence of synchronization as a by-product of a system that rewards periodic vestibular and auditory inputs, a system that is proposed to motivate infants to begin walking and reward their production of steady gaits. Larsson[49] identifies bipedal locomotion as providing an opportunity for groups to match their walking and running gaits to reduce the continuous auditory masking that unsynchronized footfalls would create. By evolving the ability to synchronize gait, windows of quiet would be available to detect other important sounds of predators and prey. This could enable groups to move around more stealthily by obscuring the size of a group and confer a survival advantage.

Theories rooted in caregiving

Bipedalism brought with it disadvantages, including the need for a smaller birth canal due to constraints on pelvic shape, which in turn necessitated giving birth to helpless infants born at an early stage of development. Dissanayake[50] proposes that a motivational system had to evolve to ensure that bipedal mothers would become committed to the extended caregiving required by their immature infants and that this selective pressure led to a structured form of rhythmic emotional bonding that depended on abilities to predict the timing of others actions and to feel bonded because of it. This initial foundation supports the continuous use of musical interactions throughout life and exemplifies the grander sweep of more holistic origin hypotheses – embedded in a supramodal framework of ritual and imitation, rhythmic synchrony becomes just one piece in the whole that combines emotion, sociality, and rhythm.

Adaptational theories focused on groups

Rhythm as facilitator or marker of social groups

Music-making is often done in groups. Brown[51] has argued core features of music, including a temporal structure that readily encourages group synchronization, are optimal for making this so. The communal participatory use of music in small-scale cultures reinforces this notion of music's central use. Not surprisingly then, many evolutionary accounts of music emphasize its ability to create cohesive groups, some going so far as to state that the capacity to synchronize is the critical developmental milestone that enabled the growth of human culture by enabling earlier humans to form larger groups, using the power of joint synchronization to ease the inevitable social tensions that forced earlier groups to fracture.[52] Many others have pointed out that music can serve as a sort of social glue and medium for group emotional regulation and communication, that builds group identity.[53]

Related to the idea that music serves to build groups is the parallel that music serves to advertise the quality of a group. Merker[54] explains the emergence of isochronous group synchronization as a modification of a behavior like the chimpanzee "carnival display," a riotous group movement and noisemaking session in response to finding a fruit tree. He supposes that if a common ancestor of chimpanzees and humans was able to develop means of synchronizing such vocalizations as a group, the summed super-voice could advertise food abundance more broadly to migrating females and draw them in. This "beacon effect" was previously used to explain group chorusing in other synchronously chorusing species. He further hypothesizes that, because of the linkage of breathing, vocalization, and locomotion, such displays might be at around the walking pace, the rate that modern humans prefer to synchronize. In contrast to Fitch,[55] Merker dismisses primate "drumming" displays as merely individual noisemaking often presented at biophysically limited maximum rates (one might think of a captive animal rattling a cage door), and thus not a promising foundation for synchronization.

Hagen and Bryant[56] suggest music is at the heart of an even higher level of human social organization: the existence of intergroup relationships in the absence of any kinship ties. They propose that music and dance enabled this more complex social organization by acting as both a group identifier and a credible indicator of group quality for the purpose of forming mutually beneficial alliances with other groups. Music and dance performances take much longer to prepare than to perform, and thus a short performance can instantly communicate a large degree of credible information about group stability and ability to act in a coordinated way. Only established groups with adequate time and traditions

could prepare impressive displays. This account is proposed to explain why humans with greater musicality in both production and discrimination of quality would be better adapted to signal group quality. This argument is quite similar to a sexual selection hypothesis, only operating at the levels of groups. While compelling ethnographic evidence for the model of using music and dance to court other groups for alliances is presented, this account seems to fit equally well with a nonadaptational account such as TTM in which cultural innovation built on preexisting abilities replaces biological adaptation.

Future directions

We have tried to lay out the wide spectrum of accounts for the origin of human beat-based rhythm. It is a fascinating, though admittedly incomplete, set of views. Each one seems to have made one or more leaps, and most focus intently on only part of the evidence available. As unsatisfying a conclusion as it might be, it seems likely that all of the foregoing accounts have some aspects that are correct: music and rich BPS are complexes of many individual components, and most accounts so far have simplified this. Every account, even nonadaptation accounts, presumes that functional aspects evolved, but disagree on what selective pressure led to this. On top of these adaptations, we have apparently invented vast and varied traditional repertoires of music and dance for a range of purposes. It remains to sharpen the conceptual account of the components of human rich BPS and to find neural mechanisms accounting for these different components. The input of percussionists would be most welcome here. Ultimately, we need an account for the evolution of each aspect of rich BPS, and to determine if they are separable, evolved for specific reasons, or are best considered as a whole. There are of course many other questions left unanswered: If the benefits of group music-making are so powerful, why have they not evolved more often? Is it that the neural change needed to link auditory and motor systems is difficult to evolve, or is it that other species lacked the social milieu and essential prerequisites for the addition of this link to be of any value? We hope the reader is sufficiently stimulated to read further and join the debate.

Notes

1. B. Nettl, "An Ethnomusicologist Contemplates Universals in Musical Sound and Musical Culture," in N. L. Wallin and B. H. Merker (eds.), *Origins of Music* (Cambridge, MA: MIT Press, 2000).

2. W. T. Fitch, "The Biology and Evolution of Rhythm: Unraveling a Paradox," in P. Rebuschat, M. Rohrmeier, J. A. Hawkins, and I. Cross (eds.), *Language and Music as Cognitive Systems* (Oxford University Press, 2012).

3. A. D. Patel and J. R. Iversen, "The Evolutionary Neuroscience of Musical Beat Perception: the Action Simulation for Auditory Prediction (ASAP) Hypothesis," *Frontiers in Systems Neuroscience*, 8 (2014) 57.

4. N. J. Conard, M. Malina, and S. C. Münzel, "New Flutes Document the Earliest Musical Tradition in Southwestern Germany," *Nature*, 460 (2009), 737–40.

5. D.-J. Povel and P. J. Essens, "Perception of Temporal Patterns," *Music Perception*, 2 (1985), 411–40.

6. For example, T. L. Bolton, "Rhythm," *The American Journal of Psychology*, 6 (2), (1894), 145–238. For comprehensive reviews, see: B. H. Repp, "Sensorimotor Synchronization: A Review of the Tapping Literature, *Psychonomic Bulletin and Review*, 12 (2005), 969–92; B. H. Repp and Y-H Su, "Sensorimotor Synchronization: A Review of Recent Research (2006–2012)," *Psychonomic Bulletin and Review*, 20 (2013), 403–53.

7. For a recent review, see L. J. Trainor and L. Cirelli, "Rhythm and Interpersonal Synchrony in Early Social Development, *Annals of the New York Academy of Science*, 1337 (2015) 45–52.

8. J. D. McAuley, M. R. Jones, S. Holub, H. M. Johnston, and N. S. Miller, "The Time of our Lives: Life Span Development of Timing and Event Tracking," *Journal of Experimental Psychology: General*, 135 (2006) 348–67.

9. T. Eerola, G. Luck, and P. Toiviainen, "An Investigation of Pre-schoolers' Corporeal Synchronization with Music," *Proceedings of the 9th International Conference on Music Perception and Cognition*, (2006).

10. S. Kirschner and M. Tomasell, "Joint Drumming: Social Context Facilitates Synchronization in Preschool Children," *Journal of Experimental Child Psychology*, 102 (2009), 299–314.

11. A. Ravignani, D. L. Bowling, and W. T. Fitch, "Chorusing, Synchrony, and the Evolutionary Functions of Rhythm," *Frontiers in Psychology*, 5 (2014), 1118.

12. B. H. Merker, "Synchronous Chorusing and Human Origins," in Wallin, et al., *The Origins of Music* (Cambridge, MA: MIT Press, Bradford Book, 2001), pp. 315–27.

13. H. Merchant and H. Honing, "Are Non-human Primates Capable of Rhythmic Entrainment? Evidence for the Gradual Audiomotor Evolution Hypothesis," *Frontiers in Neuroscience*, 7 (2014), 274.

14. A. Hasegawa, K. Okanoya, and T. Hasegawa, "Rhythmic Synchronization Tapping to an Audio-visual Metronome in Budgerigars," *Science Report*, 1 (2011), 120.

15. Y. Hattori, M. Tomonaga, and T. Matsuzawa, "Distractor Effect of Auditory Rhythms on Self-paced Tapping in Chimpanzees and Humans," *PLoS ONE*, 10 (2015), e0130682.

16. Merchant and Honing, "Non-human Primates," 274.

17. J. London, *Hearing in Time* (Oxford University Press, 2004).

18. E. E. Hannon and S. E. Trehub, "Metrical Categories in Infancy and Adulthood," *Psychological Science*, 16 (2005), 48–55.

19. P. Vuust, M. Wallentin, K. Mouridsen, L. Ostergaard, and A. Roepstorff, "Tapping Polyrhythms in Music Activates Language Areas," *Neuroscience Letters*, 494 (2011), 211–6.

20. C. E. Hagmann and R. G. Cook, "Testing Meter, Rhythm, and Tempo Discriminations in Pigeons," *Behavioral Processes*, 85 (2010), 99–110; L. J. Trainor and L. Cirelli, "Rhythm and Interpersonal Synchrony in Early Social Development," *Annals of the New York Academy of Science*, 1337 (2015), 45–52.

21. W. T. Fitch, "Rhythmic Cognition in Humans and Animals: Distinguishing Meter and Pulse Perception," *Frontiers in Systems Neuroscience*, 7 (2013), 68.

22. L. Fadiga, L. Craighero, and A. D'Ausilio, "Broca's Area in Language, Action, and Music," *Annals of the New York Academy of Science*, 1169 (2009), 448–58.

23. G. Mendoza and H. Merchant, "Motor System Evolution and the Emergence of High Cognitive Functions," *Progress in Neurobiology*, 122 (2014), 73–93.

24. A. D. Patel, J. R. Iversen, M. R. Bregman, and I. Schulz, "Experimental Evidence for Synchronization to a Musical Beat in a Non-human Animal," *Current Biology*, 19 (2009), 827–30.

25. A. Schachner, T. F. Brady, I. M. Pepperberg, and M. D. Hauser, "Spontaneous Motor Entrainment to Music in Multiple Vocal Mimicking Species," *Current Biology*, 19 (2009), 831–6.

26. P. Cook, A. Rouse, M. Wilson, and C. Reichmuth, "A California Sea Lion (Zalophus californianus) can Keep the Beat: Motor Entrainment to Rhythmic Auditory Stimuli in a Non-vocal Mimic," *Journal of Comparative Psychology*, 127 (2013), 412–27.

27. P. Toiviainen, G. Luck, and M. R. Thompson, "Embodied Meter: Hierarchical Eigenmodes in Music-Induced Movement," *Music Perception*, 28 (2010), 59–70.

28. For example, J. A. Grahn and J. B. Rowe, "Feeling the Beat: Premotor and Striatal Interactions in Musicians and Non-musicians During Beat Perception, *Journal of Neuroscience*, 29 (2009), 7540–8.

29. J. R. Iversen, B. H. Repp, and A. D. Patel, "Top-down Control of Rhythm Perception Modulates Early Auditory Responses," *Annals of the New York Academy of Science*, 1169 (2009), 58–73.

30. A. D. Patel and J. R. Iversen, "The Evolutionary Neuroscience of Musical Beat Perception: the Action Simulation for Auditory Prediction (ASAP) Hypothesis," *Frontiers in Systems Neuroscience*, 8 (2014), 57.

31. C. E. Hagmann and R. G. Cook, "Testing Meter, Rhythm, and Tempo Discriminations in Pigeons," *Behavioral Processes*, 85 (2010), 99–110; H. Honing, H. Merchant, G. P. Háden, L. Prado, and R. Bartolo, "Rhesus Monkeys (Macaca mulatta) detect Rhythmic Groups in Music, but not the Beat," *PLOS ONE*, 7 (2012), e51369.

32. A. D. Patel, J. R. Iversen, Y. Chen, and B. H. Repp, "The Influence of Metricality and Modality on Synchronization with a Beat," *Experimental Brain Research*, 163 (2005), 226–38.

33. P. Toiviainen and T. Eerola, "Where Is the Beat?: Comparison of Finnish and South-African Listeners," *Proceedings of the 5th Triennial ESCOM Conference*, (2003), 501–4.

34. S. Pinker, *How the Mind Works* (New York: Norton, 1997).

35. A. D. Patel, "Music, Biological Evolution, and the Brain," in M. Bailar (ed.), *Emerging Disciplines* (Rice University Press, 2010), pp. 91–144.

36. A. D. Patel, "Musical Rhythm, Linguistic Rhythm, and Human Evolution," *Music Perception*, 24 (2006), 99–104

37. Patel, et al., "Experimental Evidence," 827–30.

38. A. Schachner, "Auditory-motor Entrainment in Vocal Mimicking Species: Additional Ontogenetic and Phylogenetic Factors," *Communicative and Integrative Biology*, 3 (2010), 290–3.

39. Cook, et al., "A California Sea Lion," 412–27.

40. A. D. Patel, "The Evolutionary Biology of Musical Rhythm: Was Darwin Wrong?" *PLOS Biology*, 12 (2014), e1001821.

41. C. Darwin, On the Origin of Species by Means of Natural Selection, 1st ed. (London: John Murray, 1859).

42. *Ibid.*

43. C. Darwin, *The Descent of Man and Selection in Relation to Sex*, 1st ed., vol. 2 (London: John Murray, 1871), p. 333.

44. G. Miller, "Evolution of Human Music through Sexual Selection," in Wallin, et al., *The Origins of Music* (Cambridge, MA: MIT Press, Bradford Book, 2001), pp. 329–60.

45. J. G. Roederer, "The Search for a Survival Value of Music," *Music Perception*, 1 (1984), 350–6.

46. T. A. McMahon, *Muscles, Reflexes, and Locomotion* (Princeton University Press, 1984).

47. M. F. McKinney and D. Moelants, "Ambiguity in Tempo Perception: What Draws Listeners to Different Metrical Levels?" *Music Perception*, 24 (2006), 155–66.

48. M. Riggle, "A Simpler Explanation for Vestibular Influence on Beat Perception: No Specialized Unit Needed," *Empirical Musicology Review*, 4 (2009), 19–22.

49. M. Larsson, "Self-generated Sounds of Locomotion and Ventilation and the Evolution of Human Rhythmic Abilities," *Animal Cognition*, 17 (2013), 1–14.

50. E. Dissanayake, "Ritual and Ritualization: Musical Means of Conveying and Shaping Emotion in Humans and other Animals," in S. Brown and U. Voglsten (eds.), *Music and Manipulation: on the Social Uses and Social Control of Music* (Oxford: Berghahn Books, 2006), pp. 31–56.

51. S. Brown, "Evolutionary Models of Music: From Sexual Selection to Group Selection," *Perspectives in Ethology*, 13 (2000), 234–84.

52. W. H. McNeill, *Keeping Together in Time: Dance and Drill in Human History* (Harvard University Press, 1997).

53. Brown, "Evolutionary Models," 234–84; S. Mithen, *The Singing Neanderthals: The Origins of Music, Language, Mind and Body* (Harvard University Press, 2006).

54. B. H. Merker, G. S. Madison, and P. Eckerdal, "On the Role and Origin of Isochrony in Human Rhythmic Entrainment," *Cortex*, 45 (2009), 4–17.

55. Fitch, "The Biology and Evolution of Rhythm."

56. E. H. Hagen and G. A. Bryant, (2003) "Music and Dance as a Coalition Signaling System," *Human Nature*, 14 (2003), 21–51.

Select bibliography

This short bibliography contains references to books in the English language that might be useful to readers and is not intended to be comprehensive. References to journal articles and to other percussion-related publications will be found in the notes to each chapter.

Agawu, K., *African Rhythm: A Northern Ewe Perspective* (Cambridge University Press, 1995).
  Representing African Music: Postcolonial Notes, Queries, Positions (New York: Routledge, 2003).
Altenberg, J. E., *Trumpeter's and Kettledrummer's Art*, E. H. Tarr (trans.) (Nashville: Brass Press, 1974).
Arbeau, T., *Orchesography*, M. S. Evans (trans.) (New York: Dover Publications, 1967 [1589]).
Arom, S., *African Polyphony and Polyrhythm: Musical Structure and Methodology* (Cambridge University Press, 1991).
Azadehfar, M. R., *Rhythmic Structure in Iranian Music*, 2nd ed. (Tehran Arts University Press, 2011).
Bakan, M. B., *Music of Death and New Creation: Experiences in the World of Balinese Gamelan Beleganjur* (University of Chicago Press, 1999).
Baschet, F., *Les Sculptures Sonores: The Sound Sculptures of Bernard and Francois Baschet* (Chelmsford: Soundworld, 1999).
Bebey, F., *African Music: A People's Art* (Brooklyn: Lawrence Hill, 1975).
Beck, J. (ed.), *Encyclopedia of Percussion* (New York: Garland, 1995).
Becker, B. (ed.), "Contemporary Percussion: Performers' Perspectives," *Contemporary Music Review*, vol. 7, pt. 1 (1992).
Becker, B., *Rudimental Arithmetic: A Drummer's Study of Pattern and Rhythm* (Asbury Park, NJ: Keyboard Percussion Publications, 2008).
Berliner, P., *The Soul of Mbira: Music and Traditions of the Shona People of Zimbabwe* (University of California Press, 1978).
  Thinking in Jazz: the Infinite Art of Improvisation (University of Chicago Press, 1994).
Blacking, J., *Music, Culture, and Experience: Selected Papers of John Blacking* (University of Chicago Press, 1995).
Blades, J., *Drum Roll: A Professional Adventure from the Circus to the Concert Hall* (London: Faber and Faber, 1977).
  Percussion Instruments and their History (New York: Praeger, 1970).
Blades, J. and J. Montagu, *Early Percussion Instruments: from the Middle Ages to the Baroque* (Oxford University Press, 1976).
Bowles, E. A., *The Timpani: A History in Pictures and Documents* (Stuyvesant, NY: Pendragon Press, 2002).

[296]

The Timpani Supplement: More Pictures and Documents, (Hillsdale, NY: Pendragon Press, 2009).

Brend, M., *Strange Sounds: Offbeat Instruments and Sonic Experiments in Pop* (San Francisco: Backbeat Books, 2005).

Brindle, R. S., *Contemporary Percussion* (Oxford University Press, 1970).

Burton, G., *Learning to Listen: The Jazz Journey of Gary Burton* (Boston: Berklee Press, 2013).

Butler, M. J., *Unlocking the Groove: Rhythm, Meter, and Musical Design in Electronic Dance Music* (Indiana University Press, 2006).

Cage, J., *Silence: Lectures and Writings* (Wesleyan University Press, 1961).

Chapin, J., *Advanced Techniques for the Modern Drummer Vol. 1: Coordinated Independence as Applied to Jazz and Bebop* (Emeryville, CA: Alfred Music [1948] 2002).

Charry, E., *Mande Music* (University of Chicago Press, 2000).

Chenoweth, V., *The Marimbas of Guatemala* (University of Kentucky Press, 1964).

Chernoff, J. M., *African Rhythm and African Sensibility* (University of Chicago Press, 1979).

Clark, J., *Connecticut's Fife and Drum Tradition* (Wesleyan University Press, 2011).

Clayton, M., *Time in Indian Music: Rhythm, Metre, and Form in North Indian Rag Performance* (Oxford University Press, 2000).

Cowell, H., *New Musical Resources* (Cambridge University Press, 1996).

Danielsen, A. (ed.), *Musical Rhythm in the Age of Digital Reproduction* (Surrey: Ashgate Publishing, 2010).

Dean, M., *Drum: A History* (Toronto: Scarecrow Press, 2012).

Deveaux, S., *The Birth of Bebop: A Social and Musical History* (University of California Press, 1997).

Erskine, P., *No Beethoven: An Autobiography and Chronicle of Weather Report* (Emeryville, CA: Alfred Music, 2013).

Eshun, K., *More Brilliant Than the Sun: Adventures in Sonic Fiction* (London: Quartet Books, 1999).

Floyd, S. A., *The Power of Black Music: Interpreting Its History from Africa to the United States* (Oxford University Press, 1995).

Gara, L. and W. "Baby" Dodds, *The Baby Dodds Story* (Louisiana State University Press, 1992).

Gates, H. L., Jr., *The Signifying Monkey* (Oxford University Press, 1988).

Hart, M. and F. Lieberman with D. A. Sonneborn, *Planet Drum: A Celebration of Percussion and Rhythm* (New York: Harper, 1991).

Hart, M. with J. Stevens and F. Lieberman, *Drumming at the Edge of Magic: a Journey into the Spirit of Percussion* (San Francisco: Harper, 1990).

Helmholz, H., *On the Sensations of Tone* (New York: Dover, 1954).

Hinger, F. D., *Technique for the Virtuoso Timpanist* (Hackensack, NJ: Jerona Music, 1975).

Time & Motion: The Musical Snare Drum (New Haven: Cornucopia, 1991).

Holland, J., *Percussion* (London: Macdonald and Jane's, 1978).

Practical Percussion: A Guide to the Instruments and their Sources (Lanham, MD: Scarecrow Press, 2005).

Hopkin, B., *Musical Instrument Design* (Tucson, AZ: Sharp Press, 1999).

Howard, J. H., *Drums in the Americas: The History and Development of Drums in the New World from the Pre-Columbian Era to Modern Times* (New York: Oak Publications, 1967).

Jones, A. M., *Studies in African Music,* 2 vols. (Oxford University Press, 1959).

Jones, L., *Blues People* (New York: Harper Perennial, 2002).

Kaptain, L., *"The Wood that Sings": The Marimba in Chiapas, Mexico* (Everett, PA: HoneyRock, 1992).

Katz, M., *Capturing Sound: How Technology has Changed Music* (University of California Press, 2004).

Keil, C. and S. Feld, *Music Grooves* (University of Chicago Press, 1994).

Kippen, J., *Gurudev's Drumming Legacy: Music, Theory and Nationalism in the Mrdang aur Tabla Vadanpaddhati of Gurudev Patwardhan* (Surrey: Ashgate Publishing, 2006).

  The Tabla of Lucknow: A Cultural Analysis of a Musical Tradition (Cambridge University Press, 1988).

Kite, R., *Keiko Abe: A Virtuosic Life* (Leesburg, VA: GP Percussion, 2007).

Kivy, P., *The Fine Art of Repetition: Essays in the Philosophy of Music* (Cambridge University Press, 1993).

Korall, B., *Drummin' Men: The Heartbeat of Jazz, the Swing Years* (New York: Schirmer Books, 1990).

Krell, J., *Kincaidiana: A Flute Player's Notebook* (Santa Clarita, CA: National Flute Assn., 1997).

Kubik, G., *Theory of African Music,* 2 vols. (University of Chicago Press, 1994).

  Africa and the Blues (University Press of Mississippi, 1999).

Latour, B., *Reassembling the Social: An Introduction to Actor-Network Theory* (Oxford University Press, 2007).

LeVan, R. K., "African Musical Influence in Selected Art Music Works for Percussion Ensemble, 1930–1984," unpublished PhD thesis, University of Pittsburgh (1991).

Locke, D., *Drum Gahu: A Systematic Method for an African Percussion Piece* (Crown Point, IN: White Cliffs Media, 1987).

  Drum Damba: Talking Drum Lessons (Crown Point, IN: White Cliffs Media, 1990).

London, J., *Hearing in Time: Psychological Aspects of Musical Meter* (Oxford University Press, 2012).

Manual, P., *Popular Musics of the Non-western World: An Introductory Survey* (Oxford University Press, 1988).

Mattingly, R., *The Drummer's Time: Conversations with the Great Drummers of Jazz* (Cedar Grove, NJ: Modern Drummer Publications, 1998).

McGraw, A. C., *Radical Traditions: Reimagining Culture in Balinese Contemporary Music* (Oxford University Press, 2013).

McNeill, W. H., *Keeping Together in Time: Dance and Drill in Human History* (Harvard University Press, 1997).

Miller, K., *Playing Along: Digital Games, YouTube, and Virtual Performance* (Oxford University Press, 2012).

Mithen, S., *The Singing Neanderthals: The Origins of Music, Language, Mind, and Body* (Harvard University Press, 2006).

Moeller, S. A., *The Moeller Book: The Art of Snare Drumming* (Chicago: Ludwig Music Publishing Co., 1982).

Moersch, W., *New Music Marimba Concerto List* (Champaign, IL: *New Music Marimba*, 2015).

Monson, I., (ed.), *The African Diaspora: A Musical Perspective* (New York: Routledge, 2003).

Montagu, J., *Making Early Percussion Instruments* (Oxford University Press, 1976). *Timpani and Percussion* (Yale University Press, 2002).

Moody, R., *On Celestial Music and Other Adventures in Listening* (New York: Back Bay Books, 2012).

Moore, J. L., "Acoustics of Bar Percussion Instruments," unpublished PhD thesis, The Ohio State University (1970).

Mowitt, J., *Percussion: Drumming, Beating, Striking* (Duke University Press, 2002).

Negus, K., *Music Genres and Corporate Culture* (New York: Routledge, 1999).

Nketia, J. H. K., *The Music of Africa* (New York: W. W. Norton, 1974).

Partch, H., *Genesis of a Music* (New York: Da Capo, 1974).

Peinkofer, K. and F. Tannigel, *Handbook of Percussion Instruments* (London: Schott, 1976).

Peters, G., *The Drummer Man* (Wilmette, IL: Kemper-Peters, 1975).

Philip, R., *Performing Music in the Age of Recording* (Yale University Press, 2004).

Pond, S., *Head Hunters: The Making of Jazz's First Platinum Album* (University of Michigan Press, 2005).

Potter, K., *Four Musical Minimalists* (Cambridge University Press, 2000).

Rebuschat, P., M. Rohrmeier, J. A. Hawkins, and I. Cross (eds.), *Language and Music as Cognitive Systems* (Oxford University Press, 2012).

Redmond, L., *When the Drummers Were Women* (New York: Three Rivers, 1997).

Reed, T., *Progressive Steps to Syncopation for the Modern Drummer* (Emeryville, CA: Alfred Music [1958] 1997).

Reich, S., *Writings on Music, 1965–2000* (Oxford University Press, 2002).

Roberts, J. S., *Black Music of Two Worlds* (New York: Praeger, 1972).

Rossing, T. D., *Science of Percussion Instruments* (Singapore: World Scientific, 2005).

Sachs, C., *The History of Musical Instruments* (New York: W. W. Norton, 1940).

Saffle, M. (ed.), *Perspectives on American Music, 1900–1950* (New York: Garland Publishing, 2000).

Sankaran, T., *The Rhythmic Principles of South Indian Drumming* (Toronto: Lalith Publishing, 1994).
The Art of Konnakol (Solkattu) (Toronto: Lalith Publishing, 2010).

Schick, S., *The Percussionist's Art: Same Bed, Different Dreams* (University of Rochester Press, 2006).

Schweizer, S. L., *Timpani Tone and the Interpretation of Baroque and Classical Music* (Oxford University Press, 2010).

Shapiro, P., *Turn the Beat Around: The Secret History of Disco* (New York: Macmillan, 2006).

Small, C., *Musicking: The Meanings of Performing and Listening* (Hannover: University Press of New England, 1998).

Smith, G. D., *I Drum, Therefore I Am: Being and Becoming a Drummer* (Surrey: Ashgate Publishing, 2013).

Stone, G. L., *Stick Control for the Snare Drummer* (Boston: G. B. Stone, 1935).

Storch, L., *Marcel Tabuteau: How Do You Expect to Play the Oboe If You Can't Peel a Mushroom?* (Indiana University Press, 2008).

Sumarsam, *Gamelan: Cultural Interaction and Musical Development in Central Java* (University of Chicago Press, 1995).

Swiss, T., J. Sloop, and A. Herman (eds.), *Mapping the Beat: Popular Music and Contemporary Theory* (Malden, MA: Blackwell, 1998).

Tenzer, M., *Balinese Music* (Hong Kong: Periplus, 1998).
  Gamelan Gong Kebyar (University of Chicago Press, 2000).

Toussaint, G. T., *The Geometry of Musical Rhythm: What Makes a "Good" Rhythm Good?* (Boca Raton, FL: CRC Press, 2013).

Wald, E., *The Blues: A Very Short Introduction* (Oxford University Press, 2010).

Wallin, N. L., B. H. Merker, and S. Brown, (eds.), *The Origins of Music* (MIT Press, 2000).

Weium, F., and T. Boon (eds.), *Material Culture and Electronic Sound* (Smithsonian Institution Scholarly Press, 2013).

Wilcken, L., *The Drums of Vodou* (Tempe, AZ: White Cliffs Media, 1992).

Williams, B. M., "The Early Percussion Music of John Cage, 1935–1943," unpublished PhD thesis, Michigan State University (1990).
  Learning Mbira: A Beginning (Everett, PA: HoneyRock, 2001).

Wyre, J., *Touched by Sound: A Drummer's Journey* (Norland, ON: Buka Music, 2002).

Index

CPSIA information can be obtained
at www.ICGtesting.com
Printed in the USA
LVHW011058270519
619153LV00007B/259/P

McQuail's
mass communication theory

McQuail's

mass communication theory

4th edition

SAGE Publications
London • Thousand Oaks • New Delhi

This edition published 2000

First edition 1983
Second edition 1987
Third edition 1994

SAGE Publications Ltd
6 Bonhill Street
London EC2A 4PU

SAGE Publications Inc
2455 Teller Road
Thousand Oaks, California 91320

SAGE Publications India Pvt Ltd
32, M-Block Market
Greater Kailash – I
New Delhi 110 048

British Library Cataloguing in Publication data

A catalogue record for this book is
available from the British Library

ISBN 0 7619 6546 7
ISBN 0 7619 6547 5 (pbk)

Library of Congress catalog card number available

Typeset by Photoprint, Torquay, Devon
Printed in Great Britain by The Alden Press, Oxford

For Marjorie Ferguson

contents

The main aims of this revised and expanded edition have been to update the original text in the light of more recent theory and research and also in recognition of accelerating changes in the media themselves. As on the occasion of the last revision, but especially as we cross into a new century, I have not been immune to the suspicion that the concept of mass communication and the thinking surrounding it may be becoming increasingly dated. The times and the media have certainly changed very much since it was first coined. On the other hand, at the time of writing this revision, the services of the mass media were again being enlisted by governments to support military actions of uncertain wisdom, justice and popularity. The resulting propaganda war was not so different in character from its many 20th century predecessors. There is also growing evidence that the 'old' mass media, in the form of media conglomerates, are actively engaged in taking over and incorporating the 'new media' into the existing global media system, as they begin to show economic potential. The expression 'mass communication' may have a faded air and 'modernist' associations, but the reality to which it refers is much the same, only more complex and extensive.

As usual, there are too many debts to properly acknowledge, but, as before, I would single out the contribution, knowingly or not, of many colleagues and friends, especially those at the University of Amsterdam. I would particulary like to thnk the editors of, and contributors to, the book *The Media in Question*, which gave me such pleasure and stimulus while preparing this revision. They are: Kees Brants, Joke Hermes, Liesbet van Zoonen, Ien Ang, Els de Bens, Jay Blumler, Jan van Cuilenburg, Peter Dahlgren, George Gerbner, Peter Golding, Cees Hamelink, Kaarle Nordenstreng, Karen Siune, Andrew Tudor, and Jan Wieten. And not forgetting Karl Erik Rosengren for his Personal *Festschrift*.

One other special debt is owed to the Els de Bens and Monique Dedain for making available to me the resources of what is probably the best library in Europe for such a purpose, that of the Department of Communication, at the University of Gent. Julia Hall of Sage Publications has encouraged and supported this work in numerous ways and managed to ensure by its change of title a longer life in the 21st century than might otherwise be feasible. On a final, sad note, I mark by the dedication of this book, the untimely death of a colleague and friend, Marjorie Ferguson, whose pertinent and lively contributions to our field of study will be much missed.

Denis McQuail
Chandlers Ford, Hampshire, February, 2000.

THEORIES

first approaches

The term 'mass media' is shorthand to describe means of communication that operate on a large scale, reaching and involving virtually everyone in a society to a greater or lesser degree. It refers to a number of media that are now long-established and familiar, such as newspapers, magazines, film, radio, television and the phonograph (recorded music). It has an uncertain frontier with a number of new kinds of media that differ mainly in being more individual, diversified and interactive and of which the Internet is the leading example. Despite the rapid and continuing growth of these 'new media' there is little sign that the 'mass media' are actually declining, according to any criterion. Rather, they are being supplemented, extended and also challenged to adapt to the newcomers to the scene. While this book does consider the emerging theory for new media, it focuses on the ongoing phenomenon of 'mass communication', whose significance stems from the very fact of its near universality of reach, great popularity and public character.

These features have consequences for the political organization and cultural life of contemporary societies. In respect of *politics*, the mass media have gradually become:

- an essential element in the process of democratic politics by providing an arena and channel for wide debate, for making candidates for office widely known and for distributing diverse information and opinion;
- a means of exercising power by virtue of the relatively privileged access that politicians and agents of government can generally claim from the media as a legitimate right.

In respect of *culture*, the mass media:

- constitute a primary source of definitions and images of social reality and the most ubiquitous expression of shared identity;
- are the largest focus of leisure time interest, providing the shared 'cultural environment' for most people and more so than any other single institution.

In addition, the media are steadily increasing in economic significance, as media industries grow, diversify and consolidate their power in the market.

If these claims are accepted, it is not difficult to understand the great attention which the mass media have attracted since their early days, nor why they have been subject to so much public scrutiny and regulation as well as theorizing. The conduct of democratic (or undemocratic) politics, nationally and internationally, depends more and more on mass media, and there are few significant social issues which are addressed without some consideration of the role of the mass media, whether for good or ill. As will appear, the most fundamental questions of society – those concerning the distribution and exercise of power, the management of problems and the processes

of integration and change – all turn on communication. This is especially true of the messages carried by the public means of communication, whether in the form of information, opinion, stories, or entertainment.

THE MEDIA–SOCIETY RELATIONSHIP

It is hard to draw any clear line between theory of media and theory of society. The view taken in this book is that the media constitute a separate 'social institution' within society, with its own rules and practices, but subject to definition and limitation by the wider society. Thus, the media are ultimately dependent on society, although they have some scope for independent influence and they may be gaining in autonomy as their range of activity, economic significance and informal power grows. This is a potentially spiralling and self-fulfilling process, driven by ever-increasing estimation of their significance by political and cultural actors.

The nature of the relation between media and society depends on circumstances of time and place. This book largely deals with mass media and mass communication in modern, 'developed' nation states, mainly elective democracies with free-market (or mixed) economies which are integrated into a wider international set of economic and political relations of exchange, competition and also domination or conflict. The author's view is that the theory and related research discussed in this book relate generally to social contexts characterized by structured differences in economic welfare and political power between social and economic classes.

It is probable that mass media are experienced differently in societies with 'non-Western' characteristics, especially those that are less individualistic and more communal in character, less secular and more religious. There are other traditions of media theory and media practice, even if western media theory has become part a hegemonic global media project. The differences are not just a matter of more or less economic development, since profound differences of culture and long historical experience are involved. It is too large a task to try to deal with the diversity of global experience, but not too late to issue a warning to the reader about the perspective of this text. It is not just a question of unwitting ethno-centricism, since the problem also lies in the dominant social scientific tradition that has its roots in western thought. In this respect, the approach that derives from cultural studies is better able to cope with the diversity of cultural settings of media production and reception, even if it also has an undoubted western bias in its current postmodern manifestation.

The study of mass communication cannot avoid dealing with questions of values and of political and social conflict. All societies have latent or open tensions and contradictions that often extend to the international arena. The media are inevitably involved in these disputed areas as producers and disseminators of meaning about the

events and contexts of social life, private as well as public. It follows from these remarks that we cannot expect the study of mass communication to provide theoretically neutral, scientifically verified information about the 'effects' or the significance of something that is an immensely complex as well as inter-subjective set of processes. For the same reasons, it is often difficult to formulate theories about mass communication in a way that is open to empirical testing.

BASIC DIFFERENCES OF APPROACH

Not surprisingly, the field of media theory is also characterized by widely divergent perspectives. A difference of approach between the left (progressive) and right (conservative) tendencies has often been influential in structuring theory. There has also been a difference between a critical and a more applied approach to theory that does not correspond to the political axis. Lazarsfeld (1941) referred to this as a critical versus administrative orientation. Critical theory seeks to expose underlying problems and faults of media practice and to relate them in a comprehensive way to social issues, guided by certain values. Applied theory aims to harness an understanding of communication processes to solving practical problems of using mass communication more effectively (Windahl et al., 1992). However, we can also distinguish two other axes of theoretical variation.

One of these separates 'media-centric' from 'society-centric' (or 'socio-centric') approaches. The former approach attributes much more autonomy and influence to communication and concentrates on the media's own sphere of activity; the latter views the media as a reflection of political and economic forces. Theory for the media can thus be little more than a special application of broader social theory (Golding and Murdock, 1978). Media-centric theory sees mass media as primary movers in social change, driven forward by irresistible developments of communication technology. Whether or not society is driven by the media, it is certainly true that mass communication theory itself is so driven, tending to respond to each major shift of media technology and structure.

The second main dividing line is between those theorists whose interest (and conviction) lie in the realm of culture and ideas and those who emphasize material forces and factors. This divide corresponds approximately with certain other dimensions: humanistic versus scientific; qualitative versus quantitative; and subjective versus objective. While these differences may reflect only the necessity for some division of labour in a wide territory, they often involve competing and contradictory claims about how to pose questions, conduct research and provide explanations. These two alternatives are independent of each other, and between them they identify different perspectives on media and society (Figure 1.1).

theories

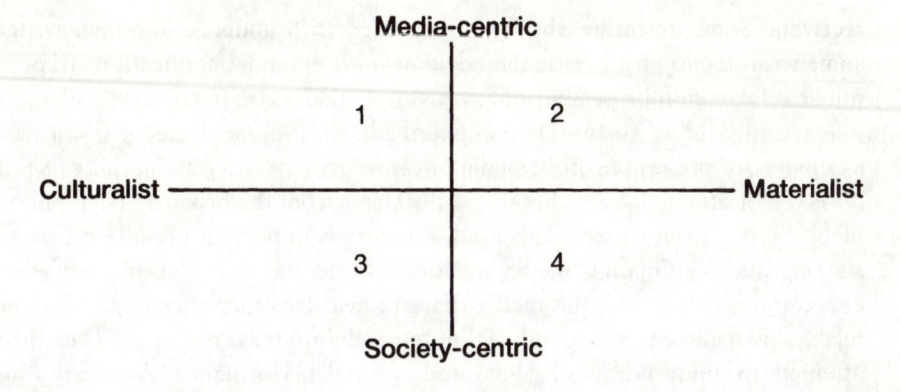

FIGURE 1.1   Dimensions and types of media theory – four main approaches can be identified according to two dimensions: media-centric versus society-centric; and culturalist versus materialist

The four types of perspective can be briefly described as follows:

1   A media-culturalist perspective involves giving primary attention to content and to the subjective reception of media messages as influenced by the immediate personal environment.
2   A media-materialist approach emphasizes the structural and technological aspects of the media.
3   A social-culturalist perspective emphasizes the influence of social factors on media production and reception and the functions of the media in social life.
4   A social-materialist perspective sees media and their contents mainly as a reflection of political-economic and material conditions of the society (e.g. class differences) as factors.

DIFFERENT KINDS OF THEORY

If theory is understood not only as a system of law-like propositions, but as any systematic set of ideas that can help make sense of a phenomenon, guide action or predict a consequence, then one can distinguish at least four kinds of theory which are relevant to mass communication. These can be described as: social scientific, normative, operational and everyday theory. The most obvious kind to be expected in a text like this consists of *social scientific* theory – general statements about the nature, working and effects of mass communication, based on systematic and objective observation of media and other relevant factors.

The body of such theory is now large, although it is loosely organized and not very clearly formulated or even very consistent. It also covers a very wide spectrum, from broad questions of society to detailed aspects of individual information sending and

receiving. Some 'scientific' theory is concerned with understanding what is going on, some with developing a critique and some with practical applications in processes of public information or persuasion.

A second kind of theory can be described as *normative*, since it is concerned with examining or prescribing how media *ought* to operate if certain social values are to be observed or attained. Such theory usually stems from the broader social philosophy or ideology of a given society. This kind of theory is important because it plays a part in shaping and legitimating media institutions and has considerable influence on the expectations concerning the media that are held by other social agencies and by the media's own audiences. A good deal of research into mass media has been the result of attempts to apply norms of social and cultural performance. A society's normative theories concerning its own media are usually to be found in laws, regulations, media policies, codes of ethics and the substance of public debate. While normative media theory is not in itself 'objective', it can be studied by the 'objective' methods of the social sciences (McQuail, 1992).

A third kind of knowledge about the media can best be described as *operational* theory, since it refers to the practical ideas assembled and applied by media practitioners in the conduct of their own media work. Similar bodies of accumulated practical wisdom are to be found in most organizational and professional settings. In the case of the media it helps to organize experience on many questions such as how to select news, please audiences, design effective advertising, keep within the limits of what society permits, and relate effectively to sources and audiences. At some points it may overlap with normative theory, for instance in matters of journalistic ethics.

Such knowledge merits the name of theory because it is usually patterned and persistent, even if never codified, and is influential in respect of behaviour. It comes to light in the study of communicators and their organizations (for example, Elliott, 1972; Tuchman, 1978; Tunstall, 1993). Katz (1977) compared the role of the researcher in relation to media production to that of the theorist of music or philosopher of science who can see regularities which a musician or scientist does not even need to be aware of.

Finally, there is *everyday* or common-sense theory of media use, referring to the knowledge we all have from our own personal experience with media. This enables us to understand what is going on, how a medium fits into our daily lives, how different genres are intended to be 'read', as well as how we like to read it, what the differences are between different media and media genres, and much more. On the basis of such theory is grounded the ability to make consistent choices, develop patterns of taste, construct life-styles and identities as media consumers. It also supports the ability to make critical judgements.

All this, in turn, shapes what the media actually offer to their audiences and sets both directions and limits to media influence. For instance, it enables us to distinguish between 'reality' and 'fiction', to 'read between the lines' or to see through the persuasive aims and techniques of advertising and other kinds of propaganda. The working of common-sense theory can be seen in the norms for use of media which

many people recognize and follow (see Chapter 16), and it can play a significant part in the outcome of public debate about the media, whether or not supported by scientific evidence. Alasuutari (1999b: 88–90) describes different images of the media held by the audience that provide a kind of 'mental map' for ease of use, but are never made explicit. The audience member has a set of repertoires and understandings, loosely related to the way the media present themselves and picking up ideas widely current about the media, such as that they can be a 'window' on the world or a forum for free speech.

This book is most directly concerned with the first and second kinds of theory, but the other two are also important. For instance, a legitimate answer to the question 'What is mass communication?', in place of a formal and abstract definition, would simply be 'What people think it is' leading to very different perceptions on the part of media communicators, their sources and clients and from the many different audiences. The social definitions that mass media acquire in this way are not established by media theorists or legislators but emerge from practice and experience. The emergence of definitions (really perceptions) of media, and their uses for individuals and society, is a complex and lengthy process. The results are often variable and hazy, as will be seen when we try to pin them down.

COMMUNICATION SCIENCE AND THE STUDY OF MASS COMMUNICATION

Mass communication is one topic among many for the social sciences and only one part of a wider field of enquiry into human communication. Under the name 'communication science' the field has been defined by Berger and Chaffee (1987: 17) as a science which 'seeks to understand the production, processing and effects of symbol and signal systems by developing testable theories, containing lawful generalizations, that explain phenomena associated with production, processing and effects'. While this was presented as a 'mainstream' definition to apply to most communication research, in fact it is very much biased towards one model of enquiry – the quantitative study of communicative behaviour and its causes. It is especially inadequate to deal with the nature of 'symbol systems' and signification, the process by which meaning is given and taken in varied social contexts.

More recently, difficulties about definition and delineation of the field have stemmed from developments of technology that have blurred the line between public and private communication and between mass and interpersonal communication. It is unlikely that we can find a single definition of the field that can adequately cover the diversity of the relevant phenomena and perspectives. It is also unlikely that any 'science of communication' can be independent and self-sufficient, given the origins of the study of communication in many disciplines and the wide-ranging nature of

the issues that arise, including matters of economics, law, politics, ethics as well as culture.

Levels of communication

A less problematic way of locating the topic of mass communication in a wider field of communication enquiry is according to different *levels* of social organization at which communication takes place. According to this criterion, mass communication can then be seen as one of several society-wide communication processes, at the apex of a pyramidal distribution of other communication processes according to this criterion (Figure 1.2).

At each descending level of the pyramid indicated there is an increasing number of cases to be found, and each level presents its own particular set of problems for research and theorizing. In an integrated modern society there will often be one large public communication network, usually depending on the mass media, which can reach and involve all citizens to varying degrees, although the media system is also usually fragmented according to regional and other social or demographic factors.

To qualify as a communication network, in the sense intended here, there has to be both a means of delivery and exchange and an active flow of messages in which most

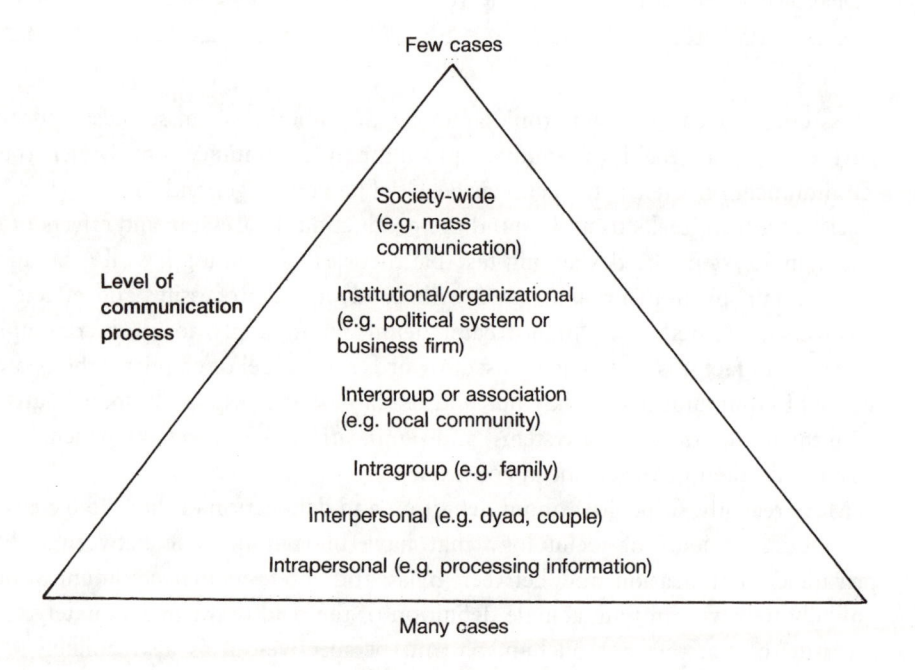

FIGURE 1.2   The pyramid of communication: mass communication is one amongst several processes of social communication

theories

or all of a relevant group actively participate. Alternative (non-mass-media) technologies for supporting society-wide networks do exist (especially the network of physical transportation, the telecommunications infrastructure and the postal system), but these usually lack the society-wide social elements and public roles which mass communication has.

In the past (and in some places still today) society-wide public networks were provided by the church or by political organizations, based on shared beliefs and usually based on a hierarchical chain of contact. This extended from the 'top' to the 'base' and employing diverse means of communication ranging from formal publications to personal contacts.

At a level below that of the whole society, there are several different kinds of communication network. One type duplicates the larger society at the level of region, city or town and may have a parallel media structure. Another is represented by the firm or work organization, which may not have a single location but is usually very integrated within its own organizational boundaries, within which much communication flow takes place. A third variety is that represented by the 'institution' – for instance, that of government, or education, or justice, or religion, or social security. The activities of a social institution are always diverse and also require correlation and much communication, following patterned routes and forms. Organizations and social institutions are distinguished from society-wide networks by being specific in their tasks. They are also bounded and relatively closed, although communication does flow across the boundaries (for example, when a bureaucracy or firm communicates with its clients, and vice versa).

Below this level, there are even more and more varied types of communication network, based on some shared feature of daily life: an environment (such as a neighbourhood), an interest (such as music), a need (such as the care of small children) or an activity (such as sport). At this level, the key questions concern attachment and identity, co-operation and norm formation. At the *intragroup* (for instance, family) and *interpersonal* levels, attention has usually been given to forms of conversation and patterns of interaction, influence, affiliation (degrees of attachment) and normative control. At the *intrapersonal* level, communication research concentrates on the processing of information (for instance, attention, perception, comprehension, recall and learning) the giving of meaning and possible effects (e.g. on knowledge, opinion, self-identity and attitude).

This seemingly neat pattern has been complicated by the growing 'globalization' of social life, in which mass communication has played some part. There is a yet higher 'level' of communication and exchange to consider – that crossing and even ignoring national frontiers, in relation to an increasing range of activities (economic, political, sport, entertainment, etc.). Organizations and institutions are less confined within national frontiers, and individuals can also satisfy communication needs outside their own society and their immediate social environments. The once strong correspondence between patterns of personal social interaction in shared space and time, on the one hand, and systems of communication, on the other, has been much weakened, and our cultural and informational choices have become much wider.

Despite the diversity of the phenomena, each level indicates a range of similar questions for communication theory and research. These can be summarized as follows.

> **Box 1.1 Concerns of communication theory and research**
>
> - Who communicates to whom? (sources and receivers)
> - Why communicate? (functions and purposes)
> - How does communication take place? (channels, languages, codes)
> - What about? (content, references, types of information)
> - What are the outcomes of communication (intended or unintended), for information, understandings, action?

ALTERNATIVE TRADITIONS OF ANALYSIS: STRUCTURAL, BEHAVIOURAL AND CULTURAL

While the questions raised at different levels are similar in this abstract form, in practice very different concepts are involved, and the reality of communication differs greatly from level to level. (For instance, a conversation between two family members takes place according to different 'rules' from those governing a news broadcast to a large audience, a television quiz show, or a chain of command in a work organization.) It is easy to appreciate from this why any 'communication science' has necessarily to be constructed from several different bodies of theory and evidence, drawn from several of the traditional 'disciplines' (especially sociology and psychology in the earlier days, but now also economics, history and literary and film studies). In this respect, the deepest and most enduring divisions separate interpersonal from mass communication, cultural from behavioural concerns, and institutional and historical perspectives from those that are cultural or behavioural. Putting the matter simply, there are essentially three main alternative approaches: the structural, the behavioural and the cultural.

The *structural* approach derives mainly from sociology but includes perspectives from history, politics law and economics. Its starting point is 'socio-centric' rather than 'media-centric', and its primary object of attention is likely to be media systems and organizations and their relationship to the wider society. In so far as questions of content arise, the focus is likely to be on the effect of social structure and media systems on patterns of content. In so far as questions of media use and effect are concerned, the approach emphasizes the consequences of mass communication for other social institutions. This includes, for instance, the influence of political marketing on the conduct of elections or the role of news management and PR in government policy. The fundamental dynamics of media phenomena are located in the exercise of power, in the economy and the socially organized application of technology.

theories

The *behavioural* approach has its principal roots in psychology and social psychology but it also has a sociological variant. In general, the primary object of interest is individual human behaviour, especially in matters to do with choosing, processing and responding to communication messages. Mass media use is generally treated as a form of rational, motivated action that has a certain function or use for the individual and also some objective consequences. Psychological approaches are more likely to use experimental methods of research based on individual subjects. The sociological variant focuses on the behaviour of members of socially defined populations and favours the multivariate analysis of representative survey data collected in natural conditions. Individuals are classified according to relevant variables of social position, disposition and behaviour, and the variables can be statistically manipulated. In the study of organizations, participant observation is commonly adopted. Content analysis is often practised as a form of behavioural research, treating media documents (texts) as the equivalent of populations that can also be sampled and submitted to statistical variable analysis.

The **cultural** approach has its roots in the humanities, in anthropology and in linguistics. While very broad in potential, it has been mainly applied to questions of meaning and language, to the minutiae of particular social contexts and cultural experiences. The study of media is part of a wider field of cultural studies. It is more likely to be 'media-centric' (although not exclusively), sensitive to differences between media and settings of media making and reception, more interested in the in-depth understanding of particular or even unique cases and situations than in generalization. Its methods favour the qualitative and depth analysis of social and human-signifying practices and the analysis and interpretation of 'texts'.

DEFINING MASS COMMUNICATION

The term 'mass communication', which was coined at the end of the 1930s, has too many connotations to allow of a simple agreed definition (see Chapter 2). The word 'mass' is itself value laden and controversial, and the term 'communication' still has no agreed definition – although Gerbner's (1967) 'social interaction through messages' is hard to beat for succinctness. Nevertheless, there is sufficient commonality in widely held 'common-sense' perceptions to provide a working definition and a general characterization. The term 'mass' denotes great volume, range or extent (of people or production), while 'communication' refers to the giving and taking of meaning, the transmission and reception of messages. One early definition (Janowitz, 1968) reads as follows: 'mass communications comprise the institutions and techniques by which specialized groups employ technological devices (press, radio, films, etc.) to disseminate symbolic content to large, heterogeneous and widely dispersed audiences'. In this

and similar definitions, the word 'communication' is really equated with 'transmission', as viewed by the sender, rather than in the fuller meaning of the term, which includes the notions of response, sharing and interaction.

The **process** of 'mass communication' is not synonymous with the 'mass media' (the organized technologies which make mass communication possible). There are other uses of the same technologies and other kinds of relationships mediated through the same networks. For instance, the basic forms and technologies of 'mass' communication are the same as those used for very local newspapers or radio. Mass media can also be used for individual, private or organizational purposes. The same media that carry public messages to large publics for public purposes can also carry personal notices, advocacy messages, charitable appeals, situations-vacant advertisements and many varied kinds of information and culture. This point is especially relevant at a time of convergence of communication technologies, when the boundaries between public and private and large-scale and individual communication networks are increasingly blurred.

Everyday experience with mass communication is extremely varied. It is also voluntary and usually shaped by culture and by the requirements of one's way of life and social environment. The notion of mass communication experience is abstract and hypothetical. Where, on occasions, it does seem to be a reality, the causes are more likely to be found in particular conditions of social life than in the media technology or contents. The diversity of technology-mediated communication relationships is increasing as a result of new technology and new applications. The general implication of these remarks is that mass communication was, from the beginning, more of an idea than a reality. The term stands for a condition and a process which is theoretically possible but rarely found in any pure form. It is an example of what the sociologist Max Weber called an 'ideal type' – a concept which accentuates key elements of an empirically occurring reality, without there necessarily being a single complete example. Where it does seem to occur, it turns out to be less massive, and less technologically determined, than appears on the surface.

THE MASS MEDIA INSTITUTION

Despite changing technology, the mass communication phenomenon persists within the whole framework of the mass media institution. This refers broadly to the set of media organizations and activities, together with their own formal or informal practices, rules of operation and sometimes legal and policy requirements set by the society. These reflect the expectations of the public as a whole and of other social institutions (such as politics, governments, law, religion and the economy). Media institutions have gradually developed around the key activities of publication and wide dissemination of information and culture. They also overlap with other institutions,

especially as these expand their public communication activities. Media institutions are internally segmented according to type of technology (print, film, television, etc.) and often within each type (such as national versus local press or broadcasting). They also change over time and differ from one country to another (see Chapter 9). Even so, there are several typical defining features, additional to the central activity of producing and distributing 'knowledge' (information, ideas, culture) on behalf of those who want to communicate and in response to individual and collective demand. The main features are as follows.

- The media institution is located in the 'public sphere', meaning especially that it is open in principle to all as receivers and senders. The media deal with public matters for public purposes – especially with issues on which public opinion can be expected to form; they are answerable for their activities to the wider society (accountability takes place via laws, regulations and pressures from state and society).
- By virtue of their main publishing activity on behalf of members of a society, the media are also endowed with a large degree of freedom in their economic, political and cultural activities.
- Although the media can exert influence and achieve effects, the media institution is formally powerless (there is a logical relation between this absence of power and the large degree of freedom).
- Participation in the media institution is voluntary and without social obligation; there is a strong association between media use and leisure time and a dissociation from work or duty.

> **Box 1.2   The mass media institution**
> - Main activity is the production and distribution of symbolic content
> - Media operate in the 'public sphere' and are regulated accordingly
> - Participation as sender or receiver is voluntary
> - Organization is professional and bureaucratic in form
> - Media are both free and powerless

FURTHER READING

DeFleur, M. and Ball-Rokeach, S. (1989) *Theories of Mass Communication*, 5th edn. New York: Longman.

Grossberg, L., Wartella, E. and Whitney, D.C. (1998) *MediaMaking*. Thousand Oaks, CA: Sage.

Mattelart, A. and Mattelart, M. (1998) *Theories of Communication: a Short Introduction*. London: Sage.

Rosengren, K.E. (1999) *Communication*. London: Sage.

Silverstone, R. (1999) *Why Study the Media?* London: Sage.

the rise of mass media

The term 'mass media' refers to the organized means for communicating openly and at a distance to many receivers within a short space of time. These criteria are relative, since the earliest forms of mass media (the printed book or pamphlet) were limited to the minority of a society that happened to be literate and relatively close to the place of publication. There has been a continuous line of development of technologies since the earliest forms of media (rock paintings) to the latest digital forms that have expanded the capacity, speed and efficiency of transmission (Schement and Curtis, 1995). It is not easy to say when a 'revolution' occurs; however, when we also take into account certain changes in societies, it does make some sense to think in such terms. Often the significant transitional moments are only appreciated in retrospect.

We have distinguished already between a *process* of mass communication and the actual media that make it possible. It is important to underline that the idea of communicating publicly over time and at a distance is much older than are the mass media now in use. This process was integral to the organization of early societies, carried out especially within religious, political and educational institutions. Even the element of large-scale (mass) dissemination of ideas was present at an early point in time, in the sharing of political and religious awareness and obligations. By the early Middle Ages, the Church had elaborate and effective means in place to ensure transmission to everyone without exception. This can be called mass communication, although it was largely independent of mass media. Nevertheless, it means that the connection was easy to make between the two. It was certainly made by authorities of church and state that reacted with alarm at the potential loss of control represented by printing, and it was also made by authors seeking to disseminate new ideas. The bitter **propaganda** struggles of the Reformation and Counter-reformation, during the 16th century are evidence enough. It was the historical moment when the link between the technology for mass communication irrevocably acquired a particular social and cultural definition.

The aim of this chapter is to set out the approximate sequence of development of the present-day set of mass media. It is also to indicate major turning points and to tell briefly something of the circumstances of time and place in which different media acquired their public definitions in the sense of their perceived utility or role in society. These definitions have tended to form early in the history of any given medium and to have become 'fixed' by circumstances as much as by any intrinsic properties as means of communication. As time has passed, definitions have also changed, especially by becoming more complex and acquiring more 'options', so that it eventually becomes difficult to speak of a single, universally current and consistent definition of any given medium.

In recounting the history of mass media we deal with three main elements that produce distinctive configurations of application and of significance in the wider life of society.

These are:

- certain communicative purposes, needs, or uses, for instance informing, enter-taining, cultural expression, education (such purposes can be found at different 'levels', ranging from individuals to the whole society);
- technologies for communicating publicly to many at a distance;
- forms of social organization that provide the skills and frameworks for deploying the technologies within the wider social context.

These are somewhat disembodied notions, and history is concrete. In practice, the way communication technologies are used depends very much on the circumstances of the time and place. It is hard to predict or even explain after the event why some developments have been of revolutionary significance. It is hard to assign any unique or essential attribute to any of the separate 'mass media' that we identify. The combinations of the above elements that actually occur are usually dependent on features of the social and cultural climate that are intangible. Even so, it seems clear that a certain measure of **freedom** of thought, expression and action has been a necessary condition for the rise of print and other media. In general, the more open the society, the more inclination there has been to develop communication technology to its fullest potential. More closed or repressive regimes either limit development or set strict boundaries to the ways in which technology can be used.

In the following summary of the history and characteristics of different media, it is almost inevitable that a 'Western' perspective and set of values is being applied. This can be justified on the grounds that both the technology and the institutional frame-works of mass media were initially mainly Western (European or North American) and that most other parts of the world have taken up and applied the same developments in a similar way. It is also arguable that the key features of openness and individual choice that are almost intrinsic to mass mediated communication are regarded as typically 'Western' ideas. Even so, there is no reason why mass media need follow only one path in the future, always converging on the western model. There are diverse possibilities, and it is quite possible that cultural differences will trump technological imperatives.

Each *medium* dealt with can be identified in respect of its technology and material form, typical formats and genres, perceived uses and its institutional setting.

PRINT MEDIA: THE BOOK AND THE LIBRARY

The history of modern media begins with the printed book – certainly a kind of revolution, yet initially only a technical device for reproducing the same, or rather a similar, range of texts to what was already being extensively copied by hand. Only gradually does printing lead to a change in content – more secular, practical and

popular works (especially in the vernacular languages), as well as political and religious pamphlets and tracts – which played a part in the transformation of the medieval world. At an early date, laws and proclamations were also printed by royal and other authorities. Thus, there occurred a revolution of society in which printing played an inseparable part.

In the early medieval period, the book was not regarded primarily as a means of communication. Rather it was a store or repository of wisdom and especially of sacred writings and religious texts that had to be kept in incorrupted form. Around the central core of religious and philosophical texts there accumulated also works of science and practical information. The main material form of the book at this time was of bound volumes of separate pages within strong covers, reflecting the requirements for safe storage, reading aloud from a lectern plus the demands of travel and transportation. Books were meant both to last and to be disseminated within limited circles. The modern book is a direct descendant of this model, and similar uses are embedded within it.

The alternative form of rolls of paper or parchment was discontinued, especially when the printing press replaced writing by hand and required the pressing of flat sheets. This ensured the triumph of the medieval manuscript book format, even when miniaturized. Another important element of continuity between pre- and post-printing is the library, a store or collection of books. This has not changed much in concept or physical arrangement, at least until the advent of digital libraries. It also reflects and confirms the idea of a book as a record or permanent work of reference. The character of the library did not change much with printing, although it stimulated the acquisition of private libraries. The later development of the library has given it some claim to be considered not only as a medium but even a mass medium. It is certainly often organized as a means of public information and was envisaged from the 19th century onwards as an important tool of mass enlightenment.

The successful application of print technology to the reproduction of texts in place of handwriting, about the mid-15th century, was only the first step in the emergence of a 'media institution'. Printing gradually became a new craft and a significant branch of commerce (Febvre and Martin, 1984). Printers were later transformed from tradespeople into publishers, and the two functions gradually became distinct. Equally important was the emergence of the idea and role of the 'author' since earlier manuscript texts were not normally authored by living individuals.

A natural further development was the role of professional author, as early as the late 16th century, typically supported by wealthy patrons. Each of these developments reflects the emergence of a market and the transformation of the book into a commodity. In fact many of the basic features of modern media are already embodied in book publishing by the end of the 16th century, including the earliest form of reading public. The book itself has shown no sign of losing its position as an important mass medium, despite the many contemporary alternative technologies. It has also retained some elements of its original 'aura' as an important cultural artefact.

PRINT MEDIA: THE NEWSPAPER

It was almost two hundred years after the invention of printing before what we now recognize as a prototypical newspaper could be distinguished from the handbills, pamphlets and newsletters of the late 16th and early 17th centuries. Its chief precursor seems, in fact, to have been the letter rather than the book – newsletters circulating through the rudimentary postal service, concerned especially with transmitting news of events relevant to international trade and commerce. It was thus an extension into the public sphere of an activity that had long taken place for governmental, diplomatic or commercial purposes. The early newspaper was marked by its regular appearance, commercial basis (openly for sale), public character and its multiple purpose. Thus, it was used for information, record, advertising, diversion and gossip.

The 17th-century commercial newspaper was not identified with any single source but was a compilation made by a printer-publisher. The official variety (as published by Crown or government) showed some of the same characteristics but was also a voice of authority and an instrument of state. The commercial paper was the form which has given most shape to the newspaper institution, and its development can be seen in retrospect as a major turning point in communication history – offering first of all a service to its anonymous readers rather than an instrument to propagandists or potentates.

In a sense the newspaper was more of an innovation than the printed book – the invention of a new literary, social and cultural form – even if it might not have been so perceived at the time. Its distinctiveness, compared with other forms of cultural communication, lies in its orientation to the individual reader, reality-orientation, utility, disposability, secularity and suitability for the needs of a new class: town-based business and professional people. Its novelty consists not in its technology or manner of distribution, but in its functions for a distinct class in a changing and more liberal social-political climate.

The later history of the newspaper can be told either as a series of struggles, advances and reverses in the cause of liberty or as a more continuous history of economic and technological progress. The most important phases in press history that

enter into the modern definition of the newspaper are described in the following paragraphs. While separate national histories differ too much to tell a single story, the elements mentioned, often intermingling and interacting, have all played a part in the development of the press institution.

Box 2.2   The newspaper medium

- Regular and frequent appearance
- Commodity form
- Informational content
- Public sphere functions
- Urban, secular audience
- Relative freedom

From its early days, the newspaper was an actual or potential adversary of established power, especially in its own self-perception. Potent images in press history refer to violence done to printers, editors and journalists. The struggle for freedom to publish, often within a broader movement for freedom, democracy and citizen rights, is emphasized. The part played by underground presses under foreign occupation or dictatorial rule has also been celebrated. Established authority has often confirmed this self-perception of the press by finding it irritating and inconvenient (although also often malleable and, in the extreme case, very vulnerable to power).

There has also been a general progression historically towards more press freedom, despite major setbacks from time to time. This progress has sometimes taken the form of greater sophistication in the means of control applied to the press. Legal restraint replaced violence, then fiscal burdens were imposed (and later reversed). Now institutionalization of the press within a market system serves as a form of control, and the modern newspaper, as a large business enterprise, is vulnerable to more kinds of pressure or intervention than its simpler forerunners were. The newspaper did not really become a true 'mass' medium until the 20th century, in the sense of directly reaching a majority of the population on a regular basis, and there are still quite large inter-country differences in the extent of newspaper reading. It has been customary and it is still useful to distinguish between certain types or genres of newspaper (and of journalism), although there is no single typology to suit all epochs and countries. The following passages describe the main variants.

The political press

One common form of the newspaper is the party-political paper dedicated to the task of activation, information and organization. The party newspaper (published by or for the party) has lost ground to commercial press forms, both as an idea and as a viable business enterprise. The idea of a party press, even so, still has its place as a

component in democratic politics. Where it does survive in Europe (and there are examples elsewhere), it is typically independent from the state (though possibly subsidized), professionally produced, serious and opinion-forming in purpose. Its uniqueness lies in the attachment of its readers by way of party allegiance, its sectionalism and its mobilizing function for party objectives. Examples include the 'vanguard press' of the Russian revolutionary movement, the party political newspapers (especially social-democratic) of several Scandinavian countries and the official party press of Communist regimes.

The prestige press

The late-19th-century bourgeois newspaper was a high point in press history and contributed much to our modern understanding of what a newspaper is or should be. The 'high-bourgeois' phase of press history, from about 1850 to the turn of the century, was the product of several events and circumstances. These included: the triumph of liberalism and the absence or ending of direct censorship or fiscal constraint; the forging of a business-professional establishment; plus many social and technological changes favouring the rise of a national or regional press of high information quality.

The new prestige or 'elite' press was independent from the state and from vested interests and often recognized as a major institution of political and social life (especially as a self-appointed former of opinion and voice of the 'national interest'). It tended to show a highly developed sense of social and ethical responsibility and it fostered the rise of a journalistic profession dedicated to the objective reporting of events. Many current expectations about what a 'quality' newspaper is, still reflect several of these ideas and provide the basis for criticisms of newspapers which deviate from the ideal by being either too partisan or too 'sensational'.

The commercial newspaper

The mass newspaper has been called 'commercial' for two main reasons: it is operated for profit by monopolistic concerns, and it is heavily dependent on product advertising revenue (which made it both possible and advantageous to develop a mass readership). The commercial aims and underpinnings of the mass newspaper have exerted considerable influence on content, in the direction of political populism as well as support for business, consumerism and free enterprise (Curran, 1986; Curran and Seaton, 1997). For present purposes, it is more relevant to see, as a result of commercialization, the emergence of a new kind of newspaper. This is: lighter and more entertaining, emphasizing human interest, more sensational in its attention to crime, violence,

scandals and entertainment, and having a very large readership in which lower-income and lower-education groups are over-represented (Hughes, 1940; Schudson, 1978; Curran et al., 1981).

This may now claim to be the dominant (in the sense of the most read) newspaper form in many countries, especially since it makes inroads into the more traditional 'serious' newspaper market in what has been called a process of **'tabloidization'** (Connell, 1998). Even so, the popular newspaper of today still effectively derives its status as a newspaper from the 'high-bourgeois' form (especially by claiming to give current political and economic information), although it seems in other respects most clearly defined by its contrast with the prestige newspaper.

FILM AS A MASS MEDIUM

Film began at the end of the 19th century as a technological novelty, but what it offered was scarcely new in content or function. It transferred to a new means of presentation and distribution an older tradition of entertainment, offering stories, spectacles, music, drama, humour and technical tricks for popular consumption. It was also almost instantly a true mass medium in the sense that it quite quickly reached a very large proportion of populations, even in rural areas. As a mass medium, film was partly a response to the 'invention' of leisure – time out of work – and an answer to the demand for economical and (usually) respectable ways of enjoying free time for the whole family. Thus it provided for the working class some of the cultural benefits already enjoyed by their social 'betters'. To judge from its phenomenal growth, the latent demand met by film was enormous. Of the main formative elements named above, it would not be the technology or the social climate but the needs met by the film for individuals that mattered most.

The characterization of the film as 'show business' in a new form for an expanded market is not the whole story. There have been three other significant strands in film history. First, the use of film for propaganda is noteworthy, especially when applied to national or societal purposes, based on its great reach, supposed realism, emotional impact and popularity. The practice of combining improving message with enter-tainment had been long established in literature and drama, but new elements in film were the capacity to reach so many people and to be able to manipulate the seeming reality of the photographic message without loss of credibility. The two other strands in film history were the emergence of several schools of film art (Huaco, 1963) and the rise of the social documentary film movement. These were different from the main-stream in having either a minority appeal or a strong element of realism (or both). Both have a link, partly fortuitous, with film-as-propaganda in that both tended to develop at times of *social crisis*.

There continue to be thinly concealed ideological and implicitly propagandist elements in many popular entertainment films, even in politically 'free' societies. This reflects a mixture of forces: deliberate attempts at social control; unthinking adoption of populist or conservative values; various marketing and PR infiltrations into entertainment; and the pursuit of mass appeal. Despite the dominance of the entertainment function in film history, films have often displayed didactic propagandistic tendencies. Film is certainly more vulnerable than other media to outside interference and may be more subject to conformist pressures because so much capital is at risk.

Three turning points in film history have been the 'Americanization' of the film industry and film culture in the years after the First World War (Tunstall, 1977), the coming of television and the separation of film from the cinema. The relative decline of nascent, but flourishing, European film industries at that time (reinforced by the Second World War) probably contributed to a homogenization of film culture and a convergence of ideas about the definition of film as a medium. Television took away a large part of the film-viewing public, especially the general family audience, leaving a much smaller and younger film audience. It also took away or diverted the social documentary stream of film development and gave it a more congenial home in television. However, it did not do the same for the art film or for film aesthetics, although the art film may have benefited from the 'demassification' and greater specialization of the film/cinema medium. For the first two generations of filmgoers, the film experience was inseparable from having an evening out, usually with friends and usually in venues that were far grander than the home. In addition, the darkened cinema offered a mixture of privacy and sociability that gave another dimension to the experience. Just as with television later, 'going to the pictures' was as or even more important than seeing any particular film.

One consequence of the multiplication of ways of delivering films has been the reduced need for 'respectability'. In principle, nearly all early films were made for everyone, with attention only to age differences, and the cinema was a public place inviting public regulation. Released from the constraint of public exhibition, the film became freer to cater to the demand for violent, horrific or pornographic content. Despite the liberation entailed in becoming a less 'mass' medium, the film has not been able to claim full rights to political and artistic self-expression, and many countries retain an apparatus of licensing, censorship and powers of control.

A last concomitant of film's subordination to television in audience appeal has been its integration with other media, especially book publishing, popular music and television itself. It has acquired a certain centrality (Jowett and Linton, 1980), despite the reduction of its immediate audience, as a showcase for other media and as a cultural source, out of which come books, strip cartoons, songs, and television 'stars' and series. Thus, film is as much as ever a mass culture creator. Even the loss of the cinema audience has been more than compensated by a new domestic film audience reached by television, video recordings, cable and satellite channels.

BROADCASTING

Radio and television have, respectively, a seventy-plus- and a forty-plus-year history as mass media, and both grew out of pre-existing technologies – telephone, telegraph, moving and still photography, and sound recording. Despite their obvious differences, now wide in content and use, radio and television can be treated together. Radio seems to have been a technology looking for a use, rather than a response to a demand for a new kind of service or content, and much the same is true of television. According to Williams (1975: 25), 'Unlike all previous communications technologies, radio and television were systems primarily designed for transmission and reception as abstract processes, with little or no definition of preceding content'. Both came to borrow from existing media, and most of the popular content forms of both are derivative from film, music, stories, news and sport.

A distinctive feature of radio and television has been their high degree of regulation, control or licensing by public authority – initially out of technical necessity, later from a mixture of democratic choice, state self-interest, economic convenience and sheer institutional custom. A second and related feature of radio and television media has been their centre–periphery pattern of distribution and the association of national television with political life and the power centres of society, as it became established as both popular and politically important. Despite, or perhaps because of, this closeness to power, radio and television have hardly anywhere acquired, as of right, the same freedom that the press enjoys, to express views and act with political independence.

Television has been continuously evolving, and it would be risky to try to summarize its features in terms of communicative purposes and effects. Initially the main genre innovation of television stemmed from its capacity to transmit many pictures and sound live and thus act as a 'window on the world' in real time. Even studio productions were live broadcasts before the days of efficient video-recording. This capacity of simultaneity has been retained for some kinds of content, including sporting events, some newscasting, and certain kinds of show. What Dayan and Katz (1992) characterize as 'media events' are often likely to have significant live coverage. Most TV content is not live, although it often aims to create an illusion of ongoing

reality. A second important feature of television is the sense of intimacy and personal involvement that it seems able to cultivate between the spectator and presenter or the actors and participants on screen.

The status of television as the most 'massive' of the media in terms of reach, time spent and popularity has barely changed over thirty years and it adds all the time to its global audience. Despite the fact that it has been denied an openly political role and is primarily considered a medium of entertainment, it is believed by many to play a vital role in modern politics. It is considered to be the main source of news and information for most people and as the main channel of communication between politicians and citizens, especially at election times. In this informally allocated role of public informer, television has generally remained credible and trusted. Another role is that of educator – for children at school and adults at home. It is also the largest single channel of advertising in nearly all countries, and this has helped to confirm its mass entertainment functions. So far, many predictions that mass television would fragment into many different channels, along the model of the magazine, have not been realized, despite the proliferation of channels on cable and satellite. It even seems as if for many people the appeal of television lies in the very fact that it is a medium for everyone in an otherwise fragmented and individuated society.

Box 2.4   Television

- Very large output, range and reach
- Audiovisual content
- Complex technology and organization
- Public character and extensive regulation
- National *and* international character
- Very diverse content forms

RECORDED MUSIC

Relatively little attention has been given to music as a mass medium in theory and research, perhaps because the implications for society have never been clear, nor have there been sharp discontinuities in the possibilities offered by successive technologies of recording and reproduction/transmission. Recorded and replayed music has not even enjoyed a convenient label to describe its numerous media manifestations, although the generic term '**phonogram**' has been suggested (Burnett, 1990, 1996) to cover music accessed via record players, tape players, compact disc players, VCRs (video cassette recorders), broadcasting and cable, etc.

The recording and replaying of music began around 1880 and were quite rapidly diffused, on the basis of the wide appeal of popular songs and melodies. Their popularity and diffusion were closely related to the already established place of the

theories

piano (and other instruments) in the home. Much radio content since the early days has consisted of music, even more so since the rise of television. While there may have been a gradual tendency for the 'phonogram' to replace private music-making, there has never been a large gap between mass mediated music and personal and direct audience enjoyment of musical performance (concerts, choirs, bands, dances, etc.). The phonogram makes music of all kinds more accessible at all times in more places to more people, but it is hard to discern a fundamental discontinuity in the general character of popular musical experience, despite changes of genre and fashion.

Even so, there have been big changes in the broad character of the phonogram, since its beginnings. The first change was the addition of radio broadcast music to phonogram records, which greatly increased the range and amount of music available and extended it to many more people than had access to gramophones. The transition of radio from a family to an individual medium in the post-war 'transistor' revolution was a second major change, which opened up a relatively new market of young people for what became a burgeoning record industry. Each development since then – portable tape players, the Sony Walkman, the compact disc and music video – has given the spiral another twist, still based on a predominantly young audience. The result has been a mass media industry which is very interrelated, concentrated in ownership and internationalized (Negus, 1992). Despite this, music media have significant radical and creative strands which have developed despite increased commercialization (Frith, 1981).

While the social significance of music has received only sporadic attention, its relationship to social events has always been recognized and occasionally celebrated or feared. Since the rise of the youth-based industry in the 1960s, mass mediated popular music has been linked to youthful idealism and political concern, to supposed degeneration and hedonism, to drug-taking, violence and antisocial attitudes. Music has also played a part in various nationalist independence movements (e.g. Ireland and Estonia). While the content of music has never been easy to regulate, its distribution has predominantly been in the hands of established institutions, and its perceived deviant tendencies subject to some sanctions. Aside from this, most popular music has continued to express and respond to rather enduring conventional values and personal needs.

Box 2.5 Recorded music (phonogram) media
- Multiple technologies of recording and dissemination
- Low degree of regulation
- High degree of internationalization
- Younger audience
- Subversive potential
- Organizational fragmentation
- Diversity of reception possibilities

The expression 'new media' has been in use since the 1960s and has had to encompass an expanding and diversifying set of applied communication technologies. However, the foundations of the current 'communications revolution' rest on two main innovations. One is satellite communication and the other is the harnessing of the computer. The key to the immense power of the computer as a communication machine lies in the process of **digitalization** that allows information of all kinds in all formats to be carried with the same efficiency and also intermingled. In principle there is no longer any need for the various different media that have been described, since all could be subsumed in the same computerized communication centre. In practice there is no sign of this happening. Alongside computer-based technologies there are other innovations that have in some degree changed some aspects of mass communication. New means of transmission by cable, satellite and radio have immensely increased the capacity to transmit. New means of storage and retrieval, including the personal video-recorder, CD-ROM, compact disc, etc. have also expanded the range of possibilities, and even the remote control device has played a part. While not directly supporting mass communication, the many new possibilities for private 'media-making' (camcorders, PCs, printers, cameras, etc.) have expanded the world of media and forged bridges between public and private communication and between the spheres of professional and amateur. Finally, we should note the new kinds of 'quasi-media' including computer games and virtual reality devices that overlap with the media in their culture and in the satisfactions of use.

The implications of all this for mass media are still far from clear, although it is certain that the 'traditional' media have also benefited greatly from new media innovations as well as acquiring new competitors. Secondly we can already conclude that the communications revolution has generally shifted the 'balance of power' from the media to the audience, in-so-far as there are more options to choose from and more active uses of media available. Traditional mass communication was essentially one-directional, while the new forms of communication are essentially *interactive*. Mass communication has in several respects become less massive and less centralized. Beyond that, it is useful to distinguish between the implications of enhanced transmission and the emergence of any new medium as such.

In respect of transmission, the main changes have been the installation of cable systems, the development of satellites for direct broadcasting or feeding into cables and the adaptation of telephone networks to carry many new kinds of traffic. The impact of these changes is still mainly limited to a relatively small proportion of the world population. The main results have been to expand the existing supply without yet fundamentally changing what is transmitted or what is consumed.

In respect of the emergence of any new medium, we can at least recognize the claim of the **Internet** (and World Wide Web) to be considered as a medium in its own right. This is based on its having a distinctive technology, manner of use, range of content

and services, and distinct own image. Its recognition as a medium has been held back by the fact that the Internet is not owned, controlled or organized by any single body, but is simply a network of internationally interconnected computers operating according to agreed protocols. Numerous organizations, but especially service providers and telecommunication bodies, contribute to its operation. The Internet as such does not exist anywhere as a legal entity and is not subject to any single set of national laws or regulations. However, those who use the Internet can be accountable to the laws and regulations of the country in which they reside as well as to international law. Despite the plausibility of counting the Internet as a mass medium, its diffusion is limited and it has not yet acquired a clear definition of its function. It began primarily as a non-commercial means of intercommunication and data exchange between professionals, but its more recent rapid advance has been fuelled by its potential as a purveyor of goods and many profitable services and as an alternative to other means of interpersonal communication. It is still very marginal as a means of *mass communication* as defined in this book (but see Chapter 6).

Box 2.6   The Internet as a medium

- Computer-based technologies
- Hybrid, non-dedicated, flexible character
- Interactive potential
- Private and public functions
- Low degree of regulation
- Interconnectedness

DIFFERENCES BETWEEN MEDIA

It is much less easy to distinguish these media from each other than it used to be. This is partly because some media forms are now distributed across different types of transmission channel, reducing the original uniqueness of form and experience in use. The clearest example is film, since the same media product is now available on many kinds of television, by way of the telephone network, on cassette and even the Internet. People can also have their own libraries of film to draw upon. Secondly, the increasing **convergence** of technology, based on digitalization, can only reinforce this tendency. Newspapers are already widely accessible as text on the Internet, and the telephone system is edging towards delivery of media content. The clear lines of regulatory regime between the media are already blurred, both recognizing and encouraging greater similarity between different media. Thirdly, *globalizing* tendencies are reducing the distinctiveness of any particular national variant of media content and institution. Fourthly, the continuing trends towards integration of national and global media

corporations has led to the housing of different media under the same roof, encouraging convergence by another route.

Nevertheless, on certain dimensions, clear differences do remain. In this connection, two enduring questions about the media are addressed here. Firstly, how *free* is a medium in relation to the wider society? Secondly, what is a medium good for and what are its perceived *uses*, from the point of view of an individual audience member?

Freedom versus control

Relations between media and society usually have both a political dimension and a normative or social-cultural aspect. Central to the political dimension is the question of freedom and control. As noted above, near-total freedom was claimed and eventually gained for the *book*, for a mixture of reasons, in which the requirements of politics, religion, science and art all played some part. This situation remains unchallenged in free societies, although the book has lost some of its once subversive potential as a result of its relative marginalization (book reading is a minority or minor form of media use). The influence of books remains considerable, but has to a large extent to be mediated through other more popular media or other institutions (education, politics, etc.).

The *newspaper* press bases its historical claim to freedom of operation much more directly on its political functions of expressing opinion and circulating political and economic information. But the newspaper is also a significant business enterprise for which freedom to produce and supply its primary product (information) is a necessary condition of successful operation. The rather limited political freedom enjoyed by broadcast *television* and *radio* derives from a claim to perform some of the same functions as the newspaper press and to serve a general 'public interest'. Formal political control has tended to diminish, as the television industry expands and becomes more like a normal business, in which market disciplines replace open political control.

The various *new media*, some using cable or telecommunications networks for distribution, still await clear definitions of their appropriate degree of political freedom. Freedom from control may be claimed on the grounds of privacy or the fact that these are not media of indiscriminate mass distribution but directed to specific users. They are so-called 'common-carriers' that generally lack control over their content. They also increasingly share the same communicative tasks as media with established editorial autonomy. The question remains in dispute for a number of reasons, among them the need for regulation for technical reasons or to prevent abuse of monopoly power.

These differences relating to *political* control (freedom means few regulations and little supervisory apparatus) follow a general pattern. First, where the communication

function involved closely affects the exercise of power in society (as with newspapers and television news and information), there is a stronger motive for scrutiny if not direct control. In general, activities in the sphere of fiction, fantasy or entertainment are more likely to escape attention than are activities that touch directly on social reality.

Virtually all media of public communication have a radical potential, in the sense of being potentially subversive of reigning systems of social control. They can provide access for new voices and perspectives on the existing order; new forms of organization and protest are made available for the subordinate or disenchanted. Even so, the institutional development of successful media has usually resulted in the elimination of the early radical potential, partly as a side-effect of commercialization, partly because authorities fear disturbance of society (Winston, 1986). According to one theory of media development, the driving logic of communication has been towards more effective social management and control, rather than towards change and emancipation (Beniger, 1986).

The *normative* dimension of control operates according to the same general principles, although sometimes with different consequences for particular media. For instance, film, which has generally escaped direct political control, has often been subject to control of its content, on grounds of its potential moral impact on the young and impressionable (especially in matters of violence, crime or sex). The widespread restrictions applied to television in matters of culture and morals stem from the same tacit assumptions. These are that media that are very popular and have a potentially strong emotional impact on many people need to be supervised in 'the public interest'.

Supervision includes positive support for 'desirable' cultural communication objectives as well as for restrictions on the undesirable. The more communication activities can be defined as either educational or 'serious' in purpose or, alternatively, as artistic and creative, the more freedom from normative restrictions can usually be claimed. There are complex reasons for this, but it is also a fact that 'art' and content of higher moral seriousness do not usually reach large numbers and are seen as marginal to power relations.

The degree of control of media by state or society may depend on the feasibility of applying it. The most regulated media have typically been those whose distribution is most easily supervised, such as centralized national radio or television broadcasting or local cinema distribution. In the last resort, books and print media generally are much less easy to monitor or to suppress. The same applies to local radio, while new possibilities for desktop publishing and photocopying and all manner of ways of reproducing sound and images have made direct censorship a very blunt and ineffective instrument. The impossibility of policing national frontiers to keep out unwanted foreign communication is another consequence of new technology that promotes more freedom. While new technology in general seems to increase the promise of freedom of communication, the continued strength of institutional controls, including those of the market, over actual flow and reception should not be underestimated.

Issues of use and reception

The increasing difficulty of typifying or distinguishing media channels in terms of content and function has undermined once-stable social definitions of media. The newspaper, for instance, may now be as much an entertainment medium, or a consumers' guide, as it is a source of information about political and social events. Cable-delivered television systems are no longer confined to offering balanced programming for all. Even so, a few dominant images and definitions of what media 'are best for' do appear to survive, the outcome of tradition, social forces and the 'bias' of certain technologies.

For instance, television, despite the many changes and extensions relating to production, transmission and reception, remains primarily a medium of family entertainment (Morley, 1986), even if the family is less likely to be viewing together (see Chapter 16). It is still a focus of public interest and a shared experience in most societies. It has both a domestic and a collective character that seems to endure. The traditional conditions of family living (shared space, time and conditions) may account for this, despite the technological trend to individuation of use and specialization of content. The expected diffusion of digital definition television might tend to reinforce the latter trend, but social and cultural factors are likely to matter more than the technology.

Box 2.8 Differentiating media use

- Inside or outside the home?
- Individual or shared experience?
- Public or private in use?
- Interactive or not?

The remarks about television in Box 2.8 indicate three relevant dimensions of media perception and reception: whether within or outside the home; whether an individual

or shared experience; and whether more public or more private. Television is typically shared, domestic and public. The newspaper, despite its changing content, conforms to a different type. It is certainly public in character, but is less purely domestic and is individual in use. Radio is now many things but often rather private, not exclusively domestic and more individual in use than television. Both the book and the music phonogram also largely follow this pattern. In general, the distinctions indicated have become less sharp as a result of changes of technology in the direction of proliferation and convergence of reception possibilities.

The newer digital media have added to the uncertainty about which medium is good for what purpose, but they have also added a new dimension according to which media can be distinguished: that of degree of **interactivity**. The more interactive media are those that allow continual motivated choice and response by users. While the video game, CD-ROM computer database and telephone chat-line are clear examples where interaction is the norm, it is also the case that multi-channel cable or satellite television increases interactive potential, as do the recording-and-replay facilities of the domestic VCR.

IMPLICATIONS OF MEDIA CHANGE FOR THE PUBLIC INTEREST

It is commonly said that we live in an 'information society', one in which work is extensively based on information and service industries and where information of all kinds is the key to wealth and power (see Chapter 6). Modern societies are increasingly dependent on complex systems of communication of which mass communication is only one part. Even so, what is happening to mass media is symptomatic of wider processes. They continue as well to be a focus of enormous interest and play a part in political, social and economic life. The significance of mass media extends beyond any real power or authority that they have or might claim.

The changes currently affecting media and society suggest that, in general, there is less need for the kind of close supervision and regulation of media which prompted many of the concerns underlying earlier media research. These concerns often stemmed from the wish to assert collective control over newly developing media, to protect vulnerable individuals and to limit the power of private capital. There has also been an agreed public interest in ensuring fair access for opposing ideological factions or political parties and generally to ensure adequate distribution of scarce and valued social and cultural goods. Greater prosperity, openness, value-relativity, individual consumerism and economic liberalism all seem to weigh in this direction, leaving aside any changes occurring in the media themselves.

It can also be argued that the increased complexity of society, the greater abundance of information flows and their centrality for the commerce, progress and social-cultural life of modern society have established new requirements of adequate

performance on the part of the media. The decline of some older structures of political and social control and sources of guidance for individuals (political parties, churches, family, community) may well be thought to increase the need for effective institutions in the public sphere to compensate for these losses. The 'public sphere' may appear to have contracted, as a result of 'privatization', individualism and secularization, but it has also been extended by globalizing trends that touch almost every aspect of daily experience.

Conditions of individualism, relativism and volatility are precisely those which increase the dependence and vulnerability of most people and thus also their need for information. This may imply a greater rather than a diminishing public interest in mass media. On the other hand, the nature of any 'public interest' may well now be more variable and uncertain, and it will need continuing redefinition. What we cannot yet discern, among the many patterns of change, is any sign of the imminent demise of the mass media in their central character as sketched in this chapter.

FURTHER READING

McCluhan, M. (1962) *The Gutenberg Galaxy.* Toronto: University of Toronto Press.
Schement, J. and Curtis, T. (1995) *Tendencies and Tensions of the Information Age.* New Brunswick, NJ: Transaction Publishers.
Williams, R. (1975) *Television: Technology and Cultural Form.* London: Fontana.
Winston, B. (1998) *Media, Technology and Society.* London: Routledge.

concepts and models

The century just ended can plausibly be described as the 'first age of mass media'. It was also marked by alternating wonder and alarm at the influence of the mass media. Despite the enormous changes in media institutions and technology and in society itself, and also the rise of a 'science of communication', the terms of public debate about the potential social significance of 'the media' seem to have changed remarkably little. A description of the issues which emerged during the first two or three decades of the century is of more than just historical interest, and early thinking provides a point of reference for understanding the present. Three sets of ideas were of particular importance from the outset. One concerned the question of the *power* of the new means of communication, a second the question of social *integration* or disintegration, and the third the question of public *enlightenment* or its opposite.

The power of mass media

A belief in the power of mass media was initially based on observation of their great reach and apparent impact, especially in relation to the new popular newspaper press. According to DeFleur and Ball-Rokeach (1989), newspaper circulation in the USA peaked in 1910, although it was a good deal later in Europe and other parts of the world. The popular press was mainly funded by commercial advertising, its content was characterized by sensational news stories and its control often concentrated in the hands of powerful press 'barons'. The First World War saw the mobilization of press and film in most of Europe and the United States for the nationalist war aims of contending states. The results seemed to leave little doubt of the potency of media influence on the 'masses', when effectively managed and directed.

This impression was yet further reinforced by what happened in the Soviet Union and, later, in Nazi Germany, where the media were pressed into the service of propaganda on behalf of ruling party elites. The use of news and entertainment media by the allies in the Second World War removed any doubts about their propagandist value. Before the century was half way on its course, there was already a strongly held and soundly based view that mass publicity was effective in shaping opinion and influencing behaviour. It could also have effects on international relations and alliances. More recent events, including the ending of the Cold War and the handling of the Gulf War and Kosovo Conflict have confirmed the media as an essential and dynamic component in any international power struggle, where public opinion is also a factor. The conditions for effective media power have generally included a national media industry capable of reaching most of the population, a degree of consensus in the message disseminated (whatever its origin) and some measure of credibility and trust on the part of audiences (also with varying foundations).

Social theorists in the late 19th and early 20th centuries were very conscious of the 'great transformation' which was taking place, as slower, traditional and communal ways gave way to fast-paced, secular, urban living and to a great expansion in the scale of social activities. Many of the themes of European and North American sociology (for example, in the work of Toennies, Spencer, Weber, Durkheim and Park) reflect this collective self-consciousness of the problems of change from small- to large-scale and from rural to urban societies. The social theory of the time posited a need for new forms of integration in the face of the problems caused by industrialization and urbanization. Crime, prostitution, dereliction and dependency were associated with the increasing anonymity, isolation and uncertainty of modern life.

While the fundamental changes were social and economic, it was possible to point to newspapers, film and other forms of popular culture (music, books, magazines, comics) as potential contributors both to individual crime and declining morality and also to rootlessness, impersonality and lack of attachment or community. In the United States, where attention to communication was first most clearly articulated, large-scale immigration from Europe in the first two decades of the century highlighted questions of social cohesion and integration. This is exemplified in the sociological work of the Chicago School and the writings of Robert Park, G.H. Mead, Thomas Dewey and others (Rogers, 1993). Hanno Hardt (1979, 1991) has reconstructed the main lines of early theory concerning communication and social integration, both in Europe and in North America.

The links between popular mass media and social integration were easy to perceive in terms both negative (more crime and immorality) and individualistic (loneliness, loss of collective beliefs), but it was also possible to envisage a positive contribution from modern communications to cohesion and community. Mass media were a potential force for a new kind of cohesion, able to connect scattered individuals in a shared national, city and local experience. They could also be supportive of the new democratic politics and of social reform movements. How the influence of media came to be interpreted was often a matter of an observer's personal attitude to modern society and the degree of optimism or pessimism in their social outlook. The early part of the century, as well as (or perhaps because of) being a high point of nationalism, revolution and social conflict, was also a time of progressive thinking, democratic advance and scientific and technological progress.

Mass communication as mass educator

The spirit of the times (modern and forward-looking) supported a third set of ideas about mass communication – that the media could be a potent force for public

enlightenment, supplementing and continuing the new institutions of universal school-ing, public libraries and popular education. Political and social reformers saw a positive potential in the media, taken as a whole, and the media also saw themselves as, on balance, making a contribution to progress by spreading information and ideas, exposing political corruption and also providing much harmless enjoyment for ordinary people. In many countries, journalists were becoming more professional and adopting codes of ethics and good practice.

The democratic task of the press in informing the newly enfranchised masses was widely recognized. The newly established radio institutions of the 1920s and 1930s, especially in Europe, were often given a public cultural, educational and informative mission, as well as the task of promoting national identity and unity. Each new mass medium has been hailed for its educational and cultural benefits, as well as feared for its disturbing influence. The potential for communication technology to promote enlightenment has been invoked once again in respect of the latest communication technologies – those based on the computer and telecommunications (for example, Neuman, 1991).

The media as problem or scapegoat

Despite these recurring hopeful scenarios, the passing of decades does not seem to have changed the tendency of public opinion both to blame the media (see Drotner, 1992) and expect them to do more to solve society's ills. There are successive instances of **moral panics** relating to the media, whenever an insoluble or inexplicable problem arises. The most constant element has been a negative perception of the media – especially the inclination to link media portrayals of crime, sex and violence with the seeming increase in social disorder. However, new ills have also been found to lay at the door of the media, especially such phenomena as violent political protest and demonstration, international terrorism and even the supposed decline of democracy and rise of political apathy and cynicism. Paradoxically or not, it has usually been the media themselves that have highlighted and amplified many of these alarmist views, perhaps because they seem to confirm the power of the media, but more likely because they are already popularly believed.

THE 'MASS' CONCEPT

This mixture of popular prejudice and social theorizing about the media has formed the background against which research has been commissioned, hypotheses have been

formulated and tested, and more precise theories about mass communication have been developed. And while the interpretations of the direction (positive or negative) of mass media influence show much divergence, the most persistent element in public estimation of the media has been a simple agreement on their strong influence. In turn, this perception owes much to various meanings of the term 'mass'. Although the concept of '**mass society**' was not fully developed until after the Second World War, the essential ideas were circulating before the end of the 19th century. The key term 'mass' in fact unites a number of concepts which are important for understanding how the process of mass communication has often been understood, right up to the present.

Early uses of the term usually carried negative associations. It referred initially to the multitude or the 'common people', usually seen as uneducated, ignorant and potentially irrational, unruly and even violent (as when the mass turned into a mob of rioters) (Bramson, 1961). It could also be used in a positive sense, however, especially in the socialist tradition, where it connotes the strength and solidarity of ordinary working people when organized for collective purposes or when having to bear oppression. The terms 'mass support', 'mass movement' and 'mass action' are examples whereby large numbers of people acting together can be seen in a positive light. As Raymond Williams (1961: 289) commented: 'there are no masses, only ways of seeing people as masses'.

The different valuations of the idea of a mass reflect varying political or personal perspectives, but they also relate to whether or not the mass in question is legitimately constituted and acting in a rational and orderly manner. Even so, the predominant attitude towards mass phenomena has been negative, even when they pose no threat to the established social order. The dominant social and cultural values of 'the West' have been individualist and elitist, biased against collective action. Aside from its political references, the word 'mass', when applied to a set of people, also has unflattering implications. It suggests an amorphous collection of individuals without much individuality. One standard dictionary definition defines the word as an 'aggregate in which individuality is lost' (*Shorter Oxford English Dictionary*). This is close to the meaning which early sociologists sometimes gave to the media audience. It was the large and seemingly undifferentiated audiences for the popular media that provided the clearest examples of the concept.

Box 3.1 The concept of mass

- Large aggregate
- Undifferentiated
- Mainly negative image
- Lacking order or organization
- Reflective of mass society

The term 'mass communication' came into use in the late 1930s, but its essential features were already well known and have not really changed since, even if the media themselves have in some ways become less massive. While even early mass media were quite diverse in their scale and conditions of operation (for instance popular films could be seen in village tents as well as metropolitan picture palaces), we can discern the typical form of mass communication according to certain general characteristics. These derive from the technologies of multiple reproduction and distribution and certain forms of organization, even if the particular reality of mass communication as experienced by audiences often diverges significantly from the typical form. The most obvious feature of the mass media is that they are designed to reach the *many*. Potential audiences are viewed as large aggregates of more or less anonymous consumers, and the relationship between sender and receiver is bound to be influenced by this fact. The 'sender' is often the organization itself or a professional communicator (journalist, presenter, producer, entertainer, etc.) whom it employs. If not this, it is another voice of society given or sold access to media channels (advertiser, politician, preacher, advocate of a cause, etc.). The relationship is inevitably one-sided and impersonal, and there is a social as well as a physical distance between sender and receiver. The former usually has more authority, prestige or expertise than the latter. The relationship is not only asymmetrical, it is often calculative or manipulative in intention. It is essentially non-moral, based on a service promised or asked for in some unwritten contract with no mutual obligation.

The symbolic content or message of mass communication is typically 'manufactured' in standardized ways (mass production) and is re-used and repeated in identical forms. We do not generally think of mass media content as unique or creative, although this may reflect a cultural bias against what is popular. In any case, the media message is mainly a product of work with an exchange value in the media market and a use value for its receiver, the media consumer. It is essentially a commodity and differs in this respect from the content of other types of human communication relationship.

The reception of mass communication is also distinctive. Audiences are generally conceived of (by media themselves, but also by popular prejudice) as large aggregates of dispersed and passive spectators, without opportunities to respond or to participate in a genuine way. Although conscious of being part of a much larger set, the media spectator has little contact with or knowledge of fellow spectators and can only interact directly with a small number. The 'mass audience' is in any case only constituted momentarily by the more or less simultaneous contact with a distant source and has no other existence except in the book-keeping of the media industries (Ang, 1991).

THE MASS AUDIENCE

Herbert Blumer (1939) was the first to define the **mass** formally as a new type of social formation in modern society, by contrasting it with other formations, especially the *group, crowd* and *public*. In a small group, all its members know each other, are aware of their common membership, share the same values, have a certain structure of relationships which is stable over time and interact to achieve some purpose. The crowd is larger but still restricted within observable boundaries in a particular space. It is, however, temporary and rarely re-forms with the same composition. It may possess a high degree of identity and share the same 'mood', but there is usually no structure or order to its moral and social composition. It can act, but its actions are often seen to have an affective and emotional, often irrational, character.

The third collectivity named by Blumer, the **public**, is likely to be relatively large, widely dispersed and enduring. It tends to form around an issue or cause in public life, and its primary purpose is to advance an interest or opinion and to achieve political change. It is an essential element in democratic politics, based on the ideal of rational discourse within an open political system and often comprising the better-informed section of the population. The rise of the public is characteristic of modern liberal democracies and related to the rise of the 'bourgeois' or party newspaper described earlier.

The term 'mass' captured several features of the new audiences for cinema and radio (and to some extent the popular press) that were not covered by any of these three concepts. The new audience was typically much larger than any group, crowd or public. It was very widely dispersed, and its members were usually unknown to each other or to whoever brought the audience into existence. It lacked self-awareness and self-identity and was incapable of acting together in an organized way to secure objectives. It was marked by a shifting composition within changing boundaries. It did not act for itself but was, rather, 'acted upon' (thus an object of manipulation). It was heterogeneous, in consisting of large numbers, from all social strata and demographic groups, but also homogeneous in its choice of some particular object of interest and according to the perception of those who would like to manipulate it.

> **Box 3.3 The mass audience**
>
> - Large numbers
> - Widely dispersed
> - Non-interactive and anonymous
> - Heterogeneous
> - Not organized or self-acting

The audience for mass media is not the only social formation that can be characterized in this way, since the word is sometimes applied to consumers in the expression 'mass market' or to large bodies of voters (the 'mass electorate'). It is significant, however, that such entities also often correspond with media audiences and that mass media are used to direct or control both consumer and political behaviour.

Within the conceptual framework sketched, media use was represented as a form of 'mass behaviour', which in turn encouraged the application of methods of 'mass research' – especially large-scale surveys and other methods for recording the reach and response of audiences to what was offered. A commercial and organizational logic for 'audience research' was furnished with theoretical underpinnings. It seemed to make sense, as well as being practical, to discuss media audiences in purely *quantitative* terms. In fact, the methods of research tended only to reinforce a biased conceptual perspective (treating the audience as a mass market). Research into ratings and the reach of press and broadcasting reinforced a view of readerships and audiences as a mass market of consumers. There has been a theoretical opposition to this view which has gradually gained ground (see Chapter 15) and led to revised views of the nature of audience experience (Ang, 1991). Even the relevance of viewing the audience as a mass has been undermined by the changes in the media that are described elsewhere (see Chapter 16)

MASS CULTURE AND POPULAR CULTURE

The typical *content* which flowed through the newly created channels to the new social formation (the mass audience) was from the start a very diverse mixture of stories, images, information, ideas, entertainment and spectacles. Even so, the single concept of '**mass culture**' was commonly used to refer to all this (see Rosenberg and White, 1957). Mass culture had a wider reference to the tastes, preferences, manners and styles of the mass (or just the majority) of people. It also had a generally pejorative connotation, mainly because of its associations with the assumed cultural preferences of 'uncultivated', non-discriminating or just lower-class audiences.

The term is now quite dated, partly because class differences are less sharply drawn and no longer separate an educated professional minority from a large, poor and ill-

educated working-class majority. It is also the case that the former hierarchy of 'cultural taste' is no longer widely acknowledged or accepted. Even when in fashion, the idea of mass culture as an exclusively 'lower class' phenomenon was not easy to validate empirically, since it referred to the normal cultural experience of almost everyone to some degree. The expression 'popular culture' is now generally preferred because it simply denotes what many or even most people like. Even so, it has some connotation of what is popular with the young. More recent developments in media and cultural studies (as well as in society) have led to a more positive valuation generally of popular culture. For some media theorists (e.g. Fiske, 1987) the very fact of popularity is a token of value in political as well as cultural terms.

Definitions and contrasts

Attempts to define mass culture often contrasted it (unfavourably) with more traditional forms of (symbolic) culture. Wilensky, for instance, compared it with the notion of 'high culture', which will refer to two characteristics of the product:

> (1) it is created by, or under the supervision of, a cultural elite operating within some aesthetic, literary, or scientific tradition . . . (2) critical standards independent of the consumer of their product are systematically applied to it. . . . 'Mass culture' will refer to cultural *products manufactured solely for the mass market*. Associated characteristics, not intrinsic to the definition, are *standardization* of product and *mass behaviour* in its use. (1964: 176)

Box 3.4 Mass culture

- Non-traditional
- Non-elite
- Mass produced
- Popular
- Commercial
- Homogenized

Mass culture was also defined by comparison with an earlier cultural form – that of folk culture or a traditional culture which more evidently comes from the people and usually pre-dates (or is independent of) mass media and the mass production of culture. Original folk culture (especially expressed as dress, customs, song, stories, dance, etc.) was being widely rediscovered in Europe during the 19th century. Often, this was for reasons connected with the rise of nationalism, otherwise as part of the 'arts and crafts' movement and the romantic reaction against industrialism. The

rediscovery (by the middle classes) was taking place at the very time that it was rapidly disappearing amongst worker and peasant classes because of social change. Folk culture was originally made unselfconsciously, using traditional forms, themes, materials and means of expression and had usually been incorporated into everyday life. Critics of mass culture often regretted the loss of the integrity and simplicity of folk art, and the issue is still alive in parts of the world where mass-produced culture has not completely triumphed. The new urban industrial working class of Western Europe and North America were the first consumers of the new mass culture after being cut off from the roots of folk culture. No doubt the mass media drew on some popular cultural streams and adapted others to the conditions of urban life to fill the cultural void created by industrialization, but intellectual critics could usually see only a cultural loss.

Dynamics of cultural forms

The rise of mass culture was open to more than one interpretation. Bauman (1972), for instance, took issue with the idea that mass communication media *caused* mass culture, arguing that they were more a tool to shape something that was happening in any case as a result of the increasing cultural homogeneity of national societies. In his view, what is often referred to as mass culture is more properly just a more universal or standardized culture. Several features of mass communication have contributed to the process of standardization, especially dependence on the market, the supremacy of large-scale organization and the application of new technology to cultural production. This more objective approach helps to defuse some of the conflict that has characterized the debate about mass culture. In some measure, the 'problem of mass culture' reflected the need to come to terms with new technological possibilities for symbolic reproduction (Benjamin, 1977) which challenged established notions of art. The issue of mass culture was fought out in social and political terms, without being resolved in aesthetic terms.

Despite the possibility of finding a seemingly value-free conception of mass culture in terms of social change, the issue remains conceptually and ideologically troublesome. As Bourdieu (1986) and others have clearly demonstrated, different conceptions of cultural merit are strongly connected with social class differences. Possession of economic capital has usually gone hand in hand with possession of 'cultural capital', which in class societies can also be 'encashed' for material advantages. Class-based value systems once strongly maintained the superiority of 'high' and traditional culture against much of the typical popular culture of the mass media. The support for such value systems (though maybe not for the class system) has weakened, although the issue of differential cultural quality remains alive as an aspect of a continuing cultural and media policy debate.

The ideas about media and society and the various sub-concepts of 'mass' that have been described, helped to shape a model of research into mass communication which has been described as 'dominant' in more than one sense. Aside from being widely taught as the correct approach it has been portrayed by its critics as somewhat hegemonic and oppressive (for example, Gitlin, 1978; Real, 1989). The description of a 'dominant paradigm' offered here is rather eclectic and mixes different elements. It is inevitably an oversimplification of a complex and not very coherent set of ideas. A somewhat similar version is to be found in other textbooks and overviews (for example, Rogers, 1986; DeFleur and Ball-Rokeach, 1989). It is counterbalanced by the description of an 'alternative paradigm' that can be compiled from various critical views of society and of the media.

One view of the good society

The 'dominant paradigm' (or dominant meaning structure) combined a view of powerful mass media in a mass society with the typical research practices of the emerging social sciences, especially social surveys, social-psychological experiments and statistical analysis. The paradigm is both an outcome of and a guide to communication research. The underlying, though rarely explicated, view of society in the dominant paradigm is essentially normative. It presumes a certain kind of normally functioning 'good society' which would be democratic (elections, universal suffrage, representation), liberal (secular, free-market conditions, individualistic, freedom of speech), pluralistic (institutionalized competition between parties and interests) and orderly (peaceful, socially integrated, fair, legitimate).

The potential or actual good or harm to be expected from mass media has largely been judged according to this model, which happens to coincide with one version of Western society. The contradictions within this view of society and its distance from social reality were largely ignored. It is by reference to this model that research has been undertaken into the socializing, informing, mobilizing and opinion-shaping activities of the media. The same is true in relation to crime, ethnic conflict and other problematic features of mass media content and effects. Most early research oriented to the media in developing or Third World countries was guided by the assumption that these societies would gradually converge on the same (more advanced and progressive) Western model.

Early international communication research was also influenced by the notion that the model of a liberal, pluralist and just society was threatened by an alternative, totalitarian form (communism), where the mass media were distorted into tools for suppressing democracy. The awareness of this alternative helped to identify and even

reinforce the norm described. This point of view could be largely shared between the media and theorists/researchers. The media often saw themselves as playing a key role in supporting and expressing the values of the 'Western way of life'.

Origins in information science and **functionalism**

The theoretical elements of a dominant paradigm were not invented for the case of the mass media but largely taken over from sociology, social psychology and an applied version of information science. This took place especially in the decade after the Second World War, when there was a largely unchallenged North American hegemony over both the social sciences and the mass media (Tunstall, 1977). The model of a good society described above leans to the mid-century US ideal. Sociology, as it matured theoretically, offered a functionalist framework of analysis for the media as for other institutions. Lasswell (1948) was the first to formulate a clear statement of the 'functions' of communication in society – meaning essential tasks performed for the maintenance of society (see Chapter 4). The general tendency of functional analysis is to assume that communication works towards the integration, continuity and normality of society, although also recognizing that mass communication can have dysfunctional (disruptive or harmful) consequences. There are many ramifications and variants of functional analysis, and, despite a much reduced intellectual appeal, the language of functions has proved difficult to eliminate from discussions of media and society.

The other important theoretical element influential in the dominant paradigm guiding media research stemmed from information theory, as developed by Shannon and Weaver (1949), which was concerned with the technical efficiency of communication channels for carrying information. They developed a model for analysing information transmission that visualized communication as a sequential process. This process begins with a *source* that selects a *message*, which is then *transmitted*, in the form of a *signal*, over a *communication channel*, to a *receiver*, who transforms the signal back into a message for a *destination*. The model was designed to account for differences between messages as sent and messages as received, these differences being considered to result from *noise or interference* affecting the channels. This 'transmission' model was not directly concerned with *mass* communication, but it was popularized as a versatile way of conceiving many human communication processes, despite its original non-human applications.

These theoretical origins were very much in line with methodological developments of the mid-century period and the nature of research issues. A combination of advances in 'mental measurement' (especially applied to individual attitudes and other attributes) and in statistical analysis appeared to offer new and powerful tools for achieving generalized and reliable knowledge of previously hidden processes and states. The methods were especially valued because they seemed able to answer

theories

questions about the influence of mass media and about their effectiveness in persuasion and attitude change.

Bias of the paradigm towards studying media effects

According to Rogers (1986: 867) this model 'was the single most important turning point in the history of communication science' and it 'led communication scientists into a linear, effects-oriented approach to human communication in the decades following 1949'. Rogers also notes that the result was to head communication scientists into 'the intellectual cul-de-sac of focusing mainly upon the *effects* of communication, especially mass communication' (1986: 88). This view of communication is compatible with, though more flexible than, the stimulus–response model, which in one variant or another was equally influential in educational research. Rogers and others have long recognized the blind spot in this model, and more recent thinking about communication research has often taken the form of a debate with the model. Even so, the linear causal approach was what many wanted, and still do want, from communication research.

Mass communication is often seen (by those with power to transmit) primarily as an efficient device for getting a message to many people whether as advertising, political propaganda or public information. The fact that communication does not usually look that way from the point of view of receivers has taken a long time to register. The theoretical materials for a very different model of (mass) communication were actually in place relatively early – based on the thinking of several earlier (North American) social scientists, especially G.H. Mead, C.H. Cooley and Robert Park. Such a 'model' would have represented human communication as essentially human, social and interactive, concerned with sharing of meaning, not impact (see Hardt, 1991). That this alternative was not taken up reflects the greater appeal of the dominant paradigm because of its assumed relevance and practicality and also the power of its methods.

Against this background, the path taken by 'mainstream' mass media research is not difficult to describe and understand. Research has mostly been concerned with the measurement of the effects of mass media, whether intended (as with political and public information campaigns) or unintended (as with crime and violence). Alternatively, it has been concerned with studying aspects of the process that could aid in the interpretation of effects – for instance, the content of media messages, or the motivations, attitudes and different characteristics of the audience. Even the study of media organizations has been justified by the light it sheds on what messages are likely to be selected for transmission. Traces of functional thinking and of the linear causal model are ubiquitous. The methodological preferences of most communication researchers within the mainstream have also been for precise measurement and quantification, usually based on observations of individual behaviour.

Mainstream research has built around this basic approach several extra elements that have helped to shore up its credibility and to resolve conflicts with the ideal model of liberal-pluralist society described above. On the face of it, the one-way model of effect appears mechanistic and deterministic, in line with the conception of mass society in which a small elite with power and money could use the powerful instruments of media channels to achieve persuasive and informational ends. The images of a hypodermic syringe or 'magic bullet' have been used to capture part of this idea (DeFleur and Ball-Rokeach, 1989). In fact, the rejection by researchers of this notion of powerful direct effect is almost as old as the idea itself (Chaffee and Hochheimer, 1982). It has been clear for fifty years that mass media simply do not have the direct effects suggested. It has always been rather difficult to prove any effects (cf. Klapper, 1960).

The simple transmission model does not work for a number of reasons which empirical research has made clear. The main reasons are as follows: signals do not reach receivers, or not the ones intended; messages are not understood as they are sent; there is much more 'noise' in the channels than can be overcome. Moreover, little communication is actually unmediated, but is typically filtered through other channels or open to checking with personal contacts. All this undermines the notion of powerful media and casts doubt on the transmission model. Despite this, the model still helps in posing and testing (null) hypotheses, and the findings that have accumulated around its 'failure' have been paradoxically supportive. By underlining the mediated and interactive nature of public communication, they have helped to sustain the positive image of the liberal-pluralist society as still in good shape and not subject to subversion by a few powerful or wealthy manipulators (Gitlin, 1978). Out of 'failed' (= no measured effect) research comes a positive message of health for the status quo and also a vindication of the empirical research tradition.

Box 3.5   The dominant paradigm of communication research

- A liberal-pluralist ideal of society
- A functionalist perspective
- A linear transmission model of effects
- Powerful media modified by group relations
- Quantitative research and variable analysis

AN ALTERNATIVE PARADIGM

What follows is also a composite picture, woven from different voices at different times and expressing different objections to the dominant paradigm, but nevertheless reasonably coherent. Of course, 'the' critical perspective has itself developed and changed over time, but its origins are as old as its chief object of attack. In varying

degrees the alternative (or 'critical') perspectives involve objections to a set of disparate but interrelated ideas and practices. The unacknowledged liberal pluralist ideology of society has been exposed (for example, Hall, 1989). The linearity of the model of effect and its generally mechanistic character has found numerous critics. So has the influence of market and military demands on research and the media (Mills, 1956). Gitlin (1978) exposed the too rosy interpretations of research findings about media effects and audience motivations. The potentially dehumanizing effects of technology (for example, Carey, 1988) and the excessively quantitative and individual-behaviourist methodologies have been singled out (for example, Smythe, 1972; Real, 1989; Jensen and Jankowski, 1991). Finally the model has been blamed for neglect by communication research of vast areas of culture and human experience (Carey, 1988).

A different view of society and media

Most broadly, the 'alternative paradigm' rests on a different view of society, one which does not accept the prevailing liberal-capitalist order as just or inevitable or the best one can hope for in the fallen state of humankind. Nor does it accept the rational-calculative, utilitarian model of social life as at all adequate or desirable. There is an alternative, idealist and sometimes Utopian ideology, but nowhere a worked-out model of an ideal social system. Nevertheless, there is a sufficient common basis for rejecting the hidden ideology of pluralism and of conservative functionalism.

There has been no shortage of vocal critics of the media themselves, from the early years of the century, especially in relation to their commercialism, low standards of truth and decency, control by unscrupulous monopolists and much more. More relevant here are the theoretical grounds for approaching the mass media in a way different from that proposed in the dominant paradigm. The original ideological inspiration for a well-grounded alternative has been socialism or Marxism in one variant or another. The first significant impulse was given by the *émigrés* from the **Frankfurt School** who went to the USA in the 1930s and helped to promote an alternative view of the dominant commercial mass culture (Jay, 1973; Hardt, 1991). Their contribution was to provide a strong intellectual base for seeing the process of mass communication as manipulative and ultimately oppressive (see Chapter 5).

C. Wright Mills followed them (in the 1950s) by articulating a clear alternative view of the media, drawing on a native North American radical tradition, eloquently exposing the liberal fallacy of pluralist control. He described the media as organized in the post-war USA (now often portrayed as a golden age) as a powerful instrument of control on behalf of an interlocked 'power elite' (Mills, 1956) and as a means of inducing total conformity to the state and the economic order. He had himself worked on the research (Katz and Lazarsfeld, 1955) which purported to establish the

importance of personal relations in insulating individuals from media power, but he came to reject the results as potentially manipulative knowledge (Mills, 1959).

Diverse sources of challenge

Despite the influence of the social-critical perspective of Mills, and later, of Marcuse (1964), a second wave of influence from Europe (where the dominant paradigm also held sway until well into the 1960s) has perhaps done most to promote the alternative paradigm internationally. This has occurred since the 1970s and has different driving forces and objectives. The main components of, and supports for, an alternative paradigm are as follows. First is a much more sophisticated notion of ideology in media content which has allowed researchers to 'decode' the ideological messages of mass-mediated entertainment and news (which tend towards legitimating established power structures and defusing opposition).

Secondly, a related development has denied the notion of fixed meanings embedded in media content and leading to predictable and measurable impact. Instead, we have to view meaning as constructed and messages as decoded according to the social situation and interests of those in the receiving audience. In particular, it is argued that the **ideology** of the 'power elite' disseminated by the media can be read in an 'oppositional' way and exposed for the propaganda which it is. This is an alternative version of the '**active audience**' discovered in the course of empirical media-effect research.

The economic and political character of mass media organizations and structures nationally and internationally has been re-examined. These institutions are no longer taken at face value but can be assessed in terms of their operational strategies, which are far from neutral or non-ideological. As the critical paradigm has developed, it has moved from an exclusive concern with working-class subordination to a wider view of other kinds of domination, especially in relation to youth, alternative subcultures, gender and ethnicity. These changes have been matched by a turn to more 'qualitative' research, whether into culture, discourse or the ethnography of mass media use. This has provided alternative routes to knowledge and forged a link back to the neglected pathways of sociological theory of symbolic interactionism and phenomenology (see Jensen and Jankowski, 1991). This is part of a more general development of cultural studies, within which mass communication can be viewed in a new light. According to Dahlgren (1995) the cultural studies tradition 'confronts the scientistic self-delusion' of the dominant paradigm, but there is an inevitable tension between textual and socio-institutional analysis.

The communication relations between the First World and the Third World, especially in the light of changing technology, has encouraged new ways of thinking about mass communication. For instance, the relationship is no longer seen as a matter of the enlightened transfer of development and democracy to 'backward' lands. It is at

least as plausibly seen as economic and cultural domination. Lastly, although it does not necessarily lead in a *critical* direction, the new means of communication have forced a re-evaluation of earlier thinking about media effects, if only because the model of one-directional mass communication can no longer be sustained.

The status of the alternative paradigm

The alternative perspective that emerges from these developments of thought and enquiry, is not just the mirror image of the dominant paradigm or a statement of opposition to the mechanistic and applied view of communication. It is based on a more complete view of communication as sharing and ritual. It is complementary as well as being an alternative. It offers its own viable avenues of enquiry, but following a different agenda. The paradigm has been especially valuable in extending the range of methods and approaches to popular culture in all its aspects. The interaction and engagement between media experiences and social-cultural experiences are central to all this. The main points are summarized in Box 3.6.

While this discussion has presented two main versions, it is arguable that the proposed 'alternative' to the 'dominant' approach brings together two distinct elements – one 'critical', the other 'interpretative' or 'qualitative'. There are some reasons in the history of theory and research why these elements are associated. In particular, early critics of society and research (such as C. Wright Mills) opposed both the methods and the thinking of empirical researchers, and the pioneers of the cultural critical school, such as Stuart Hall strongly endorsed interpretative methods. However, there are critical researchers who stand by social scientific methods, and the critical component of cultural studies of media as these have developed is at least variable (Ferguson and Golding, 1997). For some purposes it is useful to follow the suggestion of Potter et al. (1993) and apply a threefold division of research paradigms, that are identified as 'social science', 'interpretative' and 'critical analysis'. Fink and Gantz (1996) found this scheme to work well in a content analysis of published communication research.

Box 3.6 The alternative paradigm

- A critical view of society and rejection of value neutrality
- Rejection of the transmission model of communication
- A non-deterministic view of media technology and messages
- Adoption of an interpretative perspective
- Qualitative methodology
- A preference for cultural or political-economic theories
- Wide concern with inequality and sources of opposition in society

---

The success of the alternative approach to media research, backed by strong reinforcements from cultural studies and humanistic research (drawn by the magnetism of media power and centrality in cultural life), has not caused its old opponent to expire. It too has its sources of renewed vigour (for instance, the impulse to apply media to political and other forms of campaigning and the growing economic and industrial significance of media technology). There is also evidence of some overlapping and *rapprochement* (Curran, 1990; Schrøder, 1999). In particular, ideological (as opposed to intellectual) differences are no longer so salient.

The differences of approach between dominant and alternative paradigms are deep-rooted, and their existence underlines the difficulty of having any unified 'science of communication'. The differences stem also from the very nature of (mass) communication, which has to deal in ideology, values and ideas and cannot escape from being interpreted within ideological frameworks. While the reader of this book is not obliged to make a choice between the two paradigms, knowing about them will help to make sense of the diversity of theories and of disagreements about the supposed 'facts' concerning mass media.

FOUR MODELS OF COMMUNICATION

The original definition of mass communication as a process (see pages 40–1) depended on objective features of mass production, reproduction and distribution which were shared by several different media. It was very much a technologically and organizationally based definition, subordinating human considerations. Its validity has long been called into question, especially as a result of the conflicting views just discussed and, more recently, by the fact that the original mass production technology and the factory-like forms of organization have themselves been undermined by social and technological change. We have to consider alternative, though not necessarily inconsistent, models (representations) of the process of public communication. At least four such models can be distinguished, aside from the question of how the 'new media' should be conceptualized.

A transmission model

At the core of the dominant paradigm can be found (see page 46) a particular view of communication as a process of *transmission* of a fixed quantity of information – the *message* as determined by the sender or source. Simple definitions of mass communication often follow Lasswell's (1948) observation that the study of mass communication is an attempt to answer the question, 'Who says what to whom, through what channel

and with what effect?'. This represents the linear sequence already mentioned which is largely built into standard definitions of the nature of predominant forms of mass communication. A good deal of early theorizing about mass communication (see, for example, McQuail and Windahl, 1993) was an attempt to extend and to improve on this simplistic version of the process. Perhaps the most complete early version of a model of mass communication, in line with the defining features noted above and consistent with the dominant paradigm, was offered by Westley and MacLean (1957).

Their achievement was to recognize that mass communication involves the interpolation of a new 'communicator role' (such as that of the professional journalist in a formal media organization) between 'society' and 'audience'. The sequence is thus not simply: (1) sender, (2) message, (3) channel, (4) many potential receivers; but rather: (1) events and 'voices' in society, (2) channel/communicator role, (3) messages, (4) receiver. This revised version takes account of the fact that mass communicators do not usually originate 'messages' or communication. Rather they *relay* to a potential audience their own account (news) of a selection of the events occurring in the environment, or they give *access* to the views and voices of some of those (such as advocates of opinions, advertisers, performers and writers) who want to reach a wider public. There are three important features of the complete model as drawn by Westley and MacLean. One is the emphasis on the *selecting* role of mass communicators; secondly, the fact that selection is undertaken according to an assessment of what the audience will find interesting; thirdly, that communication is not purposive, beyond this last goal. The media themselves typically do not aim to persuade or educate or even to inform.

According to this model, mass communication is a self-regulating process that is guided by the interests and demands of an audience that is known only by its selections and responses to what is offered. Such a process can no longer be viewed as linear, since it is strongly shaped by 'feedback' from the audience both to the media and to the advocates and original communicators. This view of the mass media sees them as relatively open and neutral service organizations in a secular society, contributing to the work of other social institutions. It remains essentially a transmission model (from senders to receivers), although much less mechanistic than earlier versions. It also substitutes the satisfaction of the audience as a measure of efficient performance for that of information transfer. It is not accidental that this model was based on the American system of free-market media. It would not very accurately fit a state-run media system or even a European public broadcasting institution. It is also innocent of the idea that the free market might not necessarily reflect the interests of audiences or might not also conduct its own form of purposeful propaganda.

A ritual or expressive model

The transmission model remains a useful representation of the rationale and general operation of some media in some of their functions (especially general news media and

advertising). It is, however, incomplete and misleading as a representation of many other media activities and of the diversity of communication processes that are at work. One reason for its weakness is the limitation of communication to the matter of 'transmission'. This version of communication, according to James Carey (1975),

> is the commonest in our culture and is defined by such terms as sending, transmitting or giving information to others. It is formed off a metaphor of geography or transportation. . . . The centre of this idea of communication is the transmission of signals or messages over time for the purpose of control.

It implies instrumentality, cause-and-effect relations and one-directional flow. Carey pointed to the alternative view of communication as 'ritual', according to which

> communication is linked to such terms as sharing, participation, association, fellowship and the possession of a common faith. . . . A ritual view is not directed towards the extension of messages in space, but the maintenance of society in time; not the act of imparting information but the representation of shared beliefs.

This alternative can equally be called an 'expressive' model of communication, since its emphasis is also on the intrinsic satisfaction of the sender (or receiver) rather than on some instrumental purpose. Ritual or expressive communication depends on shared understandings and emotions. It is celebratory, consummatory (an end in itself) and decorative rather than utilitarian in aim and it often requires some element of 'performance' for communication to be realized. Communication is engaged in for the pleasures of reception as much as for any useful purpose. The message of ritual communication is usually latent and ambiguous, depending on associations and symbols that are not chosen by the participants but made available in the culture. Medium and message are usually hard to separate. Ritual communication is also relatively timeless and unchanging.

Although, in natural conditions, ritual communication is not instrumental, it can be said to have consequences for society (such as more integration) or for social relationships. In some planned communication campaigns – for instance, in politics or advertising – the principles of ritual communication are sometimes taken over and exploited (use of potent symbols, latent appeals to cultural values, togetherness, myths, tradition, etc.). Ritual plays a part in unifying and in mobilizing sentiment and action. Examples of the model can be found in the spheres of art, religion and public ceremonials and festivals.

Communication as display and attention: a 'publicity model'

Besides the transmission and ritual models, there is a third perspective that captures another important aspect of mass communication. This can be summarily labelled a

publicity model. Often the primary aim of mass media is neither to transmit particular information nor to unite a public in some expression of culture, belief or values, but simply to catch and hold visual or aural attention. In doing so, the media attain one direct economic goal, which is to gain audience revenue (since attention = consumption, for most practical purposes), and an indirect one, which is to sell (the probability of) audience attention to advertisers. As Elliott (1972: 164) has pointed out (implicitly adopting the transmission model as the norm), 'mass communication is liable not to be communication at all', in the sense of the 'ordered transfer of meaning'. It is more likely to be 'spectatorship', and the media audience is more often a set of spectators than participants or information receivers. The *fact* of attention often matters more than the *quality* of attention (which can rarely be adequately measured).

While those who use mass media for their own purposes do hope for some effect (such as persuasion or selling) beyond attention and publicity, gaining the latter remains the immediate goal and is often treated as a measure of success or failure. A good deal of research into media effect has been concerned with questions of image and awareness. The fact of being known is often more important than the content of what is known and is the only necessary condition for celebrity. Similarly, the supposed power of the media to set political and other 'agendas' is an example of the attention-gaining process. A good deal of effort in media production is devoted to devices for gaining and keeping attention by catching the eye, arousing emotion, stimulating interest. This is one aspect of what has been described as 'media logic' (see page 296), with the *substance* of a message often subordinated to the devices for presentation (Altheide and Snow, 1979, 1991).

The attention-seeking goal also corresponds with one important perception of the media by their audiences, who use the mass media for diversion and passing time. They seek to spend time 'with the media', to escape everyday reality. The relationship between sender and receiver according to the display–attention model is not necessarily passive or uninvolved, but it is morally neutral and does not in itself necessarily imply a transfer or creation of meaning.

Going with the notion of communication as a process of *display and attention* are several additional features that do not apply to the transmission or ritual models:

- Attention-gaining is a *zero-sum* process. The time spent attending to one media display cannot be given to another, and available audience time is finite. By contrast, there is no quantifiable limit to the amount of 'meaning' that can be transferred or to the satisfactions that can be gained from participating in ritual communication processes.
- Communication in the display–attention mode exists only in the present. There is no past that matters, and the future matters only as a continuation or amplification of the present. Questions of cause and effect relating to the receiver do not arise.

- Attention-gaining is an end in itself and in the short term *value neutral* and essentially *empty of meaning*. Form and technique take precedence over message content.

These three features can be seen as underlying, respectively, the *competitiveness*, the *actuality/transience* and the *objectivity/detachment* which are pronounced features of mass communication, especially within commercial media institutions.

Encoding and decoding of media discourse: a reception model

There is yet another version of the mass communication process, which involves an even more radical departure from the transmission model than the two variants just discussed. This depends very much on the adoption of the critical perspective described above, but it can also be understood as the view of mass communication from the position of many different receivers who do not perceive or understand the message 'as sent' or 'as expressed'. This model has its origins in critical theory, semiology and discourse analysis. It is located more in the domain of the cultural than the social sciences. It is strongly linked to the rise of 'reception analysis' (see Holub, 1984; Jensen and Rosengren, 1990). It challenges the predominant methodologies of empirical social scientific audience research and also the humanistic studies of content because both fail to take account of the 'power of the audience' in giving meaning to messages.

The essence of the 'reception approach' is to locate the attribution and construction of meaning (derived from media) with the receiver. Media messages are always open and 'polysemic' (having multiple meanings) and are interpreted according the context and the culture of receivers. Among the forerunners of reception analysis was a persuasive variant of critical theory formulated by Stuart Hall (1980) which emphasized the stages of transformation through which any media message passes on the way from its origins to its reception and interpretation. It drew from, but also challenged, the basic principles of structuralism and **semiology** which presumed that any meaningful 'message' is constructed from signs which can have denotative and connotative meanings, depending on the choices made by an encoder.

Semiology emphasizes the power of the encoded text and sees the location of meaning as firmly embedded in it. Hall accepted some elements of this approach but challenged the basic assumption, on two grounds. First, communicators choose to encode messages for ideological and institutional purposes and manipulate language and media for those ends (media messages are given a 'preferred reading', or what might now be called 'spin'). Secondly, receivers ('decoders') are not obliged to accept messages as sent but can and do resist ideological influence by applying variant or oppositional readings, according to their own experience and outlook.

In Hall's (1980) model of the process of **encoding and decoding,** he portrays the television programme (or any equivalent media text) as a *meaningful discourse*. This is encoded according the *meaning structure* of the mass media production organization and its main supports, but decoded according to the different meaning structures and frameworks of knowledge of differently situated audiences. The path followed through the stages of the model is simple in principle. Communication originates within media institutions whose typical frameworks of meaning are likely to conform to dominant power structures. Specific messages are 'encoded', often in the form of established content genres (such as 'news', 'pop music', 'sport reports', 'soap operas', 'police/detective series') which have a face-value meaning and in-built guidelines for interpretation by an audience. The media are approached by their audiences in terms of 'meaning structures', which have their origin in the ideas and experience of the audience.

While the general implication is that meaning as decoded does not necessarily (or often) correspond with meaning as encoded (despite the mediation of conventional genres and shared language systems), the most significant point is that decoding can take a different course than intended. Receivers can read between the lines and even reverse the intended direction of the message. It is clear that this model and the associated theory embody several key principles: the multiplicity of meanings of media content; the existence of varied 'interpretative' communities; and the primacy of the receiver in determining meaning. While early effect research recognized the fact of selective perception, this was seen as a limitation on, or a condition of, the transmission model, rather than part of a quite different perspective.

Comparisons

The discussion of these different models shows the inadequacy of any single concept or definition of mass communication that relies too heavily on what seem to be intrinsic characteristics or biases of the *technology* of multiple reproduction and dissemination. The human uses of technology are much more diverse and more determinant than was once assumed. Of the four models, summarized in comparative terms in Figure 3.1, the transmission model is largely taken over from older institutional contexts – education, religion, government – and is really appropriate only to media activities which are instructional, informational or propagandist in purpose. The expression or ritual model is better able to capture elements which have to do with art, drama, entertainment and the many symbolic uses of communication. The publicity or display – attention model reflects the central media goals of attracting audiences (high ratings and wide reach) for purposes of prestige or income. The reception model reminds us that the seeming power of the media to mould, express or capture is partly illusory, since the audience in the end disposes.

| | Orientation of | |
	Sender	Receiver
Transmission model	Transfer of meaning	Cognitive processing
Expression or ritual model	Performance	Consummation/ shared experience
Publicity model	Competitive display	Attention-giving spectatorship
Reception model	Preferential encoding	Differential decoding/ construction of meaning

FIGURE 3.1   Four models of the mass communication process compared: each model involves differences of orientation on the part of sender and receiver

NEW THEORETICAL PERSPECTIVES ON MEDIA AND SOCIETY

The basic concepts and models for the study of mass communication were developed on the basis of the special features indicated (scale, simultaneity, one-directionality, etc.) and under conditions of transition to the highly organized and centralized industrial society of the 20th century. Not everything has changed, since such societies are still the norm, despite trends towards internationalization and more flexible social organization, not to mention the much vaunted **postmodernism** of the times. However, we are now faced with new technological possibilities for communication that are not massive or one-directional and there is some shift away from the earlier massification and centralization of society. The potential of transition to an 'information society' is real enough (see Chapter 6). We need also take account of a decline in force of the social critical paradigm as outlined above.

These changes are already recognized in mass communication theory, although the shift is still cautious and much of the conceptual framework erected for mass communication is still relevant. We still have mass politics, mass markets and mass consumption. The media have extended their scale on a global dimension. The beliefs vested in the power of publicity, public relations and propaganda by other names are still widely held by those with economic and political power.

The 'dominant paradigm' from earlier days of mass communication is not so difficult to apply in new conditions, with a similar confidence in the manipulative

capacity of the media and the malleability of the 'masses'. The key notion of information transportation is still very much with us in the management of diverse systems. Some elements of the alternative paradigm (especially the methodological principles) are in accord with the changed social circumstances and with a postmodern *Zeitgeist*, since they are sensitive to context and to diversity of use, response and interaction.

As to the critical purpose, it is possible that the seeming current condition of 'normlessness' and loss of faith is temporary and superficial. The old problems to which critical theory was addressed have not been solved, and there are plenty of new causes to fill the gap left (temporarily) by the decline of the class struggle. The mass media themselves are organized in no postmodern spirit, whatever may be said of their content. Issues of gender definition, cultural identity, inequality, racism, environmental damage, world hunger and social chaos are examples of problems of rising salience and concern in which the media are deeply implicated, just because of their enhanced role in the organization of national and global society.

FURTHER READING

Dervin, B., Grossberg, L., O'Keefe, B.J. and Wartella, E. (eds) (1989) *Rethinking Communication*, Vol. 1: *Paradigm Issues*. Newbury Park, CA: Sage.

Hardt, H. (1991) *Critical Communication Studies*. London: Routledge.

Jensen, K.B. and Jankowski, N. (eds) (1991) *A Handbook of Qualitative Methods for Communication Research*. London: Routledge.

McQuail, D. and Windahl, S. (1993) *Communication Models for the Study of Mass Communication*. 2nd edn. London: Longman.

van Zoonen, E. (1994) *Feminist Media Studies*. London: Sage.

theory of media and theory of society

In this chapter, we look at ideas concerning the relation between mass media and society, reserving the cultural implications for Chapter 5 even though society and culture are inseparable, and the one cannot exist without the other. Treating society first also implies a primacy for society that cannot be sustained. Most media theory relates to both 'society' and 'culture' together and has to be explained in relation to both. For present purposes, the domain of 'society' refers to the material base (economic and political resources and power), to social relationships (in national societies, communities, families, etc.) and to social roles and occupations that are socially regulated (formally or informally). The domain of 'culture' refers primarily to other essential aspects of social life, especially to *symbolic expression*, *meanings* and *practices* (social customs, institutional ways of doing things and also personal habits).

While it is incorrect to view culture as secondary to society, the history of modern society has usually been written in terms of a materially driven process, with society as the 'base' and culture as 'superstructure'. In fact, this is itself an example of a 'cultural' bias in the interpretation of experience that illustrates the impossibility of separating the two concepts. We (that is, all of us) can reflect on society only through ideas which have their location (as defined above) in the sphere of culture. Society, as we experience it, is constituted out of the meanings we give to material experience.

A typology of society–culture relations

The conundrum of the relation between culture and society is no easier to resolve in respect of media than in any other context. In fact it may even be more difficult, since mass communication can be considered as both a 'societal' and a 'cultural' phenomenon. The mass media institution is part of the structure of society, and its technological infrastructure is part of the economic and power base, while the ideas, images and information disseminated by the media are evidently an important aspect of our culture (in the sense defined above).

In discussing this problem, Rosengren (1981b) has offered a simple typology which cross-tabulates two opposed propositions: 'social structure influences culture'; and its reverse, 'culture influences social structure'. This yields four main options that are available for describing the relation between mass media and society, as shown in Figure 4.1. If we consider mass media as an aspect of society (base or structure) then the option of *materialism* is presented. There is a considerable body of theory that views culture as dependent on the economic and power structure of a society. It is

theory of media and theory of society **61**

| | Social structure influences culture | |
	Yes	No
Culture influences social structure — Yes	Interdependence (two-way influence)	Idealism (strong media influence)
Culture influences social structure — No	Materialism (media are dependent)	Autonomy (no causal connection)

FIGURE 4.1   Four types of relation between culture (media content) and society

assumed that whoever owns or controls the media can choose, or set limits to, what they do.

If we consider the media primarily in the light of their contents (thus more as culture), then the option of *idealism* is indicated. The media are assumed to have a potential for significant influence, but it is the particular ideas and values conveyed by the media (in their content) which are seen as the primary causes of social change, irrespective of who owns and controls. The influence is thought to work through individual motivations and actions. This view leads to a strong belief in various potential media effects for good or ill. Examples include the promotion by the media of peace and international understanding (or having the opposite effect), of pro- or antisocial values and behaviour, and of enlightenment or the secularization and modernization of traditional societies. A form of idealism or 'mentalism' concerning media also lies behind the view that changes in media forms and technology can change our way of gaining experience in essential ways and even our relations with others (as in the theories of McLuhan).

The two options remaining – of interdependence and of autonomy – have found less distinctive theoretical development, although there is a good deal of support in common sense and in evidence for both.

Interdependence implies that mass media and society are continually interacting and influencing each other (as are society and culture). The media (as cultural industries) respond to the demand from society for information and entertainment and, at the same time, stimulate innovation and contribute to a changing social-cultural climate, which sets off new demands for communication. Clark (1969) explained how the French sociologist Gabriel Tarde, writing about 1900, envisaged a constant inter-weaving of influences: 'technological developments made newspapers possible, news-papers promote the formation of broader publics, and they, by broadening the loyalties of their members, create an extensive network of overlapping and shifting groupings'. Today, the various influences are so bound together that neither mass

communication nor modern society is conceivable without the other, and each is a necessary, though not a sufficient, condition for the other. From this point of view we have to conclude that the media may equally be considered to mould or to mirror society and social changes.

The option of *autonomy* in the relations between culture and society is not necessarily inconsistent with this view, unless interpreted very literally. It is at least very likely that society and mass media can vary independently up to a point. It does seem that societies that are culturally very similar can sometimes have very different media systems. The autonomy position also supports those who are sceptical about the power of the media to influence ideas, values and behaviour – for instance, in promoting a conformist ideology or stimulating 'modernity' or damaging the cultural identity of poorer or less powerful countries. There are different views about how much autonomy (or lack of interaction between media and society) is possible. The debate is especially relevant to the central thesis of 'internationalization' or 'globalization', which implies a convergence and homogenization of a worldwide culture, as a result of the media. The autonomy position would suggest that media culture is superficial and need not significantly touch the local culture. It follows that **cultural imperialism** is not likely to happen simply by chance or against the will of the culturally 'colonized' (see Chapter 10).

An inconclusive outcome

As with many of the issues to be discussed, there are more theories than there is solid evidence, and the questions raised by this discussion are much too broad to be settled by empirical research. According to Rosengren (1981b: 254), surveying what scattered evidence he could find, research gives only 'inconclusive, partly even contradictory, evidence about the relationship between social structure, societal values as mediated by the media, and opinions among the public'. There is a strong possibility that different theories hold under different conditions and at different levels of analysis. This applies to each of the three main issues of society which are discussed below. They relate to *power, integration* and *change*.

It seems that the media can serve to repress as well as to liberate, to unite as well as to fragment society, both to promote and to hold back change. What is also striking in the theories to be discussed is the ambiguity of the role assigned to the media. They are as often presented in a 'progressive' as in a 'reactionary' light, according to whether the dominant (pluralist) or alternative (critical, radical) perspective is adopted. Despite the uncertainty, there can be little doubt that the media, whether moulders or mirrors of society, are the main messengers *about* society, and it is around this observation that the alternative theoretical perspectives can best be organized.

A central presupposition, relating to questions both of society and of culture, is that the media institution is essentially concerned with the production and distribution of *knowledge* in the widest sense of the word. Such knowledge enables us to make some sense of our experience of the social world, even if the 'taking of meaning' occurs in relatively autonomous and very diversified ways. The information, images and ideas made available by the media may, for most people, be the main source of an awareness of a shared past time (history) and of a present social location. They are also a store of memories and a map of where we are and who we are (identity) and may also provide the materials for orientation to the future. As noted at the outset, the media to a large extent serve to constitute our perceptions and definitions of social reality and normality for purposes of a public, shared social life, and are a key source of standards, models and norms.

The main point to emphasize is the degree to which the different media have come to interpose themselves between ourselves and any experience of the world beyond our immediate personal environment and our direct sense observation. They also provide the most continuous line of contact with the main institutions of the society in which we live. In a secular society, in matters of values and ideas, the mass media tend to 'take over' from the early influences of school, parents, religion, siblings and companions. We are consequently very dependent on the media for a large part of our wider 'symbolic environment' (the 'pictures in our heads'), however much we may be able to shape our own personal version. It is the media which are likely to forge the elements which are held in common with others, since we now tend to share much the same media sources and 'media culture'. Without some degree of shared perception of reality, whatever its origin, there cannot really be an organized social life.

The mediation concept

These comments can be summed up in terms of the concept of mediation of contact with social reality. Mediation involves several different processes. As noted already, it refers to the relaying of second-hand (or third-party) versions of events and conditions which we cannot directly observe for ourselves. Secondly, it refers to the efforts of other actors and institutions in society to contact us for their own purposes (or our own supposed good). This applies to politicians and governments, advertisers, educators, experts and authorities of all kinds. It refers to the indirect way in which we form our perceptions of groups and cultures to which we do not belong.

Mediation also implies some form of *relationship*. Relationships that are mediated through mass media are likely to be more distant, more impersonal and weaker than

direct personal ties. The mass media do not monopolize the flow of information we receive, nor do they intervene in all our wider social relations, but their presence is inevitably very pervasive. Early versions of the idea of 'mediation of reality' were inclined to assume a division between a public terrain in which a widely shared view of reality was constructed by way of mass media messages and a personal sphere, where individuals could communicate freely and directly. More recent developments of technology have undermined this simple division, since a much larger share of communication and thus of our contact with others and our environmental reality is mediated via technology (telephone, computer, fax, e-mail, etc.), although on an individual and private basis. The implications of this change are still unclear and subject to diverse interpretations.

Thompson (1993, 1995) has suggested a typology of interaction to clarify the consequences of the new communication technologies that have detached social interaction and symbolic exchange from the sharing of a common locale. He notes (1993: 35) that 'it has become possible for more and more individuals to acquire information and symbolic content through mediated forms of interaction'. He distinguished two types of interaction alongside face-to-face interaction. One of these, which he calls 'mediated interaction', involves some technical medium such as paper, electrical wires, etc. which enables information or symbolic content to be transmitted to individuals who are remote in space or time or both. The participants in mediated interaction do not share the same spatio-temporal reference systems and have to consider the need to supply contextual information and make do with fewer symbolic cues than in face-to-face contact.

The other type is called 'mediated quasi-interaction' and refers to relations established by the media of mass communication. There are two main distinguishing features. Firstly in this case, participants are not oriented towards specific others, and symbolic forms are produced for an indefinite range of potential recipients. Secondly, mediated quasi-interaction is monological (rather than dialogical), in the sense that the flow of communication is one-way. There is also no direct or immediate response expected from the receiver. Despite the use of the term 'quasi-interaction', Thompson regards mass communication as involving a 'social situation in which individuals are linked together in a process of communication and symbolic exchange' (1993: 36). He argues that the 'media have created a new kind of public sphere which is despatialized and non-dialogical in character' (1993: 42) and is potentially global in scope.

Mediation metaphors

In general, the notion of mediation in the sense of media intervening between ourselves and 'reality' is no more than a metaphor, although it does point to several of the roles played by the media in connecting us to other experience. The terms that are often

used to describe this role, reflect different attributions of purposefulness, inter-activity and effectiveness. Mediation can mean different things, ranging from neutrally informing, through negotiation, to attempts at manipulation and control. The variations can be captured by a number of communication images, which express different ways in which the media may connect us with reality. These are summarized in Box 4.1.

Box 4.1   Perceptions of mediation roles

- as a **window** on events and experience, which extends our vision, enabling us to see for ourselves what is going on, without interference from others;
- as a **mirror** of events in society and the world, implying a faithful reflection (albeit with inversion and possible distortion of the image), although the angle and direction of the mirror are decided by others, and we are less free to see what we want;
- as a **filter** or **gatekeeper,** acting to select parts of experience for special attention and closing off other views and voices, whether deliberately or not;
- as a **signpost, guide** or **interpreter,** pointing the way and making sense of what is otherwise puzzling or fragmentary;
- as a **forum** or **platform** for the presentation of information and ideas to an audience, often with possibilities for response and feedback;
- as an **interlocutor** or informed partner in conversation who not only passes on information but responds to questions in a quasi-interactive way

---

Some of these images are to be found in the media's own self-definition – especially in the more positive implications of extending our view of the world, providing integration and continuity and connecting people with each other. Even the notion of filtering is often accepted in its positive sense of selecting and interpreting what would otherwise be an unmanageable and chaotic supply of information and impressions. These versions of the mediating process reflect differences of interpretation of the role of the media in social processes. They can vary on two main dimensions: one of openness versus control, another of neutrality versus being actively participant. It is noticeable that the various images discussed do not refer to the interactive possibilities of newer media, in which the 'receiver' can become a 'sender' and make use of the media in interaction with the environment. This indicates the degree to which new technology may indeed lead to revolutionary changes, with 'intermediation' replacing or supplementing the mediation process (see Chapter 6).

A FRAME OF REFERENCE FOR CONNECTING MEDIA WITH SOCIETY

The general notion that mass communication interposes in some way between 'reality' and our perceptions and knowledge of it refers to a number of specific processes at

different levels of analysis. The Westley and MacLean (1957) model (see page 53) indicates some of the additional elements needed for a more detailed frame of reference. Most significant is the idea that the media are sought out by institutional advocates as channels for reaching the general public (or chosen groups) and for conveying their chosen perspective on events and conditions. This is broadly true of competing politicians and governments, advertisers, religious leaders, some thinkers, writers and artists, etc. We are reminded that experience has always been mediated by the institutions of society (including the family), and what has happened is that a new mediator (mass communication) has been added which can extend, compete with, replace or even run counter to the efforts of social institutions. It is also the case that mass media are often acting as agents, consciously or not, of other sources.

The simple picture of a 'two-step' (or multiple) process of mediated contact with reality is complicated by the fact that mass media are not completely free agents in relation to the rest of society. They are subject to formal and informal control by the very institutions that have an interest of their own in shaping public perceptions of reality. The media are themselves an institution with their own goals, rules, conventions and mechanisms of control. Their objectives do not necessarily coincide with the primary goals of the society, nor even with the aim of relaying some objective 'truth' about reality.

An abstract view of the 'mediation of reality', based on Westley and MacLean but also reflecting these points, is sketched in Figure 4.2. The media provides their audience with a supply of information, images, stories and impressions, sometimes according to anticipated needs, sometimes guided by its own purposes (e.g. gaining revenue or influence), and sometimes following the motives of other social institutions (e.g. advertising, making propaganda, projecting favourable images, sending information). Given this diversity of underlying motivation in the *selection* and *flow* of the 'images of reality', we can see that mediation is unlikely to be a purely neutral process. The 'reality' will always be to some extent selected and constructed and there will be certain consistent biases. These will reflect especially the differential opportunities available for gaining media access and also the influence of 'media logic' in constituting reality (see page 296).

Figure 4.2 also represents the fact that experience is not completely and not always mediated by the mass media. There are still certain direct channels of contact with social institutions (e.g. political parties or churches). There is also some possibility of direct personal experience of some of the more distant events reported in media (e.g. crime, poverty, illness, war and conflict). The potentially diverse sources of information (including personal contact with others) may not be completely independent from each other, but they provide some checks on the adequacy and reliability of 'quasi-mediated interaction'.

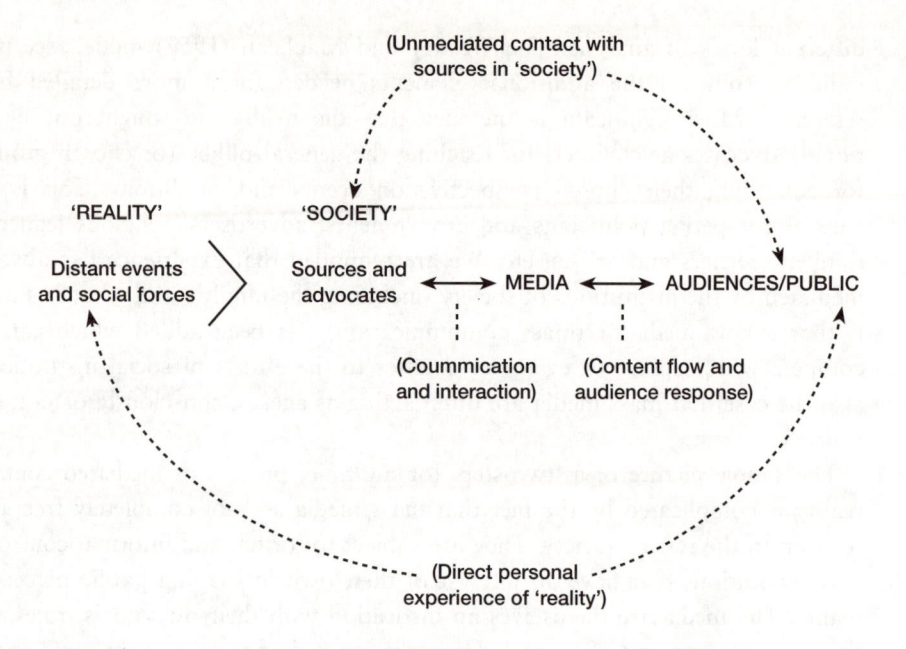

FIGURE 4.2 A frame of reference for theory-formation about media and society: media interpose between personal experience and more distant events and social forces (based on Westley and MacLean, 1957)

Types of media–society theory

In the light of this, the main varieties of theory about media and society can be accounted for as follows. First, there are 'macro-theories' concerning the relations between media and other social institutions, which bear on the extent to which the media are autonomous. Do media offer alternative visions of or simply reinforce otherwise dominant lines of power and influence? Secondly, there is theory that focuses more directly on media institutions and organizations and on how they interpret and carry out their chosen or given tasks, especially under conditions of changing technology and competition for resources and support. Thirdly, theory focuses on the perspective and needs of the audience and the consequences of their using media to gain social experience. This also covers the question of the everyday-life experience of audience members and the social context of media reception.

Of course, there is no neat system for categorizing the available theories. These are fragmentary and selective, sometimes overlapping or inconsistent, often guided by conflicting ideologies and assumptions about society. Theory-formation does not follow a systematic and logical pattern but responds to real-life problems and historical circumstances. Before describing some of the theory that has been formulated, it is necessary to consider what some of these problematic issues have been during the 'first age of mass communication'.

The media are invariably related in some way to the prevailing structure of political and economic power. It is evident, first of all, that media have an economic cost and value, are an object of competition for control and access. Secondly, they are subject to political, economic and legal regulation. Thirdly, mass media are very commonly regarded as effective instruments of power, with the potential capacity to exert influence in various ways.

> **Box 4.2 Aspects of mass media power**
>
> - Attracting and directing public attention
> - Persuasion in matters of opinion and belief
> - Influencing behaviour
> - Structuring definitions of reality
> - Conferring status and legitimacy
> - Informing quickly and extensively

These propositions about media power contained in Box 4.2 give rise to the following sub-questions:

- Who controls the media and in whose interest?
- Whose version of the world (social reality) is presented?
- How effective are the media in achieving chosen ends?
- Do mass media promote more or less equality in society?
- How is access to media organized?

In discussions of media power, two models are usually opposed to each other: one a model of dominant media, the other of pluralist media (see Figure 4.3). The former model sees media as subservient to other institutions, which are themselves inter-related. Media organizations, in this view, are likely to be owned or controlled by a small number of powerful interests and to be similar in type and purpose. They disseminate a limited and undifferentiated view of the world shaped by the per-spectives of ruling interests. Audiences are constrained or conditioned to accept the view of the world offered, with little critical response. The result is to reinforce and legitimate the prevailing structure of power and to head off change by filtering out alternative voices.

The pluralist model is, in nearly every respect, the opposite, allowing for much diversity and unpredictability. There is held to be no unified and dominant elite, and change and democratic control are both possible. Differentiated audiences are seen to initiate demand and are able to resist persuasion and react to what media offer. In general, the 'dominance' model is that deployed both by conservatives pessimistic about the 'rise of the masses' and also by critics of capitalist society disappointed by the failure of the revolution to happen. It is consistent with a view of media as an

	Dominance	Pluralism
Societal source	Ruling class or dominant elite	Competing political, social, cultural interests and groups
Media	Under concentrated ownership and of uniform type	Many and independent of each other
Production	Standardized, routinized, controlled	Creative, free, original
Content and world view	Selective and decided from 'above'	Diverse and competing views, responsive to audience demand
Audience	Dependent, passive, organized on large scale	Fragmented, selective, reactive and active
Effects	Strong and confirmative of established social order	Numerous, without consistency or predictability of direction, but often no effect

FIGURE 4.3 Two opposing models of media power (mixed versions are more likely to be encountered)

instrument of 'cultural imperialism' or tool of political propaganda. The pluralist view is an idealized version of what liberalism and the free market will lead to. While the models are described as total opposites, it is possible to envisage there being mixed versions, in which tendencies towards mass domination (such as through concentration of ownership) are subject to limits and counter-forces and are 'resisted' by their audiences. In any free society, minorities and opposition groups should be able to develop and maintain their own alternative media.

MAIN ISSUES FOR MEDIA THEORY: (II): SOCIAL INTEGRATION AND IDENTITY

A dual perspective on media

Theorists of mass communication have often shared with sociologists an interest in how social order is maintained and in the attachment of people to various kinds of social unit. The media were early-on associated with the problems of rapid urbanization, social mobility and the decline of traditional communities. They have continued to be linked with social dislocation and a supposed increase in individual immorality, crime and disorder. Mass communication as a process has often been typified as predominantly individualistic, impersonal and anomic, thus conducive to lower levels

of social control and solidarity. The media have brought messages of what is new and fashionable in terms of goods, ideas, techniques and values from city to country and from the social top to the base. They have also portrayed alternative value systems, potentially weakening the hold of traditional values.

An alternative view of the relation between mass media and social integration has also been in circulation, based on other features of mass communication. It has a capacity to unite scattered individuals within the same large audience, or integrate newcomers into urban communities by providing a common set of values, ideas and information and helping to form identities. This process can help to bind together a large-scale, differentiated modern society more effectively than would have been possible through older mechanisms of religious, family or group control. In other words, mass media seem in principle capable both of supporting and of subverting social cohesion. The positions seem far apart, the one stressing centrifugal and the other centripetal tendencies, although in fact in complex and changing society, both forces are normally at work at the same time, the one compensating to some extent for the other.

Ambivalence about social integration

The main questions that arise for theory and research can thus (much as in the case of power) be mapped out on two orthogonal dimensions. One refers to the direction of effect: either *centrifugal* or *centripetal*. The first refers to the stimulus towards social change, freedom, individualism and fragmentation. The second refers to effects in the form of more social unity, order, cohesion and integration. Both social integration and dispersal can be valued differently, depending on preference and perspective. One person's desirable social control is another person's limitation of freedom; one person's individualism is another person's non-conformity or isolation. So the second dimension can be described as normative, especially in the assessment of these two opposite tendencies of the working of mass media. The question it represents is whether the effect at issue should be viewed positively or negatively (McCormack, 1961; Carey, 1969).

In order to make sense of this complicated situation, it helps to think of the two versions of media theory – centrifugal and centripetal – each with its own dimension of evaluation, so that there are, in effect, four different theoretical positions relating to social integration (see Figure 4.4).

These are as follows:

1. *Freedom, diversity.* The positive version of the centrifugal effect stresses freedom, mobility and modernization.
2. *Integration, solidarity.* The positive version of the centrifugal effect stresses the integrative and cohesive function of the media.

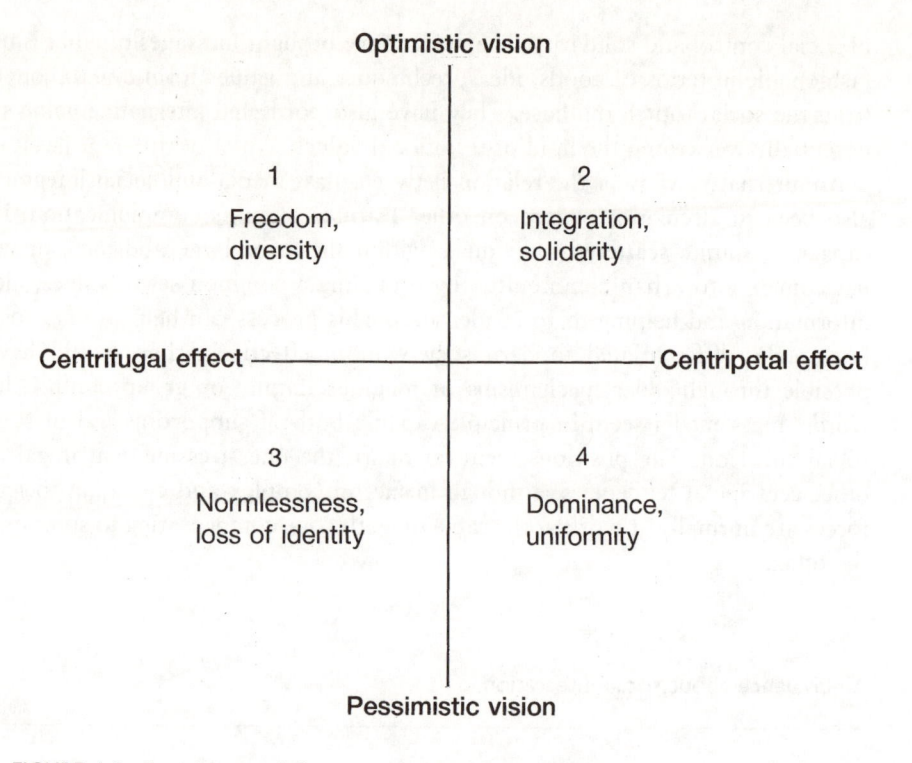

FIGURE 4.4   Four images of the consequences of mass communication for social integration

3. *Normlessness, loss of identity.* The negative view of change and individualism points to individual isolation and loss of social cohesion.
4. *Dominance, uniformity.* Society can be over-integrated and over-regulated, leading to central control and conformity.

Box 4.3   Questions about media and integration

- Do mass media increase or decrease the level of social control and conformity?
- Do media strengthen or weaken intervening social institutions, such as family, political party, local community, church, trade union?
- Do media help or hinder the formation of diverse groups and identities based on subculture, opinion, social experience, social action, etc.?

Different types and levels of integrative media effects

Leaving aside the question of evaluation, it should be an empirical matter to determine which condition is actually prevalent in society and what its causes might be. This is an extraordinarily difficult task, since we need both good indicators of integration and

evidence concerning many possible causal factors, besides the working of media. One recent attempt to account for the alleged loss of cohesion and degree of participation of American society has illustrated the difficulties without offering an answer (Putnam, 1995). To answer such questions we need to take account of different levels at which integration might be observed (such as the level of a whole society, or a local community, or the individual sense of identity). We may also have to distinguish between 'functional integration' (absence of conflict, co-operation for common tasks) and 'normative integration' (the sharing of norms and values). One can have one without the other, and communication is relevant to both (Allen, 1977).

A good deal of early media theory and research focused on questions of integration. For instance, Hanno Hardt (1979) has described the concerns of 19th- and early 20th-century German theorists with the integrative role of the press in society. Among the functions of the press he encountered were the following:

- binding society together;
- giving leadership to the public;
- helping to establish the 'public sphere';
- providing for the exchange of ideas between leaders and masses;
- satisfying needs for information;
- providing society with a mirror of itself;
- acting as the conscience of society.

In the United States, members of the Chicago School, who pioneered research into mass communication (Rogers, 1993), especially in the person of Robert Park and his pupil Herbert Blumer, emphasized the potentially positive role of mass media – for instance, in the assimilation of immigrants into their new nation (Clark, 1969). McCormack (1961) has argued that a modern, changing society is necessarily segmented, and the 'unique function of mass media is to provide both to industry and to society a coherence, a synthesis of experience, an awareness of the whole'.

The media may also be expected to help forge minority identities or to help resolve social conflicts. Much of the early literature on 'modernization', development and nation-building in the post-colonial era emphasized the contribution of media to forging a new national identity (Pye, 1963). More recently, attention has focused on the opposite effects, as increasingly internationalized media threaten to undermine national and cultural autonomy in many media-dependent societies (see Chapter 10).

MAIN ISSUES FOR MEDIA THEORY (III): SOCIAL CHANGE

A key question concerns the direction and strength of the relationship between mass communication and other changes taking place in society – in brief, are media a cause

or an effect of social change? Many issues of change have already been raised in relation to power, integration and modernization. Wherever the media exert influence they also cause change; the options of social centralization or dispersal are two main kinds of change. As we have seen, no simple answer can be expected, and different theories offer alternative versions of the relationship. At issue are the alternative ways of relating three basic elements: (a) the technology of communication and the form and content of media; (b) changes in society (social structure and institutional arrangements); and (c) the distribution among a population of opinion, beliefs, values and practices. All consequences of mass media are potentially questions about social change, but most relevant for theory have been the issues of 'technological determinism' and the potential to use media for development. The first refers to the effect on society of changing communications media. The second refers to the more practical question of whether or not (and how) mass media might be applied to economic and social development (as an 'engine of change' or 'multiplier of modernity') (see pages 83–4).

MEDIA–SOCIETY THEORY I: THE MASS SOCIETY

In the following pages, several distinctive theoretical approaches to these issues of social power, integration and change are discussed. They are presented more or less in chronological order of their formulation and they span the range from optimistic to pessimistic, critical to neutral. The first to be dealt with, mass society theory, is more interesting for historical reasons than for its current relevance, and its elements are built around the concept of 'mass' which has already been discussed on pages 38–9. The theory emphasizes the interdependence of institutions that exercise power and thus the integration of the media into the sources of social power and authority. Content is likely to serve the interests of political and economic power-holders. The media cannot be expected to offer a critical or alternative definition of the world, and their tendency will be to assist in the accommodation of the dependent public to their fate.

The 'dominant media' model sketched above reflects the mass society view. The type of society which developed out of industrialization and urban immigration is one characterized by family privatization, competitiveness and low levels of solidarity and participation. Mass society theory gives a primacy to the media as a causal factor. It rests very much on the idea that the media offer a view of the world, a substitute or pseudo-environment, which is a potent means of manipulation of people but also an aid to their psychic survival under difficult conditions. According to C. Wright Mills (1951: 333), 'Between consciousness and existence stand communications, which influence such consciousness as men have of their existence'.

This vision of society is pessimistic and more a diagnosis of the sickness of the times than a social theory, mixing elements of critical thought from the political left with a

nostalgia for a golden age of community and democracy. As a theory of the media, it strongly invokes images of control and portrays the direction of influence as flowing from above. Mass society is, paradoxically, both 'atomized' and centrally controlled. The media are seen as significantly contributing to this control in societies characterized by largeness of scale, remoteness of institutions, isolation of individuals and lack of strong local or group integration.

The theory posits that media will be controlled or run in a monopolistic way and will be an effective means of organizing people in masses as audiences, consumers, markets, electorates. Mass media are usually the voice of authority, the givers of opinion and instruction and also of psychic satisfaction. The media establish a relation of dependence on the part of ordinary citizens, in respect not only of opinion but also of self-identity and consciousness. According to the most influential and articulate theorist of mass society, C.W. Mills (1951, 1956), the mass media lead to a form of non-democratic control 'from above', with few chances to answer back.

The mass society as described is certainly integrated but not in any 'healthy' way. According to Kornhauser (1968), the lack of strong social organization and the relative isolation of individuals encourage efforts of leaders to mobilize and manipulate. Mills (1951, 1956) also pointed to the decline of the genuine public of classic democratic theory and its replacement by shifting aggregates of people who cannot formulate or realize their own aims in political action. This regret has been echoed more recently by arguments about the decline of a 'public sphere' of democratic debate and politics, in which large-scale, commercialized mass media have been implicated (Elliott, 1982; Garnham, 1986; Dahlgren, 1995).

One solution to increased massification and privatization that has been proposed has been by way of emancipatory uses of new media from below (for example, Enzensberger, 1970), or as a result of new developments of technology (Neuman, 1991). Research has helped to modify some of the large claims of mass society theory by reasserting the potential resistance of the audience to manipulation and control and demonstrating the persistence of strong influences from group, subculture, class, locality and other sources as a limitation on the power of the media.

The idea that we live in a 'mass society' persists in variety of loosely related components. These include a nostalgia (or hope) for a more 'communitarian' alternative to the present individualistic age as well as a critical attitude towards the supposed emptiness, loneliness and consumerism of life in a contemporary free-market society. The widespread public indifference (at best) towards democratic politics and lack of participation in it are also widely regretted and often attributed to the cynical and manipulative use of mass media by politicians and parties.

However, the various lines of critique are not very well organized in a central thesis, nor is the evidence beyond dispute. The notion in the original theory of there being a small elite dominating the rest of society is not widely accepted, despite the evidence of increasing social inequality, of the existence of a self-perpetuating class of very rich people and of even more powerful global corporations. The widely accepted designation of contemporary society as 'postmodernist' runs contrary to the mass society

vision, which appears as an essentially 'modernist' perspective. The actual abundance and seeming diversity of many old and new forms of media seem also to undermine the validity of mass society theory in its portrayal of mass media as one of the foundation stones of the mass society. In particular, the new electronic media give rise to a near-utopian vision of what society can become that runs counter to the central mass society thesis.

Box 4.4 Mass society theory of media: main features

- Large-scale society
- Atomized public
- Centralized media
- One-way transmission
- People depend on media for identity
- Media used for manipulation and control

MEDIA–SOCIETY THEORY 2: MARXIST PERSPECTIVES

While Karl Marx only knew the press before it was effectively a mass medium, it is still possible to analyse modern media according to his ideas, even when **Marxism** is widely thought to have failed as a guide to social change. The media as an industry conform to a general capitalist type, with factors of production (raw materials, technology and labour) and relations of production. They are likely to be in the monopolistic ownership of a capital-owning class, and to be nationally or internationally organized to serve the interests of that class. They do so by materially exploiting workers (extracting surplus labour value) and consumers (making excess profits). Media work ideologically by disseminating the ideas and world-views of the ruling class, denying access to alternative ideas that might lead to change or to a growing consciousness on the part of the working class of its interests. They also hinder the mobilization of such consciousness into active and organized political opposition. The complexity of these propositions has led to several variants of Marxist-inspired analysis of modern media, merging into the present-day 'critical political economy' (Golding and Murdock, 1996; and see pages 82–3).

The classic position

The question of power is central to Marxist interpretations of mass media. While varied, these have always emphasized the fact that ultimately they are instruments of

control for a ruling class. The founding text is Marx's *German Ideology*, where he states:

> The class that has the means of material production has control at the same time over the means of mental production so that, thereby, generally speaking, the ideas of those who lack the means of mental production are subject to it . . . Insofar, therefore, as they rule as a class and determine the extent and compass of an epoch, it is self-evident that they . . . among other things . . . regulate the production and distribution of the ideas of their age: thus their ideas are the ruling ideas of the epoch. (cited in Murdock and Golding, 1977)

Marxist theory posits a direct link between economic ownership and the dissemination of messages that affirm the legitimacy and the value of a class society. These views are supported in modern times by evidence of tendencies to great concentration of media ownership by capitalist entrepreneurs (for example, Bagdikian, 1988) and by much correlative evidence of conservative tendencies in content of media so organized (for example, Herman and Chomsky, 1988).

Neo-Marxist variants

Revised versions of Marxist media theory which concentrate more on ideas than on material structures emphasize the ideological effects of media in the interests of a ruling class, in 'reproducing' the essentially exploitative relationships and manipulation, and in legitimating the dominance of capitalism and the subordination of the working class. Louis Althusser (1971) conceived this process to work by way of what he called 'ideological state apparatuses' (all means of socialization, in effect), which, by comparison with 'repressive state apparatuses' (such as the army and police), enable the capitalist state to survive without recourse to direct violence. Gramsci's (1971) concept of **hegemony** refers to a ubiquitous and internally consistent culture and ideology which are openly or implicitly favourable to a dominant class or elite, although less closely and consciously organized.

Marcuse (1964) interpreted the media, along with other elements of mass production systems, as engaged in 'selling' or imposing a whole social system which is at the same time both desirable and repressive. The main contribution of the media is to stimulate and then satisfy 'false needs', leading to the assimilation of groups who have no real material interest in common into a 'one-dimensional society'.

All in all, the message of Marxist theory is plain, but questions remain unanswered. How might the power of the media be countered or resisted? What is the position of forms of media that are not clearly in capitalist ownership or in the power of the state (such as independent newspapers or public broadcasting)? The original Leninist model of the vanguard press leading the revolutionary class struggle is no longer realistic. Critics of mass media in the Marxist tradition either rely on the weapon of disclosure of propaganda and manipulation (for example, Herman and Chomsky, 1988) or pin

their hopes on some form of collective ownership of alternative media as a counter to the media power of the capitalist class. Although public ownership of broadcasting remains a viable alternative to private media (see, e.g. Raboy, 1996), it has also been criticized from a Marxist perspective for being another tool of the bourgeois state. This is not to rule out the possibilities for alternative forms of media or for change (not necessarily in directions endorsed by Marxists) by way of micro- or grass-roots media, especially under conditions of open repression and denial of legitimate alternative media (Downing, 1984).

Box 4.5   Marxist theory of media

- Mass media owned by bourgeois class
- Media operated in their class interest
- Media promote working-class false consciousness
- Media access denied to political opposition

MEDIA–SOCIETY THEORY 3: FUNCTIONALISM

Functionalism claims to explain social practices and institutions in terms of the 'needs' of the society and of individuals (Merton, 1957). As applied to the media institution, the presumed 'needs' have mainly to do with continuity, order, integration, motivation, guidance, socialization, adaptation, etc. Society is viewed as an ongoing system of linked working parts or subsystems, of which the mass media are one, each making an essential contribution to continuity and order. Organized social life is said to require the continued maintenance of a more or less accurate, consistent, supportive and complete picture of the working of society and of the social environment. It is by responding to the demands of individuals and institutions in consistent ways that the media achieve unintended benefits for the society as a whole.

The theory depicts media as essentially self-directing and self-correcting. While apolitical in formulation, it suits pluralist and voluntarist conceptions of the fundamental mechanisms of social life and has a conservative bias to the extent that the media are likely to be seen as a means of maintaining society as it is rather than as a source of major change.

Functionalist theory has often been criticized because of its circularity. It assumes that what exists must be in some way necessary for the working of the social system, but there is no way to verify independently whether some feature of the media is necessary or not. What part the media actually play and how it is performed vary according to the type of society. An essentially functionalist theory of 'media dependency' formulated by DeFleur and Ball Rokeach (1989) treats the relative dependency of audiences on mass media sources (compared with other information sources) as a

theories

variable to be empirically determined. The theory posits that the more an audience is reliant on the mass media for information *and* the more a society is in a state of crisis or instability, then the more power the media are likely to have (or be credited with).

Despite the many difficulties, a functional approach still seems useful for some purposes of description. It offers a language for discussing the relations between mass media and society and a set of concepts that have proved hard to escape from or to replace. This terminology has the advantage of being to a large extent shared by mass communicators themselves and by their audiences and being widely understood. A definition of media function as an explicit task, purpose or motive (whether for communicators or receivers) seems to provide most common ground and to avoid the worst of the conceptual difficulties noted above. Media function can refer both to more or less objective tasks of the media (such as news or editorializing) and to purposes or utilities as perceived by a media user (such as being informed or entertained).

Specifying the social functions of media

The main functions of communication in society, according to Lasswell (1948), were surveillance of the environment, correlation of the parts of the society in responding to its environment and the transmission of the cultural heritage. Wright (1960) developed this basic scheme to describe many of the effects of the media and added 'entertainment' as a fourth key media function. This may be part of the transmitted culture but it has another aspect – that of providing individual reward, relaxation and reduction of tension, which makes it easier for people to cope with real-life problems and for societies to avoid breakdown (Mendelsohn, 1966). With the addition of a fifth item – mobilization, designed to reflect the widespread application of mass communication to political and commercial propaganda – we can name the following set of basic ideas about media tasks (= functions) in society:

- **Information**
  - providing information about events and conditions in society and the world;
  - indicating relations of power;
  - facilitating innovation, adaptation and progress.
- **Correlation**
  - explaining, interpreting and commenting on the meaning of events and information;
  - providing support for established authority and norms;
  - socializing;

- co-ordinating separate activities;
- consensus building;
- setting orders of priority and signalling relative status.

- **Continuity**
  - expressing the dominant culture and recognizing subcultures and new cultural developments;
  - forging and maintaining commonality of values.

- **Entertainment**
  - providing amusement, diversion and the means of relaxation;
  - reducing social tension.

- **Mobilization**
  - campaigning for societal objectives in the sphere of politics, war, economic development, work and sometimes religion.

We cannot give any general rank order to these items, nor say anything about their relative frequency of occurrence. The correspondence between function (or purpose) and precise content is not exact, since one function overlaps with another, and the same content can serve different functions. The set of statements refers to functions for society and needs to be reformulated in order to take account of the perspective of the individual user of mass media, as in '**uses and gratifications**' theory and research (see Chapter 16).

The social integration function of media

Functionalist theory is really only useful for considering questions of social integration. Without integration there can be no agreement on goals and means and no co-ordinated activity to achieve them. Both 'functional' and 'normative' integration, according to the meanings noted above (page 71), are indispensable. However, in a complex society there will be a number of different ways for groups to achieve sufficient control and consensus, and mass media constitute only one institution among several that contribute towards this end.

Media tend to support the values not only of society as a whole but also of segments within it, defined in various ways. For instance, local community media have consistently been portrayed, following the work of Janowitz (1952), as helping to promote identity and social organization within the anonymity of large urban societies (Stamm, 1985). They generally support the values of the community and the maintenance of a local order (Jackson, 1971; Cox and Morgan, 1973; Murphy, 1976). These tendencies are generally attributed to a wish to please, or at least not offend, their potential audiences.

An example of a selective integration function was offered by Ferguson (1983), who

Box 4.6 Functionalist theory of media

Mass media are essential to society for:

- Integration and co-operation
- Order, control and stability
- Adaptation to change
- Mobilization
- Management of tension
- Continuity of culture and values

drew an analogy between Durkheim's concept of a religious cult and the relationship between magazines and their female readers. This involves the notion of a 'cult of femininity', of which the editors are the 'priestesses' and readers the 'devotees'. The women's magazine press is the mainstay of this cult, giving it legitimacy, defining norms, giving shape and cementing a common culture based on the importance of gender and female solidarity. Radway (1984) found a somewhat similar media function for women readers of romance fiction. This sub-theory can be extended to a variety of subcultural audiences especially perhaps in respect of music (Lull, 1992).

Studies of content have often found that large-audience media tend to be conformist and supportive rather than critical of dominant values. This support takes several forms, including: avoidance of fundamental criticism of key institutions such as business, the justice system and democratic politics; giving differential access to the 'social top'; the media also symbolically rewarding those who succeed according to the approved paths of virtue and hard work, and symbolically punishing those who fail or deviate. Media are generally found to give disproportionate attention either to those who exemplify the aspirations of the majority or to those who reject the values of society, usually by way of crime or 'extremist' politics.

There is evidence from audience research to show that one motivation for media use by individuals is to reinforce attachment to society and its values, or at least to find security and reassurance (Katz et al., 1973). Dayan and Katz (1992) argue that major social occasions portrayed on television (public or state ceremonies, major sporting events) and often drawing huge audiences world-wide help to provide otherwise missing social cement. One of the effects of what they call media events is to confer status on leading figures and issues in society. Another is on social relations: 'With almost every event, we have seen *communitas and camaraderie* emerge from normally atomized – and sometimes deeply divided – societies' (1992: 214).

In the light of these observations, it is not so surprising that research on effects has failed to lend much support to the proposition that mass media, for all their attention to crime, sensation, violence and deviant happenings, are a significant cause of social, or even individual, crime and disorganization. The more one holds to a functionalist theory of media, the less logical it is to expect socially disintegrative effects.

Political-economic theory identifies a socially critical approach that focuses primarily on the relation between the economic structure and dynamics of media industries and the ideological content of media. It directs research attention to the empirical analysis of the structure of ownership and control of media and to the way media market forces operate. From this point of view, the media institution has to be considered as part of the economic system, with close links to the political system. The predominant character of what the media produce can be largely accounted for by the exchange value of different kinds of content, under conditions of pressure to expand markets, and by the underlying economic interests of owners and decision-makers (Garnham, 1979). These interests relate to the need for profit from media operations and to the relative profitability of other branches of commerce as a result of monopolistic tendencies and processes of vertical and horizontal integration (such as into or from oil, paper, telecommunications, leisure, tourism and property).

The consequences are to be observed in the reduction of independent media sources, concentration on the largest markets, avoidance of risks, and reduced investment in less profitable media tasks (such as investigative reporting and documentary film-making). We also find neglect of smaller and poorer sectors of the potential audience and often a politically unbalanced range of news media. The effects of economic forces are not random, but (according to Murdock and Golding)

> work consistently to exclude those voices lacking economic power or resources . . . the underlying logic of cost operates systematically, consolidating the position of groups already established in the main mass-media markets and excluding those groups who lack the capital base required for successful entry. Thus the voices which survive will largely belong to those least likely to criticize the prevailing distribution of wealth and power. Conversely, those most likely to challenge these arrangements are unable to publicize their dissent or opposition because they cannot command resources needed for effective communication to a broad audience (1977: 37).

The main strength of the approach lies in its capacity for making empirically testable propositions about market determinations, although the latter are so numerous and complex that empirical demonstration is not easy. While the approach centres on media activity as an economic process leading to the commodity (the media product or content), there is a variant of the political-economic approach that suggests that the primary product of the media is really *audience*. This refers to the fact that they deliver audience attention to advertisers and shape the behaviour of media publics in certain distinctive ways (Smythe, 1977). What commercial media sell to their clients is a certain more or less guaranteed number of potential customers according to a market-relevant profile. While Marxism has been the main inspiration for the political-economic analysis of media, the approach has a much wider base in the critical analysis of media structure and economics. The tools for this are widely available in sociology, political science and economics. (See, for example, Hirsch and Gordon,

1975; Curran, 1986; Bagdikian, 1988; Ferguson, 1990; Curran and Seaton, 1997, and many other publications.)

The relevance of political-economic theory has been greatly increased by several trends in media business and technology (perhaps also enhanced by the fall from grace of a strictly Marxist analysis). First, there has been a growth in media concentration world-wide, with more and more power of ownership being concentrated in fewer hands and with tendencies for mergers between electronic hardware and software industries (Murdock, 1990). Secondly, there has been a growing global 'information economy' (Melody, 1990; Sussman, 1997), involving an increasing convergence between telecommunication and broadcasting. Thirdly, there has been a decline in the public sector of mass media and in direct public control of telecommunication (especially in Western Europe), under the banner of 'deregulation', 'privatization' or 'liberalization' (Siune and Truetzschler, 1992; McQuail and Siune, 1998). The essential propositions of political-economic theory have not changed since earlier times, but the scope for application is much wider.

Box 4.7   Critical political-economic theory

- Economic control and logic is determinant
- Media structure tends towards concentration
- Global integration of media develops
- Contents and audiences are commodified
- Diversity decreases
- Opposition and alternative voices are marginalized
- Public interest in communication is subordinated to private interests

---

Golding and Murdock (1996) indicate several tasks for the application of theory of political economy. One has to do with the impact of forms of ownership and commercial strategies (both state and commercial) on cultural production. They argue that the increasing share of large corporations in cultural production leads to a further reduction of the 'public sphere' (the open space for rational political discourse between economy and state; Garnham, 1986) and more pressure on the autonomy of those who work within the media industries. A second task is to shed light on the political economy of cultural consumption, with particular reference to material and cultural barriers to benefits from the communication 'abundance' of our time and to the potentially widening information 'gaps' between richer and poorer (see also Golding, 1990).

MEDIA–SOCIETY THEORY 5: MODERNIZATION AND DEVELOPMENT

The present overview of theory would be incomplete without reference to a body of thinking and research that flourished in the years after the Second World War. This

approach was based on the belief that mass communication could be a potent instrument in world economic and social development. The media could effectively spread the message of modernity and help transfer the institutions and practices of democratic politics and market economics to economically backward and socially traditional nations of the world, especially those outside the control of the communist sphere of influence. The global development project cannot really be understood outside the context of the Cold War, but it had several independent streams. Amongst these was a genuine wish to improve conditions in the 'underdeveloped world' and a belief in the power of mass communication to teach and to lead by example and by the stimulation of consumer demand for industrial goods.

Theory of media and development has several variants, but most assume the superiority of modern (that is, secular, materialist, Western, individualist, etc.) ways and of individual motivation as the key to change. People need to want to 'get on' (McLelland, 1961; Hagen, 1962). The contribution of mass media can take several forms. They can help to promote the diffusion and adoption of many technical and social innovations that are essential to modernization (Rogers, 1962, 1976; Rogers and Shoemaker, 1973). They can teach literacy and other essential skills and techniques. They can encourage a 'state of mind' favourable to modernity (Lerner, 1958), especially the possibility to imagine an alternative way of life. Lerner described the Western-inspired media as 'mobility multipliers'. Thirdly, mass communication was seen as essential to the development of national unity in new nations (ex-colonies) (Pye, 1963) and of participant democratic politics, especially by way of elections.

Much of this thinking has now been set aside or re-evaluated, in the light of very limited success in terms of the original development goals and increasing doubts about the underlying purpose (Hamelink, 1983; Schiller, 1989; Tomlinson, 1991). The model of media influence deployed was very much a mechanistic transmission model that did not take account of the realities of social context. Rogers (1976) has described the 'passing of a dominant paradigm' and suggested an alternative, based on participation and convergence. In general, the much greater significance of local power structures, traditional values and economic constraints, relative to what mass communication can achieve, has been recognized. Media remain one tool for implementing change in

---

Box 4.8 Mass media and development

Mass media serve as agents of development by:

- Disseminating technical know-how
- Encouraging individual change and mobility
- Spreading democracy (= elections)
- Promoting consumer demand
- Aiding literacy, education, health, population control, etc.

'developing' countries, but they are severely limited by their dependence on infra-structure and by their high costs. They are also associated in a negative way with cultural imperialism and dependancy (see Chapter 10).

MEDIA–SOCIETY THEORY 6: COMMUNICATION TECHNOLOGY DETERMINISM

There is a long and still active tradition of searching for links between the dominant communication technology of an age and key features of society, bearing on all three of the issues outlined (power, integration and change). To label this body of thinking 'determinist' does not do justice to the many differences and nuances, but there is a common element of 'media-centredness' (see page 88). There is also a tendency to concentrate on the potential for (or bias towards) social change of a particular communication technology and to subordinate other variables (Schement and Curtis, 1995). Otherwise, there may be little in common between the theories.

Any history of communication (as of other) technologies testifies to the accelerating pace of invention and of material potential as an outcome, and some theorists are inclined to identify distinct phases. Rogers (1986), for instance, locates turning points at the invention of writing, the beginning of printing in the 15th century, the mid-19th century start to the telecommunication era, and the age of interactive communication beginning in 1946 with the invention of the mainframe computer. Schement and Curtis (1995) provide us with a detailed 'timeline' of communication technology inventions, which they classify according to their being either 'conceptual/institutional' (such as writing) or 'devices for acquisition and storage' (such as paper and printing), or being related to processing and distribution (such as computers and satellites). History shows several apparent trends but especially a shift over time in the direction of more speed, greater dispersion, wider reach and greater flexibility. They underline the capacity for communication more readily to cross barriers of time and space.

The Toronto School

The first significant theorist in this tradition seems to have been the Canadian economic historian H.M. Innis, who founded the '**Toronto School**' of thinking about the media in the period after the Second World War. Innis (1950, 1951) attributed the characteristic features of successive ancient civilizations to the prevailing and dominant modes of communication, each of which will have its own 'bias' in terms of societal form. For example, he regarded the change from stone to papyrus as causing a shift from royal to priestly power. In ancient Greece, an oral tradition and a flexible

alphabet favoured inventiveness and diversity and prevented the emergence of a priesthood with a monopoly over education. The foundation and endurance of the Roman empire was assisted by a culture of writing and documents on which legal-bureaucratic institutions, capable of administering distant provinces, could be based. Printing, in its turn, challenged the bureaucratic monopoly of power and encouraged both individualism and nationalism.

There are two main organizing principles in Innis's work. First, as in the economic sphere, communication leads over time to monopolization by a group or a class of the means of production and distribution of knowledge. In turn this produces a disequilibrium that either impedes changes or leads to the competitive emergence of other forms of communication, which tend to restore equilibrium. This can also be taken to mean that new communication technologies undermine old bases of social power. Secondly, the most important dimensions of empire are *space* and *time,* and some means of communication are more suitable for one than for the other (this is the main so-called bias of communication). Thus, empires can persist either through time (such as ancient Egypt) or extensively in space (such as Rome), depending on the dominant form of communication.

McLuhan's (1962) developments of the theory offered new insights into the consequences of the rise of print media (see also Eisenstein, 1978), although his main purpose of explaining the significance of electronic media for human experience has not really been fulfilled (McLuhan, 1964) (see also Chapter 5). Of printing, McLuhan wrote: 'the typographic extension of man brought in nationalism, industrialism and mass markets and universal literacy and education'.

Technology and ideology

The sociologist Gouldner (1976) interpreted key changes in modern political history in terms of communication technology. He connects the rise of 'ideology', defined as a special form of rational discourse, to printing and the newspaper, on the grounds that (in the 18th and 19th centuries) these stimulated a supply of interpretation and ideas (ideology). He then portrays the later media of radio, film and television as having led to a decline of ideology because of the shift from 'conceptual to iconic symbolism',

---

Box 4.9   Media technological determinism (pre-new technology)

- Communication technology is fundamental to society
- Each technology has a bias to particular communication forms, contents and uses
- The sequence of invention and application of communication technology influences social change
- Communication revolutions lead to social revolutions

revealing a split between the 'cultural apparatus' (the intelligentsia), which produces ideology, and the 'consciousness industry', which controls the new mass public. This anticipates a continuing 'decline in ideology' as a result of the new computer-based networks of information (see also pages 120–4).

An interactive alternative

Most informed observers are now wary of single-factor explanations of social change and do not really believe in direct mechanistic effects from new technology. Effects occur only when inventions are taken up, developed and applied, usually to existing uses at first, then with a great extension and change of use according to the capacity of the technology and the needs of a society (see pages 120–4). Development is always shaped by the social and cultural context. It no longer makes sense to think in terms of a single dominant medium with some unique properties. This may have been justifiable in the case of the book or, in some respects, later, the telegraph and telephone. At present, very many different new media forms coexist with many of the 'old' media, none of which has disappeared. At the same time, the argument that media are converging and linking to comprise an all-encompassing network has considerable force and implications (Neuman, 1991). It may also be true that new media forms can have a particular social or cultural 'bias' (see Chapter 6) which makes certain effects more likely. These possibilities are discussed in the following section.

MEDIA–SOCIETY THEORY 7: THE INFORMATION SOCIETY

There has, if anything, been even more agreement on the impact of the 'new technology' on society, for good or ill. The assumption of a revolutionary social transition is, even so, not without its critics (for example, Leiss, 1989; Ferguson, 1992). Ferguson (1986) treats this 'neo-technological determinism' as a *belief system* which now tends to operate as a self-fulfilling prophecy. The term 'communications revolution', along with the term **'information society'**, has almost come to be accepted as an objective description of our time and of the type of society which is emerging. It is hard to escape from the deterministic element in much current thinking about the 'new media', with societal effects again being attributed to intrinsic features of technology. Rogers, who sees himself as a 'soft technological determinist', views 'technology along with other factors, as causes of change' (1986: 9) and

identifies three crucial features of the new technology. These are: their interactivity, their individualized, demassified nature and the 'asynchronous nature of the new communication systems' (they are no longer time-bound). Most commentators seem to agree on the relevance of these points, if not about the strength of influence (see Chapter 6).

The general consensus about the significance of changes occurring in communication technology is not accompanied by unanimity about the social consequences. Neuman's views, cited above, represent an informed optimism about the benefits which will follow from new communication technology if they are allowed to develop freely (see also Pool, 1983). These views are a decisive rejection of the gloomy prophecies of mass society theory (see above), in which new and more powerful mass media were represented as tools for a greater degree of subordination of the masses by powerful elites in societies characterized by homogeneity, privatization, loneliness and conformity. The concept of an information society is discussed more fully in Chapter 6, which deals with new media developments. However, certain main points are summarized in Box 4.10.

Box 4.10   Information society theory

New media technology leads to an information society, characterized by:

- Predominance of information work
- Great volume of information flow
- Interactivity of relations
- Integration and convergence of activities
- Growth and Interconnection of networks
- Globalizing tendencies
- Postmodern culture

CONFLICT VERSUS CONSENSUS, AND MEDIA-CENTRIC VERSUS SOCIETY-CENTRIC APPROACHES

These theoretical perspectives on the relation between media and society are diverse in several respects, emphasizing different causes and types of change and pointing to different paths into the future. They cannot all be reconciled, since they represent alternative philosophical positions and opposed methodological preferences. Nevertheless, we can make sense of them in terms of two main dimensions of approach: one contrasting a critical with a consensual view of society; another focusing on the difference between a 'media-centric' and a 'society-centric' view. In general, the critical approach implies a view of society as in a continual state of conflict or power struggle

theories

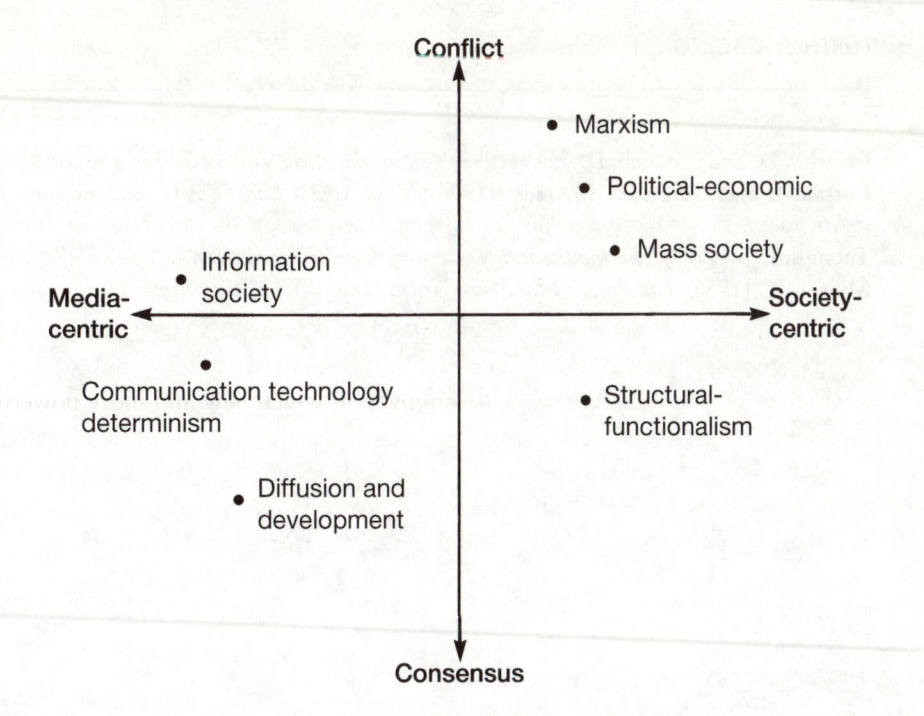

Conflict

• Marxism

• Political-economic

• Mass society

Media-
centric

Society-
centric

• Information
society

• Communication technology
determinism

• Structural-
functionalism

• Diffusion and
development

Consensus

FIGURE 4.5   An overview of theories of media and society: the main choices are between conflict and consensus and between media as moulder and media as mirror of society

between (mainly) 'haves' and 'have-nots'. By contrast, the consensual approach implies a pluralistic view of society as governed by forces of equilibrium and the hidden hand of the market and leading to the best that can be hoped for.

The second dimension is more self-explanatory, representing the difference between those who see media technology (and content) as primary movers in social change and those who consider the roots of change to lie with the society. Rosengren (1983) has drawn attention to a somewhat similar mapping of differences in sociological theory (Burrell and Morgan, 1979), which also identified four alternative paradigms on much the same lines as in Figure 4.5.

The seven types of theory discussed in this chapter are given an approximate location in terms of the two dimensions. The 'map' is really incomplete without some of the theory relating to culture that will be discussed in Chapter 5, but it gives some idea of the general structure of thinking about mass media and society. The picture is complicated by the fact that some theories are expressed in optimistic and others in pessimistic terms. This applies especially to thinking about new information technology. Both the predicted interconnectedness and the globalization of society that are seen to develop have been viewed as either positive or negative, depending on outlook. The general division of theory into a dominant paradigm and an alternative/critical view (see pages 45–52) lies at the root of this ambivalence and inconsistency.

Crowley, D. and Mitchell, D. (eds) (1993) *Communication Theory Today*. Cambridge: Polity.

Curran, J. and Gurevitch, M. (eds) (1996) *Mass Media and Society*, 2nd Edition. London: Arnold.

Thompson, J. (1995) *The Media and Modernity*. Cambridge: Polity.

Mills, C.W. (1956) *The Power Elite*. New York: Oxford University Press.

mass communication and culture

This chapter sets out to explore the more 'cultural' dimensions of the theories already discussed in Chapter 4 and to introduce some additional perspectives. The general framework of 'mediation' (see pages 64–6) remains relevant, but here the emphasis shifts to *what* is mediated (the particular meanings) and to the process by which meaning is given and taken (sometimes referred to as 'signification'). Since the earlier days of mass communication research, a distinctive 'culturalist' perspective on mass media has been developing, especially under the influence of the humanities (literature, linguistics, philosophy), as distinct from the more social scientific emphasis of 'mainstream' communication science. At some points, or on some issues, the two traditions have merged, although there remain substantial differences of thinking and method. This book, and this chapter, is written primarily from a social scientific perspective, but it aims also to benefit from some of the insights and ideas of the 'culturalists'.

It is not easy to give a simple definition of the essence of their approach, but it has generally to do with the notion of a **text** and with the construction and taking of meaning from texts. Fiske (1989: 1) defines culture as 'the constant process of producing meanings of and from our social experience'. This view of culture as an ongoing process contrasts with older versions equating culture with fixed patterns or with the *results of* cultural practices, especially valued cultural artefacts.

The taking of meaning involves the 'reading' of texts, a term which encompasses a wide range of symbolically encoded items, including commodities, clothes, language and structured social practices, as well as the more conventional notion of all kinds of media products (television programmes, books, songs, films, etc.). The culturalist approach takes in all aspects of the production, the forms and the reception of texts in this sense and the discourses that surround them. While mass media necessarily fall within the range of cultural studies, the latter has a much wider range of reference, and there is only a limited overlap of issues and theory.

COMMUNICATION AND CULTURE

James Carey (1975) proposed an alternative to the dominant view of communication as *transmission* in the form of a 'ritual' model (see page 53), and he has also advocated an approach to communication and society in which culture is allotted a more central place. 'Social life is more than power and trade . . . it also includes the sharing of aesthetic experience, religious ideas, personal values and sentiments, and intellectual notions – a ritual order' (Carey, 1988: 34). Accordingly, he defined communication as 'a symbolic process whereby reality is produced, maintained, repaired and transformed' (1988: 23).

theories

In order to take the question of the relation between *mass* communication and culture in this sense further, we need to be more precise about what presents itself as an object of study. This is made difficult by the many senses in which the term 'culture' is used, itself a reflection of the complexity of the phenomenon. Culture is defined by Carey as a *process*, but it can also refer to some *shared attribute* of a human group (such as their physical environment, tools, religion, customs and practices, or their whole way of life). Culture also can refer to *texts and symbolic artefacts* that are encoded with particular meanings by and for people with particular cultural identifications.

Towards defining culture

If we extract essential points from these different usages, it seems that culture must have all of the following attributes. It is something collective and shared with others (there is no purely individual culture). It must have some symbolic form of expression, whether intended as such or not; it has some pattern, order or regularity, and therefore some evaluative dimensions (if only degree of conformity to a culturally prescribed pattern). There is (or has been) a dynamic continuity over time (culture lives and changes, has a history and potentially a future). Perhaps the most general and essential attribute of culture is communication, since cultures could not develop, survive, extend and generally succeed without communication. Finally, in order to study culture we need to be able to recognize and locate it, and essentially there are three places to look: in people, in things (texts, artefacts) and in human practices (socially patterned behaviours).

There are some obvious implications for the study of mass communication, since every aspect of the production and use of mass media has a cultural dimension. We can focus on *people* as producers of culturally meaningful media texts, or people as 'readers of texts', from which they take cultural meanings, with implications for the rest of social life. We can focus on the texts and artefacts themselves (films, books, newspaper articles) and on their symbolic forms and possible meanings. We may want to study the *practices* of makers of media products or of *users* of the media. Media audience composition and behaviour (practices around the choice and use of media) are always culturally patterned, before, after and during the media experience.

Box 5.1   Characteristics of culture

- Collectively formed and held
- Open to symbolic expression
- Ordered and differentially valued
- Systematically patterned
- Dynamic and changing
- Communicable over time and space

This broad terrain can be narrowed down by identifying some of the main questions and theoretical issues. Historically, the first 'cultural' question on the agenda of media theory was that of the character of the new *mass culture* made possible by mass communication. It was usually posed in respect of the content (cultural texts), but it extended to the question of the *practice of* mass media use. It nearly always involved a view of *people* as a mass – the new form of social collectivity, which was otherwise often perceived as without any other culture of its own.

The rise of a distinctive 'media culture' has also stimulated rethinking about the nature of 'popular culture', which has now to be seen not just as a cheap alternative, mass-produced for mass consumption, but as a vital new branch of cultural creativity and enjoyment (Schudson, 1991; McGuigan, 1992). The issue of mass culture also stimulated the rise of *critical cultural theory*, which, among other things, has been extended to consider issues of *gender* and of *subculture* in relation to mass communication.

A second key theme, following the line opened up in Chapter 3, relates to the potential consequences of the new technologies themselves for the experience of meaning in the emerging modern world, according to the 'mediation' perspective outlined above. Communication technology has many implications for the way we may come to know our own social world and our place in it.

Thirdly, there are political-economic aspects of the organized production of culture represented by mass media industries. We have come to think of the media as a 'consciousness industry', driven by economic logic as well as by cultural changes. An important aspect is the *commodification* of culture in the form of the 'software' produced by and for communication 'hardware' that is sold and exchanged in enlarging markets. Another consequence of this (and of technology) has been the *internationalization* of production and distribution.

The typical culture (in the sense of media texts) produced by the major media industries is often globalized in form, even when it appears in the local or national variants and languages. This has led to theory and research concerning the consequences for *cultural identity* and for the autonomy and distinctiveness of pre-existing ways of life and belief systems. Similar questions of cultural identity and autonomy

---

Box 5.2   Issues for media cultural theory

- Mass culture and popular culture
- Communication technology effects
- Commodification of culture
- Globalization
- Cultural identity
- Gender and subculture

---

also arise at the level of subcultures and extend to cover the way media use and reception are integrated into and adapted according to the immediate lived cultural and social experience.

THE BEGINNINGS: THE FRANKFURT SCHOOL AND CRITICAL THEORY

A socially based critical concern with the rise of mass culture goes back at least to the mid-19th century and in the mid-20th century was represented in England in the work of F.R. Leavis and his followers in the field of social literary criticism. The latter movement has also been (indirectly) influential in the rise of more radical (and populist) critical theory as expressed in the work of Richard Hoggart, Raymond Williams and Stuart Hall. The continuing thrust of these critics has been to attack the commercial roots of cultural 'debasement' and to speak up for the working-class consumer of mass culture as the victim (and not only that) rather than the villain of the story. The initial aim was to redeem the people on whose supposedly 'low tastes' the presumed low quality of mass culture was often blamed. Since then, 'mass culture' itself has largely been rescued from the stigma of low quality, although in the course of this the original concept of mass culture has been largely abandoned.

For the wider development of ideas about mass communication and the character of 'media culture', within an internationalized framework, the various national debates about cultural quality have probably been less influential than a set of ideas, owing much to Marxist thinking, which developed and diffused in the post-war years. The term 'critical theory' serves to refer to this long and diverse tradition which owes its origins to the work of a group of post-1933 *émigré* scholars from the Marxist School of Applied Social Research in Frankfurt. The most important members of the group were Max Horkheimer and Theodor Adorno, but others, including Leo Lowenthal, Herbert Marcuse and Walter Benjamin, played an important role (see Jay, 1973; Hardt, 1991).

The school had been established originally to examine the apparent failure of revolutionary social change as predicted by Marx. In explanation of this failure they looked to the capacity of the 'superstructure' (especially ideas and ideology represented in the mass media) to subvert material and historical forces of economic change (and also the promise of the Enlightenment). History (as interpreted by Marx) seemed to have 'gone wrong', because ideologies of the dominant class had come to condition the economic base, especially by promoting a 'false consciousness' among the working masses and helping to assimilate them to capitalist society. The universal and commercialized mass culture was seen as one important means by which this success for monopoly capital had been achieved. The whole process of mass production of goods, services and ideas had more or less completely sold the system of capitalism, along with its devotion to technological rationality, consumerism, short-term gratification and the myth of the 'classless' society.

The *commodity* is the main instrument of this process since it appeared that both art and oppositional culture could be marketed for profit at the cost of losing critical power. Marcuse later (1964) gave the description 'one-dimensional' to the mass consumption society founded on commerce, advertising and spurious egalitarianism. The media and the 'culture industry' as a whole were deeply implicated in this critique. Many of these ideas were launched during the 1940s by Adorno and Horkheimer (1972, in translation), which contained a sharp and pessimistic attack on mass culture. This was criticized for its uniformity, worship of technique, monotony, escapism and production of false needs, its reduction of individuals to customers and the removal of all ideological choice (see Hardt, 1991: 140). According to Shils (1957), the very jaundiced Frankfurt School view of mass culture was not only anti-capitalist but also anti-American and mainly reflected the first impact of modern mass media on a group of displaced European intellectuals. In several respects, the critique of mass culture outlined is very close to that found in different versions of the then contemporary mass society theory.

The emphasis in critical theory on the culture of the mass media as a powerful influence for preventing fundamental change has lived on in several different lines of theory. In general, the 'consciousness industry' has been an object of sustained critical attention. More particularly, a concept of cultural **commodification** was developed as a tool for examining the **commercialization** of culture and the working of advertising, while a broader notion of 'hegemony' evolved to account for the effects of media on consciousness.

The theory of commodification originates in Marx's *Grundrisse*, in which he noted that objects are commodified by acquiring an exchange value, instead of having merely an intrinsic use value. In the same way, cultural products (in the form of images, ideas and symbols) are produced and sold in media markets as commodities. These can be exchanged by consumers for psychic satisfactions, amusement and illusory notions of our place in the world, often resulting in the obscuration of the real structure of society and our subordination in it (false consciousness). This is an ideological process largely conducted via our dependence on commercial mass media. The theory of commodification applies especially well to the interpretation of commercial advertising (Williamson, 1978), but it has a wider reference. In general, the more art and culture are commodified, the more they lose any critical potential, and intrinsic value distinctions are replaced by or equated with market criteria of cost and demand.

HEGEMONY

The concept of 'hegemony', borrowed by critical theorists from Gramsci's (1971) term for a ruling ideology, helps to bring together a lot of different ideas about how the culture of media (news, entertainment, fiction) helps to maintain the class-divided and

class-dominated society. Hegemony refers to a loosely interrelated set of ruling ideas permeating a society, but in such a way as to make the established order of power and values appear natural, taken-for-granted and commonsensical. A ruling ideology is not imposed but appears to exist by virtue of an unquestioned consensus. Hegemony tends to define unacceptable opposition to the status quo as dissident and deviant. In effect, hegemony is a constantly reasserted definition of a social situation, by way of discourse rather than political or economic power, which becomes real in its consequences (Hall, 1982). The mass media do not define reality on their own but give preferential access to the definitions of those in authority. This is a 'culturalist' correlate of the political-economy theory of control described in Chapter 4.

Ideology, in the form of a distorted definition of reality or, in the words of Althusser (1971), as 'the imaginary relationships of individuals to their real conditions of existence', is not dominant in the sense of being imposed by force by a ruling class. But it is an all-pervasive and deliberate cultural influence that serves to interpret experience of reality in a covert but consistent manner. According to Hall:

> That notion of dominance which meant the direct imposition of one framework, by overt force or ideological compulsion, on a subordinate class, was not sophisticated enough to match the complexities of the case. One had also to see that dominance was accomplished at the unconscious as well as the conscious level: to see it as a property of the system of relations involved, rather than as the overt and intentional biases of individuals in the very activity of regulation and exclusion which functioned through language and discourse. (1982: 95)

This approach directs attention at the way the relationships of capitalism have to be reproduced and legitimized according to the more or less voluntary consent of the working class itself. The tools for analysing these processes have been provided by developments in semiological and structural analysis which offer methods for the exposing of covert and underlying structures of meaning.

LATER DEVELOPMENTS OF CRITICAL CULTURAL THEORY: THE BIRMINGHAM SCHOOL

Critical cultural theory has now extended well beyond its early concerns with ideological domination, although in one way or another the study of ideology in media culture remains central. So does the significance of media culture for the experience of particular groups in society such as youth, the working class, ethnic minorities and other marginal categories. Theory posits a drive towards the assimilation and subordination of potentially deviant or oppositional elements in society. Research carried out, in particular, at the Centre for Contemporary Cultural Studies at the University of

Birmingham during the 1970s led to the identification of the '**Birmingham School**' as the main locus for the approach.

The person most associated with the work of this school, Stuart Hall, has written that the cultural studies approach:

> stands opposed to the residual and merely reflective role assigned to the "cultural". In its different ways it conceptualizes culture as interwoven with all social practices; and those practices, in turn, as a common form of human activity. . . . It is opposed to the base–superstructure way of formulating the relationship between ideal and material forces, especially where the base is defined by the determination by the "economic" in any simple sense. . . . It defines "culture" as both the means and values which arise amongst distinctive social groups and classes, on the basis of their given historical conditions and relationship, through which they "handle" and respond to the conditions of existence . . . (quoted in Gurevitch et al., 1982: 267)

The social-cultural approach seeks to attend to both messages and public, aiming to account for patterns of choice and response in relation to the media by a careful and critically directed understanding of the actual social experience of subgroups within society. The whole enterprise has also been informed by an appreciation of the efforts of power-holders to manage the recurrent crises of legitimacy and economic failure held to be endemic in industrial capitalist society (Hall et al., 1978).

The critical approach associated with the Birmingham School was also responsible for an important shift from the question of ideology embedded in media texts to the question of how this ideology might be 'read' by its audience. Stuart Hall (1980) proposed a model of '*encoding–decoding* media discourse' which represented the media text as located between its producers, who framed meaning in a certain way, and its audience, who 'decoded' the meaning according to their rather different social situations and frames of interpretation (see pages 56–7).

Drawing on the political sociology of Parkin (1972), Hall suggested that there are three basic codes in circulation – one of dominant meanings associated with power, a second 'negotiated' code, which is essentially the code of the media in their role as neutral and professional carriers of information. There is a third, 'oppositional', code, which is available to those who choose, or who are led by circumstances, to view messages about reality differently and can 'read between the lines' of official versions of events. This simple model recognizes that ideology as *sent* is not the same as ideology as *taken*. While there may be so-called 'preferred' readings offered from above, they can either be treated with some distance and subjected to objective analysis (as they may be by journalists) or be perceived as 'propaganda' and resisted or subverted accordingly.

These ideas proved a considerable stimulus to rethinking the theory of ideology and of false consciousness. They led to research on the potential for 'differential decoding' (for example, Morley, 1980), with a view, especially, to finding evidence of working-class resistance to dominant media messages. The direct results were meagre in this

respect, but indirectly the theory was very effective in 're-empowering' the audience and returning some optimism to the study of media and culture. It also led to a wider view of the social and cultural influences which mediate the experience of the media, especially ethnicity, gender and 'everyday life' (Morley, 1986, 1992). Latterly Morley (1997) has distanced himself from some interpretations of his (and others') work in this vein that have over-emphasized the degree of differential and oppositional reading of media texts. He criticizes those who presume without evidence that 'forms of interpretive resistance are more widespread than subordination, or the reproduction of dominant meanings' (page 124).

GENDER AND THE MASS MEDIA

One area where the theory of differential cultural reading of media texts has made important advances, in collaboration with feminist research, is in relation to gender. While communication studies, even of the radical critical tendency, have long seemed to be largely 'gender-blind' (perhaps more a matter of unwillingness to see), one can now justifiably speak of a 'cultural feminist media studies project' (van Zoonen, 1991, 1994). This goes far deeper and wider than the original limited agenda of matters such as the under-representation of women in media and the stereotyping and sex-role socialization which was and still is a feature of much media content. Current concerns also go beyond issues of pornographic media contents which matter to feminists (and others) not only because they are offensive and symbolically degrading but because they might be a stimulus to rape and violence. The amount of gender-related media research is now very large and, although in part it follows lines of theory pioneered with reference to social class and race, it has several other dimensions. These include an attention to Freudian psychoanalytic theory following the ideas of Jacques Lacan and Nancy Chodorov. The focus was primarily on the role of gender in 'positioning' the spectator in relation to images (film, television, photographic) of male and female. Another line of research focused on the part played by the media in transmitting a patriarchal ideology concerning the place of women in society. There are now many connections with the wider field of feminist studies (Long, 1991; Kaplan, 1992).

According to van Zoonen (1994) most of the earlier gender relevant media research, including psychoanalytic theory, implicitly at least, followed the transmission model of effect, based on the direct reaction of a receiver to a message stimulus (see page 52). She suggests that there is now emerging a new paradigm, essentially culturalist in character, which offers a better way of understanding how the media are related to gender. At the core of the new approach is the idea of 'gender as discourse, a set of overlapping and sometimes contradictory cultural descriptions and prescriptions

referring to sexual difference' (1994: 40). The second key basis is an emphasis on the active *construction* of meanings and identities by 'readers' of media texts. In general the new perspective for feminist media research, according to van Zoonen, addresses the following main questions: How are discourses of gender encoded in media texts? How do audiences use and interpret gendered media texts? How does audience reception contribute to the construction of gender at the level of individual identity?

The question of gender touches almost every aspect of the media–culture relationship. Most central is probably the question of gender definition. Van Zoonen (1991: 45) writes that the meaning of gender 'is never given but varies according to specific cultural and historical settings . . . and is subject to ongoing discursive struggle and negotiation'. Partly at issue is how gender differences and distinctiveness are signified (see Goffman, 1976). Another general aspect of the struggle is over the differential value attaching to masculinity and to femininity. Feminist perspectives on mass communication open up numerous lines of analysis, often largely neglected in the past (Rakow, 1986; Dervin, 1987). One concerns the fact that many media texts are deeply and persistently *gendered* in the way they have been encoded, usually according to a view of the anticipated audience. Fiske (1987) provides extensive evidence of what 'gendered television' means, from detailed deconstructions of numerous popular television programmes. A prominent example in his and other work is that of the *soap-opera genre* (see Brown, 1990), which may arguably be regarded as following a 'feminine aesthetic'. According to Fiske (1987: 197), soap operas 'keep patriarchy under constant interrogation, they legitimate feminine values and thus produce self-esteem for the women who live by them. They provide, in short, the means for a feminine culture . . . in constant struggle to establish and extend itself within and against a dominant patriarchy'. Livingstone (1991) refers to the theory that the typical structure of soap operas parallels the typical routine of a housewife's day (see also Modleski, 1982).

The gendering of content may also be studied at the point of production, since most media selection and production work is carried out by men (see Chapter 11). In this matter, attention has also been directed to 'the news', which for long was largely a male preserve and in its dominant forms seemed to represent a world of male concerns. In this respect, the typical agenda of news content (politics, economics, sport) was oriented more to male readers. More recently this has been changing and one of the components of contemporary critiques of the 'decline' of the news media has been an alleged trivialization, personalization and sensationalism which are (whether correctly or not, but in line with dominant stereotypes) often synonymous with 'feminization'. News media, both television and the press, are certainly actively seeking to interest female readers and also engaging in extreme competition for the elusive mass audience.

Attention to the construction of gender in media texts is only one aspect of the relevance of gender for communication theory. Studies of media audiences and the reception of media content have shown that there are relatively large differ-

ences according to gender in the manner of use of media and the meanings attached to the activity. A good deal of the evidence can be accounted for by patterned differences in social roles, by typical everyday experience and concerns of men and women, and by the way gender shapes the availability and use of time. It also relates to power roles within the family and the general nature of relationships between women and male partners or of women in the wider family (Morley, 1986). Different kinds of media content (and their production and use) are also associated with expressions of common identity based on gender (Ferguson, 1983; Radway, 1984) and with different pleasures and meanings acquired (Ang, 1985). There may also be deep roots in psychological differences between male and female (Williamson, 1978). In considering these matters, however, it is especially important to take note of van Zoonen's warning that the context is continually changing and that 'the codes that confer meaning onto the signs of femininity are culturally and historically specific and will never be completely unambiguous or consistent' (1994: 149).

A gender-based approach also raises the question of whether media choice and interpretation can provide some lever of change or element of resistance for women in a social situation still generally structured by inequality. The potential for oppositional reading and resistance has been invoked both to explain why women seem attracted to media content with overtly patriarchal messages (such as romance fiction) and to help re-evaluate the surface meaning of this attraction (Radway, 1984). One can say, in summary, that differently gendered media culture, whatever the causes and the forms taken, evokes different responses, and that differences of gender lead to alternative modes of taking meaning from media. There are also differences in selection and context of use which have wider cultural and social implications (Morley, 1986). While the greater attention to gender has been widely welcomed, there have also been warnings about reading too much into gender differences and about assuming the presence and influence of some essential gender identity (Ang and Hermes, 1991).

Feminism is a political as well as a cultural project and feminist media studies have inevitably been caught up in wider debate within cultural media studies about the political significance or not of popular culture (see page 104). This stems in part from the great attention that has been paid to popular genres like soap operas and talk shows that are oriented to female audiences. It was clear where early researchers stood on this issue, especially where popular content (romances, children's stories, women's magazines) was seen as stereotyped and carrying a predominantly patriarchal and conservative ideology or pandered to male sexuality. Things have changed in the media, with much more content by women and for women, with no inhibitions about female sexuality (e.g. McRobbie, 1996). They have also changed in media research through the 'redemption' of popular genres (e.g. Radway, 1984; Ang, 1991).

However, there remains a tension over the direction to be taken by feminist theory and research in respect of the political goal of the movement. Not all are

convinced about the relevance of the changes in the media and new popular cultural theory. Van Zoonen, for instance emphasizes the need to distinguish between news and entertainment. As to the former, she says it is 'completely justified to expect a decent, ethical and more or less accurate representation of feminist politics and politicians in news media' (1994: 152). She does not apply the same criteria to popular culture, which belongs to the realm of 'collective dreams, fantasies and fears'. Without necessarily disagreeing, Hermes takes a more positive view of the potential role of popular culture, arguing for a concept of 'cultural citizenship'. She writes (1997: 86)

> The lynch-pin of theories of the public sphere is reason . . . popular culture research (guided by postmodernist and feminist theory) has argued that emotion and feeling are just as important to our everyday lives. If democracy can be said to be about deliberation among the many about how to attain the best life possible for as many as possible, then it makes no sense to set such exclusive store by reasoned argument in our theorization of it. We need to rethink citizenship as cultural citizenship and accept that those who inhabit mass democracies use many different logics to shape their lives.

THE 'REDEMPTION' OF THE POPULAR

The mass media are largely responsible for what we call either mass culture or popular culture, and they have 'colonized' other cultural forms in the process. The most widely disseminated and enjoyed symbolic culture of our time (if it makes any sense to refer to it in the singular) is what flows in abundance by way of the media of films, television, newspapers, phonogram, video, etc. It makes little sense to go on supposing that this flood can in some way be dammed in, turned back or purified, or to view the predominant culture of our time as a deformed offspring of commerce from a once pure stock.

There is even little possibility of distinguishing an elite from a mass taste, since nearly everyone is attracted to some of the diverse elements of popular media culture. Tastes will always differ, and varying criteria of assessment can be applied, but we should at least accept the media culture of our time as an accomplished fact and treat it on its own terms. The term 'mass culture' is likely to remain in circulation, but the alternative form 'popular culture' (meaning essentially 'culture which is popular' – much enjoyed by many people) seems preferable and no longer carries a pejorative association. Popular culture in this sense is a hybrid product of numerous and never-ending efforts for expression in contemporary idiom aimed at reaching people and capturing a market, and an equally active demand by people for what Fiske (1987) would call 'meanings and pleasures'.

John Fiske (1987, 1989) has been one of the most eloquent and convincing in the effort to vindicate popular culture. An important source of his attachment to popular culture is the line of thinking, outlined above, according to which the same cultural product can be 'read' in different ways, even if a certain dominant meaning may seem to be built in. Fiske defines a media text as the *outcome* of its reading and enjoyment by an audience. He defines the plurality of meanings of a text as its 'polysemy'. The associated term **'intertextuality'** refers partly to the interconnectedness of meanings across different media artefacts (blurring any line between elite and popular culture) but also to interconnectedness of meanings across media and other cultural experiences. An example of both terms is provided by the fact that a cultural phenomenon like the pop singer Madonna can appeal to, yet have quite different meanings for, both young girls and ageing male readers of *Playboy* magazine (Schwichtenberg, 1992).

There are entirely different readings of much popular media content in different subcultures, opening the way for escape from potential social control. Fiske writes:

> The preferred meanings in television are generally those that serve the interests of the dominant classes; other meanings are structured in relations of dominance–subordination . . . the semiotic power of the subordinate to make their own meanings is the equivalent of their ability to evade, oppose, or negotiate with this social power. (1987: 126)

Much of this thinking is derived originally from Hall's theory of decoding and from new critical theory in general, according to which all texts can be read in an oppositional way and their encoded ideology readily subverted.

For Fiske, the primary virtue of popular culture is precisely that it is popular both literally 'of the people' and dependent on 'people power'. He writes: 'Popularity is here a measure of a cultural form's ability to serve the desires of its customers . . . . For a cultural commodity to become popular it must be able to meet the various interests of the people amongst whom it is popular as well as the interests of its producers' (1987: 310). Popular culture must be relevant and responsive to needs or it will fail, and success (in the market) may be the best test that culture is both; (in practice the criterion of success supersedes any notion of intrinsic quality). Fiske rejects the argument that lines of division of cultural capital follow the lines of division of economic capital (Bourdieu, 1986). Instead he argues that there are two economies, with relative autonomy, one cultural and the other social. Even if most people in a class society are subordinated, they have a degree of '*semiotic power*' in the cultural economy – that is, the power to shape meanings to their own desires.

Despite the profound re-evaluation of popular culture that has occurred and the rise of postmodernism (discussed below), several charges of the kind made by Frankfurt School critics remain on the table. Much of the content offered by media that is both popular and commercially successful still looks to many critics as if it is still open to much the same objections as in more elitist and less enlightened times. Media culture is often seen to have one or more of the following limitations. It is, variously, repetitive, undemanding, thematically limited and conformist. Many examples can be found of popular content that are ideologically tendentious, nasty and positively anti-intellectual. These judgements may be regarded as conventional and old-fashioned but it remains the case that most popular culture is produced by large corporations with an overriding view to their own profits, rather than to enriching the cultural lives of the people. Audiences are viewed as consumer markets to be manipulated and managed. Popular formulas and products tend to be used until threadbare, then discarded when they cease to be profitable, whatever the audience might demand in the 'cultural economy'.

The study of popular culture originated in a general project of reform that sought to validate what was good in the 'common culture' of the people and condemn in a reasoned way what was bad. It seems strange to survivors of the generation involved in this essentially 'modernist' project that today's critical cultural theorists can celebrate cultural forms that seem still to have a structured tendency to support an oppressive form of society, at least on the surface. The new 'cultural populism' has, not surprisingly, produced its own backlash (McGuigan, 1992; Ferguson and Golding, 1997). Gitlin sees the new cultural studies as a populist project that has simply inverted the old hierarchy of cultural values, without overthrowing it. In his view it has become anti-political, which was not its avowed intention. Instead of being against capitalism, it has come to 'echo the logic of capitalism' (1997: 32).

One of the difficulties with the 'redemption' arguments is that they largely ignore the continuing semiotic inequality whereby a more educated and better-off minority has access both to popular culture *and* to 'unpopular' culture (such as classical music, great literature and modern and avant-garde art). The majority are still limited to popular forms alone and totally dependent on the commercial media market (Gripsrud, 1989). There is nothing in the redemption arguments presented which really addresses this point or indicates how this difference can be bridged. Nor is there anything that allows one to discriminate between cultural productions in terms of any intrinsic value.

There is a risk in the 'backlash' against polemical and overstated arguments of neglecting the benefits of new ways of thinking about 'popular culture'. The traditional cultural distinctions were often surrogates for class distinctions, and cultural value came not from intrinsic aesthetic value, but from endorsement by social

clites. In Bourdieu's terms, the distinctions went with cultural capital, which in turn often came along with financial capital. One way out of the impasse, without going back to the past, is to make use of the concept of life-style, in recognition of the flux and diversity of contemporary social life, especially as cultural capital is more widely and evenly distributed by way of the educational system. For example, Andersson and Jansson (1998), in a study of Swedish media use, identify the phenomenon of a 'progressive cultural lifestyle' which combines an interest in popular with traditional culture. The social group concerned combines high cultural capital with limited economic resources. This lifestyle is identified both by preferences and by styles of media use. It is eclectic, fragmented and relaxed in style. We do not know how far these observations can be generalized but they suggest that new times produce new cultural paradigms.

The idea of 'quality' of mass media cultural provision nevertheless remains on the agenda of applied media theory, even if its meaning has shifted, because there are still relevant policy issues and also public concerns about quality. Quality no longer refers exclusively to the degree of conformity to a traditional cultural canon, but may be defined in terms of creativity, originality, diversity of cultural identity and various ethical or moral principles (Schrøder, 1992), depending on whose perspective is chosen. It is also still very relevant to a wide range of 'reality-oriented' media genres, ranging from news to talk shows. It can certainly no longer be assumed that what has most appeal has less 'quality', but the material economic dynamic of cultural production cannot be so easily distinguished from the 'semiotic' cultural economy.

COMMERCIALIZATION

Embedded in the early critique of mass culture, and still alive at the fringes of the discussion (certainly in the context of media policy), is the notion of 'commercialism' (the condition) or 'commercialization' (the process). In some uses, this term is a code for a watered-down version of the Marxist critique and may verge on the 'bourgeois' (even the snobbish and elitist). Even so, it expresses some ideas that are still relevant to current media industry dynamics and to media-cultural change and it is closely related to the critique of commodification (see page 96). The critique of commercialism is particularly difficult to reconcile with the redemption of the popular, since popularity is usually a condition of commercial success.

While at one level the term 'commercialism' may refer objectively to particular free-market arrangements, it has also come to imply consequences for the type of media content which is mass-produced and 'marketed' as a commodity, and also consequences for the relations between the suppliers and the consumers of media. The

term 'commercial', applied as an adjective to some types of media provision, identifies correlates of the competitive pursuit of large markets (Bogart, 1995). Aside from an abundance of advertising matter (commercial propaganda), commercial content is likely, from this perspective, to be more oriented to amusement and entertainment (escapism), more superficial, undemanding and conformist, more derivative and standardized.

There has been much comment on the '**tabloidization**' of newspapers as they compete for readers. The equivalent process in television has led to many new forms of 'reality' television that deal in all kinds of 'human interest' and dramatic topics in a variety of formats. The term tabloidization comes from the smaller format of the more popular (or boulevard) newspapers in some countries. Connell (1998) discusses the British variants, taking the term to mean that 'sensationalist' news discourses have displaced 'rationalist' discourses, with a strong emphasis on narrative. He does not find convincing evidence that reporting in tabloid newspapers is essentially different from 'broadsheet' variants. Bird (1998) looked at the 'tabloidization' of American *television* news and concludes from her audience study that there has been a real trend towards *personalization* and *dramatization* that does make news more accessible to the many, but it has also led to a trivialization of what people actually learn from news.

While it is true that essentially the same market arrangements can just as easily support the supply and consumption of greatly varied and high-quality cultural products, the critique of commerce has another dimension. It can be argued that commercial relationships in communication are intrinsically distancing and potentially exploitative. The commercial variant of a communicative relationship does not support the formation of ties of mutual attachment or lead to shared identity or community. It is calculative and utilitarian on both sides, reflecting essential features of the 'transmission' or 'publicity' rather than the 'ritual' model of communication in society (see pages 52–8). The commercial environment of media production also provides a straitjacket which closes off many possibilities for innovation and creativity (Blumler, 1991, 1992). The fundamental problem is that profit becomes the only motive that really counts.

Some of the severest criticisms of commercial trends and their consequences have been reserved for the consequences for democracy (e.g. Blumler and Gurevitch, 1995). The general trend towards making news entertaining before it is informative has been much commented on, as has the rise of a new media genre of 'infotainment' that is said to promote ignorance and also detachment from political participation. The problem has been accentuated in the eyes of critics by the willing co-operation of politicians for short-term ends in the general tendency of the media to popularize and personalize, at the expense of substance. As usual there is a counter-argument (e.g. Brants, 1998) that points to positive effects from popularization as well as lack of evidence that the media are the cause of perceived cultural trends. The new genres and formats may not match the standard of information value of old media but they may serve a valuable purpose alongside more traditional media forms, that have not in fact disappeared. However,

the problem remains that for many popular media there is no purpose to inform or enlighten.

COMMUNICATION TECHNOLOGY AND CULTURE

It has already been argued that numerous historical innovations in communication technology, although undoubtedly often revolutionary in their implications, cannot really be traced as causes of specific shifts in the form of society (Slack, 1984). Innovations are always taken up and adapted according to some more compelling social imperative (Winston, 1986). There are too many other powerful forces involved in social change. It is not easy to find a relation between the successes and failures of 'modernization' during the last fifty years and features of the relevant media system. It is, however, plausible to suppose that communication technology will have an effect on the process of communication itself and that culture and communication are intertwined. If our experience of the world is technologically mediated, then technology itself should have some relevance.

McLuhan's view of cultural change

McLuhan's (1964) advance on Innis (see page 85) was to look at the process by which we experience the world through different media of communication and not just at the relation between communication and social power structures. He proclaimed that all media (by which he meant anything which embodies cultural meaning and can be 'read' as such) are 'extensions of man', thus extensions of our senses. Like others, he drew attention to the implications of a shift from a purely *oral* communication to one based on a written language (by about 5000 BC). Much of cultural experience remained predominantly oral until comparatively recent times. McLuhan also focused on *how* we experience the world, not on *what* we experience (thus not on the content). Each new medium transcends the boundaries of experience reached by earlier media

and contributes to further change. McLuhan correctly saw different media working together, while perhaps less plausibly he predicted the attainment of a 'global village' in which information and experience would be freely available for all to share.

A general proposition was that, as more of our senses are engaged in the process of taking meaning (as media become increasingly 'cool', or frictionless, as against single-sense or 'hot' media), the more involving and participatory the experience is. According to this view, experiencing the world by reading printed text is isolating and non-involving (encouraging the rational, individual attitude). Television viewing is involving, although not very informing, and also conducive of a less rational and calculative attitude. No proof (or disproof) has ever been offered, and the ideas were described by McLuhan himself only as perceptions or 'probes'. As he wished, they stimulated much speculation in an era in which audiovisual media have seemed in many respects to take over from print media.

A model of technology and cultural change

Most other relevant theory of communication technology has focused on possible influences on the form or content of given media messages and thus on the meanings they make available. Even so, no technology–culture effect can be established, because the technologies themselves are also cultural artefacts, and there is no way of breaking into the circle. Such theory as we have is little more than description of observable patterns in the cultural meanings offered via mass media which may be influenced by various characteristics, not only technological, of a given medium. A general view of the process by which changing technology can influence media culture is given in Figure 5.1. Perhaps the most important point that it illustrates is that technologies are

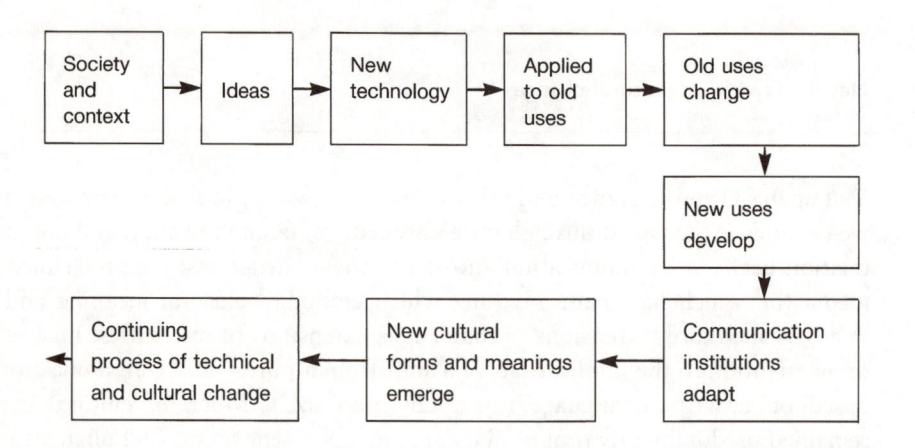

FIGURE 5.1 Interactive sequence of communication and technological and cultural change: technologies arise from society and have effects on society depending on the form of application

unlikely to have a direct impact on cultural practices, and only as mediated through a relevant institution (in this case, the mass media).

MEDIA LOGIC AND THE BIAS OF COMMUNICATION

Further to the question of technological determinism, a concept which has proved useful is that of '**media logic**', developed by Altheide and Snow (1979). This refers to the influence of media (considered both as cultured technology and formal organization) on 'real world' events themselves, as well as on their portrayal and constitution. More recently, Altheide and Snow (1991: 10) have described media logic as 'a way of seeing and interpreting social affairs. . . . Elements of this form (of communication) include the various media and the formats used by these media. Formats consist, in part, in how material is organized, the style in which it is presented, the focus or emphasis . . . and the grammar of media communication'.

Because of the increased centrality of mass media for other institutions, there is also a growing need for those in the public eye and events relating to public (and commercial) life to require high and appropriate media visibility if they are to have full effect. There is an imperative to conduct affairs and stage events in ways that conform to the needs and routines of the mass media (in respect of timing and form). The idea of a staged 'media event' (or pseudo event) belongs to the theory of media logic (Boorstin, 1961; Dayan and Katz, 1992). It has an obvious relevance to predominant modes of news coverage, in which familiar formats and routines predictably frame certain categories of event (Altheide, 1985). The general notion of media logic extends to include the influence of media requirements on a wide range of cultural happenings, including sport, entertainment and public ceremonies. There are also many examples of new kinds of format which the media have made part of everyday cultural experience (such as radio phone-ins, television talk-shows, music video films, advertising spots and never-ending serials).

In trying to account for technological influence on (media) culture, we may extend the notion of '*bias*' introduced by Innis and recognize several tendencies that follow from the characteristics of a particular media technology (and its institutional development). We can name five types of media bias as follows, without exhausting the possibilities. There is a bias of *sense experience*, following McLuhan, so that we may experience the world in more or less visual imagery (see Hartley, 1992) or in more or less of an involving and participant way. Secondly, there is a bias of form and representation, with 'messages' strongly coded (as in print) or essentially uncoded, as in photographs (Barthes, 1967). Thirdly, there is the bias of message *content* for instance, in terms of more or less realism or polysemy, more open or closed formats (other dimensions are possible).

Fourthly, there is a bias of *context of use*, with some media lending themselves to private and individualized reception, others being more collective and shared. Fifthly,

there is a bias of *relationship*, contrasting one-way with interactive media. Bias does not mean determinism, but it contains a predeliction towards certain kinds of experience and ways of mediation. Ellis's (1982) comparison of broadcast television with cinema film provides an instructive illustration of how the (unintended) bias of a medium can work in subtle but systematic and multiple ways, affecting content and probable ways of perception and reception.

Box 5.4 Five types of media technology bias

- Of sense experience
- Of content
- Of form
- Of context of use
- Of sender–receiver relationships

CULTIVATION AND THE MEDIATION OF IDENTITY

The rise of television and its enormous appeal were the source of much theorizing about the consequences for social experience. A recurring theme has been the degree to which most of our experience is literally mediated through the words and images of the dominant medium of our time. Giddens (1991) has emphasized this as one of the key features of 'high modernity'. He writes:

> In high modernity, the influence of distant happenings on proximate events, and even on the intimacies of the self, becomes more and more commonplace. The media, printed and electronic, obviously play a central role in this respect. Mediated experience, since the first experience of writing, has long influenced both self-identity and the basic organization of social relations. . . . With the development of mass communications, the interpenetration of self-development and social systems . . . becomes ever more pronounced. (1991: 4–5)

Earlier, Gerbner (1967) had identified the significance of mass communication, in terms not of the concept of 'masses', but of the transformation of society brought about by the 'extension of institutionalized public acculturation beyond the limits of face to face and any other personally mediated interaction'. He writes of 'publication' (the main action of mass media) as a transformation of private systems of knowing into public systems creating new bases of collective thought. McLuhan (1964) wrote similarly of the 'retribalizing' effects of television. Implied in this is the view that identities are drawn from the systematic and widely shared messages of the mass media.

According to Gerbner and colleagues, television is responsible for a major 'cultivating' and 'acculturating' process, according to which people are exposed systematically to a selective view of society on almost every aspect of life, a view which tends to shape

their beliefs and values accordingly. The environment is so monopolized by television that its lessons are continually learned and relearned. In a more critical vein, C.W. Mills had earlier drawn a similar lesson. He wrote: 'Between consciousness and existence stand communications which influence such consciousness as men have of their existence' (1951: 333). Subsequently (1956), he expounded on the almost total dependency of individuals on the media for their sense of identity and aspirations. This transformation brings publics into being.

The shifting boundaries of social space

A more recent theory of mass media and social change that owes something to McLuhan (with help from Goffman) also attributes great cultural influence to television. Meyrowitz's (1985) thesis is that the all-pervasiveness of electronic media has fundamentally changed social experience by breaking down the compartmentalization between social spaces that was typical of earlier times. Human experience, in his view, has traditionally been segmented by role and social situation and sharply divided between private ('backstage') and public ('onstage') domains. Segmentation was by age, gender and social status, and the 'walls' between zones of experience were high. Television appears to put all aspects of social experience on show to all, without distinction. There are no longer any secrets for instance, about adulthood, sex, death or power.

Older bases for identification and for authority are weakened or blurred, sometimes to be replaced by new group identities (such as for women, for homosexuals, and in radical movements) made possible by mediated experience and by the overcoming of limits of space (social and physical). Everyone tends to move in the same information environment, but the result is a culture without any distinct sense of socially or physically bounded place. The theory tends to explain rather too much of what has seemed to happen to (North American) society in modern times, and it cannot be tested, except mentally, but it sheds some extra light on the meaning of the 'mediation of experience'.

GLOBALIZATION OF CULTURE

One of the few effects of new communication technology on which there is wide agreement is the trend towards internationalization of mass communication. The question of potential cultural effects flowing from this trend has been much debated. The movement towards a global media culture has several sources, most notably the greatly increased capacity to transmit sounds and (moving) images at low cost across frontiers and around the world, overcoming limits of time and space. Equally potent as

a cause is the rise of global media businesses (and global markets for media products), that provides the organizational framework and driving force for **globalization**. Neither of these conditions has arrived suddenly, nor is the idea of transnational culture itself novel (it long predates the very idea of the national), but what may be new is the increased transcultural communicative potential of pictures and music. The relevant changes in the structure of media industries and global media flow, especially in relation to television, have been extensively studied, but the cultural consequences are much less open to observation and have led to much speculation and more sound than light.

The process of cultural 'transnationalization' that is assumed to be taking place has a variety of meanings and is discussed in more detail in Chapter 10. It implies some effect on the media themselves and also on those at the receiving end. It also refers to the development of interconnected infrastructures for transmission and reception and the growth of multinational ownership and operation. One of the effects on the media is the presence of certain broad *kinds* of media cultural content. The typical content will have been chosen for its wide appeal, even if originally produced for a domestic market. This will usually imply a downgrading of cultural specificity in themes and settings and a preference for formats and genres that are thought to be more universal. Because of the influence of the United States in audiovisual and music production, transnational content is sometimes considered as culturally North American, although there are other large producers and exporters in different spheres of influence, including Mexico, Japan, Egypt and India. The general direction of effect is assumed to be towards displacing or subordinating the original culture of receiving countries and/or causing it to imitate the international model. Another outcome is the emergence of a global media culture with a potential for serving a very large and disparate media market (see below).

Time, space and the media

At this point we can map out the relations between media and cultural identity in terms of two main dimensions, *time* and *space* (Figure 5.2). Time is chosen because endurance can be considered a central aspect of all cultures and degree of endurance the test of salience and significance. The most enduring identities are those based on language, religion, nationhood, etc., the most ephemeral are those based on taste, fashion and style. In this context, the capacity of media to extend in space is also the most relevant criterion of globalizing tendencies. Media channels and content can range from the very local (and nearest to home) to the most global, carrying geographically and culturally remote messages.

In the space so mapped out by plotting one dimension against another there are many possibilities of different, but not necessarily inconsistent, relations between media and identity. Different types of media can have different types of impact on the

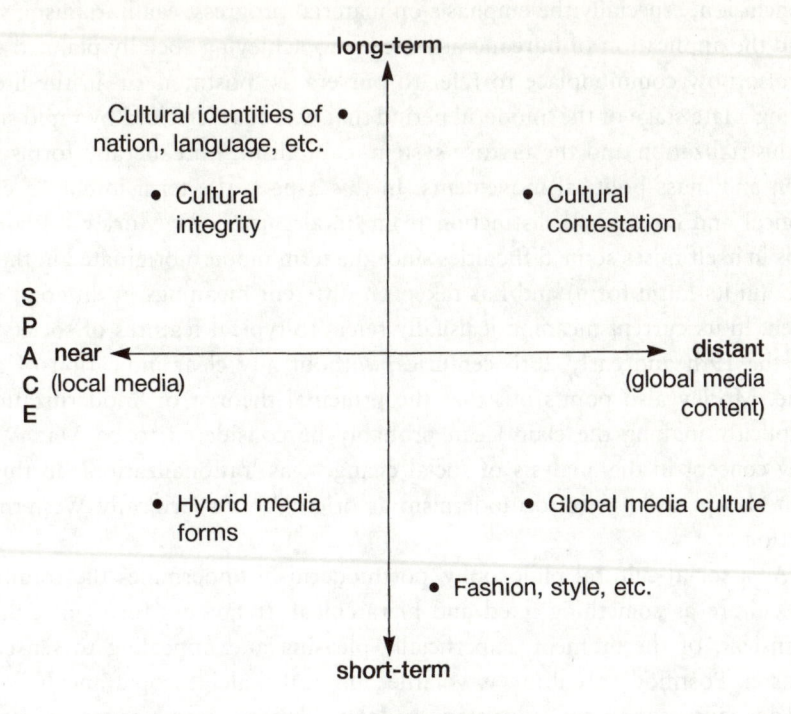

FIGURE 5.2   Media and cultural identity: the dimensions of time and space between them locate the main variants and conditions of the relationship

decay, endurance or flourishing of cultural identity and experience. In general, local, ethnic and more personal media help to support enduring identities and cultural autonomy, while international media content has more impact on superficial and short-term cultural phenomena, such as fashion, style and taste. There is no longer a single dominant media technology, so that different media can compensate for (or reinforce) each other's cultural influence. Actual effects cannot be predicted and will depend on circumstances of case, time and place.

MASS MEDIA AND POSTMODERN CULTURE

The notion of a 'postmodern condition' (Harvey, 1989) has captured the imagination of many social and cultural theorists, and it seems very much a theory for the Information Society (see Chapter 10). Despite its wide currency, it is a complex and obscure concept that involves several ideas that are relevant to the mass media. Its

political implication is that the 'Enlightenment project' has reached its historic conclusion, especially the emphasis on material progress, egalitarianism, social reform and the application of bureaucratic means to achieving socially planned objectives. It is also now commonplace to refer to our era as 'postmodern' in the literal sense of being a late stage of the 'modern' period that was characterized by rapid social change, industrialization and the factory system, capitalism, bureaucratic forms of organization and mass political movements. In this aspect, the term implies a clear chronological and conceptual distinction from 'modernism'. As Morley (1996) points out, this in itself raises some difficulties since the term modern originated in the 5th century AD (in its Latin form) and has taken on different meanings in different epochs since then. In its current meaning it usually refers to typical features of society and culture of the 19th and early 20th centuries, without any clear indication of any dividing line. Morley also points out that the principal theorist of 'modernization' (without explicitly making the claim) can probably be considered to be Max Weber, whose key concept in the analysis of social change was 'rationalization'. In this respect we can also plausibly regard modernism as originally a specifically Western (European) notion.

As a social-cultural philosophy, postmodernism undermines the traditional notion of culture as something fixed and hierarchical. It favours forms of culture that are transient, of the moment, superficially pleasing and appealing to sense rather than reason. Postmodern culture is volatile, illogical, kaleidescopic and hedonistic. Mass media culture has the advantage of appealing to many senses as well as being associated with novelty and transience. Many features of (commercial) popular media culture reflect postmodernist elements. Music video on television was hailed as the first postmodern television service (Kaplan, 1987; Grossberg, 1989; Lewis, 1992). Old ideas of quality of art and serious messages cannot be sustained, except by reference to authority, and are seen as inescapably 'bourgeois'. This is a potent set of ideas that goes much further than providing a defence for the once much maligned and patronized 'culture of the masses'. It is an entirely new representation of the situation that has turned some of the weapons of cultural critics against themselves (for instance, their claim to speak on behalf of the masses). It gains strength both from a real shift of social values and from a re-evaluation of popular culture and the probability that there has also been a real cultural revolution within the mass media, leading towards a new aesthetic. Television and popular music have become the dominant arts of the time and have shown enormous inventiveness and power to change.

The idea of postmodernism has been easier to characterize in cultural than in social terms, since the features of 'modern' society mentioned are still in evidence, maybe even reinforced if one thinks of how much the world is ruled by global financial markets that operate with inexorable and uniform logic. The term refers more to the dominant ethos or spirit of the times and to certain aesthetic and cultural trends. Docherty (1993) interprets postmodern cultural and social philosophy as a response to the post-1968 re-appraisal of revolutionary aspirations, which had, in their turn, been

based on the premise of an end to capitalism and the birth of a new utopia. This dream had been originally founded on the ideas of material progress, reason and enlightenment that were embedded in the very idea of modern society.

Viewed like this, postmodernism stands for a retreat from political ideology, a certain loss of faith in the gods of reason and science. This shapes the contemporary Zeitgeist (spirit of the age) in the sense that we no longer share any fixed belief or commitment and there is a tendency to hedonism, individualism and living in the present moment. This is in accord with another widely cited characterization of postmodernism by Lyotard (1986) to the effect that there is no longer any *grand narrative*, no organizing or explanatory framework or central project for humanity. The cultural aesthetics of postmodernism involve a rejection of tradition and a search for novelty, invention, momentary enjoyment, nostalgia, playfulness, pastiche and inconsistency. Jameson (1984) refers to postmodernism as the 'cultural logic of late capitalism', even though there is no logic to be found. Gitlin (1989) suggests that postmodernism is specifically North American, capturing many features of American culture.

Grossberg et al. (1998) associate it especially with the process of commercialization of everything. Certainly the postmodern ethos is much more favourable to commerce than were earlier cultural perspectives, since opposition to capitalism is undermined and commerce can be seen as responding to consumer wants or as actively promoting changes in fashion, style and products. However, there is scope for social and cultural optimism as well as pessimism within the range of postmodern thought. Ien Ang has also underlined the need to distinguish between conservative and critical postmodernism as an intellectual attitude. She writes 'the former does indeed succumb to an "anything goes" attitude . . . [but] . . . the latter, critical postmodernism is motivated by a deep understanding of the limits and failures of what Habermas calls the "unfinished project of modernity"' (1998: 78).

The forms of contemporary advertising, especially on television, seem to exhibit most of the cultural features mentioned above. The work of Jean Baudrillard (1983) helps us to understand the essence of postmodern culture, especially his concept of *simulacrum*, which refers to the fact that the difference between an image and the reality is no longer important. The mass media provide an inexhaustible supply of images of a pseudo-reality that serves instead of experience and becomes for many hard to distinguish form reality itself. The idea is well exemplified by the film 'The Truman Show' (1997) whose whole plot turns on the situation of a real person whose life has been lived within the plot of a long-running soap opera dealing with an imaginary community. These notions of convergence of image and reality are also expressed in virtual reality devices that substitute simulated for real experience.

The appeal of the postmodern concept is based on its helping to link many convincing perceptions of tendencies in the media (including new media) and in its summing up the essence of the media's own logic. It also seems useful as a word to connect diverse social changes (for instance the fragmentation of the class structure, decline in political ideology and globalization). But apart from that it has little

substance of its own, no analytic purchase to speak of and no intrinsic fixed meaning. Put like this it sounds like a caricature of itself.

FURTHER READING

Altheide, D.L. and Snow, R.P. (1979) *Media Logic*. Newbury Park, CA: Sage.

Carey, J. (1989) *Communication as Culture*. Boston, MA: Unwin Hyman.

Curran, J., Morley, D. and Walkerdine, V. (eds) (1996). *Cultural Studies and Communications*. London: Edward Arnold.

Ferguson, M. and Golding, P. (eds) *Cultural Studies in Question*. London: Sage.

Fiske, J. (1987) *Television Culture*. London: Routledge.

Real, M. (1989) *Supermedia*. Newbury Park, CA: Sage.

6

new media – new theory?

Theory relating to mass communication has to be continually re-assessed in the light of new technologies and their applications. In Chapter 3, we recognized the arrival of new types of media that extend and change the entire spectrum of socio-technological possibilities for public communication. No transformation has yet happened, and it is too early to predict how far and fast the process of change will go. Even so, it is important to anticipate the possibility and examine the implications for the key issues of society and culture that have already been raised. The underlying assumption in this chapter is that a medium is not just an applied technology for transmitting certain symbolic content or linking participants in some exchange. It also embodies a set of social relations that interact with features of the new technology. New theory is only likely to be required if there is a fundamental change in the forms of social organization of media technologies, in the social relations that are promoted, or in what Carey (1998) terms the 'dominant structures of taste and feeling'.

The most fundamental aspect of information and communication technology (ICT) is probably the fact of *digitalization*, the process by which all texts (symbolic meaning in all encoded and recorded forms) can be reduced to a binary code and can share the same process of production, distribution and storage. The most widely noted potential consequence for the media institution is the *convergence* between all existing media forms in terms of their organization, distribution, reception and regulation. As we have seen, many different forms of mass media have so far survived, retained their separate identity and even flourished. The general institution of mass media has also survived as a distinct element of public social life. The 'new electronic media' can be viewed initially as an addition to the existing spectrum rather than as a replacement. On the other hand, we have to consider that digitalization and convergence might have much more revolutionary consequences.

In advance of the fact we can do little more than speculate on the basis of past experience and current trends. If we consider the main features of the media institution as outlined above on page 15, it seems that the Internet in particular already deviates from that typification on three of the five points. Firstly, the Internet is not only or even mainly concerned with the production and distribution of messages, but is at least equally concerned with processing, exchange and storage. Secondly, the new media are as much an institution of private as well as of public communication and are regulated (or not) accordingly. Thirdly, their operation is not typically professional or bureaucratically organized in the same degree as mass media. These are quite significant differences that underscore the fact that the new media correspond with mass media primarily in being widely diffused, in principle available to all for communication and at least as free.

There have been numerous attempts to characterize the new media, especially as embodied in the Internet, but they are hindered by uncertainty about their future uses

and institutional forms. The computer as applied to communication has produced many variant possibilities, no one of which is dominant. Postmes et al. (1998) describe the computer as a 'uniquely undedicated' communication technology. In a similar vein, Poster (1999) describes the essence of the Internet as its very *undetermination*, not only because of the diversity and uncertainty in the future, but also because of its essentially postmodernistic character. He also points to key differences with broadcasting and print as follows.

The Internet incorporates radio, film and television and distributes them through 'push' technology. It

> transgresses the limits of the print and broadcasting models by (1) enabling many-to-many conversations; (2) enabling the simultaneous reception, alteration and redistribution of cultural objects; (3) dislocating communicative action from the posts of the nation, from the territorialized spatial relations of modernity; (4) providing instantaneous global contact; and (5) inserting the modern/late modern subject into a machine apparatus that is networked. (Poster, 1999: 15)

More succinctly, Livingstone (1999: 65) writes 'What's new about the internet may be the combination of interactivity with those features which were innovative for mass communication – the unlimited range of content, the scope of audience reach, the global nature of communication'. This view suggests extension rather than replacement.

The general differences between new and old media can be appreciated in more detail if we consider the main roles and relationship that are found within the traditional media institution, especially those concerned with authorship (and performance), publication, production and distribution, and reception. In brief, the main implications are as follows.

For authors. There is more opportunity to become an author, if posting on the Internet and desk-top publishing and similar autonomous acts count as publication. However, the status and rewards of the author as understood until now have depended on the significance and location of publication and on the degree and kind of public attention received. Writing a private letter or a poem, taking photographs is not true authorship. The conditions of public recognition and esteem have not really changed with the new technology, and the condition of having a large audience and widespread fame may even have become more difficult to achieve. It is not easy to become famous on the Internet, without the co-operation of the mass media.

For publishers, the role continues but has become more ambiguous for the same reasons that apply to authors. Until now a publisher was typically a business firm or a non-profit public institution. The new media open up alternative forms of publication and present opportunities and challenges for traditional publishing. Early indications are that the latter is quite capable of adapting to the changed situation and of embracing new technological possibilities. The role does not essentially change. The functions of *gate-keeping*, editorial intervention and validation of authorship remain and will continue to be called for in an age of abundance and diversity of forms.

Production and *distribution* roles are too diverse to encapsulate in a few remarks. Even so, it seems that fundamental change is taking place. The convergence process tends to abolish many existing functions and distinctions. Distribution of mass media was organized to solve problems created by space and time barriers so as to deliver large amounts of information physically in dispersed places at about the same time. These problems have essentially been solved and part of the institution can disappear. This does not seem to have happened, to judge from the survival power of the traditional newspaper. Even so the insubstantial and fragmentary character of the *organization* of the Internet presents a continuing challenge to established ways of doing things.

As to the *audience* role, there are large possibilities of change, especially in the direction of greater autonomy and equality in relation to sources and suppliers. The audience member is no longer really part of a mass, but is either a member of a self-chosen network or special public or is an individual. In addition, the balance of audience activity shifts from reception to searching, consulting and interacting. Despite this, there is evidence of continuity in the mass audience (see Chapter 16) and there is still a demand by the audience for gate keeping and editorial guidance. Rice (1999: 29) remarks on the paradox of the extended range of choices facing the audience: 'now individuals must makes more choices, must have more prior knowledge, and must put forth more effort to integrate and make sense of the communication. Interactivity and choice are not universal benefits; many people do not have the energy, desire, need or training to engage in such processes'.

As far as the relations between different roles are concerned, we can posit a general loosening and more independence, especially affecting authors and audiences. Rice (1999: 29) notes that 'the boundaries between publisher, producer, distributor, consumer and reviewer of content are blurring'. This casts doubt on the continued appropriateness of the idea of an *institution* in the sense of some more or less unified social organization with some core practices and shared norms. In the general meltdown it is likely that we will recognize the emergence of separate more specialized institutional complexes of media activity. These will be based either on technologies or on certain uses and content (e.g. relating to news journalism, entertainment films, business, sport, pornography, tourism, education, professions, etc.), with no shared institutional identity. In that sense, the mass media will have withered away.

THE RISE OF AN INFORMATION SOCIETY

Mass communication has always been strongly associated if not fully identified with most of the processes of public communication in contemporary large-scale society.

theories

This means an association with the diffusion of news and information, advertising of all kinds, public opinion formation, advocacy and propaganda and mass entertainment. This is a diverse spectrum that can be affected and changed by many different influences, including actions of collective agencies such as governments, institutions or firms as well as general unplanned dynamics arising from changes of technology, patterns of consumption, culture and life-style. It is not fruitful to look at all the possibilities of change separately, especially as they are likely to be inter-related with each other. The idea of the information society is the most relevant and overarching framework for understanding and expressing different forces for change in contemporary society. It is really the only well-qualified candidate. It has something to say about socio-technical as well as cultural change and has implications for all aspects of public communication as mentioned. Hence our attention to it here.

The term 'information society' seems to have originated in Japan in the 1960s (Ito, 1981), although its genealogy is usually traced to the concept of 'post-industrial' society. This was first proposed by the sociologist Daniel Bell (1973), while another source was the idea of an 'information economy' developed by the economists Machlup (1962) and Porat (1977) (see Schement and Curtis, 1995). Bell's work belonged to the tradition that relates types of society to succeeding stages of economic and social development. The main characteristics of the post-industrial society were found mainly in the rise in the service sector of the economy relative to manufacture or agriculture and thus the predominance of 'information-based' work. Theoretical knowledge (scientific, expert, data-based) was becoming the key factor in the econ-omy, outstripping physical plant and land as bases of wealth. Correlatively a 'new class' was emerging based on the possession of knowledge and personal relation skills. Most of the observed 'post-industrial' trends have been seen to accelerate in the last quarter of the 20th century. The production and distribution of information of all kinds, especially using computer-based technology has itself become a major sector of the economy.

Aside from the accumulating evidence of the significance of information in contem-porary economy and society, there has not been much agreement or clarity about the *concept* of 'information society', although useful observations have been made. Melody (1990: 26–7) describes information societies simply as those that have become 'dependent upon complex electronic information networks and which allocate a major portion of their resources to information and communication activities'.

Van Cuilenburg (1987) put the chief characteristic as the exponential increase in production and flow of information of all kinds, largely as a consequence of reduced costs, following miniaturization and computerization. Reductions in costs of transmission have continued to fuel the process of exponential growth. There is a continually decreasing sensitivity to distance as well as to cost and continually increasing speed, volume and interactivity of possibilities for communication. Despite the importance of the trends under way, it has not really been established that any revolutionary transformation in society has yet occurred, as opposed to a

new media – new theory?

further step in the development of capitalism (Schement and Curtis, 1995: 26). What is still missing is evidence of a transformation in social relationships (Webster, 1995).

Several commentators have emphasized the increased 'interconnectedness' of society as a result of Information Society trends. According to Neuman (1991), this is the underlying 'logic behind the cascade of new technologies'. He writes

> The quintessential characteristic of the new electronic media is that they all connect with one another. We are witnessing the evolution of a universal, interconnected network of audio, video and electronic text communication that will blur the distinction between interpersonal and mass communication and between public and private communication. . . . The ultimate result . . . will be intellectual pluralism and personalized control over communication. (1991: 12).

Some writers (e.g. van Dijk, 1993; Castells, 1996) choose to use the term 'network society' instead of Information Society. Van Dijk (1999) suggests that modern society is in a process of becoming a network society: 'a form of society increasingly organizing its relationships in media networks which are gradually replacing or complementing the social networks of face to face communication'. A network structure of society is contrasted with a centre–peripheral mass society. It exhibits numerous overlapping circles of communication that can have both a vertical and horizontal range. Such networks can serve to exclude as well as connect. Traditional mass media exhibited a similar structure and were inclusive of all.

The idea of interconnectedness relates to another aspect of contemporary society that has attracted comment, and that is the high degree of *dependence* on others. This is hardly a new idea, since it was the basis of Durkheim's century-old social theory concerning the division of labour. But there is arguably a qualitative change in our era resulting from the continued excursions of information technology into every aspect of life, especially where intelligent machines replace human agency. One aspect that has been emphasized by Giddens (1991) is the degree to which we have to put our trust in expert systems of all kinds for maintaining normal conditions of life. We also live with increased awareness of risks of many kinds (health, environmental, economic, military) that are both derived from the public circulation of information and also managed by reference to information. In addition, it would seem that the 'culture' of contemporary society, in the traditional sense of mental and symbolic pursuits and customary ways of passing time free from essential obligations, is largely dominated by a vast array of informational services. The mass media may still dominate, but there is an increasing number of new informational and interactive options.

A notable, although intangible dimension of the concept of 'Information Society' is the fact that it is so widely recognized and taken up by social commentators, politicians and journalists as an apt term for the sort of society we live in. It forms part

of contemporary self-consciousness, and in some versions it is almost a new world-view. For instance de Mue (1999) compares the transition taking place to the development of mechanics in the 17th and 18th centuries. He writes

> While the mechanistic world view is characterized by the postulates of analysability, lawfulness and controllability, the informationistic world view is characterized by the postulates of synthesizability, programmability and manipulability . . . it fundamentally alters human experience and the evaluation of and association with reality.

For others, informatization connotes a new vision of progress for all and a future with unlimited horizons, more or less in continuation of the model we already have. As such it carries some ideological baggage, tending to legitimate some trends of the time (e.g. faith in science and high technology as solutions to problems) and to delegitimate others (especially ideological politics about class and inequality). By emphasizing the means and processes of communication and quantitative dimensions of change it de-emphasizes the precise content and purpose of it all. In this respect, a connection with postmodernism (see pages 113–16) can also be made. It is at least apparent that very divergent interpretations are possible.

It is worth also underlining the degree to which contemporary thinking has objectified and materialized information. Schement and Curtis (1995: 212) emphasize the 'Idea of Information' as standing at the base of the Information Society and driving the language by which we make sense of it. The essence is the ease with which people have come to think of information as a *thing*. Thus, we speak of markets for information, quantify the amount of information, pay increasing attention to ownership of information and rights of access to information. We make sense of the information society predominantly in these terms. Despite scattered insights of this kind, the Information Society concept has been dominated by economic, sociological, geographical and technological considerations. The *cultural* dimension has been relatively neglected, aside from recognition of the great volume of information and symbolic production, and unless we view postmodernist thinking as filling this gap. The rise of an 'information culture' that extends into all aspects of everyday life may be easier to demonstrate than the reality of an Information Society.

The relationship between these developments and the mass media has already been considered in some aspects. It is clear that 'information economy' is much larger than the mass media on their own, and the primary information technologies involved are not those of mass production and distribution of print material for the general public or mass dissemination by broadcasting or electronic recordings. It could be argued that the birth of the 'Information Age', although presaged by mass communication, marks a new and separate historical path. Certainly, the mass media were well established before the supposed information 'revolution' and may be better considered as part of the industrial age rather than of its successor. There are

certainly many voices that have foretold the death of mass media precisely because of the rise of new information technologies that are said to render them obsolete (e.g. Maisel, 1973).

We can expect no clear answer to this theoretical conundrum in the short term, and for the time being it is sensible to consider the mass media at least as an integral part of some larger trend. As we saw in the previous chapter, there is an influential school of communication technology determinism that has posited significant consequences for the nature of content communicated, for the effects produced and the relationships established as arising from 'dominant' forms of technology of the day. This thesis was developed first in relation to printing, then extended to consider broadcast television, and it makes at least as much sense to consider the case of communication technologies that are in several respects novel. Everett Rogers, who describes himself as a 'soft technological determinist' identifies three crucial features of the new technology in terms of (1) their interactivity, (2) their individualized, demassified nature and (3) the 'asynchronous nature of the new communication systems' (1986: 9) (meaning they are no longer time-bound). Despite the differences, the 'new media' are being used and exploited in much the same way as the old mass media for selling, advertising, propaganda and persuasion and much besides.

The convergence spoken of above also means that the purposes for which the new media are used coincide often with those underlying 'old media'. It sometimes seems that it is the traditional mass media that are the most powerful promotional driving force behind the diffusion of new media. The interconnections by way of cross-references and mutual support increase all the time, and ownership and organization of old and new media also converge within multimedia businesses.

The Information Society concept has not been universally accepted as helpful for analysis, for reasons that have in part been explained. A central problem is the lack of a political dimension, since it seems to have no core of political purpose, simply an (attributed) inevitable logic of its own (van Dijk, 1999). In itself this constitutes an unspoken ideological bias towards technocratic and maybe free market outcomes. In this it may at least match the predominant spirit of the times in both popular and intellectual 'Western' circles.

THE MAIN ISSUES FOR 'NEW MEDIA THEORY'

If we assume a trajectory of change in line with the Information Society thesis as sketched above, a number of issues are highlighted. As will be evident, these are not entirely new, but they need to be looked at again in the light of media-technological change. It is also relevant to consider how far new technology creates or will create

a fundamental discontinuity such that older theory of mass communication is of decreasing relevance. In Chapter 4, mass media were looked at in the light of three very broad concerns: to do with *power and inequality, social integration and identity* and *social change*. Up to a point, theoretical perspectives on the new media can still be discussed in relation to the same themes (McQuail, 1986).

However, it soon becomes clear that on certain issues the terms of earlier theory do not fit the new media situation very well. In respect of *power*, for instance, it is much more difficult to *locate* the 'new media' in relation to the possession and exercise of power. They are not as clearly identified in terms of ownership, nor is access monopolized in such a way that the content and flow of information can be easily controlled. Communication does not flow in a predominantly vertical or centralized pattern from the 'top' or the 'centre' of society.

Access is widely available as sender, receiver, spectator or participant in some exchange or network. It is not possible to characterize the dominant 'direction' or bias of influence of information flows, although the issue of the degree of freedom available to the new 'channels' is far from settled. In some respects it is enlarging as expansion outpaces regulation, but there are also significant moves under way to bring it within the scope of law, regulation and stronger social control as well as of corporate media organization. At present, we cannot say that new media are possessed by and used in the interest of a dominant class, even though there are class-related inequalities of access and use and large corporations show great interest in acquiring property in new media.

In relation to *integration and identity* the conceptual terrain is much the same as that dealt with earlier. The same broad issue is still whether the new media are a force for fragmentation or cohesion in society. However, the specific questions that arise are empirically quite different and are also posed at different levels of analysis. It is not possible and makes little sense to characterize or quantify the predominant 'content' of new media, however these are defined, because of its diversity and the lack of 'audiences' in the old sense. Thus no hypotheses about the direction of effect can be formulated.

Older concerns about mass media took as their basis the central case of the nation state, usually coinciding with the territory served by a mass medium. Alternatively it might be a region, city or other political-administrative zone. Identity and cohesion were largely defined in geographical terms. The form of the technology (limited by physical distance and time) was partly responsible for this, but other factors were involved. The characteristics of 'new media' noted above, free them from the geographical restriction on dissemination and thus open up alternative bases for identification and network formation. The key questions are no longer confined to pre-existing social relationships and identities.

In respect of potential for social *change*, the issue of communication technology as itself an agent of change, altering social and cultural experience, remains central. However, the potential for new communications as an agent of planned economic or social change requires re-assessment. At first sight there is a big difference between

mass media that can be systematically applied to goals of planned development by way of mass information and persuasion (as in health, population, technical innovation campaigns) and the open-ended, non-purposive uses that are typical of new technology. The loss of direction and control over content by the sender seem to be crucial.

However, this is to repeat the mistake of early agents of planned development to assume that change can be achieved from outside on the basis of authority and superior expertise. It may be that more participatory media are equally or better suited to producing change, because they are more involving as well as more flexible and richer in information. This would be consistent with the more advanced models of the change process (Rogers, 1986). The problem, however, lies not in the nature of the technology, but in the continuing material barriers to access. The process of 'development' may still have to precede the deployment of new media, just as old media had to have an audience in order to have some effect.

THE POSSIBLE BASIS FOR A 'NEW MEDIA THEORY'

As Rice et al. (1983: 18) observed, the 'notion that the channel of communication might be as important a variable in the communication process as source, message, receiver and feedback, may have been overlooked'. Referring to the work of the 'Toronto School', they add that 'One need not be a technological determinist to agree that the medium may be a fundamental variable in the communication process'. Nevertheless, it is still very difficult to pin down the 'essential' characteristics of any given medium, and the ground for distinguishing between 'new' and 'old' media is not very solid.

The main problem lies in the fact that in actual experience it is hard to distinguish the channel or medium from the typical *content* that it carries or the typical *use* that is made of it or the *context of use* (for instance, home, work or public place). Precisely the same problem has bedeviled earlier research into the relative advantages and capacities of different 'traditional' media as channels of communication. However, this does not mean that there is no important difference nor some emerging discontinuity between old and new. At the moment we can do little more than make plausible suggestions.

More recently, Rice (1999) has argued that it is not very profitable to try to characterize each medium according to its specific attributes. Instead we should study the attributes of media in general and see how new media 'perform'. Contrasts and comparisons of media tend to 'idealize' certain features of a medium (e.g. face to face communication or the virtues of the traditional book), ignoring paradoxes of positive and negative consequences.

The diversity of the category 'new media' and their continually changing nature sets an obvious limit to theory-forming about their 'consequences'. The technological forms are multiplying but are also often temporary. It may be useful to think in terms of four main categories of 'new media' which share certain channel similarities and are approximately differentiated by types of use, content and context, as follows:

1. *Interpersonal communication media*. These include the telephone (increasingly mobile) and e-mail (primarily for work, but becoming more personal). In general, content is private and perishable and the relationship established and reinforced may be more important than the information conveyed.

2. *Interactive play media*. These are mainly computer based and video games, plus Virtual Reality devices. It is not certain if it makes sense to compare these with the 'old media', although they involve communication, use similar technology and may be considered as 'functional alternatives' to certain uses of media. If we do make the comparison, the main difference lies in the interactivity and perhaps the dominance of 'process' over 'use' gratifications (see p. 381).

3. *Information search media*. This is a wide category, but the Internet/WWW is the most significant example, viewed as a library and data source of unprecedented size, actuality and accessibility. However, the diversity of content (ranging from pornography to scientific information) and of motives for use defies any useful characterization, beyond the behavioural implications of using the various alternative technologies. Besides the Internet, the telephone is also increasingly a channel for information retrieval as are broadcast teletext and radio-data services. The distinction between new information channels and other available sources (new or old) is hard to establish, although the degree of *interactivity* and thus of flexibility and autonomy for the 'user' may be the most useful discriminating variable.

4. *Collective participatory media*. The category includes especially the uses of the Internet for sharing and exchanging information, ideas, experience and developing active (computer-mediated) relationships. Uses range from the purely instrumental to affective and emotional. Apart from the Internet, video and telephone conferencing are relevant here, although they are largely confined to work contexts.

The diversity indicated by this typology makes it hard to draw up any useful summary of *medium* characteristics that are unique to the 'new' media or applicable to all four categories. However, we can indicate certain dimensions or variables that are relevant and help to differentiate 'new' from 'old media', as seen from the perspective of an individual 'user'. These are:

- Degree of *interactivity*, as indicated by the ratio of response or initiative on the part of the user to the 'offer' of the source/sender.
- Degree of *social presence (or sociability)* experienced by the user, meaning the sense of personal contact with others that can be engendered by using a medium (Short et al. 1976; Rice, 1993). It also refers to the 'media richness', the extent to

which media can bridge different frames of reference, reduce ambiguity, provide more cues, involve more senses and be more personal.

- Degree of *autonomy*. The issue is whether or not a user feels in control of content and use, more or less independent of the source.
- Degree of *playfulness*, referring partly to uses for entertainment, enjoyment, as against utility and instrumentality, partly to the potential for enjoyment from the process of use of the technology in itself.
- Degree of *privacy* associated with the use of a medium and or its typical or chosen content. This includes the degree to which it is personalized and unique.

According to Perse and Dunn (1998) research into the use of home computers and other media shows the former to be little mentioned for any communication need. The conclusion is that 'computers are still not a primary channel to fill media related needs. In fact the most commonly mentioned use of mass communication was to keep busy and pass time'. These features are compared to the 'ritualistic' uses of mass media distinguished by Rubin (1984) as distinct from the gratification provided by specific content.

An attempt to conceptualize the Internet as a mass medium has been made by Morris and Ogan (1996), approaching it from the point of view of the audience. A difficulty they encountered is that the Internet is very fragmented, offering quite different kinds of communication experience. It is thus neither clearly distinct from ordinary mass media, nor itself a mass medium as usually defined. This is not only a matter of scale, but also of the lack of institutional properties of mass media, including their public identity and professionalism. Morris and Ogan place the concepts of uses and gratifications, degree and type of involvement and degree of social presence on the agenda, but find that too little research has been done to reach any firm conclusion about the essential characteristics of the Internet as a medium.

Lindlof and Schatzer (1998) offer a view of the Internet derived from audience ethnography, commenting on the diversity of its forms that include news groups, mailing lists, simulation spaces, web sites and so on. In their view, computer-mediated communication is different from other media use because it is transient, multi-modal, with few codes of conduct governing use, and allowing for such a high degree of 'end-user manipulation of content'. The condition of irrelevance of location of source 'offers new possibilities for civic life, shared learning and intercultural contact free of geographical limits, but also opens spaces for explicit sexual content, hate speech, rumor propagation, alcohol advertisements aimed at children'.

Despite the uncertainty, we can suggest that in general, new media compared with 'old' have a capacity to be more interactive, have more social presence, be more private, give more autonomy. They also have greater capacity for playfulness, in so far as play is interactive either with people or machines. There remain, however, some large question marks against the way in which rather abstract qualities should be understood in the context of media use.

A particular example is offered by the potential for sociability and interactivity. While it is true that the computer machine does connect people with other people, at the point of use it involves solitary behaviour, individualistic choices and responses and frequently anonymity. The relationships established or mediated by the new communicating machines are often transient, shallow and without commitment. They may be regarded less as an antidote to the individualism, rootlessness and loneliness associated with modern life than as a logical development towards forms of social interaction that can be achieved to order, as it were. The cultural requirements for engaging in and enjoying computer-mediated communication are thus quintessentially postmodernistic.

NEW PATTERNS OF INFORMATION TRAFFIC

Another useful way of considering the implications of the changes under discussion is to think in terms of alternative types of *information traffic* and the balance between them. Two Dutch telecommunication experts, J.L. Bordewijk and B. van Kaam (1986), have developed a model which helps to make clear and to investigate the changes under way. They describe four basic communication patterns and show how they are related to each other. The patterns are labelled 'allocution', 'conversation', 'consultation' and 'registration'.

Allocution

With allocution, information is distributed from a centre simultaneously to many peripheral receivers. This pattern applies to several familiar communication situations, ranging from a lecture, church service or concert (where listeners or spectators are physically present in an auditorium) to the situation of broadcasting, where radio or television messages are received by large numbers of scattered individuals at the same moment. Allocution (a word derived from the Latin for the address by a Roman general to assembled troops) is typically *one-way* communication to many, with relatively little personal 'feedback' opportunity (especially in the mass media situation). Another characteristic is that time and place of communication are determined by the sender or at the 'centre'. Although the concept is useful for this comparison, the gap between personal address to many and impersonal mass communication is a very large one and is not really bridgeable by a single concept.

Conversation

With conversation, individuals (in a potential communication network) interact directly with each other, bypassing a centre or intermediary and choosing their own partners as well as the time, place and topic of communication. This pattern applies in a wide range of situations, from that of an exchange of personal letters to use of electronic mail. The electronically mediated conversation does, however, often imply a centre or intermediary (such as the telephone exchange), even if this plays no active or initiatory role in the communication event.

Characteristic of the conversational pattern is the fact that parties are *equal* in the exchange. In principle, more than two can take part (for example, a small meeting or telephone conference). However, at some point, increased scale of participation leads to a merger with the allocutive situation.

Consultation

Consultation refers to a range of different communication situations in which an individual (at the periphery) looks for information at a central store of information – data bank, library, reference work, computer disc, etc. As noted, such possibilities are increasing. In principle, this pattern can also apply to the use of a newspaper (otherwise considered an allocutive mass medium), since the time and place of consultation and also the topic are determined by the receiver at the periphery and not by the centre.

Registration

The pattern of information traffic termed 'registration' is, in effect, the consultation pattern in reverse, in that a centre 'requests' and receives information from a participant at the periphery (usually without their awareness). This applies wherever central records are kept of individuals in a system and to all systems of surveillance. It relates, for instance, to the automatic recording at a central exchange of telephone calls, to electronic alarm systems and to automatic registration of television set usage in 'people-meter' audience research or for purposes of charging consumers. It also refers to the collation of personal particulars of e-commerce customers, for purposes of advertising and targeting. The accumulation of information at a centre often takes place without reference to, or knowledge of, the individual. While the pattern is not historically new, the possibilities for registration have increased enormously because of computerization and extended telecommunication connections. Typically, in this

pattern, the centre has more control than the individual at the periphery to determine the content and occurrence of communication traffic.

An integrated typology

These four patterns complement and border upon (or overlap with) each other. The authors of the model have shown how they can be related in terms of two main variables: of central versus individual control of information; and of central versus individual control of time and choice of subject (see Figure 6.1). The allocution pattern stands here for the typical 'old media' of mass communication and conforms largely to the transmission model – especially broadcasting, where a limited supply of content is made available to a mass audience. The consultation pattern has been able to grow, not only because of the telephone and new telematic media, but because of the diffusion of video- and sound-recording equipment and the sheer increase in the number of channels as a result of cable and satellite. The new media have also differentially increased the potential for 'conversational' or interactive communication between widely separated individuals. As noted, 'registration' becomes both more practicable and more likely to occur, although it is not a substitute for other types of communication traffic. It can be viewed as extending the powers of surveillance in the electronic age.

The arrows inserted in Figure 6.1 reflect the redistribution of information traffic from allocutory to conversational and consultative patterns. In general, this implies a broad shift of balance of communicative power from sender to receiver, although this may be counterbalanced by the growth of registration and a further development of the reach and appeal of mass media. Allocutory patterns have not necessarily diminished in volume, but they have taken new forms, with more small-scale provision

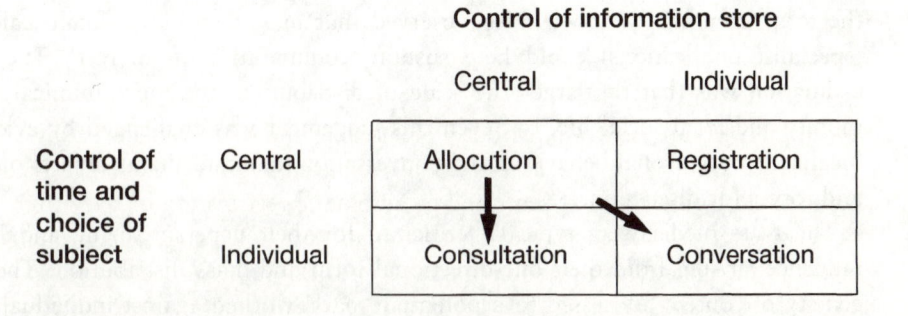

FIGURE 6.1 A typology of information traffic: communication relationships are differentiated according to the capacity to control the supply and the choice of content; the trend is from allocutory to consultative *or* conversational modes

for segmented audiences based on interest or information need ('narrowcasting'). Finally, we can conclude from this figure that patterns of information flow are not as sharply differentiated as might appear, but are subject to overlap and convergence, for technological as well as social reasons. The same technology (for example, the telecommunications infrastructure) can provide a household with facilities for each of the four patterns described.

This way of portraying the changes under way invites us to consider again the relevance of the current body of media theory concerning 'effects'. It seems that much of this only applies to the allocutory mode, where a transmission model may still be valid. For other situations we need an interactive, ritual or user-determined model. Even so, at present we do not have very adequate paradigms of theory or research for investigating possible changes in the way new media are experienced.

COMPUTER-MEDIATED COMMUNITY FORMATION

The idea of 'community' with reference to a real or ideal form of social organization has for long had an important position in social theory, especially as a tool for assessing the impact of social change and as a counterpoise to the idea of a mass. In earlier thinking a community referred to a set of people sharing a place (or some other bounded space), an identity, certain norms, values and cultural practices and usually small enough to know or interact with each other. Some elements of status and hierarchy and also social organization, if only informal, were also features.

The traditional mass media were viewed ambivalently in their relation to the typical (local) community. On the one hand, their largeness of scale and importation of outside values and culture were viewed as undermining communities based on personal interaction. On the other hand, the media in adapted localized forms could serve and reinforce community under the best conditions. Although it is another use of the term 'community' it was also observed that mass-distributed small-scale media (specialist publications) could help sustain 'communities of interest'. The general estimation was that the larger the scale of distribution, the more inimical to community and local social life, but even this judgement was challenged by evidence of localized interpersonal behaviour and conversation taking media as objects of interest and topics for discussion.

The mass media were typically criticized for their depersonalizing and isolating influence, arising from their one-directional form and mass distribution. The homogeneity of content addressed to a potential 'mass' worked against individualism and diversity. It also tended to displace local cultures and incorporate everyone into the same kind of consciousness. In this it accelerated other forces at work in industrial society (urbanism, mass politics, nationalism).

Against this background, there has been a continuing debate about the consequences of each innovation. In the 1960s and 1970s, the introduction of cable television was hailed not only as a way of evading the limits and drawbacks of mass broadcast television but as a positive means of community creation. Local cable systems could link up homes in a neighbourhood to each other and to a local centre. Programming could be chosen and made by local residents. Many extra services of information and help could be added on at low cost. In particular, access could be given to a wide variety of groups and even individual voices, with limited cost. The restricted bandwidth of broadcast television ceased to be a major practical constraint, and television by cable began to approach the abundance of print media, at least in theory.

The notions of a 'wired community' and wired city became popular (see Dutton et al., 1986) and experiments were conducted in many countries to test the potential of cable television. This was the first 'new medium' to be treated seriously as an alternative to 'old-style' mass media. In the end, the experiments were largely discontinued and failed to live up to expectations, giving rise to the expression 'the cable fable'. The more utopian hopes were based on false foundations, especially the assumption that such community-based miniature versions of large-scale professional media were really wanted enough by the people they were meant to serve. Problems of financing and organization were often unsurmountable. Cable distribution became not an alternative to mass media, but predominantly just another means of mass distribution, albeit with some space for local access in some places. Distinctive about these cable visions was the fact that a physical 'community' already existed but with unfulfilled potential that better inter-communication was supposed to realize.

A new set of expectations concerning community has developed around computer-mediated communication (CMC). The core idea is that of a **'virtual community'** that can be formed by any number of individuals by way of the Internet at their own choice or in response to some stimulus (Rheingold, 1994). Lindlof and Schatzer (1998) define a virtual community as one 'founded intentionally by people who share a set of similar interests, often revolving around certain texts or tropes imported from non-CMC venues, such as soap operas and their characters'.

Some features of real communities can be attained, including interaction, a common purpose, a sense of identity and belonging, various norms and unwritten rules, with possibilities for exclusion or rejection. There are also rites, rituals and forms of expression. Such on-line communities have the added advantage of being in principle open and accessible, while real communities are often hard to enter.

There have been numerous empirical studies of on-line 'communities', usually based on some common interest, for instance fandom for a music group or on some shared characteristic, such as sexual orientation or a particular social or health situation (see Jones, 1997, 1998). The typical conditions for the formation of a virtual community seem to include minority status, physical dispersal of members and a degree of intensity of interest. It can be appreciated that CMC offers possibilities for motivated and interactive communication that are not available from mass media nor from the

immediate physical environment. Lindlof and Schatzer (1998) use as their example a *Lesbian Café* based on a computer bulletin board system. One distinctive feature is the presence of 'lurkers' who observe but do not participate.

Proponents of the on-line community idea are usually aware that the term is a metaphor (Watson, 1997), rather than the real thing. On the other hand, the 'real thing' was generally rather elusive and sometimes mythical. Jones (1997: 17) cites Benedict Anderson's (1983) view that 'Communities are to be distinguished not by their falseness/genuineness, but by the style in which they are imagined'. Jones writes 'The Internet's communities are imagined in two ways inimical to human communities'. One is their frequent lack of significance and another the fact that there is an aimless and coincidental kind of connectedness about the experience. The term 'pseudo-community', taken from Beniger (1987), is used to express doubts about the genuine-ness of the virtual community.

The very fact of mediation by a machine tends to reduce the awareness of being in touch with other people. Even the advocates of virtual community, such as Rheingold (1994) recognize that on-line identities are often not genuine or revealed. They are adopted 'personae' often designed to conceal aspects of identity, for instance age or gender (Jones, 1997: 107). Participation in many on-line discussions and interactions is thus essentially anonymous, and this may sometimes be part of the attraction. The lack of authenticity and also commitment tends to undermine the claim to the term 'community' in its established meaning. Postman (1993) has criticized the adoption of the community metaphor because there is a lack of the essential element of account-ability and mutual obligation. Although computer-mediated communication does offer new opportunities to cross social and cultural boundaries, it can also indirectly reinforce the same boundaries. Those who want to belong to a community in cyberspace have to conform to its norms and rules in order to be recognized and accepted.

The entire terrain is still very much disputed, but it has to be recalled that there are many different kinds of on-line associations and it is not helpful to treat them as equal candidates for the same concept. The fact that many are not helpfully described by the term 'community' does not mean that there is not some real, possibly new, social formation involved.

POLITICAL PARTICIPATION, NEW MEDIA AND DEMOCRACY

The earlier mass media of press and broadcasting were widely seen as beneficial (even necessary) for the conduct of democratic politics. The benefit comes from the flow of information about public events to all citizens and the exposure of politicians and governments to the public gaze and critique. However, negative effects have also

been perceived, stemming from the dominance of channels by a few voices, the predominance of a 'vertical flow', and the heightened commercialism of the media market, leading to neglect of democratic roles. The typical organization and forms of mass communication limit access and discourage active participation and dialogue. The new electronic media have been widely hailed as a potential way of escape from the oppressive 'top-down' politics of mass democracies in which tightly organized political parties make policy unilaterally and mobilize support behind them with minimal negotiation and grass-roots input. The new media provide the means for highly differentiated provision of political information and ideas, almost unlimited access in theory for all voices, and much feedback and negotiation between leaders and followers. They promise new *fora* for the development of interest groups and formation of opinion.

Even 'old politics', it is said, might work better (and more democratically) with the aid of instant electronic polling and new tools of campaigning. The ideas concerning the public sphere and civil society discussed above have stimulated the notion that new media are ideally suited to occupy the space of civil society between the private domain and the domain of state activity (see page 157). According to conventional views, it has been difficult to identify where and what this space is, since the proverbial coffee shops are no longer adequate to the function of promoting the circulation of opinion in a modern society. The Habermasian ideal seems open to fulfilment by way of forms of communication (the Internet in particular) that make readily available vast amounts of relevant information and also allow citizens to express their views and communicate with each other and their political leaders without leaving their homes.

While conventional political communication in the form of media campaigns will continue, there is another dimension of informed participation in which dialogue takes place between politicians and active citizens, without the inevitable intervention of a party machine. Active political involvement can also operate at any desired level of office, ranging from the very local to the national. It is too early to conclude that politics has been given new life by new media, but there are emerging possibilities for 'electronic democracy' which do challenge the ritualized and scelerotic 'campaigns' that have come to dominate the political process.

Not least important, as Coleman (1999) points out, is the 'role of new media in the subversive service of free expression under conditions of authoritarian control of the means of communication'. It is certainly not easy for governments to control access to and use of the Internet by dissident citizens, but also not impossible. The threat of punishment can also be a powerful deterrent. Despite the openings towards more participatory politics promised by new media, their availability does not appear to pose any new theoretical issue or promise a new kind of politics as suggested by ideas of a 'Virtual Congress' and an 'Electronic town meeting', even a new form of electronic democracy (see Street, 1997). Essentially, in this vision the technology would solve problems of information and participation. However, it is not at all clear how the transformation of old politics can take place without other basic changes in society.

The new technology can be said to facilitate globalization, because of its capacity to overcome time and space barriers (including national frontiers) to communication. The new technologies are themselves often global in structure and in the way they work, promoting conformity in the manner of language (especially English), procedures and habits of use. They also originate in the economically dominant 'first world' and are developed in the interest of global firms and industries whose ownership is concentrated in the same countries. The United States is particularly dominant and tends to look after its own national state interest in the process of international development, seeking to apply its rules and management principles to the new technologies.

The networks, circles and connections between users of new technology based on telecommunications and computers do not have to follow the lines of national frontiers in the same way as old mass media almost invariably have done. It is therefore less appropriate to apply the centre–peripheral model of mass communication which reflects the varying degrees of dependency of poorer and smaller countries and regions on a few 'primary producers' of news and entertainment. The possession of the right technology does open doorways to new possibilities for information and intercommunication, irrespective of 'level of development' of one's own home place.

Nevertheless, the imbalance of communication still exists, and exceptions apply only to a small minority for certain purposes. The basic research has not been done to show the nature and extent of global imbalance. But there are enough data and indications to suppose that the informational 'content' made available by new technology and the rates of participation in consulting and exchanging information strongly favour the 'have' regions and nations (and especially the 'Anglo-Saxon' parts). The costs of technology and its use continue to favour the same already privileged beneficiaries as does the investment in infrastructure and management systems. The more new media become economically more interesting, the more this trend is accentuated.

In the earlier days of mass media, there was also a belief that the communicative reach and power of radio and television could help bridge the gaps in social and economic development. The reality proved to be different, and mass media, in their trans-national forms at least, were likely to do more for their originating societies and cultures than for their supposed beneficiaries in the 'third world'. The same tendency to see technology as a changer of the world is still present (Waisbord, 1998). It is hard to see how the situation is different, despite the greater potential for the 'users' and receivers of new media to claim access and to take over the means of cultural oppression. The way new communications technology has developed seems to favour specifically Western values and cultural forms including their individualism

and personal freedom. The collective interaction possibilities of the World Wide Web are posited on the obsolescence or decay of older, more firmly rooted forms of collectivity.

TECHNOLOGIES OF FREEDOM?

The words heading this section form the title of a seminal work, by Ithiel de Sola Pool (1983), that celebrated electronic means of communication because of the escape they offered from what he regarded as the illegitimate imposition of censorship and regulation on broadcast radio and television. The essence of his argument was that the only logical (though disputed) case for state control of media was spectrum shortage and the need to allocate access opportunity in semi-monopoly conditions. The emerging new era could grant the freedom enjoyed by print media and common carriers (telephone, mails, cable) to all public media. Distribution by cable, telephone line, new radio waves and satellite was rapidly removing the claim for regulation arising out of scarcity. Moreover, the increasing 'convergence of modes' of communication made it increasingly impossible as well as illogical to regulate one type of medium and not others.

The freedom that has been claimed as a feature of the new media (especially the Internet) is not precisely the same freedom as Pool was claiming for media in general. Essentially Pool wanted the freedom of the market and the 'negative freedom' (no government intervention) of the US **First Amendment** to apply to all media. The image of freedom attaching to the Internet has had more to do with its vast capacity and with the lack of structure, organization and management that characterized its earlier years when it was a freely accessible playground for allcomers, with much use subsidized by academic institutions or other public bodies. The system was there for all to use, even if the original motives for its creation were strategic and military, while the motives for its subsequent promotion and expansion were mainly economic and in the interest of telecommunication operators.

The system had an in-built resistance to attempts to control or manage it. It appeared not to be owned or managed by any one in particular, to belong to no territory of jurisdiction. In practice its 'content' and the uses made of it were not easy to control or sanction, even where jurisdiction could be established. In this it shared many features of common carrier media, such as mails and telephone. Contrary to Pool's vision of freedom, and unlike, for instance, the early experiments with videotex, there was no charge for access as sender and receiver.

Relative to most other media, the Internet remains free and unregulated. However, there have been clear tendencies, as it has grown in success and use, for its freedom to be limited (for instance in the US 1996 Communications Act). As it has become

more like a mass medium, with high penetration and a potential for reaching an important segment of the consumer market, there is a higher stake in forms of regulation and management. It is increasingly a medium for commerce (selling goods as well as information services), so that financial security has to be achieved. As it penetrates more homes, with ordinary families, rather than offices and universities, the demands for applying criteria of 'decency' and also for means of enforcement have grown, despite jurisdictional difficulties. As with earlier media, once a claim to great social impact is made, the demand for control grows and the practical obstacles to control turn out not to be so insurmountable (see Gringras, 1997). More and more of the normal legitimate accountability claims against public media are arising (e.g. about intellectual property, libel, privacy). The seeming anarchy of many service providers and content organizers is giving way to a more structured market situation. The perceived money-making potential of the Internet, reflected in the enormous rise in value of some Internet stocks, is going to mean that less and less content of value will really be 'free' in money terms. The management of the system will also have to be more transparent as well as efficient.

Police and intelligence services are paying more attention to the need for surveillance and control, especially in respect of potential trans-border crime, terrorism or domestic disaffection. Taken together the tendencies described lead to a severe modification of the Internet's anarchic and open image. The situation is too early and too unsettled to make an assessment, but not too early to say that even the most free *means* of communication cannot escape the operation of various 'laws' of social life. These include those of communication itself (which bind participants together in some mutual obligations or expectations), and especially those of economics and social pressure.

The more apocalyptic visions of the future indicate a potential for social control through electronic means that far outstrips those available in the industrial age, except where brute force could be used. The monitoring and tracking of informational traffic and interpersonal contacts is increasing, based essentially on the 'registration' pattern of computerized information traffic indicated above. Jansen wrote of the new potential for systematically eroding the privacy of the home and of interpersonal relations: 'Once the wires are in place, the Electronic Panopticon (referring to Jeremy Benthams's model prison) works automatically. Only the minimal supervision from the Tower is required' (1988: 23–4).

Rheingold (1994: 15) wrote 'the Net can also be an enormous invisible cage. Virtual communities are a hyper-realistic illusion of technical advance as a refuge from the destruction of human communities'. These visions of the future are based on real possibilities and reflect the uneven balance of power in society. However, they are not universally shared nor have they yet been realized. Green (1999), for instance, regards these fears as technologically deterministic and one-sided. He points to the potential for new media, as noted above, to reverse the direction of surveillance and to express democratic impulses by way of access to centres of power.

theories

The rhetoric surrounding new media has often embodied a claim that electronic media help to produce a more equal as well as a more liberated society. The big advantage is the ready access for all who want to speak, unmediated by the powerful interests that control the content of print media and the channels of broadcasting. You do not need to be rich and powerful to have a presence on the World Wide Web. The potential of new media to bypass established institutional channels does also seem to improve the chances for the many and reduce their dependence on the various monopolistic sources of information and influence. If all homes have the technology and the trend of expansion goes in that direction, then universal access to cultural and informational goods in a coming 'videotopia' seems to follow. The political voices urging us to develop the 'electronic highway' into homes, libraries, schools and workplaces see this as an emancipatory programme of action.

The critics have not been silent on this prospect. The school of political economy sees little reason to change a view of the world according to which the chief beneficiaries of 'electronic highways' will continue to be large electronic and tele-communication firms (Sussman, 1997). The new media are no different from old media in terms of the social stratification of ownership and access. It is the better off that first acquire and then upgrade the technology and are always ahead of the poor. They are differentially empowered and, if anything, move further ahead. Social and information gaps widen rather than narrow and there emerges an 'information underclass' as well as a social underclass.

There has also been controversy in relation to gender. Despite the general advantage that women seem to have gained in employment terms from informatization of work, there has been a persistent claim that computers have a male bias. Some theorists of feminism (e.g. Ang and Hermes, 1991) resist any idea that there is an essential difference between men and women in relation to being comfortable with computer technology. However, according to Turkle (1988) the problem is not that computers have a male bias, but that 'the computer is socially constructed as male'. It will take time to establish the truth of this matter, and there is unlikely to be any single universal truth.

In most sober assessments of the development of communication technology, it is dystopians that seem more convincing than utopians, at least in rejecting the possibility of a quick fix. Beniger's (1986) interpretative history of communication innovations since the early 19th century finds that they fit within a pattern, not of increasing libera-tion, but of increasing possibilities for management and control. He uses the term 'control revolution' to describe the communications revolution. Whatever the poten-tial, the needs of commerce, industry, the military and bureaucracy have done most to promote development and determine how innovations are actually applied.

Another chronicler of communication innovation (Winston, 1986) recognized that most new technologies have innovative potential, but the actual implementation

always depends on two factors. One is the operation of 'supervening social necessity' that dictates the degree and form of development of inventions. Secondly, there is the ' "law" of the suppression of radical potential', which acts as a brake on innovation to protect the social or corporate status quo. In general, he argues for theories of 'cultural' rather than technological determination. Carey (1998) takes a similar position about the 'new media', arguing that 'globalization, the Internet and computer communications are all underdetermined by technology and history. The final determination of these new forms is one prepared by politics'.

If the institutionalization of all technologies has led until now to the suppression of any radical tendency, there is no particular reason to suppose that this will be different with the latest inventions. Certainly the early history of the Internet has seen it evolve from a free tool and toy for students and academics to very serious big business in which applications are driven by expectations of profit. It will be 'free' only where this serves the purposes of commercial development.

CONCLUSION

This excursion in theory has been somewhat inconclusive, although generally arguing against the need as yet to recast the main frameworks of mass communication theory. Public communication continues much as before. The main values of liberalism, democracy, work, human rights and even communication ethics are evolving rather than collapsing at the end of the 20th century. Even the old problems addressed by such values are still in place, including war, injustice, inequality, crime and want. Nevertheless, there are some signs of change on the way when looked at from the communication perspective. Three aspects call for attention. One is the redrawing of social (and cultural) boundaries that formation of networks encourages. Another is the potential transformation of political communication (really of politics) in the widest sense as the old 'allocutive' means seem to perform less well. Thirdly, there is the decline of shared public space, however hard this is to quantify, in part the result of communicative developments and the 'informatization' process and also the fragmentation of once common cultural patterns.

FURTHER READING

van Dijk, J.A.G.M. (1999) *The Network Society*. London: Sage.
Jones, S. (1997) *Virtual Culture*. London: Sage.
Mackay, H. and O'Sullivan, T. (eds) (1999) *The Media Reader*. London: Sage.
Rice, R.E. and Associates (1984). *The New Media*. Newbury Park, CA: Sage.
Webster, F. (1995) *Theories of the Information Society*. London: Sage.

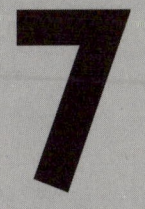

normative theory of media and society

It is already clear from earlier chapters that it is virtually impossible to separate ideas about the 'objective' relationship between media and society from 'normative' or even ideological considerations. This is partly because all the criteria and concepts used to describe and assess the way media work involve or invite some sort of value judgement, for instance when we speak of freedom, identity, integration, diversity and even information itself. In this chapter we turn quite deliberately to normative questions and especially to ideas of how the media *ought* to or are expected to be organized and to behave in the wider public interest or for the good of society as a whole. We are dealing in general with both the rights and the obligations or responsibilities of the media as these are perceived in various national societies and more widely. The forms of organization are essentially matters of media *structure*, while the 'behaviour' refers to matters of media *performance*, thus to the way media carry out their chosen or allotted tasks.

The concept of a '**public interest**' is both simple and also very contested in social and political theory. As applied to the mass media, its simple meaning is that the media carry out a number of important, even essential, tasks in a contemporary society and it is in the general interest that these are performed and performed well. It also implies that we should have a media system that is operated according to the same basic principles governing the rest of a society, especially in relation to justice, fairness, democracy and current notions of desirable social and cultural values. At the minimum, we can say that it is in the public interest that the media do not cause social problems or extreme offence. But the idea of a public interest involves positive expectations as well as certain restrictions and forms of accountability (see Chapter 8). If we have a clear idea of what the 'public interest' is in a given case, then we have the basis for an appropriate 'normative theory' that will spell out what ought and what ought not to happen.

This simple notion does not take us very far in reality. The first problem encountered is that most media are not established in order to serve the public interest as such but to follow some goal of their own choosing. The goal is sometimes defined in cultural, professional or political terms but more often it is the goal of making profit as a business. Sometimes it is both at the same time. This points to the key issue of determining just what the public interest might be and of who should decide it. There are always diverse and conflicting versions of what is good for a society as a whole, and there is even support for the view that it is better for the media not to pursue any normative goal at all. Rather, the many different media should be left free to do what they want, within the limits of the law. Where media are run on a commercial basis, as they mainly are, the media's view of what is the public interest tends to equate it with what interests the public. This shifts the responsibility for norms, ethics and values, etc. to the society. The whole dispute lies at the heart of the debate over liberalism and

collectivism (or communitarianism) that has raged for the entire 20th century and even longer, affecting all spheres of public life.

The difficulties of handling the public interest concept are inextricably connected with its high significance. In this respect, Blumler (1998: 54–5) makes three key points. Firstly, just as in the case of government, there are questions of authority as well as of power: 'In communications, the media are similarly placed. The justification for their freedoms, their wide-ranging roles in society, politics and culture, and their place in regulatory orders depends ultimately on the public interests presumed to be served thereby'. In short, the power of the media, like that of government, has to be used in a *legitimate* way, which is not far removed from the notion of *responsibility*. Secondly Blumler argues that 'a certain transcendent quality attaches to the notion of the public interest. It is different from and, in policy terms, superior to particular interests. This entails a longer-term perspective, in which the claims of successor generations and the future of society are included as well as people's immediate needs'. Thirdly 'notions of the public interest must work in an imperfect and impure world'. This means inevitable tension, compromise and improvisation according to circumstances.

Held (1970) has described two of the main versions of what constitutes the public interest and how its content might be established. One is a 'majoritarian' view, according to which the issue should be settled by reference to the popular vote. In the case of media this would tend to equate the public interest with 'giving the public what it wants', pleasing the majority of consumers in the media market. The opposing view is called 'unitarian' or absolutist, since the public interest would be decided by reference to some single dominant value or ideology. This would lead at best to a paternalist system in which decisions about what is good are decided by guardians or experts. Between the free-market version of the public interest and the paternalistic model, there are alternatives, but none offers clear guidance. The main other way is an approach that involves debate and democratic decision-making on the one hand and, on the other, *ad hoc* judicial determinations of what is or is not in the public interest in a given case. As we will see later, there are a number of different ways in which the accountability of media to society in terms of the public good can be achieved or at least pursued (see pages 180–7).

Whatever the arguments about the concept of public interest, it is quite obvious that the mass media have everywhere been subject to extensive control and regulation by law and other formal or informal means with a view to getting them to do what 'society' wants or prevent them from doing what it doesn't. The actual means and content of control varies a good deal from one national media 'system' to another, influenced by the usual political, cultural and economic determinants. They vary also from one medium to another and are rarely internally coherent or consistent.

Leaving theory aside, in the practice of media politics, law and regulation, there seems to have been quite a lot of agreement on the main components of the public interest in respect of mass media, going well beyond the minimum requirement of causing no harm. To judge from many cases where public interest has had to be

specified, the main requirements from the media are as listed in Box 7.1. More will be said of these components in this and later chapters, and it will be obvious that trying to specify the *content* of the public interest in media even at this very general level raises many thorny problems.

> **Box 7.1   Main public interest requirements from mass media**
> - Plurality of ownership of media
> - Freedom of publication
> - Diversity of information available to public
> - Diversity of expression of opinion
> - Extensive (near-universal) reach
> - Quality of information and culture available to public
> - Adequate support for the democratic political system
> - Respect for judicial system
> - Respect for individual and general human rights

In this chapter we take a broad and historical look at the main theoretical approaches to these questions and the directions of normative theory that have been the result. Before that we consider the main issues that have arisen.

MAIN ISSUES FOR SOCIAL THEORY OF THE MEDIA

As noted above, we can differentiate between norms and standards that apply to the structure and organization of media and those that apply to their behaviour or content. However, there is a logical connection between the two, and on a larger perspective the same set of principles applies to both aspects, as will be made clear in Chapter 8. Here we concentrate on the main types of problem that have surfaced in debates concerning the relation between media and society. A differentiation is made between five categories. All but the first of these raise issues of content and thus possible restrictions on freedom to publish.

Structure and ownership

The core matters relate to the degree of freedom enjoyed by the media and also the degree of freedom and access of citizens to media of their choice. The question of freedom arises both in relation to the state but also in relation to economic and other powerful interests in the society. The essential norm is that media should have a certain independence, sufficient to protect free and open public expression of ideas and

information. The second part of the issue raises the question of diversity, a norm that opposes concentration of ownership and monopoly of control, whether on the part of the state or private media industry. The guiding principle is that citizens should have access to media that reflect their ideas and meet their interests and needs. In addition, the many and diverse would-be voices in the society have wide opportunities to use media to communicate to the wider society.

Public order and the security of the state

While it is common for authoritarian regimes to use state security as an excuse for controlling or closing media, there is a widely held view in democracies (and demonstrated in public opinion surveys) that there are some legitimate limits to media freedom. The issue arises because of the potential attributed to the media to either 'harm' society by causing conflict and disorder or to benefit society by assisting in essential processes of maintaining order and the integrity of the society. The circumstances envisaged where this issue arises are usually extreme ones involving grave external threats, actual war, extreme internal conflict or violent terrorist acts. Although there is some consensus on extreme hypothetical cases, this is a disputed territory because of the inclination of governments to use public interest arguments to maintain secrecy and deny legitimate claims for information and freedom to publish.

'Public sphere' expectations

This heading refers to a wide range of positive expectations about the essential (also normal) contribution of mass media to the working of political and other social institutions. This contribution is made through: publishing full, fair and reliable information on public matters; assisting in the expression of diverse points of view; giving access to many voices in society; facilitating the participation of citizens in social and political life, etc. By implication, these points also cover certain negative aspects of media conduct, especially those associated with extreme 'commercialization' (trivialization and sensationalism) and with promoting cynical and negative images of public figures and political processes.

Cultural values

The issues that fall in this category are diverse, ranging from questions of morals and decency to matters of culture and aesthetic taste. In general the media are expected to

respect if not support the dominant values and moral standards of their own society and, though less strongly, to give expression to the culture, arts and language of their own national society. In this domain, there is more negative than positive normative theory, prohibitions rather then prescriptions (for instance in relation to violence and pornography). The application of norms varies considerably according to the range of the media involved (extent of public impact) and the degree to which there is a public or private dimension to the issue. Issues are public where significant social groups are involved (e.g. children, women, the mentally ill, ethnic minorities) and where great offence or some social harm is feared.

Rights of individuals

The media often impinge on individual rights, even where these are protected either in law or popular opinion. The most frequently occurring issues concern personal reputation (libel and slander), rights to privacy, property rights (e.g. copyright), and rights to anonymity by those accused. There is inevitably a disputed frontier zone where it can be claimed that violation of private rights is justified by a larger public interest. This arises, for instance, in the case of political scandals, or some criminal matters (e.g. exposing paedophiles), or where a public celebrity is involved.

There are, of course other issues on which content may be restricted on public interest grounds. These include some health or safety issues (for instance tobacco advertising), judicial matters (e.g. contempt of court), the working of the political system (publication of opinion poll results). These examples are sufficient to underline the point that the media, perhaps more than any other social institution, operate in the full glare of publicity and are as much watched by the rest of society as they watch society. How and with what results this public scrutiny of the public watchdog takes place is discussed later.

EARLY APPROACHES TO THEORY: THE PRESS AS 'FOURTH ESTATE'

This chapter will be mainly concerned with expectations from 'society' in the sense of the organized political community and with topics that are likely to concern the news and journalism in particular. Because of this it is permissible to use the term 'press theory', which generally refers to journalistic matters in the widest sense. The first media were print media, and the most significant freedoms are those gained and still claimed by and for print media. The historical background and/or current context for all of the perspectives to be discussed is one that assumes a general commitment to freedom of the press, meaning the right to publish without any prior censorship or

licence and without incurring penalties, within the limits of other legal obligations. In an important sense, in the times and places covered by this discussion (mostly 20th century Western type democracies) the only fully respected theory of the press has been the theory of **press freedom**. Everything else is a qualification or a limitation designed for some end of the common good. Later in this chapter, the nature of press freedom will be assessed directly in the light of these different perspectives and of changes in the media (see pages 153–6).

In the light of the above remarks we can say that the 'original' theory of the press was concerned with the role of journalism in the political process, as propounded by a variety of liberal thinkers including Thomas Paine, John Stuart Mill, Alexis de Tocqueville and many others. The term 'Fourth Estate' was reputedly coined by Edmund Burke in late 18th century England to refer to the political power possessed by the press, on a par with the other three 'estates' of power of the British realm: the Lords, Church and Commons. The power of the press arose from its ability to give or withhold publicity and from its informative capacity. The central freedom was to report and comment on the deliberations, assemblies and the acts of governments. This freedom was the cornerstone of representative democracy and of progress. All the revolutionary and reformist movements from the 18th century onwards inscribed liberty of the press on their banners and made use of it in practice to advance their causes.

In this particular, mainly Anglo-American tradition of thought, freedom of the press was closely linked with the idea of freedom of the individual and with liberal and utilitarian political philosophy. Philosophical support for press freedom was found essentially in arguments against censorship and suppression of opinion. John Stuart Mill's argument in his book *On Liberty*, states that

> the peculiar evil of silencing the expression of an opinion is, that it is robbing the human race, posterity as well as the existing generation, those who dissent from the opinion even more than those who hold it. If the opinion is right, they are deprived of the opportunity of exchanging error for truth; if wrong, they lose what is almost as great a benefit, the clearer perception and livelier impression of truth, produced by its collision with error.

These ideas were later worked into the notion of a 'self-righting' mechanism by which the freely expressed truth will surely triumph over error when both are published freely. The core idea goes back to John Milton. Another popular way of expressing the same idea is in terms of 'the free market-place of ideas', first used in 1918 by an American judge. Although used metaphorically, this phrase has had the unfortunate effect of associating freedom of the press very closely with the idea of a literal free market. The historical context of the struggle for press freedom was almost invariably one of antagonism between publication and some authority, first the Church and later government in many aspects. It is not surprising that press freedom came to be defined primarily as freedom from restriction. This was the meaning it had been given in legal terms in the United States, in the words of the First Amendment to the US Constitution (1791) to the effect that 'Congress shall make no law . . .

abridging the freedom of speech or of the press'. By contrast, reformed constitutions in many other countries have referred to a right guaranteed to citizens. For example, Article 7 of the 1848 constitution of The Netherlands says 'No-one needs advance permission in order to make public through the printing press any thoughts or feelings, aside from everyone's responsibility in law'.

By the end of the 19th century and early 20th century it was clear that press freedom in the economic sense and in purely negative terms of rejecting government interference was also a potential weapon against the liberation of the people from their economic if not their political chains. Instead of being a vehicle for advancing freedom and democracy, it was becoming (especially in the Anglo-American homeland of the ideas) more and more a means of making money and propaganda for the new and powerful capitalist classes and especially the 'press barons'.

THE 1947 COMMISSION ON FREEDOM OF THE PRESS AND THE THEORY OF SOCIAL RESPONSIBILITY

In response to widespread criticism of the American newspaper press, especially because of its sensationalism and commercialism, but also its political imbalance and monopoly tendencies, a private commission of inquiry was set up in 1942. The founder was the publisher Henry Luce and it was conducted under the high-minded chairmanship of Robert Hutchins, Chancellor of Chicago University (Blanchard, 1977). The aim of the commission was 'to examine areas and circumstances under which the press of the United States is succeeding or failing; to discover where free expression is or is not limited, whether by government censorship pressure from readers or advertisers or the unwisdom of its proprietors or the timidity of its management'.

The commission forms an important milestone in the present story for several reasons. It was the first of many such inquiries and reports, often initiated by governments in many countries, to look into the failure of the media to meet the needs of society. In the United States there has been no equivalent public inquiry into the press, but several commissions have looked at specific problems arising from the activities of the media, especially in relation to violence and civil unrest. Secondly, the 1947 Commission was perhaps the first occasion since freedom of the press was attained when the need for intervention by government to put right the ills of the press was contemplated, and this in the heartland of capitalism. Thirdly, it served as an influential example to other countries, especially in the period of reform and reconstruction that followed the Second World War. Fourthly, the findings of the report contributed something of substance to subsequent theorizing and to the practice of accountability, although there is no real evidence that it actually improved the press at the time.

The findings of the commission (Hutchins, 1947) were critical of the press for its frequent failings and for being so limited in the access it gave to voices outside the circle of a privileged and powerful minority. The report coined the notion of **social responsibility** and named the key journalistic standards that the press should seek to maintain. A responsible press should 'provide a full, truthful, comprehensive and intelligent account of the day's events in a context which gives them meaning'. It should 'serve as a forum for the exchange of comment and criticism' and be a 'common carrier of the public expression'. Thirdly, the press should give a 'representative picture of constituent groups in society' and also present and clarify the 'goals and values of society'. The report criticized the sensationalism of the press and the mixing of news with editorial opinion.

In general the Commission supported the concept of a diverse, objective, informative and independent press institution which would avoid causing offence or encouraging crime, violence or disorder. Social responsibility should be reached by self control not government intervention. However, the latter is not ruled out. Siebert et al.'s interpretation of social responsibility locates it under a concept of positive liberty – 'freedom for', rather than 'freedom from'. They write (1956: 95) 'Social responsibility theory holds that the government must not merely allow freedom; it must actively promote it. . . . When necessary, therefore, the government should act to protect the freedom of its citizens'. The acts of government mentioned include legislation to forbid 'flagrant abuses', and it may also 'enter the field of communication to supplement existing media'.

The 'theory of social responsibility' involved a view of media ownership as a form of public trust or stewardship, rather than as an unlimited private franchise. One of the members of the Commission, William Hocking (1947: 169) wrote 'Inseparable from the right of the press to be free has been the right of the people to have a free press. But the public interest has advanced beyond that point; it is now the right of the people to have *an adequate press*'. And of the two rights, he added 'it is the right of the public that now takes precedence'. This is one fundamental basis for the demand for responsibility. The other basis derives from the fact that the ownership of modern mass communications (then newspapers and broadcasting especially) was already highly concentrated, giving great power to a small number of people. This power carried with it a responsibility to exercise it with great caution and respect for others. It has been an influential idea, not only on the press but also in the legitimation of the government regulation of broadcasting, especially in the United States. Until the deregulatory moves of the 1980s, the Federal Communication Commission (FCC) often acted on the assumption that broadcasting was a public trust, subject to review and even revocation. The main principles of the theory are summarized in Box 7.2.

The social responsibility tradition that received its philosophical basis in the 1947 American Commission was actually put into practice with much more determination and effects in countries other than the United States, especially in Western Europe in the two or three decades following the Second World War. The impulse was three-fold:

the wish to make a new beginning after the war with old institutions, the general rise of more 'progressive' politics, and the experience of a wave of press concentration that revived fears of private media monopoly.

Picard (1985) coined the term 'Democratic-socialist theory of the press' to describe the European 'social welfare' model of mass media in this period, although this somewhat overstates the leftist credentials of the thinking. However, it is certainly true that in a number of countries (especially Britain and Sweden), searching public enquiries were undertaken into the state of the media (see, for instance Royal Commission on The Press, 1977). These looked at press diversity and concentration, and in a number of countries, subsidies were introduced to maintain a range of competing newspapers and especially to support ailing and minority publications. The guiding objective was certainly the health of democracy. The public interest was interpreted as justifying various forms of intervention by the state in what had been a free market although actual intervention was kept to a minimum. The European Union has to some extent inherited the mantle of the nation states and has conducted enquiries into the level of media diversity and concentration of ownership and at least contemplated the need for concerted measures to protect these important democratic values.

PROFESSIONALISM AND MEDIA ETHICS

Another significant response to the perceived failings of the mass newspaper press, especially its commercialism, but also its lack of political independence, was the development of professionalism amongst journalism. This took various forms, including the organization into associations, the formation of Press Councils and the drawing up of principles of good practice in the form of codes of practice and ethics. The historical development of journalism and the institutional forms taken are outside the scope of this discussion, but are nevertheless of great importance for the content and implementation of normative theory. Press Councils are typically voluntary, or at least non-governmental, bodies that mediate between the public and the mass media (see Sonninen and Laitila, 1995). Their main function is to adjudicate on complaints

from any party affected by the media, but especially the printed press (broadcasting has its own separate forms). This function implies the need to have some codes of standards or principles to which reference can be made, and in general press councils are instruments of self-regulation for the press that acknowledge a responsibility to the public.

A journalistic code of ethics refers to a set of principles of professional conduct that are adopted and controlled by journalists themselves. The movement towards codifying journalistic practice had already started in the USA before the Hutchins Committee Report (Hutchins, 1947), and one of the first Canons of Journalism was published by the American Society of Newspaper Editors in 1923. Codes of conduct were being introduced in Europe at around the same time, notably in France, Sweden and Finland, and eventually in nearly all countries (Laitila, 1995).

The phenomenon reflects the general process of professionalization of journalism, but also the wish of the media industry to protect itself from criticism, and especially from the threat of external intervention and reduced autonomy. The study of codes on their own can give a misleading idea of what journalism is really about, but their content provides a good idea of what it was felt that journalism *ought* to be doing. At least they reveal the values that the media publicly proclaim as guidelines for their work. To that extent they constitute a form of normative theory. Nevertheless, the codes are often little more than collections of disparate and practical prescriptions that do not express any single organizing idea about the nature of society or the overall social purpose of the institution. To discover this requires some interpretation.

The many different codes reflect differences in the conventions and traditions of the country concerned and in the relative influence of different interested parties – publishers, editors, journalists or an external regulatory body. Most codes concentrate on the provision of reliable information and on avoiding distortion, suppression, bias, sensationalism and the invasion of privacy (Harris, 1992). But some codes go further in expressing some view of the larger role of journalism in society.

A comparative study of journalistic codes in 31 European countries carried out by Laitila (1995) shows there to be a very large number of different principles, although she classified them in terms of six types of accountability. These were: to the public; to the sources and referents; to the state; to the employer; for professional integrity; for protection of the status and unity of the profession. Although there is considerable diversity of codes, especially when all the separate entries are considered, Laitila found quite a high level of agreement on certain general principles. Six in particular, all with some degree of relevance to the wider society, were found in nearly all of the 31 codes examined. These are summarized in Box 7.3.

Certain specific provisions that were common (present in more than 70% of codes) included: the prohibition of discrimination on the basis of race/ethnicity/religion, etc.; respect for privacy; prohibition of bribes or any other benefits.

Codes are nearly always national in formulation, but there has been some movement to recognize the broader significance of news in world affairs. Under the auspices

> **Box 7.3   Most frequent principles in journalistic codes**
>
> - Truthfulness of information
> - Clarity of information
> - Defence of the public's rights
> - Responsibilities in forming public opinion
> - Standards of gathering and presenting information
> - Respecting the integrity of the sources

of Unesco a set of 'International Principles of Professional Ethics in Journalism' was drawn up (Traber and Nordenstreng, 1993) that drew attention to additional matters. These included the idea of a 'Right to Information' and the need to respect universal values and the diversity of cultures. There was also emphasis on the need for journalism to promote human rights, peace, national liberation, social progress and democracy (see Nordenstreng, 1998).

On the face of it, it does look as if there is quite a lot of common ground in what journalists in different countries formally accept as the appropriate standards. In that sense there is something like a shared body of normative theory to apply to daily practice. There is much less attention to be found in most codes, if at all, to the larger purposes of journalism in society. The predominant emphasis nearly everywhere is on the standards of objective (neutral), independent and informative (factually correct) journalism. Mancini (1996) has commented on the disjunction between the widely diffused and proclaimed adherence to this liberal theory of journalism and actual practice in many countries. The 'gap' between theory and practice is found on two main points. One relates to the investigative, critical and advocacy role of the journalist that gets little notice in any code. Another relates to the supposed independence and neutrality of journalism, when in practice most journalism operates in rather close symbiosis with government, powerful economic interests and other authorities. These observations lead at least to the conclusion that journalistic codes are inadequate and incomplete as theory and perhaps to the view that they should better be regarded as a particular ideology with a particular purpose.

We should also keep in mind that quite a few media organizations, especially in television broadcasting, maintain internal codes of practice (sometimes published, sometimes not) dealing with the same and other issues to provide guidelines for editors and producers. These are somewhat different from the professional codes, because they mainly assist internal control and accountability. Sometimes they are designed to cope with the special circumstances of audiovisual media, with their greater potential for impact. They also play a part in responding to external content regulations that apply, not only to journalism, but also to fiction and dramatic representations. In those circumstances, different specific problems arise, although in the end they usually derive from the same basic principles, which include truth, fairness, openness, respect for others, decency and the need to avoid harmful public consequences.

Beyond the area of news journalism, there is extensive evidence of regulation in the form of voluntary codes designed mainly to protect the public from some possible harm or the industry from outside pressure. Advertising is nearly everywhere subject to various self-imposed restrictions and guidelines. Motion pictures have from early on been subject to forms of censorship at the point of production, the most famous and influential example being the Motion Picture Code of Conduct introduced in the USA in 1933 to deal mainly with portrayals of sex, mainly under the influence of the Catholic Church. Broadcast television has been even more restricted. These types of codification do little more than reveal a fear of the influence of the media and a fear of public disapproval.

FOUR THEORIES OF THE PRESS AND BEYOND

A significant moment in the development of theorizing about the media (again really the newspaper press) occurred through the publication of a small textbook by three American authors (Siebert et al., 1956). This set out to describe the then current alternative 'theories of the press', concerning the relation between press and society. The book has been widely sold, translated, used in education and debated ever since (Nordenstreng, 1997), perhaps because of the striking claim of its title and the gap it fills in the literature on mass media. Recently it has been subject to extensive review, criticism and effective refutation, not only because of the near demise of one of the 'four theories' – that of Soviet Communism, but for other inadequacies (Nerone, 1995). An important aspect of the whole project was the proposition that the 'press always takes on the form and coloration of the social and political structures within which it operates. Especially it reflects the system of social control' (Siebert et al., 1956: 1).

Despite this proposition, the book provides little or no evidence or illustration apart from depicting Soviet Communist theory as an integral part of the Soviet system. The three other 'theories' presented are called 'authoritarian', 'libertarian', and 'social responsibility', respectively. Furthermore, according to more recent critics (including Nerone, 1995), the book is really only about one theory, the libertarian, or at best two – libertarian and its antithesis, authoritarian, of which the Soviet model is offered as a modern example. What is described as 'authoritarian theory' is really a description of two or more centuries of control of the press by various (mostly European) repressive regimes, a situation from which the USA happily escaped by freeing itself from Britain.

Authoritarianism is mostly empty of theoretical content, although its fundamental guiding principle is summarized in the words of Dr Samuel Johnson, the 18th century English writer as follows.

"Every society has a right to preserve public peace and order, and therefore has a good right to prohibit the propagation of opinions which have a dangerous tendency". According to Johnson, it is not the magistrate that has such a right but society and he adds that the restraint of opinion may be morally wrong, but it is "politically right". (quoted in Siebert et al., 1956: 36)

Soviet communist theory is described as an example of a 'positive' theory of the media in the sense that the media had as their goal the spread and reinforcement of Marxist truth and the attainment of a classless society, after the withering away of the proletarian state. Apart from being state controlled and not privately owned, the main difference from libertarian theory is seen as the strong emphasis on the rights of the society rather than of the individual.

Libertarian theory is described both in terms of the classic struggle for freedom and democracy against various forms of tyranny but also in terms of the constitutional basis and operation of the American media system. The main principle, apart from the supreme importance of the negative freedom of absence of government control, is the appeal to the 'self-righting' process. According to this, truth triumphs over error in the end and leads to the 'free market place of ideas', which seems to bless private ownership and the free enterprise system (see page 147). Certain passages wrestle uneasily with the case of broadcasting and the cinema which were in many respects subject to government control even in the United States.

There is no doubt that the book was published at a critical moment in the Cold War when the two sides were pitted in a battle for hearts and minds of the still uncommitted world and the freedom and unfreedom of the media was a central issue. The USA was actively trying to export its own ideology of liberalism and free enterprise, and its model of press freedom was especially important in this (Blanchard, 1986). At the very least it can be said that the 'Four Theories' fitted this programme. According to Nerone (1995), the authors 'uncritically accepted the very ideological mystification the media owners propound to explain their own existence. The myth of the free press in the service of society exists because it is in the interests of media owners to perpetuate it'. Aside from being generally uncritical, the main failing that has been identified is the unspecified assumption that only government and not private capital can be a constraint on free expression. The worst it seems that private ownership can cause is some failures in performance and decline in quality.

The version of libertarian theory, based on American practice of the period, has been the object of much critical comment. As Nerone (1995) shows, it is not really a good theoretical exposition, although that was not really its pretension. More to the point are the weaknesses of substance in the libertarian theory that is the central focus of the story, although the discussion of 'social responsibility' provides some counter-argument. Firstly, the theory identifies press freedom very closely with property rights – the ownership of the means of publication, neglecting the economic barriers to access and the abuse of monopolistic publishing power. Secondly, the liberty of the press is too much framed as a negative concept – freedom *from* government. An alternative, more positive or affirmative version would endow the concept with ideas of purposes

theories

and positive benefits, which might need some social intervention. As Glasser (1986: 93) writes:

> From the perspective of a negative concept of freedom, the press is under no obligation to extend its liberty or to accommodate the liberty of others. . . . From the perspective of an affirmative understanding . . ., in contrast, freedom and responsibility stand side by side . . . [and] an individual's ability to gain the benefits of liberty must be included among the conditions definitive of liberty.

Thirdly, as we have noted, the theory does not seem to apply very well to media other than to the printed press or to many media functions other than journalism. It has much reference to opinion and belief, but much less relevance for information and many of the issues of freedom that arise in the newer conditions of an Information Society, including access, confidentiality, privacy, property rights, etc. Fourthly, the theory is vague about who has or benefits from the right to freedom. If it is the newspaper proprietor who has the right, what of the rights of editors, journalists and even the public? There are many points of detailed dispute, including the question of where the limits of freedom can come. At what point can the state legitimately intervene to protect 'essential' interests. In general, historical example has shown that states effectively adopt the authoritarian perspective when they think they need to and can get away with it, following Dr Johnson's notion of a political right (see page 154).

Despite these and other limitations, the *Four Theories* book has promoted not only counter-attack and debate, but also many attempts to rewrite or extend the 'theories' on the basis of the idea that each social system is likely to have its own 'press theory'. An extensive review can be found in Nordenstreng (1997). Several commentators, for instance, including McQuail (1983), Altschull (1984) and Hachten (1981), have suggested that we need to have a category for 'development theory' alongside the liberal and Marxist variants. This would recognize the fact that societies undergoing a transition from underdevelopment and colonialism to independence often lack the money, infrastructure, skills and audiences to sustain an extensive free-market media system. A more positive version of media theory is needed which focuses on national and developmental goals as well as the need for autonomy and solidarity with other nations in a similar situation. In the circumstances it may be legitimate for government to allocate resources selectively and to restrict journalistic freedom in some ways. Social responsibility comes before media rights and freedoms. In practice, many media systems in the developing world still qualify for the 'authoritarian' label.

While many ideas have been floated to improve the original typification of press theories, the attempt to formulate consistent and coherent 'theories of the press' in this way is bound to break down sooner or later. This is partly because of the ideological content of all such theory and the bias (whether open or unwitting) of all commentators. It also stems from the complexity and incoherence of media systems and thus the impossibility of matching a theory with a type of society. This approach has been unable to cope with the diversity of media and changing technology and times. It has

little to say about music, the cinema, or most of television that is concerned with entertainment, fiction, sport and games. In most countries today, the media do not constitute a single system with a distinctive philosophy or rationale. There are many different 'functions' and expectations. This does not invalidate the quest for normative theory, but it needs to follow another path.

THE PUBLIC SERVICE BROADCASTING ALTERNATIVE

As we have noticed, libertarian theory has found it difficult to cope with broadcasting in general and with the public broadcasting model in particular, even in its limited American manifestation. This is because it gives primacy to the needs of society or the collective needs of citizens rather than to individual rights, consumer freedom or market forces. The initial rationale for government intervention in broadcasting, as early as the 1920s, was based primarily on the need to regulate the use of limited transmission wavelengths, in the interests of both the industry and consumers. In America a system of licensing of private operators was adopted, involving regulation by the FCC, not only of technical matters but also in respect of some social and political matters. These included the need to provide (locally) relevant information, balance and fairness on controversial and political issues and, in general, diversity. Significant vestiges of these policies still remain. However, the term 'public broadcasting' in the United States generally refers to the minority network financed by viewers and listeners voluntarily and choosing to pursue certain cultural goals.

In many other countries, especially in Western Europe, **public service broadcasting** refers to a system that is set up by law and generally financed by public funds (often a compulsory licence paid by households) and given a large degree of editorial and operating independence. The general rationale for their operation is that they should serve the public interest by meeting important communication needs of the society and citizens, as decided and reviewed by way of the democratic political system.

There has never been a generally accepted 'theory' of public service broadcasting, and different national variants have somewhat different versions of the rationale and logic of operation. The general developments of audiovisual media of recent years and the expansion of the scope of media markets, globally as well as nationally, have created a crisis for institutions that have operated in a largely consensual way for decades. There has been much rethinking of aims and forms (see Blumler, 1992; Hoffmann-Riem, 1996; Atkinson and Raboy, 1997).

If there is a common theory it consists of certain goals that it is presumed can only be adequately achieved by a public form of ownership and/or regulation. The goals that recur in different systems are as listed in Box 7.4.

In general these goals are ways of filling in the notion of the 'public interest'. The other part of the 'theory' concerning the form of organization involves the view that the free market left to itself would fail to satisfy the criteria indicated by these goals because it would not be profitable to do so. The positive version of the theory holds that an effective system for meeting the public interest has to meet certain conditions. These include: some element of public financing; a high degree of independence from government as far as consistent with forms of funding and with continuous processes of accountability to the audience and to the political system. The main weakness of public broadcasting 'theory' (as distinct from the chances of survival) lies in two sources of tension. One is between the necessary independence and the necessary accountability for finance received and goals achieved. The other is between achieving the goals set by 'society' in the public interest and meeting the demands of the audience as a set of consumers in the wider media market. Without public interest goals there is no rationale for continuing, but without audiences, public service goals cannot really be achieved.

MASS MEDIA, CIVIL SOCIETY AND THE PUBLIC SPHERE

During the last decade, especially since the translation in 1989 into English of Jurgen Habermas's (1962/1989) book entitled *The Structural Transformation of the Public Sphere*, there has been much reference to the concept of a *public sphere* in speaking of the role of the mass media in political life. Elements of normative theory can be derived from the discussion that has resulted. In general the public sphere refers to a notional 'space', which provides a more or less autonomous and open arena or forum for public debate. Access to the space is free, and freedom of assembly, association and expression are guaranteed. The 'space' lies between the 'basis' and the 'top' of society, and mediation takes place between the two. The basis can also be considered the private sphere of the life of individual citizens, while the political institutions at the centre or top are part of the public life.

In Habermas's account of the rise of democracy, the historically first version of the public sphere or space was represented mainly by the 18th century coffee house or debating society, where active participants in political life met, discussed and formed political projects. An important task was to keep a check on government by way of an informed and influential public opinion. The principal means of communication was direct private conversation. The formation of this public sphere owed much to the conditions of capitalism and economic freedom and individualism, and the first form of public space was described as a 'bourgeois' public sphere. Subsequently developments included the rise of new corporate interests and other powers and also the general substitution of mass communication for the interpersonal discussion amongst elites. Habermas was generally somewhat pessimistic about the consequences for democracy in modern times since the public was more likely to be manipulated by the media than helped to form opinions in a rational way.

Despite much criticism by other scholars of the idealizing of a bygone and elitist form of political life (e.g. Curran, 1990), the idea of a public sphere has been found to have value under conditions of mature capitalism (see Dahlgren, 1996). Curran (1996: 82) writes that it offers a 'model of a public sphere as a neutral zone where access to relevant information affecting the public good is widely available, where discussion is free of domination and where all those participating in public debate do so on an equal basis. The media facilitate this process by providing an arena of public debate, and by reconstituting private citizens as a public body in the form of public opinion'.

In general, the public sphere idea fits in the wider and also current notion of a '**civil society**', where diverse 'intermediate institutions' of a voluntary involving nature provide a zone of 'protection' for citizens in their relations with the state. Dahlgren (1996: 6) cites a positive endorsement by Michael Walzer (1992: 89) of an essential 'space of uncoerced human association and also the set of relational networks – formed for the sake of family, faith, interest and ideology – that fill this space'. It is a version of the civil society that stands opposed to the 'mass society' analyzed by Mills (1956) and also at odds with various totalitarian systems. The media, when organized in an appropriate way, especially when open, free and diverse, can be considered one of the most important intermediary institutions of the civil society.

Schulz (1997) has described a model of a 'media-constructed public sphere', based on recent theory and research in political communication, which seems more negative than positive in its contribution to civil society. According to this model, under contemporary conditions, the mass media take on a central role in the working of the political system. This arises especially because of the decline of all other *fora* for political interaction, especially the political meeting. Television and the press, according to Schulz, are the most important sources of information and ideas and still a largely shared experience for citizens, despite tendencies towards fragmentation of the audience. He suggests that extensive reliance on mass media has been accompanied by an increase in cynicism and negativism towards politics in general (a view also advanced by Cappella and Jamieson, 1997). This model and its testing involve the elements of a normative theory for media in a democracy, promoting the need to

encourage citizen participation and to support the political processes in positive ways.

Indeed the positive expectations from society in relation to media have for some time been predominantly expressed in the form of much criticism of the declining journalistic standards of mass media, mainly as a result of commercialization (Bogart, 1995). The mass media are accused of failing to serve the politicians in their attempts to inform and involve the public, preferring instead to entertain, sensationalize and follow the money (Patterson, 1994; Blumler and Gurevitch, 1995; Fallows, 1996; Blumler and Kavanagh, 1999). James Carey (1999), in a scathing critique of contemporary journalistic tendencies, raises the troubling question of what becomes of journalism if it ceases to care about its democratic role. He writes 'Without the institutions or spirit of democracy journalists are reduced to propagandists or entertainers' (1999: 17). He goes on to remark that 'journalism can be destroyed by forces other than the totalitarian state; it can also be destroyed by the entertainment state'. A counter charge sometimes levelled against politicians is that they are the true source of the malaise, in being more interested in manipulation of the media to their advantage and marketing themselves than in enriching democracy. Modern campaigning tends to transform active citizens into spectators and counters in a game of numbers (Swanson and Mancini, 1996). The negative view of the current state of media and democracy is not shared by all. There are arguments in favour of contemporary, more popular, forms of political communication (e.g. Dahlgren, 1995). Moreover, the evidence for decline in standards of media performance as a result of commercialization is not very strong, at least not in a number of European countries (Brants, 1998).

RESPONSES TO THE DISCONTENTS OF THE CONTEMPORARY PUBLIC SPHERE

One of the solutions that has been proposed has come from the (American) journalist community itself, under the name of 'civic' or 'public' journalism (Glasser and Craft, 1997; Schudson, 1998; Glasser, 1999). A basic premise of the public journalism movement is that journalism has a *purpose*, that it ought to try and improve the quality of civic life, by fostering participation and debate. Schudson describes it as based on a 'Trustee model' rather than a Market or Advocacy model. He writes (1998: 136) 'in the Trustee Model, journalists should provide news according to what they as a professional group believe citizens should know'. From this we can see a basis of legitimation in the professionalism of the journalist, rather than in some more all-embracing political theory.

In Schudson's word's 'The journalists are professionals who hold citizenship in trust for us'. According to Glasser and Craft, public journalism calls for a shift from a 'journalism of information' to a 'journalism of conversation'. The public needs not only information but also engagement in the day's news that invites discussion and

debate. It should be clear that public journalism parts company with the tradition of neutrality and objective reporting, but it is not a return to politicized or advocacy journalism. The means for achieving the goals of the new 'movement' remain somewhat in dispute, since the media themselves are structurally unchanged and it is in doubt whether this version of the professional task can really transcend the constraints of a competitive media market system and counter the fundamental causes of political apathy and cynicism. However, it points to lively debate in a traditional area of concern about the performance of the media. The public journalism movement does not seem to have found much of a following in Europe. Attention has focused more on the need to strengthen existing public service media and other non-commercial media and also on the potential for harnessing new media to improve democratic participation (van Dijk, 1996; Brants and Siune, 1998).

Sometimes dissatisfaction with established media has found expression in the celebration of completely different forms, free from the established systems. The present author (McQuail, 1983) proposed a category of theory under the heading 'democratic-participant' to take account of many ideas expressed on behalf of alternative, grass-roots media that expressed and looked after the needs of citizens. The theory found expression in the 1960s and 1970s in pressure for local and community radio and television. It challenged the dominance of centralized, commercialized, state-controlled and even professionalized media. Often the key to applying this theory was seen to lie in the new technology of the times (Enzensberger, 1970). It favoured media that would be small in scale, non-commercial and often committed to a cause. Participation and interaction were key concepts. At the present time, quite a lot of expectation for re-invigorating political life is invested in the promise of new interactive media (see Chapter 6).

Curran (1996) has also advocated the need for a wide variety of types of media alongside the commercial sector. The category of 'civic media' that he proposes as one of these types includes many different publications, ranging from political party publications through the media of many minority groups and interests, to include a range of occupational and other institutional publications. The total reach of such publications is actually very large, but they usually fall outside the attention of mass communication research and theory. They are not run for profit but they are oriented to a variety of causes in the public sphere. Curran suggests that such media could be reinvigorated by getting rights of access to radio and television and getting some forms of public subsidy.

NORMATIVE MEDIA THEORY: WAYS AHEAD

This overview testifies to the abundance of flora growing in the garden of normative media theory, although jungle might be a better image. There is much theoretical

confusion and little agreement on principles or even terminology. Nevertheless, there has been more progress than appears at first sight and debate is very lively, prompted not only by the ills of old media but also by the hope engendered by new media. There is quite a high measure of agreement, for example on the basic ideas of how the media should contribute in the working of a democratic society. In the most general terms, the media are widely expected to promote at least four main goals:

- maintaining a constant surveillance of events, ideas and persons active in public life, leading both to a flow of information to the public and exposing violations of the moral and social order;
- providing an independent and radical critique of the society and its institutions;
- encouraging and providing the means for access, expression and participation by as many different actors and voices as is necessary or appropriate;
- contributing to shared consciousness and identity and real coherence of the community as a whole as well as its component groups.

We cannot expect all media to contribute equally or at all to these main goals, and beyond that we have to recognize divergent streams of thinking that cannot really co-exist. Nordenstreng (1997) has sketched the outlines of five different normative theory 'paradigms' that lead to different kinds of normative prescription. These can be summarized as follows:

1. *A liberal-pluralist paradigm.* This is based on the old libertarian theory as presented above, with an emphasis on the individual, and defining the public interest as what interests the public. Accountability to society is achieved by way of the media market and some forms of minimal self-regulation, with a minimal role for the state.
2. *A social-responsibility paradigm.* Here, the right to freedom of publication is accompanied by obligations to the wider society that go beyond self-interest. A 'positive' notion of freedom, involving some social purpose, is envisaged. This favours communitarian over individualist political theory.
3. *A critical paradigm.* Media are regarded as strategically located at the nexus of social structures, and freedom of expression is articulated in terms of repressive or hegemonic powers (of the state and business) on the one hand and the oppressed masses on the other. Media have a potential for emancipation, but only in forms that escape from dominant institutional control.
4. *An administrative paradigm.* This has its origins in the elite bourgeois press of the 19th century and exalts the notion of an objective journalism 'of record' that draws on authoritative sources to provide reliable information on matters of significance. It expresses both ideals of journalistic professionalism and also the requirements of an efficient bureaucratic state. It has an information-technocratic bias and looks to benefit and please managerial and political elites rather than the masses.

5. *A cultural negotiation paradigm.* The origins of this lie predominantly in attention to pre-modern and agrarian society and to grass-roots movements, in liberation theology and in cultural studies. The paradigm rejects a universal rationality as well as ideals of bureaucratic-professional competence and efficiency. It emphasizes the rights of subcultures with their particularistic values and promotes intersubjective understanding and a real sense of community.

FURTHER READING

Christians, C., Rotzoll, K.B. and Fackler, M. (1991) *Media Ethics*, 3rd edn. New York: Longman.

Dahlgren, P. (1995) *Television and the Public Sphere*. London: Sage.

Lichtenberg, J. (ed.) (1990) *Democracy and the Mass Media*. Cambridge: Cambridge University Press.

Nerone, J.C. (ed.) (1995) *Last Rights: Revisiting Four Theories of the Press*. Urbana, IL: University of Illinois Press.

Picard, R. (1985) *The Press and the Decline of Democracy*. Westport, CT: Greenwood Press.

STRUCTURES

8

media structure and performance: principles and accountability

This chapter sets out to provide a general statement of the principles involved in assessing media. There are many reasons for caution. The principles exist in so many specific variants, in such sensitive terrain, often with deep historical and cultural roots, that no single short account can be satisfactory. In addition, the outcome of such an exercise has the appearance of constituting something like a coherent and comprehensive set of standards for the media, when no such thing exists in any society, and if it did it would probably be inconsistent with fundamental freedoms. It also seems to advance a claim for societal control of the media (certainly it tends in this direction), even if this is not the intention.

The standards presented below, aside from lacking mutual consistency in some points, also apply in different ways to different media phenomena. Some, for instance, relate to structure and organization (such as concentration of ownership), others to actual service and performance (such as diversity as choice for consumers). Despite these reservations, it is worthwhile to try to summarize the most commonly accepted ideas, if only to provide a starting point for criticism and discussion (for a fuller treatment, see McQuail, 1992). Where relevant, the normative ideas are discussed in terms both of what they call for in respect of media structure and performance and also of the benefits they should deliver for society – the 'public interest', as discussed above (pages 142–4). The discussion is structured according to five main headings: freedom, equality, diversity, information quality, social order and solidarity, and cultural order.

MEDIA FREEDOM

Overuse has made the term 'freedom' difficult to discuss in any fresh way, but it has an obvious claim to be considered as the basic principle of any theory of public communication, from which other benefits should flow. Nevertheless, there are many versions of freedom, and the word does not speak for itself, as the earlier discussion (see page 149) has made clear. Freedom is a condition, rather than a criterion of performance, and does not readily lend itself to either prescriptive or proscriptive statements. It refers primarily to rights to free expression and the free formation of opinion. However, for these rights to be realized there must also be access to channels and opportunities to receive diverse kinds of information.

Freedom of communication has a dual aspect: offering a wide range of voices and responding to a wide-ranging demand or need. Similar remarks apply to the cultural provision of media, where independence will be associated, other things being equal, with creativity, originality and diversity. These ideas bring us to an interface and

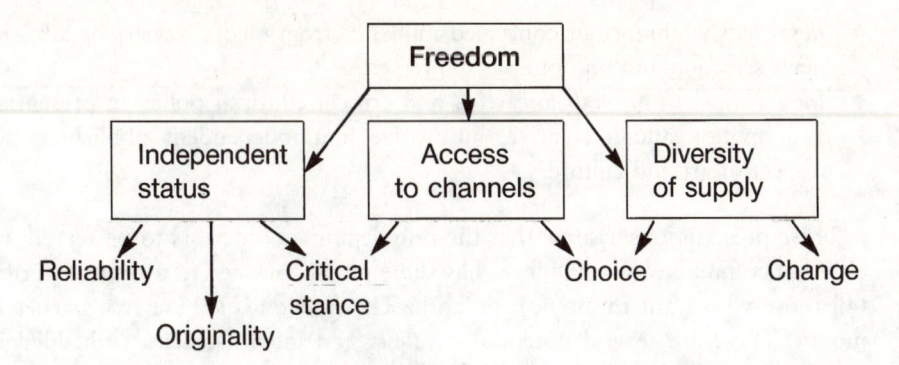

FIGURE 8.1   Freedom as a media performance principle, together with related criteria

overlap with benefits offered under the heading of 'equality'. This brief discussion has sought to make a connection between certain elements of structure, organizational conduct, media performance and output and also extra-media needs. The elements are as follows:

- structural conditions (especially the legal freedom to transmit/publish);
- operating conditions (real independence from economic and political pressures and relative autonomy for journalists and other 'communicators' within media organizations);
- opportunities for 'voices' in society to gain access to channels;
- and benefits of quality of provision for 'receivers' – according to criteria of relevance, diversity, reliability, interest, originality and personal satisfaction.

The main elements discussed can now be expressed as logically related components in a larger normative framework, as summarized in Figure 8.1.

Freedom requirements

In the institutional arrangements and in the public interest discourse referred to above, freedom of communication calls for:

- *(very clearly)* absence of censorship, licensing or other controls by government so that there is an unhindered right to publish and disseminate news and opinions and no obligation to publish what one does not wish to;
- *(also clearly)* the equal right and possibility for citizens of free reception of (and access to) news, views, education and culture (this is part of what has come to be known as a 'right to communicate');
- *(less clearly)* freedom for news media to obtain information from relevant sources;

- *(less clearly)* absence of concealed influence from media owners or advertisers on news selection and on opinions expressed;
- *(desirable but optional)* an active and critical editorial policy in presenting news and opinion and a creative, innovative and independent publishing policy in respect of art and culture.

These prescriptions assume that the only legitimate interests to be served are those either of communicators (whoever has some public message to transmit) or of citizens (all those who want to attend), or both. The freedom of these two parties is paramount. There are several potential conflicts and inconsistencies embedded in these requirements. First of all, freedom of public communication can never be absolute but has to recognize limits sometimes set by the private interests of others or by the higher collective good of a society. Secondly, there is a potential conflict of interest between owners or controllers of media channels and those who might want access to the channels but have no power (or legal right) to secure it (either as senders or receivers). Thirdly, there may be an imbalance between what communicators want to say and what others want to hear: the freedom of one to send may not coincide with the freedom of another to choose. Finally, it may be necessary for government or public power to intervene to secure some freedoms that are not, in practice, delivered by the unfettered system.

Benefits of media freedom

Media freedom also leads to positive benefits for the everyday needs of social institutions – especially a flow of reliable information and diverse points of view. Press independence is also a precondition of the exercise of the 'watchdog' role exercising public vigilance in relation to those with most power, especially government and big business. Free media will be prepared, when necessary, to offend the powerful, express controversial views and deviate from convention and from the commonplace.

Although no ideal state of communication freedom can be attained, the public benefits expected of freedom in a democratic society are easier to state and involve little internal inconsistency. The most important elements are summarized in Box 8.1.

Box 8.1   Main public benefits of media freedom

- Systematic and independent public scrutiny of those in power and an adequate supply of reliable information about their activities (this refers to the 'watchdog' or critical role of the press)
- Stimulation of an active and informed democratic system and social life
- The chance to express ideas, beliefs and views about the world
- Continued renewal and change of culture and society
- Increase in the amount and variety of freedom available

The principle of equality has to be translated into more specific meanings when it is applied to the mass media. As a principle, it underlies several of the normative expectations that have already been referred to. In relation to communication and political power, equality requires that no special favour be given to power-holders and that access to media should be given to contenders for office and, in general, to oppositional or deviant opinions, perspectives or claims. In relation to business clients of the media, equality requires that all legitimate advertisers be treated on the same basis (the same rates and conditions). Equality implies, in such matters, that the normal principles of the market should operate freely and fairly.

Equality supports policies of universal provision in broadcasting and telecommunication and of sharing out the costs of basic services. Equality will support the expectation of fair access, on equivalent terms, for alternative voices (the diversity principle in another form) that meet relevant criteria. In short, equality calls for an absence of discrimination or bias in the amount and kind of access available to senders or receivers, as far as is practicable. The real chances of equality are likely to depend on the level of social and economic development of a society and the capacity of its media system. There will have to be enough space on different and mutually independent channels for any degree of equality to be realized in practice. A consideration of equality as an evaluative principle also takes us into the territory of objectivity, although this has other meanings and potential sources of support, especially those provided by the value of independence and by trends to professionalism and autonomy (see below). The main sub-principles related to the value of equality can be expressed as shown in Figure 8.2.

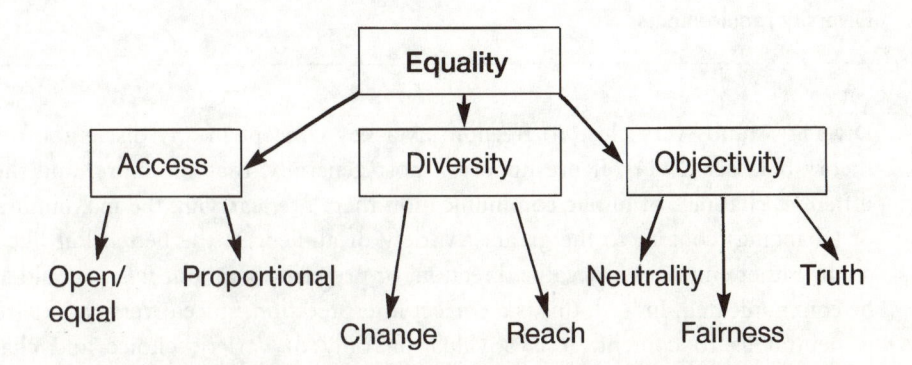

FIGURE 8.2 Equality as a media performance principle, together with related concepts

The principle of **diversity** (also identified as a major benefit of freedom and linked with the concept of access) is especially important because it underpins the normal processes of progressive change in society. This includes the periodic replacement of ruling elites, the circulation of power and office, the countervailing power of different interests) which pluralistic forms of democracy are supposed to deliver. In accounting for diversity of *provision*, the extent to which real alternatives are on offer can be registered according to several alternative yardsticks. These include: type of media (such as press, radio or television); function or type (such as entertainment or information); the level of operation (national, regional, local, etc.); the audience aimed at and reached (differentiated by income, age, etc.); language, ethnic or cultural identity; and politics or ideology. In general, a media system is more equal in character the more diverse the provision according to the criteria mentioned.

Two basic variants of the 'diversity-as-equal-treatment' principle have been identified. According to one version, a literal equality should be on offer – everyone receives the same provision or chances for access as sender. This applies, for instance, where contending parties receive equal time in an election, or in those countries (such as Canada or Belgium) where separate language groups receive an equivalent media service. An alternative and more usual version means only a 'fair', or appropriate, allocation of access and treatment. Fairness is generally assessed according to the principle of proportional representation. Media provision should proportionately reflect the actual distribution of whatever is relevant (topics, social groups, political beliefs, etc.) in the society, or reflect the varying distribution of audience demand or interest. The differentiation of media provision (content) should approximately correspond to the differences at source or to those at the receiving end.

Diversity requirements

Diversity stands very close to freedom as a key concept in any discussion of media theory (Glasser, 1984). It presupposes, most generally, that the more, and the more different, channels of public communication there are, carrying the maximum variety of (changing) content to the greatest variety of audiences, the better. Put like this, it seems rather empty of any value direction, or prescription about *what* should actually be communicated. Indeed, this is a correct interpretation, since diversity, like freedom, is neutral as to content. It is a valuation only of variety, choice and change in themselves. Nevertheless, the diversity principle applied to actual media systems and content does become more specific in its normative requirements, and the following are the main elements.

- Media should *reflect* in their structure and content the various social, economic and cultural realities of the societies (and communities) in which they operate, in a more or less proportional way.
- Media should offer more or less equal chances of *access* to the voices of various social and cultural minorities that make up the society.
- Media should serve as a *forum* for different interests and points of view in a society or community.
- Media should offer relevant *choices* of content at one point in time and also *variety* over time of a kind that corresponds to the needs and interests of their audiences.

Again, we can point to some inconsistencies and problems in these normative requirements. The degree of diversity that is possible is limited by media channel capacity and by editorial selections that have to be made. The more that media are *proportionally* reflective of society, the more likely it is that small minorities will be effectively excluded from mass media, since a small proportion of access will be divided between many claimants. Similarly, catering properly for dominant and consistent expectations and tastes in mass media limits the chance to offer a very wide choice or much change. However, the full range of many different media in a society can help to compensate for the limitations of 'traditional' mass media.

Benefits of media diversity

While diversity is sometimes regarded as a good in itself, it is also often perceived as a means to other benefits. These are summarized in Box 8.2.

> **Box 8.2 Main public benefits of diversity**
> - Opening the way for social and cultural change, especially where it takes the form of giving access to new, powerless or marginal voices
> - Providing a check on the misuse of freedom (for instance, where the free market leads to concentration of ownership)
> - Opening the opportunity for minorities to maintain their separate existence in a larger society
> - Limiting social conflicts by increasing the chances of understanding between potentially opposed groups and interests
> - Adding generally to the richness and variety of cultural and social life

INFORMATION QUALITY

While the expectation that media should provide information of reasonable quality has a more practical than philosophical or normative foundation, it is hardly less

important in modern thinking about media standards than the principles of freedom or diversity. Freedom and diversity do not necessarily produce more informative public communication. Informational requirements have a dual origin – relating to the desirability of an informed society and a skilled work-force, on the one hand, and, on the other, having a body of citizens who are in a position to participate in the choice of leaders and in democratic decision-making (Keane, 1991).

The objectivity concept

The most central concept in relation to information quality has probably been that of **objectivity**. Objectivity is a particular form of media *practice* and also a particular attitude to the task of information collection, processing and dissemination. The main features include adopting a position of detachment and neutrality towards the object of reporting. This means an absence of subjectivity or personal involvement. Secondly there is a lack of partisanship – not taking sides in matters of dispute or showing bias. Thirdly objectivity requires strict attachment to accuracy and other truth criteria (such as relevance and completeness). It also presumes a lack of ulterior motive or service to a third party. The process of observing and reporting should, thus, not be contaminated by subjectivity, nor should it interfere with the reality being reported on. In some respects it has an affinity, in theory at least, with the ideal of rational, 'undistorted' communication advocated by Habermas (1989/1962).

This version of an ideal standard of reporting practice has many advocates and has become the dominant ideal for the role of professional journalist (Weaver and Wilhoit, 1986). It has links with the principle of *freedom*, since independence is a necessary condition of detachment and truthfulness. Under some conditions (such as political oppression, crisis, war and police action), the freedom to report can only be obtained in return for a guarantee of objectivity. On the other hand, freedom also includes the right to be biased or partisan.

The link with *equality* is also strong: objectivity requires a fair and non-discriminatory attitude to sources and to objects of news reporting, all of which should be treated on equal terms. Additionally, different points of view on matters where the facts are in dispute should be treated as of equal standing and relevance, other things being equal. Objective treatment or presentation may in practice be achieved by allowing equal space or time for alternative perspectives on, or versions of, facts.

The benefits of objectivity

In the set of normative interactions that develop between media and their operating environments, objectivity may be crucial. Agencies of state and advocates of various

interests are able to speak directly to their chosen audiences by way of the media, without undue distortion or intervention by the mediators themselves and without compromising the independence of channels. Because of the established conventions of objectivity, media channels can distance their editorial content from the advertising matter that they carry, and advertisers can do likewise in respect of editorial content.

In general, media audiences appear to understand the principle of objective performance well enough, and its practice helps to increase public credence and trust in the information and opinions which the media offer. The media themselves find that objectivity gives their own news product a higher and wider market value. Finally, because the objectivity standard has such a wide currency, it is often invoked in claims and settlements concerning bias or unequal treatment. Most modern news media set a lot of store by their claim to objectivity in its several meanings. Policies for broadcasting in many countries impose, by various means, a requirement of objectivity, on their public broadcasting systems, sometimes as a condition of their independence.

A framework for objectivity research and theory

It is not easy to define objectivity, but one version of its various components has been set out by Westerstahl (1983) in the context of research into the degree of objectivity shown by the Swedish broadcasting system. This version (Figure 8.3) recognizes that objectivity has to deal with *values* as well as with facts and that facts also have evaluative implications.

In this scheme, factuality refers, first of all, to a form of reporting which deals in events and statements which can be checked against sources and are presented free from comment, or at least clearly separated from any comment. Factuality involves several other 'truth criteria': completeness of an account, accuracy and an intention not to mislead or suppress what is relevant (good faith). The second main aspect of factuality is 'relevance'. This is more difficult both to define and to achieve in an

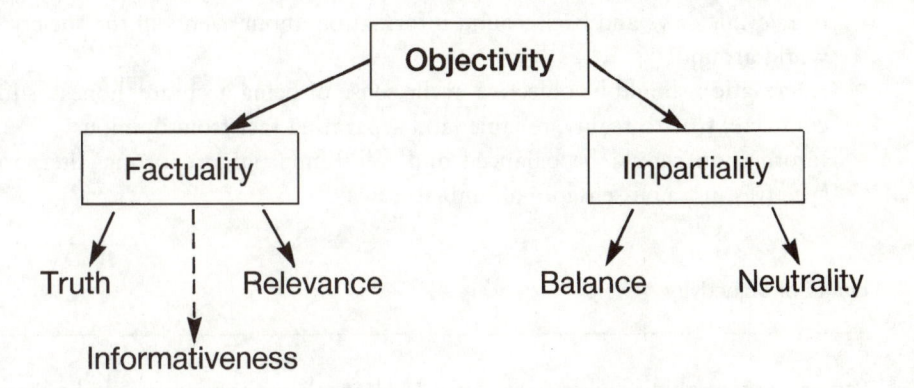

FIGURE 8.3   Component criteria of objectivity (Westerstahl, 1983)

objective way. It relates to the process of *selection* rather than to the form of presentation and requires that selection take place according to clear and coherent principles of what is significant for the intended receiver and/or the society (Nordenstreng, 1974). In general, what affects most people most immediately and most strongly is likely to be considered most relevant (though there may be a gap between what the public perceives as of interest and what experts say is significant).

According to Westerstahl's scheme, impartiality presupposes a 'neutral attitude' and has to be achieved through a combination of balance (equal or proportional time/space/emphasis), as between opposing interpretations, points of view or versions of events, and neutrality in presentation. Under conditions of 'external diversity', as described above, the impartiality component of objectivity does not apply (although that of factualness does), since the assumption is that there will be alternative media to tell the story from another point of view. For instance, a strongly partisan newspaper in a partisan system is not expected to present the reader with all *points of view*, although the reader still expects reliable information.

The scheme in Figure 8.3 has been given an extra element, that of 'informativeness', which is important to the fuller meaning of objectivity. The reference is to qualities of informational content which are likely to improve the chances of actually getting information across to an audience: being noticed, understood, remembered, etc. This is the pragmatic side of information, which is often undervalued or neglected in normative theory but is essential to the fuller notion of good informational performance.

Main information quality requirements

Some of the expected benefits of objectivity are self-evident, while others are subsumed under freedom and diversity requirements. The main 'information quality' standards which are encountered in policy prescriptions or codes of practice can be formulated as follows.

- Media (especially press and broadcasting) should provide a *comprehensive* supply *of relevant* news and background information about events in the society and the world around.
- Information should be objective in the sense of being accurate, honest, sufficiently complete, true to reality, reliable, and separating fact from opinion.
- Information should be balanced and fair (impartial), reporting alternative perspectives in a non-sensational, unbiased way.

Limits of objectivity

Several potential difficulties are embedded in these norms, especially because of uncertainty about what constitutes an adequate or relevant supply of information and

about the very nature of 'objectivity' (Hemánus, 1976; Westerstahl, 1983; Hackett, 1984). More serious are the possible inconsistencies with claims of media freedom (which does not distinguish between 'true' and 'false' expression) and diversity (which emphasizes the multiplicity and inconsistency of reality). We can also note that such criteria are more appropriate to the *totality* of media information in a society, rather than to any particular channel or sector. Not all media are equally expected by their own audiences to provide full and objective information on 'serious' topics.

Objectivity (and related standards of factuality, etc.) is far from unanimously regarded as either necessary, virtuous or even possible to achieve. But there is a good deal of force in Lichtenberg's (1991: 230) argument that 'insofar as we aim to understand the world we cannot get along without assuming both the possibility and value of objectivity'.

SOCIAL ORDER AND SOLIDARITY

The normative questions which belong under this heading are those which relate to the integration and harmony of society, as viewed from different (even opposed) perspectives. On the one hand, there is a rather consistent tendency on the part of those in authority to *look* to public communication media for at least tacit support in the task of maintaining order. On the other hand, pluralistic societies cannot be conceived as having one single dominant order which has to be maintained, and mass media have mixed and divided responsibilities, especially with reference to alternative social groups and subcultures and to the expression of the conflicts and inequalities of most societies. Problems also arise over how far the media can go in their support for opposition or potential subversion (as it may seem from 'the top'). The relevant principles concerning the media are mixed and not mutually compatible but can be expressed in something like the following way. The concept of order is used here in a rather elastic way, to apply to symbolic (cultural) orders such as religion, art and customs, as well as to forms of social order (community, society and established structures of relations). This broad distinction is also cut across by a distinction of perspective – from 'above' and 'below', as it were. This distinction is essentially that between established authority of society, on the one hand, and individuals and minority groups, on the other. It also corresponds approximately to the distinction between order in the sense of control and order in the sense of solidarity and cohesion – the one 'imposed', the other voluntary and self-chosen. These ideas about order can be arranged as shown in Figure 8.4.

Any complex and viable social system will exhibit all the sub-aspects of order shown here. There will be mechanisms of social control as well as voluntary attachments, often by way of membership of component groups in society. There will be a sharing of common meanings and definitions of experience, as well as much divergence of

		From 'above'	From 'below'
	Social	Control/ compliance	Solidarity/ attachment
Domain			
	Cultural	Conformity/ hierarchy	Autonomy/ identity

FIGURE 8.4   Ideas concerning mass media and order depend on whose order and what kind of order is involved

identity and actual experience. Shared culture and solidaristic experience tend to be mutually reinforcing. The relationship between mass communication and these different concepts has been handled in theories of media and society in divergent, though not logically inconsistent, ways (see Chapter 4). Functionalist theory attributes to mass media a latent purpose of securing the continuity and integration of a social order (Wright, 1960) by promoting co-operation and a consensus of social and cultural values.

Critical theory has usually interpreted mass media as agents of a dominant, controlling class of power-holders who seek to impose their own definitions of situations and their values and to marginalize or delegitimize opposition. The media are often seen as serving conflicting goals and interests and as offering conflicting versions of an actual or desirable social order. The question '*Whose* order?' has first to be settled. Relevant normative theory cannot be concerned only with the disruption of order (such as with conflict, crime or deviance) but should also relate to the failings of the established order as perceived by more marginal, or minority, social and cultural groups.

Expectations and norms relating to order

From the perspective of social control, the relevant norms are often applied to condemn positive portrayals of conflict, disorder and deviance or to support differential access and positive symbolic support for established 'order' institutions and authorities – the law, church, school, police, military, etc. The second sub-principle (that of solidarity) involves the recognition that society is composed of many subgroups, different bases of identity and different interests. There is no consensual good order in a modern nation state, and there can be a number of alternative ideas about what is a desirable social order. From this perspective, a viable normative expectation from mass media is that they should sympathetically recognize the alternatives and

provide access and symbolic support for relevant minority groups and views. In general, this (normative) theoretical position will encompass an outward-looking and empathic orientation to social groups and situations that are marginal, distant or deviant from the point of view of a dominant national society.

To summarize a very mixed set of normative perspectives concerning social order:

- In respect of the relevant public which they serve (at national or local level, or as defined by group and interest), the media should provide channels of inter-communication and support.
- The media may contribute to social integration by paying concerned attention to socially disadvantaged or injured individuals and groups.
- The media should not undermine the forces of law and order by encouraging or symbolically rewarding crime or social disorder.
- In matters of national security (such as war, threat of war, foreign subversion or terrorism), the freedom of action of media may be limited by considerations of national interest.
- On questions of morals, decency and taste (especially in matters of the portrayal of sex and violence and the use of language), the media should in some degree observe the reigning norms of what is broadly publicly acceptable and avoid causing grave public offence.

It is clear that these prescriptions and proscriptions are mutually inconsistent and are very much subject to variations in time and place and in the details of the case and point of view. The norms also apply very differently to different kinds of media.

CULTURAL ORDER

The domain of the 'cultural' is not easy to keep separate from that of the 'social', but here it refers to any set of symbols organized by way of language or in some other meaningful patterning. Normative media theory has typically been concerned either with matters of cultural 'quality' (of media content) or with its 'authenticity' in respect of real-life experience.

The subdivision of the sphere of the cultural for present purposes of representation in a normative framework follows a similar line to that applied in the social domain: between a 'dominant', official or established culture and a set of possible alternatives or subcultures. In practice, the former implies a hierarchical view of culture, according to which cultural values and artefacts which have been 'certified' by established cultural institutions will be relatively privileged, compared with 'alternative' cultural values and forms. Typically, such an established culture will imply a set of absolute

cultural values and certifiable quality standards. The cultural virtues of the 'alternative' perspective will, in contrast, be diverse and relative, based only on personal perceptions of attractiveness, relevance and familiarity.

Cultural quality norms

Normative theory, often expressed in wider cultural policies, gives support for very different kinds of cultural quality in the mass media. First, it often protects the 'official' cultural heritage of a nation or society, especially in education and science, art and literature. This may extend to support for innovation in the traditional arts. Secondly, it supports distinctive regional and local variants of cultural expression, on grounds of authenticity as well as of tradition (sometimes for political reasons). Thirdly, some theory recognizes the equal rights of all cultural expressions and tastes, including 'popular culture'.

Although there have been many heated discussions about the possible cultural responsibilities of mass media, there is little agreement on what to do about them, and less action. The norms involved are not usually very compelling and are always selectively applied. Even so, much the same principles tend to be invoked in different contexts. The most commonly encountered are the following.

- Media content should reflect and express the language and contemporary culture (artefacts and way of life) of the people which the media serve (nationally, regionally and locally); it should be relevant to current and typical social experience.
- Some priority should be given to the educational role of the media and to the expression and continuity of the best in the cultural heritage of a country.
- Media should encourage cultural creativity and originality and the production of work of high quality (according to aesthetic, moral, intellectual and occupational criteria).

The very uneven application of these normative principles in any form of control reflects both the primacy of freedom and also the strength of commercial imperatives. Principles of cultural quality are likely to be advanced as desirable but are rarely enforceable. There is rarely enough consensus on what criteria of cultural quality mean. Almost the only empirically demonstrable criterion of cultural quality is that of cultural *relevance* to the audience, especially as expressed in familiar, realistic and contemporary settings, events and themes. The more that media (for instance, public broadcasting institutions) are subject to policy in the interests of the public as a whole, the more likely are cultural criteria to be invoked as a guide to performance. Sometimes, national and economic self-interest can lead to support for some of the cultural principles described.

Aside from the shrinking sector of public broadcasting (see Blumler, 1992; McQuail and Sinne, 1998), most media operate on a day-to-day basis with little conscious regard for the norms described above. The desirable goals are reached or not, and the evils are avoided or not, according to the working of particular media market circumstances, the pulls and pushes of organizational circumstance, and the professional ethics, creative goals and routine decisions of those who work in the media. There are more immediate rules of law, ethics or good practice which are more likely to preoccupy people in the media on a day-to-day basis (Meyer, 1987). Only occasionally is it necessary for those within or outside the media to reflect systematically on the application of one or more of the principles outlined. Only rarely, if ever, would consideration be given to the whole range of ideas that has been summarized.

The set of principles outlined is simply one attempt to describe a universe of discourse which is available within the Western liberal-pluralist tradition as it has developed during the last forty or so years. It cannot be said to represent a consensus on what the media ought to do or not do 'in the public interest' (as defined above), although an attempt has been made to avoid extreme or controversial propositions. What may well be controversial is the degree to which a given principle is relevant to a given situation or medium. In any case, the freedom principle provides a let-out from most obligations, short of extreme antisocial forms of publication. The application of any given principle has also to be established in a relevant political forum, before it can have much weight or consequence.

A CHANGING NORMATIVE ENVIRONMENT

The changes in the media reviewed earlier have not yet fundamentally changed the *content of* the norms described, but they have affected their relative force and the priorities among them. The increasing number of alternative media channels, in particular, has reduced the pressure on seemingly 'dominant' media (for instance, the national newspaper press or broadcast television) to fulfil some perceived public roles. There is probably less fear of media monopoly, despite concentration tendencies, because the potential for competition is greater. More media channels also seem to promise more diversity, although the quality of that diversity is far from assured. Several of the norms outlined have recently come to be invoked in debates about the future of public broadcasting and about the standards to be applied when allocating new television or radio operating licences, especially to private operators. Some of the norms are also still relevant to judging whether press concentration, or cross-media ownership, works against the public interest. There is also continued pressure for

media with seeming increasing influence in cultural, social and political matters to show a degree of self-regulation. Some of the standards discussed are relevant to this matter.

We can expect that, as media institutions are reshaped in former communist states of Central and Eastern Europe, models will be sought in the West, perhaps even some coherent media 'philosophy' to replace one that has been discarded. No doubt some will find this in an unfettered libertarianism, which promises to open windows and dispose of the trappings of paternalism and control. Others will find continued value in a modified version of the former doctrines of social(ist) responsibility. The universe of ideas described above offers something to both parties, although (because of the nature of the exercise) it tends to stress the responsibilities of mass media and implicitly diminish the libertarian viewpoint. No general recommendation can be made. It will be up to the varied publics and to those who frame the new institutions to decide what they want, what is viable and what can be afforded. In respect of the last point, social theory of the media does not have to be subordinate to commerce, but it has to take account of economic reality.

THE MEANING OF ACCOUNTABILITY

It is not easy to define 'accountability' in its full sense. Feintuck (1999: 120) offers a legal definition in two parts. One of these is 'a requirement to give an account of one's actions, either directly to the public, or via public authorities'. Secondly, it means 'being liable to sanction if found in breach of some requirement or expectation attaching to the exercise of power'. This is useful, but the intention here is to widen the scope of application, given that much media activity does not fall within the legitimate scope of public power. Consequently, the core reference is to a process of public scrutiny whereby the public activities of the media (acts of publication) are confronted with legitimate expectations of society. The latter are a diverse set of expectations and claims deriving from the normative theory reviewed in Chapter 7 and expressed in terms of the criteria that have just been discussed.

We define media accountability in a provisional way as

> all the voluntary or involuntary processes by which the media answer directly or indirectly to their society for the quality and or consequences of publication, with particular reference to matters of the general public good.

Because of the complexity and sensitivity of the issues that arise, it is clear that we are not dealing with a simple or single mechanism of social control or regulation. The various elements that contribute to accountability are part of the normal operation of the media in any open society. In keeping with central tenets of normative theory, media accountability processes should meet three general criteria.

1. They should respect rights to free publication.
2. They should prevent or limit harm arising from publication to individuals as well as to society.
3. They should promote positive aspects of publication rather than merely being restrictive.

The first of these three criteria reflects the primacy of the requirement of free expression in democracies. The second implies that obligations to 'society' are in the first instance obligations to individual human beings with rights, needs and interests. The third puts the emphasis on dialogue and interaction between media and other institutions of society. The fundamental difficulty of meeting these three criteria lies in the inescapable tension between freedom and accountability, since total freedom recognizes no obligations to answer for actions to others, within the normal limits of law. Typically, constitutional law in democracies rules out any constraint on the 'freedom of the press', so the legitimate scope for avoiding accountability is very wide (see Dennis et al., 1989).

This presentation of the case is based on the assumption that there is such a thing as a 'public interest' as discussed above. Secondly, it assumes that the media are important enough to society to justify holding them to account and that effective accountability is not necessarily inconsistent with basic freedom on the ground that true freedom involves some elements of responsibility to others. The issues arising under the heading of the 'public good' have been discussed earlier (page 143) and some of the relevant criteria already indicated.

It is useful here to make a distinction between the concepts of accountability and responsibility. The latter refers to the obligations and expectations that are directed at the media. Accountability, on the other hand refers primarily to the processes by which media are called to account. As Hodges (1986) puts it

the issue of responsibility is the following: to what social needs should we expect journalists to respond? The issue of accountability is: how might society call on journalists to account for performance of the responsibilities given to them? Responsibility has to do with defining proper conduct, accountability with compelling it.

In considering processes of accountability, it is useful to distinguish between the responsibilities at issue in terms of the degree of compulsion involved. Some are entirely voluntary, some are contracted and others are required by law. In general, the more voluntary, the softer or more optional are the mechanisms of accountability. A softer mode of accountability is one that does not involve a financial or other penalty, but instead usually a verbal process of inquiry, explanation or apology. The media prefer to avoid external adjudication and penalties, for obvious reasons, hence the prevalence of self-regulatory mechanisms of accountability. These may also be more appropriate to issues of communication, where there is usually no physical or material damage.

For accountability to take place there has to be some response to what the media do (publication), and the media have to listen. Accountability means answering to *someone* for *something* according to some *criterion* and with varying degrees of obligation on the part of the media. Combining some of these ideas it becomes possible to sketch two alternative models of accountability: one that can be called a *liability* model, another an *answerability* model.

The *liability model* puts the emphasis on potential harm and danger that might arise from media publication, whether harm to individuals or society (for instance danger to morals or public order). The measures taken in line with this model will involve material penalties imposed by private or public law.

In contrast, the *answerability model* (or mode) is non-confrontational and emphasizes debate, negotiation, voluntariness and dialogue as the best means to bridge differences that arise between media and their critics or those affected. The means of accounting will be predominantly verbal rather than material, and any penalties will also be verbal (e.g. publication of apologies, corrections or replies).

It is always difficult to weigh up the balance between private (individual) harm (e.g. to the reputation of a public figure) and possible public benefit (e.g. exposure of some scandal or abuse). In practice, there are also likely to be 'chilling' effects on publication where severe material penalties might follow after the event of publication. The greatest danger is to small publishers, giving greater advantage to rich media corporations who can afford to risk financial losses in the pursuit of audiences. The 'answerability' model is generally most consistent with ideas of participant democracy and most likely to encourage diversity, independence and creativity of expression.

LINES AND RELATIONS OF ACCOUNTABILITY

By definition, accountability involves a relationship between media and some other parties. We can recognize two separate stages of accountability: one internal and the other external. The former involves a chain of control within the media, such that specific acts of publication (e.g. news items or television programmes) can be made the responsibility of the media organization and its owners. Important issues do arise in this respect concerning the degree of autonomy or freedom of expression of those who work in the media (e.g. journalists, writers, editors, producers). There is a tension between freedom and responsibility 'within the walls' of the media so to speak, which is too often resolved in favour of media owners. In any case, we cannot rely on internal

control or management to satisfy the wider social need for accountability. Internal control may either be too strict (protecting the organization from claims) and thus a form of self-censorship or too much directed at serving the interests of the media organization rather than society.

Here we are concerned with the 'external' relationships between media and those affected by, or with an interest in, publication. These are varied and overlapping, as we can appreciate from a simple enumeration of the main potential partners, as shown in Box 8.3. In addition it happens quite often that media will be held indirectly accountable to any of the following three:

- social institutions that are affected by media or depend on media for their normal operation;
- public opinion, standing here for 'society as a whole';
- various pressure and interest groups that are affected by publication.

The main 'lines of accountability' are sketched in Figure 8.5. In these circumstances, it is inevitable that accountability processes will also be multiple and diverse, in order to fit the variety of interests, situations and possible claims. The time-scale of accountability also varies greatly. Every issue of a daily newspaper and each television news bulletin is routinely 'tested' in an immediate way by a variety of potential claimants, including the audience. In the longer term, we find media systems being assessed by research and experts, reviewed by commissions or debated by politicians, especially after some social crisis.

FRAMES OF ACCOUNTABILITY

Because of the diversity of agencies involved, it is useful to think in terms of a small number of basic 'frames of accountability', each representing an alternative, although not mutually exclusive, approach to accountability, each having its own typical discourse, logic, forms and procedures. A frame in this sense involves several common

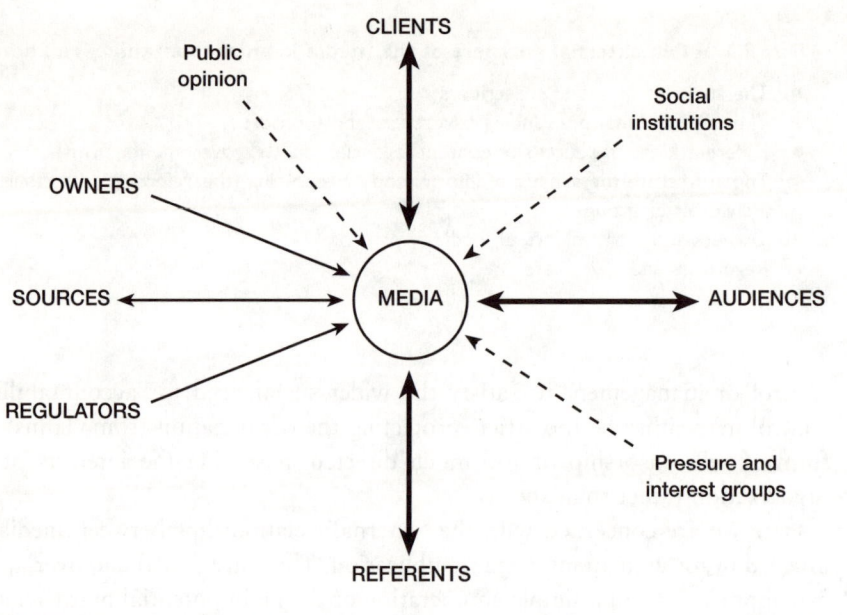

FIGURE 8.5   Lines of accountability between media and external agents in relation to publication

elements: there must be a relationship between a media 'agent' and some external 'claimant', often with a third party as an adjudicator; there are some criteria or principles of good conduct; and there are rules, procedures and forms of account.

The four most generally prevalent accountability frames in this sense can be identified respectively under the headings: *law and regulation; financial/market; public responsibility; professional responsibility*. We can briefly describe them by reference to the typical instruments and procedures; the issues they are most suited to dealing with; the degree of compulsion involved; and the relative advantages and disadvantages they have.

The frame of law and regulation

The first of these frames (*law and regulation*) refers to all public policies, laws and regulations that affect media structure and operation. The main purpose should be to create and maintain the conditions for free and extensive intercommunication in society and advance the public good as well as to limit potential harm to legitimate private and public interests.

The main *mechanisms and procedures* normally comprise regulatory documents concerning what media may and may not do, together with formal rules and procedures for implementing the provisions of any regulation.

As to the *advantages* of this approach to accountability, the first is that there is ultimately some power to compel delivery of the benefits that society claims. There is also democratic control, by way of the political system, over ends and means as a check on abuse of powers of compulsion. Any limits to freedom, as well as to the scope of any regulation, are clearly established. The *disadvantages* and limitations are quite severe, most importantly because of the potential conflict between the aim of protecting freedom of publication and making the media accountable. The fear of penalties can work in much the same way as (pre-publication) censorship, even where this is not legitimate. Law and regulation are easier to apply to structures (e.g. questions of ownership) than to content, where freedom of expression arises and where definitions are difficult. In general law and regulation give more advantage to those with power and money, even when the intention is to protect the interests of all. Finally, it has been observed that laws and regulations are often ineffective, hard to enforce, unpredictable in their wider and long-term effects and hard to change or remove when they become out of date. They can become part of a system of vested interests (e.g. in matters of subsidy or licensing).

The market frame

The *market* has not always been seen as a significant mechanism of public account-ability, but in practice it is an important means for balancing the interests of media organizations and producers and those of their clients and audiences (consumers). The *mechanisms* are the normal processes of demand and supply in a free (and therefore competitive) market that should in theory encourage 'good' and discourage 'bad' performance. Various kinds of audience and market research provide evidence, additional to sales, about the public response to what is offered by the media.

In principle a wide range of issues is covered by market accountability, although the main focus is on aspects of communication 'quality' as seen by the consumer. Quality relates not only to content, but also to technical quality. The market should encourage improvement by way of competition. There is no *compulsion* involved in control through market forces, which is one of the *advantages* of the approach. The laws of supply and demand should ensure that interests of producers and consumers are kept in balance. The system is self-regulating and self-correcting, with no need for outside regulation or control.

The *limitations* of the market have probably received more attention from critics and academics than have the advantages. From one critical perspective the main problem of the media is that they are too 'commercialized', meaning organized for ends of profit rather than communication and lacking any true standard of quality. From this point of view the market cannot serve as a check on itself. Without taking this principled standpoint, there are other arguments against the market as a means of

accounting. One is the fact that markets are rarely perfect and the theoretical advantages of competition are not realized. Where private monopoly develops, there is no effective counterweight to media policies that seek only to maximize short-term gain. Market thinking tends to confuse freedom and quality of media with freedom and welfare of media owners.

The frame of public responsibility

This refers to the fact the media organizations are also social institutions that fulfil, with varying degrees of voluntariness and explicit commitment, certain important public tasks, that go beyond their immediate goals of making profits and giving employment. Whether they acknowledge this or not, public opinion in open societies generally expects the media (taken as a whole) to serve the public interest in matters of information, publicity and culture. Aside from general public opinion, most open societies display a wide variety of pressure groups and lobbies, that seek to look after the interest of one or other group in society.

The *mechanisms and procedures* mainly consist of the activities of pressure groups, including media consumer organizations and the public opinion surveys by which general public opinion is expressed. In a number of countries there are various forms of press or broadcasting councils and procedures for public complaint that are adopted voluntarily by the media industry as a means of meeting claims from society. Some media are operated as public trusts on a non-profit basis to serve some public informational or social purpose. The very large volume of public debate, review and criticism, often carried by the media (or some of them) is an important means of informal control.

The main *advantages* of a developed public responsibility frame include the fact that the needs of society can be expressed in a direct way – by claims made, on the media, to provide for these needs. In addition, intrinsic to this frame is the idea of a continuous interactive relationship between media and society. The public can answer back to the media in their roles as citizens or members of some interest group or minority (not just as consumers or as individuals with legal rights), and the media are under pressure to respond and have the means to do so. This mode of accountability is very open and democratic by definition as well as being voluntary and therefore protective of freedom.

There are also *limitations*. An obvious weakness is the very voluntary character mentioned. Some media will use their freedom not to be responsible, and the needs of society may not be served. It is always a very fragmentary and incomplete set of provisions. There is no real 'system' here, and it works better in some countries and traditions than in others. There may be a conservative tendency, with support for an existing establishment and consensus about values, with dominance by certain elites.

The effectiveness of the frame is being threatened by trends to globalization (multinational control of media) and commercial monopolies.

The frame of professional responsibility

This refers to accountability that arises out of the self-respect and ethical development of professionals working in the media (e.g. journalists, advertisers, public relations), who set their own standards of good performance. It can also apply to associations of owners, editors, producers, etc. that aim to protect the interests of the industry by self-regulation.

The *mechanisms and procedures* generally consist of a published set of principles or code of conduct that is adopted by members of a media professional group, together with some procedures for hearing and judging complaints and claims against particular media actions. The *issues* can be any matter dealt with in the code of ethics or conduct, but invariably relating to some harm or offence caused to an individual or group. The development of professionalism in the media is often supported by government and other public institutions and assisted by improved education and training.

The *advantages* are that the system is generally likely to work because it is both voluntary and in the self-interest of the media and professionals. It has the benefit of being non-coercive and it encourages voluntary self-improvement as well as self-control. In practice, there are also considerable *limitations*. It is narrow in its application and does not usually exert strong pressure on powerful media. It is not sufficiently independent of the media, themselves and is also very fragmentary in its coverage. In general, professionalism is not very strongly developed within the media and employees have relatively little autonomy in relation to management and owners.

CONCLUDING REMARKS

It is clear that in an open society there are likely to be many overlapping processes of accountability, but no complete system, and no single one of the 'frames' described is sufficient for the task on its own or uniquely superior to the others. There are many gaps (performance issues not dealt with adequately), and some media accept no responsibility except what is imposed by market forces.

The diversity of forms and means of accountability can be considered a positive feature in itself even if the overall result is not satisfactory. In general, according to the principle of openness, we should prefer forms of accountability that are transparent, voluntary and based on active relationships and dialogue and debate. The alternatives

of external control, legal compulsion and threats of punishment may be more effective in the short term and sometimes the only way to achieve some goal, but in the long term they run counter to the spirit of the open society.

FURTHER READING

Dennis, E.E., Gilmor, D. and Glasser, T. (eds) (1989) *Media Freedom and Accountability.* New York: Greenwood Press.

McQuail, D. (1992) *Media Performance: Mass Communication and the Public Interest.* London: Sage.

Meyer, P. (1987) *Ethical Journalism.* New York: Longman.

Feinstuck, M. (1999) *Media Regulation, Public Interest and the Law.* Edinburgh: Edinburgh University Press.

9

media structures and institutions

So far, mass media have been discussed as if they were a social institution rather than an industry. They have become increasingly more of the latter without necessarily becoming less of the former, and an understanding of the main principles of structure and dynamics of the media calls for an economic as well as a political and a social-cultural analysis. Although the media have grown up in response to the social and cultural needs of individuals and societies, they are largely run as business enterprises. A trend in this direction has accelerated in recent years for several reasons, especially because of the increasing industrial and economic significance of the entire information and communication sector. Associated with this is the widespread privatization of state telecommunication enterprises and an extension of their activities nationally and internationally. The shift to free-market economies in former communist states has been an additional factor. Even where media are run as public bodies, they are more subject to financial discipline and operate in competitive environments.

A book about mass communication theory is not the place for a thorough treatment of these matters, but it is impossible to understand the social and cultural implications of mass media without at least a sketch of the wider political and economic forces at work shaping media institutions. The public regulation, the control and the economics of media embody certain general principles that belong to the sphere of theory, and the aim of this chapter is to concentrate on these principles, avoiding detail of local and temporary circumstances.

The key to the unusual character of the media institution is that its activities are inextricably both economic and political as well as being very dependent on continually changing technologies of distribution. These activities involve the production of goods and services which are often both private (consumption for individual personal satisfaction) and public (viewed as necessary for the working of society as a whole and also in the public domain). The public character of the media derives mainly from the political function of the media in a democracy but also from the fact that information, culture and ideas are considered as the collective property of all. Nor, as with other public goods like air and daylight, does their use diminish their availability for others.

More specifically, mass media have grown up historically with a strong and widely shared image as having an important part to play in public life and being essentially within the public domain. Certainly, this was and remains true of the newspaper, but it applies in different ways to most of the newer mass media. What media do or do not do has mattered to societies, and this has been reflected in complex systems of ideas about what they should or should not be doing (see Chapter 8). It is also reflected in varied mechanisms to encourage, protect or limit them on behalf of a supposed 'public interest'. Despite this, the media generally have to operate wholly or partly according

to the dictates of market economics. Even in this aspect, they may attract the attention of governments for the same reasons that other private businesses are subject to various forms of legal and economic regulation.

Alternative perspectives

Not surprisingly, there is no agreed objective description of the media institution that can be separated from the varying national/societal circumstances in which they operate. One option is to apply an *economic/industrial* perspective (see Tunstall, 1991), looking at the distinctive and varying characteristics of the media as economic enterprises, as between different media and different contexts. An alternative perspective is that offered by critical *political-economic* theory (as introduced on page 82). This provides concepts derived especially from the critique of capitalism, with reference to processes of concentration and commercialization. A third main possibility is to examine media structures according to a *public interest* perspective and in the light of normative criteria of conduct and performance that have been discussed in the last two chapters. There is a fourth possibility to look at the media institution from an *internal* or *media professional* point of view. Each of these perspectives will be drawn on for some purposes in the following pages.

We can represent the unusual position of media as at the centre of three main forces – political, economic and technological – and thereby requiring alternative modes of analysis (Figure 9.1).

The main issues

A theoretical analysis is only possible if certain general issues or problems are first identified. At a descriptive level, we focus mainly on the question of *differences*. How do media differ from each other in economic and policy terms? How and why are the economics and regulation of media untypical both of normal business and of normal public services? How and why do national media institutions vary in structure and control? This last aspect of the comparison is important precisely because media are not only businesses, responding to economic forces, but also deeply rooted (usually nationally based) social and cultural institutions.

There is also relevant theory concerning the current *dynamics* of media industries, especially the trends towards expansion, diversification and convergence of media, mainly on the basis of new technology and new economic opportunities. There are trends towards concentration, integration and internationalization of media activity. Implicated in this last point is the question of global communicative relations between the main 'media powers', mostly in the North, and the relatively dependent South. Not

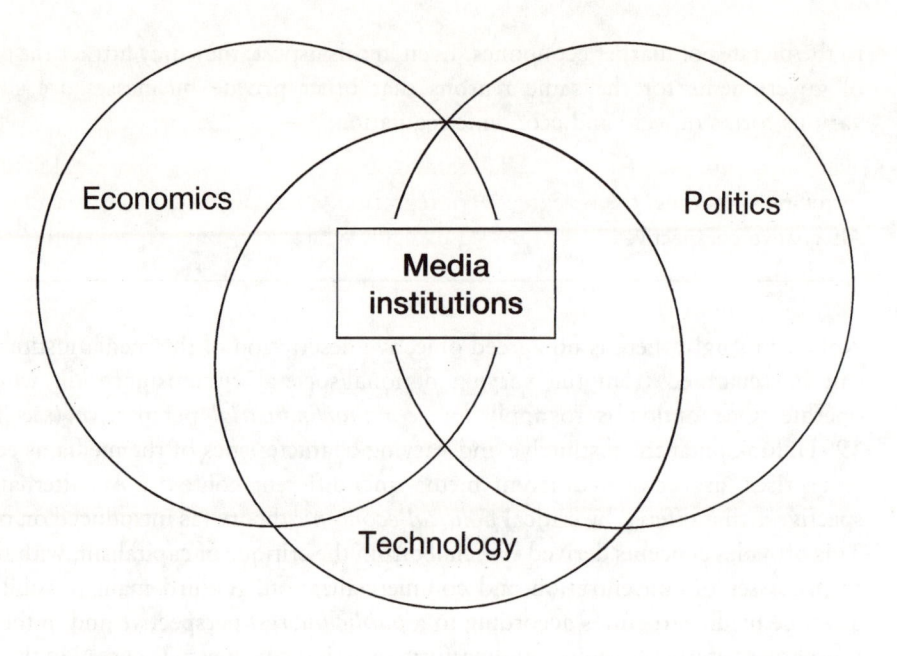

FIGURE 9.1   The media are at the centre of three overlapping kinds of pulls and pushes

all the trends mentioned seem logically consistent, and some framework is needed within which they can be made sense of.

Media policy and regulation are also both characterized by seemingly opposed trends, especially as between deregulation (and privatization) and some significant kinds of re-regulation. While it is tempting to regard our own time as a moment of communications 'revolution', the mass media have been continuously changing since their earliest days, following one technological innovation after another, and many of the forces at work are constant. They reflect two basic dynamics: the first, a wish to make money; and the other, a struggle for power in society, in which the media are deeply implicated.

THE BASICS OF MEDIA STRUCTURE AND LEVELS OF ANALYSIS

The scene can be set by a reminder of the main features of economically developed media systems. The term 'media system' refers to the actual set of mass media in a given national society, despite the fact that there may be no formal connection between the elements. Most media systems, in this sense, are the result of chance historical growth, with one new technology after another being developed and leading to the

adaptation of existing media. Sometimes a media system is linked by a shared political-economic logic, as with the free-enterprise media of the United States or the state-run media of China. Many countries have 'mixed' systems, with private and public elements, and these may well be organized according to a set of national media policy principles, leading to a degree of integration. Occasionally, there may be a single Ministry of Communications, or equivalent, which has some responsibilities across a range of different media, private or public, which adds another 'systemic' component. In most countries, broadcasting (television and radio) has a special status and is governed by some form of regulatory body closely linked to the political system (see e.g. Robillard, 1995).

The media may also be treated as a coherent system by their audiences or by advertisers, and certainly the term 'the media' is often used in this collective sense. The more that free-enterprise mass media are held in relatively few corporate hands, the more these may be thought of as a single system, although even the highest levels of concentrated private ownership still allow for some structural diversity and competition. Lastly, one may consider the media as a system in the broader sense of the whole information and communication sector, interconnected with the industries of advertising, public relations, marketing and, often, opinion and audience research as well.

Within the media system, specific different media types are to be found: newspapers, television, radio, music, telecommunications, etc. These may also be described as media 'sectors', especially in policy discourse or for purposes of economic analysis. In fact, the unity of such 'sectors' is often as illusory as is that of the whole system. There are many differentiating as well as integrating factors (especially through separate or shared distribution systems). For instance, the medium of film can refer to the cinema, video hire or sale, broadcast or subscription television, etc. These are different means of distribution, often different businesses and organizations, although there is usually some form of vertical integration. As a result of media conglomeration, we need to distinguish another unit of analysis: that of the firm or enterprise, which may constitute a significant part of a sector or have holdings which cut across boundaries of media type or geography (the multimedia, and often multinational, firm).

Major media like newspapers and broadcasting are often geographically fragmented. The daily newspaper can be any one of the following: a national mass circulation paper, a business paper, a political or religious publication, a regional morning or a city evening newspaper. Other media, such as magazines, are ranged across a wide spectrum of types, defined by topic and readership. Below the level of medium or sector we find the single-medium organization – for instance, the particular 'title' in the case of a newspaper or magazine, or the network, channel or station in the case of radio or television. Because of horizontal integration, these may well not be independent. For some purposes of structural analysis, it may also be necessary to identify a particular media product – for example, a book, film or television show – as a separate unit.

SOME ECONOMIC PRINCIPLES OF MEDIA STRUCTURE

In economic terms, 'the media' show up as very disparate, although they do have some shared features (see below). Most obviously there are a number of different, often competing, media (newspapers, television, film, radio, etc.) within the same national 'media system', each with different advantages and disadvantages for producers, advertisers and consumers. Equally obviously, media are structured geographically, with media provision geared to populations considered as international, national, regional, city or local markets.

Different media markets and sources of income

The diversity can usefully be understood in terms of several different kinds of 'market'. According to Picard (1989: 17), 'A market consists of sellers that provide the same good or service, or closely substitutable goods or services, to the same group of consumers'. In general, markets can be defined according to place, people, type of revenue and the nature of the product or service. Different media and differences of geography often identify separate media markets.

A more fundamental line of economic division in the media business is between the *consumer market* for media products and services and the *advertising market*, in which a service is sold to advertisers in the form of access to the audience. This feature of media economics – reliance on two different sources of revenue – has far-reaching significance. One can note that within the first (consumer) market there is another division, between the market for 'one-off' products, like books, tapes, videos and newspapers, sold directly to consumers and that for continuous media services like cable or broadcast television or on-line media.

Advertising versus consumer revenue – implications

The difference between the two main sources of revenue – direct product sales and advertising – (there are other sources) is an important tool for comparative

analysis and for explaining media features and trends. The distinction cuts across the difference between media types, although some media are rather unsuitable for advertising (especially the 'one-off' media), while others can operate equally in both markets (especially television, radio, newspapers and magazines). There are some 'advertising revenue only' media, with no consumer revenue – for instance, free newspapers, promotional magazines and quite a lot of commercial television.

The distinction has both an economic and a non-economic significance. In respect of the latter, it is usually believed (from the critical or public interest and professional perspectives) that the higher the dependence on advertising as a source of revenue, the less independent the content from the interests of the advertisers and business generally. This implies less credibility as an information source and less creative autonomy. In the extreme case of totally advertising-financed or sponsored media, the ostensible content is hard to distinguish from advertising, propaganda or public relations. The question of advertiser influence on media organizations is discussed again in Chapter 11. There is little doubt about certain general kinds of influence, such as the bias towards youth and higher income groups and the preference for neutral rather than politicized media (Tunstall and Machin, 1999).

From the economic perspective, operation in the different markets raises other considerations. One is the question of financing, since advertising-supported media are usually paid for in advance of production, while in the consumer market the income has to follow the outlay. Secondly, there are different criteria and methods for assessing market performance. Advertising-based media are assessed according to the number and type of consumers (who they are, where they live) reached by particular messages (for example, circulation, readership and reach/ratings). These measures are necessary for attracting would-be advertising clients and for establishing the rates that can be charged. The market performance of media content that is paid for directly by consumers is assessed by the income received from sales and subscriptions to services. Ratings of (qualitative) satisfaction and popularity may be relevant to both markets, but they count for relatively more in the consumer income market.

Performance in one market can affect performance in another, where a medium operates in both. For instance, an increase in newspaper sales (producing more consumer revenue) can lead to higher advertising rates, provided that the increase does not lead to a lower average level of social-economic composition, with a reverse effect on unit advertising rates. It is also clear that the difference of revenue base can lead to different kinds of opportunity or vulnerability to wider economic circumstances. Media that are heavily dependent on advertising are likely to be more sensitive to the negative impact of general economic downturns than media that sell (usually low-cost) products to individual consumers. The latter may also be in a better position to cut costs in the face of falls in demand (but this depends on the cost structure of production).

The difference between the two revenue markets interacts with other features of the media market. As noted above, the social composition of the audience reached (and 'sold' to advertisers) is important, because of differences in purchasing power and in type of goods advertised. There is a logic in the advertising-based media which favours a convergence of media tastes and consumption patterns (less diversity). This is because homogeneous audiences are often more cost-effective for advertisers than heterogeneous and dispersed markets (unless they are very large mass markets for mass products). This is one reason for the viability of the free newspaper that provides complete coverage of a particular area with relatively high homogeneity.

This factor matters much less in the case of 'paid content', since it does not matter *whose* money it is as long as it is received. On the other hand, even paid content has to be marketed and distributed, and this raises the question of the location and social composition of intended audiences and markets. The success of advertising-based media may also depend on the geographical location and relative dispersion of audiences. It is important for some advertisers (such as local traders) to be able to reach a high proportion of their potential customers. One result is that newspapers with a dispersed set of readers are often more at risk economically than those with a locally concentrated circulation. This is partly because of higher distribution costs, but it also stems from the relative capacity to 'cover' a particular market of consumers especially the relevant so-called 'retail trading zone'. The general effect is to reward media concentration (almost by definition, the more newspapers – or other media – which compete, the more dispersed their separate sets of readers are likely to be).

Competition for revenue

In line with this, it has been argued more generally that 'competition for a single revenue source results in imitative uniformity' (Tunstall, 1991: 182). Tunstall suggests that this is the reason for the perceived 'low taste' quality (or just 'imitative uniformity') of North American network television, which is financed almost entirely from mass *consumer* advertising (see DeFleur and Ball-Rokeach, 1989). The same applies to the alleged low standards of the British tabloid newspapers that compete for much the same mass (down-) market. Tunstall also argues that this kind of large undifferentiated market maximizes the power of the powerful (for instance, by the threat of advertising withdrawals, or simply pressure). Certainly one of the benefits argued for a public sector in European television has been that it avoids the situation where all broadcasting competes for the same revenue sources (for example, Peacock, 1986).

This argument mainly applies to a particular case (of national media financed by

consumer advertising). The effects indicated would be modified according to the diversity of types of advertising and to any factor that tends to segment the market (such as diversity of social composition or taste of the audience). Although, historically, advertising for mass consumer products has been the mainstay of genuinely 'mass' media of the kind represented by US networks and British tabloid newspapers, this type of media is in relative decline, and there have always been differentiated advertising markets. For instance, there is a significant volume of personal advertising, or advertising for employment, business and finance, corporate images and public relations, or government and public information. Apart from this, the fact that different media often compete with each other for the same advertising income can encourage diversity. The degree and kind of competition are an important modifying variable. Reliance on advertising as such need not lead to uniformity of provision.

At the turn of the 21st century, the largest question mark in this territory stands against the consequences of advertising on the Internet. There is a rapid growth in use of this new medium for advertising, although the relative share is still small and the value still unproven. Nevertheless some predictions point to rapid and alarming impacts on some established media, especially newspapers, that depend on the type of advertising that looks most suited to the new media – especially classified, personal, property, specialized, and jobs. This threat to the future of the newspaper looks more immediate than the luring away of readers to electronic competitors.

The significance of the social-economic background of the would-be audience for media financing has already been mentioned, and the reasons are obvious enough. Aside from differences of content, preferences and interests that may be linked with social class, the better-off can (and do) normally pay more for more media and are more interesting targets for high-value consumer products. There are also relations between occupational categories and media services.

Media cost structure

The issue of media cost structures was noted earlier as a variable in the economic fortunes of media. One of the peculiarities of mass media as compared with some other economic enterprises is the potential imbalance between the 'fixed costs' and the 'variable costs' of production. The former refers to such things as land, physical plant, equipment and distribution network. The variable costs refer to materials, 'software' and (sometimes) labour. The higher the ratio of fixed to variable costs, the more vulnerable a business is to a changing market environment, and traditional mass media typically have a high ratio, with heavy capital investments which have to be recouped later by sales and advertising revenue.

It is in the nature of the typical media product that it has a very high 'first copy' cost. A single daily newspaper or the first print of a film carries all the burden of the fixed

costs, while the marginal cost of additional copies may be very small. This makes traditional media like newspapers vulnerable to fluctuations in demand and in advertising revenue and also puts a premium on economies of scale and exerts a pressure towards agglomeration. It also exerts pressure towards the separation of production from distribution, since the latter often involves high fixed costs (for instance, cinemas, cable networks, satellites and transmitters). High fixed costs also erect a high barrier to would-be new entrants into the media business.

In this matter also, the new media open up new uncertainties for the established media. In general it looks as if fixed costs can be much lower than with traditional media, with much lower entry costs and therefore greater ease of entering the market. Nevertheless, content costs remain high, and the new channels still offer big advantages to established media firms that already have the content to fill them.

OWNERSHIP AND CONTROL

Fundamental to an understanding of media structure is the question of ownership and how the powers of ownership are exercised. The belief that ownership ultimately determines the nature of media is not just a Marxist theory but virtually a common-sense axiom summed up in Altschull's (1984) 'second law of journalism': 'the contents of the media always reflect the interests of those who finance them'. Not surprisingly, there are several different forms of ownership of different media, and the powers of ownership can be exercised in different ways.

As implied by Altschull's remark, it is not just ownership that counts, it is a wider question of who actually pays for the media product. Although there are media whose owners do personally pay for the privilege of influencing content, most owners just want profit, and most media are financed from different sources. These include a range of private investors (among them other media companies), advertisers, consumers, various public or private subsidy-givers, and governments. It follows that the line of influence from ownership is often indirect and complex – and it is rarely the only line of influence.

Most media belong to one of three categories of ownership: commercial companies, private non-profit bodies and the public sector. However, within each of these three there are significant divisions. For media ownership it will be relevant whether a company is public or private, a large media chain or conglomerate or a small independent. It may also matter whether or not a media enterprise is owned by a so-called 'media tycoon' or 'mogul', typified as wanting to take a personal interest in editorial policy (Tunstall and Palmer, 1991). Non-profit bodies can be neutral trusts, designed to safeguard independence of operations, or bodies with a special cultural or social task such as political parties, churches, etc. Public ownership also comes in many different forms ranging from direct state administration to elaborate and

diversified constructions designed to maximize independence of decision-making about content.

The effects of ownership

For mass communication theory, it is nearly always the ultimate publication decision that matters most. Liberal theory rests on the assumption that ownership can be effectively separated from control of editorial decisions. Larger (allocative) decisions about resources, business strategy, etc., are taken by owners or boards of owners, while editors and other decision-makers are left free to take the professional decisions about content, which is their special expertise. In some situations and countries there are intermediary institutional arrangements (such as editorial statutes) designed to safeguard the integrity of editorial policy and the freedom of journalists. Otherwise, professionalism, codes of conduct, public reputation (since media are always in the public eye) and common (business) sense are supposed to take care of the seeming problem of undue owner influence (this is discussed in Chapter 11).

The existence of checks and balances cannot, however, obscure several facts of life of media operation. One is that, ultimately, commercial media have to make profits to survive, and this often involves taking decisions which directly influence content (such as cutting costs, closing down, shedding staff, investing or not, and merging operations). Publicly owned media do not escape an equivalent economic logic. It is also a fact that most private media have a vested interest in the capitalist system and are inclined to give support to its most obvious defenders – conservative political parties. The overwhelming editorial endorsement by US newspaper editorials of Republican presidential candidates over the years (Gaziano, 1989), and similar phenomena in some European countries, are not likely to be the result of either chance or natural wisdom.

There are many less obvious ways in which a similar tendency operates, not least potential pressure from advertisers. Public ownership is thought to neutralize or balance these particular pressures, although that too means following a certain editorial line (albeit one of neutrality). The conventional wisdom of liberal theory suggests that the best or only solution to such problems lies in multiplicity of private ownership. The ideal situation would be one in which many small or medium-size media compete with each other for the interest of the public by offering a wide range of ideas, information and types of culture. The power which goes with ownership is not seen as bad in itself but only becomes so when concentrated or used selectively to deny access. This position tends to underestimate the fundamental tension between market criteria of size and profit and social-cultural criteria of quality and influence. They may simply not be reconcilable. The issue of concentration lies at the heart of the theoretical debate.

In the theory of media structure, much attention has been paid to the question of uniformity and diversity. Most social theory concerned with the 'public interest' places a value on diversity, and there is also an economic dimension involved: that of monopoly versus competition. Free competition, as noted, should lead to variety and to change of media structure, although critics point to a reverse effect: that it leads to monopoly, or at least oligopoly (undesirable on economic as well as social grounds). As far as media economics are concerned, there are three main aspects to the question: *inter-media* competition, *intra-medium* competition and *inter-firm* competition. Inter-media competition depends chiefly on whether products can be substituted for one another (such as news on radio for news on television or in the newspaper) and on whether advertising can be substituted from one medium to another. Both substitutions seem possible only up to a certain point. There always appears to be some 'niche' in which a particular medium has an advantage (Dimmick and Rothenbuhler, 1984). All media types also seem to be able to offer some distinctive advantages to advertisers: of form of message, timing, type of audience, context of reception, etc. (Picard, 1989).

Horizontal versus vertical concentration

In general, because units of the *same* medium sector are more readily substitutable than *between* media, the focus of attention is often directed at intra-medium competition (such as of one newspaper with another in the same market, geographically or otherwise defined). This is where concentration has most tended to develop, within the same medium sector (this may also in part be the result of public policies to limit 'cross-media' monopoly). In general, media concentration has been distinguished according to whether it is 'horizontal' or 'vertical'. Vertical concentration refers to a pattern of ownership which extends through different stages of production and distribution (for instance, a film studio owning a cinema chain) or geographically (a national concern buying city or local newspapers, say).

Horizontal concentration refers to mergers within the same market (for example, of two competing city or national newspaper organizations or of a telephone and a cable network). Both of these processes have happened on a large scale in a number of countries, although the effects may have been modified by continuing inter-media choice and the rise of new media. Choice is often protected by public policies against 'cross-media ownership' (different media being owned and operated by the same firm, especially in the same geographical market). The media can also become involved in horizontal concentration through the merging of firms in different industries, so that a newspaper or television channel can be owned by a non-media business (see Murdock, 1990).

This does not directly reduce media diversity but can add to the power of mass media and have wider implications for advertising.

Other types of concentration effect

Another relevant set of distinctions by type of concentration (de Ridder, 1984) relates to the *level* at which it occurs. De Ridder distinguishes between publisher/concern (ownership), editorial and audience levels. The first refers to increased powers of owners (for instance, the growth of large chains of separate newspapers, as in the USA and Canada) or of television stations (as has happened more recently in Italy). The units making up such media enterprises *can* remain editorially independent (as far as content decisions are concerned), although rationalization of business and organization often leads to sharing of certain services and reduces the difference between them. In any case, there is a separate question as to whether editorial concentration, as measured by the number of independent titles, rises or falls in line with publisher concentration. The degree of editorial independence is often hard to assess.

The second questions that of audience concentration; this refers to the concentration of audience market share, which also needs to be separately assessed. A relatively minor change of ownership can greatly increase audience concentration (in terms of 'control' by a publishing group). A large number of independent newspaper titles does not in itself set limits to media power or ensure much real choice if most of the audience is concentrated on one or two titles. The condition of the system is certainly not very diverse in that case. The reasons for concern about concentration turn on these two points.

Degrees of concentration

The degree of media concentration is usually measured by the extent to which the largest companies control production, employment, distribution and audience. Although there is no ceiling beyond which one can say the degree is undesirable, according to Picard (1989: 334) a rule of thumb threshold of acceptability is one where the top four firms in an industry control more than 50 per cent, or the top eight firms more than 70 per cent. There are several media instances where such thresholds are exceeded or approached, such as the daily newspaper press in the USA, the national daily press in Britain, Japan and France, television in Italy and the international phonogram industry.

The situation of concentration can vary from one of perfect competition to one of complete monopoly, with varying degrees in between. Different media seem inclined to take up different places on this continuum, for a variety of reasons. Perfect competition

is rare, but a relatively high level of competition is shown in many countries by book and magazine publishing. Television and national newspapers are generally oligopolistic markets, while true monopoly is now mainly confined to unusual cases of more or less 'natural' monopoly – for instance, cable and telecommunication. A 'natural monopoly' is one where the consumer is best served, on grounds of cost and efficiency, by there being a single supplier (it is usually accompanied by measures to protect the consumer).

The reasons for increasing media concentration and integration of activities are the same as for other branches of business, especially the search for economies of scale and greater market power. In the case of the media it has something to do with the advantages of vertically integrated operation, since larger profits may be made from distribution than from production. There is also an incentive for media companies to acquire media with a stable cash flow of the kind provided by conventional television channels and daily newspapers (Tunstall, 1991). Control of software production and distribution can be very helpful for electronic companies, which need to make heavy investments in product innovations (such as forms of recording) that depend for their takeoff on a good supply of software.

There are also increasing advantages in sharing services and being able to link different distribution systems and different markets. This is generally known as 'synergy'. As Murdock (1990: 8) remarks: 'In a cultural system built around "synergy" more does not mean different; it means the same basic commodity appearing in different markets and in a variety of packages'. In this kind of environment, an upward spiral to concentration is continually being applied, since the only way to survive is by growth. The unification of the Single European Market since 1993 has played a part in this spiralling effect. Often, national restrictions on growth within a single country (because of anti-monopoly or cross-media ownership regulations) have stimulated cross-national monopoly-forming (Tunstall, 1991). The setting up of the World Trade Organization (WTO) in 1994 to implement the GATT agreements has marked a new phase in media transnationalization. The media are primarily defined as a business and it is now much harder to justify public intervention in the national media.

Policy issues arising

The trend towards greater media concentration, nationally and internationally, gives rise to three main kinds of public policy issues. One relates to pricing, another to the product and a third to the position of competitors. The main pricing issue has to do with consumer protection, since the more monopoly there is the greater the power of the provider to set prices. A media example is offered by the case of cable television, which can gradually acquire a distribution monopoly for the residents of a locality, where there is limited substitutability. Competition in most other media sectors is

effective in keeping prices down. A separate question relates to rates charged to advertisers under conditions of monopoly, and similar considerations arise.

The main product issue has to do with the content of a monopoly-supplied media service, especially questions of adequate quality and choice, both for the consumer and for would-be providers of content. The third issue, concerning competitors, refers to the driving out of competitors as a result of economies of scale or advantages in the advertising market of high density of coverage or use of financial power to engage in 'ruinous competition'. Concentration will generally impinge only on competitors in the same market, but it can extend further. For all the reasons given, there has been much research directed at the consequences of concentration (whether good or bad) – especially for the newspaper sector, where concentration has been greatest (see Picard et al., 1988). The results of research have been generally inconclusive, partly because of the complexity whereby the fact of concentration is usually only one aspect of a dynamic market situation. Most attention has focused on the consequences for content, with particular reference to the adequacy of *local news and information*, the performance of the *political and opinion-forming* functions of media, the degree of *access* to different voices and the degree and kind of *choice and diversity* (McQuail, 1992). While, by definition, media concentration always reduces choice in some respects, it is possible that the profits of monopoly can be returned to the consumer or community in the form of better media. The profits can also be channelled to shareholders (Squires, 1992).

DISTINCTIVE FEATURES OF MEDIA ECONOMICS

This account of the main economic principles of media structure and dynamics can be concluded by pointing to some typical features of the economics of media, which at the same time distinguish them from other kinds of business. First, we can say that the media are typically 'hybrid' or mixed in character. Often they operate in a dual market selling a product to consumers and a service to advertisers. They are also extremely diversified in terms of the type of product sold and the range of technologies and organizational means for distribution. Secondly, media cost structures are characterized by high labour intensiveness and high fixed costs (although both dependencies are diminishing as a result of technological change and media expansion).

A third feature of the media is the high degree of uncertainty and also the uniqueness of product. Uncertainty refers to consumer evaluation (it is still difficult to predict audience tastes for music, films or books, however much manipulation through publicity is tried). Fourthly, despite standardization, many media products can be, and have to be, endlessly differentiated on a day-to-day basis and can rarely be repeatedly sold in exactly the same form. Fifthly, the media seem especially prone to concentration tendencies, perhaps because the advantages of monopoly control of advertising

markets are so evident, and perhaps because of the appeal of power and social prestige to would-be media 'tycoons'. Sixthly, many media businesses (at least those involving distribution) are unusually hard to enter without large capital resources (mainly because of high fixed costs and high launch costs). One cannot hope to start up a significant newspaper or a television channel 'in a small way', although there are always some specialist niche markets available. Finally, the media are different just because they are affected by a public interest (Melody, 1990), and thus 'not just any other business', and tend to be burdened with a considerable weight of public responsibility, whether they like it or not (sometimes they do).

DYNAMICS OF MEDIA STRUCTURE

Only a few brief remarks are possible about this large topic. All media structures are temporary arrangements, with only the appearance of solidity. The main forces at work are relatively stable and constant in the short term but produce change in the long term. They include: the pursuit of profit in a situation of supply and demand (market forces); the dominance of certain technologies for a period of time; social and economic changes in society; and the various political and policy goals which often shape the working environment of media. Of the four, the most predictable and unchanging are market forces, although the consequences are always dependent on other (more changeable) factors.

As far as market forces are concerned, commercial media are not so very different from any other business, although differences do arise when mass media have a semi-public status and role. The drive towards concentration, as we have seen, affects almost all mass media in one way or another. A second main process of change is the rise and fall of firms in a more or less cyclical pattern, reflecting variable commercial dynamism and investment as well as changes in conditions of operation. Media may be especially sensitive to changing social and cultural trends. That changing communication technology causes change needs little argument, since it is obvious that media institutions have developed around a succession of different technologies (as described in Chapter 2), which constantly open up the potential for new markets and undermine

old ones. Even this process of change is usually managed, as far as possible, to avoid major disruption to the industry. DeFleur (1970) convincingly demonstrated that the diffusion of successive new media technologies, from the press through to television, followed a similar cumulative S-shaped curve, and we can expect the same pattern to apply to the many new electronic media forms. At some point a critical mass appears to be reached which is a precondition for take-off. The rise of new technology does not usually eclipse old media entirely but causes them to adapt to the new market conditions.

The role of public policy (in effect, politics) in relation to media change is ambiguous, sometimes seeking to hold back or firmly manage change, sometimes to encourage it for economic or ideological reasons. The history of broadcasting in Western Europe since about 1980 is illustrative of this (see McQuail and Siune, 1998). Until that point in time, for half a century the development of radio and television had been kept firmly in the hands of national governments and under conditions of legal monopoly. The broadcast media were deemed too important to society to be left to the marketplace, and the intrinsically monopolistic character of broadcasting was thought to need strong public control to protect consumers.

These political arrangements were fundamentally undermined by four main kinds of change which were largely outside the control of European national governments. Technological advances in the means of transmission (satellite and cable) made the original justification of monopoly (shortage of airwaves and channels) obsolete and made it physically very difficult to maintain the system of national monopoly. There arose powerful economic arguments for opening up the market to encourage industrial development of new communication technology. Moves towards European integration, political as well as economic, also implied trans-border freedom of communication and worked against tight national control. Fourthly, the public service character of the 'old order' of broadcasting was inconsistent with a rising tide of free-market ideology.

The results can be seen in the ending of public broadcasting monopolies in Europe, the opening of frontiers to transnational television, the multiplication of television channels and the appearance of strong commercial competition for the public television and radio channels. Broadcast institutions have been radically adapted, and a new phase of (still limited) competition is under way, with further change to be expected, as the financial basis of public television is further undermined. In Central and Eastern Europe, for different reasons, there have been parallel movements from public to commercial arrangements.

The European case is illustrative both of the continuing strength and of the ultimate limits of public policy for managing media change. Richer societies with the will to do so can keep their media under national and public control, but only so far as technology and the wider political environment allow. The economically dependent countries of the Third World are much more exposed to external forces outside their control.

Salvaggio (1985) developed a model in which he compared four different types of society in relation to their communication policy goals and potential for

implementation. The four types are: competitive, free-market; public utility (the mixed or social-market economies of Western Europe); communist (as in China or the former Soviet Union); and Third World (most developing countries). Salvaggio argues that the same general factors govern policy in all four types of society, but that each society will have a more or less constant guideline of its own (the *Ideology* of the society, such as 'development' or 'free enterprise'), while at least one other variable factor will exert a dominant influence on what is done to promote or control change. In the case of free-market societies, this will be *economic forces*; and in the case of developing countries, it is *external forces* outside the control of the national society.

THE REGULATION OF MASS MEDIA: ALTERNATIVE MODELS

For reasons that have been explained, mass media institutions carry a heavy weight of rules, regulation and scrutiny. The shape and rationale of media regulation can only be sketched here. The normative basis for the principles underlying regulation has been discussed in Chapters 7 and 8. The simplest way of describing media regulation is in terms of three basic models (see Pool, 1983), which apply, approximately and respectively, to the newspaper press, to radio and television broadcasting and to telecommunication.

The free-press model

The basic model for the press is one of freedom from any government regulation and control that would imply censorship or limits on freedom of publication. Press freedom is often enshrined as a principle in national constitutions and in international charters, such as the European Treaty on Human Rights. However, the press freedom model is often modified or extended by public policy in order to guarantee the expected public interest benefits of a free and independent press. Prominent among the reasons for public policy attention to newspapers is the trend towards concentration which, although the result of free economic competition, effectively reduces access to press channels and choice for citizens. Because of this, the press often receives some legal protection as well as some economic benefits. Both imply some element of public scrutiny and supervision, however benevolent. Economic benefits can range from postal and tax concession to loan and subsidy arrangements. There may also be anti-concentration laws and rules against foreign ownership. The press freedom model applies in much the same way to book publishing (where it originates) and to most other print media. By default it also applies to music, although without any special privileges.

By contrast, radio and television broadcasting and, less directly, many newer means of audiovisual delivery have been subject from their beginning to high levels of restriction and direction, often involving direct public ownership. The initial reasons for regulation of broadcasting were mainly technical or to ensure the fair allocation of scarce resources and control of monopoly. However, regulation became deeply institutionalized, at least until the 1980s when new technologies and a new climate of opinion reversed the trend.

The general concept of public service lies at the core of the broadcasting model, although there are several variants, as well as weaker (as in the USA) or stronger forms (as in Europe) (see pages 156–7). Public service broadcasting in a fully developed form (such as in Britain) generally has several main features, supported by policy and regulation. The broadcasting model can involve many different kinds of regulation. Usually, there are specific media laws to regulate the industry and often some form of public service bureaucracy to implement the law. Quite often, the services of production and distribution may be undertaken by private enterprise concerns, operating concessions from the government and following some legally enforceable supervisory guidelines.

The decline in strength of the broadcasting model has been marked by increasing tendencies towards 'privatization' and 'commercialization' of broadcasting, especially in Europe (see McQuail and Siune, 1998). This has involved, most notably, the transfer of media channels and operation from public to private ownership, increased levels of financing from advertising and the franchising of new commercial competitors for public broadcasting channels. Despite its relative decline, however, the broadcasting model shows no sign of being abandoned, for reasons related to the presumed communicative power of audiovisual media and broader public interest concerns.

The common carrier model

The third main model of regulation predates broadcasting and is usually called the common carrier model because it relates primarily to communication services such as mail, telephone and telegraph which are purely for distribution and intended to be open to all as universal services. The main motive for regulation has been for efficient implementation and management of what are (or were) 'natural monopolies' (see page 202) in the interests of efficiency and the consumer. In general, common carrier media have involved heavy regulation of the infrastructure and of economic exploitation but only very marginal regulation of content. This is in sharp contrast to broadcasting, which is characterized by a high degree of content regulation, even where infrastructure is increasingly in private hands.

While the three models are still useful for describing and making sense of the different patterns of media regulation, the retention of these separate regimes is increasingly called into question. The main challenge comes from the technological 'convergence' between modes of communication which makes the regulatory separation between print, broadcasting and telecommunication increasingly artificial and arbitrary. The same means of distribution, especially satellites and telecommunication, can be used to deliver all three kinds of media (and others). Cable systems are now often legally permitted to offer telephone services; broadcasting can deliver newspapers; and the telephone network can provide television and other media services. For the moment, a political and regulatory logic survives, but it will not endure.

Box 9.3   Three regulatory models compared

	Print	Broadcasting	Common carrier
Regulation of infrastructure	None	High	High
Regulation of content	None	High	None
Sender access	Open	Closed	Open
Receiver access	Open	Open	Closed

MEDIA POLICY PARADIGM SHIFTS

The trend towards convergence of policy models for different media is part of a larger pattern of change in approaches to media policy. Some elements of this have already been noted, including the early attempts to make the mass media more accountable to society, and more recently the influence of globalization, the trend to 'deregulation' and privatization of media. Following van Cuilenburg and McQuail (1998), over the longer term of a century of communication development we can detect three main phases of communication policy, in different parts of the world. The first can be described as a phase of *emerging media policy* lasting from the later 19th century until the introduction of broadcasting in the 1920s. There is no coherent policy goal beyond those of protecting the strategic interests of governments and nation and promoting the industrial and economic development of new communication systems (telephony, cable, wireless telegraphy, radio, etc.). The general assumption was that the book would be the main medium of culture and education and the newspaper the instrument of political life and both should be as free from control as possible and therefore outside the scope of public policy.

The second main phase can be described as one of *public service*. It begins with the recognition of a need to legislate for broadcasting, but this time with a new awareness

structures

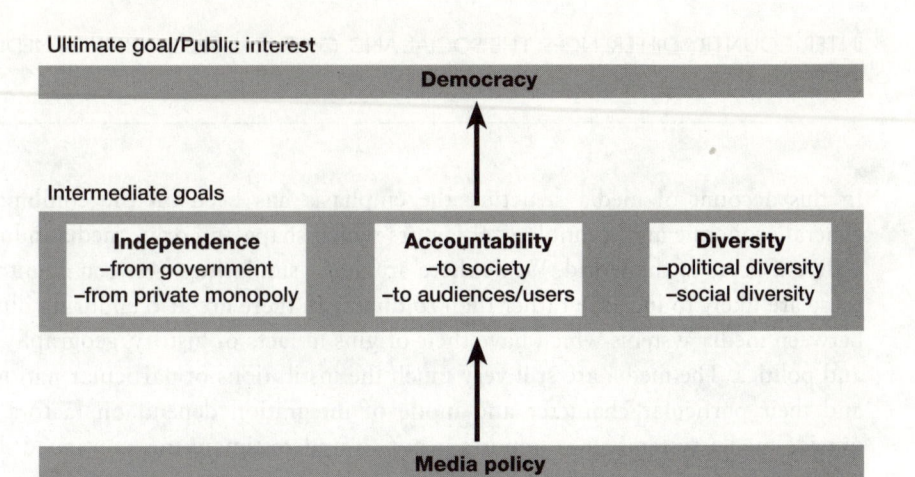

Democracy

| **Independence** –from government –from private monopoly | **Accountability** –to society –to audiences/users | **Diversity** –political diversity –social diversity |

Media policy

FIGURE 9.2   The public service policy paradigm (from van Cuilenberg and McQuail, 1998: 67)

of the social significance of the medium for political, social and cultural life. Communications were seen as much more than technologies. New ideas of 'communication welfare' were introduced that went much further than the requirement of controlled allocation of scarce frequencies. Policy was positive in promoting certain cultural and social goals as well as negative in the sense of forbidding certain kinds of harm to 'society'. For the first time, the press came within the scope of public policy, in order to limit the power of monopoly owners and maintain 'standards' in the face of commercial pressures. This phase reached its apex in Europe in the 1970s and has been in relative decline ever since, though important elements remain. The main structural features were some form of public service television and some measures to ensure a socially responsible newspaper press. The main features are summarized in Figure 9.2. In this model, social normative concerns are the main driving force, especially those associating with the needs of democracy. It is also bounded by the national territory and shaped by 'national interests'. It legitimates government intervention in communication markets for social purposes.

A third phase of policy is now clearly developing as a result of many of the trends that have already been discussed, but especially the trends of internationalization, digitalization and convergence. The key events have been the move to centre stage of telecommunications. The period into which we have moved is one of intense innovation, growth and competition on a global scale. Policy still exists, but the '*new paradigm*' is guided by different goals and values. The dominant values are no longer those of 'social welfare' in its wide sense (nor even 'communication welfare'), but include especially openness and transparency of ownership and control, maximum access for all and choice for consumers, continuation of commercial competition and technological innovation. In general the economic goal has displaced those of social and political welfare, while the values of the latter have also been redefined.

media structures and institutions

In this account of media structure the emphasis has been on the combination of general economic and technological factors which shape and drive media industries in different parts of the world. While there are many similarities between countries, and these are likely to increase rather than to diminish, there are also enduring differences between media systems which have their origins in facts of history, geography, culture and politics. The media are still very much the institutions of particular nation states, and their particular character and mode of integration depend on factors that lie outside media systems. It is important not to underestimate this continued diversity, nor to assume that we can properly understand the media of a particular society in terms of a few more or less universal features of structure and dynamics. It is not only *systems* which differ markedly from country to country, but also patterns of cultural preference and of actual media use behaviour.

It is impossible to summarize the full diversity of media structure, but we can point to a few of the dimensions that differentiate national media systems. These are summarized in Box 9.4.

Box 9.4   Main dimensions of media system difference

- Scale and centralization
- Degree of politicization
- Diversity profile
- Sources of finance
- Degree of public regulation and control

These dimensions are of interest because it is widely assumed that media systems are converging towards a common destination on these very points. In general, the media are thought to be becoming not only more 'globalized' but also less massified, more decentralized, more oriented to popular taste and culture, less (or more) diverse (according to perspective), less politicized, less regulated and more commercial in funding. The reality is not so simple.

All national media systems appear to be in a state of permanent flux, mainly as a result of the same technological changes. Even so, neither the media practices nor the established economic and regulatory patterns have yet converged on anything like a single model, despite superficially similar trends. A simple reason for this is that the technological changes imply very different consequences according to the specific national situation. The differences are rooted not only in politics, culture and history but also in varying market circumstances (reflecting the great complexity of the media business). Economics as much as culture inhibits the convergence which technology is

supposed to produce. Media markets are still very culturally specific. The same forces that are at work nearly everywhere are as much inclined to differentiate as they are to unify in their consequences. Commonly experienced trends (such as that of media globalization) do not logically have to lead to the same outcomes.

MEDIA SYSTEMS AND POLITICAL SYSTEMS

Much of foregoing discussion of media policy and regulation, as well as earlier chapters on normative theories of the media, leaves little doubt about the complex and powerful links between mass media and the national political system even where there is formally little or no connection. The very fact of limited overt connections makes it easy to ignore the degree to which the institutions are intertwined and helps to support one of the widespread myths about mass media in Western democracies – that, because they claim political independence, they are somehow detached from politics.

This is not the place to correct the myth or make good the omission (beyond what has already been said in the previous two chapters). This is partly because the links between political and media systems do show large intercultural differences. Nevertheless, it is useful to mention some connections that are related to structure, conduct and performance. First of all, there is a body of law, regulation and policy in every country that has been negotiated through the political system that guarantees rights, freedoms and sets obligations and limits even to the most free of public media. Necessary changes in the light of circumstances will have to be decided on by politicians, who will be aware of their needs and that of the political institutions. There are acts of law and regulation in every country that touch specifically on the role of media in democratic process and the relation between the two. In many countries there is a public sector of the media (usually broadcasting) over which governments have some ultimate control and there are diverse ways in which the management of these organizations is penetrated by political interests, even where they have some autonomy.

In the case of privately owned media, the links to the political system are usually less transparent, but not always so. Media proprietors generally have financial and strategic interests that call for continuous influence on political decision-making. Not infrequently they have open ideological positions and even political ambitions of their own. The endorsement of political parties by newspapers is probably more common than not. Broadcasting, including private systems, has generally abstained from open political involvement, by custom, choice or necessity, but they cannot help being potential political players, and even on the mundane question of gaining and keeping licences they have to take good care of their political relationships.

media structures and institutions

Finally, at the level of performance, the content of most daily media is still penetrated by politics, not normally because it is so fascinating. There is no easy explanation, which is part of the oddity of what is supposed in many places to be a consumer market. While citizens need to be informed and advised in the longer term they do not need what they are offered every day. We have to assume that the reasons lie either in the advantages for news media in terms of a staple commodity or in the enormous efforts made by political interests (in the widest sense) to gain access to the public for their diverse ends. It is probably this connection between the two institutions that serves to hold them together in an embrace that cannot be broken.

POST-COMMUNIST CHANGES IN MEDIA STRUCTURE

During the last decade, fundamental changes have affected a very large part of world media systems – virtually all the countries within the old Communist 'bloc', involving three or four hundred million people, the old 'Second World'. It is impossible to leave this great sea-change unremarked in a chapter on media structure in a book on media theory. At the same time, the changes have been so extensive and sudden, the countries involved so much more diverse than imagined in Cold War frames, and the course of change so incomplete that it is still early to derive clear lessons. This is not for lack of attention from inside and without by scholars and media themselves, and we know almost too much to assess clearly what has happened. The comments that follow are an attempt to sketch still-early impressions.

The fall of communism came too quickly and unexpectedly for there to be much preparation in theory for explaining either the role of the media in change or predicting the consequences for the media. In the general explanation of the societal transformation, it does not seem that the media played a very active role, although they were important at the margins, especially in literal sense, when the liberation movement got under way in the Baltic states (Lauristin and Vihalemm, 1997). In the case of the DDR, which may be considered a catalyst of further change, there is reason to think that exposure to West German media was important. Even so, the change of system in the end seems on the whole to have been more 'top-down' than 'bottom-up', accompanied by an 'implosion' of the old order, rather than revolution (Jakubowitz, 1995) and as if it were waiting to happen.

The old media systems exhibited formal structures that looked superficially like those of Western Europe, with separate press and television organizations. However, virtually all major media of East and Central Europe and the Soviet Union were distinctive in being subject to central, government or party control and censorship, albeit with a fair degree of editorial autonomy on matters not politically sensitive. The economic foundations of the media system were not based on a free market. There was

very limited paid advertising and audience payments had little relation to costs of production and distribution.

The diversity of circumstances as between the old Soviet Union, some of its republics (like the Baltic States), the big Central European countries, and the smaller and poorer Balkan region, make broad generalizations impossible. This applies especially to the early stages of the process, and to the various ideological components, which included nationalism, religion and liberty of expression and of economic enterprise. Looking back and from a distance, however, we can make some general points about what has happened.

First of all, and in virtually all affected countries, there was a great outpouring of new publications and forms of expression in response to the lifting of censorship around the start of the 1990s. This exuberant use of new freedoms was curtailed in the end by several factors. There was no longer any political or cultural door to push against, and coping with the sometimes harsh realities of free market society prompted new priorities. A certain routinization set into the media as elsewhere and media had to find economic feet. There was extreme competition for limited income and other resources and these were not easy to come by in markets only partially established or liberated.

The second main and obvious point to make concerns the privatization or commercialization process itself. This not only applied financial disciplines where they had not been experienced, especially the need to attract advertising and sell something beyond ideas and opinions to audiences of consumers. Aside from the major effort of restructuring of ownership and management, this meant catering for new tastes, adopting styles and methods of Western media, and opening to Western content and ownership. In addition, media were often flooded with advertising to a degree and of a kind intolerable in Western Europe. If nothing else the idealized notion of free media expressing free ideas was somewhat unrealized in the experience that became normal after a short time.

Thirdly, there is a good deal of evidence from later accounts (e.g. Paletz et al., 1995; Sparks and Reading, 1998) that the *politicization* of the media did not end with communism, even though it has taken new forms. This is not surprising, since politics did not end. One early manifestation of the new political situation was the tendency for newspapers and journalists to prove their new freedom by attacking governments and being more partisan than the media in the West. Another form has been the survival in most of the countries concerned of public broadcasting organizations that are generally regarded as instruments of support for the government of the day and dependent on government. There are also private broadcasters in each country that often require or court political patronage in order to get and keep licences and/or which happen to be funded by financial groups with political agendas. In the difficult economic and other circumstances, it has been virtually impossible to avoid this. The situation of the printed press is much more variable, but it too either adopts a purely 'commercial' and apolitical formula or newspapers become allied to some political-financial interest. The whole process of establishing a legal as well as economic basis for a new and more diversified media order out of the ruins of the older has been an

immensely contested event. It is not surprising that in several countries we hear of 'media wars' taking place in the early 1990s.

There are many unstable elements in the media situations referred to here, and many influences that do not play much part in the structure and dynamic of western media. These include the inheritance from the past of quite different practices and the love–hate relationship with 'western' ideas, practices and finance. It is not clear that the vast 'experiment' in media transformation has produced or been guided by any new theory of media structure or norms, but the question remains open (see de Smaele, 1999). We can still learn a great deal from the experiences about the working of cultural, political and economic forces that often lie beneath the surface of media 'normality' or are concealed by myths. The events have shed light, albeit unevenly, on the relationship between free media and democratic society. This has prompted one commentator to ask, with special reference to Russia, whether 'conventional wisdom is correct that press freedom is a pre-condition for the democratic, law-based state? Or is the democratic law-based state a precondition for press freedom?' (Price, 1995: 127). From the perspective of the norms and ideals sketched in Chapters 7 and 8, the lessons seem to be inspiring and depressing in equal measure, but much the same could be said of the (unreformed) 'old order' of Western media.

FURTHER READING

Hoffmann-Riem, W. (1996) *Regulating Media*. New York: Guilford Press.

McQuail, D. and Siune, K. (1998) *Media Policy: Convergence, Concentration, Commerce*. London: Sage.

de Sola Pool, I. (1983) *Technologies of Freedom*. Cambridge, MA: Harvard University Press.

Picard, R. (1989) *Media Economics*. Beverly Hills, CA: Sage.

Turow, J. (1984) *Media Industries*. White Plains, NY: Longman.

Tunstall, J. and Palmer, M. (eds) (1991) *Media Moguls*. London: Routledge.

10

global mass communication

Books and printing were in their origins quite international, since they predated the era of nation states and served cultural, political and commercial worlds that extended throughout Europe and beyond. Many early printed books were in Latin or were translated from another language, and the earliest newspapers were often compiled from newsletters that circulated widely throughout Europe. Nevertheless, the newspaper as it developed became very much a national institution, and national boundaries largely delineated the circulation of print media in general. The national character of early mass media was reinforced by the exclusiveness of language as well as by cultural and political factors.

The technology of production and distribution often limited wider circulation, and in many countries newspapers did not even attain the status of being truly national. When film was invented, it too was largely confined within national frontiers at least until after the 1914–18 war. Its subsequent diffusion, especially in the form of the Hollywood film, is the first real example of a transnational mass medium, much aided by the war-time collapse of European film-making (Tunstall, 1977). When radio was widely introduced during the 1920s, it was once more an essentially national medium, not only because of the spoken word in different languages, but also because transmission was generally organized to encompass the national territory and not further. Political developments in Europe (the rise of communism and Nazism) and depression everywhere, encouraged nations to look inward.

By comparison, we are now being constantly reminded of how international the media have become and how the flow of news and culture encompasses the globe and draws us into a single 'global village', to use the words of McLuhan (1964). Before considering this proposition, it is worth putting the current globalization of mass media into some historical perspective. Media internationalism is not new. The major newspapers from the mid-19th century onwards were well served by powerful and well-organized news agencies that made use of the international telegraph system, and foreign news was a staple commodity of many newspapers across the world. The predominant features of the geopolitical scene, especially nationalism itself and also imperialism, encouraged an interest in international events, especially where war and conflict provided good news copy (this predates the 19th century, e.g. Wilke, 1995). In the early part of the 20th century, governments began to discover the advantages of the media for international as well as domestic propaganda purposes. Since the Second World War a good many countries have used radio to provide a world-wide service of information and culture designed to foster a positive national image, promote the national culture and maintain contact with expatriates. This is hardly mass communication, but it is an overt expression of motives that lie behind the management of global news flow.

As noted already, the American film in particular became a potent bearer of images

of modernity and other aspects of American life and culture. Early recorded music also had a quasi-international character, firstly because of the classical repertoire and secondly because of the increasing diffusion of American popular songs, sometimes associated with musical films. A balanced view of the early history of mass media would suggest that, in many countries, there has always been a real or potential tension between the desire to maintain a national cultural and political hegemony and also to share in cultural and technological innovations. There are also many instances of national minorities trying to assert a cultural identity in the face of imperialist cultural domination in the literal sense (for instance within the British, Austrian and Russian empires). The United States was a late-comer in this role.

Nevertheless, some features of the current media situation point without much doubt to an accelerating trend of trans-nationalization affecting news, music, film, entertainment and sport and virtually all forms of media. Television is still probably the single most potent influence in this media globalization process, partly because, as with the cinema film, its visual character helps it to pass barriers of language. Just as important, however, is the fact that its predominant form of organization and means of transmission are such that it cannot easily be contained within national frontiers nor kept out. This was not so in its early days, when the range of terrestrial transmission was easily limited to national frontiers in most countries.

NEW DRIVING FORCES: TECHNOLOGY AND MONEY

Technology has certainly given a powerful push to the globalization of television. The arrival of television satellites in the late 1970s broke the principle of national sovereignty of broadcasting space and made it difficult and ultimately impossible to offer effective resistance to television transmission from outside the national territory. But the extent to which satellites reach global audiences directly is often exaggerated. There are other means of diffusion that work in the same direction – for instance by connecting cable systems and simply by physically transporting cassettes. But the main route is by exports channelled through nationally based media.

While technology has been a necessary condition of extensive globalization, and the truly global medium of the Internet illustrates this most clearly, the most immediate and enduring driving forces behind globalization have been economic. Television was established on the model of radio broadcasting, as a continuous service at least during the evening, later during the day and ultimately on a continuous basis. The cost of filling broadcasting time with original or domestic material has always strained the capacity of production organizations, even in wealthy countries. It is virtually impossible without great repetition or extensive importing. This pressure has operated

on public systems as well as commercial organizations, but more especially on the latter.

The expansion of television since the 1980s, made possible by new efficient and low-cost transmission technologies, has been driven by commercial motives and has fuelled demand for imports. It has also stimulated new audio visual production industries in many countries that look, in their turn, for new markets. The main beneficiary and the main exporter has been the United States, which has a large and surplus production of popular entertainment and an entrée into many markets secured by the cultural familiarity of its products mainly as a result of decades of American films. The English language is an added advantage but not decisive, since most TV exports have always been dubbed or subtitled when transmitted.

An important component of international mass communication is advertising, linked to the globalization of many product markets and reflecting the international character of many advertising agencies and the dominance of the market by a small number of firms (see Chapter 9). One outcome is the appearance of the same advertising message in different countries, but there is also an indirect internationalizing effect on the media that carry the advertising. Advertising also often carries images of other countries and parts of the world, usually in a way that reinforces stereotypes, albeit mainly positive ones.

MULTINATIONAL MEDIA OWNERSHIP AND CONTROL

The recent phase of the 'communications revolution' has been marked by a new phenomenon of media concentration – both transnational and multimedia, leading to the world media industry's being increasingly dominated by a small number of very large media firms. In some cases, these developments are the achievement of a fairly traditional breed of media 'moguls' (Tunstall and Palmer, 1991), though with new names. Despite the high visibility of larger-than-life media moguls, it is likely that the trend is rather towards more impersonal patterns of ownership and operation, as befits such large global enterprises.

Certain types of media content lend themselves to globalization of ownership and control of production and distribution. These include 'foreign news', feature films, popular music recordings, television serials and books. Tunstall (1991) refers to these as 'one-off' media, by contrast with the 'cash-flow' media of newspapers and television stations, which have generally resisted multinational ownership. The 'one-off' product can be more easily designed for an international market and lends itself to more flexible marketing and distribution over a longer time span. 'News' was the first product to be 'commodified' in the way indicated, by way of the main

international news agencies. These are, in effect, 'wholesale' suppliers of news as a commodity, and it is easy to see why national news media find it much more convenient and economical to 'buy in' news about the rest of the world than to collect it themselves.

The rise of the global news agencies of the 20th century was made possible by technology (telegraph and radio-telephony) and stimulated by war, trade, imperialism and industrial expansion (Boyd-Barrett, 1980; Boyd-Barrett and Rantanen, 1998). Government involvement was quite common. For these reasons, the main press agencies in the post-war era were North American (UPI and Associated Press), or British (Reuters), French (AFP) or Russian (Tass). Since then, the US predominance has declined in relative terms with the virtual demise of UPI, while other agencies have grown (such as the German DPA and the Japanese Kyodo). Tass has been replaced by Itar-Tass, still a state agency. According to Tunstall (1992), despite general American media dominance, Europe had become the largest producer and consumer of foreign news. Paterson (1998: 79) writes that the three television news agencies originate much of the international news used by the world's broadcasters are Reuters, World Television News (WTN) and Associated Press Television News (APTV). Tunstall and Machin (1999: 77) refer to a virtual 'world news duopoly' controlled by the US Associated Press and the British Reuters. The French AFP, German DPA and Spanish EFE are also big players. It is clear that predominance is shaped by the domestic strength of the media organizations concerned, in terms of market size, degree of concentration and economic resources. The English language confers an extra advantage.

The foremost example of internationalization of media ownership, production and distribution is that of the popular music industry (a development of the last fifty years), with a high proportion of several major markets being in the hands of the 'big five' companies (Burnett, 1990, 1996; Negus, 1992). These were (as of 1993): Columbia (a former US company bought by Sony of Japan), Time-Warner (the world's largest media conglomerate), RCA (now owned by the German company Bertelsmann), EMl (Britain's Thorn Electronics) and Polygram (now Dutch and German owned, by Philips and Siemens). Advertising provides another example of very high concentration and internationalization. According to Tunstall and Machin (1999), about ten leading advertising groups place about half the world"s advertising expenditure. Advertising agencies tend also to control market research and public relations companies.

Globalization and concentration of large media companies tend also to lead to cartel forming, and the very large firms co-operate in various ways as well as compete. They also exhibit ownership connections. Tunstall and Machin (1999) report a complex pattern of interrelated interests amongst the leading three American media firms (Time-Warner, Disney and Viacom) and also four foreign firms with a big stake in the US market: Seagram (Canada), Bertelsmann (Germany), Sony (Japan) and News Corporation (Australia). Companies also co-operate by sharing revenue, co-production, co-purchasing of movies, and dividing up local outlets.

These remarks make it clear that 'global mass communication' is a multifaceted phenomenon that takes a variety of forms. These include:

- Direct transmission or distribution of media channels or complete publications from one country to audiences in other countries. This covers foreign sales of newspapers (sometimes in special editions) and books, certain satellite television channels, officially sponsored international radio broadcast services;
- Certain specifically international media, such as MTV Europe, CNN International, BBC World, TVCinq, etc.;
- Content items of many kinds (films, music, TV programmes, journalistic items, etc.) that are imported to make up part of domestic media output;
- Formats and genres of foreign origin that are adapted or remade to suit domestic audiences;
- International news items, whether about a foreign country or made in a foreign country, that appear in domestic media;
- Miscellaneous content such as sporting events, advertising and pictures that have a foreign reference or origin.

It is clear from these examples that there is no sharp dividing line between media content that is 'global' and that which is 'national' or local. Mass communication is almost by definition 'global' in character, and only the United States and a few isolated societies can claim to have a purely domestic media supply. The United States produces much and imports little, but even in this case the content of American media culture is international by virtue of the fact that it is shared with the rest of the world. It is also indirectly globalized by the orientation of much of its own production towards world markets.

Despite the many manifestations of media globalization, there are few media outlets (channels, publications, etc.) that give much guaranteed access for a given source to any significant foreign audience. At most we can predict that certain successful products (e.g. a hit film or TV show, a music recording, a sporting event) will receive a world-wide audience in the end. This implies that 'receiving' countries still have a considerable capacity to influence the 'national' media experience. We have to consider how far the 'foreign' content has been subject to 'gate-keeping' controls at the point of import (for instance edited, screened and selected, dubbed or translated, given a familiar context). The main mechanism of 'control' is not usually policy or law, or even economics (which usually encourages imports), but the audience demand for their 'own' media content in their own language. There are natural barriers of language and culture that resist globalization (Biltereyst, 1992). Economics can limit as well as

stimulate imports. In general the wealthier a country, even when small in population, the more chance it has to afford its media autonomy.

CULTURAL IMPERIALISM AND BEYOND

In the era immediately following the Second World War, when communication research was largely an American monopoly, the mass media were commonly viewed as one of the most promising channels of modernization (= Westernization) and especially a potent tool for overcoming traditional attitudes (see page 83). From this perspective, the flow of mass media from the developed or capitalist West to the less developed world was seen as both good for its recipients and also beneficial in combating the alternative model of modernization based on socialism, planning and government control. The kinds of media flow envisaged were not direct propaganda or instruction, but the ordinary entertainment (plus news and advertising) that was presumed to show a prosperous way of life and the social institutions of liberal democracy at work. The flood of American print, music and television provided the main example and testing of the theory.

This was undoubtedly a very ethnocentric way of looking at global communication flow and it eventually provoked a critical reaction from scholars and political activists and also from those at the receiving end. Before long the issue was inescapably caught up in Cold War polemics and left-wing resistance movements in semi-colonial situations (especially in Latin America). Unlike the international propaganda efforts of previous times the new 'media imperialism' seemed to be carried out at the willing request of the mass audience for popular culture and was thus much more likely to 'succeed'. Of course, it was not the audience making a direct choice, but domestic media firms choosing on their behalf, for economic rather than ideological reasons.

Most of the issues surrounding global mass communication have a direct or indirect connection with the thesis of 'cultural imperialism', or the more limited notion of 'media imperialism'. Both concepts imply a deliberate attempt to dominate, invade or subvert the 'cultural space' of others and suggest a degree of coercion in the relationship. It is certainly a very unequal relationship in terms of power. It also implies some kind of overall cultural or ideological pattern in what is transmitted, which has often been interpreted in terms of 'Western values', especially those of individualism, secularism, materialism. It has a political as well as a cultural content, however, in the first case essentially a submission to the global project of American capitalism (Schiller, 1969). In the case of relations with Latin America noted already, the idea of an American 'imperialist' project for the hemisphere, certainly in the 1960s and 1970s was not fanciful (Dorfman and Mattelart, 1975). Critical theorists have not

always agreed on whether it was the economic aims of global market control or the cultural and political aims of 'Westernization' that took precedence, although the two aspects are obviously connected. The (critical) political economy theorists emphasize the economic dynamics of global media markets that work blindly to shape the flows of media commodities. Not surprisingly, such dynamics favour the free market model and in general promote capitalism.

The critics of global media imperialism have generally been countered by a mixed set of supporters of the free market or just pragmatists who see the imbalance of flow as a normal feature of the media market. In their view it has benefits for all and is not necessarily problematic (e.g. Pool, 1974; Noam, 1991; Hoskins and Mirus, 1988; Wildman, 1991). It may even be temporary or reversed under some circumstances. Biltereyst (1995) has described these as two dominant and opposed paradigms under the heading of *dependency* and *free-flow*. In his view both paradigms rest on somewhat weak grounds empirically. The critical dependency model is based very largely on evidence of quantity of flow and some limited interpretation of ideological tendencies of content. There is little or no research on the posited effects. The free-flow theorists tend to assume minimal effects on the grounds that the audience is voluntary, and they make large assumptions about the cultural neutrality and ideological innocence of the globally traded content. It is also quite possible to view the ongoing globalization of media as having no ultimate goal or purpose and no real effect (in line with the 'cultural autonomy' position signalled in Chapter 4 (page 62). It is simply an unplanned outcome of current political, cultural and technological changes.

If the process of global mass communication is framed from the point of view of the national societies at the receiving end, according to the media imperialist thesis, there are at least four propositions to consider. These are listed in Box 10.1 and will be discussed later in the chapter. However, there has been a shift in thinking about globalization that has moved on from the overwhelmingly negative perspective of media imperialism. It is not a return to the 'optimism' of the modernization phase, but more a reflection of postmodern ideas and new cultural theory that avoids the normative judgements of earlier theory.

Box 10.1   Media imperialism thesis: the effects of globalization

- Global media promote relations of dependency rather than economic growth
- The imbalance in the flow of mass media content undermines cultural autonomy or holds back its development
- The unequal relationship in the flow of news increases the relative global power of large and wealthy news-producing countries and hinders the growth of an appropriate national identity and self-image
- Global media flows give rise to a state of cultural homogenization or synchronization, leading to a dominant form of culture that has no specific connection with real experience for most people

The cultural imperialism thesis has been largely abandoned in the more recent tendency to frame many of the same issues in terms of 'globalization' (Sreberny-Mohammadi, 1996; Golding and Harris, 1998: 4). As we have seen (page 102), there has been a strong challenge to the critique of popular mass media and its general cultural pessimism. This has also affected thinking about the effects of global cultural exchange, although perhaps not about the global flow of news. Certainly, we quite often encounter positive, even celebratory views of the global inclusiveness brought about by mass media. The shared symbolic space can be extended, and the constraints of place and time that are associated with nationally compartmentalized media systems can be evaded. Globalization of culture can even look good compared with the ethnocentrism, nationalism and even xenophobia that has characterized some national media systems. The new era of international peace ('New World Order') that was supposed to have been ushered in by the end of the Cold War could be thought to require a significant presence of internationalist media (Ferguson, 1992).

The negative bias of the theory literature concerning international media flows may be viewed as a reflection of an earlier tradition in media research that dealt with mass media primarily in terms of problems for society. But it was also the result of the mixing of several lines of critique relating to national identity and integrity, global capitalism and Third World dependency (Tomlinson, 1991). Sreberny-Mohammadi (1996) suggests that the 'cultural imperialism' model 'was based on a situation of comparative global media scarcity, limited global media players and embryonic media systems in much of the Third World'. These conditions have changed in some degree, and in any case the situation is much more complex than it was twenty or more years ago.

Most of the propositions arising from the media imperialism thesis also tend to frame global mass communication as a process of cause and effect, as if the media were 'transmitting' ideas, meaning, cultural forms from place to place, sender to receiver. To that extent, the critics use much the same language as the original 'theorists of development'. There is a general consensus that this 'transportation' model (see page 52) of how media work is not very appropriate outside certain cases of planned communication. If nothing else, we need to take much more account of the active participation of the audience in shaping any 'meaning' that is taken from mass media (Liebes and Katz, 1990).

This revised and more positive perspective on globalization rests on the observation that the international flow of media generally responds to demand, and has to be understood in terms of the wants and needs of receivers and not just the actual or supposed motives of the suppliers. This fact does not in itself invalidate the media imperialist critique, given the constraints in the global media market. Nor does the 'new revisionism' satisfy many critics who see only a new ideology or mythology in the contemporary euphoria about the global (Ferguson, 1992). Many features of the

world media situation attest to the even more powerful grip of the capitalist apparatus and ethos on media nearly everywhere, with no place to hide (not even a Soviet Union).

THE MEDIA TRANSNATIONALIZATION PROCESS

Under this heading we look at the process by which content and audience experience are in some sense globalized. It is an effect process (if there is one) with two stages: first, transformation of content, and second, impact on audiences. In his analysis of the international flows of television, Sepstrup (1989) has suggested that we differentiate *flows* in the following way:

- **national** – where foreign (not home-produced) content is distributed in the national television system;
- **bilateral** – where content originating in and intended for one country is received directly in a neighbouring country;
- **multilateral** – where content is produced or disseminated without a specific national audience in mind.

In the *national* case, all content is distributed by the home media, but some of the items will be of foreign origin (films, TV shows, news stories, etc.). The *bilateral* case refers mainly to direct cross-border transmission or reception, where audiences in a neighbouring country are reached on a regular basis. This is common, for example, in respect of the USA and Canada, Britain and Ireland, The Netherlands and Belgium. The *multilateral* type covers most examples of overtly international media channels (MTV, CNN, etc.). The first type of internationalization is by far the most important in terms of volume of flow and reach to audiences, yet at the same time, as we have noted, it is potentially open to national control. Despite the variety of ways in which mass communication has become internationalized, it is worth keeping in mind that only a small proportion of media content is actually produced primarily for an international market and relatively little is directly aimed at non-national audiences. Internationalism of media is thus largely unintended and incidental, despite its prevalence.

The model of transnationalizing *effects* proposed by Sepstrup (1989) on the basis of this characterization is reproduced in Figure 10.1. This shows the relationship between three notional countries, in which X is a major producer and exporter of media content and Y and Z are importers. There are three main lines of transnationalizing effect: *national, bilateral* and *multilateral*. The first of these operates on the basis of imports and is really a process by which a national media *system* is internationalized by way of borrowing content. The next step in the process, if there is one, is that the national system becomes the agent for influencing its audiences in an 'international'

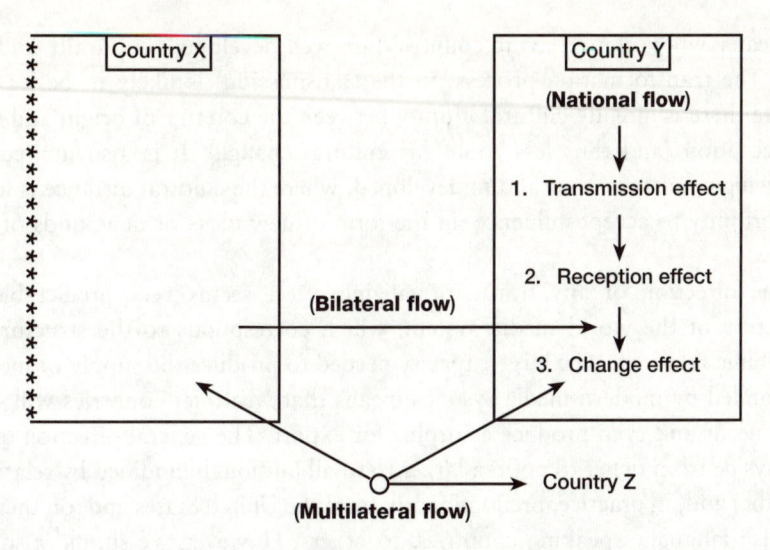

FIGURE 10.1   Internationalization of television: three types of flow (from McQuail and Windahl, 1993: 225, based on theory in Sepstrup, 1989)

direction, for good or ill. For this to take place, the content not only has to be transmitted, but it has to be received and responded to in a positive way. Only if this happens can we speak of a process of internationalization that affects the culture and the society.

Of the other two processes, the case of bilateral flow (direct cross border transmission) most often occurs when neighbouring countries already have much in common in terms of culture, experience and often language. In these circumstances it is not easy to distinguish the role of the media from many other kinds of contact. The case of multilateral flow from one country direct to many others is still relatively unimportant as far as conventional mass media are concerned, because the audiences affected are small. However, it is growing in importance with the growth of the Internet, which encourages multiple multilateral flows.

Sepstrup warns against drawing conclusions of cultural *effect* from these processes of transnational flow. We need to distinguish between 'international' media content or 'internationalized' systems on the one hand and what is actually received (or received from any consequence for the receiving culture) on the other. It is a long way from the transmission of foreign produced content to any predictable 'foreign' influence achieved. There are many steps and obstacles on the way. Language is a very large barrier to certain kinds of content or to direct transmission of any message. Cultural differences are another obstacle since they cause selective perception and interpretation of content received, thus diverting the supposed message in unpredictable directions (see page 56).

The more that content is filtered through the national media system, the more it is subject to selection and adapted, re-framed and recontextualized to fit local tastes, attitudes and expectations. The chance of 'culture clash' is diminished. This transformation

is greater where the receiving countries are well developed, culturally and economically. The transformation process (in the transmission) is likely to be least operative where there is already cultural affinity between the country of origin and the country of reception (and thus less room for cultural change). It is also limited where the receiving country is poor and undeveloped, where the cultural distance is high and the opportunity to accept influence (in the form of new ideas or new kinds of behaviour) is low.

The direction of any transnationalizing effect seems very predictable from the structure of the world media system, which corresponds to the structure of global economic relations. The large capacity needed to produce the supply of media content demanded by modern media systems means that wealthier countries will satisfy their own needs and even produce a surplus for export. The general direction of effect will always be from richer to poorer, larger to small (although modified by relative national income) and, in practice, predominantly from the United States and, on their coat tails, English language speaking countries, to others. However, we should also note some reverse effects. The more media content is produced with a view to wider markets, the more culturally inclusive and less ethnocentric (and specific) it is likely to be. Gerbner (1995) has deplored the fact that American film and television production is in some respects debased by the demand in world markets for violence, sex and action to help sell the typical American product.

Referring back to the fact of voluntary import or reception of international flow, it is worth noting that the arrival and growth of the Internet does widen the possibility of access to global information and cultural resources. Access is now possible without reliance on the various gatekeepers that always restrict and control the flow of content in more traditional media. These gatekeepers operate at both the sending and receiving end of distribution channels. The Internet (and World Wide Web) is a genuinely international medium and potentially opens a vast new resource to all. However, it remains another fact that Internet 'content' is dominated by 'western' (and English language) originators, however diverse, and access is dependent on expensive equipment, significant costs for poor people, and language and other skills.

INTERNATIONAL MEDIA DEPENDENCY

It is a well- and long-established fact that a few countries, with the USA most prominent, do dominate the global trade in news and entertainment. The other countries are often dependent not only for the supply of media content, but in economic terms as well. According to dependency theorists, a necessary condition for throwing off dependent relations is to have some self-sufficiency in the realm of

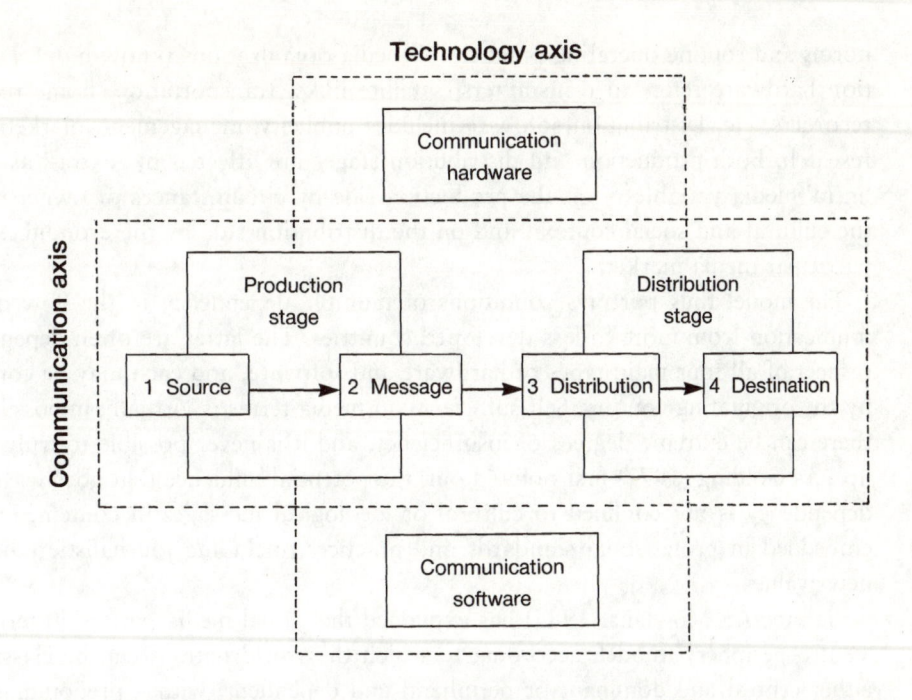

FIGURE 10.2   International communication dependency (Mowlana, 1985): each stage of the mass communication process can be identified as having a hardware and a software aspect of potential dependancy

information, ideas and culture. Mowlana (1985) has analysed all forms of inter-national communication and proposed a model in which two dimensions are the most important determinants of the degree of dependence or autonomy. These are the *technology* axis (hardware versus software) and the *communication* axis (production versus distribution). The main features of the model are shown in Figure 10.2.

The model represents a now familiar sequence from sender (1) to receiver (4), mediated by a technologically based production (2) and distribution (3) system. In international communication, contrary to the typical national media situation the four stages of origination, production, distribution and reception can be (and often are) spatially, organizationally and culturally separated from each other. Media products from one country are typically imported and incorporated into a quite different distribution system and reach audiences for which they were not originally intended. Quite commonly, especially in respect of film and television, the entire origination and production of products occurs in one country and the distribution in another. This is how the 'North' is often related to the 'South' in media terms.

This typically extended and discontinuous process is cross-cut by the technology axis, which reminds us that each stage is dependent on two kinds of expertise (and also of property), one relating to hardware, the other to software. Production hardware includes cameras, studios, printing plants, computers, etc. Production software includes not only actual content items but also performance rights, management, professional

norms and routine operating practices of media organizations (know-how). Distribution hardware refers to transmitters, satellite links, transportation, home receivers, recorders, etc. Distribution software includes publicity, management, marketing and research. Both production and distribution stages are affected by 'extra-' as well as 'intra'-media variables – on the production side by circumstances of ownership and the cultural and social context, and on the distribution side by the economics of the particular media market.

The model thus portrays conditions of multiple dependency in the flow of communication from more to less developed countries. The latter are often dependent in respect of all four main types of hardware and software, and each may be controlled by the originating country. Self-sufficiency in media terms is virtually impossible, but there can be extreme degrees of insufficiency, and it is never possible to truly 'catch-up'. As Golding (1977) first pointed out, the potential influence that goes with media dependency is not confined to cultural or ideological messages in content, it is also embedded in professional standards and practices, including journalistic ethics and news values.

Galtung (in Mowlana, 1985) has explained the global media pattern in terms of a 'centre–periphery' model, according to which the world nations can be classified as either central and dominant or peripheral and dependent, with a predominant flow from the former towards the latter. Certain larger, more 'central' countries originate news and other media content and distribute it to their own 'satellites'. In general, it is the United States and the larger countries of Western Europe (France, Britain, Italy, Germany, Spain) that are more 'central' and have media satellites in tow. But China and Japan have their own 'satellites' and the Arab world its own small galaxy. The former Soviet Union was another 'central' media power whose influence has been dissipated. The particular configuration changes with time and differs somewhat from medium to medium (press, television, music, film). A feature of this model is that there is only limited flow between the peripheral countries themselves, although there are regional and language-based patterns of exchange, which are probably growing rather than diminishing in significance.

The limited interchange at the periphery has been held to increase dependency by preventing the development of any common cause or collective action in relation to richer countries. The centre–periphery model does not rest on the idea of there being one single centre, and the complexities of media development and opening of opportunities for intercommunication undermine the view that there is a rigid and well-organized system of domination in the relations between states. However, the project for the development of a global telecommunications and media infrastructure that will connect individuals everywhere suggests that we may be entering a new phase where the older dependency models are inadequate to the task (Baldwin et al., 1996; Sussman, 1997).

In the emerging and still unclear 'system' of global communication flows, it is probable that the nation state will be less significant as a unit of analysis. It is more difficult to assign information and culture to a country of origin. Multinational

production and marketing in the control of large corporations and multilateral media flows will establish their own patterns of dominance and dependency.

INTERNATIONAL NEWS FLOW

As noted earlier, the globalization of news really began in earnest with the rise of the international news agencies in the 19th century (see Boyd-Barrett and Rantanen, 1998), and news was the first media product to be effectively commodified for international trade. The reasons for this are not altogether clear, although the history of mass media shows the early and perennial importance of a service of current information for attracting audiences. The 'news' has become a more or less standardized and universal genre as a component of print and electronic media and along with it the 'news story'. The news story can have a value as useful information or can satisfy curiosity and human interest, regardless of where it is heard.

The televising of news has accelerated the cross-cultural appeal of news by telling the story in pictures to which can be added words in any language or with any 'angle'. Television news film agencies followed in the footsteps of the print news agencies. The picture may well tell a story but the words pin down the intended meaning. Television news film, like print news, has been based on the principle of journalistic 'objectivity' that is designed to guarantee the reliability and credibility of accounts of events. In some ways it is easier to export purely verbal news because of the greater ambiguity of pictures. While earlier international 'foreign' news concentrated on politics, war, diplomacy and trade, there has been an enormous expansion of the scope for international news, with particular reference to sport, the world of media and entertainment, finance, tourism, fashion and much more.

The original debate about the unbalanced global flow of news echoed the terms of the dependency debate as discussed above. One of the earliest empirical studies of news imbalance (Schramm, 1964) showed that the news media in all 'developing' countries were heavy importers of news, while news audiences in developed countries were largely supplied with home-produced news, even when it was about foreign events. It was argued that the lack of autonomy in news production limited national cultural development (especially, for example, in new nations, often ex-colonies) and limited their full independence and sovereignty.

The fundamental reasons for news dependency were thought to lie in insufficient resources plus the ease of supply of the surplus news product of richer countries, mainly by way of international news agencies. At the same time the countries that were self-sufficient in news could be seen as restricted in their own view of the world. Not only was the supply of news reaching audiences in the developed world very selective and incomplete, it also involved seeing the rest of the world only through the perspective of domestic concerns.

The debate over news imbalance that raged for much of the 1970s did not bring the contesting parties much closer together, since they were separated by quite different interests and commitments. One of the parties was the news industry itself, generally opposed to anything that might hinder the press or the news market from continuing to operate as always, in the name of press freedom. There is evidence to suggest that this self-interest coloured reporting of the issue in the Unesco context (see Giffard, 1989). Another party consisted of the news-dependent countries who wanted at the very least to change the terms of international news reporting by establishing some normative guidelines (see the 1978 Unesco Mass Media Declaration). They also claimed some rights to control reporting within their own frontiers in the national interest and in the name of equity. The Cold War provided two parties. One was the Soviet bloc claiming the right to keep its news space clear of unwanted foreign influence, in the name of sovereignty. Another was the American or Western bloc that wanted unlimited 'free flow', safe in the knowledge that this would work in its own political and commercial interest. The goal of a New World Information and Communication Order (NWICO) that would replace the inequity of the free market in news was eventually abandoned in the aftermath of Unesco's defeat. The McBride Report (1980) that made recommendations for implementing the new principles was largely ignored. According to Hamelink (1998), the failure of the McBride Committee was at least partly due to its inadequate understanding of social reality.

Along the way, however, much light was shed by research and by the public debate on the actual structure of news flow and the underlying dynamics of the global news industry. It was repeatedly confirmed that news (whether press or TV) in more developed countries did not typically give a great deal of space to foreign news (except in specialist or elite publications). Foreign news was largely devoted to events in other countries that were large, nearby and rich, or connected by language and culture. It was also narrowly focused on the interests of the receiving country. Most foreign news could often be accounted for by attention to a small number of ongoing crises (e.g. conflict in the Middle East or in South East Asia) of relevance to the developed world. Large areas of the physical world were found to be systematically absent or miniscule on the implied 'map' of the world represented by the universe of news event locations (e.g. Gerbner and Marvanyi, 1977; Womack, 1981). In particular, developing countries were only likely to enter the news frame of developed countries when some events there were threatening to the economic or strategic interests of the 'great powers'. Alternatively, news was made when problems and disasters reached a scale so as to interest audiences in distant and safer lands.

The reasons for the 'bias' of international news selection that still largely persists are not hard to find or to understand. In the first place they result from the organization of news flow by way of agencies and each news medium's own gatekeeping. The ultimate arbiter is the average news consumer in some American or European suburb who is usually thought of as not very interested in distant events. Agencies collect news 'abroad' with a view to what will interest the ultimate 'home' audience, and the

foreign news editors of home media apply an even more precise set of criteria of a similar kind. The result is largely to eliminate news of distant places that is not dramatic or directly relevant to the receiving nation. The basic dynamics have not changed since these explanations were first offered, and 'foreign news' receives even lower attention than ever. However, the world market has gradually enlarged and diversified to make the range of choice offered by news agencies wider than it was twenty years ago and to improve conditions for independent news agencies (Boyd-Barrett and Rantanen, 1998).

In an early model of factors influencing foreign news selection, based on Norwegian newspapers, Galtung and Ruge (1965) indicated three main types of factor that played a part: *organizational*; *genre-related*; and *socio-cultural*. The organizational factors are the most universal and least escapable, and they also have some ideological consequences. The collection of news has to be organized, and there is a bias towards events and news stories that fit the machinery of selection and retransmission. This favours events that occur near the reporting facilities (often in cosmopolitan centres with good communications).

Genre-related factors include: a preference for news events that fit advance audience expectations (consonance with past news) and that can be readily placed within a familiar interpretative 'frame' for instance, frames of underdevelopment and endemic crisis. The social-cultural influences on foreign news selection stem from certain Western values that focus on individuals and involve an interest in elite people and also negative, violent or dramatic happenings. The outcome of these factors is to consistently disadvantage developing countries. They are not important enough to be intrinsically interesting, their news events are often slow and complex, they are not peopled by prominent and known personalities. They typically enter the range of vision of Western news media on grounds of some sudden negative event and then just as quickly disappear from sight. There is little chance of any insight or understanding developing as a result.

Other analyses of patterns of attention in foreign news have largely confirmed the validity of this analysis. News will tend not to deal with distant and politically unimportant nations (except in some temporary crisis), with non-elites or with ideas, structures and institutions. Long-term processes (such as development or dependency) are not easy to turn into news, as normally understood. Apart from the explanations given, it seems from other research that the existence of economic and political relations (as well as geographic and cultural propinquity) between countries is associated with more equitable news exchange relations (Rosengren, 1974; Ito and Koshevar, 1983).

These findings suggest that international news communication in action is less likely to be an independent cause of change than some theories of mass communication imply. It is more likely to reflect the world as it is and to reinforce rather than change existing global relationships. This conclusion diminishes the claim that media are themselves a potent force for globalization. However, we should keep in mind that most studies of news have concentrated on 'serious' (i.e. political and economic) content

and hard news. Less attention has been given to areas that may be quantitatively and in other ways more significant, in particular material about sport, music, entertainment, gossip and other human interest matters, which may easily find itself into the 'news'.

THE GLOBAL TRADE IN MEDIA CULTURE

While the international flow of news was problematized mainly on political grounds (with economics in the background), the import and export of cultural goods has been a bone of contention primarily on cultural grounds. Attention was focused on the issue especially by research into the global flow of films and of television programmes (especially Varis, 1974, 1984). Subsequent research has confirmed the main conclusions in relation to television (Mowlana, 1985; Kivikuru and Varis, 1985; Sepstrup, 1989; Wallis and Baran, 1990) and extended the findings to music (Negus, 1992; Burnett, 1996). In general the results of research show that the international flow of entertainment and fiction programming follows essentially the same pattern as the flow of news.

The core findings of most early research could well be summarized in terms of the title of Tunstall's (1977) seminal study of the issue: *The Media are American*. While the USA remains the predominant global exporter of films and television, this assessment is no longer so accurate. Television news, for instance, has moved its centre of gravity to Europe, with the three main television film news agencies based in London (Tunstall and Machin, 1999; Paterson, 1998). But the main reason for change is the enormous expansion of television production and transmission outside the United States since the 1970s. The USA is relatively less important in global media terms than it was twenty-five years ago. This means that more countries can satisfy more of their own needs from home production. Sreberny-Mohammadi (1996) cites findings from more up-to-date inventories that show unexpectedly high levels of local production. For instance, India and Korea produced about 92% of their televised programming, and 99% of Indian daily viewing is of home-produced content. But there are still high levels of penetration, especially in respect of American films and television drama nearly everywhere. Sreberny-Mohammadi warns against over-interpretation of the evidence of 'indigenization', since much is produced by large corporations operating in exactly the same logic as the former villains of cultural imperialism.

The classification of content in terms of its 'global' rather than local origin is not simple, and the underlying reasons for a particular structure of programming or audience selection are often complex. A side-effect of the general expansion has been the increased demand for extra content to fill the new channels that have emerged in

the wake of cable and satellite developments and general deregulation of broadcasting. This is particularly evident in Western Europe, where many new cable and satellite channels depend on a supply of cheap imports, despite regulatory efforts to limit this. In practice, for European countries the main source of supply remains the United States (for which Europe is the main export market), although there are growing options of importing from other European countries and elsewhere (e.g. Australia). Many of the newer satellite channels with a large amount of imported programming have very small audiences.

The advantage of the United States as source is that it has a large and well organized output of culturally familiar content at prices which reflect the market situation of the importer. The cultural distances between any two European countries are often larger than between either and the United States, as far as media content is concerned, since television is still largely produced in national systems for home audiences and is very culture-specific. Problems of dubbing and subtitling are also likely to be greater. Ironically, the very virtues of home production (own language, cultural relevance) are a barrier to exports and indirectly assist the international trade in American products.

Despite this, there are also increased opportunities for European television productions (for instance to Latin America, Africa and the former Soviet Union, although the trade is not very profitable). The global trade in audio-visual content varies according to economic and political as well as cultural circumstances. Before the end of the Soviet Union, the flow of Western cultural content into Eastern parts was very restricted, although still greater than the flow from East to West. China imports, but still closely controls content. Language determines some patterns (for instance in relations with former colonies). In general, Islamic media systems are very restrictive on imports of Western content and try to prevent direct access to foreign sources (e.g. by satellite).

The situation of Western Europe is not typical, but it illustrates some of the issues and problems that arise (see van Hemel, 1996). In the background to the European case there is a long history of grumbling (usually by cultural elites) about the threat of 'Americanization' to cultural values and even civilization. In the aftermath of the Second World War, the dominance of American media was an accomplished fact, but impoverished countries still restricted film imports and supported nascent national film industries. In general, television services were developed on the basis of national public service models that gave some priority to promoting and protecting the national cultural identity

More recent attitudes in Western Europe to importing audio-visual content have been shaped by two main factors, aside from expansion and privatization. One has been the political-cultural project of a more united Europe (see below). The second has been the goal of creating a large internal European market, in which European audio-visual industries should have their place in the sun. Both goals were perceived to be undermined by the one-directional transatlantic flow of content. American television content was standing in the way of intermingling of European culture, and the single

market was creating opportunities for American imports, to judge from the unacceptably large trade deficit in media products. According to Tunstall and Machin (1999) the attempts to enlarge the market have mainly benefited American exporters.

The mixing of cultural and economic motives and arguments confused the issue considerably, especially when it became an obstacle to concluding the GATT agreements for greater world free trade in late 1993. The resulting compromise has allowed principles of free trade and cultural sovereignty to survive, though without much practical effect on the course of events. The European Union retains some policies that give some protection to European television and film industries, but the trading deficit in such goods continues. Despite the dynamics of media markets which always give a potential edge to countries with the largest home markets and to the English language, there is much evidence of real limitations to cultural and even economic 'subversion' (Dupagne and Waterman, 1998).

Although media imports to Europe basically arise from the general attractiveness of the product to the media audience, it is also clear that, in any given country, the most popular television programmes (highest ratings) are nearly always home produced (even if based on international media formats). Leading American imports generally come second in order of preference, but there is also a large amount of imported content that is used to fill day-time or late-night schedules with small audiences or to stock new low-budget satellite and cable channels.

The price of US exports is always adjusted to the particular market situation, and there is a 'cultural discount' factor in operation that relates the price to degree of cultural affinity between exporter and importer (the lower the affinity the lower the price) (Hoskins and Mirus, 1988). Much imported content may thus be marginal in many senses. But it will always be present in large quantities around the world because there is so much of it available, if need be at give-away prices, since production costs have already been covered.

Secondly, imported content from the USA falls largely into the category of drama and fiction and reflects the high cost of own production on the part of other countries rather than the overwhelming appeal or superior quality of the product. This does not lessen the potential significance, although there is nothing very new in this and the cultural consequences are debatable (see below). For one thing, most of the content that is most relevant for the formation of identity and extension of local experience is home-made and the local language always 'dominates' the screen.

In a 1994 study of the output of five main Dutch television channels (McQuail, 1996), a distinction was made between five categories of content, as follows: 'high media market value'; 'high cultural value'; 'minority provision'; 'reality' content (news, information, sport); and 'staple entertainment' (game-shows, comedy, music, serial fiction, etc.). The first category accounted for 24% of output and was two-thirds imported (mainly American). High cultural, minority and 'reality' content (45% of output) was overwhelmingly home-made or European. The 'staple entertainment' category was divided about equally between Dutch and imported (mainly American) products. The total imported content was around 30% and the study suggests that

America will always do well at the top end of the market, due to the strength of Hollywood. At the lower end it will have a place for economic reasons, but there is good potential for local substitution.

The transnationalization of audiovisual media in Europe has proceeded at a much more limited pace than was predicted on the basis of the potential from the technology. In respect of ownership, there has been little sign of American acquisition of major media players in Europe, aside from the case of Britain-based Murdoch. Instead, Europe has produced its own tycoons and conglomerates, typically with their own national base and sphere of influence (e.g. Berlusconi, Bertelsmann) (Tunstall and Palmer, 1991). Europe initiated its common television space project in 1989 under the slogan 'Television without frontiers', but there has since been only limited cross-border reception of television, mainly affecting small countries that can borrow from their larger neighbours (already with cultural affinity).

Most television is still nationally produced and viewed. The much heralded transnational (multilateral) satellite channels such as CNN and MTV have had limited success in reaching mass audiences in Europe and have been forced to regionalize and adapt their content and format to cope with local requirements. The story of MTV Europe as told by Roe and de Meyer (2000) is indicative of what happened more generally over time to the transnational satellite television channels that spearheaded the 'invasion' of Europe in the 1980s and 1990s. MTV was initially very successful in gaining a new youth audience for mainly Anglo-American pop music. However, competing channels in Germany, the Netherlands and elsewhere forced MTV to respond with a policy of regionalization, employing the 'local' language, but not changing the music significantly. This struggle continues and the lesson does seem to be that, while the English language is an asset because it is the language of pop music, it is not in general an advantage for channel presentation.

CONCEPTS OF NATIONAL AND CULTURAL IDENTITY

A recurring theme of debate and research arising out of media globalization is that concerning **cultural identity**. The opposition has frequently been based on the view that an imported media culture holds back the development of the native culture of the receiving country, or even many local and regional cultures within a country. A new issue has been added by the concern with a specifically *European* cultural identity (in the context of European political and economic unification) (Schlesinger, 1987; van Hemel, 1996). It has been suggested that 'European culture' (and different national cultures within Europe) might be undermined by transnational (especially North American) cultural importation (Thomsen, 1989). On the other hand, cultural transnationalization *within the boundaries of Europe* would support the unification

project, helping to create a more distinctive and homogeneous European culture. The framing of the issue and the motivations (in part economic and political) behind it are not so very different in essence from the case of North–South cultural flow. Cultural relations between Canada and the USA have also long been treated in similar terms.

Underlying the above issues is a strong 'belief system' holding that cultures are both valuable collective properties of nations and places and also very vulnerable to alien influences. The value attributed to a national culture is rooted in ideas developed during the 19th and 20th centuries, when national independence movements were often intimately connected with the rediscovery of distinctive national cultural traditions (for example, in Greece, Ireland and Finland). The frequent lack of correlation between newly established national boundaries (often invented) and 'natural' cultural divisions of peoples has done little to modify the rhetoric about the intrinsic value of national culture. 'National identity' is thus a different and more questionable concept than cultural identity in general, and the notion of a 'European cultural identity' is even weaker and even more an 'imagined community', the term applied by Anderson (1983) to the idea of nation, since it is promoted for political reasons.

In view of the high degree of conceptual confusion, it is not surprising that the question of the cultural *impact* of the international flow remains unsettled. Schlesinger (1987) recommends starting at the other end, with a clearer idea of what cultural identity means, before trying to assess the effect of mass media on it, although he is sceptical about the whole business, at least in the European context. He suggests an approach by way of a general concept of 'collective identity'. A collective identity, in this sense, persists in *time* and is resistant to change, although survival also requires that it be consciously expressed, reinforced and transmitted. For this reason, having access to and support from relevant communications media is evidently important. The concept could well apply to what are called cultural identities in the debate about transnationalization, since there is assumed to be a set of people sharing some significant cultural features of ethnicity, language, way of life, etc., and also sharing the same place and time.

However, while it is useful for some purposes (such as determining if a cultural identity exists or not), this conceptualization may be too *strong* for the problem at issue (media transnationalization). Most of the collective identities which qualify according to this concept are enduring, have deep roots and are resistant to the relatively superficial 'impact' of, for example, watching or listening to foreign (especially Anglo-American) media. They depend on shared histories, religion and language. The media are more likely to have an influence, for good or ill, on cultural identities of a more voluntary, transient and also multiple (overlapping) kind. These may be collectively held but are based on taste, lifestyle and other transient features. These are more like *subcultural* identities, which are not necessarily *exclusive* and whose growth may even be stimulated and helped by (international) media.

The European case highlighted important issues, stimulated research and has

allowed some wider lessons to be drawn. On the whole, the claim for nations to have full cultural sovereignty and to be able to control their own 'audio-visual' space has been sidelined. European states have accepted the principle that their citizens should have free access to the cultural information of other European countries, and by implication of all countries. The exploration of notions of 'cultural identity' has largely exposed the rhetorical and imprecise nature of this concept. Whatever it is, it is not something that is easy to manipulate by acting on the mass media, nor does it seem to be much influenced by media culture. It survives and flourishes in many forms, and the general expansion of television, music and other media have added some widely (internationally) shared cultural elements without evidently diminishing the uniqueness of cultural experience in different nations, regions and localities of Europe.

Cultural invasion: resistance, subversion and **hybridization**

From this perspective, the media may appear even to help in the process of cultural growth, diffusion, invention and creativity, and are not just undermining existing culture. Much modern theory and evidence supports the view that media-cultural 'invasion' can sometimes be *resisted* or redefined according to local culture and experience. Often the 'internationalization' involved is self-chosen and not the result of imperialism (in Western Europe, for instance). Lull and Wallis (1992) use the term 'transculturation' to describe a process of 'mediated cultural interaction' in which Vietnamese music was crossed with North American strains to produce a new cultural *hybrid*. There are likely to be many examples of a similar process. Secondly, alternative 'readings' of the same 'alien' content are, as we have seen, quite possible. 'Semiotic power' can also be exercised in this context, and media content can be decoded differentially according to the culture of receivers (Liebes and Katz, 1986). This is probably too optimistic a view to bear much weight, and the evidence is not yet very strong. Foreign cultural content may also be received with a different, more distant attitude (Biltereyst, 1991) than home-made media culture. Despite the attractions of global media culture, language differences still present a real barrier to cultural 'subversion' (Biltereyst, 1992). Evidence concerning the reception of foreign news (aside from its availability) is still very fragmentary, but there is some evidence and good theory to support the view that foreign news events are framed by audiences in terms of possible relevance to the home country but also according to personal circumstance. They are understood, or 'decoded' according to more familiar social and cultural contexts (Jensen, 1998).

The 'problem' of potential cultural damage from transnationalized media may well be exaggerated (in Europe at least). In the case of Europe, most cultural imports are from cultures with historic affinity to European culture, and the media do relatively

little to diffuse the really different cultures (of Asia, Islam, etc.). Many distinct national (and sub-national) cultures within Europe are still strong and resistant. Audiences can probably tolerate several different and inconsistent worlds of cultural experiences (such as local, national, sub-group and global), without the one having to destroy the other. The media can extend cultural choices in a creative way, and internationalization can work creatively. Cultural 'invasion' of Third World cultures is different because it is accompanied by other material changes and occurs in situations of dependence and less free choice. Many parts of the Third World, even so, have still not yet been reached very significantly by the international media 'invasion'; large parts of Asia can and do look after themselves, or are protected by cultural distinctiveness.

This debate reflects the two contradictory trends at work, globally as well as nationally – one (centripetal) towards cohesion, the other (centrifugal) towards fragmentation (see page 72). The media can promote both, and which effect is stronger depends on the particular context and circumstances. Strong cultural identities will survive and weaker ones give way. A weak cultural identity such as that of 'Europe' is not likely to be much affected one way or another by current levels of 'Americanization'; though, if it is to get any stronger, it may need media recognition and policy support. This is to suggest that media may be a necessary, but are unlikely to be a sufficient, condition for cultural resistance or submission. This relativizing of the problem does not abolish it, and there are circumstances under which cultural loss does occur.

Towards a global media culture?

One cultural consequence of media globalization may be overlooked because it is obvious: the rise of a globalized media culture as such. Media internationalization probably does lead to more homogenization or 'cultural synchronization'. According to Hamelink (1983: 22), this process 'implies that the decisions regarding the cultural development of a given country are made in accordance with the interests and needs of a powerful central nation. They are then imposed with subtle but devastating effectiveness without regard for the adaptive necessities of the dependent nation'. As a result, cultures are less distinctive and cohesive and also less exclusive.

Another commentator observes that we increasingly encounter a form of culture that is tied to no place or period.

> It is contextless, a true melange of disparate components drawn from everywhere and nowhere, borne upon the chariots of the global telecommunications system . . . . There is something equally timeless about the concept of a global culture. Widely diffused in space, a global culture is cut off from any past . . . it has no history. (Smith, 1990: 177)

Some of these points can be seen to connect with the characterization of a postmodern culture, of which McLuhan has been hailed as precursor (Docherty, 1993) (see below). Postmodern culture is by definition detached from any fixed time and place, and has no moral standpoint or fixed meaning. Not by chance, the international media are given some credit (or blame) for promoting this type of culture. While such a global media culture may appear value-free, in fact it embodies a good many of the values of Western capitalism, including individualism and consumerism, hedonism and commercialism. It may add to the cultural options and open horizons for some, but it may also challenge and invade the cultural space of pre-existing local, indigenous, traditional and minority cultures.

CONCLUSION

Global mass communication is a reality, and during the second half of the century there has almost certainly been a steady strengthening of the conditions that allow the media audience to receive information and cultural content from other countries and parts of the world. The main conditions are: the existence of a free market in media products; the existence and respect for an effective 'right to information', thus political freedom and freedom of speech; the technologies that can offer fast, capacious and low-cost channels of transmission across borders and large distances. Nevertheless, the real chances for global sending or receiving and the probability of it taking place depend on more mundane matters, especially those relating to the national media system and its degree of connectedness to other systems.

Paradoxically, the country endowed with all three of the conditions mentioned (the USA) is one of the least likely to be a beneficiary by way of the media of culture and information coming from outside its own frontiers. The means are there but the will is missing in this case. The countries most favoured by a real experience of international media are likely to be small and wealthy enough both to sustain a viable national culture and enjoy the eclectic fruits of the global information society. There has to be an appreciation of these fruits, or some pressing need, for global mass communication to prosper, and the main hope for this lies now with the Internet and World Wide Web.

A condition for global communication to become a more significant component of public communication (as opposed to an important element of media markets) will be some movement towards a global political order and some forms of international government. The supposed 'New order' that followed the fall of communism has not made much progress in this direction. For the foreseeable future, mass communication will continue to be dominated by the nation state and the small group of rich and powerful countries that arbitrates world events.

FURTHER READING

Boyd-Barrett, O. and Rantanen, T. (eds) (1998) *The Globalization of News*. London: Sage.

Hamelink, C. (1994) *The Politics of World Communication*. London: Sage.

Sepstrup, P. (1990) *The Transnationalization of Television in Western Europe*. London: John Libbey.

Tomlinson, J. (1991) *Cultural Imperialism*. London: Pinter.

Tunstall, J. (1977) *The Media are American*. London: Constable.

III

the media organization in its context

The media organization, where media content is 'made', is an essential link in the process of mediation by which 'society addresses itself'. In this chapter we look at the forces at work within organizations, the external influences upon their activity and the influence of particular organizational features on what they produce and disseminate in the way of 'media culture'. There is by now a large body of empirical research, dating back to the 1950s, which in one way or another sheds light on the nature and working processes of media organizations. There has been a gradual shift of interest from media effects to the characteristic features of media content and then to the organizational sources and 'causes' of these features. Research has also moved on from the study of the personal attitudes and social background of 'mass communicators' (Rosten, 1937, 1941). There is much more appreciation today of the requirements of the formal work organization and recurrent routines and practices within it. Only by knowing how the media themselves operate can we understand how society influences the media and vice versa.

During the 1970s, in particular, there was a flood of research into 'news-making', stimulated initially by evidence of patterning and selective attention (sometimes called 'bias') in news content and by debates over news objectivity and the nature of 'news values'. The largely consistent findings showed the news product to be, in one sense or another, both a routine product of a 'news factory' (Bantz et al., 1980) and also a very predictable symbolic 'construction' of reality. It is here that the choice of critical perspective (and wider social theory) comes into play. Gradually, more attention began to be paid to the production of non-journalistic content, especially drama, music and entertainment (e.g. Cantor, 1971; Ettema and Whitney, 1982; Turow, 1991; Tunstall, 1993). Even so, this has remained a relatively undeveloped area of research.

New life has been given to organizational research by major changes in the structure of media industries, especially the processes of globalization, ownership conglomeration and organizational fragmentation. New means of distribution (such as cable, satellite and telecommunication networks) have also given rise to new kinds of media organization.

FRAMEWORKS AND PERSPECTIVES

One very simple and general framework within which questions can be posed takes as its starting point the institutional structures as described in Chapter 9. *Structural* features (for instance, size, forms of ownership and media-industrial function) can be seen as having direct consequences for the *conduct* of particular media organizations. Conduct refers to all the systematic activities that in turn affect *performance*, in the

sense of the type and relative amount of media content produced and offered to audiences. According to this model, we need to look not only at internal features of media organizations but also at their relations with other organizations and with the wider society.

Most of the research and theory discussed in the following pages is 'media-centric' rather than 'society-centric' (see Chapter 3), taking or recording the view from within the media. This may lead to an overestimation of the significance of organizational influences on content. From a 'society-centric' point of view, much of what media organizations do is determined by external social forces, including, of course, the requirements of media audiences. The question of 'paradigm choice' (see page 45) has not been very sharply posed in relation to research on media organizations, since it tends to call for a mixture of both qualitative and quantitative methods and attracts critical as well as neutral perspectives. There is also scope for applying structural, behavioural and cultural analysis, since all three are relevant. The predominant method of research has been participant observation of media people at work or depth interviewing of involved informants. On some points, survey research has provided essential additional information (for instance, on questions of occupational role and social composition).

In general, the theory that has been formulated on the basis of research into media organizations, while fragmentary, has been fairly consistent. It supports the view that content is systematically and distinctively influenced by organizational routines, practices and goals rather than either personal or ideological factors. However, this proposition is itself open to alternative interpretations. It could be taken either to support the view that ownership and control influences content or that any kind of standardized or mass production process involves some systematic influence on content. It is on the first of these alternatives that the society-centric critical perspective generally focuses. The more or less consistent 'bias' of the media in terms of values, beliefs and the selective portrayal of 'reality' is regarded as the planned outcome of the strategies of those who own and control the media.

ORGANIZATIONAL INFLUENCES ON CONTENT: THE MAIN ISSUES

It is possible to channel nearly all the main theoretical questions about media and society through an examination of media organizations, although in the end this is not very helpful, and it is better to concentrate on a few central issues of structure and conduct. Two such overarching issues can be identified:

- What degree of freedom does a media organization possess in relation to the wider society, and how much freedom is possible within the organization?
- How do media-organizational routines and procedures for selecting and processing content influence what is produced?

These two questions roughly correspond to the duality noted above of structural effect on organizational conduct and the effect of the latter, in its turn, on content produced. Both questions, for instance, lead to consideration of the tension arising from the following oppositions at the heart of media-making:

- constraint versus autonomy;
- routine production versus creativity;
- commerce versus art;
- profit versus social purpose.

The broad range of issues which arise can be appreciated when one takes an overview of theoretical perspectives organized around the question of 'influences on media content', as posed by Shoemaker and Reese (1991). Drawing on suggestions from Gans (1979) and Gitlin (1980), they name five main hypotheses:

1 Content reflects social reality (mass media as mirror of society);
2 Content is influenced by media workers' socialization and attitudes (a communicator-centred approach);
3 Content is influenced by media-organizational routines;
4 Content is influenced by social institutions and forces;
5 Content is a function of ideological positions and maintains the status quo (the hegemonic approach).

The first of these hypotheses is not directly discussed in this chapter, although the degree of 'reflection of reality' is certainly affected by a number of organizational factors. One example is the low representation of women in media work that is associated with a predominantly 'man's view' of what is important in the world as portrayed in the news. Another example is provided by the occupational routines that influence the selection of content in very predictable ways. The most directly relevant of the five hypotheses are numbers 2, 3 and 4. Hypothesis 5 largely lies outside the scope of this chapter because it is so broad. However, in general it presumes that media organizations are not autonomous, but are penetrated by other sources of power (especially political and economic). The more it appears that outside forces shape the operation of media, the more plausible this hypothesis becomes. Some light will be shed on this matter.

LEVELS OF ANALYSIS

It is increasingly difficult to speak of a 'media organization' as if there were a single ideal-typical form. The original term was largely based on the model of an independent newspaper, within which all the principal activities of management, financial

control, news collection and processing, printing and distribution took place more or less under one roof. This model was always untypical of media in general, not applying, for instance, to the film, book publishing or music industries and applying only variably to radio and television. It is virtually impossible to apply it to most of the so-called new media, which interrelate several separate and disparate organizational functions. As a model, it is best suited to studying news production, which takes place (in its final stage) within a unity of time and space. It is least suited to the spheres of fiction, music and entertainment, where creation, selection, processing, production and distribution are often organizationally very separate from each other.

The diversity of organizational forms is matched by the diversity of occupational groups that might qualify as 'mass communicators'. These have been taken as including movie moguls and press tycoons, actors, television producers, film directors, script-writers, book authors, newspaper and broadcast journalists, song-writers, disc-jockeys, musicians, literary agents, newspaper and magazine editors, advertisers and public relations people, campaign managers, and many more. Most of these categories are also subdividable according to type of medium and size or status of the work organization, employment status, etc. A good deal of media work takes place on a freelance or entrepreneurial basis (such as film-making – Boorman, 1987), and many media workers (notably writers and actors) belong to no single production organization, even if they may belong to professional or craft associations. As a result, the concepts of 'mass communicator' and of 'media profession' are almost as leaky as that of media organization.

Despite this diversity, it still makes sense to try to contain questions of media production within a common framework of analysis. One useful step is to think in terms of levels of analysis, so that the different phases of media work and the significant relations between units of organizational activity and between media and the 'outside world' can be identified for study. Dimmick and Coit (1982), for instance, describe a hierarchy with nine different levels at which influence or power may be exercised. The main levels and associated sources of influence are:

- supra-national (international regulation agencies or multinational firms);
- society (for instance, government or national social institutions, such as political parties);
- media industry (competing media firms, advertisers, etc.);
- supra-organizational (chains, conglomerates);
- community (city, local business);
- intra-organizational (groups or departments within an organization);
- individual (role, social background, personal attitude, gender, ethnic origin).

Shoemaker and Reese (1991) employ a somewhat similar hierarchy of levels of influences on media content, which they label (in descending order) as ideological, extra-media, organizational, media routines and individual.

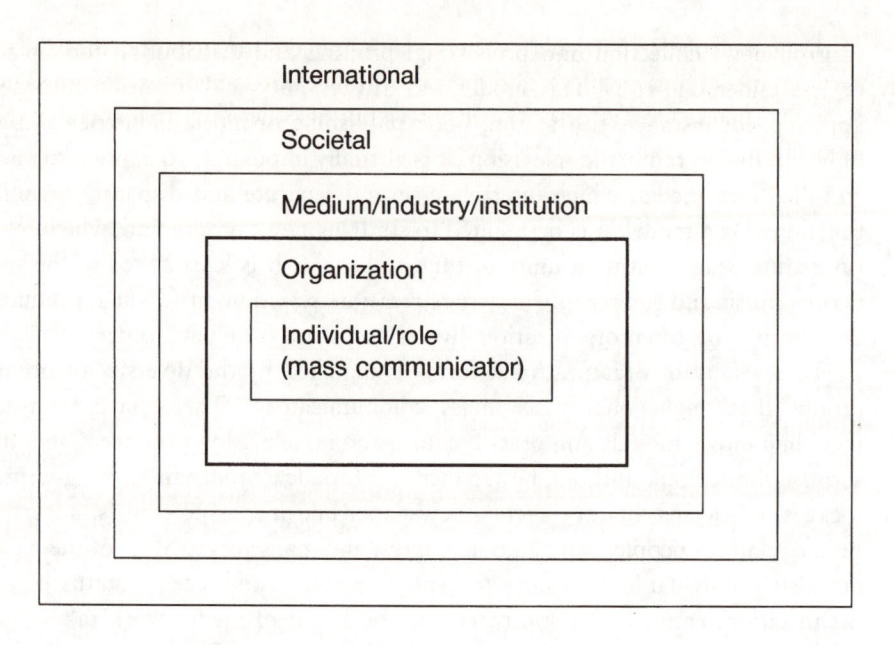

FIGURE 11.1   Mass media organizations: levels of analysis

For the purposes of this chapter, a similar but modified hierarchy is employed, as shown in Figure 11.1. The hierarchical presentation implies that the 'higher-order' influence has primacy in terms of strength and direction. This is not necessarily the case in reality, although it does serve to represent the society-centric perspective, according to which media are dependent on their society. It also corresponds to the most likely general balance of power in society. Even so, it is more appropriate to consider the relations between media communicators and their environment as, in principle, interactive and negotiable. It is also appropriate to emphasize that the media organization operates within and maintains its own 'boundaries' (however permeable) and has some degree of autonomy and freedom of choice.

The arrangement of entries recognizes the significance of the individual who carries out media work and is subject to the requirements of the organization, but also has some freedom to define his or her place in it. Most of the discussion which follows relates to the central area of the 'organizational level', but also takes account of the relations across the boundary between the work organization and other agents and agencies of the wider media institution and society. The nature of media institutions as providers and definers of the context of organizational activity has already been discussed (Chapter 9).

It is also clear from Chapter 7 that media organizations in their relations with the wider society are formally or informally regulated or governed by normative expectations on either side. Such matters as the essential freedoms of publication and the ethical guidelines for many professional activities are laid down by the 'rules

of the game' of the particular society. This implies, for instance, that the relations between media organizations and their operating environment are governed not solely by naked market forces or political power but also by unwritten social and cultural guidelines.

THE MEDIA ORGANIZATION IN A FIELD OF SOCIAL FORCES

It follows from what has been said that any theoretical account of media organizations and occupations has to take account of a number of different relationships within and across the boundaries of the organization. These relationships are often active negotiations and exchanges and sometimes conflicts, latent or actual. The influential model of mass communication drawn by Westley and MacLean (1957), which has already been discussed (page 53), represents the communicator role as that of a broker between, on the one hand, would-be 'advocates' in society with messages to send and, on the other, the public seeking to satisfy its information and other communication needs and interests.

Gerbner (1969) portrayed mass communicators as operating under pressure from various external 'power roles', including clients (such as advertisers), competitors (other media in the main), authorities (especially legal and political), experts, other institutions and the audience. He wrote:

> While analytically distinct, obviously neither power roles nor types of leverage are in reality separate or isolated. On the contrary, they often combine, overlap and telescope. . . . the accumulation of power roles and possibilities of leverage gives certain institutions dominant positions in the mass communication of their societies.

Clearly, in the case of agents of government or business, these can represent powerful leverage and at the same time be 'advocates' in the sense used above (self-interested communicators) and also important *sources* for the media themselves. Not only are they often major would-be communicators, they are also *avoiders* of communication attention, except on their own terms. The media have to try to manage the supply of source material in competition with other would-be managers and in latent competition with some of their own sources.

Using these ideas and relying on the wide support for such a view in the research literature (see also Dimmick and Coit, 1982), we can portray the position of the media organization in general terms as follows. Those within it have to make decisions at the centre of a field of different constraints, demands or attempted uses of power and influence, as in Figure 11.2. The general hierarchy shown in Figure 11.1 has been converted into a view of more specific actors and agencies in the environment of a media organization. This representation is primarily derived from research on news

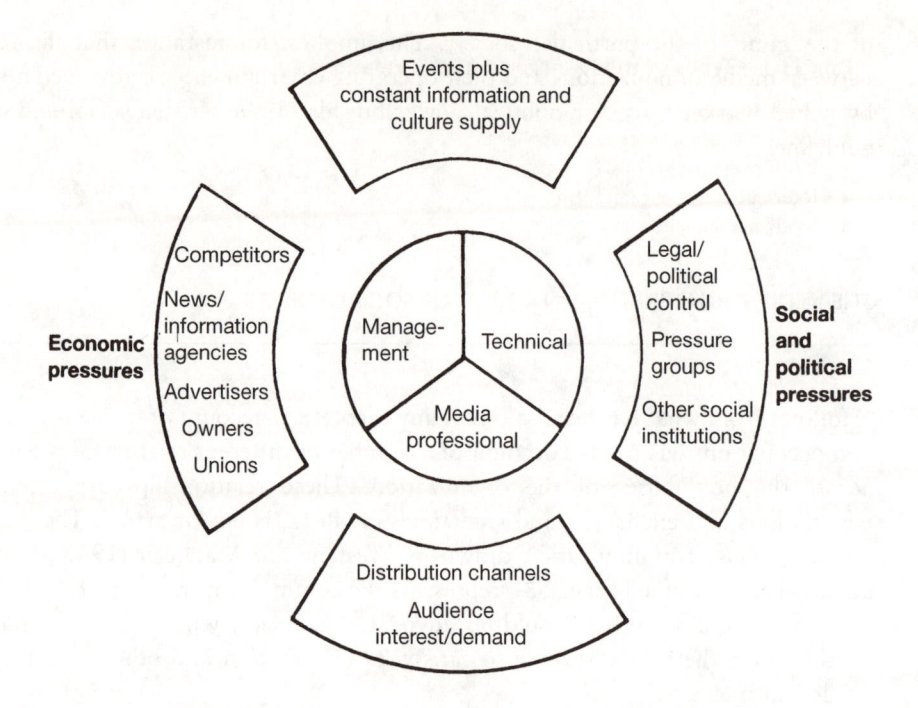

FIGURE 11.2   The media organization in a field of social forces

media (especially newspapers), but the picture would be much the same for many similar 'self-contained' and multi-purpose media including broadcast television (see, for example, Wallis and Baran, 1990).

The pressures and demands illustrated in Figure 11.2 are not all necessarily *constraining* on media organizations. Some can be sources of liberation (for instance, by way of alternative sources of income, or government policy protection for their task). Some of the forces cancel or balance each other (such as audience support against advertiser pressure, or media institutional prestige against external institutional or source pressure). Lack of external pressure would probably indicate social marginality or insignificance.

A further refinement of this scheme, based on the work of Engwall (1978), involves the internal division of the media organization into three dominant work cultures, indicating the main sources of tension and lines of demarcation which have been found to exist within media organizations (see page 271). This presentation allows one to identify six main kinds of relationship which need to be examined in order to gain some understanding of the conditions affecting organizational activity and the mass communicator role. These are shown in Box 11.1, and each type is discussed *inter alia* the following pages. One additional matter that remains to be dealt with is the influence, not of relationships, but of the typical structure and composition of media organizations. This sheds some light on the possibility that the work of organizations is also affected in a general way by the kind of people that are employed.

RELATIONS WITH SOCIETY

A good deal has already been said on this matter, especially in Chapters 7 and 9. The influence of society is ubiquitous and continuous and arises in virtually all of the external relationships that media have. In liberal-democratic societies, the media are free to operate within the limits of the law, but conflicts still occur in relations with government and with powerful social institutions. The media are also continually engaged, sometimes in an antagonistic way, with their main sources and with organized pressure groups. How these issues are defined and handled depends in part on the self-defined goals of the media organization. There are likely to be large differences, for instance, between media that adopt or are given a significant social, cultural or political task (true of many news organizations) and those that are primarily concerned with making profits. The outcome also depends on the degree and kind of professionalization of the relevant media occupations. In general, we can expect that higher levels of professionalism go with more autonomy and with developed views about responsibility to society (see especially Chapters 7 and 8). In addition to the question of the media's own goals with respect to society, we need to take into account the expectations about access to the media on its own behalf which 'society' may express, especially through the political system.

Goals of media organizations

Most organizations have mixed goals, and rarely are they all openly stated. Mass media are no exception, and they may even be particularly ambiguous in this respect. In organizational theory, a differentiation is often made between utilitarian and normative organizational goals (for example, Etzioni, 1961). The utilitarian organization aims to produce or provide material goods or services for financial ends, while the normative organization aims to advance some value or achieve a valued condition, based on the voluntary commitment of its participants. The position of mass media organizations in respect of this typology is ambiguous, since they often have a mixture

of utilitarian and normative goals and forms of operation. Most media are run as businesses but often with some 'ideal' goals, and some media are run primarily for 'idealistic' social or cultural purposes, without seeking profit. For instance, public broadcasting organizations (in Europe especially) have generally had a bureaucratic form of organization but with non-profit social and cultural goals.

Another suggested basis for organizational classification distinguishes according to *type of beneficiary*. Blau and Scott (1963) ask: 'Is it the society as a whole, a particular set of clients, the owners, the audience, or the employees of the organization, whose welfare or good is being served?' Again, no single answer can be given for the media as a whole, and particular organizations often have several actual or potential beneficiaries. Nevertheless, there is some reason to hold that the general public (not always the direct audience) should be the chief beneficiary (see the discussion of public interest on page 142).

A common element in all the normative press theories discussed (in Chapter 7) is that the media should meet the needs and interests of their audience in the first instance and the interests of clients and the state only secondarily. Since media depend on the continuous voluntary choices of their audiences if they are to be either effective or profitable, this principle has a common-sense basis. It is also a view that is often expressed by mass communicators.

Drawing from evidence of newspaper journalists, Tunstall (1971) described the organizational goals in economic terms, distinguishing between revenue goals and non-revenue goals. The latter refer to purposes without a direct financial aspect, such as gaining prestige, exercising influence or power in society, or achieving some normative end (for instance, serving the community). Revenue goals are of two main kinds – gaining income from direct sales to consumers and from selling space to advertisers. Different kinds of publication policy go with the variation of goals in these terms. While the audience appears to be subordinate in this typology, in practice the satisfaction of advertisers and the gaining of revenue from sales both depend on pleasing the audience, and non-revenue goals are often shaped by some conception of wider public interest. Furthermore, Tunstall indicates that in a case of conflict of goals within the newspaper, the audience revenue goals (increasing the circulation by pleasing the audience) provide the 'coalition goal' on which most can agree (especially management and journalists).

THE JOURNALIST'S ROLE: ENGAGEMENT OR NEUTRALITY?

Some media organizations (especially public service media and those with an opinion-forming or informational purpose) clearly do seek to play some part in society, but the nature of this role is also open to diverse interpretations. Certain kinds of publication,

espccially prestige or elite newspapers (such as Le *Monde*, the *Financial Times* and the *Washington Post*), have set out deliberately to be influential through the quality of their information or the authority of their opinion (Padioleau, 1985). There are several other options for the exercise of influence, and it is not the exclusive property of an internationally known elite press. Small-scale media can be influential in more restricted spheres, and influence can obviously be exercised by mass circulation newspapers and popular television.

There is, nevertheless, a broad choice to be made between a more active and participant, or a more neutral, role for the **journalist** in society. Cohen (1963: 191) was one of the first to make the critical distinction along these lines when he distinguished two separate self-conceptions of the reporter's role as that of 'neutral reporter' or 'participant'. The first refers to ideas of the press as informer, interpreter and instrument of government (lending itself as channel or mirror), the second to the traditional 'fourth estate' notion, covering ideas of the press as representative of the public, critic of government, advocate of policy and policy-maker.

The weight of evidence (for example, Johnstone et al., 1976) is that the neutral, informative role is most preferred by journalists, and it goes with the importance attached by most journalists to objectivity as a core professional value (Lippmann, 1922; Carey, 1969; Janowitz, 1975; Roshco, 1975; Phillips, 1977; Schudson, 1978; Tuchman, 1978; Hetherington, 1985; Morrison and Tumber, 1988; Weaver and Wilhoit, 1996). Strong political commitment (and active engagement) is by definition not easy to reconcile with even-handed neutral reporting, and many news organizations have guidelines designed to limit the influence of personal beliefs on reporting. However, the preference for 'objectivity' also stems from the self-interests and commercial logic of media businesses, since partisanship tends to narrow the audience appeal.

The underlying differentiation of press roles was clarified in a study of regional newspaper journalists in Sweden. Fjaestad and Holmlov (1976) identified two main kinds of purpose, each endorsed by over 70 per cent of respondents: those of 'watchdog' (such as control of local government) and of 'educator' (providing a forum, aid to consumers, social and political information, etc.). They also named some secondary or minor functions recognized by a third or fewer of respondents (especially 'political mobilization', 'entertainment' and 'forging a local consensus').

Studies of journalists and editors in the United States have tended to reveal a clear preference for non-engagement and objectivity; but even so, Johnstone et al. (1976) found that 76 per cent of US journalists thought it extremely important that media should 'investigate claims and statements made by government'. Although the date (1971) when these data were collected was favourable to the adoption of a somewhat critical role by the press, the finding is consistent with several elements in the North American journalistic tradition. These include the political philosophy of 'reformism' (Gans, 1979), the choice of an 'adversary role' vis-à-vis government (Weaver and Wilhoit, 1986) or, more generally, the idea that media should look out for the interests of their audience, whom they claim to represent. This is different from partisan

advocacy of a particular point of view, which still seems to be in decline as a journalistic philosophy.

A survey of US journalists by Weaver and Wilhoit (1986), using the same questions and design as Johnstone et al. (1976), confirmed some enduring features of the situation and added some new elements. The research showed that in 1982–3 there had been some withdrawal from the critical perspective held by journalists of 1971, although they remained somewhat reformist in spirit and, on balance, politically more left-inclined than right. Endorsement of the questionnaire item on the 'extreme importance' of media investigating claims and statements made by government had dropped from 76 to 66 per cent, and there was more support for neutral-informative than for participant elements of the journalist's role. Nevertheless, there was also significant minority support for an 'adversary' role.

A similar enquiry in the early 1990s found approximately the same balance of views on journalists' roles (Weaver and Wilhoit, 1996: 133–41). A majority of journalists still thought that investigating government claims and getting information quickly to the public were extremely important. One change over the decade seemed to be an increased tolerance on the part of journalists of the use of some forms of deception or espionage in gaining information and also of using information without permission. There was also a lower degree of autonomy as perceived by journalists themselves.

Perhaps the most interesting change from the early 1970s emerged from a reassessment of the 'neutral versus participant' dichotomy. Weaver and Wilhoit (1986) opted for a tripartite division of roles as interpreter, disseminator, or adversary, in that order of prominence. The *interpreter* role was based on the same items as were previously used to produce the label 'participant': analysing and interpreting complex questions, investigating claims made by government and discussing national policy as it happens. The second type – that of *disseminator* – mainly relates to 'getting information to the public quickly' and 'concentrating on the largest possible audience'. The third, *adversary*, role (applying to both government and business) was much weaker but was still recognized in some degree by a majority of journalists. The resulting scheme of role perceptions is reproduced in Figure 11.3, showing the main overlap between them.

Public broadcasting institutions, such as the BBC, are under a particular obligation to be neutral and balanced, and the chief aim of BBC decision-makers in news and actuality has been described as 'holding the middle ground' (Kumar, 1975), acting as a broker between disputants, rather than being a participant. The question as to whether this lends itself to supporting the established social order has often been discussed. Hall (1977) thought that it does, and we would not expect a public institution to undermine its own foundations. However, this does not prevent fundamental criticism being reported or carried. A wide-ranging investigation of the BBC by Burns (1977) reached a more cautious conclusion than Hall but spoke nevertheless of a 'collusion thus forged with both the establishment and the "silent (and invisible, perhaps imaginary) majority" . . . against any disturbance of the peace' (1977: 209). While times have changed, the forces at work are likely to be similarly balanced. In general

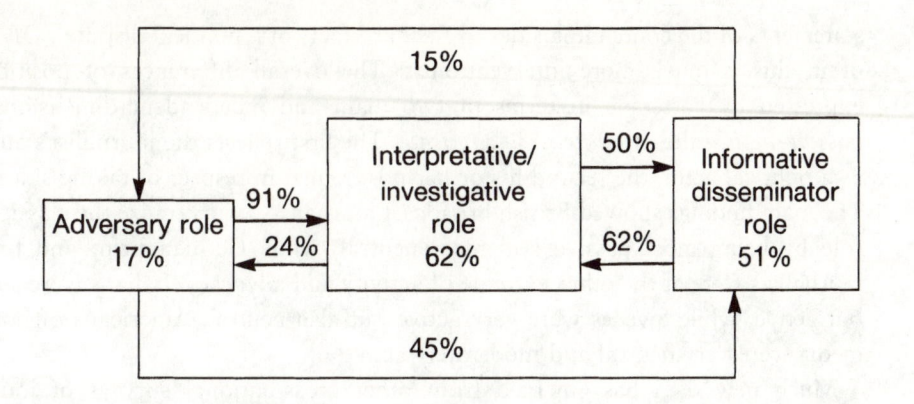

FIGURE 11.3   Journalists' role perceptions (Weaver and Wilhoit, 1986): interpretation and information come first, with opposition a clear but distinctive third option

public broadcasting organizations in continental Europe provide more legitimate recognition of different political and ideological streams. Even so, there has been a general trend towards the norm of neutrality.

The *plurality* of role conceptions held by journalists is also stressed by Weaver and Wilhoit, who write (1986: 116): 'only about 2 percent of the respondents are exclusively one-role oriented'. They also remind us that, on such matters as role perception and journalistic ethics, there seem to be large cross-cultural differences. For instance, Donsbach (1983) showed British journalists to be much more committed to a purely informative role than were German journalists, and they were much less particular about a range of dubious journalistic practices. Köcher (1986) offers more evidence on this matter, referring to the alternative roles of 'bloodhound' or 'missionary' which, respectively, typified British and German journalists.

More recently, Patterson (1998) compared journalistic cultures of five countries, the United States, Britain, Germany, Italy and Sweden, based on surveys with journalists in each country. One of the main differences stemmed from the wide variation in the degree of partisanship of media systems as a whole, according to journalists' own perceptions. In particular, the United States was exceptional in the degree to which its major news organizations were perceived as concentrated in the middle of the political spectrum. Even broadcasting in Europe is subject to partisan tendencies, though in Britain least of all.

Journalists themselves acknowledged that partisan leanings affected news decisions, most strongly in Germany. German journalists believed in the superiority of opinions over news. While objectivity as a norm was regarded as of some importance in each country, its meaning varied quite a lot. The predominant meaning ascribed by American journalists was as 'expressing fairly the position of each side in a political dispute'. In Germany and Sweden much more weight attached to getting 'beyond the

statements of the contending sides to the hard facts of a political dispute'. On the face of it, this is much more interventionist. The overall differences of position were expressed by Patterson in terms of two main and independent dimensions – one *passive–active*; the other *neutral–advocate*. The first reflects the journalist's autonomy as a political actor, the second his or her positioning in respect of taking sides or not. The main findings showed British broadcast journalists to maximize the classic neutral role by being most passive and most neutral, while German print and broadcast journalists were at the other extreme of activity and advocacy. Italians were advocates but active, while Swedes were very active but also neutral. Americans of both main media were very neutral and moderately active.

Much new data has emerged from other cross-national surveys of journalists, especially research reported in Weaver (1996). The findings are too diverse to summarize, but it looks as if role conceptions are both variable and quite strongly related to political culture and the degree to which democracy is firmly established. For instance, in countries where democracy is weaker, there is less emphasis on the watchdog role. Weaver (1996: 87) remarks that 'political system similarities and differences are far more important than cultural similarities and differences, organizational constraints or individual characteristics in predicting the variance in perceptions of three roles (timely information, interpretation, and entertainment) by journalists in these countries'. A new dimension to research has been added by the opportunity to compare role conceptions of journalists after the fall of Communism in Europe. An example is Wu et al.'s (1996) survey of American and Russian journalists. On most points, especially in relation to information dissemination, objectivity and expressing public opinion, the two populations were similar, but Russian journalists opted for a more politically active role.

Professionalism

At the heart of Burns's study of the BBC was a discussion of 'professionalism' in broadcasting and of alternative orientations to the work task which forms one source of the statement of occupational dilemmas made above. Burns found two main attitudes to the occupational task. One was a deep loyalty to the traditional goals of public broadcasting as an instrument of cultural and social betterment and for the defence of 'standards'. The second was 'professionalism', sometimes 'television for television's sake', but always involving a deep commitment to the task and the craft of making 'good television'. This concept of media professionalism has several components standing opposed to 'amateurism' and to external interference, resting on the judgement of work by fellow professionals and leading to some insulation from the pressures of both public and management.

For most members of professions, the appropriate wider social role which they

perform is usually 'taken care of' by the institution – as in medicine or teaching – leaving individuals to concentrate on the practice of their skills. To a certain extent, this is true of mass communicators, but full professionalization has been held back, perhaps by the internal diversity of media and the recency and flux of some of the occupations involved. There is also a continued uncertainty about what is actually the central professional skill of the journalist (and this is possibly even more in question for other media occupations). The sociologist Max Weber (1948) referred to the journalist as belonging to 'a sort of pariah caste' and, like the artist, lacking a fixed social classification. Schudson (1978) aptly characterized journalism as an 'uninsulated profession', because of the lack of clear boundaries.

The general import of Tuchman's (1978) study of news work is towards the conclusion that professionalism in news has largely come to be defined according to the needs of the news organization itself. The height of professional skill is the exercise of a practical craft, which delivers the required informational product, characterized by a high degree of *objectivity*, key marks of which are obsessive facticity and neutrality of attitude. The objectivity of news has become, in her view, the equivalent of a professional ideology. This analysis is consistent with other indications from media work that professionalism is a degree of accomplishment which cannot be measured by tests or examinations and can only be recognized by fellow professionals. The question of whether journalism should be considered as a profession remains in dispute, both within and without the media world.

Windhal et al. (1992: 128) conclude that the knowledge base of journalists does not command the same respect as that of occupational groups that are acknowledged to be professions. Kepplinger and Koecher (1990) maintain that 'journalists cannot really be counted among the professional class', largely on the ground that they behave very selectively with those they have to deal with and professionals should treat everyone equally. Journalists also 'deny a moral responsibility for unintentionally negative consequence of their reports' (1990: 307), while applying a stronger standard to others. However, Kepplinger and Koecher also observe that 'this selectivity is a basis for the reputation of journalism and a prerequisite for its success'. Olen (1988) makes a similar point by contending that journalism *should not* become a profession, since it involves the exercise of a right to freedom of expression that cannot be monopolized by an institution (that of journalism). In this respect, it can also be argued that the critical role of the press may oblige it at times to act in an 'irresponsible' way, as defined by established institutions. The possible increased tolerance for 'unethical' practices noted above can reflect vigilance on behalf of society as well as the pressures of commercialism. Some light is shed on this issue by Brodasson's (1994: 242) contention that journalism does at times at least have one important attribute of other professions – that of 'sacredness'. Journalists do have occasion to perform altruistic services. He writes that while journalism 'falls short on some traditional criteria . . . it is evident that both its perceived functions as a vital service and its sacred aspect are present in at least some sectors of journalism'. He also comments that it is intimately connected with democracy, but paradoxically is most likely to display its altruism

and sacredness under non-democratic conditions, when it requires dedication and bravery.

PRESSURE AND INTEREST GROUPS

Relations between media and society are often mediated through a wide range of more or less informal, but often organized, pressure groups which seek to influence directly what the media do – especially by trying to set limits to what they publish. There are many examples of established bodies, such as religious, occupational or political bodies, complaining and lobbying on a range of issues, often to do with matters of morality, perceived political bias or minority representation (Shoemaker and Reese, 1991). In many countries there is legal and social pressure on the media to be positive towards minorities of all kinds, including ethnic groups, women, gays and lesbians, and more sensitive to the needs of vulnerable groups like children, poor, disabled and homeless people and the mentally ill.

While the media are usually cautious in handling such pressures and are reluctant to yield their autonomy (the pressures often tend to cancel each other out), there is evidence of success by outside agencies in influencing content. This happens when the media's commercial interests might be threatened or where bad publicity is feared for other reasons. According to an extensive (US) study by Montgomery (1989: 217), the most effective advocacy groups 'were those whose goals were most compatible with the TV network system and whose strategies were fashioned with a keen sense of how that system functioned'. Success also depends on the degree of support among the general public for a particular advocacy position. The general effect is likely to show up in entertainment television as blandness, conformity and a blurring of controversy. In general, the media are less open to external pressures of this kind in relation to 'hard' news.

It is usually impossible to distinguish unacceptable pressure (or the act of yielding to it) from the general tendency of the media to try to please as many of their audiences (and advertisers) as possible and to avoid hurting minorities or encouraging antisocial activities. The media are also wary of legal reprisal (Tuchman, 1978) and inclined to avoid unnecessary controversy or departures from verifiable facts which are in the public domain. Organizational avoidance behaviour in response to social or legal pressure has to be accepted as legitimate, within the rules of the media-institutional 'game', but the general result is to ensure a differentially more positive treatment for the better-organized and more socially central minorities and causes (Shoemaker, 1984). Weaker and more deviant groups get a worse press and exert little influence. Paletz and Entman (1981: 125) exemplified such marginal groups with little positive access to, or control over, media coverage as 'unofficial strikers, urban rioters, welfare mothers, student militants, radicals and impoverished reactionaries'. The composition

of this category will vary, but the general principle remains the same. For instance, Lubbers et al. (1998) showed that Dutch press reports relating to minorities appeared to operate within an implicit hierarchy of favourability of treatment that ranged from most established to the newest kinds of immigrant group.

RELATIONS WITH OWNERS AND CLIENTS

The central issue which arises under this heading is the extent to which media organizations can claim to exercise autonomy in relation, first of all, to their owners and, secondly, to other direct economic agencies in their environment, especially those which provide operating funds: investors, advertisers, sponsors. According to Altschull's (1984) dictum that 'The content of the news media always reflects the interests of those who finance the press', the answer is fairly clear and also consistent with the principles of free press theory in its 'market' version. Nevertheless, there is usually some scope for autonomy on the part of 'communicators' employed by media owners (especially freedom based on professionalism or the requirements for creativity), and there are many different kinds of media and several different kinds of paymaster. Of the latter, the most important (leaving the paying audience aside) are media owners and advertisers.

Proprietor influence

There is no doubt that owners in market-based media have ultimate power over content and can ask for what they want to be included or left out. There is plenty of circumstantial evidence to show that this power is used (Curran and Seaton, 1997; Shoemaker and Reese, 1991) (see also Chapter 9, page 198) Even so, there are quite strong conventions relating to journalism which protect the decision-making autonomy of editors on particular news stories. Meyer's (1987) survey evidence confirmed that US journalistic ethics frowned on owner intervention, although editors reported a fair degree of autonomy in practice. Similar evidence was obtained in Britain by the Royal Commission on the Press (1977). It is not too surprising that journalists should claim more autonomy nor that editors of established newspapers are reluctant to admit being told what to do by proprietors.

Nevertheless, there is an inevitable tendency for owners of news media to set broad lines of policy, which are likely to be followed by the editorial staff they employ. There may also be informal and indirect pressure on particular issues that matter to owners

(for instance, relating to their other business interests) (Turow, 1994). Much credible, but often anecdotal, evidence supports this conclusion, and, in the end, the theory of economically free press legitimates this state of affairs. Newspaper owners are free to use their papers to make propaganda, if they wish to do so, provided they accept the risk of losing readers and credibility. There is a widely held view, though one difficult to prove, that increased size and conglomeration of the media industry have reduced the relevance of this issue. Media have simply become too big a business to be run for personal whims, and decisions have to be taken impersonally on grounds of managerial and market considerations.

Aside from direct proprietorial intervention on particular matters, there are likely to be pressures that arise from the growth of chains and conglomerates. These often involve a high degree of co-operation between different editorial units and implementation of a group-wide policy on some issues. There is some evidence in the United States, for instance, that certain newspaper groups are more likely to consistently support Republican rather than Democratic candidates for the Presidency (most newspaper editorials do this anyway – Wackman et al., 1975; Gaziano, 1989). Giffard (1989) showed that reporting of UNESCO has consistently followed lines laid dawn by publishers' interests (see also Preston et al., 1989). While no conspiracy can be proved, it happens that editors and owners of newspapers belong to national and international newspaper trade associations whose aims are to protect the financial interests of the industry and are inevitably political. It would be unlikely if content were not in some way influenced on some issues.

The general effect of monopoly media ownership on content has proved difficult to pin down (see, for example, Picard et al., 1988), although there is little doubt that a condition of monopoly would be harmful for freedom of expression and consumer choice. Shoemaker and Reese conclude (1991) that those who work for large chains are likely to have a lower attachment to and involvement in the community in which they work. For them, the (larger) media organization takes precedence over community influence. Correlatively, locally based media may gain strength and independence from ties with the community or city that they serve. The commercial newspaper business is, of course, not the only branch of the media industry. In the case of most entertainment industries – the non-news branch of broadcasting, popular music, film, etc. – there are few conventions which set limits to the power of owners, although organizational decisions are assumed to be largely driven by market considerations (including public demand and response). There is also no 'community' to connect with.

The situation of public broadcasting is more complex. There are no owners, only managers, controllers and guardians appointed by democratically elected governments, who are usually accountable for their decisions according to a specific version of the public interest. The degree of freedom for journalists, producers, writers and entertainers may be less than in market-based media (although this is not necessarily so), but the limits are normally clear and not subject to arbitrary breach or suspension. There has usually been a relatively high degree of artistic and professional freedom,

with limits from bureaucratic and budgetary control (and organization policy) rather than from market forces. Currently, public broadcasting operates everywhere in a competitive environment, and the risk of censorship, except that sanctioned by public opinion, is small. As a media sector that is not directly governed by market forces, its existence helps to set limits to any general increase in media monopoly.

The influence of advertisers

The consequences of advertising financing for media content are perennially discussed. On the one hand, it is obvious that the *structure* of much of the mass media industry in most capitalist countries reflects the interests of advertisers – something that has developed historically along with other social and economic changes. It is no accident that media markets often coincide with other consumer divisions. Most free-market media are finely tuned to jointly maximizing the needs of advertisers and their own interests as a normal condition of operation. The 'normal' influence extends to the matching of media content patterns according to the consumption patterns of targeted audiences. Media design, layout, planning and scheduling often reflect advertiser interests. What is less easy to demonstrate is that particular advertisers can directly intervene to influence significant publication decisions in their own interests, beyond what is already provided for in the system.

As with proprietorial intervention in news, there is little doubt that it happens from time to time on a local or specific basis (for example, Shoemaker and Reese, 1991). McManus (1994) provides a number of cases of commercial influences on reporting. Baker (1994: 99) observes that 'advertisers, not governments are the primary censors of media content in the United States today'. He cites evidence of advertisers using their market power to attempt to block particular communications that damage their interests and also of advertiser pressure that influences personnel as well as editorial decisions in the media. But influence comes in diverse forms that are often hard to detect and not necessarily illegitimate (for instance providing information that has a promotional value, product placement, sponsoring, etc.). Bogart (1995: 93–4) summarizes the (in his view, considerable) influence of advertising on media content in terms of five key points, as follows.

- Advertisers rarely try to buy journalists to slant news in their favour; more often they try to suppress news they don't like.
- They are sensitive about the environment for their messages and edgy about controversy.
- When advertisers yield to vigilante pressure, media producers veer towards self-censorship.

- Advertisers shape content when they sponsor broadcast programmes.
- The virtual end of local press competition shows how advertisers determine the life and death of media.

Advertiser influence is generally ethically disapproved, especially when it affects news (Meyer, 1987), and in general it may not even be in the interests either of media (especially news media) or of advertisers to be seen to be too close to each other. Both can lose credibility and effectiveness if a form of conspiracy against the media public is suspected. In general it seems that economically strong and 'elite' media are best in a position to resist undue pressure (see Gans, 1979). But the same is true of media that are supported by balanced sources of revenue (that is, subscriber payments as well as advertisers, or, in Europe especially, broadcast licence revenue plus advertising income). Media organizations most likely to be influenced by advertiser pressure are those whose sole source of revenue is advertising, especially where the competition is heavy. The most frequently cited example of intense competition for advertising revenue that is fed rapidly into editorial decisions of all kinds is probably that of US network television (Blumler, 1991; Tunstall, 1991).

Several organizational factors limit the power of outside economic agencies and promote autonomy, although they offer only uncertain and variable protection (see Elliott, 1977). For instance, there are some sources of finance, whether public or private, which are intended to support non-profit, cultural or professional goals, most obviously in public media, but also through private sponsorship. Secondly, media as much as (if not more than) other business enterprises have to take risks, which means sometimes giving creative and professional people their own way. New ideas and an oversupply of products are continually needed to match an insatiable demand for products which rapidly become obsolescent (Hirsch, 1973). An important key to potential freedom lies in the most unpredictable of the sources of support, the audience. If media organizations succeed with the public, they attract other financial benefits. Since there is no known way of buying or predicting this success, the prediction or attainment of audience interest counts as a professional/organizational secret, whose possession gives leverage in economic bargaining.

Some organizational studies suggest an alternative view to that advanced above about financial constraints – namely, that a competitive commercial environment can have positive effects on creativity and innovation. Ettema and Whitney (1982), for instance, in a study of US public television, report the view that struggling against organizational and financial limits sets puzzles for solution by creative workers. Turow's (1982) comparison of 'unconventional' US television projects with 'conventional' projects, also concluded that innovation was likely to come not from attempts to meet audience demand but from a series of essentially conflict-laden factors. These included aggressive competition from other media or channels, technical change, enforced internal economy or power struggles between individuals within media organizations.

Although the audience is, by conventional wisdom, the most important of the clients and influences in the environment of any media organization, research tends to show the audience as having a low salience for many mass communicators, however closely ratings and sales figures are followed by management. Media professionals display a high degree of 'autism' (Burns, 1969), consistent perhaps with the general attitude of professionals, whose very status depends on their knowing better than their clients what is good for them. Burns extended the comparison to service occupations in general, whose members 'carry with them a countervailing and ordinarily concealed posture of invidious hostility' (towards their clients).

Hostility to the audience

Altheide (1974: 59) comments that the pursuit of large audiences by the television stations which he studied 'led to a cynical view of the audience as stupid, incompetent and unappreciative'. Elliott (1972), Burns (1977) and Schlesinger (1978) found something of the same to be true of British television. Schlesinger (1978: 111) attributed this partly to the nature of professionalism: 'a tension is set up between the professionalism of the communicator, with its implied autonomy, and the meeting of apparent audience demands and desires, with their implication for limiting autonomy'. Ferguson (1983) also reported a somewhat arrogant attitude to the audience on the part of women's magazine editors.

The situation may also stem from the fact that the mass communicator is offering a professional service and a product, while the dominant criterion applied by the organization is nearly always the ratings (= volume of sales of the product, the size of the audience sold to the advertiser). As Ferguson (1983) pointed out, editors in commercial media all agreed that professional success has to be demonstrated in terms of rising circulation and advertising revenues. However, most people in the media, with some justification, will not recognize ratings as a very reliable measure of intrinsic quality. For instance, Gans (1979: 232) noted that 'When a network audience-research unit presented findings on how a sample of viewers evaluated a set of television news films, the journalists were appalled because the sample liked the films which the journalists deemed to be low quality and disliked the "good stories" '.

An alternative view

It is possible that hostility towards the audience is somewhat exaggerated by media respondents themselves, since there is contrary evidence that media people have a

strong positive attitude to their audience in the abstract. Ferguson, again, notes that women's magazine editors showed a strong sense of responsibility to their audience and want to provide a helpful service (1983: 140). Weaver and Wilhoit (1986) found that the single most important factor contributing to work satisfaction of journalists was the possibility of helping people (endorsed by 61 per cent). They also found that the single most frequent source of feedback to journalists is from individual members of the audience. The resistance to ratings and other audience statistics, which are largely a management tool with little to say about actual audiences (Ang, 1991), should not necessarily be equated with negative views of the audience.

Insulation and uncertainty

On a day-to-day or item-by-item basis, most mass communicators in established media do not need to be concerned about the immediate response of the audience, and they have to take decisions about content in advance of any response. This, coupled with the intrinsic difficulty of 'knowing' a large and very disparate audience, contributes to the relative insulation described above. The most common institutional device for making contact with the audience, that of audience research, serves an essential management function and relates media to the surrounding financial and political system, but seems to convey little that is meaningful to the individual mass communicator (Burns, 1977; Gans, 1979). Attitudes to the audience tend to be guided and differentiated according to the role orientations set out above.

Among communicators, if one follows the line of Burns's findings, the 'pragmatic' are happy with the ratings which also satisfy the organization. The craft-oriented are content with the judgements of their fellow-professionals. Those committed to the goals of the organization (for instance, carrying out a cultural mission, or political or commercial propaganda) are content with these goals as internally assessed. Those wishing to have influence in society look to their influential contacts in relevant social contexts. For everyone there are friends, relatives and casual contacts who can provide feedback of a more comprehensible kind.

Images of the audience

There remains a continuing problem of uncertainty for those who do want to communicate, who do want to change or to influence the general public and use media for this purpose, or who direct themselves at minorities or for minority causes where impact matters (see Hagen, 1999). One readily available solution is the construction of an abstract image of the kind of people they would like to reach (Bauer, 1958; Pool and Shulman, 1959). According to Gans (1957: 318), 'The audience participates in the making of a movie through the audience image held by the creator'. Shoemaker and

Reese (1991: 96) conclude that 'Journalists write primarily for themselves, for their editors, and for other journalists'. Nevertheless, communicating to a large and amorphous audience 'out there' is bound to remain problematic for those who care about 'getting a message across'. Audiences are mainly just spectators, who observe and applaud but do not interact with the senders and performers (Elliott, 1972).

Media organizations, as distinct from the individual 'communicators' within them, are to a large extent in the business of producing spectacles as a way of creating audiences and generating profit and employment (see the 'publicity model' on pages 54–6). They need some firm basis on which to predict the interests and likely degree of attention of an audience. As Pekurny (1982) points out, feedback from ratings cannot tell you how to improve television programmes, nor are they often available until long after a programme is made. Pekurny says that the 'real feedback system' is not the home viewing audience but the writers, producers, cast and network executives themselves. In addition, there is strong reliance on 'track records' of particular producers and production companies and on reusing successful past formulas. This conclusion is supported by Ryan and Peterson (1982), who tell us that in popular music the most important factor guiding selection in the production process (see page 297) is the search for a good 'product image', which means essentially trying to match the characteristics of previously successful songs.

ASPECTS OF INTERNAL STRUCTURE AND DYNAMICS

The analysis made so far, in line with the scheme in Figure 11.1, points to a degree of differentiation and division within the boundaries of the organization. There are several sources of division. One of the most obvious is the diversity of function (such as news, entertainment or advertising) of many media organizations, with different interests competing for status and finance. Another is the fact that the personnel of media organizations come from different social backgrounds and vary according to age, gender, ethnicity and other attributes. We have already noted the duality of purpose of many media (both material and ideal) and the endemic conflict between creative ends (which have no practical limits) and the need to organize, plan, finance and 'sell' media products. Most accounts of media-organizational goals point to differences of orientation and purpose that can be a source of latent conflict.

Internal diversity of purpose

The fact that mass media organizations have mixed goals is important for locating the media in their social context, understanding some of the pressures under which they

operate and helping to differentiate the main occupational choices available to media workers. It is one essential aspect of a general ambiguity over social role that has already been discussed. Some further light on this question is shed by the characterization of the newspaper as a 'hybrid organization' (Engwall, 1978), in the sense that it cannot be clearly placed on either of two key organizational dimensions: the manufacture–service dimension, and the dimension of variability of product and technology and use. The newspaper organization is engaged in both making a product and providing a service. It also uses a wide variety of production technology, from the simple to the complex.

In varying degrees, this holds true of other mass media organizations, certainly of broadcasting. Engwall found that several different 'work cultures' flourish, each justified according to a different goal or work task – namely, the news-oriented culture, the politically oriented, the economically oriented and the technically oriented. The first two tend to go together and are expressed by the professional or creative category, noted above (also closer to the 'normative' type), while the second two are essentially 'utilitarian'. Those holding to the news-oriented culture are likely to be journalists collecting and processing news, while the politically oriented will generally comprise editorial staff and senior political correspondents. The economically and technically oriented consist of those involved in financial management and in solving problems of production, and they will have much in common with their counterparts in other business organizations.

In so far as this situation can be generalized, it seems that media organizations are likely to be as internally divided as to purpose as they are different from each other. It is hard to think of another category of organization that is as likely to pursue simultaneously such diverse objectives and serve such divergent values. That this should happen without excessive conflict suggests some fairly stable forms of accommodation to the attendant problems. Such an accommodation may be essential in what Tunstall (1971) has characterized by the paradoxical term of 'non-routine bureaucracy'. It may also indicate the presence in media of an above-average degree of compromise, uncertainty and 'displacement of goals' by comparison with other types of complex organization.

THE INFLUENCE OF PERSONAL CHARACTERISTICS OF 'MASS COMMUNICATORS'

Many studies of media organizations or occupations include, as a matter of course, an examination of the social background and outlook on society of the group of respondents under study (early examples are Rosten, 1937, 1941; a more recent example is Tunstall, 1993). This is sometimes because of an assumption that the personal characteristics of those most directly responsible for media production will influence content. It is a hypothesis that accords well with the ideology or mythology

of the media themselves and stands opposed to the notion of organizational or technological determinism. It is also a familiar idea amongst audiences that the personality and values of the author, for instance of a novel or a film, will give the work its primary meaning, despite being processed in a media industry. The expectation that media will 'reflect society' (the first hypothesis considered on page 246) can be supported on the grounds either that it is what their audiences want or that those who work in the media are a cross-section of society, at least in their values and beliefs.

However, these views need to be modified to allow for the influence of organizational goals and settings. Most media products are not the work of a single author, but of teams, and ideas of personal authorship are not very relevant, despite the tendency of media to promote individual stars and celebrities. Shoemaker and Reese (1991) suggest that lines of influence can follow one or other of the paths shown in Figure 11.4. In essence, what is shown are two alternative paths – one in which organizational role subordinates or conceals personal characteristics, and another in which having power or status in an organization permits an individual communicator to express their personal beliefs and values in public communication.

The first question to arise is whether there is any distinctive pattern of social experience or personal values to be found among media communicators. Inevitably there are as many descriptions of social background as there are studies, and even though most concern journalists, there is no single pattern to report. However, a few general remarks are in order, taking as a starting point the findings of Weaver and Wilhoit (1986) concerning the social composition of their sample of US journalists.

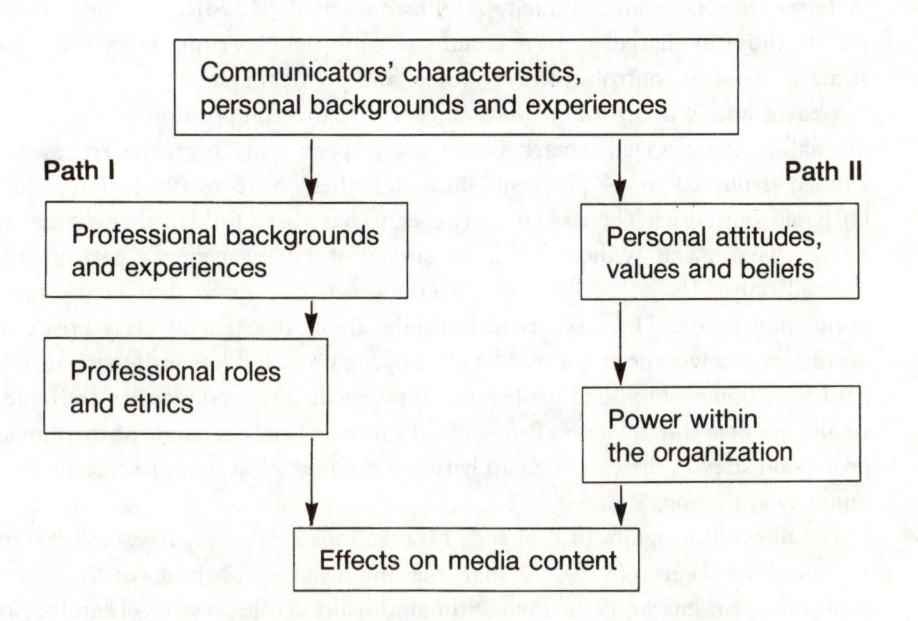

FIGURE 11.4 How factors intrinsic to the communicator may influence media content: institutional versus professional pathways (Shoemaker and Reese, 1991)

For the purpose, journalists were defined as 'those who have editorial responsibility for the preparation or transmission of news stories or other information, including full-time reporters, correspondents, columnists, newsmen and editors' (1986: 168). It is clear that US journalists, however marginal their role in society, are not marginal in income terms but belong on average to the middle category, thus within the economically secure sector of society, without being rich. This mirrors the earlier findings of Johnstone et al. (1976) and the data from Britain afforded by Tunstall (1971).

More recent evidence from Weaver and Wilhoit (1992) suggests that the social composition of the occupation in America is fairly stable and that US journalists are fairly average in respect of many aspects of social background. The same authors report, from a contemporary cross-national study of 21 countries that the 'demographic profile of US journalists is similar in some ways to the profiles of journalists in other areas of the world' (Weaver, 1996: 84). The main similarities include an over-representation of men in newsrooms (about 66% across the board), and a bias towards youth. The main difference was the generally higher level of education of US journalists.

There are evidently big variations between the stars of journalism and the ordinary salariat, as in other branches of media business. Lichter and Rothman (1986), for instance, painted a portrait of 240 personnel of elite US news media showing them to be not only well off but demographically unrepresentative in being more white and more male than the country as a whole and less likely to hold a religious belief. One can probably assume that people who work for less elite media are also less of an elite themselves, although they may still be demographically unrepresentative (for instance, in terms of gender and ethnicity). Johnstone et al. (1976) concluded that 'in any society those in charge of mass communication tend to come from the same social strata as those in control of the economic and political systems'.

Weaver and Wilhoit found that, since 1971, the composition of the corps of US journalists had changed remarkably in one respect: a much greater representation of women (from 20 to 34 per cent), although there were relatively fewer black and Hispanic journalists. There seems, however, to have been little further change up to the 1990s (Weaver and Wilhoit, 1992). A survey of American media personnel in 1996 showed only 11% to be of minority ethnic origin, a good deal below the general population figure. There seems little doubt about the general class position of the average media worker: it is a middle-class occupation, but less professionalized or well paid than other established professions (law, medicine, accountancy, etc.) and with a small elite of well-paid stars. Peters and Cantor's (1982) account of the movie acting profession stresses the extreme gap between the powerless and insecure many and the minority at the top.

The theoretical significance of such observations is less easy to establish. One view, advanced by Gans (1979), is that the middle-class position of the journalistic profession is a guarantee of their ultimate loyalty to the system. Therefore they are free, in the US system, because they can be trusted to see and interpret the world in much the same way as the real holders of power, holding the same basic ideology and

values. Gans concluded that news journalists generally hold what are called 'motherhood' values, including support for the family and a nostalgia for small-town pastoralism. They also tend to be ethnocentric, pro-Democratic, individualistic and in favour of 'responsible capitalism', moderatism, social order and leadership.

Such values, according to Gans, include elements of both conservative and liberal ideologies. It is a persuasive view, more so than the alternative idea that they are not only an elite but a left-leaning one, according to Lichter and Rothman (1986), with subversive motives and a penchant for supporting deviance and extremist movements. Their main argument was based on case studies of news reporting of controversial issues in elite media. Gans's view of journalists as 'safe' but not reactionary is also perhaps more convincing than the other extreme view that they are a conservative elite, mainly serving the interests of the state, the governing class and big business (as inferred by Herman and Chomsky, 1988).

More significant than evidence of the values of journalists (but not inconsistent with it) may be the finding that media personnel owe most of their relevant attitudes and tendencies to socialization from the immediate work environment (for example, Breed, 1955; Weaver and Wilhoit, 1986: 127–8). This view, while not discounting the influence of social background and personal belief, returns us to the greater probability of organizational, rather than individual and subjective, determination. Even so, the possibility for personal influence by mass communicators varies according to the genre and the type of organization. Non-news genres offer more scope for expressing personal beliefs, and there is probably more scope where commercial and financial pressures are less (Tunstall, 1993).

The review of evidence by Shoemaker and Reese (1991) relating to the influence of personal beliefs and values is inconclusive. Even so, to conclude that there is no influence would seem to rule out any real degree of personal autonomy and to overestimate the power of work socialization (see page 271). Shoemaker and Reese (1991: 72) see the relation as variable: 'it is possible that when communicators have more power over their messages and work under fewer constraints, their personal attitudes, values and beliefs have more opportunity to influence content' (see Figure 7.4). It is fairly evident, for instance, that individuals who reach high status in different media (journalism, film, television, music) do have and use opportunities for expressing personal opinions and beliefs. The 'logic of media', which favours personalization, often supports this tendency, as long as it does not also conflict with commercial logic.

WOMEN IN NEWS ORGANIZATIONS

The case of gender seems to promise a good test of the proposition that personal characteristics will influence content, since it has been one claim of part of the feminist

movement that the media have been in various ways on the 'other side' in various campaigns of the gender war. As usual it turns out not to be so easy to reach a conclusion. There is an empirical correlation between the relatively low numbers and lower occupational status of women in news media organizations (Gallagher, 1981; Thoveron, 1986; *Media Studies Journal*, 1993; European Commission, 1999) on the one hand and the underrepresentation or stereotyping of women in the news (for instance, in terms of topic and context, as well as the more obvious use of female 'sex symbols') on the other. A European Commission report (1999) cites studies showing that in French news media only 17% of those cited or interviewed were women. Similar figures were 22% for Finnish news and 13% in the United Kingdom. The same source concludes that women 'portrayed in the media are younger, more likely to be shown as married, less likely to be shown as in paid employment', compared with men (1999: 12).

The issue is not confined to the question of news, but news is often singled out as of particular significance for the wider question of gender inequality and construction in society. The correlation between male domination (in power positions if not always numerically) of virtually all media organizations and male-oriented themes or patriarchal values offers strong prima facie support for the view that greater media occupational equality would make a difference to content (see Chapter 5). The evidence for this remains weak, however. Baehr (1996) says that decisions about content are much more influenced by financial necessity than by personal preference. The European Commission report (1999) cited above is also doubtful about any automatic connection between numbers of women employed in media (even in senior positions) and the way women are portrayed.

According to evidence from the Netherlands reported by van Zoonen (1994), the typical lesson learnt in journalism schools was that 'feminism – even moderately defined – and professional journalism were at odds with each other'. In other words, socialization worked to induce conformity in practice to traditional ways of making news, even though many young women journalists felt they had autonomy. One general conclusion to be drawn from this and other evidence is that gender always interacts with the organizational context. The results may be different from case to case.

Van Zoonen (1988, 1991) has also argued that a more fundamental approach to the construction of gender is needed. She points to basic inconsistencies in the assumption that having more women in the newsroom would change the news (for the better). For one thing, on closer inspection the available evidence does not give good empirical support for this assumption. There have been significant increases in female participation in the work force (see, for example, Weaver and Wilhoit, 1986, 1996; *Media Studies Journal*, 1993) without any noticeable changes in the 'nature of news'. An American case study by Zoch and van Slyke Turk (1998) examined one thousand news stories over ten years to see if female reporters were more likely to choose female sources. They found a small tendency in this direction, mainly due to the kind of stories that women were still more likely to be asked to cover. The theory takes for

granted that journalists have enough autonomy to have influence as individuals, whereas this has to be treated as problematic and variable.

There are also divergent views as to what constitutes 'change'. Should the news become 'feminized', or should 'femininity' itself be redefined (perhaps in the direction of masculinity)? The European Commission report (1999: 11) cites French research by Erik Neveu that showed 'signs of a feminine tone or slant among women journalists in terms of a tendency to report on "ordinary lives", a less deferential attitude towards authorities, and the use of psychological approaches in the reporting of political lives'. However, this was not evidence of a 'feminine habitus' within journalism, but the result a circular process following the allocation of certain topics to men or women.

There are two distinct issues here: that of journalistic autonomy versus determination (by external forces or the organizational hierarchy or 'media logic') and that of the desirability of change in the nature of news and the direction which it might take. None of this is an argument against the fact of there being gender differences, or against more equal employment for women, or against change, but the various issues are separate and cannot all be bundled together under the general heading of having more women in news organizations. If the central matter is the way gender is constructed then a broader approach is needed. It is also the case that broad changes in media, including efforts to attract more female readers for the press and the differentially growing purchasing power of women are leading to certain 'feminizing' trends, perhaps independently of the number of women employed or their degree of managerial responsibility.

It would follow that a necessary condition for more equitable treatment of women in news will be a gradual rise of women to positions of power within media organizations. Tunstall's (1993) evidence concerning television producers in Britain describes a situation of increasingly significant representation of women in production (and decision-making) roles (especially in the BBC), against a background of strong gender segmentation in television work. The producer role is also sketched as one that seems designed to suit men or unmarried women. The study produced some evidence of a belief on the part of producers themselves that, in several fields, gender could affect the choice of topics.

LATENT CONFLICTS

Not surprisingly, most studies of media organizations reveal many different kinds of latent conflict, based on a variety of factors, although quite often reflecting a tension between the aspirations of 'lower-level' participants and those in control of media. The influence of proprietors on news has already been discussed (p. 259). Turow (1994)

suggests that media organizational theory originally over-emphasized the degree of consensus that obtains in new organizations as a result of strong social control and socialization and later tended to over-emphasize conflict as being endemic and even normal. An early study by Breed (1955) detailed the (mainly informal) socializing mechanisms that helped to ensure the maintenance of policy. Young reporters would be expected to read the newspaper they work for and sit in on editorial conferences. Policy is also learned through informal gossip with colleagues. Deviations from publication 'policy' were discouraged by feelings of obligation to superiors, by the satisfactions of belonging to the in-group and sometimes by management sanctions and rewards in giving assignments. In general, according to Breed's research, what policy actually was, remained covert.

Research by Bantz (1985), however, led to the conclusion that the organizational culture of news organizations is intrinsically oriented towards conflict, if one defines organizational culture as 'patterns of meanings that define action'. He suggests five factors that promote conflict within the news organization. One is the natural tendency of the journalist to distrust any external source, to be suspicious and vigilant. Two others are accounted for by the conflict between professional norms and both business and entertainment norms. Fourthly there is the permanent state of internal and inter-media competition over stories. Finally, and more speculatively is the fact that news content always places a high premium on conflict.

Returning to the question of conflict based on hierarchy, Muriel Cantor's (1971) study of a group of producers employed in making films for major television networks indicated the existence of three main types. First, there were 'film-makers', mainly younger, well-educated people ambitious to become feature film directors and comparable to the 'professional' category of broadcasters which Burns (1977) singled out. Secondly, there was a group of writer-producers, whose chosen purpose was to make stories with a worthwhile message and to communicate with a wide public. Thirdly, there were older, less well-educated career producers, whose main orientation was to the network and their career within it.

Not surprisingly, the last-mentioned group was least likely to have conflicts with management, since their main aim of reaching the biggest possible audience was shared by the networks. The film-makers, for different reasons, were prepared to accept network goals because they wanted to practise their craft, accumulate money and move on to feature films. It was the writer-producers who came most into conflict with the networks (management) because of their different attitude to the content that they were required to produce. Management wanted a saleable, risk-free product, while the writers still retained some ideals of the craft and wanted to convey a worthwhile message. The chance to reach a large audience was essential to their purpose, but the price, in terms of conforming to commercial goals, was a high one to have to pay.

The lessons of other research on communicators (mainly journalists) seem to lead to a similar conclusion that where conflict occurs between media organization and employee, it is likely to be where the political tendency or economic self-interest of

the organization gets in the way of individual freedom of expression. An early study of an American regional newspaper by Stark (1982) showed a general potential tension between conservative management and reporters. Some locally oriented reporters supported management, while a group of more professionalized and cosmopolitan journalists used their skills and knowledge of their beat to counter management pressure and retain enough autonomy. Flegel and Chaffee (1971) support the view that a devotion to the craft and a 'technical orientation' towards a quality product, requiring cooperation, helps to reduce conflict and promote a sense of autonomy.

According to Sigelman (1973), the potential problem of conflict on grounds of beliefs is usually avoided by selective recruitment and self-selection by entrants into media organizations with compatible work environments. Studies of newspapers indicate a strong sense on the part of journalists that editors and publishers have a 'policy', which tends to dictate either the kind of story to be chosen or the manner of treatment. Aside from initial selection, the main way of achieving conformity seems to be by way of socialization 'on the job', as described by Breed (1955; see above). Perhaps most significant in news media is the fact that being able to handle the news according to the reigning policy becomes a skill and even a value in itself. The objective of getting the news overrides personal feelings. Presumably similar processes occur in other media organizations.

Turow (1994) raises the possibility of an increasing potential for internal conflict and even a need for it as a result of more and more concentration of ownership. In particular, conflicts of interest arise when news events actually concern media themselves (increasingly common) and the media concerned happen to belong to the same overall corporation. Professional journalistic values call for freedom to report on controversies that might damage the commercial interests of the parent company and editorial permission may be denied. Turow's evidence shows that this does happen and that there is already a tendency for 'silent bargains' to be made that encourage conformity and co-operation with overall company policy. A covert reward system exists that stresses caution and loyalty.

It is not clear how much the power of owners and chief editors to influence content is a source of conflict. Gans's account of several US news media (1979: 95) is somewhat ambiguous about the power of corporate executives over reporters. On the one hand, they do make 'policy', conduct frequent and regular briefings, look after the commercial and political interests of the firm and can 'suggest, select and veto news stories whenever they choose'. On the other hand, they do not use their power on a day-to-day basis, and there are countervailing powers that lie with television news producers and editors, if not with individual reporters. Survey evidence tends to support the view that journalists mainly regard themselves as having a reasonable degree of autonomy, even if the problem of pressure from 'policy' does arise (see Meyer, 1987). Weaver and Wilhoit (1986) reported that 60 per cent of their journalists thought they had almost complete freedom in selecting stories they wanted to work on, and 66 per cent in deciding which aspects of a news story to emphasize.

Media occupations are weakly 'institutionalized' compared, for instance, with law, medicine or accountancy, and professional success will often depend on unaccountable ups and downs of public taste or on personal and unique qualities which cannot be imitated or transmitted. Apart from certain performance skills it is hard to pin down an essential or 'core' media accomplishment. This may variously be presented as an ability to attract attention and arouse interest, assess public taste, be understood or 'communicate' well, be liked, 'know the media business' or 'have a nose for news'. None of these seems comparable to the skills, based on recognized and required training, that underlie most other professions. It may be that the freedom, creativity and critical approach that many media personnel still cherish, despite the bureaucratic setting of their work, are ultimately incompatible with full professionalization in the traditional sense.

It would, in any case, as noted above, be very difficult, even allowing for the division of labour in any complex organization, to identify a general occupational type or archetypal 'mass communicator' profession. There may well be a central core consisting especially of those with a directly creative or communicative task, such as editors, journalists, writers and film-makers. But even the core professionals rarely seem unanimous about how they see their professional task. Perhaps the most fundamental dilemma is one of freedom versus constraint in an institution whose own ideology places a value on originality and freedom, yet whose organizational setting requires relatively strict control.

> **Box 11.2   Media-occupational role dilemmas**
>
> - Active participatory versus neutral, informational
> - Creative and independent versus bureaucratic, routine
> - Communicative purpose versus meeting consumer demand

FURTHER READING

Berkowitz, D. (ed.) (1997) *Social Meanings of News*. Thousand Oaks, CA: Sage.

Elliott, P. (1972) *The Making of a Television Series*. London: Constable.

Ettema, J. and Whitney, D.C. (eds) (1982) *Individuals in Mass Media Institutions*. Beverly Hills, CA: Sage.

McManus, J. (1994) *Market Driven Journalism*. Thousand Oaks, CA: Sage.

Shoemaker, P.J. and Reese, S.D. (1996) *Mediating the Message*, 2nd edn. New York: Longman.

Weaver, D. and Wilhoit, G.C. (1986) *The American Journalist*. Bloomington: University of Indiana Press.

the production of media culture

We have looked up to now at a range of more or less static or constant factors that shape the work of media organizations. These relate, in particular, to the composition and internal social structure of the media workforce and the relations that are maintained, under a variety of economic and social pressures, with the world outside the organization. The context of the media is never really static, but it may appear stable as a result of a balance achieved between outside forces and organizational goals. In the following sections we focus mainly on two interrelated aspects of organizational activity, which can be described respectively as 'selecting' and 'processing'. The first refers to the sequence of decisions which extends from the choice of 'raw material', as it were, to delivering the finished product. The second refers to the application of work routines and organizational criteria (including both professional and business aspects) that affect the nature of this product as it passes through the 'chain' of decision-making.

This way of describing media-organizational work originates primarily from research on news production, but it can apply more or less equally to a range of other media products and media settings (Hirsch, 1977). In the case of news, the chain extends from 'noticing' an event in the world, through writing about or filming it and preparing a news item for transmission. In the case of a book, a movie, a television show or a piece of popular music, a similar chain extends from an idea in someone's head, through an editorial selection process and many phases of transformation into the final product (Ryan and Peterson, 1982).

In general all phases of media production involve a large volume of work that becomes routinized as a matter of necessity. Even the starting point – a news event or 'creative idea' – is strongly (perhaps most strongly) influenced by convention and prior experience that defines an event as 'newsworthy'. The regularities of behaviour and thinking that result from these routines give rise to empirical generalizations and to the possibility of theorizing about what is going on. The routines also reflect the 'operational' theories in the heads of media professionals (see page 8).

MEDIA-ORGANIZATIONAL ACTIVITIES: GATEKEEPING AND SELECTION

The term **gatekeeping** has been widely used as a metaphor to describe the process by which selections are made in media work, especially decisions whether or not to admit a particular news report to pass through the 'gates' of a news medium into the news channels (see White, 1950; Shoemaker, 1991). However, the idea of gatekeeping has a much wider potential application since it can apply to the work of literary agents and publishers, to many kinds of editorial and production work in print and television. It

applies to decisions about distribution and marketing of existing media products (for instance of films). In a wider sense it refers to the power to give or withhold access to different voices in society and is often a locus of conflict. One common tension in democratic societies is between governments (and politicians) and the media over the amount and kind of attention they receive in mass media. Another example relates to the kind of representation and amount of access given to minorities.

Despite its appeal and plausibility, the gatekeeping concept has a number of weaknesses and has been continuously revised since its first applications. Weak points are its implication of there being one (initial) gate area and one main set of selection criteria, its simple view of the 'supply' of news, and its tendency to individualize decision-making. In a comprehensive overview of the concept and related research, Shoemaker (1991) has extended the original model to take account of the wider social context and many factors at work. She draws attention to the role of advertisers, public relations, pressure groups plus varied sources and 'news managers' in influencing decisions. In her model, gatekeeping usually involves multiple and succeeding acts of selection over the period of news production. Often group decision-making is involved. Reference is made not only to aspects of content but also to the kind of audience expected and to questions of cost. The main points of this model were largely confirmed in a case study of local television news by Berkowitz (1990). News selection can vary considerably in the degree of activity involved, and the concept as generally understood seems more suitable for the more passive kinds of 'news discovery' (McManus, 1994) than the more enterprising variety.

IDEOLOGICAL VERSUS ORGANIZATIONAL INFLUENCES

In early studies of news gatekeeping (White, 1950; Gieber, 1956) most interest was focused on the large number of items that failed to gain entry and on the reasons for exclusion. In the nature of the early research, there was a tendency to emphasize the subjective character of news selection decisions. Later, more attention was given to systematic influences on selection that can be considered as either 'organizational' or 'ideological'. The former refers primarily to bureaucratic routines, the second to values and cultural influences which are not purely individual and personal but which stem also from the social (and national) setting of news activity. The necessity for normal processes of news selection to be strongly influenced by routine was recognized long ago by Walter Lippmann (1922: 123), when he wrote: 'without standardization, without stereotypes, without routine judgements, without a fairly ruthless disregard of subtlety, the editor would soon die of excitement'.

Subsequent research demonstrated that the content of news media tends consistently to follow a predictable pattern and that different organizations behave in a similar way when confronted by the same events and under equivalent conditions (Glasgow Media

Group, 1976; McQuail, 1977; Shoemaker and Reese, 1991). There appears to be a stable perception on the part of news decision makers about what is likely to interest an audience and a good deal of consensus within the same social-cultural settings (Hetherington, 1985).

An alternative explanation to that of subjective individual judgement is to be found in the concept of *news values*, which refers to the criteria of relevance and interest to the news public (see also Chapter 14, page 341). While the general idea of news values was already familiar, a study of foreign news in the Norwegian press by Galtung and Ruge (1965) led to the first clear statement of the news values (or 'news factors') that influence selection.

Galtung and Ruge hypothesized that events would become news the more they fitted certain organizational and also some cultural or 'ideological' criteria. This idea surfaces widely in research on media organizations, though with different notions of what counts as ideological. Hall (1973), for instance, used it in a political sense to refer to the substance of news photos, even though technical quality and dramatic or sensational character also played a part. The notion of a 'media logic' (see page 296) also embraces the twin ideas of organizational and technical suitability plus a media-cultural component. The 'ideological' news factors described by Galtung and Ruge refer mainly to values that are embedded in Western society – especially those which stem from an individualist and materialist philosophy.

Aside from their intrinsic content, some events are more likely to become news than others, because they lend themselves to the formal procedures of gathering and processing which often operate on a 24-hour (or more frequent) production cycle. For this reason, news organizations prefer events that fit a number of criteria related to time, place and potential audience demand (see below and also Chapter 14, page 338). In addition to suitability for routine processing, it is obvious that access to events and the presence or absence of the *facilities* for recording and transmission play a major part in selection. There is a self-fulfilling effect from the location of reporters and equipment in particular places.

FACTORS IN NEWS SELECTION

The gatekeeping concept, as already noted, has a built-in limitation in its implication that news arrives in ready-made and unproblematic event-story form at the 'gates' of the media, where it is either admitted or excluded. This does apply to the large volume of news that arrives from news agencies, but does not account for the whole selection process. Manheim (1998) describes the 'myth structure of journalism' of which one component is the idea that news is a 'naturally occurring product' of the political environment and the visible content of events. Following this, he typifies journalistic news gathering according to two dominant and two subsidiary types. The main

types are that of 'hunter-gathering', referring to the collection of surface phenomena as potential stories, and that of 'cultivation', referring to the 'beat' system for planned collection of news and clever use of familiar sources. This involves more positive activity. The other two types are relatively rare and refer to 'investigative' and 'enterprise' journalism, but these also share the assumption that news occurs naturally.

The gatekeeping framework is also largely based on the assumption that there is a given, finite, knowable reality of events in the 'real world', from which it is the task of the media to select according to appropriate criteria of reality-reflection, significance, or relevance. As Fishman (1980: 13), writes, 'most researchers assumed that news either reflects or distorts reality and that reality consists of facts and events out there which exist independently of how news workers think of them and treat them in the news production process'. For Fishman, the central concern should be the 'creation of news', and in this he has been followed by a number of other influential theorists.

It is clear that the eventual news content of the media arrives by several different routes and in different forms. It may have to be sought out or ordered in advance, or its 'discovery' may have to be systematically planned. At times it also has to be internally manufactured or constructed. Such a process of construction, like the selection of news, is not random and subjective. It takes place largely according to schemes of interpretation and of relevance which are those of the bureaucratic institutions that either are sources of news or process events (police departments, courts, welfare agencies, government committees, etc.). According to Fishman (1982), 'what is known and knowable by the media depends on the information-gathering and information-processing resources' of these agencies. The main factors that influence eventual choice can be considered under the headings of 'people', 'place' and 'time', usually in one combination or another. Alongside or built into these features, however, are questions of cost and of audience appeal.

People and selection

In general, it is clear that 'Western media' at least like news events that involve personal actions even if only making statements and also like to 'personalize' abstract topics to make them more concrete and interesting to the audience. There is a general tendency to look for well-known people, stars and celebrities around which to construct news. The more prominent the person involved in any sphere, the more attention and privileged access as a source can be expected. News is often reports of what prominent people say about events rather than reports of the events themselves.

Probably the best-known case of 'person as event' is that of the US President, a power figure supported by a large and effective publicity machine. As one study (Grossman and Kumar, 1981) noted, in all the variety of possibilities for reporting the

President there is one constant imperative – closeness to senior officials and, if possible, the President in person on as exclusive a basis as possible. Other kinds of celebrity figure that fit the same picture can readily be imagined. World events tend to be told as stories about heroes and villains, for instance heroes of the fall of communism such as Gorbachev and Walesa or of the new figures threatening the West such as Saddam Hussein or Slobodan Milosevic. This reflects the fact that a great deal of news gathering revolves around people, especially since people are more permanently available than events, and (unlike institutions) they can speak. It is often from prominent individuals that exclusives and scoops can be obtained by well-connected journalists.

The significance of personal contacts with anyone close to those inside circles of power in any kind of media work involving attention to current social reality has been underlined by research as well as by informal accounts of news producers. Reese et al.'s (1994) study of various 'sources' appearing or cited on American mainstream news media in the late 1980s showed a remarkable concentration on a relatively small number of inter-connected individuals whose views were used to validate the news.

What we see of the world through media eyes is often the result of chance encounters or informal communication networks developed by people in the media. The power to make news that attaches to certain offices also helps to account for the differential influence of certain sources and the potential for 'pseudo-events' to be assembled around the activities of prominent people (Dayan and Katz, 1992). The relative status of people in the news is one of the elements of 'media logic', discussed below (page 296).

Location and selection

The nearer the location of news events is to the city, region or nation of the intended audience, the more likely it is to be noticed. Nearness may, however, be overridden as a factor by other considerations, such as power or the intrinsic character of events (for instance, scale and negativity) (Galtung and Ruge, 1965). Westerstahl and Johansson (1994) show, from a large scale cross-national study of foreign news selection, that two attributes of news account for a large amount of selection. These are the 'importance' of the event country and the 'proximity' to the home media. These authors trace the origin of this observation to a German author writing in 1695! The fact that recognition of events as news has to involve a specific location helps to explain the success with which authorities (especially in war situations) can manage news, by virtue of their control over physical access to the site of events. Aside from the simple need to be able to observe, the conventions of objective news require evidence of location, and what has no verifiable location is a 'non-event'.

The importance of location was emphasized by Walter Lippmann (1922) in his account of the routinization of news gathering. He wrote that news consists of events

which 'obtrude', above what is normal, and which can be anticipated by observation at those places where past newsworthy events have happened or been made public – such as courts, police stations, parliaments, airports and hospitals. News media are normally linked to a 'net' that covers the globe, its nodal points marked by the presence of an agency or a correspondent. The idea of a *news net* was developed by Tuchman (1978) as an image of a device designed to 'catch' news, like fish. Its capacity depends on the fineness of the mesh and the strength of its fibre. The finer strands of the net (for small fish) are provided by 'stringers', while reporters and the wire services provide the larger mesh. There is a hierarchy involved, with status in the news net determining whose information is more likely to be identified as news (preference goes to seniority and to own reporters rather than news agencies):

> The spatial anchoring of the news net at centralized institutions is one element of the frame delineating strips of everyday reality as news. . . . The news net imposes a frame upon occurrences through the co-operation of the complex bureaucracy associated with the dispersion of reporters. . . . Finally, the news net incorporates three assumptions about readers' interests: readers are interested in occurrences at specific localities; they are concerned with the activities of specific organizations; they are interested in specific topics. (Tuchman, 1978: 23, 25)

The news net has a very tight weave at places where power is concentrated, like the Washington–New-York corridor or the Paris–Berlin–London triangle. The advance planning of news coverage in spatial terms thus involves a set of presuppositions about where news is likely to happen, which will have a certain self-fulfilling tendency. This tendency is witnessed by the great continuity of flow of news from regions like the Middle East and Eastern Europe in recent years, once these have been established as sites for events and as foci of political concern. The corollary of this is that news flow can usually be less easily generated from locations where sudden and unexpected events take place.

The influence of location on reporting occurs initially through the assignment of reporters to places where 'news events' are likely to occur. The identification of such events depends on beliefs about what will interest the audience (an aspect of typification). Most news organizations have a structure of desks or departments which is partly based on location such as city news, crime news (courts and police) and politics. Traditionally, on local media at least, this was expressed in terms of a series of 'beats'.

The news beat, as explained by Fishman (1980), is not only *territorial* and *topical* (subject-defined), it is also a social setting, a network of social relations involving reporters and sources who frequent particular places. The news beat is established in order to facilitate the uncovering of 'news events', but it inevitably leads to the construction of events. What happens in a certain place (on the news beat) is much more likely to be defined as news just because it is observed (compared with a 'non-event', which is another event which is not observed).

Not surprisingly, since it is built into the definition of news, time has enormous influence as a consideration on selection. Timeliness is an essential ingredient of both novelty and relevance, both of which are highly prized in news. It also depends on and amplifies one of the most significant properties of communication technology – its capacity to overcome barriers of time (as well as space). As well as a net to capture space, there is also a frame for dealing with time. Tuchman (1978) has illuminated the nature of this particular aspect of the 'news net', since time underlies the typification of events as news. The net she describes, distributed in space and time, is designed to maximize the chance of capturing news events when and where they are likely to occur and the efficiency of dealing with them. Typifying events according to their time scale, especially in relation to the news production cycle, increases the chance of actually reporting as news those events that fit the conventional definitions of news. News people implicitly operate with a time-based typology of news which helps in planning their work (see Figure 12.1).

The main types are 'hard news', dealing with immediate events, and 'soft news', mainly background or time-free news. In addition there are three other categories: 'spot' (very new, immediate, just breaking) news, 'developing' news, and 'continuing' news. There is also a time dimension, according to which news can be classified as 'pre-scheduled', 'unscheduled' or 'non-scheduled'. The first refers to 'diary' events that are known about in advance and for which coverage can be planned. The second refers to news of events that happen unexpectedly and need to be immediately disseminated – the most difficult for routine handling, but not the largest category of news. The third relates to news (usually soft) that is not tied to any particular time and can be stored and released at the convenience of the news organization. The typification of

	Time dimension		
News type	Pre-scheduled	Unexpected	Non-scheduled
Hard	•	•	
Soft			•
Spot		•	
Developing		•	
Continuing	•	•	

FIGURE 12.1 Time and types of news (Tuchman, 1978)

events in this way narrows the range of uncertainty, but also encourages the tendency to rely on 'continuing' news and on pre-scheduled or non-scheduled event news, thus telling against uniqueness and novelty. The extraordinary influence of time in the news operation has been especially noticed in broadcasting. Schlesinger (1978: 105) refers to a 'stopwatch culture', which goes beyond what is needed for practical purposes: 'It is a form of fetishism in which to be obsessed about time is to be professional in a way which newsmen have made peculiarly their own'. Its consequence, in his view, is to do some violence to history and reduce the meaningfulness of news.

Although pre-planned (diary) events make up a large part of the routine news coverage, there are occasions when planned events of a non-routine kind can take on a special significance. There may be occasions when either event organizers or the media themselves are in a position to influence the way news is reported by fulfilling their own wishes or expectations. There are various accounts of how the planning of expected event coverage strongly influences the eventual content of coverage. Following an idea of Lang and Lang (1953), Halloran et al. (1970) studied the sequence of events preceding a planned demonstration and protest march in London in 1968, directed against US war policy in Vietnam. They showed how media stories in the weeks before the event predefined it as both significant and violent, fomented by foreigners and with potential threats to property and even the social order (it was supposedly a 'year of revolution'). One result of this 'pre-structuring' of the meaning and course of the event was to shape the organizational and physical arrangements for event coverage as well as the interpretations of its significance. In fact, the planned event was relatively peaceful, but the news apparatus was committed in advance to an alternative version and found it difficult to reconcile the reality with the established expectation. The result was distortion and unbalanced reporting. Similar phenomena have been noticed in relation to planned military events, like the 1982 British expedition to the Falklands, the Gulf War of 1991 and the initially peaceful US 'invasion' of Somalia in 1992. More commonly, the problem for the media organization is a reverse one of catching up with unplanned events in unexpected locations.

Molotch and Lester (1974) proposed a fourfold typology of events of which the largest category is that of 'routine events', the three others being 'accidents', 'scandals' and 'serendipity' (chance). Routine events, however, are divided into three types:

- those where 'event promoters have habitual access to the news assemblers';
- those where 'event promoters seek to disrupt the routine access of others in order to make events of their own';
- and those where 'the access is afforded by the fact that the promoter and news assemblers are identical'.

The first category refers to normal situations, such as the reporting of national politics, the second to demonstrations and publicity-gaining acts of 'outsiders'. The last

category relates to 'media events' and 'pseudo-events', in which the media are closely implicated. This typology also has implications for the exercise of source power.

> **Box 12.1 News selection factors**
>
> ● Power and fame of individuals involved in events
> ● Personal contacts of reporters
> ● Location of events
> ● Location of power
> ● Predictability and routine
> ● Proximity to the audience of people and events in the news
> ● Recency and timeliness of events
> ● Timing in relation to the news cycle

THE STRUGGLE FOR ACCESS

The question of access to the media (and thus to society itself as audience) by any one institutional element of the society has already been raised at several points. The initial frame of reference in Chapter 4 represents the media as creating (or occupying) channels 'between' the institutions of society and its members. One of the main kinds of pressure on media organizations shown in Figure 11.2 is that for access by social and political interests. Much of the normative theory discussed in Chapter 7 turns in the end on the question of who in society should have access and on what terms.

Even in democratic societies, offering a high degree of freedom to their media, there are clear expectations, sometimes backed by considerable pressure, that mass media will make channels available for society-wide communication, especially 'downwards' from leaders or elites to the base of society. This may be achieved by legal provision, by purchase of time/space in a free market or by the media voluntarily serving as an open means of public communication. It matters a good deal to the media how 'access for society' is achieved, since freedom of the press is generally held to include the right not to publish and thus to withhold access. In practice, the operation of normal news values and the dependence of media on influential sources generally ensures that access is available to the social 'top' at least.

A continuum of media autonomy

The situation can be understood in terms of a continuum, at one extreme of which the media are totally 'penetrated' by, or assimilated to, outside interests, whether state or

not; at the other end, the media are totally in control and free to exclude or allow in as they will. Pluralistic theory presupposes that the diversity of organizations and possibilities for access will ensure an adequate mix of opportunity for 'official' voices of society and for critical and alternative views.

'Access for society' means more, however, than giving a platform for opinions, information, etc. It also relates to the *manner* in which media portray what passes for the reality of society. They may do this in ways that alter, distort or challenge it. In the end, the question of societal access involves a very complex set of conventions over the terms according to which media freedoms and societal claims can be exercised and reconciled. Much depends on the standardized characteristics of formats and genres and on the manner in which they are intended to portray social reality or are understood to do so by their audiences.

This question has been illuminated for the case of television production in one country (Britain) by Elliott (1972), but his ideas could be developed to apply to press media and to other national media systems. His typology (Figure 12.2) shows the variability of competence of the media organization over the giving or withholding of access to other would-be communicators. It portrays an inverse relationship between the degree of freedom of access available to society and the degree of extensiveness of control and action by media. The larger the scope of control by the media themselves (scope of production), the more limited the direct access by the society. There is a varying degree of intervention or mediation by the media as between the 'voice of society' or social reality on the one hand and the society as audience on the other. This

Scope of production	Production function	Directness of access by society	Type of access	Television example
Limited ↑	1 Technical facilitation	Total ↑	1 Direct	Party broadcast
	2 Facilitation and selection		2 Modified direct	Education
	3 Selection and presentation		3 Filtered	News
	4 Selection and compilation		4 Remade	Documentary
	5 Realization and creation	↓	5 Advisory	Realistic social drama
↓ Extensive	6 Imaginative creation	Zero	6 No control by society	Original television drama

FIGURE 12.2 A typology of production scope and directness of access by society (Elliott, 1972): access by society is inversely related to communicator (editorial) autonomy

formulation underlines the basic conflict between media autonomy and social control. Access is bound to be a site of struggle.

Actuality content as a contested zone

Figure 12.2 shows the variable degree to which social 'reality' is filtered by the media, with news and documentary falling at a midpoint on the scale. The scope for producers to select and shape is more or less balanced against the scope for society to claim direct access to the audience. Editorial freedom is also in balance with the scope for the audience to achieve a view of reality. Such 'actuality' material generally promises the audience a valid reflection of reality, but also retains the right of the media to set criteria of selection and presentation. Apart from its other merits, this typology reminds us that news, on which so much study of media selection has been concentrated, is only one of several kinds of message about reality that have to pass through the 'gates' of the media.

In practice, it is at the intermediate stages of the continuum (the sphere of actuality) where most potential for conflict arises and where media organizations have to defend their choices and priorities in relation to both society and public. This area extends beyond news and documentaries to encompass 'docu-dramas', historical dramas and many 'realistic' serials that portray police, medicine, the military, etc. It also covers what is now often referred to as 'infotainment' (Brants, 1998). The more sensitive and powerful the external representatives of these domains of reality happen to be, the more careful the media have to be and the more obliged they are to avoid sensitive areas or to employ irony, allegory, fantasy and other long-known devices for evading direct accountability. It is not only self-interested authority that has a restraining influence, but also the possibility of unintended and unwanted effects on reality itself (such as causing panic, crime, suicide or terrorism).

Since Elliott's construction of this typology, there have been significant developments in broadcasting that do not invalidate the principles, but introduce new possibilities and issues. The most important single innovation has been that of audience participation in radio and television shows (Munson, 1993; Livingstone and Lunt, 1994; Shen, 1999). The phenomenon occurred first by way of radio-call-in shows, usually in response to some expert, public figure or celebrity. There has since been an explosion of new formats and volume of output. The main variants of the new forms of 'reality television' are shown in Box 12.2.

The specific examples as well as the types are quite diverse and vary cross-culturally. In terms of the foregoing discussion of access, we can draw at least three conclusions. One is that there are novel forms of access for aspects of reality that were previously kept hidden, for instance the 'confessional' or sensational talk-show. Secondly, we can conclude that there is a 'third voice' to be heard alongside the media professionals and

the official or expert voices of society, and it is the voice of ordinary people. Thirdly, there is a large expansion of the intermediate types of access as shown in Figure 12.2. In this territory the line between reality and fiction is very blurred and meanings are much more filtered and negotiated.

THE INFLUENCE OF SOURCES ON NEWS

Media of all kinds depend on having a readily available supply of source material, whether this is book manuscripts to publish, scripts to film, or reports of events to fill newspapers and television. Relations with news sources are essential to news media and they often constitute a very active two-way process. The news media are always looking for suitable content, and content (not always suitable) is always looking for an outlet in the news.

News people also have their own preferred sources and are also linked to prominent figures by institutional means – press conferences, publicity agents, etc. Studies of news reporters (for example, Tuchman, 1978; Fishman, 1980) make clear that one thing which they do not share with their colleagues is their sources and contacts. Elliott's (1972) study of the making of a television documentary about racial prejudice showed the importance of the 'contact chain'. This refers to the use by researchers and producers of the knowledge of their own personal contacts to find source material. One result was that eventual content on screen was shaped by ideas and preconceptions held initially within the production team and by the personal contacts they happened to have. This small example of one common organizational practice supports the idea that the characteristics and personal values of media personnel may be influential after all. There is a difference, however, between news and documentary. In fact, as Tunstall (1993) shows, British television producers do often exercise their personal preferences, although the scope varies according to 'market' conditions.

Several news studies have demonstrated that the kind of source or authority cited to back up news stories does tend to influence the implicit direction of content even

when it is supposed to be neutral. The practice of validating news reports generally gives most weight to established authority and conventional wisdom. This is an almost inevitable form of bias in mainstream news media, but it can end up as a consistent ideological bias, concealed behind the mask of objectivity. In the study of US television news content by Reese (1994) referred to above (page 280) the three main types of 'source' interviewed or cited were either institutional spokespersons, 'experts' and other journalists. The main finding of the study was the very high degree of interrelation between the same limited set of sources, making it difficult for a plurality of viewpoints to emerge. Reese (1994: 85) writes, 'By relying on a common and often narrow network of sources . . . the news media contribute to [a] systematic convergence on the conventional wisdom, the largely unquestioned consensus views held by journalists, power-holders and many audience members'.

The Westley–MacLean model described above (page 53) shows communication organizations as brokers between would-be 'advocates' trying to convey their view of social reality and a public interested in reliable information about this reality. For their own purposes, news media establish regular contacts with informed insiders and experts, in order to secure timely, authoritative or otherwise inaccessible information, especially in advance of competitors. Correspondingly, regular contacts are initiated and maintained by would-be sources themselves, in order to secure favourable access. This applies especially to political actors, large firms, public institutions, show-business personalities, etc. One general result has been an inevitable degree of symbiosis between media and their sources.

Even this does not exhaust the possibilities, especially by leaving out of account the degree to which media serve as sources for each other in unchartable combinations and permutations. Any given medium tends to regard other media as the best initial guide to newsworthiness and celebrity status in making selections. Aside from the continuous feeding on each other by press and television, both as sources and as objects of information and comment, there are important relations of content provision from the film industry to television and from music to radio. This is one aspect of the '**intertextuality**' of media (see page 350). Research on mass communication has signalled a number of factors that result in an inevitable symbiosis between media and their sources, as follows.

The planning of supply

Ericson et al. (1987) even designate a special category of 'source media' whose main activity is to supply journalists with what they are looking for on behalf of source organizations of the kind mentioned. Source media consist of press conferences, press releases, public relations, etc. In addition, the media are continually collecting their

own material by direct observation, information-gathering and reporting on a day-to-day and event-guided basis. They also routinely use the services of information suppliers, especially national or international news agencies, news film agencies, television exchange arrangements, etc.

There are several aspects to note. First, there is the matter of the high degree of *planning* and predictability that goes with any large-scale continuous media production operation. The media have to have an assured supply for their own needs and thus have to 'order' content in advance, whether of news, fiction or other entertainment. This need is reflected in the growth of secondary organizations (such as news agencies) which provide content regularly. It also implies some inconsistency with the notion of media as neutral carriers or mirrors of the ongoing culture and news of the society. It conflicts with the ideals of novelty, spontaneity and creativity that are often part of the media self-image. If supply has to be planned well in advance according to advance specifications, the reality is very far from this ideal.

Secondly, there is the question of *imbalance* between information suppliers and media takers of information or other content. Some sources are more powerful than others or have more bargaining power because of their status, market dominance or intrinsic market value. Gandy (1982) has referred to the 'information subsidies' that are given selectively by powerful interest groups in order to advance their causes. This situation is reflected, for instance, in the privileged access of the more politically and economically powerful and the favoured position of richer media and media systems in the world. Media organizations are far from equal in their degree of access to sources that can further enhance their position.

According to Gans (1979), the sources who are most successful in gaining access to (elite) news media are likely to be powerful, well resourced and well organized for supplying journalists with the kind of 'news' they want at the right moment in time. Such sources are both 'authoritative' and 'efficient' and they often enjoy 'habitual access' to the news media, in the sense meant by Molotch and Lester (1974). There is a potential limit to the independence and diversity of news media posed by the difficulty they have in turning away such source material.

Thirdly, there is the question of *assimilation* that arises when there exists a mutual interest on the part of the media and would-be external communicators (advocates or sources). There are obvious examples when political leaders want to reach large publics, but less obvious collusion arises in routine news coverage where reporters depend on sources likely to have both inside information and an interest in the way it is published. This applies to sources such as politicians, officials and the police.

Assimilation can be said to occur if the degree of collaboration which exists for mutual benefit between reporter and source reaches a point where it conflicts with the 'distributive' role normally expected from those who claim to inform the public (Gieber and Johnson, 1961). Although this type of relationship may be justified by its success in meeting the needs of the public as well as those of the media organization, it also conflicts with expectations of critical independence and professional norms. It can lend itself to the suppression or manipulation of information

in the interest of certain actors or institutions (Murphy, 1976; Chibnall, 1977; Fishman, 1980).

Public relations and news management

Molotch and Lester (1974) showed how news could be controlled by those in a position to manage publicity about events, if not the events themselves (see page 283). They call these 'event promoters' and argue that with reference to 'routine events' the event promoters have several opportunities for gaining access on their own terms. They can claim habitual access to the 'news assemblers' (that is, journalists), or they can use their power to disrupt the routine access of others and create 'pseudo-events' of their own which gain media attention. There is often a more or less institutionalized collusive relationship between politicians or officials and press which may serve a range of purposes without necessarily being manipulative in its effect (Whale, 1969; Tunstall, 1970; Sigal, 1973). This is especially evident in election campaigns, which lend themselves to the staging of 'pseudo-events' ranging from press conferences to major policy statements or demonstrations (Swanson and Mancini, 1996). In some spheres assimilation between news media and sources is virtually complete. Politics, government and law enforcement are three prime examples, but major sports provides another, and big business is not far behind in being able to claim uncritical media attention more or less at will and in having a good deal of control over the content and flow of information.

Assimilation in the sense used above is also promoted by the activities of professional public relations agencies. There is considerable evidence to suggest that well-organized suppliers of information can be effective and that a good deal of what is supplied by public relations agencies to the news media does get used (Turow, 1989; Shoemaker and Reese, 1991; Glenn et al., 1997). A study by Baerns (1987), for instance, found that political reporting in one German *Land* was predominantly based on official press releases and news conferences. This is probably not exceptional, but it reflects the fact that journalists tend differentially to rely on official or bureaucratic sources for certain kinds of news (see Fishman, 1980), and the same pattern would not apply to all kinds of news. Journalists would normally be suspicious of self-serving public relations handouts. In the end, however, it does seem that rather little of the news we receive is the outcome of enterprise and investigation on the part of journalists (Sigal, 1973), though it may still be both reliable and relevant.

If anything, the process of attempting to influence news has accelerated in line with modern techniques of campaigning and opinion measurement (Swanson and Mancini, 1996). Political parties, government agencies and all major institutions employ news managers and 'spin doctors' whose task is to maximize the favourable presentation of policy and action and minimize any negative aspect. The overriding goal is to have either a positive or an unconcerned public opinion, while truth and even 'reality' take

second place. It is hard to say if the media are actually more influenced than in the past, but it has probably become harder for the media to make any independent assessment of their own of the value of information provided to them in such volume. As a result, the responsibility for truth is left to the source, more often than not.

It is not only in political campaigns that news management plays an increasing role. Manheim (1998) has drawn attention to what he calls a 'third force in news making' – the practice of 'strategic communication'. The earlier two forces were those of the actors in the political environment and the real observable actions and events. Strategic communication is carried out by paid experts on behalf of well-resourced institutions, lobbies and interests. Strategic communicators use all forms of intelligence gathering and techniques of influence as well as mass media and they are often operating outside the sphere of publicity. They may include governmental and political agencies, but also major corporations, well-funded parties to law-suits, labour unions and foreign governments. Not insignificantly, they try to influence foreign policy.

Box 12.3   Source access to news

Source access depends on:

- Efficient supply of suitable material
- Power and influence of source
- Good public relations
- Dependency of media on limited source
- Mutual self-interest in news coverage

MEDIA-ORGANIZATIONAL ACTIVITY: PROCESSING AND PRESENTATION

The processing of the 'raw material' of news, which usually consists of data about a supposed reality, begins at the first moment of selection. It can be considered in terms of a series of decisions and choices directed towards the achievement of a product that fits the goals of the organization. As we have seen, many media have mixed goals, so this process is a very complex one, involving a good deal of bargaining and substitution of one goal for another. The general aim, nevertheless, is to produce something which meets professional or craft standards of quality and has a good chance of success with the audience. The organizational processes involved are typically very hierarchical rather than democratic or collegial, although *within* particular production units the latter may apply.

Most accounts of the structure of formal media organizations, especially relating to news (for example, Tunstall, 1971, 1993; Hetherington, 1985; Ericson et al., 1987, Shoemaker and Reese, 1991), report a fairly similar hierarchical form of control. In

large commercial media corporations, the board of directors, representing share-holders, has initial and final power, while executive management is subdivided according to different operations. Shoemaker and Reese (1991), for instance, show an organizational chart for the *Wall Street Journal*, headed by the board of the controlling company (Dow Jones Inc.). Top management supervises the work of two levels of editorships, classified by a topic (such as foreign, investment, media and enter-tainment, and law) or by function (such as page-one editor, spot news desk editor and enterprise editor). These different editorial desks are served by reporters. Such formal charts primarily reflect and serve the need to allocate and control the use of resources and plan the division of labour.

Internal processing of information

It takes a different kind of chart to see how the media product is actually processed. Ericson et al. (1987) have shown how news organizations arrange the sequence of inputs and decisions. There are two main lines of activity, which start with 'ideas' for news (originating in other media, routine observations, agencies, etc.). Ideas lead to one line – that of story development, and ideas are also fed by a second 'sources' line. Sources can be reactive (routine) or proactive (enterprise). The two lines are closely connected since particular stories lead to the development of and search for sources. The two lines correspond more or less to the two stages of the 'double action' model of news flow described by Bass (1969) – essentially news gathering and news pro-cessing. The processing line follows from story assignments made by the assignment editor and goes through a sequence of news conference, play decisions (prominence and timing), layout or line-up, final news editing, content page make-up or television anchor script, and final line-up. This sequence can be fed up to the penultimate stage by source input. A schematic version of this is given in Figure 12.3.

In general, the sequence extends from a phase where a universe of substantive ideas is considered, through a narrowing down, according to news judgements and to what is fed from the source channel, to a third phase, where format, design and presentation decisions are taken. In the final phase, technical decisions are likely to be paramount.

This model for news processing is compatible with what seems to occur in other situations, where reality content is also processed, although over a longer time scale and with more scope for production to influence content (see Figure 12.2, page 285). For instance, Elliott (1972), in his study of the making of a television documentary series, distinguishes three 'chains':

- a *subject* chain concerned with assembling programme ideas for the series;
- a *contact* chain connecting producer, director and researcher with their contacts and sources;

- and a *presentation* chain in which realities of time-slot and budget were related to customary ideas for effective presentation.

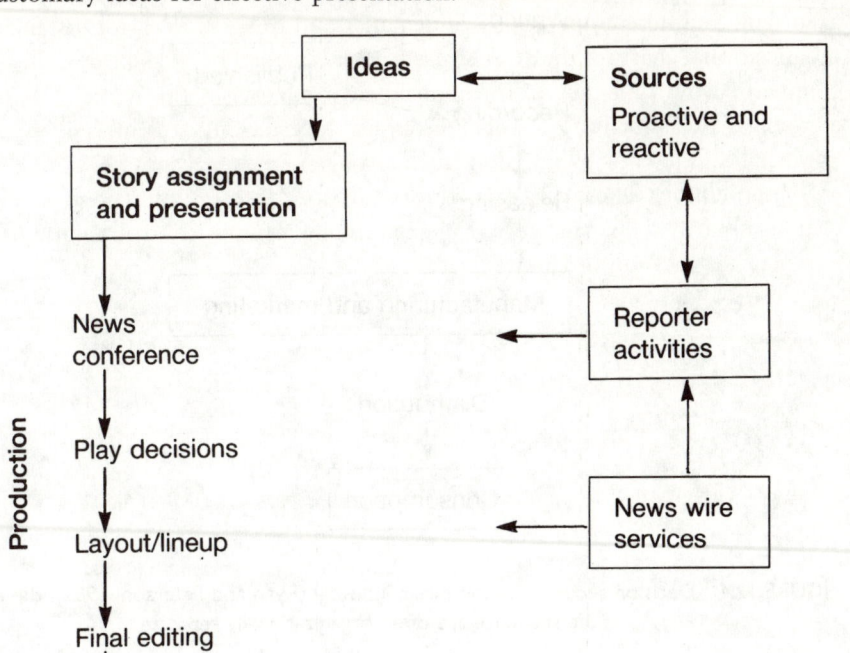

FIGURE 12.3   Intra-organizational processing, from ideas to the news (based on Ericson et al., 1987): news as published has internal as well as external origins, and both types are processed jointly

The latter included having plenty of illustrative film and having a well-known television personality to act as presenter. The first two correspond to the 'Ideas' and the 'Sources' routes in Figure 12.3, while presentation matters arise at the later stages of the 'production line'.

An alternative model of organizational selection

These examples apply to cases where media processing takes place within the boundaries of the same organization. The music industry offers a different model, although there is still a sequence from ideas to transmission. Ryan and Peterson (1982) have drawn a model of the 'decision chain' in the popular music industry, which

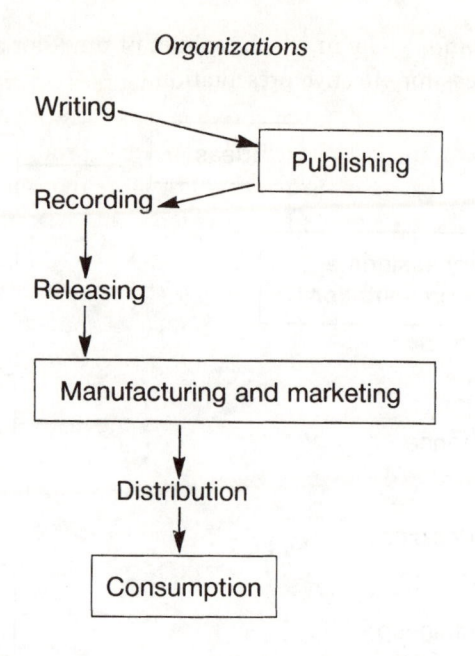

FIGURE 12.4   Decision sequence in the music industry (Ryan and Peterson, 1982): the elements in the sequence are often organizationally separate

consists of six separate links. These are: (1) from song writing to publishing; (2) from demo tape to recording (where producer and artist are selected); (3) and (4) from recording to manufacturing and marketing; (5) and (6) from there to consumption via radio, juke-box, live performance or direct sales (see Figure 12.4). In this case, the original ideas of song-writers are filtered through music publishers' ideas concerning presentation (especially artist and style), which then play a part in promoting the product in several different markets. Different from the previous examples is the linkage between several organizationally separate agencies and tasks. Processing takes place on the basis of a prediction about what the next 'gatekeeper' in the chain will think, the key being the overall 'product image'.

Bias as a result of internal processing

When content is subjected to organizational routines there is often an accentuation of the characteristics of any initial selection bias. This seems to happen not only to news but to other kinds of content as well, since a high proportion of content acquired or started as projects never reaches distribution (this is especially true of the film industry, which is profligate with creative talent). This accentuation can mainly be accounted for by the wish to maximize output according to a tried and trusted product image. Some media products live on for years and are resold, remade or recycled indefinitely.

Media organizations tend to reproduce selectively according to criteria that suit their own goals and interests. These may sometimes be professional and craft criteria, but more weight is usually given to what sells most or gets highest ratings. Among commercially relevant criteria, cheap and easy production according to a proven formula of success carries most weight. The more that the same criteria are applied at successive stages of decision-making, the more pre-existing biases of form and content are likely to endure while variety, uniqueness and unpredictability will take second place. Bias in this sense may mean no more than favouring products which are both easy to reproduce and popular with audiences, but it also differentially reinforces certain elements of the media culture and increases conformity with organizational policy.

The tendency of media to look to other media for content and format ideas, for evidence of success and for validation of celebrity also has a reinforcing effect on existing values. There is a spiralling and self-fulfilling effect that tends to work against experimentation and innovation, despite the necessity for innovation at some point.

Standardization and organizational logics

Although mass communication is a form of mass production, the standardization implied in this term relates in the first instance to multiple reproduction and distribution. The individual items of media content do not have to share all the characteristics of mass-produced products. They can easily be original, unique and highly differentiated (for instance, the one-off performance of a sports event, a television talk-show or a news programme, which will never be repeated identically). In practice, however, the technology and organization of mass media production are not neutral and do exert a standardizing influence. Initial diverse and unique content items or ideas are fitted to forms that are both familiar to media producers and thought to be familiar to audiences. These forms are those most suitable for efficient production according to specifications laid down by the organization.

These specifications are of an *economic*, a *technological* and a *cultural* kind and each entails a certain logic of its own, which leaves a distinctive mark on the cultural product through its influence on production decisions. Pressures for *economic* efficiency stem from the need to minimize cost, reduce conflict and ensure continuity and sufficiency of supply. Cost reduction exerts pressure according to different time schemes – in the long run it may lead to the introduction of new technology, in the short run to maximizing output from existing staff resources and equipment and avoiding expensive or loss-making activities. The main pressures on media processors – to save time, use technology efficiently, save money and meet deadlines – are so interrelated that it is easier to see them in their combined consequences than in their separate operation. McManus (1994) in his study of local television news showed that

the lower the budget and smaller the staff, the greater the proportion of news that was 'discovered' in a 'passive' rather than 'active' way (meaning reliance on other media, agency and public relations material, lack of initiative or investigation).

The *technological* logic is quite obvious in its effects, which keep changing as a succession of major new inventions has affected different media industries. There is an almost irresistible pressure sooner or later to adopt the latest innovations. Film was changed by the coming of sound and colour; the newspaper industry by continuous advances in printing and information transmission; and television by the portable video camera, satellites and now digitalization.

The pressure of technology is experienced mainly as a result of inventions which set higher technical standards for lower prices and which progressive media organizations have to keep up with (whether audiences know or care or not) in order to compete. The investment in technical facilities leads to pressure for their maximum use, and prestige as well as utility becomes a factor. New technology often means more speed, flexibility and capacity, but it establishes norms that put pressure on all media organizations to conform and eventually influences audience expectations about what is most professional or acceptable.

THE LOGIC OF MEDIA CULTURE

The processing of media raw material requires a form of cultural standardization. It has already been suggested that media are constrained by their 'definitions' and associated expectations as to what they are 'good for' in general and what sort of content they can best offer and in what form. Within the media, the main types of content – news, sports, drama, entertainment, advertising – also follow standard-ized formats which are rooted in traditions (media-made or culturally inherited), ways of work, ideas about audience taste and interest, and pressures of time or space. Altheide and Snow (1979) were the first to use the term **'media logic'** to capture the systematic nature of pre-existing definitions of what a given type of content should be like.

The concept has been especially useful for identifying the predilection of media producers for factors that they believe will increase audience attention and satisfac-tion. In relation to informational content, media logic places a premium on immediacy, such as dramatic illustrative film or photos, on fast tempo and short 'sound bites' (Hallin, 1992), and on personally attractive presenters and relaxed formats (such as the so-called 'happy news' format). Media logic also operates on the level of content – for instance, in political campaigns it leads to a preference for personalization, for controversiality and for attention to the 'horse race' (for example, as measured by opinion polls) rather than the issues (Graber, 1976b; Hallin and Mancini, 1984; Mazzoleni, 1987b). The 'bias' of media logic is predictable and systematic, embedded

in media-organizational working arrangements and forward planning. Hallin (1992) demonstrated that there was a clear correlation in US news coverage of elections between 'horse-race coverage' and *soundbite news* – the more of the former, the shorter the latter.

Altheide (1985: 14) advanced the concept of 'media format' to refer to 'the internal organization or logic of any shared symbolic activity'. The idea is of a *dominant form*, to which mass communicators are more or less constrained to conform. Formats refer not only to broad categories of content but also to unit ideas and representations of reality – akin to stereotypes. They are useful not only to producers but also to audiences, who learn to differentiate within the mosaic of what is offered according to formats which they have learned. According to Altheide (1985), formats are not only a key to understanding much media production but also relevant to questions of effect on society, since they shape the perception of reality acquired from media.

ALTERNATIVE MODELS OF DECISION-MAKING

In a review of the mechanisms according to which culture is produced in the commercial–industrial world of mass media, Ryan and Peterson (1982) describe five main frameworks for explaining how decisions are made in the media arts. Their first model is that of the *assembly line*, which compares the media production process to the factory, with all skills and decisions built into the machinery and with clear procedural rules. Because media-cultural products, unlike material goods, have to be marginally different from each other, the answer is overproduction at each stage.

The second model is that of *craft and entrepreneurship*, in which powerful figures, with established reputations for judging talent, raising finance and putting things together, manage all the creative inputs of artists, musicians, engineers, etc., in innovative ways. This model applies especially to the film business but could also hold for publications in which editors may play the role of personally charismatic and powerful figures with a supposed flair for picking winners.

The third model is that of *convention and formula*, in which members of a relevant 'art world' agree on a 'recipe', a set of widely held principles which tell workers how to combine elements to produce works in the particular genre. Fourthly, there is the model of *audience image and conflict*, which sees the creative production process as a matter of fitting production to an image of what the audience will like. Here decisions about the latter are central, and powerful competing entrepreneurs come into conflict over them.

The final model is that of the *product image*. Its essence is summarized as follows:

> Having a product image is to shape a piece of work so that it is most likely to be accepted by decision makers at the next link in the chain. The most common way of doing this is to

produce works that are much like the products that have most recently passed through all the links in the decision chain to become successful. (Ryan and Peterson, 1982: 25)

This model does not assume there to be a consensus among all involved, or an entrepreneur, or an agreed audience image. It is a model which seems closest to the notion of 'professionalism', defined as the special knowledge of what is a good piece of media work, in contrast to the prediction of what will succeed commercially.

Most studies of media production seem to confirm the strong feeling held by established professionals that they know how best to combine all the available factors of production within the inevitable constraints. This may be achieved at the cost of not actually communicating with the audience, but it does secure the integrity of the product.

Box 12.4   Five models of media decision-making

- The assembly line
- Craft and entrepreneurship
- Convention and formula
- Audience image
- Product image

Ryan and Peterson's typology is especially useful in stressing the *diversity* of frameworks within which a degree of regularity and predictability can be achieved in the production of cultural goods (including news). There are different ways of handling uncertainty, responding to outside pressures and reconciling the need for continuous production with artistic originality or journalistic freedom. The concepts of manufacturing or routine bureaucracy, often invoked to apply to media production, should be used with caution.

THE ATTENTION-GAINING IMPERATIVE

We need to recall the dominant influence of the 'publicity' model, compared with the 'transmission' or 'ritual' models of communication (as described in Chapter 3). The transmission model captures one image of the media organization – as a system for efficiently turning events into comprehensible information, or ideas into familiar cultural packages. The ritual model implies a private world in which routines are followed largely for the benefit of the participants and their clients. Both capture some element of the reality (which is itself very heterogeneous). The publicity model helps to remind us that mass communication is often primarily a business, and show business at that. Its roots are as much in the theatre and the showground as in politics, art or education. Appearance, artifice and surprise (the fundamentals of 'media logic') often

count for more than substance, reality, truth or relevance. At the core of many media organizations, there are contrary tendencies that are often in tension, if not at open war, with each other, making illusory the search for any comprehensive theory of their work.

FURTHER READING

Elliott, P. (1972) *The Making of a Television Series*. London: Constable.
Fishman, M. (1980) *Manufacturing News*. Austin, TX: University of Texas Press.
Gans, H.J. (1979) *Deciding What's News*. New York: Vintage Books.
Tuchman, G. (1978) *Making News: a Study in the Construction of Reality*. New York: Free Press.

CONTENT

media content: issues, concepts and methods of analysis

The most accessible evidence of how mass communication works is provided by the vast body of 'messages' and 'meanings' which are continuously being transmitted and received from all kinds of different media. In a very literal sense we can equate the media with the message, although it would be extremely misleading to do so. In this respect, the distinction between message and meaning is a significant one. The physical text of the message in print, sound or pictorial image is what we can directly observe and is in a sense 'fixed'. But we cannot simply 'read off' the meanings that are somehow 'embedded' in the texts or transmitted to audiences. These meanings are not self-evident and certainly not fixed. They are also very diverse and often ambiguous.

Theory and research concerning mass media content are fissured by this distinction between message and meaning, which largely parallels the choice between a 'transport' and a 'ritual' (or cultural) model of communication (see pages 53–4). This remark exposes the difficulty in speaking about content at all. Even so, we often encounter generalizations about the content of mass media as a whole, or a particular type of content, especially with reference to matters of media intention, 'bias', or probable effect. The tendency to generalize about these matters has been encouraged by the patterned and standardized forms which media content often takes.

The reasons for studying media content in a systematic way stemmed initially either from an interest in the potential effects of mass communication, whether intended or unintended, or from a wish to understand the appeal of content for the audience. Both perspectives have a practical basis, from the point of view of mass communicators, but they have gradually been widened and supplemented to embrace a larger range of theoretical issues. Early studies of content reflected concern about the portrayal of crime, violence and sex in popular entertainment, the use of media as propaganda and the performance of media in respect of racial or other kinds of prejudice. The range of purposes was gradually extended to cover news, information and much entertainment content.

Most early research was based on the assumption that content reflected the purposes and values of its originators, more or less directly, that 'meaning' could be discovered or inferred from messages, and that receivers would understand messages more or less as intended by producers. It was even thought that 'effects' could be discovered from the seeming 'message' built into content. More broadly, the content of mass media has often been regarded as more or less reliable evidence about the culture and society in which it is produced. All of these assumptions, except perhaps the last, have been called into question, and the study of content has become correspondingly complex and challenging. It may not go too far to say that the most interesting aspects of media content are not the overt messages, but the many more or less concealed and uncertain meanings that are present in media texts.

Despite these various complications it is useful at this point to review the main motives that have guided the study of media content. These help to structure the field of inquiry and account for the development of certain kinds of method and theory.

- *Describing and comparing media output.* For many purposes of analysis of mass communication (for instance, assessing change or criticizing performance), we need to be able to characterize the content of particular media and channels. This means having reliable and meaningful categories of content that are not simply those provided by the media themselves.
- *Comparing media with 'social reality'.* A recurrent issue in media research has been the relation between media messages and 'reality'. There are several alternative ways in which this relationship can be interpreted (as noted below, pages 323–4), but most basic is the question of whether media content does, or should, reflect the social reality, and if so, which or whose reality? The issue is complicated not only by the uncertainty over what constitutes meaning (both of messages and of 'reality') but also by the great range of types of content, with their widely varying 'reality claims' (see pages 284–6).
- *Media content as reflection of social and cultural values and beliefs.* Historians, anthropologists and sociologists have referred to the content of media as evidence of values and beliefs of a particular time and place or social group, on the assumption that it generally responds to the prevailing hopes, fears or beliefs of the people and reflects common values. Media content has been considered as a 'cultural' indicator, in more or less the same way as have social and economic indicators in describing conditions.
- *Functions and effects of media.* Although perspectives have varied considerably, from a Marxist to a positive-functionalist view, there is still a widespread view that media do have effects and a tendency to interpret content in terms of its probable consequences, whether good or bad, intended or unintended. Attention is directed both at overt intentions of media and at unintended bias and hidden ideology. Although content on its own cannot be taken as evidence of effect, it is difficult to study effects without intelligent reference to content (as cause). This means having relevant theoretical formulations as well as descriptions.
- *Evaluating media performance.* Krippendorf (1980) uses the term 'performance analysis' to refer to research designed to find answers about the *quality* of the media as judged by certain criteria. In Chapter 8, we can find a number of more or less objectifiable indicators for judging media in terms of such principles as diversity, independence, objectivity, fairness, cultural quality.
- *Assessing organizational bias.* As we have seen in the preceding chapters, there are reasons for believing that the social composition of media professions and the manner of media production can have systematic biasing effects on content. Examples include: the representation of women in media work and in output; the

media content: issues, concepts and methods of analysis

dependence on official news sources and the conformity of content to established power.

- *Audience analysis*. Since audiences are always defined at least in part by media content, we cannot study audiences without studying content. This means having methods for classifying audience output in ways relevant to audiences' perceptions and selections and also for coping with the interpretation (attributed meanings) of content by audiences. The relationship between texts and readers is a large and complex topic in itself.
- *Questions of genre, textual and discourse analysis, narrative and other formats*. In this context, the text itself is the object of study, with a view to understanding how it 'works' to produce effects desired by authors and readers. The topic embraces the question of the language, grammar and syntax of film (Monaco, 1981) and of video. Structural and semiological analysis of more or less hidden meanings plays a key part.

In taking some of these issues further, we begin with a short explanation of the main relevant perspectives on content and continue with a review of methodological issues. There is no coherent theory of media content and no consensus on the best method of analysis, since alternative methods are needed for different purposes and for different kinds of content and different media **genres**. The concept of genre is an essential tool in the study of media content, since it provides an organizing framework to cope with the enormous volume of what the media offer and a path to understanding how meaning may be constructed out of the experience of reading, listening and viewing. At times we use the term **discourse** for convenience rather than in a technical sense. Fiske (1987: 14), for instance, describes discourse as 'a language or system of representation that has developed socially in order to make and circulate a coherent set of meanings about a topic area'. In this chapter, after looking at semiological approaches, we deal with discourse around *information science* and *performance analysis*. The main purpose is to illustrate and introduce the main themes and to define key concepts.

CRITICAL PERSPECTIVES ON CONTENT

While performance assessment as described above involves taking a critical view of the media, what is at issue here is not just criticism of the media for failing in their (often self-chosen) tasks but fundamental criticism of the established media. There are several sources of criticism, but the most significant relate to social class, gender and ethnicity. Also relevant is the perspective from, or on behalf of, the Third World, with reference to established Western media. Each of these critical perspectives has been well represented in the media theory and research literature.

The main critical tradition has been based on Marxist theory of ideology which relates mainly to class inequality but can also deal with some other issues. Grossberg (1991) has pointed to several variations of Marxist cultural interpretation, that deal with the 'politics of textuality'. He identifies three 'classical' Marxist approaches, of which the most relevant derive from the Frankfurt School and ideas concerning 'false consciousness'. The original Marxist critique presumed that an image of the world favourable to the ruling class or the capitalist system would be embedded in media texts and be more or less taken over uncritically by their subordinated audiences. As a result audiences would fail to develop the will to resist. Two later approaches distinguished by Grossberg are 'hermeneutic' (interpretative) and 'discursive' in character, and again there are several variants. Compared with classical approaches, however, the main differences are, first, that 'decoding' is recognized as problematic and, secondly, that texts are seen as not just 'mediating' reality but actually constructing experience and acquiring identity.

The Marxist tradition has probably paid most attention to news and actuality, because of its direct ideological significance in defining the social world and the world of events. Drawing on various sources, including Barthes and Althusser, Stuart Hall (1977) argued that the practice of signification through language establishes maps of cultural meaning which promote the dominance of a ruling-class ideology, especially by establishing a hegemony. This involves containing subordinate classes within superstructures of meaning which frame all competing definitions of reality within the range of a single hegemonic view of things.

News contributes to this task in several ways. One is by 'masking' aspects of reality – especially by ignoring the exploitative nature of class society or by taking it for granted as 'natural'. Secondly, news produces a 'fragmentation' of interests, which undermines the solidarity of subordinate classes. Thirdly, news imposes an 'imaginary unity or coherence' – for instance, by invoking concepts of community, nation, public opinion and consensus. There is a good deal of news analysis (for example, Glasgow Media Group, 1976, 1980, 1985) which lends support to this critical interpretation of how (and why) news is the way it is. A good deal of critical content analysis interprets evidence of deviations of representation from reality in terms of ideology and manipulation by dominant social classes.

Critique of advertising and commercialism

There is a long tradition of critical attention to advertising that sometimes adopts the Marxist approach as described, but also derives from other cultural or humanistic

values. Williamson (1978) in her study of advertising applies the familiar concept of 'ideology', which is defined (by Althusser, 1971) as representing 'the imaginary relationship of individuals to their real conditions of existence'. Althusser also says that 'All ideology has the function (which defines it) of "constituting" individuals as subjects'. For Williamson, the ideological work of advertising is accomplished (with the active co-operation of the 'reader' of the advertisement) by transferring significant meanings and ideas (sometimes myths) from experience (such as beauty, success, happiness, nature and science) to commercial products and by that route to ourselves.

The commercial product becomes a way to achieve the social or cultural state and to be the kind of person we would like to be. We are 'reconstituted' by advertising but end up with an imaginary (and thus false) sense of our real selves and of our relation to the real conditions of our life. This has the same ideological tendency as that attributed to news in critical theory – masking real exploitation and fragmenting solidarity. A very similar process is described by Williamson (1978) in terms of 'commodification', referring to the way advertising converts the 'use value' of products into an 'exchange value', allowing us (in our aspiration) to acquire (buy) happiness or other ideal states.

The ideological work of advertising is essentially achieved by constituting our environment for us and telling us who we are and what we really want (see Mills, 1951). In the critical perspective, all this is illusory and diversionary. What the effect of advertising might actually be is beyond the scope of any analysis of content, but it is possible to work back from content to intention, and the critical terminology of 'manipulation' and 'exploitation' is easier to justify than is the case with ideology in news. In general, 'commodification' in relation to culture implies that something is taken away from people by the commercial 'consciousness industry' and then sold back to them. It is one expression of the process of 'alienation' whereby we lose touch with our own nature (and culture).

On the question of cultural quality

The original members of the Frankfurt School viewed most forms of mass culture (see page 95) as both alienating and exploitative – encouraging false consciousness and concealing the reality of social division. At the same time it kept the working class, when not working, in a soporific state of escapism: the new 'opium of the people' to replace religion. This critique of mass culture largely replaced the original more elitist or moralistic critique of industrialized popular culture. However, it also seems now to be both out of fashion and fundamentally flawed. There are several reasons for this, apart from the ultimate impossibility of proving the intrinsic superiority of any particular taste preferences (see above, page 102) or demonstrating the harm caused by mass culture.

There have been a number of attempts to assess the quality of television in particular in recent years and in different countries. The reasons lie primarily in a response to the expansion and privatization of media. Perhaps the most notable example is the Quality Assessment of Broadcasting project of the Japanese public broadcaster, NHK (Ishikawa, 1996). Notable in this project is the attempt to evaluate quality of output from different perspectives, namely that of 'society', of the professional broadcasters and of the audience. Most relevant here and most problematic is the assessment made by programme makers themselves. We find a number of criteria being applied. These relate especially to: degree and type of craft skill; resources and production values; originality; relevance and cultural authenticity; values expressed; integrity of purpose; audience appeal. There are other criteria and other ways of assessing quality, because the range of content is so wide.

It has been suggested (by Schrøder, 1992) that there are essentially three kinds of cultural standards to be applied: the aesthetic (there are many dimensions), the ethical (questions of values, integrity, intended meaning, etc.) and the 'ecstatic' (measured by popularity, pleasure and performative value, essentially aspects of consumption). In brief, one can say that developments of cultural theory have significantly extended the scope of critical cultural study, even for those who remain convinced of the existence of more or less universal and absolute standards of quality.

Mass media and violence

In terms of sheer volume of words written and salience in the public mind, the foremost critical perspective on mass media would probably belong under this heading. From the earliest days of true mass media, they were attacked for their potential contribution to crime, violence and aggression, and in the absence of much evidence of any causal connection critics focused on the *content* of popular media. It has always been much easier to demonstrate that media portrayed violence and aggression in news and fiction to a degree quite disproportionate to real life experience than to show any effects. Many studies have produced seemingly shocking statistics of average exposure to mediated violence. The argument of critics has been not just that it might cause violence and crime, especially by the young, but that it is often intrinsically undesirable, producing emotional disturbance, fear, anxiety and deviant tastes.

Accepting that thrills and action are a staple part of popular entertainment that cannot simply be banned (although some degree of censorship has been widely legitimated in this matter), content research has often been devoted to understanding the more or less harmful ways in which violence can be depicted. This has led to attention to the context of occurrence and the different ways in which violence may be rewarded, punished or legitimated in plots. Associated value systems and styles and genres of 'violent' content are also at issue. Non-physical violence embedded in plots and dramatic situations has also been examined.

At a more recent point in time (since the 1970s) the scope of criticism has been widened to include not only the questions of socialization of children, but also the issue of violent aggression directed at women. This occurs frequently in non-pornographic content. The causes of vocal concern lie both in the development of feminist thinking and a probable real increase in the public display of this kind of content. Here the issue is not only the possibility of stimulating violence against women but also the symbolic degradation of and offence to women by the very fact of publication.

Gender-based critique

There are several other varieties of critical *feminist* perspective on media content (Rakow, 1986; van Zoonen, 1994). Initially these were mainly concerned with the stereotyping, neglect and marginalization of women that was common in the 1970s (see, for example, Tuchman et al., 1978). As Rakow points out, media content can never be a true account of reality, and it is less important to change media representations (such as having more female characters) than to challenge the underlying sexist ideology of much media content. An example of a new basis for critique (Long, 1991) is the very fact that theory and research have tended to 'over-valorize' the public sphere as distinct from the private or domestic sphere. This shows up, for instance, in differential attention (given by researchers) to politics, war, business and sports, in which men are more likely than women to be active and prominent (Brown, 1990). Forms of media content which are most popular with women have been relatively neglected (gendered texts are also rank-ordered texts). Such media forms as romances (Radway, 1984), magazines (Hermes, 1995) and soap operas (Hobson, 1982) have had to be rescued from obscurity and assumed irrelevance (Modleski, 1982).

Most central to critical feminist analysis is probably the broad question (going beyond stereotypes) of how texts 'position' the female subject in narratives and textual interactions and in so doing contribute to a definition of femininity in collaboration with the 'reader'. Essentially the same applies to masculinity, and both fall under the heading of 'gender construction'. For the feminist critique, two issues necessarily arise. First, the extent to which 'commercial' media texts intended for the entertainment of women (like soap operas or romances) can ever be liberating when they embody the realities of patriarchal society and family institutions (Radway, 1984; Ang, 1985). Secondly, the degree to which new kinds of mass media texts which challenge gender stereotyping and try to introduce positive role models can have any 'empowering' effect for women (while remaining within the dominant commercial media system).

Ultimately the answers to these questions depend on how the texts are received by their audiences. Radway's (1984) study of romantic fiction argued that there is some

clement of liberation, if not empowerment, through what is essentially a woman's (own) genre, but she also acknowledged the patriarchal ideology of the form:

> the romance also provides a symbolic portrait of the womanly sensibility that is created and required by patriarchal marriage and its sexual division of labour. . . . [It] underscores and shores up the very psychological structure that guarantees women's commitment to marriage and motherhood. (1984: 149)

A variety of literary, discourse and psychoanalytic methods have been used in the critical feminist study of content. There seems to be no dominant theory or method, rather a unity of research concerns and a methodological eclecticism, placing a strong emphasis on interpretation rather than quantification. In general, also, the 'false consciousness' model, implying a more or less automatic 'transfer' of gender positioning, has been discarded, and even content study has to look back to encoding and forward to alternative possibilities for 'decoding'.

STRUCTURALISM AND SEMIOLOGY

One influential way of thinking about media content has origins in the general study of language. Basically, *structuralism* refers to the way meaning is constructed in texts, the term applying to certain 'structures of language', consisting of signs, narrative or myths. In general, languages have been said to work because of in-built structures. The term 'structure' implies a constant and ordered relation of elements, although this may not be apparent on the surface and requires decoding. In general, it has been assumed that such structures are located in and governed by particular cultures – much wider systems of meaning, reference and signification. **Semiology** is a more specific version of the general structuralist approach. There are several classic explications of the structuralist or semiological approach to media content (for example, Barthes, 1967, 1977; Eco, 1977) and now several useful introductions and commentaries (such as Burgelin, 1972; Hawkes, 1977; Fiske, 1982).

Structuralism is a development of the linguistics of de Saussure (1915) and combines with it some principles from structural anthropology. It differs from linguistics in two main ways. First, it is concerned not only with conventional verbal languages but also with any sign-system that has language-like properties Secondly, it directs attention less to the sign-system itself than to chosen texts and the meaning of texts in the light of the 'host' culture. It is thus concerned with the elucidation of cultural as well as linguistic meaning, an activity for which a knowledge of the sign-system is instrumental but insufficient on its own.

North American (C.S. Peirce, 1931–35) and British (C.K. Ogden and I.A. Richards, 1923) scholars subsequently worked towards the goal of establishing a 'general science of signs' (semiology or semiotics). This field was to encompass structuralism and other things besides, thus all things to do with *signification* (the giving of meaning by means of language), however loosely structured, diverse and fragmentary. The concepts of 'sign-system' and 'signification' common to linguistics, structuralism and semiology derive mainly from de Saussure. The same basic concepts were used in somewhat different ways by the three theorists mentioned, but the following are the essentials.

A *sign* is the basic physical vehicle of meaning in a language – any 'sound-image' that we can hear or see and which usually *refers* to some object or aspect of reality, about which we wish to communicate, which is known as the *referent*. In human communication, we use signs to convey meanings about objects in the world of experience to others, who interpret the signs we use, on the basis of sharing the same language or knowledge of the sign-system we are using (for instance, non-verbal communication). According to de Saussure, the process of signification is accomplished by two elements of the sign. He called the physical element (word, image, sound) the *signifier* and used the term *signified* to refer to the mental concept invoked by a physical sign in a given language code (Figure 13.1).

Normally in (western) language systems, the connection between a physical signifier (such as a word) and a particular referent is arbitrary, but the relation between signifier and signified (meaning or concept conveyed) is governed by the rules of culture and has to be learned by the particular 'interpretative community'. In principle, anything which can make a sense-impression can act as a sign, and this sense-impression has no necessary correspondence with the sense-impression made by the thing signified (for instance, the word 'tree' does not look at all like a representation of an actual tree). What matters is the sign-system or 'referent-system' that governs and interrelates the whole process of signification.

Generally, the separate signs gain their meaning from the systematic differences, contrasts and choices which are regulated in the linguistic or sign-system code and from the values (positive or negative valence) which are given by the rules of the

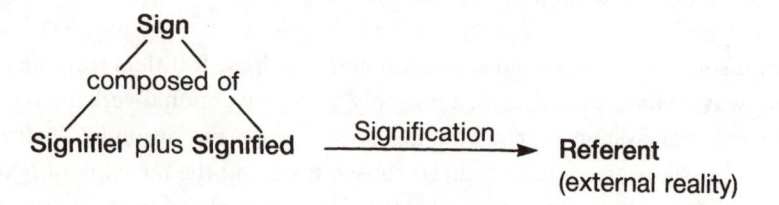

FIGURE 13.1   Elements of semiology: signs in meaning systems have two elements – physical plus associated meanings in the culture and in use

culture and the sign-system. Semiology has sought to explore the nature of sign-systems that go beyond the rules of grammar and syntax and regulate complex, latent and culturally dependent meanings of texts.

Connotation and denotation

This has led to a concern with *connotative* as well as *denotative* meaning – the associations and images invoked and expressed by certain usages and combinations of signs. *Denotation* has been described as the 'first order of signification' (Barthes, 1967), because it describes the relationship within a sign between the signifier (physical aspect) and signified (mental concept). The obvious straightforward meaning of a sign is its denotation. Williamson (1978) gives an example of an advertisement in which a photo of the film star Catherine Deneuve is used to advertise a French brand of perfume. The photo denotes Catherine Deneuve.

Connotation relates to a second order of signification, referring to the associated meaning that may be conjured up by the object signified. In the example of the advertisement, Catherine Deneuve is generally associated by members of the relevant language (and cultural) community with French 'chicness'. The relevance of this to advertisers is that the connotation of the chosen model (here a film star) is transferred by association to a perfume which she uses or recommends.

A seminal demonstration of this approach to text analysis was provided by Barthes (1977) in his analysis of a magazine advertisement for Panzani foods. This showed an image of a shopping bag containing groceries (the physical signifier), but these in turn were expected to invoke positive images of freshness and domesticity (the level of connotation). In addition, the red and green colours also signified 'Italianness' and could invoke a myth of culinary tradition and excellence. Thus, signification commonly works at two levels (or orders) of meaning: the surface level of literal meaning, and the second level of associated or connoted meaning. The activation of the second level requires some deeper knowledge or familiarity with the culture on the part of the reader.

Barthes extended this basic idea by introducing the concept of a *myth*. Often the thing signified by a sign will have a place in a larger discrete system of meaning, which is also available to the member of a particular culture. Myths are pre-existing and value-laden sets of ideas derived from the culture and transmitted by communication. For instance, there are likely to be myths about national character or national greatness, or concerning science or nature (its purity and goodness), that can be invoked for communicative purposes (as they often are in advertising).

Denotative meaning has the characteristics of universality (the same fixed meaning for all) and objectivity (references are true and do not imply evaluation), while connotation involves both variable meaning according to the culture of the recipient and elements of evaluation (positive or negative direction). The relevance of all this for

the study of mass communication should be evident. Media content consists of a large number of 'texts' (in the physical sense), often of a standardized and repetitive kind, that are composed on the basis of certain stylized conventions and codes. These often draw on familiar or latent myths and images present in the culture of the makers and receivers of texts (Barthes, 1972).

Uses of semiology

The application of semiological analysis opens the possibility of revealing more of the underlying meaning of a text, taken as a whole, than would be possible by simply following the grammatical rules of the language or consulting the dictionary meaning of separate words. It has the special advantage of being applicable to 'texts' that involve more than one sign- system and to signs (such as visual images and sounds) for which there is no established 'grammar' and no available dictionary. Without semiology, for instance, it would hardly have been possible for Williamson (1978) to have carried out her seminal study of advertisements.

Much media content is of a similar kind. However, semiological analysis presupposes a thorough knowledge of the originating culture and of the particular genre. According to Burgelin (1972: 317), 'the mass media clearly do not form a complete culture on their own . . . but simply a fraction of such a system which is, of necessity, the culture to which they belong'. Moreover, it follows from the theory summarized above that a text has its own immanent, intrinsic, more or less given and thus objective meaning, apart from the overt intention of sender or the selective interpretation of the receiver. As Burgelin also comments (1972: 316), 'there is nobody, and nothing, outside the message which can supply us with the meaning of one of its elements'.

This body of theory supplies us with an approach, if not exactly a method, for helping to establish the 'cultural meaning' of media content. It certainly offers a way of describing content: it can shed light on those who produce and transmit a set of messages; it has a special application in opening up layers of meaning which lie beneath the surface of texts and deny simple description at the 'first level' of signification. It is also useful in certain kinds of evaluative research, especially as directed at uncovering the latent ideology and 'bias' of media content.

Box 13.1   Structuralism/semiology

- Texts have meanings built in by way of language
- Meanings depend on a wider cultural and linguistic frame of reference
- Texts represent processes of signification
- Sign-systems can be 'decoded' on the basis of knowledge of culture and sign-system
- Meanings of texts are connotative, denotative or mythical

A completely different discourse around media content originates in the **information theory** approaches popularized by the work of Shannon and Weaver (1949). The roots are intermingled with the basic transmission model (see pages 52–3), which conceives communication as essentially the intentional transfer of information from sender to receiver by way of (physical) channels which are subject to noise and interference. According to this model, communication is judged by the efficiency (volume and cost) and effectiveness in achieving the planned 'transfer'. The concept of **information** has proved difficult to define, because it can be viewed in different ways, but the central element is probably the capacity to 'reduce uncertainty'. Information is thus defined by its opposite (randomness or chaos).

Information theory

According to Frick (1959), the insight that led to the development of information theory was the realization that 'all the processes that might be said to convey information are basically selection processes'. The mathematical theory of communication provided an objective approach to the analysis of communication texts. The basis for objectivity (quantification) is the binary (yes/no) coding system, which forms the basis for digital computing. All problems of uncertainty can ultimately be reduced to a series of either/or questions, and the number of questions required to solve a problem of meaning equals the number of items of information and is a measure of information quantity.

This line of thinking provides a tool for the analysis of the informative content of texts and opens up several lines of research. There is an in-built bias to a view of communication content as embodying rational purposes of the producers and to an instrumental view of media messages (the transmission model again). The approach is also fundamentally *behaviourist* in its assumptions. For obvious reasons, most application of this kind of theory has been to 'informative' kinds of content (such as news). Nevertheless, all media texts that are systematically encoded in known 'languages' are open in principle to analysis in terms of information and uncertainty reduction. Photographs, for instance, at the level of denotation, often present a series of 'iconic' items of information, signs that can be read as references to objects in the 'real world'.

Up to a point, iconic images are as informative as words, sometimes more so, and can also indicate certain kinds of relations between objects (such as relative distance) and give detailed information about colour, size, texture, etc. Fictional narratives can also be treated as informational texts, by assuming what they represent to be informative. For purposes of quantifying the amount of information that is sent or

received and for measuring some aspects of the quality of messages, it need not matter which type of media content is at issue.

Applications of information theory in the study of content

Examples of how the assumptions of information theory can be used in the analysis of media content can be found in certain measures of *informativeness, readability, diversity* and *information flow*. There are a number of different ways of measuring the '*information value*' (in the sense of capacity to reduce uncertainty) of media texts. The simplest approach is to count the number of 'facts' in a text, with alternative possibilities for defining what constitutes a fact (often it is conceived as a basic verifiable unit of objective information). Research by Asp (1981) involved a measure of 'information value' (or informativity) of news on certain controversial issues, based on three different indicators of news content, having first established a universe of relevant factual points in all news reports.

One measure was of *density*: the proportion of all relevant points in a given report. A second was of *breadth*: the number of different points as a proportion of the total possible. The third was *depth*: the number of facts and reported motives helping to explain the basic points (some subjective judgement may be involved here). An *information value index* was calculated by multiplying the density score by the breadth score. While factualness can be formally measured in this and similar ways, it cannot be assumed that information density or richness will make communication any more effective, although it may represent (good) intentions on the part of the reporters and a potential for being informative.

An alternative is to measure *readability*, another valued quality of journalistic texts. Approaches to measurement have mainly followed the idea that news is more readable when there is more *redundancy* (the reverse of information density). The simple idea is that an 'information-rich' text packed full of factual information which has a high potential for reducing uncertainty is also likely to be very challenging to a (not very highly motivated) reader. This is also related to the variable of being closed or open – information-rich texts are generally closed, not leaving much room for interpretation.

There is experimental support for the view that the less information in a text, the easier it generally is to read and understand. The main (experimental) tool for measuring readability is called the *cloze procedure* (Taylor, 1953) and involves a process whereby a reader has to substitute words for systematically omitted words. The ease of substitution is the measure of ease of reading, since texts with many redundant words give rise to fewer problems. This is not the only measure of readability, since measures of *sensationalism* achieve much the same result, though without the same basis in information theory (Tannenbaum and Lynch, 1960).

If we can measure the information in media content, and if we can categorize items

of information in a relevant way, it follows that we can also measure the (internal) *diversity* of texts. A typical diversity question (see below) might be the degree to which news gave equal or proportionate attention to the views of several different political parties or candidates. Chaffee (1981), for instance, suggested using Schramm's (1955) measure of *entropy*, which involved calculating the number of categories and the evenness of distribution of media space/time between categories (of information or opinion). There is more diversity where we find more categories (a wide range of opinion) and less diversity where there is very unequal attention to different categories (one opinion tends to dominate news coverage).

As noted, the informational approach can be used for measuring the volume of *flow of information*. This arises in theory and research concerning the 'information society'. For instance, Ito (1981) describes the methods by which communication flow (through all channels) in Japan and some other countries has been continuously measured. This comparative 'census' of information requires a common unit measure for information volume, and this is achieved by measuring 'words' and finding equivalents for words for other kinds of media content (such as television picture or music). Certain assumptions were made to convert all media forms to the word unit, based on the normal flow of speech (so many words per minute). In this way, the time taken by music can be given a word equivalent score, while still and moving pictures are converted to words by noting the number of visible words that could be written on a picture. This is obviously a very crude measure of information volume, but it is practical for purposes of comparison between media forms, between countries and over time. It also illustrates another aspect of the 'informational discourse'.

The evaluative dimension of information

From the examples given of the informational approach it looks as if it is very one-dimensional and hard to apply to non-factual aspects of content. It seems insensitive to the different levels of meaning that have already been mentioned and offers no place for alternative interpretations of a message. From the informational perspective, ambiguous or open texts are simply more redundant or chaotic. It is also unclear how this kind of objective analysis can cope with the *evaluative* dimension of information (which is always present in news).

While this critique is valid, there are possibilities for the objective analysis of the value direction of texts. These depend on the assumption (which can be empirically supported) that signs often carry positive or negative loadings in their own natural languages or code systems, certainly for those who are members of the relevant 'interpretative community'. It follows that references to people, objects or events can objectively convey values.

The work of Osgood et al. (1957) on the evaluative structure of meaning in a language laid the basis for developing objective measures of value direction in texts.

The essence of the approach (see van Cuilenburg et al., 1986) is to identify frequently-recurring words according to their 'common meaning' (their relative positive or negative weight in everyday use). Next we record the extent to which words of different value direction are (semantically) connected with relevant attitude objects in the news (such as political leaders, policies, countries and events). In principle, by such procedures, it is possible to quantify the 'inscribed' evaluative direction of attitude in media content.

Moreover it is possible to uncover *networks* of semantically associated 'attitude objects', and this sheds further light on value patterns (implied by association) in texts. This method does have the potential to allocate an evaluative meaning to whole texts, as well as to 'facts' or items of information, within a particular culture and society. Contextual knowledge is, however, a necessary condition, and the method departs from the purity of information theory.

Box 13.2   Communication as information

- Communication is to be defined as transfer of information from sender to individual receiver
- Media texts are bodies of information
- Information is essentially the reduction of uncertainty
- Information quality and the informativeness of texts are measurable
- The evaluative direction of information is measurable

MEDIA PERFORMANCE DISCOURSE

There is an extensive body of research into mass media content according to a number of normative criteria, especially those discussed in Chapter 8. This tradition of research is usually based on some conception of the public interest (or good of society) that provides the point of reference and the relevant content criteria (McQuail, 1992). Although a given set of values provide the starting point for analysis of media, the *procedures* adopted are those of a neutral scientific observer, and the aim is to find independent evidence which will be relevant to public debate about the role of media in society (Stone, 1987; Lemert, 1989). The NHK Quality Assessment project mentioned earlier (Ishikawa, 1996) is a good example of such work. The evidence sought should relate to particular media but needs also to have a general character.

It could be said that this particular discourse is about the politics of media content. It adjoins and occasionally overlaps with the critical tradition, discussed earlier, but differs in that it stays within the boundaries of the system itself, accepting the goals of the media in society more or less on their own terms (or at least the more idealistic goals). The normative background and the general nature of the principles have

content

already been sketched (Chapter 8). What follows are some examples of the testable expectations about the quality of media provision which are implied in the various performance principles.

Freedom and independence

Perhaps the foremost expectation about media content is that it should reflect or embody the spirit of free expression, despite the many institutional and organizational pressures that have already been described. It is not easy to see how the quality of freedom (and here the reference is primarily to news, information and opinion functions of media) can be recognized in content. Several general aspects of content can, even so, be identified as indicating more or less freedom (from commercial, political or social pressure). For example, there is the general question of editorial 'vigour' or activity, which should be a sign of using freedom and shows itself in a number of ways. These include: actually expressing opinions, especially on controversial issues; willingness to report conflict and controversy; following a 'pro-active' policy in relation to sources (thus not relying on press handouts and public relations, or being too cosy with the powerful); and giving background and interpretation as well as facts.

The concept of 'editorial vigour' was coined by Thrift (1977) to refer to several related aspects of content, especially dealing with *relevant* and significant local matters, adopting an argumentative form and providing 'mobilizing information' the latter referring to information which helps people to *act* on their opinions (Lemert, 1989). Some critics and commentators also look for a measure of advocacy and of support for 'underdogs' as evidence of free media (Entman, 1989). Investigative reporting may also be regarded as a sign of news media using their freedom.

In one way or another, most mass media content could be assessed in terms of the 'degree of freedom' exhibited. Outside the sphere of news, one would look for innovation and unexpectedness, non-conformity and experimentation in cultural matters. The most free media are also likely to deviate from conformity in matters of taste and be willing to be unpopular with audiences as well as with authorities. However, if so, they are not likely to remain mass media.

Content diversity

After freedom, probably the most frequently encountered term in the 'performance discourse' is diversity. It refers essentially to three main features of content:

- a wide range of *choice* for audiences, on all conceivable dimensions of interest and preference;

- many and different opportunities for *access* for voices and sources in society;
- and a true or sufficient *reflection* in media of the varied reality of experience in society.

Each of these concepts is open to measurement. In this context we can really only speak of content diversity if we apply some external standard to media texts whether of audience preference, social reality or (would-be) sources in society. Lack of diversity can be established only by identifying sources, references, events, types of content, etc., which are missing or underrepresented. In themselves, media texts cannot be said to be diverse in any absolute sense.

Objectivity in news

The standard of news objectivity (see page 172) has given rise to much discussion of journalistic media content, under various headings, especially in relation to some form of **bias,** which is the reverse of objectivity. As indicated already, the ruling norms of most Western media call for a certain practice of neutral, informative reporting of events, and it is against this positive expectation that much news has been found deficient. However, objectivity is a relatively complex notion when one goes beyond the simple idea that news should reliably (therefore honestly) report what is really going on in the world (Hackett, 1984). On the one hand, there are several sub-components of the idea that news tells us about reality. On the other hand, the expectation of *neutral* reporting is also open to various interpretations.

The simplest version of the idea that news tells us about the real world can be referred to as *factuality* (see Chapter 8). This refers to texts made up of distinct units of information that are necessary for understanding or acting upon a news 'event'. In journalistic terms it means at least providing dependable (correct) answers to the questions Who?, What?, Where?, When? and maybe Why?, and going on from there. A systematic approach to the assessment of factuality in the sense of 'information value' has already been discussed. News can be more or less 'information rich' in terms of the number of facts offered.

For analysing news quality, however, one needs more refined criteria. In particular, one asks if the facts given are *accurate* and whether they are sufficient to constitute an adequate account of the criterion of *completeness.* Accuracy itself can mean several things, since it cannot be directly 'read' or 'measured' from inspection of texts alone. One meaning of accuracy is conformity to independent records of events, whether in documents, other media or eyewitness accounts. Another meaning is more subjective – accuracy is conformity of reports to the perception of the source of news or the subject of the news (object of reporting). Accuracy may also be a matter of internal consistency within news texts.

Completeness is equally difficult to pin down or measure, since complete accounts of even simple events are not possible or necessary. Although one can always make assessments and comparisons of news in terms of more or less information, the question really turns on how much information is needed or can reasonably be expected, which is a subjective matter. We are quickly into another dimension of factuality – that of the *relevance* of the facts offered. Again it is a simple notion that news information is relevant only if it is interesting and useful (and vice versa), but there are competing notions and criteria of what counts as relevant. One source of criteria is what *theory* says news ought to be like. Another is what professional *journalists* decide is most relevant, and a third is what an *audience* actually finds interesting and useful. These three perspectives are unlikely to coincide on the same criteria or on the assessment of content.

Theory tends to equate relevance with what is *really* significant in the longer perspective of history and what contributes to the working of society (for instance, informed democracy). From this point of view, a good deal of news, such as about personalities, 'human interest', sport or entertainment, is not regarded as relevant. Journalists tend to apply professional criteria and a feel for news values that balance the longer-term significance with what they think their public is interested in.

One study of US journalists (Burgoon, quoted in McQuail, 1992: 218) showed a decided split between perceptions of 'significance' and 'interest' as factors in news judgement. Relevance was seen as having to do first of all with things 'which affect people's lives', secondly with things which are interesting or unusual, thirdly with facts which are timely or relate to nearby or large-scale happenings. In the end, it is the audience that decides what is relevant, and there are too many different audiences for a generalization to be useful. Even so, it is clear that much of what theory says is relevant is not perceived as such by much of the audience much of the time.

The issue of what counts as *impartiality* in news seems relatively simple but can also be complex in practice, not least because there is little chance of achieving a value-free assessment of value freedom. Impartiality is appreciated mainly because many events involve conflict and are open to alternative interpretations and evaluations (this is most obviously true of political news, but much the same could be said of sports). Most generally, the normal standard of impartiality calls for balance in the choice and use of sources, so as to reflect different points of view, and also neutrality in the presentation of news – separating facts from opinion, avoiding value judgements or emotive language or pictures. The term 'sensationalism' has been used to refer to forms of presentation which depart from the objectivity ideal, and measures of news text sensationalism have been developed (for example, Tannenbaum and Lynch, 1960).

There have also been attempts to show how the choice of words can reflect and imply value judgements in reporting on sensitive matters, for instance relating to patriotism (Glasgow Media Group, 1985) or race (Hartman and Husband, 1974; van Dijk, 1991). There are also indications that particular uses of visuals and camera shots can lead the viewer in certain evaluative directions (Tuchman, 1978; Kepplinger,

1983). Impartiality often comes down in the end simply to the absence of intentional or avoidable 'bias' and 'sensationalism'.

Reality reflection or distortion?

Bias in news content can refer, especially, to distorting reality, giving a negative picture of minority groups of many kinds, neglecting or misconstruing the role of women in society, or differentially favouring a particular political party or philosophy (see Shoemaker and Reese, 1991). There are many such kinds of news bias which stop short of lies, propaganda or ideology but often overlap with and reinforce similar tendencies in fictional content. While the territory of media bias is now almost boundless and still extending, we can summarize the most significant and best-documented generalizations in the following statements, first about news (Box 13.3) and then about fiction (Box 13.4).

Box 13.3 Typical examples of news 'bias'

- Media news over-represents the social 'top' and official voices in its sources
- News attention is differentially bestowed on members of political and social elites
- The social values which are most underlined are consensual and supportive of the status quo
- Foreign news concentrates on nearer, richer and more powerful nations
- News has a nationalistic (patriotic) and ethnocentric bias in the choice of topics and opinions expressed and in the view of the world assumed or portrayed
- News reflects the values and power distribution of a male-dominated society
- Minorities are differentially marginalized, ignored or stigmatized
- News about crime over-represents violent and personal crime and neglects many of the realities of risk in society

---

Box 13.4 Typical deviations of fictional texts from 'social reality'

- Occupational distribution of characters is highly skewed to the higher-status occupations, especially in law enforcement, medicine, the military, show business, etc.
- Ethnic minorities have tended to be in lower-status or dubious social roles although this may be modified, without necessarily becoming more realistic
- Women have tended to appear in stereotyped occupational and domestic roles and are generally more passive and in the background
- Fictional violence, just as crime in the news, is portrayed in a very unrealistic light, on almost all conceivable dimensions
- Fiction which deals with social or political conflict tends either to support consensual values or to avoid the issues
- Homosexuality tends to be shown covertly, ignored or treated stereotypically (rarely positively)

An analysis of the fictional content of mass media, from a similar perspective of trueness to reality or implicit (unwitting) bias, leads to the main generalizations listed in Box 13.4. Here the evidence has normally been derived by applying methods of quantitative analysis to the overt content of texts, on the assumption that relative frequency of references will be taken as reflecting the 'real world'.

A critique of the reality-reflection norm

It is striking how much the evaluation of media content comes down to the question of relation to reality, as if media ought to reflect more or less proportionately some empirical reality and ought always be 'fair' as between the advantaged and the disadvantaged. This is referred to by Kepplinger and Habermeier (1995) as the 'correspondence assumption' often attributed to the audience. The assumption that media ought to reflect reality in some direct and proportional way has been the basis for much criticism of media performance and has often been a key ingredient in research on media effects (for instance, in cultivation analysis) but is itself open to question. According to Schulz (1988), it derives from an antiquated 'mechanistic' view of the relationship between media and society, more or less akin to the 'transportation model' of communication effects. It fails to recognize the essential specificity, arbitrariness and, sometimes, autonomy of media texts and neglects the active participation of the audience in the making of meaning. Perhaps most telling is the absence of evidence that the audience does actually assume any statistical correspondence between media content and reality.

Apart from this fundamental doubt about the expectation of proportional reality-reflection, there are several reasons why media content should *not* normally be expected to 'reflect' reality in any literal (statistically representative) way. Functionalist theory of media as agents of social control, for instance, would lead us to expect that media content would over-represent the dominant social and economic values of the society. We would also expect social elites and authorities to have more visibility and access. Indeed, the media do reflect the social reality of inequality when they tip the scales of attention towards the powerful in society and towards powerful nations in the world. The complaint is really that in so doing they may reinforce it.

The analysis of media organizations has shown how unlikely it is that news will match some 'average' of reality. The need for authoritative news sources and the requirements of 'news values' are an obvious source of statistical 'distortion'. In addition, fictional media often deliberately seek to attract an audience by over-populating their stories with characters who lead more exciting lives and are richer, younger, more fashionable and more beautiful than the typical audience member (Martel and McCall, 1964). The study of 'key events' and 'framing' of news makes it both clear and also understandable that 'reality' cannot be treated as if all happenings were of equal significance, even within the same category.

The simple fact that mass media are generally oriented to the interests of their audiences as 'consumers' of information and entertainment can easily account for most of the evidence of reality distortion summarized above. It is clear that audiences like many things which are inconsistent with reality-reflection, especially fiction, fantasy, the unusual and bizarre, myths, nostalgia and amusement. The media are often sought out precisely as an alternative to and an escape from reality. When people look for models to follow or for objects of identification, they are as likely to seek an idealized as a realistic object or model. Viewed from this point of view, the reality 'distortions' observed in content are not in themselves surprising or necessarily regrettable.

QUESTIONS OF RESEARCH METHOD

The various frameworks and perspectives for theorizing about media content that have been discussed, often imply sharp divergences of methods of research. The full range of alternatives cannot be discussed here, since there are many different methods for different purposes (several have already been introduced). Methods range from simple and extensive classifications of types of content for organizational or descriptive purposes to deeply interpretative enquiries into specific examples of content, designed to uncover subtle and hidden potential meanings. Following the line of theoretical demarcation introduced in Chapter 3, we can broadly distinguish between quantitative and descriptive enquiry into overt meaning, on the one hand, and more qualitative, deeper and more interpretative enquiry, on the other. There are also enquiries directed to understanding the very nature of the various 'media languages' and how they work, especially in relation to visual imagery and sounds.

Where is meaning?

Theory has been perennially preoccupied with the question of the 'location' of meaning. Does meaning coincide with the intention of the sender, or is it embedded in the language, or is it primarily a matter of the receivers' interpretation (Jensen, 1991)? As we have seen from the previous chapters, mass-communicated information and culture are produced by complex organizations, whose purposes are usually not very specific and yet often predominate over the aims of individual communicators. This makes it hard to know what the 'sender's' intention really is – who can say, for instance, what the purpose of news is, or whose purpose it is? The option of concentrating on the message itself as the source of meaning has been the most attractive one, partly for reasons of practicality. The physical texts themselves are

always available for direct analysis, and they have the advantage (compared with human respondents) of being 'non-reactive' to the investigator. They do not decay with time, although their context does decay and with it the possibility of really knowing what they originally meant to senders or to receivers.

It is impossible to 'extract' meaning from media content texts without also making assumptions which themselves shape the meaning extracted – for instance, the assumption that the amount or frequency of attention to something is a reliable guide to message meaning, intention and effect. The findings of content analysis can never 'speak for themselves'. In addition, the 'languages' of media are far from simple and still only partially understood, especially where they involve music and visual images (both still and moving) in many combinations, drawing on numerous and varied codes and conventions.

Dominant versus alternative paradigms again

The choices of research method generally follow the division between a dominant empirically oriented paradigm and a more qualitative (and often critical) variant (see Chapter 3). The former is mainly represented by traditional **content analysis,** which was defined by Berelson (1952: 18) as 'a research technique for the objective, systematic and quantitative description of the manifest content of communication'. This assumes that the surface meaning of a text is fairly unambiguous and can be read by the investigator and expressed in quantitative terms. In fact, it is assumed that the numerical balance of elements in the text (such as the number of words or space/time allocated to a set of topics) is a reliable guide to the overall meaning. Several relatively sophisticated forms of quantitative content analysis have been developed which go well beyond the simple counting and classifying of units of content that were characteristic of early research. There remains, even so, a fundamental assumption that media content is encoded according to the same language as the reality to which it refers.

The alternative approach is based on precisely the reverse assumption – that the concealed or latent meanings are the most significant, and these cannot be directly read from the numerical data. In particular, we have to take account not just of relative frequency but of links and relationships between elements in the text, and also to take note of what is missing or taken for granted. We need to identify and understand the particular discourse in which a text is encoded. In general we need to be aware of the conventions and codes of any genre that we study, since these indicate at a higher level what is going on in the text (Jensen and Jankowski, 1991). In contrast, content analysis may permit the conflation of several different kinds of media text, ignoring discursive variety.

Both varieties of analysis can claim some measure of scientific reliability. They deploy methods which can, in principle, be replicated by different people, and the

'findings' should be open to challenge according to some (not always the same) canons of scientific procedure. Secondly, they are both designed to deal with regularity and recurrence in cultural artefacts rather than with the unique and non-reproducible. They are thus more appropriate for application to the symbolic products of the culture industries than to those of the 'cultural elite' (such as 'works of art'). Thirdly, they avoid judgements of moral or aesthetic value (another sense of being objective). Fourthly, all such methods are, in principle, instrumental means to other ends. They can be used to answer questions about the links between content, creators, social context and receivers.

TRADITIONAL CONTENT ANALYSIS

Basics

'Traditional' content analysis, following Berelson's (1952) definition (see above), is the earliest, most central and still most widely practised method of research. Its use goes back to the early decades of the century (cf. Kingsbury and Hart, 1937). The basic sequence in applying the technique is set out in Box 13.5.

Box 13.5   Content analysis: basic sequence

1.   Choose a universe or sample of content
2.   Establish a category frame of external referents relevant to the purpose of the enquiry (such as a set of political parties or countries which may be referred to in content)
3.   Choose a 'unit of analysis' from the content (this could be a word, a sentence, an item, a whole news story, a picture, a sequence, etc.)
4.   Seek to match the content to the category frame by counting the frequency of the references to relevant items in the category frame, per chosen unit of content
5.   Express the results as an overall distribution of the complete universe or chosen content sample in terms of the frequency of occurrence of the sought-for referents

---

The procedure is based on two main assumptions. First, that the link between the external object of reference and the reference to it in the text will be reasonably clear and unambiguous. Secondly, that the frequency of occurrence of chosen references will validly express the predominant 'meaning' of the text in an objective way. The approach is, in principle, no different from that adopted in surveys of people. One chooses a population (here a media type or subset), draws a sample within it for respondents representative of the whole (the units of analysis), collects data about individuals according to variables and assigns values to these variables. As with the survey, content analysis is held to be reliable (reproducible) and not unique to

the investigator. The method produces a statistical summary of a much larger media reality. It has been used for many purposes but especially for comparing media content with a known frequency distribution in 'social reality'.

Limits to content analysis

The traditional approach has many limitations and pitfalls, which are of some theoretical interest as well as practical relevance. The usual practice of constructing a category system before applying it involves the risk of an investigator imposing a meaning-system rather than discovering it in the content. Even when care is taken to avoid this, any such category system must be selective and potentially distorting. The outcome of content analysis is itself a new text, the meaning of which may, or even must, diverge from the original source material. This result is also based on a form of 'reading' of content that no actual 'reader' would ever, under natural circumstances, undertake. The new 'meaning' is neither that of the original sender, nor that of the text itself, nor that of the audience, but a fourth construct, one particular interpretation. Account cannot easily be taken of the context of a reference within a text or of the text as a whole. Internal relationships between references in texts may also be neglected in the process of abstraction. There is an assumption that 'coders' can be trained to make reliable judgements about categories and meanings.

The boundaries of the kind of content analysis described are, in fact, rather elastic, and many variants can be accommodated within the same basic framework. The more one relaxes requirements of reliability, the easier it is to introduce categories and variables that will be useful for interpretation but 'low' in 'objectivity' and somewhat ambiguous. This is especially true of attempts to capture references to values, themes, settings, style and interpretative frameworks. Content analyses often display a wide range of reliability, because of attempts to include some more subjective indicators of meaning.

QUANTITATIVE AND QUALITATIVE ANALYSIS COMPARED

The contrast between traditional content analysis and interpretative approaches can now be summarized. Some differences are self-evident. First, structuralism and semiology (the main interpretative approaches; see pages 311–14 above) do not involve quantification, and there is even an antipathy to counting as a way of arriving at significance, since meaning derives from textual relationships, oppositions and context rather than from number and balance of references. Secondly, attention is directed to latent rather than to manifest content, and latent (thus deeper) meaning is

regarded as actually more essential. Thirdly, structuralism is systematic in a different way from content analysis, giving no weight to procedures of sampling and rejecting the notion that all 'units' of content should be treated equally.

Fourthly, structuralism does not allow the assumption that the world of social and cultural 'reality', the message and the receiver all involve the same basic system of meanings. Social reality consists of numerous more or less discrete universes of meaning, each requiring separate elucidation. The 'audience' also divides up into 'interpretative communities', each possessing some unique possibilities for attributing meaning. Media content, as we have seen, is also composed on the basis of more than one code, language or sign-system. All this makes it impossible, even absurd, to assume that any category system of references can be constructed in which a given element is likely to mean precisely the same in the 'reality', in the content, to the audience member and to the media analyst. It follows from structuralist theory that it is very difficult to carry out research that relates findings in one of these 'spheres' to findings in another.

Mixed methods are possible

This comparison does not indicate the superiority of one approach over the other, since, despite the claim at the outset that these methods have something in common, they are essentially good for different purposes. Structuralism does not offer a systematic method and is not accountable in its results according to normal standards of reliability, nor is it easy to generalize from the results to other texts, except perhaps in relation to form (for instance, comparing one genre with another). It is certainly not a way of summarizing content, as content analysis often can be.

For some purposes, it may be permissible and necessary to depart from the pure form of either 'Berelsonian' or 'Barthian' analysis, and a number of studies have used combinations of both approaches, despite their divergent assumptions. An example of such a hybrid approach is the work on British television news of the Glasgow Media Group (1976, 1980, 1985), which combined rigorous and detailed quantitative analysis of industrial news with an attempt to 'unpack' the deeper cultural meaning of specific news stories. The school of 'cultural indicators', as represented by Gerbner and colleagues (see pages 110–11), has also sought to arrive at the 'meaning structure' of dominant forms of television output by way of systematic quantitative analysis of overt elements of television representation.

There are methods that do not easily belong to either of the main approaches described. One is the psychoanalytic approach favoured at an early stage of content study. This focuses on the motivation of 'characters' and the underlying meaning of dominant themes in the popular (or less so) culture of a given society or period (for example, Wolfenstein and Leites, 1947; McGranahan and Wayne, 1948; Kracauer, 1949). It was also taken up for studying gender issues and the meaning and influence of advertising (e.g. Williamson, 1978).

Other variants of analysis method have already been noted – for instance, the analysis of narrative structure (Radway, 1984) or the study of content functions. Thus, Graber (1976a) named the following set of functions of political communication: to gain attention; to establish linkages and define situations; to make commitments; to create policy-relevant moods; to stimulate action (mobilize); to act directly (words as actions); and to use words as symbolic rewards for actual or potential supporters.

Such possibilities are a reminder of the *relative* character of most analysis of content, in that there has always to be some outside point of reference or purpose according to which one chooses one form of classification rather than another. Even semiology can supply meaning only in terms of a much larger system of cultural meanings and sense-making practices.

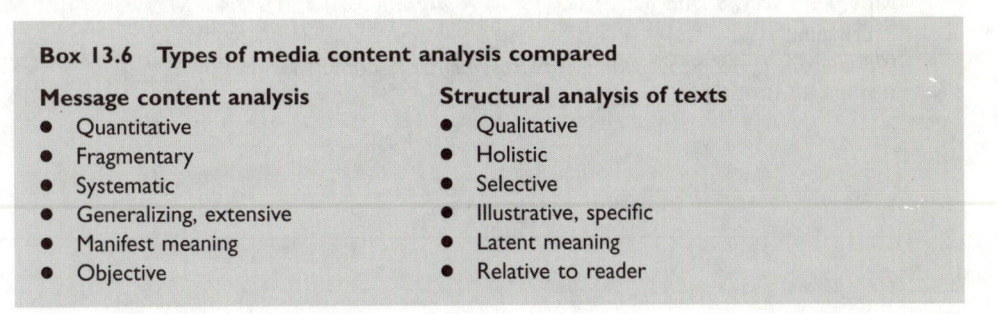

Box 13.6   Types of media content analysis compared

Message content analysis	Structural analysis of texts
● Quantitative	● Qualitative
● Fragmentary	● Holistic
● Systematic	● Selective
● Generalizing, extensive	● Illustrative, specific
● Manifest meaning	● Latent meaning
● Objective	● Relative to reader

One recurrent problem with all methods and approaches is the gap that often exists between the outcome of content analysis and the perceptions of the creators or the audience. The creators tend to think of what is unique and distinctive in what they do, while the audience is inclined to think of content in terms of a mixture of conventional genre or type labels and a set of satisfactions which have been experienced or are expected. The version extracted by the content analyst is thus not very recognizable to the two main sets of participants in the mass communication enterprise (producers and receivers) and often remains a scientific or literary abstraction.

CONCLUSION

The future of content analysis, one way or another, has to lie in relating 'content' as sent to the wider structures of meaning in a society. This path can probably best be followed by way of discourse analysis that takes account of other meaning systems in the originating culture or by way of audience reception analysis that takes seriously the notion that readers also make meanings. Both are necessary in some degree for an adequate study of media. The various frameworks and perspectives for theorizing about media content that have been introduced often imply sharp divergences of

methods of research as well as differences of purpose. The full range of alternative methods cannot be discussed here, but the main options will be set out in Chapter 14.

FURTHER READING

Barthes, R. (1967) *Elements of Semiology.* London: Jonathan Cape.
Glasgow Media Group (1976) *Bad News.* London: Routledge.
Lemert, J. (1989) *Criticizing the Media.* Beverly Hills, CA: Sage.
Riffe, D., Lacey, S. and Fico, F.G. (1998) *Analyzing Media Messages.* Mahwah, NJ: Lawrence Erlbaum.
Williamson, J. (1978) *Decoding Advertisements.* London: Marion Boyars.

media genres and texts

In general use, the term genre simply means a kind or type and it is often loosely applied to any distinctive category of cultural product. In film theory, where it originates, the term has been controversial, because of the tension between individual creative authorship and location in a genre (Andrew, 1984). An emphasis on the genre tends to credit the value of a work to a cultural tradition rather than to an individual artist, who simply follows the rules laid down by the particular school of production. In relation to most mass media content, however, the concept of genre is useful and not especially controversial, since the question of artistic authorship does not usually arise.

Defining genre

For our purpose, genre can refer to any *category* of content that has the following characteristics:

- It has a *collective* identity recognized more or less equally by its producers (the media) and its consumers (media audiences).
- This identity (or definition) relates to purposes (such as information, entertainment or sub-variants), form (length, pace, structure, language, etc.) and meaning (reality reference).
- The identity has been established over time and observes familiar conventions; cultural forms are preserved, although these can also change and develop within the framework of the original genre.
- A particular genre, as already implied, will follow an expected structure of narrative or sequence of action, draw on a predictable stock of images and have a repertoire of variants of basic themes.

The genre may be considered as a practical device for helping any mass medium to produce consistently and efficiently and to relate its production to the expectations of its audience. Since it helps individual media users to plan their choices, it can also be considered as a mechanism for ordering the relations between producers and consumers. According to Andrew (1984: 110), genres (of film).

> are specific networks of formulas that deliver a certified product to a waiting customer. They ensure the production of meaning by regulating the viewers' relation to the image and narrative construction for him or her. In fact, genres construct the proper spectators for their own consumption. They build the desires and then represent the satisfaction of what they have triggered.

This view overrates the extent to which the media can determine the response of an audience, but it is at least consistent with the aspirations of media themselves to control the environments in which they operate.

The origin of genre analysis is credited by Berger (1992) to Suart Kaminsky, who wrote that

> genre study of the film is based in the realization that certain popular narrative forms have both cultural and universal roots, that the Western of today is related to archetypes of the past 200 years in the United States and to the folk tale and the myth. (1974: 3)

Stuart Hall (1980) also applied the genre idea to the 'B-movie western'. In his analysis, genre depends on the use of a particular 'code' or meaning system, which can draw on some consensus about meaning among users of the code (whether encoders or decoders) in a given culture. According to Hall, we can speak of a genre where coding and decoding are very close and where meaning is consequently relatively unambiguous, in the sense of being received much as it is sent.

The classic western movie is then said to derive from a particular myth concerning the conquest of the US west and involving such elements as displays of masculine prowess and womanly courage, the working out of destiny in the wide open spaces and the struggle of good versus evil. The particular strength of the western genre is that it can generate many variant forms that can also be readily understood in relation to the original basic form. For instance, we have seen the psychological western, the parody western, the 'spaghetti' western, the comedy western and the soap opera western. The meaning of the variant forms often depends on the reversal of elements in the original code.

Many familiar examples of media content can be subjected to a genre analysis designed either to uncover their essential recurring features or formulas, as Radway (1984) has done for the romance story or to classify the different variants of the same genre, and as Berger (1992) does for the detective mystery. According to Berger, the 'formula' is a sub-category or genre and involves the conventions of the genre, with particular reference to time, place, plots, costumes, types of hero, heroine and villain, etc. A 'Western', for instance has a certain range of possibilities for the formulaic elements that will be known to experienced audience members. This knowledge enables the content to be read correctly when certain signs appear: for instance, white hats identifying good guys, and the music that heralds the approaching cavalry.

More recent developments of media-cultural studies have given prominence to several familiar television genres and provided the boundaries for new fields of enquiry. A noteworthy example is the attention paid to soap operas, partly on account of their identification as a *gendered* form of television (Modleski, 1982; Allen, 1987, 1989; Hobson, 1989; Geraghty, 1991). The more feminine characteristics of the soap opera genre were said to reside in its form of narrative, preference for dialogue over action and attention to values of extended families and the role of mothers and housewives.

The soap opera is also a very typical example of a serial form of narrative. The great interest in the serial *Dallas* during the 1980s (Ang, 1985; Liebes and Katz, 1990), for somewhat different reasons, also drew attention to the soap opera as a genre. The particular example also stretched the meaning of the term to include a media product which was very different from the early North American radio or television daytime serial. Even so, the wide and long currency of the term 'soap opera' applied to different kinds of drama confirms, in some measure, the validity and utility of the concepts of genre and soap opera. One of the strengths of the genre idea is its capacity to adapt and extend to cope with dynamic developments. This is well represented in the even more recent rise of the 'talk-show' genre, which began as entertainment interviews with celebrities and as a 'breakfast television' format and has expanded luxuriously through the world in manifestations that range from the sensationalist knock-about to very serious occasions for political participation. The common elements holding the genre together are not easy to identify, apart from the centrality of talk and the presence of a key anchor personality. But they often included some audience presence or participation, some conflict or drama, some degree or illusion of actuality, a strong dose of personalization and illusion of intimacy (see Munson, 1993).

A typology of genres

So far it has seemed that genre analysis can only be applied to discrete categories of *analysis*, each with certain key dimensions. At least one attempt has been made at a more meta-analysis. Berger (1992) suggests that all television output can be classified according to four basic types, produced by two dimensions: degree of emotionality and degree of objectivity. The typology is shown in Figure 14.1. The explanation of the terms is as follows.

- *Contests* are programmes with competition involving real players, including game shows, quizzes and sports. They are both real and emotionally involving (in intention).
- *Actualities* include all news, documentary and reality programming. They are objective and unemotional in principle.

		Objectivity	
		High	Low
Emotionality	Strong	**Contests**	**Dramas**
	Weak	**Actualities**	**Persuasions**

FIGURE 14.1   The structure of television genres: a typology (Berger, 1992: 7)

- *Persuasions* are low on both dimensions and reflect an intention of a sender to persuade, especially by advertising or some form of advocacy or propaganda.
- *Dramas* cover almost all fictional story-telling and a wide range of genres.

As Berger notes, the application of this scheme is complicated by the fact that new and mixed genres are continually being created that do not belong to a unique category. Familiar examples are those of 'docudrama' and other kinds of 'infotainment'. But this is also a feature of individual genres and can be helpful in tracking and analysing what is happening.

While genre is a useful concept for finding one's way in the luxuriant abundance of media output and for helping to describe and categorize content, it is not a very powerful tool of analysis, since there are simply too many possibilities for applying it. The distinction between one genre and another is not easy to ascertain objectively, and the correspondence of recognition and understanding by producers and audience, named above as a characteristic of a genre, is not easy to demonstrate. It may be a more useful term in relation to films and books, where individual acts of choice are made and paid for, guided by experience, taste and publicity, and lead to established preference. It has also been shown that inter-genre differences can be used to differentiate types of television producer (Tunstall, 1993).

> **Box 14.1   Mass media genres**
> - Genres are defined equally by producers and readers of media content
> - Genres are identified by function, form and content
> - Genres both preserve and help to develop textual forms
> - Genres are aids to production and to reading of texts
> - Genres are characterized by their own logics, formats and language

MEDIA FORMAT AND LOGIC

The genre concept has also been useful in a somewhat adapted form for analysing media formats. Altheide and Snow (1979), for instance, developed a mode of analysis of media content, employing the terms *media logic* and *media format*. The first refers essentially to a set of implicit rules and norms that govern how content should be processed and presented to take most advantage of the characteristics of a given medium (see page 296). This includes fitting the needs of the media organization (including the media's perception of the needs of the audience). The operation of a media logic, according to Altheide (1985), implies the existence of a 'media grammar' which governs how time should be used, how items of content should be sequenced and what devices of verbal and non-verbal communication (codes) should be used.

Altheide sees content as tailored to fit media formats, and formats as tailored to fit listener/viewer preferences and assumed capacities.

The formats are essentially subroutines for dealing with specific themes within a genre. For instance, Altheide (1985) describes a 'format for crisis' in television news, which transcends the particularities of events and gives a common shape to the handling of different news stories. The main conditions necessary for the news handling of a crisis on a continuing basis are accessibility (to information or to the site of the crisis), visual quality (of film or tape), drama and action, relevance to the audience and thematic unity.

Following the same line of thought, Mazzoleni (1987b) has suggested that, in the field of political communication, a 'media logic' has tended to encroach on a 'political logic' in the selection and presentation of politics. During campaigns especially, this shows itself in a concentration on personalities and details of campaign events rather than on abstract political ideas. He has applied the hypothesis to the case of a traditionally very politicized television system, that of Italy (see also Hallin and Mancini, 1984). Without using the same terminology, a very similar hypothesis had already been applied to the study of election campaigns in the United States (Graber, 1976b) and in Denmark (Siune, 1981).

Graber (for example, 1981) has made notable contributions to the study of political languages in general and its television versions in particular. She confirms the points made by Altheide in her comment that 'television journalists have developed repertoires – another possible term for frames, logics or sub-genre formats of highly stereotyped cues for many specific situations in politics'. She argues convincingly that the encoding and decoding of audiovisual languages is essentially *different* from that of verbal languages in being more associational, connotative and unstructured and less logical, clearly defined and delimited. The systematic analysis of audiovisual languages is, nevertheless, still at an early stage.

Visual language

An exploration of this fertile terrain lies outside the scope of this book, but a few more remarks are in order on the distinctive features of audiovisual 'languages', if the term is allowable (see Adams and Schreibman, 1978; Geis, 1987). A comparison between print media and film/television media suggests the following contrasts, which derive from language rather than social factors. Television (and film) is, in general, less regulated by agreed (linguistic) codes, more ambiguous in meaning, lacking in clear authorship (or indication of source), more open, more concrete, more universal and more information rich.

It does not appear that the distinctive features of television have yet been harnessed to achieve more communicative effectiveness. Both print and audiovisual media have their own in-built inefficiencies and both are severely limited by human information-processing capacity. It may be the case that the full potential of audiovisual languages

(and the same applies to alphanumeric–pictorial forms) has simply not yet been realized in a period of rapid change of technology and experimentation with new forms and purposes of communication media.

Before leaving the subject of genres, formats and related concepts, it is worth emphasizing that they can, in principle, cut across the conventional content categories of media output, including the divide between fiction and non-fiction. Fiske (1987) underlines the essential *intertextuality* of genres. This is not too surprising, given the long tradition that allows fiction to draw on real-life situations or historical events for its subject matter, although it may undermine the reality claims of media news and information. Schlesinger et al. (1983) provide a demonstration by analysing the portrayal of terrorism on British television both in news and current affairs and in dramatic fiction (see also pages 350–51).

THE NEWS GENRE

In the following sections, attention focuses on the news genre, partly because it has such a long history and is so central in accounting for the position of the media as a privileged social institution. The newspaper is, arguably, the archetype as well as the prototype of all modern mass media (Tunstall, 1977: 23), and 'news' is the central ingredient of the newspaper (though far from the only one). To some extent, radio and television were modelled on the newspaper, with regular news as their chief anchor point. News merits special attention in a discussion of media content just because it is one of the few original contributions of the mass media to the range of cultural forms of expression. It is also the core activity according to which a large part of the journalistic (and thus media) occupation defines itself.

News provides the component that distinguishes something called a newspaper from other kinds of print media and often earns it a special status or protection in society, allowing it to express opinion in the name of the public. Media institutions could barely exist without news, and news could not exist without media institutions. Unlike almost all other forms of authorship or cultural creation, news-making cannot be done privately or even individually. The institution provides both the machinery for distribution and the guarantee of credibility and authority.

What is news?

Despite the central position of news in the media, the question 'What is news?' is one which journalists themselves seem to find distinctly metaphysical and difficult to answer except in terms of their intuition, 'feel' and innate judgement. Attempts to

answer it by analysis of media content have not been very revealing. It happens that the two 'founding fathers' of the sociology of news were both former or practising journalists and drew on their own experience in tackling the question of the nature of the news. Walter Lippmann (1922: 216) focused on the process of news gathering, which he saw as a search for the 'objective clear signal which signifies an event'. Hence, 'news is not a mirror of social conditions, but the report of an aspect that has obtruded itself'.

The second early commentator on news, Robert Park (1940), paid more attention to the essential properties of the news report. His starting point was to compare it with another 'form of knowledge', history, which is also a record of past events, and to place news on a continuum that ranges from 'acquaintance with' to 'knowledge about'. News is located somewhere in the middle of this continuum. The result of Park's comparison of news with history can be distilled into a few main points, as follows:

- News is timely; it is about very recent or recurrent events.
- News is unsystematic; it deals with discrete events and happenings, and the world seen through news alone consists of unrelated happenings, which it is not the primary task of news itself to interpret.
- News is perishable – it lives only when the events themselves are current, and for purposes of record and later reference other forms of knowledge will replace news.
- Events reported as news should be unusual or at least unexpected, qualities that are more important than their 'real significance'.
- Apart from unexpectedness, news events are characterized by other 'news values' that are always relative and involve subjective judgements about likely audience interest.
- News is mainly for orientation and attention-direction and not a substitute for knowledge.
- News is predictable.

This last paradoxical and provocative point was explained by Park as follows:

> if it is the unexpected that happens it is not the wholly unexpected which gets into the news. The events that have made news in the past, as in the present, are actually the expected things . . . it is on the whole the accidents and incidents that the public is prepared for . . . the things that one fears and that one hopes for that make news. (1940: 45)

A similar point was put more succinctly by Galtung and Ruge (1965) in the remark that 'news' are actually 'olds'. Warren Breed (1956) listed the following terms as descriptive of news: 'saleable', 'superficial', 'simple', 'objective', 'action centred', 'interesting' (as distinct from significant), 'stylized' and 'prudent'. He also suggested dimensions along which an item of news might be placed: news versus truth; difficult versus routine (in terms of news gathering); and information versus human interest.

Much depends on whether the events which make news are 'visible' or not to the public or to news producers. According to Hall (1973), there are three basic 'rules of

news visibility': (1) its link to an event or occurrence (the component of action); (2) its recency; and (3) its newsworthiness or link to some important thing or person. Noteworthy, in Hall's view, is that news is itself responsible for creating over time the 'consensus' knowledge by which newsworthiness is recognized by newspeople and accepted as such by the public. He writes:

> the ideological concepts embodied in photos and texts in a newspaper do not produce new knowledge about the world. They produce recognition of the world as we have already learnt to appropriate it.

This essentially coincides with Park's claim that news is predictable.

Box 14.2   Main attributes of news

- Timeliness and recency
- Unexpectedness
- Predictability of type
- Fragmentary nature
- Perishability
- Signalling
- Shaped by values
- Interesting
- Factualness

News and human interest

In Breed's characterization of news, it is at one point contrasted with **human interest**, implying that the former has to do with serious information, the latter with something else perhaps entertaining, personalized or sensational. In practice it seems hard to separate the two, and both have been elements in the newspaper since its earliest appearances. A classic study by a pupil of Park, Helen McGill Hughes (1940), examined the relationship between the two forms of content and concluded that the (US) newspaper had been 'transformed from a more or less sober record into a form of popular literature'. In her view, a human interest story is not intrinsically different from other news stories but takes its character from the particular attitude which the writer adopts towards the reader. It is a story that is intended to divert, but also one which is told, as it were, from the reader's point of view. As a result, it can only be told by a reporter who is 'able to see the world as his or her readers do'. Hence it is more akin to gossip or the folk tale. The characteristics of news are derived in part from much older traditions of storytelling (Darnton, 1975). Certainly readers are often more attracted to 'human interest' than to 'news' about politics, economics and society (Curran et al., 1981; Dahlgren and Sparks, 1992). From this point of view, it has a positive contribution to make to democratic communication.

media genres and texts

As with other genres, there are several variants that depend on the central code of the news. One example is that of gossip, especially concerning media stars or other celebrities, which purports to offer objective information but usually has no deep significance or any material relevance. The conventions and codes of the news genre can also be used in advertising or in satirical media performances, which outwardly observe the news form, but are totally inverted. So-called 'tabloid television' – sensational, gossipy, weird information – is another example of the stretching of a genre. The news genre is also capable of adaptation and extension to new circumstances. News had to be in some degree reinvented for radio, television and pictorial possibilities. The 'happy news format' of television news, which was introduced in the 1970s for greater audience appeal has been widely adopted (Dominick et al., 1975).

Types of journalism

In practice, the provision of news is also structured in genre terms according to different types of publication and channel. Thus, there are basically different types of journalism. Journalism itself first needs to be identified as something separate from its product – the news. This is not very easy, especially because of the limited degree of professionalization. A working, if awkward, definition might read: 'paid writing (and the audiovisual equivalent) for public media with reference to actual and ongoing events of public relevance'. We can also differentiate types of journalistic media, aside from inter-media differences, according to audience markets. We can, for instance, identify 'prestige' newspapers, as well as publications that are popular, 'tabloid' or boulevard. We can also distinguish these from local and specialist (e.g. sport or business) forms. Beyond, or alongside, this, we can distinguish journalism according to certain stylistic or theoretical traditions. These include: 'new journalism' (personal and committed); civic or public journalism (see page 159); development journalism (see page 155); investigative journalism; journalism of record; advocacy journalism; alternative journalism; gossip journalism. For analytical purposes it is useful to be clear about the different levels and cross-cutting dimensions of the varieties of the journalistic genre.

NEWS VALUES AND THE STRUCTURE OF NEWS

One general conclusion from the many content studies is that news exhibits a rather stable and predictable overall pattern when measured according to conventional categories of subject matter. Many of the reasons for this have already been discussed

in relation to the production of news (Chapters 11 and 12). There are variations from one country to another and one medium type to another, and the pattern is naturally responsive to major events, such as war and world crisis. Nevertheless, the stability of news content is often remarkable.

One obvious explanation for this state of affairs is firmly embedded in ideas about the nature of news that have just been discussed, especially the fact that news has to attract attention and interest the audience. Interest is likely to stem either from relevance and utility or from some intrinsic appeal. The concept of **news values** has been frequently used to capture this idea (see Park's characterization of news, above). Essentially a news value is some attribute of a news event that is thought by journalists to have a potential for transforming the facts into an interesting 'story' for the audience or which give it some compelling significance.

There have been numerous attempts to distil the essence of such qualities of events, although there are some fundamental reasons why it is impossible to reach any definitive account of 'news values' that has great predictive or explanatory value in accounting for any particular example of news selection. One problem lies in the fact that value has to be attributed and there are competing sources of perception. Although by definition, journalists and editors are the most influential judges of value (since they *decide* on relative value), the *actual* perceptions of diverse audiences cannot be ignored, nor can the views of powerful sources and others affected by news. Secondly, most events are complex enough to have a potential 'score' for value on more than one attribute (e.g. not only the chief actor in an event, but what the event is and where it takes place, etc.). Thirdly, there is a tension between values that are related to 'human interest', as discussed above (page 339) and those that are defined by real-world (potential) consequences. Fourthly, news values are not only relative in relation to each other, but according to very variable time scale. Events may be rapidly (or even instantly) eclipsed by other events with greater 'value'.

The most influential explanation of news values is probably that offered by Galtung and Ruge (1965) and already mentioned (pages 277–8). They identified socio-cultural influences that derive from 'Northern European' culture. From this perspective, news values tend to favour events that are about elite people, elite nations and negative happenings. Events scoring high on all these values are believed to produce most audience interest, and these values are consistent with several of the organizational and genre-related selection requirements. Thus 'bigness' goes with eliteness; personal actions fit the short time scale and are least ambiguous and most 'bounded'; negative events often fit the production time schedule, are unambiguous and can be personalized (such as disasters, killings and crimes).

The approach to explaining news in terms of news values also depends on the assumption of a highly routinized process of 'news discovery'. However, sometimes events break through routines, and the really dramatic and unexpected dominates the news. This is captured by what Tuchman (1978) refers to as the news typification of 'What a story!'. Events in this category are extremely diverse, united only by their unexpectedness, significance, and strain on credibility of all concerned (see also Berkowitz, 1992). The fact of a news medium having a scoop on a story that is less

than world-shattering can also make it a 'What a story'. The main point is to remind us that the reporting of events is a dynamic process, while the 'news value' assessment approach may miss the dynamic.

An aspect of news work that is related to the 'What a story' phenomenon is the notion of a 'key event'. This refers to the kind of event that becomes a big news story not only because of scale, unexpectedness and dramatic quality, but because of some unusual degree of public resonance and significance in symbolizing some deeper public crisis or anxiety. The original idea was provided by Fishman (1982) who referred to a particular account of a crime as triggering a wave of news coverage about crime. Other examples that have been mentioned include the Chernobyl disaster, the death of Princess Diana, etc. Key events are real happenings and not at all the same as 'media events'. Kepplinger and Habermeier (1995) investigated the hypothesis that *key events* can have a powerful effect on the representation of reality by triggering a wave of reporting that is quite disproportionate to the reality of occurrence of events. An example close to home for them was the wave of reports about racial attacks on immigrants in Germany that occurred in 1992 and 1993. Their study of news reporting in Germany before and after certain significant events confirmed the hypothesis that key events do stimulate much enhanced attention to certain topics over a certain period, without there being any change in the reality of these topics. One way in which the media coped with the fact that there was no changed reality was to report about other similar events in the past. This is not the normal role of the newspaper. In general, the findings underline the risk of treatment frequency or prominence of news as a reliable guide to the reality of events. We can also link these findings to theory of 'framing' and 'agenda-setting' (see pages 454–7).

> **Box 14.3   Primary news values in Western media**
>
> - Scale of events
> - Closeness
> - Clarity
> - Short time scale
> - Relevance
> - Consonance
> - Personification
> - Negativity
> - Significance
> - Drama and action

News bias and the **framing** of news

The interpretative framework suggested by Galtung and Ruge (page 278) has been found to apply fairly widely and not only to foreign news. It tells us a certain amount

about the kind of event that will tend to be reported and, by implication, about what will be neglected. Thus it is predictive of a pattern of one general kind of news 'bias'. The theory does not offer a complete explanation of all regularities of news composition, however, and an alternative, less psychological and more structural approach to explanation has been recommended by Rosengren (1974), who argues that several features of news flows can be accounted for by political and economic factors. He demonstrates that flows of trade between countries are good predictors of mutual news attention. The same has been found to be true of international treaty relationships (Ito and Koshevar, 1983). With respect to domestic news, it is plausible that the giving or withholding of news attention has as much to do with political and economic factors as with the news values of individual news selectors or the news value attached to events.

The question of news *structure* has often been discussed in terms of *bias*, although we should not assume any deliberate tendency to mislead. Organizational explanations or the influence of hidden cultural elements are often at the root of apparent bias. In addition, since judgements of news value are often relative and based on a journalistic 'feel for the news' at the particular moment, there will usually be strong elements of subjectivity. The standards of objectivity which are built into the news code are more likely to be expressed in the manner of handling and reporting events than in the selection or the neutrality of presentation.

In the light of research into how media organizations influence the choice of content and especially with a view to possible influence on audiences, much attention has been paid to the question of how news information is presented or 'framed'. Tuchman (1978) referred to Goffman (1974) as the originator of the idea that a frame is needed to organize otherwise fragmentary items of experience or information. The idea of 'frame' in relation to news has been widely and loosely used in place of terms such as 'frame of reference', 'context', 'theme', or even 'news angle'. In a journalistic context, stories are given meaning by reference to some particular 'news value' that connects one event with other similar ones. While it is a common-sense notion, it is also useful to use the term with some precision, especially when the aim is to study possible effects of framing of news. In that case the content frame has to be compared with the frame of reference in the mind of an audience member. According to Entman (1993) 'Framing involves *selection* and *salience*'. He summarizes the main aspects of framing by saying that frames *define problems*, *diagnose causes*, *make moral judgements*, *suggest remedies*. It is clear that a very large number of textual devices can be used to perform these activities. They include the use of certain words or phrases, making certain contextual references, choosing certain pictures or film, referring to certain sources and so on.

Framing is a way of giving some interpretation to isolated items of fact. It is almost unavoidable for journalists to do this and in so doing departing from pure 'objectivity' and introducing some (albeit unintended) bias. When information is supplied to news media by sources (as much often is), then it often arrives with a built-in frame that suits the purpose of the source and is unlikely to be purely objective. There are numerous examples of framing in the literature of content analysis, a few of which can

be mentioned. Race relations issues have often been presented as problematic for society rather than for immigrant minorities (Hartman and Husband, 1974). Almost all news about the Soviet Union and Eastern Europe was for decades reported in terms of the 'Cold War' and the Soviet 'enemy' (McNair, 1988). Up to the present moment the situation in Northern Ireland has been reported, by the British media at least, in terms of the threat posed by the IRA, as if they were the only cause of the conflict (Elliott, 1982; Curtis, 1984) and the British the only victims. The list is a long one and generally seems to suggest that the more powerful the source and the more control of information flow, the more extra-media influence there is on the framing process.

The general reasons why frames are employed are clear enough from organizational factors and from the need to communicate efficiently with audiences, but the reasons for particular frames need to be assessed on a case-by-case basis. An important question is the degree to which frames are fragmentary and diverse or monopolistic in terms of meaning. Where large political or strategic influences are involved there are very active efforts to determine how events are framed. The more distant the events, the easier it is to achieve some consensual framing, since the sources of alternative views have less access and the audience is less personally involved.

Manheim (1998) describes the public relations campaign designed to gain American public support for action to liberate Kuwait in 1990 and 1991. Research established that an appeal to justice did not help as much as the demonization of Saddam Hussein as a latter-day Hitler. In the recent Kosovo conflict, NATO propaganda aimed from the start of the air attack on Yugoslavia to frame the event as both a necessary and 'humanitarian' war against 'genocide', also calling up images of the Holocaust, comparing Milosovic to Hitler and generally demonizing the Serbs. The purpose was to raise and keep support in public opinion and to combat alternative available frames according to which the attack was perceived as illegal, excessively brutal or an inappropriate way to deal with an internal ethnic conflict. The materials for framing were readily available to the media from the previous years of savage Balkan conflict, and on the whole the propaganda offensive was successful with European media, although it did not prevent official criticism of those media that occasionally offered some alternative or just more balanced perspective.

The form of the news report

The strength of the news genre is attested to by the extent to which certain basic features are found across the different media of print, radio and television, despite the very different possibilities and limitations of each. The shared elements of form can be summarized as having to do with *recurrence*, *neutrality* and *facticity*. Newspapers and news bulletins show great constancy over time in appearance, in length or duration

and in the balance of types of content, such as foreign, political, sports, economic, or human interest news (McQuail, 1977).

Much the same is true of television news, so that the number of items does not vary much from one bulletin to another with the same news service. There is even a steady relationship between type of content and average length (Glasgow Media Group, 1976). Some of these features of regularity are found to be much the same in different countries (Rositi, 1976; Heinderyckx, 1993). What is striking is the extent to which a presumably unpredictable universe of events seems open to incorporation, day after day, into much the same temporal, spatial and topic frame. It is true that deviations occur, at times of crisis or exceptional events, but the news form is posited on the normality and predictability of the world of events.

Another main aspect of news form has to do with indications of relative significance of events and of types of content and with ways of structuring the whole. Significance is mainly indicated by the sequencing of content and by the relative amount of space or time allocated. According to what the Glasgow Media Group (1980) calls 'viewers' maxims', it will be understood that first-appearing items in television news are most 'important' and that, generally, items receiving more time are also more important. However, it has not been easy to turn daily observation into systematic theory or general statement. Television news bulletins are generally constructed with a view to arousing initial interest, by highlighting some event, maintaining interest through diversity and human interest and holding back some vital information to the end (sports results and weather forecast), then sending the viewer away at the close with a light touch.

The Glasgow Media Group argued that the hidden purpose or effect of this is to reinforce a 'primary framework' of normality and control and a view of the world that is essentially ideological. The world is 'naturalized' (see also Tuchman, 1978). Rositi's (1976) search for the latent organization in the television news of four European countries led to rather modest but interesting results. He concluded that 'perhaps the only latent organization to be found at the level of the entire news program is that described as the movement from a fragmented image of society to its recomposition through the homogeneity of interests and political representation'.

The regularities described characterize the dominant Western news form, and it is possible that media operating under different 'press theories' will exert different kinds of regularity. There are almost certainly significant and systematic differences between television news-giving in different societies, although these are more likely to follow cultural and institutional lines of demarcation which are different from national and language frontiers. A comparison of US and Italian television news, for instance, led to the conclusion that each system's news gives a significantly different conception of what politics is about (Hallin and Mancini, 1984). The main differences were attributed to the much larger space occupied by a public sphere, other than the state, in the case of Italy. As a result, journalists in the USA have a much larger role as representatives of the public than they adopt, or are credited with, in Italy. A comparison of the basic news formats of seventeen main evening television

news bulletins in Western Europe found relatively minor deviations of practice (Heinderyckx, 1993).

NEWS AS NARRATIVE

The text as narrative has for long been an object of study, and the narrative concept has proved useful in understanding a variety of media contents. Basic narrative forms span a wide range of types, including advertisements and news 'stories' as well as the more obvious candidates of drama and fiction. In one way or another, most media content tells stories, which take rather patterned and predictable forms. The main function of narrative is to help make sense of reports of experience. It does this in two main ways: by linking actions and events in a logical sequential or causal way; and by providing the elements of people and places that have a fixed and recognizable (realistic) character. Narrative helps to provide the logic of human motive that makes sense of fragmentary observations, whether fictional or realistic. When news is considered as narrative, we can appreciate the way in which it draws on and retells the recurrent and dominant myths of a society, inevitably with some 'ideological' loading (Bird and Dardenne, 1988).

Darnton (1975) argues that our conception of news results from 'ancient ways of telling stories'. News accounts are typically cast in narrative form, with principal and minor actors, connected sequences, heroes and villains, beginning, middle and end, signalling of dramatic turns and a reliance on familiar plots. The analysis of news narrative structure has been formalized in the 'discourse analysis' tradition, especially by van Dijk (1983, 1985), who has developed an empirically based framework for the analysis of news based on the concept of 'news schemata', which provide a syntax of news stories.

The general categories are followed implicitly by news producers (part of their 'working theory'). Bell has extended and applied van Dijk's framework, which he summarizes as follows:

> A news text will normally consist of an abstract, attribution and the story proper . . . . A story consists of one or more episodes, which in turn consist of one or more events. Events must contain actors and action, usually express setting, and may have explicit attribution . . . . As well as those elements which present the central action, we recognize three additional categories that can contribute to an event: follow-up; commentary and background. (1991: 169)

Bell remarks that 'the most striking character of news discourse comes from the non-chronological order of its elements', which he attributes to the need to obey news

content

values rather than ordinary narrative norms. Fragments of information are selected by a journalist and reassembled in newsworthy order.

Factual reporting versus storytelling

Many aspects of news form are clearly related to the pursuit of objectivity in the sense of facticity or factualness. The language of news is 'linear', elaborating an event report along a single dimension with added information, illustration, quotation and discussion. Tuchman (1978) describes some of the familiar features of news narrative – for instance the fact that it is told in the past tense, with headlines in the present tense and also that it avoids conventions associated with fiction. She also observes an equivalent narrative style for television news film as follows.

> News film casts an aura of representation by [the fact that] . . . its uses of time and space announce that the tempo of events and spatial arrangements have *not* been tampered with to tell this story. By seeming *not* to arrange time and space, news films claim to present facts, not interpretations. That is, the web of facticity is embedded in a supposedly neutral, not distorted, synchronization of film with the rhythm of everyday life. (1991: 109–10)

According to the Glasgow Media Group (1980: 160) 'the language of news seems to be in a form which would allow of a fairly simple test of its truth or falsity. It has the appearance of being entirely constative (propositional and capable of being shown to be true or false) and not *performative*'. Both terms are taken from J.L. Austin and were used by Morin (1976) in an attempt to describe the basic ambiguity of the news discourse. According to her (structuralist) analysis of the news form, an event has to be rendered into a 'story about an event'. This process involves a negotiation between two opposed modes: that of the 'performative', which is also the interpretative and the 'fabulative' (storytelling) mode, and that of the 'constative', which is also the 'demonstrative' and factual mode. Thus 'pure facts' have no meaning, and 'pure performance' stands far removed from the irreversible, rationally known fact of history, which news is generally supposed to purvey. In Morin's view, different kinds of story involve different combinations of both and can be plotted against the two 'axes' of the television discourse.

There is little doubt of the vital nature of facticity to the news genre. Tuchman (1978) tells us that a key element of facticity is attribution to very credible or positively verified sources. As Smith puts it, 'The whole idea of news is that it is beyond a plurality of viewpoints' (1973: 174). In his view, without an attribution of credibility by the audience, news could not be distinguished from entertainment or propaganda. This may point to one reason why Gans's (1979) seemingly reasonable plea for 'multi-perspectival news' was unlikely to receive universal acclaim and why the secular trend in news development has been away from ideology and towards neutrality. Despite this, there is little reason to modify Gerbner's (1964) conclusion from a study of the

media genres and texts

French press that 'there is no fundamentally non-ideological, apolitical, non-partisan news-gathering and reporting system'.

ALTERNATIVE VERSIONS OF THE NEWS SEQUENCE

Despite the progress of media research and theory there remains a gap between two different conceptions of the news-making process – a gap that separates the 'common-sense' journalistic view from media theory. Four elements are related in a different sequence in the two views: events, criteria of news selection (news values), news interests of the public, and news report. The 'view from the media' emphasizes the reality-responsive quality of news, and the theoretical viewpoint the structured and autistic nature of the news selection process. According to the former (journalistic) view, the normal news sequence is as follows:

1. events
2. news criteria
3. news report
4. news interest.

This sequence begins with the world of unpredictable happenings which 'obtrude' and break the normality and to which news media respond by applying criteria concerning relative significance for their public. They compile objective news reports of the chosen events, and the public responds with attention and interest or not, a datum which feeds into subsequent selection behaviour.

The alternative (theoretical) model of the sequence is:

1. news interest
2. news criteria
3. events
4. news report.

Here the starting point is experience of what gains the attention of the public, which contributes to a rather stable and enduring set of news criteria, including the organizational and genre requirements. News events are only recognized as news-worthy if they conform to these selection criteria. News reports are then written, guided more by the news organization's own requirements and routine practices than by reference to the 'real world' of events or what audiences 'really' want or need.

It is not necessary to make an absolute choice between the models, but they cannot both be true to what happens. The second version is a further illustration of the influence of the 'publicity' (attention-gaining) model described in Chapter 3.

A new form of discourse concerning media texts has appeared, especially with the rise of cultural studies and its convergence on an existing tradition of mass communication research. The origins of cultural studies are somewhat mixed, including traditional literary and linguistic analysis of texts, semiology and Marxist theory. A convincing effort has been made by Fiske (1987) to bring much disparate theory together, especially for the purpose of analysing and understanding popular (television) culture. New definitions of the media text have been introduced along with ways of identifying some key features.

The concept of text

The term **text** has been mainly used in two basic senses, one of them to refer very generally to the physical message itself – the printed document, film, television programme or musical score, as noted above. An alternative usage, recommended by Fiske, is to reserve the term 'text' for the meaningful outcome of the encounter between content and reader. For instance, a television programme 'becomes a text at the moment of reading, that is, when its interaction with one of its many audiences activates some of the meanings/pleasures that it is capable of provoking' (1987: 14). It follows from this definition that the same television programme can produce many different texts in the sense of accomplished meanings. Summing up this point, Fiske tells us that 'a programme is produced by the industry, a text by its readers' (ibid.). It is important, from this perspective, to see that the word 'production' applies to the activities of both the 'mass communicators' and the audiences.

This is a central point in what is essentially a theory of media content viewed from the point of view of its reception rather than its production or intrinsic meaning. Other essential elements in this approach are to emphasize that the media text (in the first or 'programme' sense) has many potential alternative meanings that can result in different readings. Mass media content is thus in principle *polysemic*, having multiple potential meanings for its 'readers' (in the generic sense of audience members). Fiske argues that polysemy is a necessary feature of truly popular media culture, since the more potential meanings there are, the greater the chance of appeal to different audiences and to different social categories within the total audience.

Multiplicity of textual meaning has an additional dimension, as Newcomb (1991) reminds us. Texts are constituted out of many different languages and systems of meaning. These include the codes of dress, physical appearance, class and occupation, religion, ethnicity, region, social circles and many more. Any words in a spoken

language or interactions in a drama can have different meanings in relation to any or several of these other languages.

Differential encoding

Despite this polysemic character, the discourses of particular examples of media content are often designed or inclined to control, confine or direct the taking of meaning, which may in turn be resisted by the reader. This discussion relates to Hall's (1973/1980) model of *encoding/decoding* (discussed in Chapter 3), according to which there is usually a *preferred reading* encoded in a text – the meaning which the message producer would like the receiver to take. On the whole, it is the 'preferred readings' that are identified by analysis of overt content – the literal or surface meaning plus the ideology. As Fiske (1987) also reminds us, the text as produced by the reader is not confined in its meaning by the boundaries that are set on the production side between programmes or between content categories. A 'reader' of media texts can easily combine, for instance, the experience of a programme with that of advertisements inserted in it, or with adjoining programmes.

This is one aspect of the intertextuality of media, and it applies also to crossing boundaries between media (such as film, books and radio). Intertextuality is not only an accomplishment of the reader but also a feature of media themselves, which are continually cross-referencing from one medium to another, and the same 'message', story or type of narrative can be found in very different media forms and genres. The expansion of marketing based on media images has extended the range of inter-textuality from media content 'texts' to all kind of consumption articles. Television, according to Fiske (1987), gives rise to a 'third level of intertextuality' – referring to the texts that viewers make themselves and reproduce in conversation or in writing about the media experience. Ethnographic researchers into media audiences draw on such 'third-level' texts when they listen in on conversations or organize group discussions to hear about how the media are experienced (for example, Radway, 1984; Ang, 1985; Liebes and Katz, 1986).

Codes are systems of meaning whose rules and conventions are shared by members of a culture or by what has been called an 'interpretative community' (for instance, a set of fans of the same media genre, author or performer). Codes help to provide the links between media producers and media audiences by laying the foundation for interpretation. We make sense of the world by drawing on our understanding of communicative codes and conventions. Particular gestures, expressions, forms of dress and images, for example, carry more or less unambiguous meanings within particular cultures that have been established by usage and familiarity. An example of a film code (Monaco, 1981) is an image combining a weeping woman, a pillow and money, to symbolize shame.

In the particular discourse about media content under discussion, the content may be considered to be more or less 'open' or 'closed' in its meanings. According to Eco (1979), an open text is one whose discourse does not try to constrain the reader to one particular meaning or interpretation. Different kinds and actual examples of media text can be differentiated according to their degree of openness. For instance, in general, news reports are intended not to be open but to lead to a uniform informational end, while serials and soap operas are often loosely articulated and lend themselves to varied 'readings'. This differentiation is not always consistent between genres, and there can be large variations within genres in the degree of textual openness. In the case of commercial advertisements, while they are intended to achieve a long-term goal benefiting the product advertised, the form of advertisement can range from the playful and ambiguous to the one-dimensional 'hard sell' or simple announcement. It has also been argued that television in general has a more open and ambiguous text than cinema film (Ellis, 1982).

The distinction between open and closed texts has a potential ideological significance. In their discussion of the television portrayal of terrorism, for instance, Schlesinger et al. (1983) argued that a more open portrayal also leads to alternative viewpoints, while a closed portrayal tends to reinforce the dominant or consensual view. They make another distinction between a 'tight' or 'loose' storyline, reinforcing the tendency of the closed versus open choice. They conclude that television news is in general both closed and tight, while documentary and fiction are more variable. They observe that, in the case of fiction, the larger the (expected) audience, the more closed and tight the representation of terrorism, thus converging on the 'official' picture of reality as portrayed on the news. This suggests some form of ideological control (probably self-censorship), with risks not being taken with a mass audience.

Seriality

There has been a revival of interest in narrative theory (Oltean, 1993), especially as a result of the great attention given to television drama, serials and series in media studies (for example, Seiter et al., 1989). The topic of **seriality** now has a place in narrative theory. Narrative theory itself owes much to the work of Propp (1968), who uncovered the basic similarity of narrative structure of Russian folk tales. Modern popular media fiction also testifies to the high degree of constancy and similarity of a basic plot. For instance, Radway (1984) described the basic narrative logic of mass-produced romance stories for women in terms of a series of stages. It starts with a disturbance for the heroine, through an antagonistic encounter with an aristocratic

male, by way of a separation, to a reconciliation and a sexual union, concluding with a restoration of identity for the heroine.

While basic plots can be found in many different genres, with a range of established but familiar variations, there are other narrative differences to note. Television *series* can, for instance, be clearly differentiated from *serials*, using narrative theory. The series consists of a set of discrete stories which are terminated in each episode. In the cases of serials, the story continues without end from one episode to the next. In both cases there is continuity, primarily achieved by retaining the same principal characters. However, there is a difference: in series, the heroes and heroines (subjects) remain constant, while the villains (objects) differ from one episode to another. The same characters go through different narrative sequences in the same settings. In between episodes, as Oltean (1993) remarks, 'the marionettes stay put in a cabin placed outside the fictional reality'.

By contrast, with serials (such as normal soap operas, which in their original form were broadcast daily) the same cast of characters appears each time, and an illusion is fostered that they continue their life actively between episodes. They 'remain fictively active' (Oltean, 1993). Another aspect of narrative underlined by Oltean is the difference between 'linear' and 'parallel' processing. In serials there is a transition from one storyline to the next, while in series there is a 'meta-story' (concerning the permanent characters), with several different storylines as they encounter their new adventures week by week. The series organizes stories according to a principle of linearity, while serials (such as soap operas) prefer parallel processing with a network of concurrent storylines involving different sub-groups of the permanent cast of characters interacting and interweaving on varying time scales.

Realism

Narrative often depends on assumptions about realism and helps to reinforce a sense of reality, by invoking the logic, normality and predictability of human behaviour. The conventions of realistic fiction were established by the early forms of the novel, although they were preceded by realism in other arts. On the one hand, realism of media depends on a certain attitude that what is portrayed is 'true to life', if not literally true in the sense of having actually occurred. Realistic fiction depends on the belief that it *could* occur or might have done so. Even fantastic stories can be made realistic if they use actual settings and social backgrounds and gain verisimilitude from applying plausible logics of action.

There are also techniques of writing and filming that emphasize realism. In the former case, accurate documentary-like descriptions and concrete, logical and sequential storytelling achieve the result. In filming, aside from representing real places, a continuous flow of action serves to create a realistic illusion. Sometimes black and white film stock is inserted (for instance in flash-backs) to indicate that scenes have a real or documentary character. There are also classic realistic stylistic devices

(Monaco, 1981). One of these is the 'shot-reverse-shot', which moves the camera from one speaker to a partner in a dialogue to create the illusion for the spectator of involvement in the ongoing conversation (Fiske, 1987).

Film and television can also employ in fiction the 'documentary' mode or style, which is established on the basis of learned conventions. In general, documentary style relies on real places and social settings to create the illusion of actuality. According to Fiske (1987), media realism leads in a 'reactionary' (rather than a radical) direction because it 'naturalizes' the status quo – makes it seem normal and therefore inevitable. In the terms used above, realism goes in the direction of 'closure', since the more real-seeming the portrayal, the more difficult for the reader, who is likely to take the reality of the world for granted, to establish any alternative meanings. This relates back to Schlesinger et al.'s (1983) evidence about differing degrees of openness and closure in news and fiction.

Differential 'reading' of texts

Although the broad approach to media content under review does assume that meaning is variable, according to an interpretation by the reader, there is also a recognition of the 'bias of encoding' in the form of 'preferred meanings'. One aspect of this relates to the notion of the 'inscribed reader' (Sparks and Campbell, 1987). Particular media contents can be said, in line with the theory of Bourdieu (1986), to 'construct' a reader, a construction which can to some extent be 'read back' by an analyst on the basis of the set of concerns in the text as written. The 'inscribed reader' is also the kind of reader who is primarily *addressed* by a message. A similar concept is that of the 'implied audience' (Deming, 1991).

The process by which this works has also been called *interpellation* or appellation, and usually refers back to the ideology theories of Althusser (1971). According to Fiske (1987: 53), 'interpellation refers to the way any use of discourse "hails" the addressee. In responding . . . we implicitly accept the discourse's definition of "us", or . . . we adopt the subject position proposed for us by the discourse'. This feature of discourse is widely exploited in advertising (Williamson, 1978), where advertisements commonly construct and project their image of a model consumer of the product in question. They then invite 'readers' to recognize themselves in these images. Such images normally associate certain desirable qualities (such as chicness, cleverness, youth or beauty) with using the product, and generally this is flattering to the consumer as well as to the product.

Gendered media texts

The concept of an inscribed (written-into) or interpellated reader can be used to analyse the audience image sought by particular media, in terms of class, cultural taste,

age or lifestyle (Sparks and Campbell, 1987). It is widely argued that many kinds of media content, following the same line of argument, are differentially gendered. They have built in some bias towards the supposed characteristics of one or other gender, presumably for reasons of appealing to a chosen audience, or simply because many language codes are innately gendered.

Fiske gives an example based on the television police series *Cagney and Lacey*, which features two women as the chief protagonists. In the series, 'the discourse of gender . . . underwrites a number of codes to discourage us from adopting the masculine point of view that is normal in patriarchal television'. The female active role is 'represented as a controlling, active person upon whom the camera dwells not in order to display her sexual attractiveness, but to explore and convey the manner in which she is controlling the scene' (1987: 53).

A number of writers (for example, Geraghty, 1991) have argued that the soap opera as a genre is intrinsically 'gendered' as female narrative, by way of its characterization, settings and dialogue and the positioning of male and female roles. Modleski (1982) suggested that the loose structure of the typical soap opera matches the fragmented pattern of the housewife's daily work. By contrast, television action serials can often be said to be gendered in a masculine way. Some of the differences (as with advertising) are certainly caused by simply planning to appeal to different audience groups, following conventional and often stereotyped ideas about male–female differences. Mass-produced romances of the kind described by Radway (1984) are clearly 'gendered' from the start and mostly written by women as well as openly for women. However, this is not likely to be the whole explanation, and 'gendering' can take subtle and not always intended forms, which makes the pursuit of the topic worthwhile.

For example, a study of female and male film directors by Patsy Winsor, reported by Real (1989), showed a number of significant differences in the content of popular films made by men and women. Female film directors were noticeably less inclined to include acts of physical aggression or to associate them so strongly with men. They showed women in more active roles, and in several different and less predictable ways produced distinctive texts. The study concluded that, notwithstanding the constraints of popular film-making, there was some evidence of the emergence of a 'women's aesthetic'.

Studying the popular

The approach to content which has been reviewed has seemed especially suited to the study of popular mass entertainment, especially fictional and dramatic forms, which seek to involve the reader in a fantasy, but usually in realistic settings. The aim of such media content is to convey not any specific meaning but simply 'entertainment' – taking people out of themselves and into other worlds of the imagination, caught up in dramatic actions and emotions. The texts employed for this purpose tend to be relatively 'open' and do not have to work hard at the cognitive level.

Outside the sphere of popular fiction, there is likely to be a greater tension between the postulate of *polysemy* and the view that texts are structured in certain ways to achieve their audience and their effect. The inscribed texts of media news, for instance, are much more closed and determinate in their informational purpose, even if they also can be differentially or even aberrantly 'decoded' (Eco, 1979).

Box 14.4   The cultural text approach

- Media texts are jointly produced with their readers
- Texts may be differentially encoded
- Texts are 'polysemic' – many potential meanings
- Media texts are related to other texts (intertextual)
- Media texts employ different narrative forms

FURTHER READING

Altheide, D.L. and Snow, R.P. (1979) *Media Logic*. Beverly Hills, CA: Sage.

Berger, A.A. (1992) *Popular Culture Genres*. Newbury Park, CA: Sage.

Curran, B.J., Morley, D. and Walkerdine, V. (eds) (1996) *Cultural Studies and Communications*. London: Edward Arnold.

Newcomb, C.H. (ed.) *Television: the Critical View*. New York: Oxford University Press.

Radway, D.J. (1984) *Reading the Romance*. Chapel, NC: University of North Carolina Press.

AUDIENCES

15

audience theory and research traditions

The word 'audience' is very familiar as the collective term for the 'receivers' in the simple sequential model of the mass communication process (source, channel, message, receiver, effect) that was deployed by pioneers in the field of media research (see, e.g. Schramm, 1955). It is a term that is understood by media practitioners as well as theorists and is recognized by media users as an unambiguous description of themselves. Nevertheless, beyond common-sense usage, there is much room for differences of meaning and theoretical disputes. These stem mainly from the fact that a single word is being applied to an increasingly diverse and complex reality, open to alternative and competing theoretical formulations. One commentator has gone as far as to suggest that 'what is occurring is the breakdown of the *referent* for the word audience in communication research from both the humanities and the social sciences' (Biocca, 1988a: 103). In other words, we keep the familiar word, but the thing itself is disappearing.

The audience for most mass media is not usually observable, except in fragmentary or indirect ways. According to Allor (1988) 'The audience exists nowhere; it inhabits no real space, only positions within analytic discourses'. As a result, the term 'audience' has an abstract and debatable character and the reality to which the term refers is also diverse and constantly changing.

Audiences are both a product of social context (which leads to shared cultural interests, understandings and information needs) and a response to a particular pattern of media provision. Often they are both at the same time, as when a medium sets out to appeal to the members of a social category or the residents of a certain place. Media use also reflects broader patterns of time use, availability, lifestyle and everyday routines.

An audience can thus be defined in different and overlapping ways: by *place* (as in the case of local media); by *people* (as when a medium is characterized by an appeal to a certain age group, gender, political belief or income category); by the particular type of *medium* or *channel* involved (technology and organization combined); by the *content* of its messages (genres, subject matter, styles); by *time* (as when one speaks of the 'daytime' or 'primetime' audience, or an audience that is fleeting and short term compared with one that endures).

ORIGINS OF THE AUDIENCE

The early origins of today's media audience lie in public theatrical and musical performances as well as in the games and spectacles of ancient times. Our earliest notions of audience are of a physical gathering in a certain place. A Greek or Roman

city would have a theatre or arena, and it was no doubt preceded by informal gatherings for similar events and for religious or state occasions. The Graeco-Roman audience had many features that are familiar today, including:

- planning and *organization* of viewing and listening as well as of the performances themselves;
- events with a *public* and 'popular' character;
- *secular* (thus not religious) content of performance – for entertainment, education and vicarious emotional experience;
- *voluntary*, individual acts of choice and attention;
- *specialization of roles* of authors, performers and spectators;
- physical *locatedness* of performance and spectator experience.

The audience, thus, as a set of spectators for public events of a secular kind, was already institutionalized more than two thousand years ago. It had its own customs, rules and expectations about the time, place and content of performances, conditions for admission, and so forth. It was typically an urban phenomenon, often with a commercial basis, and content varied according to social class and status. Because of its public character, audience behaviour was subject to surveillance and social control.

The modern mass media audience shares some of these features but is also very different. There has been a proliferation of audience forms, but media technological inventions have also brought the social innovation of a new dominant form, one that retains some of the meaning of the early 'audience', but which is no longer the same. It differs especially in being much larger, much more dispersed, individualized and privatized.

FROM MASS TO MARKET

Although many observers commented on the amazing new possibilities for reaching so many disparate people so quickly by the press, film or radio, the first theoretical formulation of the media audience concept stemmed from a wider consideration of the changing nature of social life in modern society. As recounted in Chapter 3, Herbert Blumer (1939) first provided an explicit framework in which the audience could be exemplified as a new form of collectivity made possible by the conditions of modern societies. He called this phenomenon a 'mass' and differentiated it from older social forms – especially the group, the crowd and the public.

This concept of a mass seemed to capture several essential features of the audiences attracted to the commercial newspaper and the cinema. The mass audience was large and widely dispersed, and its members did not and could not know each other. Its

composition was always shifting and it lacked any sense of self-identity, because of its dispersion and heterogeneity. The audience cannot easily 'talk back' to the producers and senders of mass-media messages. The communicative relationship involved is typically calculative and non-moral, with no real commitment or attachment on either side. There is also often a large **social** distance between a more powerful, expert or prestigious media source and the audience member.

This view of the mass audience is less a description of reality, than an accentuation of features typical of conditions of mass production and distribution of news and entertainment. When used by early commentators, the term generally had a pejorative connotation, reflecting Western values of individualism and a pessimistic view of modern industrial society, by contrast with an image of a more communal and satisfying way of life. Calling an audience a mass, reflected fears of depersonalization, irrationality, manipulation and of a general decline in cultural or moral standards.

Rediscovery of the audience as a group

The reality of people's experience of mass print and film was always very diverse. While impersonality, anonymity and vastness of scale might describe the phenomenon in general, much actual audience experience is personal, small-scale and integrated into social life and familiar ways. Many media operate in local environments and are embedded in local cultures. Since most people make their own media choices freely, they do not typically feel manipulated by remote powers. The social interaction that develops around media use helps people to incorporate it into everyday life as a friendly rather than an alienating presence.

There was a significant turning point in the history of mass communication theory, during the 1940s and 1950s (Delia, 1987), when the atomistic conception of a mass audience was challenged by researchers (see especially Katz and Lazarsfeld, 1955). Research hailed the 'rediscovery of the group', finding evidence that it had never really disappeared, even in the seemingly unfavourable conditions of the large industrial city (Janowitz, 1952). Actual audiences were shown to consist of many overlapping networks of social relations based on locality and common interests, and the 'mass' media were incorporated into these networks in different ways. The communal and social group character of audiences was restored to conceptual prominence (e.g. Merton, 1949; Janowitz, 1952).

Audience as market

However one interprets the early history of broadcasting, there is no doubt that the radio and television audience rapidly developed into an important consumer

market for hardware and software. At first sight, the widely used expression 'media market' might seem to offer a more objective alternative to other, more value-laden, terms to describe the audience phenomenon. As the media have become bigger business, the term 'market' has gained in currency. It can designate regions served by media, social-demographic categories, or the actual or potential consumers of particular media services or products. It may be defined as an 'aggregate of actual or potential consumers of media services and products, with a known social-economic profile'.

While the market concept is a pragmatic and useful one for media industries and for analysing media economics, it can also be problematic and it is not really value-free. It links sender and receiver in a 'calculative' rather than a normative or social relationship, as a cash transaction between producer and consumer rather than a communication relationship. It ignores the internal relations between consumers, since these are of little interest to service providers. It privileges social-economic criteria and focuses on media *consumption* rather than reception.

Effective communication and the quality of audience experience are of secondary importance in market thinking. The significance of audience experience for the wider public sphere is also de-emphasized. The view of the audience as market is inevitably the view 'from the media' (especially of their owners and managers), and within the terms of the media industries' discourse. People in audiences do not normally have any awareness of themselves as belonging to markets, and the market discourse in relation to the audience is implicitly manipulative.

Box 15.1   The audience as market

- Members are an aggregate of individual consumers
- Boundaries are based mainly on economic criteria
- Members are unrelated to each other
- Members have no shared identity
- The formation is temporary

CRITICAL PERSPECTIVES

Perceptions of the audience have often been influenced by negative views about mass media in general and have ranged from simple prejudice and snobbery to sophisticated exercises in media analysis. The first category is exemplified by the view that equates large media audiences with the 'lowest common denominator' of taste and which assumes that 'mass culture', 'low-taste' and 'mass audience' are more or less synonymous. This way of thinking has been described as an 'ideology of

mass culture' (Ang, 1985), according to which, much popular entertainment is automatically condemned as inferior, and those who like it as lacking in taste and discrimination.

The main thrust of critique from the Left was grounded in an attack on the commercial exploiters of more or less vulnerable media consumers. According to Gitlin (1978), the representation in communication research of the audience as active and resistant (as noted above) was itself largely an ideological move designed to obscure the continuing reality and to deflect the attack on monopolist, capitalist media. The school of audience research (especially the 'uses and gratifications' approach) which emphasized the audience as being 'in charge' of their media experience (see pages 366–7) was also attacked for overstating the real autonomy of the audience (Elliott, 1974).

In an innovative and sophisticated move, the Canadian Dallas Smythe (1977) gave birth to the theory that audiences actually *work* for advertisers (thus, for their ultimate oppressors). They do so by giving their free time to watch media, which labour is then packaged and sold by the media to advertisers as a new kind of 'commodity'. The whole system of commercial television and the press rests on this extraction of surplus value from an economically exploited audience.

The same audience has to pay yet again for its media, by way of the extra cost added to the advertised goods. It was an ingenious and convincing piece of theorizing which revealed the mass audience phenomenon in quite a new light (see Jhally and Livant, 1986). It is plausible to suppose that the media need their audience more than audiences need their media, and there is also reason to view audience research as primarily a tool for the close control and management (call it manipulation) of media audiences.

A more recent critical view charges the media industry with routinely transforming the actual television audience into a piece of commercial information called 'ratings' (Ang, 1991). Ratings are described as forming 'the basis for the agreed-upon standard by which advertisers and network buy and sell the audience commodity' (1991: 54). Ang reminds us that 'watching television is an ongoing, day-to-day cultural practice engaged in by millions of people' and the 'ratings discourse' serves to 'capture and encompass the viewing practice of all these people in a singular, object-ified, streamlined construct of "television audience" '. These comments essentially label the industry view of the audience as intrinsically dehumanizing and exploitative. Again, it reflects the view that commercial mass media are served by their audiences rather than vice versa.

Ang (1991) criticized the 'mainstream' audience research tradition for adopting an 'institutional' view which aims to produce commercial and institutional knowledge of an abstraction of the audience for purposes of control and manipulation. She argued that media institutions have no real interest in *knowing* their audiences, only in being able to prove there is one, by way of systems and techniques of measurement (e.g. 'people meters') which convince their clients, but which can never begin to capture the true essence of 'audiencehood'.

Since the audience has always been a contested category, it is not surprising that the purposes of doing research into audiences are varied and often inconsistent. All research shares the general characteristic that it helps to 'construct', 'locate' or 'identify' an otherwise amorphous, shifting or unknowable social entity. But the methods used, the constructions of the audience arrived at, and the uses to which they are put all diverge considerably. Leaving aside the purpose of theory-building, we can classify research goals in terms of the main uses to which information about the audience can be put. These are shown in Box 15.2.

> **Box 15.2   Main goals of audience research**
>
> - Accounting for sales (book-keeping)
> - Measuring actual and potential reach for purposes of advertising
> - Manipulating and channelling audience choice behaviour
> - Looking for audience market opportunities
> - Product-testing and improving communication effectiveness
> - Meeting responsibilities to serve an audience
> - Evaluating media performance in a number of ways (for instance, to test allegations of harmful effects)

Perhaps the most fundamental division of purpose is that between media industry goals and those that take the perspective and 'side' of the audience. Research can, as it were, represent the voice of the audience, or speak on its behalf. The goal of meeting responsibilities to the audience often guides research carried out by public broadcasters (e.g. Emmett, 1968). Although it is not at all sure that audience research can ever truly serve the audience alone, we can provisionally view the different purposes of research as extending along a dimension ranging from audience control to audience autonomy. Eastman (1998) has sketched the history of audience research as a permanent tug-of-war between the media industry seeking to manage audience behaviour, and people seeking to satisfy their media needs.

By far the greatest quantity of audience research belongs at the Control end of the spectrum, since this is what the industry wants and pays for (Beniger, 1986; Eastman, 1998). Few of the results of industry research appear in the public domain, and they are consequently neglected in academic accounts of the audience. Curiously enough, according to Eastman (1998), scholarly research on the audience has made no impact on the media industry. Despite this overall imbalance and general disconnection of research effort, the clearest line of development in audience theory has been a move away from the perspective of the media communicator and towards that of the receiver. It seems as if media industry has also accepted this as a pragmatic trend as a result of the steadily increasing competition for audience attention. Accounts of audience research have increasingly tended to emphasize the 'rediscovery' of people, and

the notion of an active and obstinate audience in the face of attempted manipulation. The preferences of audiences seem to keep ahead as the driving forces of media use.

ALTERNATIVE TRADITIONS OF RESEARCH

Jensen and Rosengren (1990) distinguished five traditions of audience research, which can be summarized as having to do with: effects; uses and gratifications; literary criticism; cultural studies; and reception analysis. For present purposes, it is convenient to deploy a somewhat more economical typology of audience research, by identifying three main variant approaches under the headings 'structural', 'behavioural' and 'social-cultural'. The first of these is not well covered by Jensen and Rosengren's scheme, and the 'literary criticism' heading is of little relevance here.

The structural tradition of audience measurement

The needs of media industries gave rise to the earliest and simplest kinds of research, which were designed to obtain reliable estimates of what were otherwise unknown quantities. These were especially the size and reach of radio audiences and the 'reach' of print publications (the number of potential readers as opposed to the circulation or print-run). These data were essential to management, especially for gaining paid advertising. In addition to size it was important to know about the social composition of audiences in basic terms – the Who and Where of the audience. These elementary needs gave rise to an immense industry interconnected with that of advertising and market research.

The behaviourist tradition: media effects and media uses

Early mass communication research was mainly pre-occupied with media effects, especially on children and young people and with an emphasis on potential harm (see Klapper, 1960). Nearly every serious effects study has also been an audience study, in which the audience is conceptualized as 'exposed' to influence or impact, whether of a persuasive, learning or behavioural kind. The typical effects model was a one-way process in which the audience was conceived as an unwitting target or a passive recipient of media stimuli. The second main type of 'behavioural' audience research was in many ways a reaction from the model of direct effects. Media *use* was now

central, and the audience was viewed as a more or less active and motivated set of media users/consumers, who were 'in charge' of their media experience, rather than passive 'victims'. Research focused on the origin, nature and degree of motives for choice of media and media content. Audiences were also permitted to provide the definitions of their own behaviour (see Blumler and Katz, 1974). The 'uses and gratifications' approach is not strictly 'behavioural', since its main emphasis is on the social origins of media gratifications and on the wider social functions of media, for instance in facilitating social contact and interaction or in reducing tension and anxiety.

The cultural tradition and reception analysis

The cultural studies tradition also occupies a borderland between social science and the humanities. It has been almost exclusively concerned with works of popular culture in contrast to an early literary tradition. It emphasizes media use as a reflection of a particular social-cultural context and as a process of giving meaning to cultural products and experiences in everyday life. This school of research rejects both the stimulus–response model of effects and the notion of an all-powerful text or message. It involves a view of media use as in itself a significant aspect of 'everyday life'. Media reception research emphasized the study of audiences as 'interpretive communities' (Lindlof, 1988). Reception analysis is effectively the audience research arm of modern cultural studies, rather than an independent tradition.

The main features of the culturalist (reception) tradition of audience research can be summarized as follows (though not all are exclusive to this approach).

- The media text has to be 'read' through the perceptions of its audience, which constructs meanings and pleasures from the media texts offered (and these are never fixed or predictable).
- The very process of media use and the way in which it unfolds in a particular context are central objects of interest.
- Media use is typically situation-specific and oriented to social tasks which evolve out of participation in 'interpretative communities'.
- Audiences for particular media genres often comprise separate 'interpretative communities' which share much the same forms of discourse and frameworks for making sense of media.
- Audiences are never passive, nor are all their members equal, since some will be more experienced, or more active fans than others.
- Methods have to be 'qualitative' and deep, often ethnographic, taking account of content, act of reception and context together.

It is fairly obvious that this tradition has little in common with either the structuralist or behaviourist approaches. Behaviourist and psychological approaches

	Structural	*Behavioural*	*Cultural*
Main aims:	Describe composition; enumerate; relate to society	Explain and predict choices, reactions, effects	Understand meaning of content received and of use in context
Main data:	Social-demographic, media and time use	Motives; acts of choice; reactions	Perceptions of meaning re social and cultural context
Main methods:	Survey and statistical analysis	Survey; experiment; mental measurement	Ethnographic; qualitative

FIGURE 15.1 Three audience research traditions compared

may get nearer to the goal of describing the nature of audience experience, but from the cultural perspective the outcomes of research remain abstract, individualized and desiccated renderings which can only lend themselves to manipulative purposes. The three traditions are summarily compared in Figure 15.1.

There are some indications of increasing convergence in research approaches (Schrøder, 1987; Curran, 1990), especially in the combination of quantitative and qualitative methods, but large differences of underlying philosophy and conceptualization remain between the alternative schools. These differences have implications for the goals of research and for the choice of methods.

ISSUES ARISING

This brief review of alternative research approaches helps us to identify the main issues and problems that have shaped thinking and research about mass media audiences, aside from the obvious practical need to have basic information about the audience. As we will see, the transformation of a straight question about the audience into an 'issue' or a social problem normally requires the injection of some value judgements, as described in the following paragraphs.

Media use as addiction

'Excessive' media use has often been viewed as harmful and unhealthy (especially for children), leading to addiction, dissociation from reality, reduced social contacts and diversion from education (Maccoby, 1954; McLeod et al., 1965). Television has been the most usual suspect, but before television, films and comics were regarded similarly, while video games and computers have become the latest perpetrators.

The oldest as well as the most general theoretical question about the audience is whether or not it should be treated as a social group (or public, in the sense outlined earlier) or simply as a mass of isolated individuals. To qualify as the former, an audience would need to show conditions of having boundaries, self-awareness, internal interaction, and systems of normative control (Ennis, 1961). The more an audience is viewed as an aggregate of isolated individuals (or a market of consumers), the more it can be considered as a mass. Many subsidiary questions flow from this, including the issue of whether new interactive media possibilities can help to restore group-like collective features to audience experience.

Audience behaviour as active or passive?

Another broad theoretical issue concerns the degree of 'activity' or 'passivity' that can be attributed to the audience (see Eastman, 1998). By definition, the audience as a mass is passive, because it is incapable of collective action, while any true social group has the means and may have the inclination to be active in the sense of choosing a shared goal and participating in its pursuit. Individual acts of media choice, attention and response can also be more or less active, in terms of degree of motivation, attention, involvement, pleasure, critical or creative response, connection with the rest of life, etc. There has always been a tendency, whether explicitly or not, to view active media use as 'better' than passive.

Alternative media perceptions of the audience

At one extreme, we find a view of the audience as either a consumer market or a commodity to be sold on to advertisers, at so much per thousand. What counts are numbers and purchasing power. Alternatively, the audience can be approached in normative and relational terms, with a genuine communicative purpose. What matters then is its composition, its engagement with communicators and content, the quality of attention and response, its loyalty, commitment and continuity. Also at issue here is the dilemma referred to above, between research for control or for liberation and protection of the audience. Whose side is the researcher on? This question has become inextricably mixed up with the question of methods and the in-built bias of different research approaches. The history of research into audiences has been troubled by a fundamental conflict of view between practitioners of quantitative, survey or experimental, research and advocates of alternative, more qualitative and intensive research.

The former seems more inclined to serve the goals of management, the latter claims to take the point of view, and to 'be on the side', of the audience.

The implications of new media technology

Finally, there is the question of the future of media, especially as a result of the changes in communication technology described above (see Chapter 6), which have led to opposing predictions and valuations. One proposition is that audiences will become more and more fragmented and will lose their national, local or cultural identity. There will also be an increasing gap between the media rich and the media poor. Another negative view of new electronic media is that they strengthen the potential for social control and surveillance (Gandy, 1989; Spears & Lea, 1994). On the other hand, new kinds of integration may compensate for the loss of older forms, more options for audience formation are available to more people and there could be more freedom and diversity of communication and reception.

TYPES OF AUDIENCE

In general, audiences can originate both in society and in media and their contents: either people stimulate an appropriate supply of content, or the media attract people to the content they offer. If we take the first view, we can consider media as responding to the general needs of a national society, local community, pre-existing social group or some category of individuals that the media choose as a 'target group'. Alternatively, if we consider audiences as primarily created by the media, we can see that they are often brought into being by some new technology (as with the invention of film, radio or television) or they are attracted by some additional 'channel', such as a new magazine or radio station. In this case, the audience is defined by the media source (e.g. the 'television audience' or the 'readers of newspaper X') rather than by their shared characteristics.

The media are continuously seeking to develop and hold new audiences, and in doing so they anticipate what might otherwise be a spontaneous demand, or identify potential needs and interests which have not yet surfaced. In the continual flux of media audience formation and change, the sharp distinction made at the outset is not easy to demonstrate. Over time, media provision to pre-existing social groups has become hard to distinguish from media recruitment of social categories to the content offered. Media-created needs have also become indistinguishable from 'spontaneous' needs, or both have fused inextricably. Nevertheless, the theoretical distinction between receiver- and sender-created demand is a useful one for mapping out different

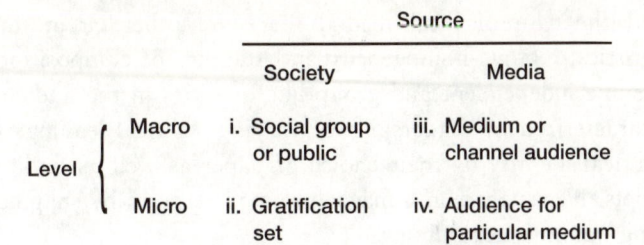

FIGURE 15.2   A typology of mass media audience formation

versions of audience that have been introduced. The distinction is set out in Figure 15.2, first of all between society- and media-created needs and, secondly, between the different levels at which the process operates, whether at macro- or micro-level.

The four main types that are identified in Figure 15.2 are further described in the following sections.

THE AUDIENCE AS A GROUP OR PUBLIC

This type of audience has an independent existence prior to its identification as an audience. The clearest examples are now likely to be either historical or small-scale, since it is increasingly hard for the group-like conditions of interactivity, normative regulation and 'boundedness' to be met in a modern society, let alone for them to define an audience. However, publications set up by political or religious bodies or other associations to serve the purposes of their own organization and members still meet the criteria.

Today, the most common example of a media audience which is also in some sense a social group is probably the readership of a local newspaper or the listener group of a community radio station. Here the audience shares at least one significant social/cultural identifying characteristic – that of shared space and membership of a residential community. Local media can contribute significantly to local awareness and sense of belonging (Janowitz, 1952; Stamm, 1985 and 1997; McLeod et al., 1996; Rothenbuhler et al., 1996). Local residence defines and maintains a wide range of media-relevant interests (e.g. leisure, environmental, work-related, social networks, etc.) and local media advertising serves local retail trade and labour markets as well as residents of the area. Social and economic forces together reinforce the integrative role of local media. Even if a local medium goes out of business, the local community that forms its audience will persist.

audience theory and research traditions   371

Beyond the case of local media, there are other circumstances where shared characteristics, relative homogeneity and stability of composition indicate the existence of some independent and group-like qualities in the audience. Newspapers are often characterized by readerships of varying political leaning, and readers express their political identity by their choice of paper as well as finding reinforcement for their beliefs. Newspapers and magazines may respond by shaping their contents and expressing opinions accordingly.

Public service broadcasting, where it exists, also attracts an audience with some of the features of a genuine public. It is accountable to the general public through a variety of institutional means, including audience participation, and it has an obligation to serve various social groups and minorities in the society. In the case of public television (PBS) in the USA, viewer/listener donations are supposed to forge a bond between media and audience (Avery, 1993).

The conditions of society that militate against the formation of audiences as groups and publics, include especially totalitarian government and very high levels of commercially monopolized media. In the one case, there is no autonomy for social groups, and in the second, audience members are treated as customers and consumers, but with little power in the media market to realize their diverse wants. There are some other relevant examples of audience groups and special publics. For example, the broad term 'alternative' media (Downing, 1984) embraces a wide range of more or less oppositional media channels which can be considered to carry on the tradition of the early radical and party press, especially in developing countries. Many such media are 'micro-media', operating at grass roots level, discontinuous, non-professional, sometimes persecuted or just illegal. The 'samizdat' publications, forbidden under communism, the opposition press in Pinochet's Chile, or the underground press of occupied Europe during the Second World War, are well-known examples. The publics for such media are often small, but they are likely to be intensely committed. They usually have clear social and political goals. Less unusual and more enduring examples are provided by the many minority ethnic and linguistic publications and channels that have grown up in many countries to serve immigrant groups.

One more familiar type of audience which fits the social group criteria named relates to publications (it usually has been print media) which serve or support professional and social identifications, often circulating within a particular, though widely dispersed, network. Here, the audience shares certain goals, interests or understandings, sometimes it forms around a particular public issue. At some point, a notional line divides those 'audiences' which are in the public sphere from those in private, expert or professional circles.

While the trends of the time, especially the great expansion and increased commercialization of big media, seem to work against the formation of social group audiences, many of the new technologies have actually helped to promote such audiences. This has been illustrated by the growth of local and community radio and television (Kleinsteuber and Sonnenberg, 1990; Jankowski et al., 1992). Cable television also made a contribution to challenging the hold of mass broadcasting, and currently

the Internet and World Wide Web are actively promoting new kinds of group-like audiences (see Chapter 6).

THE GRATIFICATION SET AS AUDIENCE

This term is chosen to refer to multiple possibilities for audiences to form and re-form on the basis of some media-related interest, need or preference. The use of the word 'set' implies that such audiences are typically aggregates of dispersed individuals, without mutual ties. While the audience as 'public' often has a wide range of media needs and interests and derives its unity from shared social characteristics, the 'gratification set' is identified by a particular need or type of need (which may, nevertheless, derive from social experience). To a certain degree, this type of audience has gradually supplanted the older kind of public, the result of differentiation of media production and supply to meet distinctive consumer demands. Instead of each public (whether based on place, social class, religion or party) having its own dedicated medium, many self-perceived needs have stimulated their own corresponding supply.

The phenomenon is not new, since early popular newspapers, as well as gossip, fashion and 'family' magazines have long catered for a diverse range of specific but overlapping audience interests. More recently, the range of interests covered has widened, with each type of medium (film, book, magazine, radio, phonogram, etc.) packaging its potential audience appeal in a variety of ways. The sets of readers/viewers/listeners that result from a highly differentiated and 'customized' supply are unlikely to have any sense of collective identity, despite some shared social-demographic characteristics.

Relevant here is the concept of 'taste culture' which was coined by Herbert Gans (1957) to describe something like the audience brought into being by the media, based on a convergence of interests, rather than by shared locality or social background. He defined it as 'an aggregate of similar content chosen by the same people' (in Lewis, 1981: 204). Taste cultures are less sets of people than sets of similar media products – an outcome of form, style of presentation and genre which are intended to match the life-style of a segment of the audience. The more this happens, the more there is likely to be a distinctive social-demographic profile of a taste culture.

Research in the tradition of 'media uses and gratifications' has shed light on the nature of the underlying audience demands and on the way in which they are structured (see below). The motivations expressed for choice of media content and the ways in which this content is interpreted and evaluated by the audience point to the existence of a fairly stable and consistent structure of demand. The *idea* of an audience as characterized by some particular social or psychological need arising out of experience is significant in the 'discourse' about audiences and is helpful in describing

audiences as well as providing the media themselves with guidelines for developing new media services and coping with competition.

THE MEDIUM AUDIENCE

The third version of the audience concept (in Figure 15.2) is the one that identifies it by the choice of a particular type of medium – as in the 'television audience' or the 'cinema-going public'. The earliest such usage was in the expression the 'reading public' – the small minority who could and did read books, when literacy was not very common. The reference is usually to those whose behaviour or self-perception identifies them as regular and attracted 'users' of the medium concerned.

Each medium – newspaper, magazine, cinema, radio, television, phonogram – has had to establish a new set of consumers or devotees, and the process continues with the diffusion of 'new media' such as the Internet or multimedia. It is not especially problematic to locate relevant sets of people in this way, but the further character-ization of these audiences is often crude and imprecise, based on broad social-demographic categories.

This type of audience is close to the idea of a 'mass audience' as described above (page 366), since it is often very large, dispersed and heterogeneous, with no internal organization or structure. It also corresponds to the general notion of a 'market' for a particular kind of consumer service. By now most such audiences are so overlapping that there is little differentiation involved, except in terms of subjective affinity and relative frequency or intensity of use. The audience for any one mass medium is often identical with the audience for another.

Even so, this version of the audience concept retains some relevance, as media forms change and succeed one another. Being a 'member' of the audience for film, for instance, involves learning some elements of a role, certain habits as well as particular understandings and perceptions of a medium and its genres. These are things that develop in social interaction in a particular cultural setting. The full meaning of a particular medium audience varies from place to place and time to time. For example, the 'film audience' of today no longer coincides with the 'cinema-going audience'. It is more home-bound and diverse, older than the cinema audience, accustomed to endless choice from the film archives of the past and stocks of the present, little troubled by censors, hardly limited by cost, supplied by home video and television. There is no longer such a thing as a 'film fan', though there are 'cult films', which can now have a larger following than in the days of dependence on cinema exhibition.

The audience continues to distinguish between media, according to their particular social uses and functions or according to their perceived advantages and disadvantages. Media have fairly distinctive images (Perse and Courtright, 1992). Research has shown that some media are substitutable for each other for certain purposes, while others

have distinctive uses (Katz et al., 1973). Competition between different media for audience and advertising income is intense and these differences play a part. The 'medium audience' is an important concept for those who want to use the media for purposes of advertising and other campaigns, despite the lack of exclusivity. A key decision in advertising is often that concerning the 'media-mix', the division of an advertising budget between the alternatives, taking into account the characteristics of each medium, the audience it reaches and the conditions of reception.

In media economics, the issue of media *substitutability* continues to be important and often turns on the extent to which distinctive medium audiences persist (Picard, 1989). Several considerations come into play, aside from the questions of audience size and demographics. Some messages are best delivered in a domestic or family context, indicating a choice of television, while others may be individual and more risque, indicating posters or magazines. Some may be appropriate in an informational context, others against a background of relaxation and entertainment. From this perspective, the medium audience as target is chosen not only on the basis of socio-economic characteristics, but with reference to typical content carried and the social-cultural associations and context of the media behaviours concerned.

AUDIENCE AS DEFINED BY CHANNEL OR CONTENT

The identification of an audience as the readers, viewers, listeners of a *particular* book, author, film, newspaper title or television programme is relatively straightforward. It is the usage, with which audience research in the 'book-keeping' tradition is most comfortable, and it seems to pose few problems of empirical measurement. There are no hidden dimensions of group relations or consciousness to take account of, no psychological variables of motivation that need to be measured. It is the audience in this very concrete sense, on which the business of the media turns most of all. For this reason, specific content or channel has usually been privileged as a basis for defining audiences, especially in industry-related research.

This version of audience is also consistent with market thinking, according to which audiences are sets of consumers for particular media products. The audience consists either of paying customers or the heads and pockets delivered to advertisers per unit of media product and charged for accordingly. It is expressed as the 'ratings', the 'numbers' which are central to the media business. It provides the main criteria of success in any game of media politics, even where profit is not involved. Increasingly, it is the dominant meaning of the term audience, the only one with immediate practical significance and clear market value. It also involves a view of the audience as a *product* of the media – the first and indubitable *effect* of any medium.

Despite the seeming lack of ambiguity, there are some hidden complications. For instance, the complete audience can never be measured in practice, only reconstructed or estimated after the event. Such an audience can also be defined alternatively in terms of subscribers, or households reached, or readers. Audiences vary in their degree of attention and involvement. In many media situations, choices of content are not made by the individuals that compose the measured audience in this sense. It turns out that this version of the audience concept is hardly less of an abstraction than any other. The great advantage, nevertheless, is the fact that it can be quantified, and once this has been done the rules of mathematics are ultimately unassailable.

This sense of audience is a valid one, but we cannot be limited to it. There are, for instance, audiences in the sense of 'followers' or fans of television or radio serials and series, which cannot be unambiguously measured. There are also audiences for particular films, books, songs and also for stars, writers, performers which only accumulate over time to a significant number or proportionate reach. All of these are relevant aspects of the audience experience, though they usually evade any but the most approximate measurement.

This brings us to the yet more complex question of fans and *fandom*. The term can refer to any set of extremely devoted followers of a media star or performer, performance or text (Lewis, 1992). They are usually identified by great, even obsessive attachment to their object of attraction. Often they show a strong sense of awareness and fellow-feeling with other fans. Being a fan also involves a pattern of supplementary behaviour, in dress, speech, other media use, consumption, etc.

Fandom is often associated in the view of critics with immaturity and mindlessness, an outcome of mass culture and an example of mass behaviour. It has also been interpreted as evidence of manipulation and exploitation – something encouraged by the media to strengthen ties with products and performers, to help with publicity and in order to make extra money from merchandising and other media 'spin-offs'. It helps in extending the life of products and to maximize profit. While this is true, there is an alternative perspective, according to which fandom shows not manipulation by the media but the 'productive power' of audiences (Fiske, 1992). According to this view, the fans actively create new meaning out of the materials offered, building up systems of cultural discrimination, stylistic display, social identification and association which serve to detach the fan group from the manipulative grip of the media.

ALTERNATIVE MODELS OF THE AUDIENCE–SENDER RELATIONSHIP

There is another path towards a typification of the audience and of audience experience that depends on the relationship between source and receiver. It can best be explained in terms of the three alternative models of the communicative relationship

that were introduced in Chapter 3. One can be described as a *transmission* model, another as an *expressive* or *ritual* model and a third as an *attention* model.

The three modes of (mutual) audience orientation and related experiences can be approximately summed up as follows: *cognitive processing*; *sharing and normative commitment*; *attention giving*.

Audience as target

In the transmission model, the communication process is considered primarily as the sending of signals or messages over time for the purposes of control or influence. The receiver, and thus the audience, is perceived as a *destination* or *target* for the purposeful transfer of meaning. This model applies, for example, to education and many kinds of public information campaign, as well as some kinds of advertising. Its basic process is one of 'cognitive processing'.

Audience as participants

According to the 'ritual' or 'expressive' model (Carey, 1975), communication is defined in terms of sharing and participation, increasing the commonality between sender and receiver, rather than in terms of changing 'receivers' in line with the purpose of the 'sender'. Communication is not primarily instrumental or utilitarian, but normative. Audience members are essentially participants.

Audience as spectators

The third audience type arises in a model of communication in which the source does not seek to transmit information or beliefs, but simply to capture the attention of an audience, regardless of communicative effect. Audience attention as 'spectatorship' is involving, but not for long. It implies no 'transfer of meaning' or sharing or deepening of ties between sender and receiver (Elliott, 1972).

QUESTIONS OF AUDIENCE REACH

The least problematic version of the audience concept is probably that which underlies the 'ratings' in their various forms. Media providers need to know a great deal about the extent of media reach (which is at the same time a measure of audience attention),

for reasons of finance or policy or for organization and planning. These concerns create a strong vested interest in the 'canonical audience' referred to by Biocca (1988b: 127). This concept derives from the theatre and cinema and refers to a physical body of identifiable and attentive 'spectators'. A belief in the existence of such an audience is essential to the routine operation of media and provides a shared goal for the media organization (Tunstall, 1971). The fact of having an audience, and the right one as well, is a necessary condition of media organizational survival and it has to be continually demonstrated.

However, this requirement is less easy to meet than it seems, because of the differences between media and different ways of defining the 'reach' of a given medium or message. Leaving inter-media differences aside, there are at least six relevant concepts of audience reach, as follows.

- The 'available' (or potential) audience: all with the basic skills (e.g. literacy) and/or reception capability.
- The 'paying' audience: those who actually pay for a media product – whether newspaper, film entrance, video rental, CD or book.
- The 'attentive' audience: those that actually read, watch, listen, etc. to particular content.
- The 'internal' audience: those who pay attention to particular sections, types or single items of content.
- The 'cumulative' audience: the overall proportion of the potential audience that is reached over a particular period of time.
- The 'target' audience: that section of a potential audience singled out for reach by a particular source (e.g. an advertiser).

There is also the question of listening or viewing as primary or secondary activity, since both can and do accompany other activities, radio more so than television. Conceptually, this is not very crucial, but it matters greatly for measurement (see Twyman, 1994). Other less conventional audiences can also be distinguished, for instance for outdoor billboards and video screens, direct mail, audiotext, telephone selling campaigns, etc. 'Old media' also change their content and uses of old media also change. The terms and definitions presented here are not fixed. However, the principles of classification remain much the same and we can adapt these to new circumstances.

A GENERALIZED VIEW OF AUDIENCE REACH AND IMPACT

The basic features of audience reach, as viewed by the would-be communicator, are shown in Figure 15.3, derived from the work of the Belgian researcher, Roger Clausse (1968).

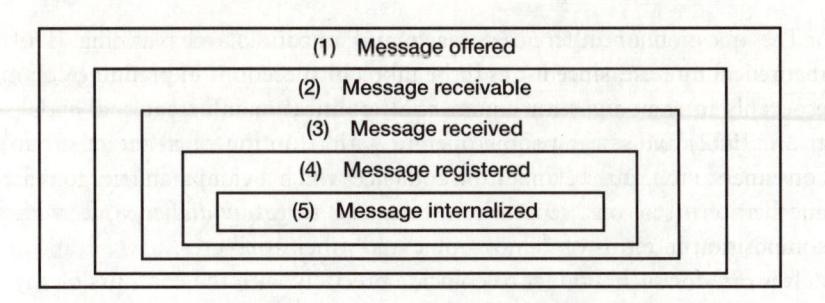

FIGURE 15.3   A schema of differential audience reach (Clausse, 1968)

Although this model was developed for the case of broadcasting, it can apply, in principle, to all mass media to cover most of the distinctions made above. The outer band represents the almost unlimited potential for the reception of broadcast messages. In effect it equates audience with a near-universal distribution system. The second band indicates the realistic maximum limits which apply to reception – delineating the *potential* media public, which is defined by residence in a geographical area of reception, and by possession of the necessary apparatus to receive, or the means to purchase or borrow publications, phonograms, video recordings, etc. It is also determined by the degree of literacy and possession of other necessary skills.

Definitions of availability or eligibility also play a part. For instance, the potential audience might exclude children under a certain age and certain other categories of viewers or listeners (e.g. foreigners or people in institutions). We may also limit the notion of potential audience to those having an affinity with the media concerned as well as habits of use. For some purposes the 'potential audience' has also to take account of time of day – distinguishing, for instance, between an early morning, a daytime and an evening audience.

The third band identifies another level of media public – the *actual* audience reached by a radio or television channel or programme or any other medium. This is what is usually measured by sales, admission and subscription figures, reading surveys and audience ratings (often expressed as a percentage of the potential audience), etc. The fourth and the central band relates to the *quality* of attention, degree of impact and potential effect, some of which are empirically measurable. In practice, only a small fragment of the total of *actual* audience behaviour can ever be measured and the rest is extrapolation, estimate or guesswork.

Clausse commented on the extraordinary degree of instability of audiences and also on the 'wastage' represented by this diagram, since most communication receives only a small fraction of its potential attention and impact. He also drew attention to the qualitative differences between media publics. These range from a condition of 'communion' where scattered individuals may be brought together by the medium in an intense and shared experience, through one of coherent togetherness, to a mass condition (conglomeration of individuals), represented by the varied, casual or habitual uses of the media for unplanned diversion.

The question of differential reach and impact of mass media is of more than theoretical interest, since it has to be taken into account in planning communication – especially in campaigns for commercial, political or informational ends (see Windahl et al., 1992). Most campaigns operate with a notion of a 'target group' (of voters, consumers, etc.), that becomes the audience which a campaign tries to reach. This adds another term to our repertoire – that of *target audience*, one with a specified composition in terms of demographic and other attributes.

It is rare for such a target to coincide precisely with the contours of any of the types of audience (or actual audiences) mentioned earlier. However, the aim of a campaign source is to maximize the correspondence between the actual audience reached by different media and the target audience as conceived in the campaign plan. The more this is achieved the more cost-efficient is the campaign (although not necessarily more effective). The target audience is much the same as what has been called in humanistic enquiry the 'inscribed' or 'implied' audience – that for whom an author writes (Sparks and Campbell, 1987). In this tradition, the inscribed audience can be identified from media 'texts', which usually contain clues to the tastes, interests and capabilities of intended recipients, not to mention the stereotypes ('media images') held by media providers.

ACTIVITY AND SELECTIVITY

Research into audience selectivity was originally stimulated by fears about the effects of mass communication. Critics of mass culture feared that a large and *passive* audience would be exploited and culturally harmed and that passive and unselective attention, especially by children, should be discouraged. In addition the media, especially television, were thought to encourage passivity in children and adults alike (e.g. Himmelweit et al., 1958; Schramm et al., 1961). The whole issue has been defined in a clear normative way, with passivity as harmful, and active use of media as good. However, there are significant industry interests at stake, since too much audience activity can be interpreted as trouble for those who seek to control the audience by manipulation of programming and exploiting the routine character and inertia of much media use (Eastman, 1998).

There has continued to be controversy about how active the typical media audience really is and about what activity means. There is quite a lot of evidence (see, for instance, Kubey, 1986; Kubey and Csikszentmihalyi, 1991) to show that television viewing, at least, is not a very salient activity, nor an object of strong feelings. On the other hand, reading and film-going are likely to be more personally involving.

Biocca (1988a) has reviewed the different meanings and concepts of *audience activity*, proposing five different versions that are to be found in the literature, as follows.

1. *Selectivity.* We can describe an audience as active the more that choice and discrimination are exercised in relation to media and content within media. This is mainly likely to show up in evidence of planning of media use and in consistent patterns of choice. Very heavy media use (especially of television) is likely to be accounted as by definition 'unselective' and therefore inactive.

   In television research a distinction has been made between 'ritualized' and 'instrumental' patterns of use (Rubin, 1984). The former refers to habitual and frequent viewing by people with a strong affinity with the medium. Instrumental use is purposeful and selective, thus more likely to qualify as active. Use of other media, especially radio, music and newspapers can be similarly patterned. This version of the activity concept seems to imply that more active users are more sparing with their time. It is a very weak notion of activity since selectivity can sometimes just be the response to a large number of media options. Channel switching and 'grazing' with a remote control appear to indicate selectivity, although they also imply indecision and lack of close attention. Many other kinds of media behaviour are by definition 'selective': renting videos, buying books and records, borrowing from a library, etc., but there may be also much chance involved.

2. *Utilitarianism.* Here the audience is the 'embodiment of the self-interested consumer'. Media consumption represents the satisfaction of some more or less conscious need, such as those postulated in the 'uses and gratifications' approach. By definition it subsumes 'selectivity', although there can be selectivity without utilitarianism.

3. *Intentionality.* An active audience according to this definition is one which engages in active cognitive processing of incoming information and experience. This type of activity accompanies, rather than precedes, media use although it is often implied by the various forms of subscription to media. Thus, regular subscribers to a publication or media service can be viewed as more active.

4. *Resistance to influence.* Following the lines of the 'obstinate audience' concept (Bauer, 1964), the activity concept here emphasizes the limits set by members of the audience to unwanted influence or learning. The reader, viewer or listener remains 'in control' and unaffected, except as determined by personal choice.

5. *Involvement.* There are different versions of what this means and how it might be measured, but in general, the more an audience member is 'caught up' or 'engrossed' in the ongoing media experience, the more we can speak of involvement. This can be also called 'affective arousal'. Involvement may also be indicated by such signs as 'talking back' to the television, or even talking about it to fellow viewers while it is on.

These different versions of the audience activity concept do not all relate to the same moment in the sequence of media exposure. As Levy and Windahl (1985) point out, they may relate to *advance* expectations and choice, or to activity *during* the experience, or to the *post exposure* situation, for instance the transfer of satisfactions

gained from the media to personal and social life (e.g. in conversation about media, or based upon media-derived topics).

There are some other aspects of active media use that may be missed by the five variants outlined. For instance, audience activity can take the form of direct response by letter or telephone, whether or not encouraged by the media. Local or community media, whether print or broadcast, may generally have more active audiences, or they have more opportunity to do so. Critical reflection on media experience, whether openly expressed in 'feedback' or not, is another example of audience activity, as is conscious membership of a fan club.

In the case of television, audience appreciation ratings, which are either unusually high or low, often indicate the presence within a programme audience of a set of active viewers who respond very positively or very negatively. The act of recording and replaying from radio or television is another indication of above-average engagement. Finally, we can note the view, examined later in more detail, that audiences often participate in the media experience by giving meaning to it, thus actively *producing* the eventual media 'text' (Fiske, 1987, 1992).

The general notion of 'audience activity' is evidently an unsatisfactory concept. It is open to diverse definitions, its indicators are very mixed and ambiguous and it means different things with different media. It is sometimes manifested in behaviour, but sometimes it is only a mentalistic construct (an attitude or feeling). According to Biocca, it is almost empty of meaning in general, because it is *unfalsifiable*: 'It is, by definition, nearly impossible for the audience *not* to be active' (1988a: 59). Despite the inadequacy of activity as a single general concept, there continue to be valid theoretical and practical reasons for retaining it, but only when the chosen version can be clearly defined and empirically tested.

FURTHER READING

Ang, I. (1991) *Desperately Seeking the Audience*. London: Routledge.
Alasuutari, P. (ed.) (1999) *Rethinking the Media Audience*. London: Sage.
McQuail, D. (1997) *Audience Analysis*. Thousand Oaks, CA: Sage.
Morley, D. (1992) *Television, Audiences and Cultural Studies*. London: Routledge.

16

audience formation and experience

In line with earlier remarks, we can approach the question of accounting for media use either from the 'side' of the audience, asking what influences individual choices and behaviours, or from the side of the media, asking what factors of content, presentation and circumstance help to draw and keep audience attention. There is no sharp division between the two, since questions of personal motivation cannot be answered without some reference to media products and contents.

We can also choose to follow one or more of the audience research schools described earlier (Chapter 15), each of which suggests a somewhat different kind of explanation for media use behaviour. The 'structural' tradition emphasizes the media system and the social system as primary determinants. The behavioural (functionalist) approach takes individual needs, motives and circumstances as the starting point, while the social-cultural approach emphasizes the particular context in which an audience member is located and the way in which media alternatives are valued and given meaning. As we have seen, each approach has different theoretical foundations and entails different kinds of research strategy and methods.

A good deal is known about the general factors shaping audience behaviour, which is usually marked by considerable stability and predictability (see e.g. Bryant and Zillman, 1986). Broad patterns of attention to media change only slowly and usually for obvious reasons, such as a change in media structure (for instance the rise of a new medium) or because of some wider social change (e.g. the development of a youth culture or the transition from communism to capitalism). There are always random influences and chance combinations of factors, but audience research is mostly a matter of routine recording of very predictable outcomes. Such mystery as there is relates to questions of detailed choice within a media sector, between channels or products, or concerning the success or failure of some specific innovation or item of content. If there were no mystery, the media business would not be as risky as it is and every film, song, book or show could be a hit.

These remarks are a reminder that there has always been something of a disjunction between the *general* pattern of mass media use and what happens on a day-to-day basis. In one respect this can be understood as the difference between an average based on extensive aggregate data and observation of a single case, where the case might be one day's pattern or one person's habitual media use. As individuals we usually have a fairly stable pattern of media preferences, choices and time use (although one 'pattern' may be of instability), but each day's media experience is unique and affected by varying and unpredictable circumstances.

In the following sections we look at some alternative theoretical models for accounting for the recruitment and composition of media audiences.

The basic premise, as indicated already, is that media use is largely shaped by certain relatively constant elements of social structure and media structure. Social structure refers to 'social facts' such as those of education, income, gender, place of residence, position in the life-cycle, etc. which have a strong determining influence on general outlook and social behaviour. Media structure refers to the relatively constant array of channels, choices and content that is available in a given place and time. The media system responds to pressures and to feedback from audiences, so as to maintain a stable self-regulating balance between supply and demand.

The processes at work are sketched in a model (Figure 16.1), slightly adapted from Weibull (1985), which depicts the relationship between that habitual pattern of media use behaviour and the particular choices, for instance on a given day. In Figure 16.1, the upper section shows an individual's habitual pattern of media use as an outcome of

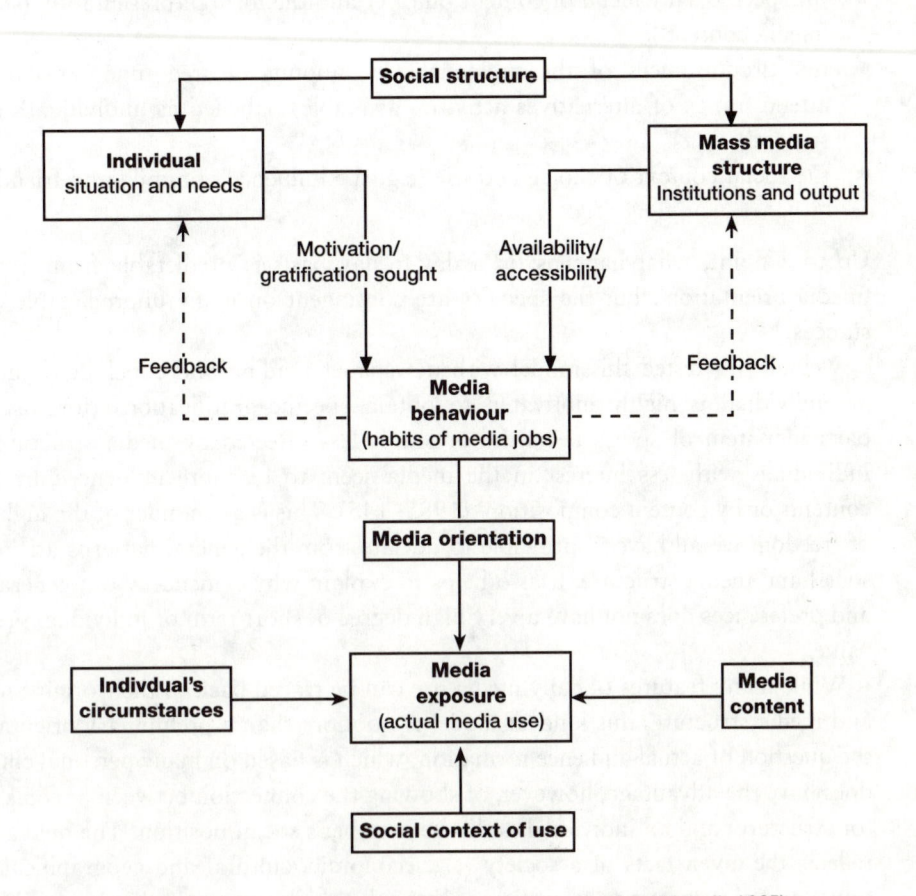

FIGURE 16.1   A structural model of media use (after Weibull, 1985)
(source: McQuail, 1997: 69)

two main factors which themselves reflect the overall social structure. One is the more or less fixed *social situation* in which a person is located along with the associated media-related *needs* (e.g. for certain information, relaxation, social contact, etc.). The second factor (shown as 'mass media structure') consists of the available media possibilities in the particular place, given a person's economic and educational circumstances. Between them, these two factors lead not only to a regular pattern of *behaviour*, but also to a fairly constant disposition, tendency or 'set', which is called a person's '*media* **orientation**'. This is a joint outcome of social background and past media experience and takes the form of an affinity for certain media, specific preferences and interests, habits of use, expectations of what the media are good for, etc. (see McLeod and McDonald, 1985; McDonald, 1990). This provides the connection to what is contained in the lower part of the figure. Here we find the particular daily situation in which specific choices of media and content are made. These are likely to be influenced by three main variables:

- the specific daily menu of content on offer and the form of presentation (shown as 'media content');
- the circumstances of the moment (e.g. amount of free time, availability to attend, range of alternatives activities available) (labelled as 'individual's circumstances');
- the social context of choice and use (e.g. the influence of family and friends).

Up to a point, what happens on a day-to-day basis is predictable from a person's 'media orientation', but the specifics are contingent on many unpredictable circumstances.

Weibull has tested this model with newspaper reading and concluded that 'when an individual is highly motivated to obtain specific gratifications (for instance, a particular item of sports news) he or she is less affected by media structure . . . . Individuals with less interest in the media seem to be more influenced by specific contents or by content composition' (1985: 145). This is a reminder of the high degree of freedom we all have in principle to deviate from the general patterns arising from social and media structure. It also helps to explain why evidence about general tastes and preferences does not have a very high degree of short-term or individual predictive value.

While many features of daily media use can be traced back to their origins in social and media structure, this kind of model is no more than a preliminary orientation to the question of actual audience formation, which is based on many personal choices. It does have the advantage, however, of showing the connection between a media system (or structure) and an individual audience member's social position. The media system reflects the given facts of a society (e.g. economic, cultural and geographical conditions) and also responds to audience demands which are partly determined by social background factors, partly idiosyncratic and contingent.

The idea that media use depends on the perceived satisfactions, needs, wishes or motives of the prospective audience member is almost as old as media research itself. As noted in Chapter 15, audiences are often formed on the basis of similarities of individual need, interest and taste. Many of these appear to have a social or psychological origin. Typical of such 'needs' are those for information, relaxation, companionship, diversion or 'escape'. Audiences for particular media and kinds of media content can often be typified according to such broad motivational types. The approach has also been applied to studying the appeal of new electronic media (Perse, 1990) and even to uses of the telephone (Dimmick and Rothenbuhler, 1984). Relative affinity with different media is associated with differences of expectation and gratifications sought.

This way of thinking belongs to a research school which became known as the 'uses and gratifications approach', the origins of which lie in the search for explanations of the great appeal of certain staple media contents. The central question posed is: *Why do people use media and what do they use them for?* Functionalist sociology (see Wright, 1974) viewed the media as serving various needs of the society – e.g. for cohesion, cultural continuity, social control and for a large circulation of public information of all kinds. This, in turn, presupposes that individuals also use media for related purposes such as personal guidance, relaxation, adjustment, information and identity-formation.

The first such research dates from the early 1940s, and focused on the reasons for the popular appeal of different radio programmes, especially 'soap operas' and quizzes and also of daily newspaper reading (Lazarsfeld and Stanton, 1944, 1949). These studies led to some unexpected findings, for instance that daytime radio soap operas, although often dismissed as superficial and mindless stories to fill time, were often found significant by their (women) listeners. They provided a source of advice and support, a role model of housewife and mother, or an occasion for emotional release through laughter or tears (Herzog, 1944; Warner and Henry, 1948). From talking to newspaper readers, it was also discovered that these were more than just sources of useful information, but also important for giving readers a sense of security, shared topics of conversation and a structure to the daily routine (Berelson, 1949).

Uses and gratifications rediscovered

The basic assumptions of the approach when it was rediscovered and elaborated twenty years later (in the 1960s and 1970s) were as follows.

- Media and content choice is generally rational and directed towards certain specific goals and satisfactions (thus the audience is active and audience formation can be logically explained).

- Audience members are conscious of the media-related needs which arise in personal (individual) and social (shared) circumstances and can voice these in terms of motivations.
- Broadly speaking, personal utility is a more significant determinant of audience formation than aesthetic or cultural factors.
- All or most of the relevant factors for audience formation (motives, perceived or obtained satisfactions, media choices, background variables) can, in principle, be measured.

In line with these assumptions, the process of media selection was described by Katz et al. (1974: 20) as being concerned with: '(1) the social and psychological origins of (2) needs which generate (3) expectations of (4) the mass media or other sources which lead to (5) differential exposure (or engaging in other activities), resulting in (6) need gratification and (7) other consequences . . .'.

A longer-term aim of the research school was to reach some general theoretical framework within which to place the many particular findings about audience motivations. McQuail et al. (1972), after studying a number of different radio and TV programmes in Britain, proposed a scheme of 'media–person interactions' (a term which reflects the dual origin of the media gratification concept), which capture the most important media satisfactions. This is shown in Box 16.1.

Box 16.1   A typology of media–person interactions (McQuail et al., 1972)

1. *Diversion*: escape from routine or problems; emotional release
2. *Personal relationships*: Companionship; social utility
3. *Personal identity*: self reference; reality exploration; value reinforcement
4. *Surveillance* (forms of information seeking)

A more psychological version of the theory of audience motivation was suggested by McGuire (1974), based on general theory of human needs. He distinguished firstly between cognitive and affective needs, then adding three further dimensions: 'active' versus 'passive' initiation; 'external' versus 'internal' goal orientation; and orientation to 'growth' or to 'stability'. When interrelated these factors yield sixteen different types of motivation which apply to media use. Examples include the 'search for cognitive consistency' by reading a newspaper (this belongs to a cognitive, active, external, stability-oriented type) or the motive for watching television drama in 'order to find models of personal behaviour' (an affective, active, internal, growth-oriented type). In the nature of psychological theory of this kind, the media user is unlikely to be conscious of the underlying causes of motivations. Even so, there has been some research which shows a relationship between the McGuire factors and different motivational patterns of television use (Conway and Rubin, 1991).

This theoretical approach was criticized in its own time both because of its behaviourist and functionalist leanings and also because it has not provided much successful prediction or causal explanation of media choice and use (McQuail, 1984). The reasons for poor prediction may lie partly in difficulties of measurement and partly in the fact that much media use is actually very circumstantial and weakly motivated. The approach seems to work best in relation to specific types of content where motivation might be present, for example in relation to political content (Blumler and McQuail, 1968) or news (Levy, 1977 and 1978), or erotica (Perse, 1994). In general, the connection between attitude to the media and media use behaviour is weak and the direction of the relationship is uncertain. Typologies of 'motives' often fail to match patterns of actual selection or use, and it is hard to find a logical and consistent relation between the three sequentially ordered factors of: *liking/preference*; actual *choosing*; and subsequent *evaluation*.

The extent to which audience behaviour is guided by specific and conscious motives has always been in dispute. Babrow (1988) shares the doubts and has proposed that we think more in terms of 'interpretive frameworks', based on experience. Thus, some audience choice is meaningful in terms of such frameworks, while other exposure is based only on habit and reflex and may be considered unmotivated (Rubin, 1984). These ideas are in line with the concept of 'media orientation' introduced earlier in this chapter and the idea of a general preference set included in Figure 16.3 below.

In discussing the status of 'uses and gratifications' theory, Blumler (1985) made a distinction, based on extensive evidence, between 'social origins' and ongoing social experience. The former seems to go with predictable constraints on the range of choice as well as with compensatory, adjustment-oriented, media expectations and uses. The second (ongoing experience and current social situation) are much less predictable in their effects. They often go with 'facilitatory' media uses – with positive choice, and application, of media for personally chosen ends. This means that media use is an outcome of forces in society, of the personal biography of the individual and also of immediate circumstances. The *causes* of audience formation are located in the past as well as in the very immediate present and at points in between. It is not surprising that attempts at general *explanation* of actual audience realities have had so little success.

Expectancy value theory

Essential to most theory concerning personal motivations for media use is the idea that the media offer rewards which are expected (thus predicted) by potential members of

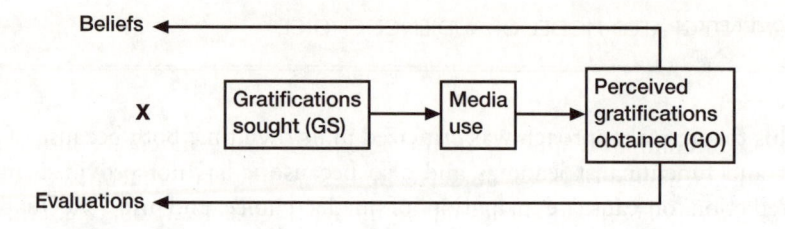

FIGURE 16.2 An expectancy-value model of media gratifications sought and obtained (Palmgreen and Rayburn, 1985)

an audience, on the basis of relevant past experience. These rewards can be thought of as experienced psychological effects which are valued by individuals (they are sometimes called media 'gratifications'). Such rewards can be derived from media use as such (e.g. 'having a good read') or from certain favourite genres (e.g. detective stories) or actual items of content (a particular film) and they provide guidance (or feedback) for subsequent choices, adding to the stock of media-relevant information. A model of the process involved has been proposed by Palmgreen and Rayburn (1985), based on the principle that attitudes (towards media) are an outcome of empirically located beliefs and also of values (and personal preferences). The resulting 'expectancy-value' model is depicted in Figure 16.2.

The elements in the model are formally related as follows:

$$GS_i = b_i e_i$$

where GS_i is the ith gratification sought from some media object X (medium, programme or content type); b_i = the belief (subjective probability) that X possesses some attribute or that a behaviour related to X will have a particular outcome; and e_i = the affective evaluation of the particular attribute or outcome.

In general the model expresses the proposition that media use is accounted for by a combination of *perception* of benefits offered by the medium and the differential *value* of these benefits for the individual audience member. This helps to cover the fact that media use is shaped by *avoidance* as well as by varying degrees of positive choice amongst the potential gratifications expected from the media. The model distinguishes between expectation (gratifications sought) and satisfaction (gratifications obtained) and identifies an *increment* over time from media use behaviour. Thus, where GO (gratifications obtained) is noticeably higher than GS (gratifications sought) we are likely to be dealing with situations of high audience satisfaction and high ratings of appreciation and attention. The reverse pattern can also occur, providing clues to falling circulation, sales or ratings, and channel switching in the case of television. This theoretical refinement has not altered the fact that audience motivational theory is not easy to translate into a sharp empirical tool.

audiences

We can combine a number of the influences on media choice into a single heuristic model, which provides a guide to understanding the sequential process of audience formation. The main entries in the model (Figure 16.3) operate either on the 'audience side' of the media–person interaction or on the 'media side'. While described separately, the two sets of factors are not independent of each other but the result of a continuing process of mutual orientation and adjustment. The form of the model as presented here was influenced initially by the work of Webster and Wakshlag (1983), who sought to explain television viewer choice in a similar way. The version shown here is intended, in principle, to apply to all mass media and not just television. First, the main explanatory factors can be introduced.

'Audience side' factors

1   *Social background and milieu*, especially as reflected in social class, education, religious, cultural, political and family environment and region or locality of residence. We can also refer here to what Bourdieu (1986) calls 'cultural capital' – learnt cultural skills and tastes, often transmitted inter-generationally by way of family, education and the class system.
2   *Personal attributes* of age, gender, family position, study and work situation, level of income; also 'life-style', if relevant. There is some indication that personality differences may play a part (see Finn, 1997).
3   *Media-related needs*, of the kind discussed above, for such personal benefits as company, distraction, information, etc. These needs are widely experienced, but the particular balance between them depends on personal background and circumstances.
4   *Personal tastes and preferences* for certain genres, formats or specific items of content.
5   *General habits of leisure time media use* and availability to be in the audience at a particular time. Since media are used in space as well as time, availability also refers to being in the appropriate places to receive (e.g. at home, in trains, driving, etc.). Availability also refers to the economic potential to be in an audience, for instance being able and willing to pay the price of a cinema ticket or a music recording.
6   *Awareness* of the choices available and the amount and kind of information possessed also play a part in audience formation. More active audience members can be expected to plan their media use accordingly.
7   *Specific context of use*. This varies according to medium but generally refers to sociability and location of use. Most relevant is whether one is alone or in

company (friends, family, others). Where media are used (e.g. at home, work, travelling, in a cinema, etc.) can also influence the character of the experience as well as the process of choice-making.

8   *Chance* often plays a part in media exposure, and its intervention reduces the ability to really *explain* choice or audience composition.

'Media side' factors

A   *The media system.* Preferences and choices are influenced by the make-up of the (national) media system (number, reach and type of media available) and by the specific characteristics of different media outlets.

B   *Structure of media provision.* This refers to the general pattern of what the media provide in a given society, which exerts a long-term influence on audience expectations.

C   *Available content options.* The specific formats and genres that are on offer to the potential audience at particular times and places.

D   *Media publicity.* This includes advertising and image-making by the media on their own behalf as well as intensive marketing of some media products.

E   *Timing and presentation.* Media selection and use are likely to be influenced by specific strategies of timing, scheduling, placement or design of content, of media message according to competitive audience-gaining strategies.

Figure 16.3 represents the general process of choice-making, in which influences of both kinds (from society and from media) are shown sequentially according to their relative 'distance' from the moment of choice or attention (*media use*). Most distant (and more or less fixed) are social and cultural background and (for most adults at least) general sets of tastes and preferences, likes and interests. Thus, our social background has a strongly orienting and dispositional influence on our choice behaviour. The other, almost equally distant (but less constant) factor is the general make-up of different media and the mix of genres, of which we have accumulated knowledge and experience. There is both a cognitive and an evaluative aspect to our dispositions (see the expectancy-value model above).

Personal knowledge of this kind and the related attitudes shape our tastes and preferences. The combination of the two (perception and evaluation) leads to a *general content preference set*. This is a hypothetical construct, but it shows up in consistent and thus predictable patterns of choice-making and also in more or less coherent patterns and types of media usage (these are close to what are sometimes called 'taste cultures'). We can think of it in terms of the 'repertoire' of available sources and content types with which we are familiar and from which we make actual choices (see Heeter, 1988). It is also very close to Weibull's 'media orientation' in the structural model (see Figure 16.1) and includes affinity for media as well as for types of content. Patterns of choice-making are, of course, always adapted according to changes in

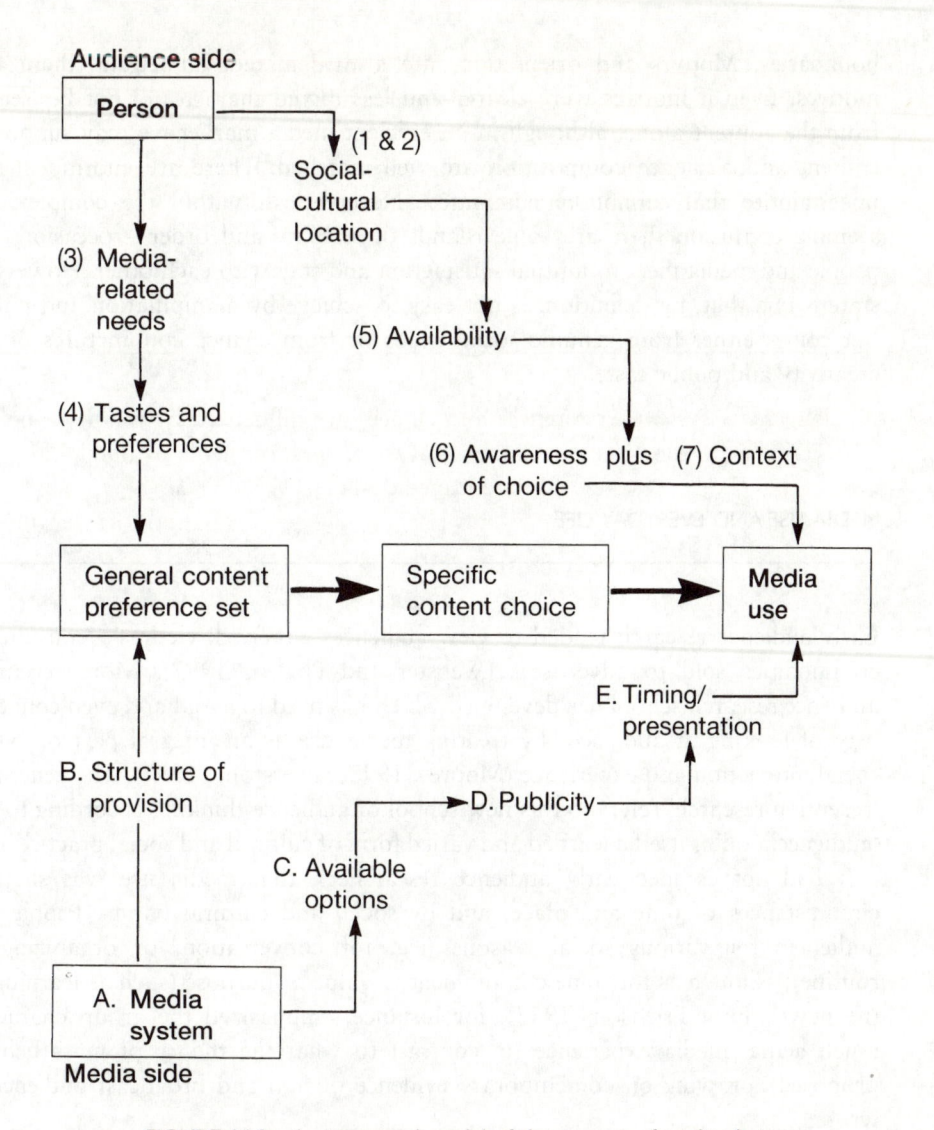

Audience side

Person

(1 & 2)
Social-
cultural
location

(3) Media-
related
needs

(5) Availability

(4) Tastes and
preferences

(6) Awareness plus (7) Context
of choice

General content
preference set → Specific
content choice → **Media
use**

E. Timing/
presentation

B. Structure of
provision

D. Publicity

C. Available
options

A. **Media
system**

Media side

FIGURE 16.3   An integrated model of the process of media choice

circumstances and experience with the media. There is a continuous process of response, feedback, learning and evaluation.

At a point much closer in time or place to media use, the circumstances of the potential audience member and the availability of the media coincide, resulting in actual audiences. These are never fully predictable, although the broad shape in aggregate terms is, as noted above, rather constant. It is the internal composition that is always shifting, since individual choice behaviour is affected by circumstances.

The complexity and multiplicity of audience formation precludes any simple descriptions or single theoretical explanation. We can certainly conclude that audiences are rarely what they seem. They are often shifting aggregates without clear

audience formation and experience   393

boundaries. Motives and orientations are always mixed. Sometimes there are no motives. Even if motives were clearer and less mixed they would not be 'readable' from the content alone, although in an efficient media market we may suppose that content and audience composition are well matched. There are enormous in-built uncertainties that cannot be eliminated. Nevertheless, within the complexity and seeming confusion there are some islands of stability and order – occasions where people and media meet to mutual satisfaction and stay with each other. However, this state is one that, by definition, is not easy to achieve by manipulation and publicity, but comes either from genuine social needs or from chance conjunctures of media creativity and public taste.

MEDIA USE AND EVERYDAY LIFE

Early audience research tended to view audiences either as 'victims', 'consumers' or commodities sold to advertisers (Webster and Phalen, 1997). More recently, an audience research school has developed which has tried to avoid and even counter this way of looking at audiences by treating media use as an integral part of everyday social interaction and experience (Moores, 1993; Silverstone, 1994). The general term 'reception research' refers to this new school of audience thinking according to which 'audiencehood' is itself a learned and varied form of cultural and social practice.

It had not escaped early audience researchers, that media use was shaped by circumstances of time and place, and by social and cultural habits. People joined audiences for various social reasons (e.g. for conversation, or organizing daily routine), as much as for some communicative value or purpose (such as learning from the news). Eliot Friedson (1953), for instance, emphasized the group character of much actual media experience (in contrast to what the theory of mass behaviour proposed), drawing on contemporary evidence of film and broadcast audiences. He wrote:

> Much audience behavior, then, takes place in a complex network of local social activity. Certain time of day, certain days, certain seasons are the appropriate times for engaging in particular activities connected with various mass media. The individual is frequently accompanied by others of his social group . . . [and] participates in an interpersonal grid of spectators who discuss the meaning of past experience with mass communication and the anticipated significance of future experience.

'Going to the movies' has nearly always been viewed more as a social activity than as an occasion for seeing particular films (Handel, 1950). It represents a continuation of the original 'audience', made up of those who went out to a public social event, usually in the company of others. The occasion had a significance beyond that of any 'message' communicated or any individual gratification obtained. Seeing a 'bad' movie

could be just as satisfying as seeing a 'good' one. Much the same could be said of radio, phonograph listening and television viewing, although, unlike the cinema, these have nearly always taken a secondary place in complex patterns of family life. 'Watching television' is generally a more accurate description of what is going on than 'watching television programmes', but it too overstates the significance of the ubiquitous flickering screen. The extensive and detailed studies of time use by Kubey and Csikszentmihalyi (1991), based on self-reports, leave little doubt about the generally uninvolving and secondary character of television viewing, although this should not be confused with lack of significance. The untidiness and chanciness which characterize media use, as noted above, are in fact only a matter of perception, since there is always a certain logic, although not usually the logic of the 'media exposure' model.

PUBLIC AND PRIVATE SPHERES OF MEDIA USE

As noted, certain forms of media use have a distinctly public character, both in the sense of taking place outside the home (as with cinema or concerts) and also in having a wider significance as a shared response to public performances and to public events. Saenz (1994: 576) refers to the continued significance of a 'widely shared, collectively appreciated performance, an immediate delivery . . . to a large and general audience'. He adds 'the sense of performance and cultural currency in television programming constitutes an important dimension in viewers' appreciation of television drama as a prominent cultural event'. The term 'public' can have a reference to the type of content, the location of an event and also to the degree of shared, collective, experience.

Mass media which are located in their use primarily in the home (especially television, video, music and books) can be considered to bridge the gap between the private, domestic, world and the concerns and activities of the wider society. Under some conditions, being a member of an audience has the meaning of sharing in the wider life of society, while in other circumstances, it is a self-initiated experience which may be entirely personal or shared only by a small circle of friends or family members. It is not so much the physical location of the audience experience (for instance cinema and theatre versus home) which matters as the definition of its meaning as more public or more private.

The public type of audiencehood is typified by occasions of consciously motivated attention to reports of events which are of wide social significance (e.g. election results, major disasters, world crises), or which involve watching of major live sporting events on television (Rothenbuhler, 1987) or big entertainment events (e.g. live concerts). Public audience experience normally involves some degree of identification with a wider social grouping – whether defined as fans, or citizens, or a local population or a

taste culture. It may also be experience associated with some more or less public role, for instance citizen, voter or worker.

In their study of 'media events', Dayan and Katz (1992) draw attention to a special category of occasions, when the media (especially television) unite a population in a near-ritual manner to celebrate and join in some wider national or global experience. Such media events are always special and constitute interruptions of routine. Aside from their significance, they are typically preplanned, remote and live. The examples cited include the Olympic Games, Sadat's journey to Israel in 1978, major papal visits, coronations and royal weddings. To be in the (media) audience for such events is to participate more fully in the public life of the nation or other significant membership group. This research reminds us again of the collective character of 'audiencehood'.

The private type of audience experience is constructed according to personal mood and circumstance and does not involve any reference to society or even to other people. When not purely introspective, it is likely to be concerned with self-comparison and matching with a media model, role or personality in the search for an acceptable identity for public self-presentation. The difference between the public and the private type of audience experience depends on a combination of factors: the type of medium and content and the frame of mind of (or definition supplied by) the audience member. Expansion and development of media seem to be opening up relatively more possibilities for private audiencehood, by bringing more of media experience within the control of the individual to choose at will (see Neuman, 1991).

SUBCULTURE AND AUDIENCE

Early critics of 'mass society' theory pointed to the high degree of social differentiation of the seemingly homogeneous 'mass' audience. As media industries have developed and sought more new and 'niche' audience markets they have needed no persuasion on this point and have even entered the business of trying to define and create new social and cultural subgroups, based on taste or life-style, with which potential media consumers might identify. There is a continuous process of creating media-based styles or pseudo-identities which are intended to strike a responsive chord in an audience.

Nevertheless, media use is always likely to be shaped predominantly according to early experience and identifications forged in personal social life or in line with the social context of the moment. After the particular social milieu of one's family, comes the peer group of school classmates or neighbourhood friends which influence taste and media consumption, especially in respect of music and television – the two most popular media for the young. There are many layers of differentiation, aside from the sometimes fine age-grading of youthful preferences (von Feilitzen, 1976) and the

general separation out of a 'youth culture' as distinct from that of adults. Young adult experience is reshaped by social contacts at work and in leisure. Such general environmental influences are cross-cut by many other specific factors, not least that of gender.

There is much evidence that media use can play an important role in the expression and reinforcement of identity for subgroups of different kinds (Hebdige, 1978). This is not surprising, since media are part of 'culture', but there is a particular point in noting the strong connection between more deviant and alternative subcultures in modern society and, especially, youth musical taste (Avery, 1979; Roe, 1992). The focus of resistance to dominant forces of society has often been musical and dance forms which are appropriated by subcultures and become a symbol of resistance (Hall and Jefferson, 1975; Lull, 1992). Much modern music adopted by youth is anathema to parents, teachers and to established society generally. Murdock and Phelps (1973), for instance, showed how young people expressed their distance from official school and middle class values by way of musical tastes.

LIFE-STYLE

The concept of **life-style** has often been used in describing and categorizing different patterns of media use, often as part of a constellation of other attitudes and behaviour (e.g. Eastman, 1979; Frank and Greenberg, 1980; Donohew et al., 1987). The pioneering work of the French sociologist Pierre Bourdieu (1986) represents a long tradition of inquiry relating various expressions of cultural taste with social and family background. In one respect, the life-style concept offers an escape from the presumption that media taste (unlike traditional aesthetic and artistic taste) is determined by social class and education, since life-styles are, to some extent, self-chosen patterns of behaviour and media use choice.

In commercial marketing research the life-style concept is helpful for classifying consumers into various types in ways which assist the targeting and design of advertising. For such purposes it is desirable to go beyond basic social-demographic categories and to make finer distinctions, especially with psychological dimensions. Life-style research involves studying a wide range of social positional variables, behaviours (including media use and other leisure and consumption practices) and attitudes, tastes and values. There is in fact no limit to the potential scope of such research nor, perhaps, to the number of media-relevant 'life-styles' which can be identified. It is also often possible to choose alternative ways of describing the same research findings, for instance by emphasizing different causal factors. These can be social (e.g. class and income) or cultural, attitudinal or psychological (see Finn, 1997).

One of the main problems with the concept is finding an appropriate level of analysis. Johansson and Miegel (1992) distinguish three levels: that of the whole society (for international comparisons), that of differences within societies and cultures and, finally, the individual level. Of the latter they say the 'lifestyles are expressions of individuals' ambitions to create their own specific, personal, social and cultural identities' (1992: 23). The second level is the most commonly applied, often with rather confusing results. At the third level, there are potentially as many life-styles as there are individuals. Nevertheless, the concept is helpful in understanding the many different ways in which media are meaningfully interrelated with social and cultural experience.

GENDERED AUDIENCES

The idea that media use is notably and persistently 'gendered' has also been developed in reception research, under the influence of feminist theory (Seiter et al., 1989). The differentiation of media use according to sex has long been recognized, and certain types of media are specifically produced for female audiences, often by women, especially perhaps certain magazines (Ferguson, 1983) and types of fiction (e.g. romance). Male audiences are also served by distinctive media types and genres.

What is new is a greater curiosity about the meaning of these differences and a search for an understanding of how the social construction of gender also influences media choice and vice versa. Gendered audience experience is a complex outcome of a certain kind of media content, typical everyday routines and the wider structure of what may still be described as 'patriarchal society' – or a 'man's world' as far as power is concerned. A much-cited example is Radway's (1984) research into one set of devoted (really addicted) women readers of mass-produced romance fiction. Radway set out to account for the compulsive appeal of romance fiction by accepting in the first instance the main explanations offered by women readers themselves. From this perspective, romances offer an escape specifically designed for women, first of all by way of the act of reading which establishes a private 'space' and time, protected from incursion by husbands and family duties. Secondly, romances offer versions, albeit in fantasy form, of the ideal romance, which can be emotionally nurturing. Radway's evidence suggested that alternatives and images found by women readers in their fiction were at least mildly empowering and supportive, notwithstanding the tendency of critical feminism to view romance fiction as delusory and reactionary in tendency.

The notion of gendered audience has also been invoked in relation to another genre which attracts a largely female audience – that of radio and television 'soap operas' (e.g. Allen, 1989; Hobson, 1982, 1989; Geraghty, 1991). Studies have linked their narrative form (continuity, indeterminacy) to typical features of the housewife's daily

routine, which is fragmented and distracted (preventing continuous attention) but also flexible. Soap operas in general are significantly preferred and more watched by women, even when they recognize the low status of the genre (e.g. Alasuutari, 1992). Ethnographic research into female soap opera viewers indicates that the genre is widely appropriated as especially meant for women and often serves for conversation and reflection about viewers' own everyday experiences (Livingstone, 1988).

In respect of the audience for women's magazines, Hermes (1995) has identified a set of interpretative 'repertoires' or structures of meaning in terms of which women readers account for their reading behaviour and their relative attraction to the different varieties of the genre (ranging from feminist to traditional publications). Repertoires refer, for instance, to the sense of duty to support the cause of women or the mild guilt at reading traditional women's magazines. These sets of ideas are often mutually inconsistent or in dialogue with each other, but contradictions are made easier to handle by the relative lack of significance attached to the magazine medium by even their most faithful readers.

The essence of a gendered audience is not the sex ratio of its composition, but the degree to which conscious membership of an audience (audiencehood) is given some distinct meaning in terms of specific female or male experience. There are numerous indications in research into media use that gendered differences are associated with different preferences and satisfactions. For instance, Anderson et al. (1996) found that stressed women watched more game and variety shows, while stressed men watched more action and violent programming, thus accentuating differences which show up in the general audience. This is not to suggest that most mass media experience can be accounted for in gender terms, since there is much evidence of shared purpose and understanding across gender lines.

Another aspect of audience gendering is the degree to which the complex social act of using a domestic medium such as television is influenced by relations between the sexes and by particular sex roles. The classic exploration is probably that of Morley (1986), whose ethnographic study of family viewing emphasized the many unwritten rules, understandings and patterns of behaviour that develop in the micro-audience environment of even one family. Typically, the power to control (evening) viewing was exercised by the man (see also Lull, 1982).

Women, in general, were found less likely to plan viewing or to watch continuously. They were more likely to do other things while viewing, to give way to the preferences of other family members for social reasons, to talk while viewing, to feel guilty for viewing alone. Women would be inclined to treat television as a resource for easing family tensions, reconciling quarrels, and encouraging varying degrees of privacy or sociability in a viewing situation. Morley (1986) cites the example of men using their power of control to 'get even' with their wives in some dispute, for instance by watching sport exclusively. Presumably women do something similar in return, when they get the chance. Finally, there is now an expanding field of research addressed to the influence of gender on the acquisition and use of new communication technologies in the home (Frissen, 1992; Moores, 1993).

Early thinking about mass media use often associated it with forms of social isolation, and there have been similar anxieties about computer games and the Internet. There are obviously many individuals who are both socially isolated and also strongly addicted to media use behaviours that might reinforce their isolation. However, there is no decisive evidence of any general decline in social contact as a direct result of mass media use. An understandable concern about addiction to media has diverted attention from the more typical meanings of media attractiveness. Most uses of the media have been effectively rendered sociable. Media use is itself a ubiquitous form of normal social behaviour and an acceptable substitute for actual social interaction. It is also widely perceived as a significant 'agent of socialization' – an occasion for social learning and a means towards participation in the wider society.

The sociability of the audience experience is indicated by certain familiar (and well-attested) features of media use. We often attend to the media with others, especially in the case of film and television. The media (e.g. television or music) are often used to entertain other people or to ease social interaction. Attending to the media is often accompanied by talk about the ongoing experience. The content of media (news items, stories, performances) provides an object of shared attention for many as well as topics of conversation. Media-related talk is especially useful in providing a non-intrusive basis of contact with strangers. Media in the home are frequently a background to virtually every other kind of activity, without necessarily impeding or displacing these activities. Kubey and Csikszentmihalyi (1991: 75), for instance, reported that '63.5% of the time television was being viewed, people reported doing something else as well'.

There is no clear evidence that the classic forms of interpersonal 'sociability', such as conversation and 'hanging out', have disappeared, although it is very likely that some domestic entertainments, which were sociable, like card-playing, musical parties and family games have declined (although for other reasons as well). Rosengren et al., in their overview of findings of the long-term Swedish Media Panel research into child development, have found much evidence of varied and complex patterns linking media use with other social activities. They find (1989: 200) 'on the whole positive relations between children's television viewing and their social inter-action'. Age (grade in school), gender and social class all played a part in mediating the link.

It appears that the patterns of everyday socializing are both complex and changing as a result of new means of passing time. Most media use can be as sociable or not as one chooses, depending on our real-life resources (in terms of money, mobility, available friends and social contacts). This is what Rosengren and Windahl (1972) termed 'interaction potential'. In providing a substitute to 'real-life' social contact, which might simply not be available, especially in modern urban living, the media often help to alleviate loneliness and stress caused by isolation.

Mass-mediated social contact can supplement and complement, as well as displace, real personal contacts with others. As a result, the potential for social interaction can as well be enlarged by mass media as reduced. Evidence of a causal relation between media use and social isolation is hard to come by (see Finn and Gomm, 1988; Rubin et al., 1990; Perse and Rubin, 1990; Canary and Spitzberg, 1993). In so far as there is a general empirical answer to the question of relationship between social interaction and media use, it seems that higher levels of 'real' social contact are often accompanied by above average levels of contact with the media. This finding does not settle the issue, but the correlation can be understood as supporting the claim that being in an audience is most correctly to be defined as 'social' rather than 'non-social'. On the other hand, the accumulating evidence of television use in multi-channel (and multi-receiver) circumstances, indicates that a very high proportion of use is actually by individuals on their own. A study of German television use in 1992 by Krotz and Hasebrink (1998), using people-meter data, showed that 61% of television use time involved only one person watching.

There are a variety of ways in which media use becomes intertwined with everyday life, especially in the case of television, which is such a ubiquitous accompaniment to domesticity. James Lull (1982) has suggested a typology of social uses of television, based on participant observation of families. Some of the points also apply to other media. The first type is referred to as *structural* and identifies the numerous ways in which the media provide a time frame for daily activities. This begins with an early news bulletin, an accompaniment to breakfast, and continues, according to the daily schedule, to mark breaks from work, meal-times, the return from work and evening relaxation with familiar and suitable programming on radio and television. This is what Mendelsohn (1964) referred to as the function of radio in 'bracketing the day'. A media-derived structure of this kind provides a sense of companionship and marks off phases of the day, helping to establish appropriate moods. A second type is called *relational* and covers the points made earlier about content as a conversational 'coin of exchange' and a way of easing social contacts of an informal but not intimate kind.

The third category is summarized in terms of *affiliation* and *avoidance*, referring to the fluctuating dynamics of social relations in which people want to be, by turns, socially close to, or separate from, others with whom they share the same physical space. Different media offer different opportunities for one or the other option. Affiliation is expressed by joining in the same spectatorship (e.g. a football match on TV) in varying degrees of participation.

Avoidance takes more diverse forms. Some involve the use of particular media that are by definition solitary in use, like books or headphone music. In public as well as private places, reading newspapers often expresses a wish to be left alone. Having separate television and radio receivers in different parts of a house helps in the dispersal of members of a household. These social devices are usually understood and accepted as legitimate, thus avoiding offence to others. It is impossible to separate out the more 'legitimate' media use motives from the less acceptable aspect of self-

isolation. In families, as children grow up, there is a fairly clear pattern of increasing dispersal of individual activities, which is closely related to the use of different media (von Feilitzen, 1976).

Of the remaining social uses named by Lull, one – *social learning* – covers a wide range of socializing aspects of media use (e.g. adopting certain role models) and a fifth carries the label *competence/dominance*. This refers to the socially structured power to control media use in a household, ranging from a decision to choose a daily newspaper to the use of the TV remote control, and including decision-making over the acquisition of media hardware and software. It also refers to uses made of media-derived information and expertise to play the role of opinion-leader in social contacts with family and friends (Katz and Lazarsfeld, 1955). Ethnographic research in domestic settings makes it clear that media use is often governed by quite complex, usually unspoken, rules and understandings which vary from one family to another (see Morley, 1986).

NORMATIVE FRAMING OF MEDIA USE

The preceding discussion is a reminder of the extent to which research into the media audience has taken place within a normative, even judgemental, framework (see Barwise and Ehrenberg, 1988: 138ff.), itself a sign that media use has been thoroughly incorporated in the socialization process. Although, as we have seen, high media use does not in itself have to be viewed as harmful, the most basic norm applied to the media has been that you can have too much, even of a good thing. The normative framing of media use seems at first to run counter to the view that media use is a voluntary, free-time, 'out-of-role' and generally pleasurable activity, more or less unrelated to any social obligation. Yet audience research continually uncovers the existence of value systems which informally serve to regulate media behaviour. As Krcmar (1996: 251) observes, 'families have as many rules and disagreements about TV viewing as they do about such diverse topics as homework, eating habits and religious obligations'. It is from the imposition of norms for media use in family contexts (with reference to parental responsibility) that we are most aware of normative control of media (Geiger and Sokol, 1959; Brown and Linné, 1976; Hedinsson, 1981; Rosengren and Windahl, 1989).

There is plenty of evidence that the media are widely regarded by their own audiences as potentially influential for good or ill and thus in need of direction and control by society. At the very least they should be supervised by parents. For instance, Gunter and Winstone (1993) reported that 90% of a British sample thought parents should discourage their children from watching too much TV, and large majorities support control over viewing in general. In the same survey, about 50% thought

British television was strongly regulated, and 75% were satisfied with this or wanted even more control than was exercised at present.

There is also evidence that public opinion in several countries favours quite strong regulation for a range of media, including print, on a variety of grounds (see Golding and van Snippenburg, 1995). Audiences are broadly concerned about media standards and feel that maintaining these standards can often require intervention. Public opinion does not generally allocate as much freedom to media as they often claim for themselves.

While no doubt much of the normative concern about media stems from fears of unwanted influences, media use in itself can be regarded as morally dubious (as noted above). For instance, Steiner (1963) found a tendency for viewers to show guilt over their own high levels of television use, which he attributed to a legacy from the protestant ethic, which frowns on 'unproductive' uses of time. Among middle-class audiences, especially, a sensitivity to this value persists. Radway found similar kinds of guilt feelings amongst keen female readers of romantic fiction and for similar reasons: 'guilt is the understandable result of their socialization within a culture that continues to value work above leisure and play' (1994: 105). In both examples, guilt was more evidenced in words than in behaviour, reflecting the influence of social desirability.

In her study of readers of women's magazines, Hermes (1995) found that within the 'interpretative repertoires' (ideas which frame reading experiences) of women readers, there was a place both for feelings of duty to read a feminist publication and guilt at enjoying traditional women's magazines. Barwise and Ehrenberg (1988) and Kubey and Csikszentmihalyi (1991) suggest that such guilt feelings (in relation to television) are typically quite weak (Hermes would probably agree in respect of magazines), but their persistence and ubiquity is nevertheless striking in a supposedly hedonistic age and about such a harmless pleasure.

AUDIENCE NORMS FOR CONTENT

Normative expectations relate not only to media use behaviour, but also to aspects of media content. People voice complaints about, as well as appreciation of, the media. Positive response usually outweighs criticism, but what is striking is the fact that the performance of the media is so widely regarded as a proper topic for the expression of public attitudes, judgements and opinion. Audiences expect media to conform to certain norms of good taste and morality, sometimes also to other values, such as those of the local community, patriotism and democracy. Norms for what is appropriate in fiction and entertainment usually refer to bad language, violence, sex and the models of behaviour offered by media. Here family life, the protection of children and the personal susceptibilities and moral standards of adults are the main point of reference.

Morals aside, it is notable also that audiences are sensitive to the quality of media on grounds of political bias and fairness, often placing more emphasis on impartiality and reliability than on the media's own rights to freedom of expression (e.g. Comstock, 1988; Gunter and Winstone, 1993). Audiences can often seem intolerant of the public expression in the mainstream media of extreme or deviant political views. The norms applied by the audience to media information commonly refer to completeness and accuracy, balance and diversity of opinion. News sources are often judged according to their relative credibility (Gaziano and McGrath, 1987).

Despite the evidence of critical public attitudes, rather few people seem personally offended by the media, and actual use behaviour shows a state of relative normlessness (see, e.g. Gunter and Winstone, 1993). This paradox may reflect the existence of private norms based on personal taste and preferences which, as with many aspects of behaviour, do not corresspond with the public norm. It also suggests that evaluative attitudes expressed towards media are somewhat superficial and learnt as socially desirable rather than deeply internalized. This is not to say that personal preferences in choosing and responding to media content will not be influenced by an individual's own personal values (see Johansson and Miegel, 1992). Rather, these value influences are often implicit and beneath the surface.

Values applied to content often involve fine distinctions between one medium and another and one genre and another. For example, Alasuutari (1992) showed that Finnish television viewers deployed a sort of 'moral hierarchy', according to which news and information were highly regarded and soap operas were seen as a 'low' form of content. This applied even to fans of soap operas (this perception is quite widespread; see, e.g., Ang, 1985; Morley, 1986; Seiter et al., 1989). They were expressing a consensus of judgement that they were aware of, without feeling personally bound to follow it. The nature of the hierarchy is not very surprising, since it reflects traditional cultural values and tastes, especially a respect for reality and information.

Other forms of critical distance include an objection to some aspects of content on moral or ideological grounds. In other words, it seems that 'experienced' audience members (these kinds of data came from regular and articulate viewers) have a fairly extensive repertoire of positions they can take up in respect of particular media contents. Similar general conclusions about women's magazines were drawn by Hermes (1995), and the complexity of audience response does not seem limited by the relative lack of reader involvement or the acknowledged superficiality of the content concerned.

THE VIEW FROM THE AUDIENCE

As noted in Chapter 12, mass communicators solve the 'problem' of orientation to an essentially unknown audience in a variety of ways, depending on their particular role

conception and type of medium or concept. Here we look briefly at the communicator–audience relationship from the other 'end', having already described normative concerns about content. In general, the audience does not experience its relations with the media and media communicators as problematic on a day-to-day basis. Under conditions of freedom and diversity, audiences choose their own media sources according to personal likes and perceptions of what is relevant and interesting. Nevertheless some effort is required on the part of the audience and some discomfort may be entailed. The first dimension to consider in audience–source relations is that of *affective direction*.

Although media are freely chosen by their audiences, actual people in audiences may not have personally chosen their media or the specific content to which they find themselves exposed. This applies where members of families, households or other groups are subject to the choices of others about what is available to read, view or listen to. Such media 'micro-gatekeepers' may be parents, partners, friends, etc. It also applies where there are few or no real alternatives, for instance where there is only one city or local newspaper which is hard in practice to ignore.

There is usually a large flow of unrequested and often unwanted media messages by way of media advertising of all kinds, mail, telephone, etc. which gives rise to a similar situation. Even where we do choose our own media channel, source and content, we can easily be dissatisfied with some aspects of media performance and there is much scope for negative responses to the media. We are continually faced with the need to select and evaluate, and this includes making choices *against* what we dislike.

Apart from the existence of positive or negative feelings towards source, medium or message, we need to consider the degree of audience *involvement* or *attachment*, which can vary from that of casual spectatorship to a high sense of personal commitment to a media person or performance. From the earliest days of radio, communicators sought to establish an illusion of personal contact and intimacy with the invisible audience by using familiar forms of address, using sound effects to simulate the presence of audiences or by encouraging audience participation. There has always been much pseudo-participation associated with radio and television, more now than ever, and it is not surprising that it evokes some response in the audience, as shown by the phenomenon of fandom (page 406). In practice it is difficult to empirically distinguish 'real' attachment from 'artificial' attachment. But, as Hermes (1999: 74) points out, 'Seeing media figures as real and as part of our everyday cultural and emotional experience is part and parcel of how media texts come to have meaning'.

The concept of **para-social interaction** was introduced by Horton and Wohl (1956) to describe the displacement of a human interlocutor by a media character or personality, treating it by implication as less satisfactory than real social interaction. However, it may be considered as better than nothing, or as a reaction to lack of real social contact. Scales have been developed to measure the degree of para-social interaction (PSI) (Austin, 1992), following a definition of PSI by Rubin et al. as 'the

degree to which audience members feel they interact with their favourite TV news persona' (1990: 250).

Rosengren et al. (1989) proposed a four-fold typology of 'television relations', which they derived from two main dimensions of audience relations with the media. One of these they call *interaction* – having the feeling of interacting with actors on the screen. The second is the variable of degree of *identification* (involvement with some media figure). The extreme case of attachment to media occurs when a high degree of interaction coincides with a high degree of identification. Rosengren et al. refer to this situation as one of *capture*. The reverse condition, with low identification and low involvement, is referred to as 'detachment'. Earlier research by Noble into children's use of television provided evidence of strong audience attachment to television personalities. He reported that: 'these [TV] characters serve as something akin to a screen community with whom the viewer regularly talks and interacts . . . . this serves for many as an extended kin grouping' (1975: 63–4). He identified different degrees of involvement with media personalities and characters. One version can be described as 'recognition', where a viewer has a very positive attachment, but does not lose a sense of reality. Against this, there is the phenomenon of 'identification' which leads to sharing the emotions of the character and a loss of contact with reality.

MEDIA FANDOM

Audiences are connected to 'distant' media sources in several different ways, perhaps especially through the mediation of their family, friends and others in their social milieux. It is also relevant to include institutionalized 'fandom' in this same category, even if often it is not very spontaneous and is engineered or manipulated by the media. Audience experience has always been characterized by occasions of greatly accentuated and specified attachment to particular performers (most especially), but also to certain kinds of performance (types of music, genres of film or fiction). The weakest kind of fandom is simply an attraction to a medium (as in the old expression 'film fan'). The strongest version involves a high degree of emotional investment and activity centring on a media personality. Something rather similar, but less intense, can occur with followers of a particular television series, when attachment to a fictional character gets mixed up with attachment to the actor, or when the distinction between fiction and reality is lost sight of.

Fandom is best considered as something collective – a consciously shared feeling of more or less intense attraction. There are individual fans, of course, but it would be hard to be a lone fan, and the concept would be redundant. Fandom has always been promoted and stimulated by the media publicity arm for obvious reason (see Sabal in Lewis, 1992) and by numerous means. It is also generated by fans themselves, when

they associate with each other and express their attachment in public ways (T-shirts, fanzines style, etc.) (see Lewis, 1992). According to recent cultural theory (e.g. Fiske, 1992) fandom involves an element of actual media 'production' by the audience itself, since the activities of fans extend the media event.

By definition fandom defines relations with the media in a satisfying way and bridges the inevitable real 'distance' between star and star-gazer. Nevertheless, it can also be a painful experience, involving high expectations and vicarious emotional attachments that make the fan potentially vulnerable. Presumably, any such 'costs' incurred though fandom are not normally disproportionate to the satisfactions obtained, although in some cases a loss of contact with reality can go too far. Fandom can also have a downside for the object of affection since fans can be fickle and unforgiving and will ultimately desert. They also treat stars as objects of gossip, envy and dislike (Alberoni, 1972), often encouraged in this by other media.

THE END OF THE AUDIENCE?

As we noted at the beginning of Chapter 15, the audience concept has always been more problematic than it seems, because it can be defined and constructed in so many ways and has no fixed existence. The problems are compounded the more we take the view of the audience itself rather than the media industry. New and different audiences can be constituted by people themselves based on some shared interest or identity. New technologies are bringing in to question the clear distinction between sender and receiver which is crucial to the original idea of the media audience, as well as introducing new forms of use of media (see Chapter 6). Interactive and consultative uses of media take away the spectatorship that was so characteristic of the original mass audience. Aside from radically new communication technologies there are many changes to the 'old technologies' and to media industries that have implications for the audience.

The effects of change are quite mixed, however. On the one hand they increase the size of audiences in some respects, as a result of concentration and monopoly forming and the exploitation of the same content in many different markets. Internationalization is also a route towards much larger (cumulative) audiences for certain high-profile types of content. On the other hand, 'actual' audiences are being diversified as a result of channel multiplication and specialization. There are many more, but often smaller and more homogeneous, audiences. Instead of audiences being recruited from a given geographic area or social class, they are based more on tastes and life-styles. The term *segmentation* is used to refer to the process by which media supply is matched more precisely to a relevant set of media consumers, and the process is aided by the greater possibility of selection on the part of consumers themselves. Evidence

from the USA already indicates that the homogeneity of composition of cable channel audiences is much greater than for national broadcast channels (Barnes and Thomson, 1994: 89).

Another process, that of *fragmentation*, involves the dispersal of the same amount of audience attention over more and more media sources. Ultimately, nearly all choices could be individualized, spelling the end of the audience as a significant social collectivity. Media users will come to have no more in common with each other than owners of any other consumer article. Along with fragmentation of audiences and individualization of use comes a decline in the strength of ties that bind people to their chosen media source and loss of any sense of identity as an audience.

The analysis of electronically collected data by people-meters is beginning to shed new light on patterns of television use in the age of 'media abundance', providing evidence for some of these generalizations. Studies of German and Swiss audiences reported by Krotz and von Hasebrink (1998) and von Hasebrink (1997) have captured some of the changes taking place in television use behaviour in Europe, even if longtitudinal data are not available. The data from German house- holds indicates four important trends. One is decline of the 'typical' collective family viewing situation, since the overwhelming amount of viewing is by one or only two persons. Secondly, there is a very prevalent type of viewing that involves 'many and short' viewing periods, especially amongst children and younger people. Thirdly, despite much greater choice, there is still quite a strong channel loyalty, with many viewers using a limited number of channels and having an identifiable 'home base' to return to. Fourthly, there is clear evidence of content preferences playing a part in selection, contrary to evidence from the days of limited television provision, when preference for content seemed to play a minimal role (Goodhart et al., 1975; Eastman, 1998).

We can summarize the audience trends discussed in terms of four succeeding stages, as shown in Figure 16.4. This applies especially to television, but it has a wider reference. In the early years of television (1950s and 1960s) most viewers in most countries had a very limited choice of up to three national channels (the USA had somewhat more choice). The same media experience was widely shared by nearly everyone. This Unitary Model implies a single audience more or less co- extensive with the general public. As supply of content and channels increase, there is more diversity, and more distinctive options begin to emerge within the framework of a unitary model (e.g. daytime and night-time television, regional variations, more private television in Europe). This pattern of limited internal diversification can be called a Pluralism Model. The third, Core–Periphery, Model is one in which the multiplication of channels undermines the unity of the framework. It becomes possible, as a result of the VCR, cable and satellite transmission and other new media to enjoy a television diet that differs significantly from the majority or mainstream. We are already in that situation in most developed countries. The final stage envisaged in Figure 16.4 is that of Break-Up, where fragmentation accelerates and there is no longer any 'centre', just very many and very diverse sets of media users.

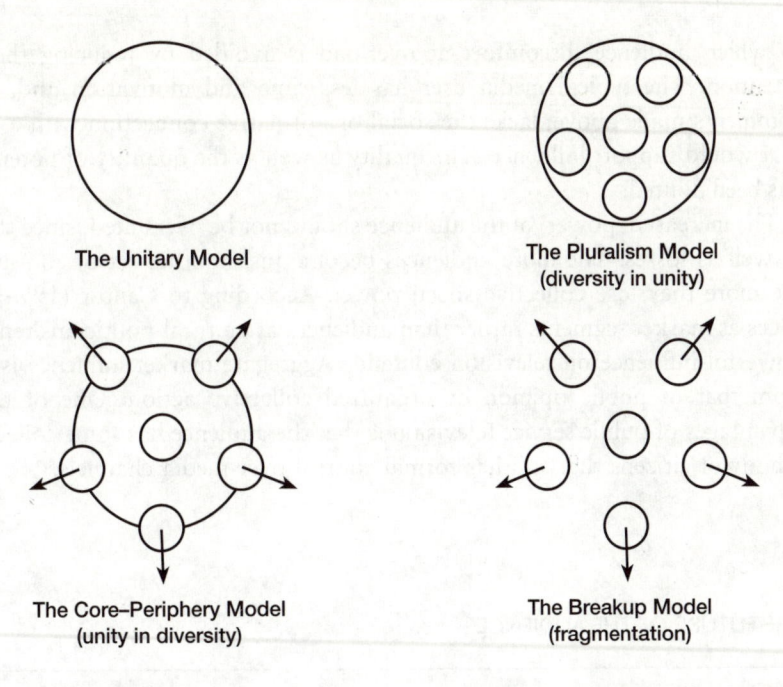

The Unitary Model

The Pluralism Model
(diversity in unity)

The Core–Periphery Model
(unity in diversity)

The Breakup Model
(fragmentation)

FIGURE 16.4   Four stages of audience fragmentation (source: McQuail, 1997: 138)

THE 'ESCAPE' OF THE AUDIENCE

The apparent changes in the general character of audiences can be assessed in different ways. The problems for the media industry are well summed up by the title of Ien Ang's (1991) book, *Desperately Seeking the Audience*. It has become more difficult to keep track of the audience, to manage or predict its composition and the direction of its interests, even if new technology such as that of the people-meter and other forms of computer analysis of system users also improve the flow of information back to the media. However, the potential 'escape' of the audience from management and control, as well as the greatly increased choice, seem to be entries on the credit side in the balance of audience power.

On the face of it there has been such a shift in favour of media consumers in the market place and even perhaps as individual citizens. There are more channels of relevant political and civic information and less likelihood of a mass audience being the object of semi-monopolistic propaganda or biased information. It is generally harder for would-be persuaders, whether political or commercial, to reach any large general public. If Neuman and Pool (1986) are correct, the audience is also less attentive to messages received than was the case in the early days of radio and television. The overabundance of supply outstrips the capacity of people to notice or make use of it. Even when attention is given, the likelihood of influence is lower than it used to be. Neuman and Pool invoke the idea of an equilibrium model according

to which audience discomfort at overload is avoided by reducing the 'quality' of attention. The typical media user has less time and motivation and, according to comments made above, lacks the social or normative connection with a media source that would support influence. The quality as well as the quantity of potential influence has been diluted.

The increased 'power' of the audience should not be overstated, since there are gains as well as losses. The more audiences become just another set of consumer markets, the more they lose collective social power. According to Cantor (1994: 168) 'Audiences as market segments rather than audiences as cultural-politicians remain the most powerful influence on television content'. Aggregate market influence is far removed from that of public opinion or organized collective action. One of the continued advantages of public service television is that the audience has some collective rights as a body of citizens that still has formal control over media channels.

THE FUTURE OF THE AUDIENCE

At the present time, despite the trends discussed, it is too early to conclude that the mass audience will fade away. It still exists, albeit in somewhat new forms, and the mass media industries have shown a remarkable capacity to survive in familiar forms. Despite the multiplication of channels for television and the greater ease of publication with new technology, the overall structure of media audiences has not yet changed fundamentally. Webster and Phalen (1997: 114) noted that 'traditional mass appeal network television still dominates media consumption in the United States'. In most European countries, the multiplication of channels has not yet led to a general fragmentation of audiences, although there are warning signs. Change has been very gradual, and much the same can be said of the newspaper press in most countries.

It is still very plausible to conclude, along with Neuman (1991), that there is a very considerable inertial force that limits fundamental change in audience formation. One aspect of the resistance is attributable to 'the social psychology of media use', expressed in 'deeply ingrained habits of passive, half-attentive use (1991: 42). The other pressure is the communications industry itself. According to Neuman (ibid.) 'Economies of scale push in the direction of common-denominator, one-way mass communications, rather than promoting narrowcasting and two-way communications'. There are also powerful and varied social forces influencing media production and use that have deep roots and are resistant to the influence of technological change on its own. The shape of audiences reflects the structure, dynamics and needs of social formations ranging from national societies to small groups. These forces do not all work in the same direction to support the mass audience, and some are likely to favour new uses of new media and thus new audience realities. As a result, we cannot make any certain predictions, even about the strength and direction of broad trends.

Sufficient reasons have already been given to wonder whether the term 'audience' is still a useful one, especially as there are so many kinds of use of many different communications media. The term 'audience' cannot easily be divested of its strong connotation of 'spectatorship' – of rather passive watching and listening. It is also closely tied in meaning to the reception of some 'message', despite the fact that we know audience behaviour to involve several equally important motives or satisfactions – for instance, social togetherness and the pleasures of actual use of a medium, regardless of content. Despite this, there seems to be no viable alternative term, and we will probably have to go on using it to cover very diverse occasions.

Even so, we can always differentiate for specific purposes. By way of indicating and summarizing the diverse possibilities, Box 16.2 offers a list of the main dimensions of audience. Each variable shown can be used to describe and classify one or other of the many types of audience that now exist, and each has a history in theory and research.

Box 16.2   The main dimensions of the audience

- Degree of activity or passivity
- Degree of interactivity and interchangeability
- Size and duration
- Locatedness in space
- Group character (social/cultural identity)
- Simultaneity of contact with source
- Heterogeneity of composition
- Social relations between sender and receiver
- Message vs social/behavioural definition of situation
- Degree of perceived 'social presence'
- Sociability of context of use

FURTHER READING

Neuman, W.R. (1991) *The Future of the Mass Audience*. Cambridge: Cambridge University Press.

Webster, J.G. and Phalen, P.F. (1997) *The Mass Audience: Rediscovering the Dominant model*. Mahawa, NJ: Lawrence Erlbaum.

Ettema, J.S. and Whitney, D.C. (eds) (1994) *Audiencemaking: How the Media Create the Audience*. Thousand Oaks, CA: Sage.

VI

EFFECTS

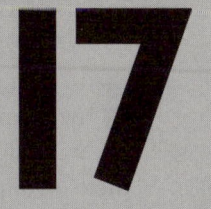

17

the effect research tradition

The entire study of mass communication is based on the assumption that the media have significant effects, yet there is little agreement on the nature and extent of these assumed effects. This uncertainty is the more surprising since everyday experience provides countless, if minor, examples of influence. We dress for the weather as forecast, buy something because of an advertisement, go to a film mentioned in a newspaper, react in countless ways to media news, to films, to music on the radio, and so on. There are many reported cases of negative media publicity concerning, for instance, food contamination or adulteration, leading to significant changes in food consumption behaviour, sometimes with large economic impact. Acts of violence or suicide appear to be copied or stimulated by media portrayals. Much policy and regulation is directed at preventing the media from causing harm.

Our minds are full of media-derived information and impressions. We live in a world saturated by media sounds and images, where politics, government and business operate on the assumption that we know what is going on in the wider world. Few of us cannot think of some personal instance of gaining significant information or of forming an opinion because of the media. Much money and effort is also spent on directing the media to achieve such effects. Despite the uncertainties mentioned, there seems to be sufficient pragmatic knowledge, based on experience, to enable the media and their clients to continue to behave as if they knew how to achieve effects.

And yet considerable doubt remains. The paradox can partly be explained in terms of the difference between the general and the particular. We can be sure that particular effects are occurring all the time without being able to see or predict the aggregate outcome or to know after the event how much is attributable to the media. There can be many effects, without any overall pattern or direction. The media are rarely likely to be the only necessary or sufficient cause of an effect, and their relative contribution is extremely hard to assess. There are many good theoretical reasons for this uncertainty, and even common sense and 'practical knowledge' waver when faced with questions of media effect in the contested areas of morals, opinion and deviant behaviour which have attracted most public notice. On many such matters there can be no question of the media being a primary cause, and we have no real 'explanation' of patterns of thought, culture and behaviour which have deep social and historical roots. Furthermore, it makes little sense to speak of 'the media' as if they were one thing rather than the carriers of an enormously diverse set of messages, images and ideas. Most of this material does not originate with the media themselves but 'comes from society' and is 'sent back' to society by way of the media.

The attention to media 'effects' has sometimes been viewed as rather puzzling, since we do not ask similar questions about the effects of other major social institutions, such as education, or religion or the law, each of which is in the business of communicating. Nowak (1997) has suggested one reason for this in the fact that

research questions in other fields have been raised from *within* the institution, directed to particular, not global issues of effect. In the case of mass media, most research was initiated from *outside*, especially by academics, social critics, politicians, interest groups, etc. The underlying premise was that mass media were some kind of 'problem' for the rest of society. He goes on to suggest that this has changed very much over the last 25 years, as the media began to study themselves (from inside) and as the field of 'media and communication studies' has itself grown and matured. This has led to much less focus on 'effects' in general and more on understanding how mass media work, what their significance is and how we can read their texts. There is much truth in this. Even so, despite the obstacles mentioned above and the inevitable inconclusiveness, the quest for media effects continues to prove fascinating. A belief in crucial short-term as well as deep and long-term consequences from the media will not easily be extinguished.

THE NATURAL HISTORY OF MEDIA EFFECT RESEARCH AND THEORY: FOUR PHASES

The development of thinking about media effects may be said to have a 'natural history', in the sense of its being strongly shaped by the circumstances of time and place. It has also been influenced by several 'environmental' factors, including the interests of governments and law-makers, changing technology, the events of history, the activities of pressure groups and propagandists, the ongoing concerns of public opinion, and even the findings and the fashions of social science. Such influences are interactive in the sense that they themselves are never quite independent of the media. It is not surprising that no straight path of cumulative development of knowledge can be discerned. Even so, we can distinguish a number of stages in the history of the field which indicate some degree of ordered progression and reflect the accumulation of knowledge.

Phase I: all-powerful media

In the first phase, which extends from the turn of the century until the late 1930s, the media were credited with considerable power to shape opinion and belief, to change habits of life and to mould behaviour more or less according to the will of their controllers (Bauer and Bauer, 1960). This view was based not on scientific investigation but on observation of the enormous popularity of the press and of the new media of film and radio that intruded into many aspects of everyday life as well as public affairs.

In Europe, the use of media by advertisers, by First World War propagandists, by dictatorial states in the inter-war years and by the new revolutionary regime in Russia, all appeared to confirm what people were already inclined to believe – that the media could be immensely powerful. Against the background of such beliefs, systematic research using survey and experimental methods, and drawing heavily on social psychology, was begun during the 1920s and 1930s. Many books were written about the power of propaganda in this period (e.g. Lasswell, 1927; see also Jowett and O'Donnell, 1986). Often the motives for concern were of a reformist or progressive kind, aiming at improving the media or harnessing them to some desirable 'pro-social' goal, such as education, combating prejudice or increasing public information.

Phase 2: theory of powerful media put to the test

This transition to empirical enquiry led to a second phase of thinking about media effect. Its beginning is well exemplified in the research literature by the series of Payne Fund studies in the United States in the early 1930s (Blumer, 1933; Blumer and Hauser, 1933; Peterson and Thurstone, 1933). These studies were primarily concerned with the influence of films on children and young people. This era of research into media effects continued until the early 1960s. Many separate studies were carried out into the effects of different types of content and media, of particular films or programmes and of entire campaigns. Attention was mainly concentrated on the possibilities of using film and other media for planned persuasion or information. Hovland et al. (1949), for instance, reported a series of large-scale experimental studies that assessed the value of using film material to 'indocrinate' American military recruits into awareness of and support for the aims of the Second World War. Star and Hughes (1950) reported a campaign designed to improve public support for the United Nations. Lazarsfeld et al. (1944) and Berelson et al. (1954) initiated a long tradition of investigating the effectiveness of democratic election campaigns. There continued to be research into the possible harmful effects of media on children, especially television when it arrived in the 1950s.

Over the course of time the nature of research changed, as methods developed and evidence and theory suggested new kinds of variable that should be taken into account. Initially, researchers began to differentiate possible effects according to social and psychological characteristics; subsequently they introduced variables relating to intervening effects from personal contacts and social environment, and latterly according to types of motive for attending to media.

What now seems like the end of an era was marked by expressions of disillusion with the outcome of this kind of media effect research (e.g. Berelson, 1959). There were new statements of conventional wisdom which assigned a much more modest role to media in causing any planned or unintended effects. The still influential and

useful summary of early research by Joseph Klapper, published in 1960 (though dating from 1949), appeared to set the seal on this research phase. It concluded that 'mass communication does not ordinarily serve as a necessary or sufficient cause of audience effects, but rather functions through a nexus of mediating factors' (1960: 8).

It was not that the media had been found to be without effects or influence; rather there was no direct or one-to-one link to be expected between media stimulus and audience response. Media were shown to operate within a pre-existing structure of social relationships and a particular social and cultural context. These factors took primacy in shaping the opinions, attitudes and behaviour under study and also in shaping media choice, attention and response on the part of audiences. It was also clear that information acquisition could occur without related attitude change, and attitude change without changes in behaviour (for example, Hovland et al., 1949; Trenaman and McQuail, 1961).

The new sobriety of assessment was slow to modify opinion outside the social scientific community. It was particularly hard to accept for those who made a living from advertising and propaganda and for those in the media who valued the myth of their great potency (see Key, 1961). Those with political or commercial motives for using or controlling the media did not feel they could risk accepting the message of relative media impotence which research had produced. There was still room for varying assessments, since the message of limited effect was heavily qualified and was itself a reaction against unrealistic claims. The failure of research to find powerful effects could well be attributed to the complexity of the processes and the inadequacy of research designs and methods.

Phase 3: powerful media rediscovered

Hardly had the 'no (or minimal) effect' conclusion been written into the textbooks when it was being challenged by those who doubted that the whole story had been written. There was plenty of contemporary evidence of a circumstantial nature that the media could indeed have important social effects and be an instrument for exercising social and political power. Authoritative retrospective accounts of the period (for example, Lang and Lang, 1981; McGuire, 1973; McLeod et al., 1991) shed considerable doubt on whether there ever was a watershed at this time between a belief in media power and one in media impotence.

In relation to public opinion effects, Lang and Lang (1981) argue that the 'minimal effect' conclusion is only one particular interpretation which has gained undue currency (see also Chaffee and Hochheimer, 1982). Lang and Lang write: 'The evidence available by the end of the 1950s, even when balanced against some of the negative findings, gives no justification for an overall verdict of "media impotence" ' (1981: 659). In their view, the 'no effect' myth was due to a combination of factors. Most notable was the undue concentration on a limited range of effects, especially short-term effects

on individuals (for instance, during elections), instead of on broader social and institutional effects, and undue weight given to two publications: Katz and Lazarsfeld's *Personal Influence* (1955) and Klapper's *The Effects of Mass Communication* (1960). Nevertheless, they conceded that the myth was influential enough to close off certain avenues of research temporarily.

One reason for the reluctance to accept a 'minimal effect' conclusion was the arrival of television in the 1950s and 1960s as a new medium with even more power of attraction (if not necessarily of effect) than its predecessors and with seemingly major implications for social life. The third phase of theory and research was one in which potential effects were still being sought, but according to revised conceptions of the social and media processes likely to be involved. Early investigation had relied very heavily on a model (borrowed from psychology) in which correlations were sought between degree of 'exposure' to media stimuli and measured changes of, or variations in, attitude, opinion, information or behaviour, taking account of numerous intervening variables.

The renewal of effect research was marked by a shift of attention towards long-term change, cognitions rather than attitude and affect, and towards collective phenomena such as climates of opinion, structures of belief, ideologies, cultural patterns and institutional forms of media provision. Attention also focused on intervening variables of context, disposition and motivation. In addition, effect research benefited from growing interest in how media organizations processed and shaped 'content' before it was delivered to audiences (for example, in Halloran et al., 1970; Elliott, 1972).

Much of what follows is taken up with a review of these newer theories of effect and of modifications of early direct-effect models. While there are many contributors to, and causes of, the revival of interest, it was Noelle-Neumann (1973) who coined the slogan 'return to the concept of powerful mass media' which serves to identify this research phase. The upsurge of left-wing political thinking in the 1960s (the New Left) also made an important contribution by crediting the media with powerful legitimating and controlling effects in the interests of capitalist or bureaucratic states.

Phase 4: negotiated media influence

Work on media texts (especially news) and audiences, and also on media organizations, beginning in the late 1970s, brought about a new approach to media effects which can best be termed 'social constructivist' (Gamson and Modigliani, 1989). In essence, this involves a view of media as having their most significant effects by constructing meanings. These constructs are then offered in a systematic way to audiences, where they are incorporated (or not), on the basis of some form of negotiation,

into personal meaning structures, often shaped by prior collective identifications. Meanings (thus effects) are constructed by receivers themselves. This mediating process often involves strong influence from the immediate social context of the receiver. The break with 'all-powerful media' is also marked by a methodological shift, especially away from quantitative survey methods. An early practitioner of effect research has even referred to the 'bankruptcy of behaviourism' as an explanation of media effects (Mendelsohn, 1989).

The origins of the new research phase are diverse and lie quite deep in the past. The new thinking also retains some points of similarity with early 'powerful media' theory, including, for example, theory of ideology and false consciousness, Gerbner's cultivation theory (Signorielli and Morgan, 1990) and the ideas elaborated by Noelle-Neumann (1974) in her 'spiral of silence' theory. This emerging paradigm of effects has two main thrusts. First, media 'construct' social formations and even history itself by framing images of reality (in fiction as well as news) in predictable and patterned ways. Secondly, people in audiences construct for themselves their own view of social reality and their place in it, in interaction with the symbolic constructions offered by the media. The approach allows both for the power of media and for the power of people to choose, with a terrain of continuous negotiation in between, as it were. In general, it is a formulation of the effect process which accords well with the mediation perspective outlined in Chapter 4.

There are by now a good many research studies which operate within this framework, with attention often directed at how media interact with significant social movements which are active in society (for instance, in relation to the environment, peace and the advance of women and minorities). One example is offered by Gitlin's (1980) account of the US students' movement in the late 1960s. Another is Gamson and Modigliani's (1989) analysis of opinion formation concerning nuclear power. A more recent study by van Zoonen (1992) of the rise of the women's movement in the Netherlands has adopted a 'social constructivist' approach to assessing the contribution of the media to the events. She explains the perspective essentially as follows. The media are more than plain transmitters of movement messages and activities, but they do this selectively; it is not the transmission which counts so much as 'a particular *construction* of the movement's ideas and activities', influenced by many negotiations and conflicts within the news organization. She comments: 'The media image of the movement is the result of an intricate *interaction* between movement and media', leading to a certain *public identity* and *definition*.

The constructivist approach does not replace all earlier formulations of the effect process – for instance, in matters of attention-gaining, direct stimulus to individual behaviour or emotional response. It is also consistent with a good deal of earlier theory, although it departs radically in terms of method and research design by calling for much deeper, broader and more qualitative kinds of evidence, especially about the context of 'critical events' during which constructions are forged. It clearly owes more to the cultural than to the structural and behavioural traditions outlined earlier (Chapter 3). But it does not stand entirely apart from the latter, since

investigation has to be located in a societal context and it assumes that eventual constructions are the outcome of numerous behaviours and cognitions by many participants in complex social events. The approach can be applied to a good many situations of presumed media influence, especially in relation to public opinion, social attitudes, political choice, ideology and many cognitions. The various formulations of frame and schema theory (Graber, 1984) can usefully be located under the same general heading.

Media power can vary with the times

Before leaving the historical aspect of research into media effects, it is worth reflecting on a suggestion by Carey (1988) that variations in *belief* in the power of mass communications may have a historical explanation. He writes 'it can be argued that the basic reason behind the shift in the argument about the effects from a powerful to a limited to a more powerful model is that the social world was being transformed over this period'. Powerful effects were indeed signalled in a time of world upheaval around the two world wars, while the quieter 1950s and 1960s seemed more stable, until peace was again upset by social upheaval. It does seem that whenever the stability of society is disturbed, by crime, war, economic malaise or some 'moral panic', the mass media are given some of the responsibility.

We can only speculate about the reasons for such associations in time, but we cannot rule out the possibility that media *are* actually more influential in certain ways at times of crisis or heightened awareness. This might apply to the impact of the fall of communism in Europe or of international conflicts such as the Gulf and Balkan wars of the 1990s. There are several reasons for this possibility. People often know about the more significant historical events only through the media and may associate the message with the medium. In times of change and uncertainty it is also highly probable that people are more dependent on media as a source of information and guidance (Ball-Rokeach and DeFleur, 1976; Ball-Rokeach, 1985). Media have also been shown to be more influential on matters outside immediate personal experience. Under conditions of tension and uncertainty, government, business and other elites and interests often try to use media to influence and control opinion.

All these are arguments for the view that the power (potential effect) of media may indeed vary according to historical conditions. In a somewhat different context (that of the socializing effects of television on children), Rosengren and Windahl (1989) suggest that variations in evidence about the influence of television itself may reflect the fact that television was actually different in content and as a social experience in the 1980s compared with the 1950s when the first research was undertaken. If that was true then it has implications for today when television experience has again changed in many ways. The important if obvious point that the media are not constant

as a potential influence, over time and between places, is often overlooked in the search for generalization.

LEVELS AND KINDS OF EFFECTS

Media 'effects' are simply the consequences of what the mass media do, whether intended or not. The expression 'media power', on the other hand, refers to a general potential on the part of the media to have effects, especially of a planned kind. 'Media effectiveness' is a statement about the *efficiency* of media in achieving a given aim and always implies intention or some planned communication goal. Such distinctions are important for precision, although it is hard to keep to a consistent usage. Even more essential for research and theory is to observe the distinction between 'levels' of occurrence, especially the levels of individual, group or organization, social institution, whole society, and culture. Each or all can be affected by mass communication, and effects at any one level (especially a 'higher' level) often imply some effects at other levels. Most media effect research has been carried out, methodologically, at the individual level, though often with the aim of drawing conclusions relating to collective or higher levels.

Perhaps the most confusing aspect of research on effects is the multiplicity and complexity of the phenomena involved. Broad distinctions are normally made between effects which are cognitive (to do with knowledge and opinion), those which are affectual (relating to attitude and feelings) and effects on behaviour. This threefold distinction was treated in early research as following a logical order, from the first to the third and with an implied increase in significance (behaviour counting more than knowledge). In fact, it is no longer easy to sustain the distinction between the three concepts or to accept the unique logic of that particular order of occurrence (see page 432). Nor is behaviour (such as acts of voting or purchasing) necessarily more significant than other kinds of effect. To add to the complexity, much of our evidence comes from replies to questionnaires which are themselves individual acts of verbal behaviour from which we hope to reconstruct collective phenomena, often with an inextricable mixture of cognitive and affectual elements.

There are several ways of differentiating between the types of media effect. Klapper (1960) distinguished between *conversion, minor change* and *reinforcement* – respectively: change of opinion or belief according to the intention of the communicator; change in form or intensity of cognition, belief or behaviour; and confirmation by the receiver of an existing belief, opinion or behaviour pattern. This threefold distinction needs to be widened to include other possibilities, especially at levels above that of the individual (see Chapter 2). The main options are listed in Box 17.1. The categories of effect are mainly self-explanatory, but the facilitation of change refers to the mediating

Box 17.1   Main kinds of media-induced change

The media can:

- Cause intended change
- Cause unintended change
- Cause minor change (form or intensity)
- Facilitate change (intended or not)
- Reinforce what exists (no change)
- Prevent change

Any of these changes may occur at the level of the individual, society, institution or culture

role of media in the construction of meanings and in wider processes of change in society, in line with the most recent paradigm of media effect (phase 4, page 420). The two effect types that imply absence of any effect involve different conceptions of media processes. In the case of an individual, reinforcement is a probable consequence of selective and persistent attention on the part of the receiver to content that is congruent with his or her existing views.

'Preventing change', on the other hand, implies the deliberate supply of one-sided or ideologically shaped content in order to inhibit change in a conforming public. Often this just refers to the repetition of consensual views and absence of any challenge. The 'no change' effect from the media, of which we have so much evidence, requires very close attention because of its long-term implications. It is a somewhat misleading expression, since anything that alters the probability of opinion or belief distribution in the future is an intervention into social process and thus an effect.

These distinctions are not exhaustive, and new distinctions may have to be made for purposes of studying particular problems. Windahl et al. (1992) describe a proposal by Kent Asp to classify types of effect according to three variables: level, time frame and source. The level may be individual or the system; time can be short or long; the source, most generally, can be the mass medium, its message and content, or the original source of the message (such as a political party).

Lang and Lang (1981) pointed to yet other types of effect which have been observed, including 'reciprocal', 'boomerang' and 'third-party' effects. The first refers to the consequences for a person or even an institution of becoming the object of media coverage. A planned event, for instance, is often changed by the very fact of being televised. There is often an interaction between media and the objects of reporting. Gitlin (1980) showed, for example how the US student movement in the 1960s was influenced by its own publicity. A 'boomerang' effect, causing change in the opposite direction to that intended, is a very familiar phenomenon (or risk) in campaigning. A 'third-party' effect refers to the belief, often encountered, that other people are likely to be influenced but not oneself. The term 'sleeper' effect has also been used to refer to effects that do not show up until much later.

In their discussion of dimensions of effects, McLeod et al. (1991) also point to the difference between effects which are diffuse or general (such as the supposed effects of television as a medium) and those which are content specific. In the latter case, a certain in-built structure or tendency (for instance, a political bias) is singled out as the potential cause of change.

PROCESSES OF MEDIA EFFECT: A TYPOLOGY

In order to provide an outline of developments in theory and research, we begin by interrelating two of the distinctions already mentioned: between the intended and the unintended, and between the short-term and the long-term. This device was suggested by Golding (1981) to help distinguish different concepts of news and its effects. He argued that, in the case of news, intended short-term effects may be considered as 'bias'; unintended short-term effects fall under the heading of 'unwitting bias'; intended long-term effects indicate 'policy' (of the medium concerned); while unintended long-term effects of news are 'ideology'. Something of the same way of thinking helps us to map out, in terms of these two co-ordinates, the main kinds of media effect process which have been dealt with in the research literature. The result is given in Figure 17.1.

The main entries in the figure can be briefly described, although their meaning will be made more explicit in the discussion of theory that follows.

- *Propaganda*: defined as 'the deliberate and systematic attempt to shape perceptions, manipulate cognitions, and direct behaviour to achieve a response that furthers the desired intent of the propagandist' (Jowett and O'Donnell, 1986).
- *Individual response*: the process by which individuals change, or resist change, following exposure to messages designed to influence attitude, knowledge or behaviour.
- *Media campaign*: the situation in which a number of media are used in an organized way, to achieve a persuasive or informational purpose with a chosen population. The most common examples are found in politics, advertising, fund-raising, and public information for health and safety. Campaigns tend to have the following additional characteristics. They have specific and overt aims and a limited time span and are thus open to assessment as to effectiveness. They have authoritative (legitimate) sponsorship, and their purposes tend to be in line with consensual values and with the aims of established institutions; and the population targeted for influence is usually large and dispersed.
- *News learning*: the short-term cognitive effect of exposure to mass media news, as measured by tests of audience recall, recognition or comprehension.

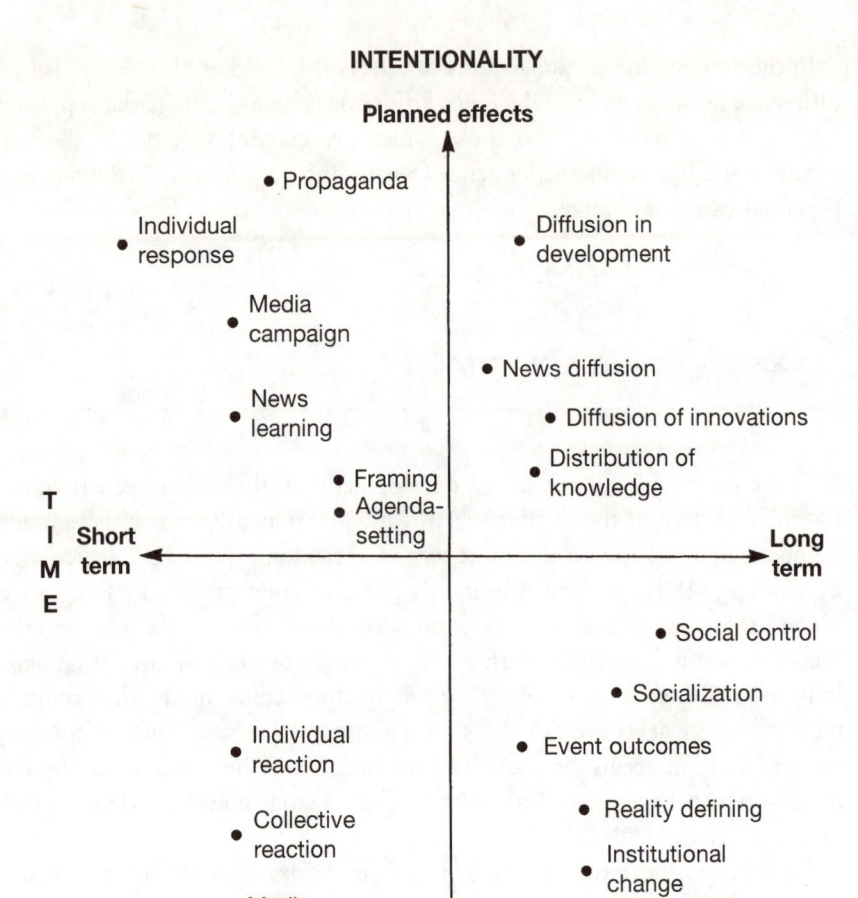

INTENTIONALITY

Planned effects

- Propaganda
- Individual response
- Diffusion in development
- Media campaign
- News diffusion
- News learning
- Diffusion of innovations
- Distribution of knowledge
- Framing
- Agenda-setting

T I M E   **Short term** ←——————————→ **Long term**

- Social control
- Socialization
- Individual reaction
- Event outcomes
- Collective reaction
- Reality defining
- Institutional change
- Media 'violence'
- Cultural change

Unplanned effects

FIGURE 17.1   A typology of media effects; Effects can be located on two dimensions: that of time span and that of intentionality

- *Agenda-setting*: process by which the relative attention given to items or issues in news coverage influences the rank order of public awareness of issues and attribution of significance. As an extension, effects on public policy may occur.
- *Framing*: as a media *effect* this describes the influence on the public of the news angles, interpretative frameworks and 'spin' that contextualize news reports and event accounts. An associated process is that of *priming*.
- *Individual reaction*: unplanned or unpredicted consequences of individual exposure to a media stimulus. This has mainly been noticed in the form of imitation and learning, especially of aggressive or deviant acts (including suicide), but also of 'pro-social' ideas and behaviour. The term 'triggering' has also been used. Other

related types of effect include strong emotional responses, the displacement of other activities, the imitation of styles and fashions, the identification with heroes or stars, sexual arousal, and reactions of fear or anxiety.

- *Collective reaction*: here some of the same individual effects are experienced simultaneously by many people in a shared situation or context, leading to joint action, usually of an unregulated and non-institutional kind. Fear, anxiety and anger are the most potent reactions, which can lead to panic or civil disturbance.
- *Development communication*: the planned use of communication for purposes of long-term development (often in Third World countries), using a series of campaigns and other means of influence, especially the interpersonal network and authority structure of the community or society. Object is to disseminate 'modern' practices in health, agriculture, etc.
- *News diffusion*: the spread of awareness of particular (news) events through a given population over time, with particular reference to the extent of penetration (proportion ultimately knowing) and the means by which information is received (personal versus media sources).
- *Diffusion of innovations*: the most common reference is to the process of take-up of technological innovations within a given population, often on the basis of advertising or general publicity. It can be an unintended as well as an intended effect. The process often follows a characteristic S-curve pattern with predictable features relating to sources of influence and types of motive. Early and late innovators also tend to show different characteristics.
- *Distribution of knowledge*: the consequences of media news and information for the distribution of knowledge as between social groups, with particular reference to different kinds of media source and to the social origins of variation. The main reference is to the closing or widening of '**knowledge gaps**'.
- *Socialization*: the informal contribution of media to the learning and adoption of norms, values and expectations of behaviour in particular social roles and situations.
- *Social control*: refers here to systematic tendencies to promote conformity to an established order or a pattern of behaviour. The main effect is to support the legitimacy of existing authority, by way of ideology and the 'consciousness industry'. Depending on one's social theory, this can be considered either as a deliberate or as an unintended extension of socialization. Because of this ambiguity, it is 'located' in Figure 17.1 near the midpoint of the vertical co-ordinate.
- *Event outcomes*: referring to the part played by media in conjunction with institutional forces in the course and resolution of major 'critical' events (see Lang and Lang, 1981). Examples could include revolution, major domestic political upheavals and matters of war and peace. Less significant events, such as elections, could also figure here (Chaffee, 1975).
- *Reality defining and construction of meaning*: a similar process to social control, but different in having more to do with broad structures of cognitions and frames of interpretation than with behaviour. This (very extensive) kind of effect is also

different in requiring the more or less active participation of receivers in the process of constructing their own meaning.

- *Institutional change*: the unplanned adaptation by existing institutions to developments in the media, especially those affecting their own communication functions (cf. the notion of 'reciprocal effects'.
- *Cultural change*: shifts in the overall pattern of values, behaviours and symbolic forms characterizing a sector of society (such as youth), a whole society or a set of societies. The alternative tendencies, referred to as 'centrifugal' or 'centripetal' are relevant to this point. The possible strengthening or weakening of cultural identity may also be an example of effect.
- *Effect on social integration*, as posited in much mass communication theory. Integration (or its absence) may be observed at different levels, especially local community or nation, which also correspond with the distribution areas of media.

The entries in Figure 17.1 are intended to stand for processes of effect differentiated according to level, time span, complexity and several other conditions that have been briefly indicated. In some cases, the same basic model may apply to more than one of the processes.

FURTHER READING

Bryant, J. and Zillman, D. (eds) (1994) *Perspectives on Media Effects*, 2nd edn. Hillsdale, NJ: Lawrence Erlbaum.

Iyengar, S. and Reeves, R. (eds) (1997) *Do the Media Govern?* Thousand Oaks, CA: Sage.

Lowery, S.A. and DeFleur, M.L. (eds) (1995) *Milestones in Mass Communication Research*, 3rd edn. New York: Longman.

18

processes of short-term effect

The dimensions according to which types of effect were classified in Figure 17.1 are not the only possibilities, and the resulting typology may not always seem completely logical. At the heart of the problem is the fact that all media effects must begin with attention, or 'exposure' to some media message by an individual. The results of this event extend through time and take different, often collective forms. The effects themselves, for instance acquiring knowledge of events by way of news, are not uniquely short- or long-term, but can be treated as both. Because the 'inputs' from media are so numerous, varied and interrelated, we cannot in practice separate them, although we have to do so for purposes of analysis. In this and the following chapter the treatment of topics has largely been based on the way effects have been studied rather than on essential differences in the effects themselves. The subheadings reflect the names that media researchers have given to different theories, models, concepts, processes and perspectives that have been singled out for study.

The stimulus–response model

Two of the entries in Figure 17.1 – *individual response* and *individual reaction* – can be dealt with together under this heading, since they share the same underlying behavioural model, that of **stimulus–response** or conditioning. Although appropriate here, the model also has a much wider potential application. The model's main features can be simply represented as follows:

$$\text{single message} \rightarrow \text{individual receiver} \rightarrow \text{reaction}$$

It applies more or less equally to intended and to unintended effects, although there is a significant difference between a *response* (implying some interaction with the receiver and also a learning process) and a *reaction* (which implies no choice or interaction on the part of the receiver). A more extended version of the basic response and learning process as it occurs in persuasion and opinion formation is indicated by McGuire (1973) in the form of six stages in sequence: presentation, attention, comprehension, yielding, retention, overt behaviour.

This elaboration is sufficient to show why stimulus–response theory has had to be modified to take account of selective attention, interpretation, response and recall. The model, in whatever form, is highly pragmatic, predicting, other things being equal, the occurrence of a response (verbal or behavioural act) according to the presence or absence of an appropriate stimulus (message). It presumes a more or less direct behavioural effect in line with the intention of the initiator and consistent with some overt stimulus to act in a certain way which is built into the message. In discussions of

media effect, this has sometimes been referred to as the 'bullet' or 'hypodermic' theory, terms that far exaggerate the probability of effect and the vulnerability of the receiver to influence.

Much has been written of the inadequacy of such a theory, and DeFleur (1970) showed how this model was modified in the light of growing experience and research. First, account had to be taken of individual differences, since, even where expected reactions have been observed, their incidence varies according to difference of personality, attitude, intelligence, interest, etc. As DeFleur wrote: 'media messages contain particular stimulus attributes that have differential interaction with personality characteristics of audience members' (1970: 122). This is especially relevant, given the complexity of most media messages compared with the kind of stimulus used in most psychological experiments. Secondly, it became clear that response varies systematically according to social categories within which the receiver can be placed, thus according to age, occupation, life-style, gender, religion, etc. DeFleur notes that 'members of a particular category will select more or less the same communication content and will respond to it in roughly equal ways' (1970: 123).

Mediating conditions

The revision of the stimulus–response model involved the identification of the conditions that mediate effects. McGuire (1973) indicated the main kinds of variable as having to do with source, content, channel, receivers and destination. There is reason to believe that messages stemming from an authoritative and credible source will be relatively more effective, as will those from sources that are attractive or close (similar) to the receiver. As to content, effectiveness is associated with repetition, consistency and lack of alternatives (monopoly situation). It is also more likely where the subject matter is unambiguous and concrete (Trenaman, 1967).

In general, effect as intended is also likely to be greater on topics that are distant from, or less important for, the receiver (lower degree of ego-involvement or prior commitment). Variables of style (such as personalization), types of appeal (such as emotional versus rational) and order and balance of argument have been found to play a part, but too variably to sustain any general prediction. Channel (medium) factors have often been investigated, with mixed results, mainly because content and receiver factors dominate learning outcomes. It is also hard to discriminate between intrinsic channel differences and the differences between media in which channels are embedded (such as press versus television).

Generally, research has failed to establish clearly the relative value of different modes (audio, visual, etc.) in any consistent way, although the written or spoken verbal message seems to take primacy over pictorial images, according to measures of recall or comprehension (for example, Katz et al., 1977). As we have seen, a number of obvious receiver variables can be relevant to effect, but special notice should perhaps

be given to variables of motivation, interest and level of prior knowledge. The degree of motivation or involvement has often been singled out as of particular importance in the influence process and in determining the sequence in which different kinds of effect occur (Krugman, 1965).

According to Ray (1973), the normal 'effect hierarchy' as found, for instance, in the work of Hovland et al. (1949) is a process leading from cognitive learning (the most common effect) to affective response (like or dislike, opinion, attitude) to 'conative' effect (behaviour or action). Ray argues, with some supporting evidence, that this model is normal only under conditions of high involvement (high interest and attention). With low involvement (common in many television viewing situations and especially with advertising) the sequence may go from cognition directly to behaviour, with affective adjustment occurring later to bring attitude into line with behaviour (reduction of dissonance – Festinger, 1957).

In itself, this formulation casts doubt on the logic and design of many persuasive communication campaigns which assume attitude to be an unambiguous correlate and predictor of behaviour. There is also a question mark against campaign evaluations based on measures of attitude change alone. The question of consistency between the three elements is also at issue. According to Chaffee and Roser (1986), high involvement is also likely to be a necessary condition for consistency of effects, and thus for a stable and enduring influence. Their preferred model of media effect involves a repetitive sequence from low involvement, through perception of dissonance and then to learning, with cumulative results. In this view, shallow and easily forgotten information can develop into a reasoned set of ideas and into action, especially under conditions of repeated exposure (as in a systematic campaign).

In any natural (non-laboratory) media situation, individual receivers will choose which stimulus to attend to or to avoid, will interpret its meaning variably and will react or not behaviourally, according to choice (Bauer, 1964). This seriously undermines the validity of the conditioning model, since the factors influencing selectivity are bound to be strongly related to the nature of the stimulus, working for or against the occurrence of an effect. Our attention should consequently be drawn away from the simple fact of experiencing a stimulus and towards the mediating conditions described above, especially in their totality and mutual interaction. This approach to the effect problem is more or less what Klapper (1960: 5) recommended and described as a 'phenomenistic' approach – one which sees 'media as influences working amid other influences in a total situation'.

Source–receiver relations and effect

As has been noted, trust in and respect for the source can be conducive to influence. There have been several attempts to develop theories of influence taking account of relationships between sender (or message sent) and receiver. Most of these theories

refer to interpersonal relations. One framework has been suggested by French and Raven (1953), indicating five alternative forms of communication relationship in which social power may be exercised by a sender and influence accepted by a receiver. The underlying proposition is that influence through communication is a form of exercise of power that depends on certain assets or properties of the agent of influence (the communicator).

The first two types of power asset are classified as *reward* and *coercion*, respectively. The former depends on there being gratification for the recipient from a message (enjoyment, for instance, or useful advice); the latter depends on some negative consequence of non-compliance (uncommon in mass communication). A third type is described as *referent* power and refers to the attraction or prestige of the sender, such that the receiver identifies with the person and is willingly influenced, for affective reasons.

Fourthly, there is *legitimate* power, according to which influence is accepted on the assumption that a sender has a strong claim to expect to be followed or respected. This is not very common in mass communication but may occur where authoritative messages are transmitted from political sources or other relevant institutional leaders. This type of power presumes an established relationship between source and receiver that predates and survives any particular instance of mass communication. Finally, there is *expert* power, which operates where superior knowledge is attributed to the source or sender by the receiver. This situation is not uncommon in the spheres of media news and advertising, where experts are often brought in for explanation, comment or endorsement. Examples of exploitation of all five types of media power can be found in advertising and informational campaigns, and more than one of these power sources is likely to be operative on any one given occasion.

A rather similar attempt to account for effects (especially on individual opinion) was made by Kelman (1961). He named three processes of influence. One of these, *compliance*, refers to the acceptance of influence in expectation of some reward or to avoid punishment. Another, *identification*, occurs when an individual wishes to be more like the source and imitates or adopts behaviour accordingly (similar to 'referent' power). A third, *internalization*, describes influence that is guided by the receiver's own pre-existing needs and values. This last-named process may also be described as a 'functional' explanation of influence (or effect), since change is mainly explicable in terms of the receiver's own motives, needs and wishes.

Katz (1960) recommended this approach to explaining the influence of mass communication in preference to what he considered to have been dominant modes of explanation in the past. One of these he described as an 'irrational model' of humanity, which represents people as a prey to any form of powerful suggestion. An alternative view depends on a 'rational model', according to which people use their critical and reasoning faculty to arrive at opinions and acquire information. This would be consistent with a view of the individual as sovereign against propaganda and deception. Katz found both views mistaken and less likely than a 'functional' approach to account for communicative effect, thus giving most weight to the needs of receivers

and to their motives for attending to communication. He argued that communication use helps individuals to achieve their objectives, maintain a consistent outlook and their self-esteem.

THE MEDIA AND VIOLENCE

The practical issue of media effects identified by the violence and aggression portrayed in content has been the object of so much research that it requires to be treated separately at this point. The kinds of effect that are generally suspected are mainly of an unintended and short-term character, although longer-term consequences in the way of behaviour patterns and cultural change are also possible. In its earliest days media research was strongly driven by the search for evidence of harm to young people from the frequent representation of crime and aggression. Each new popular medium has given rise to a new wave of alarm about its possible effects.

At the same time, alarm in society at actual or supposed increases in crime and violence or at certain forms or extreme incidents of violence has led to the media being identified as a suspect. This phenomenon is an example of the 'moral panic' referred to above. A recent example was the tendency to implicate the Internet in the cases of school mass murders in the United States in the later 1990s. Aside from the 'problem' posed by new media outside the control of society and parents, there has been a general change in media that has encouraged a fresh look at an old issue. The main concern is about the proliferation of television channels and decline of regulation, which has made it likely that young children will have a much larger diet of televised violence (and also pornography). This concern may be greatest in Europe, especially Eastern Europe, where the end of communism has exposed the media to the forces of commercialism and greatly weakened cultural policy.

The recurrent belief that screen violence (especially) is a cause of actual violence and aggression has led to many thousand research studies, but no great agreement on the degree of causal influence from the media. The programme of research carried out for the US Surgeon General at the end of the 1960s resulted, according to Lowery and DeFleur (1995), in three main conclusions:

1. Television content is heavily saturated with violence.
2. Children are spending more and more time exposed to violent content.
3. Overall, the evidence supports the hypothesis that the viewing of violent entertainment increases the likelihood of aggressive behaviour.

The main components of hypotheses about violent effects have remained fairly constant. Wartella et al. (1998: 58–9) outline three basic theoretical models for describing the process of learning and imitation of television violence. One is the

'social learning theory' of Albert Bandura, according to which children learn from media models what behaviour will be rewarded and what punished. Secondly, there are 'priming' effects (Berkowitz, 1984). When people view violence it activates or 'primes' other related thoughts and evaluations, leading to a greater predisposition to use violence in interpersonal situations. Thirdly, Huesmann's (1986) script theory holds that social behaviour is controlled by 'scripts' that indicate how to respond to events. Violence on television is encoded in such a way as to lead to violence, as a result of aggressive scripts. In addition to learning and modelling effects, there is a widespread belief that exposure to portrayals of violence leads to a general 'desensitization' that lowers inhibitions against and increases tolerance of violent behaviour. As with all such theories there are many variables influencing the disposition of a person and several relating to the depiction of violence. Wartella et al. (1998: 59–60) list the main contextual factors (in content) influencing audience reactions. These are shown in Box 18.1. In addition to variables of personal disposition and content there are also variables of the viewing situation that are important, especially being alone or being with parents or peers.

Box 18.1   Contextual factors in the portrayal of violence

- The nature of the perpetrator
- The nature of the target
- The reason for violence
- The presence of weapons
- The extent and graphicness of the violence
- The degree of realism of the violence
- Whether the violence is rewarded or punished
- The consequence of the violence
- Whether humour is involved in the violence

The main findings of the Surgeon General's report as summarized above have often been confirmed (see, e.g. Bryant and Zillman, 1986; Comstock, 1988). There has continued to be a great deal of violence portrayed on television, and it has continued to exert a great attraction for the young. It is less easy to say if the average degree of exposure has increased or not over time, but the potential to see screen violence has gradually extended to other parts of the world, along with the means of viewing. Groebel (1998), reporting on a global survey of violence on television, on behalf of Unesco, involving five thousand children in 23 countries, commented on the universality of media violence and on the widespread fascination with aggressive media hero figures, especially amongst boys. For instance, he found that 88% of the world's children knew Arnold Schwarznegger's Terminator (1998: 182).

The third finding noted above, concerning effects on behaviour, is much less unanimous and has always been controversial because of the industry and policy implications. It is not easy to be certain on this matter, and any general authoritative statement takes on a political character. The American Psychological Association

(1993) concluded that 'there is absolutely no doubt that those who are heavy viewers of this [television] violence demonstrate increased acceptance of aggressive attitudes and increased aggressive behavior' (cited in Wartella et al., 1998). However, even this falls short of a clear statement of causation and leaves aside the question of other influences such as environment. Groebel (1998) noticed in his finding that children from high-aggression environments (crime and war) and who were in a 'problematic emotional state' were much more likely to view and be attracted by aggressive violence than were others.

In her survey of the views of European academic researchers into media and violence, Linné (1998) asked what their opinion was of the causal link between violence in the media and violence in society. Twenty-two per cent thought there was an 'evident causal link', 33% a 'vague causal link and only for some children' and 4% said 'no causal link'. The remainder found the issue too problematic to be given such a simple answer. In general, Linne found that research had shifted from the question of causation towards that of understanding the appeal of violence that undoubtedly exists.

From Groebel's research (see above) comes the observation (1998: 195) that 'children's aggressive behaviour patterns and perceptions are a mirror of what they experience in their real environment: frustration; aggression; problematic circumstances'. He goes on to say (1998: 198) 'Media violence . . . is primarily presented in a rewarding context . . . [and] satisfies different needs. It "compensates" own frustrations and deficits in problem areas'. It offers 'thrills for children in a less problematic environment. For boys it creates a frame of reference for "attractive role models". . . . The "reward characteristics" of aggression are more systematically promoted than non-aggressive ways of coping with one's life'. These findings are not novel and echo the lessons of much earlier research. We know for sure that undesirable effects occur following attention to television violence, although they are generally mediated by way of other factors that may well be the 'real' or fundamental cause.

A MODEL OF BEHAVIOURAL EFFECT

These developments of theory take one a good way from the simple conditioning model and help to account for some of the complexities encountered in research. It is obvious that in situations of unintended effect, some individuals will be more prone than others to react or respond to stimuli, 'more at risk' when harmful effects are involved. An elaboration of the basic stimulus–response model for the case of television viewing has been developed by Comstock et al. (1978) to help organize the results of research in this field, especially relating to violence. It rests on the presupposition that media experience is no different in essence from any other experience, act or observation which might have consequences for learning or behaviour.

The process depicted by the model, and shown in Figure 18.1, takes the form of a sequence following the initial act of 'exposure' to a form of behaviour on television ('TV act'). This is the first and main 'input' to learning or imitating the behaviour concerned. Other relevant inputs (enclosed within the box in Figure 18.1) are the degree of excitement and arousal ('TV arousal') and the degree to which alternative behaviours ('TV alternatives') are depicted: the more arousal and the fewer behaviours (or more repetition), the more likely learning is to take place. Two other conditions (inputs) have to do with the portrayal of consequences ('TV perceived consequences')

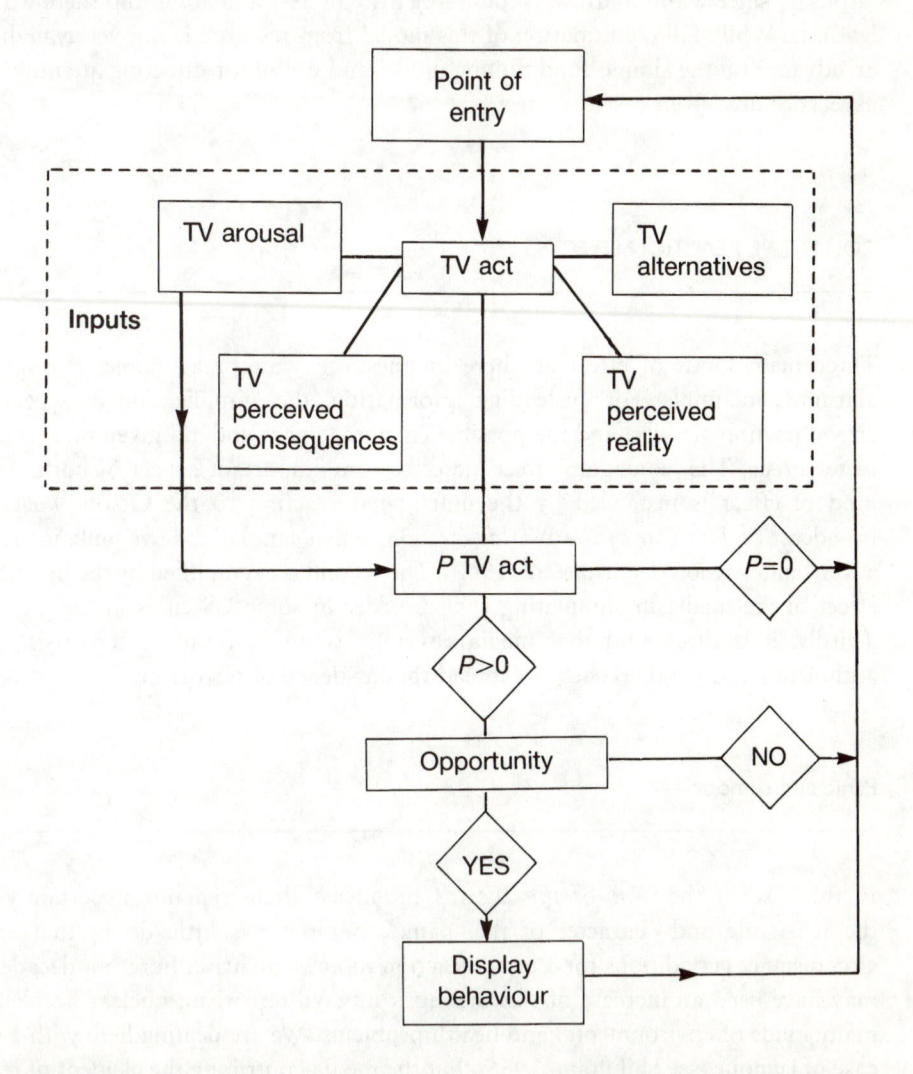

FIGURE 18.1   A simplified version of Comstock et al.'s (1978) model of television effects on individual behaviour (from McQuail and Windahl, 1993). The effect process is a continuous sequence of repeated exposure to representations of behaviour ('TV acts'); effects depend on the way the behaviour is perceived, on inputs from the situation and on opportunities to act out and display the behaviour concerned

processes of short-term effect

and the degree of reality ('TV perceived reality'): the more that positive consequences seem to exceed negative ones and the more true to life the television behaviour, the more likely is learning ('P TV act') to take place. Where the conditions for effect are not met ($P = 0$) the individual returns to the start of the process; where some probability of effect exists ($P > 0$), the question of opportunity to act arises.

All the inputs mentioned affect the probability of learning the action (the effect), but ultimately any resulting behaviour is conditional on there being an opportunity to put the act into practice. Apart from opportunity, the most important condition is 'arousal', since without arousal (connoting also interest and attention) there will be no learning. While full confirmation of this model from research is not yet available, it is an advance on the simple conditioning model and useful for directing attention to key aspects of any given case.

COLLECTIVE REACTION EFFECTS

Three main kinds of effect are here in question: widespread panic in response to alarming, incomplete or misleading information; the amplification or spreading of crowd or mob activity; and the possible encouragement and aid given unintentionally to terrorists. The 'contagion effect' describes one important aspect of both. The first kind of effect is instanced by the much-cited reaction to the Orson Welles radio broadcast of *The War of the Worlds* in 1938, when simulated news bulletins reported a Martian invasion (Cantril et al., 1940). The second is exemplified by the hypothesized effect of the media in stimulating civil disorder in some US cities in the late 1960s. Thirdly, it is often said that media coverage is more useful to terrorists than to authorities and may also help to spread the incidence of terrorism.

Panic and rumour

In the case of the *War of the Worlds* broadcast there remains uncertainty about the real scale and character of the 'panic', but there is little doubt that in some circumstances conditions for a panic reaction to news do arise. In recent decades there may have been an increase of risk arising from civil terrorism, nuclear accidents and many kinds of environmental and health problems. We are dealing here with a special case of **rumour** (see Shibutani, 1966), but the media contribute the element of reaching large numbers of separate people at the same moment with the same item of news (which may not be open to independent verification). The other related conditions for a panic response are anxiety, fear and uncertainty. Beyond this, precipitating features of panic seem to be incompleteness or inaccuracy of information, leading to the urgent

search for information, usually through personal channels, thus giving further currency to the original message (Rosengren, 1976).

Civil disorder

Because of the potential threat to the established order, non-institutionalized and violent collective behaviour has been extensively studied, and the media have been implicated in the search for causes of such behaviour. It has been suggested that the media, variously, can provoke a riot, create a culture of rioting, provide lessons on how to riot, and spread a disturbance from place to place. The evidence for or against these propositions is thin and fragmentary, although it seems to be acknowledged that personal contact plays a larger part than media in any riot situation. There is some evidence, even so, that the media can contribute by simply signalling the occurrence and location of a riot event (Singer, 1970), by publicizing incidents which are themselves causes of riot behaviour or by giving advance publicity to the likely occurrence of rioting. In general, it seems likely that the media do have a capacity to define the nature of events, and even if they are ultimately 'on the side' of established order they can unintentionally increase the degree of polarization in particular cases.

While the media have not been shown to be a primary or main cause of rioting (see, for example, Kerner et al., 1968; Tumber, 1982), they may influence the timing or form of riot behaviour. Spilerman (1976) lends some support to this and other hypotheses, on the basis of rather negative evidence. Despite extensive research, he failed to find a satisfactory structural explanation of many urban riots in the United States (that is, explanations in terms of community conditions). He concluded that television and its network news structure were primarily responsible, especially by creating a 'black solidarity that would transcend the boundaries of community'.

In treating together the topic of panic and rioting, it is worth noting that the most canvassed solution to the dangers just signalled, the control or silencing of news (Paletz and Dunn, 1969), might itself entail a local panic through lack of any explanation for observable neighbourhood disturbances.

Media and terrorism

Much terrorist violence is either planned, threatened or carried out for political objectives by people seeking, however indirectly, to use the media, and giving rise to a complex interaction between the two. The main potential benefit for terrorists is either to gain attention for a cause or to arouse public fear and alarm, which will in turn bring pressure to bear on a government. Terrorism has been said to be stimulated by the 'oxygen of publicity'. Schmid and de Graaf (1982) have also argued that violence

is often a means of access to mass communication and even a message in itself. The media are inevitably implicated in this process, communicating the 'message of terrorism' because of the weight they attach to reporting violence. There are numerous interacting possibilities for effects of media coverage on terrorism, including effects on terrorists themselves, on governments, on the public and on victims of terrorists. These potential effects can be portrayed as helping either terrorists or the authorities (Alali and Eke, 1991; Paletz and Schmid, 1992).

Despite the salience of the issue, there is little research evidence of any effect beyond what is obvious. Schmid and de Graaf (1982) find evidence of strong beliefs by police and a moderate belief by media personnel that live coverage of terrorist acts does encourage terrorism. However, Picard (1991) has dismissed the seeming evidence for contagion as both pseudo-scientific and threatening to media freedom. At most, the arguments seem about evenly divided (Paletz and Schmid, 1992). More difficult to assess are the consequences of refusing such coverage.

Contagion and imitation

An example of possible contagion effects is the sequence of aircraft hijacking crimes in 1971–2, which showed clear signs of being modelled on news reports. Holden (1986) reported correlational evidence of a similar kind that seems to point to an influence from media publicity. There has been other empirical support for the theory that press reports can 'trigger' individual but widespread actions of a pathological kind. Phillips (1980) showed that suicides, motor vehicle fatalities and commercial and non-commercial plane fatalities had a tendency to increase following press publicity for suicides or murder-suicides. He was also (1982) able to link the portrayal of suicide in television fiction (statistically) to the real-life occurrence of suicide, although the findings have been challenged on methodological grounds (Hessler and Stipp, 1985). There seems, at least, some evidence to make a plausible case for an imitation or 'contagion' effect.

THE CAMPAIGN

Basic features

The defining characteristics of a campaign have already been indicated, but we should pay special attention to the fact that campaigns have typically dealt with well-institutionalized behaviour that is likely to be in line with established norms and values. The summary presentation in Box 18.2 draws attention to key features of the

process. First, the originator of the campaign is almost always not an individual but a collectivity: a political party, government, church, charity, pressure group, business firm, etc. The known position in society of the source will strongly affect its chances of success in a campaign.

Secondly, campaigns are also often concerned with directing, reinforcing and activating existing tendencies towards socially approved objectives like voting, buying goods, raising money for good causes or achieving better health and safety. The scope for novelty of effect or major change is thus often intrinsically limited, and the media are employed to assist other institutional forces. We know relatively little about such campaigns that exist to promote objectives that are controversial or ill defined (but experience is growing as a result of AIDS-related publicity).

Box 18.2   Typical elements and sequence of a public campaign

- Collective source
- Socially approved goals
- Several channels
- Many messages
- Variable reach of target group
- Filter conditions
- Variable information processing
- Effects achieved

Thirdly, a campaign usually consists of many messages distributed through several media, with the chances of reach and effect varying according to the established nature of the channels and the message content. A key consideration is the degree to which the identified target group within the public as a whole is actually reached. A distinctive feature of many campaigns is that they aim to *redistribute* a limited amount of public attention, action or money (thus a zero-sum condition). This applies especially to advertising, but it is also true of politics and, in practice, to most fund-raising for charitable purposes (see Benthall, 1993). The question of varying 'filter conditions', 'processing' and 'effects' is taken up below.

Filter conditions

There is a set of 'filter conditions' or potential barriers that can facilitate or hinder the flow of messages to the whole or chosen public. Several of these have already been discussed and they are to some extent predictable in their operation, although only in very broad terms. *Attention* is important because without it there can be no effect, and it will depend on the interest and relevance of content for the receivers, on their motives and pre-dispositions and on channel-related factors. *Perception* matters

because messages are open to alternative interpretations, and the success of a campaign depends to some extent on its message being interpreted in the same way as intended by the campaign source. Research has indicated the occurrence of 'boomerang' effects – for instance, in attempts to modify prejudice (for example, Cooper and Jahoda, 1947; Vidmar and Rokeach, 1974), and it is a constant preoccupation of commercial and political campaigners to try to avoid counter-effects which will aid the 'opposition'. Unwanted side-effects also occur in campaigns to raise money for good causes. For instance, appeals on behalf of the Third World may also create an image of incompetence and inferiority of the region or peoples involved (Benthall, 1993).

Much has been written of the part played by the *group situation* of the receiver in mediating the effects of campaigns (see page 443). Here we need note only that campaigns usually come from 'outside' the many groups to which people belong, according to age, life circumstances, work, neighbourhood, interest, religion, etc. Thus, much of the history of media campaign research has been a struggle to come to terms with the fact that societies are not so conveniently 'atomized' and individuated as the first media campaigners expected. Group allegiance, or its absence, has consequences for whether messages are noticed and then accepted or rejected.

Motivation also plays a part, especially the variable of type and degree of expected satisfaction on the part of the audience member that can influence either learning or attitude change. The revival of an interest in audience motives and in the 'uses and gratifications' approach more generally was influenced by the search for better prediction and explanation of effect processes (Blumler and McQuail, 1968). These 'filter conditions' together determine the composition of the public reached, and the success of a campaign is ultimately dependent on a reasonable 'fit' between composition of the planned 'target' public and the actual public reached.

Diversity of campaign effects

Finally, the entry in Box 18.2 for 'effects' reminds us of the enormous diversity of possible effects, some of which will be intended and others not, some short-term and others long-term. A basic typology of effects divides them into those that are 'cognitive', or 'affective' or 'behavioural', respectively referring to information, feelings and action. Again, a successful or 'effective' campaign will depend on the match between planned effects and those achieved. The criteria for effectiveness have thus to be set by the sender, but evaluation should also take account of side-effects which have to be weighed in the overall balance. The model is a reminder of the complexity of campaigns and the ease with which they can go wrong. There is a very large literature on political campaigns (well reviewed in Kraus and Davis, 1976) and on other kinds of campaign (Rice and Paisley, 1981; Rice and Atkin, 1989).

effects

There is no easy way of summarizing the results of campaign research, beyond remarking that some campaigns do seem to succeed (Mendelsohn, 1973) and others to fail (Hyman and Sheatsley, 1947). Partial failures and partial successes account for most cases in the research literature and probably in reality (Windahl et al., 1992). Rogers and Storey (1987: 831) conclude in relation to campaigns that the 'shifting conceptualization of communication effects and communication process has led to recognition that communication operates within a complex social, political and economic matrix and that communication could not be expected to generate effects all by itself'.

Personal influence in campaign situations

In the study of mass media effects the concept of **'personal influence'** has acquired such a high status that it has been referred to as an essential part of the 'dominant paradigm' (Gitlin, 1978). While the concept is relevant to any effect, it originated in the study of campaigns, and the circumstances of medium-term and deliberate attempts to persuade and inform are most conducive to the intervention of personal contacts as sources of influence. The underlying idea of personal influence is a simple one; its originators expressed it, in the course of their research into the 1940 US presidential election campaign (Lazarsfeld et al., 1944: 151), as follows: 'ideas often flow from radio and print to the opinion leaders and from them to the less active sections of the population'.

Thus, two elements are involved. First, the notion of a population stratified according to interest and activity in relation to media and to the topics dealt with by mass media (in brief, 'opinion leaders' and 'others'). Secondly, the notion of a 'two-step flow' of influence rather than direct contact between 'stimulus' and 'respondent'. These ideas were further developed and elaborated by Katz and Lazarsfeld (1955). Since that time many students of campaigns have tried to incorporate the role of personal influence as a 'variable' in their research, and more sophisticated campaign managers have tried to apply the ideas for the more successful management of the commercial, political or social campaign purpose.

Not only has the 'personal influence' hypothesis had a strong effect on research and on campaigning itself, it has also played an important part in mass communication theory and even in media ideology. It has been invoked to explain the paucity of evidence of direct media effect and to counter the view, advanced first by mass society theorists and later by proponents of ideological determinism, that the media are powerful and rather inescapable shapers of knowledge, opinion and belief in modern societies. The 'ideological component' of personal influence theory lies in the supposition that individuals are 'protected' from manipulation by the strength of personal ties and by the group structure within which they acquire knowledge and form judgements (Gitlin, 1978). Much research and thought devoted to the question has gradually led

to a lower degree of emphasis on the simple proposition as expressed above (for example, Okada, 1986).

While confirming the importance of conversation and personal contact as accompaniment to and perhaps modifier of media influence, research has not yet clearly shown that personal influence always acts as a strong independent or *counteractive* source of influence on the matters normally affected by mass media. Some of the evidence originally advanced by the proponents of the concept has also been re-examined, with differing conclusions (Gitlin, 1978). Secondly, it has become clear that the division between 'leaders' and 'followers' is variable from topic to topic; the roles are interchangeable, and there are many who cannot be classified as either one or the other (and may thus be outside the scope of group influence) (Robinson, 1976). Thirdly, it seems probable that what occurs is as likely to be a multi-step as a two-step flow.

It is clear that direct effects from the media can and do occur without 'intervention' from opinion leaders, and it is highly probable that personal influence is as likely to reinforce the effects of media as to counteract them. Despite these qualifications and comments on the personal influence thesis, there are circumstances where inter-personal influence can be stronger than the media: the overthrow of the Shah of Iran seems to provide a well-documented case in point (Teheranian, 1979). There are reasons for supposing that the same applied on several key occasions during the events surrounding the fall of Communism in Eastern Europe between 1989–1991.

The influence process

There are a number of models that represent the way that information and impressions are processed in any attempt at influence or persuasion, leaving aside the different variants of conditioning. One cognitive processing model in particular that has often been applied is Petty and Cacioppo's (1986) Elaboration Likelihood Model (ELM). This deals with the different ways in which we engage in thinking about issues relevant to a given message. Elaboration refers to the extent to which a person thinks about the issue and about relevant arguments contained in a message. The essence of the idea is that a recipient of a persuasive message can either pay attention to information in the message itself or other 'peripheral' matters, such as the credibility of the source or aspects of presentation, image and form that have no direct cognitive input. The distinction is between *central* (high elaboration) and *peripheral* processing,

As far as persuasive effects on public opinion are concerned, the ELM model indicates two alternative ways to produce the desired changes. One is to encourage thought and analysis by way of information provided (the *central* route). The other is by encouraging people to focus on simple cues and associations (the *peripheral* route). In the case of commercial advertising, the difference is between informational copy and attempts to influence by suggestion and association.

A related, but different, aspect of processing incoming information is discussed by Capella and Jamieson (1997). This is the distinction between 'on-line' and 'memory-based' approaches. The first of these assumes that the key information (e.g. in a news story) is all provided in the message itself as it is viewed or read. The second refers to the fact that any message (informational or persuasive) will tap into an existing store of information, impressions, beliefs, evaluations, etc. It will activate pre-disposition rather than provide something entirely new. This is a complex matter and in reality both on-line input and memory are likely to be active during processing. However, it has implications for strategies and probabilities of influence. In general, the more that memory-based processing operates, the more 'peripheral' is the route and also the greater is the chance of effects such as framing and priming that are discussed in the following chapter (pages 454–5).

Reflections on the campaign

While success or failure can usually be accounted for in terms of the various conditions that have been named, a few extra remarks are in order. First, in many areas of social life, especially in politics and commerce, the campaign has become deeply institutionalized and has acquired something of a ritual character. The question that then arises is not whether campaigns produce this or that marginal advantage but whether it would be possible *not* to campaign (or to advertise) without disastrous results. This applies especially in election campaigns and in advertising. Secondly, campaigners do not usually control the reality of a situation or reports about it, and circumstances may intervene to destroy or invalidate the message of a campaign. However, the greater the power to manipulate the reality (such as held by governments through policy-making or information giving), the more control there is over the outcome of a campaign.

Thirdly, most campaigns that have been studied take place under conditions of competition (counter-campaigning or with alternative courses argued). Rather too much of the theory that we have has been influenced by these circumstances, and we know relatively little about campaigning for objectives that are not contested, under conditions that make it difficult to avoid otherwise trusted media sources.

Ultimately, campaigns depend rather heavily on the relationship between sender and receiver, and there are several ways in which relations favourable to successful campaigning are forged. Several aspects have been discussed in the context of individual-level effects, but attention should be paid to the attractiveness, authority and credibility of media and sources. Especially important are moral or affective ties between audiences and media and audience belief in the objectivity and disinterest of sources.

Another dimension that should also be kept in mind is that campaigns can differ according to what Rogers and Storey (1987) call the 'locus of benefit'. Some campaigns purport to be in the interests of the recipient (such as health and public

information campaigns), while others are clearly on behalf of the sender – most commercial advertising and most 'propaganda'. This does not necessarily give the former a decisive advantage, if they fail to meet other basic conditions of success (like reaching the intended target audience or choosing the right message), though it may endow them with advantages of receiver trust and goodwill.

There is a good deal more public knowledge available about public information campaigns than there is about advertising campaigns, although the latter are far more numerous. There is still not enough representative evidence to assess claims that the persuasive power of advertising is greatly overrated. The evidence of effectiveness is often indirect, coming mainly from the persistent behaviour of campaigners themselves.

PROPAGANDA

The term has many applications, but also some recurrent features in common use. The definition given above (page 425) is a rather neutral version, since the connotations have generally been negative. It is the 'enemy' that makes propaganda, while 'our side' provides information, evidence and argument. In our time the first association of propaganda is generally with conflict between states, but the term can be applied to religion, politics and other matters of strong belief. It differs in some respects from simple persuasion attempts. It usually occurs on some strongly contested issue; it is often coercive and aggressive in manner; it is not objective and has little regard for truth, even if not necessarily false. It comes in a range of types from 'black' (deceptive, frightening and unscrupulous) to 'white' (soft and with a selective use of truth). Finally, it is always carried out to further some interest of the propagandist, not the target audience.

The mass media are now regarded as essential to successful propaganda, since they are the only channels guaranteed to reach the whole public and have the advantage (in open societies) of being regarded as trustworthy. This advantage is also a drawback, since journalists generally have an aversion to what they perceive as attempts to use them for propaganda purposes. This means they cannot always be trusted to carry the message as originated and uncritically, and they may also carry counter-propaganda. Especially since the Vietnam War which has widely (but not very correctly) been regarded as a propaganda failure for the American authorities, every military action in the Western sphere of influence has been conducted with great regard for effective propaganda. In the Falklands Islands expedition, the Persian Gulf War, the Arab–Israel conflict and many minor skirmishes, the authorities have controlled the flow of military information and ensured that they were the best (relevant and helpful) source of news for the world press (see Morrison and Tumber, 1988; Kellner, 1992; Iyengar and Simon, 1997; Taylor, 1992). The events of the recent Kosovo Conflict followed a

effects

similar path and reports suggest that Russia learnt lessons to apply in the Chechnya war of 1999.

In the cases mentioned, the strategy of becoming the main or only source of useful news content was largely successful in the main propaganda aim of maintaining at least tolerant support from domestic and significant world public opinion. The factors working for success were the general docility of the press (Dorman, 1997); the upsurge of patriotic feelings engendered by military action (Zaller, 1997); the distance (physical and mental) of the scene of conflict from home that inhibits the formation of opposition or of alternative interpretations of events. The main conditions in support of successful propaganda have thus been present: near monopoly of supply of information and images and a wide consensus on goals. In most of the recent instances, 'enemy' propaganda has been largely unable to reach its targets in the 'home' country or internationally.

In the case of the Kosovo conflict in 1999, many of these conditions were also present, but there was more need of active propaganda efforts by Nato countries because of the moral and legal dubiousness of the air attack on civilian targets in Yugoslavia. Public opinion in many allied (i.e. Nato) countries as well as internationally was also very divided. The attempts to demonize the Serb enemy (see page 344 above) and promote the war were hindered by the readiness of the media in Nato countries to give some access to reasoned opposition voices and to give credible reports of tragic or horrific effects of the bombing. While there seems little evidence of change of opinion during the conflict, a 'blacker' side of 'Western' mass mediated propaganda was revealed than had been the case for some time.

The main lessons to be learnt from historical examples of propaganda in action are that that there is no single formula, since all depends on the contingent circumstances. The one certain thing is that for propaganda to work it has to reach people and be accepted (if not believed). Acceptance depends on the absence of alternative objective information, the inherent plausibility of the content in the light of information available and on the emotional and ideological climate of the time. It is difficult to sustain the blacker and more aggressive type of media coverage over the long term. Despite the special character of propaganda, all the normal rules for ensuring communication effectiveness still apply.

CONCLUSION

If one goes back to the premise of media effects in the light of the theory and evidence discussed, the main message is that a simple assumption of some effect from mass media is a sound one. However, the direction, degree, durability and predictability of effect are each uncertain and have to be established case by case, with only limited possibilities for generalization.

Capella, J.A. and Jamieson, K.H. (1997) *The Spiral of Cynicism*. New York: Oxford University Press.

Hovland, C.I., Lumsdaine, A.A. and Sheffield, F.D. (1949) *Experiments in Mass Communication*. Princeton, NJ: Princeton University Press.

Lazarsfeld, P.F., Berelson, B. and Gaudet, H. (1944) *The People's Choice*. New York: Columbia University Press.

Windhal, S., Signitzer, B. and Olson, J. (1991) *Using Communication Theory*. London: Sage.

19

longer-term and indirect effects

This chapter begins with a consideration of longer-term effects of mass media that are deliberately planned. In fact, relevant examples are hard to come by. The main case is that of communication in the field of (mainly Third World) economic and social development, where the media are consciously applied to promote long-term change. Most evidence relates to the many attempts since the Second World War to harness mass media to campaigns for technical advance or for health and educational purposes in developing countries, often following models developed in the rural United States (Katz et al., 1963). Early theory of media and development (for example, Lerner, 1958) portrayed the influence of media as 'modernizing' simply by virtue of promoting Western ideas and appetites. The mainstream view of media effect has been as a mass educator in alliance with officials, experts and local leaders, applied to specific objectives of change.

A principal chronicler of this tradition has been Everett Rogers (1962; Rogers and Shoemaker, 1973), whose model of information diffusion envisaged four stages: information, persuasion, decision or adoption, and confirmation. This sequence is close to McGuire's (1973) stages of persuasion (see page 430). However, the role of the media is concentrated on the first (information and awareness) stage, after which personal contacts, organized expertise and advice, and actual experience take over in the adoption process. The early diffusionist school tended to emphasize organization and planning, linearity of effect, hierarchy (of status and expertise), social structure (thus also personal experience), reinforcement and feedback. Rogers (1976) has himself signalled the 'passing' of this 'dominant paradigm', its weakness lying in these same characteristics and its over-reliance on 'manipulation' from above. Rogers and Kincaid (1981) have put forward an alternative 'convergence model' of communication which emphasizes the need for a continual process of interpretation and response, leading to an increased degree of mutual understanding between sender and receiver (see also Rogers, 1986). Newer theories of development allot to mass media a more limited role, with success depending on their remaining close to the base of the society and to its native culture. It is worth noting that mass communication is itself an innovation which has to be diffused before it can play a part in diffusion processes of the kind familiar in modern or developed societies (DeFleur, 1970; Rogers, 1986). For media to be effective, other conditions of modernity may also have to be present – such as individuation, trust in bureaucracies and in technology, and understanding of the basis of media authority, legitimacy and objectivity.

While development aid continues to be given by donor countries for communication projects and the improvement of mass media infrastructure, there is now much less expectations of direct large-scale effects on levels of development. There is more awareness of the limitations of information-technological solutions and of the unequal distribution of any benefits. There is also more emphasis on the need to improve public

communication for the mass of the people and communication freedom as a human right as preconditions of progress (Linden, 1998).

THE DISTRIBUTION OF KNOWLEDGE

As we enter a new area of our media effect typology (see Figure 17.1) we have to deal with a set of topics and concepts which are difficult to locate in terms of the two main variables of time scale of effect and intentionality, especially the second. The topics are, however, united by a concern with cognition: each has to do with information or knowledge in the conventional sense. One has to do with a major media activity: news provision. Another deals with differential attention to issues and objects in the world: agenda-setting. A third covers the general distribution of opinion and information in society, potentially leading to the variable distribution of knowledge.

These different kinds of media effect are included under the rather neutral label 'distribution of knowledge', since the media do actually distribute information and the result can be expressed as a distribution in the statistical sense. The kinds of effect dealt with here cannot be accommodated within any of the models so far presented, but various models have been developed to explain the processes at work (see McQuail and Windahl, 1993).

NEWS DIFFUSION AND LEARNING FROM NEWS

The diffusion of news in the sense of its take-up and incorporation into what people 'know' is mainly a short- or medium-term matter but with long-term and often systematic consequences. It is also open to alternative formulations as to purpose: the media do intend in general that their audiences will learn about events, but they do not normally try to *teach* people what is in the news. The question of how much people understand and remember from the news has not received very systematic attention, and most early news effect research focused on 'diffusion' – the spread of news as measured by the capacity to recall certain named events.

Four main variables have been at the centre of attention in this matter. They are the extent to which people (in a given population) know about a given event, the relative importance or perceived salience of the event concerned, and the volume of information about it that is transmitted. The fourth variable was the extent to which knowledge of an event comes first from news media or from personal contact. The possible interactions between these four are complex, but one model of the interaction is expressed by the J-curved relationship between the proportion who are aware of an

event and the proportion who heard of the same event from an interpersonal source (Greenberg, 1964).

Patterns of diffusion

The J-shape expresses the following findings: when an event is known about by virtually everyone (such as the assassination of J.F. Kennedy in 1963 or the death of Princess Diana in 1997), a very high proportion (over half) are likely to have been told by a personal contact (associated conditions here being high event salience and rapid diffusion). When events are known by decreasing proportions of the population, the *percentage* of personal contact origination falls and that of media source rises (associated conditions are lower salience and slower diffusion rates). However, there is a category of events which is known about ultimately only by rather small proportions of a whole population. These comprise minorities for whom the event or topic is highly salient, and the proportion of knowledge from personal contact rises again in relation to media sources, because personal contact networks are activated in these circumstances.

The pattern of news information diffusion has been shown to take a variety of forms which deviate from the 'normal' S-curve of diffusion (a slow start, then an acceleration, then a flattening as the upper limit is reached). The J-curve, just described, is one important variant type. Chaffee (1975) has suggested three alternative patterns that are sometimes found: cases of incomplete diffusion, of very rapid early acceleration and of unduly slow acceleration. We should look for different explanations in terms of either 'content-specific' factors or source variables or receiver variables, often working in combination.

Theory about news diffusion is still held back by the bias of research towards a certain class of events, especially towards 'hard news', which has a high measure of unexpectedness (Rosengren, 1973, 1987). In order to have a fuller picture of processes of news diffusion we would need more evidence about 'soft news' and more about routine or anticipated events. We are also limited by the difficulty of estimating event importance independently of the amount of attention given by the media, bearing in mind the varying interests of different sectors of the society.

Learning and comprehension

News learning research (both advanced and reviewed by Robinson and Levy, 1986) has been increasing, especially in respect of television and with particular reference to possible lessons for the improvement of the informative capacity of news. Contributions have been made, especially, by Findahl and Hoijer, 1981, 1985; Robinson and

Levy, 1986; Woodall, 1986; Gunter, 1987, 1999; Davis and Robinson, 1989; Robinson and Davis, 1990; Newhagen and Reeves, 1992). The results so far have tended to confirm the outcome of much basic communication research of decades past (Trenaman, 1967). Thus the interest, relevance and concreteness of news stories aid comprehension, and both prior knowledge and the habit of discussion of news topics with others are still important, in addition to favourable educational background. Robinson and Levy (1986) considered television to be overrated as a source of knowledge of public affairs, and also that several common news production and presentation practices often work against adequate comprehension of news by audiences.

A promising approach to the study of news comprehension and learning has been built on other media research into content and audiences. News content research has shown that much news is presented within frameworks of meaning which derive from the way news is gathered and processed. News is topically and thematically 'framed' for easier understanding, and it is reasonable to suppose that audiences employ some of the same frames in *their* processing of incoming news. Gurevitch and Levy (1986: 132) described the frames of interpretation brought by viewers to television news as 'metamessages', 'latent meanings that are embedded in audience decodings', which help to link individual sense-making to larger stories. They assume that audiences, much as journalists, have 'tacit theories' to frame their understanding of events in the world and to help in their processing of information.

Graber (1984) has developed this line of thinking to explore news processing. The interpretative frames or schemas (see Chapter 14, p. 342) provide guides to selection, relevance and cognition and are collectively constructed and often widely shared. She defined a schema as a 'cognitive structure consisting of organized knowledge about situations and individuals that has been abstracted from prior experiences. It is used for processing new information and retrieving stored information' (1984: 23). Schemas help in evaluating information and filling gaps when information is missing or ambiguous.

The broadest and most enduring frames may have an international currency (for instance, 'the Cold War', 'international terrorism' or 'threat to world environment'), but others may be local and specific. Graber found the actual 'schemata in people's minds' were very diverse, fragmentary and poorly organized. The ways in which schemas were used in responding to news information were also varied, with several different strategies being observed. Despite the provisional evidence and the plausibility of this approach, Woodall (1986) has warned against relying too much on it.

Other research, in the tradition of 'reception analysis', has supported the view that actual interpretations of news are strongly influenced at the point of reception by the circumstances, outlook and prejudices of the individual audience member in a domestic and 'everyday life' situation (see Jensen, 1986, 1998). The perspectives arising often cut across the actual topics of the news. The earliest types of news reception research (see Alasuutari, 1999a) were based on the encoding/decoding

model of Stuart Hall and involved the hypothesis that news could be decoded in 'hegemonic', 'negotiated' or 'oppositional' ways according to outlook. The evidence for this was not easy to come by, but a study of Palestinian and Jewish responses to news of the 'Intifada' seems to offer clear support (Liebes and Riback, 1994). 'Extremists' on both sides tended to read the news in either a 'hegemonic' or an 'oppositional' way, while moderates on both sides applied a 'negotiated' mode of interpretation.

FRAMING EFFECTS

The idea of framing is an attractive one, but how it works as an effect process is less easy to account for. As Cappella and Jamieson put it (1997: 98) 'The way the news is framed by journalists and how the audience frames news may be similar or different'. The same authors proposed a model of framing effects, with the central idea that news frames activate certain inferences, ideas, judgements and contrasts concerning issues, policies and politicians. Their particular concern was to assess whether consistent framing of political news as either 'strategic' (dealing with attempts to gain campaign advantage) or 'conflict-oriented' (as opposed to objectively reporting substance) would contribute to greater public cynicism about politics.

In response to the view that media effects have generally been hard to detect they observe (1997: 208) that:

> The answer in part is the simple idea that successful persuasion occurs when the message takes advantage of pre-existing beliefs in the audience. A public that has accepted the idea that officials are acting in their own self-interest . . . can be easily primed to see self-promotion in every political act. When journalists frame political events strategically, they activate existing beliefs and understandings; they do not need to create them.

Their evidence supports the idea of a cumulative (spiralling) process of increased cynicism as a media effect.

Scheufele (1999) has suggested a process model of framing effects that recognizes them as outcomes of interaction between three different kinds of actor: interested sources and media organizations; journalists (media); audiences. As he notes, we are dealing with two kinds of frame: media frames and individual (receiver) frames. Both kinds of frame can be either independent (a cause) or dependent (an effect). According to the model, there are four interrelated framing processes involving these actors. Firstly, there is the construction and use of media frames by journalists and others working in news organizations under routine pressures, constantly dealing with

sources and applying 'news values' and 'news angles' to event reports. Secondly, there is the transmission of 'framed' news reports (e.g. a cynical view of politicians) to the audience. Thirdly, there is an acceptance of certain frames by members of the audience, with consequences for their attitudes, outlook (e.g. cynicism) and behaviour (e.g. non-participation). On a longer time scale there is an additional stage, where media perceptions of, and feedback from, their audience may reinforce the original organizational and journalistic tendencies and lead to repeated transmission of the same kind of content.

AGENDA-SETTING

The term 'agenda-setting' was coined by McCombs and Shaw (1972, 1993) to describe a phenomenon which had long been noticed and studied in the context of election campaigns. Dearing and Rogers (1996) define the process as 'an ongoing competition among issue protagonists to gain the attention of media professionals, the public and policy elites'.

Lazarsfeld et al. (1944) referred to it as the power to 'structure issues'. An example would be a situation in which politicians seek to convince voters as to what, from their party standpoint, are the most important issues. This is an essential part of advocacy and attempts at influencing public opinion. As a hypothesis, it seems to have escaped the general conclusion that persuasive campaigns have small or no effects. As Trenaman and McQuail pointed out, 'The evidence strongly suggests that people think *about* what they are told but at no level do they think *what* they are told' (1961: 178). The evidence collected at that time and since consists of data showing a correspondence between the order of importance given in the media to 'issues' and the order of significance attached to the same issues by the public and politicians.

This is the essence of the agenda-setting hypothesis, but such evidence is insufficient to show a causal connection between the various issue 'agendas'. For that we need to know the content of party programmes, evidence of opinion change over time in a given section of the public (preferably with panel data), plus content analysis showing media attention to different issues in the relevant period. We also need some indication of relevant media use by the public concerned. Such data have rarely, if ever, been produced at the same time in support of the hypothesis of agenda-setting. The further one moves from the general notion that media direct attention and shape cognitions and towards examining actual cases, the more uncertain it becomes whether such an effect actually occurs.

Davis and Robinson (1986) have also criticized previous agenda-setting research for neglecting possible effects on what people think concerning: *who* is important, *where* important things happen, and *why* things are important. According to Rogers and

Dearing (1987), we need to distinguish clearly between three different agendas: the priorities of the media, those of the public and those of policy. These interact in complex ways and may have effects in different directions. The same authors also note that media vary in their credibility, that personal experience and the media picture may diverge, and that the public may not share the same values about news events as the media. In addition, 'real world events' may intervene in unexpected ways to upset previous agendas (Iyengar and Kinder, 1987). Reese (1991) has pointed out that much depends on the relative balance of power between media and sources, a factor that varies considerably from case to case.

Each of these comments introduces new sources of variation. Despite the difficulties, agenda-setting has attracted mass communication researchers because it seems to offer an alternative to the search for directional media effects on individual attitudes and behaviour change. Dearing and Rogers (1996: 15) write that agenda-setting is related to several other kinds of effects, including: the bandwagon effect, the spiral of silence, diffusion of news, and media gatekeeping.

Most evidence (for example, Behr and Iyengar, 1985) is inconclusive, and assessments (among them by Kraus and Davis, 1976; Becker, 1982; Reese, 1991; Rogers et al., 1993) tend to leave agenda-setting with the status of a plausible but unproven idea. The doubts stem not only from the strict methodological demands for proof of a causal connection, but also from theoretical ambiguities. The hypothesis presupposes a process of influence, from the priorities of political or other interest groups to the news priorities of media, in which news values and audience interests play a strong part, and from there to the opinions of the public. There are certainly alternative models of this relationship, of which the main one would reverse the flow and state that underlying concerns of the public will shape both issue definition by political elites and that by the media. Such a process is fundamental to political theory and to the logic of free media. It is likely that the media do contribute to a *convergence of the three 'agendas'* mentioned above, but that is a different matter from setting any particular one of them.

Aside from the general issue of validation, Dearing and Rogers (1996) conclude with several generalizations about agenda-setting. One is that different media do tend to agree about the relative salience of a set of issues. Secondly, media agendas do not closely match 'real world' indicators. It is not the absolute significance of an issue that counts but the relative strength of forces and people trying to define and promote an issue. Finally, the 'position of an issue on the media agenda importantly determines that issue's salience in the public agenda' (1996: 192).

Reference is sometimes made (especially in political communication research) to 'media priming' effects, as a more specific aspect of agenda-setting. It also has a long history in election campaign research in the attempts by politicians to be associated with the issues on which they have the strongest reputation. The authors of the idea (Iyengar and Kinder, 1987) show that the political issues that receive most attention (highest on the agenda) also figure more prominently in public assessments of the performance of political actors. The general assessment of a party or a politician thus

depends on the perception of how they do in the most salient issues. The priming 'effect' is essentially one of promoting certain evaluative criteria and it plays a part in attempts to manage news. For instance, the often suspected attempts of national leaders to divert attention from domestic failure by some foreign policy success, or even military adventure, is an extreme example of priming. Like agenda-setting, although it seems true to what is going on, it is difficult to prove in practice. Pan and Kosicki (1997) investigated the process in relation to public assessments of the US President's media performance and concluded that any priming effect of media is too weak in relation to other influences to be demonstrated.

Box 19.1   The agenda-setting hypothesis

- Public debate is represented by a set of salient issues (an agenda for action)
- The agenda originates from public opinion and proposals of political elites
- Competing interests seek to promote the salience of 'their' issues
- Mass media news selects issues for more or less attention according to several pressures, especially those from interested elites, public opinion and 'real-world' events
- The outcome in media (relative degree of prominence of issues) both gives public recognition to the current agenda and has further effects on opinion and the evaluation of the political scene

---

KNOWLEDGE GAPS

It has long been assumed that the press and broadcasting have added so greatly to the flow of public information that they will have helped to modify differences of knowledge resulting from inequalities of education and social position (Gaziano, 1983). There is some evidence from political campaign studies to show that such 'information gap-closing' between social groups can occur in the short-term (for example, Blumler and McQuail, 1968). However, there has also been evidence of the reverse effect, showing that an attentive minority gains much more information than the rest, thus widening the gap between certain sectors of the public.

Tichenor et al. (1970) wrote of the 'knowledge gap hypothesis' that it 'does not hold that lower status population segments remain completely uninformed (or that the poorer in knowledge get poorer in an absolute sense). Instead the proposition is that growth of knowledge is relatively greater among the higher status segments'. There is certainly a class bias in attention to 'information-rich' sources, and strong correlations are persistently found between social class, attention to these sources and being able to answer information questions on political, social or economic matters.

There are two main aspects to the knowledge gap hypothesis: one concerning the general distribution of aggregate information in society between social classes, the other relating to specific subjects or topics on which some are better informed than others. As to the first 'gap', it is likely to have roots in fundamental social inequalities which the media alone cannot modify. As to the second, there are many possibilities for opening and closing gaps, and it is likely that the media do close some and open others. A number of factors can be named as relevant to the direction of media effect. Donohue et al. (1975) put special emphasis on the fact that media operate to close gaps on issues that are of wide concern to small communities, especially under conditions of conflict, which promote attention and learning.

Nowak (1977) paid particular attention to the links between information gaps and divisions of social and economic power, focusing on practical solutions which would be helpful to specific groups with identifiable 'information needs'. He developed the concept of 'communication potential' to refer to the various resources which help people to achieve goals through communication activity. Useful in Nowak's contribution is the emphasis not only on form, presentation and manner of distribution in the 'gap-closing' enterprise but also on the kind of information involved, since not all information is equally useful to all groups.

In general, motivation and perceived utility influence information seeking and learning, and these factors come more from the social context than from the media. It has, however, been argued that different media may work in different ways and that print media are more likely to lead to a widening of gaps than is television (Robinson, 1972), because these are the favoured sources for the favoured classes. The suggestion that television can have a reverse effect (benefiting the less privileged) is based on the fact that it tends to reach a higher proportion of a given population with much the same news and information and is widely regarded as trustworthy. However, much depends on the institutional forms adopted in a given society.

Public broadcasting arrangements in Western Europe and, to a lesser extent, the national network system in the USA used to ensure (in part due to their *de facto* oligopoly) that television would provide a popular and homogeneous source of shared information about national and international concerns. Under more recent trends towards channel multiplication, a greater competition and audience fragmentation, the homogeneous audience for information is disappearing. Television is becoming a more differentiated source of information more akin to print media.

The differential diffusion of new computer-based information technology also works towards increasing the division between the information-rich and the information-poor. Knowledge gap theory would indicate a widening of the gaps as a result, since people who are already information-rich, with higher information skills and more resources, would move even further ahead of informationally poorer strata.

Robinson and Levy's (1986) evidence concerning news learning does not increase confidence in the capacity of television to close knowledge gaps. A review by Gaziano (1997) of thirty nine studies of the knowledge gap hypothesis concluded that the effect

of the media on closing or narrowing gaps remains uncertain, but the gaps continue (see also Visvanath and Finnegan, 1996).

LONG-TERM UNPLANNED CHANGE: A MODEL

We enter an area where there is much theory and speculation but little firm evidence of confirmed relationships between the mass media and matters of values, beliefs, opinions and social attitudes. The reasons for this uncertainty are familiar: the phenomena at issue are too wide-ranging and complex to investigate reliably or fully; they call for broad historical and ideological judgements; and the flow of influence between media and social events is often reciprocal. Where evidence exists, it does little more than to illustrate and add to the plausibility of a given theory, and it may be unrealistic ever to expect more. Nevertheless, we are dealing with one of the most interesting and important aspects of the working of mass communication and can at least try to develop an intelligent way of talking about what might happen.

Each of the effect processes to be discussed can occur without planning or organization. Yet these same processes are central to social change, to normative and ideological control and to the construction and maintenance of public belief systems, climates of opinion, value patterns and forms of collective awareness as posited by many social theorists. It is hard to conceive of a society without such processes, however difficult they are to specify and quantify. More important than the question of intention (which cannot be resolved) is that of direction. Do particular processes favour conservation or change and, in either eventuality, in whose interest? Without some consideration of this question, however provisional and beyond the scope of 'media theory' alone to answer, the examination of media effects would be incomplete.

The model, sketched on page 460, indicates some key aspects of various types of unplanned and long-term effects that have been attributed to mass media, irrespective of purpose or direction. First, the processes at issue all presume some pattern and consistency over time in media output. Secondly, they presuppose some initial learning effects of the kind already discussed. Thus the media provide materials for recognizing and interpreting reality beyond what is available from personal experience. What is termed in the model the 'second effect' refers to the encounter between media content and people in audiences. Here the set of 'filter conditions' signalled in the case of the campaign (Box 18.3) operate in much the same way, but especially those which have to do with social group and cultural environment. Beyond this, the processes listed as 'third effect' need to be discussed separately. The question of 'distribution of knowledge' has already been dealt with. The main processes of long-term change relate to socialization, the formation of opinion climates, the structuring

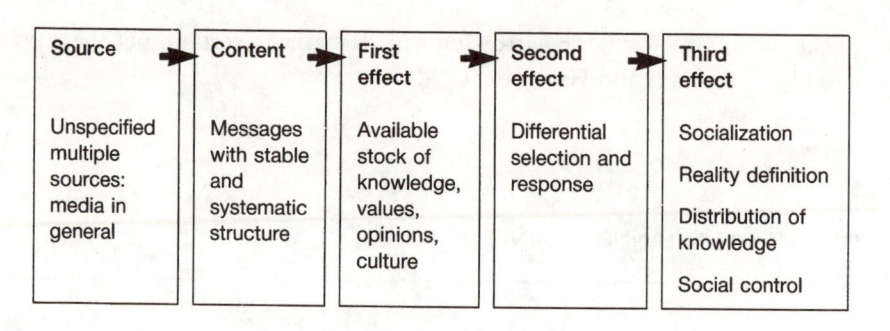

Source	Content	First effect	Second effect	Third effect
Unspecified multiple sources: media in general	Messages with stable and systematic structure	Available stock of knowledge, values, opinions, culture	Differential selection and response	Socialization Reality definition Distribution of knowledge Social control

FIGURE 19.1   The process of long-term unplanned media influence

of perceptions of reality, cultivation and acculturation, and social control and consciousness forming.

SOCIALIZATION

That the media play a part in the early socialization of children and the long-term
socialization of adults is widely believed, although in the nature of the case it is
difficult to prove. This is partly just because it is such a long-term process and partly
because any effect from media interacts with other social background influences and
variable modes of socialization within families (Hedinsson, 1981). Rare longitudinal
studies of development have sometimes produced strong prima facie evidence of
socialization from media (for example, Rosengren and Windahl, 1989). Nevertheless,
certain basic assumptions about the potential socialization effects from media are
often built into policies for control of the media, decisions by media themselves and
the norms and expectations which parents apply or hold in relation to the media use of
their own children. The thesis of media socialization has, in fact, two sides to it: on the
one hand, the media can reinforce and support other agencies of socialization; on the
other, they are also viewed as a potential threat to the values set by parents, educators
and other agents of social control.

The main logic underlying the thesis is that the media can teach norms and values
by way of symbolic reward and punishment for different kinds of behaviour as
represented in the media. An alternative view is that it is a learning process whereby
we all learn how to behave in certain situations and learn the expectations which go
with a given role or status in society. Thus the media are continually offering pictures
of life and models of behaviour in advance of actual experience.

Early studies of children's use of media (for example, Wolfe and Fiske, 1949;
Himmelweit et al., 1958; Noble, 1975; Brown, 1976) have confirmed a tendency for
children to find lessons about life and to connect these with their own experience.
Studies of content also drew attention to the systematic presentation of images of

effects

social life which could strongly shape children's expectations and aspirations. McCron (1976) pointed to a basic divergence of theory, one strand emphasizing the consensual nature of social norms and values and another viewing media along with other agencies of social control as tending to impose on subordinate groups the values of dominant classes. The latter perspective emphasizes the central conflicts of society and the possibility of change through resistance and renegotiation of meanings. In this view, the media are neither 'pro-social' nor 'antisocial' but tend to favour the values of an established order. In whichever formulation, the general proposition that media have a socialization effect is clear, but it is only indirectly founded on empirical evidence.

REALITY-DEFINING AND CONSTRUCTING

That media offer many representations of the reality of society has already been argued, and some aspects of the nature of this 'media reality' have been discussed. The process of 'agenda-setting' is one way in which a frame of reference for viewing the world is constructed. If the media can convey an impression about priorities and direct attention selectively among issues and problems, they can do much more. The step from such a ranking process to wider opinion-forming is not a large one, and the theory of media socialization assumes that lessons about reality are taught and learned. The basic process at work may be described by the general term 'defining the situation', and its importance rests on the familiar sociological dictum of W.I. Thomas that 'if men define situations as real they are real in their consequences'. Another general term for the same process is the 'creation of a symbolic environment' (Lang and Lang, 1981).

THE SPIRAL OF SILENCE: THE FORMATION OF CLIMATES OF OPINION

The concept of the '**spiral of silence**' derives from a larger body of theory of public opinion that was developed and tested by Noelle-Neumann over a number of years (Noelle-Neumann, 1974, 1984, 1991). The relevant theory concerns the interplay between four elements: mass media; interpersonal communication and social relations; individual expressions of opinion; and the perceptions which individuals have of the surrounding 'climate of opinion' in their own social environment. The main assumptions of the theory (Noelle-Neumann, 1991) are as follows:

- Society threatens deviant individuals with isolation.
- Individuals experience fear of isolation continuously.

- This fear of isolation causes individuals to try to assess the climate of opinion at all times.
- The results of this estimate affect their behaviour in public, especially their willingness or not to express opinions openly.

In brief, the theory proposes that, in order to avoid isolation on important public issues (like political party support), many people are guided by what they think to be the dominant or declining opinions in their environment. People tend to conceal their views if they feel they are in a minority and are more willing to express them if they think they are dominant. The result is that those views that are perceived to be dominant gain even more ground and alternatives retreat still further. This is the *spiralling* effect referred to.

In the present context, the main point is that the mass media are the most readily accessible source for assessing the prevailing climate, and if a certain view predominates in the media it will tend to be magnified in the subsequent stages of personal opinion formation and expression. The theory was first formulated and tested to explain puzzling findings in German politics where opinion poll findings were inconsistent with other data concerning expectations of who would win an election and signally failed to predict the result. The explanation offered was that the media were offering a misleading view of the opinion consensus. They were said to be leaning in a leftist direction, against the underlying opinion of the (silent) majority.

A somewhat similar view of opinion shaping by the US media in the 1970s, although with a politically different tendency, was offered by Paletz and Entman (1981). They reported the propagation by the mass media of a 'conservative myth': the conventional journalistic wisdom that the USA had turned sharply away from the radicalism of the 1960s. As they showed, however, there was no support for this interpretation from opinion polls taken over the period in question, thus failing to uphold the 'spiral of silence' thesis.

Two Swedish studies reported in Rosengren (1981a) compared trends both in newspaper editorial opinion and in public opinion. One of these, by Rikardsson (1981), showed a very close relationship between Swedish public opinion on the Middle East issue and that of the Swedish press, both of them deviating from 'world opinion' as measured by opinion polls in several other nations. There was no time lag, however, on which to base a conclusion about the direction of effect. Another study, by Carlsson et al. (1981), on the relationship over time between party support, economic conditions and editorial direction of the press, concluded that political opinions are probably moulded first by economic conditions and second by media content. However, their data tended to support the standpoint of Noelle-Neumann and other proponents of 'powerful mass media'. A more recent and different test of the theory concerned the issue of nuclear energy. Noelle-Neumann (1991) found evidence of increasing press attention to the issue, accompanied by a steady increase in negative reporting. Over time, public support for nuclear energy also declined markedly, and the timing and sequence of changes suggested an interactive spiralling effect as predicted in the theory.

The spiral of silence theory is a close neighbour to mass society theory and involves a similar, somewhat pessimistic, view of the quality of social relations (Taylor, 1982). According to Katz (1983), its validity will depend on the extent to which alternative reference groups are still alive and well in social life. The more that is the case, the less scope there is for the process described to operate, since there will be support for minority or deviant views. Moscovici (1991) also suggests that, in general, we should pay less attention in public opinion formation to silent majorities and more to 'loud minorities', which often play a larger part in opinion change.

The spiral of silence theory is much more than a theory of media effect and involves several dimensions that need to be investigated in conjunction. It is not surprising that it remains in a hypothetical form or that evidence is weak and inconsistent from one context to another. For instance, Glynn et al. (1997) concluded from a recent meta-analysis of survey studies that there was little evidence that perception of support or not for one's own opinion is related to willingness to speak out. Even so, there is supportive evidence (e.g. Mutz and Soss, 1997; Gunther, 1998) for a simpler version of the theory that media coverage does shape individual perceptions of public sentiment on current issues (opinion about opinion).

STRUCTURING REALITY AND UNWITTING BIAS

Common to much theory in this area is the view that long-term media effects occur unintentionally, as a result of media organizational tendencies, occupational practices, technical limitations and the systematic application of certain news values, frames and formats. Thus, as noted above, Paletz and Entman (1981) attributed the propagation of a 'conservative myth' by US media during the 1970s mainly to 'pack journalism', the tendency of journalists to work together, arrive at a consensus, cover the same stories and use the same news sources. It is probable that during the Gulf Crisis of 1990–91 the tendency of most Western media to frame the news in a way which was both consensual and supportive of the United Nations coalition (see *Nordicom Review*, 1992) reflects this tendency. It was probably also the result of successful news management by the military that capitalized on the news media's own routine needs for a supply of suitable information.

The notion that media 'structure reality' in a way that is often guided by their own needs and interests has been demonstrated. An early example of research was the study by Lang and Lang (1953) of the television coverage of the return of General McArthur from Korea after his recall. This showed how a relatively small-scale and muted occasion was turned (in its reporting) into something approaching a mass demonstration of welcome and support by the selective attention of cameras and commentary to points of most activity and interest. The reportage was seeking to reproduce from

rather unsatisfactory materials a suitable version of what had been predicted as a major occasion.

The media coverage of a large demonstration in London against the Vietnam War in 1968 followed much the same pattern (Halloran et al., 1970). The coverage was planned for an event pre-defined (largely by the media themselves) as potentially violent and dramatic, and the actual coverage strained to match this pre-definition, despite the scarcity of suitable reality material. The same research supported the conclusion that audiences perceived the event more in line with its framing on television than as it actually transpired.

Evidence of an actual effect from such media practices on how people define reality is not easy to find. However, in their study of how children came to define the 'problem' of race and immigration, Hartman and Husband (1974) showed that dominant media definitions were picked up, especially where personal experience was lacking. A different kind of effect was documented by Gitlin (1980) in relation to media coverage of the US radical student movement in the late 1960s. Here the media played a major part in shaping the image of this movement for the North American public. The line of effect generally accorded with the media's own needs (such as needs for dramatic action, celebrities, personalities and conflict), and caused the student movement itself to respond to this image and adapt and develop accordingly. A more recent study of the definition by the media of the women's movement in the Netherlands in its early days (van Zoonen, 1992) provides another example of a similar process at work. These cases show a hidden dimension of media bias that stems from real-life adaptation to the logic of the media (Altheide and Snow, 1991).

Most of the effects referred to here derive from 'unwitting bias' in the media, but the potential to define reality is often exploited knowingly. The term 'pseudo-events' has been used to refer to a category of event more or less manufactured to gain attention or create a particular impression (Boorstin, 1961; McGinnis, 1969). The staging of pseudo-events is now a familiar tactic in many election (and other) campaigns, but more significant is the possibility that a high percentage of media coverage of 'actuality' really consists of planned events which are intended to shape impressions in favour of one interest or another. Those most able to manipulate actuality coverage are those with most power; so the bias, if it exists, may be unwitting on the part of the media but is certainly not so for those trying to shape their own 'image'.

CULTIVATION

Among theories of long-term media effect, the cultivation hypothesis of Gerbner (1973) remains probably the best documented and most investigated (see Signorielli and Morgan, 1990). It holds that television, among modern media, has acquired such a central place in daily life that it dominates our 'symbolic environment', substituting

its (distorted) message about reality for personal experience and other means of knowing about the world. Television is also described as the 'cultural arm of the established industrial order [which] serves primarily to maintain, stabilize and reinforce rather than to alter, threaten or weaken conventional beliefs and behaviours' (Gross, 1977: 180). This statement brings the cultivation effect very close to that posited by the critical theorists of the Frankfurt School and not far from later Marxist analysis. According to Signorielli and Morgan (1990: 15):

> **Cultivation analysis** is the third component of a research paradigm called 'Cultural Indicators' that investigates (1) the institutional processes underlying the production of media content, (2) images in media content, and (3) relationships between exposure to television's message and audience beliefs and behaviors.

The theory

The central hypothesis of the research was that viewing television gradually leads to the adoption of beliefs about the nature of the social world which conform to the stereotyped, distorted and very selective view of reality as portrayed in a systematic way in television fiction and news. Cultivation is said to differ from a direct stimulus–response effect process mainly because of its gradual and cumulative character. It involves, first, learning and, secondly, the construction of a view of social reality dependent on personal circumstances and experience (such as of poverty, race or gender) and also on reference-group membership. It is also seen as an interactive process between messages and audiences.

In this theory of media effect, television provides many people with a consistent and near-total symbolic environment that supplies norms for conduct and beliefs about a wide range of real-life situations. It is not a window on or a reflection of the world but a world in itself. The resulting research has two main thrusts: one directed to testing the assumption about the consistency (and distortion) of the television 'message system', the other designed to test, by way of survey analysis, a variety of public beliefs about social reality, especially ones which can be tested against empirical indicators. The core of the ensuing analysis is the comparison between beliefs about reality and actual reality, taking account of varying degrees of habitual exposure to television. There is some basic similarity to the ideas underlying the 'agenda-setting' hypothesis (see page 455).

Testing the theory

Those who watch increasing amounts of television are predicted to show increasing divergence of perceptions of reality away from the known picture of the social world

and towards the 'television' picture of the world. A major focus of the research has always been on questions concerning violence and crime, with cultivation research paying attention to its television portrayal, its actual incidence and differential risks, on the one hand, and to public awareness of and attitudes towards crime, on the other. Other topics of political and social concern have also been studied.

In an extensive review of numerous studies of the television construction of reality, Hawkins and Pingree (1983) found many scattered indications of the expected relationships, but no conclusive proof of the *direction* of the relationship between television viewing and ideas about social reality. They say that 'television *can* teach about social reality and that the relationship between viewing and social reality may be reciprocal: Television viewing causes a social reality to be constructed in a certain way, but this construction of social reality may also direct viewing behaviour. In a recent extensive overview of cultivation research Morgan and Shanahan (1997) draw the conclusion that cultivation effects do occur but are on average quite small.

Doubts and questions

Research into the cultivation process has been somewhat limited by its assumptions about the contents of television and the nature of television viewing. The television experience is probably more differentiated and non-cumulative than allowed for in the theory and may be becoming more so as production and supply increase (both in the USA and elsewhere). Developments of thinking concerning the active construction of meaning by individuals and the diminished power of the text (see Chapter 14) also undermine the assumption of the long-term cumulative effect of powerful 'message systems'.

Several authors have raised doubts about the interpretation of the television message (for example, Newcomb, 1978) and about the causal relationship posited between television use data and survey data concerning values and opinions (Hirsch, 1980, 1981; Hughes, 1980). There is also some reason to doubt whether the 'cultivation' effect would occur elsewhere than in the United States, partly because television content and use (as well as the 'real world') are often different.

The evidence from other countries is still mixed, despite the amount of work that has been done. In relation to images of a violent society, Wober (1978) found no support from British data, and Doob and McDonald (1979) reported similarly from Canada. A longitudinal study of Swedish children (Hedinsson, 1981: 188) concluded, however, that evidence amounted to, 'if not a direct support, at least a non-refutation of Gerbner's theory'. Rosengren and Windahl (1989) report a number of findings of longer-term changes in relation to the television experience of the young that could be taken as support for the cultivation hypothesis. One example appears in the 'mental maps' of the world that differ significantly according to the amount of television

viewing. For high viewing adolescent boys the world outside Sweden consists of little apart from North America.

However plausible the theory, it is almost impossible to deal convincingly with the complexity of posited relationships between symbolic structures, audience behaviour and audience views, given the many intervening variables. It is also hard to separate out any process of 'cultivation' from general socialization. Despite all this, it appears that the line of enquiry represented by cultural indicators and cultivation research is not a spent force and can lend itself to more specified and nuanced enquiries on particular topics (Signorielli and Morgan, 1990).

SOCIAL CONTROL AND CONSCIOUSNESS FORMATION

A number of media effects have already been discussed which might belong under this heading, since the idea of socialization includes an element of social control, and some, at least, of the reality-defining tendencies that have been discussed seem to work in favour of an established social order. However, it is difficult to determine when 'social control' is to be accounted as intended or unintended. Generally the answer depends on the theory of society which one chooses to adopt. If control effects are long-term but unintended, they are accounted as 'ideology' in the terms used by Golding (1981) (as discussed in Chapter 13). If they are planned effects they are what Golding calls 'policy', but they could also be called propaganda (on behalf of some third party or agent of influence outside the media).

There is a continuum of theoretical positions. One commonly held view is that the media act non-purposively to support the values dominant in a community or nation, through a mixture of personal and institutional choice, external pressure and anticipation of what a large and heterogeneous audience expects and wants. A stronger and more critical version of this position sees the media as essentially conservative because of a combination of market forces, operational requirements and established work practices. An extreme version of this position holds that the media are actively engaged on behalf of a ruling (and often media-owning) class or bourgeois state in suppressing or diverting opposition and constraining political and social deviance. This is essentially the Marxist view of media as an instrument for the legitimation of capitalism (Miliband, 1969; Westergaard, 1977).

These alternative theories vary in their precision, in their specification of the mechanisms by which control is exercised and in the attribution of conscious purpose and power to the media. However, they tend to draw on much the same kind of evidence, most of it relating to systematic tendencies in content, with very little directly about effects. A hybrid critical theory of systematic long-term effect has been developed by Herman and Chomsky (1988) in the form of a 'propaganda model'. This says that news in capitalist countries has to be 'strained' through several 'filters',

especially the financial integration of the media with the rest of the economy, advertising, news management campaigns, the dominant (anti-communist) ideology of the society and reliance on official sources of information. Herman and Chomsky found a good deal of circumstantial evidence of the last-named filter at work, as have other researchers, for instance Reese (1994) and Manheim (1998).

Herman and Chomsky take the title of their book, *Manufacturing of Consent*, from Walter Lippmann, who wrote (1922: 158) that the 'manufacture of consent is capable of great refinements . . . and the opportunities for manipulation open to anyone who understands the process are plain enough'. Lippmann's views exemplify what was referred to above as the first phase (that of 'all-powerful media') in the evolution of thinking about the power of the media, and the weakness of the Herman and Chomsky position is that they take so little account of later research and evidence.

In considering the often eloquent and plausible theoretical arguments for the ideological role of the media, we should also keep in mind the other equally plausible theories (and sometimes evidence) concerning the limited effects and potential effectiveness of the media. Media still need to be credible if their message is to be taken over, and there is quite a lot of evidence that audiences are quite sceptical and perhaps becoming more so. Equally important are the implications of the model of 'differential decoding' (Jensen 1986, 1998; Liebes and Riback, 1994) (see pages 56–7). Most of the theories about ideological or hegemonic effects are based on observation of media and content, not of audience or 'effects'. The lessons of 'reception' research offer a counterweight, even though they derive originally from the same critical school.

Consensus maintenance: selective attention and omission

A good deal of the content-based evidence for long-term social control effects has already been discussed. The content of media with the largest audiences does appear broadly supportive of reigning social norms and conventions (an aspect of socialization and of 'cultivation'). Fundamental challenges to the national state or its established institutions are hard to find in the mass media. The argument that mass media tend towards the confirmation of the status quo is thus based on evidence both about what is present and about what is missing in media content. The former includes the rewarding (in fiction) of 'conformist' or patriotic behaviour, the high degree of attention and privileged (often direct) access given to established elites and points of view, and the often negative or unequal treatment of non-institutional or deviant behaviour. The mass media are repeatedly shown as supportive of national or community consensus, and as tending to show problems as soluble within the established 'rules' of society and culture. One outcome of 'cultivation' research is evidence of a link between dependence on television and the adoption of consensual or middle-of-the-road political views (Gerbner et al., 1984).

The evidence of media omission is, in the nature of things, harder to assemble. An early effort to explore selective inattention was made by Warren Breed (1958). On the basis of what he called a 'reverse content analysis' (comparing press content with sociological community studies), Breed concluded that US newspapers consistently omitted news which would offend the values of religion, family, community, business and patriotism. He concluded that 'power' and 'class' are protected by media performance. Comparative content analyses of news in several countries have added evidence of systematic omission in the attention given to certain issues and parts of the world.

Detailed studies of news content such as those by the Glasgow Media Group (1976, 1980, 1985) or by Golding and Elliott (1979) have documented some significant patterns of omission. More importantly, perhaps, they have shown a pattern of selection that is so consistent and predictable that a corresponding pattern of news rejection can be inferred. The view that media are systematically used for purposes of legitimation of the state in capitalist society has relied heavily on evidence of what is missing in the media. Stuart Hall (1977: 366), drawing on the work of both Poulantzas and Althusser, named those ideological processes in the media as 'masking and displacing', 'fragmentation' and 'imposition of imaginary unity or coherence'. The first is the failure to admit or report the facts of class exploitation and conflict. The second refers to the tendency to deny or ignore common working-class interests and to emphasize the plurality, disconnection and individuality of social life. The third refers to the taking-for-granted of a national consensus, common to all classes and people of goodwill and common sense.

The construction of conformity

An additional element in the theory of conservative ideological formation by the media lies in the observation that the media define certain kinds of behaviours and groups as both deviant from, and dangerous to, society. Apart from the obviously criminal, these include groups such as teenage gangs, drug-takers, 'football hooligans' and some sexual deviants. It has been argued that the media often demonstrably exaggerate the real danger and significance of such groups and their activities (Cohen and Young, 1973) and tend to create 'moral panics' (Cohen, 1972). The effect is to provide society with scapegoats and objects of indignation, to divert attention from real evils with causes lying in the institutions of society and to rally support for the agencies of law and order.

It has also been suggested that the media tend to widen the scope of their disapproval by associating together very different kinds of behaviour threatening to society. In the pattern of coverage of terrorism, rioting or political violence they help to provide a symbolic bridge between the clearly delinquent and those engaged in non-institutionalized forms of political behaviour like demonstrations or the spreading of

strikes for political reasons. In some kinds of popular press treatment, according to Hall et al. (1978), it is hard to distinguish the criminal outsider from the political 'extremist'. Within the category of antisocial elements those who rely on state benefit payments may also come to be included under the label of 'welfare scroungers' (Golding and Middleton, 1982), and the same can happen to immigrants, refugees or travelling people. The process has been called 'blaming the victim' and is a familiar feature of collective opinion forming to which the media can make an important contribution.

Media power – who benefits?

It is almost impossible to give any useful assessment of the degree to which the effects posited by this body of theory and research actually occur. First, the evidence of content is incomplete, relating only to some media in some places and times. Secondly, it has not really been demonstrated that the media in any Western country offer a coherent ideology, even if there are significant elements of consistency in selection and omission and forces that work towards convergence of views. Thirdly, many of the processes, especially those of selective use and perception, by which people resist or ignore propaganda apply here as well as in campaign situations.

Nevertheless, it would be difficult to argue that the media are, on balance, a force for major change in society, or to deny that a large part of popular content is generally conformist in tendency. In so far as media capture attention, occupy time and disseminate images of reality and of potential alternatives, they fail to promote any oppositional identity among the less advantaged sectors of society or support radical change. The media are mainly owned and controlled either by (often large) business interests or (however indirectly) by the state – thus by the interests which also have most political and economic power. Media concentration is probably still increasing as well as extending internationally, and it remains entirely plausible that owners will pursue their long-term interests, which includes the stability of the world market system, through their own media, even if in an indirect way. As one small example, Dreier (1982) concluded that the two main elite newspapers in the USA were also the most integrated into the capitalist system and most inclined to adopt a 'corporate-liberal' perspective, an attitude of 'responsible capitalism'. He regarded this level of control to be more significant for power than any tendency to bias selection at newsroom level. There is no reason to think the situation has fundamentally changed.

There is a good deal of prima-facie evidence that such controlling power over the media is valued (by its possessors) beyond its immediate economic yield, especially for political and social influence and status. In any case, it is no secret that most media most of the time do not see it as their task to promote fundamental change in the social

system. They work within the arrangements that exist, often sharing the consensual goal of gradual social improvement. Gans's judgement (1979: 68) that 'news is not so much conservative or liberal as it is reformist' probably applies very widely. The media are committed by their own self-defined task and their ideology to serve as a carrier for messages (for instance, about scandals, crises and social ills) which can be an impulse to change. They probably do stimulate much activity, agitation and anxiety that disturb the existing order, within the limits of systems which have some capacity for generating change. Ultimately, the questions involved turn on how dynamic societies are and on the division of social power within them, and these take us well beyond the scope of media-centred theory.

EFFECTS ON OTHER SOCIAL INSTITUTIONS

As the media have developed, they have, without doubt, achieved two things: diverted time and attention from other activities, and become a channel for reaching more people with more information than was available under 'pre-mass-media' conditions. These facts have implications for any social institution that needs to gain public attention and to communicate to the society at large. Other institutions are under pressure to adapt or respond in some way to the mass media, or to make their own use of mass media channels. In doing so, they are likely to change their own practices, especially by adapting to what has been called a 'media logic' (see page 335). According to Altheide and Snow (1991: ix), 'today all social institutions are media institutions'. Because the transition is usually gradual, occurring along with other kinds of change, the specific contribution of the mass media to institutional change cannot be accounted for with any certainty.

The case of politics provides fairly clear evidence of adaptation to the rise of mass media, especially to the fact that the media have become a (if not *the*) main source of information and opinion for the public (see Blumler, 1970; Seymour-Ure, 1974; Graber, 1976b; Paletz and Entman, 1981; Robinson and Levy, 1986). The challenge to politics from mass media institutions has taken several forms. The diversion of time from political activity to watching television may be one of these. More important is the diversion of attention away from politically committed and partisan sources of information and ideology and towards media sources, which are more neutral, less differentiated in political terms, more commercial and more entertainment-oriented. The mass media seem increasingly to 'set the agenda' and to define political problems on a continuous day-to-day basis, but guided by a more objective and informational logic. Political parties and politicians increasingly have to react to this flow of information and also come to terms with a more consensual form of public opinion.

Ideas about the influence of 'media logic' on political institutions (see Mazzoleni, 1987) include the following: that personalities (leaders) have become relatively more important; that attention has been diverted from the local and regional to the national stage; that face-to-face political campaigning has declined; that opinion polls have gained in influence. Electorates have also become more volatile (more inclined to change allegiance), partly as a result of less active participation. General news values have influenced the attention-gaining activities of political parties as they seek to gain media access, and internal party channels of communication have been attenuated. Mass media gatekeepers are thought, rightly or wrongly, to have increased their power over who gets access and over terms of access for politicians to the public. In addition to all this, 'trial by media' has become a fact of public life in most countries.

The triumph of media logic over political logic also finds expression in the greater interest in personalities and elections as 'horse-races' than as occasions for learning about issues and policies (Graber, 1976b). There is little doubt that election campaigns have been widely transformed into skilfully and professionally managed events more akin to advertising, public relations and marketing than traditional politics (Blumler and Gurevitch, 1995; Swanson and Mancini, 1996). As always, it is hard to separate out the effects of media change from broad changes in society working both on the media and on political institutions, and there is much room for dispute about the real cause of any given institutional effect. Some of these matters have been discussed in Chapter 9.

EVENT OUTCOMES

The case for studying the role of the media in the outcome of significant societal events has been persuasively put by Lang and Lang (1981), and they applied their own advice by studying the Watergate affair and the downfall of President Nixon (Lang and Lang, 1983). Other researchers (Kraus et al., 1975) have also recommended the study of what they term 'critical events', mainly elections but also other occasions of significance for society. The mass media may rarely initiate change independently, but they do provide the channels, the means and an arena for the playing-out of events in which many actors and interests are involved, often in competition with each other. The primary object of influence may not be the general media public itself but other specific organized interest groups, elites, influential minorities, etc.

The media provide horizontal channels (especially between elites) as well as vertical channels for communicating in either direction. Influence flows from the top down, but politicians often treat the media as a source of intelligence about the mood of the country. Lang and Lang (1983) noted that the media 'present political actors with a "looking-glass image" of how they appear to outsiders'. What they call

the 'bystander public' (referring to the general media public) provides a significant reference group for political actors, and it is often for the benefit of a bystander public that they frame many of their actions. This is a part of a process of 'coalition-building'.

The kind of event in which the media play an active and significant part, as it unfolds, is likely to be characterized by having a public and collective character, a historic significance and a long time scale in which media and key actors interact with each other. Major international crises often meet these criteria, and there is steady growth in interest in the part played by the media in such events as the fall of the Berlin Wall, the crises in the Gulf and former Yugoslavia and the many aid missions to Third World countries.

Many other events with a shorter time scale or more local relevance might benefit from a similar research perspective. Ideally, one needs to be able to identify the main actors and agents in the affair (as distinct from media and the general public), examine their motives and the means at their disposal, record their interactions and the sequence of events in which they take part, and assess how actors and events are reported in public. No conclusion is likely to be possible until an outcome is arrived at and has entered history. No unambiguous assessment of the precise contribution of mass media can be expected, but the task cannot be avoided if the effects of media in society are to be understood.

MEDIA AND CULTURAL CHANGE

The theories discussed in Chapter 5 set out a number of possibilities for significant effects of mass media on long-term cultural change, and the same ground need not be covered again. Despite the plausibility of many of the ideas developed about the influence of mass media on culture, there is little firm evidence of the effects posited. It is almost tautological to pose the problem, since the media (in their definitions, their contents and the practices that surround them) are by now an integral part of the cultures of 'modern' societies. It might seem easier to investigate the cultural impact of Western media on developing countries, and it makes more sense to try, but this too poses almost insurmountable problems of conceptualization and research design. The problem presented for investigation is a very large example of a recurring situation in which meanings are constructed amid continuous interaction between the receiving culture and the transmitted messages of global media. We can try to speak of processes such as 'globalization', 'cultural synchronization' and 'homogenization', but what is really there and what causes what, have first to be an object of good conceptualization and theorizing before sense can be made of data (Tomlinson, 1991).

CONCLUSION

The influence of mass media on long-term change can never be measured, because the processes at work are interactive and often open-ended. But much can be learned about the way the media become involved in social and cultural events and changes. The spread of media influence through a range of institutional processes, such as those of international politics, development and emergency aid, environmental control, business and markets, makes the work of enquiry, however inconclusive, of continued relevance. It also calls for a continual refocusing and updating of theory.

FURTHER READING

Gitlin, T. (1980) *The Whole World is Watching – Mass Media in the Making and Unmaking of the New Left*. Berkeley, CA: University of California Press.

Glynn, C.J., Herbst, S., O'Keefe, G.J. and Shapiro, R.Y. (1999) *Public Opinion*. Boulder, CO: Westview Press.

Iyengar, S. and Kinder, D.R. (1987) *News that Matters*. Chicago: University of Chicago Press.

Rosengren, K.E. and Windahl, S. (1989) *Media Matter*. Norwood, NJ: Ablex.

EPILOGUE

20

the state of the art

It would be unlikely if in the space of six years since the last edition of this book was written the end of 'mass communication' were to have arrived or even become noticeably closer. Despite the associations of media with all things novel and fashionable the mass media institution has never shown a great tendency towards fundamental change, unless it comes from the surrounding society. Speculation continues about the imminent demise of the mass media, because of the advance of alternative technologies, but they show an immense capacity to adapt and survive. The genuinely new media have begun to develop quite strongly but have made little impact as yet on the imperium of the old media, except, perhaps, by inviting colonization.

It is too early to be certain, but it seems at least likely that several of the characteristics of the 'old' media are simply not substitutable in the short or medium term. The technologies and forms may change, but only mass communication can meet the *collective* requirements of political, economic and social life, which are relatively stable and enduring. National and international politics still depends on the existence of effective publicity machines and on the dissemination of 'mass' information (that is, reaching large majorities). Global economics still depends on the large-scale manipulation of demand (by advertising, marketing, etc.) and on large units of production, of both hardware and software. Media industries themselves have a vested interest in maximizing the reach of their products and extracting the maximum value with the aid of multiple as well as large-scale channels of transmission. Social-cultural convergence on a global scale is occurring in several ways but it is not simply a consequence of the media. It is a self-generating and sustaining tendency that is supported by mass media, but in turn it supports mass media as a multinational industry and moulder of culture.

To draw these conclusions is to presume that mass media, as we know them, are driven less by technology than by their users and their ultimate masters. In any case, it states a strong claim for the continued relevance of the category 'mass communication' as an object of theorizing, without neglecting new growth areas which are much more clearly the result of a genuine communications revolution. In these areas, other bodies of communication theory have to be developed, which may or may not directly relate to the field of mass communication as outlined in this book.

THE STATE OF THEORY

It is impossible here to give an adequate evaluation of what passes for theory in relation to mass communication, but one has to admit that the corpus of work

described in a summary way in this book is still very fragmentary and also variable in quality. It often amounts to little more than a posing of many questions plus some empirical generalizations based on a disparate set of observations that are not fully representative of the enormous range of situations where the media are at work. Included in our assemblage of theory is much that is speculative and also essentially normative, prompting value judgements rather than providing explanations or a basis for prediction.

In respect of the normative tendencies of theory, there is no reason to apologize. The workings of mass media are deeply involved with political, social ethical and moral issues that range from our personal lives to global issues. Research and theory have always been driven by moral and political concerns and generally in a critical spirit. They represent in part the informed concerns expressed on behalf of the public, as well as seeking to advance understanding. There is certainly no less reason for public concern about the media than in the past. The media are being used more and perhaps more effectively than ever for control, for making propaganda and for managing and manipulating the social environment on behalf of the already powerful and the contenders for power, nationally and internationally.

The reasons for slow theoretical development are much the same as in other fields – especially the essentially intersubjective character of the practices and activities involved in mass communication, their multiplicity and variety and the diversity of the constant flux of the social environment in which they take place. Having conceded this much, there does also appear to have been some genuine accumulation of knowledge and progression of thinking about a phenomenon that has remained essentially the same over a long period. Theorizing as practised in the mainstream tradition of the social sciences remains the most practical path towards setting priorities for enquiry, directing research and helping to make some overall sense of many fragmentary and diverse findings. One of the signs of progress has been the increased degree of co-operation and mutual tolerance between adherents of different paradigms, especially that based on quantification and systematic measurement and that based on hermeneutic methods, interpretation, deep description and critical perspectives.

There can be no full reconciliation on this last point, since fundamental values are at stake, but there can be agreement to differ within a common framework. Where researchers can speak to and understand each other, there can also be complementary lines of enquiry on topics of agreed interest. The dispute between 'culturalists' and 'scientific-empiricists' has generated light as well as heat, and the same is true of the disagreements between radical-critical researchers and conservative functionalists. As Rosengren comments, in a phrase which compares the search for reconciliation between theoretical opposites to the pursuit of the mythical 'tulip rose':

much as our hearts may ache for it, we shall never see the tulip rose. But roses and tulips may grow and blossom together, just as the individual researcher may alternate between

phases of, say, particular observation and more stringent methods, and just as members of different schools and traditions may draw upon each other's work. (1989: 28)

In the nature of these things, however, the cessation of hostilities on one front may be a sign only of the sidelining of the conflict or the outbreak of hostilities elsewhere. In this particular case, the broader social climate does seem to have changed in a way which has essentially damped the fires of radical-critical thought, and a new agenda is in the making. The references made to postmodern thinking give some clue to the way things are going. Most briefly, we seem to be entering an age of pronounced disbelief in which the certainties and the equivalent of moral imperatives of progressive rationalism are themselves being undermined or abandoned. This development is very relevant for a body of theory (about mass communication) which has always had normative sub-themes, even when at its seemingly most empirical (such as in the study of media effects). In keeping with the spirit of postmodernism, the new theoretical battle lines are not clearly drawn, and friends and enemies have not yet found a consistent way to identify each other.

NEW THEORY NEEDED?

Despite the continuity of mass media, the introduction of new forms of electronic media does represent a challenge to theory, as well as to existing traditional media industries. The 'new media' are now increasingly being used for tasks of public communication as well as for communication in the sphere of personal life and in many professional and business contexts. They have become a supplementary and also deeper source of information, a potentially effective advertising medium, a platform for minority voices and an alternative channel for delivering familiar 'mass media' products, services and satisfactions. In respect of most of these tendencies, the new media can be accommodated with reasonable ease within the existing frameworks of media theory and research.

In very general terms the new media can be examined in respect of social *integration* and other matters of social structure, much as have the existing mass media. The notion of *convergence*, as a result of digitalization, prompts hypotheses about the re-division of tasks and functions between media, although as yet we seem to see only more differentiation than coming together. Other general frameworks are indicated by the familiar theses of *globalization* and *technological determinism*. Critical perspectives from *political economic theory* apply as much to 'new' as to 'old' media, especially given their global character and the part by played by global capital and business interests in their development. At a less elevated level of theory, it seems that new media are continuing rather than initiating a trend towards *demassification* and *fragmentation* of audiences. Their interactive properties are real enough, but it was

already established that media use and processes of influence were effectively interactive, given the power of the receiver to select, interpret and construct preferred meanings. Some at least of the familiar issues of social and normative theory that have been prompted by the rise of new media are already on the agenda of policy discussions. These include especially matters concerning freedom and control and fears of 'harm' of various kinds stemming from the uncontrolled development and use of new means of communication.

> **Box 20.1 Old frames of theory for new media**
>
> - Social integration and social structure
> - Political economy approach
> - Convergence thesis
> - Globalization
> - Technological determinism
> - Demassification

While all this is quite reassuring, it would be foolish to ignore the real uncertainties that exist about how the potential of new media will be developed and used. They could easily have a distinct social and cultural effect that is equal to that of the 'old' media, something still not properly assessed. There are several gaps and deficiencies in the theoretical apparatus at our disposal and there is some risk in placing new developments too quickly within old frameworks. We may miss things that are not obviously new, but may work gradually to transform communication and society. The organization of society still largely corresponds to 'modernist' forms in structural terms. It is still generally centralized and hierarchical with continuing or growing social inequality and class divisions. We still live with and in potentially antagonistic and self-centred nation states. These structural forms are probably best served by mass communication of the traditional type. At the same time there is more social fluidity and a loosening and mingling of cultures. New kinds of social network are emerging and may grow in importance, served and encouraged by certain properties of the 'new media'.

At this point, one can only suggest an agenda for theory that might help to repair or extend existing frameworks. The most general need is to develop ideas about an *information society* or a *network society* which would be less speculative and more analytically useful than those currently in circulation. We need to know what the relevant networks are and how they are organized. Are they replacing the older bases of identification, culture and significant social relations? Secondly, we need to explore the question of *freedom* as promised by certain features of new media. Are they really 'technologies of freedom', or will they be subject to the same constraints as the old media and serve as even more effective means of control and social containment? Thirdly, we may ask what the *interactivity* of new media really amounts to, beyond its technological aspects. Does it really mean much for more significant kinds of communication, as opposed to being an effective way of delivering certain services,

such as shopping and banking? Fourthly, are the new media really a basis for developing more meaningful *social relationships* than old media, given the continued absence of face-to-face contact and other social supports?

In addition to these questions, we need to know more about the actual *experience of use* of new media, especially the gratifications provided by distinctive features such as interactivity, searching at will through a universe of content and involvement in communities of interest. While certain normative issues are clearly much the same for new as for old media, there are some new dimensions for theoretical consideration. Amongst these are the implications for different communication professions, including that of journalism. There is also the matter of *responsibility to society* that is often acknowledged, however grudgingly, by established mass media, but hardly arises in the case of the Internet. If providers of new media are not responsible or accountable, there can be no continuous relations of trust or loyalty and correspondingly less chance of influence or social power.

Box 20.2 New headings of theory for new media

- Information society
- Social and communication networks
- Freedom or containment?
- Interactivity
- Experience of use
- Responsibility and trust
- New critical theory?

In the early days of study of mass media, inquiry was driven by critical as much as by 'functional' objectives. This seems less to be the case today. 'New media watchers' still tend to divide into (many) utopians or (few) dystopians, although we are getting past that simplistic pair of attitudes, as the reality, extent and irreversibility of media change is acknowledged. But we still lack a developed set of critical perspectives and tools of analysis that theory should be able to provide, even in these postmodern times.

THE MULTIPLE LOGICS OF MASS COMMUNICATION

One of the achievements of theory is the identification of several different 'logics' according to which the process of mass communication is actually conducted and can be analysed by the detached observer. We have escaped, at least, from the assumption that there must be one dominant perspective or standpoint from which mass communication can be analysed (for instance, according to the 'power of the mass media'

or the social integration/disintegration dimension). A logic here refers to a framework of meaning in which elements of a phenomenon are coherently related to each other and a consistent pattern of action and thinking can be identified. A logic in this sense indicates priorities and draws attention to what is significant. For the observer it is a guide to selective attention and also to interpretation. The main relevant 'logics' can be named and described as follows.

It is hard not to be aware of a general *commercial* logic, as more and more aspects of media operation seem to be driven by market forces rather than social or cultural considerations. This extends well beyond matters of structure (for instance the decline of public broadcasting) and affects the standards and values of content and the wider role of the media in society.

There is an *industrial* logic that places media phenomena within the broader framework of a larger media industry and institution. Production processes, content selections, audience formation and technological innovations can be made sense of in economic or broader institutional terms. The key to the logic is what makes sense in terms of the wider political-economic context of the firm.

An *organizational* logic operates on some of the same questions of production and selection, but within much more circumscribed limits and according to different goals. The key to this particular logic is the smooth running of the media organization, according to traditional or laid-down conventions and familiar routines of a co-operative work process which is either satisfying to those engaged in it or seen as the best way to achieve the immediate work goals.

A *technological* logic refers to the perceived capacities and qualities of a particular technology for collecting, processing, producing or transmitting media content. The key is to be found in what communication technologies are supposed to be 'good for', in respect of any of the things which mass media normally do: reporting reality, conveying information, telling stories, capturing attention, etc. The technological logic may be embedded within the organizational logic, but it has a wider currency: among would-be media communicators and audiences. The wider theoretical significance of this logic is a related tendency to media-determinism and media-centricity.

The notion of *cultural* logic is more complex and difficult to pin down. It can refer broadly to the culture of the mass media, in which case it accords with (or underlies and explains) recurring features of media practice – for instance, certain forms of storytelling or the appeal to senses of hearing and sight (sensationalism). In this sense, media-cultural logic is also exemplified by the star system, the production and recycling of celebrities of all kinds, and by the world of advertising, with its rather limited set of aims and techniques, but with changing modes and styles. Personalization, immediacy and novelty reflect the application of media-cultural logic. There is another sense of cultural logic, which derives from the culture of the society or the recipients of media. Socially defined audiences, taste cultures and subcultures supply the key to consistency and to an alternative path of analysis.

Some of these points overlap with the idea of a *political* logic which refers especially to the demands made on the media by powerful and organized interests in society,

both inside and outside the formal political institution. The political logic is directed towards harnessing the media to the chosen ends of contenders for office and holders of power. This may sometimes mean trying to impose democratic control (for instance, in matters of culture or service to the political system), sometimes bending the media to strategic economic goals of a national society. In general the political logic works against the autonomy of mass media, however much freedom of media is proclaimed as a high principle.

Finally, there is an *informational* logic which applies to the media in some of their activities (not so much the 'news' as more basic informational functions, such as stock-market reports, sports results, weather, listings, public notices and job advertisements). This view of the media is linked to a definition of communication as 'transfer of information' and implies criteria of effectiveness and efficiency which can be applied. Many specialized media operate largely according to this model, and it plays a part in public perceptions of mass media, even when they fail to live up to expectations.

While these logics can be analytically separated, they really operate concurrently and in combination with each other. What has been referred to earlier in this book as 'media logic', for instance, describes a combination of elements drawn from the technological, organizational and cultural categories. The idea of a guiding logic is primarily a tool of analysis, but it helps to clarify the multiplicity of purposes and practices involved in this complex phenomenon. It also offers alternative and new paths for theoretical exploration.

MASS MEDIA AS A (DEFECTIVE) MEANING MACHINE

One of the least ambiguous results of revised or alternative paradigms is the conclusion that mass communication is centrally about the giving and taking of meaning, although the outcomes are enormously varied and unpredictable. In part this inefficiency stems from the multiplicity of purposes served by mass media, but it also derives from the lack of fixed or unitary meanings in any media 'text' or 'message', whatever the intention of a sender might be, or the shaping by rules of language and discourse. Attempts can be made for some purposes to 'decode' the probable direction of intention or effect of media content, but there is no 'scientific' route towards an objective result of such decoding. We cannot draw sure conclusions about producers, audiences or possible effects from such research. Most fundamentally, this uncertainty derives from the essentially creative, interactive and open-ended nature of communication, in which meaningful outcomes are always negotiated and unpredictable.

Despite the undeniable personal 'power of the reader', there is also plenty of evidence that audience 'readings' do often follow conventional and predictable lines of interpretation and that familiar media genres such as news and television series are

probably read, as often as not, more or less as intended. The meanings of media content and of the acts of media use are multiple – alternative interpretative communities do exist – but many media genres are understood by most of their receivers most of the time in predictable ways and much meaning is denotational and unambiguous. There is a power of the text that it is foolish to ignore.

Domains of meaning

There is clearly no general answer to questions of meaning construction, but media research and theory have indicated several elements in a more general framework of social and personal meanings, within which media play an important part. These elements can be described in terms of several recurrent dimensions or oppositions which help to answer the questions, 'What meanings?' and 'Meanings for what?'. The following headings provide a tentative guide to matters on which there is both a supply of and a search for meanings. They identify, at a very general level, the topics and domains of meaning in which mass media operate for individuals and wider collectivities.

Significance. The media provide clues to what is more or less important, salient or relevant in many different contexts, from personal sex lives to global politics. Everyday life is problematic without having some kinds of answer to questions of this kind.

Reality and real-life contexts. The dimension at issue is that of reality versus fantasy, fact versus fiction, truth versus falsehood. The underlying question often lies at the heart of media genres and languages and helps initially to frame much response. This is not to assume the possibility of any absolute answer about the 'reality' of texts or interpretations.

Public versus private space. To say that media operate in the public sphere is already to privilege a domain of meaning in which the mass media carry much weight. We are likely to look to media for a guide to public meanings and definitions most widely shared or accepted. However, it is also arguable that media increasingly break down the conventional distinctions between private and public spaces in social life. The general notion persists that there is some boundary separating what is personal, domestic and private from what is open to view and accountable in the public sphere. This is a key matter of definition, in which mass communication plays a role.

Identity. The very large matter of social and cultural identity – who and what we are and how we are different from others – lies at the heart of many questions concerning meaning construction by the media. The media reflect and reinforce many conventional markers and boundary systems in relation to gender, class, ethnicity, religion, nationality, subculture, etc. Equally, the media do much to undermine boundaries maintained by circumstances or by other institutions. The messages of the

media can also be mined for alternatives and for support for self-chosen definitions of identity.

Space and location. Related to identity but also independent is the question of location. Media meanings are structured by many clues to place. Both news and fiction can usually be understood only when they are furnished with an answer to the question, 'Where?'. The media themselves are usually located at a specific point of origin and are intended for an audience which is territorially located in a nation, region or city (though perhaps decreasingly so). Much content provides implicit answers to what 'here' is like as opposed to 'there', what is near compared with what is distant. The globalization of media may confuse the message and undermine the locatedness of meanings, but it also leads to an enriched supply of place-related meanings (Gould et al., 1984).

Time. A rather similar set of remarks relates to the question of time, with media content often accountable in terms of the present and the past, actuality and history, what is recalled compared with what is going on now or projected into the future. The media have been said to provide a collective memory, especially of the relevant past of a people, culture or society. The whole rhythm of mass media production and dissemination is guided by time in terms of the daily, weekly, seasonal and historical cycle of events, in itself an influential contribution to the taking of meaning.

All the terms mentioned here have featured at some point in the theories discussed in the book, and they are repeated now to suggest a wealth of theoretical lines of development in respect of meaning construction which have hardly been followed in any systematic way. These paths will be easier to follow if the notion of fixed, objective, encoded meaning is rejected, but they still require respect for the text and the context of production.

POWER, INFLUENCE AND EFFECT

Do the media have any?

For reasons which have been made clear, most direct questions about 'the power of the media' either make no sense or cannot be answered (Nowak, 1997). This does not make the issue less important, but it has to be approached indirectly. It is fairly clear that the media are everywhere dependent on the rest of society, reactive to more fundamental impulses and subordinate to sources of real economic and political power. The media are nowhere expected to exercise direct power in their own interest, outside the sphere of gaining attention, communicating, informing, entertaining, making money, etc. The principle of free expression does legitimate the voicing of opposition, criticism and advocacy of alternatives, but this can better be accounted

under the heading of 'influence'. Any consequences are the result of other circumstances outside the control of media themselves. Similarly, the 'power' to influence consumer behaviour by way of advertising is ultimately dependent on consumers themselves.

Whose side are the media on?

The concept of media power is open to a variety of definitions. Often it is used to refer to the question of effectiveness for achieving a given power objective, such as persuasion, mobilization or information. Media theory, in the behaviourist tradition, has quite a lot to say about the conditions of effective performance in such matters. Both evidence and theory support the view that media often can and do achieve delimited objectives and can be effective according to a chosen purpose, although within strict limits. Another formulation of power, more at home in the social-structuralist tradition, concerns the question of *whose* power the media might exercise or facilitate. Is it that of society as a whole, or a particular class or interest group?

Most theory (and evidence) seems again to support the view that media, more often than not, by commission or omission, do tend to serve the interests of those who already have disproportionate political and economic power in society. This is not simply to say that the power of the media is that of a dominant class, but it is consistent with that position, if one can only locate the class. It does mean that the media are not an independent source of power of their own and that political and economic influence which flows through the media has origins in the power centres of society. The established media, in liberal societies, often do support forces of progressive social change and express popular demands for change. However, they also sometimes support forces of reaction and aggression, and their normal operating requirements do not require them to be in the vanguard of fundamental change or make them reliable guardians of morality. The very stance of neutrality which most media adopt, makes them more vulnerable to assimilation by existing power-holders and more effective instruments of influence and manipulation, just because they are trusted.

The mass media are so integrated into the life of most societies that it makes little sense to view them as an independent source of power or influence. Their activities are geared to the needs, interests and purposes of innumerable other actors in society. The proposition that the media are ultimately dependent on other institutional arrangements in society is not inconsistent with the fact that other institutions may also be dependent on the media, certainly in the short-term. The media are often the only practical means available for transmitting information quickly and efficiently to many and for purveying propaganda.

the state of the art   **487**

More to the point is that the media have a virtual monopoly over a commodity which is often a necessary condition for the effective exercise of power: that of status and celebrity in the wider society. While the media are not entirely free agents in delivering this – it is their audiences that really supply the vital commodity of attention and interest – they have the means and generally the skill to deliver and signal public esteem for most practical purposes, at least in the short-term. Fame is, however, a zero-sum commodity – there is only so much to go around before it becomes diluted (see the 'publicity model', pages 54–6) – and subject to intense competition between media as well as between the would-be famous. One way in which the supply can be expanded is by turning fame into infamy, as when a prominent or popular figure falls into disgrace. The limits are still set by the amount of public attention (in terms of time), which is not in elastic supply.

Dealing in celebrity is generally a matter of mutual self-interest, since the media themselves need to provide their audiences with images of celebrity. Fame and celebrity usually depend on wider systems of meaning that have developed over time and which the mass media did not create nor completely control. They also depend on social networks and hierarchies in the society and on interpersonal processes of discourse, rumour and gossip. In some circles, media recognition is not a necessary condition of celebrity. But the range of media control is extending and leading to a collapsing of different categories of fame for specific achievements and to the rise of the notion of 'the fame of being famous'. While the famous may increasingly need the media, the media constantly need the famous in order to attract attention and certify their own importance. Without famous or celebrated performers there are unlikely to be devoted fans. There is a good deal of scope for developing theory in relation to these matters.

QUESTIONS OF CULTURE

Mass communication theory has shown a healthy capacity to extend its scope to cover many aspects of culture, especially in relation to the links with everyday life and by opening up the endlessly complex subject of the nature of 'media culture'. Media theory has on the whole benefited from the work of cultural theorists who have colonized the once rather limited territory founded mainly upon psychology, sociology and politics. Even so, there are many actively contested frontier zones, among them the question of intrinsic *cultural quality*, a notion once strongly upheld by humanistic traditions but now called into question by adherents of new populism, subculturalists, relativists of many shades and followers of postmodern cultural theory. The core issues

will continue to be debated, not least because of their relevance to decisions in the field of media-cultural politics. The question of *cultural identity* and the relevance of media to its many manifestations will be one of the central issues for some time and has not yet received the analysis it deserves.

In relation to the theory of an *information society*, itself in a very uneasy state, there are several largely unexplored cultural questions which are relevant to media theory. The information society has been largely defined up to now in technological, economic and sociological terms. The *cultural* dimension of information societies seems to have been largely neglected, although postmodernistic thinking is one of the main forms in which exploration is taking place. If there is a recognizable 'information culture' corresponding to the information society (a plausible supposition), then the mass media are bound to be an important element and also an influence.

If we think of a culture as comprising a certain symbolic content, then it is media which fill much of the cultural space with images and sounds. Where the notion of culture refers to social practices, then media and communication technology are clearly influential. Where culture refers to an attitude of mind, the mass media seem to encourage attitudes both of 'modernity' and of 'postmodernity'. They also encourage confidence in science and technique and a belief (even if illusory) in the power to control reality through symbolic manipulation. If not control, they offer escape or symbolic substitutes (see 'virtual reality'). Many of the foundations of the information society (including trust in expert systems, Giddens, 1991) are dependent on the media for sustaining confidence. The terrain that opens up is very extensive, and its exploration will probably require much better instruments for mapping and for analysis than have been brought by the cultural theorists who were the first colonists.

LAST WORDS

If mass communication as a process is set to endure, so obviously are the institutions that carry it on. These are undergoing continual and profound changes for reasons which have been described – especially because of changing technology, which alters what is both possible and profitable. Theory of media institutions is still relatively primitive, and there is much scope for development on the basis of existing concepts and modes of analysis, largely corresponding to the different logics described above. Mass communication is alive and well, whether we like it or not, and the arrival of new media only adds to the pile of work in the theory workshop.

Note: glossary entries appear in bold type on their first use. Cross references to other glossary entries are in italics.

Access. In a communication process or system, it can refer either to the possibility for a sender to reach a chosen audience or for an audience to receive certain messages or channels. In practice it mainly relates to the degree of openness of media channels to a wide range of voices, especially those with little power or limited resources. An example is a 'public access' channel provided in a cable system for community or non-profit purposes. As a general principle it is related to *media diversity*.

Active audience. The term arose in the context of revised ideas about the mass audience. Research established early on that media audiences are in varying degrees selective, motivated and resistant to influence. The kind and degree of audience activity is very relevant to the possibility of any effect from media. Audience activity has been studied in more detail within the tradition of *uses and gratifications* research as well as *reception analysis*. In the latter case, activity is mainly found to reside in differential interpretation.

Advertising. Paid publicity in media for goods or services directed at consumers. It has various aims including the creation of awareness, making brand images, forming positive associations and encouraging consumer behaviour. There are many different categories of advertising, which are linked to different media forms (classified, display, personal, etc.). For some major media, advertising provides the greater part of income. All advertising content shares the fact of being paid for by its source. Advertising has been controversial for several reasons, especially the following. It is not generally wanted by its receivers; it has a *propagandist* character and is suspected of deception and manipulation; it has a distorting effect on the relation between media and audience; its content is stereotyped and misleading; the presence of advertising influences other non-advertising content. The general effectiveness of advertising for its purposes

is more or less accepted, but certain evidence of success or of reasons for success is hard to come by. Advertising is integrated into a very large industry of market research, *public relations* and marketing.

Agenda-setting. A process of media influence (intended or unintended) by which the relative importance of news events, issues or personages in the public mind is affected by the order of presentation (or relative salience) in news reports. It is assumed that the more the media attention, the greater is the importance attributed by the news audience. The media influence is not on the *direction* of opinion but only on *what people think about*. The concept has been mainly applied to political communication and election campaigns especially. Despite the near certainty that the process does occur as hypothesized, it is not easy to prove, because media take their priorities from public opinion as well as from politicians. See also *framing*.

Audience. All those who are actually reached by particular media content or media 'channels'. The audience can also exist as an imagined 'target' or intended group of receivers. It may coincide with a real social group or *public*. Audiences can be defined according to the relevant media and content or in terms of their social composition, location or time of day. Media audiences are not fixed entities and may only be known after the event as statistical abstractions (e.g. 'the ratings'), with a known probability of recurrence. This is typically the view 'from the media', but there is an equally valid alternative perspective on the audience as a collective social-cultural entity.

Bias. Any tendency in a news report to deviate from an accurate, neutral, balanced and impartial representation of the 'reality' of events and social world according to stated criteria. A distinction is usually made between intended and unintended bias. The former stems mainly from partisanship, advocacy and the ideological standpoint of the media or source. The latter is generally attributed to organizational and routine factors in selection and processing of news. See also *objectivity*.

Birmingham School. Name used to denote a number of authors associated with the centre for Contemporary Cultural Studies (CCCS) at the University of Birmingham, England, established in the mid-1960s. Original founder was Richard Hoggart, in association with Stuart Hall. The work of the school was a major influence in the development of critical cultural studies, including *reception* research and *feminist media studies*.

Broadcasting. The transmission of radio and television signals over air from fixed terrestrial transmitters and with limited range, before the advent of cable and satellite systems from the 1970s onwards. Broadcasting was intended for open reception by all within the transmission range and was mainly financed either by advertising or by receiver set/household licences. It was and remains governed by legal and regulatory regimes designed to allocate licences and supervise performance. It is virtually the only major medium in public or government ownership in non-socialist societies. See *public service broadcasting*.

Campaign. The planned attempt to influence public opinion, behaviour, attitudes and knowledge on behalf of some cause, person, institution or topic, using different media over a specific period of time. The main types of campaign are: advertising; political; public informational; fund-raising. Public campaigns are usually directed towards socially approved goals. They are often based on research and subject to evaluation of success.

Catharsis. A type of effect of tragic or violent fiction and drama that leaves the audience purged of emotion and released of any urge to be affected by the actions portrayed. Originally suggested by Aristotle and taken up by researchers into media violence to account for seeming lack of behavioural effects. Although theoretically plausible, it does not seem to have been specifically demonstrated or measured.

Civil society. The term has been widely used in recent social theory to refer to forms of social organization that offer alternatives to totalitarianism, especially communist rule. The key aspect is the existence of an intermediate 'zone' between private life and the state, where independent voluntary collective associations and organizations can operate freely. A precondition for this is freedom of association and expression, including the necessary means, amongst which the media are very important. Free media can thus be regarded as an institution of civil society. See also *public sphere*.

Coding (or encoding) and decoding. Broad terms for the production and 'reading' of texts of all kinds. The reference is less to the use of specific language (verbal or visual) than to structures of meaning embedded in or extracted from texts. The terms were popularized by Stuart Hall and incorporated in a much cited model of the relationship between media and audience. An important feature of the associated theory is that meaning is 'decoded' according to the social and cultural position of the receiver'. Most texts 'as sent' are also held to carry some 'preferred reading', that is essentially ideological, but we can usually expect alternative readings. In the case of news, Stuart Hall suggested that interpretations could either take up the preferred 'hegemonic' meanings, follow some more distanced 'negotiated' variant or reverse the intended meaning in an 'oppositional' reading. See also *polysemy* and *ideology*.

Commercialization. A process by which media structures and contents come to reflect the profit-seeking goals of media industries and are governed by market considerations. The main reference is usually to cultural consequences, and these always have a negative connotation. Commercialized media content is believed to be in varying degrees 'inauthentic', standardized and stereotypical, given to *sensationalism* and personalization. It promotes values of materialism and consumerism. It is also thought to be less creative and trustworthy. Commercial media are suspected of lacking full independence from their owners and advertisers. In some contexts the process is also referred to as 'Americanization', on the grounds that imports of American content are involved, usually coupled with American production standards and values. See *advertising, tabloidization, commodification, sensationalism*.

Commodification. The word originates in marxist theory according to which all entities have a material cash value. In relation to media, two aspects stand out. One is the treatment of all media messages as 'product' to be bought or sold in the media market, without reference to other criteria of value. Secondly, the audience can also be treated as a commodity to be sold by media to advertisers at so much per head, according to ratings and other market criteria. See *Marxism*.

Communication. The term has many different meanings and definitions but the central idea is of a process of increased commonality or sharing between participants, on the basis of sending and receiving 'messages'. Theoretical disagreement exists about whether we should count as communication the transmission or expression of some message, on its own, without evidence of reception or effect or completion of a sequence. The most important dimensions of communication concern two points: the degree of response or feedback (one-way versus interactive

process); and the degree to which a communication relationship is also a social relationship. In general, modern technologies increase the possibility and likelihood of detaching communication (message transmission or exchange) from any social basis.

Content analysis. A technique for the systematic, quantitative and objective description of media texts, that is useful for certain purposes of classifying output, looking for effects and making comparisons between media and over time or between content and 'reality'. Content analysis is not well suited to uncovering the underlying meaning of content, although it can provide certain indicators of 'quality' of media.

Convergence. The process of coming together or becoming more alike. It is usually applied to the convergence of media technologies as a result of *digitalization* (computerization). The distinctive physical characteristics of media cease to matter at least for purposes of production, processing and transmission. The contemporary increase in convergence has been used as an argument for media deregulation, since most regulatory regimes are linked to specific technologies (e.g. printing, broadcasting, cable, projection, etc.). Despite the potential, at the reception 'end' for convergence on a single apparatus, diversification seems to increase.

Critical theory. A general term for late Marxist versions of the part played by the mass media in maintaining a dominant *ideology* or *hegemony*. The origins are usually found in the work of the *Frankfurt School*, but there are several variants, especially the cultural and the political economy forms. The first of these has been associated with structuralist and semiological interpretations of texts (hermeneutics generally) and also with audience *reception analysis* and ethnography. The second has generally engaged with issues of structure and ownership and control of the media. Critical theory is often regarded as an alternative to empirical, behaviourist or 'scientific' approaches to the study of mass media. It is by definition normative, involving notions of an alternative and better form of society and media system.

Cultivation analysis. Term given to a particular type of media effect research, developed by George Gerbner. The underlying process is one of 'acculturation', meaning that people gradually come to accept the view of the world as portrayed on television (in particular) as a true representation of reality and adapt their hopes, fears and understandings accordingly. The main method of cultivation analysis is to chart the dominant 'television view of reality' in fiction and news and compare this with the views expressed by audience members, according to their degree of habitual exposure. The hypothesis is that the more people view television, the more their ideas correspond with the 'television view'.

Cultural imperialism. A general expression for the tendency of global media industry exporters (especially from the USA) to dominate the media consumption in other smaller and poorer countries and in so doing impose their own cultural and other values on audiences elsewhere. Not only content is exported, but also technology, production values, professional ideologies and ownership. The analogy is with historical imperialism where the means were military and economic power. Explicitly or implicitly, it is assumed that cultural imperialism leads to dependence, loss of autonomy and a decline in national or local cultures. Some latitude exists as to whether the process is deliberate and about the degree to which it is involuntary at the receiving end. The concept is a fairly crude one, but it has a strong resonance.

Cultural studies. A branch of theory and research that overlaps with the media and communication field but has a much wider reference to all forms of cultural experience and symbolic expression. It has been distinguished by a *critical* and humanistic orientation and also a strong focus on 'popular culture', especially of youth. It originated in Britain, but is now international in scope, very diverse and largely independent of media and communication studies.

Culture. In the present context it has a primary reference to the symbolic artefacts produced by media industries, but it also has a wider reference to customs, practices and meanings associated with the mass communication process (production and reception). It is sometimes used to refer to the wider framework of beliefs, ideology etc. of society (the 'superstructure') that provides the context of media operation.

Diffusion of innovations. The process of spreading any kind of new technical device, idea or useful information. It generally follows an S-shaped pattern, with a slow start, an acceleration of adoption and a long tail. The 'early adopters' tend to be untypical in terms of social composition and communication behaviour. The mass media have been found to play a secondary role in influencing diffusion, with personal example and known authority sources being primary. The media themselves provide typical examples of innovations that fit the S-curve pattern of diffusion.

Diffusion of news. Process whereby awareness of 'events' is spread through a population either by mass media or via personal, word of mouth contact with or without media involvement. Key questions concern the degree and speed of public diffusion in relation to actual or types of events and also the relative weight of media and personal sources in achieving the outcome.

Digitalization. General word for the computerization of all data transmission, storage and processing, employing the binary code and as such the basis for *convergence* of media. It is currently best known in reference to the replacement of analogue by digital transmission of television signals, leading to a large increase in potential channel capacity and scope for interactivity.

Discourse analysis. Applies to all forms of language use and textual forms, but the essential idea is that communication occurs by way of forms of 'text and talk', adapted to particular social locations, topics and kinds of participant. These are sometimes known as 'interpretative communities'. 'Critical discourse analysis' investigates the dominance exerted and expressed through linguistic forms that are vehicles for carrying socially prevailing sentiments and ideologies.

Diversity. In simple terms, it is no more than the degree or range of difference on any chosen dimension – the more difference the more diversity. When applied to mass media it can relate to structures of ownership and control, to content as produced and transmitted and to audience composition and content choices. Each of these can be empirically assessed in terms of diversity. Diversity is associated with access, freedom, choice, change and equality. It stands as a positive value in opposition to monopoly, uniformity, conformity and consensus.

Effects of media. The consequences or outcomes of the working of, or exposure to, mass media, whether or not intended. They can be sought at different levels of social analysis. There are many types of effect, but it is usual to distinguish at least between effects that are behavioural,

attitudinal (or affective) and cognitive. Effects are distinct from 'effectiveness', which relates to the efficiency of achieving a given communicative objective.

Entertainment. Describes a main branch of media production and consumption, covering a range of formats that generally share the qualities of attracting, amusing, diverting and 'taking people out of themselves'. It also refers to the process of diversion itself, and in this sense it can also relate to the genres that are not usually regarded as entertaining, such as news, advertising or education. It is often perceived as problematic when addiction to entertainment excludes informational uses of media or when the 'entertainment' mode invades the sphere of reality content – especially news, information and politics, as it seems increasingly to do. The term 'infotainment' has been coined to describe the result.

First Amendment. The First Amendment to the Constitution of the United States was enacted in 1791 and it outlawed Congressional (i.e. federal government) interference in or regulation of freedom of speech, religion and the press, etc. It has become a shorthand term to cover all matters of freedom of expression and opinion in the United States, often involving the mass media. Many other countries have equivalent constitutional provisions, although they are usually expressed in terms of the rights of citizens. The way the First Amendment is formulated has tended to identify government as the arch enemy of freedom, strongly associating free media with the free market. See *freedom of the press*.

Fourth estate. A term attributed by the historian Thomas Carlyle to the 18th century polemicist Edmund Burke and applicable to the press gallery of the English House of Commons. Burke asserted that the power of the press was at least equal to that of the other three 'estates of the Realm' – Lords, Commons and Clergy. It became a conventional term for journalists in their role as reporters of and watchdogs on government.

Framing. A term with two main meanings. One refers to the way in which news content is typically shaped and contextualized by journalists within some familiar frame of reference and according to some latent structure of meaning. A second, related, meaning concerns the effect of framing on the public. The audience is thought to adopt the frames of reference offered by journalists and see the world in a similar way. This process is related to *agenda-setting*.

Frankfurt School. The name applied to the group of scholars who originally worked in the Frankfurt Institute of Social Research and emigrated to the USA after the Nazis came to power. The central project of the group was the critical analysis of modern culture and society in the Marxist tradition. The main figures included Theodor Adorno, Max Horkheimer, Herbert Marcuse and Leo Lowenthal. They were all very influential in the development of critical theory in North America and Europe after World War Two and especially in media and cultural studies. Their pessimistic view of 'mass culture' was, paradoxically, one stimulus to a later re-validation of popular cultural forms.

Freedom of information (or communication). Freedom of information has a broad meaning that covers all aspects of public expression and transmission of, and access to, all manner of content. It has been advanced as a human right that should be guaranteed internationally and not just within a society. In a narrow sense it usually refers to public rights of access to information of public interest or relevance held by various kinds of authority or official agency.

Freedom of the press. A fundamental principle of individual, political and human rights that guarantees in law the right to all citizens to publish without advance censorship or permission by authority, or fear of reprisal. It has to be exercised within the limits of law and to respect the rights of others. In practice, freedom of the press is often limited by (economic) barriers of access to the means of publication. The right is usually regarded as fundamental to political democracy. It is related to, but distinct from, freedom of expression, opinion or belief and also *freedom of information* and *First Amendment*.

Functional analysis. In relation to mass communication, this mode of early 20th century sociological theory treats the working of mass media as in some sense necessary to the 'normal' operation of any social system (society). The main 'function' attributed to the media is to contribute to social cohesion and integration. In this light, the effects of media can be treated as either functional (positive) or dysfunctional (negative) for individuals, groups or society. The theory has largely been discarded as offering no analytic purchase and being unable to deal adequately with social conflict and change, when 'normality' is itself problematic. Even so, it still provides a general orientation to some larger questions of social process, such as integration and interdependence.

Gatekeeping. General term for the role of initial selection and later editorial processing of event reports in news organizations. News media have to decide what 'events' to admit through the 'gates' of the media on grounds of their 'newsworthiness' and other criteria. Key questions concern the criteria applied and the systematic *bias* that has been discerned in the exercise of the role.

Genre. Essentially just a word for any main type or category of media content. It can also apply to certain subcategories of theme or plot in fiction, film, drama, etc. It is useful for analysis because many genres embody certain 'rules of encoding' that can be manipulated by their producers and also certain 'rules for decoding' that allow audiences to develop appropriate expectations and 'read' texts as intended.

Globalization. The overall process whereby the location of production, transmission and reception of media content ceases to be geographically fixed, partly as a result of technology, but also through international media structure and organization. Many cultural consequences are predicted to follow, especially the delocalizing of content and undermining of local cultures. These may be regarded as positive when local cultures are enriched by new impulses and creative *hybridization* occurs. More often they are viewed as negative because of threats to cultural *identity*, autonomy and integrity. The *new media* are widely thought to be accelerating the process of globalization.

Hegemony. A term introduced by the early 20th century Italian Marxist theorist, Antonio Gramsci, to describe a certain kind of power that arises from all-embracing ideological tendencies of mass media to support the established power system and exclude opposition and competing values. In brief it is a kind of dominant consensus that works in a concealed way without direct coercion.

Human interest. A type of news story or format that focuses on personal actions and consequences, employs dramatic, humorous or narrative styles and usually deals with matters close to everyday emotions and experience. It is associated with *commercialization* and also with *tabloidization*.

Hybridization. The process whereby new cultural forms are forged out of disparate elements, especially a combination of alien or imported forms and local or traditional cultures. Associated with *globalization*.

Identity. Specific characterization of person, place, etc. by self or others, according to biographical, social, cultural or other features. Communication is a necessary condition for forming and maintaining identity. By the same token, it can weaken or undermine it. Mass communication is only one amongst several contributory factors.

Ideology. Generally refers to some organized belief system or set of values that is disseminated or reinforced by communication. While mass media do not typically set out deliberately to propagate ideology, in practice most media content (of all kinds) does so implicitly by selectively emphasizing certain values and norms. This is referred to as a 'preferred reading' in the theory of *encoding and decoding*. Often these reflect the national culture that provides the context of the media system, but also the class position and the outlook of those who own, control and make media.

Information. In a broad sense the content (messages) of all meaningful communication is information. More narrowly (but still loosely), information usually refers to verifiable and thus reliable factual data about the 'real world'. This includes opinions as well as reports about the facts of the world. Even more narrowly and precisely, information may be equated with communicated 'data' that do (or can) enable discriminations to be made in some domain of reality and thus 'reduce uncertainty' for the receiver.

Information Society. A term widely used to describe contemporary society in terms of what is thought to be its most central driving force or source of productive power, namely information of all kinds. The justification for this assumption derives from the seeming dependence of much of modern life, materially as well as culturally, on the production, handling and application of information and on the operation of complex networks of communication. The information and communication technology sector appears to have become the chief source of wealth in more economically advanced societies.

Interactivity. The capacity for reciprocal, two-way communication attributable to a communication medium or relationship. Interactivity allows for mutual adjustment, co-orientation, finer control and greater efficiency in most communication relationships and processes. The single most defining feature of 'new media' is their degree of interactivity, made increasingly possible by *digitalization*.

Internet. The worldwide system of interconnected networks, using the telecommunications infrastructure that now supports a large number of types of computer-based communication exchanges, including consultation of databases, web sites and home pages, conversational interactions, e-mail, many kinds of electronic commerce and financial transactions. The Internet is gradually taking over many functions of 'traditional' mass media (e.g. advertising, news and information). Access to the Internet is still restricted by costs to the user, plus barriers of language, culture and computer literacy.

Intertextuality. Refers to the tendency for different media texts to refer to each other at different levels and across genres and also the process by which 'readers' make meaningful connections

across formal boundaries of texts and genres. The connections extend from media texts to material objects of consumption by way of branding and merchandising. Advertising makes much deliberate use of intertextual connections. Conversational texts of media audiences extend the influence of the original texts into everyday life and language.

Journalism. Literally taken, this refers to the product or the work of professional 'news-people'. As product it typically means informational reports of recent or current events of interest to the public. In this sense, journalism is another word for 'news', with its many typical and familiar features, especially the aim of being up to date, relevant, credible and interesting to a chosen audience. As a work process, journalism has mixed connotations, reflecting uncertainty about the status of the profession. There are several styles and schools of journalism differentiated by purpose and audience and also by national media cultures.

Knowledge gaps. A term coined to refer to the structured differences in information levels between groups in society. The original promise of mass communication was that it would help to close the gaps between the 'information-rich' and the 'information-poor'. The concept has stimulated research to investigate how far this has happened and what types of media use and other conditions are associated with such an 'effect' (or its reversal). The dominant outcome has been that newspapers have been better at closing gaps than television. Current expectations are that new media are more likely to widen than to close gaps because of their differential availability to the already better informed.

Life-style. The idea has a long history in commercial market research and has affinities with theories of taste and family background developed by Pierre Bourdieu. It refers to patterns of personal consumption and tastes of all kinds that are generally self-chosen but also shared with some others. They can be relatively independent of social class and material circumstances although they are likely to be shaped by a number of external factors, amongst which income is certainly one, along with age, education, social milieu and outlook. A life-style may be a way of expressing an individual identity, but for media it can also be a way of constructing and managing consumer markets. See also *taste culture*.

Marxism. Theory of society based on work of Karl Marx, according to whom human progress takes place on the basis of conflict between succeeding 'classes', whose dominant power depends on ownership of the current main factor of production (e.g. land, raw material, capital or labour). The dominant class exploits other classes in order to maximize profit and output. The relevance for mass communication lies in the proposition that the media are an ideological asset that can be used to defend, or attack, a dominant class position. In Marx's own time and later, the mass media were owned and operated in the interests of the dominant class. This remains an issue to be determined.

Mass. The term describes a very large but amorphous set of individuals that engage in similar behaviour, under external influence, and are viewed by their would-be manipulators as having little or no separate identity, forms of organization or power, autonomy, integrity or self-determination. It represents one view of the media audience. It is used with the same negative connotations in a number of related expressions, including mass behaviour, mass opinion, mass consumption, *mass culture, mass society*, etc. and of course 'mass communication' itself.

Mass culture. When current (approximately 1930–70), this term described the 'culture of the masses', generally meaning 'lower' forms of entertainment and fiction appealing to the uneducated and 'uncultured' majority, as opposed to the 'high culture' of the majority. Cultural change and new perceptions of popular culture have changed the meaning of the term and made it largely redundant or undesirable. When current it was more ideological (upholding elite cultural values) than empirically valid, since all but a small minority tended to participate in at least some aspects of 'mass culture'.

Mass society. A form of society theoretically identified as dominated by a small number of interconnected elites who control the conditions of life of the many, often by means of persuasion and manipulation. The term was first applied both to the post-war United States by radical critics (especially C. Wright Mills) and also by political theorists to the European societies that fell under the spell of fascism and communism. Large-scale and centralized forms of social organization are typical, accompanied by feelings of anomie and powerlessness. The mass media are necessary instruments for achieving and maintaining mass society.

Media accountability. A composite term for the idea, and the associated processes for realizing it, that media can and should be held to account for the quality, means and consequences of their publishing activities to society in general and/or to other interests that may be affected. This brings accountability into potential conflict with freedom. The idea of media accountability is sometimes, though not necessarily, associated with ideas of *social responsibility*. It does presuppose some mutual relationship between media senders and receivers. It is also closely linked to the idea of there being a *public interest* in the media.

Media concentration. The coming together of media organizations to form larger units either by vertical or horizontal integration of firms. The former refers to joining of various sequences in the media process (e.g. paper production, printing, publishing and selling of books), the latter to conglomeration of firms at the same stage in the sequence. Both lead to greater monopoly and less *diversity*. Concentration can also take place within the same national market or transnationally. The usual main reference is to concentration of ownership, although it is possible for there to be varying levels of concentration of different work processes in a media conglomerate.

Media ethics. Principles of good conduct for media practitioners, bearing in mind the public role of the media in a given society, as well as the claims of individuals. The relevant conduct relates especially to the ways in which information is obtained and to decisions about what and how to publish, especially bearing in mind the consequences that might follow for all concerned. In non-informational content areas, there are also numerous ethical issues, although these are less likely to have been codified or play a part in decision making. The claim of *journalism* to be a profession depends in some degree on the voluntary development and acceptance of ethical standards. See *media accountability*.

Moral panic. The term was first applied by the criminologist Jock Young to apply to sudden expressions of often irrational mass anxiety and alarm directed at supposed 'crime waves' or other supposed evidence of disorder and social breakdown (including promiscuity and immigration). The media are implicated through their tendency to amplify such 'panics'. They are also sometimes objects of moral panics, when alarm at their harmful effects suddenly gains currency

(e.g. in the form of crime waves, suicides, or rioting). New media, such as computer games and the Internet, tend to generate some degree of panic at alleged harm to their (young) users.

Network. Any interconnected set of points, which could be persons, places, organizations, machines, etc. In communication, interest focuses on the flow of information through the 'lines' of a network, with particular reference to their carrying capacity and interactivity, and of course to who or what is connected more or less tightly and exclusively. The term 'network society' has been coined by theorists (e.g. Castells and Van Dyke) as an alternative way of expressing the reality of the *Information Society*.

News. The main form in which current information about public events is carried by media of all kinds. There is a great diversity of types and formats as well as cross-cultural differences, but defining characteristics are generally held to be timeliness, relevance and reliability (truth value). See also *journalism*.

Newspaper. Traditionally this has referred to a print media form appearing regularly (usually not less than once a week), containing (at least) reliable reports of recent or ongoing events of general interest and offered for public sale. Associated characteristics are usually independence or transparency of ownership and editing and a geographical range of coverage and circulation. Variant forms have emerged, including the 'free newspaper', paid for by advertising, and more recently the 'electronic newspaper' that is offered on-line and lacks the limits of time and location of the traditional newspaper.

News values. The criteria applied by journalists and editors in news organizations to determine whether or not to carry particular items of *news*. In commercial media, the consensus 'value' is whether or not the item concerned is likely to interest a potential audience. However, there are other sources of value, including a judgement of intrinsic significance or the pull or pressure of influential interests other than the audience.

Objectivity. A theoretically contested term applied to *news*, although in 'common-sense' terms it sums up a number of the qualities that make for trust and reliability on the part of the news audience. These include factual accuracy, lack of *bias*, separation of fact from comment, transparency about sources, not taking sides. The reasons for controversy about the term stem mainly from the view that true objectivity is unattainable and it is misleading to pretend otherwise. In brief, all news is said to be ideological, and objectivity is held by critics to be another ideology. The requirements of objectivity make it possible for sources to manipulate the news and only serve to conceal 'bias', whether this is intended or unintended.

Opinion leader. A term introduced by Elihu Katz and Paul Lazarsfeld, in early research into the influence of mass media, to describe the social role of persons who influence the thinking or behaviour of others in informal social relationships. The identifying characteristics vary according to the 'topic' of influence and social setting, but the people concerned are generally better informed, make more use of mass media and other sources, are gregarious and likely to be respected by those they influence. The failure of early research to find 'direct' effects from mass media was attributed in part to the variable and often invisible contribution of opinion leaders (known as *personal influence*).

Para-social interaction. A term for the pseudo-interaction that can take place between individuals in audiences and fictional characters or media personalities. Some degree of loss of contact with reality is involved, and it may be the basis for influence on behaviour.

Phonogram. A convenient, though not very much used, term for all forms of recorded and personally replayed music, which were originally (almost) only available via the 'gramophone', previously 'phonograph', later 'record-player'. The word covers records, tapes and discs of all kinds.

Political economy. The original word for theoretical economics but for some time used by critical theorists working in the neo-Marxist tradition to refer to a general view of media and society in which material (economic) factors play a determining role and in which politics is primarily about economic power.

Postmodernism. A widely current (cultural) theory that underwrites the view that the 'age of ideology' is over along with the 'industrial society' and its massive forms of social organization and control and dedication to rationality. Instead we are living in an era of unstructured diversity, uncertainty, contradictions, open-ended creativity and individual freedom from imposed rules and social constraint. It has become fashionable to discern in the exuberant growth of mass media forms as the essence of popular postmodern culture. Neither the material conditions of contemporary society nor forms of organization of mass media exhibit clear signs of postmodernism. Much as with earlier critical cultural theory, postmodern thinking can support divergent optimistic and pessimistic outlooks.

Propaganda. The process and product of deliberate attempts to influence collective behaviour and opinion by the use of multiple means of communication in ways that are systematic and one-sided. Propaganda is carried in the interest of the source or sender, not the recipient. It is almost certain to be in some respects misleading or not fully truthful and can be entirely untrue, as with certain kinds of disinformation. It can also be pyschologically aggressive and distorted in its representation of reality. Its effectiveness is variable depending on the context and dispositions of the target audience more than on 'message' characteristics. See *advertising* and *campaign*.

Public. As a noun it refers to the general body of free citizens of a given society or some smaller geographical space. Its connotations are strongly influenced by democratic theory, since freedom and equality (of rights) are generally only available in a democracy. The members of a genuine public in a democracy are free to associate, converse, organize and express themselves on all subjects, and government is ultimately accountable to the will of the 'public as a whole' according to agreed procedures. This large notion of what constitutes the public is one reason why public communication has a certain claim to protection and to respect in a democracy. See also *public opinion*; *public interest*; *public sphere*.

Public interest. Expresses the idea that expectations from, and claims against, the mass media on grounds of the wider and longer term good of society, can be legitimately expressed and may lead to constraints on the structure or activity of media. The content of what is 'in the public interest' takes various forms. Its most minimal interpretation is that media should meet the

needs of their audiences, but ethical, ideological, political and legal considerations may also lead to much stronger definitions. The expression of public interest also takes place in many ways, including *public opinion*, politicians, critics and many interest groups affected by public communication. See also *media accountability*.

Public opinion. The collective views of a significant part of any *public* as defined above. This part is sometimes taken to mean a numerical majority as measured by polling, but this far overstates the capacity of the measuring instruments and misses the essential point that opinion is always diverse, dynamic and variable in strength. Historically and in certain contexts public opinion may be taken to refer to 'informed opinion', or the general view of the more educated and aware members of the society. No statement concerning public opinion is likely to be unambiguous or beyond dispute without some clear definition. See *spiral of silence*.

Public relations. Now a reference to all forms of influence carried out by professional paid communicators on behalf of some 'client' and designed primarily to project a favourable image and to counter negative views that might exist. The means are various, ranging from direct communication to providing gifts and hospitality. Public relations is often a source of supply for news media or seeks to influence news in other ways. See also *advertising* and *propaganda*.

Public service broadcasting (PSB). The (mainly European) system of broadcasting that is publicly funded and operated in a non-profit way in order to meet various public communication needs of all citizens. These were originally virtually all needs (i.e. inclusive of entertainment), and the justification for PSB lay in the 'natural monopoly' character of broadcasting distribution. This justification is no longer valid, and PSB survives on grounds of general *public interest* and because it can meet certain communication needs that tend to be neglected in commercial systems because they are unprofitable. These include universal service, special needs of certain minorities, certain kinds of educational provision, and services to the democratic political system by giving some degree of open and diverse access supporting general informational aims and meeting the specific needs of politicians in the electoral and government process.

Public sphere. The conceptual 'space' that exists in a society outside the immediate circle of private life and the walls of enclosed institutions and organizations pursuing their own (albeit sometimes public) goals. In this space, the possibility exists for public association and debate leading to the formation of public opinion and political movements and parties that can hold private interests accountable. The media are now probably the key institution of the public sphere, and its 'quality' will depend on the quality of media. Taken to extremes, certain structural tendencies of media, including concentration, commercialization and globalization, are harmful to the public sphere.

Reception analysis. An alternative to traditional audience research (concerned with counting and effect) that takes the perspective of the audience rather than the media sender and looks at the immediate contextual influences on media use and the interpretation and meaning of the whole experience as seen by the recipient. Ethnographic and qualitative methods are required.

Rumour. Communication that takes place mainly by word of mouth in the absence of reliable or complete information about events of great concern to those involved. Mass media can feed rumour (e.g. early reports of some disaster) or replace rumour. Rumour develops where mass

media are generally inadequate or unreliable (as in totalitarian societies or under conditions of war). Networks of personal relations facilitate rumour, but under extreme conditions are not necessary.

Semiology. The 'science of sign systems' or 'signification'. Originally founded on the study of general linguistics by Ferdinand de Saussure, it was developed into a method for the systematic analysis and interpretation of all symbolic texts. Systems of signs are organized within larger cultural and ideological systems that ultimately determine meaning. A key element of semiology is the idea that any (meaningful) sign (of any kind) has a conceptual element that carries meaning as well as a physical manifestation (word, image, etc.).

Sensationalism. At one level an everyday word for all aspects of media content that is likely to attract attention, excite or inflame emotions. In this sense it is related to *commercialization* and *tabloidization*. It has also been deployed as a concept in content analysis, defined in terms of some 'indicators' for measuring the degree of sensationalism. The reason for doing so is a concern at the inconsistency between sensational and *objective* news reporting.

Spin doctor. Contemporary expression to refer to all those who have the job of managing (or massaging) the public presentation of information or ideas (especially on behalf of politicians) to maximum advantage. Their work results in the manipulation of news and is related to *public relations* and *propaganda*. The term 'flak' has also been used in this connection. The role of spin doctor has been greatly enhanced in a time of political marketing and professional management of campaigns. Its prominence also reflects the media's own attraction to 'horse-race' or 'strategic' rather than substantive reporting of politics.

Socialization. The general process of social formation of the young under the influence of so-called agencies of socialization – traditionally the family, neighbourhood school, religion and now mass media.

Social responsibility. Attributed to the mass media in certain normative theories of the press and based on propositions about the needs of (democratic) society, the unwritten obligations implicit in the freedom of publication as well as general ethical and moral principles relating to truth and justice.

Spiral of silence. Concept that describes one version of the 'third-party' effect in opinion-formation – the tendency for people to be influenced in what they think (or say they do) or by what they think other people think. The term was first applied by Elizabeth Noelle-Neumann to refer to the tendency for those who think they hold a minority or deviant view to refrain from expressing it in public, thus accelerating the dominance of the supposed consensus (the spiralling effect). The hypothesis is based on a presumed 'fear of isolation'. The main thrust of the theory is to attribute to the (leftist) media a powerful effect, since they are the main source of what people *think* is the dominant opinion of the moment. Also related to the better known 'bandwagon effect' whereby apparent front runners pick up support on this basis alone.

Stimulus–response. A psychological process by which an experimental subject learns to perform some action in response to a message stimulus that has become associated with the action in question. It underlies a large body of learning theory that was applied in early research into the effects of communication and media. It has not proved a very good guide to reality.

Tabloidization. A term derived from the common tabloid format for sensationalist (i.e. gossip and scandal-mongering) newspapers, to refer to the alleged process of 'dumbing down' or going 'down-market' of the more serious press in many countries. The main believed cause was commercialization and intense competition for readers. The process has also affected television news and 'actuality' formats in general, especially in the United States, and caused alarm at the decline of journalistic standards, rise in public ignorance and risk of confusion between fiction and reality (e.g. 'infotainment').

Taste culture. A more or less organized and semi-autonomous set of cultural preferences based on certain shared tastes, although independent of actual social organization. In this the concept differs from the earlier approaches to taste patterns that were mainly explained in terms of social background, class or milieu. Related to *life-style*.

Toronto School. Describes a body of work mainly derived from theories of Marshall McLuhan, and in turn derived from an earlier scholar at the University of Toronto, the economic historian Harold Innis. At the core is a form of communication technology determinism that attributes distinctive social and cultural effects to the dominant form and vehicle of communication, independent of the actual content.

Uses and gratifications approach. A version of individualist functional theory and research that seeks to explain media use and the satisfactions derived from them in terms of the motives and self-perceived needs of audience members. This is also one verson of 'active audience' theory and has been applied in the study of media effects on the grounds that any effect has to be consistent with the needs of the audience.

Virtual community. Describes the group or close personal associations formed on-line by participants in Internet exchanges and discussions. A virtual community is thought to have many of the features of a real community, including identification, bonding, shared norms and outlook, even without any physical contact or real personal knowledge of other members.

Adams, W.C. and Schreibman, F. (eds) (1978) *Television Networks: Issues in Content Research*. Washington, DC: George Washington University.

Adorno, T. and Horkheimer, M. (1972) 'The culture industry: enlightenment as mass deception', in *The Dialectic of Enlightenment*. New York: Herder and Herder.

Alali, A.O. and Eke, K.K. (eds) (1991) *Media Coverage of Television*. Newbury Park, CA: Sage.

Alasuutari, P. (1992) ' "I'm ashamed to admit it but I have watched *Dallas*": the moral hierarchy of television programmes', *Media, Culture and Society*, 14 (1): 561–82.

Alasuutari, P. (ed.) (1999a) *Rethinking the Media Audience*. London: Sage.

Alasuutari, P. (1999b) 'Cultural images of the media', in P. Alasuutari (ed.), *Rethinking the Media Audience*, pp. 86–104. London: Sage.

Alberoni, F. (1972) 'The "powerless elite": theory and sociological research on the phenomenon of the stars', in D. McQuail (ed.), *Sociology of Mass Communication*, pp. 75–98. Harmondsworth: Penguin.

Allen, I.L (1977) 'Social integration as an organizing principle', in G. Gerbner (ed.), *Mass Media Policies in Changing Cultures*, pp. 235–50. New York: Wiley.

Allen, R.C. (ed.) (1987) *Channels of Discourse*. London: Allen and Unwin.

Allen, R.C. (1989) ' "Soap opera", audiences and the limits of genre', in F. Seiter et al. (eds), *Remote Control*, pp. 4–55. London: Routledge.

Allor, M. (1988) 'Relocating the site of the audience', *Critical Studies in Mass Communication*, 5 (3): 217–33.

Altheide, D.L. (1974) *Creating Reality*. Beverly Hills, CA: Sage.

Altheide, D.L. (1985) *Media Power*. Beverly Hills, CA: Sage.

Altheide, D.L. and Snow, R.P. (1979) *Media Logic*. Beverly Hills, CA: London: Sage.

Altheide, D.L. and Snow, R.P. (1991) *Media Worlds in the Postjournalism Era*. New York: Aldine/de Gruyter.

Althusser, L. (1971) 'Ideology and ideological state apparatuses', in *Lenin and Philosophy and Other Essays*. London: New Left Books.

Altschull, J.H. (1984) *Agents of Power: The Role of the News Media in Human Affairs*. New York: Longman.

Anderson, B. (1983) *Imagined Communities*. London: Verso.

Anderson, J., Collins, P.A., Schmitt, R.S. and Jacobowitz, R.S. (1996) 'Stressful life events and television viewing', *Communication Research*, 23 (2): 243–60.

Andersson, M. and Jansson, A. (1998) 'Media use and the progressive cultural lifestyle', *Nordicom Review*, 19 (2): 63–77.

Andrew, D. (1984) *Concepts in Film Theory*. New York: Oxford University Press.

Ang, I. (1985) *Watching 'Dallas': Soap Opera and the Melodramatic Imagination*. London: Methuen.

Ang, I. (1991) *Desperately Seeking the Audience*. London: Routledge.

Ang, I. (1998) 'The performance of the sponge: mass communication theory enters the postmodern world', in K. Brants, J. Hermes and L. van Zoonen (eds), *The Media in Question*, pp. 77–88. London: Sage.

Ang, I. and Hermes, J. (1991) 'Gender and/in media consumption', in J. Curran and M. Gurevitch (eds), *Media and Society*, pp. 307–28. London: Edward Arnold.

Asp, K. (1981) 'Mass media as molders of opinion and suppliers of information', in C.G. Wilhoit and H. de Back (eds), *Mass Communication Review Yearbook*, Vol. 2, pp. 332–54. Beverly Hills, CA: Sage.

Atkinson, D. and Raboy, M. (eds) (1997) *Public Service Broadcasting: the Challenges of the Twenty-first Century*. Paris: UNESCO.

Austin, P.J. (1992) 'Television that talks back: an experimental validation of a PSI scale', *Journal of Broadcasting and Electronic Media*, 36 (1): 173–81.

Avery, R. (1979) 'Adolescents' use of the mass media', *American Behavioral Scientist*, 23: 53–70.

Avery, R. (1993) *Public Service Broadcasting*. New York: Longman.

Babrow, A.S. (1988) 'Theory and method in research on audience motives', *Journal of Broadcasting and Electronic Media*, 32 (4): 471–87.

Baehr, H. (1996) *Women in Television*. London: University of Westminster Press.

Baerns, B. (1987) 'Journalism versus public relations in the Federal Republic of Germany', in D.L. Paletz (ed.), *Political Communication Research*, pp. 88–107. Norwood, NJ: Ablex.

Bagdikian, B. (1988) *The Media Monopoly*. Boston, MA: Beacon.

Baker, C.E. (1994) *Advertising and a Democratic Press*. Princeton, NJ: Princeton University Press.

Baldwin, T.F., McVoy, D.S. and Steinfield, C. (1996) *Convergence: Integrating Media, Information and Communication*. Thousand Oaks, CA: Sage.

Ball-Rokeach, S.J. (1985) 'The origins of individual media-system dependency', *Communication Research*, 12 (4): 485–510.

Ball-Rokeach, S.J. and DeFleur, M.L. (1976) 'A dependency model of mass media effects', *Communication Research*, 3: 3–21.

Bantz, C. (1985) 'News organizations: conflict as crafted cultural norm', *Communication*, 8: 225–44.

Bantz, C.R., McCorkle, S. and Baade, R.C. (1980) 'The news factory', *Communication Research*, 7 (1): 45–68.

Barnes, B.E. and Thomson, L.M. (1994). 'Power to the people (meter): audience measurement technology and media specialization', in J.S. Ettema and D.C. Whitney (eds), *Audience-making: How the Media Create the Audience*, pp. 75–94. Thousand Oaks, CA: Sage.

Barthes, R. (1967) *Elements of Semiology*. London: Jonathan Cape.

Barthes, R. (1972) *Mythologies*. London: Jonathan Cape.

Barthes, R. (1977) *Image, Music, Text: Essays*, selected and translated by Stephen Heath. London: Fontana.

Barwise, T.P. and Ehrenberg, A.S.C. (1988) *Television and its Audience*. Newbury Park, CA: Sage.

Bass, A.Z. (1969) 'Refining the gatekeeper concept', *Journalism Quarterly*, 46: 69–72.

Baudrillard, J. (1983) *Simulations*. New York: Semiotext.

Bauer, R.A. (1958) 'The communicator and the audience', *Journal of Conflict Resolution*, 2 (1): 67–77. Also in L.A. Dexter and D.M. White (eds), *People, Society and Mass Communication*, pp. 125–39. New York: Free Press.

Bauer, R.A. (1964) 'The obstinate audience', *American Psychologist*, 19: 319–28.

Bauer, R.A. and Bauer, A. (1960) 'America, mass society and mass media', *Journal of Social Issues*, 10 (3): 366.

Bauman, Z. (1972) 'A note on mass culture: on infrastructure', in D. McQuail (ed.), *Sociology of Mass Communication*, pp. 61–74. Harmondsworth: Penguin.

Becker, L. (1982) 'The mass media and citizen assessment of issue importance', in D.C. Whitney et al. (eds), *Mass Communication Review Yearbook*, Vol. 3, pp. 521–36. Beverly Hills, CA: Sage.

Behr, R.L. and Iyengar, S. (1985) 'TV news, real world cues and changes in the public agenda', *Public Opinion Quarterly*, 49 (1): 38–57.

Bell, A. (1991) *The Language of News Media*. Oxford: Blackwell.

Bell, D. (1973) *The Coming of Post-Industrial Society*. New York: Basic Books.

Beniger, J.R. (1986) *The Control Revolution*. Cambridge, MA: Harvard University Press.

Beniger, J.R. (1987) 'Personalization of mass media and the growth of pseudo-community', *Communication Research*, 14 (3): 352–71.

Benjamin, W. (1977) 'The work of art in an age of mechanical reproduction', in J. Curran et al. (eds), *Mass Communication and Society*, pp. 384–408. London: Edward Arnold.

Benthall, J. (1993) *Disasters, Relief and the Media*. London: I.B. Taurus.

Berelson, B. (1949) 'What missing the newspaper means', in P.F. Lazarsfeld and F.M. Stanton (eds), *Communication Research 1948–9*, pp. 111–29. New York: Duell, Sloan and Pearce.

Berelson, B. (1952) *Content Analysis in Communication Research*. Glencoe, IL: Free Press.

Berelson, B. (1959) 'The state of communication research', *Public Opinion Quarterly*, 23 (1): 16.

Berelson, B., Lazarsfeld, P.J. and McPhee, W.N. (1954) *Voting: A Study of Opinion Formation in a Presidential Campaign*. Chicago: Chicago University Press.

Berger, A.A. (1992) *Popular Genres*. Newbury Park, CA: Sage.

Berger, C.R. and Chaffee, S.H. (1987) 'The study of communication as a science', in C.R. Berger and S.H. Chaffee (eds), *Handbook of Communication Science*, pp. 15–19. Beverly Hills, CA: Sage.

Berkowitz, D. (1990) 'Refining the gatekeeping concept for local television news', *Journal of Broadcasting and Electronic Media*, 34 (1): 55–68.

Berkowitz, D. (1992) 'Non-routine and news work', *Journal of Communication*, 42 (1): 82–94.

Berkowitz, L. (1984) 'Some effects of thoughts on anti- and prosocial influence of media events: a cognitive neoassociationistic analysis', *Psychological Bulletin*, 95 (3): 410–27.

Biltereyst, D. (1991) 'Resisting American hegemony: a comparative analysis of the reception of domestic and US fiction', *European Journal of Communication*, 6 (4): 469–97.

Biltereyst, D. (1992) 'Language and culture as ultimate barriers?', *European Journal of Communication*, 7 (4): 517–40.

Biltereyst, D. (1995) 'Qualitative audience research and transnational media effects: a new paradigm?', *European Journal of Communication*, 10 (2): 245–70.

Biocca, F.A. (1988a) 'The breakdown of the canonical audience'. in J. Anderson (ed.), *Communication Yearbook 11*, pp. 127–32. Newbury Park, CA: Sage.

Biocca, F.A. (1988b) 'Opposing conceptions of the audience', in J. Anderson (ed.), *Communication Yearbook 11*, pp. 51–80. Newbury Park, CA: Sage Publications.

Bird, S.E. (1998) 'An audience perspective on the tabloidisation of news', *The Public*, 5 (3): 33–50.

Bird, S.E. and Dardenne, R.W. (1988) 'Myth, chronicle and story', in J.W. Carey (ed.), *Media, Myths and Narratives: Television and the Press*, pp. 67–86. Beverly Hills, CA: Sage.

Blanchard, M.A. (1977) 'The Hutchins Commission, the Press and the Responsibility Concept', *Journalism Monographs*, 49.

Blanchard, M.A. (1986) *Exporting the First Amendment: The Press–Government Crusade of 1945–1952*. New York: Longman.

Blau, P. and Scott, W. (1963) *Formal Organizations*. London: Routledge and Kegan Paul.

Blumer, H. (1933) *Movies and Conduct*. New York: Macmillan.

Blumer, H. (1939) 'The mass, the public and public opinion', in A.M. Lee (ed.), *New Outlines of the Principles of Sociology*. New York: Barnes and Noble.

Blumer, H. and Hauser, P.M. (1933) *Movies, Delinquency and Crime*. New York: Macmillan.

Blumler, J.G. (1970) 'The political effects of television', in J.D. Halloran (ed.), *The Effects of Television*, pp. 69–104. Leicester: Leicester University Press.

Blumler, J.G. (1985) 'The social character of media gratifications', in K.E. Rosengren et al. (eds), *Media Gratification Research: Current Perspectives*, pp. 41–59. Beverly Hills, CA: Sage Publications.

Blumler, J.G. (1991) 'The new television marketplace', in J. Curran and M. Gurevitch (eds), *Mass Media and Society*, pp. 194–215. London: Edward Arnold.

Blumler, J.G. (ed.) (1992) *Television and the Public Interest*. London: Sage.

Blumler, J.G. (1998) 'Wrestling with public interest in organized communications', in K. Brants, J. Hermes and L. van Zoonen (eds), *The Media in Question*, pp. 51–63. London: Sage.

Blumler, J.G. and Gurevitch, M. (1995) *The Crisis of Public Communication*. London: Routledge.

Blumler, J.G. and Katz, E. (eds) (1974) *The Uses of Mass Communications*. Beverly Hills, CA: Sage.

Blumler, J.G. and Kavanagh, D. (1999) 'The third age of political communication: influences and fears', *Political Communication*, 16 (3): 209–30.

Blumler, J.G. and McQuail, D. (1968) *Television in Politics: Its Uses and Influence*. London: Faber.

Bogart, L. (1995) *Commercial Culture*. New York: Oxford University Press.

Boorman, J. (1987) *Money into Light*. London: Faber.

Boorstin, D. (1961) *The Image: A Guide to Pseudo-Events in America*. New York: Atheneum.

Bordewijk, J.L and van Kaam, B. (1986) 'Towards a new classification of tele-information services', *Intermedia* 14 (1): 1621. Originally published in *Allocutie*. Baarn: Bosch and Keuning, 1982.

Bourdieu, P. (1986) *Distinction: A Social Critique of the Judgement of Taste*. London: Routledge.

Boyd-Barrett, O. (1980) *The International News Agencies*. London: Constable.

Boyd-Barrett, O. and Rantanen, T. (eds) (1998) *The Globalization of News*. London: Sage.

Bramson, L. (1961) *The Political Context of Sociology*. Princeton, NJ: Princeton University Press.

Brants, K. (1998) 'Who's afraid of infotainment?', *European Journal of Communication*, 13 (3): 315–36.

Brants, K. and Siune, K. (1998) 'Politicisation in decline', in D. McQuail and K. Siune (eds), *Media Policy*, pp. 128–43. London. Sage.

Brants, K., Hermes, J. and Zoonen, L. van (eds) (1998) *The Media in Question* (1988). London: Sage.

Breed, W. (1955) 'Social control in the newsroom: a functional analysis', *Social Forces*, 33: 326–55.

Breed, W. (1956) 'Analysing news: some questions for research', *Journalism Quarterly*, 33: 467–77.

Breed, W. (1958) 'Mass communication and socio-cultural integration', *Social Forces*, 37: 109–16.

Brodasson, T. (1994) 'The sacred side of professional journalism', *European Journal of Communication*, 9 (3): 227–48.

Brown, J.R. (ed.) (1976) *Children and Television*. London: Collier-Macmillan.

Brown, J.R. and Linné, O. (1976) 'The family as a mediator of television's effects', in J.R. Brown (ed.), *Children and Television*, pp. 184–98. London: Collier-Macmillan.

Brown, M.E. (ed.) (1990) *Television and Women's Culture*. Newbury Park, CA: Sage.

Bryant, J. and Zillman, D. (eds) (1986) *Perspectives on Media Effects*. Hillsdale, NJ: Laurence Erlbaum.

Burgelin, O. (1972) 'Structural analysis and mass communication', in D. McQuail (ed.), *Sociology of Mass Communications*, pp. 313–28. Harmondsworth: Penguin.

Burnett, R. (1990) *Concentration and Diversity in the International Phonogram Industry*. Gothenburg: University of Gothenburg.

Burnett, R. (1996) *The Global Jukebox*. London: Routledge.

Burns, T. (1969) 'Public service and private world', in P. Halmos (ed.), *The Sociology of Mass Media Communicators*, pp. 53–73. Keele: University of Keele.

Burns, T. (1977) *The BBC: Public Institution and Private World*. London: Macmillan.

Burrell, G. and Morgan, G. (1979) *Sociological Paradigms and Organizational Analysis*. London: Heinemann.

Canary, D.J. and Spitzberg, R.H. (1993) 'Loneliness and media gratifications', *Communication Research*, 20 (6): 800–21.

Cantor, M. (1971) *The Hollywood Television Producers*. New York: Basic Books.

Cantor, M. (1994) 'The role of the audience in the production of culture', in J.S. Ettema and D.C. Whitney (eds), *Audiencemaking*, pp. 159–70. Thousand Oaks, CA: Sage.

Cantril, H., Gaudet, H. and Hertzog, H. (1940) *The Invasion from Mars*. Princeton, NJ: Princeton University Press.

Cappella, J.N. and Jamieson, K.H. (1997) *The Spiral of Cynicism: the Press and the Public Good*. New York: Oxford University Press.

Carey, J. (1969) 'The communication revolution and the professional communicator', in P. Halmos (ed.), The *Sociology of Mass Media Communicators*, pp. 23–38. Keele: University of Keele.

Carey, J. (1975) 'A cultural approach to communication', *Communication*, 2: 1–22.

Carey, J. (1988) *Communication as Culture*. Boston, MA: Unwin Hyman.

Carey, J.W. (1998) 'Marshall McLuhan: Genealogy and Legacy', *Canadian Journal of Communication*, 23: 293–306.

Carey, J.W. (1999) 'Lawyers, voyeurs and vigilantes', *Media Studies Journal*, Spring/Summer: 16–22.

Carlsson, G., Dahlberg, A. and Rosengren, K.E. (1981) 'Mass media content, public opinion and social change', in K. Rosengren (ed.), *Advances in Content Analysis*, pp. 227–40. Beverly Hills, CA: Sage.

Castells, M. (1996) *The Information Age*, Vol. I: *The Rise of the Network Society*. Oxford: Blackwell.

Chaffee, S.H. (1975) 'The diffusion of political information', in S.H. Chaffee (ed.), *Political Communication*, pp. 85–128. Beverly Hills, CA: Sage.

Chaffee, S.H. (1981) 'Mass media effects: new research perspectives', in C.G. Wilhoit and H. de Back (eds), *Mass Communication Review Yearbook*, vol. 2, pp. 77–108. Beverly Hills CA: Sage.

Chaffee, S.H. and Hochheimer, J.L. (1982) 'The beginnings of political communication research in the US: origins of the limited effects model', in E.M. Rogers and F. Balle (eds), *The Media Revolution in America and Europe*, pp. 263–83. Norwood, NJ: Ablex.

Chaffee, S.H. and Roser, C. (1986) 'Involvement and the consistency of knowledge, attitudes and behavior', *Communication Research*, 3: 373–99.

Chibnall, S. (1977) *Law and Order News*. London: Tavistock.

Clark, T.N. (ed.) (1969) *On Communication and Social Influence*. Collected essays of Gabriel Tarde. Chicago: Chicago University Press.

Clausse, R. (1968) 'The mass public at grips with mass communication', *International Social Science Journal*, 20 (4): 625–43.

Cohen, B. (1963) *The Press and Foreign Policy*. Princeton, NJ: Princeton University Press.

Cohen, S. (1972) *Folk Devils and Moral Panics*. London: McGibban and Kee.

Cohen, S. and Young, J. (eds) (1973) *The Manufacture of News*. London: Constable.

Coleman, S. (1999) 'The new media and democratic politics', *New Media and Society*, 1 (1): 67–74.

Comstock, G. (ed.) (1988) *Public Communication and Behavior*. New York: Academic Press.

Comstock, G., Chaffee, S., Katzman, N., McCombs, M. and Roberts, D. (1978) *Television and Human Behaviour*. New York: Columbia University Press.

Connell, I. (1998) 'Mistaken identities: tabloid and broadsheet news discourses', *The Public*, 5 (3): 11–31.

Conway, J.C. and Rubin, A.M. (1991) 'Psychological predictors of television viewing motivation', *Communication Research*, 18 (4): 443–63.

Cooper, E. and Jahoda, M. (1947) 'The evasion of propaganda', *Journal of Psychology*, 23: 15–25.

Cox, H. and Morgan, D. (1973) *City Politics and the Press*. Cambridge: Cambridge University Press.

Cuilenberg, J.J. van (1987) 'The information society: some trends and implications', *European Journal of Communication*, 2 (1): 105–21.

Cuilenburg, J.J. van and McQuail, D. (1998) 'Media policy paradigm shifts: in search of a new communications policy paradigm', in G. Picard (ed.), *Evolving Media Markets: Effects of Economic and Policy Changes*. Turku, Finland: Economic Research Foundation for Mass Communication.

Cuilenburg, J.J. van, de Ridder, J. and Kleinnijenhuis, J. (1986) 'A theory of evaluative discourse', *European Journal of Communication*, 1 (1): 65–96.

Curran, J. (1986) 'The impact of advertising on the British mass media', in R. Collins et al. (eds), *Media, Culture and Society*, pp. 309–35. Beverly Hills, CA: Sage.

Curran, J. (1990) 'The new revisionism in mass communication research: a reappraisal', *European Journal of Communication*, 5 (2/3): 135–64.

Curran, J. (1996) 'Mass media and democracy revisited', in J. Curran and M. Gurevitch (eds), *Mass Media and Society*, 2nd edn, pp. 81–119. London: Edward Arnold.

Curran, J. and Seaton, J. (1997) *Power without Responsibility*, 5th edn. London: Fontana.

Curran, J., Gurevitch, M. and Woollacott, J. (eds) (1977) *Mass Communication and Society*. London: Edward Arnold.

Curran, J., Douglas, A. and Whannel, G. (1981) 'The political economy of the human interest story', in A. Smith (ed.), *Newspapers and Democracy*, pp. 288–316. Cambridge, MA: MIT Press.

Curtis, L. (1984) *Ireland: the Propaganda War*. London: Pluto.

Dahlgren, P. (1995) *Television and the Public Sphere*. London: Sage.

Dahlgren, P. and Sparks, C.S. (eds) (1992) *Journalism and Popular Culture*. London: Sage.

Darnton, R. (1975) 'Writing news and telling stories', *Daedalus*, Spring: 175–94.

Davis, D.K. and Robinson, J.P. (1986) 'News story attributes and comprehension', in J.P. Robinson and M. Levy (eds), *The Main Source*, pp. 179–210. Beverly Hills, CA: Sage Publications.

Davis, D.K. and Robinson, J.P. (1989) 'Newsflow and democratic society', in G. Comstock (ed.), *Public Communication and Behavior*, Vol. 2. Orlando, FL: Academic Press.

Dayan, D. and Katz, E. (1992) *Media Events*. Cambridge, MA: Harvard University Press.

Dearing, J.W. and Rogers, E.M. (1996) *Agenda-Setting*. Thousand Oaks, CA: Sage.

DeFleur, M.L. (1970) *Theories of Mass Communication*, 2nd edn. New York: David McKay.

DeFleur, M.L. and Ball-Rokeach, S. (1989) *Theories of Mass Communication*, 5th edn. New York: Longman.

Delia, J.G. (1987) 'Communication research: a history', in S.H. Chaffee and C. Berger (eds), *Handbook of Communication Science*, pp. 20–98. Newbury Park, CA: Sage.

Deming, C.J. (1991) 'Hill Street Blues as narrative', in R. Avery and D. Eason (eds), *Critical Perspectives on Media and Society*, pp. 240–64. New York: Guilford.

Dennis, E., Gilmor, D. and Glasser, T. (eds) (1989) *Media Freedom and Accountability*. New York: Greenwood.

Dervin, B. (1987) 'The potential contribution of feminist scholarship to the field of communication', *Journal of Communication*, 37 (4): 107–14.

Dijk, J.A.G.M. van (1993) *De Netwerk maatschappij*. Houten, The Netherlands: Bohn Staflen von Loghum.

Dijk, J.A.G.M. van (1996) 'Models of democracy: behind the design and use of new media in politics', *The Public*, 3 (1): 43–56.

Dijk, J.A.G.M. van (1999) *Network Society: Social Aspects of New Media*. London: Sage.

Dijk, T. van (1983) 'Discourse analysis: its development and application to the structure of news', *Journal of Communication*, 33 (3): 20–43.

Dijk, T. van (1985) *Discourse and Communication*. Berlin: de Gruyter.

Dijk, T. van (1991) *Racism and the Press*. London: Routledge.

Dimmick, J. and Coit, P. (1982) 'Levels of analysis in mass media decision-making', *Communication Research*, 9 (1): 3–32.

Dimmick, J. and Rothenbuhler, E. (1984) 'The theory of the niche: quantifying competition among media industries', *Journal of Communication*, 34 (3): 103–19.

Docherty, T. (ed.) (1993) *Postmodernism*. New York: Harvester/Wheatsheaf.

Dominick, J.R., Wurtzel, A. and Lometti, G. (1975) 'TV journalism as show business: a content analysis of eyewitness news', *Journalism Quarterly*, 52: 213–18.

Donohue, G.A., Tichenor, P. and Olien, C.N. (1975) 'Mass media and the knowledge gap', *Communication Research*, 2: 3–23.

Donohew, L., Palmgreen, P. and Rayburn, J.D. (1987) 'Social and psychological origins of media use: a lifestyle analysis', *Journal of Broadcasting and Electronic Media*, 31 (3): 255–78.

Donsbach, W. (1983) 'Journalists' conception of their role', *Gazette*, 32 (1): 19–36.

Doob, A. and McDonald, G.E. (1979) 'Television viewing and the fear of victimization: is the relationship causal?', *Journal of Social Psychology and Personality*, 37: 170–9. Reprinted in G.C. Wilhoit and H. de Back (eds), *Mass Communication Review Yearbook*, Vol. 1, 1980, pp. 479–88. Beverly Hills: Sage.

Dorfman, A. and Mattelart, A. (1975) *How to Read Donald Duck: Imperialist Ideology in the Disney Comic*. New York: International General.

Dorman, W.A. (1997) 'Press theory and journalistic practice: the case of the Gulf War', in S. Iyengar and R. Reeves (eds), *Do the Media Govern?*, pp. 118–25. Thousand Oaks, CA: Sage.

Downing, J. (1984) *Radical Media*. Boston, MA: South End Press.

Dreier, P. (1982) 'The position of the press in the US power structure', *Social Problems*, 29 (3): 298–310.

Drotner, K. (1992) 'Modernity and media panics', in M. Skovmand and K. Schrøder (eds), *Media Cultures*, pp. 42–62. London: Routledge.

Dupagne, M. and Waterman, D. (1998) 'Determinants of US TV fiction imports in West Europe', *Journal of Broadcasting and Electronic Media*, 42 (2): 208–20.

Dutton, W.H., Blumler, J.G. and Kraemar, K.L. (eds) (1986) *Wired Cities: Shaping the Future of Communications*. Boston, MA: G.K. Hall.

Eastman, S.T. (1979) 'Uses of television and consumer lifestyles: a multivariate analysis', *Journal of Broadcasting*, 23 (3): 491–500.

Eastman, S.T. (1998) 'Programming theory under strain: the active industry and the active audience', in M.E. Roloff and G.D. Paulson (eds), *Communication Yearbook 21*, pp. 323–77. Thousand Oaks, CA: Sage.

Eco, U. (1977) *A Theory of Semiotics*. London: Macmillan.

Eco, U. (1979) *The Role of the Reader*. Bloomington, IN: University of Indiana Press.

Eisenstein, E. (1978) *The Printing Press as an Agent of Change*, 2 vols. New York: Cambridge University Press.

Elliott, P. (1972) *The Making of a Television Series – a Case Study in the Production of Culture*. London: Constable.

Elliott, P. (1974) 'Uses and gratifications research: a critique and a sociological alternative', in J.G. Blumler and E. Katz (eds), The *Uses of Mass Communications*, pp. 249–68. Beverly Hills, CA: Sage.

Elliott, P. (1977) 'Media organizations and occupations – an overview', in J. Curran et al. (eds), *Mass Communication and Society*, pp. 142–73. London: Edward Arnold.

Elliott, P. (1982) 'Intellectuals, the "information society" and the disappearance of the public sphere', *Media, Culture and Society*, 4: 243–53.

Ellis, J. (1982) *Visible Fictions*. London: Routledge and Kegan Paul.

Emmett, B.P. (1968) 'A new role for research in broadcasting', *Public Opinion Quarterly*, 32: 654–65.

Engwall, L. (1978) *Newspapers as Organizations*. Farnborough, Hants: Saxon House.

Ennis, P.H. (1961) 'The social structure of communication systems', *Studies in Public Communication*, 3: 120–44.

Entman, R.M. (1989) *Democracy without Citizens: Media and the Decay of American Politics*. New York: Oxford University Press.

Entman, R.M. (1993) 'Framing: towards clarification of a fractured paradigm', *Journal of Communication* 43 (4): 51–8.

Enzensberger, H.M. (1970) 'Constituents of a theory of the media', *New Left Review*, 64: 13–36. Also in D. McQuail (ed.), *Sociology of Mass Communications*, pp. 99–116. Harmondsworth: Penguin.

Ericson, R.V., Baranek, P.M. and Chan, J.B.L. (1987) *Visualizing Deviance*. Toronto: University of Toronto Press.

Ettema, J.S. and Whitney, D.C. (eds) (1982) *Individuals in Mass Media Organizations*. Beverly Hills, CA: Sage.

Ettema, J.S. and Whitney, D.C., with Wackman, D.B. (1987) 'Professional mass communicators', in C. Berger and S.H. Chaffee (eds), *Handbook of Communication Science*, pp. 747–80. Beverly Hills, CA: Sage.

Ettema, J.S. and Whitney, D.C. (eds) (1994) *Audiencemaking: How the Media Create the Audience*. Thousand Oaks, CA: Sage.

Etzioni, A. (1961) *Complex Organizations*. Glencoe, IL: Free Press.

European Commission (1999) *Images of Women in the Media*. Luxembourg: European Commission.

Fallows, J. (1996) *Breaking the News*. New York: Pantheon.

Febvre, L. and Martin, H.J. (1984) *The Coming of the Book*. London: Verso.

Feilitzen, C. von (1976) 'The functions served by the mass media', in J.W. Brown (ed.), *Children and Television*, pp. 90–115. London: Collier-Macmillan.

Feintuck, M. (1999) *Media Regulation, Public Interest and the Law*. Edinburgh: University of Edinburgh Press.

Ferguson, M. (1983) *Forever Feminine: Women's Magazines and the Cult of Femininity*. London: Heinemann.

Ferguson, M. (1986) 'The challenge of neo-technological determinism for communication systems of industry and culture', in M. Ferguson (ed.), *New Communication Technologies and the Public Interest*, pp. 52–70. London: Sage.

Ferguson, M. (ed.) (1990) *Public Communication: the New Imperatives*. London: Sage.

Ferguson, M. (ed.) (1992) 'The mythology about globalization', *European Journal of Communication*, 7: 69–93.

Ferguson, M. and Golding, P. (1997) *Cultural Studies in Question*. London: Sage.

Festinger, L.A. (1957) *A Theory of Cognitive Dissonance*. New York: Row Peterson.

Findahl, O. and Hoijer, B. (1981) 'Studies of news from the perspective of human comprehension', in G.C. Wilhoit and H. de Back (eds), *Mass Communication Review Yearbook*, Vol. 2, pp. 393–403. Beverly Hills, CA: Sage.

Findahl, O. and Hoijer, B. (1985) 'Some characteristics of news memory and comprehension', *Journal of Broadcasting and Electronic Media*, 29 (4): 379–98.

Fink, E.J. and Gantz, W. (1996) 'A content analysis of three mass communication research traditions: social science; interpretive studies; and critical analysis', *Journalism and Mass Communication Quarterly*, 73 (1): 114–34.

Finn, S. (1997) 'Origins of media exposure: linking personality traits to TV, radio, print and film use', *Communication Research*, 24 (5); 507–29.

Finn, S. and Gomm, M.B. (1988) 'Social isolation and social support as correlates of television viewing motivations', *Communication Research*, 15 (2): 135–58.

Fishman, J. (1980) *Manufacturing News*. Austin, TX: University of Texas Press.

Fishman, M. (1982) 'News and non-events: making the visible invisible', in J.S. Ettema and D.C. Whitney (eds), *Individuals in Mass Media Organizations*, pp. 219–40. Beverly Hills, CA: Sage.

Fiske, J. (1982) *Introduction to Communication Studies*. London: Methuen.

Fiske, J. (1987) *Television Culture*. London: Methuen.

Fiske, J. (1989) *Reading the Popular*. Boston, MA: Unwin and Hyman.

Fiske, J. (1992) 'The cultural economy of fandom', in L. Lewis (ed.), *The Adoring Audience*, pp. 30–49. London: Routledge.

Fjaestad, B. and Holmlov, P.G. (1976) 'The journalist's view', *Journal of Communication*, 2: 108–14.

Flegel, R.C. and Chaffee, S.H. (1971) 'Influences of editors, readers and personal opinion on reporters', *Journalism Quarterly*, 48: 645–51.

Frank, R.E. and Greenberg, B. (1980) *The Public's View of Television*. Beverly Hills, CA: Sage.

French, J.R.P. and Raven, B.H. (1953) 'The bases of social power', in D. Cartwright and A. Zander (eds), *Group Dynamics*, pp. 259–69. London: Tavistock.

Frick, F.C. (1959) 'Information theory', in S. Koch (ed.), *Psychology: A Study of a Science*, pp. 611–36. New York: McGraw-Hill.

Friedson, E. (1953) 'Communications research and the concept of the mass', *American Sociological Review*, 18 (3): 313–17.

Frissen, V. (1992) 'Trapped in electronic cages? Gender and new information technology', *Media, Culture and Society*, 14: 31–50.

Frith, S. (1981) *Sound Effects*. New York: Pantheon.

Gallagher, M. (1981) *Unequal Opportunities: the Case of Women and the Media*. Paris: UNESCO.

Galtung, J. and Ruge, M. (1965) 'The structure of foreign news', *Journal of Peace Research*, 1: 64–90. Also in J. Tunstall (ed.), *Media Sociology*, pp. 259–98. London: Constable.

Gamson, W. and Modigliani, A. (1989) 'Media discourse and public opinion on nuclear power: a constructivist approach', *American Journal of Sociology*, 95: 1–37.

Gandy, O. (1982) *Beyond Agenda Setting*. Norwood, NJ: Ablex.

Gandy, O. (1989) 'The surveillance society: information technologies and bureaucratic social control', *Journal of Communication*, 39 (3): 61–76.

Gans, H.J. (1957) 'The creator-audience relationship in the mass media', in B. Rosenberg and D.M. White (eds), *Mass Culture*, pp. 315–24. New York: Free Press.

Gans, H.J. (1979) *Deciding What's News*. New York: Vintage Books.

Garnham, N. (1979) 'Contribution to a political economy of mass communication', *Media, Culture and Society*, 1 (2): 123–46.

Garnham, N. (1986) 'The media and the public sphere', in P. Golding and G. Murdock (eds), *Communicating Politics*, pp. 37–54. Leicester: Leicester University Press.

Gaziano, C. (1983) 'The "knowledge gap": an analytical review of media effects', *Communication Research*, 10 (4): 447–86.

Gaziano, C. (1989) 'Chain newspaper homogeneity and presidential endorsements 1971–1988', *Journalism Quarterly*, 66 (4): 836–45.

Gaziano, C. (1997) 'Forecast 2000: widening knowledge gaps', *Journalism and Mass Communication Quarterly*, 74 (2): 237–64.

Gaziano, C. and McGrath, K. (1987) 'Newspaper credibility and relationships of newspaper journalists to communities', *Journalism Quarterly*, 64 (2): 317–28.

Geiger, K. and Sokol, R. (1959) 'Social norms in watching television', *American Journal of Sociology*, 65 (3): 178–81.

Geis, M.L. (1987) *The Language of Politics*. Berlin: Springer.

Geraghty, C. (1991) *Women and Soap Operas*. Cambridge: Polity.

Gerbner, G. (1964) 'Ideological perspectives and political tendencies in news reporting', *Journalism Quarterly*, 41: 495–506.

Gerbner, G. (1967) 'Mass media and human communication theory', in F.E.X. Dance (ed.), *Human Communication Theory*, pp. 40–57. New York: Holt, Rinehart and Winston.

Gerbner, G. (1969) 'Institutional pressures on mass communicators', in P. Halmos (ed.), *The Sociology of Mass Media Communicators*, pp. 205–48. Keele: University of Keele.

Gerbner, G. (1973) 'Cultural indicators – the third voice', in G. Gerbner, L. Gross and W. Melody (eds), *Communications Technology and Social Policy*, pp. 553–73. New York: Wiley.

Gerbner, G. (1995) 'Marketing Global Mayhem', *The Public*, 2 (2): 71–6.

Gerbner, G. and Marvanyi, G. (1977) 'The many worlds of the world's press', *Journal of Communication*, 27 (1): 52–66.

Gerbner, G., Gross, L., Morgan, M. and Signorielli, N. (1984) 'The political correlates of TV viewing', *Public Opinion Quarterly*, 48: 283–300.

Giddens, A. (1991) *Modernity and Self-Identity*. Oxford: Polity.

Gieber, W. (1956) 'Across the desk: a study of 16 Telegraph editors', *Journalism Quarterly*, 33: 423–33.

Gieber, W. and Johnson, W. (1961) 'The City Hall beat: a study of reporter and source roles', *Journalism Quarterly*, 38: 289–97.

Giffard, C.A. (1989) *UNESCO and the Media*. White Plains, NY: Longman.

Giner, S. (1976) *Mass Society*. London: Martin Robertson.

Gitlin, T. (1978) 'Media sociology: the dominant paradigm', *Theory and Society*, 6: 205–53. Reprinted in G.C. Wilhoit and H. de Back (eds), *Mass Communication Review Yearbook*, Vol. 2, 1981, pp. 73–122. Beverly Hills, CA: Sage.

Gitlin, T. (1980) *The Whole World Is Watching – Mass Media in the Making and Unmaking of the New Left*. Berkeley, CA: University of California Press.

Gitlin, T. (1989) 'Postmodernism: roots and politics', in I. Angus and S. Jhally (eds), *Cultural Politics in Contemporary America*, pp. 347–60. New York: Routledge.

Gitlin, T. (1997) 'The anti-political populism of cultural studies', in M. Ferguson and P. Golding (eds), *Cultural Studies in Question*, pp. 25–38. London: Sage.

Glasgow Media Group (1976) *Bad News*. London: Routledge and Kegan Paul.

Glasgow Media Group (1980) *More Bad News*. London: Routledge and Kegan Paul.

Glasgow Media Group (1985) *War and Peace News*. Milton Keynes: Open University Press.

Glasser, T. (1984) 'Competition among Radio Formats', *Journal of Broadcasting*, 28 (2): 127–42.

Glasser, T. (1986) 'Press responsibility and First Amendment values', in D. Eliott (ed.), *Responsible Journalism*, pp. 81–9. Newbury Park, CA: Sage.

Glasser, T.L. (ed.) (1999) *The Idea of Public Journalism*. New York: Guilford Press.

Glasser, T.L. and Craft, S. (1997) 'Public journalism and the search for democratic ideals'. Stanford, CA: Stanford University Department of Communication.

Glenn, T.C., Sallot, L.M. and Curtin, P.A. (1997) 'Public relations and the production of news'. In *Communication Yearbook, 20*, pp. 111–15. Thousand Oaks, CA: Sage.

Glynn, C.J., Hayes, A.F. and Shanahan, J. (1997) 'Perceived support for one's opinion and willingness to speak out', *Public Opinion Quarterly*, 61 (3): 452–63.

Goffman, E. (1974) *Frame Analysis: an Essay on the Organization of Experience*. New York: Harper and Row.

Goffman, E. (1976) *Gender Advertisements*. London: Macmillan.

Golding, P. (1977) 'Media professionalism in the Third World: the transfer of an ideology', in J. Curran, M. Gurevitch and J. Woollacott (eds), *Mass Communication and Society*, pp. 291–308. London: Arnold.

Golding, P. (1981) 'The missing dimensions: news media and the management of change', in E. Katz and T. Szecskb (eds), *Mass Media and Social Change*. London: Sage.

Golding, P. (1990) 'Political communication and citizenship', in M. Ferguson (ed.), *Public Communication: The New Imperatives*, pp. 84–100. London: Sage.

Golding, P. and Elliott, P. (1979) *Making the News*. London: Longman.

Golding, P. and Harris, P. (1998) *Beyond Cultural Imperialism*. London: Sage.

Golding, P. and Middleton, S. (1982) *Images of Welfare – Press and Public Attitudes to Poverty*. Oxford: Blackwell and Martin Robertson.

Golding, P. and Murdock, G. (1978) 'Theories of communication and theories of society', *Communication Research*, 5 (3): 339–56.

Golding, P. and Murdock, G. (1996) 'Culture, communications and political economy', in J. Curran and M. Gurevitch (eds), *Mass Media and Society*, pp. 11–30. London: Edward Arnold.

Golding, P. and Snippenburg, L. van (1995) 'Government communications and the media', in *Beliefs in Government*, Vol. 30. London: Oxford University Press.

Goodhart, G.J., Ehrenberg, A.S.C. and Collins, M. (1975) *The Television Audience: Patterns of Viewing*. Westmead: Saxon House.

Gould, P., Johnson, J. and Chapman, G. (1984) *The Structure of Television*. London: Pion.

Gouldner, A. (1976) *The Dialectic of Ideology and Technology*. London: Macmillan.

Graber, D. (1976a) 'Press and television as opinion resources in presidential campaigns', *Public Opinion Quarterly*, 40 (3): 285–303.

Graber, D. (1976b) *Verbal Behavior and Politics*. Urbana, IL: University of Illinois Press.

Graber, D. (1981) 'Political language', in D.D. Nimmo and D. Sanders (eds), *Handbook of Political Communication*, pp. 195–224. Beverly Hills, CA: Sage.

Graber, D. (1984) *Processing the News*. New York: Longman.

Gramsci, A. (1971) *Selections from the Prison Notebooks*. London: Lawrence and Wishart.

Green, S. (1999) 'A plague on the panopticon: surveillance and power in the global information society', *Information, Communication and Society*, 2 (1): 26–44.

Greenberg, B.S. (1964) 'Person-to-person communication in the diffusion of a news event', *Journalism Quarterly*, 41: 489–94.

Gringras, C. (1997) *The Laws of the Internet*. London: Butterworths.

Gripsrud, J. (1989) 'High culture revisited', *Cultural Studies*, 3 (2): 194–7.

Groebel, J. (1998) 'The UNESCO global study on media violence', in U. Carlsson and C. von Feilitzen (eds), *Children and Media Violence*, pp. 155–80. Göteborg: University of Göteborg.

Gross, L.P. (1977) 'Television as a Trojan horse', *School Media Quarterly*, Spring: 175–80.

Grossberg, L. (1989) 'MTV: swinging on the (postmodern) star', in I. Angus and S. Jhally (eds), *Cultural Politics in Contemporary Politics*, pp. 254–68. New York: Routledge.

Grossberg, L. (1991) 'Strategies of Marxist cultural interpretation', in R.K. Avery and D. Eason (eds), *Critical Perspectives on Media and Society*, pp. 126–59. New York and London: Guilford.

Grossberg, L., Wartella, E. and Whitney, D.C. (1998) *MediaMaking: Mass Media in a Popular Culture*. Thousand Oaks, CA: Sage.

Grossman, M.B. and Kumar, M.J. (1981) *Portraying the President*. Baltimore, MD: Johns Hopkins University Press.

Gunter, B. (1987) *Poor Reception: Misunderstanding and Forgetting Broadcast News*. Hillsdale, NJ: Laurence Erlbaum.

Gunter, B. (1999) 'Television news and the audience in Europe', *The European Journal of Communication Research*, 24 (1): 5–38.

Gunter, B. and Winstone, P. (1993) *Public Attitudes to Television*, London: John Libbey.

Gunther, A.C. (1998) 'The persuasive press inference: effects of the media on perceived public opinion', *Communication Research*, 25 (5): 486–504.

Gurevitch, M. and Levy, M. (1986) 'Information and meaning: audience explanations of social issues', in J.P. Robinson and M. Levy (eds), *The Main Source*, pp. 159–75. Beverly Hills, CA: Sage.

Gurevitch, M., Bennet, T., Curran, J. and Woollacott, J. (1982) (eds) *Culture, Society and the Media*. London: Methuen.

Habermas, J. (1989/1962) *The Structural Transformation of the Public Sphere*. Cambridge, MA: MIT Press.

Hachten, W.A. (1981) *The World News Prism: Changing Media, Changing Ideologies*. Ames, IA: Iowa State University Press.

Hackett, R.A. (1984) 'Decline of a paradigm? Bias and objectivity in news media studies', *Critical Studies in Mass Communication*, 1: 229–59.

Hagen, E. (1962) *On the Theory of Social Change*. Homewood, IL: Dorsey Press.

Hagen, I. (1999) 'Slaves of the ratings tyranny? Media images of the audience', in Alasuutari, P. (ed.), *Rethinking the Media Audience*, pp. 130–50. London: Sage.

Hall, S. (1973) 'The determination of news photographs', in S. Cohen and J. Young (eds), *The Manufacture of News*, pp. 176–90. London: Constable.

Hall, S. (1977) 'Culture, the media and the ideological effect', in J. Curran et al. (eds), *Mass Communication and Society*, pp. 315–48. London: Edward Arnold.

Hall, S. (1980) 'Coding and encoding in the television discourse', in S. Hall et al. (eds), *Culture, Media, Language*, pp. 197–208. London: Hutchinson.

Hall, S. (1982) 'The rediscovery of ideology: return of the repressed in media studies', in M. Gurevitch et al. (eds), *Culture, Society and the Media*, pp. 56–90. London: Methuen.

Hall, S. (1989) 'Ideology and communication theory', in B. Dervin et al. (eds), *Rethinking Communication*, Vol. 1: *Paradigm Issues*, pp. 40–52. Newbury Park, CA: Sage.

Hall, S. and Jefferson, T. (1975) *Resistance through Rituals*. London: Hutchinson.

Hall, S., Clarke, J., Critcher, C., Jefferson, T. and Roberts, B. (1978) *Policing the Crisis*. London: Macmillan.

Hallin, D.C. (1992) 'Sound bite news: TV coverage of elections 1968–1988', *Journal of Communication*, 42 (2): 5–24.

Hallin, D.C. and Mancini, P. (1984) 'Political structure and representational form in US and Italian TV news', *Theory and Society*, 13 (40): 829–50.

Halloran, J.D., Elliott, P. and Murdock, G. (1970) *Communications and Demonstrations*. Harmondsworth: Penguin.

Hamelink, C. (1983) *Cultural Autonomy in Global Communications*. Norwood, NJ: Ablex.

Hamelink, C.J. (1998) 'New realities in the politics of world communication', *The Public*, 5 (4): 71–4.

Handel, L. (1950) *Hollywood Looks at its Audience*. Urbana, IL: University of Illinois Press.

Hardt, H. (1979) *Social Theories of the Press: Early German and American Perspectives*. Beverly Hills, CA: Sage.

Hardt, H. (1991) *Critical Communication Studies*. London and New York: Routledge.

Harris, N.G.E. (1992) 'Codes of conduct for journalists', in A. Belsey and R. Chadwick (eds), *Ethical Issues in Journalism*, pp. 62–76. London: Routledge.

Hartley, J. (1992) *The Politics of Pictures*. London: Routledge.

Hartman, P. and Husband, C. (1974) *Racism and Mass Media*. London: Davis Poynter.

Harvey, D. (1989) *The Condition of Postmodernity*. Oxford: Blackwell.

Hasebrink, U. von (1997) 'In search of patterns of individual media use', in U. Carlsson (ed.), *Beyond Media Uses and Effects*, pp. 99–112. Göteborg University: Nordicom.

Hawkes, T. (1977) *Structuralism and Semiology*. London: Methuen.

Hawkins, R.P. and Pingree, S. (1983) 'TV's influence on social reality', in E. Wartrella et al. (eds), *Mass Communication Review Year Book*, Vol. 4, pp. 53–76. Beverly Hills, CA: Sage.

Hebdige, D. (1978) *Subculture: the Meaning of Style*. London: Methuen.

Hedinsson, E. (1981) *Television, Family and Society – the Social Origins and Effects of Adolescent TV Use*. Stockholm: Almqvist and Wiksell.

Heeter, C. (1988) 'The choice process model', in C. Heeter and B.S. Greenberg (eds), *Cable Viewing*, pp. 11–32. Norwood, NJ: Ablex.

Heinderyckx, F. (1993) 'TV news programmes in West Europe: a comparative study', *European Journal of Communication*, 8 (4): 425–50.

Held, V. (1970) *The Public Interest and Individual Interests*. New York: Basic Books.

Hemánus, P. (1976) 'Objectivity in news transmission', *Journal of Communication*, 26: 102–7.

Hemel, van, A. (ed.) (1996) *Trading Culture: Gatt, European Cultural Policies and the Transatlantic Market*. Amsterdam: Boekmansstichting.

Herman, E. and Chomsky, N. (1988) *Manufacturing Consent: the Political Economy of Mass Media*. New York: Pantheon.

Hermes, J. (1995) *Reading Womens' Magazines*. Cambridge: Polity.

Hermes, J. (1997) 'Gender and media studies: no woman, no cry', in J. Corner, P. Schlesinger and R. Silverstone (eds), *International Media Research*, pp. 65–95. London: Routledge.

Hermes, J. (1999) 'Media figures in identity construction', in P. Alasuutari (ed.) *Rethinking the Media Audience*, pp. 69–85. London: Sage.

Herzog, H. (1944) 'What do we really know about daytime serial listeners?', in P.F. Lazarsfeld (ed.), *Radio Research 1942–3*, pp. 2–23. New York: Duell, Sloan and Pearce.

Hessler, R.C. and Stipp, H. (1985) 'The impact of fictional suicide stories on US fatalities: a replication', *American Journal of Sociology*, 90 (1): 151–67.

Hetherington, A. (1985) *News, Newspapers and Television*. London: Macmillan.

Himmelweit, H.T., Vince, P. and Oppenheim, A.N. (1958) *Television and the Child*. London: Oxford University Press.

Hirsch, F. and Gordon, D. (1975) *Newspaper Money*. London: Hutchinson.

Hirsch, P.M. (1973) 'Processing fads and fashions: an organization-set analysis of culture industry systems', *American Journal of Sociology*, 77: 639–59.

Hirsch, P.M. (1977) 'Occupational, organizational and institutional models in mass communication', in P.M. Hirsch et al. (eds), *Strategies for Communication Research*, pp. 13–42. Beverly Hills, CA: Sage.

Hirsch, P.M. (1980) 'The "scary world" of the non-viewer and other anomalies – a reanalysis of gerbner et al.'s findings in Cultivation Analysis, Part 1', *Communication Research*, 7 (4): 403–56.

Hirsch, P.M. (1981) 'On not learning from one's mistakes, Part II', *Communication Research*, 8 (1): 3–38.

Hobson, D. (1982) *Crossroads: The Drama of Soap Opera*. London: Methuen.

Hobson, D. (1989) 'Soap operas at work', in F. Seiter et al. (eds), *Remote Control*, pp. 130–49. London: Routledge.

Hocking, W.E. (1947) *Freedom of The Press: a Framework of Principle*. Chicago: University of Chicago Press.

Hodges, L.W. (1986) 'Defining press responsibility: a functional approach', in D. Elliot (ed.), *Responsible Journalism*, pp. 13–31. Beverly Hills, CA: Sage.

Hoffmann-Riem, W. (1996) *Regulating Media*. London: Guilford.

Holden, R.T. (1986) 'The contagiousness of aircraft hijacking', *American Journal of Sociology*, 91 (4): 876–904.

Holub, R. (1984) *Reception Theory*. London: Methuen.

Horton, D. and Wohl, R.R. (1956) 'Mass communication and para-social interaction', *Psychiatry*, 19: 215–29.

Hoskins, C. and Mirus, R. (1988) 'Reasons for the US dominance of the international trade in television programmes', *Media, Culture and Society*, 10: 499–515.

Hovland, C.I., Lumsdaine, A.A. and Sheffield, F.D. (1949) *Experiments in Mass Communication*. Princeton, NJ: Princeton University Press.

Huaco, G.A. (1963) *The Sociology of Film Art*. New York: Basic Books.

Huesmann, L.R. (1986) 'Psychological processes prompting the relation between exposure to

media violence and aggressive behavior by the viewer', *Journal of Social Issues*, 42 (3): 125–39.

Hughes, H.M. (1940) *News and the Human Interest Story*. Chicago: University of Chicago Press.

Hughes, M. (1980) 'The fruits of cultivation analysis: a re-examination of some effects of TV viewing', *Public Opinion Quarterly*, 44 (3): 287–302.

Hutchins, R. (1947) 'Commission on freedom of the press', *A Free and Responsible Press*. Chicago: University of Chicago Press.

Hyman, H. and Sheatsley, P. (1947) 'Some reasons why information campaigns fail', *Public Opinion Quarterly*, II: 412–23.

Innis, H. (1950) *Empire and Communication*. Oxford: Clarendon Press.

Innis, H. (1951) *The Bias of Communication*. Toronto: University of Toronto Press.

Ishikawa, S. (ed.) (1996) *Quality Assessment of Television*. Luton: Luton University Press.

Ito, Y. (1981) 'The "Johoka Shakai" approach to the study of communication in Japan', in G.C. Wilhoit and H. de Bock (eds), *Mass Communication Review Yearbook*, Vol. 2. Beverly Hills, CA: Sage.

Ito, Y. and Koshevar, I.J. (1983) 'Factors accounting for the flow of international communications', *Keio Communication Review*, 4: 13–38.

Iyengar, S. and Kinder, D.R. (1987) *News That Matters: Television and American Opinion*. Chicago: University of Chicago Press.

Iyengar, S. and Simon, A. (1997) 'News coverage of the Gulf crisis and public opinion', in S. Iyengar and R. Reeves (eds), *Do the Media Govern?*, pp. 248–57. Thousand Oaks, CA: Sage.

Jackson, I. (1971) *The Provincial Press and the Community*. Manchester: Manchester University Press.

Jakubowitz, K. (1995) 'Poland: what mix of continuity and change?', *The Public*, 2 (3): 61–80.

Jameson, F. (1984) 'Postmodernism: the cultural logic of late capitalism', *New Left Review*, 146 (July–August): 53–92.

Jankowski, N., Prehn, O. and Stappers, J. (eds) (1992), *The People's Voice*. London: John Libbey.

Janowitz, M. (1952) *The Community Press in an Urban Setting*. Glencoe, IL: Free Press.

Janowitz, M. (1968) 'The study of mass communication', in *International Encyclopedia of the Social Sciences*, Vol. 3, pp. 41–53. New York: Macmillan and Free Press.

Janowitz, M. (1975) 'Professional models in journalism: the gatekeeper and advocate', *Journalism Quarterly*, 52 (4): 618–26.

Jansen, S.C. (1988) *Censorship*. New York: Oxford University Press.

Jay, M. (1973) *The Dialectical Imagination*. London: Heinemann.

Jensen, K.B. (1986) *Making Sense of the News*. Aarhus: Aarhus University Press.

Jensen, K.B. (1991) 'When is meaning? Communication theory, pragmatism and mass media reception', in J. Anderson (ed.), *Communication Yearbook 14*, pp. 3–32. Newbury Park, CA: Sage.

Jensen, K.B. (1998) 'Local empiricism, global theory: problems and potentials of comparative research on news reception', *The European Journal of Communication Research*, 23 (4): 427–45.

Jensen, K.B. and Jankowski, N. (eds) (1991) *A Handbook of Qualitative Methodologies*. London: Routledge.

Jensen, K.B. and Rosengren, K.E. (1990) 'Five traditions in search of the audience', *European Journal of Communication*, 5 (2/3): 207–38.

Jhally, S. and Livant, B. (1986) 'Watching as working: the valorization of audience conscious-ness', *Journal of Communication*, 36 (2): 124–63.

Johansson, T. and Miegel, F. (1992) *Do the Right Thing*. Stockholm: Almqvist and Wiksell International.

Johnstone, J.W.L., Slawski, E.J. and Bowman, W.W. (1976) *The News People*. Urbana, IL: University of Illinois Press.

Jones, S.G. (ed.) (1997) *Virtual Culture: Identity and Communication in Cybersociety*. London: Sage.

Jones, S.G. (ed.) (1998) *Cybersociety 2.0: Revisiting Computer-Mediated Communication and Community*. London: Sage.

Jowett, G. and Linton, J.M. (1980) *Movies as Mass Communication*. Beverly Hills, CA: Sage.

Jowett, G. and O'Donnell, V. (1986) *Propaganda and Persuasion*. Beverly Hills. CA: Sage.

Kaminsky, S.M. (1974) *American Film Genres*. Dayton, OH: Pflaum.

Kaplan, E.A. (1987) *Rocking Around the Clock: Music Television, Postmodernism and Con-sumer Culture*. London: Methuen.

Kaplan, E.A. (1992) 'Feminist critiques and television', in R.C. Allen (ed.), *Channels of Discourse Reassembled*, pp. 247–83. London: Routledge.

Katz, D. (1960) 'The functional approach to the study of attitudes', *Public Opinion Quarterly*, 24: 163–204.

Katz, E. (1977) *Social Research and Broadcasting: Proposals for Further Development*. London: BBC.

Katz, E. (1983) 'Publicity and pluralistic ignorance: notes on the spiral of silence', in E. Wartella et al. (eds), *Mass Communication Review Yearbook*, Vol. 4, pp. 89–99. Beverly Hills, CA: Sage.

Katz, E. and Lazarsfeld, P.F. (1955) *Personal Influence*. Glencoe, IL: Free Press.

Katz, E., Lewin, M.L. and Hamilton, H. (1963) 'Traditions of research on the diffusion of innovations', *American Sociological Review*, 28: 237–52.

Katz, E., Gurevitch, M. and Haas, H. (1973) 'On the use of mass media for important things', *American Sociological Review*, 38: 164–81.

Katz, E., Blumler, J.G. and Gurevitch, M. (1974) 'Utilization of mass communication by the individual', in J.G. Blumler and E. Katz (eds), *The Uses of Mass Communication*, pp. 19–32. Beverly Hills, CA: Sage.

Katz, E., Adoni, H. and Parness, P. (1977) 'Remembering the news – what the picture adds to the sound', *Journalism Quarterly*, 54: 231–9.

Keane, J. (1991) *The Media and Democracy*. Oxford: Polity.

Kellner, D. (1990) *Television and the Crisis of Democracy*. Boulder, CO: Westview.

Kellner, D. (1992) *The Persian Gulf War*. Boulder, CO: Westview.

Kelman, H. (1961) 'Processes of opinion change', *Public Opinion Quarterly*, 25: 57–78.

Kepplinger, H.M. (1983) 'Visual biases in TV Campaign coverage', in E. Wartella et al. (eds), *Mass Communication Review Yearbook*, Vol. 4, pp. 391–405. Beverly Hills, CA: Sage.

Kepplinger, H.M. and Habermeier, J. (1995) 'The impact of key events on the presentation of reality', *European Journal of Communication*, 10 (3): 371–90.

Kepplinger, H.M. and Koecher, R. (1990) 'Professionalism in the media world?', *European Journal of Communication*, 5 (2/3): 285–311.

Kerner, O. et al. (1968) *Report of the National Advisory Committee on Civil Disorders*. Washington, DC: GPO.

Key, V.O. (1961) *Public Opinion and American Democracy*. New York: Alfred Knopf.

Kingsbury, S.M. and Hart, M. (1937) *Newspapers and the News*. New York: Putnams.

Kivikuru, U. and Varis, T. (eds) (1985) *Approaches to International Communication*. Helsinki: Finnish National UNESCO Commission.

Klapper, J. (1960) *The Effects of Mass Communication*. New York: Free Press.

Kleinsteuber, H. and Sonnenberg, U. (1990) 'Beyond public service and private profit: international experience with non-commercial local radio', *European Journal of Communication*, 5 (1): 87–106.

Köcher, R. (1986) 'Bloodhounds or missionaries: role definitions of German and British journalists', *European Journal of Communication*, 1 (1): 43–64.

Kornhauser, W. (1968) 'The theory of mass society', in *International Encyclopedia of the Social Sciences*, Vol. 10, pp. 58–64. New York: Macmillan and Free Press.

Kracauer, S. (1949) 'National types as Hollywood represents them', *Public Opinion Quarterly*, 13: 53–72.

Kraus, S. and Davis, D.K. (1976) *The Effects of Mass Communication on Political Behavior*. University Park, PA: Pennsylvania State University Press.

Kraus, S., Davis, D.K., Lang, G.E. and Lang, K. (1975) 'Critical events analysis', in S.H. Chaffee (ed.), *Political Communication Research*, pp. 195–216. Beverly Hills, CA: Sage.

Krcmar, M. (1996) 'Family communication patterns, discourse behavior and child TV viewing', *Human Communication Research*, 23 (2): 251–77.

Krippendorf, K. (1980) *Content Analysis*. Beverly Hills, CA: Sage.

Krotz, F. and Hasebrink, U, von (1998) 'The analysis of people-meter data: individual patterns of viewing behavior and viewers' cultural background', *The European Journal of Communication Research*, 23 (2): 151–74.

Krugman, H.E. (1965) 'The impact of television advertising: learning without involvement', *Public Opinion Quarterly*, 29: 349–56.

Kubey, R.W. (1986) 'Television use in everyday life: coping with unstructured time', *Journal of Communication*, 36 (1): 108–23.

Kubey, R.W. and Csikszentmihalyi, M. (1991) *Television and the Quality of Life*. Hillsdale, NJ: Lawrence Erlbaum.

Kumar, C. (1975) 'Holding the middle ground', *Sociology*, 9 (3): 67–88. Reprinted in J. Curran et al. (eds), *Mass Communication and Society*, pp. 231–48. London: Edward Arnold.

Laitila, T. (1995) 'Journalistic codes of ethics in Europe', *European Journal of Communication*, 10 (4): 513–26.

Lang, G. and Lang, K. (1981) 'Mass communication and public opinion: strategies for research', in M. Rosenberg and R.H. Turner (eds), *Social Psychology: Sociological Perspectives*, pp. 653–82. New York: Basic Books.

Lang, G. and Lang, K. (1983) *The Battle for Public Opinion*. New York: Columbia University Press.

Lang, K. and Lang, G.E. (1953) 'The unique perspective of television and its effect', *American Sociological Review*, 18 (1): 103–12.

Lasswell, H. (1927) *Propaganda Techniques in the First World War*. New York: Alfred Knopf.

Lasswell, H. (1948) 'The structure and function of communication in society', in L. Bryson (ed.), *The Communication of Ideas*, pp. 32–51. New York: Harper.

Lauriston, M. and Vihalemm, P. (eds) (1997) *Return to the Western World*. Tartu: Tartu University Press.

Lazarsfeld, P.F. (1941) 'Remarks on administrative and critical communication research studies', *Philosophy and Social Science*, Vol. IX, No. 2.

Lazarsfeld, P.F. and Stanton, F. (1944) *Radio Research 1942–3*. New York: Duell, Sloan and Pearce.

Lazarsfeld, P.F. and Stanton, F. (1949) *Communication Research 1948–9*. New York: Harper and Row.

Lazarsfeld, P.F., Berelson, B. and Gaudet, H. (1944) *The People's Choice*. New York: Duell, Sloan and Pearce.

Leiss, W. (1989) 'The myth of the information society', in I. Angus and S. Jhally (eds), *Cultural Politics in Contemporary America*, pp. 282–98. New York: Routledge.

Lemert, J.B. (1989) *Criticizing the Media*. Newbury Park, CA: Sage.

Lerner, D. (1958) *The Passing of Traditional Society*. New York: Free Press.

Levy, M.R. (1977) 'Experiencing television news', *Journal of Communication*, 27: 112–17.

Levy, M.R. (1978) 'The audience experience with television news', *Journalism Monographs*, 55.

Levy, M. and Windahl, S. (1985) 'The concept of audience activity', in K.E. Rosengren et al. (eds), *Media Gratification Research*, pp. 109–22. Beverly Hills, CA: Sage.

Lewin, K. (1947) 'Channels of Group Life', *Human Relations*, 1: 143–53.

Lewis, G.H. (1981) 'Taste cultures and their composition: towards a new theoretical perspective', in E. Katz and T. Szecskö (eds), *Mass Media and Social Change*, pp. 201–17. Newbury Park, CA: Sage.

Lewis, G.H. (1992) 'Who do you love? The dimensions of musical taste', in J. Lull (ed.), *Popular Music and Communication*, 2nd edn, pp. 134–51. Newbury Park, CA: Sage.

Lewis, L. (ed.) (1992) *The Adoring Audience*. London: Routledge.

Lichtenberg, J. (1991) 'In defense of objectivity', in J. Curran and M. Gurevitch (eds), *Mass Media and Society*, pp. 216–31. London: Edward Arnold.

Lichter, S.R. and Rothman, S. (1986) *The Media Elite: America's New Power Brokers*. Bethesda, MD: Adler and Adler.

Liebes, T. and Katz, E. (1986) 'Patterns of involvement in television fiction: a comparative analysis', *European Journal of Communication*, 1 (2): 151–72.

Liebes, T. and Katz, E. (1989) 'Critical abilities of TV viewers', in F. Seiter et al. (eds), *Remote Control*, pp. 204–22. London: Routledge.

Liebes, T. and Katz, E. (1990) *The Export of Meaning: Cross-Cultural Readings of 'Dallas'*. Oxford: Oxford University Press.

Liebes, T. and Riback, R. (1994) 'In defense of negotiated readings: how moderates on each side of the conflict interpret Intifada news', *Journal of Communication*, 44 (2): 108–24.

Linden, A. (1998) *Communication Policies and Human Rights in Developing Countries*. Amsterdam: University of Amsterdam.

Lindlof, T. (1988) 'Media audiences as interpretive communities', in J. Anderson (ed.), *Communication Yearbook 11*, pp. 81–107. Newbury Park, CA: Sage.

Lindlof, T.R. and Shatzer, J. (1998) 'Media ethnography in virtual space: strategies, limits and possibilities', *Journal of Broadcasting and Electronic Media*, 42 (2): 170–89.

Linné, O. (1998) 'What do we know about European research on violence in the media', in U. Carlsson and C. von Feilitzen (eds), *Children and Media Violence*, pp. 139–54. Göteborg: University of Göteborg.

Lippmann, W. (1922) *Public Opinion*. New York: Harcourt Brace.

Livingstone, S. (1988) 'Why people watch soap opera: an analysis of the explanations of British viewers', *European Journal of Communication*, 31 (1): 55–80.

Livingstone, S. (1991) 'Audience reception: the role of the viewer in retelling romantic drama', in J. Curran and M. Gurevitch (eds), *Mass Media and Society*, pp. 285–306. London: Edward Arnold.

Livingstone, S. (1999) 'New media, new audiences?', *New Media and Society*, 1 (1): 59–66.

Livingstone, S. and Lunt, P. (1994) *Talk on Television: Audience Participation and Public Debate*. London: Routledge.

Long, E. (1991) 'Feminism and cultural studies', in R. Avery and D. Eason (eds), *Cultural Perspectives on Media and Society*, pp. 114–25. New York: Guilford.

Lowery, S.A. and DeFleur, M.L. (1995) *Milestones in Mass Communication Research*, 3rd edn. New York: Longman.

Lubbers, M., Scheeper, P. and Wester, F. (1998) 'Minorities in Dutch newspapers 1990–5', *Gazette*, 60 (5): 415–31.

Lull, J. (1982) 'The social uses of television', in D.C. Whitney et al. (eds), *Mass Communication Review Yearbook*, Vol. 3, pp. 397–409. Beverly Hills, CA: Sage.

Lull, J. (ed.) (1992) *Popular Music and Communication*. Newbury Park, CA: Sage.

Lull, J. and Wallis, R. (1992) 'The beat of Vietnam', in J. Lull (ed.), *Popular Music and Communication*, pp. 207–36. Newbury Park, CA: Sage.

Lyotard, F. (1986) *The Postmodern Condition: a Report on Knowledge*. Manchester: Manchester University Press.

McBride, S. et al. (1980) *Many Voices, One World*. Report by the International Commission for the Study of Communication Problems. Paris: UNESCO; London: Kogan Page.

McCombs, M.E. and Shaw, D.L. (1972) 'The agenda-setting function of the press', *Public Opinion Quarterly*, 36: 176–87.

McCombs, M.E. and Shaw, D.L. (1993) 'The evolution of agenda-setting theory: 25 years in the marketplace of ideas', *Journal of Communication*, 43 (2): 58–66.

McCormack, T. (1961) 'Social theory and the mass media', *Canadian Journal of Economics and Political Science*, 4: 479–89.

McCron, R. (1976) 'Changing perspectives in the study of mass media and socialization', in J. Halloran (ed.), *Mass Media and Socialization*, pp. 13–44. Leicester: International Association for Mass Communication Research.

McDonald, D.G. (1990) 'Media orientation and television news viewing', *Journalism Quarterly*, 67 (1): 11–20.

McGinnis, J. (1969) *The Selling of the President*. New York: Trident Press.

McGranahan, D.V. and Wayne, L. (1948) 'German and American traits reflected in popular drama', *Human Relations*, 1 (4): 429–55.

McGuigan, J. (1992) *Cultural Populism*. London: Routledge.

McGuire, W.J. (1973) 'Persuasion, resistance and attitude change', in I. de Sola Pool et al. (eds), *Handbook of Communication*, pp. 216–52. Chicago: Rand McNally.

McGuire, W.J. (1974) 'Psychological motives and communication gratifications', in J.G. Blumler and E. Katz (eds), *The Uses of Mass Communications*, pp. 167–96. Beverly Hills, CA: Sage.

McLelland, D.W. (1961) *The Achieving Society*. Princeton, NJ: Van Nostrand.

McLeod, J.M, Ward, L.S. and Tancill, K. (1965) 'Alienation and uses of mass media', *Public Opinion Quarterly*, 29: 583–94.

McLeod, J. and McDonald, D.G. (1985). 'Beyond simple exposure: media orientations and their impact on political processes', *Communication Research*, 12 (1): 3–32.

McLeod, J.M., Kosicki, G.M. and Pan, Z. (1991) 'On understanding and not understanding media effects', in J. Curran and M. Gurevitch (eds), *Mass Media and Society*, pp. 235–66. London: Edward Arnold.

McLeod, J.M., Daily, K., Guo, Z., Eveland, W.P., Bayer, J., Yang, S. and Wang, H. (1996) 'Community integration, local media use and democratic processes', *Communication Research*, 23 (2): 179–209.

McLuhan, M. (1962) *The Gutenberg Galaxy*. Toronto: Toronto University Press.

McLuhan, M. (1964) *Understanding Media*. London: Routledge and Kegan Paul.

McManus, J.H. (1994) *Market-Driven Journalism: Let the Citizen Beware*. Thousand Oaks, CA: Sage.

McNair, B. (1988) *Images of the Enemy*. London: Routledge.

McQuail, D. (ed.) (1972) *Sociology of Mass Communications*. Harmondsworth: Penguin.

McQuail, D. (1977) *Analysis of Newspaper Content*. Royal Commission on the Press, Research Series 4. London: HMSO.

McQuail, D. (1983) *Mass Communication Theory: an Introduction*. London: Sage.

McQuail, D. (1984) 'With the benefit of hindsight: reflections on uses and gratifications research', *Critical Studies in Mass Communication*, 1: 177–93.

McQuail, D. (1986) 'Is media theory adequate to the challenge of the new communications technologies?', in M. Ferguson (ed.), *New Communication Technologies and the Public Interest*, pp. 1–17. Beverly Hills, CA: Sage.

McQuail, D. (1992) *Media Performance: Mass Communication and the Public Interest*. London: Sage.

McQuail, D. (1996) 'Transatlantic TV flow: another look at cultural cost-accounting', in Hemel, A. van (ed.), *Trading Culture: Gatt, European Cultural policies and the Transatlantic Market*, pp. 111–25. Amsterdam: Boekmansstichting.

McQuail, D. and Siune, K. (1998) *Media Policy: Convergence, Concentration and Commerce*. London: Sage.

McQuail, D. and Windahl, S. (1993) *Communication Models*, 2nd edn. London: Longman.

McQuail, D., Blumler, J.G. and Brown, J. (1972) 'The television audience: a revised perspective', in D. McQuail (ed.), *Sociology of Mass Communication*, pp. 135–65. Harmondsworth: Penguin.

McRobbie, A. (1996) '*More!* New sexualities in girls' and women's magazines', in J. Curran, D. Morley and V. Walkerdine (eds), *Cultural Studies and Communications*, pp. 172–94. London: Arnold.

Maccoby, E. (1954) 'Why do children watch TV?', *Public Opinion Quarterly*, 18: 239–44.

Machlup, F. (1962) *The Production and Distribution of Knowledge in the United States*. Princeton, NJ: Princeton University Press.

Maisel, R. (1973) 'The decline of mass media', *Public Opinion Quarterly*, 37: 159–70.

Mancini, P. (1996) 'Do we need normative theories of journalism?', Paper, Joan Shorenstein Center on Press, Politics and Public Opinion, JFK School of Government, Harvard University.

Manheim, J.B. (1998) 'The news shapers: strategic communication as third force in news-making', in D. Graber, D. McQuail and P. Norris (eds), *The Politics of News: the News of Politics*, pp. 94–109. Washington, DC: Congressional Quarterly Press.

Marcuse, H. (1964) *One-Dimensional Man*. London: Routledge and Kegan Paul.

Martel, M.U. and McCall, G.J. (1964) 'Reality-orientation and the pleasure principle', in L.A. Dexter and D.M. White (eds), *People, Society and Mass Communication*, pp. 283–333. New York: Free Press.

Mazzoleni, G. (1987a) 'Mass telematics: facts and fiction', in D. McQuail and K. Siune (eds), *New Media Politics*, pp. 100–14. London: Sage.

Mazzoleni, G. (1987b) 'Media logic and party logic in campaign coverage: the Italian general election of 1983', *European Journal of Communication*, 2 (1): 55–80.

Media Studies Journal (1993) 'The media and women without apology', Special Issue, 7 (1): 1/2.

Melody, W.H. (1990) 'Communications policy in the global information economy', in M.F. Ferguson (ed.), *Public Communication: The New Imperatives*, pp. 16–39. London and Newbury Park, CA: Sage.

Mendelsohn, H. (1964) 'Listening to radio', in L.A. Dexter and D.M. White (eds), *People, Society and Mass Communication*, pp. 239–48. New York: Free Press.

Mendelsohn, H. (1966) *Mass Entertainment*. New Haven, CT: College and University Press.

Mendelsohn, H. (1973) 'Some reasons why information campaigns can succeed', *Public Opinion Quarterly*, 37: 50–61.

Mendelsohn, H. (1989) 'Phenomenistic alternatives', *Communication Research*, 16 (4): 82–7.

Merton, R.K. (1949) 'Patterns of influence', in *Social Theory and Social Structure*, pp. 387–470. Glencoe, IL: Free Press.

Merton, R.K. (1957) *Social Theory and Social Structure*. Glencoe, IL: Free Press.

Meyer, P. (1987) *Ethical Journalism*. New York: Longman.

Meyrowitz, J. (1985) *No Sense of Place*. New York: Oxford University Press.

Miliband, R. (1969) *The State in Capitalist Society*. London: Weidenfeld and Nicolson.

Mills, C.W. (1951) *White Collar*. New York: Oxford University Press.

Mills, C.W. (1956) *The Power Elite*. New York: Oxford University Press.

Mills, C.W. (1959) *The Sociological Imagination*. New York: Oxford University Press.

Modleski, T. (1982) *Loving with a Vengeance: Mass-Produced Fantasies for Women*. London: Methuen.

Molotch, H.L. and Lester, M.J. (1974) 'News as purposive behavior', *American Sociological Review*, 39: 101–12.

Monaco, J. (1981) *How to Read a Film*. New York: Oxford University Press.

Montgomery, K.C. (1989) *Target: Prime-Time*. New York: Oxford University Press.

Moores, S. (1993) *Interpreting Audiences*. London: Sage.

Morgan, M. and Shanahan, J. (1997) 'Two decades of cultivation research: an appraisal and meta-analysis', *Communication Yearbook 20*, pp. 1–46.

Morin, V. (1976) 'Televised current events sequences or a rhetoric of ambiguity', in *News and Current Events on TV*. Rome: Edizioni RAI.

Morley, D. (1980) *The 'Nationwide' Audience: Structure and Decoding*. BFI TV Monographs No. 11. London: British Film Institute.

Morley, D. (1986) *Family Television*. London: Comedia.

Morley, D. (1992) *Television, Audiences and Cultural Studies*. London: Routledge.

Morley, D. (1996) 'Postmodernism: the rough guide', in J. Curran, D. Morley and V. Walkerdine (eds), *Cultural Studies and Communication*, pp. 50–65. London: Arnold.

Morley, D. (1997) 'Theoretical orthodoxies: textualism, constructivism and the "new ethnography" in cultural studies', in M. Ferguson and P. Golding (eds), *Cultural Studies in Question*, pp. 121–37. London: Sage.

Morris, M. and Ogan, C. (1996) 'The Internet as mass medium', *Journal of Communication*, 46 (1): 39–50.

Morrison, D. and Tumber, H. (1988) *Journalists at War*. London: Sage.

Moscovici, S. (1991) 'Silent Majorities and loud minorities', in J. Anderson (ed.), *Communication Yearbook 14*, pp. 298–308. Newbury Park, CA: Sage.

Mowlana, H. (1985) *International Flows of Information*. Paris: UNESCO.

Mue, J. de, (1999) 'The informatization of the world view', *Information, Communication and Society*, 2 (1): 69–94.

Munson, W. (1993) *All Talk: the Talkshow in Media Culture*. Philadelphia: University of Temple Press.

Murdock, G. (1990) 'Redrawing the map of the communication industries', in M. Ferguson (ed.), *Public Communication*, pp. 1–15. London: Sage.

Murdock, G. and Golding, P. (1977) 'Capitalism, communication and class relations', in J. Curran et al. (eds), *Mass Communication and Society*, pp. 12–43. London: Edward Arnold.

Murdock, G. and Phelps, P. (1973) *Mass Media and the Secondary School*. London: Macmillan.

Murphy, D. (1976) *The Silent Watchdog*. London: Constable.

Mutz, D.C. and Soss, J. (1997) 'Reading public opinion: the influence of news coverage on perceptions of public sentiment', *Public Opinion Quarterly*, 61 (3): 431–51.

Negus, K. (1992) *Producing Pop*. London: Edward Arnold.

Nerone, J.C. (ed.) (1995) *Last Rights: Revisiting Four Theories of the Press*. Urbana and Chicago: University of Illinois Press.

Neuman, W.R. (1991) *The Future of the Mass Audience*. Cambridge: Cambridge University Press.

Neuman, W.R. and Pool, I. de Sola (1986). 'The flow of communication into the home', in

S. Ball-Rokeach and M. Cantor (eds), *Media, Audience and Social Structure*, pp. 71–86. Newbury Park, CA: Sage.

Newcomb, H. (1978) 'Assessing the violence profile on Gerbner and Gross: a humanistic critique and suggestion', *Communication Research, 5* (3): 264–82.

Newcomb, H. (1991) 'On the dialogic aspects of mass communication', in R. Avery and D. Easton (eds), *Critical Perspectives on Media and Society*, pp. 69–87. New York: Guilford.

Newhagen, J.E. and Reeves, B. (1992) 'The evening's bad news', *Journal of Communication*, 42 (2): 25–41.

Noam, E. (1991) *Television in Europe*. New York: Oxford University Press.

Noble, G. (1975) *Children in Front of the Small Screen*. London: Constable.

Noelle-Neumann, E. (1973) 'Return to the concept of powerful mass media', *Studies of Broadcasting*, 9: 66–112.

Noelle-Neumann, E. (1974) 'The spiral of silence: a theory of public opinion', *Journal of Communication*, 24: 24–51.

Noelle-Neumann, E. (1984) *The Spiral of Silence*. Chicago: University of Chicago Press.

Noelle-Neumann, E. (1991) 'The theory of public opinion: the concept of the spiral of silence', in J. Anderson (ed.), *Communication Yearbook 14*, pp. 256–87. Newbury Park, CA: Sage.

Nordenstreng, K. (1974) *Informational Mass Communication*. Helsinki: Tammi.

Nordenstreng, K. (1997) 'Beyond the four theories of the press', in J. Servaes and R. Lie (eds), *Media and Politics in Transition*. Leuven: Acco.

Nordenstreng, K. (1998) 'Professional ethics: between fortress journalism and cosmopolitan democracy', in K. Brants, J. Hermes and L. van Zoonen (eds), *The Media in Question*, pp. 124–34. London: Sage.

Nordicom Review (1992) 'The Gulf War in the media', Special Issue No. 2.

Nowak, K. (1977) 'From information caps to communication potential', in M. Berg et al. (eds), *Current Theories in Scandinavian Mass Communication*, pp. 230–58. Grenaa, Denmark: GMT.

Nowak, K. (1997) 'Effects no more?', in U. Carlsson (ed.), *Beyong Media Uses and Effects*, pp. 31–40. Göteborg University: Nordicom.

Ogden, C.K. and Richards, I.A. (1923) *The Meaning of Meaning*. Reprinted 1985. London: Routledge and Kegan Paul.

Okada, N. (1986) 'The process of mass communication: a review of studies of the two-step flow hypothesis', *Studies of Broadcasting*, 22: 57–78.

Olen, J. (1988) *Ethics in Journalism*. Englewood Cliffs, NJ: Prentice-Hall.

Oltean, O. (1993) 'Series and seriality in media culture', *European Journal of Communication*, 8 (1): 5–31.

Osgood, K., Suci, S. and Tannenbaum, P. (1957) *The Measurement of Meaning*. Urbana, IL: University of Illinois Press.

Padioleau, J. (1985) *Le Monde et le Washington Post*. Paris: PUF.

Paletz, D.L. and Dunn, R. (1969) 'Press coverage of civil disorders: a case-study of Winston-Salem', *Public Opinion Quarterly*, 33: 328–45.

Paletz, D.L. and Entman, R. (1981) *Media, Power, Politics*. New York: Free Press.

Paletz, D. and Schmid, A. (eds) (1992) *Terrorism and the Media*. Newbury Park, CA: Sage.

Paletz, D.L., Jakubowitz, K. and Novosel, P. (eds) (1995) *Glasnost and After*. Cresskill, NJ: Hampton Press.

Palmgreen, P. and Rayburn, J.D. (1985) 'An expectancy-value approach to media gratifications', in K.E. Rosengren et al. (eds), *Media Gratification Research*, pp. 61–72. Beverly Hills, CA: Sage.

Pan, Z. and Kosicki, G.M. (1997) 'Priming and media impact on the evaluation of the President's media perfomance', *Communication Research*, 24 (1): 3–30.

Park, R. (1940) 'News as a form of knowledge', in R.H. Turner (ed.), *On Social Control and Collective Behavior*, pp. 32 52. Chicago: Chicago University Press, 1967.

Parkin, F. (1972) *Class Inequality and Political Order*. London: Paladin.

Paterson, C. (1998) 'Global battlefields', in O. Boyd-Barrett and T. Rantanen (eds), *The Gobalization of News*, pp. 79–103.

Patterson, T. (1994) *Out of Order*. New York: Vintage.

Patterson, T. (1998) 'Political roles of the journalist', in D. Graber, D. McQuail and P. Norris (eds), *The Politics of News: the News of Politics*, pp. 17–32. Washington, DC: Congressional Quarterly Press.

Peacock, A. (1986) *Report of the Committee on Financing the BBC*. Cmnd 9824. London: HMSO.

Peirce, C.S. (1931–35) *Collected Papers*, edited by C. Harteshorne and P. Weiss, Vols II and V. Cambridge, MA: Harvard University Press.

Pekurny, R. (1982) 'Coping with television production', in J.S. Ettema and D.C. Whitney (eds), *Individuals in Mass Media Organizations*, pp. 131–43. Beverly Hills, CA: Sage.

Perse, E.M. (1990) 'Audience selectivity and involvement in the newer media environment', *Communication Research*, 17: 675–97.

Perse, E.M. (1994) 'Uses of erotica', *Communication Research*, 20 (4): 488–515.

Perse, E.M. and Courtright, J.A. (1992) 'Normative images of communication media: mass and interpersonal channels in the new media environment', *Human Communication Research*, 19: 485–503.

Perse, E.M. and Dunn, D.G. (1998) 'The utility of home computers and media use: implications of multimedia and connectivity', *Journal of Broadcasting and Electronic Media*, 42 (4): 435–56.

Perse, E.M. and Rubin, A.L. (1990) 'Chronic loneliness and television', *Journal of Broadcasting and Electronic Media*, 34 (1): 37–53.

Peters, A.K. and Cantor, M.G. (1982) 'Screen acting as work', in J.S. Ettema and D.C. Whitney (eds), *Individuals in Mass Media Organizations*, pp. 53–68. Beverly Hills, CA: Sage.

Peterson, R.C. and Thurstone, L.L. (1933) *Motion Pictures and Social Attitudes*. New York: Macmillan.

Petty, R.E. and Cacioppo, J.T. (1986) 'The elaboration likelihood model of persuasion', in L. Berkowitz (ed.), *Advances in Experimental Social Psychology*, pp. 132–205. San Diego: Academic Press.

Phillips, D.P. (1980) 'Airplane accidents, murder and the mass media', *Social Forces*, 58 (4): 1001–24.

Phillips, D.P. (1982) 'The impact of fictional TV stories in adult programming on adult fatalities', *American Journal of Sociology*, 87: 1346–59.

Phillips, E.B. (1977) 'Approaches to objectivity', in P.M. Hirsch et al. (eds), *Strategies for Communication Research*, pp. 63–77. Beverly Hills, CA: Sage.

Picard, R.G. (1985) *The Press and the Decline of Democracy*. Westport, CT: Greenwood.

Picard, R.G. (1989) *Media Economics*. Newbury Park, CA: Sage.

Picard, R.G. (1991) 'News coverage as the contagion of terrorism', in A.A. Alali and K.K. Ede (eds), *Media Coverage of Terrorism*, pp. 49–62. London: Sage.

Picard, R.G., McCombs, M., Winter, J.P. and Lacy, S. (eds) (1988) *Press Concentration and Monopoly*. Norwood, NJ: Ablex.

Pool, I. de Sola (1974) *Direct Broadcasting and the Integrity of National Cultures*. New York: Aspen Institute.

Pool, I. de Sola (1983) *Technologies of Freedom*. Cambridge, MA: Belknap Press of Harvard University Press.

Pool, I. de Sola and Shulman, I. (1959) 'Newsmen's fantasies, audiences and newswriting', *Public Opinion Quarterly*, 23 (2): 145–58.

Porat, M. (1977) *The Information Economy: Definitions and Measurement*. Washington DC: Department of Commerce.

Poster, M. (1999) 'Underdetermination', *New Media and Society*, 1 (1): 12–17.

Postman, N. (1993) *Technopoly: the Surrender of Culture to Technology*. New York: Vintage Books.

Postmes, T., Spears, R. and Lea, M. (1998) 'Breaching or building social boundaries? SIDE-effects of computer mediated communication', *Communication Research*, 25 (6): 689–715.

Potter, W.J. Cooper, R. and Dupagne, M. (1993) 'The three paradigms of mass media research in mass communication journals', *Communication Theory*, 3: 317–35.

Preston, W., Herman, E.S. and Schiller, H.I. (1989) *Hope and Folly: The US and UNESCO 1945–85*. Minneapolis, MN: University of Minnesota Press.

Price, M.E. (1995) *Television, the Public Sphere and National Identity*. Oxford: Oxford University Press.

Propp, V. (1968) *The Morphology of Folk Tales*. Austin, TX: University of Texas Press.

Putnam, R.D. (1995) 'Bowling alone: America's declining social capital', *The American Prospect*, 23: 65–78.

Pye, L.W. (1963) *Communications and Political Development*. Princeton, NJ: Princeton University Press.

Raboy, M. (1996) 'Public service broadcasting in the context of globalization', in D. Atkinson and M. Raboy (eds), pp. 77–88. *Public Service Broadcasting: the Challenges of the Twenty-first Century*. Paris: UNESCO.

Radway, J. (1984) *Reading the Romance*. Chapel Hill, NC: University of North Carolina Press.

Rakow, L. (1986) 'Rethinking gender research in communication', *Journal of Communication*, 36 (1): 11–26.

Ray, M.L. (1973) 'Marketing communication and the hierarchy of effects', in P. Clarke (ed.), *New Models for Communication Research*, pp. 147–76. Beverly Hills, CA: Sage.

Real, M. (1989) *Supermedia*. Newbury Park, CA: Sage.

Reese, S.D. (1991) 'Setting the media's agenda: a power balance perspective', in J. Anderson (ed.), *Communication Yearbook* 14, pp. 309–40. Newbury Park, CA: Sage.

Reese, S.D., Grant, A. and Danielian, L.H. (1994) 'The structure of news sources on television: a network analysis of "CBS News", "Nightline", "McNeil/Lehrer" and "This Week With David Brinkley" ', *Journal of Communication*, 44 (2): 64–83.

Rheingold, H. (1994) *The Virtual Community*. London: Secker and Warburg.

Rice, R.E. (1993) 'Media appropriateness: using social presence theory to compare traditional and new organizational media', *Human Communication Research*, 19: 451–84.

Rice, R.E. (1999) 'Artifacts and paradoxes in new media', *New Media and Society*, 1 (1): 24–32.

Rice, R.E. and Associates (1983) *The New Media*. Beverly Hills, CA: Sage.

Rice, R.E. and Atkin, C. (eds) (1989) *Public Communication Campaigns*, 2nd edn. Newbury Park, CA: Sage.

Rice, R.E. and Paisley, W.J. (eds) (1981) *Public Communication Campaigns*. Beverly Hills, CA: Sage.

Ridder, J. de (1984) *Persconcentratie in Nederland*. Amsterdam: VU Uitgeverij.

Rikardsson, G. (1981) 'Newspaper opinion and public opinion', in K.E. Rosengren (ed.), *Advances in Content Analysis*, pp. 215–26. Beverly Hills, CA: Sage.

Robillard, S. (1995) *Television in Europe: Regulatory Bodies*. European Institute for the Media. London: John Libbey.

Robinson, J.P. (1972) 'Mass communication and information diffusion', in F.G. Kline and P.J. Tichenor (eds), *Current Perspectives in Mass Communication Research*, pp. 71–93. Beverly Hills, CA: Sage.

Robinson, J.P. (1976) 'Interpersonal influence in election campaigns: 2-step flow hypotheses', *Public Opinion Quarterly*, 40: 304–19.

Robinson, J.P. and Davis, D.K. (1990) 'Television news and the informed public: an information processing approach', *Journal of Communication*, 40 (3): 106–19.

Robinson, J.P. and Levy, M. (1986) *The Main Source*. Beverly Hills, CA: Sage.

Roe, K. (1992) 'Different destinies – different melodies: school achievement, anticipated status and adolescents' tastes in music', *European Journal of Communication*, 7 (3): 335–58.

Roe, K. and de Meyer, G. (2000) 'MTV: one music – many languages', in P. Dahlgren et al. (eds), *Television Across Europe*. London: Sage.

Rogers, E.M. (1962) *The Diffusion of Innovations*. Glencoe, IL: Free Press.

Rogers, E.M. (1976) 'Communication and development: the passing of a dominant paradigm', *Communication Research*, 3: 213–40.

Rogers, E.M. (1986) *Communication Technology*. New York: Free Press.

Rogers, E.M. (1993) 'Looking back, looking forward: a century of communication research', in P. Gaunt (ed.), *Beyond Agendas: New Directions in Communication Research*, pp. 19–40. Newhaven, CT: Greenwood.

Rogers, E.M. and Dearing, J.W. (1987) 'Agenda-setting research: Where has it been? Where is it going?', in J. Anderson (ed.), *Communication Yearbook 11*, pp. 555–94. Newbury Park, CA: Sage.

Rogers, E.M. and Kincaid, D.L. (1981) *Communication Networks: Towards a New Paradigm for Research*. New York: Free Press.

Rogers, E.M. and Shoemaker, F. (1973) *Communication of Innovations*. New York: Free Press.

Rogers, E.M. and Storey, D. (1987) 'Communication Campaigns', in C.R. Berger and S.H. Chaffee (eds), *Handbook of Communication Science*, pp. 817–46. Beverly Hills, CA: Sage.

Rogers, E.M., Dearing, J.W. and Bregman, D. (1993) 'The anatomy of agenda-setting research', *Journal of Communication*, 43 (2): 68–84.

Rosenberg, B. and White, D.M. (eds) (1957) *Mass Culture*. New York: Free Press.

Rosengren, K.E. (1973) 'News diffusion: an overview', *Journalism Quarterly*, 50: 83–91.

Rosengren, K.E. (1974) 'International news: methods, data, theory', *Journal of Peace Research*, II: 45–56.

Rosengren, K.E. (1976) 'The barseback "panic"'. Unpublished research report, Lund University.

Rosengren, K.E. (ed.) (1981a) *Advances in Content Analysis*. Beverly Hills, CA: Sage.

Rosengren, K.E. (1981b) 'Mass media and social change: some current approaches', in E. Katz and T. Szecskö (eds), *Mass Media and Social Change*, pp. 247–63. Beverly Hills, CA: Sage.

Rosengren, K.E. (1983) 'Communication research: one paradigm or four?', *Journal of Communication*, 33 (3): 185–207.

Rosengren, K.E. (1987) 'The comparative study of news diffusion', *European Journal of Communication*, 2 (2): 136–57.

Rosengren, K.E. (1989) 'Paradigms lost and regained', in B. Dervin et al. (eds), *Rethinking Communication*, pp. 21–39. Newbury Park, CA: Sage.

Rosengren, K.E. and Windahl, S. (1972) 'Mass media consumption as a functional alternative', in D. McQuail (ed.), *Sociology of Mass Communications*, pp. 166–94. Harmondsworth: Penguin.

Rosengren, K.E. and Windahl, S. (1989) *Media Matter*. Norwood, NJ: Ablex.

Roshco, B. (1975) *Newsmaking*. Chicago: University of Chicago Press.

Rositi, F. (1976) 'The television news programme: fragmentation and recomposition of our image of society', in *News and Current Events on TV*. Rome: Edizioni RAI.

Rosten, L.C. (1937) *The Washington Correspondents*. New York: Harcourt Brace.

Rosten, L.C. (1941) *Hollywood: The Movie Colony, the Movie Makers*. New York: Harcourt Brace.

Rothenbuhler, E.W. (1987) 'The living room celebration of the Olympic Games', *Journal of Communication*, 38 (4): 61–8.

Rothenbuhler, E.W., Mullen, L.J., DeCarell, R. and Ryan, C.R. (1996) 'Community, community attachment and involvement', *Journalism and Mass Communication Quarterly*, 73 (2): 445–66.

Royal Commission on the Press (1977) *Report*. Cmnd 6810. London: HMSO.

Rubin, A.M. (1984) 'Ritualized and instrumental television viewing', *Journal of Communication, 34* (3): 67–77.

Rubin, A.M., Perse, E.M. and Powell, E. (1990) 'Loneliness, parasocial interaction and local TV news viewing', *Communication Research*, 14 (2): 246–68.

Ryan, J. and Peterson, R.A. (1982) 'The product image: the fate of creativity in country music song writing', in J.S. Ettema and D.C. Whitney (eds), *Individuals in Mass Media Organizations*, pp. 11–32. Beverly Hills, CA: Sage.

Saenz, M.K. (1994) 'Television viewing and cultural practice', in H. Newcomb (ed.), *Television: the Critical View*, 5th edn, pp. 573–86. New York: Oxford University Press.

Salvaggio, J.L. (1985) 'Information technology and social problems: four international models', in B.D. Ruben (ed.), *Information and Behavior*, Vol. I, pp. 428–54. Rutgers, NJ: Transaction Books.

Saussure, F. de (1915) *Course in General Linguistics*. English trans. London: Peter Owen, 1960.

Schement, J. and Curtis, T. (1995) *Tendencies and Tension of the Information Age*. New Brunswick: Transaction Publishers.

Scheufele, D.A. (1999) 'Framing as a theory of media effects', *Journal of Communication*, 49 (1): 103–22.

Schiller, H. (1969) *Mass Communication and American Empire*. New York: Augustus M. Kelly.

Schiller, H. (1989) *Information and the Crisis Economy*. Norwood, NJ: Ablex.

Schlesinger, P. (1978) *Putting 'Reality' Together: BBC News*. London: Constable.

Schlesinger, P. (1987) 'On national identity', *Social Science Information*, 25 (2): 219–64.

Schlesinger, P., Murdock, G. and Elliott, P. (1983) *Televising Terrorism*. London: Comedia.

Schmid, A.P. and de Graaf, J. (1982) *Violence as Communication*. Beverly Hills, CA: Sage.

Schramm, W. (1955) 'Information theory and mass communication', *Journalism Quarterly*, 32: 131–46.

Schramm, W. (1964) *Mass Media and National Development*. Stanford, CA: Stanford University Press.

Schramm, W., Lyle, J. and Parker, E. (1961) *Television in the Lives of Our Children*. Stanford, CA: Stanford University Press.

Schrøder, K.C. (1987) 'Convergence of antagonistic traditions?', *European Journal of Communication*, 2 (1): 7–31.

Schrøder, K.C. (1992) 'Cultural quality: search for a phantom?', in M. Skovmand and K.C. Schrøder (eds), *Media Cultures: Reappraising Transnational Media*, pp. 161–80. London: Routledge.

Schrøder, K.C. (1999) 'The best of both worlds? Media audience research between rival paradigms', in P. Alasuutari (ed.), *Rethinking the Media Audience*, pp. 38–68. London: Sage.

Schudson, M. (1978) *Discovering the News*. New York: Basic Books.

Schudson, M. (1991) 'The new validation of popular culture', in R.K. Avery and D. Eason (eds), *Critical Perspectives on Media and Society*, pp. 49–68. New York: Guilford.

Schudson, M. (1998) 'The public journalism movement and its problems', in D. Graber, D. McQuail and P. Norris (eds), *The Politics of News; the News of Politics*, pp. 132–49. Washington, DC: Congressional Quarterly Press.

Schulz, W. (1988) 'Media and reality'. Unpublished paper for Sommatie Conference, Veldhoven, the Netherlands.

Schulz, W. (1997) 'Changes of the mass media and the public sphere', *The Public*, 4 (2): 57–70.

Schwichtenberg, C. (1992) 'Music Video', in J. Lull (ed.), *Popular Music and Communication*, pp. 116–33. Newbury Park, CA: Sage.

Seiter, F., Borchers, H. and Warth, E.-M. (eds) (1989) *Remote Control*. London: Routledge.

Sepstrup, P. (1989) 'Research into international TV flows', *European Journal of Communication*, 4 (4): 393–408.

Seymour-Ure, C. (1974) *The Political Impact of the Mass Media*. London: Cole.

Shannon, C. and Weaver, W. (eds) (1949) *The Mathematical Theory of Communication*. Urbana, IL: University of Illinois Press.

Shelton, P. and Gunaratne, S.A. (1998) 'Old wine in a new bottle: public journalism, developmental journalism and social responsibility', in M.E. Roloff and G.D. Paulson (eds), *Communication Yearbook 21*, pp. 277–321. Thousand Oaks, CA: Sage.

Shen, M.C.H. (1999) *Current-Affairs Talkshows: Public Communication Revitalized on Television*. Amsterdam: University of Amsterdam.

Shibutani, T. (1966) *Improvised News*. New York: Bobbs Merrill.

Shils, E. (1957) 'Daydreams and nightmares: reflections on the criticism of mass culture', *Sewanee Review*, 65 (4): 586–608.

Shoemaker, P. (1991) *Gatekeeping*. Thousand Oaks, CA: Sage.

Shoemaker, P.J. (1984) 'Media treatment of deviant political groups', *Journalism Quarterly*, 61 (1): 66–75, 82.

Shoemaker, P.J. and Reese, S.D. (1991) *Mediating the Message*. New York: Longman.

Short, J., Williams, E. and Christie, B. (1976) *The Social Psychology of Telecommunications*. New York: Wiley.

Siebert, F., Peterson, T. and Schramm, W. (1956) *Four Theories of the Press*. Urbana, IL: University of Illinois Press.

Sigal, L.V. (1973) *Reporters and Officials*. Lexington, MA: Lexington Books.

Sigelman, L. (1973) 'Reporting the news: an organizational analysis', *American Journal of Sociology*, 79: 132–51.

Signorielli, N. and Morgan, M. (eds) (1990) *Cultivation Analysis*. Newbury Park, CA: Sage.

Silverstone, R. (1994) *Television and Everyday Life*. London: Routledge.

Singer, B.D. (1970) 'Mass media and communications processes in the Detroit riots of 1967', *Public Opinion Quarterly*, 34: 236–45.

Siune, K. (1981) 'Broadcast election campaigns in a multiparty system', in K.E. Rosengren (ed.), *Advances in Content Analysis*, pp. 177–96. Beverly Hills, CA: Sage.

Siune, K. and Truetzschler, W. (1992) *Dynamics of Media Politics*. London: Sage.

Slack, J.D. (1984) *Communication Technology and Society*. Norwood, NJ: Ablex.

Smaele, H. de (1999) 'The application of Western models to the Russian media system', *European Journal of Communication*, 14 (2): 173–89.

Smith, A. (1973) *The Shadow in the Cave*. London: Allen and Unwin.

Smith, A.D. (1990) 'Towards a global culture', *Theory, Culture and Society*, 7 (2/3): 171–91.

Smythe, D.W. (1972) 'Some observations on communications theory', in D. McQuail (ed.), *Sociology of Mass Communications*, pp. 19–34. Harmondsworth: Penguin.

Smythe, D.W. (1977) 'Communications: blindspot of Western Marxism', *Canadian Journal of Political and Social Theory*, I: 120–7.

Sonninen, P. and Laitila, T. (1995) 'Press councils in Europe', in K. Nordenstreng (ed.), *Reports on Media Ethics*, pp. 3–22. Tampere: Department of Journalism and Mass Communication.

Sparks, C. and Campbell, M. (1987) 'The inscribed reader of the British quality press', *European Journal of Communication*, 2 (4): 455–72.

Sparks, C. and Reading, A. (1998) *Communism, Capitalism and the Mass Media*. London: Sage.

Spears, R. and Lea, M. (1994) 'Panacea or panopticon? The hidden power in computer-mediated communication', *Communication Research*, 21 (4): 427–59.

Spilerman, S. (1976) 'Structural characteristics and severity of racial disorders', *American Sociological Review*, 41: 771–92.

Squires, J.D. (1992) 'Plundering the newsroom', *Washington Journalism Review*, 14 (10): 18–24.

Sreberny-Mohammadi, A. (1996) 'The global and the local in international communication', in J. Curran and M. Gurevitch (eds), *Mass Media and Society*, pp. 177–203.

Stamm, K.R. (1985) *Newspaper Use and Community Ties: Towards a Dynamic Theory*. Norwood, NJ: Ablex.

Stamm, K., Emig, A.G. and Heuse, M.B. (1997) 'The contribution of local media to community involvement', *Journalism and Mass Communication Quarterly*, 74 (1): 97–107.

Star, S.A. and Hughes, H.M. (1950) 'Report on an education campaign: the Cincinnati plan for the UN', *American Sociological Review*, 41: 771–92.

Stark, R. (1982) 'Policy and pros: an organizational analysis of a metropolitan newspaper', *Berkeley Journal of Sociology*, 7 (11): 11–31.

Steiner, G. (1963) *The People Look at Television*. New York: Alfred Knopf.

Stone, G.C. (1987) *Examining Newspapers*. Beverly Hills, CA: Sage.

Street, J. (1997) 'Remote control? Politics, technology and "electronic democracy" ', *European Journal of Communication*, 12 (1): 27–42.

Surgeon General's Scientific Advisory Committee (1972) *Television and Growing Up: The Impact of Televised Violence*. Washington, DC: GPO.

Sussman, G. (1997) *Communication, Technology and Politics in the Information Age*. Thousand Oaks, CA: Sage.

Swanson, D. and Mancini, P. (eds) (1996) *Politics, Media and Modern Democracy*. Westport, CT: Praeger.

Tannenbaum, P.H. and Lynch, M.D. (1960) 'Sensationalism: the concept and its measurement', *Journalism Quarterly*, 30: 381–93.

Taylor, D.G. (1982) 'Pluralistic ignorance and the spiral of silence', *Public Opinion Quarterly*, 46: 311–55.

Taylor, P. (1992) *War and the Media*. Manchester: Manchester University Press.

Taylor, W.L. (1953) 'Cloze procedure: a new tool for measuring readability', *Journalism Quarterly*, 30: 415–33.

Teheranian, M. (1979) 'Iran: communication, alienation, revolution', *Intermedia*, 7 (2): 6–12.

Thomsen, C.W. (ed.), (1989) *Cultural Transfer or Electronic Imperialism*. Heidelberg: Carl Winter Universitätsverlag.

Thompson, J.B. (1993) 'Social theory and the media', in D. Crowley and D. Mitchell (eds), *Communication Theory Today*, pp. 27–49. Cambridge: Polity.

Thompson, J.B. (1995) *The Media and Modernity*. Cambridge: Polity.

Thoveron, G. (1986) 'European televised women', *European Journal of Communication*, 1 (3): 289–300.

Thrift, R.R. (1977) 'How chain ownership affects editorial vigor of newspapers', *Journalism Quarterly*, 54: 327–31.

Tichenor, P.J., Donahue, G.A. and Olien, C.N. (1970) 'Mass media and the differential growth in knowledge', *Public Opinion Quarterly*, 34: 158–70.

Tomlinson, J. (1991) *Cultural Imperialism*. London: Pinter.

Traber, M. and Nordenstreng, K. (1993) *Few Voices, Many Worlds*. London: World Association for Christian Communication.

Trenaman, J.S.M. (1967) *Communication and Comprehension*. London: Longman.

Trenaman, J.S.M. and McQuail, D. (1961) *Television and the Political Image*. London: Methuen.

Tuchman, G. (1978) *Making News: A Study in the Construction of Reality*. New York: Free Press.

Tuchman, G., Daniels, A.K. and Benet, J. (eds) (1978) *Hearth and Home: Images of Women in Mass Media*. New York: Oxford University Press.

Tumber, H. (1982) *Television and the Riots*. London: British Film Institute.

Tunstall, J. (1970) *The Westminster Lobby Correspondents*. London: Routledge and Kegan Paul.

Tunstall, J. (1971) *Journalists at Work*. London: Constable.

Tunstall, J. (1977) *The Media Are American*. London: Constable.

Tunstall, J. (1991) 'A media industry perspective', in J. Anderson (ed.), *Communication Yearbook 14*, pp. 163–86. Newbury Park, CA: Sage.

Tunstall, J. (1992) 'Europe as a world news leader', *Journal of Communication*, 42 (3): 84–99.

Tunstall, J. (1993) *Television Producers*. London: Routledge.

Tunstall, J. and Machin, D. (1999) *The Anglo-American Media Connection*. Oxford: Oxford University Press.

Tunstall, J. and Palmer, M. (eds) (1991) *Media Moguls*. London: Routledge.

Turkle, S. (1988) 'Computational reticence: why women fear the intimate machine', in C. Kramarae (ed.), *Technology and Women's Voices: Keeping in Touch'*, pp. 41–62. London: Routledge.

Turow, J. (1982) 'Unconventional programs on commercial television: an organizational perspective', in J.S. Ettema and D.C. Whitney (eds), *Individuals in Mass Media Organizations*, pp. 107–29. Beverly Hills, CA: Sage.

Turow, J. (1989) 'PR and newswork: a neglected relationship', *American Behavioral Scientist*, 33: 206–12.

Turow, J. (1991) 'A mass communication perspective on entertainment', in J. Curran and M. Gurevitch (eds), *Mass Media and Society*, pp. 160–77. London: Edward Arnold.

Turow, J. (1994) 'Hidden conflicts and journalistic norms: the case of self-coverage', *Journal of Communication*, 44 (2): 29–46.

Twyman, T. (1994) 'Measuring audiences', in R. Kent (ed.), *Measuring Media Audiences*, pp. 88–104. London: Routledge.

Varis, T. (1974) 'Television traffic – a one-way street'. Paris: UNESCO.

Varis, T. (1984) 'The international flow of television programs', *Journal of Communication*, 34 (1): 143–52.

Vidmar, N. and Rokeach, M. (1974) 'Archie Bunker's bigotry: a study of selective perception and exposure', *Journal of Communication*, 24: 36–47.

Visvanath, K. and Finnegan, J.R. (1996) 'The knowledge gap hypothesis 25 years later', in *Communication Yearbook 19*, pp. 187–227.

Wackman, D.B., Gilmor, D.M., Gaziano, C. and Dennis, E.E. (1975) 'Chain newspaper autonomy as reflected in presidential campaign endorsements', *Journalism Quarterly*, 52: 511–20.

Waisbord, S. (1998) 'When the cart of media is put before the horse of identity – a critique of technology-centered views on globalization', *Communication Research*, 25 (4): 377–98.

Wallis, R. and Baran, S. (1990) *The World of Broadcast News*. London: Routledge.

Walzer, M. (1992) 'The civil society argument', in C. Mouffe, *Dimensions of Radical Democracy*. London: Verso.

Warner, W.L. and Henry, W.E. (1948) 'The radio day-time serial: a symbolic analysis', *Psychological Monographs*, 37 (1): 7–13, 55–64.

Wartella, E., Olivarez, A. and Jennings, N. (1998) 'Children and television violence in the United States', in U. Carlsson and C. von Feilitzen (eds), *Children and Media Violence*, pp. 55–62. Göteborg; University of Göteborg.

Watson, N. (1997) 'Why we argue about virtual community: a case study of the Phish.Net fan community', in S.G. Jones (ed.), *Virtual Culture*, pp. 102–32. London: Sage.

Weaver, D. (1996) 'Journalists in comparative perspective', *The Public* 3 (4): 83–91.

Weaver, D. and Wilhoit, C.G. (1986) *The American Journalist*. Bloomington, IN: University of Indiana Press.

Weaver, D. and Wilhoit, C.G. (1992) 'Journalists – who are they really?', *Media Studies Journal*, 6 (4): 63–80.

Weaver, D. and Wilhoit, C.G. (1996) *The American Journalist in the 1990s: US News People at the End of an Era*. Mahwah, NJ: Lawrence Erlbaum.

Weber, M. (1948) 'Politics as a vocation', in H. Gerth and C.W. Mills (eds), *Max Weber: Essays*. London: Routledge and Kegan Paul.

Webster, F. (1995) *Images of the Information Society*. London: Routledge.

Webster, J.G. and Wakshlag, J.J. (1983) 'A theory of TV program choice', *Communication Research*, 10 (4): 430–46.

Webster, J.G. and Phalen, P.F. (1997) *The Mass Audience: Rediscovering the Dominant Model*. Mahawa, NJ: Lawrence Erlbaum.

Weibull, L. (1985) 'Structural factors in gratifications research', in K.E. Rosengren, P. Palmgreen and L. Wenner (eds), *Media Gratification Research: Current Perspectives*, pp. 123–47. Beverly Hills, CA: Sage.

Westergaard, J. (1977) 'Power, class and the media', in J. Curran et al. (eds), *Mass Communication and Society*, pp. 95–215. London: Edward Arnold.

Westerstahl, J. (1983) 'Objective news reporting', *Communication Research*, 10 (3): 403–24.

Westerstahl, J. and Johansson, F. (1994) 'Foreign news: values and ideologies', *European Journal of Communication*, 9 (1): 71–89.

Westley, B. and MacLean, M. (1957) 'A conceptual model for mass communication research', *Journalism Quarterly*, 34: 31–8.

Whale, J. (1969) *The Half-Shut Eye*. London: Macmillan.

White, D.M. (1950) 'The gatekeeper: a case-study in the selection of news', *Journalism Quarterly*, 27: 383–90.

Wildman, S.S. (1991) 'Explaining trade in films and programs', *Journal of Communication*, 41: 190–2.

Wilhoit, G.C. and de Bock, H. (eds) (1980 and 1981) *Mass Communication Review Yearbook*, Vols 1 and 2. Beverly Hills, CA: Sage.

Wilke, J. (1995) 'Agenda-setting in an historical perspective: the coverage of the American revolution in the German press (1773–83)', *European Journal of Communication*, 10 (1): 63–86.

Williams, R. (1961) *Culture and Society*. Harmondsworth: Penguin.

Williams, R. (1975) *Television, Technology and Cultural Form*. London: Fontana.

Williamson, J. (1978) *Decoding Advertisements*. London: Marion Boyars.

Windahl, S., Signitzer, B. and Olson, J. (1992) *Using Communication Theory*. London and Newbury Park, CA: Sage.

Winsor, P. (1989) 'Gender in film directing', in M. Real, *Supermedia*, pp. 132–64. Newbury Park, CA: Sage.

Winston, B. (1986) *Misunderstanding Media*. Cambridge, MA: Harvard University Press.

Wober, J.M. (1978) 'Televised violence and the paranoid perception: the view from Great Britain', *Public Opinion Quarterly*, 42: 315–21.

Wolfe, K.M. and Fiske, M. (1949) 'Why they read comics', in P.F. Lazersfeld and F.M. Stanton (eds), *Communication Research 1948–9*, pp. 3–50. New York: Harper and Brothers.

Wolfenstein, M. and Leites, N. (1947) 'An analysis of themes and plots in motion pictures', *Annals of the American Academy of Political and Social Sciences*, 254: 41–8.

Womack, B. (1981) 'Attention maps of ten major newspapers', *Journalism Quarterly*, 58 (2): 260–5.

Woodall, G. (1986) 'Information processing theory and television news', in J.P. Robinson and M. Levy, *The Main Source*, pp. 133–58. Beverly Hills, CA: Sage.

Wright, C.R. (1960) 'Functional analysis and mass communication', *Public Opinion Quarterly*, 24: 606–20.

Wright, C.R. (1974) 'Functional analysis and mass communication revisited', in J.G. Blumler and E. Katz (eds), *The Uses of Mass Communications*, pp. 197–212. Beverly Hills, CA: Sage.

Wu, W., Weaver, D., Owen, D. and Johnstone, J.W.L. (1996) 'Professional rules of Russian and US journalists: a comparative study', *Journalism and Mass Communication Quarterly*, 73 (3): 534–48.

Zaller, J.R. (1997) 'A model of communication effects at the outbreak of the Gulf War', in S. Iyengar and R. Reeves (eds), *Do the Media Govern?* pp. 296–311. Thousand Oaks, CA: Sage.

Zoch, L.M. and Slyke Turk, J. van (1998) 'Women making news: gender as a variable in source selection and use', 75 (4): 776–88.

Zoonen, L. van (1988) 'Rethinking women and the news', *European Journal of Communication*, 3 (1): 35–52.

Zoonen, L. van (1991) 'Feminist perspectives on the media', in J. Curran and M. Gurevitch (eds), *Mass Media and Society*, pp. 33–51. London: Edward Arnold.

Zoonen, L. van (1992) 'The women's movement and the media: constructing a public identity', *European Journal of Communication*, 7 (4): 453–76.

Zoonen, L. van (1994) *Feminist Media Studies*. London: Sage.

Page numbers in *italics* refer to figures.

Page numbers in **bold** indicate main discussion, *g* denotes glossary definition.

influence processes, 433–4, 444–5
information, 79, 497g: evaluative dimension of, 317–18
information and communication technology, 118
information culture, 123
'information economy', 121, 123
information flows, 33–4, 316, 317: new patterns, 129–32
information quality, 171–5
information search media, 127
information society, 87–8, **120–4**, 481, 497g
information theory, 315–16: in study of media content, 316–17
informational logic, 484
infotainment, 106, 286, 335
institutional change, 120, 428
institutionalization of press, 21
integration of new media, 125, 480
interaction typology, 65
interactive play media, 127
interactivity, 33, 127, 129, 131, 407, 481–2, 497g
'interconnectedness', 122, 124
interdependence, 62–3
international media dependency, 226–9
international news flow, 229–32
internationalization, 94, 209, 224–6, 407: see also globalization
Internet, 28–9, 118–19, 120, 127–8, 135, **137–40**, 226, 372–3, 497g: advertising on, 197; and violence, 434
intertextuality of media, 350, 498–9g

journalism, 498g: 'myth structure' of, 278–9; professionalism, 256–8; professionalization of, 22, 150–3; public, 159–60; types of, 340
journalists, 265, 321: autonomy, 270–1; conflicts with organizations, 272–3; role, 252–8; social composition, 267–9; socialization of, 271–2, 273; women, 268, 270

knowledge, distribution of, 15, 64, 86, 121, 427, 451
knowledge gaps, 457–9, 498g

language: barriers, 220, 225; English, 136, 218, 226, 235; visual, 336–7; see also semiology
leisure-time, 23
liberal-pluralist paradigm, 161
liberal-pluralist society, 45, 48, 49
liberalism, 20, 22, 33, 70: vs collectivism, 142–3
libertarian theory of press, 154, 156, 180
licensing, 24, 25, 156, 185
life-style, 397–8, 498g

location: and identity, 486; in news selection, 280–1

magazines, 37, 193, 201–2: women's, 263, 264, 310, 399, 403, 404
Marxism, 49, 76–8, 82–3, 95, 105, 154, 307, 498g
mass audience, 41–2, 369, 374
mass communication: definitions, 13–14, 52–3; mediation of social relations, 64–6; multiple logics of, 482–4; process, 40–1; theory, 478–82
mass communicators, 266–9
mass, concept of, 38–9, 361–2, 498g
mass culture, 42–4, 94, 95, 499g: see also popular culture
mass society theory, 39, 74–6, 463, 499g
materialism, 61: vs culturalist approaches, 6–7
meaning: connotation and denotation, 313–14, 315; location of, 324–5, 485–6; and media, 484–6
media addiction, 368
media content, 62, 105, 126, 218, 304–6: critical perspectives, 306–11; gendering of, 100–1; as information, 315–18; organizational influences, 245–6; research methods, 324–9
media culture, 94, 95: global, 232–5, 238–9
media effect, 47–8, 72–3, 305, 416–17, 494–5g: levels and kinds, 423–5; research and theory, 417–23; typology of processes, 425–8
media institutions, 14–15, 68, 190–2
media logic, 55, 269, 271, 278, 280, **296–7**, 299: and communication bias, 109–10; components, 484; and format, 335–7; influence of, 471–2
media, new and old, 87–8, 119–20, 127–9, 204–5
media organization: factors in foreign news selection, 231; frameworks and perspectives, 244–5; gatekeeping and selection, 276–7, 293–4; goals, 251–2; influences on content, 245–6; internal structure and dynamics, 271–3; latent conflicts, 271–3; levels of analysis, 246–9; processing and presentation, 291–6; research tradition, 244; and social forces, 249–51; vs ideological influences, 277–8
media orientation, 386, 389
media performance, 212, 305, **318–24**

media policy paradigm shifts, 208–9
media (pseudo) events, 25–6, 81, 109, 280, 283–4, 290, 396, 464
media structure/system, 192–3: dynamics, 204–6; economic principles of, 194–8; and political system, 211–12; post-communist changes, 212–14; social and cultural specificity, 210–11
media theory issues, 69–74
media use, 32–3, 384–6, 394–6, 400–2: changing patterns of, 407–8; and gratifications, 387–90, 442, 504g; normative framing of, 402–3
media-centric approach, 13: vs socio-centric approach, 6, 7, **88–9**, 245
media-induced change, 423–5
media-occupational role dilemmas, 274
media-society relationship, 5–6, 33–4, 36–8: connections and conflicts, 61–3; frame of reference, 66–8; mediation, 64–6
media-society theory, 74–88
mediation, 64–6
mobilization function of media, 79, 80
modernization, 83–5
monopoly, 201–4, 205, 207, 260
moral panic, 38, 434, 469, 499–500g
music industry, 26–7, 33, 193, 217, 265, 293–4: internationalization of, 219, 235
music videos, 114

neo-Marxism, 77–8
'network society', 122, 481, 500g
neutrality see objectivity
new media: categories, 127; and mass media institution, 118–20
new media theory, 480–2: main issues, 124–6; possible basis for, 126–9
new technology see electronic media
news: bias, 230–1, 320, 322, 342–3, 425; definitions, 337–9, 500g; diffusion, 427, 451–2, 494g; framing, 343–4; gendered, 100; and human interest, 339–40; learning, 425, 452–4; as narrative, 346–8; objectivity, 173, 255–6, 257, 320–2; report format, 344–6; representation of women, 102
news agencies, 218–19, 289, 992
news events, 281
news net, 281, 282
news organizations, 269–71, 272
news production, 276
news selection, 277–84
news sequence models, 348
news sources, influence of, 287–91

news values, 278, 323, 341, **342**, 343, 500g
newspapers, 20–3, 30, 216, 500g: organizations, 266; owners, 202, 259–60; prestige, 22, 252–3, 340; tabloid, 106, 196, 197, 340; use, 32, 33, 386
normative framing of media use, 402–3
normative theory, 8, 45, 158–62, 176–80, 252: range of application, 179; of social control, 31, 71, 176–7

objectivity, 500g: benefits of, 172–3; concept, 172; framework for research and theory, 173–4; interpretations of, 255–6; limits, 174–5; of news, 173, 255–6, 257, 320–2; vs engagement, 66, 252–8
operational theory, 8
organizational logic, 483
owner influences, 259–61, 273
ownership, 149, 154, 169, 193, 211: and control, 82, **198–9**, 218–19; and media structure, 144–5; see also concentration; monopoly

para-social interaction, 405–6, 501g
person as event, 279–80
personal characteristics of mass communicators, 266–9
personal influence theory, 43–4
phonogram, 26, 27, 33, 501g
pluralism see liberal-pluralist paradigm; liberal-pluralist society
pluralist vs dominance model of media power, 69–70
political actors, 472–3
political campaigns, 290–1, 418, 443, 455, 472
political control, 30–1
political logic, 483–4: vs media logic, 471–2
political and media systems, 211–12
political participation, 73, 75, 134–5
political press, 21–2
political-economy, 82–3, 94, 139, 191, 222, 501g
politicization of media, 213–14
politics, 4: 'media-priming' effects, 456–7; role of broadcasting in, 26; selection and presentation, 336
popular culture, 37, 42–4, 94, 178: gender issues, 101–2; postmodern elements, 114; 'redemption' of, 102–5; role of, 102
postmodern culture, 113–16, 238–9
postmodernism, 58, 76, 123, 488, 489, 501g: and Internet, 119
power elite, 49, 50
power of media, 36, 69–70, 125, 470–1, 486–7: models, 417–20;

power of media, cont.
negotiated influence, 420–2; variation in, 422–3
power, types of, 433
press: as 'fourth estate', 146–8, 253, 495g; freedom, 147–50, 206, 496g; functions of, 73; theories, 153–6
Press Councils, 150–1
pressure/interest groups, 258–9, 289, 421, 472
prestige press, 22, 252–3, 340
print media, 18–23, 86
product image, 294, 297–8
production, 276: cycle, 278; process, 279; typology, 285–6
professionalism: and accountability, 187; and autonomy, 263; decision-making, 298; in journalism, 256–8
propaganda, 425, **446–7**, 501g: film-as-, 23–4
propaganda model, 467–8
pseudo events see media (pseudo) events
public, 501g: audience as, 41, 371–3
public benefits, 168, 171
public interest, 30, 33–4, 142–4, 157, 181, 191, 501–2g
public opinion, 461–4, 502g
public ownership, 78, 198–9
public policy issues, 202–3, 205
public and private spheres of media use, 395–6
public relations, 502g: and news management, 290–1
public service broadcasting, 156–7, 254–5, 260–1, 372, 502g
public sphere, 15, 34, 65, 75, 83, 102, **157–9**, 502g: expectations, 145; public journalism movement, 159–60
publicity model, 54–6, 57, 106, 298–9, 348, 488: audience as spectators, 377, 378

qualitative approaches, 50, 51, 325: vs qualitative approaches, 327–9
quality: of attention, 55; cultural, 105, 177–8, 308–9, 488–9
radio, 30, 31, 33, 38, 41, 193, 216: call-in shows, 286; local, 160
ratings, 195, 263, 264, 265, 364, 377–8, 382
realism, 279, 352–3
reality: mediation of, 65, 66–7, 322–4, 428, 461, 463–4; of society, 285, 286–7, 288, 305; vs fantasy, 485
reception analysis, 453–4, 502g
reception model, 56–7
regulation, 24, 184–5: models, 206–8
revenue sources, 194–5: competition for, 196–7

ritual model, 53–4, 57, 92, 106: audience as participants, 377
romantic fiction, 310–11, 333, 351–2, 398, 403

satellite, 131, 217, 232–3, 234, 235, 408
segmentation, 407–8
selection, 276–7, 293–4
semiology, 503g: and structuralism, 311–14, 327–8; uses of, 314
semiotic power (of the people), 103, 104, 105
sensationalism, 316, 321–2, 503g
seriality, 351–2
signification, 9, 92, 307, 312, 313
soap operas, 100, 101, 115, 310, 333–4, 351, 354, 398–9, 404
social change, 73–4, 125–6
social class, 20, 42–4, 97, 104–5, 197, 458
social control, 427: and consciousness formation, 467–71; and solidarity, 175–7; vs freedom, 31–2, 71–2
social forces, 249–51
social functions of media, 79–80
social integration, 37, 80–1, 428: and identity, 71–3
social relationships: globalization of, 11–12; mediation of, 64–6; transformation of, 122, 127–8, 129, 482
social responsibility, 149, 154–5, 482, 503g: of press, 148–50, 154–5, 180
social responsibility paradigm, 161
social scientific theory, 7–8
social theory of media, 144–8
socialization, 503g: of children, 310, 460–1; of journalists, 271–2, 273; media as agent of, 400, 427, 460–1, 467
society-culture relations typology, 61–3
socio-centric approach, 12, 248: vs media-centric approach, 6, 7, 88–9, 245
space/time conceptions, 65, 86, 112–13, 136, 486
'spin doctors', 290, 503g
spiral of silence, 461–4, 503g
structural analysis, 12–13, 366, 368, 385–6
structuralism, 311–14, 327–8
subcultural audiences, 81, 94–5, 236, 237–8, **396–7**
symbolism, 9, 40, 54, 65, 81, 93, 464–5

tabloid press, 470
tabloidization, 23, 106, 340, 504g
talk-shows, 101, 334
taste culture, 373

technological convergence, 14, 29–30, 118, 124, 208, 209, 480, 493g
technological determinism, 74, 85–7, 480
technological logic, 295, 296, 483
technology: bias, 109–10; and cultural change, 107–9, 204–5; and ideology, 86–7
telephone chat-lines, 33
television, 30–1, 81, 108, 110, 114, 193, 202: and children, 26, 400, 402–3, 408, 434–5, 466–7; codes of ethics, 152; cultivation hypothesis, 464–7; as educator, 26, 458; gendered, 100, 333–4; globalization of, 217–18, 232–5; influence of, 422–3; international flows of, 224–5; local, 160; network, 196, 197; news, 229, 345–6; production typology, 285–6; 'reality', 286, 287; tabloidization of news, 106, 340; typology of genres, 334–5; typology of relations, 406;

television, *cont.*
uses and reception, 32–3, 400, 401–2, 408, 410; violence, 434–8, 466
terrorism, 351, **439–40**
text analysis, 313, 314, 316–18, 320, 325
text(s), 92, 93, 100, 103, 315, 382: concept of, 349–50; differential 'reading', 353; gendered, 353–4; open vs closed, 351
Third World, 50–1, 84–5, 136, 205, 206: cultural invasion of, 238; development communication, 427, 450–1
Toronto School, 126, 504g
transmission model, 46, 48, 52–3, 55, 57, 84, 106: audience as target, 377
transnationalization *see* globalization; internationalization

UNESCO, 152
United States: Commission on Freedom of the Press (1947),

United States, *cont.*
148–50; Federal Communication Commission, 149
uses and gratifications of media, 387–90, 442, 504g

values, 71, 80, 145–6, 269, 305, 404: *see also* Western values
video, 33, 114
violence, 309–10, 434–8, 439, 466
virtual community, 133–4, 138, 504g

Western perspective, 18, 45–6, 130, 362
Western values, 39, 84, 136–7, 221, 231, 239: *see also* cultural imperialism; hegemony
women: cult of femininity, 81; journalists, 268, 270; magazines for, 263, 264, 310, 399, 403, 404; in news organizations, 269–71; representation in news, 102; violence against, 310
World Wide Web *see* Internet

youth culture, 27, 235, 396–7, 418